PHILIP'S

STREET

Lincolnshire

Boston, Grantham, Grimsby, Lincoln, Peterborough, Scunthorpe

www.philips-maps.co.uk

First published in 2002 by Philip's
a division of Octopus Publishing Group Ltd
www.octopusbooks.co.uk
Endeavour House
189 Shaftesbury Avenue
London WC2H 8JY
An Hachette UK Company
www.hachette.co.uk

Second edition 2007
Third impression 2013

LINBB

ISBN 978-0-540-09484-4 (spiral)

© Philip's 2012

Ordnance Survey®

This product includes mapping data licensed
from Ordnance Survey® with the permission
of the Controller of Her Majesty's Stationery
Office. © Crown copyright 2008. All rights
reserved. Licence number 100011710.

Speed camera data provided by
PocketGPSWorld.com Ltd

Post Office is a trade mark of Post Office Ltd in
the UK and other countries.

Printed in China

Contents

II Mobile safety cameras

III Key to map symbols

IV Key to map pages

VI Route planning

X Major administrative and Postcode boundaries

1 Street maps at 1¾ inches to 1 mile

178 Street maps at 3½ inches to 1 mile

234 Street maps of Lincoln city centre at 7 inches to 1 mile

235 Index of towns, villages, streets, hospitals, industrial estates, railway stations, schools, shopping centres, universities and places of interest

Digital Data

The exceptionally high-quality mapping found in this atlas is available as digital data in TIFF format, which is easily convertible to other bitmapped (raster) image formats.

The index is also available in digital form as a standard database table. It contains all the details found in the printed index together with the National Grid reference for the map square in which each entry is named.

For further information and to discuss your requirements, please contact
philips@mapsinternational.co.uk

Mobile safety cameras

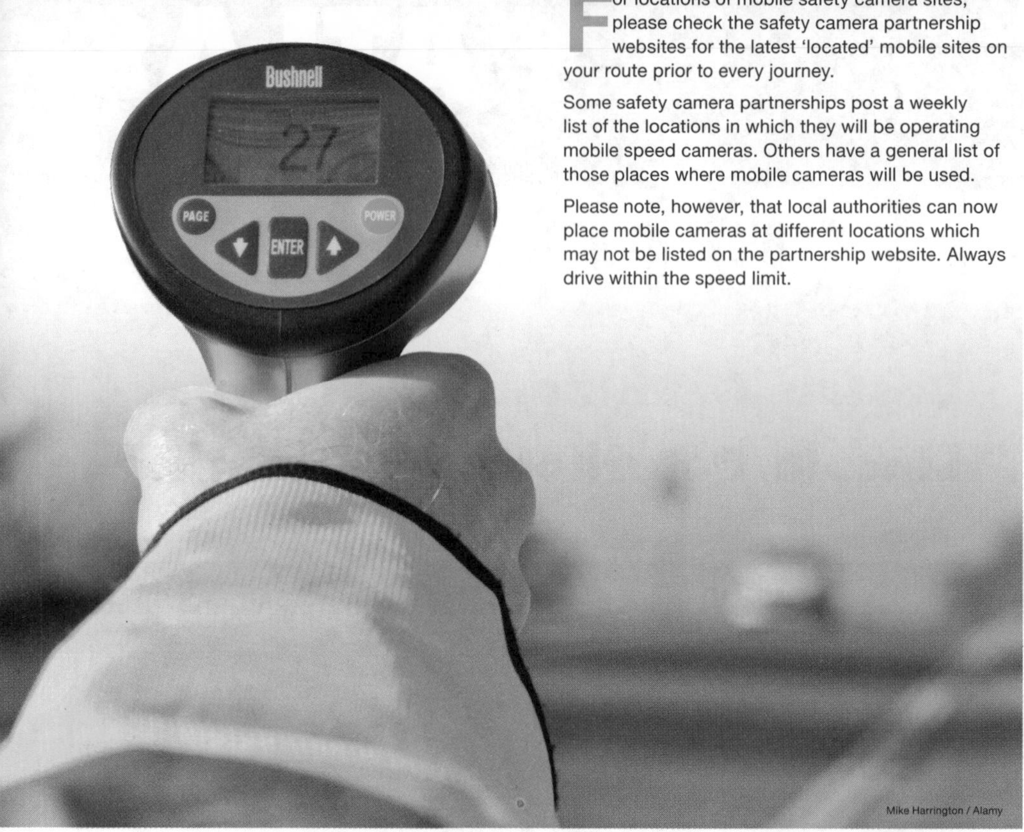

For locations of mobile safety camera sites, please check the safety camera partnership websites for the latest 'located' mobile sites on your route prior to every journey.

Some safety camera partnerships post a weekly list of the locations in which they will be operating mobile speed cameras. Others have a general list of those places where mobile cameras will be used.

Please note, however, that local authorities can now place mobile cameras at different locations which may not be listed on the partnership website. Always drive within the speed limit.

Mike Harrington / Alamy

Useful websites

Lincolnshire Road Safety Partnership
http://microsites.lincolnshire.gov.uk/LRSP/

Norfolk Safety Camera Partnership
www.norfolk-safety-camera.org.uk/

Cambridge and Peterborough Road Safety Partnership
www.cprsp.gov.uk

Cambridgeshire Safety Camera Partnership
www.cambs.police.uk/roadsafety/safetyCameras.asp

Northamptonshire safety cameras
www.northamptonshire.gov.uk/en/councilservices/Transport/roads/Pages/SafetyCameraSites.aspx

Leicester, Leicestershire & Rutland Safety Camera Scheme
www.speedorsafety.com

Nottinghamshire Safety Camera Partnership
www.nottspeed.com

South Yorkshire Safety Camera partnership
www.safetycamera.org

Safer Roads Humber
http://saferroadshumber.eastriding.gov.uk

Further information
www.dvla.gov.uk

www.thinkroadsafety.gov.uk

www.dft.gov.uk

www.road-safe.org

Key to map symbols

Motorway with junction number (22)	
Primary route – dual/single carriageway	
A road – dual/single carriageway	
B road – dual/single carriageway	
Minor road – dual/single carriageway	
Other minor road – dual/single carriageway	
Road under construction	
Tunnel, covered road	
Speed cameras – single, multiple	
Rural track, private road or narrow road in urban area	
Gate or obstruction to traffic – may not apply at all times or to all vehicles	
Path, bridleway, byway open to all traffic, restricted byway	
Pedestrianised area	
Postcode boundaries BS22	
County and unitary authority boundaries	
Railway with station	
Tunnel	
Railway under construction	
Metro station	
Private railway station	
Miniature railway	
Tramway, tram stop	
Tramway, tram stop under construction	
Bus, coach station	

Ambulance station	
Coastguard station	
Fire station	
Police station	
Accident and Emergency entrance to hospital	
Hospital	
Place of worship	
Information centre – open all year	
Shopping centre, parking	
Park and Ride, Post Office	
Camping site, caravan site	
Golf course, picnic site	
Non-Roman antiquity, Roman antiquity	

Church   ROMAN FORT

Univ	Important buildings, schools, colleges, universities and hospitals
	Woods, built-up area
River Medway	Water name
	River, weir
	Stream
	Canal, lock, tunnel
	Water
	Tidal water

Adjoining page indicators and overlap bands – the colour of the arrow and band indicates the scale of the adjoining or overlapping page (see scales below)

58 87
246

The dark grey border on the inside edge of some pages indicates that the mapping does not continue onto the adjacent page

The small numbers around the edges of the maps identify the 1-kilometre National Grid lines

Acad	Academy	Meml	Memorial
Allot Gdns	Allotments	Mon	Monument
Cemy	Cemetery	Mus	Museum
C Ctr	Civic centre	Obsy	Observatory
CH	Club house	Pal	Royal palace
Coll	College	PH	Public house
Crem	Crematorium	Recn Gd	Recreation ground
Ent	Enterprise		
Ex H	Exhibition hall	Resr	Reservoir
Ind Est	Industrial Estate	Ret Pk	Retail park
IRB Sta	Inshore rescue boat station	Sch	School
		Sh Ctr	Shopping centre
Inst	Institute	TH	Town hall / house
Ct	Law court	Trad Est	Trading estate
L Ctr	Leisure centre	Univ	University
LC	Level crossing	W Twr	Water tower
Liby	Library	Wks	Works
Mkt	Market	YH	Youth hostel

Enlarged maps only

	Railway or bus station building
	Place of interest
	Parkland

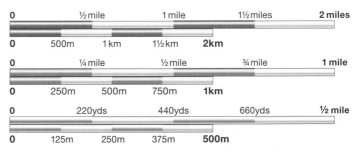

The map scale on the pages numbered in green is 1¾ inches to 1 mile
2.76 cm to 1 km • 1:36 206

0   ½ mile   1 mile   1½ miles   2 miles
0   500m   1 km   1½ km   2km

The map scale on the pages numbered in blue is 3½ inches to 1 mile
5.52 cm to 1 km • 1:18 103

0   ¼ mile   ½ mile   ¾ mile   1 mile
0   250m   500m   750m   1km

The map scale on the pages numbered in red is 7 inches to 1 mile
11.04 cm to 1 km • 1:9 051

0   220yds   440yds   660yds   ½ mile
0   125m   250m   375m   500m

IV

Key to map pages

136	Map pages at 1¾ inches to 1 mile
206	Map pages at 3½ inches to 1 mile
234	Map pages at 7 inches to 1 mile

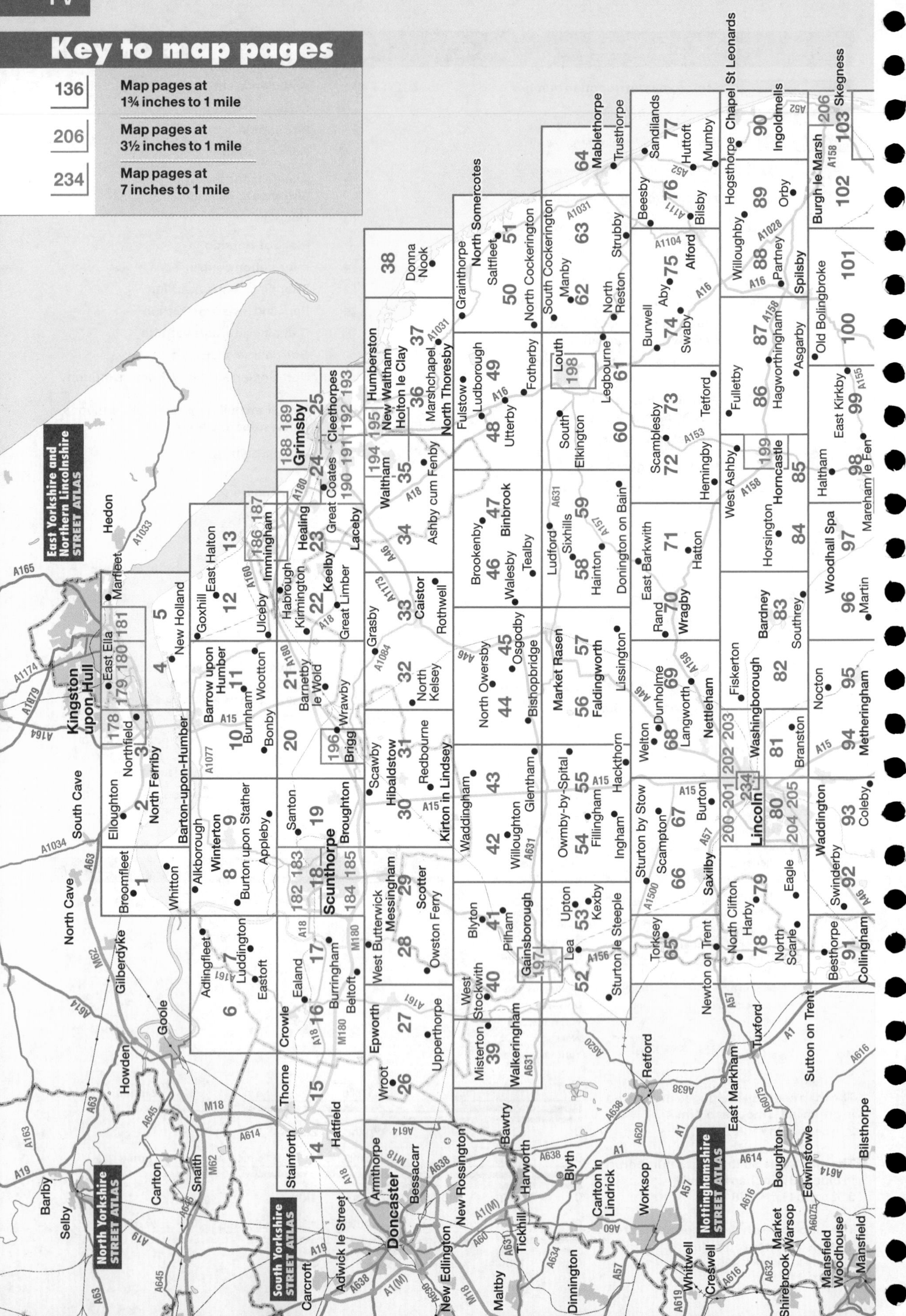

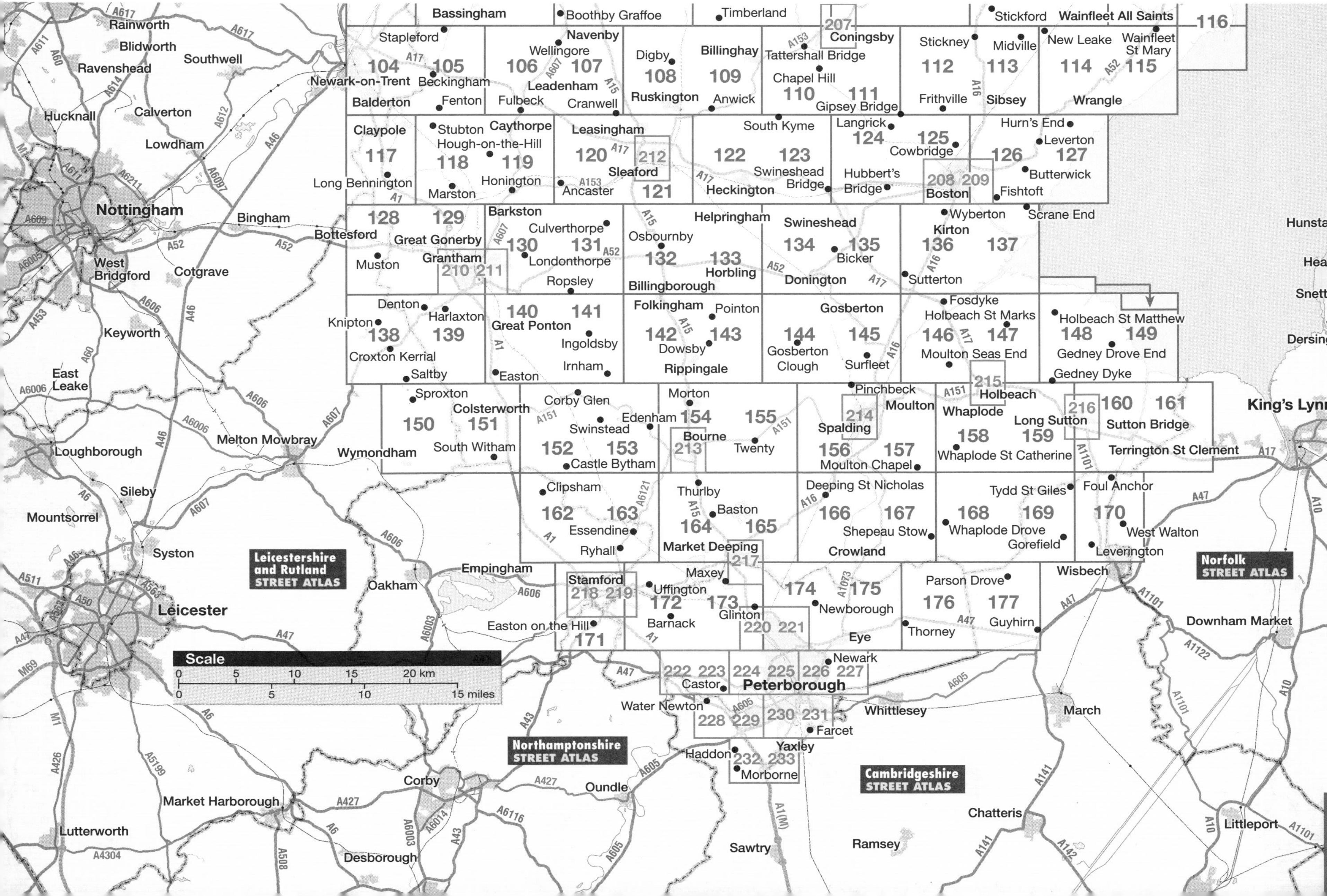

Norfolk STREET ATLAS

Cambridgeshire STREET ATLAS

Northamptonshire STREET ATLAS

Leicestershire and Rutland STREET ATLAS

King's Lynn

Hunstanton, Heacham, Snettisham, Dersingham, Downham Market, Littleport, Chatteris, Ramsey, March, Wisbech, Sawtry, Oundle, Corby, Desborough, Market Harborough, Lutterworth, Leicester, Syston, Sileby, Mountsorrel, Loughborough, East Leake, Keyworth, West Bridgford, Nottingham, Cotgrave, Bingham, Lowdham, Calverton, Southwell, Blidworth, Rainworth, Ravenshead, Hucknall, Blidworth

Stapleford, Bassingham, Boothby Graffoe, Timberland, Coningsby, Stickford, Wainfleet All Saints, Wainfleet St Mary, Midville, New Leake, Wrangle, Sibsey, Butterwick, Fishtoft, Leverton, Hurn's End, Scrane End, Gedney Dyke, Gedney Drove End, Holbeach St Matthew, Terrington St Clement, Sutton Bridge, West Walton, Leverington, Foul Anchor, Guyhirn, Parson Drove, Thorney, Whittlesey, Farcet, Yaxley, Morborne, Haddon, Castor, Water Newton, Newborough, Eye, Newark, Glinton, Peterborough, Maxey, Barnack, Uffington, Market Deeping, Thurlby, Baston, Deeping St Nicholas, Crowland, Shepeau Stow, Whaplode Drove, Gorefield, Tydd St Giles, Whaplode St Catherine, Long Sutton, Holbeach, Holbeach St Marks, Moulton Seas End, Fosdyke, Surfleet, Pinchbeck, Spalding, Moulton, Moulton Chapel, Gosberton Clough, Gosberton, Donington, Bicker, Swineshead, Swineshead Bridge, Helpringham, Heckington, Hubbert's Bridge, Cowbridge, Boston, Wyberton, Kirton, Sutterton, Langrick, Gipsey Bridge, Frithville, Stickney, Billinghay, Digby, Ruskington, Anwick, South Kyme, Leasingham, Sleaford, Ancaster, Cranwell, Leadenham, Wellingore, Navenby, Beckingham, Fenton, Stubton, Caythorpe, Hough-on-the-Hill, Honington, Marston, Barkston, Ropsley, Londonthorpe, Culverthorpe, Osbournby, Billingborough, Horbling, Folkingham, Pointon, Dowsby, Rippingale, Morton, Twenty, Bourne, Thurlby, Edenham, Swinstead, Corby Glen, Castle Bytham, Clipsham, Essendine, Ryhall, Stamford, Easton on the Hill, Empingham, Oakham, Great Ponton, Ingoldsby, Irnham, Great Gonerby, Grantham, Harlaxton, Denton, Knipton, Croxton Kerrial, Saltby, Sproxton, Colsterworth, South Witham, Wymondham, Muston, Bottesford, Long Bennington, Balderton, Newark-on-Trent, Claypole, Melton Mowbray

Grid numbers: 104, 105, 106, 107, 108, 109, 110, 111, 112, 113, 114, 115, 116, 117, 118, 119, 120, 121, 122, 123, 124, 125, 126, 127, 128, 129, 130, 131, 132, 133, 134, 135, 136, 137, 138, 139, 140, 141, 142, 143, 144, 145, 146, 147, 148, 149, 150, 151, 152, 153, 154, 155, 156, 157, 158, 159, 160, 161, 162, 163, 164, 165, 166, 167, 168, 169, 170, 171, 172, 173, 174, 175, 176, 177, 207, 208, 209, 210, 211, 212, 213, 214, 215, 216, 217, 218, 219, 220, 221, 222, 223, 224, 225, 226, 227, 228, 229, 230, 231, 232, 233

Scale: 0 5 10 15 miles / 0 5 10 15 20 km

Route planning

Scale

0 — 5 — 10 km

0 1 2 3 4 5 6 miles

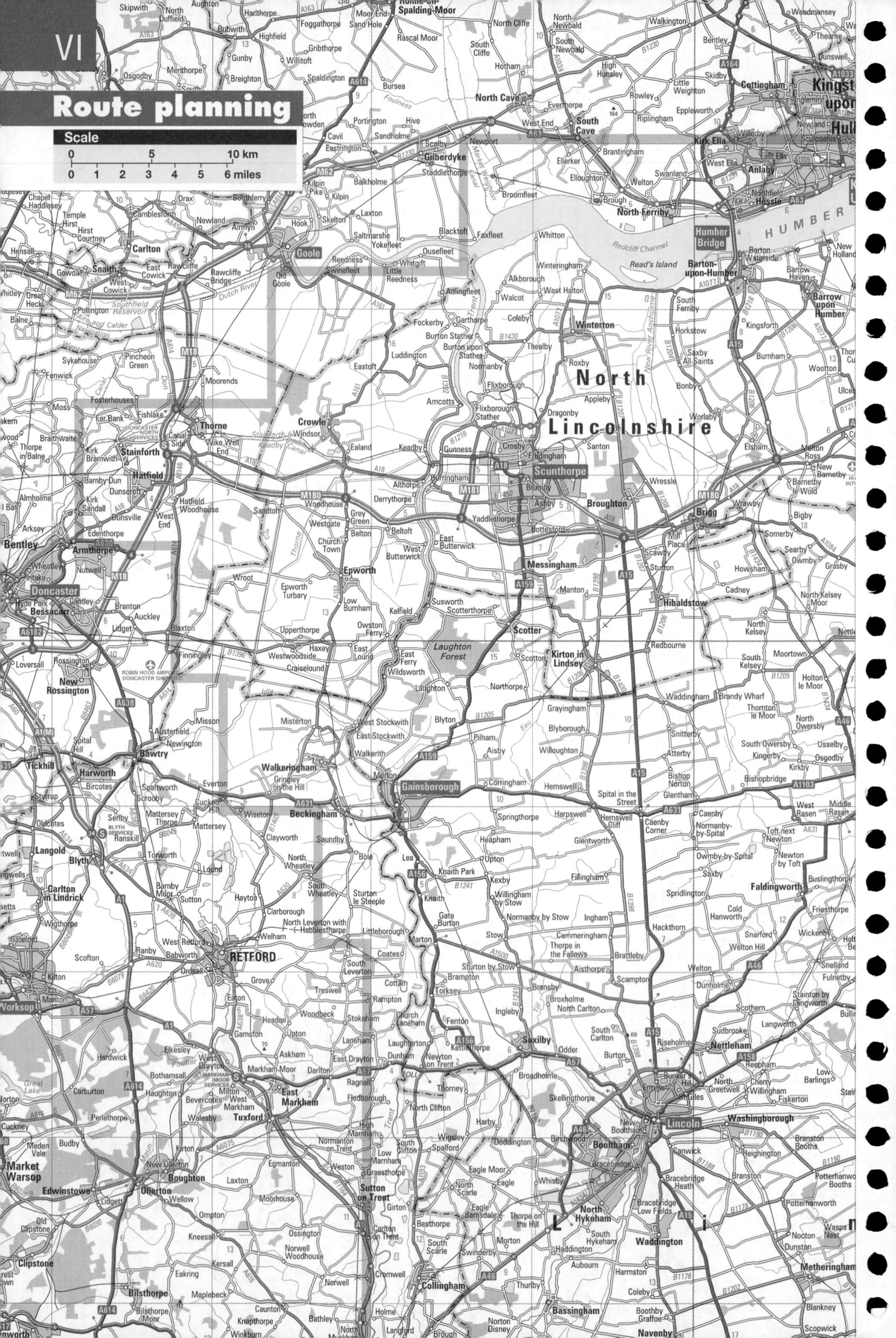

North Lincolnshire

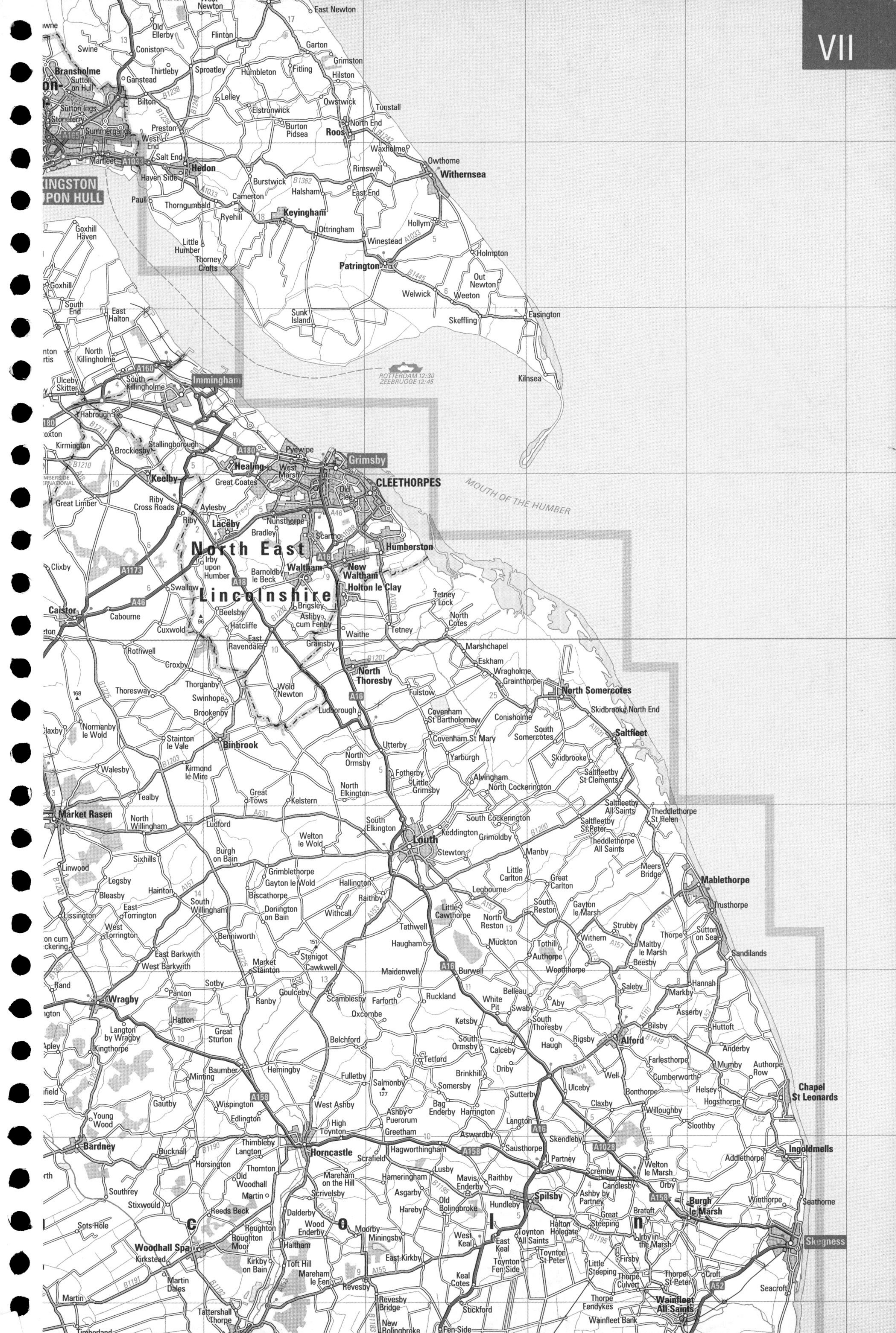
VII
East Newton
Old Ellerby
Flinton
Swine
Coniston
Garton
Grimston
Bransholme
Sutton on Hull
Thirtleby
Sproatley
Humbleton
Fitling
Hilston
Ganstead
Bilton
Lelley
Owstwick
Tunstall
Sutton Ings
Stoneferry
Elstronwick
North End
Summergangs
Preston
Burton Pidsea
Roos
West End
Waxholme
Salt End
Marfleet
Hedon
Owthorne
Withernsea
Rimswell
Haven Side
KINGSTON UPON HULL
Burstwick
Halsham
East End
Paull
Camerton
Thorngumbald
Ryehill
Keyingham
Hollym
Goxhill Haven
Ottringham
Winestead
Little Humber
Thorney Crofts
Holmpton
Patrington
Out Newton
Goxhill
Welwick
Weeton
South End
East Halton
Sunk Island
Skeffling
Easington
North Killingholme
South Killingholme
Immingham
ROTTERDAM 12:30
ZEEBRUGGE 12:45
Kilnsea
Ulceby Skitter
Habrough
Kirmington
Brocklesby
Stallingborough
Pyewipe
Grimsby
Healing
West Marsh
Keelby
Great Coates
Old Clee
CLEETHORPES
MOUTH OF THE HUMBER
Great Limber
Riby Cross Roads
Aylesby
Riby
Laceby
Nunsthorpe
Bradley
Scartho
Humberston
North East Lincolnshire
Clixby
Irby upon Humber
Barnoldby le Beck
Waltham
New Waltham
Holton le Clay
Swallow
Brigsley
Tetney Lock
Caistor
Cabourne
Beelsby
Ashby cum Fenby
North Cotes
Cuxwold
Hatcliffe
Waithe
Tetney
East Ravendale
Grainsby
Marshchapel
Rothwell
Croxby
North Thoresby
Eskham
Wragholme
Grainthorpe
Thorganby
Thoresway
Wold Newton
Swinhope
Fulstow
North Somercotes
Brookenby
Ludborough
Covenham St Bartholomew
Conisholme
Skidbrooke North End
Normanby le Wold
Stainton le Vale
Binbrook
Covenham St Mary
South Somercotes
Saltfleet
Utterby
Kirmond le Mire
Walesby
North Ormsby
Yarburgh
Skidbrooke
Fotherby
Alvingham
Saltfleetby St Clements
Little Grimsby
North Cockerington
Tealby
Great Tows
Kelstern
North Elkington
Saltfleetby All Saints
Theddlethorpe St Helen
Market Rasen
North Willingham
Ludford
South Elkington
South Cockerington
Saltfleetby St Peter
Keddington
Grimoldby
Louth
Welton le Wold
Theddlethorpe All Saints
Stewton
Burgh on Bain
Sixhills
Manby
Meers Bridge
Linwood
Little Carlton
Great Carlton
Mablethorpe
Grimblethorpe
Gayton le Wold
Legsby
Hallington
Legbourne
Hainton
Bleasby
Biscathorpe
Raithby
South Reston
Trusthorpe
Gayton le Marsh
South Willingham
East Torrington
Donington on Bain
Withcall
Little Cawthorpe
North Reston
Lissington
Strubby
West Torrington
Tathwell
Sutton on Sea
Benniworth
Thorpe
Withern
Tothill
Haugham
Muckton
Maltby le Marsh
Sandilands
East Barkwith
Market Stainton
Stenigot
Authorpe
West Barkwith
Cawkwell
Beesby
Woodthorpe
Burwell
Maidenwell
Rand
Hannah
Saleby
Sotby
Markby
Panton
Goulceby
Ruckland
Belleau
Wragby
Ranby
Scamblesby
Farforth
White Pit
Aby
Swaby
Asserby
Oxcombe
Hatton
Langton by Wragby
Ketsby
South Thoresby
Bilsby
Huttoft
Great Sturton
Belchford
South Ormsby
Rigsby
Apley
Kingthorpe
Alford
Haugh
Calceby
Anderby
Tetford
Farlesthorpe
Baumber
Minting
Hemingby
Brinkhill
Driby
Mumby
Authorpe Row
Cumberworth
Fulletby
Salmonby
Somersby
Well
Chapel St Leonards
Sutterby
Ulceby
Bonthorpe
Helsey
Gautby
Wispington
West Ashby
Hogsthorpe
Bag Enderby
Harrington
Claxby
Young Wood
Ashby Puerorum
Edlington
High Toynton
Willoughby
Langton
Greetham
Sloothby
Aswardby
Skendleby
Bardney
Thimbleby
Horncastle
Hagworthingham
Sausthorpe
Ingoldmells
Bucknall
Langton
Addlethorpe
Scrafield
Partney
Horsington
Thornton
Lusby
Scremby
Welton le Marsh
Old Woodhall
Mareham on the Hill
Hameringham
Mavis Enderby
Raithby
Candlesby
Orby
Southrey
Martin
Scrivelsby
Asgarby
Ashby by Partney
Hundleby
Spilsby
Burgh le Marsh
Winthorpe
Stixwould
Seathorne
Reeds Beck
Old Bolingbroke
Hareby
Bratoft
Dalderby
Great Steeping
Sots Hole
Roughton
Wood Enderby
Moorby
Halton Holegate
Toynton All Saints
Irby in the Marsh
Skegness
Roughton Moor
Miningsby
West Keal
East Keal
Woodhall Spa
Haltham
Toynton St Peter
Firsby
Kirkstead
Kirkby on Bain
Toft Hill
East Kirkby
Toynton Fen Side
Little Steeping
Croft
Mareham le Fen
Keal Cotes
Thorpe Culvert
Thorpe St Peter
Seacroft
Martin Dales
Revesby
Martin
Revesby Bridge
Thorpe Fendykes
Wainfleet All Saints
Tattershall Thorpe
Stickford
Wainfleet Bank
Timberland
New Bolingbroke
Fen Side
A1033
A165
A160
A180
A18
A1173
A46
A16
A1031
A631
A157
A153
A158
A1104
A52
A1028
A155
B1362
B1445
B1242
B1201
B1200
B1225
B1203
B1202
B1190
B1183
B1195
B1196
B1449
B1191
B1192

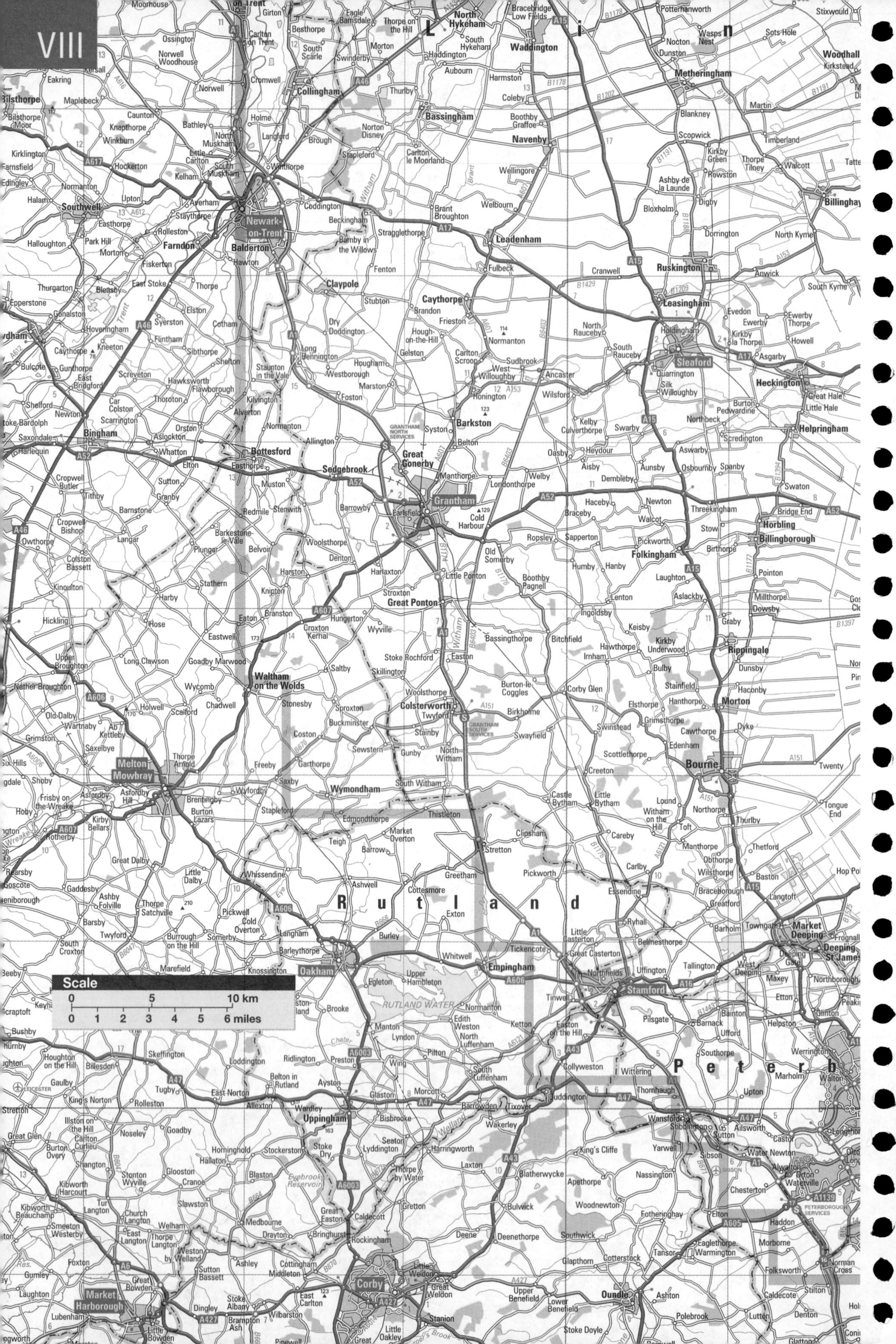
Moorhouse
Girton
Eagle Barnsdale
Thorpe on the Hill
North Hykeham
Bracebridge Low Fields
Potterhanworth
Stixwould
Ossington
Carlton on Trent
Besthorpe
South Scarle
Morton
South Hykeham
Waddington
Nocton
Wasps Nest
Sots Hole
Woodhall
Kirkstead
Norwell Woodhouse
Swinderby
Haddington
Dunston
Metheringham
Eakring
Cromwell
Collingham
Aubourn
Harmston
Norwell
Thurlby
Coleby
Bilsthorpe
Maplebeck
Bassingham
Boothby Graffoe
Blankney
Martin
Bilsthorpe Moor
Caunton
Bathley
Holme
Norton Disney
Knapthorpe
Winkburn
North Muskham
Langford
Brough
Navenby
Scopwick
Timberland
Kirklington
Little Carlton
South Muskham
Stapleford
Carlton le Moorland
Kirkby Green
Thorpe Tilney
Walcott
Farnsfield
Hockerton
Kelham
Winthorpe
Wellingore
Rowston
Edingley
Normanton
Ashby de la Launde
Halam
Upton
Averham
Coddington
Brant Broughton
Welbourn
Bloxholm
Digby
Billinghay
Southwell
Staythorpe
Newark-on-Trent
Beckingham
Easthorpe
Rolleston
Stragglethorpe
Leadenham
Dorrington
North Kyme
Halloughton
Park Hill
Morton
Farndon
Balderton
Barnby in the Willows
Fiskerton
Hawton
Fenton
Fulbeck
Cranwell
Ruskington
Anwick
Thurgarton
Bleasby
East Stoke
Thorpe
Claypole
South Kyme
Epperstone
Elston
Stubton
Caythorpe
Leasingham
Evedon
Gonalston
Syerston
Cotham
Brandon
Dry Doddington
Frieston
Normanton
North Rauceby
Holdingham
Ewerby
Ewerby Thorpe
Hoveringham
Flintham
Hough-on-the-Hill
Kirkby la Thorpe
Caythorpe
Kneeton
Sibthorpe
Long Bennington
Gelston
Carlton Scroop
South Rauceby
Sleaford
Asgarby
Howell
Bulcote
Gunthorpe
Shelton
Staunton in the Vale
Hougham
Sudbrook
West Willoughby
Ancaster
Quarrington
Heckington
East Bridgford
Screveton
Hawksworth
Westborough
Marston
Honington
Silk Willoughby
Shelford
Car Colston
Flawborough
Kilvington
Foston
Wilsford
Burton Pedwardine
Great Hale
Little Hale
Newton
Thoroton
Alverton
Barkston
Kelby
Culverthorpe
Swarby
Northbeck
Helpringham
Stoke Bardolph
Scarrington
Orston
Normanton
Syston
Saxondale
Bingham
Aslockton
Allington
Great Gonerby
Belton
Heydour
Aswarby
Scredington
Harlequin
Whatton
Bottesford
Sedgebrook
Oasby
Aisby
Aunsby
Osbournby
Spanby
Elton
Easthorpe
Manthorpe
Welby
Dembleby
Cropwell Butler
Sutton
Muston
Londonthorpe
Swaton
Tithby
Granby
Grantham
Haceby
Newton
Threekingham
Bridge End
Barnstone
Redmile
Stenwith
Barrowby
Earlsfield
Cold Harbour
Braceby
Walcot
Horbling
Cropwell Bishop
Stow
Billingborough
Langar
Barkestone-le-Vale
Ropsley
Sapperton
Pickworth
Owthorpe
Woolsthorpe
Old Somerby
Folkingham
Birthorpe
Plungar
Belvoir
Denton
Humby
Hanby
Colston Bassett
Harston
Harlaxton
Little Ponton
Boothby Pagnell
Laughton
Pointon
Kinoulton
Stathern
Knipton
Stroxton
Lenton
Aslackby
Millthorpe
Great Ponton
Dowsby
Harby
Branston
Ingoldsby
Hickling
Hose
Eaton
Hungerton
Croxton Kerrial
Wyville
Keisby
Graby
Eastwell
Bassingthorpe
Bitchfield
Hawthorpe
Kirkby Underwood
Rippingale
Upper Broughton
Long Clawson
Goadby Marwood
Stoke Rochford
Easton
Irnham
Bulby
Dunsby
Skillington
Nether Broughton
Waltham on the Wolds
Saltby
Burton-le-Coggles
Corby Glen
Stainfield
Haconby
Wycomb
Chadwell
Woolsthorpe
Colsterworth
Elsthorpe
Hanthorpe
Morton
Holwell
Scalford
Stonesby
Sproxton
Twyford
Birkholme
Grimsthorpe
Dyke
Old Dalby
Wartnaby
Ab Kettleby
Buckminster
Stainby
Swayfield
Swinstead
Cawthorpe
Grimston
Saxelbye
Coston
Sewstern
Gunby
North Witham
Edenham
Scottlethorpe
Six Hills
Thorpe Arnold
Freeby
Garthorpe
Bourne
Twenty
Shoby
Melton Mowbray
Saxby
Creeton
Frisby on the Wreake
Asfordby
Asfordby Hill
Brentingby
Wyfordby
Wymondham
South Witham
Castle Bytham
Little Bytham
Tongue End
Hoby
Kirby Bellars
Burton Lazars
Stapleford
Edmondthorpe
Thistleton
Lound
Witham on the Hill
Northorpe
Thurlby
Rotherby
Market Overton
Clipsham
Careby
Toft
Teigh
Barrow
Stretton
Manthorpe
Thetford
Rearsby
Great Dalby
Little Dalby
Whissendine
Greetham
Pickworth
Carlby
Obthorpe
Wilsthorpe
Baston
Gaddesby
Ashwell
Cottesmore
Essendine
Braceborough
Langtoft
Ashby Folville
Thorpe Satchville
Pickwell
Cold Overton
Exton
Greatford
Rutland
Barsby
Twyford
Burrough on the Hill
Somerby
Langham
Burley
Ryhall
Barholm
Towngate
Market Deeping
Frognall
Deeping St James
Croxton
Barleythorpe
Little Casterton
Belmesthorpe
South Croxton
Marefield
Knossington
Oakham
Whitwell
Tickencote
Empingham
Great Casterton
Uffington
Tallington
West Deeping
Deeping Gate
Northborough
Egleton
Upper Hambleton
Northfields
Stamford
Maxey
Scale
0 5 10 km
0 1 2 3 4 5 6 miles
Keyham
Braunston
Rutland Water
Normanton
Tinwell
Etton
Peakirk
Brooke
Edith Weston
Pilsgate
Bainton
Glinton
Bushby
Manton
Ketton
Easton on the Hill
Barnack
Ufford
Helpston
Lyndon
North Luffenham
Southorpe
Werrington
Skeffington
Chater
Houghton on the Hill
Billesdon
Loddington
Ridlington
Preston
Wing
Pilton
South Luffenham
Collyweston
Wittering
Peterb
Marholm
Walton
Gaulby
Tugby
East Norton
Belton in Rutland
Ayston
Glaston
Morcott
Thornhaugh
Upton
Leicester
King's Norton
Rolleston
Allexton
Wardley
Barrowden
Tixover
Duddington
Wansford
Stibbington
Ailsworth
Stretton
Illston on the Hill
Noseley
Goadby
Uppingham
Bisbrooke
Seaton
Wakerley
Sutton
Castor
Longthorpe
Great Glen
Carlton Curlieu
Burton Overy
Horninghold
Stockerston
Stoke Dry
Lyddington
Harringworth
King's Cliffe
Yarwell
Sibson
Water Newton
Welland
Shangton
Hallaton
Laxton
Nassington
Alwalton
Orton Waterville
Stonton Wyville
Glooston
Cranoe
Blaston
Eyebrook Reservoir
Thorpe by Water
Blatherwycke
Apethorpe
Chesterton
Kibworth Harcourt
Slawston
Gretton
Bulwick
Woodnewton
Kibworth Beauchamp
Tur Langton
Church Langton
Medbourne
Great Easton
Caldecott
Fotheringhay
Elton
Haddon
Peterborough Services
Smeeton Westerby
Welham
East Langton
Thorpe Langton
Drayton
Bringhurst
Rockingham
Deene
Deenethorpe
Southwick
Eaglethorpe
Warmington
Tansor
Morborne
Norman Cross
Foxton
Weston by Welland
Sutton Bassett
Ashley
Cottingham
Middleton
Little Weldon
Glapthorn
Cotterstock
Folksworth
Gumley
Great Bowden
Corby
Great Weldon
Upper Benefield
Oundle
Ashton
Stilton
Laughton
Market Harborough
Dingley
Stoke Albany
East Carlton
Lower Benefield
Caldecote
Lubenham
Brampton Ash
Wilbarston
Stanion
Polebrook
Lutton
Denton
Little Bowden
Little Oakley
Great Oakley
Stoke Doyle
Pipewell
Glatton
A1
A15
A17
A46
A52
A606
A607
A47
A43
A6003
A427
A6
A16
A151
A153
A612
A617
A6121
A1139
A605
B1178
B1202
B1191
B1429
B1209
B6403
B1176
B1177
B1394
B1397
B1443
B664
B670
B6047
B676
B668
Trent
Witham
Brant
Eye
Wreake
Grantham North Services
Grantham South Services

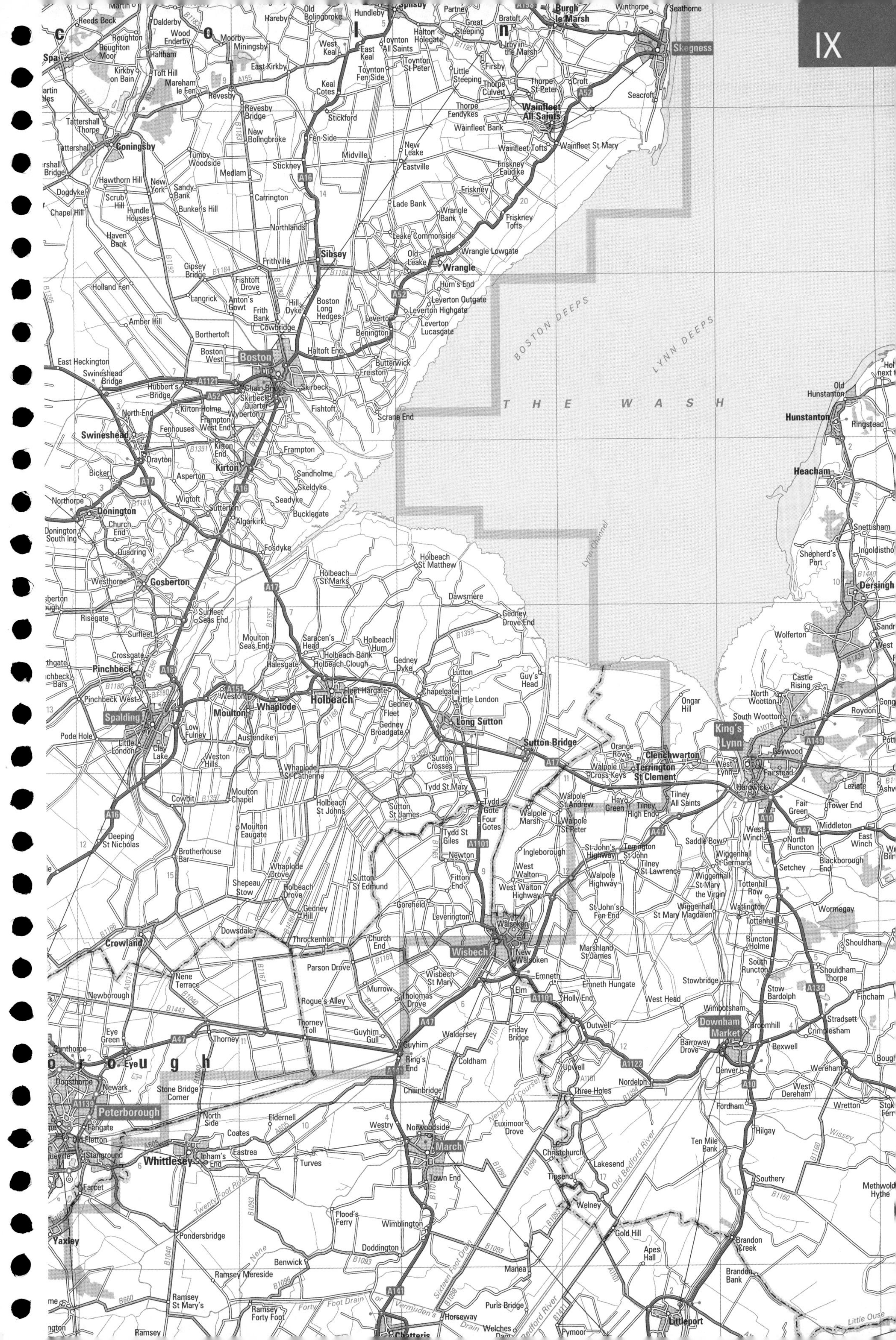
Skegness
Burgh le Marsh
Spilsby
Hundleby
Old Bolingbroke
Hareby
Partney
Bratoft
Winthorpe
Seathorne
Reeds Beck
Dalderby
Roughton
Roughton Moor
Wood Enderby
Moorby
Miningsby
West Keal
East Keal
Toynton All Saints
Halton Holegate
Great Steeping
Irby in the Marsh
Haltham
Kirkby on Bain
Toft Hill
Mareham le Fen
Revesby
East Kirkby
Toynton Fen Side
Toynton St Peter
Little Steeping
Firsby
Thorpe Culvert
Thorpe St Peter
Croft
Seacroft
Keal Cotes
Stickford
Revesby Bridge
New Bolingbroke
Tattershall Thorpe
Tattershall
Coningsby
Thorpe Fendykes
Wainfleet All Saints
Wainfleet Bank
Wainfleet Tofts
Wainfleet St Mary
Fen Side
Midville
New Leake
Eastville
Tumby Woodside
Medlam
Stickney
Friskney Eaudike
Friskney
Friskney Tofts
Hawthorn Hill
New York
Sandy Bank
Dogdyke
Scrub Hill
Hundle Houses
Bunker's Hill
Carrington
Lade Bank
Wrangle Bank
Chapel Hill
Haven Bank
Northlands
Leake Commonside
Sibsey
Old Leake
Wrangle
Wrangle Lowgate
Frithville
Gipsey Bridge
Holland Fen
Fishtoft Drove
Langrick
Anton's Gowt
Frith Bank
Hill Dyke
Boston Long Hedges
Hurn's End
Leverton Outgate
Leverton Highgate
Leverton
Leverton Lucasgate
Benington
Amber Hill
Cowbridge
Borthertoft
Boston West
Boston
Haltoft End
Butterwick
Freiston
East Heckington
Swineshead Bridge
Hubbert's Bridge
Chain Bridge
Skirbeck
Skirbeck Quarter
Fishtoft
Scrane End
North End
Kirton Holme
Wyberton
Frampton West End
Fenhouses
Swineshead
Drayton
Kirton End
Frampton
Kirton
Bicker
Asperton
Sandholme
Skeldyke
Northorpe
Wigtoft
Seadyke
Donington
Sutterton
Bucklegate
Algarkirk
Donington South Ing
Church End
Quadring
Fosdyke
Westhorpe
Gosberton
Holbeach St Matthew
Holbeach St Marks
Surfleet Seas End
Surfleet
Risegate
Dawsmere
Gedney Drove End
Moulton Seas End
Saracen's Head
Holbeach Hurn
Holbeach Bank
Holbeach Clough
Halesgate
Crossgate
Pinchbeck
Pinchbeck West
Gedney Dyke
Lutton
Guy's Head
Fleet Hargate
Holbeach
Whaplode
Weston
Moulton
Spalding
Gedney
Fleet
Chapelgate
Little London
Long Sutton
Gedney Broadgate
Low Fulney
Austendike
Pode Hole
Little London
Clay Lake
Weston Hills
Sutton Crosses
Sutton Bridge
Whaplode St Catherine
Tydd St Mary
Cowbit
Moulton Chapel
Holbeach St Johns
Sutton St James
Tydd Gote
Four Gotes
Deeping St Nicholas
Moulton Eaugate
Tydd St Giles
Newton
Brotherhouse Bar
Whaplode Drove
Shepeau Stow
Holbeach Drove
Sutton St Edmund
Fitton End
Gedney Hill
Gorefield
Leverington
Dowsdale
Crowland
Throckenholt
Church End
Parson Drove
Wisbech
Wisbech St Mary
Murrow
Nene Terrace
Newborough
Rogue's Alley
Tholomas Drove
Thorney Toll
Eye Green
Thorney
Guyhirn Gull
Guyhirn
Ring's End
Waldersey
Coldham
Gunthorpe
Eye
Dogsthorpe
Newark
Stone Bridge Corner
Chainbridge
Peterborough
North Side
Eldernell
Fengate
Old Fletton
Coates
Westry
Norwoodside
Stanground
Whittlesey
Inham's End
Eastrea
Turves
March
Farcet
Town End
Twenty Foot River
Flood's Ferry
Wimblington
Pondersbridge
Yaxley
Doddington
Nene
Benwick
Ramsey Mereside
Ramsey St Mary's
Ramsey Forty Foot
Ramsey
Forty Foot Drain
Vermuden's Drain
Sixteen Foot Drain
Chatteris
Horseway
Welches Dam
Manea
Purls Bridge
Old Bedford River
Pymoor
Littleport
Little Ouse
Apes Hall
Gold Hill
Welney
Tipsend
Lakesend
Christchurch
Euximoor Drove
Nene (Old Course)
Three Holes
Upwell
Nordelph
Outwell
Friday Bridge
Elm
Emneth
Emneth Hungate
Holly End
New Walsoken
Walsoken
Marshland St James
West Walton Highway
West Walton
Ingleborough
Walpole Highway
St John's Fen End
St John's Highway
Terrington St John
Tilney St Lawrence
Walpole St Peter
Walpole St Andrew
Walpole Marsh
Walpole Cross Keys
Orange Row
Terrington St Clement
Clenchwarton
Hay Green
Tilney High End
Tilney All Saints
Ongar Hill
King's Lynn
West Lynn
Gaywood
Fairstead
Hardwick
South Wootton
North Wootton
Castle Rising
Roydon
Wolferton
Sandringham
West Newton
Dersingham
Ingoldisthorpe
Shepherd's Port
Snettisham
Heacham
Hunstanton
Old Hunstanton
Ringstead
Holme next the Sea
Leziate
Ashwicken
Tower End
Fair Green
Middleton
East Winch
West Winch
North Runcton
Saddle Bow
Wiggenhall St Germans
Wiggenhall St Mary the Virgin
Wiggenhall St Mary Magdalen
Tottenhill Row
Tottenhill
Watlington
Setchey
Blackborough End
Wormegay
Runcton Holme
South Runcton
Shouldham
Shouldham Thorpe
Stowbridge
West Head
Stow Bardolph
Fincham
Wimbotsham
Downham Market
Stradsett
Crimplesham
Barroway Drove
Bexwell
Denver
Wereham
Boughton
West Dereham
Fordham
Wretton
Stoke Ferry
Hilgay
Wissey
Ten Mile Bank
Southery
Methwold Hythe
Brandon Creek
Brandon Bank
BOSTON DEEPS
LYNN DEEPS
THE WASH
Lynn Channel
A16
A52
A17
A151
A1121
A47
A1101
A1122
A10
A149
A148
A1078
A134
A141
A605
A1139
A1073
A155
A153
A158
B1183
B1184
B1192
B1195
B1391
B1397
B1357
B1359
B1356
B1180
B1168
B1165
B1166
B1169
B1187
B1167
B1443
B1040
B1093
B1099
B1098
B1096
B1101
B1160
B1439
B1440
B1411
B1094
B660
A1101

Major administrative and Postcode boundaries

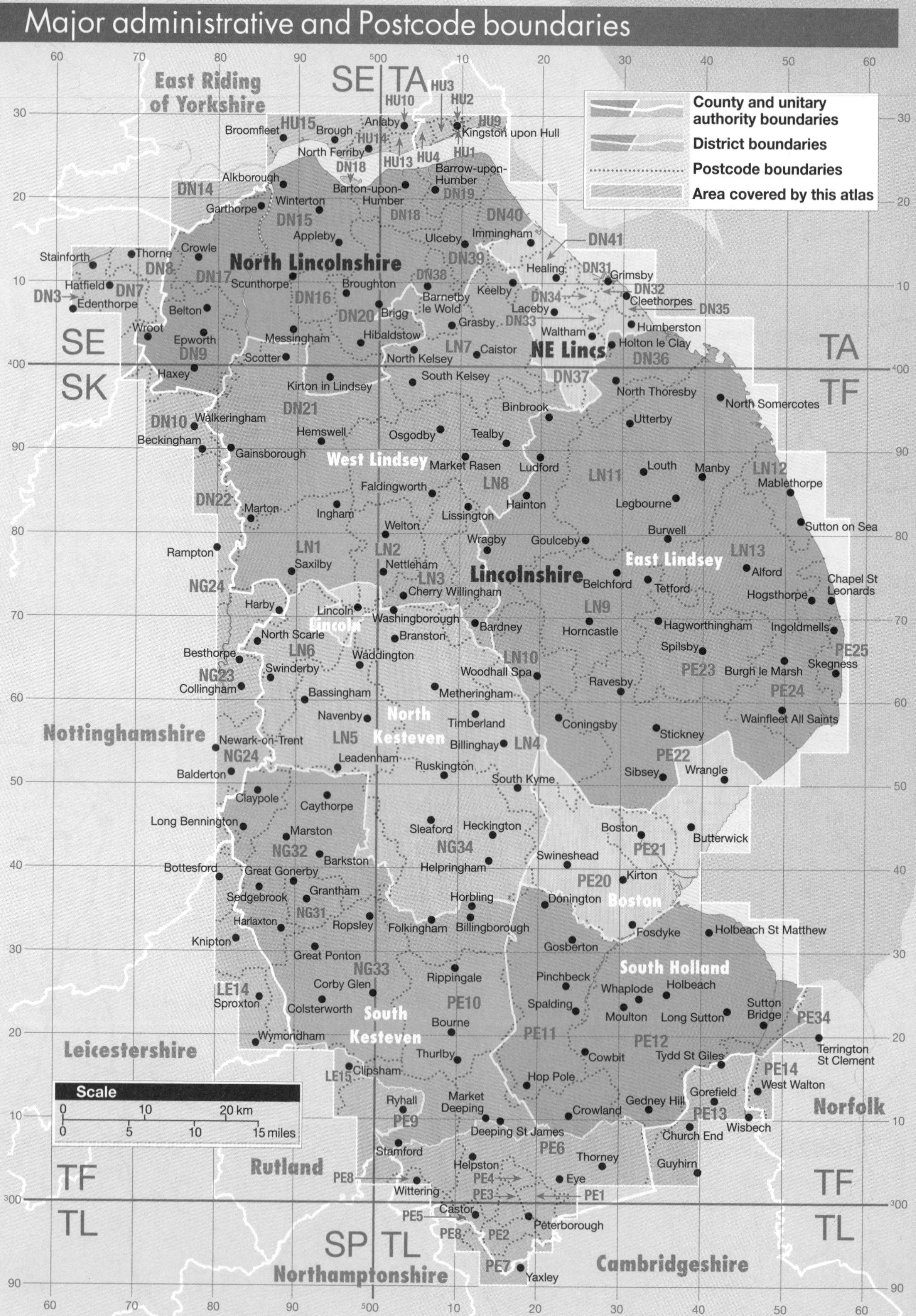

Legend:
- County and unitary authority boundaries
- District boundaries
- Postcode boundaries
- Area covered by this atlas

Scale
0   10   20 km
0   5   10   15 miles

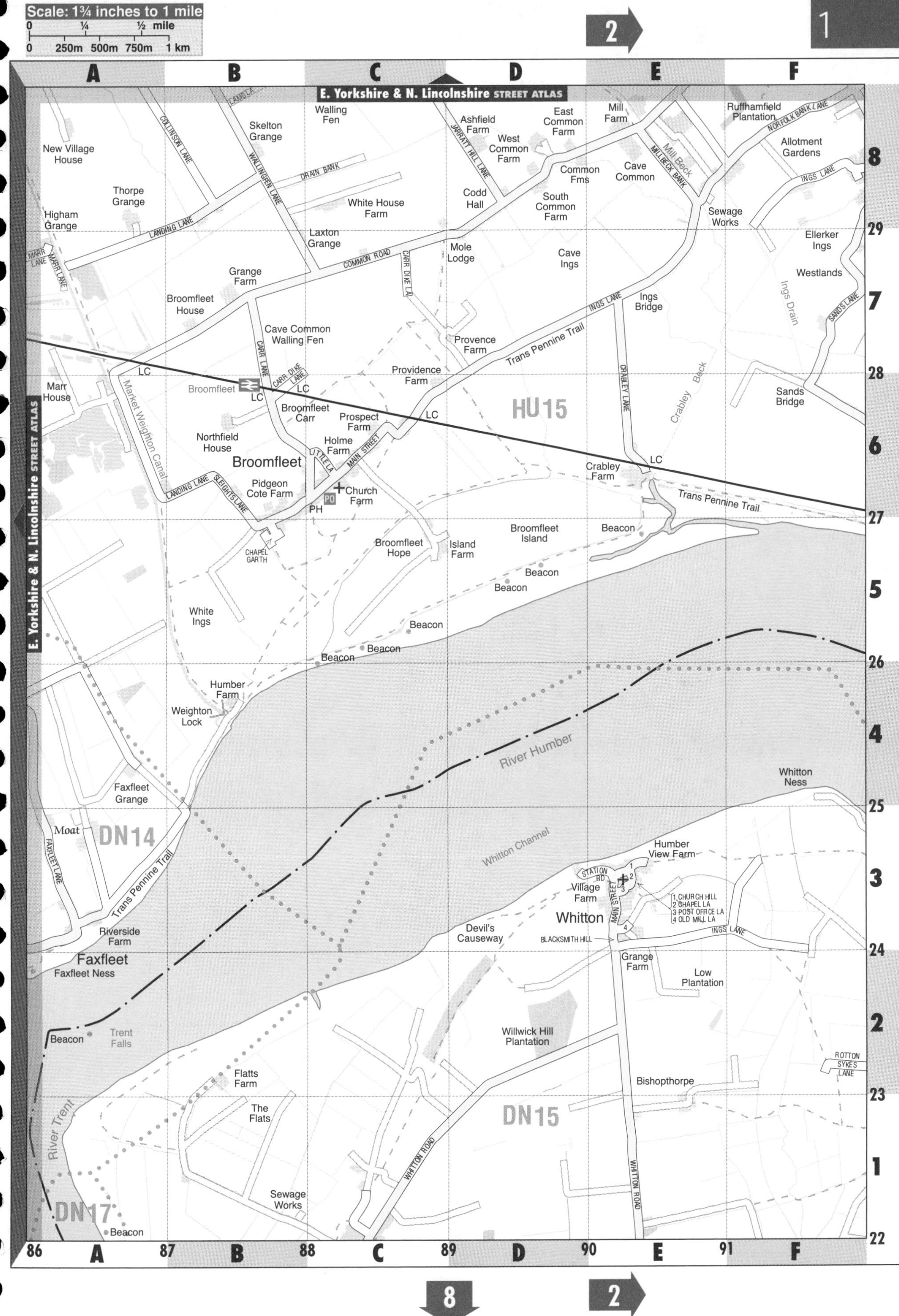

Scale: 1¾ inches to 1 mile

0   ¼   ½ mile

0   250m   500m   750m   1 km

New Village House

Higham Grange

Thorpe Grange

Skelton Grange

LEADS LA

Walling Fen

COLLINSON LANE

DRAIN BANK

WALLINGFEN LANE

LANDING LANE

MARR LANE

White House Farm

Laxton Grange

Ashfield Farm

West Common Farm

Codd Hall

JIBRATT HILL LANE

COMMON ROAD

East Common Farm

Common Fms

South Common Farm

Mill Farm

Cave Common

Mole Lodge

CARR DYKE LA

Ruffhamfield Plantation

NORFOLK BANK LANE

Allotment Gardens

INGS LANE

MILL BECK BANK

Mill Beck

Sewage Works

Ellerker Ings

Westlands

8

29

Grange Farm

Broomfleet House

Cave Common Walling Fen

CARR DYKE LANE

Provence Farm

Providence Farm

Trans Pennine Trail

INGS LANE

Ings Bridge

Ings Lane

Ings Drain

SANDS LANE

7

28

Marr House

Broomfleet

LC

Market Weighton Canal

LC

Broomfleet Carr

LC

Prospect Farm

LC

CRABLEY LANE

Crabley Beck

HU 15

Sands Bridge

Northfield House

Holme Farm

LITTLE LA

MAIN STREET

LC

Crabley Farm

LC

Trans Pennine Trail

6

27

Broomfleet

Pidgeon Cote Farm

LANDING LANE

SLEIGHTS LANE

Church Farm

PO

PH

Broomfleet Hope

Island Farm

Broomfleet Island

Beacon

Beacon

5

CHAPEL GARTH

Beacon

Beacon

White Ings

Beacon

Beacon

26

Humber Farm

Weighton Lock

Whitton Ness

4

Faxfleet Grange

Moat

DN 14

FAXFLEET LANE

Trans Pennine Trail

River Humber

25

Whitton Channel

Humber View Farm

3

Riverside Farm

STATION RD

Village Farm

Whitton

1 2 3 4

1 CHURCH HILL
2 CHAPEL LA
3 POST OFFICE LA
4 OLD MILL LA

INGS LANE

MAIN STREET

Faxfleet

Faxfleet Ness

Devil's Causeway

BLACKSMITH HILL

Grange Farm

Low Plantation

24

Beacon

Trent Falls

Flatts Farm

Willwick Hill Plantation

Bishopthorpe

ROTTON SYKES LANE

2

River Trent

The Flats

Sewage Works

WHITTON ROAD

DN 15

WHITTON ROAD

23

1

DN 17

Beacon

22

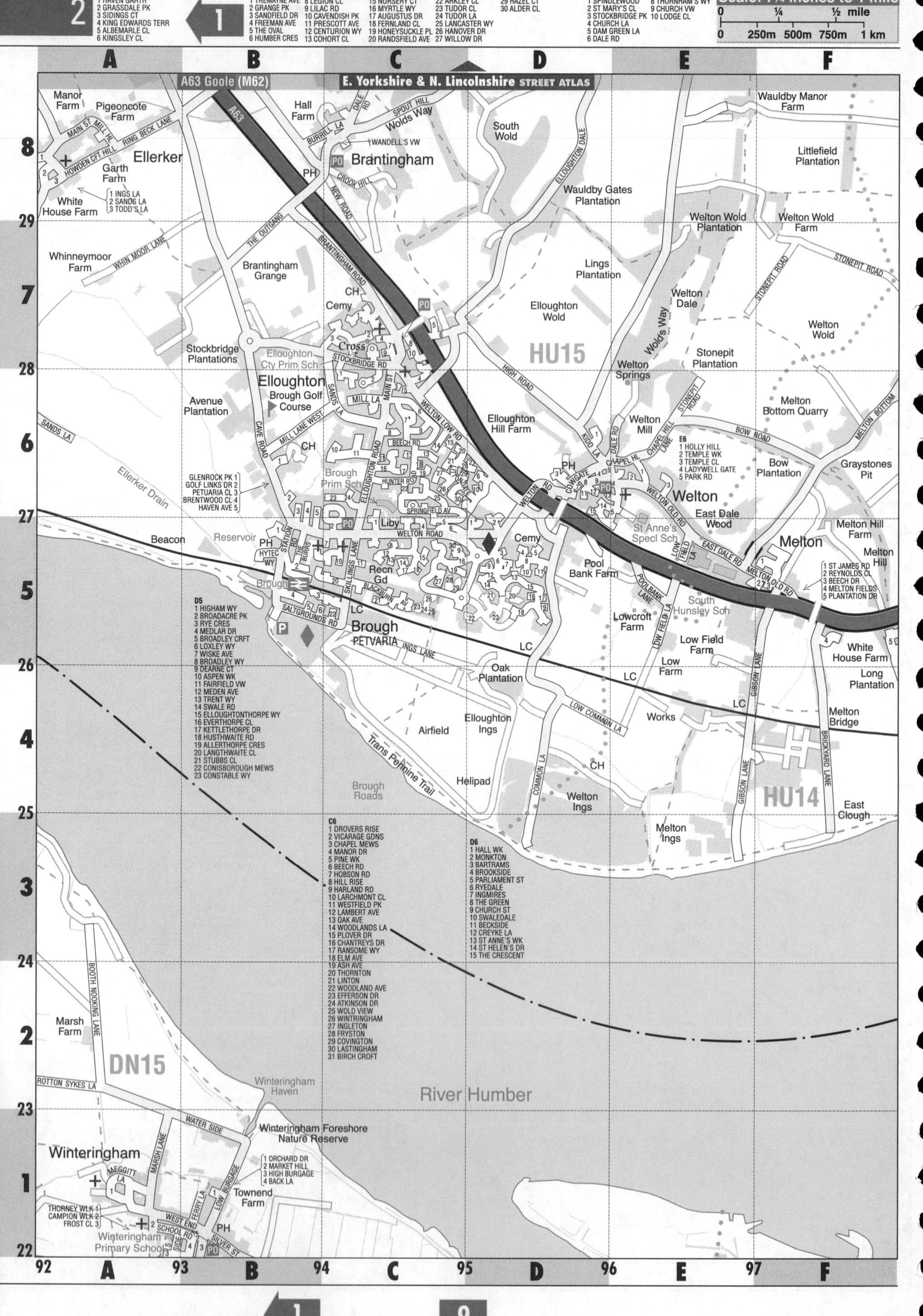

Scale: 1¾ inches to 1 mile

B5
1 HAVEN GARTH
2 GRASSDALE PK
3 SIDINGS CT
4 KING EDWARDS TERR
5 ALBEMARLE CL
6 KINGSLEY CL

C5
1 TREMAYNE AVE
2 GRANGE PK
3 SANDFIELD DR
4 FREEMAN AVE
5 THE OVAL
6 HUMBER CRES
7 WRYGARTH AVE
8 LEGION CL
9 LILAC RD
10 CAVENDISH PK
11 PRESCOTT AVE
12 CENTURION WY
13 COHORT CL
14 FRESH FIELDS
15 NURSERY CT
16 MYRTLE WY
17 AUGUSTUS DR
18 FERNLAND CL
19 HONEYSUCKLE PL
20 RANDSFIELD AVE
21 BUCCANEER WY
22 ARKLEY CL
23 TUDOR CL
24 TUDOR LA
25 LANCASTER WY
26 HANOVER DR
27 WILLOW DR
28 BIRCH CL
29 HAZEL CT
30 ALDER CL

C7
1 SPINDLEWOOD
2 ST MARY'S CL
3 STOCKBRIDGE PK
4 CHURCH LA
5 DAM GREEN LA
6 DALE RD
7 CHURCH ST
8 THORNHAM'S WY
9 CHURCH VW
10 LODGE CL

D5
1 HIGHAM WY
2 BROADACRE PK
3 RYE CRES
4 MEDLAR DR
5 BROADLEY CRFT
6 LOXLEY WY
7 WISKE AVE
8 BROADLEY WY
9 DEARNE CT
10 ASPEN WK
11 FAIRFIELD VW
12 MEDEN AVE
13 TRENT WY
14 SWALE RD
15 ELLOUGHTONTHORPE WY
16 EVERTHORPE CL
17 KETTLETHORPE DR
18 HUSTHWAITE RD
19 ALLERTHORPE CRES
20 LANGTHWAITE CL
21 STUBBS CL
22 CONISBOROUGH MEWS
23 CONSTABLE WY

C6
1 DROVERS RISE
2 VICARAGE GDNS
3 CHAPEL MEWS
4 MANOR DR
5 PINE WK
6 BEECH WK
7 HOBSON RD
8 HILL RISE
9 HARLAND RD
10 LARCHMONT CL
11 WESTFIELD PK
12 LAMBERT AVE
13 OAK AVE
14 WOODLANDS LA
15 PLOVER DR
16 CHANTREYS DR
17 RANSOME WY
18 ELM AVE
19 ASH AVE
20 THORNTON
21 LINTON
22 WOODLAND AVE
23 EFFERSON DR
24 ATKINSON DR
25 WOLD VIEW
26 WINTRINGHAM
27 INGLETON
28 FRYSTON
29 COVINGTON
30 LASTINGHAM
31 BIRCH CROFT

D6
1 HALL WK
2 MONKTON
3 BARTRAMS
4 BROOKSIDE
5 PARLIAMENT ST
6 RYEDALE
7 INGMIRES
8 THE GREEN
9 CHURCH ST
10 SWALEDALE
11 BECKSIDE
12 CREYKE LA
13 ST ANNE'S WK
14 ST HELEN'S DR
15 THE CRESCENT

E6
1 HOLLY HILL
2 TEMPLE WK
3 TEMPLE CL
4 LADYWELL GATE
5 PARK RD

F5
1 ST JAMES RD
2 REYNOLDS CL
3 BEECH DR
4 MELTON FIELDS
5 PLANTATION DR

E. Yorkshire & N. Lincolnshire STREET ATLAS

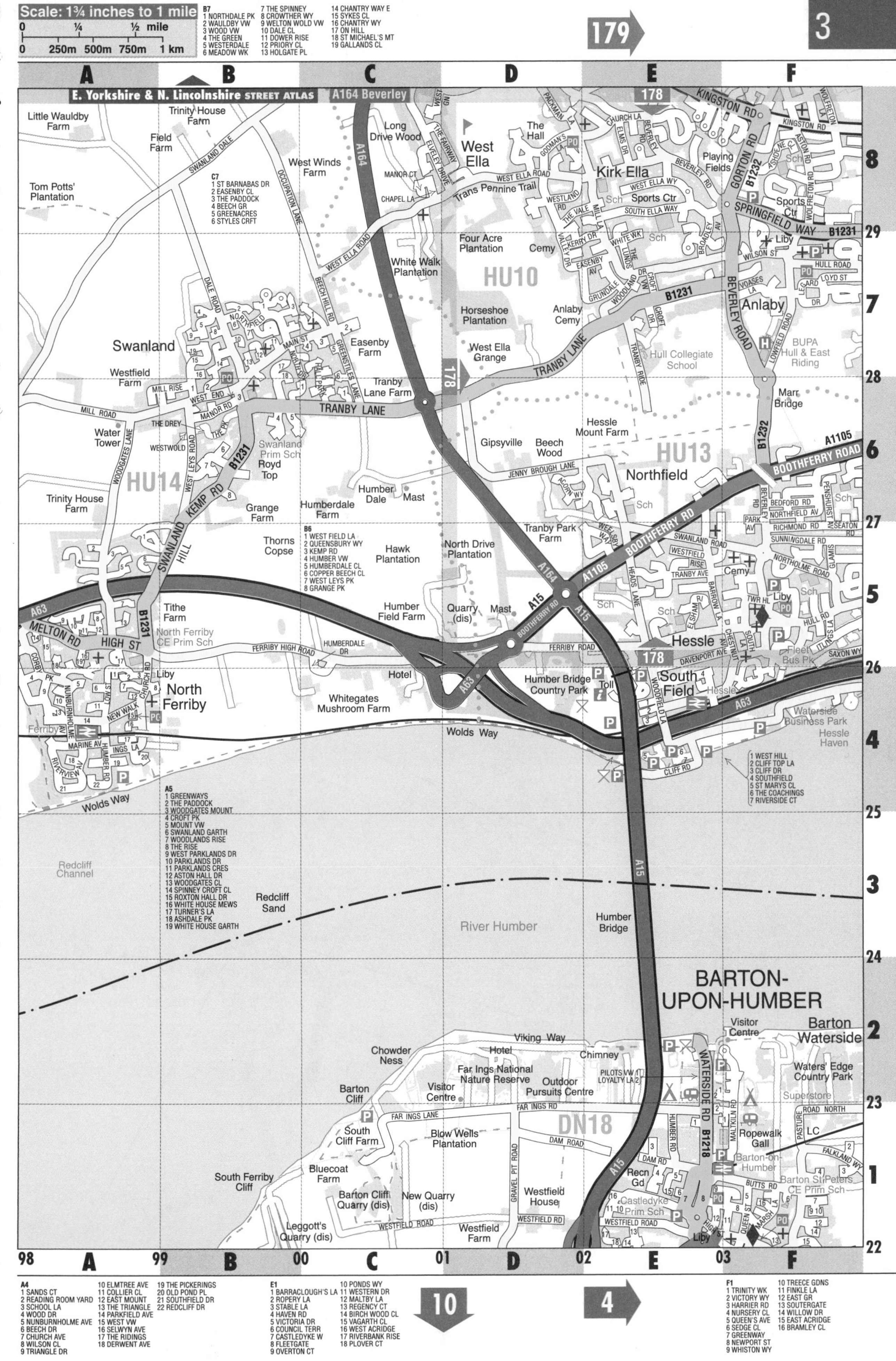

Scale: 1¾ inches to 1 mile
0 ¼ ½ mile
0 250m 500m 750m 1 km
B7
1 NORTHDALE PK
2 WAULDBY VW
3 WOOD VW
4 THE GREEN
5 WESTERDALE
6 MEADOW WK
7 THE SPINNEY
8 CROWTHER WY
9 WELTON WOLD VW
10 DALE CL
11 DOWER RISE
12 PRIORY CL
13 HOLGATE PL
14 CHANTRY WAY E
15 SYKES CL
16 CHANTRY WY
17 ON HILL
18 ST MICHAEL'S MT
19 GALLANDS CL
179
3
A B C D E F
E. Yorkshire & N. Lincolnshire STREET ATLAS
A164 Beverley
178
Little Wauldby Farm
Trinity House Farm
Field Farm
SWANLAND DALE
Tom Potts' Plantation
C7
1 ST BARNABAS DR
2 EASENBY CL
3 THE PADDOCK
4 BEECH GR
5 GREENACRES
6 STYLES CRFT
West Winds Farm
OCCUPATION LANE
Long Drive Wood
West Ella
The Hall
Kirk Ella
Playing Fields
KINGSTON RD
CHURCH LA
WEST ELLA ROAD
Trans Pennine Trail
WEST ELLA WY
Sports Ctr
SOUTH ELLA WAY
SPRINGFIELD WAY
B1231
GORTON RD
B1232
Sports Ctr
Liby
HULL ROAD
LOYD ST
Anlaby
WEST ELLA ROAD
White Walk Plantation
Four Acre Plantation
Cemy
HU10
BEVERLEY ROAD
Horseshoe Plantation
Anlaby Cemy
Swanland
Easenby Farm
West Ella Grange
TRANBY LANE
Hull Collegiate School
BUPA Hull & East Riding
Westfield Farm
Tranby Lane Farm
MILL RISE
WEST END
MANOR RD
TRANBY LANE
Marr Bridge
MILL ROAD
THE DREY
Water Tower
WESTWOLD
Swanland Prim Sch
Royd Top
Gipsyville
Beech Wood
Hessle Mount Farm
HU13
A1105
BOOTHFERRY ROAD
JENNY BROUGH LANE
Northfield
HU14
KEMP RD
B1231
Trinity House Farm
Humber Dale
Mast
Humberdale Farm
Grange Farm
Tranby Park Farm
BOOTHFERRY RD
SWANLAND HILL
Thorns Copse
B6
1 WEST FIELD LA
2 QUEENSBURY WY
3 KEMP RD
4 HUMBER VW
5 HUMBERDALE CL
6 COPPER BEECH CL
7 WEST LEYS PK
8 GRANGE PK
Hawk Plantation
North Drive Plantation
A164
A1105
Cemy
A63
Tithe Farm
Humber Field Farm
Quarry (dis)
Mast
A15
Liby
MELTON RD
HIGH ST
B1231
North Ferriby CE Prim Sch
FERRIBY HIGH ROAD
HUMBERDALE DR
FERRIBY ROAD
Hessle
178
DAVENPORT AVE
Fleet Bus Pk
SAXON WY
Liby
North Ferriby
Hotel
Humber Bridge Country Park
Toll
South Field
Hessle
Whitegates Mushroom Farm
A63
Waterside Business Park
Hessle Haven
Ferriby
MARINE AV
Wolds Way
CLIFF RD
1 WEST HILL
2 CLIFF TOP LA
3 CLIFF DR
4 SOUTHFIELD
5 ST MARYS CL
6 THE COACHINGS
7 RIVERSIDE CT
Wolds Way
A5
1 GREENWAYS
2 THE PADDOCK
3 WOODGATES MOUNT
4 CROFT PK
5 MOUNT VW
6 SWANLAND GARTH
7 WOODLANDS RISE
8 THE RISE
9 WEST PARKLANDS DR
10 PARKLANDS DR
11 PARKLANDS CRES
12 ASTON HALL DR
13 WOODGATES CL
14 SPINNEY CROFT CL
15 ROXTON HALL DR
16 WHITE HOUSE MEWS
17 TURNER'S LA
18 ASHDALE PK
19 WHITE HOUSE GARTH
Redcliff Channel
Redcliff Sand
River Humber
Humber Bridge
A15
BARTON-UPON-HUMBER
Visitor Centre
Barton Waterside
Chowder Ness
Viking Way
Hotel
Chimney
Far Ings National Nature Reserve
Waters' Edge Country Park
Barton Cliff
Visitor Centre
Outdoor Pursuits Centre
WATERSIDE RD
Superstore
FAR INGS RD
FAR INGS LANE
DN18
South Cliff Farm
Blow Wells Plantation
DAM ROAD
Ropewalk Gall
LC
South Ferriby Cliff
Bluecoat Farm
Barton Cliff Quarry (dis)
New Quarry (dis)
GRAVEL PIT ROAD
Westfield House
Recn Gd
Barton-on-Humber
B1218
Barton St Peters CE Prim Sch
Castledyke Prim Sch
WESTFIELD RD
WESTFIELD ROAD
Leggott's Quarry (dis)
Westfield Farm
Liby
8 29 7 28 6 27 5 26 4 25 3 24 2 23 1 22
98 99 00 01 02 03
10
4
A4
1 SANDS CT
2 READING ROOM YARD
3 SCHOOL LA
4 WOOD DR
5 NUNBURNHOLME AVE
6 BEECH GR
7 CHURCH AVE
8 WILSON CL
9 TRIANGLE DR
10 ELMTREE AVE
11 COLLIER CL
12 EAST MOUNT
13 THE TRIANGLE
14 PARKFIELD AVE
15 WEST VW
16 SELWYN AVE
17 THE RIDINGS
18 DERWENT AVE
19 THE PICKERINGS
20 OLD POND PL
21 SOUTHFIELD DR
22 REDCLIFF DR
E1
1 BARRACLOUGH'S LA
2 ROPERY LA
3 STABLE LA
4 HAVEN RD
5 VICTORIA DR
6 COUNCIL TERR
7 CASTLEDYKE W
8 FLEETGATE
9 OVERTON CT
10 PONDS WY
11 WESTERN DR
12 MALTBY LA
13 REGENCY CT
14 BIRCH WOOD CL
15 VAGARTH CL
16 WEST ACRIDGE
17 RIVERBANK RISE
18 PLOVER CT
F1
1 TRINITY WK
2 VICTORY WY
3 HARRIER RD
4 NURSERY CL
5 QUEEN'S AVE
6 SEDGE CL
7 GREENWAY
8 NEWPORT ST
9 WHISTON WY
10 TREECE GDNS
11 FINKLE LA
12 EAST GR
13 SOUTERGATE
14 WILLOW DR
15 EAST ACRIDGE
16 BRAMLEY CL

Scale: 1¾ inches to 1 mile

0   ¼   ½   mile
0   250m 500m 750m 1 km

E. Yorkshire & N. Lincolnshire STREET ATLAS

179   180   A1079 Beverley (A1174)

A   B   C   D   E   F

HU5

HU2

CH
HOTHAM RD S
KINGSTON ROAD   WESTLANDS RD   WILLERBY
WOLD ROAD   Liby   CALVERT RD   ROSEDALE GR   LOMOND ROAD   BROOKLANDS RD
PERTH ST   PERTH STRERET   BELVOIR ST   NEWSTEAD ST   THORESBY ST   WHARNCLIFFE   WELBECK ST
PRINCES AV   LOUIS ST   ALBANY ST   PEEL ST   HUTT ST
GREEN LA   SCOTT ST
Sch

HELMSLEY GROVE   Spring Bank W   Spring Bank West   SUNNY BANK   Cemy   Chy
P   East
Liby   ALBION ST   GEORGE ST   H

East Ella   West Park   Sports Gd
SPRINGFIELD WY   HULL RD   COLVILLE AV   ANLABY ROAD   A1105   ANLABY ROAD   A1105

HU10

HU3

CASTLE ST

Anlaby Park   Sports Ctr   GT THORNTON ST   ADELAIDE ST   CAVILL PL   A63   Mus

BOOTHFERRY ROAD   A1105   ASKEW AVENUE   HESSLE RD   A1106   HESSLE ROAD   Liby   Hull Arena   Victoria Pier Locks

Pickering Park   Gipsyville   WEST DOCK ST   Albert Dock   HU1

Priory Bridge   St Andrews Quay   Trans PennineTrail

HU4   CLIVE SULLIVAN WAY   A63

Waterside Business Park   P&R   Mast   Priory Park   P&R

CLIVE SULLIVAN WY

179   180

New Holland Pier

Fairfield Pit Nature Reserve   New Holland Mere

New Holland CE Methodist Prim Sch   New Holland   Summercroft Farm   OXMARSH LANE

Pasture Wharf Nature Reserve   Barrow Haven Reedbed Nature Reserve   Oxford Grange Farm   LINCOLN CASTLE WAY

Sailing Club   Chy   Barrow Haven   WEST MARSH LA   MARSH LANE

Barrow Haven   PH   Windmill   The Castles (Motte & Baileys)   DN19   Hann Farm   Field Farm   Leys Farm

Mill Farm   Castle Farm   WEST HANN LANE   West Hann Farm   Coulbeck Farm   Barrow Road   EAST HANN LANE   Mill Farm

DN18   West Marsh Farm   Spring Farm   The Beck   Barrow Blow Wells Nature Reserve   B1206   NEW HOLLAND RD   Barrow Hann

FALKLAND WAY
1 PASTURE RD N
2 ARDENT RD
3 PASTURE RD S
4 ANTELOPE RD

04   A   05   B   06   C   07   D   08   E   09   F

For full street detail of the highlighted area see pages 179 & 180.

3   11

E2
1 SCHOOL LA
2 WENTWORTH CR
3 FULFORD CRES
4 WESTBURN AVE
5 MORGAN WY
6 GLENEAGLES CRES
7 ALBERT ST
8 MOUNT PL
9 PEPLOE LA
10 PEPLOE CRES
11 DANESGATE

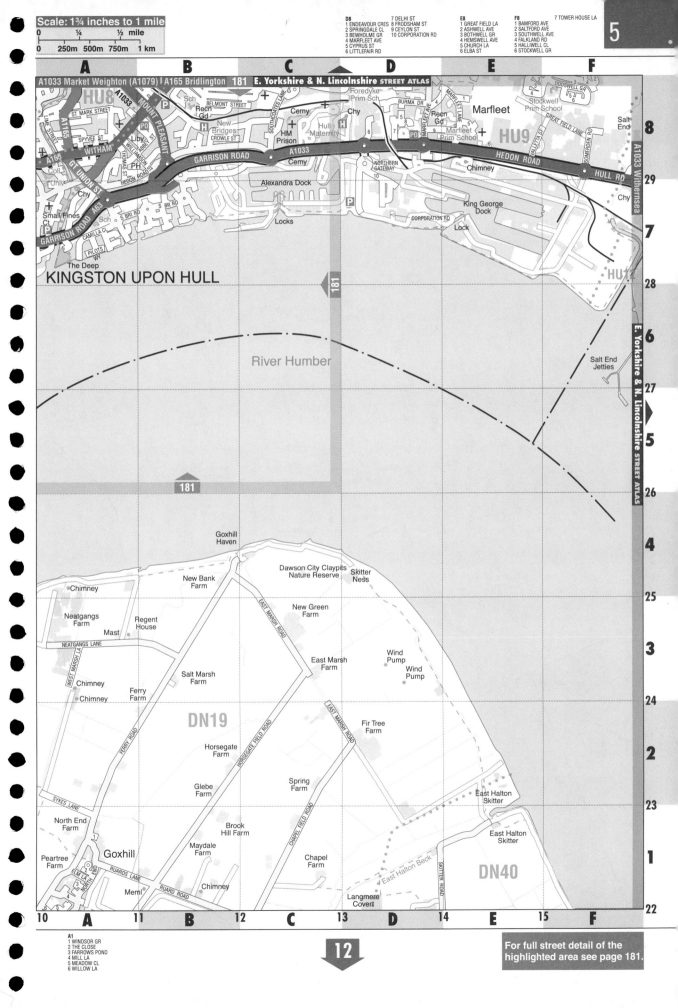

Scale: 1¾ inches to 1 mile

0   ¼   ½ mile
0   250m 500m 750m 1 km

D8
1 ENDEAVOUR CRES
2 SPRINGDALE CL
3 BEWHOLME GR
4 MARFLEET AVE
5 CYPRUS ST
6 LITTLEFAIR RD

7 DELHI ST
8 FRODSHAM ST
9 CEYLON ST
10 CORPORATION RD

E8
1 GREAT FIELD LA
2 ASHWELL AVE
3 BOTHWELL GR
4 HEMSWELL AVE
5 CHURCH ST
6 ELBA ST

F8
1 BAMFORD AVE
2 SALTFORD AVE
3 SOUTHWELL AVE
4 FALKLAND RD
5 HALLIWELL CL
6 STOCKWELL GR

7 TOWER HOUSE LA

A   B   C   D   E   F

A1033 Market Weighton (A1079)   A165 Bridlington   181   E. Yorkshire & N. Lincolnshire STREET ATLAS

HU8
A1033
Sch
BELMONT STREET
Foredyke Prim Sch
BURMA DR
Marfleet
Stockwell Prim School
GREAT FIELD LANE
DODSWELL GR
Salt End
8

ST MARK STREET
New Bridges
CROWLE ST
Recn Gd
Cemy
Chy
Recn Gd
Marfleet Prim School
HU9
DODSWELL GR

LIME STREET
SPYVEE ST
HM Prison
Hull Maternity
PO
VALLETTA ST
SOMERDEN RD
A1033 Withernsea
29

Liby
WITHAM
A1033
GARRISON ROAD   A1033
Cemy
HEDON ROAD
HULL RD
Chy
7

A166
Coll of Univ
Chy
Northern Gateway
Chimney

Small Fines Ct
Sch
P
Alexandra Dock
King George Dock
Chy
HU12

GARRISON ROAD   A63
CAMILLA CL
PILOTS WY
Locks
CORPORATION RD
Lock
28

The Deep
KINGSTON UPON HULL
181
Salt End Jetties
6

River Humber
27

E. Yorkshire & N. Lincolnshire STREET ATLAS
5

181
26

Goxhill Haven
4

Chimney
New Bank Farm
Dawson City Claypits Nature Reserve
Skitter Ness
25

Neatgangs Farm
Regent House
New Green Farm
3

NEATGANGS LANE
Mast
EAST MARSH ROAD
Wind Pump

Chimney
WEST MARSH LA
Salt Marsh Farm
East Marsh Farm
Wind Pump
24

Chimney
Ferry Farm
DN19
EAST MARSH ROAD
Fir Tree Farm
2

FERRY ROAD
Horsegate Farm
HORSEGATE FIELD ROAD
East Halton Skitter

SYKES LANE
Glebe Farm
Spring Farm
CHAPEL FIELD ROAD
East Halton Skitter
23

North End Farm
Brook Hill Farm
SKITTER ROAD
DN40
1

Peartree Farm
Goxhill
Maydale Farm
Chapel Farm
East Halton Beck

ELM LA
RUARDS LANE
RUARD ROAD
Chimney
Langmere Covert
22

10   A   11   B   12   C   13   D   14   E   15   F

A1
1 WINDSOR GR
2 THE CLOSE
3 FARROWS POND
4 MILL LA
5 MEADOW CL
6 WILLOW LA

For full street detail of the highlighted area see page 181.

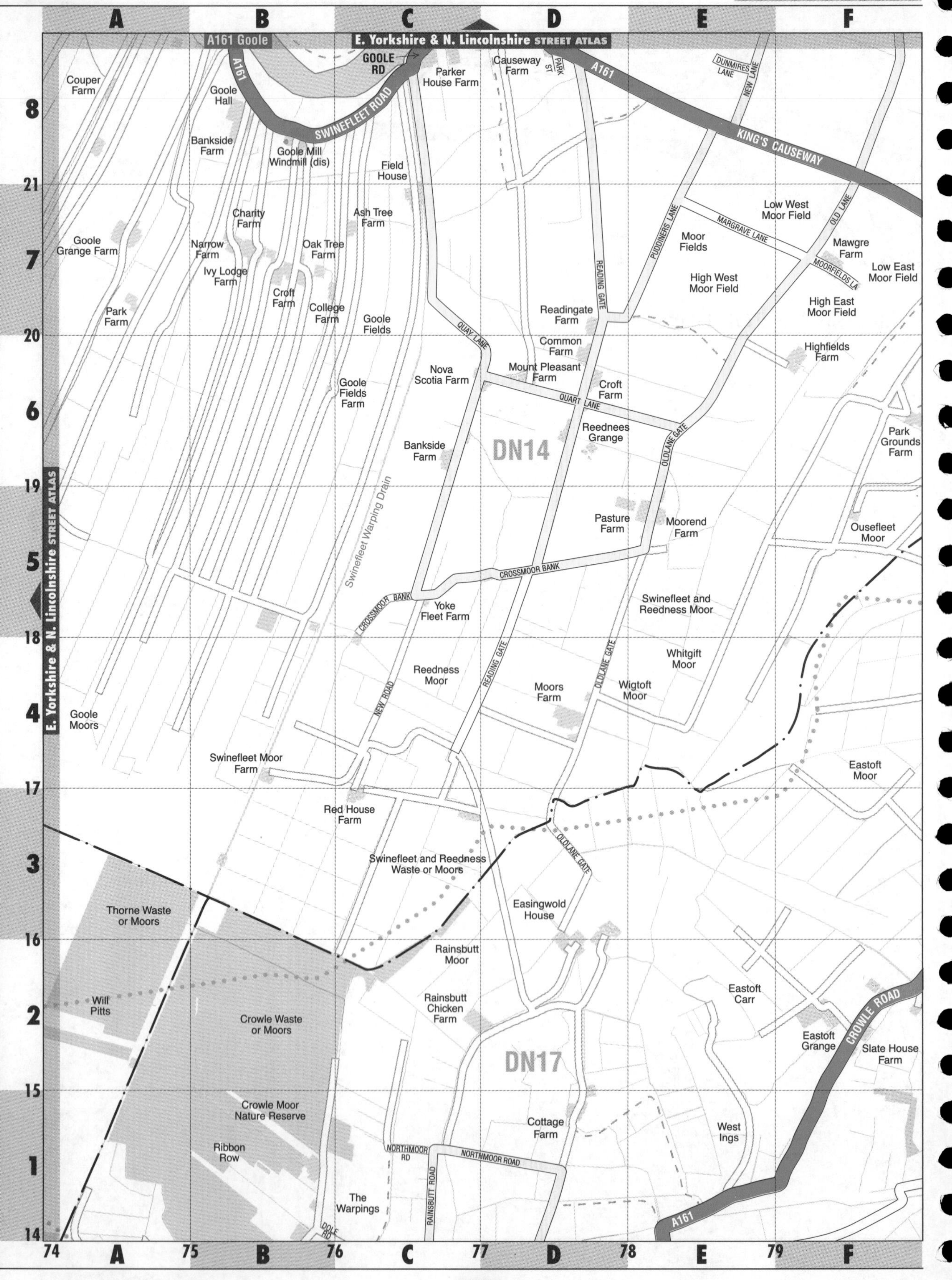

Scale: 1¾ inches to 1 mile

A161 Goole
GOOLE RD

Couper Farm
Goole Hall
Parker House Farm
Causeway Farm
PARK ST
A161
DUNMIRES LANE
NEW LANE

SWINEFLEET ROAD
KING'S CAUSEWAY

Bankside Farm
Goole Mill Windmill (dis)
Field House

OLD LANE

Goole Grange Farm
Charity Farm
Ash Tree Farm
PUDDINERS LANE
MARGRAVE LANE
Low West Moor Field

Narrow Farm
Oak Tree Farm
Moor Fields
Mawgre Farm
MOORFIELDS LA
Low East Moor Field

Ivy Lodge Farm
READING GATE
High West Moor Field

Park Farm
Croft Farm
College Farm
Goole Fields
Readingate Farm
High East Moor Field

Goole Fields Farm
Nova Scotia Farm
Common Farm
Mount Pleasant Farm
QUART LANE
Croft Farm
Highfields Farm

QUAY LANE

DN14
Reednees Grange
OLD LANE GATE
Park Grounds Farm

Bankside Farm

Swinefleet Warping Drain

Pasture Farm
Moorend Farm
Ousefleet Moor

CROSSMOOR BANK

CROSSMOOR BANK
Yoke Fleet Farm
Swinefleet and Reedness Moor

READING GATE
Whitgift Moor

NEW ROAD
Reedness Moor
Moors Farm
OLD LANE GATE
Wigtoft Moor

Goole Moors
Swinefleet Moor Farm
Eastoft Moor

Red House Farm
Swinefleet and Reedness Waste or Moors
OLD LANE GATE

Will Pitts
Thorne Waste or Moors
Easingwold House
Eastoft Carr

Rainsbutt Moor
CROWLE ROAD

Crowle Waste or Moors
Rainsbutt Chicken Farm
DN17
Eastoft Grange
Slate House Farm

Crowle Moor Nature Reserve
West Ings

Ribbon Row
Cottage Farm

NORTHMOOR RD
NORTHMOOR ROAD

The Warpings
RAINSBUTT ROAD
A161

GOLE RD

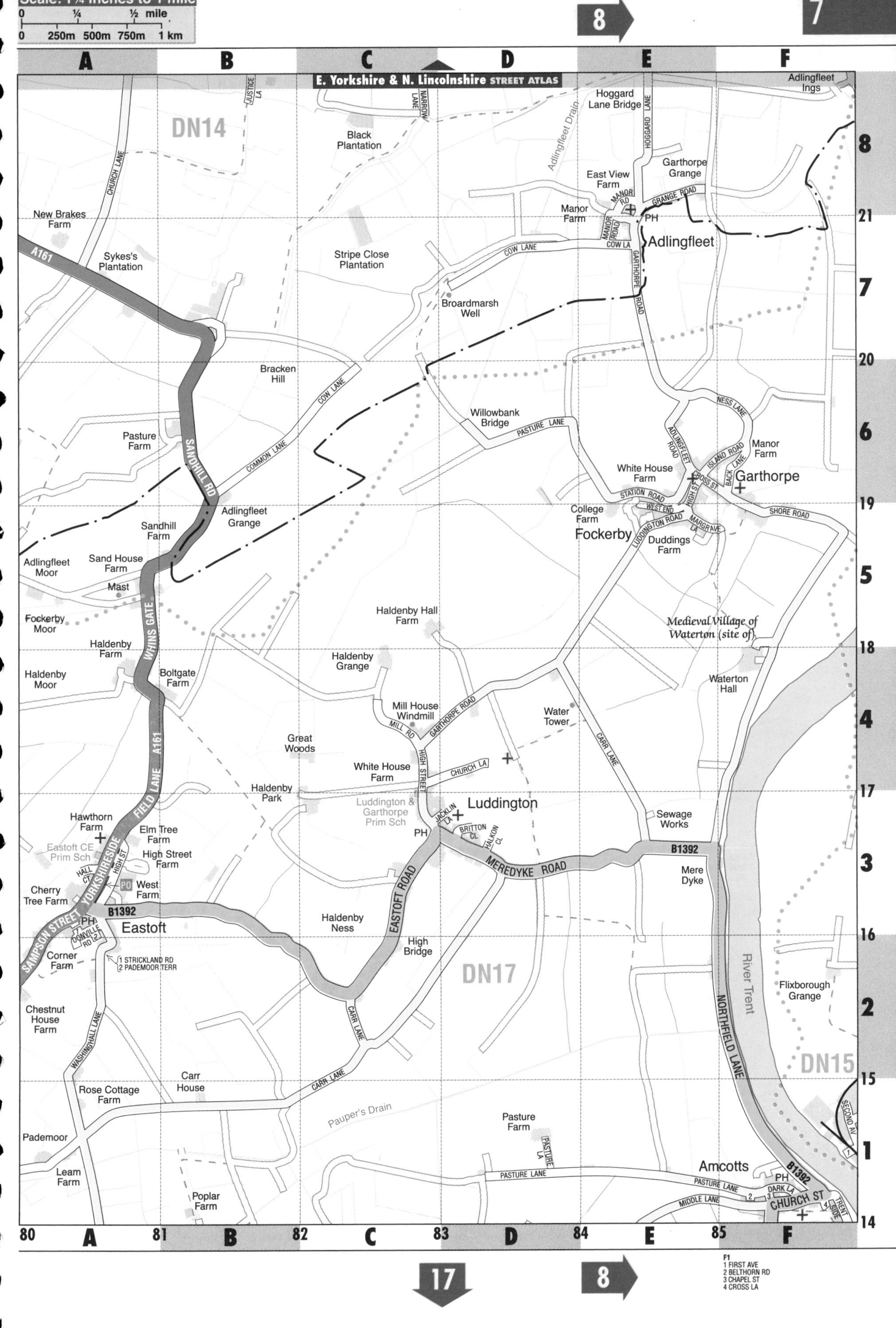

E. Yorkshire & N. Lincolnshire STREET ATLAS

DN14

New Brakes Farm

A161

Sykes's Plantation

CHURCH LANE

Pasture Farm

SANDHILL RD

COMMON LANE

Bracken Hill

COW LANE

Adlingfleet Grange

Sandhill Farm

Adlingfleet Moor

Sand House Farm

Mast

WHINS GATE

Fockerby Moor

Haldenby Farm

Boltgate Farm

Haldenby Moor

FIELD LANE

A161

Hawthorn Farm

Eastoft CE Prim Sch

Elm Tree Farm

High Street Farm

YORKSHIRESIDE

HIGH ST

HALL CT

West Farm

PO

B1392

DONVILLE RD

PH

Eastoft

Cherry Tree Farm

SAMPSON STREET

Corner Farm

1 STRICKLAND RD
2 PADEMOOR TERR

Chestnut House Farm

WASHINGHALL LANE

Rose Cottage Farm

Carr House

CARR LANE

Pademoor

Leam Farm

Poplar Farm

JUSTICE LA

Black Plantation

NARROW LANE

Stripe Close Plantation

Broadmarsh Well

Willowbank Bridge

PASTURE LANE

COW LANE

Haldenby Hall Farm

Haldenby Grange

Mill House Windmill

MILL RD

Great Woods

Haldenby Park

White House Farm

Luddington & Garthorpe Prim Sch

HIGH STREET

PH

GARTHORPE ROAD

CHURCH LA

JACKLIN LA

Luddington

BRITTON CL

HALKON CL

EASTOFT ROAD

Haldenby Ness

High Bridge

CARR LANE

DN17

MEREDYKE ROAD

B1392

Pauper's Drain

Pasture Farm

PASTURE LA

PASTURE LANE

Amcotts

MIDDLE LANE

Adlingfleet Drain

Hoggard Lane Bridge

HOGGARD LANE

East View Farm

Manor Farm

MANOR RD

GRANGE ROAD

COW LANE

GARTHORPE ROAD

Adlingfleet Ings

Hoggard Farm

Garthorpe Grange

PH

Adlingfleet

NESS LANE

ISLAND ROAD

BACK LANE

Manor Farm

White House Farm

STATION ROAD

HIGH ST

CROSS ST

Garthorpe

College Farm

WEST END

LUDDINGTON ROAD

MARGR AVE

SHORE ROAD

Fockerby

Duddings Farm

Medieval Village of Waterton (site of)

Waterton Hall

Water Tower

CARR LANE

Sewage Works

Mere Dyke

NORTHFIELD LANE

River Trent

DN15

Flixborough Grange

SECOND AV

B1392

PH

DARK LA

CHURCH ST

TRENT SIDE

F1
1 FIRST AVE
1 BELTHORN RD
2 CHAPEL ST
3 CROSS LA

7
1

Scale: 1¾ inches to 1 mile

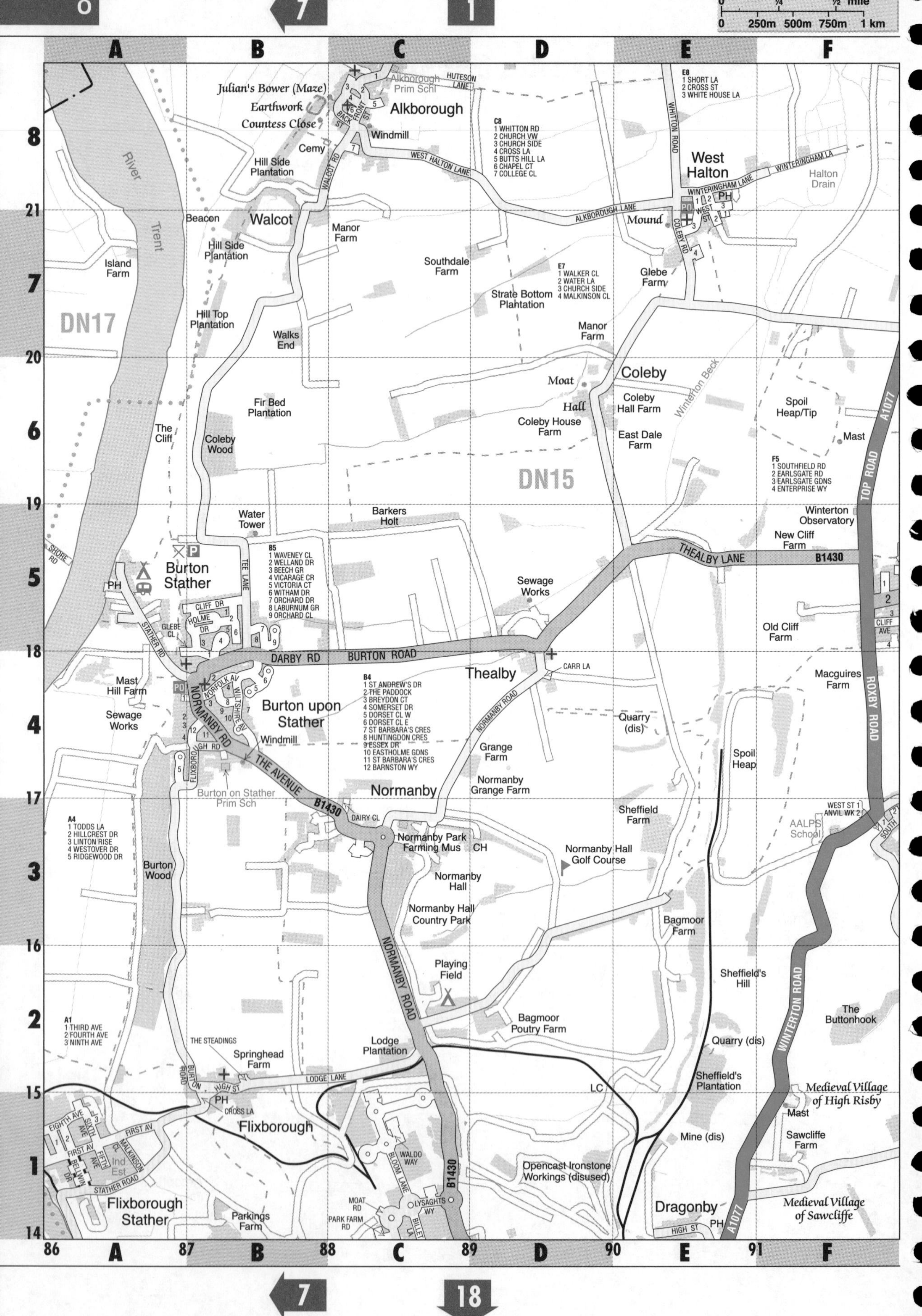
A
B
C
D
E
F
Julian's Bower (Maze)
Earthwork
Countess Close
Alkborough
Alkborough Prim Schl
HUTESON LANE
Windmill
Cemy
Hill Side Plantation
WALCOT RD
WEST HALTON LANE
C8
1 WHITTON RD
2 CHURCH VW
3 CHURCH SIDE
4 CROSS LA
5 BUTTS HILL LA
6 CHAPEL CT
7 COLLEGE CL
E8
1 SHORT LA
2 CROSS ST
3 WHITE HOUSE LA
WHITTON ROAD
West Halton
WINTERINGHAM LANE
WINTERINGHAM LA
Halton Drain
River Trent
Beacon
Walcot
Manor Farm
ALKBOROUGH LANE
Mound
COLEBY RD
Island Farm
Hill Side Plantation
Southdale Farm
E7
1 WALKER CL
2 WATER LA
3 CHURCH SIDE
4 MALKINSON CL
Glebe Farm
Strate Bottom Plantation
DN17
Hill Top Plantation
Walks End
Manor Farm
Coleby
Moat
Hall
Fir Bed Plantation
Coleby Hall Farm
Winterton Beck
Spoil Heap/Tip
The Cliff
Coleby Wood
Coleby House Farm
East Dale Farm
Mast
A1077
TOP ROAD
DN15
F5
1 SOUTHFIELD RD
2 EARLSGATE RD
3 EARLSGATE GDNS
4 ENTERPRISE WY
Water Tower
Barkers Holt
Winterton Observatory
New Cliff Farm
SHORE RD
Burton Stather
TEE LANE
B5
1 WAVENEY CL
2 WELLAND DR
3 BEECH GR
4 VICARAGE CR
5 VICTORIA CT
6 WITHAM DR
7 ORCHARD DR
8 LABURNUM GR
9 ORCHARD CL
THEALBY LANE
B1430
Sewage Works
PH
CLIFF DR
HOLME DR
GLEBE CL
STATHER RD
Old Cliff Farm
CLIFF AVE
DARBY RD
BURTON ROAD
Mast Hill Farm
NORFOLK AV
WILTSHIRE AV
B4
1 ST ANDREW'S DR
2 THE PADDOCK
3 BREYDON CT
4 SOMERSET DR
5 DORSET CL W
6 DORSET CL E
7 ST BARBARA'S CRES
8 HUNTINGDON CRES
9 ESSEX DR
10 EASTHOLME GDNS
11 ST BARBARA'S CRES
12 BARNSTON WY
Thealby
CARR LA
Macguires Farm
ROXBY ROAD
Sewage Works
Burton upon Stather
NORMANBY RD
NORMANBY ROAD
Quarry (dis)
Windmill
GH RD
THE AVENUE
Grange Farm
Spoil Heap
FLIXBOROUGH RD
Burton on Stather Prim Sch
Normanby
Normanby Grange Farm
A4
1 TODDS LA
2 HILLCREST DR
3 LINTON RISE
4 WESTOVER DR
5 RIDGEWOOD DR
DAIRY CL
Normanby Park Farming Mus
CH
Sheffield Farm
WEST ST
ANVIL WK
AALPS School
SOUTH
Burton Wood
Normanby Hall
Normanby Hall Golf Course
Normanby Hall Country Park
Bagmoor Farm
Playing Field
Sheffield's Hill
WINTERTON ROAD
A1
1 THIRD AVE
2 FOURTH AVE
3 NINTH AVE
Bagmoor Poutry Farm
The Buttonhook
THE STEADINGS
Springhead Farm
Lodge Plantation
Quarry (dis)
BURTON ROAD
LODGE LANE
Sheffield's Plantation
LC
Medieval Village of High Risby
HIGH ST
CROSS LA
Flixborough
EIGHTH AVE
SIXTH AVE
FIRST AV
FIRST AV
FIFTH AVE
MALKINSON CL
BELWIN DR
Ind Est
STATHER ROAD
WALDO WAY
BLOOM LANE
Mast
Sawcliffe Farm
Mine (dis)
Opencast Ironstone Workings (disused)
Flixborough Stather
MOAT RD
PARK FARM RD
LYSAGHTS WY
BILLET LA
Parkings Farm
Dragonby
HIGH ST
Medieval Village of Sawcliffe
86
87
88
89
90
91
8
21
7
20
6
19
5
18
4
17
3
16
2
15
1
14

7
18

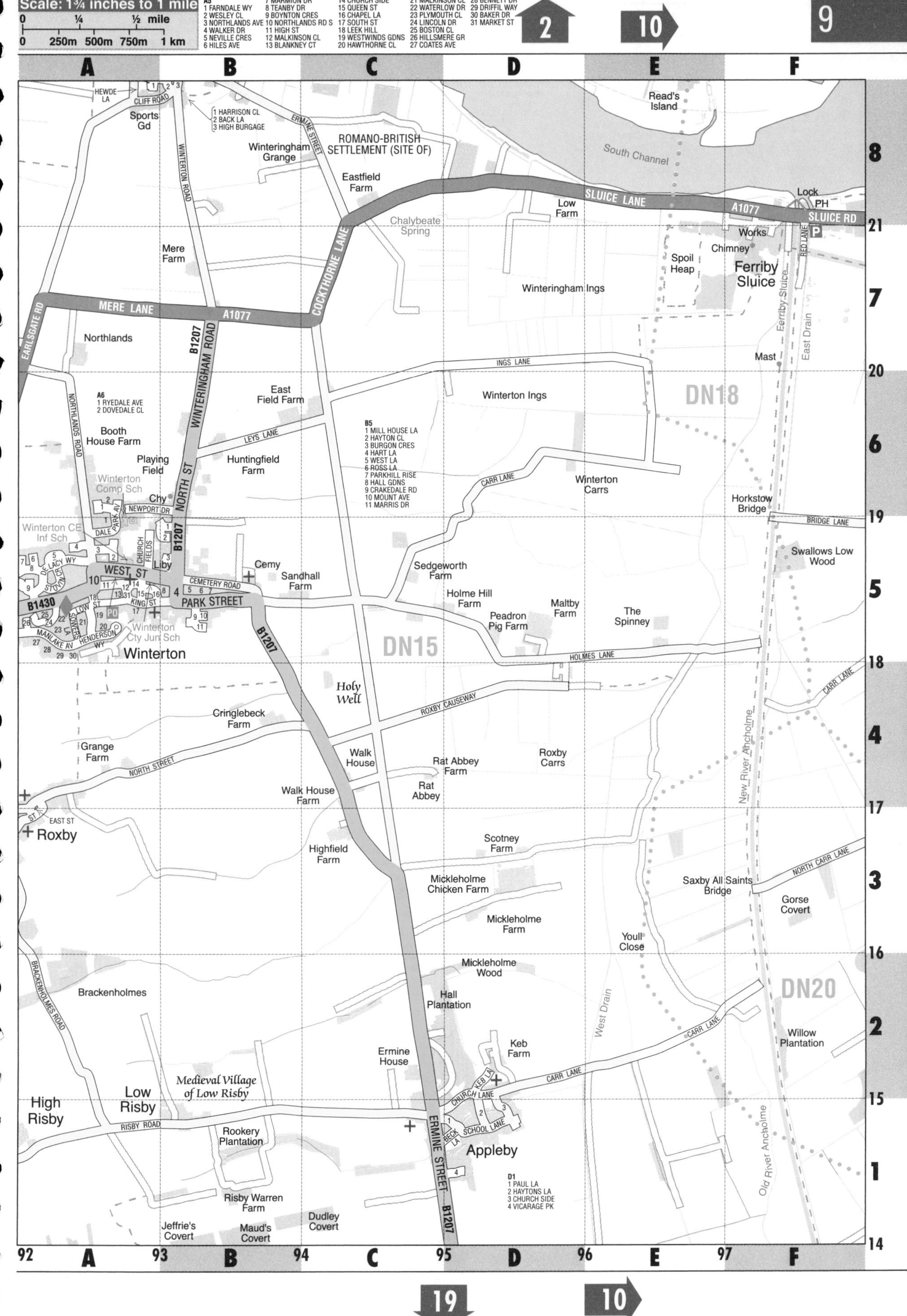

A5
1 FARNDALE WY
2 WESLEY CL
3 NORTHLANDS AVE
4 WALKER DR
5 NEVILLE CRES
6 HILES AVE

7 MARMION DR
8 TEANBY DR
9 BOYNTON CRES
10 NORTHLANDS RD S
11 HIGH ST
12 MALKINSON CL
13 BLANKNEY CT

14 CHURCH SIDE
15 QUEEN ST
16 CHAPEL LA
17 SOUTH ST
18 LEEK HILL
19 WESTWINDS GDNS
20 HAWTHORNE CL

21 MALKINSON CL
22 WATERLOW DR
23 PLYMOUTH CL
24 LINCOLN DR
25 BOSTON CL
26 HILLSMERE GR
27 COATES AVE

28 BENNETT DR
29 DRIFFIL WAY
30 BAKER DR
31 MARKET ST

A6
1 RYEDALE AVE
2 DOVEDALE CL

B5
1 MILL HOUSE LA
2 HAYTON CL
3 BURGON CRES
4 HART LA
5 WEST LA
6 ROSS LA
7 PARKHILL RISE
8 HALL GDNS
9 CRAKEDALE RD
10 MOUNT AVE
11 MARRIS DR

1 HARRISON CL
2 BACK LA
3 HIGH BURGAGE

D1
1 PAUL LA
2 HAYTONS LA
3 CHURCH SIDE
4 VICARAGE PK

ROMANO-BRITISH SETTLEMENT (SITE OF)

Read's Island

South Channel

SLUICE LANE

Lock PH

A1077

SLUICE RD

Works

Chimney

Ferriby Sluice

Spoil Heap

Winteringham Grange

Eastfield Farm

Low Farm

Chalybeate Spring

Mere Farm

Winteringham Ings

MERE LANE

A1077

Northlands

Mast

East Drain

INGS LANE

DN18

East Field Farm

Winterton Ings

Booth House Farm

Playing Field

Winterton Comp Sch

Huntingfield Farm

LEYS LANE

CARR LANE

Winterton Carrs

Horkstow Bridge

BRIDGE LANE

Winterton CE Inf Sch

Cemy

Sandhall Farm

Sedgeworth Farm

Swallows Low Wood

WEST ST

Liby

CEMETERY ROAD

PARK STREET

Holme Hill Farm

Maltby Farm

The Spinney

B1430

Winterton Cty Jun Sch

Peadron Pig Farm

Winterton

DN15

HOLMES LANE

CARR LANE

Holy Well

ROXBY CAUSEWAY

Cringlebeck Farm

Walk House

Rat Abbey Farm

Roxby Carrs

New River Ancholme

Grange Farm

NORTH STREET

Walk House Farm

Rat Abbey

Roxby

EAST ST

Highfield Farm

Scotney Farm

Saxby All Saints Bridge

NORTH CARR LANE

Gorse Covert

Mickleholme Chicken Farm

Mickleholme Farm

Youll Close

Brackenholmes

Mickleholme Wood

DN20

Hall Plantation

West Drain

Willow Plantation

CARR LANE

Ermine House

Keb Farm

CARR LANE

High Risby

Low Risby

Medieval Village of Low Risby

RISBY ROAD

Rookery Plantation

ERMINE STREET

School LANE

Appleby

Risby Warren Farm

Dudley Covert

Jeffrie's Covert

Maud's Covert

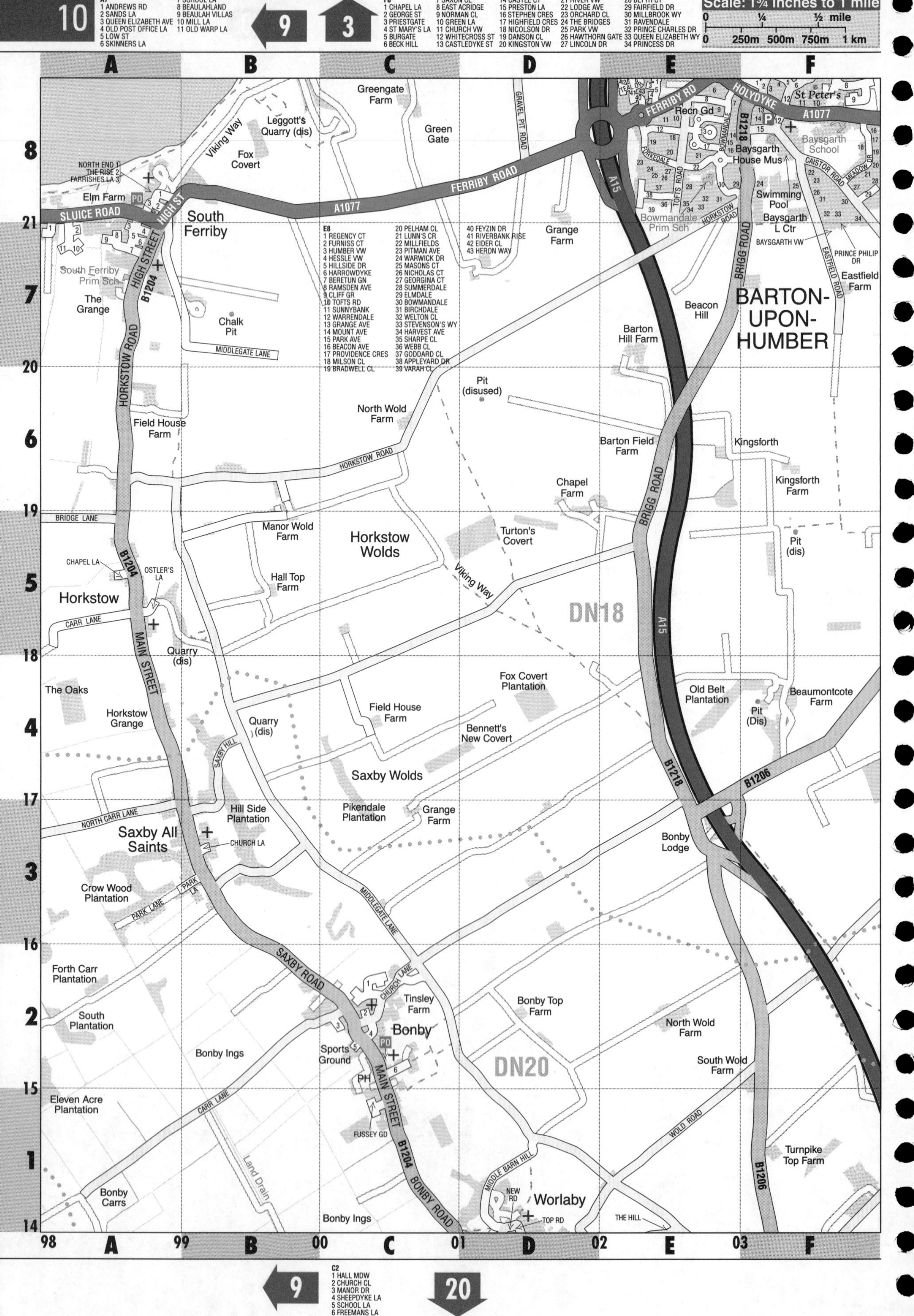
A7
1 ANDREWS RD
2 SANDS LA
3 QUEEN ELIZABETH AVE
4 OLD POST OFFICE LA
5 LOW ST
6 SKINNERS LA
7 SCHOOL LA
8 BEAULAHLAND
9 BEAULAH VILLAS
10 MILL LA
11 OLD WARP LA
9
3
F8
1 CHAPEL LA
2 GEORGE ST
3 PRIESTGATE
4 ST MARY'S LA
5 BURGATE
6 BECK HILL
7 SAXON CL
8 EAST ACRIDGE
9 NORMAN CL
10 GREEN LA
11 CHURCH VW
12 WHITECROSS ST
13 CASTLEDYKE ST
14 CASTLE CT
15 PRESTON LA
16 STEPHEN CRES
17 HIGHFIELD CRES
18 NICOLSON DR
19 DANSON CL
20 KINGSTON VW
21 RIVER VW
22 LODGE AVE
23 ORCHARD CL
24 THE BRIDGES
25 PARK VW
26 HAWTHORN GATE
27 LINCOLN DR
28 BLYTH CT
29 FAIRFIELD DR
30 MILLBROOK WY
31 RAVENDALE
32 PRINCE CHARLES DR
33 QUEEN ELIZABETH WY
34 PRINCESS DR
Scale: 1¾ inches to 1 mile
0 ¼ ½ mile
0 250m 500m 750m 1 km
A B C D E F
8 21 7 20 6 19 5 18 4 17 3 16 2 15 1 14
E8
1 REGENCY CT
2 FURNISS CT
3 HUMBER VW
4 HESSLE VW
5 HILLSIDE DR
6 HARROWDYKE
7 BERETUN GN
8 RAMSDEN AVE
9 CLIFF GR
10 TOFTS RD
11 SUNNYBANK
12 WARRENDALE
13 GRANGE AVE
14 MOUNT AVE
15 PARK AVE
16 BEACON AVE
17 PROVIDENCE CRES
18 MILSON CL
19 BRADWELL CL
20 PELHAM CL
21 LUNN'S CR
22 MILLFIELDS
23 PITMAN AVE
24 WARWICK DR
25 MASONS CT
26 NICHOLAS CT
27 GEORGINA CT
28 SUMMERDALE
29 ELMDALE
30 BOWMANDALE
31 BIRCHDALE
32 WELTON CL
33 STEVENSON'S WY
34 HARVEST AVE
35 SHARPE CL
36 WEBB CL
37 GODDARD CL
38 APPLEYARD DR
39 VARAH CL
40 FEYZIN DR
41 RIVERBANK RISE
42 EIDER CL
43 HERON WAY
Greengate Farm
Leggott's Quarry (dis)
Green Gate
GRAVEL PIT ROAD
Viking Way
Fox Covert
NORTH END
THE RISE
FARRISHES LA
Elm Farm
PO
SLUICE ROAD
HIGH ST
South Ferriby
A1077
FERRIBY ROAD
South Ferriby Prim Sch
HIGH STREET
B1204
The Grange
Chalk Pit
MIDDLEGATE LANE
HORKSTOW ROAD
Field House Farm
North Wold Farm
Pit (disused)
HORKSTOW ROAD
BRIDGE LANE
Manor Wold Farm
Horkstow Wolds
CHAPEL LA
OSTLER'S LA
Hall Top Farm
Horkstow
CARR LANE
MAIN STREET
Quarry (dis)
Turton's Covert
Viking Way
DN18
The Oaks
Horkstow Grange
Quarry (dis)
Field House Farm
Fox Covert Plantation
Bennett's New Covert
SAXBY HILL
Saxby Wolds
NORTH CARR LANE
Hill Side Plantation
Pikendale Plantation
Grange Farm
Saxby All Saints
CHURCH LA
Crow Wood Plantation
PARK LA
PARK LANE
MIDDLEGATE LANE
Forth Carr Plantation
SAXBY ROAD
CHURCH LANE
Tinsley Farm
Bonby Top Farm
South Plantation
Bonby
Bonby Ings
Sports Ground
PO
PH
MAIN STREET
DN20
Eleven Acre Plantation
CARR LANE
FUSSEY GD
B1204
Land Drain
MIDDLE BARN HILL
NEW RD
Worlaby
TOP RD
THE HILL
Bonby Carrs
BONBY ROAD
Bonby Ings
FERRIBY RD
HOLYDYKE
St Peter's
Recn Gd
A1077
B1218
P
A15
Baysgarth School
FORKEDALE
BOWMANDALE
Baysgarth House Mus
TOFTS ROAD
CAISTOR ROAD
MEADOW DR
Swimming Pool
Bowmandale Prim Sch
HORKSTOW ROAD
Baysgarth L Ctr
BAYSGARTH VW
Grange Farm
BRIGG ROAD
PRINCE PHILIP DR
EASTFIELD ROAD
Eastfield Farm
Beacon Hill
BARTON-UPON-HUMBER
Barton Hill Farm
Barton Field Farm
Kingsforth
Chapel Farm
BRIGG ROAD
Kingsforth Farm
Pit (dis)
A15
Old Belt Plantation
Pit (Dis)
Beaumontcote Farm
B1218
B1206
Bonby Lodge
North Wold Farm
South Wold Farm
WOLD ROAD
Turnpike Top Farm
B1206
98 99 00 01 02 03
9
20
C2
1 HALL MDW
2 CHURCH CL
3 MANOR DR
4 SHEEPDYKE LA
5 SCHOOL LA
6 FREEMANS LA

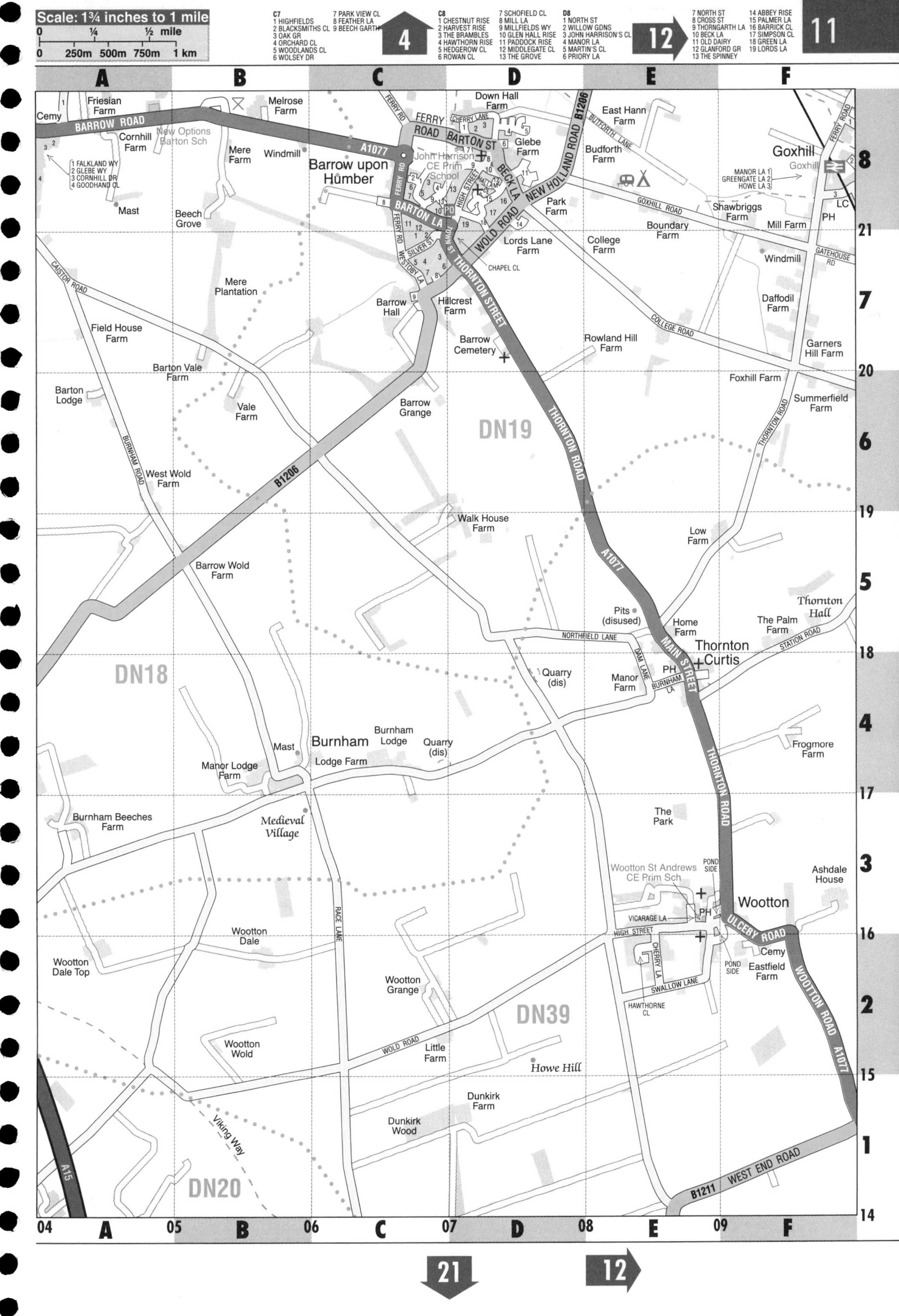

Cemy
Friesian Farm
BARROW ROAD
Cornhill Farm
1 FALKLAND WY
2 GLEBE WY
3 CORNHILL DR
4 GOODHAND CL
Mast

New Options Barton Sch
Mere Farm
Windmill
Melrose Farm

Barrow upon Humber

Beech Grove

FERRY RD
FERRY ROAD
A1077

BARTON ST
Down Hall Farm
CHERRY LANE
Glebe Farm
East Hann Farm

John Harrison CE Prim School
BARTON LA
SILVER ST
HIGH STREET
MATT LANE
PO

BECK LA
Park Farm
WOLD ROAD
NEW HOLLAND ROAD
B1206
BUTFORTH LANE
Budforth Farm

Goxhill
Goxhill
MANOR LA 1
GREENGATE LA 2
HOWE LA 3
LC
PH

Mast
Shawbriggs Farm
Mill Farm
GATEHOUSE RD

Mere Plantation

THORNTON STREET
CHAPEL CL
Lords Lane Farm
College Farm
Boundary Farm
Windmill

Field House Farm
Barrow Hall
Hillcrest Farm
Barrow Cemetery
Rowland Hill Farm
COLLEGE ROAD
Daffodil Farm

Barton Vale Farm
Vale Farm
Barrow Grange
DN19
Foxhill Farm
Garners Hill Farm
Summerfield Farm

Barton Lodge

THORNTON ROAD

West Wold Farm
BURNHAM ROAD
B1206
Barrow Wold Farm
Walk House Farm

A1077
Low Farm

Pits (disused)
NORTHFIELD LANE
Home Farm
Thornton Hall
The Palm Farm
MAIN STREET
Thornton Curtis
STATION ROAD

DN18
Quarry (dis)
DAM LANE
Manor Farm
PH
BURNHAM LA

Mast
Burnham
Burnham Lodge
Quarry (dis)
Lodge Farm

Manor Lodge Farm
Frogmore Farm

Burnham Beeches Farm
Medieval Village
THORNTON ROAD
The Park
Wootton St Andrews CE Prim Sch
POND SIDE
Ashdale House

Wootton Dale
RACE LANE
VICARAGE LA
PH
Wootton
High Street
ULCEBY ROAD
Cemy
Eastfield Farm
POND SIDE

Wootton Dale Top
Wootton Grange
CHERRY LA
SWALLOW LANE
HAWTHORNE CL

DN39
WOLD ROAD
Little Farm
Howe Hill
WOOTTON ROAD
A1077

Viking Way
Dunkirk Farm
Dunkirk Wood

A15
DN20
B1211   WEST END ROAD

4
12
21
12

12

A8
1 WILLOW LA
2 JASMINE CT
3 ROWAN CT
4 CHESNUT WY
5 NORTH END
6 MANOR LA
7 STOTHARDS LA
8 HAWTHORNE GDNS
9 LIME GR
10 TRINITY CL
11 THE BRIDLES
12 THE SQUARE
13 WESTFIELD RD
14 GREENGATE LA
15 KING ST
16 CHURCH ST
17 ALL SAINTS' CL
18 SCHOOL LA
19 CHURCH SIDE
20 PIDGEON COTE LA
21 ST JOHNS CL
22 ST MICHAEL'S CT

11   5

Scale: 1¾ inches to 1 mile
0   ¼   ½   mile
0   250m   500m   750m   1 km

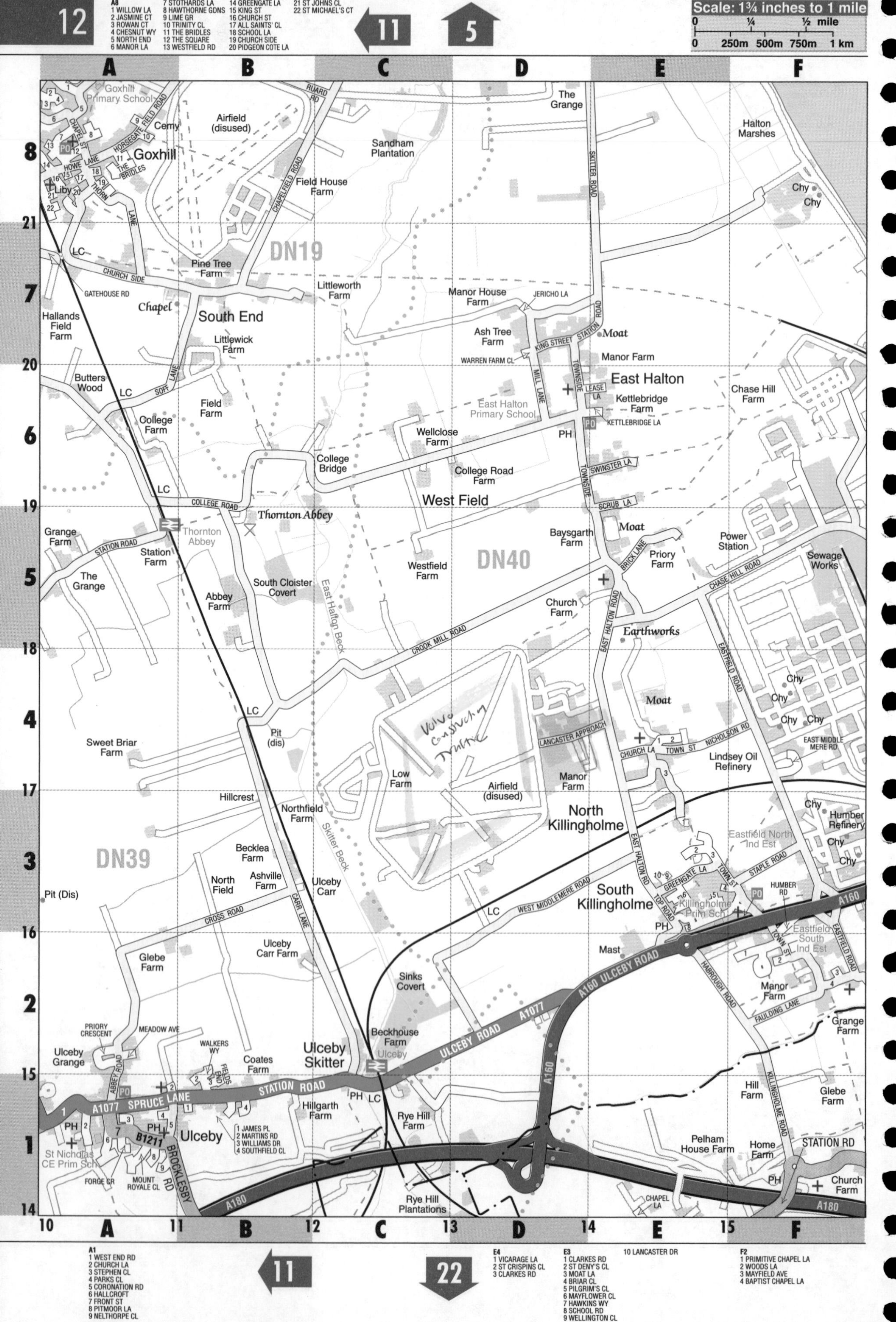

A1
1 WEST END RD
2 CHURCH LA
3 STEPHEN CL
4 PARKS CL
5 CORONATION RD
6 HALLCROFT
7 FRONT ST
8 PITMOOR LA
9 NELTHORPE CL

E4
1 VICARAGE LA
2 ST CRISPINS CL
3 CLARKES RD

E3
1 CLARKES RD
2 ST DENY'S CL
3 MOAT LA
4 BRIAR CL
5 PILGRIM'S CL
6 MAYFLOWER CL
7 HAWKINS WY
8 SCHOOL RD
9 WELLINGTON CL

10 LANCASTER DR

F2
1 PRIMITIVE CHAPEL LA
2 WOODS LA
3 MAYFIELD AVE
4 BAPTIST CHAPEL LA

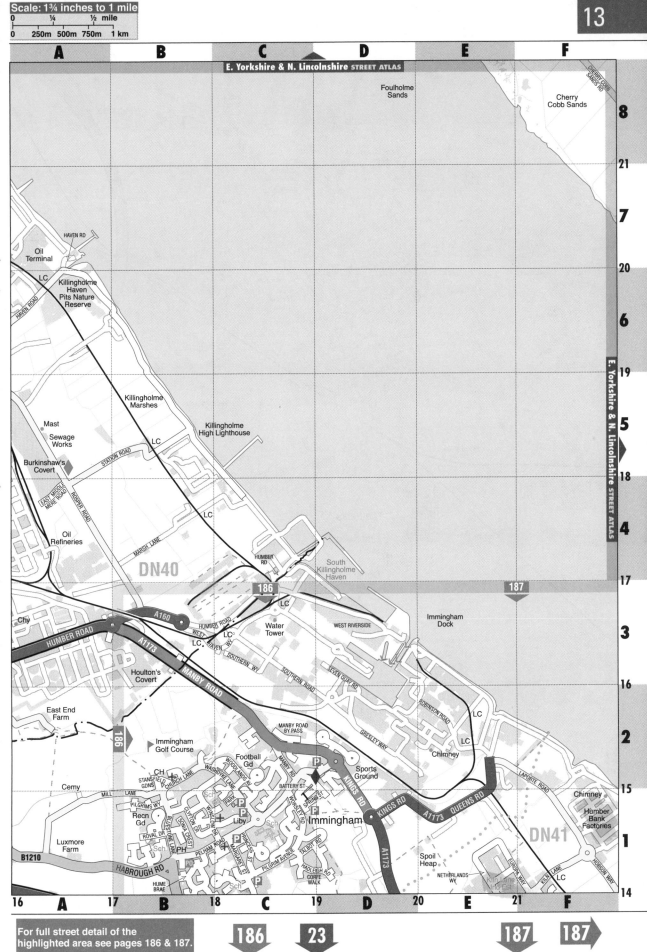

Scale: 1¾ inches to 1 mile

0   ¼   ½   mile
0   250m   500m   750m   1 km

A   B   C   D   E   F

E. Yorkshire & N. Lincolnshire STREET ATLAS

Foulholme Sands

Cherry Cobb Sands

CHERRY COBB SANDS RD

8

21

7

20

E. Yorkshire & N. Lincolnshire STREET ATLAS

19

Oil Terminal

HAVEN RD

LC

Killingholme Haven Pits Nature Reserve

HAVEN ROAD

6

Mast

Killingholme Marshes

5

Sewage Works

LC

Killingholme High Lighthouse

18

Burkinshaw's Covert

STATION ROAD

EAST MIDDLE MERE ROAD

ROSPER ROAD

LC

4

Oil Refineries

MARSH LANE

DN40

HUMBER RD

LC

South Killingholme Haven

17

187

186

Chy

A160

Water Tower

LC

West Riverside

Immingham Dock

3

HUMBER ROAD

A1173

Houlton's Covert

WEST HAVEN WY

LC

LC

SOUTHERN WY

SOUTHERN ROAD

WEST RIVERSIDE

SEVEN QUAY RD

MANBY ROAD

16

East End Farm

186

Immingham Golf Course

Manby Road By Pass

GRESLEY WAY

ROBINSON ROAD

LC

LC

2

Cemy

CH

STANSFIELD GDNS

CHURCH LANE

WASHDYKE LANE

WOODLAND AV

Football Gd

MANBY RD

Sports Ground

Chimney

15

MILL LANE

PILGRIMS WY

Recn Gd

BLUESTONE LANE

SONIA CREST

CLIFTON CR

WINSLOW DR

PARK

Liby

BATTERY ST

WORSLEY RD

SPRING ST

KINGS RD

A1173

QUEENS RD

Immingham

Chimney

Humber Bank Factories

DN41

1

Luxmore Farm

B1210

ROYAL DR

Sch

PO

PELHAM ROAD

PRINCESS ST

MARGARET ST

PILGRIM AVENUE

TALBOT RD

HADLEIGH RD

CORFE WALK

A1173

Spoil Heap

NETHERLANDS WY

Kiln Lane Ind Est

EUROPA WAY

KILN LANE

LC

LAPORTE ROAD

HOBSON WAY

HABROUGH RD

HUME BRAE

Sch

16   A   17   B   18   C   19   D   20   E   21   F   14

For full street detail of the highlighted area see pages 186 & 187.

186   23   187   187

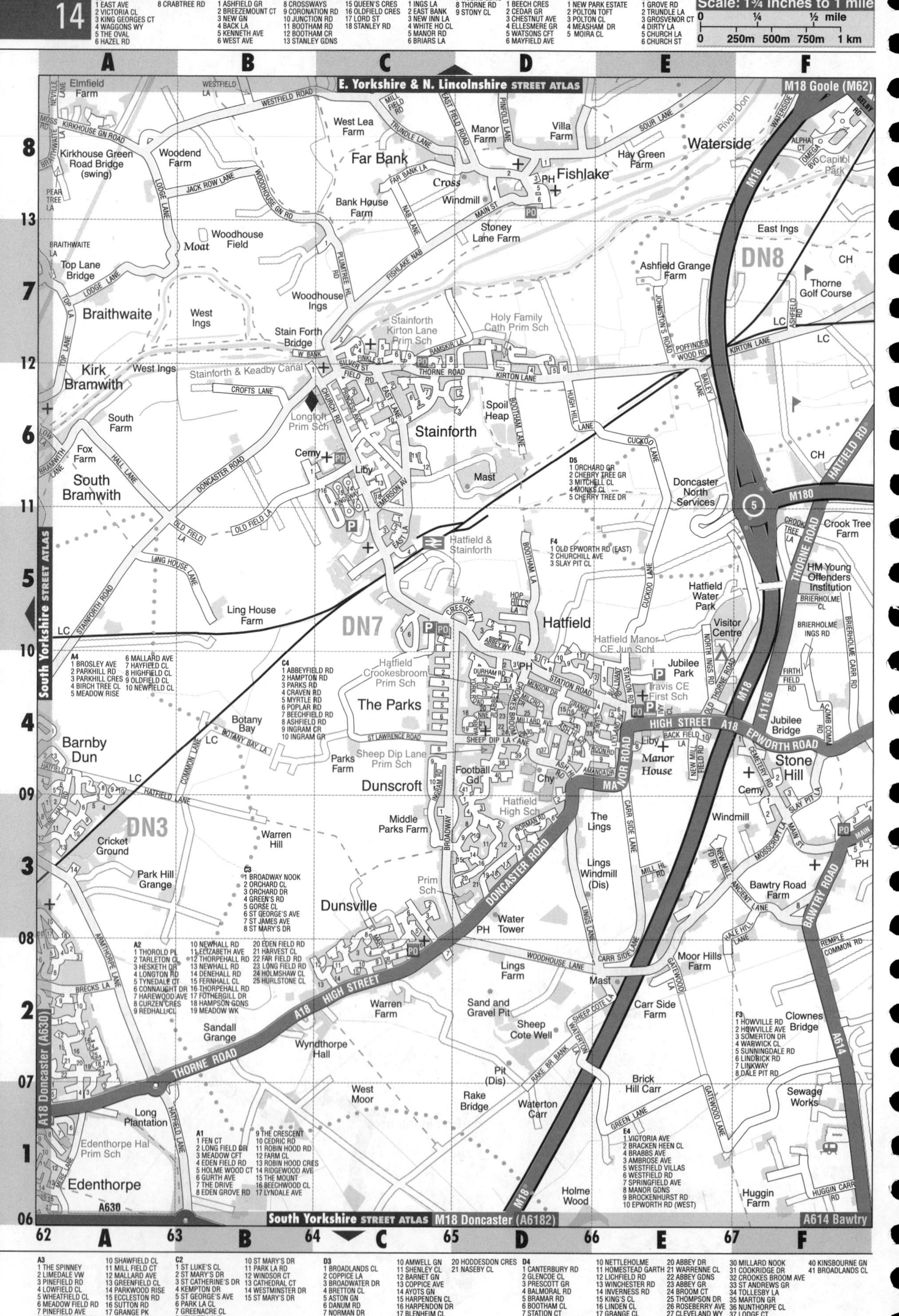

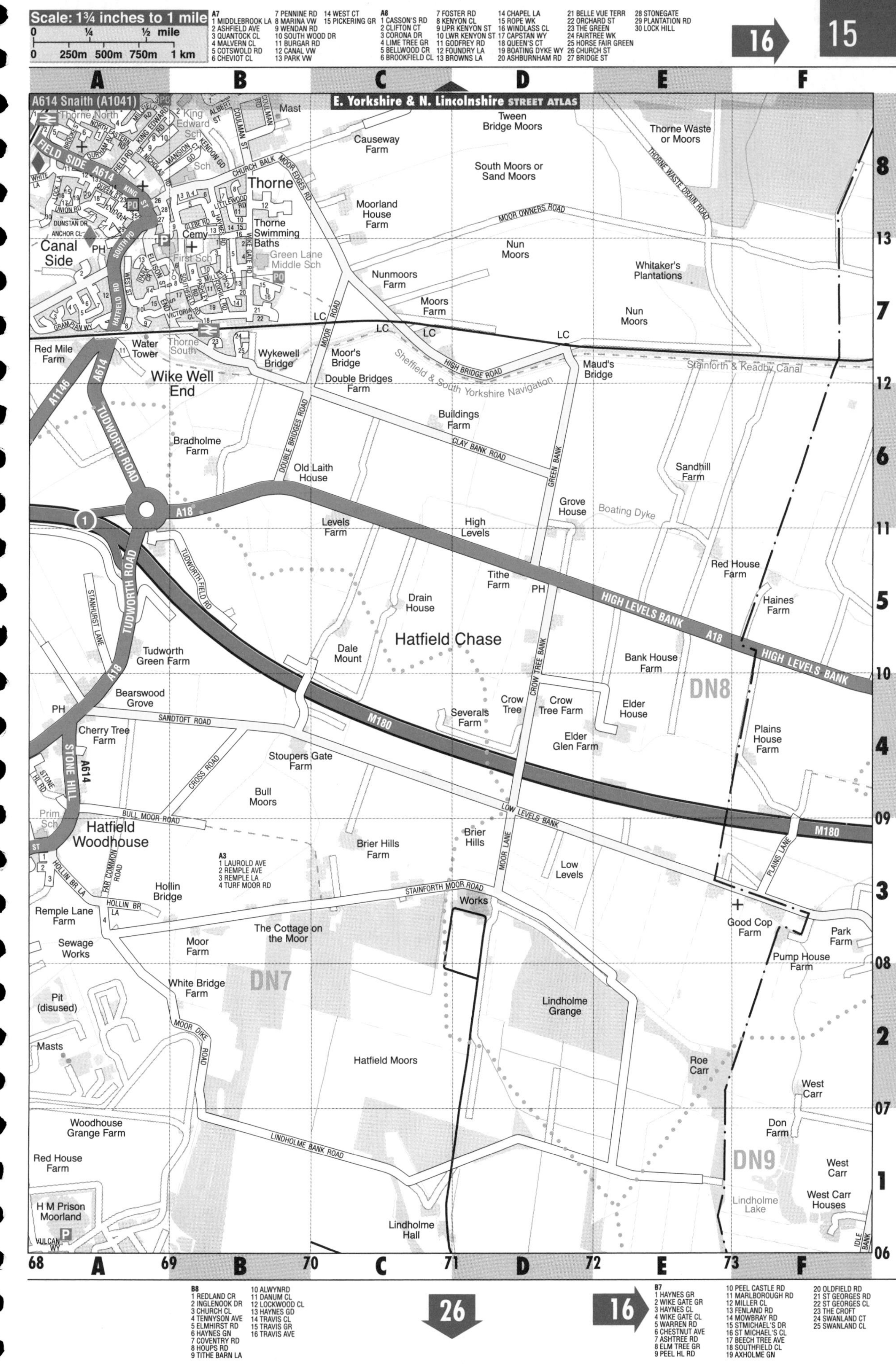

Scale: 1¾ inches to 1 mile
0 ¼ ½ mile
0 250m 500m 750m 1 km
A7
1 MIDDLEBROOK LA
2 ASHFIELD AVE
3 QUANTOCK CL
4 MALVERN CL
5 COTSWOLD RD
6 CHEVIOT CL
7 PENNINE RD
8 MARINA VW
9 WENDAN RD
10 SOUTH WOOD DR
11 BURGAR RD
12 CANAL VW
13 PARK VW
14 WEST CT
15 PICKERING GR
A8
1 CASSON'S RD
2 CLIFTON CT
3 CORONA DR
4 LIME TREE GR
5 BELLWOOD CR
6 BROOKFIELD CL
7 FOSTER RD
8 KENYON CL
9 UPR KENYON ST
10 LWR KENYON ST
11 GODFREY RD
12 FOUNDRY LA
13 BROWNS LA
14 CHAPEL LA
15 ROPE WK
16 WINDLASS CL
17 CAPSTAN WY
18 QUEEN'S CT
19 BOATING DYKE WY
20 ASHBURNHAM RD
21 BELLE VUE TERR
22 ORCHARD ST
23 THE GREEN
24 FAIRTREE WK
25 HORSE FAIR GREEN
26 CHURCH ST
27 BRIDGE ST
28 STONEGATE
29 PLANTATION RD
30 LOCK HILL
16
15
A B C D E F
A614 Snaith (A1041)
E. Yorkshire & N. Lincolnshire STREET ATLAS
Thorne North
Mast
Causeway Farm
Tween Bridge Moors
Thorne Waste or Moors
South Moors or Sand Moors
Thorne
Moorland House Farm
Thorne Swimming Baths
Green Lane Middle Sch
Canal Side
Cemy
First Sch
Nun Moors
Nunmoors Farm
Whitaker's Plantations
Moors Farm
Nun Moors
MOOR OWNERS ROAD
THORNE WASTE DRAIN ROAD
FIELD SIDE A614
CHURCH BALK
MOOR EDGES RD
HATFIELD RD
MOOR ROAD
LC
Red Mile Farm
Water Tower
Thorne South
Wykewell Bridge
Moor's Bridge
Double Bridges Farm
Wike Well End
Maud's Bridge
Stainforth & Keadby Canal
Sheffield & South Yorkshire Navigation
HIGH BRIDGE ROAD
A1146
A614
TUDWORTH ROAD
Bradholme Farm
Buildings Farm
CLAY BANK ROAD
DOUBLE BRIDGES ROAD
Old Laith House
GREEN BANK
Sandhill Farm
Grove House
Boating Dyke
A18
Levels Farm
High Levels
Red House Farm
TUDWORTH FIELD RD
STANHURST LANE
Tithe Farm
PH
Drain House
Haines Farm
HIGH LEVELS BANK
Hatfield Chase
Tudworth Green Farm
Dale Mount
Bank House Farm
CROW TREE BANK
DN8
Bearswood Grove
M180
Crow Tree
Crow Tree Farm
Elder House
Severals Farm
Cherry Tree Farm
SANDTOFT ROAD
Elder Glen Farm
Plains House Farm
Stoupers Gate Farm
CROSS ROAD
STONE HILL
Bull Moors
Prim Sch
BULL MOOR ROAD
LOW LEVELS BANK
Hatfield Woodhouse
Brier Hills
Brier Hills Farm
MOOR LANE
Low Levels
PLAINS LANE
A3
1 LAUROLD AVE
2 REMPLE AVE
3 REMPLE LA
4 TURF MOOR RD
HOLLIN BR LA
FAR COMMON ROAD
Hollin Bridge
STAINFORTH MOOR ROAD
Works
Good Cop Farm
Remple Lane Farm
Park Farm
Sewage Works
The Cottage on the Moor
Moor Farm
Pump House Farm
White Bridge Farm
DN7
Pit (disused)
MOOR DIKE ROAD
Lindholme Grange
Masts
Hatfield Moors
Roe Carr
West Carr
Woodhouse Grange Farm
Don Farm
LINDHOLME BANK ROAD
Red House Farm
DN9
West Carr
West Carr Houses
H M Prison Moorland
Lindholme Lake
Lindholme Hall
VULCAN WY
IDLE BANK
8 13 7 12 6 11 5 10 4 09 3 08 2 07 1 06
68 69 70 71 72 73
B8
1 REDLAND CR
2 INGLENOOK DR
3 CHURCH CL
4 TENNYSON AVE
5 ELMHIRST RD
6 HAYNES GN
7 COVENTRY RD
8 HOUPS RD
9 TITHE BARN LA
10 ALWYNRD
11 DANUM CL
12 LOCKWOOD CL
13 HAYNES GD
14 TRAVIS CL
15 TRAVIS GR
16 TRAVIS AVE
26
16
B7
1 HAYNES GR
2 WIKE GATE GR
3 HAYNES CL
4 WIKE GATE CL
5 WARREN RD
6 CHESTNUT AVE
7 ASHTREE RD
8 ELM TREE GR
9 PEEL HL RD
10 PEEL CASTLE RD
11 MARLBOROUGH RD
12 MILLER CL
13 FENLAND RD
14 MOWBRAY RD
15 ST MICHAEL'S DR
16 ST MICHAEL'S CL
17 BEECH TREE AVE
18 SOUTHFIELD CL
19 AXHOLME GN
20 OLDFIELD RD
21 ST GEORGES RD
22 ST GEORGES CL
23 THE CROFT
24 SWANLAND CT
25 SWANLAND CL

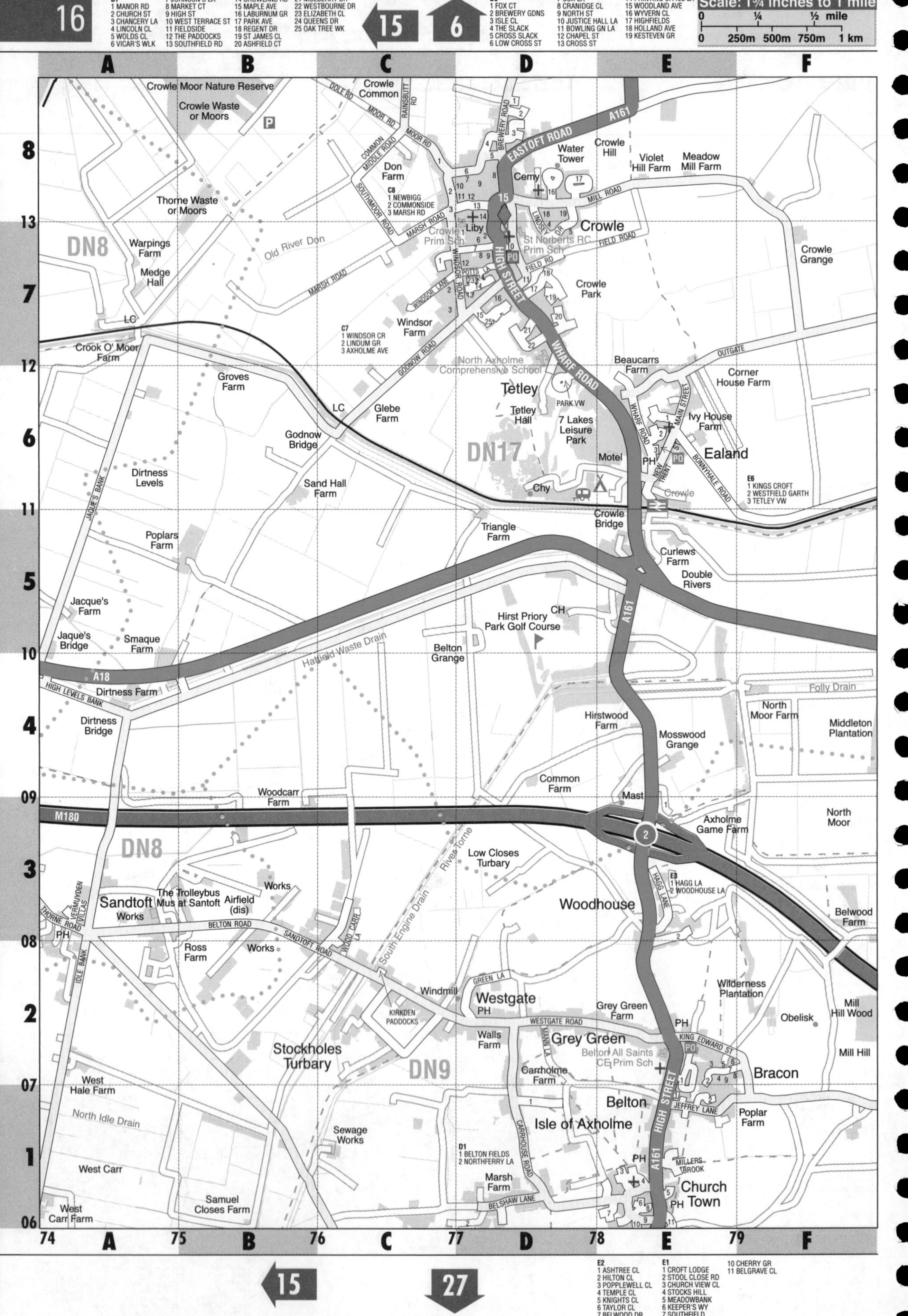
D7
1 MANOR RD
2 CHURCH ST
3 CHANCERY LA
4 LINCOLN CL
5 WOLDS CL
6 VICAR'S WLK
7 JOHNSON'S LA
8 MARKET CT
9 HIGH ST
10 WEST TERRACE ST
11 FIELDSIDE
12 THE PADDOCKS
13 SOUTHFIELD RD
14 CROWLAND RD
15 MAPLE AVE
16 LABURNUM GR
17 PARK AVE
18 REGENT DR
19 ST JAMES CL
20 ASHFIELD CT
21 MULBERRY DR
22 WESTBOURNE DR
23 ELIZABETH CL
24 QUEENS DR
25 OAK TREE WK
15
6
D8
1 FOX CT
2 BREWERY GDNS
3 ISLE CL
4 THE SLACK
5 CROSS SLACK
6 LOW CROSS ST
7 COX LA
8 CRANIDGE CL
9 NORTH ST
10 JUSTICE HALL LA
11 BOWLING GN LA
12 CHAPEL ST
13 CROSS ST
14 PRINTING OFFICE LA
15 WOODLAND AVE
16 WYVERN CL
17 HIGHFIELDS
18 HOLLAND AVE
19 KESTEVEN GR
Scale: 1¾ inches to 1 mile
0 ¼ ½ mile
0 250m 500m 750m 1 km
A B C D E F
8
13
7
12
6
11
5
10
4
09
3
08
2
07
1
06
74 75 76 77 78 79
Crowle Moor Nature Reserve
Crowle Waste or Moors
Crowle Common
DOLE RD
MOOR RD
RAINSBUTT RD
COMMON MIDDLE ROAD
SOUTHMOOR ROAD
BREWERY ROAD
EASTOFT ROAD
A161
Water Tower
Crowle Hill
Violet Hill Farm
Meadow Mill Farm
Don Farm
Cemy
MILL ROAD
C8
1 NEWBIGG
2 COMMONSIDE
3 MARSH RD
Thorne Waste or Moors
MARSH ROAD
Liby
Crowle Prim Sch
LINDSEY GR
Crowle
St Norberts RC Prim Sch
FIELD ROAD
DN8
Warpings Farm
Old River Don
HIGH STREET
WINDSOR ROAD
POTTS LA
FIELD RD
Crowle Grange
Medge Hall
WINDSOR LANE
Crowle Park
LC
C7
1 WINDSOR CR
2 LINDUM GR
3 AXHOLME AVE
Windsor Farm
Crook O' Moor Farm
WHARF ROAD
GODNOW ROAD
North Axholme Comprehensive School
Beaucarrs Farm
OUTGATE
Corner House Farm
Groves Farm
Tetley
PARK VW
MAIN STREET
Glebe Farm
Tetley Hall
7 Lakes Leisure Park
Ivy House Farm
Godnow Bridge
DN17
Motel
PH
PO
NEW TRENT ST
BONNYHALE ROAD
Ealand
Dirtness Levels
Sand Hall Farm
Chy
Crowle
E6
1 KINGS CROFT
2 WESTFIELD GARTH
3 TETLEY VW
JAQUE'S BANK
Crowle Bridge
Triangle Farm
Poplars Farm
Curlews Farm
Double Rivers
Jacque's Farm
CH
Hirst Priory Park Golf Course
Jaque's Bridge
Smaque Farm
Hatfield Waste Drain
Belton Grange
A18
Dirtness Farm
HIGH LEVELS BANK
Folly Drain
Hirstwood Farm
North Moor Farm
Middleton Plantation
Dirtness Bridge
Mosswood Grange
Common Farm
Woodcarr Farm
Mast
North Moor
M180
Axholme Game Farm
2
DN8
Low Closes Turbary
River Torne
E3
1 HAGG LA
2 WOODHOUSE LA
HAGG LANE
Works
Sandtoft Works
The Trolleybus Mus at Santoft
Airfield (dis)
Woodhouse
Belwood Farm
VERMUYDEN VILLAS
THORNE ROAD
PH
BELTON ROAD
SANDTOFT ROAD
WOOD CARR LA
South Engine Drain
Ross Farm
Works
IDLE BANK
GREEN LA
Windmill
Wilderness Plantation
Westgate
PH
Grey Green Farm
Mill Hill Wood
Obelisk
KIRKDEN PADDOCKS
WESTGATE ROAD
MANN LA
KING EDWARD ST
Walls Farm
Grey Green
Stockholes Turbary
Belton All Saints CE Prim Sch
Mill Hill
DN9
Bracon
West Hale Farm
Carrholme Farm
Belton
JEFFREY LANE
Poplar Farm
North Idle Drain
Isle of Axholme
CARRHOUSE ROAD
Sewage Works
D1
1 BELTON FIELDS
2 NORTHFERRY LA
MILLERS BROOK
Church Town
West Carr
Marsh Farm
Samuel Closes Farm
BELSHAW LANE
West Carr Farm
E2
1 ASHTREE CL
2 HILTON CL
3 POPPLEWELL CL
4 TEMPLE CL
5 KNIGHTS CL
6 TAYLOR CL
7 BELWOOD DR
8 JOHNSON CL
9 BRACON CL
E1
1 CROFT LODGE
2 STOOL CLOSE RD
3 CHURCH VIEW CL
4 STOCKS HILL
5 MEADOWBANK
6 KEEPER'S WY
7 SOUTHFIELD
8 POACHER'S CRFT
9 CHURCHTOWN
10 CHERRY GR
11 BELGRAVE CL
15
27

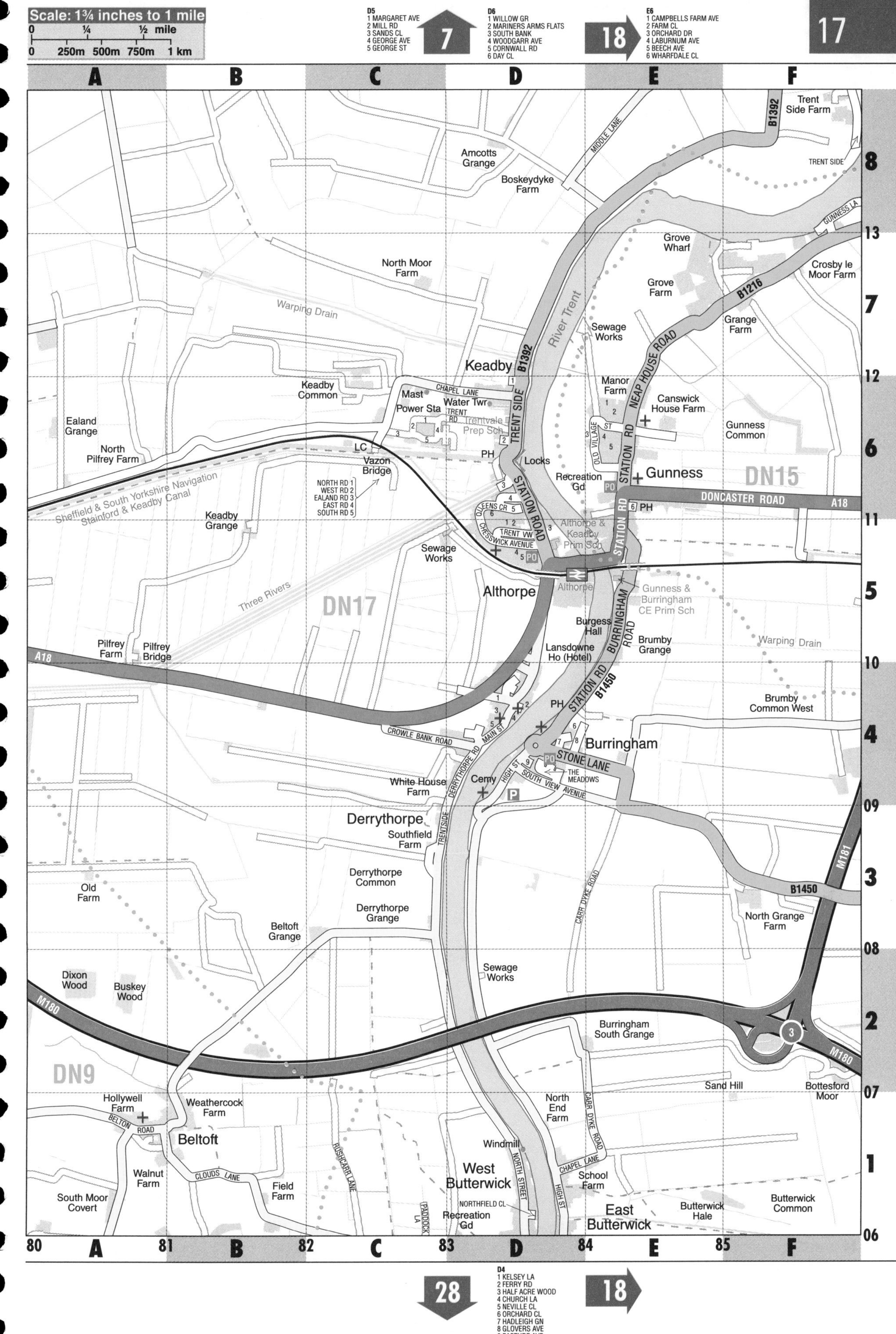

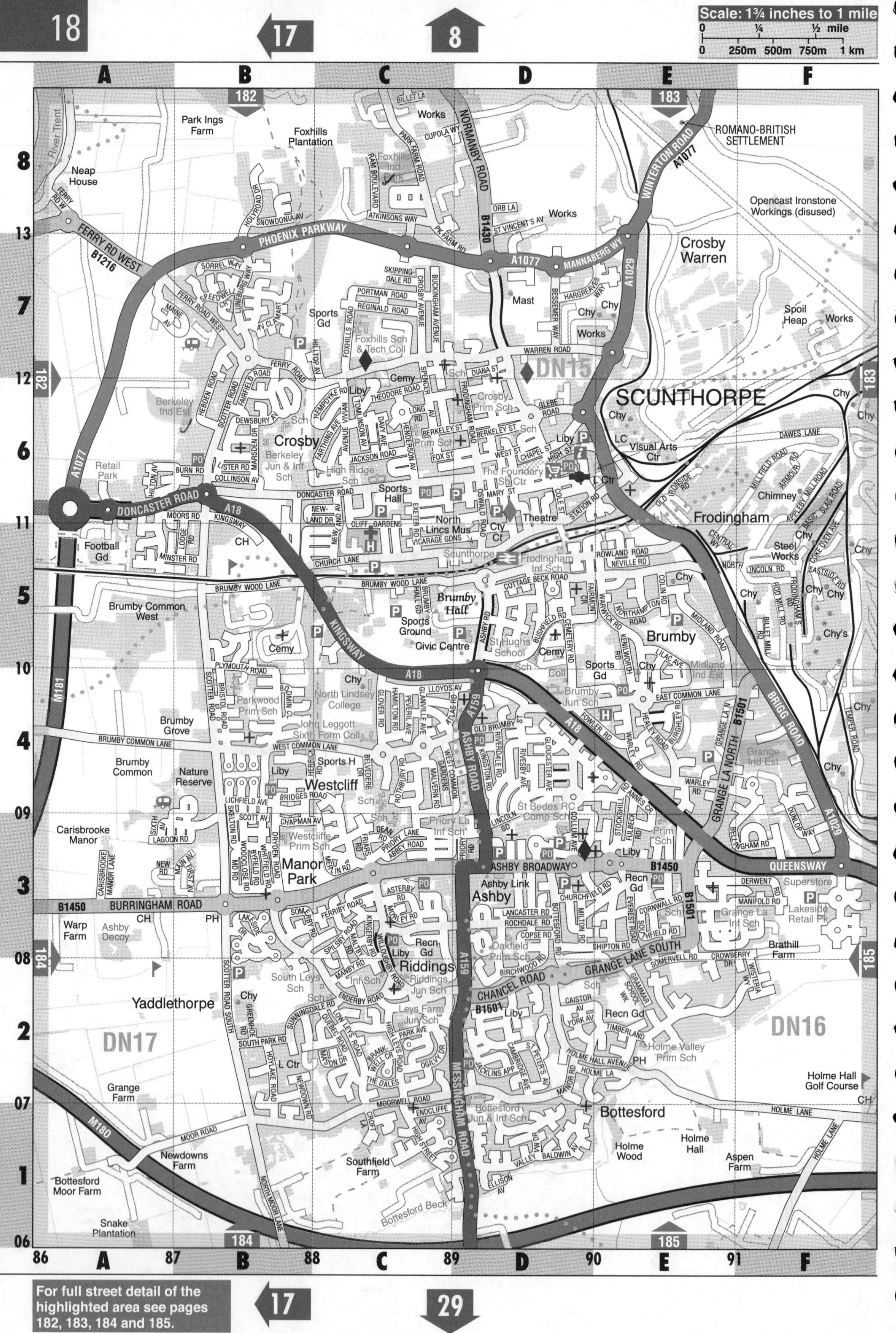

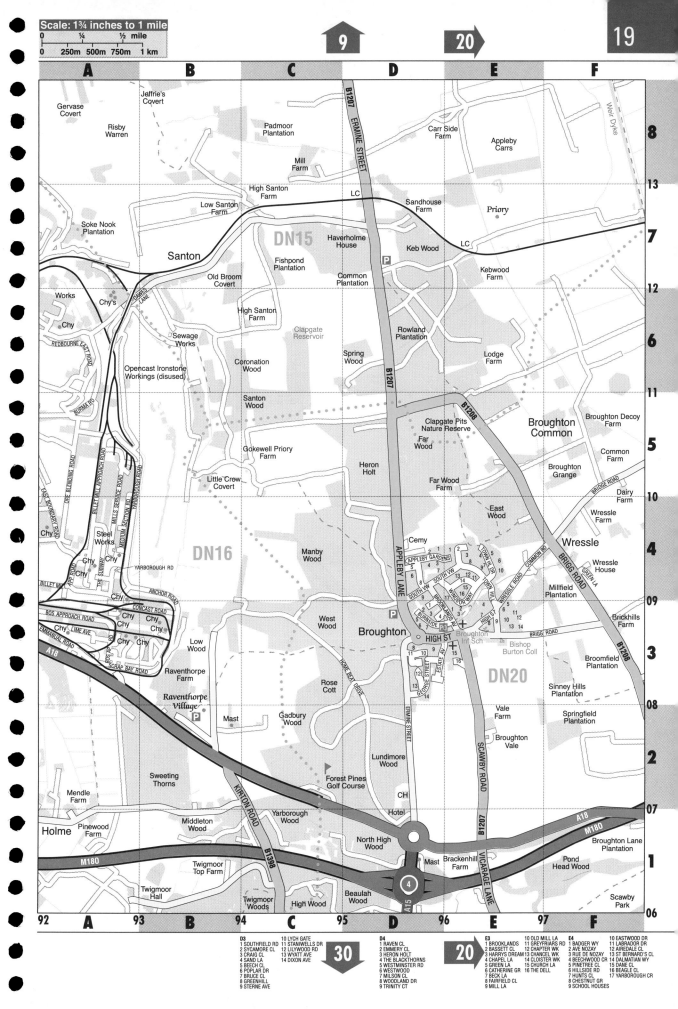

D3
1 SOUTHFIELD RD
2 SYCAMORE CL
3 CRAIG CL
4 SAND LA
5 BEECH CL
6 POPLAR DR
7 BRUCE CL
8 GREENHILL
9 STERNE AVE
10 LYCH GATE
11 STANIWELLS DR
12 LILYWOOD RD
13 WYATT AVE
14 DIXON AVE

D4
1 RAVEN CL
2 EMMERY CL
3 HERON HOLT
4 THE BLACKTHORNS
5 WESTMINSTER RD
6 WESTWOOD
7 MILSON CL
8 WOODLAND DR
9 TRINITY CT

E3
1 BROOKLANDS
2 BASSETT CL
3 HARRYS DREAM
4 CHAPEL LA
5 GREEN LA
6 CATHERINE GR
7 BECK LA
8 FAIRFIELD CL
9 MILL LA
10 OLD MILL LA
11 GREYFRIARS RD
12 CHAPTER WK
13 CHANCEL WK
14 CLOISTER WK
15 CHURCH LA
16 THE DELL

E4
1 BADGER WY
2 AVE NOZAY
3 RUE DE NOZAY
4 BEECHWOOD CR
5 PINETREE CL
6 HILLSIDE RD
7 HUNTS CL
8 CHESTNUT GR
9 SCHOOL HOUSES
10 EASTWOOD DR
11 LABRADOR DR
12 AIREDALE CL
13 ST BERNARD'S CL
14 DALMATIAN WY
15 DANE CL
16 BEAGLE CL
17 YARBOROUGH CR

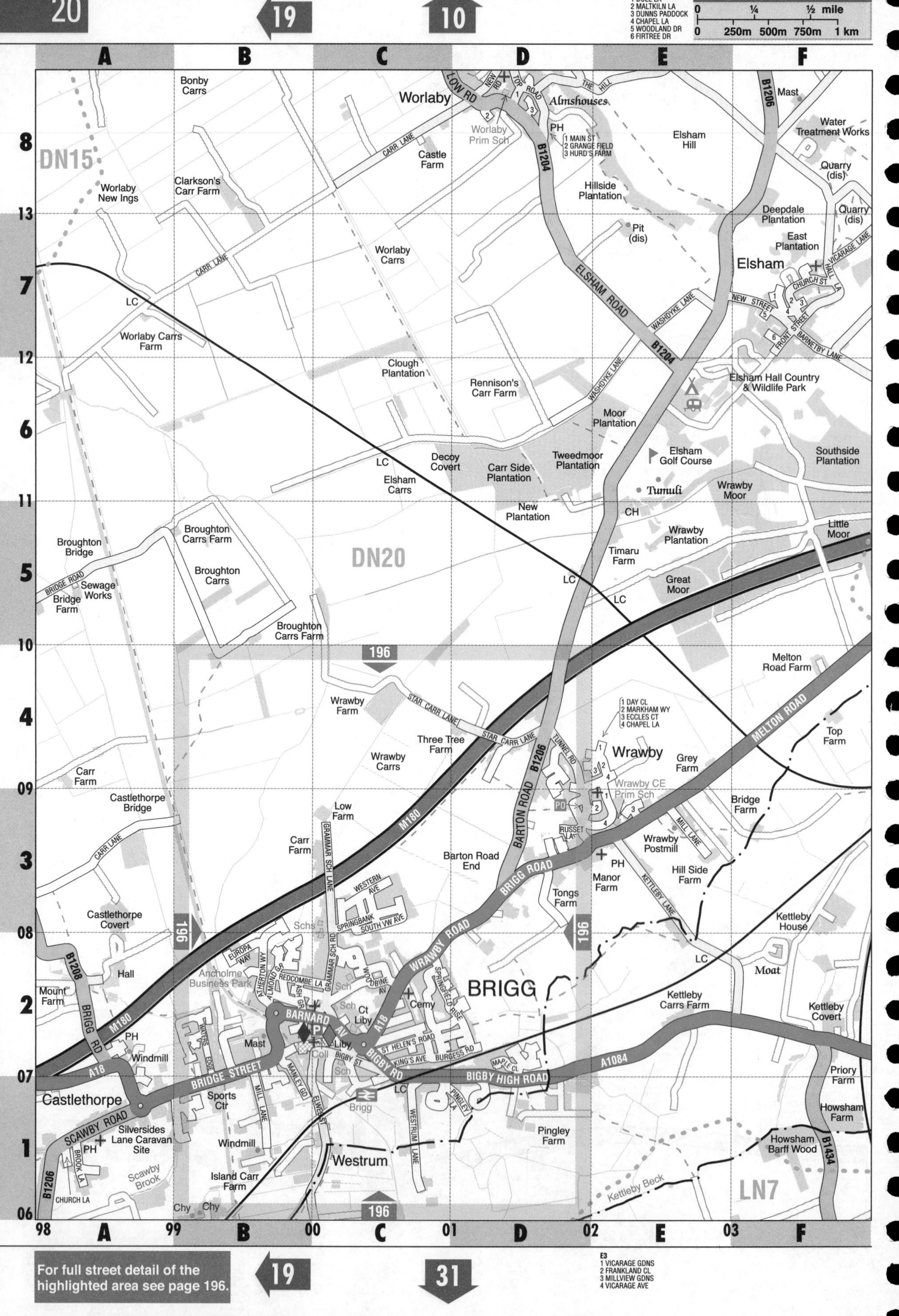

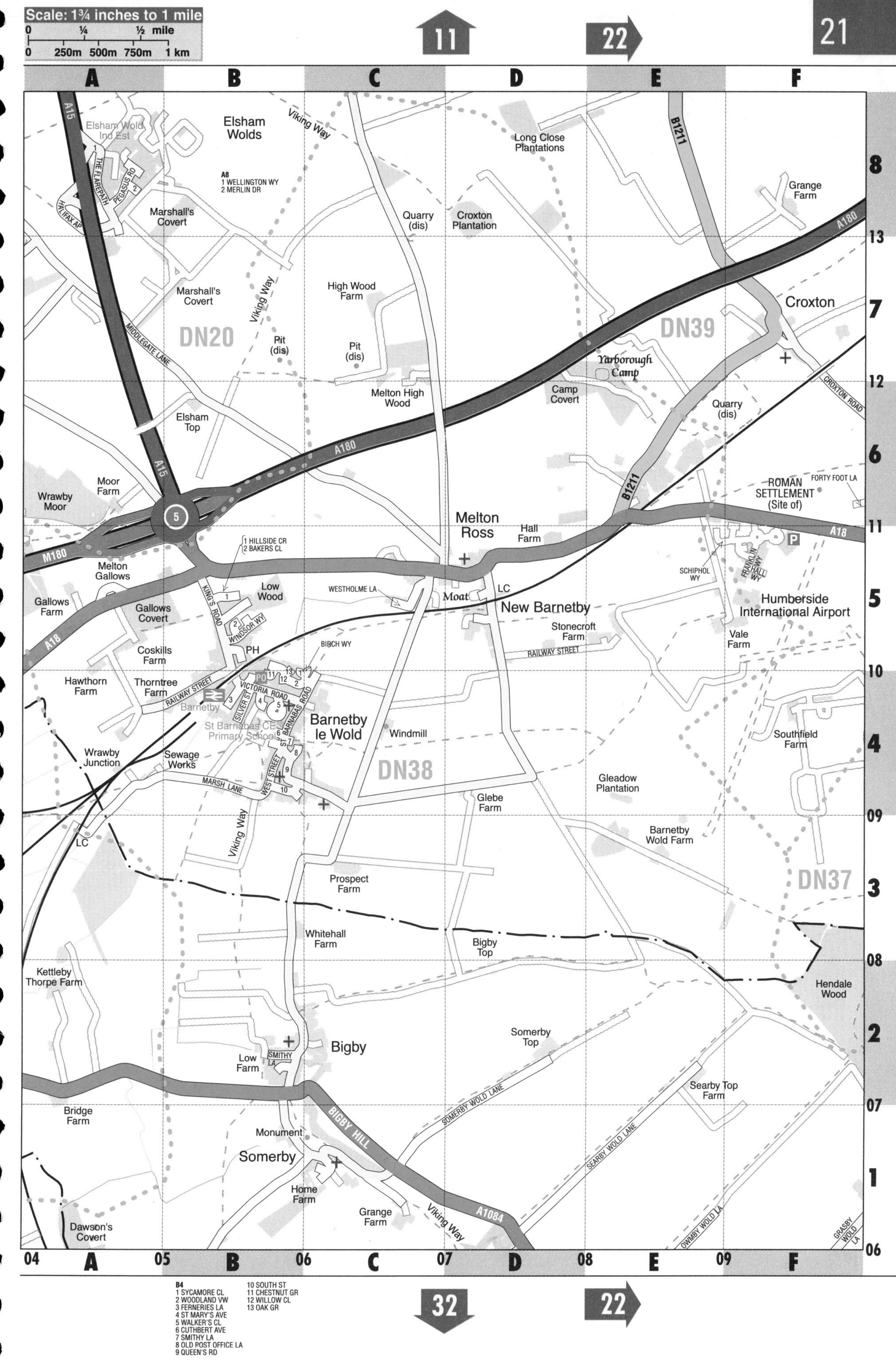

Scale: 1¾ inches to 1 mile
0 ¼ ½ mile
0 250m 500m 750m 1 km
11
22
21
A B C D E F
8 13 7 12 6 11 5 10 4 09 3 08 2 07 1 06
04 05 06 07 08 09
Elsham Wold Ind Est
Elsham Wolds
A8
1 WELLINGTON WY
2 MERLIN DR
THE FLAREPATH
PEGASUS RD
HALIFAX AP
Viking Way
Long Close Plantations
B1211
Grange Farm
A15
Marshall's Covert
Quarry (dis)
Croxton Plantation
A180
High Wood Farm
Croxton
DN20
DN39
MIDDLEGATE LANE
Pit (dis)
Yarborough Camp
CROXTON ROAD
Melton High Wood
Camp Covert
Quarry (dis)
Elsham Top
Moor Farm
Wrawby Moor
ROMAN SETTLEMENT (Site of)
FORTY FOOT LA
Melton Ross
Hall Farm
A18
M180
Melton Gallows
1 HILLSIDE CR
2 BAKERS CL
SCHIPHOL WY
FRANKLIN WY
HALL WY
P
Gallows Farm
Gallows Covert
Low Wood
KING'S ROAD
WESTHOLME LA
Moat
LC
New Barnetby
WINDSOR WY
Humberside International Airport
Stonecroft Farm
Vale Farm
Coskills Farm
PH
BIRCH WY
RAILWAY STREET
Hawthorn Farm
Thorntree Farm
PO
VICTORIA ROAD
Barnetby
SILVER ST
ST BARNABAS ROAD
St Barnabas CE Primary School
Barnetby le Wold
Windmill
Southfield Farm
Wrawby Junction
Sewage Works
DN38
MARSH LANE
WEST STREET
Gleadow Plantation
Glebe Farm
LC
Barnetby Wold Farm
Prospect Farm
DN37
Whitehall Farm
Bigby Top
Kettleby Thorpe Farm
Hendale Wood
Somerby Top
Bigby
Low Farm
SMITHY LA
Searby Top Farm
Bridge Farm
SOMERBY WOLD LANE
BIGBY HILL
Monument
Somerby
SEARBY WOLD LANE
Home Farm
Grange Farm
A1084
Dawson's Covert
OWMBY WOLD LA
GRASBY WOLD LA
B4
1 SYCAMORE CL
2 WOODLAND VW
3 FERNERIES LA
4 ST MARY'S AVE
5 WALKER'S CL
6 CUTHBERT AVE
7 SMITHY LA
8 OLD POST OFFICE LA
9 QUEEN'S RD
10 SOUTH ST
11 CHESTNUT GR
12 WILLOW CL
13 OAK GR
32
22

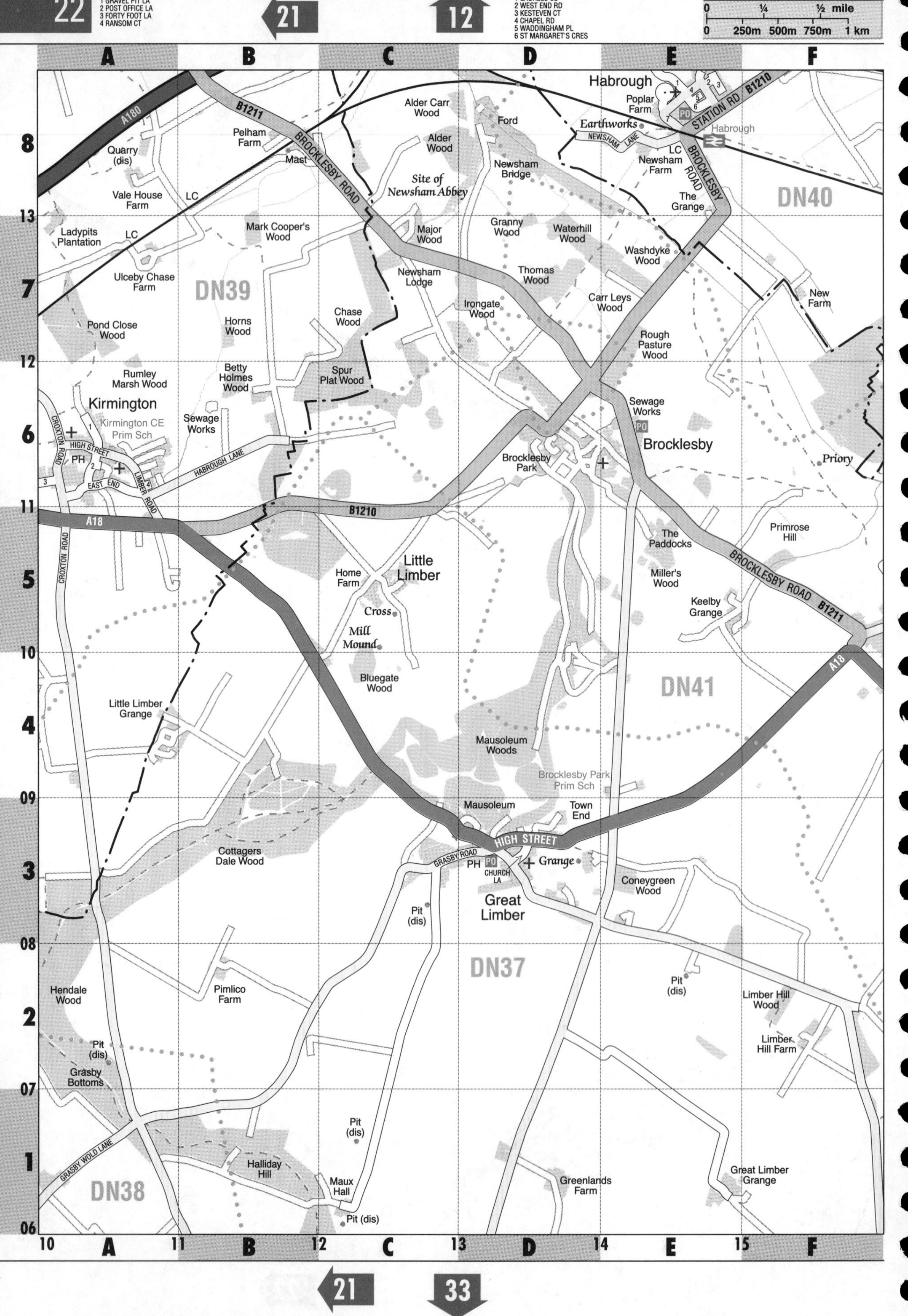

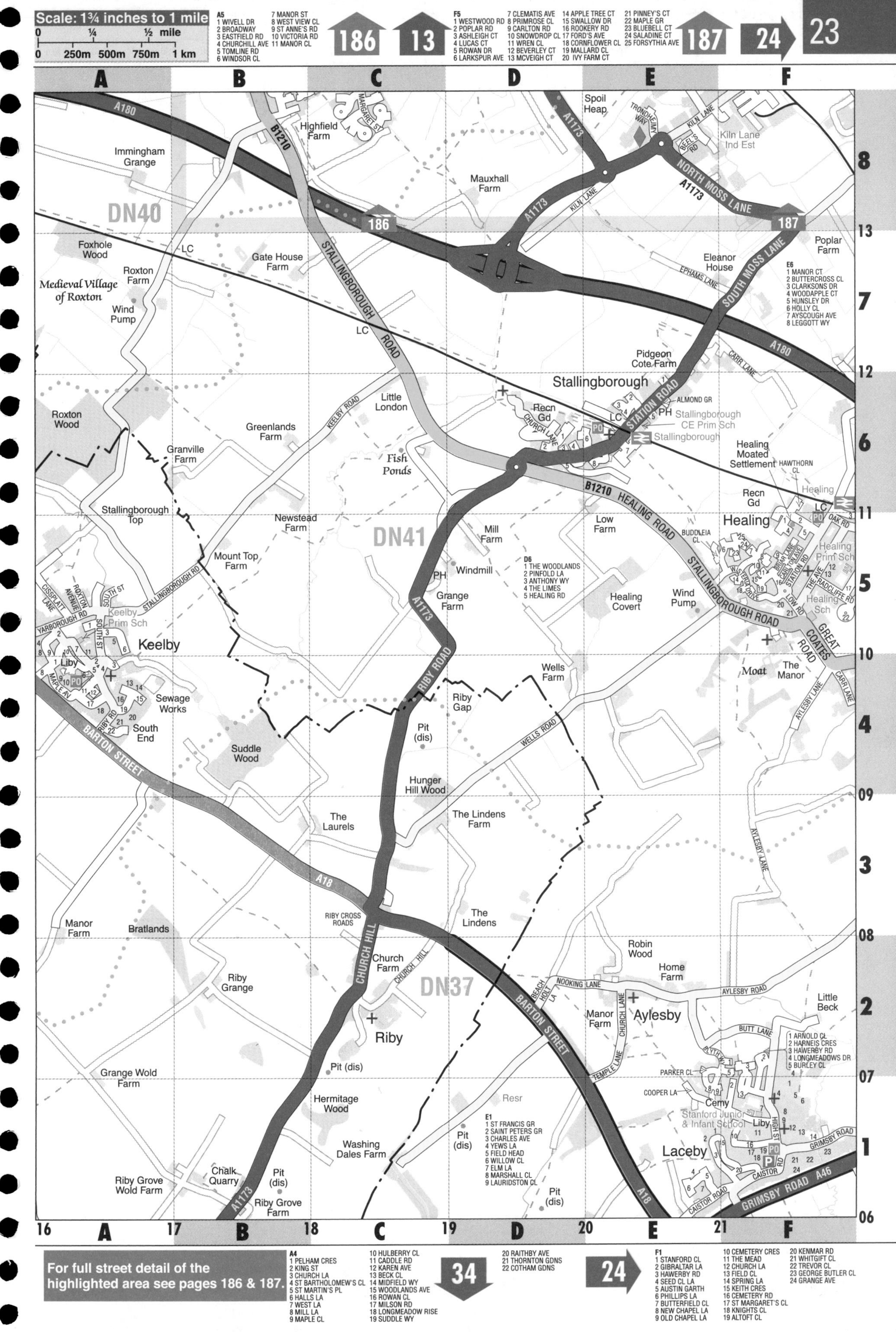

Scale: 1¾ inches to 1 mile
0 ¼ ½ mile
0 250m 500m 750m 1 km
A5
1 WIVELL DR
2 BROADWAY
3 EASTFIELD RD
4 CHURCHILL AVE
5 TOMLINE RD
6 WINDSOR CL
7 MANOR ST
8 WEST VIEW CL
9 ST ANNE'S RD
10 VICTORIA RD
11 MANOR CL
186
13
F5
1 WESTWOOD RD
2 POPLAR RD
3 ASHLEIGH CT
4 LUCAS CT
5 ROWAN DR
6 LARKSPUR AVE
7 CLEMATIS AVE
8 PRIMROSE CL
9 CARLTON RD
10 SNOWDROP CL
11 WREN CL
12 BEVERLEY CT
13 MCVEIGH CT
14 APPLE TREE CT
15 SWALLOW DR
16 ROOKERY RD
17 FORD'S AVE
18 CORNFLOWER CL
19 MALLARD CL
20 IVY FARM CT
21 PINNEY'S CT
22 MAPLE GR
23 BLUEBELL CT
24 SALADINE CT
25 FORSYTHIA AVE
187
24
23
A B C D E F
8
13
7
12
6
11
5
10
4
09
3
08
2
07
1
06
16 17 18 19 20 21
A180
B1210
Immingham Grange
Highfield Farm
Spoil Heap
A1173
TRONDHEIM WAY
KILN LANE
BEEL'S RD
Kiln Lane Ind Est
NORTH MOSS LANE
Mauxhall Farm
DN40
Foxhole Wood
LC
Gate House Farm
Roxton Farm
Medieval Village of Roxton
Wind Pump
STALLINGBOROUGH ROAD
Eleanor House
EPHAMS LANE
SOUTH MOSS LANE
Poplar Farm
E6
1 MANOR CT
2 BUTTERCROSS CL
3 CLARKSONS DR
4 WOODAPPLE CT
5 HUNSLEY DR
6 HOLLY CL
7 AYSCOUGH AVE
8 LEGGOTT WY
Pidgeon Cote Farm
CARR LANE
Stallingborough
STATION ROAD
ALMOND GR
Stallingborough CE Prim Sch
Roxton Wood
Little London
KEELBY ROAD
Greenlands Farm
Recn Gd
CHURCH LANE
PO
PH
Granville Farm
Fish Ponds
Healing Moated Settlement
HAWTHORN CL
Recn Gd
Healing
OAK RD
Stallingborough Top
Newstead Farm
DN41
Mill Farm
Low Farm
HEALING ROAD
BUDDLEIA CL
Healing Prim Sch
Mount Top Farm
STALLINGBOROUGH RD
Windmill
D6
1 THE WOODLANDS
2 PINFOLD LA
3 ANTHONY WY
4 THE LIMES
5 HEALING RD
CISSPLATT LANE
ROXTON AVENUE
SOUTH ST
Keelby Prim Sch
Grange Farm
Healing Covert
Wind Pump
STATION RD
RADCLIFFE RD
Healing Sch
YARBOROUGH RD
Keelby
Liby
MAPLE AV
Sewage Works
RIBY ROAD
Wells Farm
GREAT COATES ROAD
Moat
The Manor
CARR LANE
AYLESBY LANE
South End
Riby Gap
Pit (dis)
BARTON STREET
Suddle Wood
WELLS ROAD
Hunger Hill Wood
The Laurels
The Lindens Farm
AYLESBY LANE
A18
Manor Farm
Bratlands
RIBY CROSS ROADS
The Lindens
CHURCH HILL
Church Farm
Robin Wood
Home Farm
Riby Grange
DN37
BEACH HOLT LA
NOOKING LANE
AYLESBY ROAD
Little Beck
Manor Farm
CHURCH LANE
Aylesby
BUTT LANE
1 ARNOLD CL
2 HARNEIS CRES
3 HAWERBY RD
4 LONGMEADOWS DR
5 BURLEY CL
Riby
Pit (dis)
TEMPLE LANE
PARKER CL
Grange Wold Farm
COOPER LA
Cemy
Hermitage Wood
Resr
Stanford Junior & Infant School
Liby
HIGH ST
E1
1 ST FRANCIS GR
2 SAINT PETERS GR
3 CHARLES AVE
4 YEWS LA
5 FIELD HEAD
6 WILLOW CL
7 ELM LA
8 MARSHALL CL
9 LAURISTON CL
Washing Dales Farm
Pit (dis)
GRIMSBY ROAD
Laceby
CAISTOR RD
Riby Grove Wold Farm
Chalk Quarry
Pit (dis)
Riby Grove Farm
CAISTOR ROAD
GRIMSBY ROAD A46
For full street detail of the highlighted area see pages 186 & 187.
A4
1 PELHAM CRES
2 KING ST
3 CHURCH LA
4 ST BARTHOLOMEW'S CL
5 ST MARTIN'S PL
6 HALLS LA
7 WEST LA
8 MILL LA
9 MAPLE CL
10 HULBERRY CL
11 CADDLE RD
12 KAREN AVE
13 BECK CL
14 MIDFIELD WY
15 WOODLANDS AVE
16 ROWAN CL
17 MILSON RD
18 LONGMEADOW RISE
19 SUDDLE WY
34
20 RAITHBY AVE
21 THORNTON GDNS
22 COTHAM GDNS
24
F1
1 STANFORD CL
2 GIBRALTAR LA
3 HAWERBY RD
4 SEED CL LA
5 AUSTIN GARTH
6 PHILLIPS LA
7 BUTTERFIELD CL
8 NEW CHAPEL LA
9 OLD CHAPEL LA
10 CEMETERY CRES
11 THE MEAD
12 CHURCH LA
13 FIELD CL
14 SPRING LA
15 KEITH CRES
16 CEMETERY RD
17 ST MARGARET'S CL
18 KNIGHTS CL
19 ALTOFT CL
20 KENMAR RD
21 WHITGIFT CL
22 TREVOR CL
23 GEORGE BUTLER CL
24 GRANGE AVE

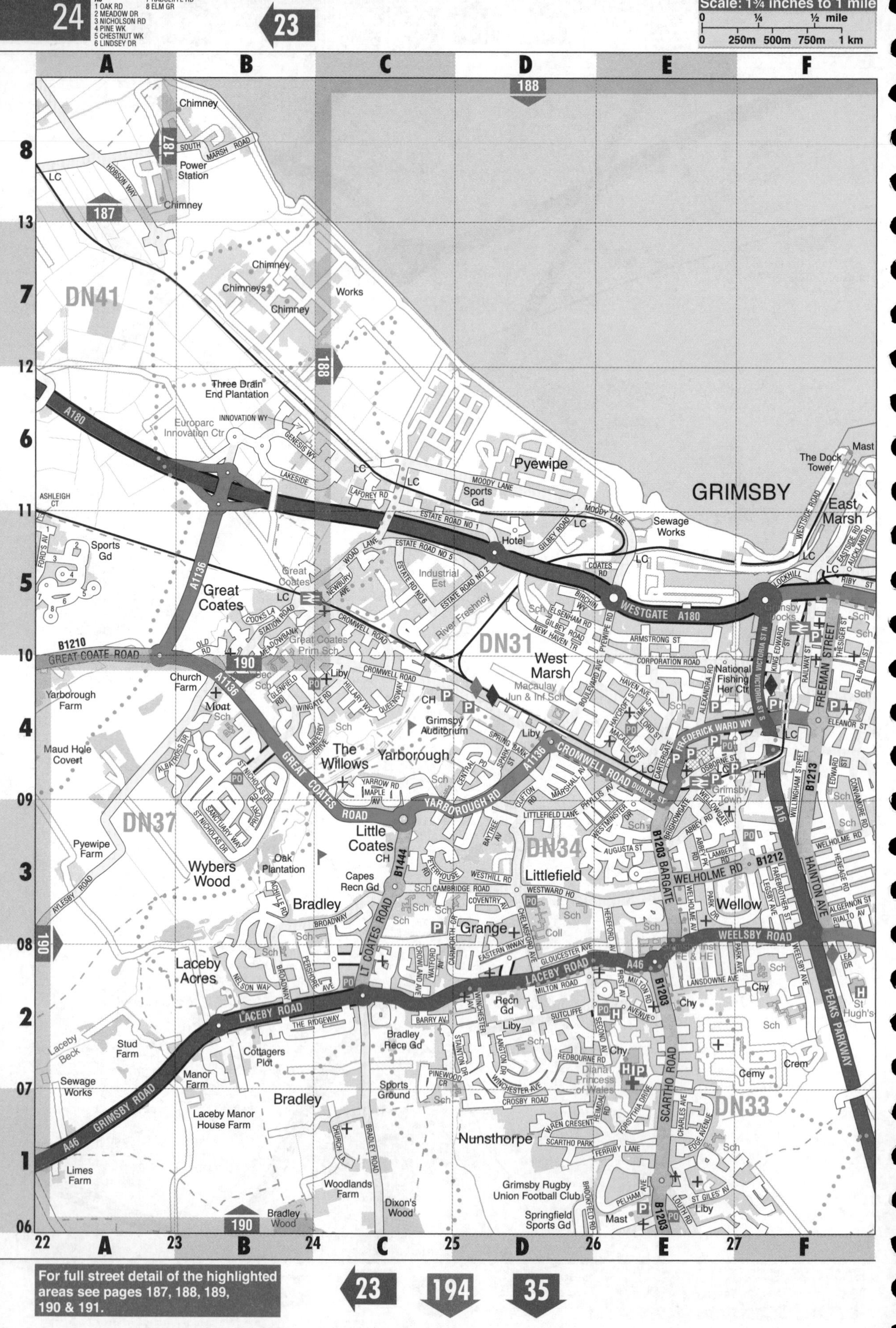

Scale: 1¾ inches to 1 mile

0   ¼   ½   mile
0   250m   500m   750m   1 km

A   B   C   D   E   F

189

189

8

13

Grimsby Roads

7

189

12

6

11

Marina

KEMP ROAD
NORTH QUAY

5

WICKHAM RD
WICKHAM RD
ROSS
RIVER BR RD
New Clee
MARSDEN RD
THOROLD ST

CLEETHORPE ROAD
A180

10

192   193   4

OLIVER ST
SIGGILT LA
Water
Twr
NORTH PROMENADE

CLEETHORPES

Grant
Thorold

GRIMSBY RD
A46

BRERETON AVE
LESTRANGE ST
FREETON ST
PRESTON AV
PARK VW

ST HELIER'S RD
POPLAR RD

Cleethorpes

Wellington Street
ROBERTS ST
Liby

QUEEN MARY AVENUE

Allotment
Gardens

REYNOLDS ST

Sch

Cleethorpes
Pier   09

JULIAN ST
DURBAN RD
FAIRMONT RD
COLUMBIA RD
CARR LA

RUNSWICK ROAD

COLIN ST

DN32

MILLER AVE
HOLYOAKE RD

Old Clee

ISAAC'S HL
ST PETER'S AV
BURSAR
CROW

ALEXANDRA RD   3

LADYSMITH ROAD

BEELEY RD

CLEE CR

CLEE ROAD

A46

BENTLEY AVE

MILL ROAD

SLIPWAY

Weelsby

CEMY

BEACON AVENUE
DAVENPORT DR
NORMA NID
RD

TRINITY ROAD
HIGHGATE
GEORGE ST

OXFORD ST

KINGS PARADE
KINGS
WAY

WEELSBY ROAD
A46

SCHOOL WK
WINDSOR RD
A1031

WARWICK ROAD
CURZON AV
PENSHURST RD

BRAEMAR AV

TAYLOR'S AVENUE

SHERBURN ST

LINDUM RD
HAD'S AV
SIGNHILLS AV
CROMWELL RD

KINGS ROAD

Kingsway   08

VAUGHAN AV
TRANSPT

PHILIP

BRIAN AV
SNABY DR

SANDRINGHAM ROAD

ALDRICH RD

CHICHESTER RD
PEARSON RD

DAGGET RD

Cleethorpes
Discovery Centre   2

Villa
Plantation

HUMBERSTON RD
A1031

MIDDLE THORPE
HIGH THORPE CR
ITTERBY CR

Coll

FLIMINGHAM
CR

LINKS RD
THORGANBY RD

BOLINGBROKE RD

PH
The Jungle

Pumping
Station

Mus

07

Carr
Plantation

Old
Hall Farm

DN35

HEWITT'S AV
A1031

OAK
WY

BECFORD RD

Visitor
Centre

Lakeside

Cleethorpes

Miniature
Railway

DN36

A1088
GRIMSBY ROAD

Superstore

WILTON ROAD

ROSEMARY WY
PRIMROSE
WY

CHELTENHAM
WY
MARLBOROUGH WAY

Cleethorpes
Country Park

Humberston

WALDORF
RD
CLYDE
RD

SEAFORD RD

CH

Pleasure
Island   1

WESTBURY
WY

BEDFORD RD

HALE
RD

LIDGARD RD

NORTH SEA LANE
BROOK VW

Thorpe Park

A16

193   06

28   A   29   B   30   C   31   D   32   E   33   F

195   36   For full street detail of the highlighted
areas see pages 189, 192 & 193.

A8
1 CUNNINGHAM RD
2 GIBSON RD
3 HAMPDEN CR
4 VARSITY CL

Scale: 1¾ inches to 1 mile
0   ¼   ½ mile
0   250m   500m   750m   1 km

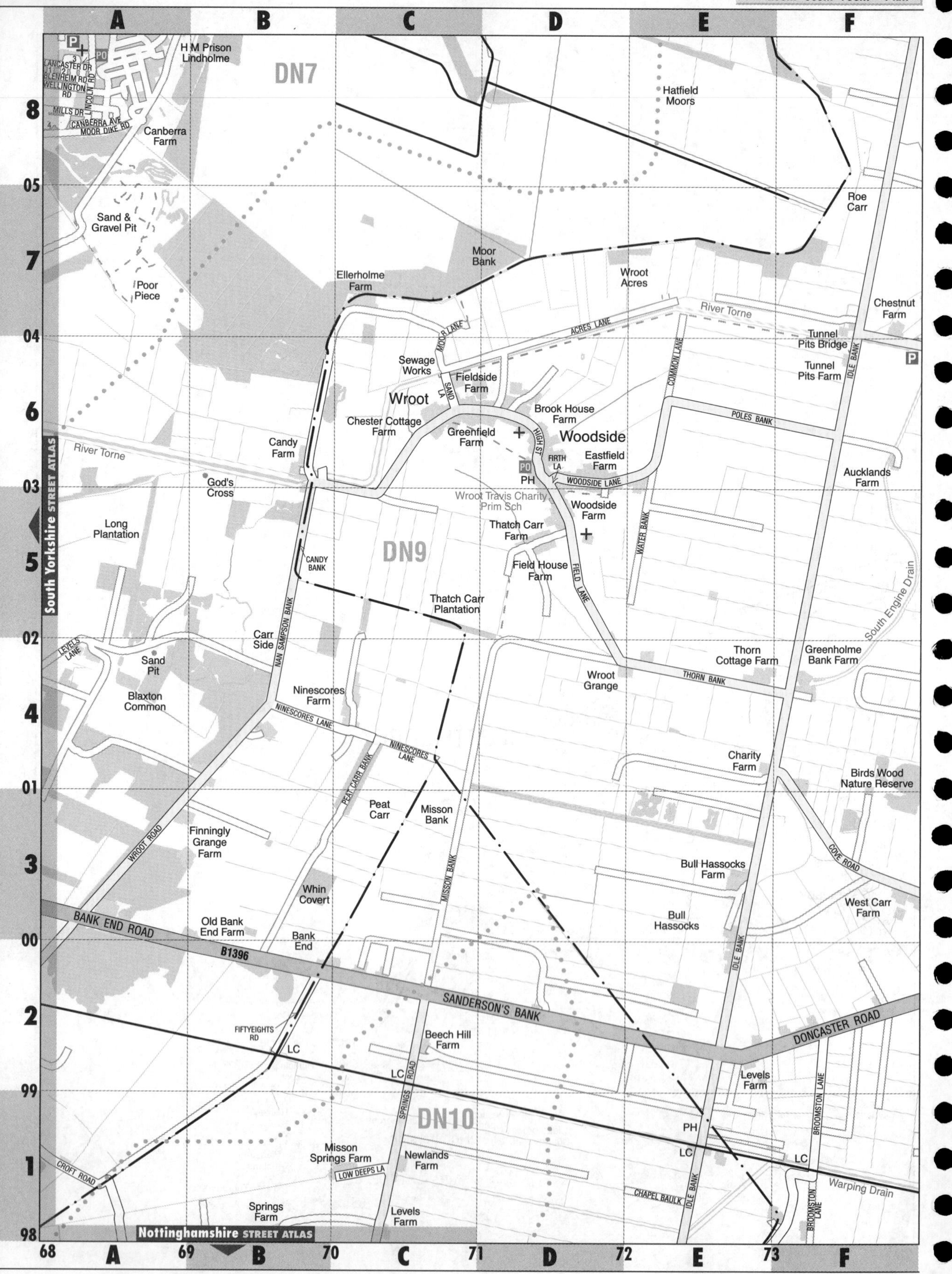

H M Prison
Lindholme

DN7

Canberra
Farm

Sand &
Gravel Pit

Poor
Piece

Ellerholme
Farm

Moor
Bank

Hatfield
Moors

Wroot
Acres

Roe
Carr

River Torne

Chestnut
Farm

Sewage
Works

Fieldside
Farm

Tunnel
Pits Bridge

Tunnel
Pits Farm

Wroot

Chester Cottage
Farm

Greenfield
Farm

Brook House
Farm

Woodside

Poles Bank

Candy
Farm

River Torne

God's
Cross

Eastfield
Farm

Aucklands
Farm

PO
PH

Wroot Travis Charity
Prim Sch

Woodside Lane

Long
Plantation

DN9

CANDY
BANK

Thatch Carr
Farm

Woodside
Farm

Field House
Farm

South Engine Drain

Thatch Carr
Plantation

Carr
Side

Thorn
Cottage Farm

Greenholme
Bank Farm

Sand
Pit

Blaxton
Common

Ninescores
Farm

Wroot
Grange

Thorn Bank

NINESCORES LANE

Charity
Farm

Birds Wood
Nature Reserve

Peat
Carr

Misson
Bank

Bull Hassocks
Farm

West Carr
Farm

Finninghay
Grange
Farm

Whin
Covert

Bull
Hassocks

Bank End Road

Old Bank
End Farm

Bank
End

B1396

Sanderson's Bank

Doncaster Road

FIFTYEIGHTS
RD
LC

Beech Hill
Farm

Levels
Farm

LC

DN10

PH
LC

Misson
Springs Farm

Newlands
Farm

Levels
Farm

LC

Croft Road

LOW DEEPS LA

Springs
Farm

Levels
Farm

Warping Drain

CHAPEL BAULK

South Yorkshire STREET ATLAS

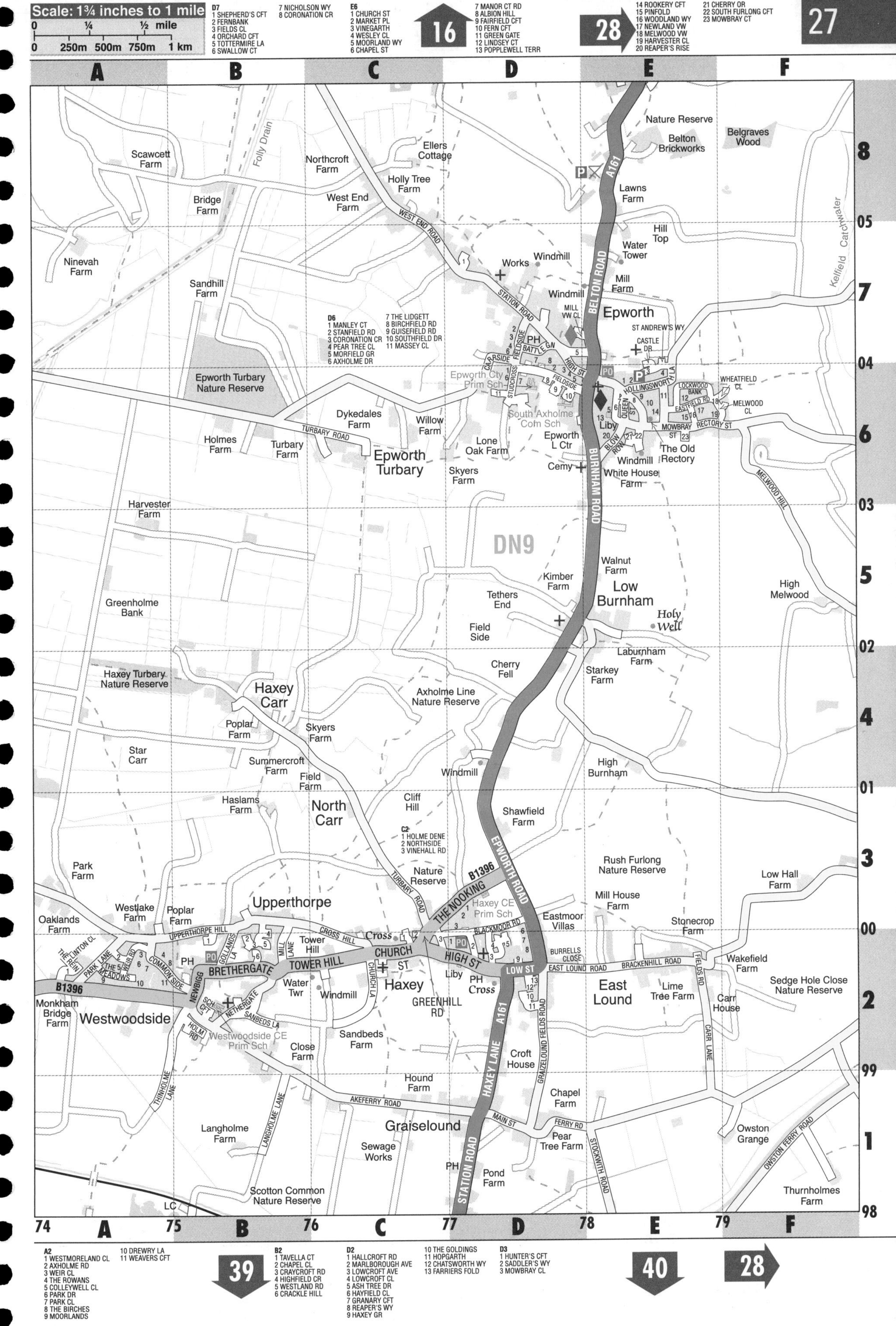

Scale: 1¾ inches to 1 mile

0   ¼   ½   mile
0   250m 500m 750m 1 km

D7
1 SHEPHERD'S CFT
2 FERNBANK
3 FIELDS CL
4 ORCHARD CFT
5 TOTTERMIRE LA
6 SWALLOW CT

7 NICHOLSON WY
8 CORONATION CR

E6
1 CHURCH ST
2 MARKET PL
3 VINEGARTH
4 WESLEY CL
5 MOORLAND WY
6 CHAPEL ST

7 MANOR CT RD
8 ALBION HILL
9 FAIRFIELD CFT
10 FERN CFT
11 GREEN GATE
12 LINDSEY CT
13 POPPLEWELL TERR

14 ROOKERY CFT
15 PINFOLD
16 WOODLAND WY
17 NEWLAND VW
18 MELWOOD VW
19 HARVESTER CL
20 REAPER'S RISE

21 CHERRY OR
22 SOUTH FURLONG CFT
23 MOWBRAY CT

D6
1 MANLEY CT
2 STANFIELD RD
3 CORONATION CR
4 PEAR TREE CL
5 MORFIELD GR
6 AXHOLME DR

7 THE LIDGETT
8 BIRCHFIELD RD
9 GUISEFIELD RD
10 SOUTHFIELD DR
11 MASSEY CL

C2
1 HOLME DENE
2 NORTHSIDE
3 VINEHALL RD

Grid references: A B C D E F
Row numbers: 8 05 7 04 6 03 5 02 4 01 3 00 2 99 1 98

Column numbers: 74 A 75 B 76 C 77 D 78 E 79 F

DN9

Scawcett Farm, Ninevah Farm, Folly Drain, Northcroft Farm, Ellers Cottage, Bridge Farm, Sandhill Farm, West End Farm, Holly Tree Farm, WEST END ROAD, Works, Windmill, Windmill, Belton Brickworks, Belgraves Wood, Nature Reserve, Lawns Farm, Kelfield Catchwater, Hill Top, Water Tower, Mill Farm, Epworth, St ANDREW'S WY, CASTLE DR, Epworth Turbary Nature Reserve, Dykedales Farm, Willow Farm, Epworth Turbary, Holmes Farm, TURBARY ROAD, Turbary Farm, Lone Oak Farm, Skyers Farm, Epworth L Ctr, Cemy, Windmill White House Farm, The Old Rectory, STATION ROAD, BELTON ROAD, BURNHAM ROAD, Harvester Farm, Greenholme Bank, Walnut Farm, Low Burnham, Holy Well, High Melwood, MELWOOD HILL, Kimber Farm, Tethers End, Field Side, Laburnham Farm, Starkey Farm, Haxey Turbary Nature Reserve, Haxey Carr, Cherry Fell, Axholme Line Nature Reserve, Poplar Farm, Skyers Farm, Star Carr, Summercroft Farm, Field Farm, Haslams Farm, North Carr, Cliff Hill, Windmill, High Burnham, Shawfield Farm, Rush Furlong Nature Reserve, Mill House Farm, Low Hall Farm, Park Farm, Westlake Farm, Poplar Farm, Oaklands Farm, Upperthorpe, UPPERTHORPE HILL, THE NOOKING, TURBARY ROAD, Nature Reserve, B1396, Haxey CE Prim Sch, BLACKMOOR RD, EPWORTH ROAD, Eastmoor Villas, Mill House Farm, Stonecrop Farm, CROSS HILL, Cross, Tower Hill, CHURCH ST, HIGH ST, LOW ST, BURRELLS CLOSE, EAST LOUND ROAD, BRACKENHILL ROAD, Wakefield Farm, THE GREEN, CLINTON CL, PARK LANE, COMMON SIDE, PH, BRETHERGATE, TOWER HILL, MILL LANE, Water Twr, CHURCH LA, Windmill, Haxey, Liby, PH, Cross, GREENHILL RD, Lime Tree Farm, Carr House, Sedge Hole Close Nature Reserve, CARR LANE, FIELDS RD, B1396, Monkham Bridge Farm, Westwoodside, THRONHOLME LANE, NEWBIGG, NETHERGATE, HOLM RD, Westwoodside CE Prim Sch, SANBEDS LA, Close Farm, Sandbeds Farm, Hound Farm, East Lound, Croft House, GRAISELOUND FIELDS ROAD, STOCKWITH ROAD, Chapel Farm, FERRY RD, OWSTON FERRY ROAD, Owston Grange, Langholme Farm, LANGHOLME LANE, AKEFERRY ROAD, Graiselound, MAIN ST, Sewage Works, PH, Pear Tree Farm, Pond Farm, STATION ROAD, HAXEY LANE, A161, Scotton Common Nature Reserve, LC, Thurnholmes Farm

A2
1 WESTMORELAND CL
2 AXHOLME RD
3 WEIR CL
4 THE ROWANS
5 COLLEYWELL CL
6 PARK DR
7 PARK CL
8 THE BIRCHES
9 MOORLANDS

10 DREWRY LA
11 WEAVERS CFT

B2
1 TAVELLA CT
2 CHAPEL CL
3 CRAYCROFT RD
4 HIGHFIELD CR
5 WESTLAND RD
6 CRACKLE HILL

D2
1 HALLCROFT RD
2 MARLBOROUGH AVE
3 LOWCROFT AVE
4 LOWCROFT CL
5 ASH TREE DR
6 HAYFIELD CL
7 GRANARY CFT
8 REAPER'S WY
9 HAXEY GR

10 THE GOLDINGS
11 HOPGARTH
12 CHATSWORTH WY
13 FARRIERS FOLD

D3
1 HUNTER'S CFT
2 SADDLER'S WY
3 MOWBRAY CL

Scale: 1¾ inches to 1 mile

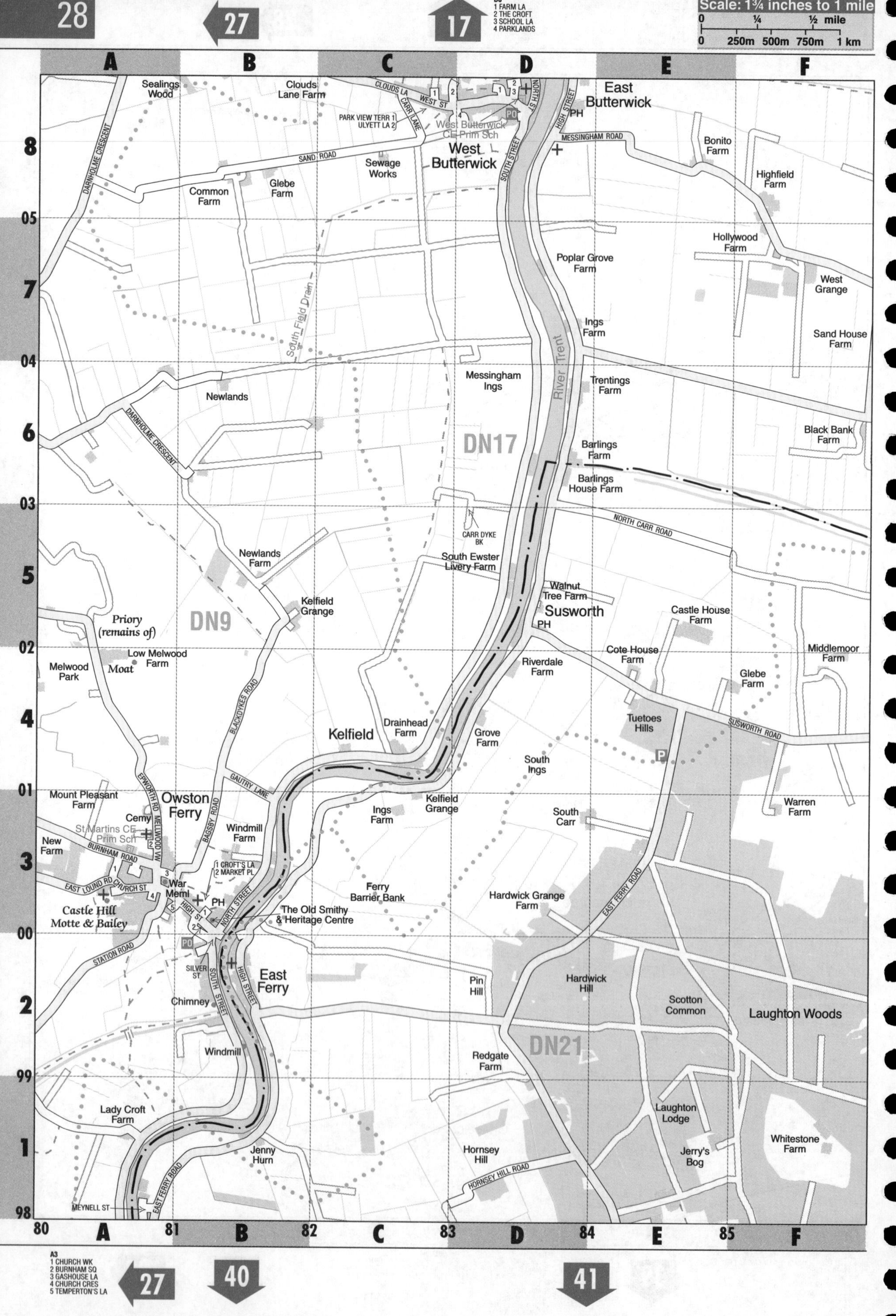
A
B
C
D
E
F
Sealings Wood
Clouds Lane Farm
CLOUDS LA
WEST ST
CARR LANE
PARK VIEW TERR 1
ULYETT LA 2
West Butterwick CE Prim Sch
West Butterwick
East Butterwick
PH
NORTH ST
HIGH STREET
MESSINGHAM ROAD
SOUTH STREET
SAND ROAD
DARNHOLME CRESCENT
Common Farm
Glebe Farm
Sewage Works
Bonito Farm
Highfield Farm
Hollywood Farm
Poplar Grove Farm
West Grange
South Field Drain
Ings Farm
Sand House Farm
Messingham Ings
River Trent
Trentings Farm
Newlands
Black Bank Farm
DN17
Barlings Farm
Barlings House Farm
NORTH CARR ROAD
CARR DYKE BK
Newlands Farm
South Ewster Livery Farm
Walnut Tree Farm
Susworth
Kelfield Grange
Castle House Farm
Priory (remains of)
DN9
Low Melwood Farm
Melwood Park
Moat
Cote House Farm
Riverdale Farm
Middlemoor Farm
Glebe Farm
BLACKDYKES ROAD
Tuetoes Hills
SUSWORTH ROAD
Drainhead Farm
Kelfield
Grove Farm
South Ings
GAUTRY LANE
EPWORTH RD
MELWOOD VW
Mount Pleasant Farm
Owston Ferry
Kelfield Grange
Ings Farm
Warren Farm
South Carr
Cemy
St Martins CE Prim Sch
Windmill Farm
BAGSBY ROAD
New Farm
BURNHAM ROAD
1 CROFT'S LA
2 MARKET PL
EAST LOUND RD
CHURCH ST
War Meml
PH
NORTH STREET
HIGH ST
Ferry Barrier Bank
Hardwick Grange Farm
EAST FERRY ROAD
Castle Hill Motte & Bailey
The Old Smithy & Heritage Centre
STATION ROAD
SILVER ST
SOUTH STREET
HIGH STREET
East Ferry
Pin Hill
Hardwick Hill
Scotton Common
Laughton Woods
Chimney
Windmill
DN21
Redgate Farm
Lady Croft Farm
Laughton Lodge
Whitestone Farm
Jenny Hurn
Hornsey Hill
Jerry's Bog
HORNSEY HILL ROAD
EAST FERRY ROAD
MEYNELL ST
8
05
7
04
6
03
5
02
4
01
3
00
2
99
1
98
80
81
82
83
84
85

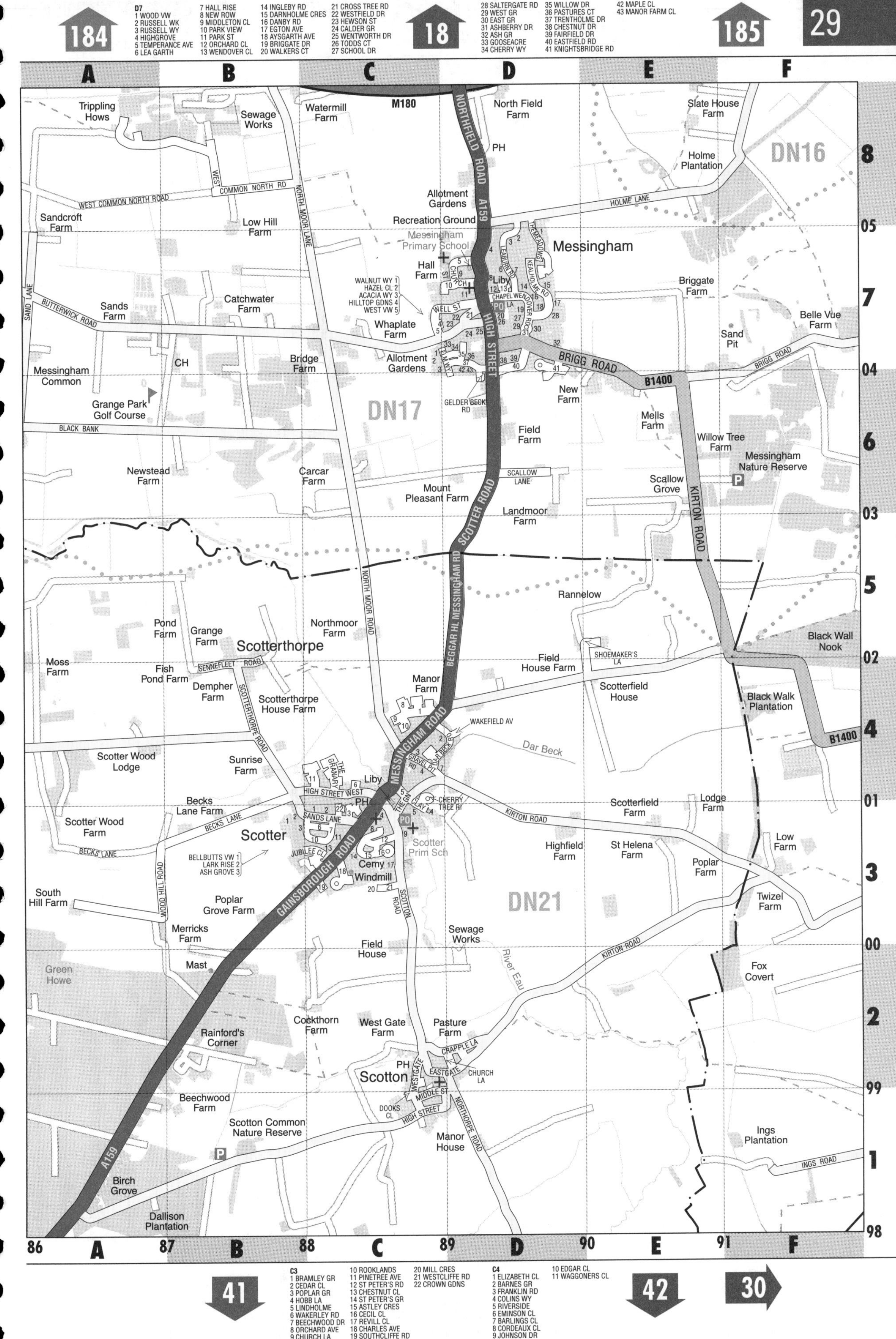
184
D7
1 WOOD VW
2 RUSSELL WK
3 RUSSELL WY
4 HIGHGROVE
5 TEMPERANCE AVE
6 LEA GARTH
7 HALL RISE
8 NEW ROW
9 MIDDLETON CL
10 PARK VIEW
11 PARK ST
12 ORCHARD CL
13 WENDOVER CL
14 INGLEBY RD
15 DARNHOLME CRES
16 DANBY RD
17 EGTON AVE
18 AYSGARTH AVE
19 BRIGGATE DR
20 WALKERS CT
21 CROSS TREE RD
22 WESTFIELD DR
23 HEWSON ST
24 CALDER GR
25 WENTWORTH DR
26 TODDS CT
27 SCHOOL DR
18
28 SALTERGATE RD
29 WEST GR
30 EAST GR
31 ASHBERRY DR
32 ASH GR
33 GOOSEACRE
34 CHERRY WY
35 WILLOW DR
36 PASTURES CT
37 TRENTHOLME DR
38 CHESTNUT DR
39 FAIRFIELD DR
40 EASTFIELD RD
41 KNIGHTSBRIDGE RD
42 MAPLE CL
43 MANOR FARM CL
185
A
B
C
D
E
F
Trippling Hows
Sewage Works
Watermill Farm
M180
NORTHFIELD ROAD
North Field Farm
Slate House Farm
PH
Holme Plantation
DN16
8
WEST COMMON NORTH ROAD
NORTH MOOR LANE
Allotment Gardens
A159
HOLME LANE
Sandcroft Farm
Low Hill Farm
Recreation Ground
05
Messingham Primary School
Messingham
Hall Farm
Liby
Briggate Farm
WALNUT WY 1
HAZEL CL 2
ACACIA WY 3
HILLTOP GDNS 4
WEST VW 5
Catchwater Farm
7
SAND LANE
BUTTERWICK ROAD
Sands Farm
WELL ST
CHAPEL
Whaplate Farm
HIGH STREET
Belle Vue Farm
Sand Pit
CH
Bridge Farm
Allotment Gardens
BRIGG ROAD
B1400
Messingham Common
04
New Farm
Grange Park Golf Course
DN17
GELDER BECK RD
Mells Farm
BLACK BANK
Field Farm
Willow Tree Farm
6
Newstead Farm
Carcar Farm
SCALLOW LANE
Messingham Nature Reserve
Mount Pleasant Farm
Scallow Grove
SCOTTER ROAD
KIRTON ROAD
Landmoor Farm
03
MESSINGHAM RD
5
Rannelow
NORTH MOOR ROAD
Pond Farm
Grange Farm
Northmoor Farm
Black Wall Nook
Scotterthorpe
BEGGAR HL
Moss Farm
SHOEMAKER'S LA
02
Fish Pond Farm
SENNEFLEET ROAD
Field House Farm
Dempher Farm
Manor Farm
Scotterfield House
Black Walk Plantation
SCOTTERTHORPE ROAD
Scotterthorpe House Farm
WAKEFIELD AV
MESSINGHAM ROAD
4
Dar Beck
B1400
Scotter Wood Lodge
Sunrise Farm
THE GRANARY
GRAVEL PIT RD
Liby
HIGH STREET WEST
PH
CHERRY TREE RI
01
Becks Lane Farm
Scotterfield Farm
Lodge Farm
KIRTON ROAD
Scotter Wood Farm
BECKS LANE
SANDS LANE
PO
Scotter
Scotter Prim Sch
BECKS LANE
Highfield Farm
St Helena Farm
Low Farm
BELLBUTTS VW 1
LARK RISE 2
ASH GROVE 3
JUBILEE CL
Cemy
Windmill
Poplar Farm
3
WOOD HILL ROAD
GAINSBOROUGH ROAD
SCOTTON ROAD
South Hill Farm
Poplar Grove Farm
DN21
Twizel Farm
Merricks Farm
Sewage Works
00
Field House
River Eau
KIRTON ROAD
Green Howe
Mast
Fox Covert
Cockthorn Farm
West Gate Farm
Pasture Farm
2
Rainford's Corner
CRAPPLE LA
PH
Scotton
EASTGATE
CHURCH LA
WESTGATE
99
MIDDLE ST
Beechwood Farm
DOOKS CL
HIGH STREET
NORTHORPE ROAD
Scotton Common Nature Reserve
Manor House
Ings Plantation
1
INGS ROAD
A159
P
Birch Grove
Dallison Plantation
98
86
87
88
89
90
91
41
C3
1 BRAMLEY GR
2 CEDAR CL
3 POPLAR GR
4 HOBB LA
5 LINDHOLME
6 WAKERLEY RD
7 BEECHWOOD DR
8 ORCHARD AVE
9 CHURCH LA
10 ROOKLANDS
11 PINETREE AVE
12 ST PETER'S RD
13 CHESTNUT CL
14 ST PETER'S GR
15 ASTLEY CRES
16 CECIL CL
17 REVILL CL
18 CHARLES AVE
19 SOUTHCLIFFE RD
20 MILL CRES
21 WESTCLIFFE RD
22 CROWN GDNS
C4
1 ELIZABETH CL
2 BARNES GR
3 FRANKLIN RD
4 COLINS WY
5 RIVERSIDE
6 EMINSON CL
7 BARLINGS CL
8 CORDEAUX CL
9 JOHNSON DR
10 EDGAR CL
11 WAGGONERS CL
42
30

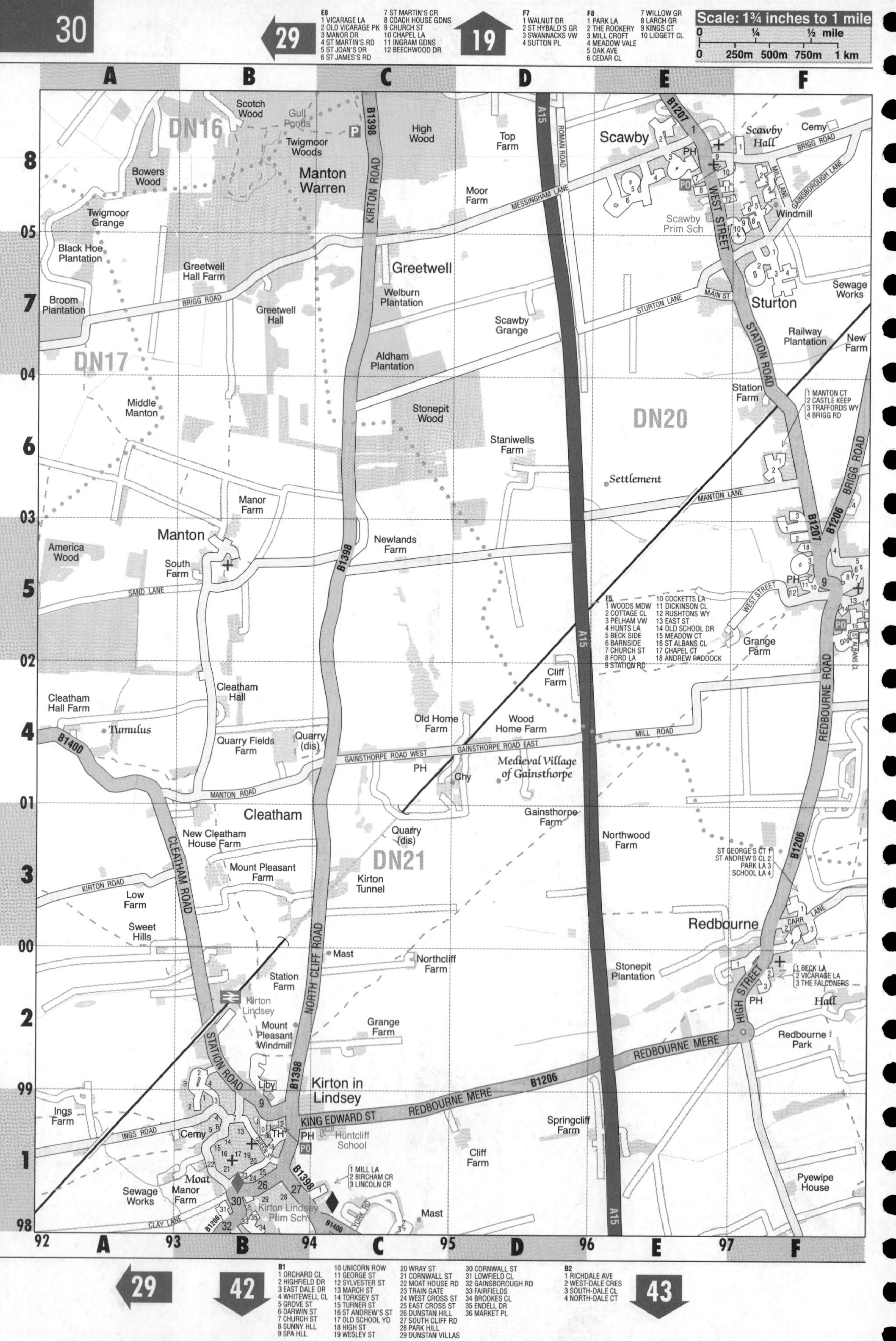

Scale: 1¾ inches to 1 mile

0   ¼   ½   mile
0   250m 500m 750m 1 km

29
19
29   42   43

E8
1 VICARAGE LA
2 OLD VICARAGE PK
3 MANOR DR
4 ST MARTIN'S RD
5 ST JOAN'S DR
6 ST JAMES'S RD
7 ST MARTIN'S CR
8 COACH HOUSE GDNS
9 CHURCH ST
10 CHAPEL LA
11 INGRAM GDNS
12 BEECHWOOD DR

F7
1 WALNUT DR
2 ST HYBALD'S GR
3 SWANNACKS VW
4 SUTTON PL

F8
1 PARK LA
2 THE ROOKERY
3 MILL CROFT
4 MEADOW VALE
5 OAK AVE
6 CEDAR CL
7 WILLOW GR
8 LARCH GR
9 KINGS CT
10 LIDGETT CL

DN16

Scotch Wood

Gull Ponds

Twigmoor Woods

High Wood

Top Farm

Scawby
Scawby Hall
Cemy
PH
PO
Scawby Prim Sch

Manton Warren

Moor Farm

Windmill

Bowers Wood

Messingham Lane

Sturton Lane
Main St
Sturton
Sewage Works

Twigmoor Grange

Greetwell

Welburn Plantation

Station Road
Railway Plantation
New Farm

Black Hoe Plantation

Brigg Road

Greetwell Hall Farm

Greetwell Hall

Scawby Grange

West Street

Broom Plantation

DN17

Aldham Plantation

Station Farm

1 MANTON CT
2 CASTLE KEEP
3 TRAFFORDS WY
4 BRIGG RD

Middle Manton

Stonepit Wood

Staniwells Farm

DN20

Settlement

Manton Lane

B1207
B1206

Manor Farm

Manton

South Farm

Newlands Farm

Sand Lane

PH

West Street
Grange Farm

Cleatham Hall Farm

Cleatham Hall

Quarry (dis)

Old Home Farm

Cliff Farm

Wood Home Farm

PO
St Albans Pl

E5
1 WOODS MDW
2 COTTAGE CL
3 PELHAM VW
4 HUNTS LA
5 BECK SIDE
6 BARNSIDE
7 CHURCH ST
8 FORD LA
9 STATION RD
10 COCKETTS LA
11 DICKINSON CL
12 RUSHTONS WY
13 EAST ST
14 OLD SCHOOL DR
15 MEADOW CT
16 ST ALBANS CL
17 CHAPEL CT
18 ANDREW PADDOCK

Tumulus
B1400

Quarry Fields Farm

Quarry (dis)

Gainsthorpe Road West   Gainsthorpe Road East

PH

Chy

Medieval Village of Gainsthorpe

Mill Road

Cleatham
New Cleatham House Farm

Manton Road

Quarry (dis)

Gainsthorpe Farm

Northwood Farm

Redbourne Road

St GEORGE'S CT 1
St ANDREW'S CL 2
PARK LA 3
SCHOOL LA 4

DN21

Kirton Tunnel

Northcliff Farm

Stonepit Plantation

Redbourne

CARR LANE
PH

Kirton Road
Low Farm

Mount Pleasant Farm

Sweet Hills

Mast

Hall

1 BECK LA
2 VICARAGE LA
3 THE FALCONERS

Station Lindsey
Kirton Lindsey

Mount Pleasant Windmill

Grange Farm

High Street
PH

Redbourne Park

Ings Farm

Liby
9

Kirton in Lindsey

Redbourne Mere

Springcliff Farm

Redbourne Mere

B1206

Ings Road

Cemy
TH
PH
PO
Huntcliff School

King Edward St

Cliff Farm

Pyewipe House

Moat Manor Farm

1 MILL LA
2 BIRCHAM CR
3 LINCOLN CR

Mast

Sewage Works

Kirton Lindsey Prim Sch

Clay Lane
B1206

York Rd
B1400

A15

B1
1 ORCHARD CL
2 HIGHFIELD DR
3 EAST DALE DR
4 WHITEWELL CL
5 GROVE ST
6 DARWIN ST
7 CHURCH ST
8 SUNNY HLL
9 SPA HLL
10 UNICORN ROW
11 GEORGE ST
12 SYLVESTER ST
13 MARCH ST
14 TORKSEY ST
15 TURNER ST
16 ST ANDREW'S ST
17 OLD SCHOOL YD
18 HIGH ST
19 WESLEY ST
20 WRAY ST
21 CORNWALL ST
22 MOAT HOUSE RD
23 TRAIN GATE
24 WEST CROSS ST
25 EAST CROSS ST
26 DUNSTAN HILL
27 SOUTH CLIFF RD
28 PARK HILL
29 DUNSTAN VILLAS
30 CORNWALL ST
31 LOWFIELD CL
32 GAINSBOROUGH RD
33 FAIRFIELDS
34 BROOKES CL
35 ENDELL DR
36 MARKET PL

B2
1 RICHDALE AVE
2 WEST-DALE CRES
3 SOUTH-DALE CT
4 NORTH-DALE CT

A B C D E F

92 93 94 95 96 97

8 05 7 04 6 03 5 02 4 01 3 00 2 99 1 98

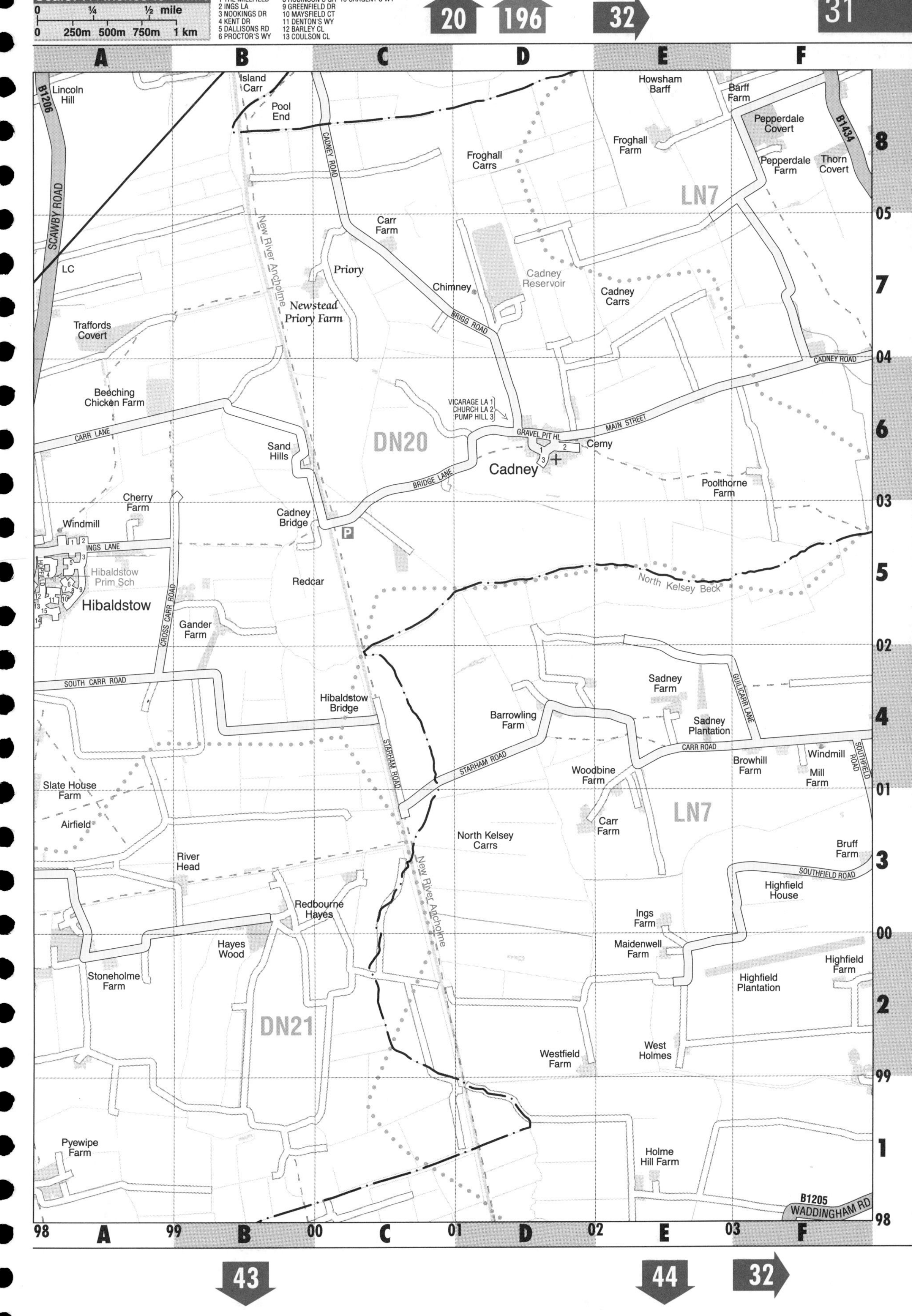
Scale: 1¾ inches to 1 mile
0 ¼ ½ mile
0 250m 500m 750m 1 km
A5
1 THE MILLFIELD
2 INGS LA
3 NOOKINGS DR
4 KENT DR
5 DALLISONS RD
6 PROCTOR'S WY
7 COX'S CT
8 ROBINSON'S GR
9 GREENFIELD DR
10 MAYSFIELD CT
11 DENTON'S WY
12 BARLEY CL
13 COULSON CL
14 WILLOUGHBY RD
15 SARGENT'S WY
20
196
32
A B C D E F
8 05 7 04 6 03 5 02 4 01 3 00 2 99 1 98
98 99 00 01 02 03
Lincoln Hill
B1206
Island Carr
Pool End
Howsham Barff
Barff Farm
Pepperdale Covert
B1434
Froghall Farm
Froghall Carrs
CADNEY ROAD
Pepperdale Farm
Thorn Covert
LN7
SCAWBY ROAD
Carr Farm
New River Ancholme
Priory
LC
Chimney
Cadney Reservoir
Cadney Carrs
Newstead Priory Farm
Traffords Covert
BRIGG ROAD
CADNEY ROAD
Beeching Chicken Farm
VICARAGE LA 1
CHURCH LA 2
PUMP HILL 3
MAIN STREET
CARR LANE
DN20
GRAVEL PIT HL
Sand Hills
Cemy
Cadney
BRIDGE LANE
Poolthorne Farm
Cherry Farm
Cadney Bridge
Windmill
P
INGS LANE
HOPFIELD
Hibaldstow Prim Sch
Redcar
North Kelsey Beck
Hibaldstow
CROSS CARR ROAD
Gander Farm
SOUTH CARR ROAD
Sadney Farm
Hibaldstow Bridge
GUILICARR LANE
Barrowling Farm
Sadney Plantation
CARR ROAD
STARHAM ROAD
Browhill Farm
Windmill
SOUTHFIELD ROAD
Slate House Farm
Woodbine Farm
Mill Farm
Airfield
Carr Farm
LN7
North Kelsey Carrs
River Head
Bruff Farm
SOUTHFIELD ROAD
Highfield House
Redbourne Hayes
Ings Farm
Hayes Wood
Maidenwell Farm
Highfield Farm
Stoneholme Farm
Highfield Plantation
DN21
Westfield Farm
West Holmes
Pyewipe Farm
Holme Hill Farm
B1205
WADDINGHAM RD
43
44
32

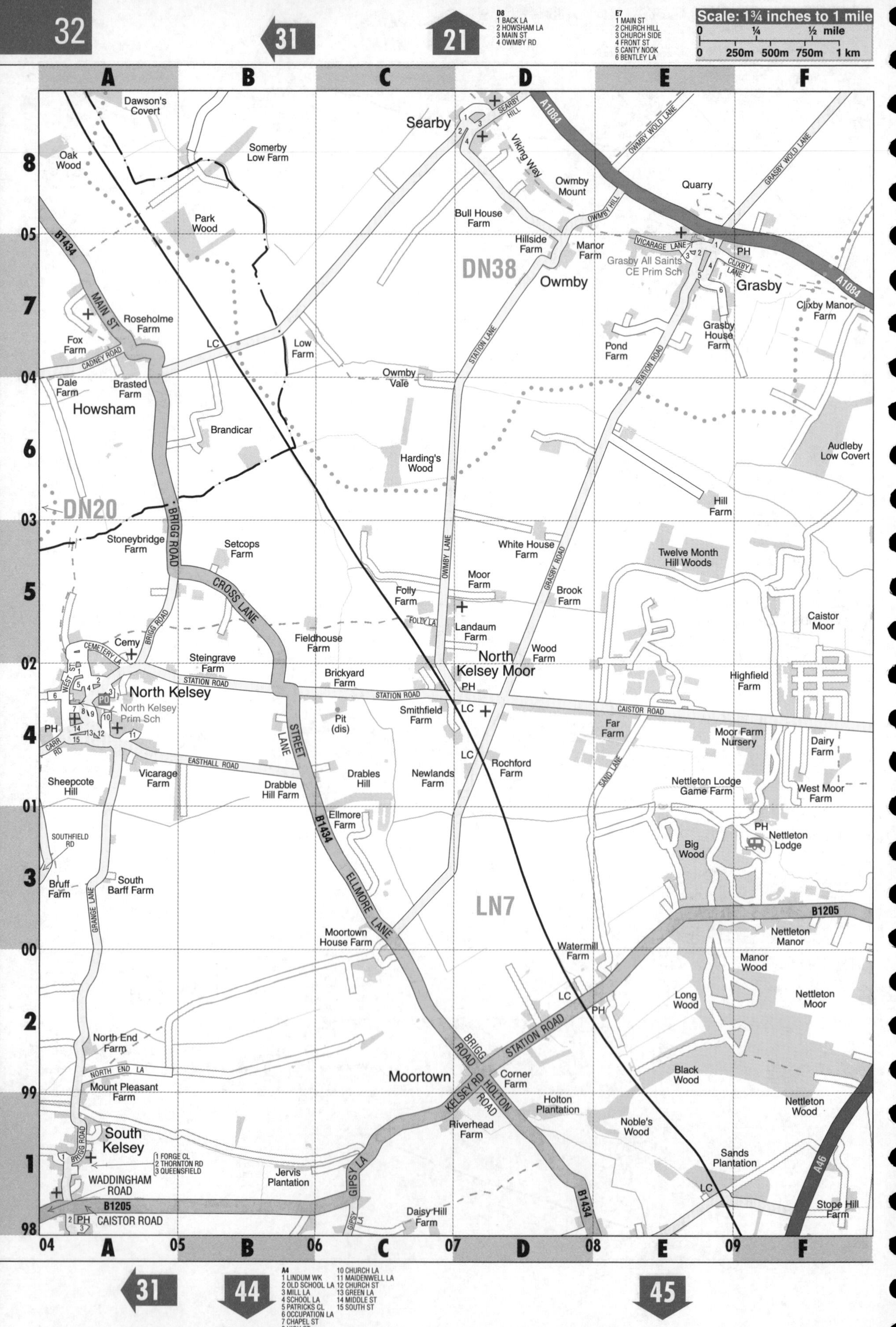
31
21
D8
1 BACK LA
2 HOWSHAM LA
3 MAIN ST
4 OWMBY RD
E7
1 MAIN ST
2 CHURCH HILL
3 CHURCH SIDE
4 FRONT ST
5 CANTY NOOK
6 BENTLEY LA
Scale: 1¾ inches to 1 mile
0 ¼ ½ mile
0 250m 500m 750m 1 km
A B C D E F
8 05 7 04 6 03 5 02 4 01 3 00 2 99 1 98
Dawson's Covert
Searby
SEARBY HILL
A1084
OWMBY WOLD LANE
GRASBY WOLD LANE
Oak Wood
Somerby Low Farm
Viking Way
Owmby Mount
Quarry
Park Wood
Bull House Farm
OWMBY HILL
B1434
Hillside Farm
Manor Farm
VICARAGE LANE
PH
CLIXBY LANE
DN38
Grasby All Saints CE Prim Sch
Owmby
Grasby
MAIN ST
Roseholme Farm
Clixby Manor Farm
Fox Farm
LC
Low Farm
STATION LANE
Grasby House Farm
STATION ROAD
Pond Farm
CADNEY ROAD
Owmby Vale
Dale Farm
Brasted Farm
Howsham
Brandicar
Harding's Wood
Audleby Low Covert
DN20
BRIGG ROAD
Hill Farm
Stoneybridge Farm
Setcops Farm
OWMBY LANE
White House Farm
GRASBY ROAD
Twelve Month Hill Woods
CROSS LANE
Moor Farm
Folly Farm
Brook Farm
FOLLY LA
Caistor Moor
Landaum Farm
Fieldhouse Farm
Wood Farm
Cemy
CEMETERY LA
Steingrave Farm
North Kelsey Moor
Highfield Farm
WEST ST
Brickyard Farm
STATION ROAD
North Kelsey
PO
STATION ROAD
PH
North Kelsey Prim Sch
Smithfield Farm
CAISTOR ROAD
Pit (dis)
Far Farm
PH
CARR RD
STREET LANE
Moor Farm Nursery
Dairy Farm
EASTHALL ROAD
Rochford Farm
Sheepcote Hill
Vicarage Farm
Drables Hill
Newlands Farm
SAND LANE
Drabble Hill Farm
Nettleton Lodge Game Farm
West Moor Farm
Ellmore Farm
SOUTHFIELD RD
Big Wood
Nettleton Lodge
Bruff Farm
South Barff Farm
ELLMORE LANE
LN7
GRANGE LANE
B1205
Moortown House Farm
Nettleton Manor
Watermill Farm
Manor Wood
Long Wood
Nettleton Moor
North End Farm
BRIGG ROAD
STATION ROAD
NORTH END LA
Moortown
Corner Farm
Black Wood
Mount Pleasant Farm
KELSEY RD
HOLTON ROAD
Holton Plantation
Nettleton Wood
Riverhead Farm
Noble's Wood
South Kelsey
1 FORGE CL
2 THORNTON RD
3 QUEENSFIELD
Sands Plantation
A46
Jervis Plantation
GIPSY LA
WADDINGHAM ROAD
B1205
Stope Hill Farm
CAISTOR ROAD
Daisy Hill Farm
04 05 06 07 08 09
31
44
A4
1 LINDUM WK
2 OLD SCHOOL LA
3 MILL LA
4 SCHOOL LA
5 PATRICKS CL
6 OCCUPATION LA
7 CHAPEL ST
8 HIGH ST
9 HALLS LA
10 CHURCH LA
11 MAIDENWELL LA
12 CHURCH ST
13 GREEN LA
14 MIDDLE ST
15 SOUTH ST
45

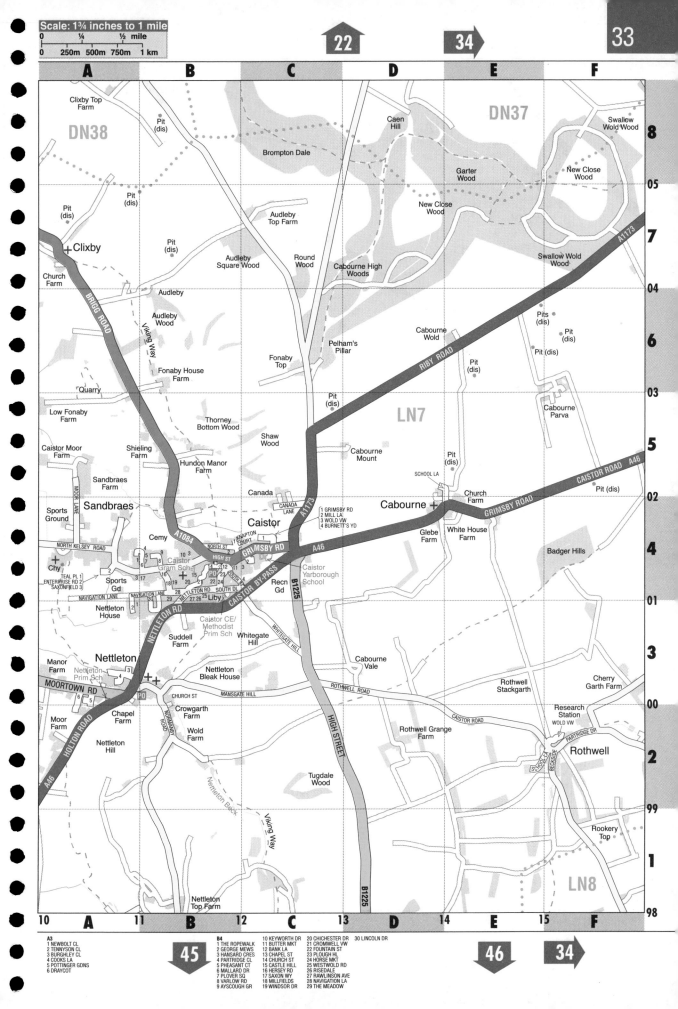

DN38

Clixby Top Farm
Pit (dis)
Brompton Dale

DN37

Caen Hill
Swallow Wold Wood

New Close Wood

Garter Wood

Pit (dis)
Pit (dis)

Clixby

Church Farm

BRIGG ROAD

Audleby Top Farm

Audleby Square Wood

Round Wood

Cabourne High Woods

New Close Wood

Swallow Wold Wood

A1173

Viking Way

Audleby

Audleby Wood

Fonaby Top

Pelham's Pillar

Cabourne Wold

Pits (dis)
Pit (dis)
Pit (dis)

RIBY ROAD

Quarry

Fonaby House Farm

Pit (dis)

LN7

Cabourne Parva

Low Fonaby Farm

Thorney Bottom Wood

Shaw Wood

Pit (dis)

A1173

Caistor Moor Farm

Shieling Farm

Hundon Manor Farm

Cabourne Mount

Pit (dis)

CAISTOR ROAD A46

Pit (dis)

Sandbraes Farm

Canada

CANADA LANE

Cabourne

Church Farm

Badger Hills

Sports Ground

Sandbraes

Cemy

Caistor

1 GRIMSBY RD
2 MILL LA
3 WOLD VW
4 BURNETT'S YD

Glebe Farm

White House Farm

GRIMSBY RD
A46
GRIMSBY ROAD

MOOR LANE

A1084

NORTH ST
KNAPTON COURT
HIGH ST

NORTH KELSEY ROAD

Chy

Caistor Gram Sch

Sports Gd

TEAL PL 1
ENTERPRISE RD 2
SAXONFIELD 3

PO

CAISTOR BY-PASS

Caistor Yarborough School

Recn Gd

B1225

NAVIGATION LANE

NAVIGATION LANE

SOUTH DL
Liby

NETTLETON RD

Nettleton House

Caistor CE/ Methodist Prim Sch

Whitegate Hill

WHITEGATE HILL

Cabourne Vale

Manor Farm

Nettleton Prim Sch

Suddell Farm

Nettleton Bleak House

Rothwell Stackgarth

Cherry Garth Farm

Nettleton

MOORTOWN RD

PO

CHURCH ST

MANSGATE HILL

ROTHWELL ROAD

Research Station
WOLD VW

CAISTOR ROAD

Rothwell

Moor Farm

Chapel Farm

Crowgarth Farm

Wold Farm

HIGH STREET

Rothwell Grange Farm

PARTRIDGE DR

SCHOOL LA
BECKSIDE

HOLTON ROAD

A46

NORMANBY ROAD

Nettleton Hill

Viking Way

Nettleton Beck

Tugdale Wood

Rookery Top

LN8

B1225

Nettleton Top Farm

A3
1 NEWBOLT CL
2 TENNYSON CL
3 BURGHLEY CL
4 COOKS LA
5 POTTINGER GDNS
6 DRAYCOT

B4
1 THE ROPEWALK
2 GEORGE MEWS
3 HANSARD CRES
4 PARTRIDGE CL
5 PHEASANT CT
6 MALLARD DR
7 PLOVER SQ
8 VARLOW RD
9 AYSCOUGH GR

10 KEYWORTH DR
11 BUTTER MKT
12 BANK LA
13 CHAPEL ST
14 CHURCH ST
15 CASTLE HILL
16 HERSEY RD
17 SAXON WY
18 MILLFIELDS
19 WINDSOR DR

20 CHICHESTER DR
21 CROMWELL VW
22 FOUNTAIN ST
23 PLOUGH HL
24 HORSE MKT
25 WESTWOLD RD
26 RISEDALE
27 RAWLINSON AVE
28 NAVIGATION LA
29 THE MEADOW

30 LINCOLN DR

33 23

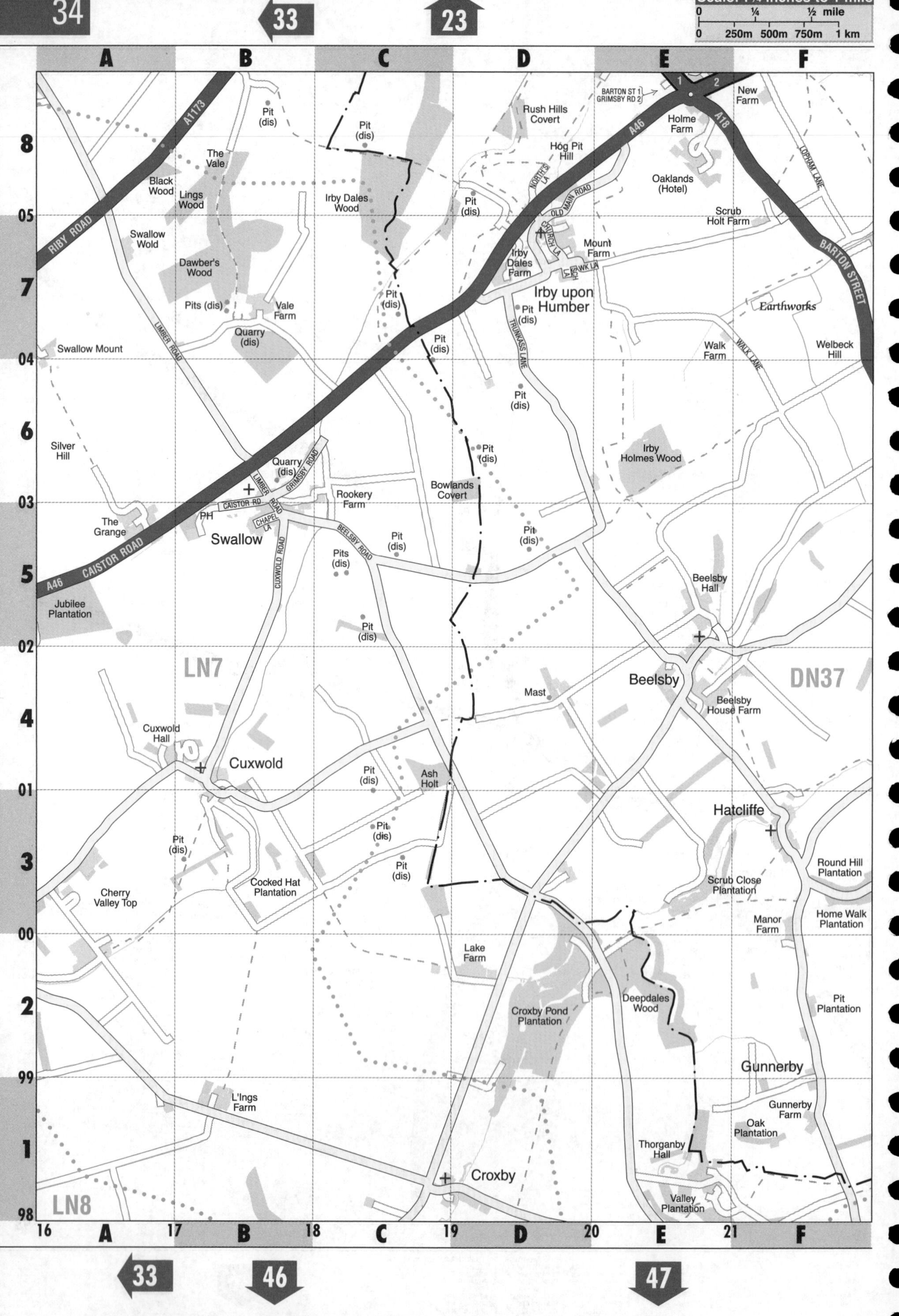

Scale: 1¾ inches to 1 mile
0 ¼ ½ mile
0 250m 500m 750m 1 km
A B C D E F
8 05 7 04 6 03 5 02 4 01 3 00 2 99 1 98
16 17 18 19 20 21
RIBY ROAD
A1173
Pit (dis)
The Vale
Black Wood
Lings Wood
Irby Dales Wood
Swallow Wold
Dawber's Wood
Pits (dis)
Vale Farm
Quarry (dis)
Swallow Mount
LIMBER ROAD
Silver Hill
Quarry (dis)
GRIMSBY ROAD
LIMBER ROAD
CAISTOR RD
CHAPEL LA
PH
The Grange
Swallow
A46 CAISTOR ROAD
Jubilee Plantation
CUXWOLD ROAD
BEELSBY ROAD
Rookery Farm
Pits (dis)
Bowlands Covert
LN7
Cuxwold Hall
Cuxwold
Ash Holt
Cherry Valley Top
Cocked Hat Plantation
Lake Farm
L'Ings Farm
Croxby
LN8
Rush Hills Covert
Hog Pit Hill
BARTON ST 1
GRIMSBY RD 2
A46
A18
New Farm
Holme Farm
LOPHAM LANE
Oaklands (Hotel)
NORTH'S LA
OLD MAIN ROAD
CHURCH LA
Scrub Holt Farm
Irby Dales Farm
Mount Farm
HAWK LA
Irby upon Humber
TRUNKASS LANE
Earthworks
BARTON STREET
Walk Farm
WALK LANE
Welbeck Hill
Irby Holmes Wood
Beelsby Hall
Mast
Beelsby
DN37
Beelsby House Farm
Hatcliffe
Round Hill Plantation
Scrub Close Plantation
Manor Farm
Home Walk Plantation
Deepdales Wood
Croxby Pond Plantation
Pit Plantation
Gunnerby
Gunnerby Farm
Oak Plantation
Thorganby Hall
Valley Plantation

33 46 47

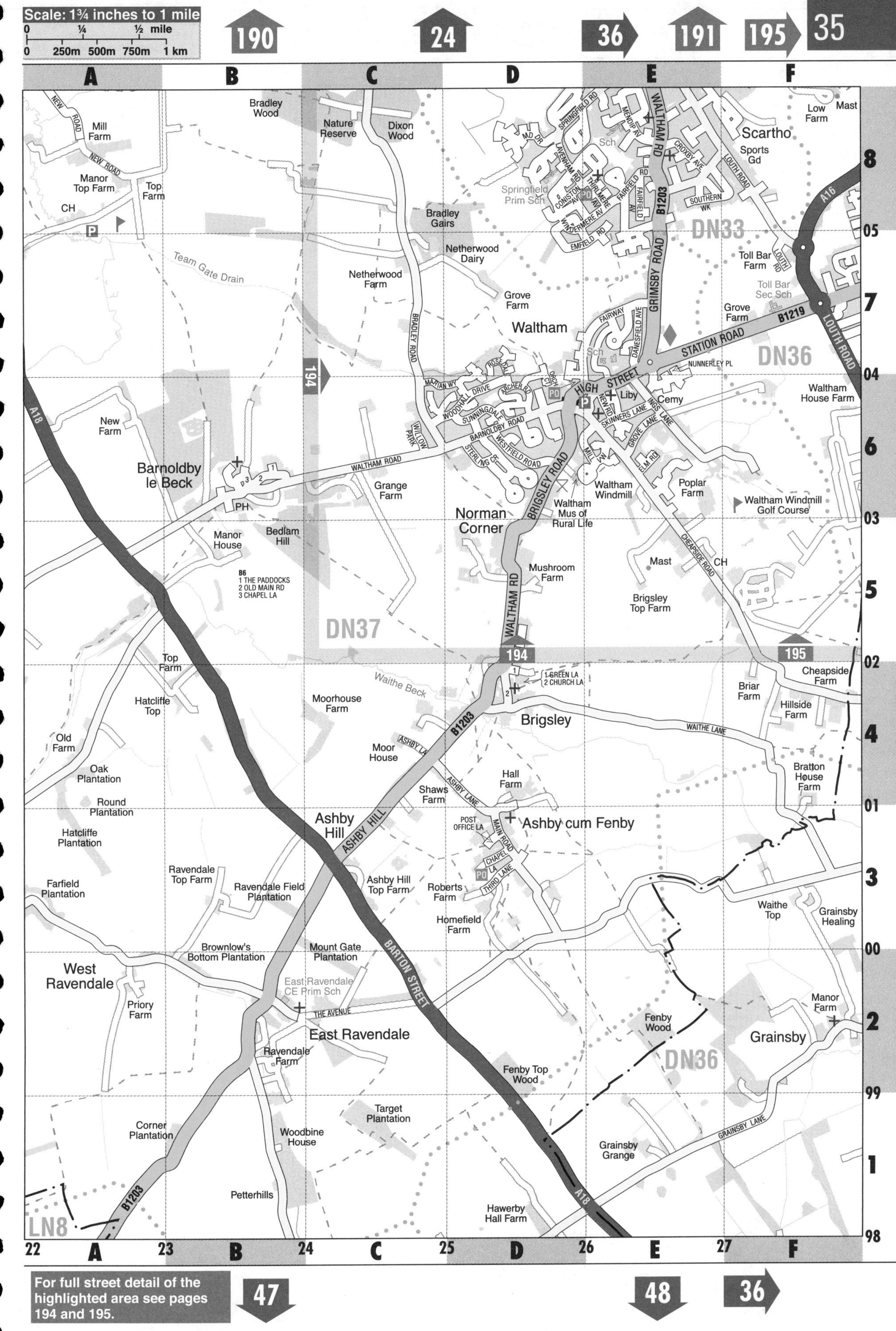

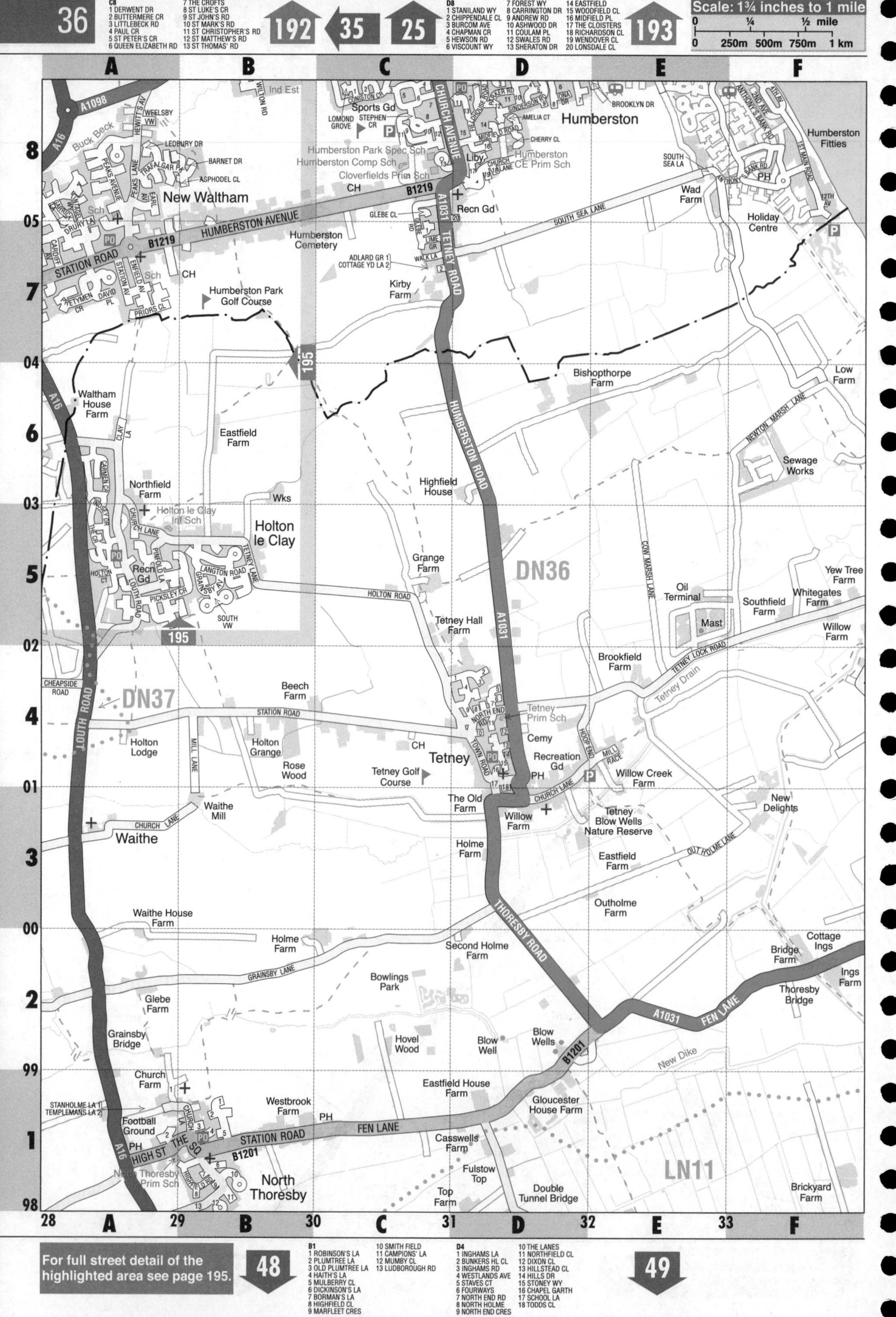

36
C8
1 DERWENT DR
2 BUTTERMERE CR
3 LITTLEBECK RD
4 PAUL CR
5 ST PETER'S CR
6 QUEEN ELIZABETH RD
7 THE CROFTS
8 ST LUKE'S CR
9 ST JOHN'S RD
10 ST MARK'S RD
11 ST CHRISTOPHER'S RD
12 ST MATTHEW'S RD
13 ST THOMAS' RD
192
35
25
D8
1 STANILAND WY
2 CHIPPENDALE CL
3 BURCOM AVE
4 CHAPMAN CR
5 HEWSON RD
6 VISCOUNT WY
7 FOREST WY
8 CARRINGTON DR
9 ANDREW RD
10 ASHWOOD DR
11 COULAM PL
12 SWALES RD
13 SHERATON DR
14 EASTFIELD
15 WOODFIELD CL
16 MIDFIELD PL
17 THE CLOISTERS
18 RICHARDSON CL
19 WENDOVER CL
20 LONSDALE CL
193
Scale: 1¾ inches to 1 mile
0 ¼ ½ mile
0 250m 500m 750m 1 km
A B C D E F
8 05 7 04 6 03 5 02 4 01 3 00 2 99 1 98
28 29 30 31 32 33
A1098
A16
Buck Beck
WEELSBY VW
HEWITT'S AV
LEDBURY DR
BARNET DR
ASPHODEL CL
TRAFALGAR PK
PEAKS AVENUE
PEAKS LANE
New Waltham
Sch
DRURY LA
CARDIFF AV
STATION ROAD
B1219
HUMBERSTON AVENUE
ENFIELD AV
STATION AV
CH
PETYMEN CR
DAVID PL
PRIORS CL
Ind Est
WILTON RD
Sports Gd
LOMOND GROVE
STEPHEN CR
CONISTON CR
Humberston Park Spec Sch
Humberston Comp Sch
Cloverfields Prim Sch
CHURCH AVENUE
Liby
Recn Gd
GLEBE CL
GLEBE RD
LIME GR
WALK LA
ADLARD GR 1
COTTAGE YD LA 2
A1031
TETNEY ROAD
Humberston Cemetery
Humberston Park Golf Course
Kirby Farm
195
FIELDHOUSE ROAD
PARKER RD
SINDERSON RD
MIDFIELD ROAD
AMELIA CT
CHERRY CL
CHURCH LANE
Humberston
Humberston CE Prim Sch
BROOKLYN DR
SOUTH SEA LA
SOUTH SEA LANE
Wad Farm
ANTHONY'S BANK RD
2ND AVE
1ST MAIN RD
12TH AV
PH
Humberston Fitties
Holiday Centre
Waltham House Farm
Eastfield Farm
CLAY LA
Bishopthorpe Farm
Low Farm
NEWTON MARSH LANE
HUMBERSTON ROAD
Sewage Works
Highfield House
Northfield Farm
CARMEN CR
LINDSEY DR
Holton le Clay Inf Sch
CHURCH LANE
Wks
Holton le Clay
PINFOLD LA
LANGTON ROAD
GRAINSBY AV
TETNEY LANE
Recn Gd
HOLTON CT
LOUTH ROAD
PICKSLEY CR
SOUTH VW
HOLTON ROAD
Grange Farm
DN36
COW MARSH LANE
Oil Terminal
Mast
Southfield Farm
Whitegates Farm
Yew Tree Farm
Willow Farm
Tetney Hall Farm
Brookfield Farm
TETNEY LOCK ROAD
Tetney Drain
CHEAPSIDE ROAD
DN37
LOUTH ROAD
Beech Farm
STATION ROAD
NORTH END RD
Tetney Prim Sch
Cemy
Holton Lodge
MILL LANE
Holton Grange
Rose Wood
CH
Tetney
TOWN ROAD
Tetney Golf Course
Recreation Gd
HOOP END
MILL RACE
Willow Creek Farm
PH
The Old Farm
Waithe Mill
CHURCH LANE
Waithe
CHURCH LANE
Willow Farm
Tetney Blow Wells Nature Reserve
New Delights
Holme Farm
Eastfield Farm
OUT HOLME LANE
THORESBY ROAD
Outholme Farm
Waithe House Farm
Holme Farm
Second Holme Farm
Cottage Ings
Bridge Farm
GRAINSBY LANE
Bowlings Park
Ings Farm
Thoresby Bridge
Glebe Farm
A1031
FEN LANE
Grainsby Bridge
Hovel Wood
Blow Well
Blow Wells
B1201
New Dike
Church Farm
Eastfield House Farm
STANHOLME LA 1
TEMPLEMANS LA 2
Westbrook Farm
Gloucester House Farm
Football Ground
CHURCH LA
PH
STATION ROAD
FEN LANE
HIGH ST
THE SQ
B1201
Casswells Farm
North Thoresby Prim Sch
North Thoresby
Fulstow Top
LN11
Top Farm
Double Tunnel Bridge
Brickyard Farm
For full street detail of the highlighted area see page 195.
48
B1
1 ROBINSON'S LA
2 PLUMTREE LA
3 OLD PLUMTREE LA
4 HAITH'S LA
5 MULBERRY CL
6 DICKINSON'S LA
7 BORMAN'S LA
8 HIGHFIELD CL
9 MARFLEET CRES
10 SMITH FIELD
11 CAMPIONS' LA
12 MUMBY CL
13 LUDBOROUGH RD
D4
1 INGHAMS LA
2 BUNKERS HL CL
3 INGHAMS RD
4 WESTLANDS AVE
5 STAVES CT
6 FOURWAYS
7 NORTH END RD
8 NORTH HOLME
9 NORTH END CRES
10 THE LANES
11 NORTHFIELD CL
12 DIXON CL
13 HILLSTEAD CL
14 HILLS DR
15 STONEY WY
16 CHAPEL GARTH
17 SCHOOL LA
18 TODDS CL
49

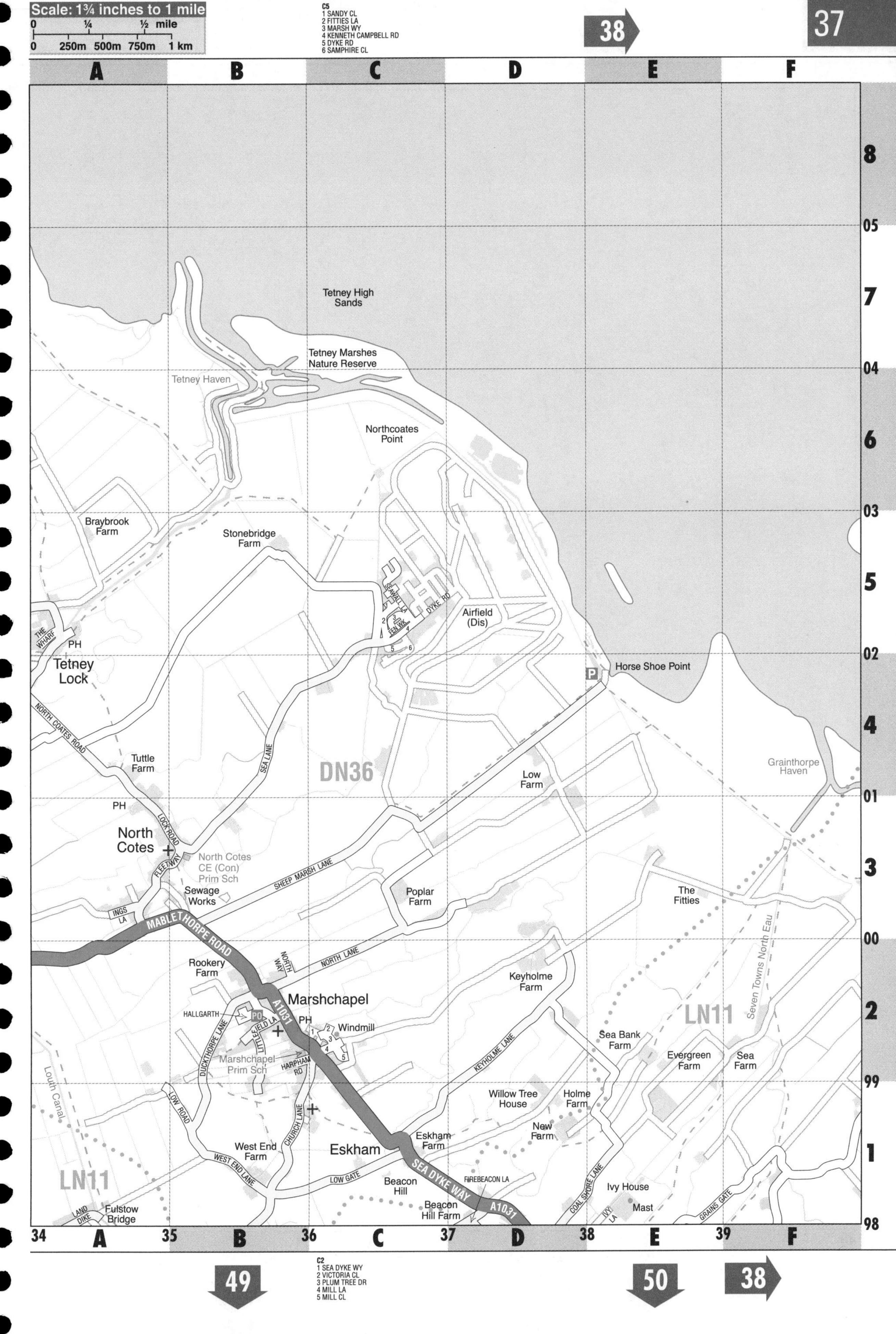
Scale: 1¾ inches to 1 mile
0 ¼ ½ mile
0 250m 500m 750m 1 km
C5
1 SANDY CL
2 FITTIES LA
3 MARSH WY
4 KENNETH CAMPBELL RD
5 DYKE RD
6 SAMPHIRE CL
38
A B C D E F
8
05
7
Tetney High Sands
Tetney Marshes Nature Reserve
Tetney Haven
04
Northcoates Point
6
03
Braybrook Farm
Stonebridge Farm
5
Airfield (Dis)
DYKE RD
THE WHARF
PH
Tetney Lock
02
Horse Shoe Point
NORTH COATES ROAD
4
Tuttle Farm
SEA LANE
DN36
Low Farm
Grainthorpe Haven
PH
01
LOCK ROAD
North Cotes
North Cotes CE (Con) Prim Sch
3
FLEET WAY
Sewage Works
SHEEP MARSH LANE
Poplar Farm
The Fitties
INGS LA
MABLETHORPE ROAD
00
NORTH WAY
NORTH LANE
Rookery Farm
Keyholme Farm
Seven Towns North Eau
Marshchapel
HALLGARTH
PO
A1031
PH
Windmill
LN11
2
DUCKTHORPE LANE
LITTLEFIELD LA
Marshchapel Prim Sch
HARPHAM RD
KEYHOLME LANE
Sea Bank Farm
Evergreen Farm
Sea Farm
Louth Canal
LOW ROAD
99
Willow Tree House
Holme Farm
CHURCH LANE
New Farm
West End Farm
Eskham
Eskham Farm
1
WEST END LANE
LN11
SEA DYKE WAY
LOW GATE
Beacon Hill
FIREBEACON LA
COAL SHORE LANE
Ivy House
LAND DIKE
Fulstow Bridge
Beacon Hill Farm
A1031
IVY LA
Mast
GRAINS GATE
98
34 35 36 37 38 39
C2
1 SEA DYKE WY
2 VICTORIA CL
3 PLUM TREE DR
4 MILL LA
5 MILL CL
49
50
38

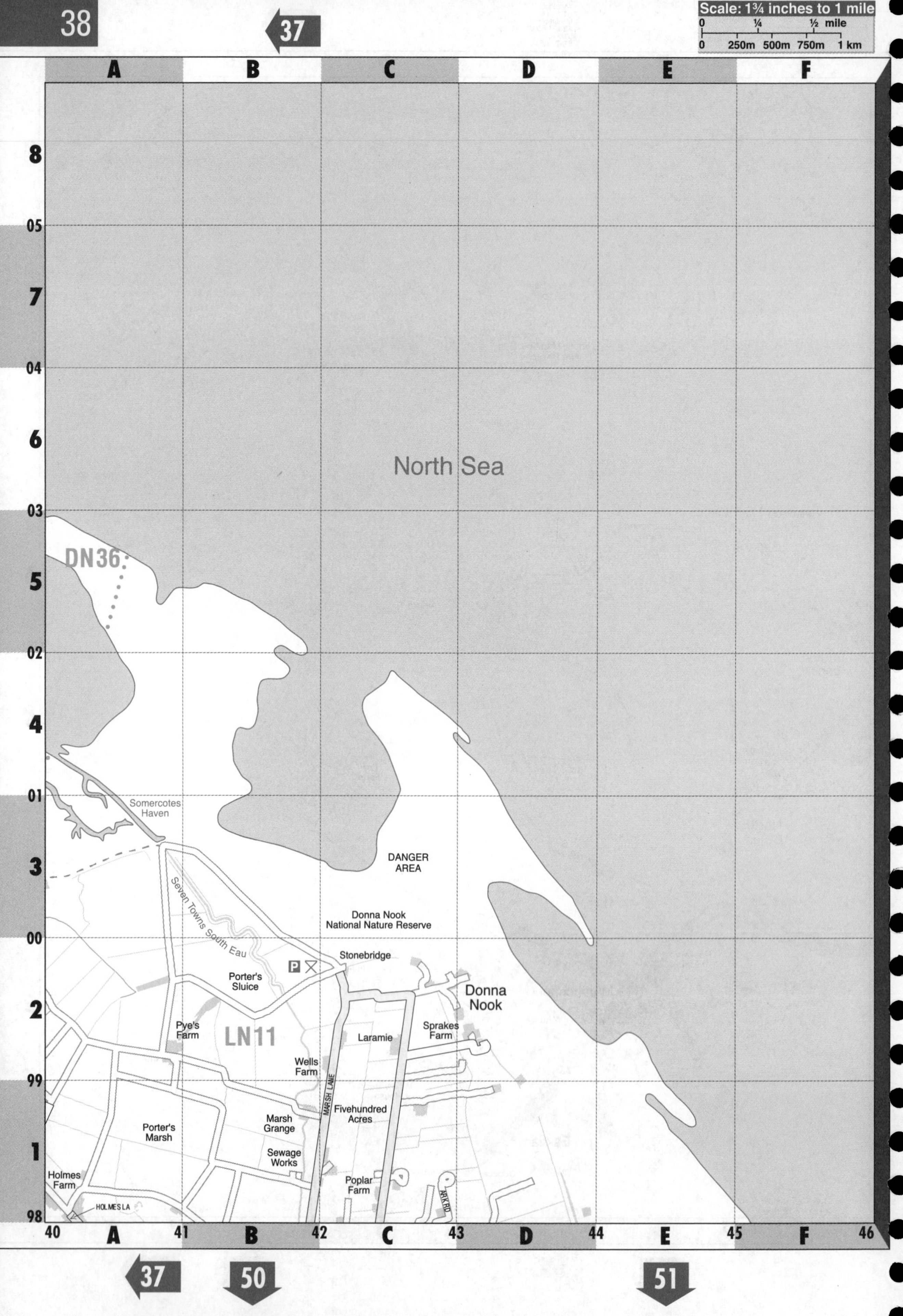

Scale: 1¾ inches to 1 mile
0   ¼   ½ mile
0 250m 500m 750m 1 km

8
05
7
04
6   North Sea
03
DN36
5
02
4
01
Somercotes
Haven
3   DANGER
AREA
Donna Nook
National Nature Reserve
00   Stonebridge
P ✕
Porter's   Donna
Sluice   Nook
2   Pye's
Farm   Sprakes
LN11   Laramie   Farm
Wells
Farm
99
Marsh
Porter's   Grange Fivehundred
Marsh   Acres
1   Sewage
Works
Holmes   Poplar
Farm   Farm
98
40   A   41   B   42   C   43   D   44   E   45   F   46

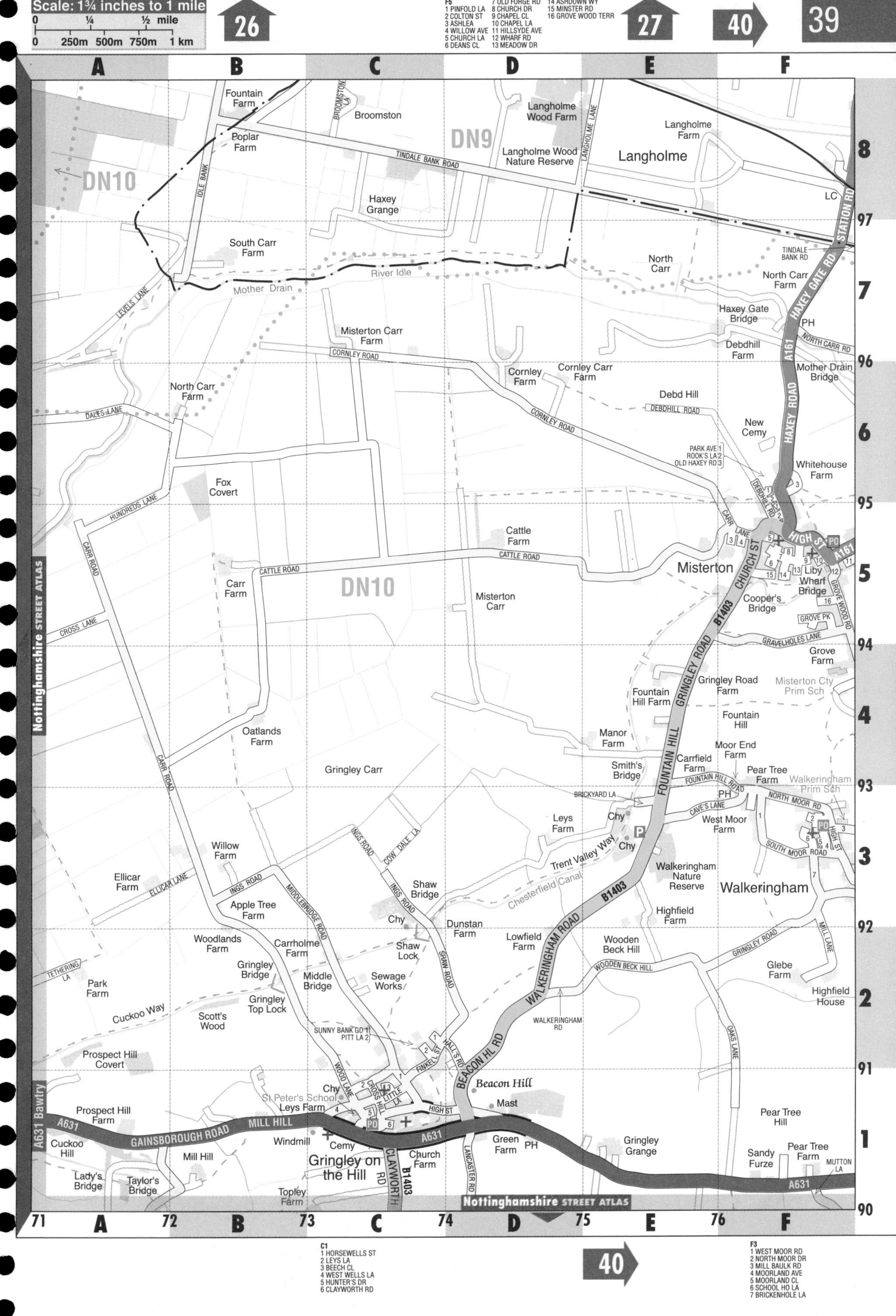

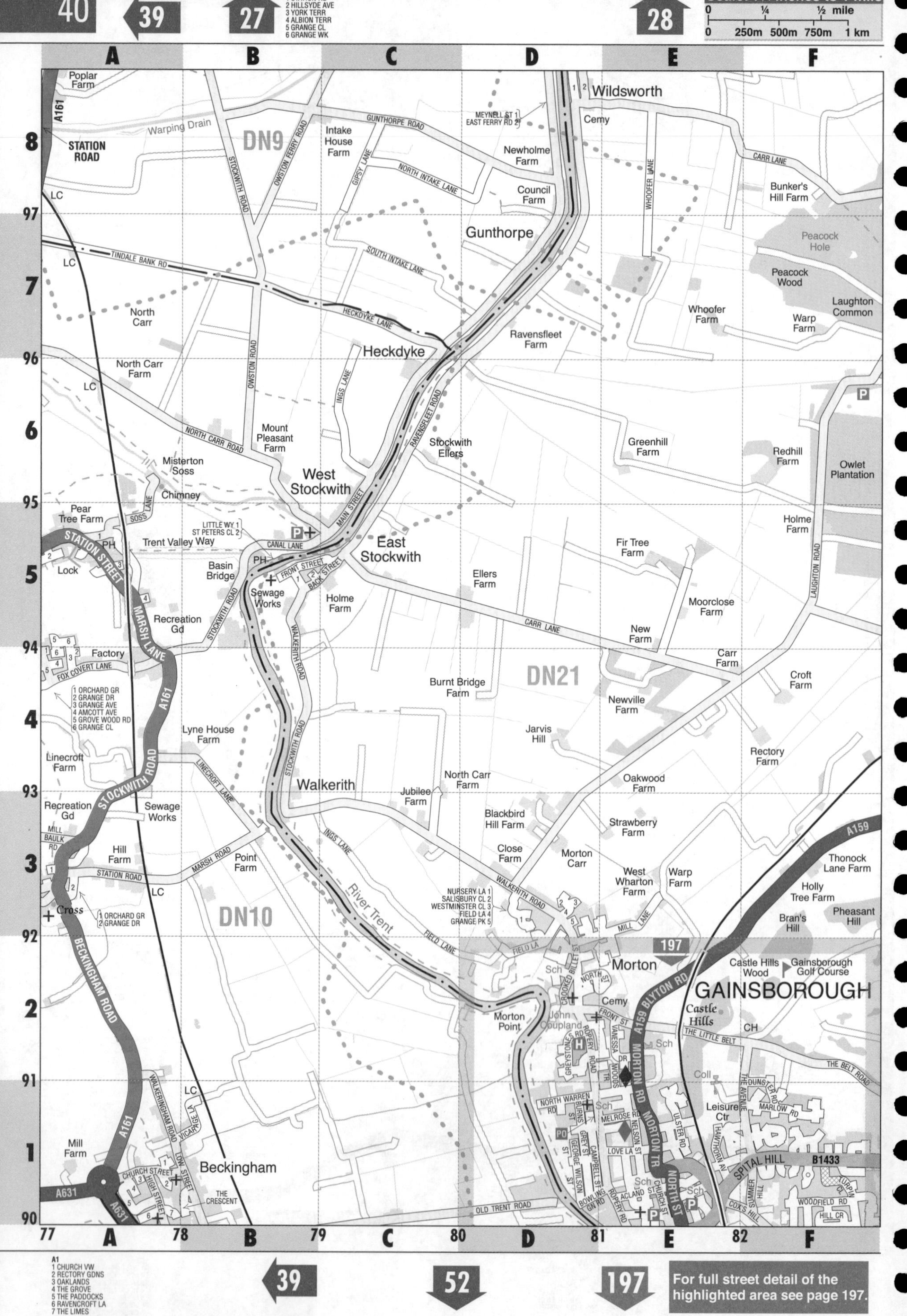

40 ◀ **39** ▲ **27** ▲ **28**

A5
1 STATION RD
2 HILLSYDE AVE
3 YORK TERR
4 ALBION TERR
5 GRANGE CL
6 GRANGE WK

Scale: 1¾ inches to 1 mile
0   ¼   ½ mile
0   250m 500m 750m 1 km

A   B   C   D   E   F

8
Poplar Farm
STATION ROAD
Warping Drain
DN9
Intake House Farm
GUNTHORPE ROAD
NORTH INTAKE LANE
MEYNELL ST 1
EAST FERRY RD 2
Wildsworth
Cemy
CARR LANE
Bunker's Hill Farm

97
LC
Council Farm
Peacock Hole

7
LC
TINDALE BANK RD
SOUTH INTAKE LANE
Gunthorpe
WHOOFER LANE
Peacock Wood
Laughton Common
North Carr
HECKDYKE LANE
OWSTON FERRY ROAD
OWSTON ROAD
STOCKWITH ROAD
GIPSY LANE
Ravensfleet Farm
Whoofer Farm
Warp Farm

96
LC
North Carr Farm
Heckdyke
INGS LANE
RAVENSFLEET ROAD
Stockwith Ellers
Greenhill Farm
Redhill Farm
Owlet Plantation

6
NORTH CARR ROAD
Mount Pleasant Farm
West Stockwith
Holme Farm
LAUGHTON ROAD

95
Misterton Soss
Chimney
SOSS LANE
Pear Tree Farm
Trent Valley Way
LITTLE WY 1
ST PETERS CL 2
CANAL LANE
MAIN STREET
East Stockwith
Fir Tree Farm

5
STATION STREET
PH
Lock
Basin Bridge
PH
FRONT STREET
BACK STREET
Sewage Works
Holme Farm
Ellers Farm
Moorclose Farm
Holme Farm

94
Factory
FOX COVERT LANE
Recreation Gd
MARSH LANE
STOCKWITH ROAD
WALKERITH ROAD
CARR LANE
New Farm
Carr Farm
Croft Farm
1 ORCHARD GR
2 GRANGE DR
3 GRANGE AVE
4 AMCOTT AVE
5 GROVE WOOD RD
6 GRANGE CL
DN21

4
A161
Lyne House Farm
LINECROFT LANE
Burnt Bridge Farm
Newville Farm
Jarvis Hill
Rectory Farm
Linecroft Farm

93
Recreation Gd
STOCKWITH ROAD
Sewage Works
Walkerith
Jubilee Farm
North Carr Farm
Oakwood Farm
Strawberry Farm
A159

3
MILL BAULK RD
Hill Farm
STATION ROAD
MARSH LANE
Point Farm
River Trent
INGS LANE
Blackbird Hill Farm
Close Farm
WALKERITH ROAD
Morton Carr
West Wharton Farm
Warp Farm
Thonock Lane Farm
Holly Tree Farm
Pheasant Hill
Cross
1 ORCHARD GR
2 GRANGE DR
DN10
NURSERY LA 1
SALISBURY CL 2
WESTMINSTER CL 3
FIELD LA 4
GRANGE PK 5
MILL LANE
Bran's Hill

92
BECKINGHAM ROAD
FIELD LANE
FIELD LA
Morton Point
197
Morton
Castle Hills Wood
Gainsborough Golf Course
GAINSBOROUGH

2
WALKENINGHAM ROAD
Sch
John Coupland
A159 BLYTON RD
MORTON ROAD
Cemy
FRONT ST
Castle Hills
THE LITTLE BELT
CH

91
LC
NORTH WARREN RD
MORTON TR
Sch
Coll
THE BELT ROAD
Mill Farm
PO
MELROSE RD
Leisure Ctr
MARLOW RD

1
A161
WALKENINGHAM ROAD
LOW STREET
VICARAGE
Beckingham
Sch
NORTH ST
SPITAL HILL
B1433
WOODFIELD RD
HILL CR

90
A631
CHURCH STREET
HIGH STREET
THE CRESCENT
OLD TRENT ROAD
COX'S HILL

77   78   79   80   81   82
A   B   C   D   E   F

A1
1 CHURCH VW
2 RECTORY GDNS
3 OAKLANDS
4 THE GROVE
5 THE PADDOCKS
6 RAVENCROFT LA
7 THE LIMES

▲ **39**   ▲ **52**   ▲ **197**

For full street detail of the highlighted area see page 197.

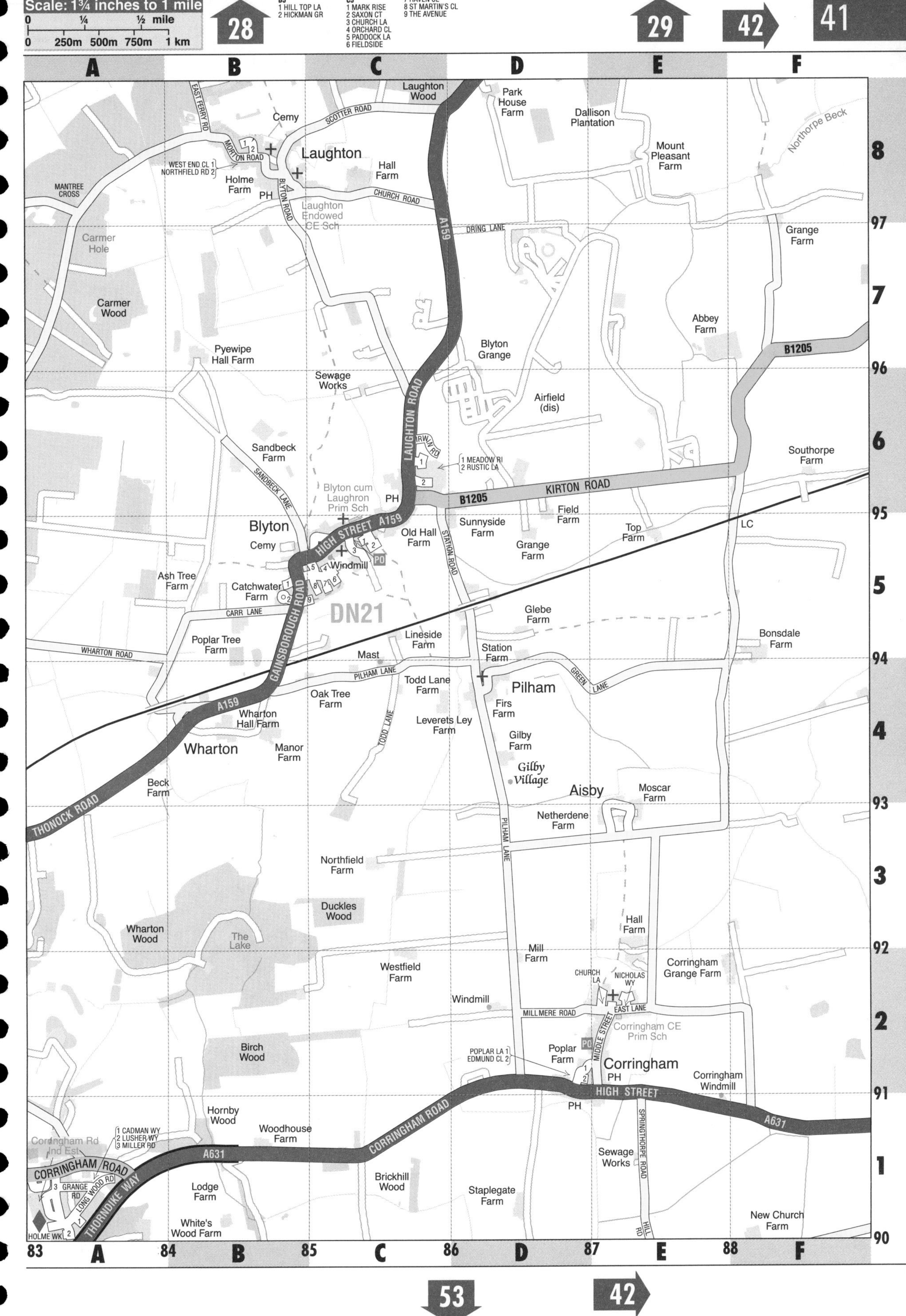
Scale: 1¾ inches to 1 mile
0 ¼ ½ mile
0 250m 500m 750m 1 km
28
B5
1 HILL TOP LA
2 HICKMAN GR
C5
1 MARK RISE
2 SAXON CT
3 CHURCH LA
4 ORCHARD CL
5 PADDOCK LA
6 FIELDSIDE
7 HAVEN CL
8 ST MARTIN'S CL
9 THE AVENUE
29
42
Laughton Wood
Park House Farm
Dallison Plantation
Cemy
Laughton
SCOTTER ROAD
EAST FERRY RD
MORTON ROAD
WEST END CL 1
NORTHFIELD RD 2
Holme Farm
PH
Hall Farm
Mount Pleasant Farm
Northorpe Beck
MANTREE CROSS
BLYTON ROAD
CHURCH ROAD
Laughton Endowed CE Sch
A159
DRING LANE
Grange Farm
Carmer Hole
Carmer Wood
Abbey Farm
Pyewipe Hall Farm
Blyton Grange
B1205
Sewage Works
LAUGHTON ROAD
Airfield (dis)
Sandbeck Farm
SANDBECK LANE
IRWIN RD
1 MEADOW RI
2 RUSTIC LA
Southorpe Farm
Blyton cum Laughton Prim Sch
PH
B1205
KIRTON ROAD
Field Farm
Blyton
HIGH STREET
Old Hall Farm
Sunnyside Farm
Top Farm
LC
Cemy
STATION ROAD
Grange Farm
Windmill
PO
Ash Tree Farm
Catchwater Farm
GAINSBOROUGH ROAD
DN21
Glebe Farm
CARR LANE
Poplar Tree Farm
Lineside Farm
Bonsdale Farm
WHARTON ROAD
Mast
Station Farm
PILHAM LANE
Todd Lane Farm
Pilham
GREEN LANE
Oak Tree Farm
Firs Farm
Wharton Hall Farm
Leverets Ley Farm
TODD LANE
Wharton
Manor Farm
Gilby Farm
Gilby Village
Beck Farm
Aisby
Moscar Farm
THONOCK ROAD
Netherdene Farm
PILHAM LANE
Northfield Farm
Duckles Wood
Hall Farm
Wharton Wood
The Lake
Mill Farm
Corringham Grange Farm
Westfield Farm
CHURCH LA
NICHOLAS WY
Windmill
MILL MERE ROAD
EAST LANE
Corringham CE Prim Sch
MIDDLE STREET
Birch Wood
POPLAR LA 1
EDMUND CL 2
Poplar Farm
Corringham
PH
Corringham Windmill
HIGH STREET
PH
A631
Hornby Wood
1 CADMAN WY
2 LUSHER WY
3 MILLER RD
Woodhouse Farm
CORRINGHAM ROAD
Corringham Rd Ind Est
CORRINGHAM ROAD
A631
Sewage Works
SPRINGTHORPE ROAD
3 GRANGE RD
LONG WOOD RD
THORNDIKE WAY
Lodge Farm
Brickhill Wood
Staplegate Farm
New Church Farm
White's Wood Farm
HOLME WK
HILL RD
A B C D E F
8 97 7 96 6 95 5 94 4 93 3 92 2 91 1 90
83 84 85 86 87 88
53
42

41 29 30

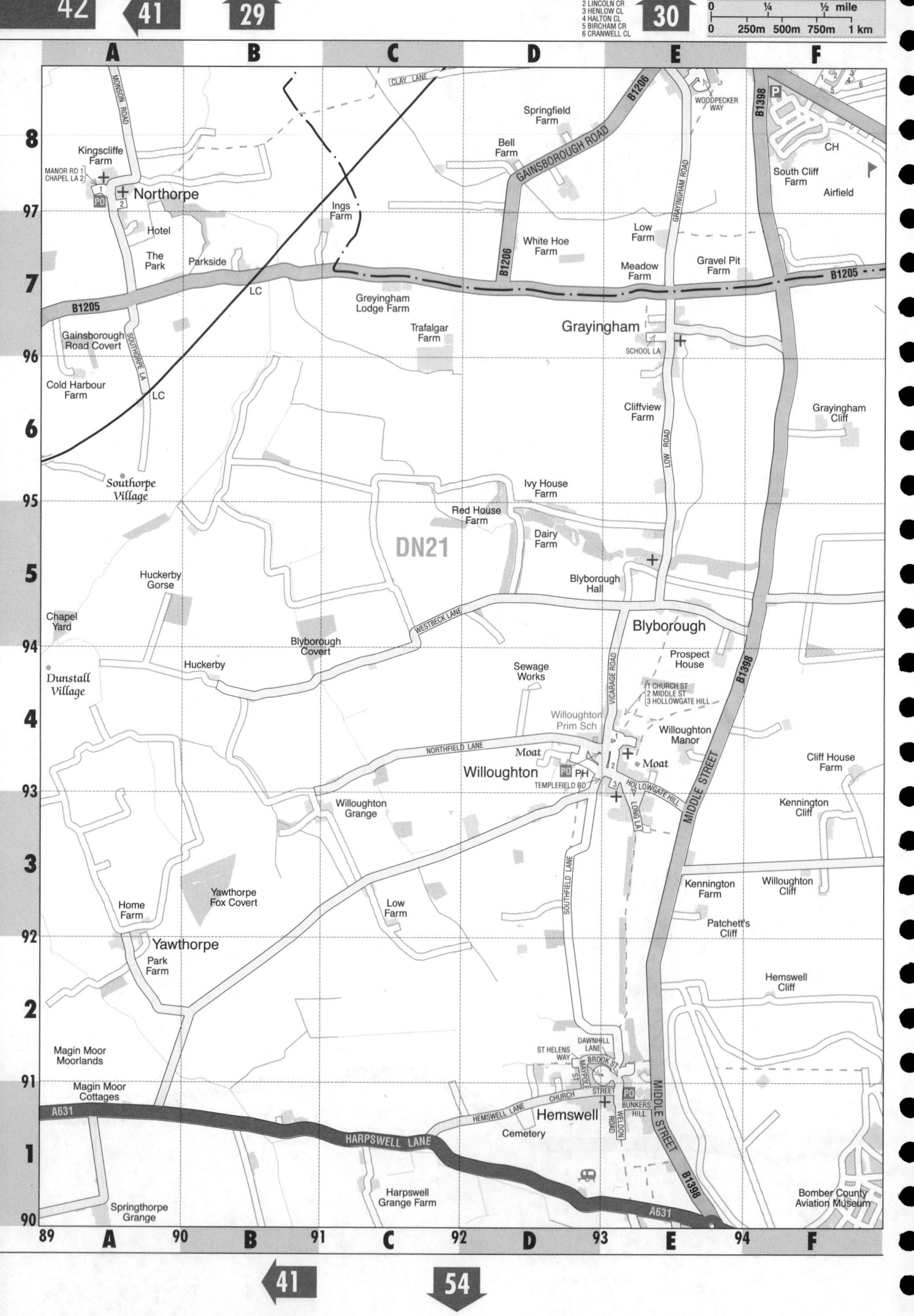
F8
1 YORK RD
2 LINCOLN CR
3 HENLOW CL
4 HALTON CL
5 BIRCHAM CR
6 CRANWELL CL
Scale: 1¾ inches to 1 mile
0 ¼ ½ mile
0 250m 500m 750m 1 km
Kingscliffe Farm
Northorpe
Hotel
The Park
Parkside
Ings Farm
Springfield Farm
Bell Farm
GAINSBOROUGH ROAD
B1206
White Hoe Farm
Low Farm
Meadow Farm
Gravel Pit Farm
GRAYINGHAM ROAD
WOODPECKER WAY
B1398
South Cliff Farm
CH
Airfield
B1205
LC
Greyingham Lodge Farm
Trafalgar Farm
Grayingham
SCHOOL LA
Gainsborough Road Covert
SOUTHORPE LA
Cold Harbour Farm
Cliffview Farm
Grayingham Cliff
LOW ROAD
Southorpe Village
Ivy House Farm
Red House Farm
Dairy Farm
DN21
Blyborough Hall
Huckerby Gorse
Chapel Yard
WESTBECK LANE
Blyborough
Blyborough Covert
Huckerby
Prospect House
Sewage Works
Dunstall Village
VICARAGE ROAD
1 CHURCH ST
2 MIDDLE ST
3 HOLLOWGATE HILL
Willoughton Prim Sch
Willoughton Manor
NORTHFIELD LANE
Moat
Willoughton
PO PH
TEMPLEFIELD RD
HOLLOWGATE HILL
LONG LA
MIDDLE STREET
Cliff House Farm
Kennington Cliff
Willoughton Grange
SOUTHFIELD LANE
Kennington Farm
Willoughton Cliff
Yawthorpe Fox Covert
Low Farm
Home Farm
Patchett's Cliff
Yawthorpe
Park Farm
Hemswell Cliff
Magin Moor Moorlands
ST HELENS WAY
DAWNHILL LANE
BROOK ST
MAYPOLE ST
STREET
Magin Moor Cottages
A631
CHURCH
HEMSWELL LANE
Hemswell
BUNKERS HILL
WELDON ROAD
Cemetery
HARPSWELL LANE
Harpswell Grange Farm
Springthorpe Grange
Bomber County Aviation Museum
A B C D E F
89 90 91 92 93 94
8 97 7 96 6 95 5 94 4 93 3 92 2 91 1 90

41 54

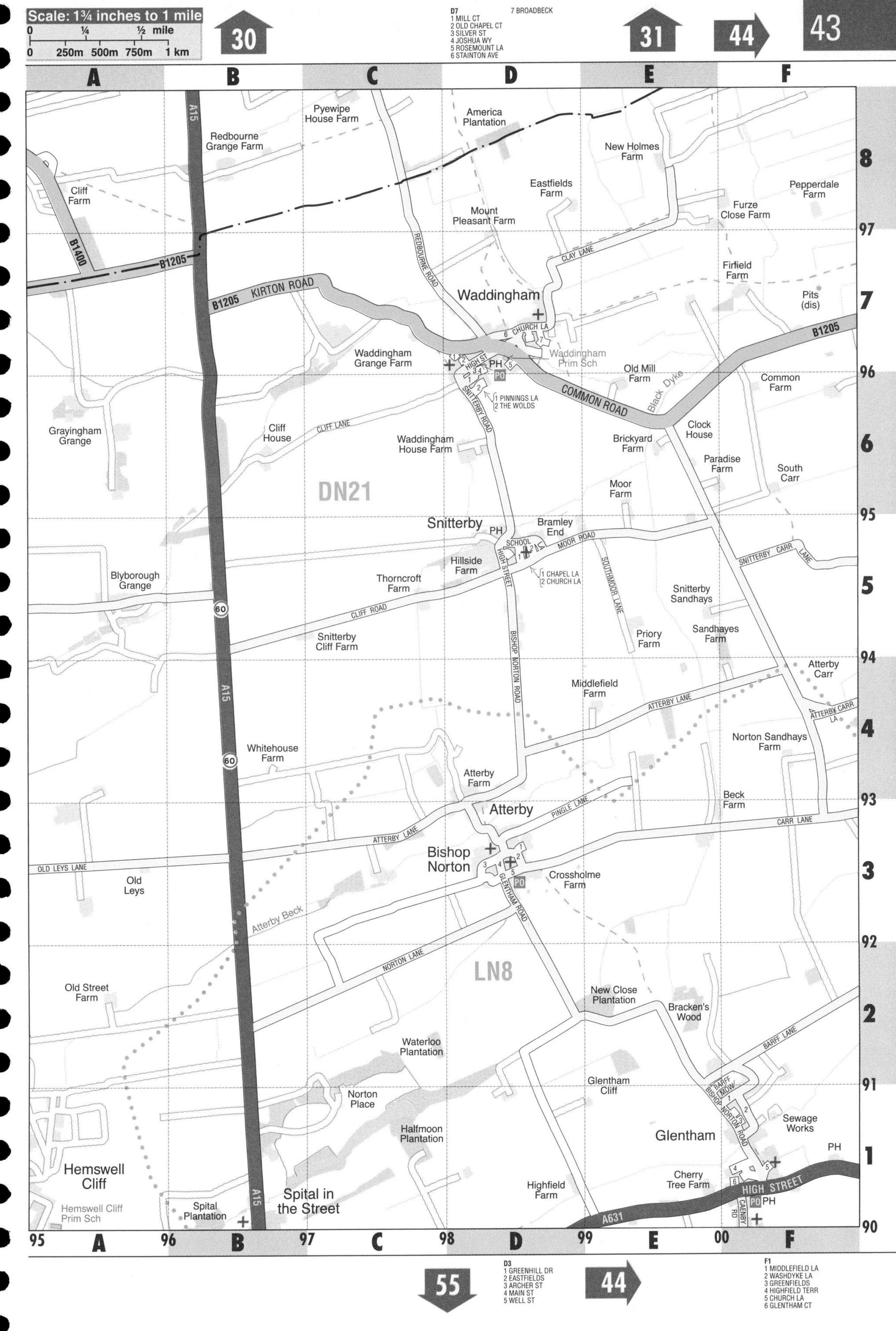

43 31 32

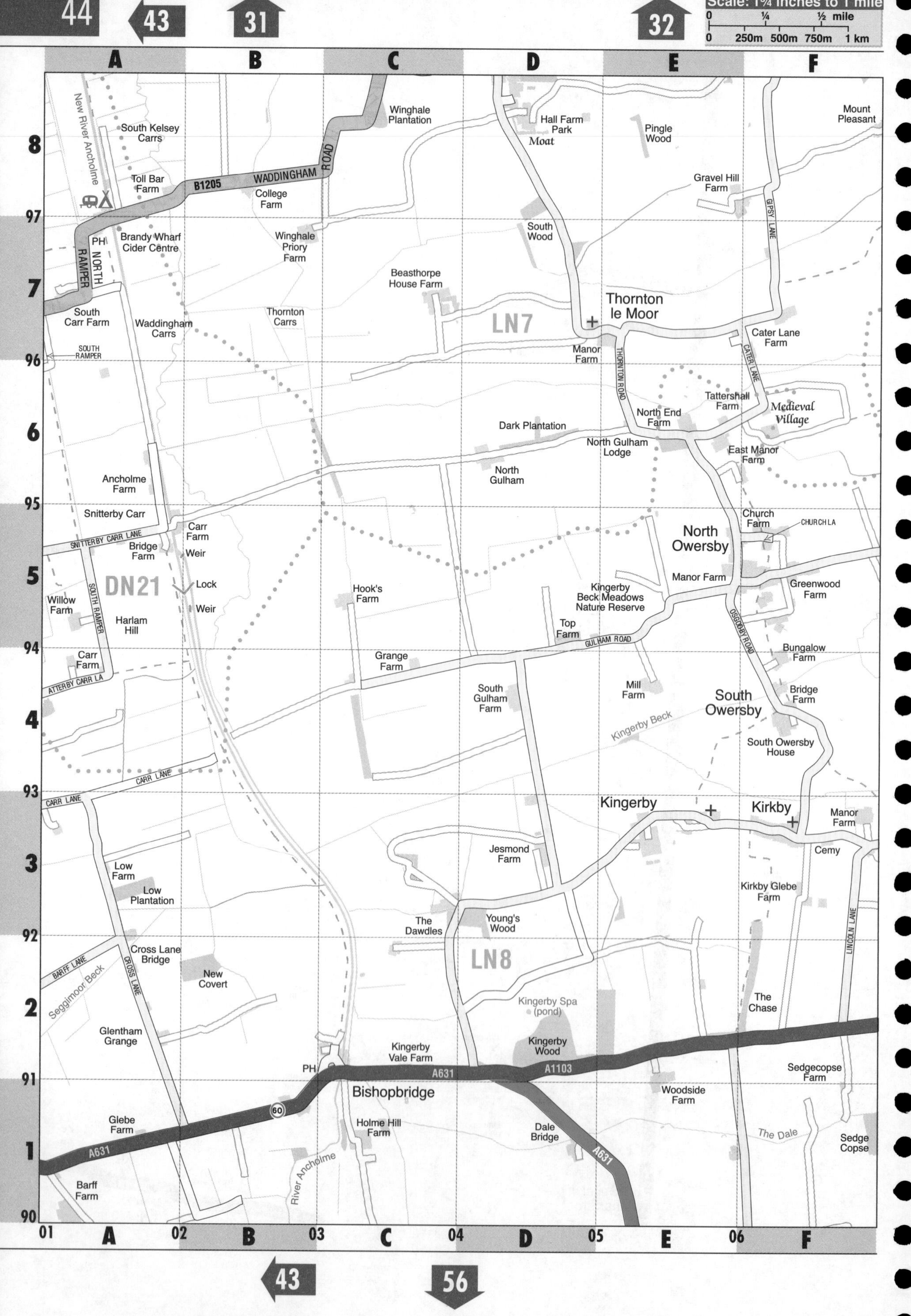
Scale: 1¾ inches to 1 mile
¼ ½ mile
0 250m 500m 750m 1 km
A B C D E F
8 97 7 96 6 95 5 94 4 93 3 92 2 91 1 90
01 02 03 04 05 06
New River Ancholme
South Kelsey Carrs
Toll Bar Farm
B1205
WADDINGHAM ROAD
College Farm
Winghale Plantation
Hall Farm Park
Moat
Pingle Wood
Mount Pleasant
Gravel Hill Farm
GIPSY LANE
PH
NORTH RAMPER
Brandy Wharf Cider Centre
Winghale Priory Farm
South Wood
Beasthorpe House Farm
Thornton le Moor
South Carr Farm
Waddingham Carrs
Thornton Carrs
LN7
SOUTH RAMPER
Manor Farm
THORNTON ROAD
Cater Lane Farm
CATER LANE
Tattershall Farm
Medieval Village
North End Farm
Dark Plantation
North Gulham Lodge
East Manor Farm
North Gulham
Ancholme Farm
Snitterby Carr
Carr Farm
Church Farm
CHURCH LA
North Owersby
SNITTERBY CARR LANE
Bridge Farm
Weir
Lock
Weir
DN21
Hook's Farm
Manor Farm
Greenwood Farm
Willow Farm
SOUTH RAMPER
Harlam Hill
Kingerby Beck Meadows Nature Reserve
OSGODBY ROAD
Top Farm
GULHAM ROAD
Bungalow Farm
Carr Farm
ATTERBY CARR LA
Grange Farm
South Gulham Farm
Mill Farm
South Owersby
Bridge Farm
Kingerby Beck
South Owersby House
CARR LANE
CARR LANE
Kingerby
Kirkby
Manor Farm
Jesmond Farm
Cemy
Low Farm
Low Plantation
Kirkby Glebe Farm
The Dawdles
Young's Wood
LN8
LINCOLN LANE
Cross Lane Bridge
BARFF LANE
CROSS LANE
Seggimoor Beck
New Covert
Kingerby Spa (pond)
The Chase
Glentham Grange
Kingerby Wood
Kingerby Vale Farm
PH
A631
A1103
Bishopbridge
Sedgecopse Farm
Woodside Farm
60
Glebe Farm
Holme Hill Farm
Dale Bridge
The Dale
A631
A631
Sedge Copse
River Ancholme
Barff Farm

43 56

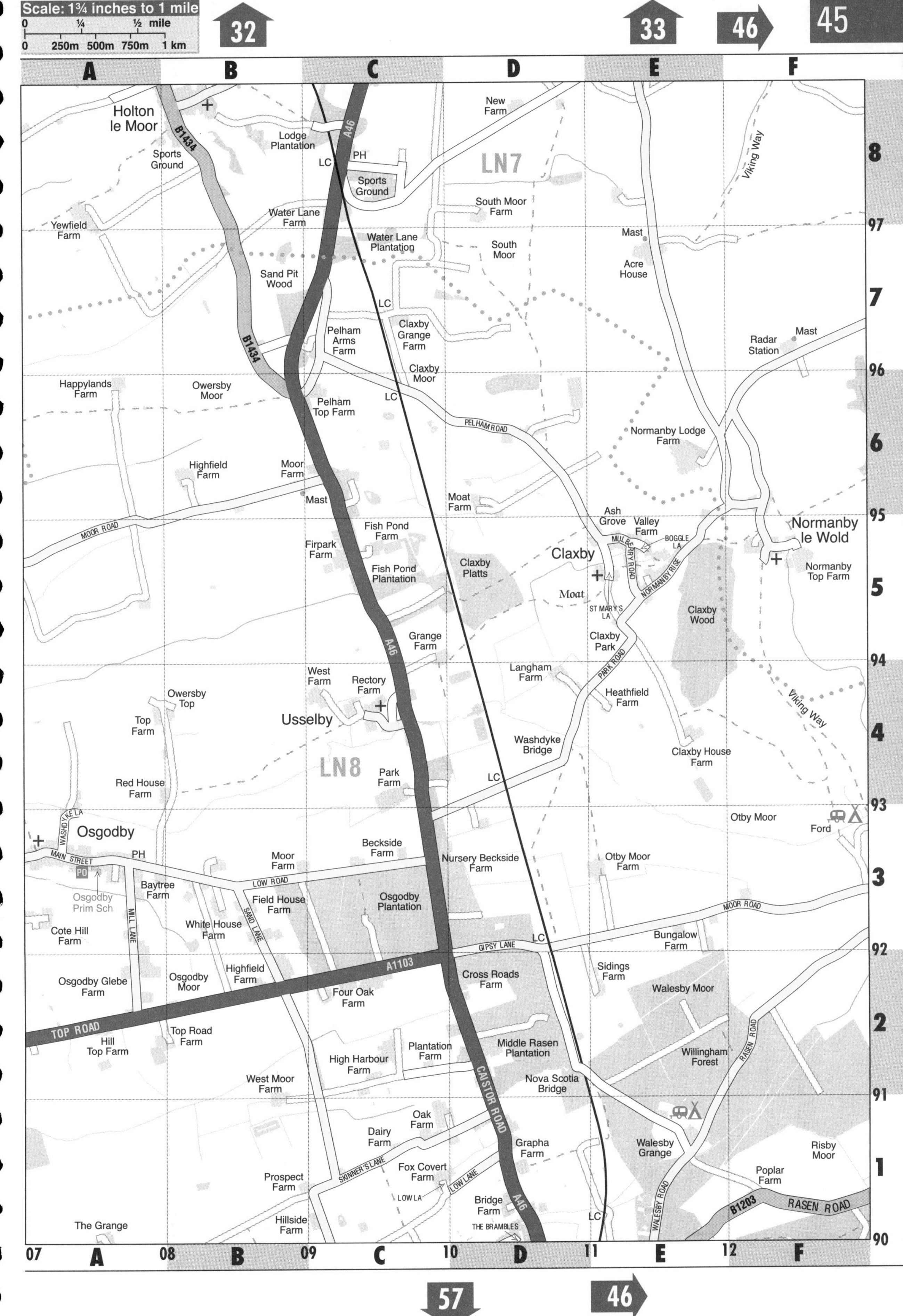
Scale: 1¾ inches to 1 mile
0 ¼ ½ mile
0 250m 500m 750m 1 km
32
33
46
A B C D E F
Holton le Moor
B1434
A46
Lodge Plantation
Sports Ground
LC
PH
Sports Ground
New Farm
LN7
South Moor Farm
Viking Way
8
97
Yewfield Farm
Water Lane Farm
Water Lane Plantation
South Moor
Mast
Acre House
Sand Pit Wood
7
LC
Claxby Grange Farm
Radar Station
Mast
Pelham Arms Farm
Claxby Moor
96
Happylands Farm
Owersby Moor
Pelham Top Farm
LC
PELHAM ROAD
Normanby Lodge Farm
6
Highfield Farm
Moor Farm
Mast
Moat Farm
95
Ash Grove
Valley Farm
Normanby le Wold
MOOR ROAD
Fish Pond Farm
Firpark Farm
Claxby
MULBERRY ROAD
BOGGLE LA
Normanby Top Farm
Fish Pond Plantation
Claxby Platts
Moat
NORMANBY RISE
ST MARY'S LA
Claxby Wood
5
Grange Farm
Claxby Park
PARK ROAD
94
West Farm
Rectory Farm
Langham Farm
Heathfield Farm
Owersby Top
Top Farm
Usselby
Washdyke Bridge
Claxby House Farm
4
LN8
Park Farm
Red House Farm
LC
93
Otby Moor
Ford
WASHDYKE LA
Osgodby
Beckside Farm
MAIN STREET
PH
Moor Farm
Nursery Beckside Farm
Otby Moor Farm
3
PO
LOW ROAD
Baytree Farm
Osgodby Prim Sch
Field House Farm
Osgodby Plantation
MOOR ROAD
MILL LANE
SAND LANE
Cote Hill Farm
White House Farm
GIPSY LANE
LC
Bungalow Farm
92
A1103
Sidings Farm
Osgodby Glebe Farm
Osgodby Moor
Highfield Farm
Cross Roads Farm
Walesby Moor
Four Oak Farm
2
TOP ROAD
Top Road Farm
Hill Top Farm
Middle Rasen Plantation
RASEN ROAD
Plantation Farm
Willingham Forest
High Harbour Farm
CAISTOR ROAD
West Moor Farm
Nova Scotia Bridge
91
Oak Farm
Dairy Farm
Grapha Farm
Walesby Grange
Risby Moor
1
Prospect Farm
SKINNER'S LANE
Fox Covert Farm
Poplar Farm
LOW LANE
LOW LA
WALESBY ROAD
B1203
RASEN ROAD
Bridge Farm
Hillside Farm
LC
The Grange
THE BRAMBLES
90
07 A 08 B 09 C 10 D 11 E 12 F
57
46

45
33
34

Scale: 1¾ inches to 1 mile

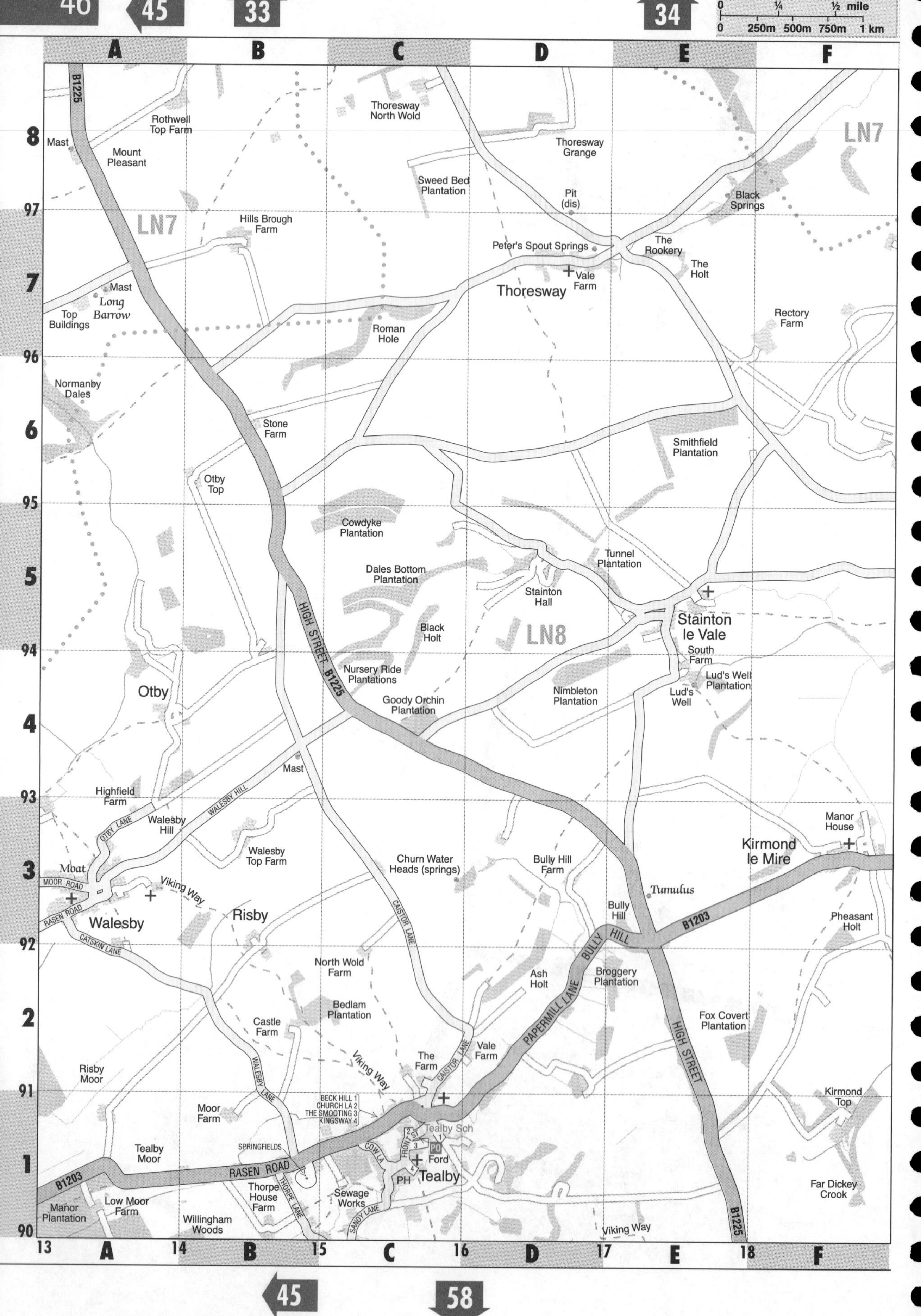
B1225
Rothwell Top Farm
Mast
Mount Pleasant
Thoresway North Wold
Thoresway Grange
Sweed Bed Plantation
LN7
Pit (dis)
Black Springs
Hills Brough Farm
Peter's Spout Springs
The Rookery
The Holt
Vale Farm
Thoresway
Mast
Long Barrow
Top Buildings
Roman Hole
Rectory Farm
Normanby Dales
Stone Farm
Smithfield Plantation
Otby Top
Cowdyke Plantation
Tunnel Plantation
Dales Bottom Plantation
Stainton Hall
Stainton le Vale
HIGH STREET B1225
Black Holt
LN8
South Farm
Nursery Ride Plantations
Lud's Well Plantation
Lud's Well
Nimbleton Plantation
Otby
Goody Orchin Plantation
Mast
Highfield Farm
Walesby Hill
WALESBY HILL
OTBY LANE
Manor House
Kirmond le Mire
Walesby Top Farm
Churn Water Heads (springs)
Bully Hill Farm
Moat
MOOR ROAD
Viking Way
Tumulus
RASEN ROAD
Walesby
Risby
CAISTOR LANE
Bully Hill
B1203
Pheasant Holt
CATSKIN LANE
BULLY HILL
North Wold Farm
Ash Holt
Broggery Plantation
Bedlam Plantation
PAPERMILL LANE
Castle Farm
Fox Covert Plantation
HIGH STREET
Vale Farm
The Farm
Risby Moor
Viking Way
WALESBY LANE
CAISTOR LANE
BECK HILL 1
CHURCH LA 2
THE SMOOTHING 3
KINGSWAY 4
Kirmond Top
Moor Farm
Tealby Sch
Tealby Moor
SPRINGFIELDS
FRONT ST
COW LA
PO
Ford
Tealby
PH
RASEN ROAD
B1203
Thorpe House Farm
THORPE LANE
Sewage Works
SANDY LANE
Far Dickey Crook
Manor Plantation
Low Moor Farm
Willingham Woods
Viking Way
B1225
A B C D E F
8 97 7 96 6 95 5 94 4 93 3 92 2 91 1 90
13 14 15 16 17 18

45
58

Scale: 1¾ inches to 1 mile

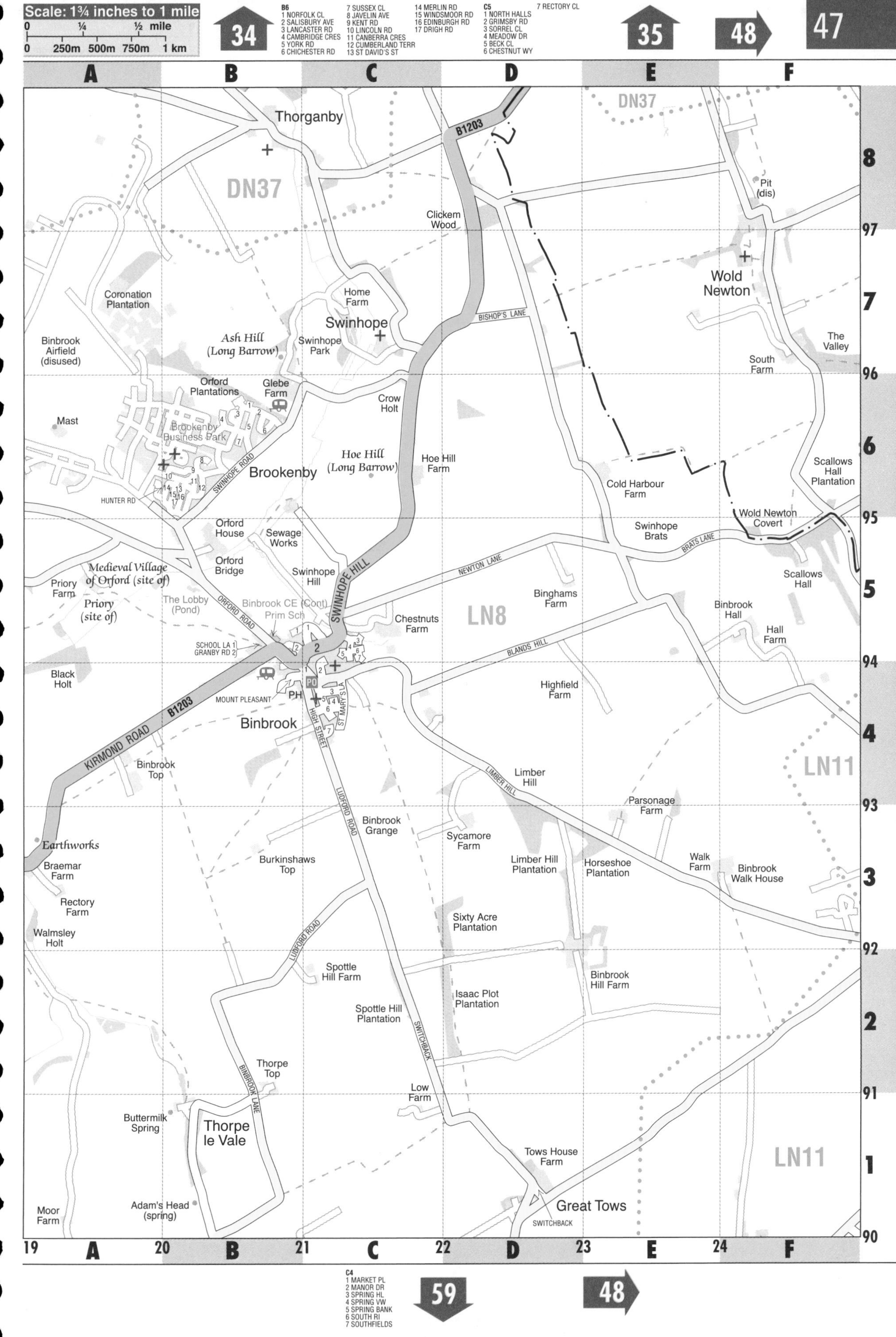

34
35
48
B6
1 NORFOLK CL
2 SALISBURY AVE
3 LANCASTER RD
4 CAMBRIDGE CRES
5 YORK RD
6 CHICHESTER RD
7 SUSSEX CL
8 JAVELIN AVE
9 KENT RD
10 LINCOLN RD
11 CANBERRA CRES
12 CUMBERLAND TERR
13 ST DAVID'S ST
14 MERLIN RD
15 WINDSMOOR RD
16 EDINBURGH RD
17 DRIGH RD
C5
1 NORTH HALLS
2 GRIMSBY RD
3 SORREL CL
4 MEADOW DR
5 BECK CL
6 CHESTNUT WY
7 RECTORY CL
Thorganby
DN37
B1203
Clickem Wood
Pit (dis)
Wold Newton
Coronation Plantation
Home Farm
Swinhope
Swinhope Park
Ash Hill (Long Barrow)
Binbrook Airfield (disused)
BISHOP'S LANE
The Valley
South Farm
Orford Plantations
Glebe Farm
Crow Holt
Mast
Brookenby Business Park
Hoe Hill (Long Barrow)
Hoe Hill Farm
Brookenby
SWINHOPE ROAD
HUNTER RD
Scallows Hall Plantation
Cold Harbour Farm
Wold Newton Covert
Orford House
Sewage Works
Swinhope Brats
BRATS LANE
NEWTON LANE
Orford Bridge
Medieval Village of Orford (site of)
Priory Farm
Priory (site of)
Swinhope Hill
SWINHOPE HILL
Binghams Farm
Scallows Hall
The Lobby (Pond)
Binbrook CE (Cont) Prim Sch
ORFORD ROAD
Chestnuts Farm
LN8
Binbrook Hall
Hall Farm
SCHOOL LA 1
GRANBY RD 2
BLANDS HILL
Black Holt
PO
PH
MOUNT PLEASANT
Highfield Farm
ST MARY'S LA
HIGH STREET
Binbrook
KIRMOND ROAD
Binbrook Top
Limber Hill
LIMBER HILL
LN11
Parsonage Farm
LUDFORD ROAD
Binbrook Grange
Sycamore Farm
Earthworks
Braemar Farm
Burkinshaws Top
Limber Hill Plantation
Horseshoe Plantation
Walk Farm
Binbrook Walk House
Rectory Farm
Sixty Acre Plantation
Walmsley Holt
Spottle Hill Farm
Binbrook Hill Farm
Isaac Plot Plantation
Spottle Hill Plantation
SWITCHBACK
Thorpe Top
BINBROOK LANE
Low Farm
Buttermilk Spring
Thorpe le Vale
Tows House Farm
Adam's Head (spring)
Moor Farm
Great Tows
SWITCHBACK
A B C D E F
19 20 21 22 23 24
8 97 7 96 6 95 5 94 4 93 3 92 2 91 1 90
C4
1 MARKET PL
2 MANOR DR
3 SPRING HL
4 SPRING VW
5 SPRING BANK
6 SOUTH RI
7 SOUTHFIELDS
59
48

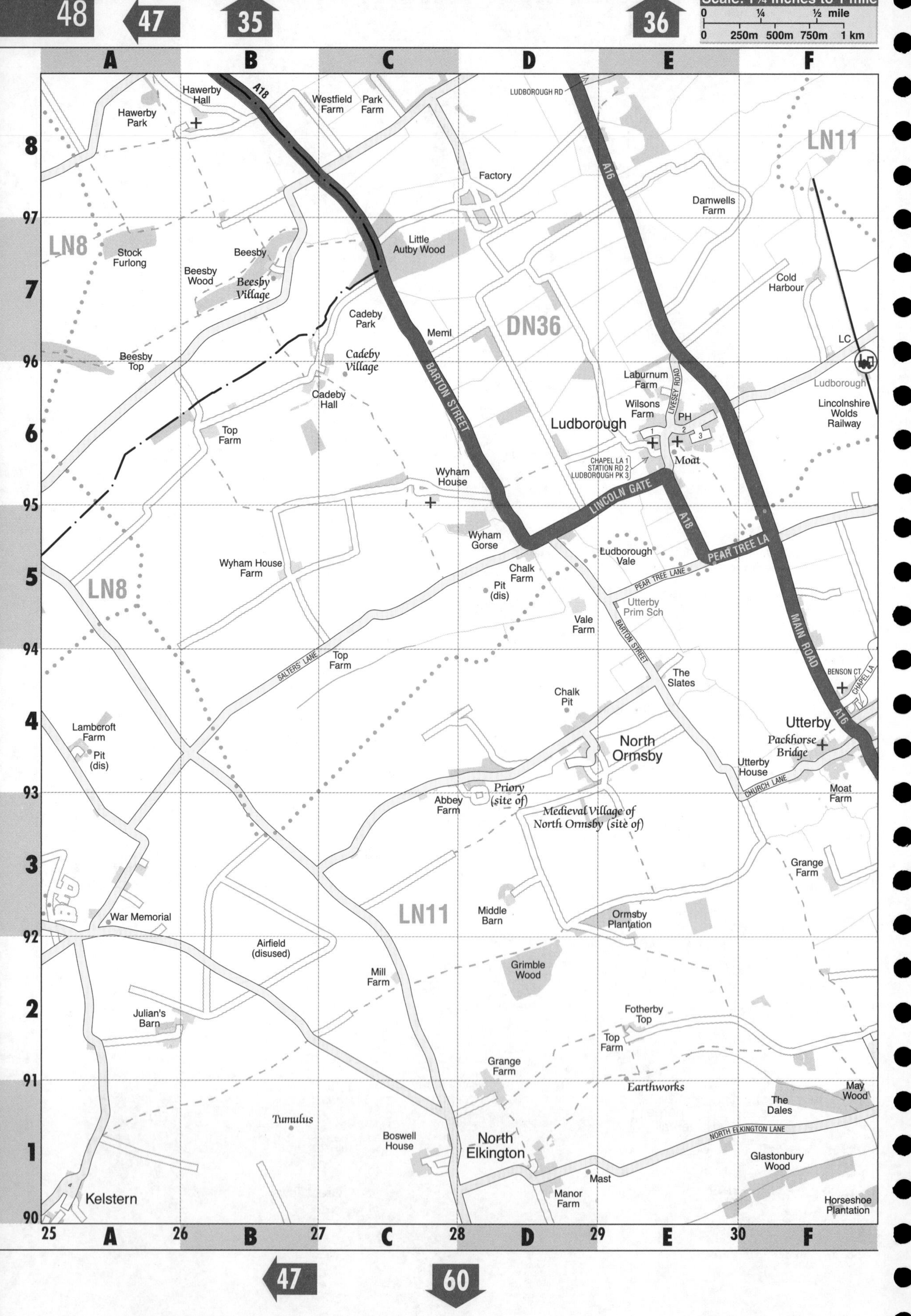
47
35
36
Scale: 1¾ inches to 1 mile
0 ¼ ½ mile
0 250m 500m 750m 1 km
A B C D E F
8 97 7 96 6 95 5 94 4 93 3 92 2 91 1 90
25 26 27 28 29 30
Hawerby Hall
Hawerby Park
Westfield Farm
Park Farm
LUDBOROUGH RD
A18
A16
LN11
Factory
Damwells Farm
LN8
Stock Furlong
Beesby
Beesby Wood
Beesby Village
Little Autby Wood
Cold Harbour
Cadeby Park
Meml
DN36
Beesby Top
Cadeby Village
Cadeby Hall
LC
Ludborough
Lincolnshire Wolds Railway
Laburnum Farm
LIVESEY ROAD
Wilsons Farm
PH
Ludborough
Top Farm
BARTON STREET
Moat
CHAPEL LA 1
STATION RD 2
LUDBOROUGH PK 3
Wyham House
LINCOLN GATE
Wyham Gorse
Ludborough Vale
PEAR TREE LA
PEAR TREE LANE
Wyham House Farm
Chalk Farm
Pit (dis)
Utterby Prim Sch
Vale Farm
MAIN ROAD
SALTERS' LANE
Top Farm
The Slates
BENSON CT
CHAPEL LA
Chalk Pit
Lambcroft Farm
Pit (dis)
North Ormsby
Utterby
Packhorse Bridge
Utterby House
CHURCH LANE
Priory (site of)
Abbey Farm
Moat Farm
Medieval Village of North Ormsby (site of)
Grange Farm
War Memorial
LN11
Middle Barn
Ormsby Plantation
Airfield (disused)
Grimble Wood
Mill Farm
Julian's Barn
Fotherby Top
Top Farm
Grange Farm
Earthworks
May Wood
The Dales
Tumulus
Boswell House
North Elkington
NORTH ELKINGTON LANE
Glastonbury Wood
Mast
Manor Farm
Kelstern
Horseshoe Plantation
47
60

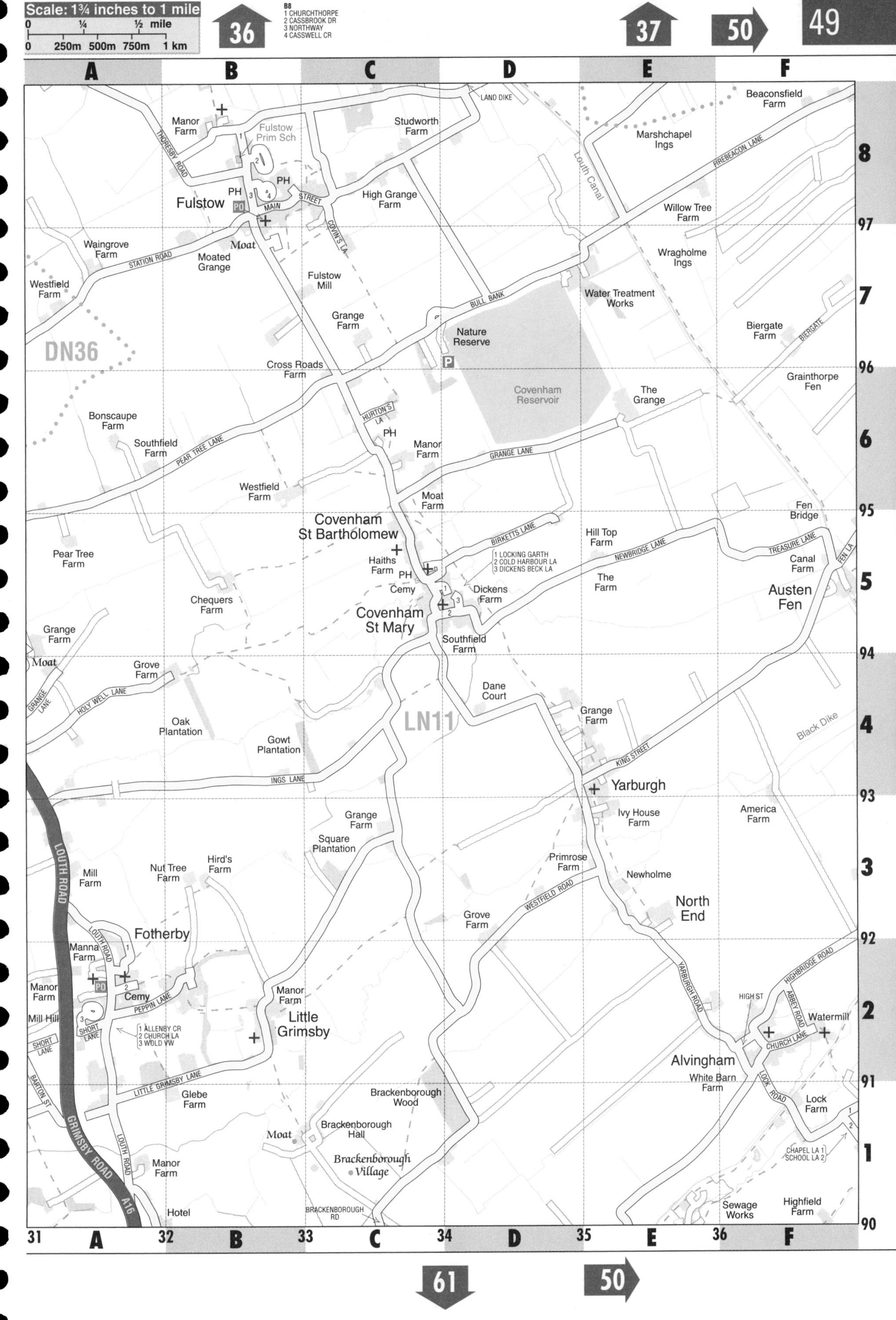
Scale: 1¾ inches to 1 mile
0 ¼ ½ mile
0 250m 500m 750m 1 km
36
B8
1 CHURCHTHORPE
2 CASSBROOK DR
3 NORTHWAY
4 CASSWELL CR
37
50
Fulstow
Fulstow Prim Sch
Manor Farm
Studworth Farm
Marshchapel Ings
Beaconsfield Farm
High Grange Farm
Willow Tree Farm
Wragholme Ings
Waingrove Farm
Moated Grange
Moat
Westfield Farm
Fulstow Mill
Grange Farm
Water Treatment Works
Nature Reserve
Biergate Farm
DN36
Cross Roads Farm
Covenham Reservoir
The Grange
Grainthorpe Fen
Bonscaupe Farm
Southfield Farm
Manor Farm
Westfield Farm
Moat Farm
Fen Bridge
Covenham St Bartholomew
Haiths Farm
Cemy
Pear Tree Farm
Hill Top Farm
Canal Farm
1 LOCKING GARTH
2 COLD HARBOUR LA
3 DICKENS BECK LA
The Farm
Dickens Farm
Austen Fen
Chequers Farm
Covenham St Mary
Southfield Farm
Grange Farm
Moat
Grove Farm
Dane Court
Grange Farm
LN11
Oak Plantation
Gowt Plantation
Black Dike
Yarburgh
Ivy House Farm
America Farm
Grange Farm
Square Plantation
Mill Farm
Nut Tree Farm
Hird's Farm
Primrose Farm
Newholme
North End
Grove Farm
Fotherby
Manna Farm
Manor Farm
Cemy
Manor Farm
Little Grimsby
Mill Hill
1 ALLENBY CR
2 CHURCH LA
3 WOLD VW
Watermill
Alvingham
White Barn Farm
Glebe Farm
Brackenborough Wood
Lock Farm
Moat
Brackenborough Hall
Brackenborough Village
CHAPEL LA 1
SCHOOL LA 2
Manor Farm
Hotel
Sewage Works
Highfield Farm
THORESBY ROAD
MAIN STREET
COVIN'S LA
LAND DIKE
Louth Canal
FIREBEACON LANE
STATION ROAD
BULL BANK
BIERGATE
HURTON'S LA
PEAR TREE LANE
GRANGE LANE
BIRKETTS LANE
NEWBRIDGE LANE
TREASURE LANE
FEN LA
HOLY WELL LANE
GRANGE LANE
INGS LANE
KING STREET
LOUTH ROAD
WESTFIELD ROAD
YARBURGH ROAD
HIGHBRIDGE ROAD
HIGH ST
ABBEY ROAD
CHURCH LANE
PEPPIN LANE
SHORT LANE
LITTLE GRIMSBY LANE
BARTON ST
LOCK ROAD
GRIMSBY ROAD
A16
BRACKENBOROUGH RD
A B C D E F
8 97 7 96 6 95 5 94 4 93 3 92 2 91 1 90
31 32 33 34 35 36
61
50

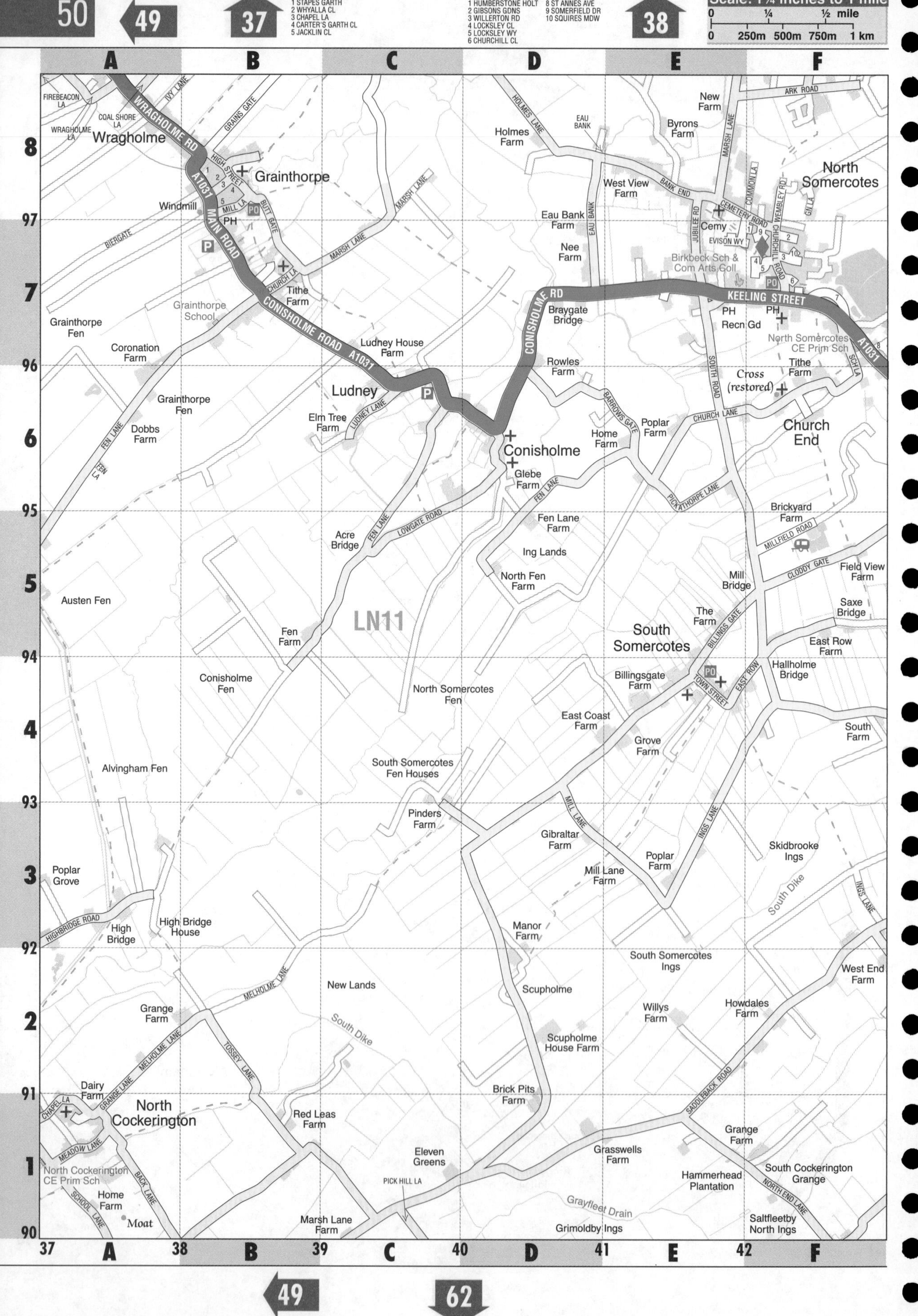
50
49
37
B8
1 STAPES GARTH
2 WHYALLA CL
3 CHAPEL LA
4 CARTER'S GARTH CL
5 JACKLIN CL
F7
1 HUMBERSTONE HOLT
2 GIBSONS GDNS
3 WILLERTON RD
4 LOCKSLEY CL
5 LOCKSLEY WY
6 CHURCHILL CL
7 KEELING ST
8 ST ANNES AVE
9 SOMERFIELD DR
10 SQUIRES MDW
38
Scale: 1¾ inches to 1 mile
0 ¼ ½ mile
0 250m 500m 750m 1 km
A B C D E F
8 97 7 96 6 95 5 94 4 93 3 92 2 91 1 90
37 38 39 40 41 42
FIREBEACON LA
COAL SHORE LA
WRAGHOLME LA
Wragholme
WRAGHOLME RD
IVY LANE
GRAINS GATE
HIGH STREET
Grainthorpe
A1031
MAIN ROAD
Windmill
MILL LA
PO
PH
BUTT GATE
BIERGATE
MARSH LANE
CHURCH LA
Tithe Farm
Grainthorpe School
Grainthorpe Fen
Coronation Farm
CONISHOLME ROAD
Ludney House Farm
Ludney
LUDNEY LANE
Elm Tree Farm
Grainthorpe Fen
Dobbs Farm
FEN LANE
FEN LA
HOLMES LANE
Holmes Farm
EAU BANK
West View Farm
Eau Bank Farm
Nee Farm
CONISHOLME RD
Braygate Bridge
Rowles Farm
Conisholme
Glebe Farm
BARROWS GATE
Home Farm
Poplar Farm
New Farm
Byrons Farm
ARK ROAD
MARSH LANE
BANK END
North Somercotes
COMMON LA
WEMBLEY RD
JUBILEE RD
Cemy
CEMETERY ROAD
EVISON WY
CHURCHILL ROAD
Birkbeck Sch & Com Arts Coll
KEELING STREET
PH
Recn Gd
North Somercotes CE Prim Sch
SCH LA
Tithe Farm
SOUTH ROAD
Cross (restored)
CHURCH LANE
Church End
PICKATHORPE LANE
Brickyard Farm
MILLFIELD ROAD
CLODDY GATE
Field View Farm
Saxe Bridge
Mill Bridge
The Farm
BILLINGS GATE
South Somercotes
East Row Farm
Hallholme Bridge
EAST ROW
TOWN STREET
Billingsgate Farm
FEN LANE
Fen Lane Farm
Ing Lands
North Fen Farm
Acre Bridge
LOWGATE ROAD
LN11
Fen Farm
Austen Fen
Conisholme Fen
North Somercotes Fen
East Coast Farm
Grove Farm
South Farm
Alvingham Fen
South Somercotes Fen Houses
Pinders Farm
MILL LANE
Gibraltar Farm
Mill Lane Farm
Poplar Farm
INGS LANE
Skidbrooke Ings
South Dike
INGS LANE
Poplar Grove
HIGHBRIDGE ROAD
High Bridge
High Bridge House
Manor Farm
South Somercotes Ings
West End Farm
New Lands
Scupholme
Willys Farm
Howdales Farm
MELHOLME LANE
Grange Farm
South Dike
Scupholme House Farm
TOSSEY LANE
MELHOLME LANE
GRANGE LANE
Dairy Farm
CHAPEL LA
North Cockerington
Brick Pits Farm
SADDLEBACK ROAD
Red Leas Farm
Grasswells Farm
Grange Farm
MEADOW LANE
Eleven Greens
North Cockerington CE Prim Sch
Hammerhead Plantation
South Cockerington Grange
NORTH END LANE
BACK LANE
SCHOOL LANE
Home Farm
Moat
PICK HILL LA
Grayfleet Drain
Marsh Lane Farm
Grimoldby Ings
Saltfleetby North Ings
49
62

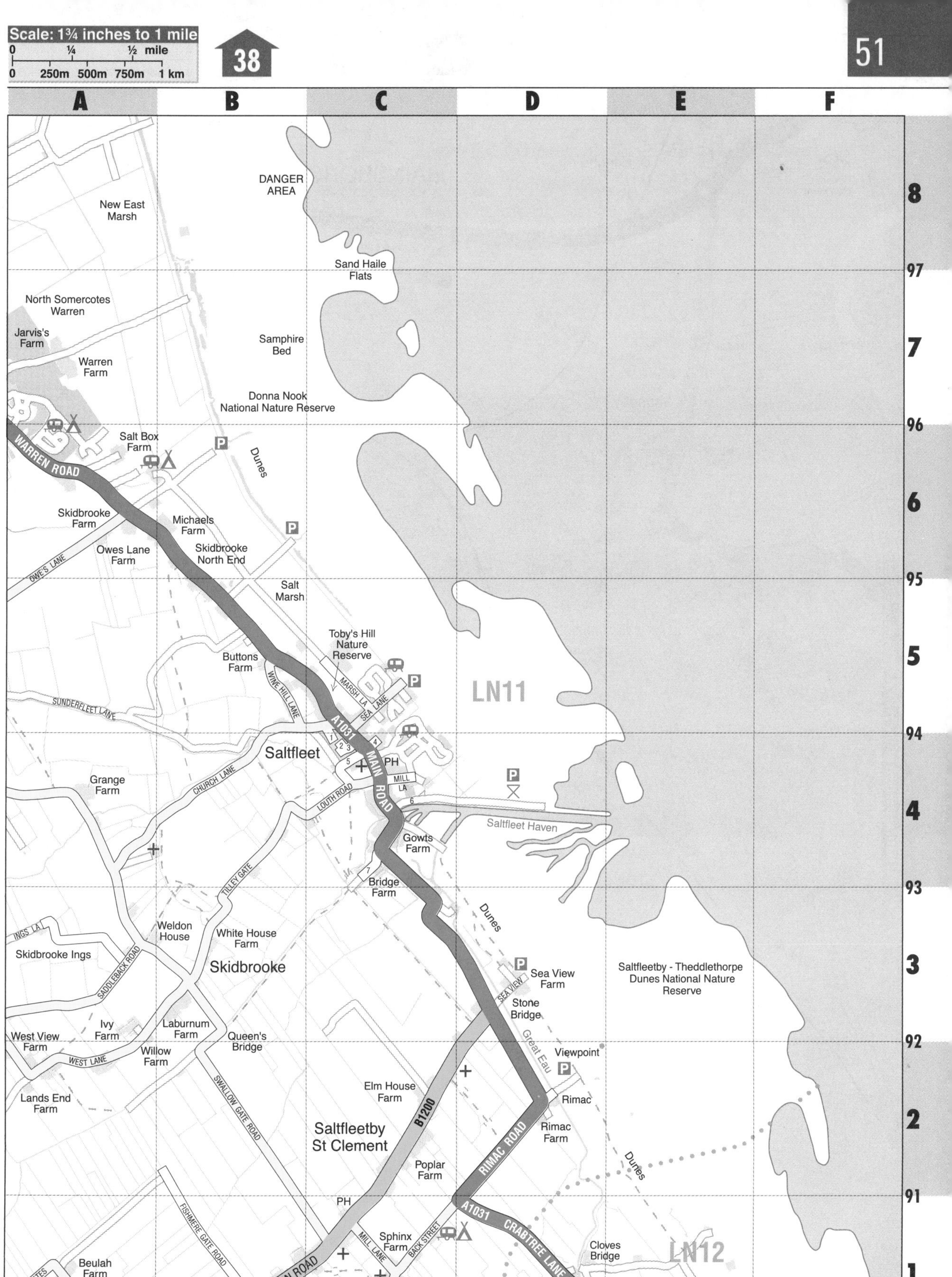

A   B   C   D   E   F

8
97
7
96
6
95
5
94
4
93
3
92
2
91
1
90

DANGER AREA

New East Marsh

Sand Haile Flats

North Somercotes Warren

Jarvis's Farm

Samphire Bed

Warren Farm

Donna Nook National Nature Reserve

WARREN ROAD

Salt Box Farm

Dunes

P

Skidbrooke Farm

Michaels Farm

Owes Lane Farm

Skidbrooke North End

OWE'S LANE

P

Salt Marsh

Toby's Hill Nature Reserve

SUNDERFLEET LANE

Buttons Farm

WIRE HILL LANE

MARSH LA

SEA LANE

LN11

A1031

Saltfleet

MAIN ROAD

1 2 3
4
5

PH

MILL LA

P

Saltfleet Haven

Grange Farm

CHURCH LANE

LOUTH ROAD

6

Gowts Farm

INGS LA.

SADDLEBACK ROAD

Weldon House

TILLEY GATE

White House Farm

Bridge Farm

7

Dunes

P

Sea View Farm

SEA VIEW

Saltfleetby - Theddlethorpe Dunes National Nature Reserve

Skidbrooke Ings

Skidbrooke

Stone Bridge

Great Eau

Ivy Farm

Laburnum Farm

Queen's Bridge

West View Farm

WEST LANE

Willow Farm

Viewpoint

P

Lands End Farm

SWALLOW GATE ROAD

Elm House Farm

B1200

P

Rimac

RIMAC ROAD

Rimac Farm

Dunes

Saltfleetby St Clement

Poplar Farm

FISHMERE GATE ROAD

PH

A1031

CRABTREE LANE

LN12

Beulah Farm

LONG GATES

SALTER GATE

MILL LANE

Sphinx Farm

BACK STREET

P

SALTFLEET RD

Cloves Bridge

Sturdys Farm

MAIN ROAD

Saltfleetby All Saints

CHURCHILL LA

P

Saltfleetby - Theddlethorpe Dunes National Nature Reserve

B1200

White House Farm

43 A 44 B 45 C 46 D 47 E 48 F

C4
1 BOTOLPH'S VW
2 HOLMES CL
3 JACKLIN DR
4 THE HILL
5 PUMP LA
6 HAVEN BANK
7 GREYFLEET BANK

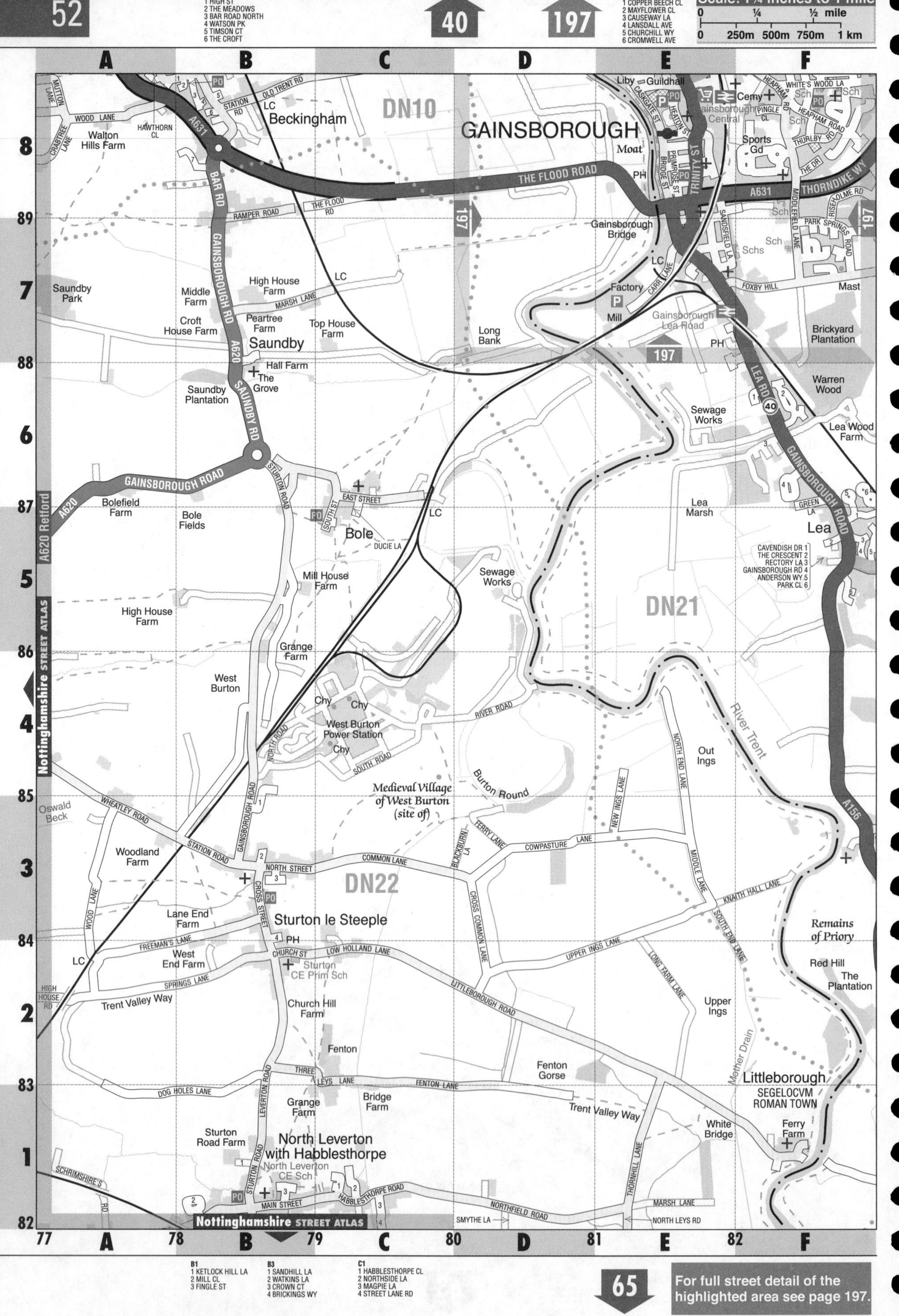

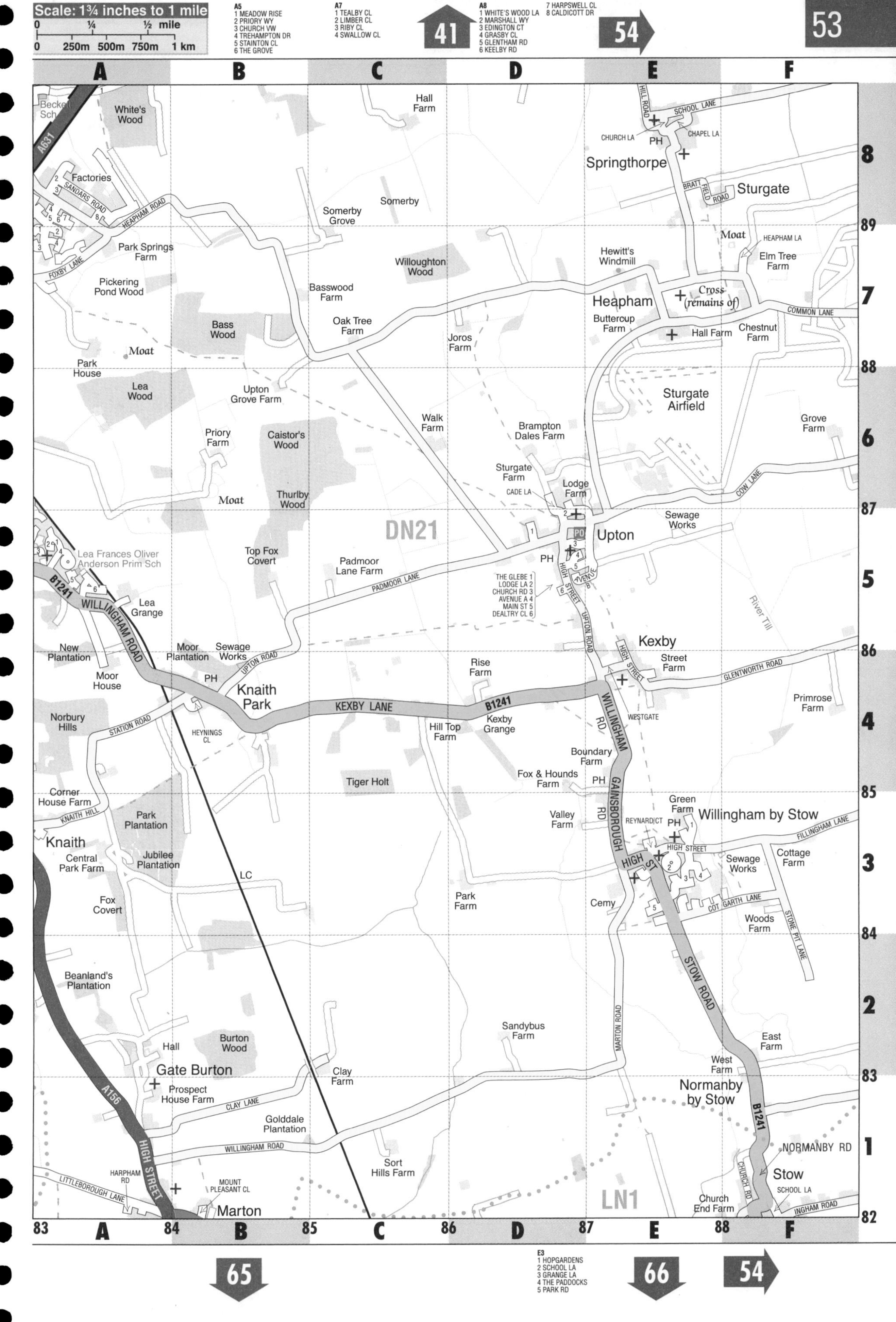
A B C D E F
8 89 7 88 6 87 5 86 4 85 3 84 2 83 1 82
Beckett Sch
White's Wood
A631
Factories
SANDARS ROAD
HEAPHAM ROAD
FOXBY LANE
Park Springs Farm
Pickering Pond Wood
Bass Wood
Moat
Park House
Lea Wood
Upton Grove Farm
Priory Farm
Caistor's Wood
Thurlby Wood
Moat
Top Fox Covert
Lea Frances Oliver Anderson Prim Sch
B1241
WILLINGHAM ROAD
Lea Grange
New Plantation
Moor Plantation
Sewage Works
UPTON ROAD
PH
Moor House
Knaith Park
Norbury Hills
STATION ROAD
HEYNINGS CL
Corner House Farm
KNAITH HILL
Knaith
Park Plantation
Central Park Farm
Jubilee Plantation
Fox Covert
LC
Beanland's Plantation
Hall
Burton Wood
Gate Burton
Prospect House Farm
CLAY LANE
A156
HIGH STREET
Golddale Plantation
WILLINGHAM ROAD
HARPHAM RD
LITTLEBOROUGH LANE
MOUNT PLEASANT CL
Marton
Hall Farm
Somerby Grove
Somerby
Willoughton Wood
Basswood Farm
Oak Tree Farm
Joros Farm
Walk Farm
DN21
Padmoor Lane Farm
PADMOOR LANE
KEXBY LANE
B1241
Rise Farm
Hill Top Farm
Kexby Grange
Tiger Holt
Park Farm
Clay Farm
Sort Hills Farm
Sandybus Farm
LN1
HILL ROAD
SCHOOL LANE
CHURCH LA
PH
CHAPEL LA
Springthorpe
BRATT FIELD ROAD
Sturgate
Moat
HEAPHAM LA
Elm Tree Farm
Hewitt's Windmill
Heapham
Cross (remains of)
COMMON LANE
Buttercup Farm
Hall Farm
Chestnut Farm
Sturgate Airfield
Grove Farm
Brampton Dales Farm
Sturgate Farm
Lodge Farm
CADE LA
COW LANE
Sewage Works
PO
Upton
PH
HIGH STREET
AVENUE
THE GLEBE 1
LODGE LA 2
CHURCH RD 3
AVENUE A 4
MAIN ST 5
DEALTRY CL 6
UPTON ROAD
River Till
Kexby
HIGH STREET
Street Farm
GLENTWORTH ROAD
Primrose Farm
WESTGATE
WILLINGHAM RD
Boundary Farm
Fox & Hounds Farm
PH
GAINSBOROUGH RD
Valley Farm
REYNARD CT
PH
Green Farm
Willingham by Stow
FILLINGHAM LANE
HIGH STREET
HIGH ST
Sewage Works
Cottage Farm
Cemy
COT GARTH LANE
Woods Farm
STONE PIT LANE
STOW ROAD
MARTON ROAD
East Farm
West Farm
Normanby by Stow
B1241
NORMANBY RD
Stow
SCHOOL LA
CHURCH RD
Church End Farm
INGHAM ROAD
83 84 85 86 87 88

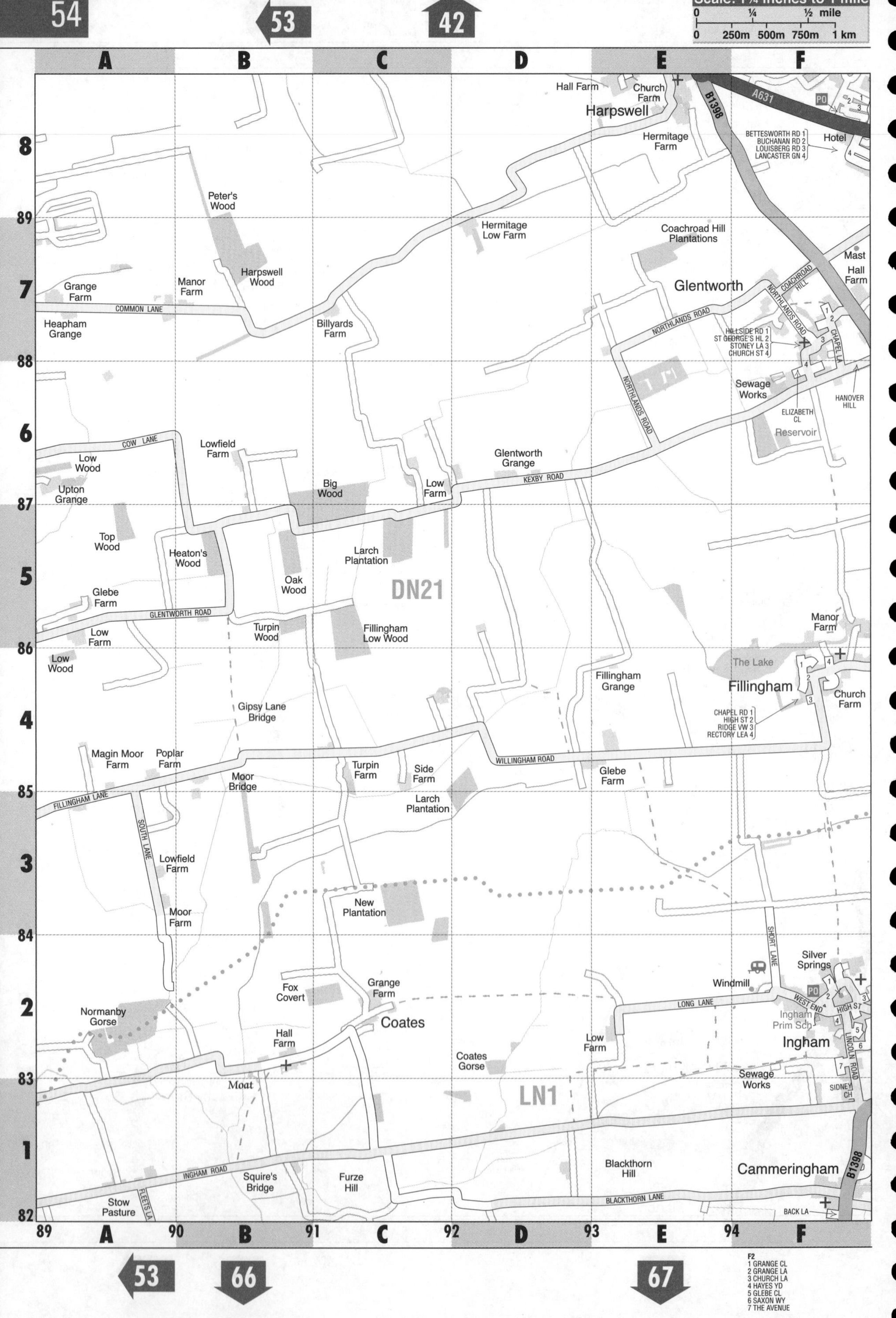

Scale: 1¾ inches to 1 mile

Harpswell
Hall Farm
Church Farm
Hermitage Farm
A631
B1398
PO

BETTESWORTH RD 1
BUCHANAN RD 2
LOUISBERG RD 3
LANCASTER GN 4
Hotel

Peter's Wood

Hermitage Low Farm

Coachroad Hill Plantations

Mast Hall Farm

Grange Farm

Manor Farm

Harpswell Wood

Glentworth

Billyards Farm

COMMON LANE

Heapham Grange

HILLSIDE RD 1
ST GEORGE'S HL 2
STONEY LA 3
CHURCH ST 4

NORTHLANDS ROAD

COACHROAD HILL

CHAPEL LA

Low Wood

COW LANE

Lowfield Farm

Sewage Works

HANOVER HILL

ELIZABETH CL

Reservoir

Upton Grange

Big Wood

Low Farm

Glentworth Grange

KEXBY ROAD

NORTHLANDS ROAD

Top Wood

Heaton's Wood

Oak Wood

Larch Plantation

DN21

Glebe Farm

GLENTWORTH ROAD

Turpin Wood

Fillingham Low Wood

Manor Farm

Low Farm

Low Wood

Gipsy Lane Bridge

Fillingham Grange

The Lake

Fillingham

CHAPEL RD 1
HIGH ST 2
RIDGE VW 3
RECTORY LEA 4

Church Farm

Magin Moor Farm

Poplar Farm

Moor Bridge

Turpin Farm

Side Farm

WILLINGHAM ROAD

Glebe Farm

FILLINGHAM LANE

SOUTH LANE

Larch Plantation

Lowfield Farm

New Plantation

SHORT LANE

Silver Springs

Moor Farm

Windmill

PO

WEST END

Fox Covert

Grange Farm

LONG LANE

Ingham Prim Sch

HIGH ST

LINCOLN ROAD

Ingham

Normanby Gorse

Coates

Low Farm

Hall Farm

Coates Gorse

LN1

Sewage Works

SIDNEY CH

Moat

INGHAM ROAD

KEALS LA

Squire's Bridge

Furze Hill

Blackthorn Hill

Cammeringham

B1398

Stow Pasture

BLACKTHORN LANE

BACK LA

F2
1 GRANGE CL
2 GRANGE LA
3 CHURCH LA
4 HAYES YD
5 GLEBE CL
6 SAXON WY
7 THE AVENUE

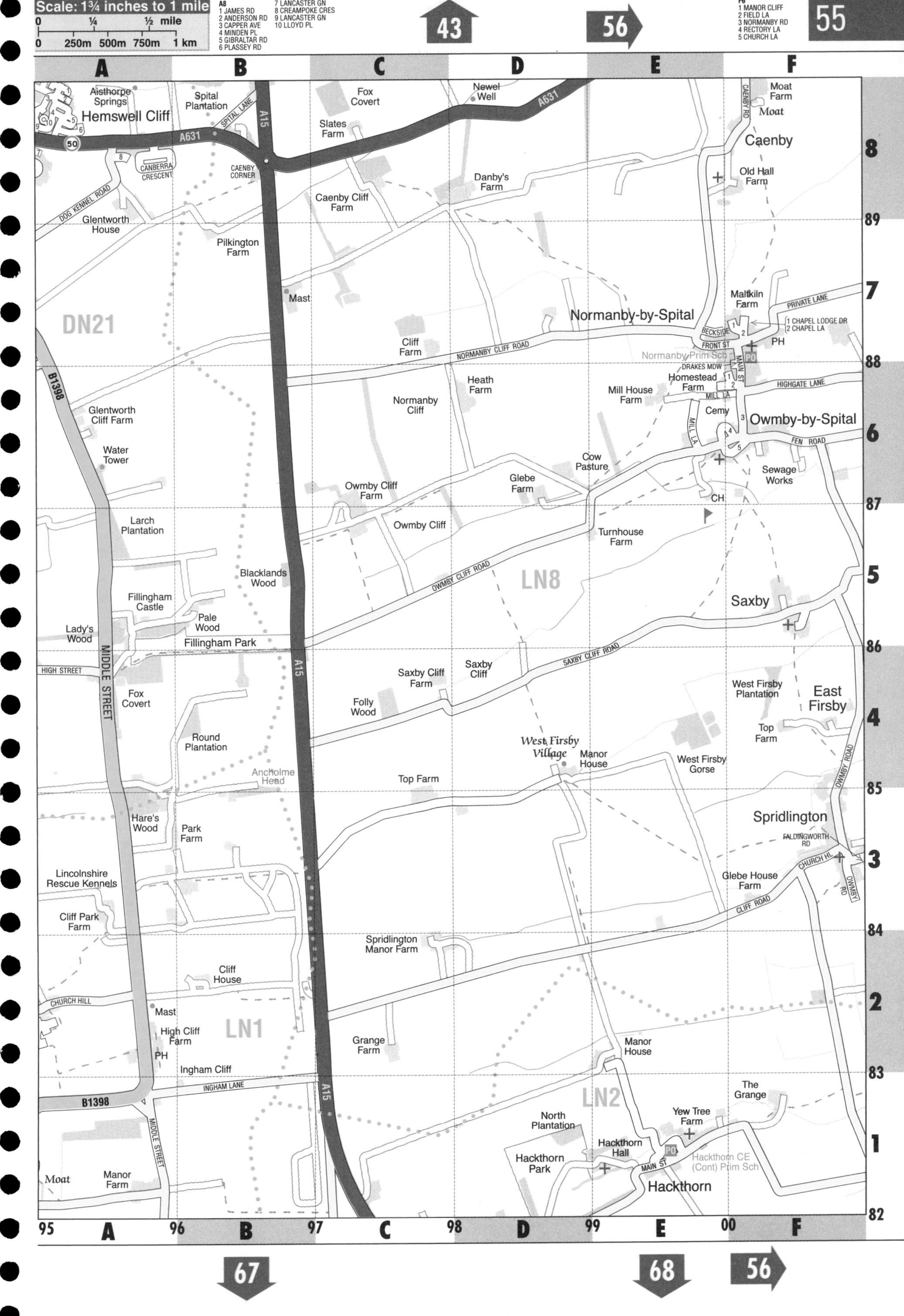
Scale: 1¾ inches to 1 mile
0 ¼ ½ mile
0 250m 500m 750m 1 km
A8
1 JAMES RD
2 ANDERSON RD
3 CAPPER AVE
4 MINDEN PL
5 GIBRALTAR RD
6 PLASSEY RD
7 LANCASTER GN
8 CREAMPOKE CRES
9 LANCASTER GN
10 LLOYD PL
43
56
F6
1 MANOR CLIFF
2 FIELD LA
3 NORMANBY RD
4 RECTORY LA
5 CHURCH LA
A
B
C
D
E
F
Aisthorpe Springs
Hemswell Cliff
Spital Plantation
SPITAL LANE
A15
A631
50
CANBERRA CRESCENT
CAENBY CORNER
Fox Covert
Slates Farm
Newel Well
CAENBY RD
Moat Farm
Moat
Caenby
Old Hall Farm
DOG KENNEL ROAD
Glentworth House
Caenby Cliff Farm
Danby's Farm
Pilkington Farm
Mast
Maltkiln Farm
PRIVATE LANE
Normanby-by-Spital
BECKSIDE
FRONT ST
1 CHAPEL LODGE DR
2 CHAPEL LA
PH
DN21
Cliff Farm
NORMANBY CLIFF ROAD
Normanby Prim Sch
PO
DRAKES MDW
MAIN ST
Homestead Farm
HIGHGATE LANE
B1398
Heath Farm
Mill House Farm
MILL LA
Glentworth Cliff Farm
Normanby Cliff
Cemy
Owmby-by-Spital
MILL LA
FEN ROAD
Water Tower
Cow Pasture
Sewage Works
Owmby Cliff Farm
Glebe Farm
CH
Larch Plantation
Owmby Cliff
Turnhouse Farm
OWMBY CLIFF ROAD
LN8
Blacklands Wood
Fillingham Castle
Pale Wood
Saxby
Lady's Wood
Fillingham Park
HIGH STREET
MIDDLE STREET
SAXBY CLIFF ROAD
Saxby Cliff
Saxby Cliff Farm
Fox Covert
West Firsby Plantation
East Firsby
Folly Wood
Round Plantation
West Firsby Village
Manor House
West Firsby Gorse
Top Farm
Ancholme Head
Top Farm
OWMBY ROAD
Spridlington
FALDINGWORTH RD
Hare's Wood
Park Farm
CHURCH HL
Lincolnshire Rescue Kennels
Glebe House Farm
OWMBY RD
CLIFF ROAD
Cliff Park Farm
Spridlington Manor Farm
Cliff House
CHURCH HILL
Mast
High Cliff Farm
LN1
Grange Farm
Manor House
PH
Ingham Cliff
INGHAM LANE
B1398
LN2
The Grange
North Plantation
Yew Tree Farm
MIDDLE STREET
Hackthorn Hall
Hackthorn Park
MAIN ST
Hackthorn CE (Cont) Prim Sch
Moat
Manor Farm
Hackthorn
8
89
7
88
6
87
5
86
4
85
3
84
2
83
1
82
95
96
97
98
99
00
67
68
56

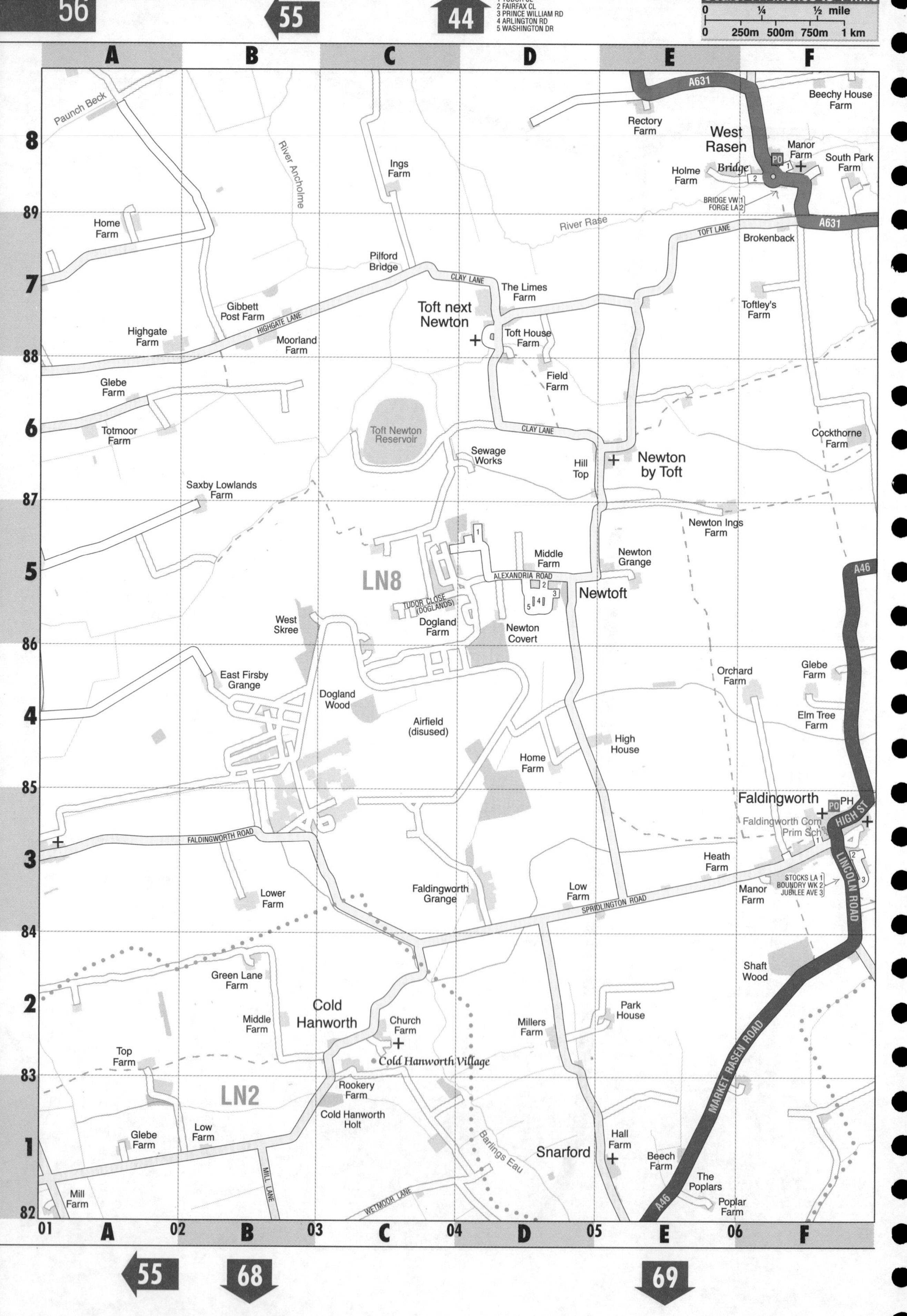

Scale: 1¾ inches to 1 mile
0   ¼   ½   mile
0   250m   500m   750m   1 km

A   B   C   D   E   F

8

Paunch Beck

A631

Beechy House
Farm

Rectory
Farm

West
Rasen

Manor
Farm

South Park
Farm

PO

Bridge

Holme
Farm

89

Home
Farm

River Rase

BRIDGE VW 1
FORGE LA 2

Brokenback

TOFT LANE

A631

7

Pilford
Bridge

Gibbett
Post Farm

CLAY LANE

The Limes
Farm

Toft next
Newton

Toftley's
Farm

Highgate
Farm

HIGHGATE LANE

Moorland
Farm

Toft House
Farm

88

Glebe
Farm

Field
Farm

6

Totmoor
Farm

Toft Newton
Reservoir

CLAY LANE

Sewage
Works

Hill
Top

Newton
by Toft

Cockthorne
Farm

87

Saxby Lowlands
Farm

Newton Ings
Farm

5

LN8

Middle
Farm

ALEXANDRIA ROAD

Newton
Grange

A46

West
Skree

TUDOR CLOSE
(DOGLANDS)

Dogland
Farm

Newtoft

Newton
Covert

86

East Firsby
Grange

Orchard
Farm

Glebe
Farm

4

Dogland
Wood

Elm Tree
Farm

Airfield
(disused)

High
House

85

Home
Farm

Faldingworth

PO PH

Faldingworth Com
Prim Sch

HIGH ST

3

FALDINGWORTH ROAD

Heath
Farm

Low
Farm

SPRIDLINGTON ROAD

Manor
Farm

STOCKS LA 1
BOUNDRY WK 2
JUBILEE AVE 3

LINCOLN ROAD

84

Lower
Farm

Faldingworth
Grange

Shaft
Wood

2

Green Lane
Farm

Park
House

Middle
Farm

Cold
Hanworth

Church
Farm

Millers
Farm

MARKET RASEN ROAD

Top
Farm

Cold Hanworth Village

83

LN2

Rookery
Farm

1

Glebe
Farm

Low
Farm

Cold Hanworth
Holt

MILL LANE

Barlings Eau

Snarford

Hall
Farm

Beech
Farm

The
Poplars

Mill
Farm

WETMOOR LANE

A46

Poplar
Farm

82

01   A   02   B   03   C   04   D   05   E   06   F

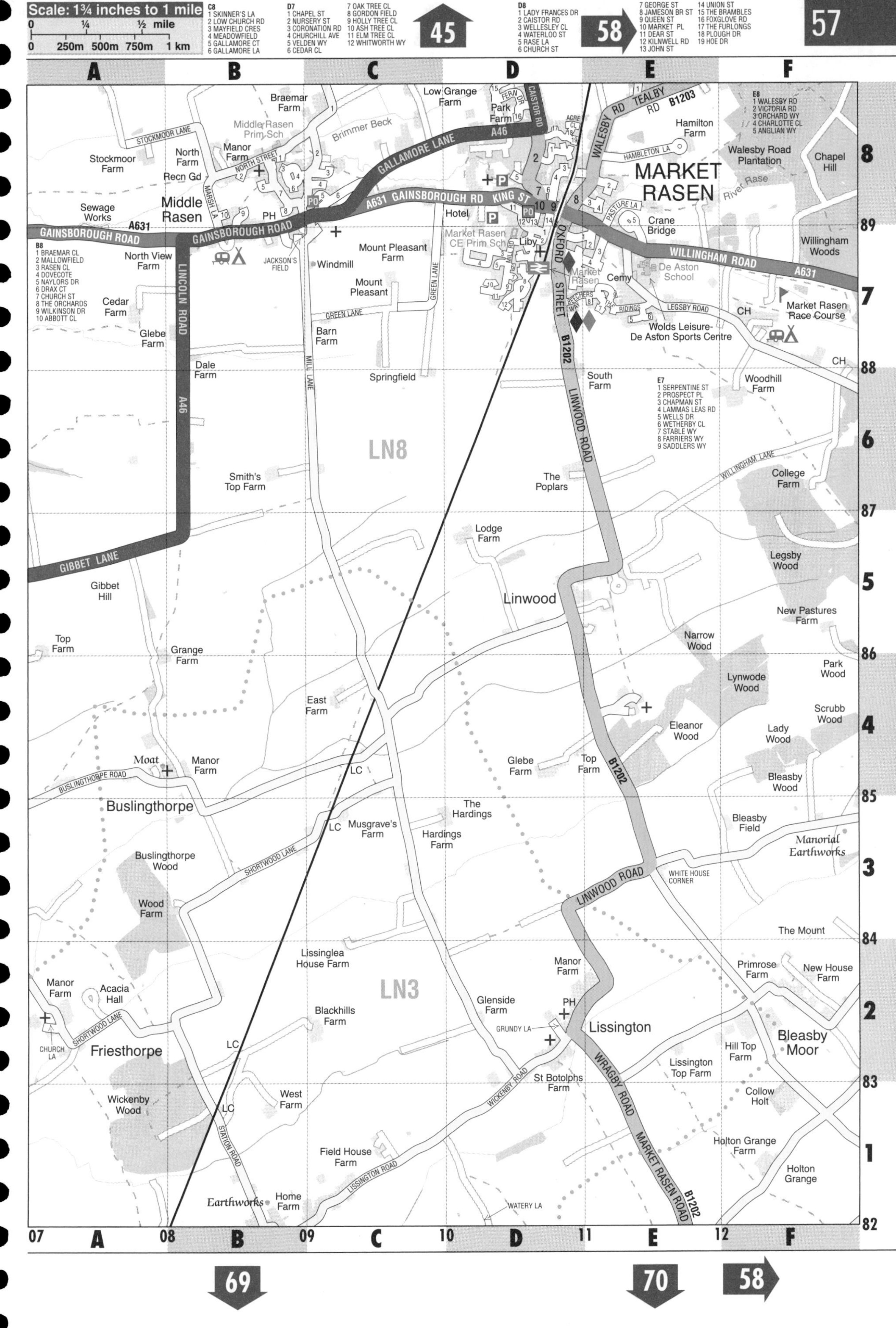
Scale: 1¾ inches to 1 mile
0 ¼ ½ mile
0 250m 500m 750m 1 km
C8
1 SKINNER'S LA
2 LOW CHURCH RD
3 MAYFIELD CRES
4 MEADOWFIELD
5 GALLAMORE CT
6 GALLAMORE LA
D7
1 CHAPEL ST
2 NURSERY ST
3 CORONATION RD
4 CHURCHILL AVE
5 VELDEN WY
6 CEDAR CL
7 OAK TREE CL
8 GORDON FIELD
9 HOLLY TREE CL
10 ASH TREE CL
11 ELM TREE CL
12 WHITWORTH WY
45
D8
1 LADY FRANCES DR
2 CAISTOR RD
3 WELLESLEY CL
4 WATERLOO ST
5 RASE LA
6 CHURCH ST
58
7 GEORGE ST
8 JAMESON BR ST
9 QUEEN ST
10 MARKET PL
11 DEAR ST
12 KILNWELL RD
13 JOHN ST
14 UNION ST
15 THE BRAMBLES
16 FOXGLOVE RD
17 THE FURLONGS
18 PLOUGH DR
19 HOE DR
E8
1 WALESBY RD
2 VICTORIA RD
3 ORCHARD WY
4 CHARLOTTE CL
5 ANGLIAN WY
B8
1 BRAEMAR CL
2 MALLOWFIELD
3 RASEN CL
4 DOVECOTE
5 NAYLORS DR
6 DRAX CT
7 CHURCH ST
8 THE ORCHARDS
9 WILKINSON DR
10 ABBOTT CL
E7
1 SERPENTINE ST
2 PROSPECT PL
3 CHAPMAN ST
4 LAMMAS LEAS RD
5 WELLS DR
6 WETHERBY CL
7 STABLE WY
8 FARRIERS WY
9 SADDLERS WY
MARKET RASEN
Middle Rasen
Linwood
Buslingthorpe
Friesthorpe
Lissington
Bleasby Moor
LN8
LN3
GAINSBOROUGH ROAD
A631 GAINSBOROUGH RD
GALLAMORE LANE
A46
LINCOLN ROAD
GIBBET LANE
WILLINGHAM ROAD
LINWOOD ROAD
B1202
WRAGBY ROAD
MARKET RASEN ROAD
OXFORD STREET
WALESBY RD
TEALBY RD
B1203
CAISTOR RD
MILL LANE
GREEN LANE
STATION ROAD
SHORTWOOD LANE
BUSLINGTHORPE ROAD
LISSINGTON ROAD
WICKENBY ROAD
WILLINGHAM LANE
LEGSBY ROAD
Stockmoor Farm
Braemar Farm
Low Grange Farm
Park Farm
Hamilton Farm
Walesby Road Plantation
Chapel Hill
Sewage Works
North View Farm
Cedar Farm
Glebe Farm
Dale Farm
Windmill
Mount Pleasant Farm
Mount Pleasant
Barn Farm
Springfield
South Farm
Woodhill Farm
De Aston School
Wolds Leisure-De Aston Sports Centre
Market Rasen Race Course
Willingham Woods
Crane Bridge
River Rase
Smith's Top Farm
The Poplars
College Farm
Lodge Farm
Legsby Wood
Gibbet Hill
New Pastures Farm
Top Farm
Grange Farm
Narrow Wood
Park Wood
Lynwode Wood
East Farm
Eleanor Wood
Scrubb Wood
Lady Wood
Moat
Manor Farm
Glebe Farm
Top Farm
Bleasby Wood
The Hardings
Musgrave's Farm
Hardings Farm
Bleasby Field
Manorial Earthworks
Buslingthorpe Wood
White House Corner
Wood Farm
The Mount
Lissinglea House Farm
Primrose Farm
New House Farm
Acacia Hall
Blackhills Farm
Glenside Farm
Hill Top Farm
Lissington Top Farm
St Botolphs Farm
Wickenby Wood
West Farm
Collow Holt
Holton Grange Farm
Field House Farm
Holton Grange
Earthworks
Home Farm
WATERY LA
GRUNDY LA
CHURCH LA
07 08 09 10 11 12
82 83 84 85 86 87 88 89
A B C D E F
69
70
58

57 46

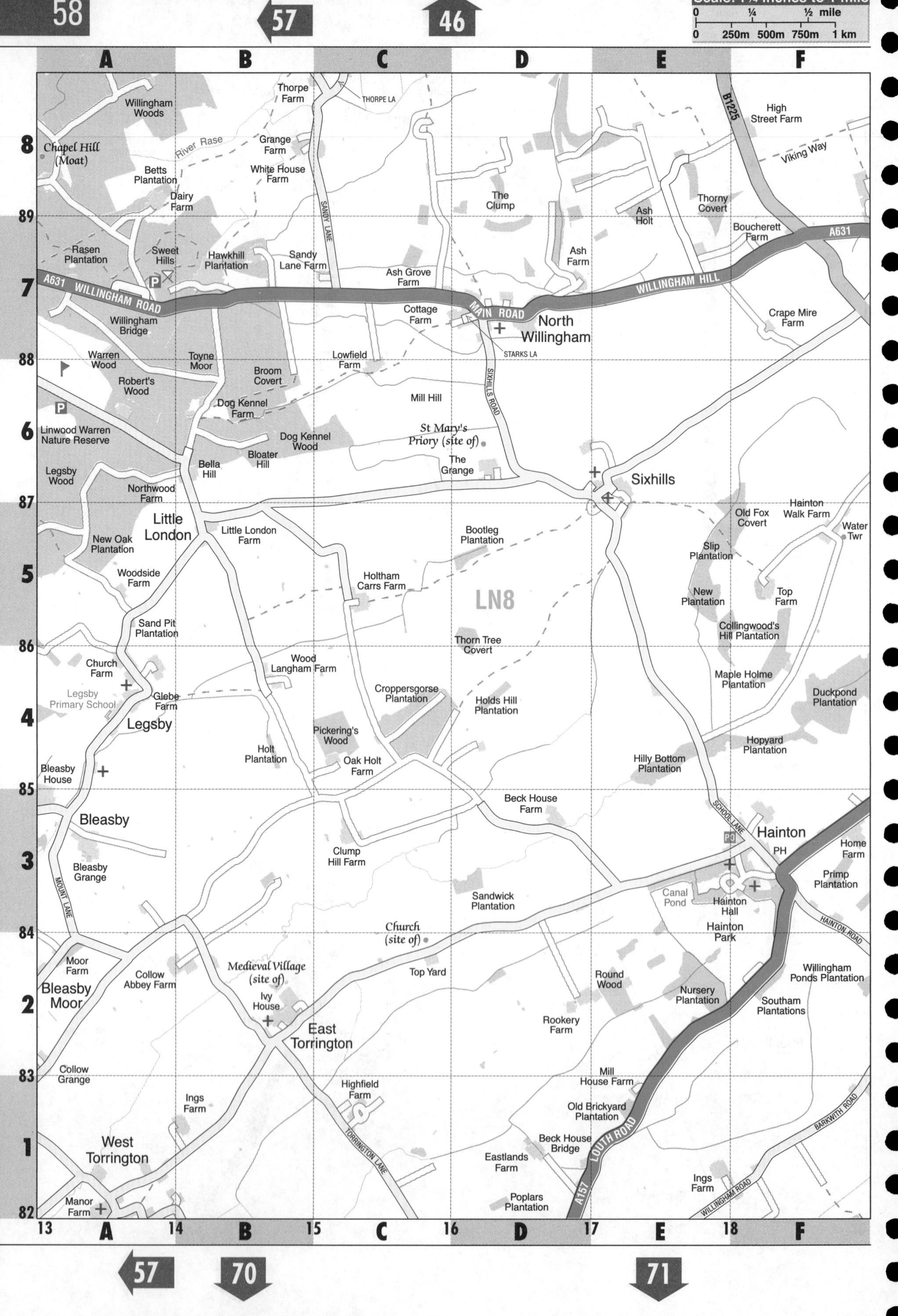
Scale: 1¾ inches to 1 mile
0 ¼ ½ mile
0 250m 500m 750m 1 km
Willingham Woods
Thorpe Farm
THORPE LA
High Street Farm
Chapel Hill (Moat)
River Rase
Grange Farm
White House Farm
Viking Way
Betts Plantation
Dairy Farm
SANDY LANE
The Clump
Ash Holt
Thorny Covert
Boucherett Farm
A631
Rasen Plantation
Sweet Hills
Hawkhill Plantation
Sandy Lane Farm
Ash Grove Farm
Ash Farm
A631 WILLINGHAM ROAD
WILLINGHAM HILL
B1225
Willingham Bridge
Cottage Farm
MAIN ROAD
North Willingham
Crape Mire Farm
STARKS LA
Warren Wood
Toyne Moor
Broom Covert
Lowfield Farm
Robert's Wood
Dog Kennel Farm
Mill Hill
SIXHILLS ROAD
Linwood Warren Nature Reserve
Dog Kennel Wood
St Mary's Priory (site of)
Bloater Hill
Bella Hill
The Grange
Sixhills
Legsby Wood
Northwood Farm
Little London
Little London Farm
Bootleg Plantation
Old Fox Covert
Hainton Walk Farm
Water Twr
New Oak Plantation
Slip Plantation
Woodside Farm
Holtham Carrs Farm
LN8
New Plantation
Top Farm
Sand Pit Plantation
Collingwood's Hill Plantation
Thorn Tree Covert
Church Farm
Wood Langham Farm
Maple Holme Plantation
Legsby Primary School
Glebe Farm
Croppersgorse Plantation
Holds Hill Plantation
Duckpond Plantation
Legsby
Pickering's Wood
Hopyard Plantation
Holt Plantation
Oak Holt Farm
Hilly Bottom Plantation
Bleasby House
Beck House Farm
SCHOOL LANE
Bleasby
Hainton
PO
PH
Home Farm
Bleasby Grange
Clump Hill Farm
Primp Plantation
MOUNT LANE
Canal Pond
Sandwick Plantation
Hainton Hall
Hainton Park
HAINTON ROAD
Church (site of)
Moor Farm
Collow Abbey Farm
Medieval Village (site of)
Top Yard
Round Wood
Willingham Ponds Plantation
Bleasby Moor
Ivy House
Nursery Plantation
Southam Plantations
East Torrington
Rookery Farm
Collow Grange
Mill House Farm
Highfield Farm
Ings Farm
Old Brickyard Plantation
BARKWITH ROAD
West Torrington
TORRINGTON LANE
Beck House Bridge
LOUTH ROAD
Eastlands Farm
A157
Ings Farm
WILLINGHAM ROAD
Manor Farm
Poplars Plantation
A B C D E F
8 89 7 88 6 87 5 86 4 85 3 84 2 83 1 82
13 14 15 16 17 18

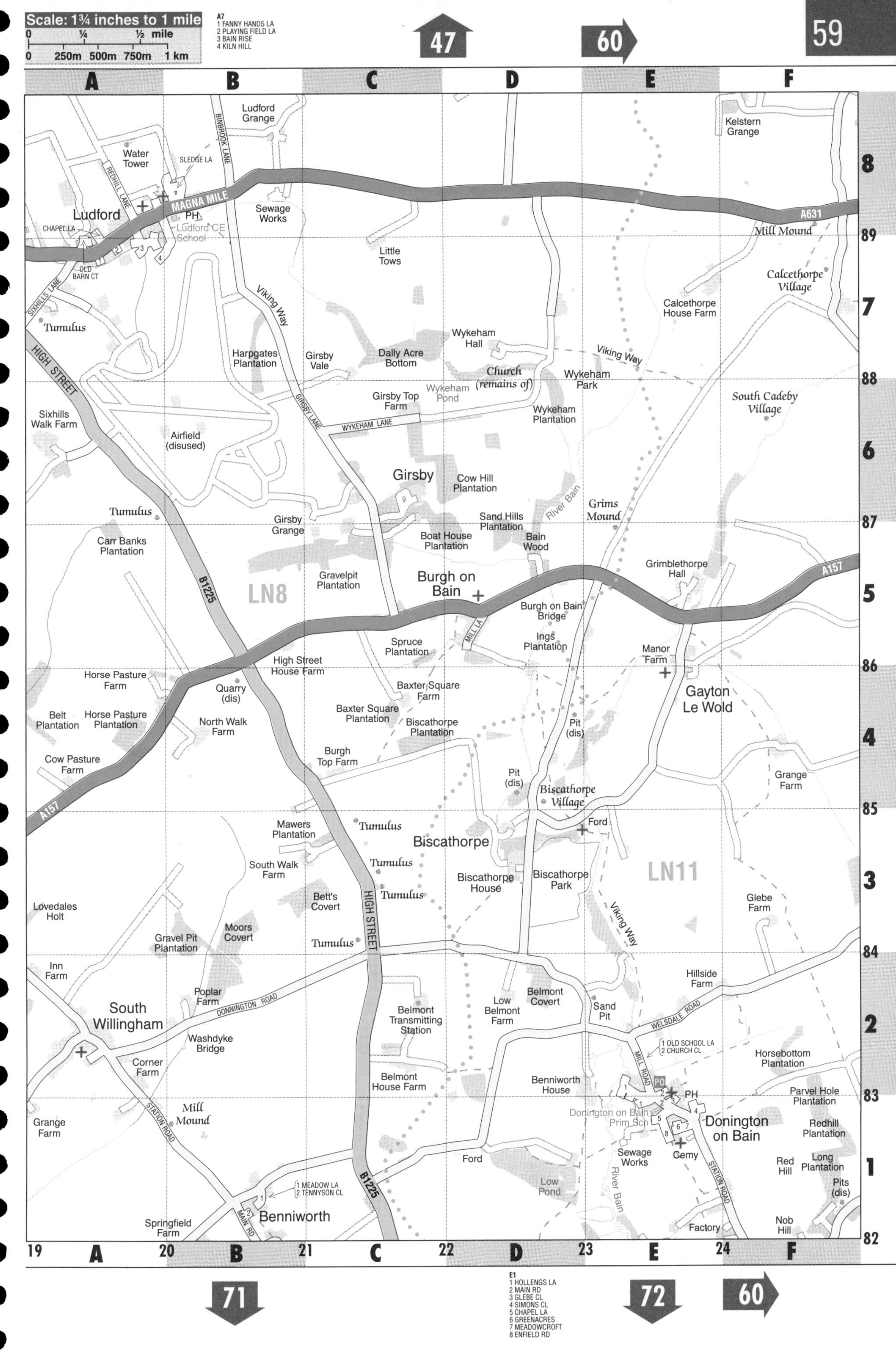
Scale: 1¾ inches to 1 mile
0 ¼ ½ mile
0 250m 500m 750m 1 km
A7
1 FANNY HANDS LA
2 PLAYING FIELD LA
3 BAIN RISE
4 KILN HILL
47
60
A B C D E F
8
89
7
88
6
87
5
86
4
85
3
84
2
83
1
82
19 A 20 B 21 C 22 D 23 E 24 F
Ludford Grange
Water Tower
SLEDGE LA
REDHILL LANE
BINBROOK LANE
MAGNA MILE
Ludford
PH
Ludford CE School
CHAPEL LA
OLD BARN CT
Sewage Works
Little Tows
Kelstern Grange
A631
Mill Mound
Calcethorpe Village
Calcethorpe House Farm
SIXHILLS LANE
Tumulus
Viking Way
Harpgates Plantation
Girsby Vale
Dally Acre Bottom
Wykeham Hall
Church (remains of)
Wykeham Pond
Wykeham Park
Wykeham Plantation
HIGH STREET
Girsby Top Farm
GIRSBY LANE
WYKEHAM LANE
South Cadeby Village
Sixhills Walk Farm
Airfield (disused)
Girsby
Cow Hill Plantation
River Bain
Grims Mound
Tumulus
Girsby Grange
Sand Hills Plantation
Boat House Plantation
Bain Wood
Carr Banks Plantation
Gravelpit Plantation
Burgh on Bain
Grimblethorpe Hall
A157
LN8
B1225
MILL LA
Burgh on Bain Bridge
Ings Plantation
Spruce Plantation
High Street House Farm
Manor Farm
Horse Pasture Farm
Quarry (dis)
Baxter Square Farm
Gayton Le Wold
Belt Plantation
Horse Pasture Plantation
North Walk Farm
Baxter Square Plantation
Biscathorpe Plantation
Pit (dis)
Cow Pasture Farm
Burgh Top Farm
Pit (dis)
Biscathorpe Village
Grange Farm
A157
Mawers Plantation
Tumulus
Biscathorpe
Ford
South Walk Farm
Tumulus
LN11
Biscathorpe House
Biscathorpe Park
Lovedales Holt
Bett's Covert
Tumulus
HIGH STREET
Viking Way
Glebe Farm
Gravel Pit Plantation
Moors Covert
Tumulus
Inn Farm
Belmont Covert
Hillside Farm
Poplar Farm
Low Belmont Farm
Sand Pit
South Willingham
DONNINGTON ROAD
Belmont Transmitting Station
WELSDALE ROAD
Washdyke Bridge
1 OLD SCHOOL LA
2 CHURCH CL
Horsebottom Plantation
Corner Farm
MILL ROAD
Belmont House Farm
Benniworth House
PO
PH
Parvel Hole Plantation
Mill Mound
Donington on Bain Prim Sch
Donington on Bain
Grange Farm
STATION ROAD
Redhill Plantation
Ford
Sewage Works
Cemy
Red Hill
Long Plantation
1 MEADOW LA
2 TENNYSON CL
B1225
Low Pond
River Bain
STATION ROAD
Pits (dis)
Springfield Farm
MAIN RD
Benniworth
Factory
Nob Hill
71
72
60
E1
1 HOLLENGS LA
2 MAIN RD
3 GLEBE CL
4 SIMONS CL
5 CHAPEL LA
6 GREENACRES
7 MEADOWCROFT
8 ENFIELD RD

59
48

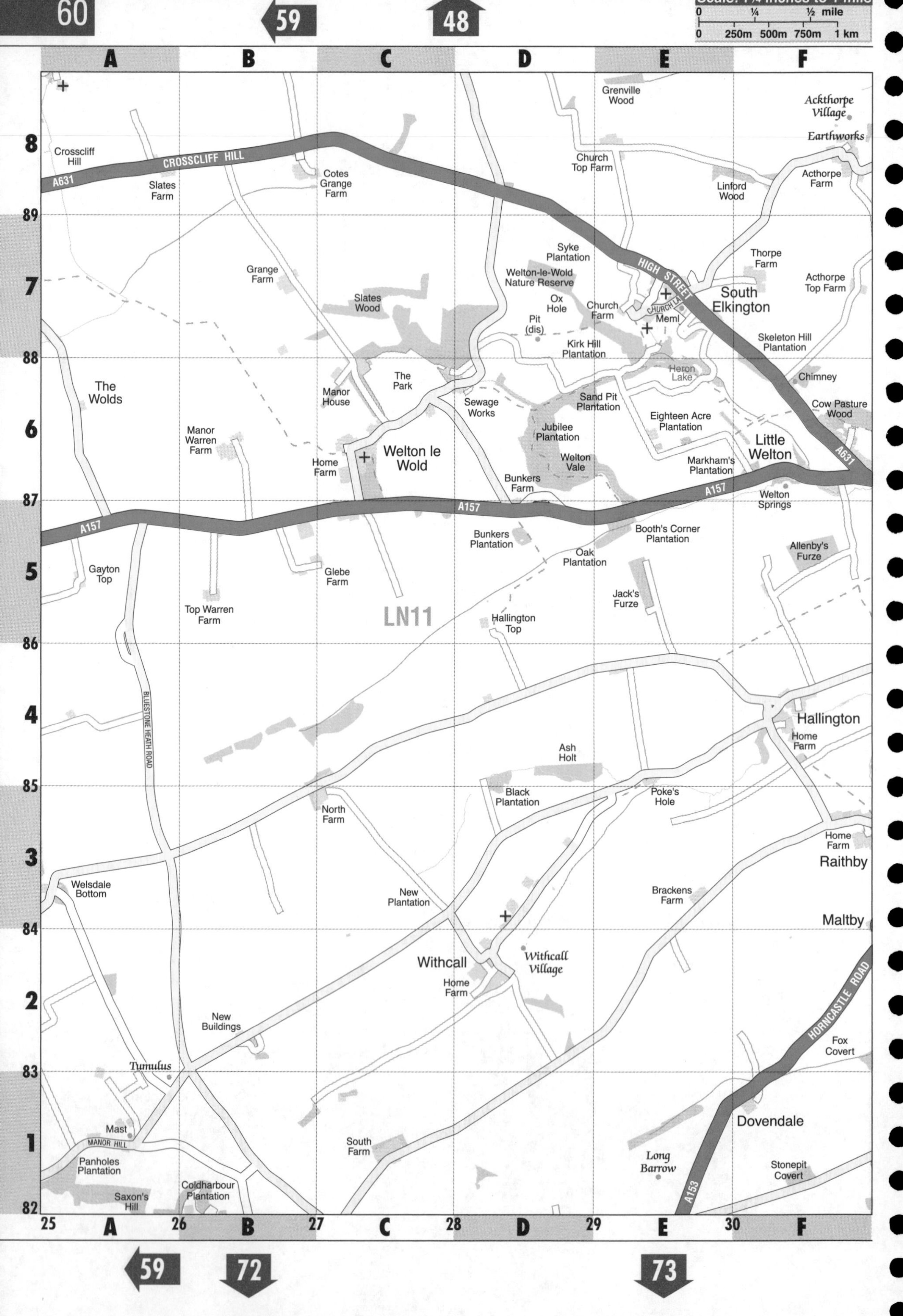
Scale: 1¾ inches to 1 mile
0 ¼ ½ mile
0 250m 500m 750m 1 km
A B C D E F
8 89 7 88 6 87 5 86 4 85 3 84 2 83 1 82
25 26 27 28 29 30
Crosscliff Hill
CROSSCLIFF HILL
A631
Slates Farm
Cotes Grange Farm
Grenville Wood
Ackthorpe Village
Earthworks
Church Top Farm
Linford Wood
Acthorpe Farm
Syke Plantation
HIGH STREET
Thorpe Farm
Acthorpe Top Farm
Grange Farm
Welton-le-Wold Nature Reserve
Slates Wood
Ox Hole
Church Farm
CHURCH LA
Meml
South Elkington
Pit (dis)
Kirk Hill Plantation
Skeleton Hill Plantation
Heron Lake
Chimney
The Park
The Wolds
Manor House
Sewage Works
Sand Pit Plantation
Eighteen Acre Plantation
Cow Pasture Wood
Jubilee Plantation
Manor Warren Farm
Welton le Wold
Home Farm
Welton Vale
Markham's Plantation
Little Welton
Bunkers Farm
A157
Welton Springs
Bunkers Plantation
Booth's Corner Plantation
Gayton Top
Glebe Farm
Oak Plantation
Allenby's Furze
Jack's Furze
Top Warren Farm
LN11
Hallington Top
BLUESTONE HEATH ROAD
Hallington
Home Farm
Ash Holt
Black Plantation
Poke's Hole
North Farm
Home Farm
Raithby
Welsdale Bottom
Brackens Farm
New Plantation
Maltby
Withcall
Withcall Village
Home Farm
New Buildings
HORNCASTLE ROAD
Fox Covert
Tumulus
Mast
MANOR HILL
Dovendale
South Farm
Long Barrow
A153
Panholes Plantation
Coldharbour Plantation
Stonepit Covert
Saxon's Hill

59
72
73

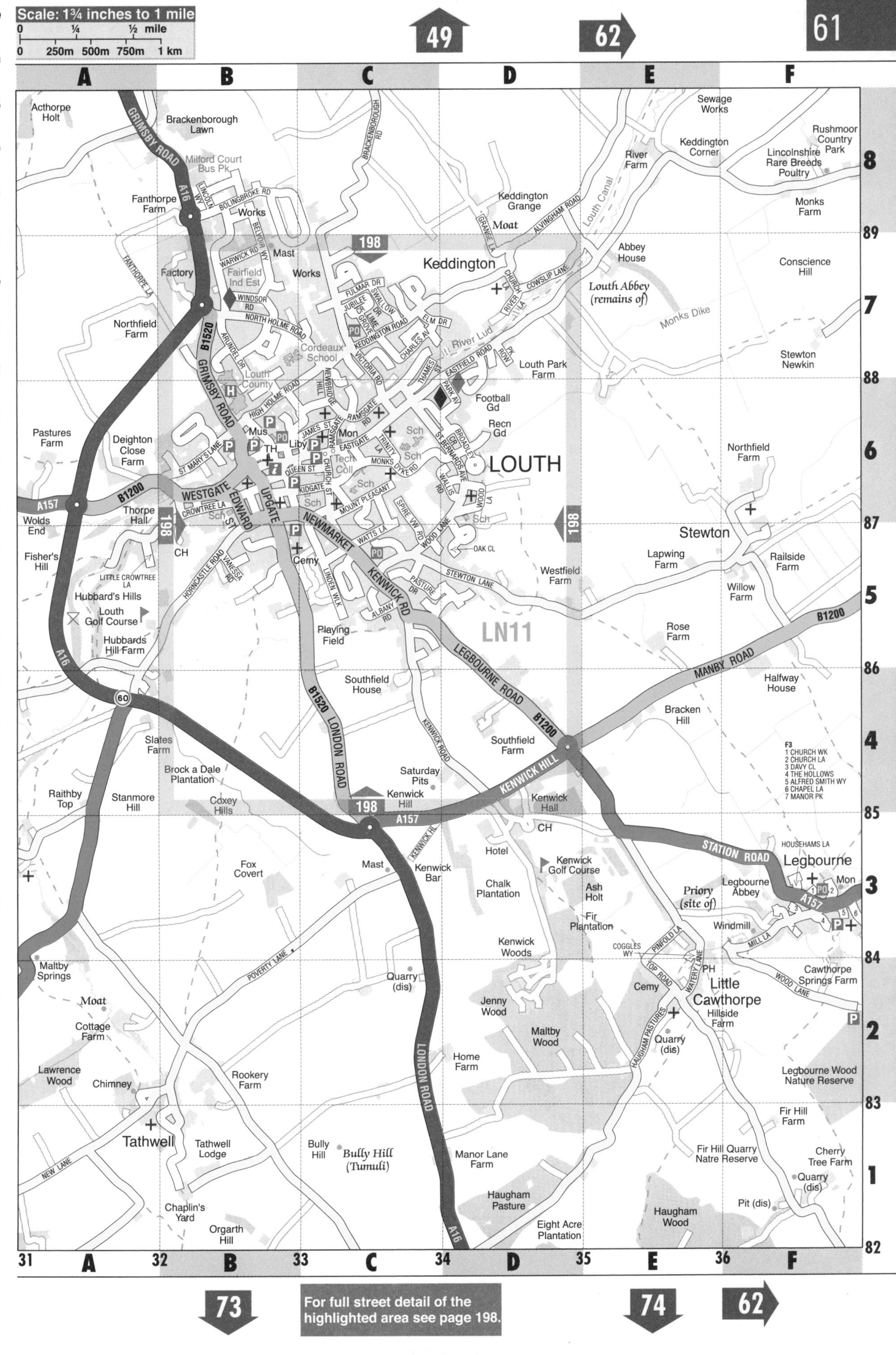

Scale: 1¾ inches to 1 mile
0 ¼ ½ mile
0 250m 500m 750m 1 km
49
62
LOUTH
Keddington
Stewton
Legbourne
Little Cawthorpe
Tathwell
LN11
Louth Abbey (remains of)
Priory (site of)
Bully Hill (Tumuli)
F3
1 CHURCH WK
2 CHURCH LA
3 DAVY CL
4 THE HOLLOWS
5 ALFRED SMITH WY
6 CHAPEL LA
7 MANOR PK
73
74
62
For full street detail of the highlighted area see page 198.

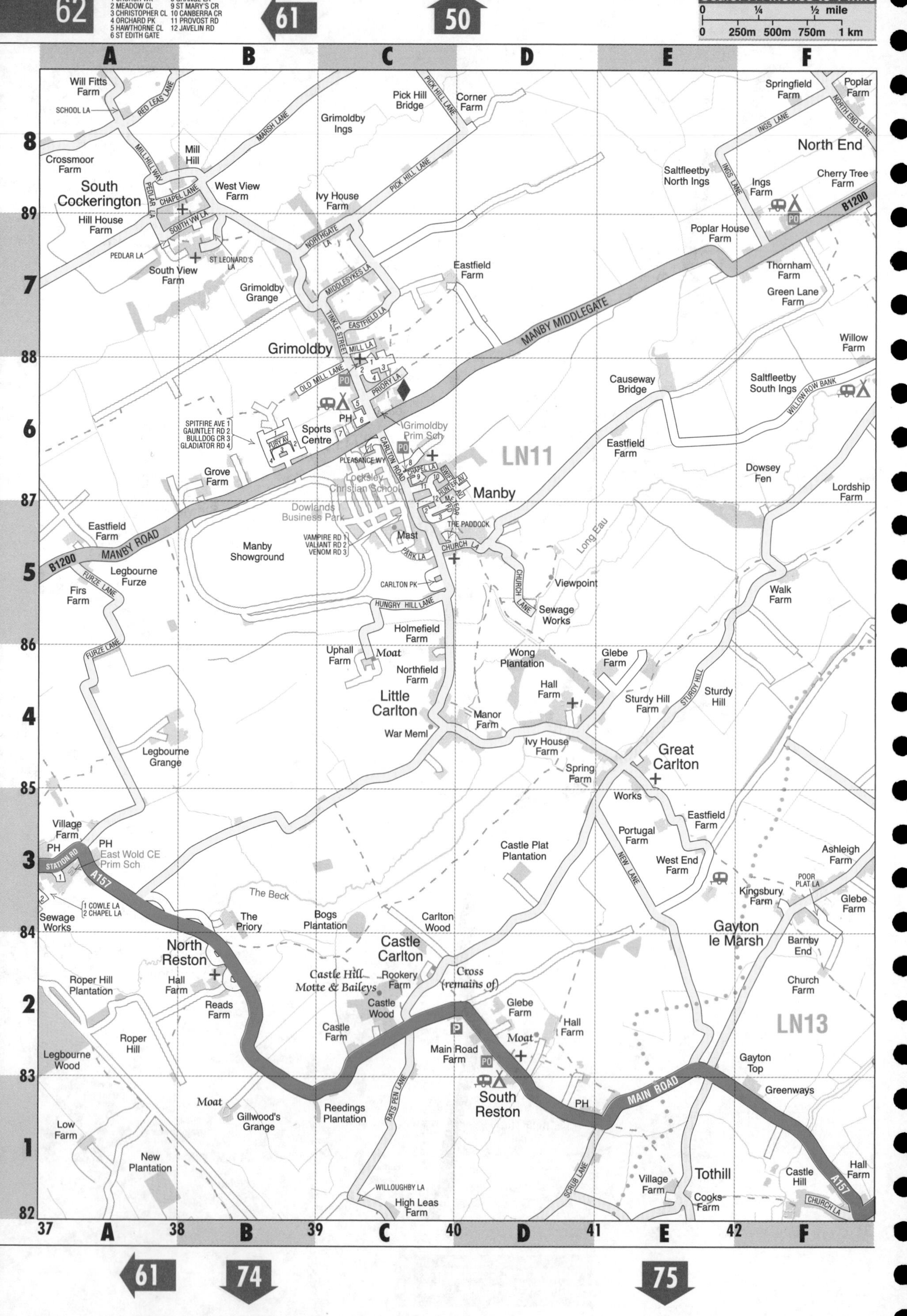
C6
1 CHURCH WK
2 MEADOW CL
3 CHRISTOPHER CL
4 ORCHARD PK
5 HAWTHORNE CL
6 ST EDITH GATE
7 SPINNEY CL
8 GRANGE LA
9 ST MARY'S CR
10 CANBERRA CR
11 PROVOST RD
12 JAVELIN RD
61
50
Scale: 1¾ inches to 1 mile
0 ¼ ½ mile
0 250m 500m 750m 1 km
A B C D E F
Will Fitts Farm
SCHOOL LA
RED LEAS LANE
MARSH LANE
Mill Hill
Crossmoor Farm
South Cockerington
Hill House Farm
PEDLAR LA
MILL HILL WAY
CHAPEL LANE
SOUTH VW LA
ST LEONARD'S LA
South View Farm
West View Farm
Grimoldby Ings
Pick Hill Bridge
PICK HILL LANE
Corner Farm
Ivy House Farm
NORTHGATE LA
MIDDLESYKES LA
Grimoldby Grange
TINKLE STREET
EASTFIELD LA
MILL LA
Grimoldby
OLD MILL LANE
PRIORY LA
PO
PH
Sports Centre
SPITFIRE AVE 1
GAUNTLET RD 2
BULLDOG CR 3
GLADIATOR RD 4
FURY AV
Grimoldby Prim Sch
CARLTON ROAD
PLEASANCE WY
CHAPEL LA
SWIFT AV
HUNTER AV
MEDOR
Locksley Christian School
Manby
LN11
Grove Farm
Eastfield Farm
Dowlands Business Park
MANBY ROAD
B1200
Manby Showground
VAMPIRE RD 1
VALIANT RD 2
VENOM RD 3
Mast
THE PADDOCK
CHURCH LA
PARK LA
CARLTON PK
HUNGRY HILL LANE
Legbourne Furze
FURZE LANE
Firs Farm
Eastfield Farm
MANBY MIDDLEGATE
Long Eau
Viewpoint
CHURCH LANE
Sewage Works
Holmefield Farm
Uphall Farm
Moat
Northfield Farm
Little Carlton
War Meml
Wong Plantation
Hall Farm
Manor Farm
Ivy House Farm
Glebe Farm
Sturdy Hill Farm
STURDY HILL
Sturdy Hill
Great Carlton
Spring Farm
Works
Springfield Farm
Poplar Farm
NORTH END LANE
INGS LANE
North End
Saltfleetby North Ings
Ings Farm
Cherry Tree Farm
Poplar House Farm
Thornham Farm
Green Lane Farm
Willow Farm
Causeway Bridge
Saltfleetby South Ings
WILLOW ROW BANK
Eastfield Farm
Dowsey Fen
Lordship Farm
Walk Farm
Legbourne Grange
Village Farm
PH
STATION RD
East Wold CE Prim Sch
A157
1 COWLE LA
2 CHAPEL LA
Sewage Works
The Beck
The Priory
Bogs Plantation
Carlton Wood
North Reston
Castle Carlton
Castle Hill Motte & Baileys
Rookery Farm
Cross (remains of)
Roper Hill Plantation
Hall Farm
Reads Farm
Castle Wood
Castle Farm
Glebe Farm
Moat
Hall Farm
Roper Hill
Legbourne Wood
Main Road Farm
P
PO
South Reston
MAIN ROAD
PH
Castle Plat Plantation
Portugal Farm
NEW LANE
Eastfield Farm
West End Farm
Ashleigh Farm
POOR PLAT LA
Kingsbury Farm
Glebe Farm
Gayton le Marsh
Barnby End
Church Farm
LN13
Gayton Top
Greenways
Moat
Gillwood's Grange
Reedings Plantation
RATS PEN LANE
Low Farm
New Plantation
WILLOUGHBY LA
High Leas Farm
SCRUB LANE
Village Farm
Tothill
Cooks Farm
Castle Hill
Hall Farm
CHURCH LA
8 89 7 88 6 87 5 86 4 85 3 84 2 83 1 82
37 38 39 40 41 42
61
74
75

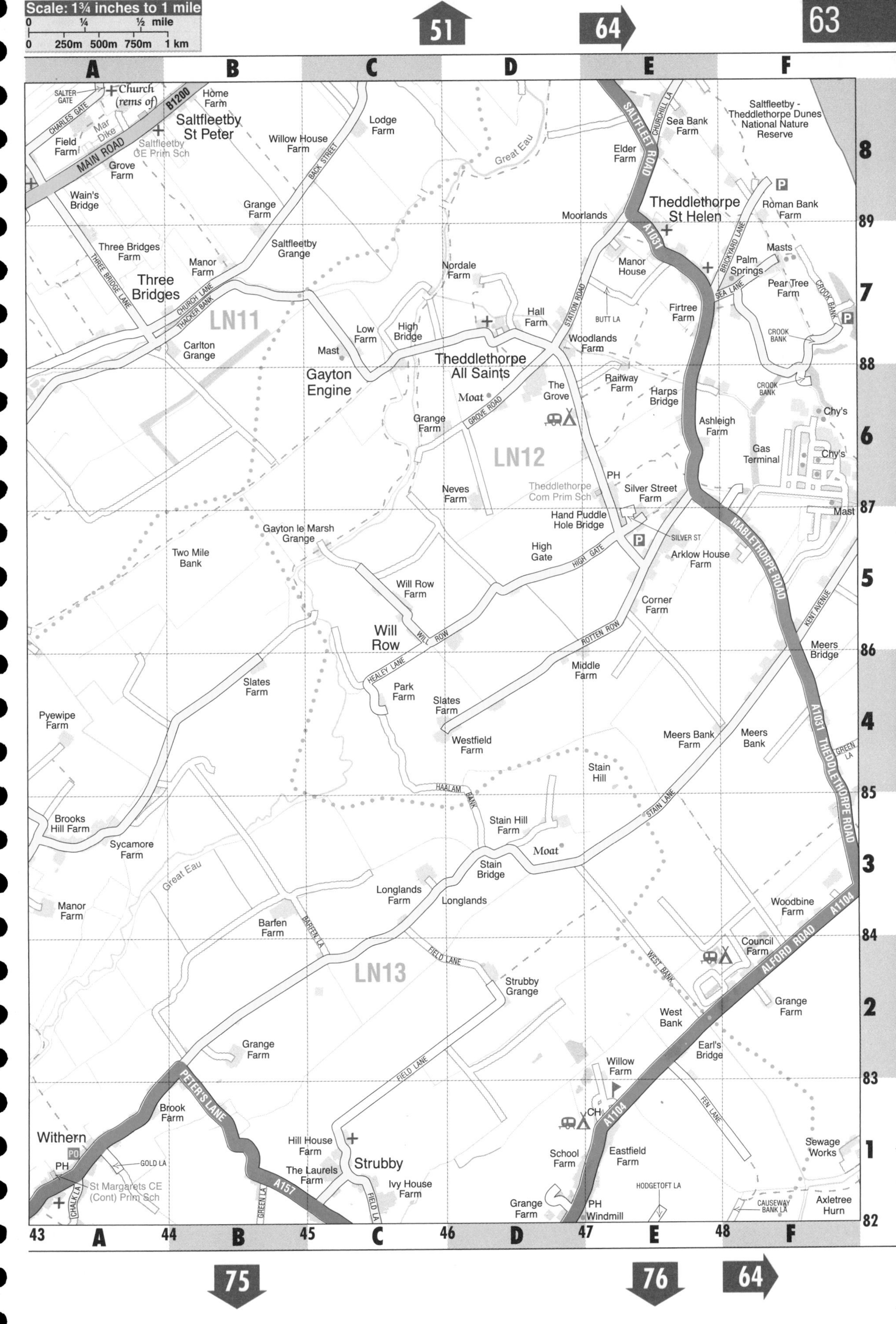
Scale: 1¾ inches to 1 mile
51
64
Saltfleetby St Peter
Three Bridges
Gayton Engine
Theddlethorpe All Saints
Theddlethorpe St Helen
Will Row
Strubby
Withern
LN11
LN12
LN13
Saltfleetby - Theddlethorpe Dunes National Nature Reserve
MABLETHORPE ROAD
A1031 THEDDLETHORPE ROAD
ALFORD ROAD
SALTFLEET ROAD
MAIN ROAD
PETER'S LANE
75
76
64

B5
1 CAMBRIDGE RD N
2 LINKS AVE
3 CAMBRIDGE RD S
4 IVEL GR
5 WHITEHEAD CL
6 IVEL CL

← 63

Scale: 1¾ inches to 1 mile
0   ¼   ½   mile
0   250m   500m   750m   1 km

Saltfleetby - Theddlethorpe Dunes National Nature Reserve

North End Farm
CROOK BANK
MEERS BANK
PH
KENT AVE
MEERS BANK
P
The Seal Sanctuary & Nature Centre

POPLAR AVE 1
CHALFONT AVE 2

A4
1 THE FAIRWAY
2 THE DRIVE
3 FALDOS WY
4 GOLF RD
5 LYLE CL
6 THE GREEN
7 EAGLE CL

GREEN LANE
GOLF ROAD
QUEBEC ROAD
ENTERPRISE ROAD
P
PO

The Dunes Family Entertainment Centre

Station Sports Ctr
i
Fun Fair
PO
Mon
Liby
IRB Station
Olde Curiosity Mus

Mablethorpe Com Prim Sch
HIGH STREET
VICTORIA RD
MABLETHORPE

Mablethorpe Hall
Moat
ALFORD ROAD
A1104
PH
CHURCH LANE
Art Gall
The Tennyson High School
THE STRAND
PH
SEAHOLME ROAD

LN12

Seahaven Springs

AQUA DR 1
MARIAN AVE 2
MEDINA GD 3
CHAMPION WY 4

Trusthorpe
Masts   Masts
SUTTON RD

C3
1 QUEENS PK CL
2 NEWSTEAD RD
3 DYMOKE CL
4 BROOKE DR
5 DYMOKE RD
6 ARDEN CL

C2
1 MILL FIELD
2 CAMPLING WY
3 BARTON CL
4 AUBREY PARKER CL
5 PARKINSON'S WY
6 JAMES AVE
7 ST PETER'S LA
8 BRAY AVE
9 ETON RD

Poplar Farm
MILE LANE
Bambers Farm
Bamber's Bridge
Elder Farm
Bridge Farm
Thorpe Farm
Sewage Works
NORTH ROAD
Bourne Farm
Crossing Farm
A52
TRUSTHORPE ROAD
WHITE ROW LA
HIGHGATE

Thorpe
FEN LA
Trusthorpe Hall
MAIN STREET
Boswell Farm

1 PARK RD E
2 CROMER AVE
3 HIGH ST
4 PROMENADE
5 YORK RD

A3
1 ORCHARD WY
2 ORCHARD CL
3 CHURCH RD
4 MALBROROUGH DR
5 OAKHAM AVE
6 WINCHESTER DR
7 CHELTENHAM WY

← 63   76

B3
1 HAWTHORN DR
2 MAYFLOWER WY
3 TRENCHARD RD
4 NELSON RD
5 STANLEY AVE
6 MAXWELL DR
7 KENSINGTON GDNS
8 STRAND CL
9 TOWER CL

10 HARLEQUIN DR
11 MARIAN AVE
12 HARRIS BOULEVARD
13 ELM AVE
14 KING ST
15 MARINA RD
16 ANCASTER RD
17 RIPON PL
18 VYNER CL
19 FOXE END

20 KNOWLE ST
21 PARK AVE
22 PARRY RD
23 THE BOULEVARD

B4
1 LONG ACRE
2 ST ANDREWS RD
3 SHERWOOD RD
4 RUGBY RD
5 MALVERN RD
6 HARROW RD
7 REPTON RD
8 QUEENSWAY
9 SOMERSBY AVE

10 FITZWILLIAM ST
11 WELLINGTON AVE
12 CHAUCER AVE
13 RUSKIN RD
14 KINGSLEY RD
15 CHARLES WRIGHT CL
16 TENNYSON AVE
17 TENNYSON RD
18 HIGH ST
19 ADMIRALTY RD

20 STATION RD
21 ALEXANDRA ST
22 ALEXANDRA PK

77

C1
1 HALL LEAS DR
2 TRUSTHORPE RD
3 HIGHGATE CL
4 HIGHFIELD AVE
5 OUNDLE RD
6 UPPINGHAM RD
7 WILLOUGHBY RD
8 MARINE AVE
9 HARDING CL

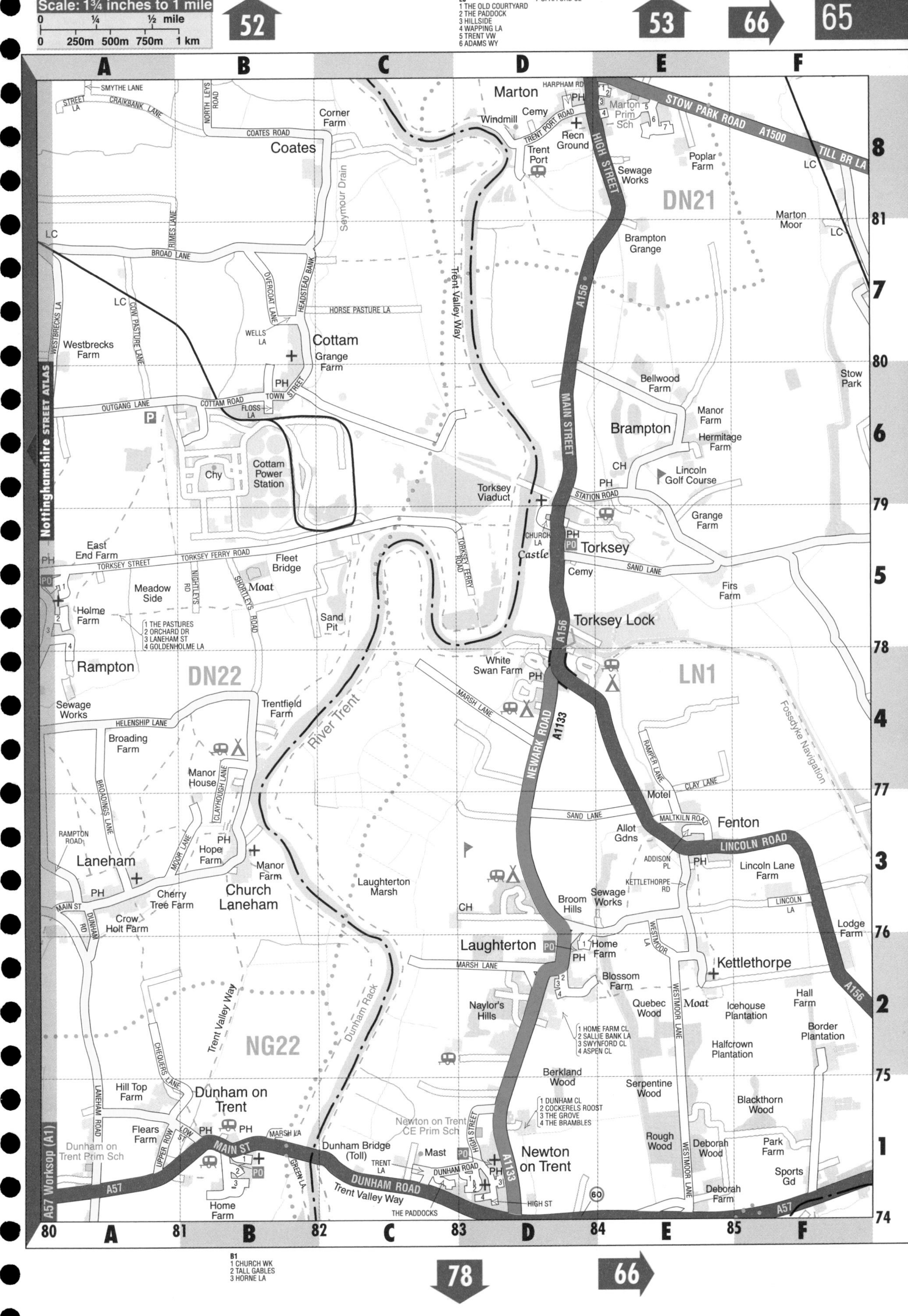

Scale: 1¾ inches to 1 mile
52
53
66
E8
1 THE OLD COURTYARD
2 THE PADDOCK
3 HILLSIDE
4 WAPPING LA
5 TRENT VW
6 ADAMS WY
7 SPAFFORD CL
Marton
Coates
Corner Farm
Windmill
Cemy
Trent Port
Recn Ground
HIGH STREET
STOW PARK ROAD A1500
TILL BR LA
Poplar Farm
Sewage Works
DN21
Marton Moor
Brampton Grange
Seymour Drain
BROAD LANE
COATES ROAD
Trent Valley Way
HORSE PASTURE LA
Westbrecks Farm
Cottam
Grange Farm
A156
Bellwood Farm
Stow Park
Manor Farm
Brampton
Hermitage Farm
OUTGANG LANE
COTTAM ROAD
Cottam Power Station
Chy
MAIN STREET
Lincoln Golf Course
Torksey Viaduct
STATION ROAD
Grange Farm
East End Farm
TORKSEY STREET
TORKSEY FERRY ROAD
Fleet Bridge
Torksey
Castle
Cemy
SAND LANE
Meadow Side
Moat
Firs Farm
Holme Farm
1 THE PASTURES
2 ORCHARD DR
3 LANEHAM ST
4 GOLDENHOLME LA
Sand Pit
Torksey Lock
Rampton
DN22
White Swan Farm
LN1
Sewage Works
HELENSHIP LANE
Trentfield Farm
MARSH LANE
Broading Farm
River Trent
NEWARK ROAD
A1133
Fossdyke Navigation
Manor House
RAMPER LANE
CLAY LANE
Motel
SAND LANE
MALTKILN ROAD
Fenton
LINCOLN ROAD
Allot Gdns
Laneham
Hope Farm
Manor Farm
Laughterton Marsh
Lincoln Lane Farm
Church Laneham
Cherry Tree Farm
Crow Holt Farm
Broom Hills
Sewage Works
Lodge Farm
Laughterton
Home Farm
Kettlethorpe
MARSH LANE
Blossom Farm
Hall Farm
Naylor's Hills
Quebec Wood
Moat
Icehouse Plantation
Border Plantation
Trent Valley Way
NG22
Dunham Rack
1 HOME FARM CL
2 SALLIE BANK LA
3 SWYNFORD CL
4 ASPEN CL
Halfcrown Plantation
Berkland Wood
Serpentine Wood
Blackthorn Wood
Hill Top Farm
Dunham on Trent
1 DUNHAM CL
2 COCKERELS ROOST
3 THE GROVE
4 THE BRAMBLES
Flears Farm
Newton on Trent CE Prim Sch
Rough Wood
Deborah Wood
Park Farm
Dunham on Trent Prim Sch
Dunham Bridge (Toll)
Mast
Newton on Trent
Sports Gd
A57 Worksop (A1)
MAIN ST
DUNHAM ROAD
Trent Valley Way
Deborah Farm
Home Farm
THE PADDOCKS
HIGH ST
Nottinghamshire STREET ATLAS
B1
1 CHURCH WK
2 TALL GABLES
3 HORNE LA
78
66

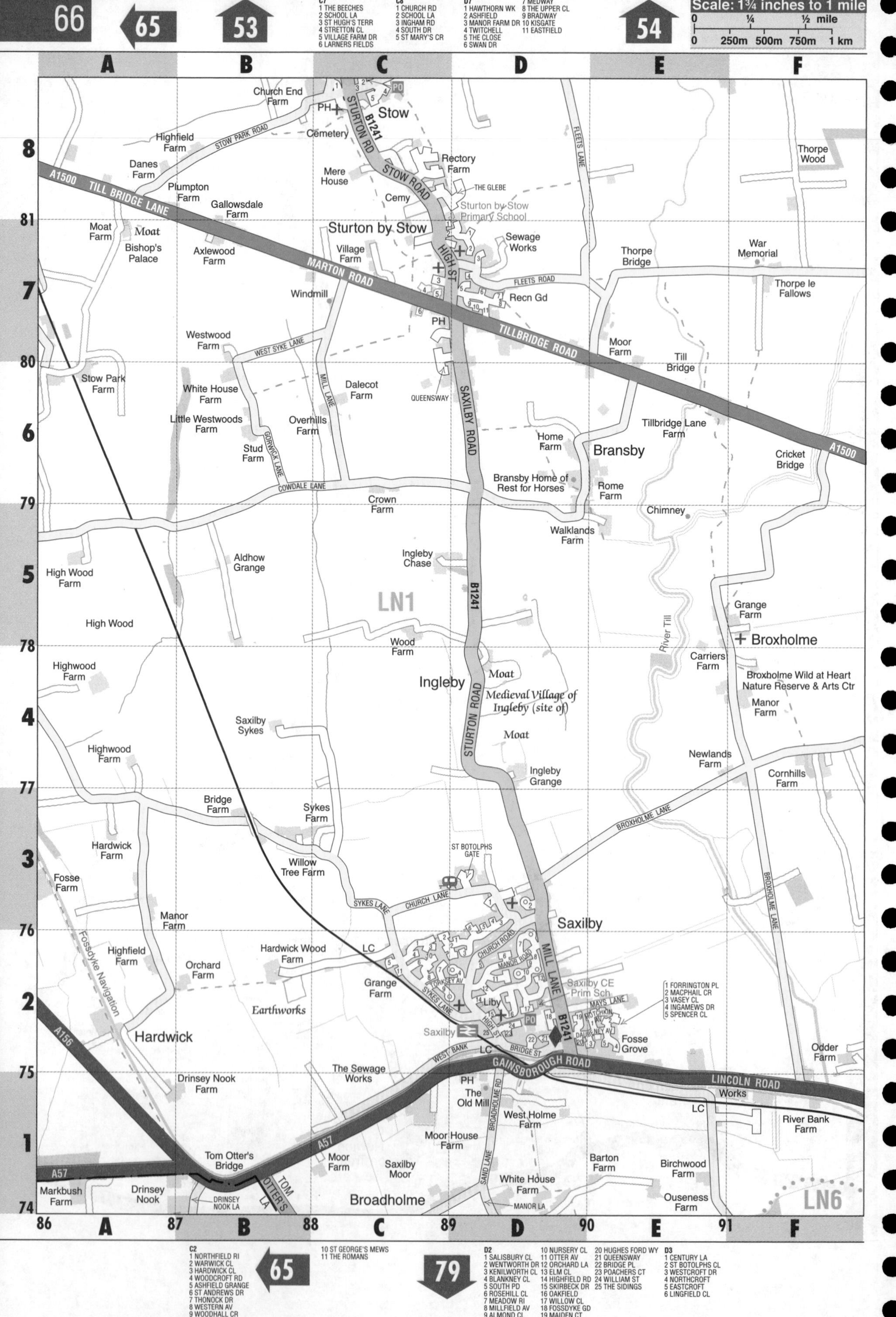

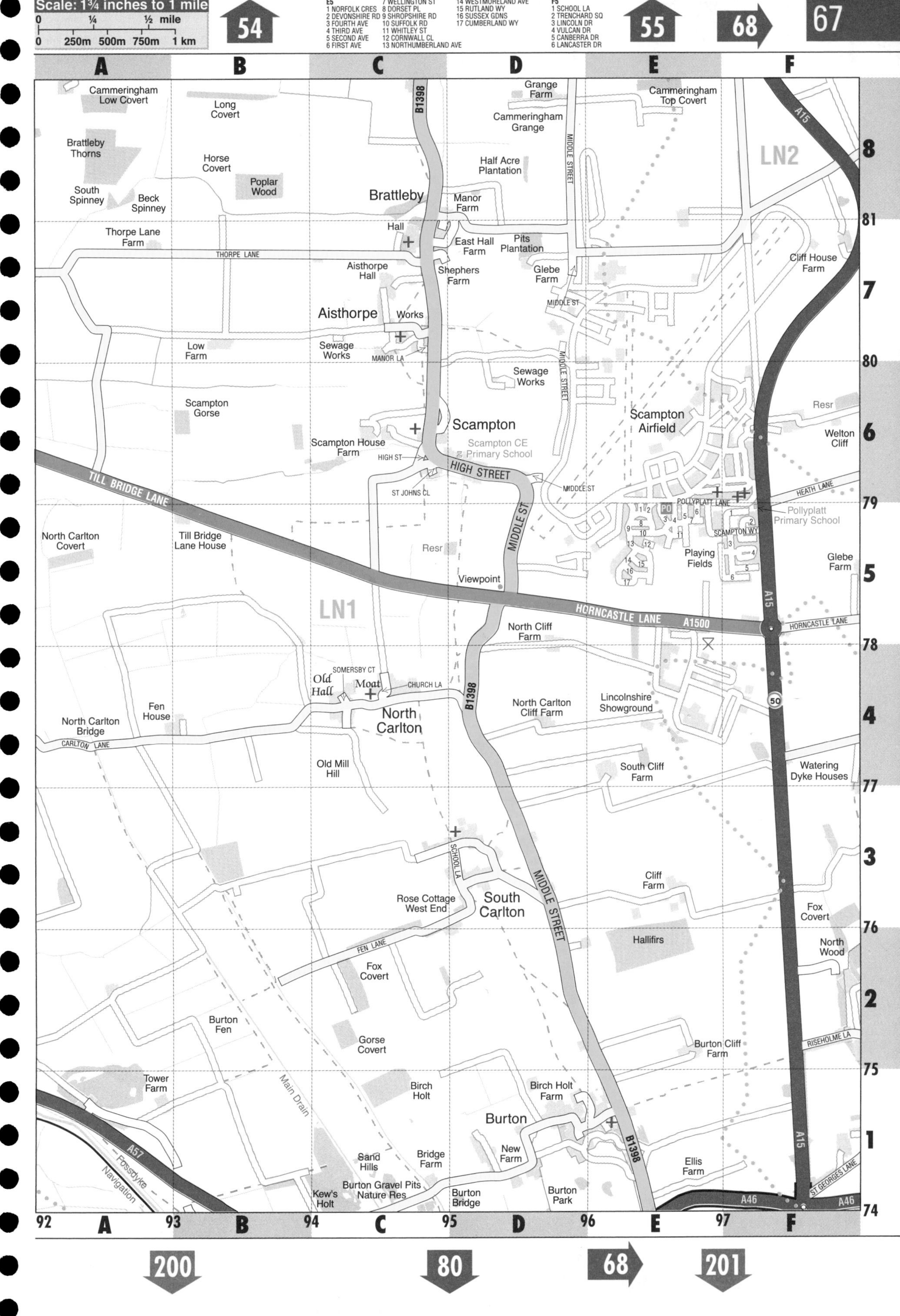

Scale: 1¾ inches to 1 mile
0 ¼ ½ mile
0 250m 500m 750m 1 km
54
E5
1 NORFOLK CRES
2 DEVONSHIRE RD
3 FOURTH AVE
4 THIRD AVE
5 SECOND AVE
6 FIRST AVE
7 WELLINGTON ST
8 DORSET PL
9 SHROPSHIRE RD
10 SUFFOLK RD
11 WHITLEY ST
12 CORNWALL CL
13 NORTHUMBERLAND AVE
14 WESTMORELAND AVE
15 RUTLAND WY
16 SUSSEX GDNS
17 CUMBERLAND WY
F5
1 SCHOOL LA
2 TRENCHARD SQ
3 LINCOLN DR
4 VULCAN DR
5 CANBERRA DR
6 LANCASTER DR
55
68
A B C D E F
Cammeringham Low Covert
Long Covert
Grange Farm
Cammeringham Grange
Cammeringham Top Covert
Brattleby Thorns
Horse Covert
Poplar Wood
Half Acre Plantation
LN2
South Spinney
Beck Spinney
Brattleby
Manor Farm
MIDDLE STREET
Thorpe Lane Farm
Hall
East Hall Farm
Pits Plantation
THORPE LANE
Aisthorpe Hall
Shephers Farm
Glebe Farm
Cliff House Farm
Aisthorpe
Works
MIDDLE ST
Low Farm
Sewage Works
MANOR LA
Sewage Works
Scampton Gorse
Scampton
Scampton Airfield
Resr
Welton Cliff
Scampton House Farm
Scampton CE Primary School
HIGH ST
HIGH STREET
TILL BRIDGE LANE
ST JOHNS CL
MIDDLE ST
POLLYPLATT LANE
HEATH LANE
Pollyplatt Primary School
SCAMPTON WY
North Carlton Covert
Till Bridge Lane House
Resr
Playing Fields
Glebe Farm
Viewpoint
LN1
HORNCASTLE LANE
A1500
North Cliff Farm
SOMERSBY CT
Old Hall
Moat
CHURCH LA
B1398
North Carlton Cliff Farm
Lincolnshire Showground
Fen House
North Carlton Bridge
North Carlton
CARLTON LANE
Old Mill Hill
South Cliff Farm
Watering Dyke Houses
SCHOOL LA
Rose Cottage West End
South Carlton
Cliff Farm
Fox Covert
North Wood
Hallifirs
FEN LANE
Fox Covert
Burton Fen
Gorse Covert
Burton Cliff Farm
RISEHOLME LA
Tower Farm
Main Drain
Birch Holt
Birch Holt Farm
Burton
A57
Fossdyke Navigation
Sand Hills
Bridge Farm
New Farm
Ellis Farm
Kew's Holt
Burton Gravel Pits Nature Res
Burton Bridge
Burton Park
A46
ST GEORGES LANE
A15
50
8 81 7 80 6 79 5 78 4 77 3 76 2 75 1 74
92 93 94 95 96 97
200
80
68
201

D7
1 FIELD CL
2 KEEPERS CL
3 POACHERS REST
4 BRAMBLE CL
5 THE SPINNEYS
6 LODGE CL

7 RIVEHALL AVE
8 EAGLE DR
9 BRINKHALL WY
10 GOREHALL DR
11 PAINSHALL CL
12 ST MARY'S AVE
13 SPRING CT

14 LANCASTER CT
15 BARNES WALLIS CT
16 WESTHALL RD
17 SWEN CL
18 FARM VW
19 HALFPENNY CL
20 THE HARDINGS

D6
1 MANOR LA
2 CHURCH LA
3 TINKERMERE CL
4 THE GROVE
5 AYAM CL
6 MEADOW WY

7 ORCHARD CL
8 ROSELEA AVE
9 DUNHOLME RD
10 RYLAND GDNS
11 DUNHOLME CL
12 THE PASTURES
13 THE WELLS

14 RIDGE CL
15 THE HARROWS
16 FURROW CL
17 SUDBECK LA
18 GREEN LA
19 POND CL
20 ALLWOOD RD

21 MORRIS CL
22 TENNYSON DR
23 PAYNELL
24 KNEELAND

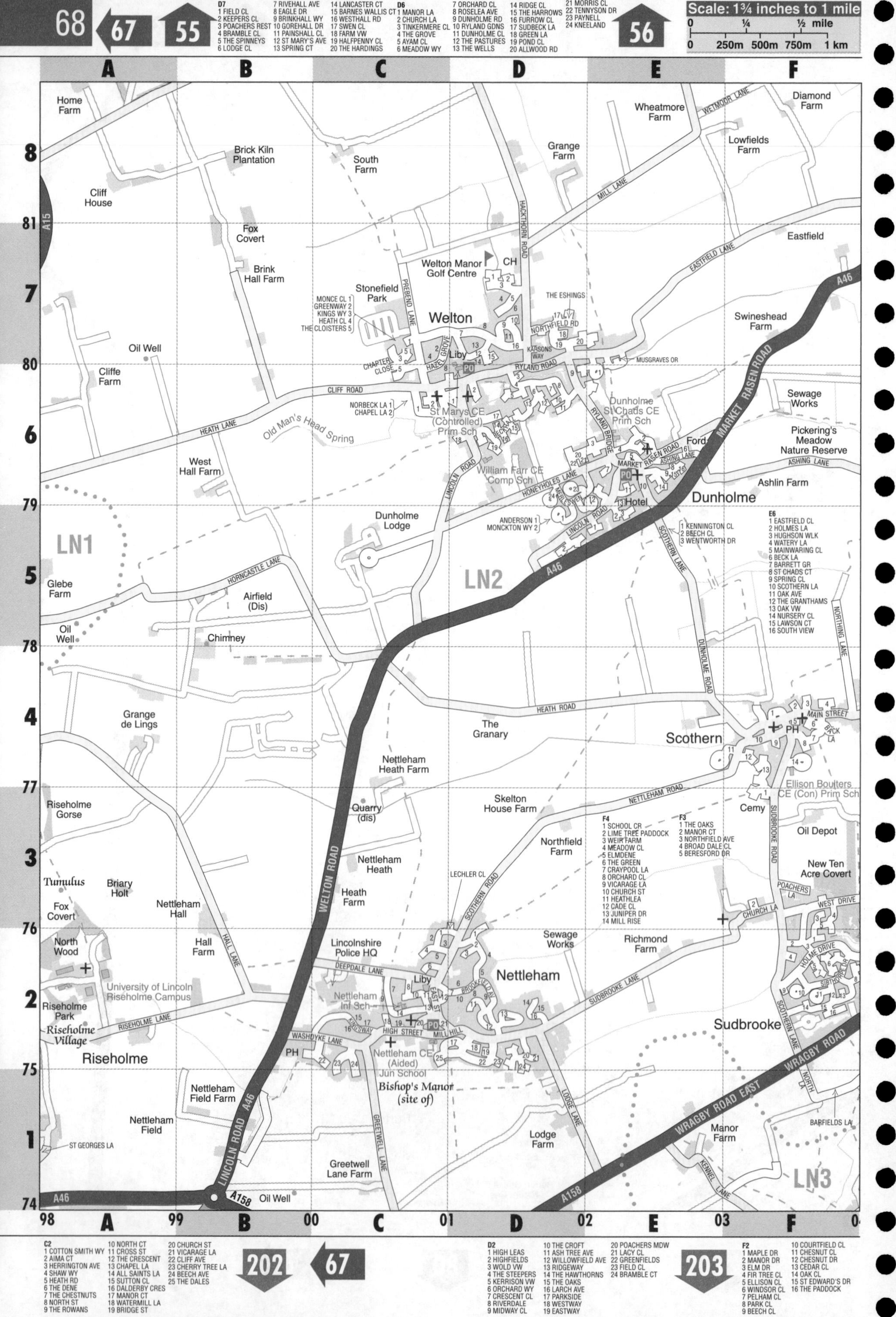

C2
1 COTTON SMITH WY
2 AIMA CT
3 HERRINGTON AVE
4 SHAW WY
5 HEATH RD
6 THE DENE
7 THE CHESTNUTS
8 NORTH ST
9 THE ROWANS

10 NORTH CT
11 CROSS ST
12 THE CRESCENT
13 CHAPEL LA
14 ALL SAINTS LA
15 SUTTON CL
16 DALDERBY CRES
17 MANOR CT
18 WATERMILL CL
19 BRIDGE ST

20 CHURCH ST
21 VICARAGE LA
22 CLIFF AVE
23 CHERRY TREE LA
24 BEECH AVE
25 THE DALES

D2
1 HIGH LEAS
2 HIGHFIELDS
3 WOLD VW
4 THE STEEPERS
5 KERRISON VW
6 ORCHARD WY
7 CRESCENT CL
8 RIVERDALE
9 MIDWAY CL

10 THE CROFT
11 ASH TREE AVE
12 WILLOWFIELD AVE
13 RIDGEWAY
14 THE HAWTHORNS
15 THE OAKS
16 LARCH AVE
17 PARKSIDE
18 WESTWAY
19 EASTWAY

20 POACHERS MDW
21 LACY CL
22 GREENFIELDS
23 FIELD CL
24 BRAMBLE CT

F2
1 MAPLE DR
2 MANOR DR
3 ELM DR
4 FIR TREE CL
5 ELLISON CL
6 WINDSOR CL
7 PELHAM CL
8 PARK CL
9 BEECH CL

10 COURTFIELD CL
11 CHESNUT CL
12 CHESNUT DR
13 CEDAR CL
14 OAK CL
15 ST EDWARD'S DR
16 THE PADDOCK

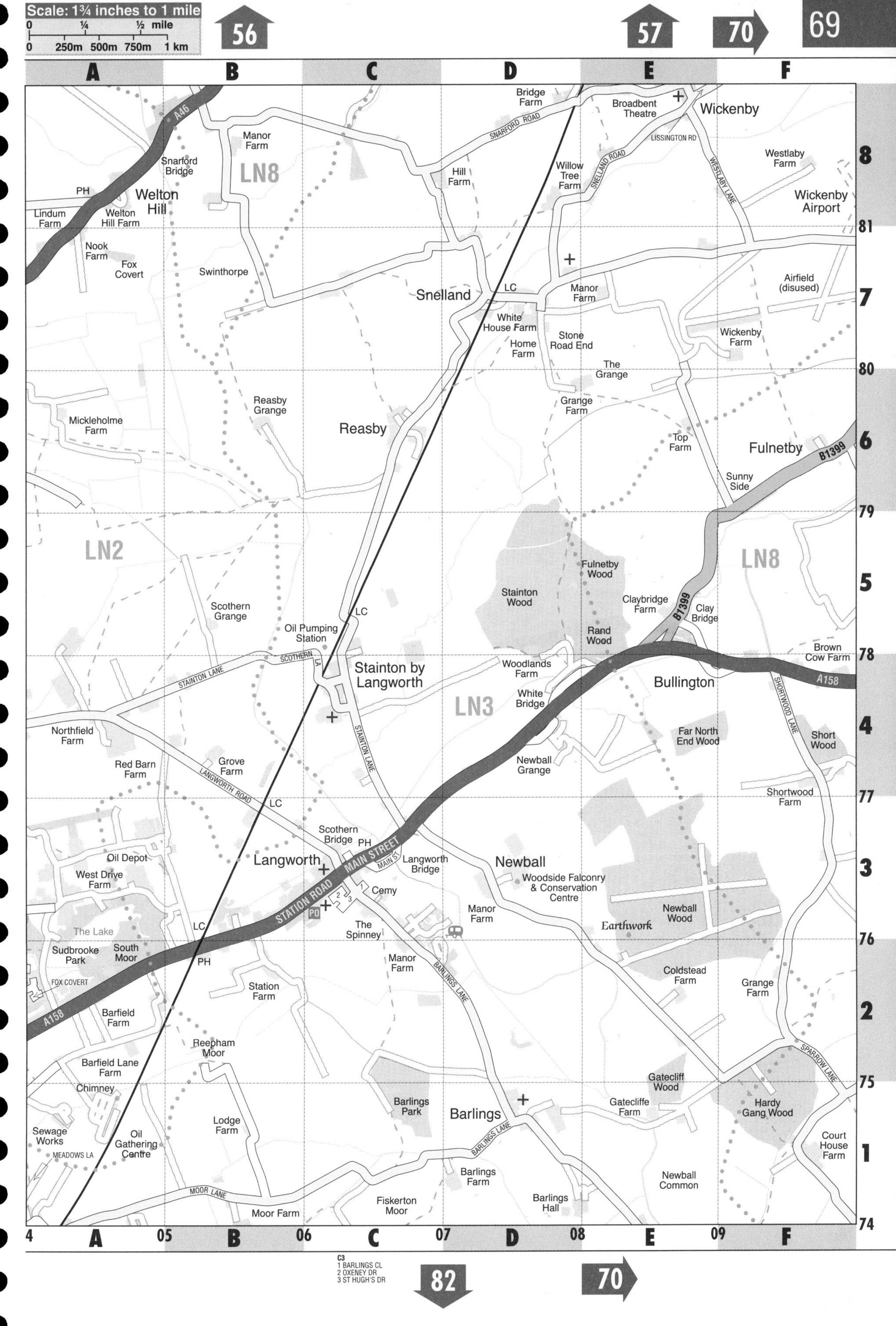

Scale: 1¾ inches to 1 mile
0 ¼ ½ mile
0 250m 500m 750m 1 km
56
57
70
A B C D E F
8 81 7 80 6 79 5 78 4 77 3 76 2 75 1 74
4 05 06 07 08 09
Bridge Farm
Broadbent Theatre
Wickenby
SNARFORD ROAD
LISSINGTON RD
A46
Manor Farm
Snarford Bridge
LN8
Hill Farm
Willow Tree Farm
SNELLAND ROAD
WESTLABY LANE
Westlaby Farm
Wickenby Airport
PH
Welton Hill
Lindum Farm
Welton Hill Farm
Nook Farm
Fox Covert
Swinthorpe
Snelland
LC
Manor Farm
Airfield (disused)
White House Farm
Stone Road End
Home Farm
Wickenby Farm
The Grange
Grange Farm
Mickleholme Farm
Reasby Grange
Reasby
Top Farm
Fulnetby
B1399
Sunny Side
LN2
LN8
Fulnetby Wood
Stainton Wood
Claybridge Farm
Scothern Grange
LC
B1399
Clay Bridge
Oil Pumping Station
Rand Wood
Brown Cow Farm
SCOTHERN LA
STAINTON LANE
Stainton by Langworth
Woodlands Farm
Bullington
A158
SHORTWOOD LANE
White Bridge
LN3
Northfield Farm
STAINTON LANE
Far North End Wood
Short Wood
Red Barn Farm
Grove Farm
LANGWORTH ROAD
Newball Grange
Shortwood Farm
LC
Scothern Bridge
PH
MAIN STREET
Oil Depot
Langworth
MAIN ST
Langworth Bridge
Newball
West Drive Farm
STATION ROAD
Cemy
Woodside Falconry & Conservation Centre
PO
Manor Farm
Newball Wood
The Lake
LC
The Spinney
Earthwork
Sudbrooke Park
South Moor
PH
Manor Farm
Coldstead Farm
FOX COVERT
BARLINGS LANE
Station Farm
Grange Farm
A158
Barfield Farm
Reepham Moor
SPARROW LANE
Barfield Lane Farm
Gatecliff Wood
Chimney
Barlings Park
Barlings
Gatecliffe Farm
Hardy Gang Wood
Lodge Farm
Sewage Works
Oil Gathering Centre
BARLINGS LANE
Court House Farm
MEADOWS LA
Barlings Farm
Newball Common
MOOR LANE
Fiskerton Moor
Barlings Hall
Moor Farm
C3
1 BARLINGS CL
2 OXENEY DR
3 ST HUGH'S DR
82
70

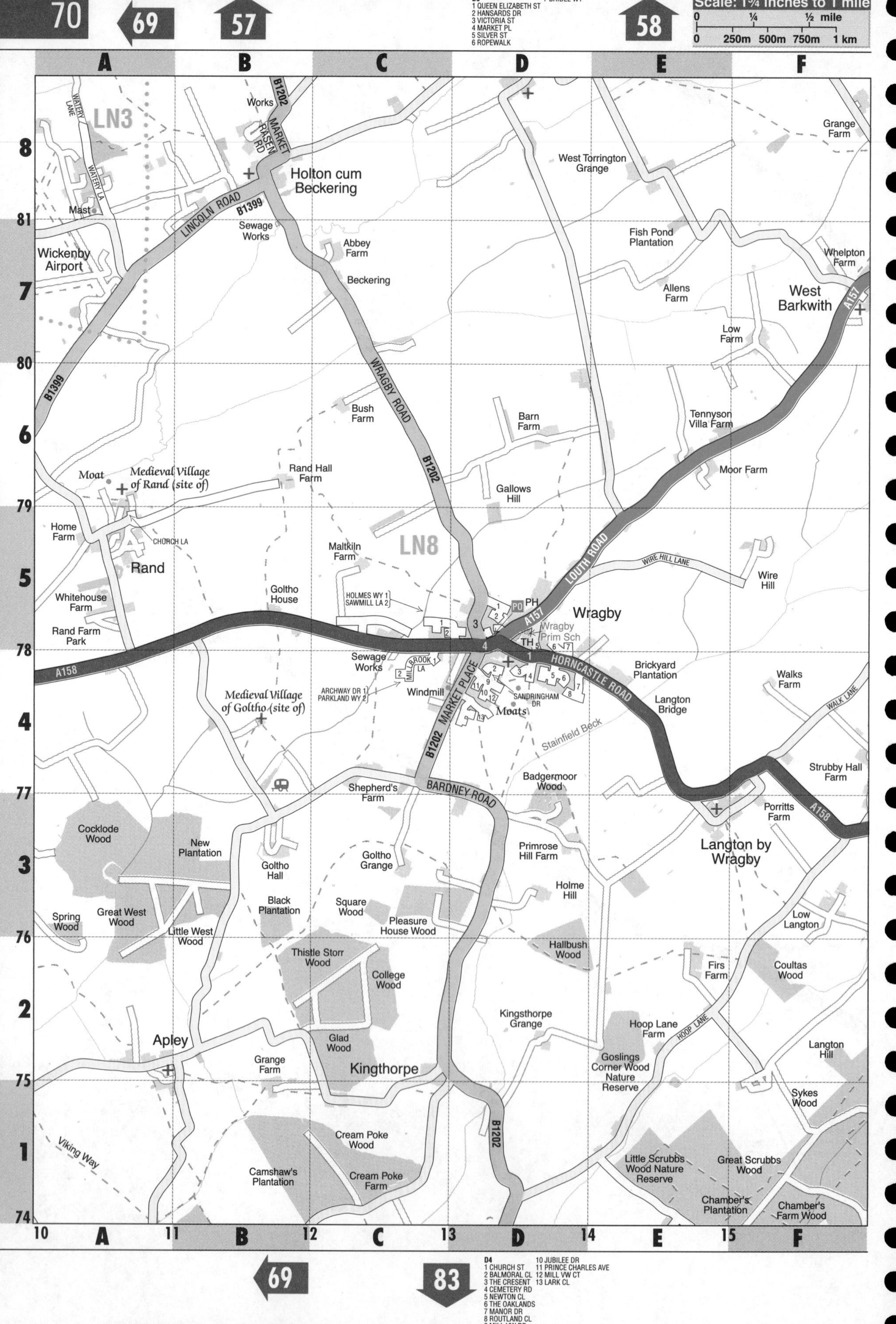

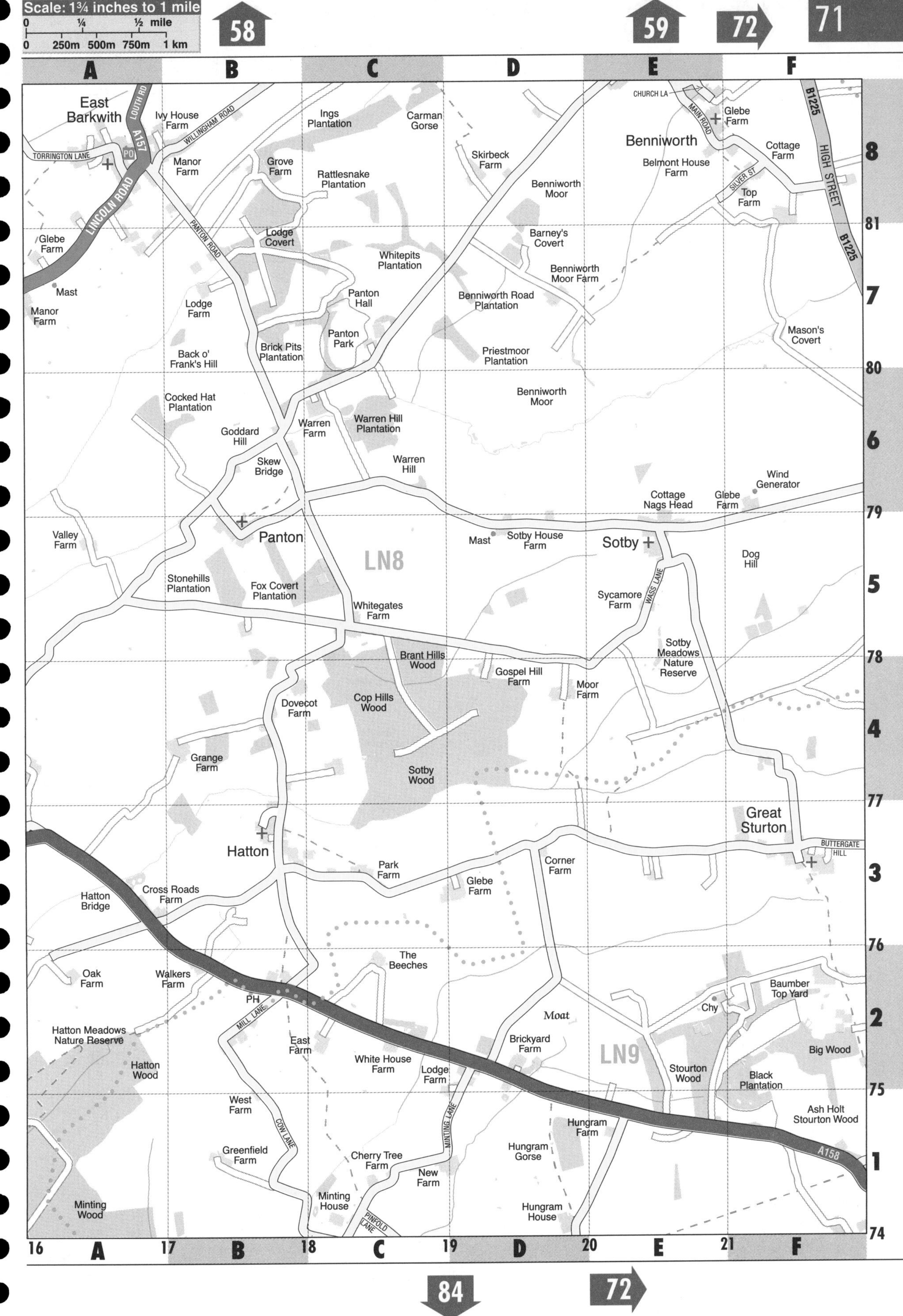
Scale: 1¾ inches to 1 mile
58
59
72
East Barkwith
Ivy House Farm
Manor Farm
Ings Plantation
Carman Gorse
Grove Farm
Rattlesnake Plantation
Skirbeck Farm
Benniworth Moor
Benniworth
Glebe Farm
Cottage Farm
Belmont House Farm
Top Farm
Glebe Farm
Mast
Manor Farm
Lodge Covert
Whitepits Plantation
Barney's Covert
Benniworth Moor Farm
Lodge Farm
Panton Hall
Benniworth Road Plantation
Mason's Covert
Panton Park
Brick Pits Plantation
Back o' Frank's Hill
Priestmoor Plantation
Benniworth Moor
Cocked Hat Plantation
Warren Farm
Warren Hill Plantation
Goddard Hill
Skew Bridge
Warren Hill
Wind Generator
Cottage
Nags Head
Glebe Farm
Valley Farm
Panton
Mast
Sotby House Farm
Sotby
Dog Hill
LN8
Stonehills Plantation
Fox Covert Plantation
Whitegates Farm
Sycamore Farm
Sotby Meadows Nature Reserve
Brant Hills Wood
Gospel Hill Farm
Moor Farm
Dovecot Farm
Cop Hills Wood
Grange Farm
Sotby Wood
Great Sturton
Hatton
Park Farm
Corner Farm
Glebe Farm
Hatton Bridge
Cross Roads Farm
Oak Farm
Walkers Farm
The Beeches
Baumber Top Yard
Chy
Moat
PH
Hatton Meadows Nature Reserve
East Farm
Brickyard Farm
LN9
Big Wood
Hatton Wood
White House Farm
Lodge Farm
Stourton Wood
Black Plantation
West Farm
Hungram Farm
Ash Holt Stourton Wood
Greenfield Farm
Cherry Tree Farm
Hungram Gorse
New Farm
Minting Wood
Minting House
Hungram House
TORRINGTON LANE
LOUTH RD
A157
LINCOLN ROAD
WILLINGHAM ROAD
PANTON ROAD
CHURCH LA
MAIN ROAD
SILVER ST
B1225
HIGH STREET
WASS LANE
BUTTERGATE HILL
MILL LANE
COW LANE
MINTING LANE
PINFOLD LANE
A158
A B C D E F
8 81 7 80 6 79 5 78 4 77 3 76 2 75 1 74
16 17 18 19 20 21
84
72

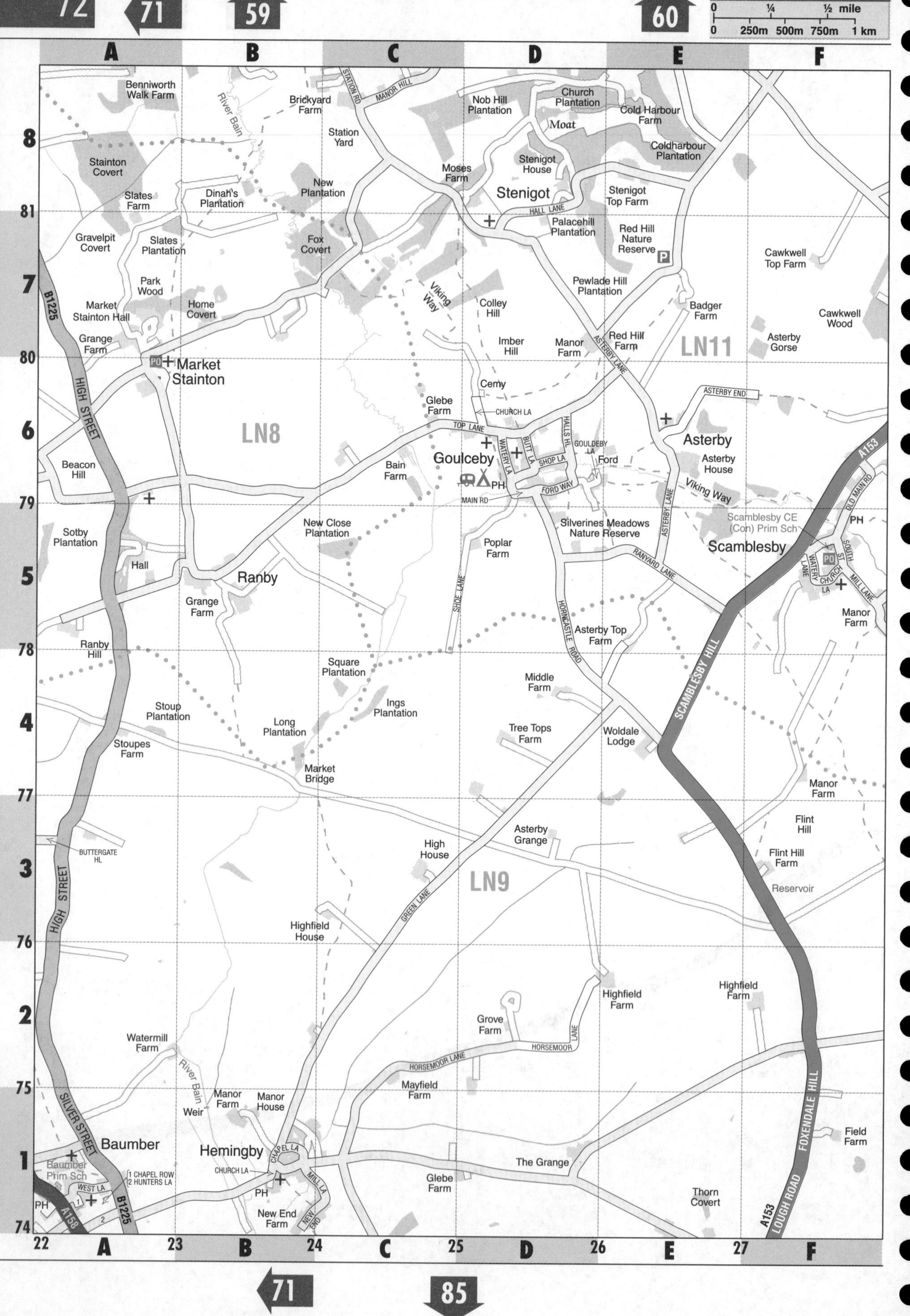

A   B   C   D   E   F

8
Benniworth Walk Farm
River Bain
Brickyard Farm
Station Yard
Manor Hill
Nob Hill Plantation
Church Plantation
Moat
Cold Harbour Farm
Coldharbour Plantation

81
Stainton Covert
Dinah's Plantation
New Plantation
Moses Farm
Stenigot House
Stenigot
HALL LANE
Stenigot Top Farm
Slates Farm

7
Gravelpit Covert
Slates Plantation
Fox Covert
Viking Way
Colley Hill
Palacehill Plantation
Red Hill Nature Reserve
Pewlade Hill Plantation
P
Cawkwell Top Farm
B1225
Park Wood
Market Stainton Hall
Home Covert
Badger Farm
Cawkwell Wood
Asterby Gorse

80
Grange Farm
PO
Market Stainton
Imber Hill
Manor Farm
Red Hill Farm
ASTERBY LANE
LN11
ASTERBY END

6
Beacon Hill
LN8
Glebe Farm
Cemy
CHURCH LA
TOP LANE
HALLS HILL
Goulceby
SHOP LA
GOULDEBY LA
Ford
Asterby
Asterby House
HIGH STREET
Bain Farm
WATERY LA
BUTT LA
PH
FORD WAY
Viking Way
Scamblesby CE (Con) Prim Sch

79
Sotby Plantation
New Close Plantation
MAIN RD
Silverines Meadows Nature Reserve
ASTERBY LANE
Scamblesby
OLD MAIN RD
A153
PH

5
Hall
Ranby
Grange Farm
SIDE LANE
Poplar Farm
RANYARD LANE
HORNCASTLE ROAD
SCAMBLESBY HILL
WATERY LA
CHURCH LA
PO
Manor Farm
SOUTH MILL LANE

78
Ranby Hill
Square Plantation
Asterby Top Farm

4
Stoup Plantation
Long Plantation
Ings Plantation
Middle Farm
Tree Tops Farm
Woldale Lodge
Manor Farm

77
Stoupes Farm
Market Bridge
Asterby Grange
Flint Hill
Flint Hill Farm
Reservoir

3
HIGH STREET
BUTTERGATE HL
High House
LN9
Highfield House
Highfield Farm
FOXENDALE HILL

76
GREEN LANE

2
Watermill Farm
Grove Farm
HORSEMOOR LANE
Mayfield Farm
Highfield Farm
Highfield Farm
Field Farm

75
River Bain
Manor Farm
Weir
Manor House
HORSEMOOR LANE
A153 LOUGH ROAD

1
SILVER STREET
Baumber
Baumber Prim Sch
PH
WEST LA
A158
B1225
Hemingby
CHAPEL LA
CHURCH LA
PH
1 CHAPEL ROW
2 HUNTERS LA
MILL LA
NEW END
New End Farm
Glebe Farm
The Grange
Thorn Covert

74
A158
A2
B1225

Scale: 1¾ inches to 1 mile

60 61 74

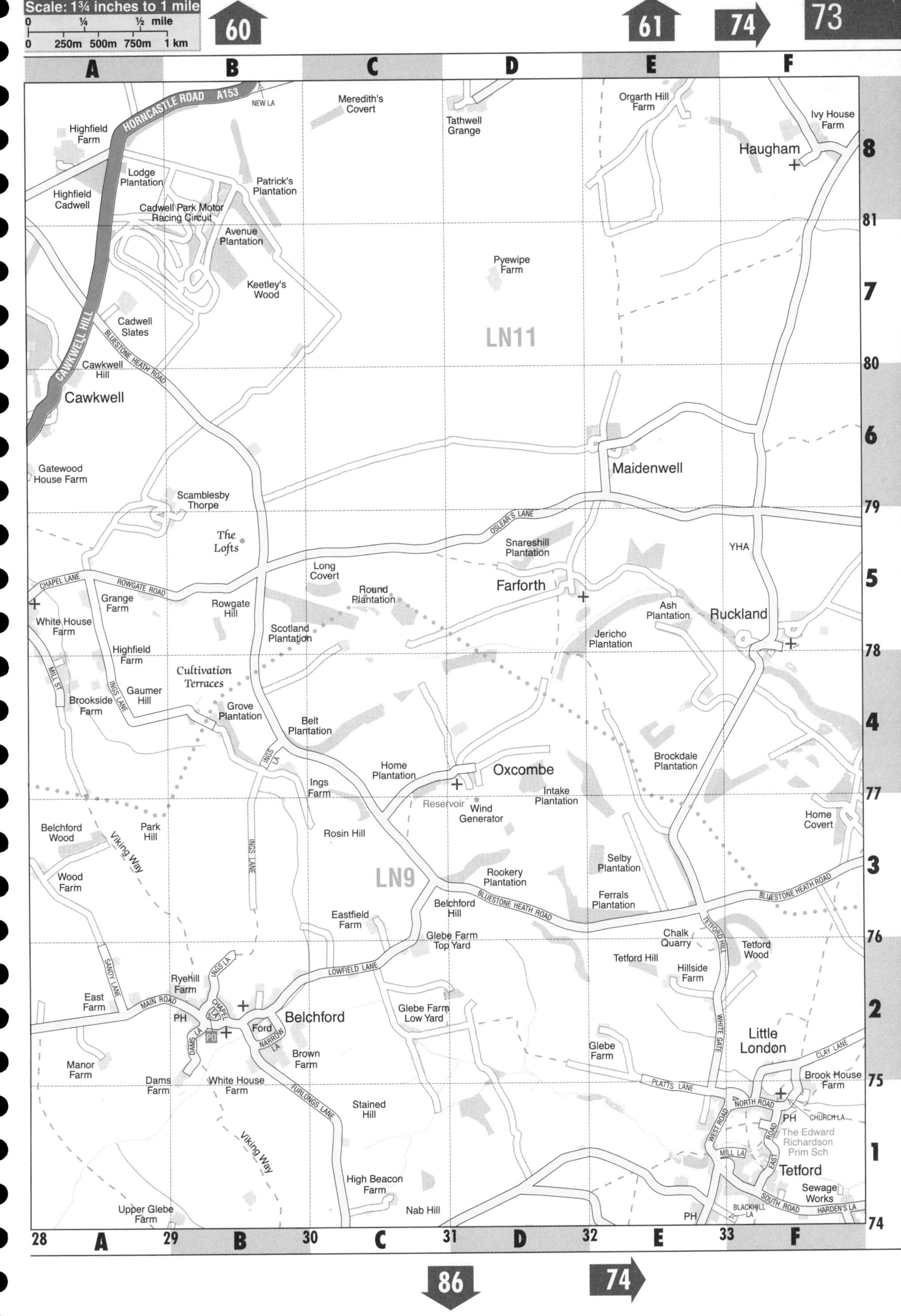

HORNCASTLE ROAD A153
NEW LA
Meredith's Covert
Tathwell Grange
Orgarth Hill Farm
Ivy House Farm
Haugham
Highfield Farm
Lodge Plantation
Patrick's Plantation
Highfield Cadwell
Cadwell Park Motor Racing Circuit
Avenue Plantation
Pyewipe Farm
Keetley's Wood
Cadwell Slates
CAWKWELL HILL
BLUESTONE HEATH ROAD
LN11
Cawkwell Hill
Cawkwell
Maidenwell
Gatewood House Farm
Scamblesby Thorpe
OSLEAR'S LANE
The Lofts
Snareshill Plantation
YHA
CHAPEL LANE
ROWGATE ROAD
Long Covert
Farforth
Grange Farm
Round Plantation
Rowgate Hill
Ash Plantation
Ruckland
White House Farm
Scotland Plantation
Jericho Plantation
Highfield Farm
MILL ST
Cultivation Terraces
Gaumer Hill
INGS LANE
Brookside Farm
Grove Plantation
Belt Plantation
Brockdale Plantation
INGS LA
Home Plantation
Oxcombe
Ings Farm
Intake Plantation
Reservoir
Wind Generator
Home Covert
Belchford Wood
Park Hill
Rosin Hill
Viking Way
INGS LANE
Selby Plantation
Wood Farm
LN9
Rookery Plantation
BLUESTONE HEATH ROAD
Ferrals Plantation
Belchford Hill
BLUESTONE HEATH ROAD
Eastfield Farm
Chalk Quarry
TETFORD HILL
Glebe Farm Top Yard
Tetford Wood
Tetford Hill
SANDY LANE
LOWFIELD LANE
Hillside Farm
INGS LA
Ryehill Farm
East Farm
MAIN ROAD
CHAPEL LA
Glebe Farm Low Yard
Belchford
PH
PO
Ford
NARROW LA
DAMS LA
WHITE GATE
Little London
CLAY LANE
Brown Farm
Manor Farm
Glebe Farm
Brook House Farm
Dams Farm
White House Farm
PLATTS LANE
NORTH ROAD
FURLONGS LANE
PH
CHURCH LA
Stained Hill
WEST ROAD
The Edward Richardson Prim Sch
MILL LA
EAST ROAD
Viking Way
Tetford
High Beacon Farm
Sewage Works
SOUTH ROAD
Upper Glebe Farm
Nab Hill
BLACKHILL LA
PH
HARDEN'S LA
A B C D E F
8 81 7 80 6 79 5 78 4 77 3 76 2 75 1 74
28 29 30 31 32 33

86 74

73 61 62

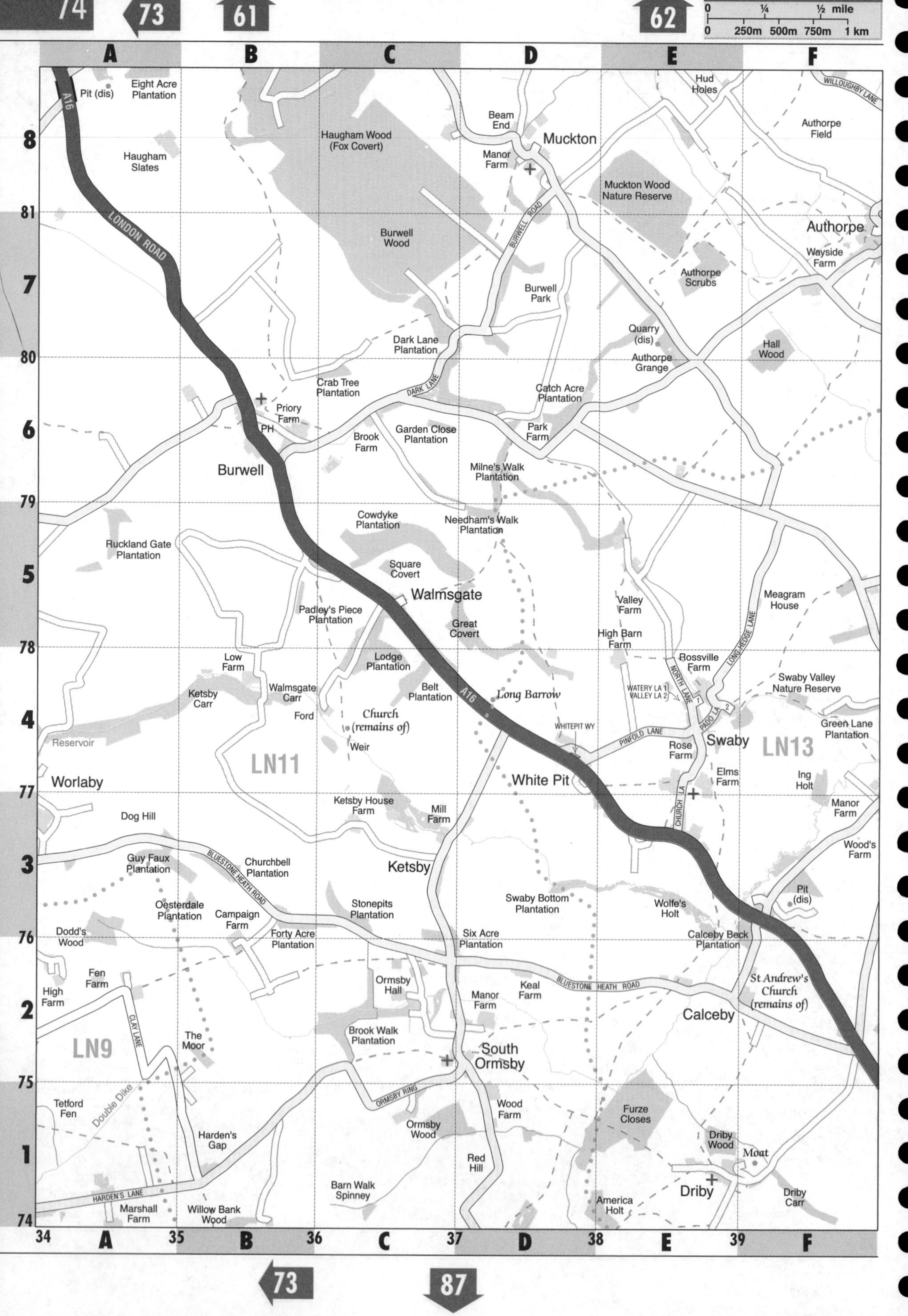
Scale: 1¾ inches to 1 mile
0 ¼ ½ mile
0 250m 500m 750m 1 km
A B C D E F
8
81
7
80
6
79
5
78
4
77
3
76
2
75
1
74
34 35 36 37 38 39
Pit (dis)
Eight Acre Plantation
A16
Haugham Slates
Haugham Wood (Fox Covert)
Beam End
Manor Farm
Muckton
Hud Holes
WILLOUGHBY LANE
Authorpe Field
Muckton Wood Nature Reserve
LONDON ROAD
Burwell Wood
BURWELL ROAD
Authorpe
Wayside Farm
Authorpe Scrubs
Burwell Park
Quarry (dis)
Dark Lane Plantation
Hall Wood
Authorpe Grange
Crab Tree Plantation
DARK LANE
Catch Acre Plantation
Priory Farm
PH
Brook Farm
Garden Close Plantation
Park Farm
Burwell
Milne's Walk Plantation
Cowdyke Plantation
Needham's Walk Plantation
Ruckland Gate Plantation
Square Covert
Walmsgate
Padley's Piece Plantation
Great Covert
Valley Farm
Meagram House
High Barn Farm
LONG HEDGE LANE
Low Farm
Lodge Plantation
Rossville Farm
NORTH LANE
Swaby Valley Nature Reserve
Ketsby Carr
Walmsgate Carr
Belt Plantation
Long Barrow
WATERY LA 1
VALLEY LA 2
PADO LA
Ford
Church (remains of)
WHITEPIT WY
PINFOLD LANE
Green Lane Plantation
Reservoir
Weir
Rose Farm
Swaby
LN13
LN11
White Pit
Elms Farm
Worlaby
Ing Holt
Ketsby House Farm
Mill Farm
CHURCH LA
Dog Hill
Manor Farm
Wood's Farm
Guy Faux Plantation
BLUESTONE HEATH ROAD
Churchbell Plantation
Ketsby
Pit (dis)
Oesterdale Plantation
Stonepits Plantation
Swaby Bottom Plantation
Wolfe's Holt
Campaign Farm
Dodd's Wood
Forty Acre Plantation
Six Acre Plantation
Calceby Beck Plantation
Fen Farm
Ormsby Hall
Keal Farm
BLUESTONE HEATH ROAD
St Andrew's Church (remains of)
High Farm
Manor Farm
CLAY LANE
Calceby
LN9
Brook Walk Plantation
The Moor
South Ormsby
Double Dike
ORMSBY RING
Tetford Fen
Wood Farm
Furze Closes
Ormsby Wood
Harden's Gap
Driby Wood
Moat
Red Hill
Barn Walk Spinney
Driby
Driby Carr
HARDEN'S LANE
America Holt
Marshall Farm
Willow Bank Wood

73 87

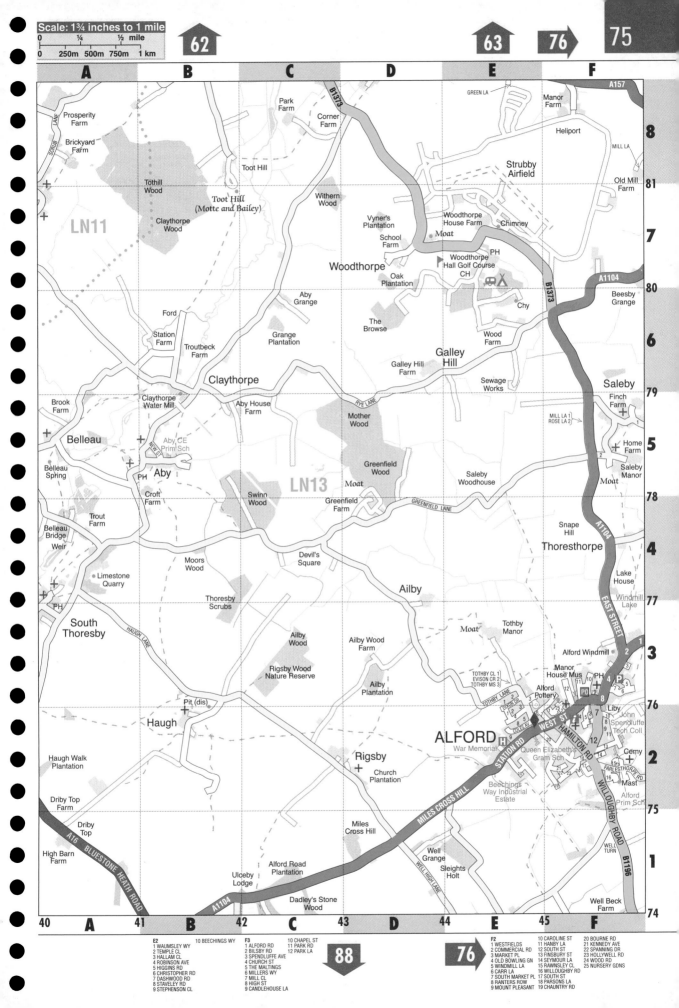

A157
LN11
Prosperity Farm
Brickyard Farm
SCRUB LANE
Toot Hill
Tothill Wood
Toot Hill (Motte and Bailey)
Claythorpe Wood
Park Farm
Corner Farm
B1373
Withern Wood
GREEN LA
Manor Farm
Heliport
MILL LA
Strubby Airfield
Old Mill Farm
Vyner's Plantation
Woodthorpe House Farm
Chimney
Moat
School Farm
Woodthorpe
Oak Plantation
Woodthorpe Hall Golf Course
PH
CH
Chy
A1104
Beesby Grange
Aby Grange
The Browse
Wood Farm
Galley Hill
Galley Hill Farm
Saleby
B1373
Ford
Station Farm
Troutbeck Farm
Claythorpe
Claythorpe Water Mill
Grange Plantation
RYE LANE
Sewage Works
Finch Farm
Brook Farm
Aby House Farm
Belleau
Aby CE Prim Sch
NEW ST
PH
Aby
Croft Farm
Mother Wood
LN13
Greenfield Wood
Moat
Saleby Woodhouse
MILL LA 1
ROSE LA 2
Home Farm
Saleby Manor
Moat
Belleau Spring
Trout Farm
Swinn Wood
Greenfield Farm
Greenfield Lane
GREENFIELD LANE
A1104
Belleau Bridge Weir
Limestone Quarry
PH
Moors Wood
Devil's Square
Snape Hill
Thoresthorpe
South Thoresby
HAUGH LANE
Thoresby Scrubs
Ailby
Lake House
Windmill Lake
Ailby Wood
Rigsby Wood Nature Reserve
Ailby Wood Farm
Moat
Tothby Manor
Alford Windmill
EAST STREET
Ailby Plantation
TOTHBY LANE
TOTHBY CL 1
EVISON CR 2
TOTHBY MS 3
DIXON DR
Manor House Mus
Alford Pottery
PO
PH
P
Liby
John Spendluffe Tech Coll
Pit (dis)
Haugh
Rigsby
Church Plantation
ALFORD
War Memorial
H
STATION RD
WEST ST
HAMILTON RD
COLES AV
Queen Elizabeth's Gram Sch
Cemy
Mast
FARLESTHORPE RD
Alford Prim Sch
Haugh Walk Plantation
Beechings Way Industrial Estate
WILLOUGHBY ROAD
Driby Top Farm
Driby Top
MILES CROSS HILL
Ulceby Lodge
Alford Road Plantation
Miles Cross Hill
Well Grange
WELL HIGH LANE
Sleights Holt
WELL TURN
High Barn Farm
A16 BLUESTONE HEATH ROAD
A1104
Dadley's Stone Wood
B1196
Well Beck Farm

E2
1 WAUMSLEY WY
2 TEMPLE CL
3 HALLAM CL
4 ROBINSON AVE
5 HIGGINS RD
6 CHRISTOPHER RD
7 DASHWOOD RD
8 STAVELEY RD
9 STEPHENSON CL
10 BEECHINGS WY

F3
1 ALFORD RD
2 BILSBY RD
3 SPENDLUFFE AVE
4 CHURCH ST
5 THE MALTINGS
6 MILLERS WY
7 MILL CL
8 HIGH ST
9 CANDLEHOUSE LA
10 CHAPEL ST
11 PARK RD
12 PARK LA

F2
1 WESTFIELDS
2 COMMERCIAL RD
3 MARKET PL
4 OLD BOWLING GN
5 WINDMILL LA
6 CARR LA
7 SOUTH MARKET PL
8 RANTERS ROW
9 MOUNT PLEASANT
10 CAROLINE ST
11 HANBY LA
12 SOUTH ST
13 FINSBURY ST
14 SEYMOUR LA
15 RAWNSLEY CL
16 WILLOUGHBY RD
17 SOUTH ST
18 PARSONS LA
19 CHAUNTRY RD
20 BOURNE RD
21 KENNEDY AVE
22 SPANNING DR
23 HOLLYWELL RD
24 WOOD RD
25 NURSERY GDNS

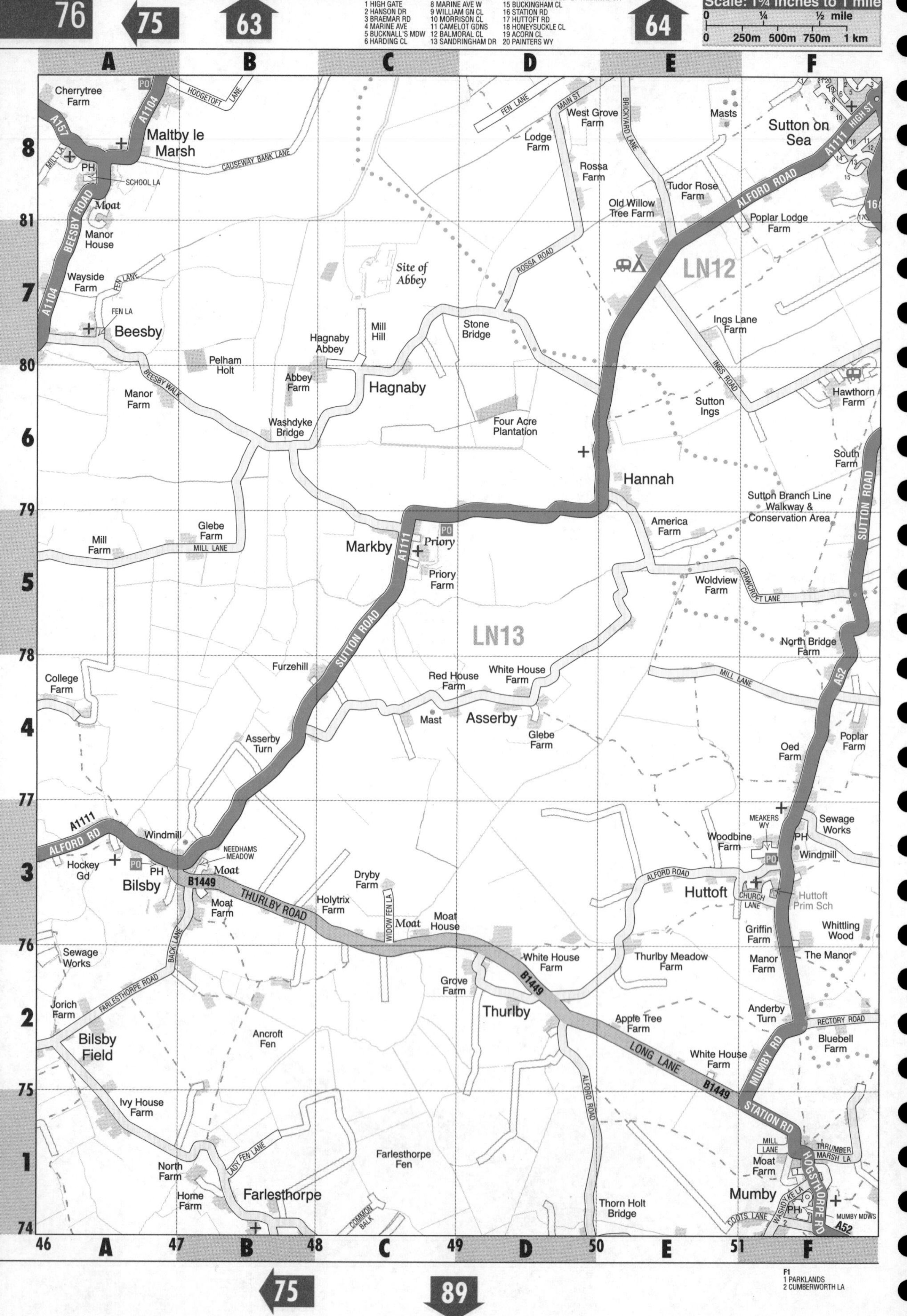

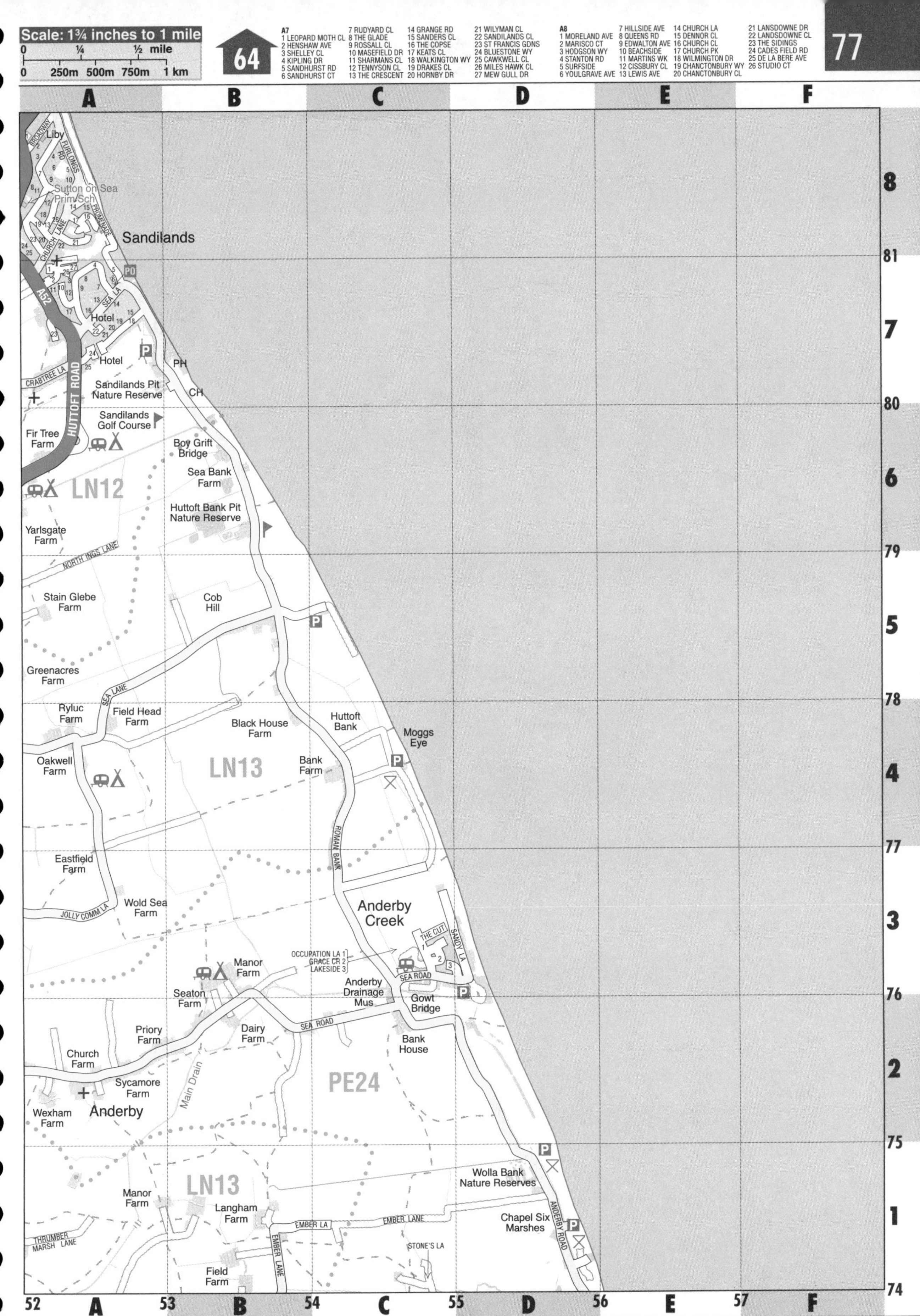

Scale: 1¾ inches to 1 mile
0 ¼ ½ mile
0 250m 500m 750m 1 km
64
A7
1 LEOPARD MOTH CL
2 HENSHAW AVE
3 SHELLEY CL
4 KIPLING DR
5 SANDHURST RD
6 SANDHURST CT
7 RUDYARD CL
8 THE GLADE
9 ROSSALL CL
10 MASEFIELD DR
11 SHARMANS CL
12 TENNYSON CL
13 THE CRESCENT
14 GRANGE RD
15 SANDERS CL
16 THE COPSE
17 KEATS CL
18 WALKINGTON WY
19 DRAKES CL
20 HORNBY DR
21 WILYMAN CL
22 SANDILANDS CL
23 ST FRANCIS GDNS
24 BLUESTONE WY
25 CAWKWELL CL
26 MILES HAWK CL
27 MEW GULL DR
A8
1 MORELAND AVE
2 MARISCO CT
3 HODGSON WY
4 STANTON RD
5 SURFSIDE
6 YOULGRAVE AVE
7 HILLSIDE AVE
8 QUEENS RD
9 EDWALTON AVE
10 BEACHSIDE
11 MARTINS WK
12 CISSBURY CL
13 LEWIS AVE
14 CHURCH LA
15 DENNOR CL
16 CHURCH CL
17 CHURCH PK
18 WILMINGTON DR
19 CHANCTONBURY WY
20 CHANCTONBURY CL
21 LANSDOWNE DR
22 LANDSDOWNE CL
23 THE SIDINGS
24 CADES FIELD RD
25 DE LA BERE AVE
26 STUDIO CT
A B C D E F
8 81 7 80 6 79 5 78 4 77 3 76 2 75 1 74
Liby
BROADWAY
FURLONGS RD
Sutton on Sea Prim Sch
PROMENADE
CHURCH LANE
Sandilands
A52
SEA LA
Hotel
Hotel
PH
CH
CRABTREE LA
HUTTOFT ROAD
Sandilands Pit Nature Reserve
Sandilands Golf Course
Fir Tree Farm
Boy Grift Bridge
Sea Bank Farm
LN12
Huttoft Bank Pit Nature Reserve
Yarlsgate Farm
NORTH INGS LANE
Stain Glebe Farm
Cob Hill
Greenacres Farm
SEA LANE
Ryluc Farm
Field Head Farm
Black House Farm
Huttoft Bank
Moggs Eye
Oakwell Farm
LN13
Bank Farm
ROMAN BANK
Eastfield Farm
Wold Sea Farm
JOLLY COMM LA
Anderby Creek
THE CUT
SANDY LA
OCCUPATION LA 1
GRACE CR 2
LAKESIDE 3
Manor Farm
SEA ROAD
Seaton Farm
Anderby Drainage Mus
Gowt Bridge
Priory Farm
Dairy Farm
SEA ROAD
Bank House
Church Farm
Main Drain
PE24
Sycamore Farm
Wexham Farm
Anderby
Wolla Bank Nature Reserves
LN13
Manor Farm
Langham Farm
Chapel Six Marshes
ANDERBY ROAD
EMBER LA
EMBER LANE
THRUMBER MARSH LANE
EMBER LANE
STONE'S LA
Field Farm
52 A 53 B 54 C 55 D 56 E 57 F

90

A   B   C   D   E   F

8

ROMAN FORT

Roberts Farm
Ragnall
Chestnut Farm

A1133

A57

60

SOUTHMOOR RD

LN1

Lodge Farm
Thorney Gate Farm
Road Wood
ROADWOOD LANE

WEST ROAD

73

NG22

Trent Valley Way

North Clifton

California Farm

Westwood Farm

West Wood

Thorney

MAIN STREET

Firs Farm

7

Fledborough

Trentholme Farm
BACK LA
SILVER ST
Riverbank Farm

CHURCH LANE

HIGH ST

MILL LANE

Lounds Farm
Hall Farm

Northfield Farm

NORTHFIELD LA

NORTHFIELD

MILL LANE

Hawthorn Farm

Brownwood Farm

72

Manor House

The Hall

COTTAGE LA

MILL LANE

MOOR LANE

Carr Wood

Moor Farm

Moor Farm

Carr Farm

Fledborough House

Trent Viaduct
Sewage Works
Sewage Works

North Clifton Prim Sch

WHEATHOLME LANE

Moor Farm

MOOR LANE

6

LC's

Church Farm

Clifton Plantation

Wheatholme Farm

South Clifton Moor

BIRKLAND LANE

PARK LANE

Manor Farm

Mast

71

P
Chy's

High Marnham Power Station

SPARROW LANE

CHURCH LANE

Manor Farm

BACK ST

FRONT ST

South Clifton

VICARAGE LANE

Birkland Farm

Rome Farm

Wigsley Wood

Wigsley

Mill Lane Farm

MILL LANE

5

HOLLOWGATE LANE

Hill Farm

PH

TRENT LANE

River Trent

HIGH ST

PH

COAL YARD LANE

Clifton Hill

NG23

Hazelnut Farm

70

High Marnham

Low Marnham

Manor Farm

Spalford

CHAPEL LA

Manor Farm

EAGLE ROAD

GRACEFIELD LA

Holme Farm

Church Farm

HOLME LA

Trent Valley Way

White Thorn Farm

4

69

Holly Farm

Field Farm

Home Farm

Windmill Farm

SPALFORD ROAD

Low Moor Farm

Broomhills Farm

HOPYARD LA

BROTTS RD

MEADOW LANE

HOLME LANE

Grange Farm

Girton Grange

P

RABBITHILL LANE

Sand & Gravel Pit

Whitfield Farm

WIGSLEY ROAD

3

Oaktree Farm

Manor Farm

68

Normanton Holme

GREEN LANE

MEADOW LA

Spalford Warren Nature Reserve

White Gate Farm

Housham Farm

SPALFORD LANE

Field House Farm

LN6

2

HOLME LANE

Sand & Gravel Pit

Highfield Farm

NEW LANE

Tomkin's Farm

North Scarle

CHAPEL LANE

HIVES LANE

Hunt's Bridge

North Scarle Prim Sch

SCHOOL LANE

PH

P

EAGLE ROAD

Mill House Farm

67

INGRAM LANE

North Holme

TRENT LANE

A1133 GAINSBOROUGH ROAD

HIGH ST

GREEN LANE

Sandy Croft Farm

GIRTON LANE

Cemy

EYRE'S LA

HIGH ST

SOUTH SCARLE LANE

Eastfield Farm

SWINDERBY ROAD

Clog Bridge

North Scarle Miniature Railway

1

1 BULHAM LA
2 CHURCH ST

Cemy

Smithy Marsh

Weecar

Baxter Bridge

Humberlands Farm

Poplar Farm

BESTHORPE ROAD

CHURCH LA 1
BLACKSMITHS LA 2

EYRE'S LA

66

WEST LA 1
PROCTERS DR 2

Girton

80   A   81   B   82   C   83   D   84   E   85   F

Nottinghamshire STREET ATLAS

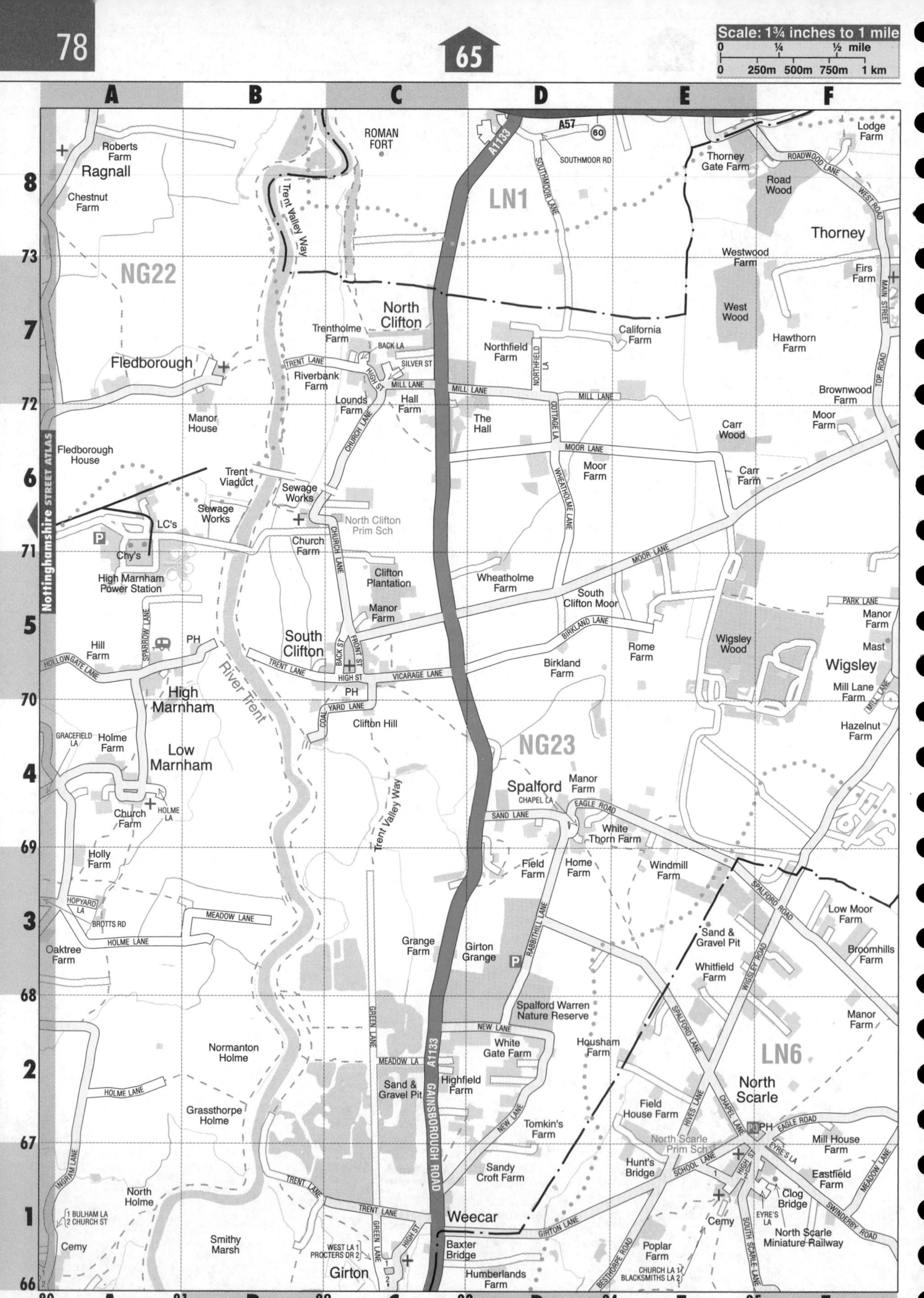

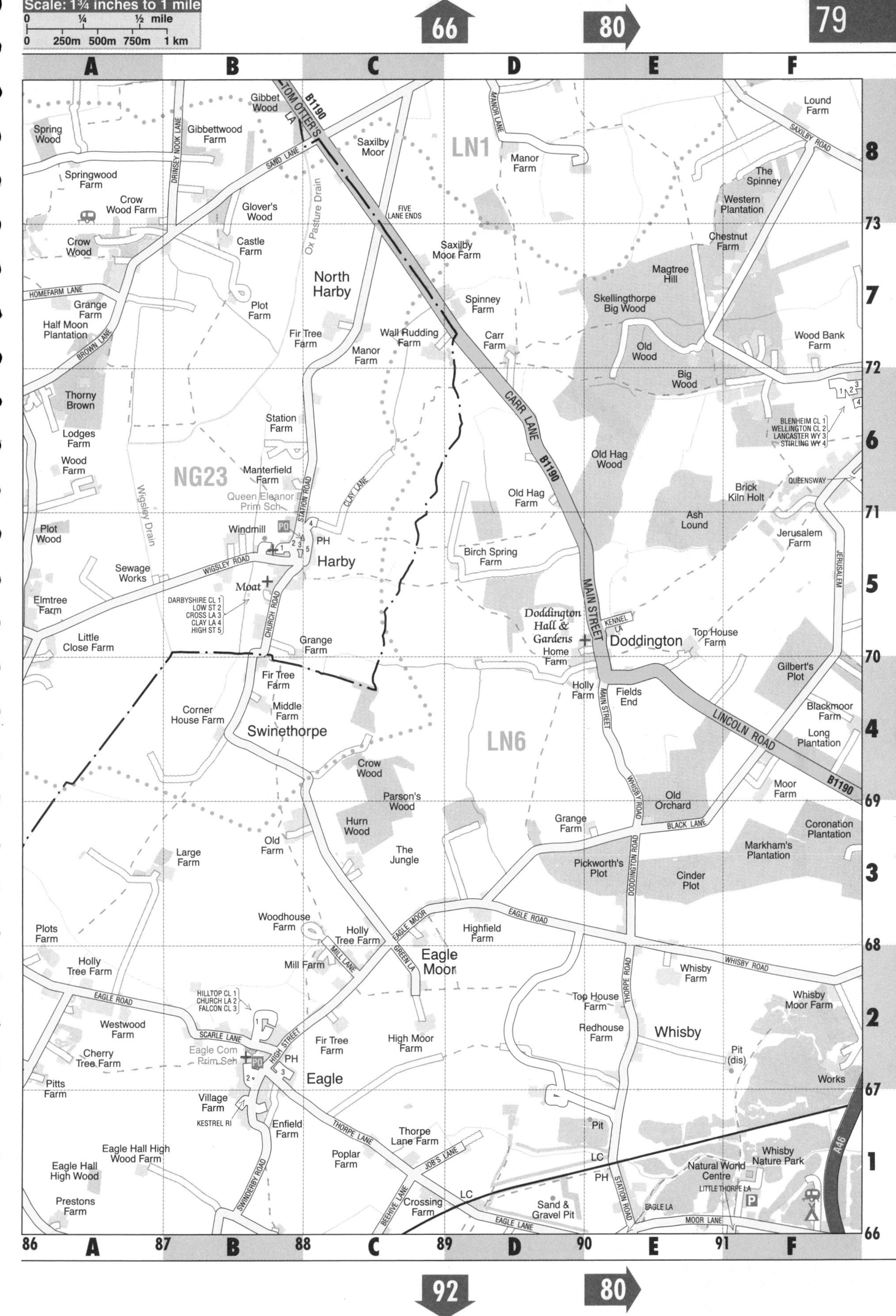
Scale: 1¾ inches to 1 mile
66
80
Gibbet Wood
Spring Wood
Gibbettwood Farm
TOM OTTER'S LA
B1190
Saxilby Moor
LN1
Manor Farm
Lound Farm
The Spinney
Western Plantation
Springwood Farm
Crow Wood Farm
Glover's Wood
FIVE LANE ENDS
Crow Wood
Castle Farm
Ox Pasture Drain
Saxilby Moor Farm
Chestnut Farm
Magtree Hill
North Harby
Grange Farm
Half Moon Plantation
Plot Farm
Skellingthorpe Big Wood
Spinney Farm
Fir Tree Farm
Wall Rudding Farm
Manor Farm
Carr Farm
Old Wood
Wood Bank Farm
Big Wood
Thorny Brown
Lodges Farm
Station Farm
CARR LANE
BLENHEIM CL 1
WELLINGTON CL 2
LANCASTER WY 3
STIRLING WY 4
Wood Farm
NG23
Manterfield Farm
Old Hag Wood
Queen Eleanor Prim Sch
Wigsley Drain
CLAY LANE
Old Hag Farm
Brick Kiln Holt
QUEENSWAY
Plot Wood
Windmill
PO
PH
Ash Lound
Jerusalem Farm
Sewage Works
WIGSLEY ROAD
Harby
Birch Spring Farm
Moat
Elmtree Farm
DARBYSHIRE CL 1
LOW ST 2
CROSS LA 3
CLAY LA 4
HIGH ST 5
CHURCH ROAD
Doddington Hall & Gardens
MAIN STREET
KENNEL LA
Doddington
Top House Farm
Little Close Farm
Grange Farm
Home Farm
Gilbert's Plot
Fir Tree Farm
Holly Farm
Fields End
Corner House Farm
Middle Farm
Blackmoor Farm
Swinethorpe
LN6
LINCOLN ROAD
Long Plantation
Crow Wood
Parson's Wood
Old Orchard
Moor Farm
B1190
Hurn Wood
Grange Farm
BLACK LANE
Coronation Plantation
Large Farm
Old Farm
The Jungle
Pickworth's Plot
Markham's Plantation
Cinder Plot
DODDINGTON ROAD
Woodhouse Farm
Highfield Farm
EAGLE ROAD
Plots Farm
Holly Tree Farm
EAGLE MOOR
Holly Tree Farm
Mill Farm
MILL LANE
GREEN LA
Eagle Moor
Whisby Farm
WHISBY ROAD
EAGLE ROAD
HILLTOP CL 1
CHURCH LA 2
FALCON CL 3
Top House Farm
THORPE ROAD
Whisby Moor Farm
Westwood Farm
SCARLE LANE
Redhouse Farm
Whisby
Cherry Tree Farm
Fir Tree Farm
High Moor Farm
Pit (dis)
Eagle Com Prim Sch
HIGH STREET
Eagle
Works
Pitts Farm
Village Farm
KESTREL RI
Enfield Farm
Pit
THORPE LANE
Thorpe Lane Farm
A46
Eagle Hall High Wood Farm
Poplar Farm
LC
Whisby Nature Park
Eagle Hall High Wood
SWINDERBY ROAD
JOB'S LANE
PH
Natural World Centre
LITTLE THORPE LA
Prestons Farm
BEEHIVE LANE
Crossing Farm
LC
Sand & Gravel Pit
STATION ROAD
EAGLE LA
MOOR LANE
EAGLE LANE
A B C D E F
86 87 88 89 90 91
66 67 68 69 70 71 72 73
1 2 3 4 5 6 7 8
92
80

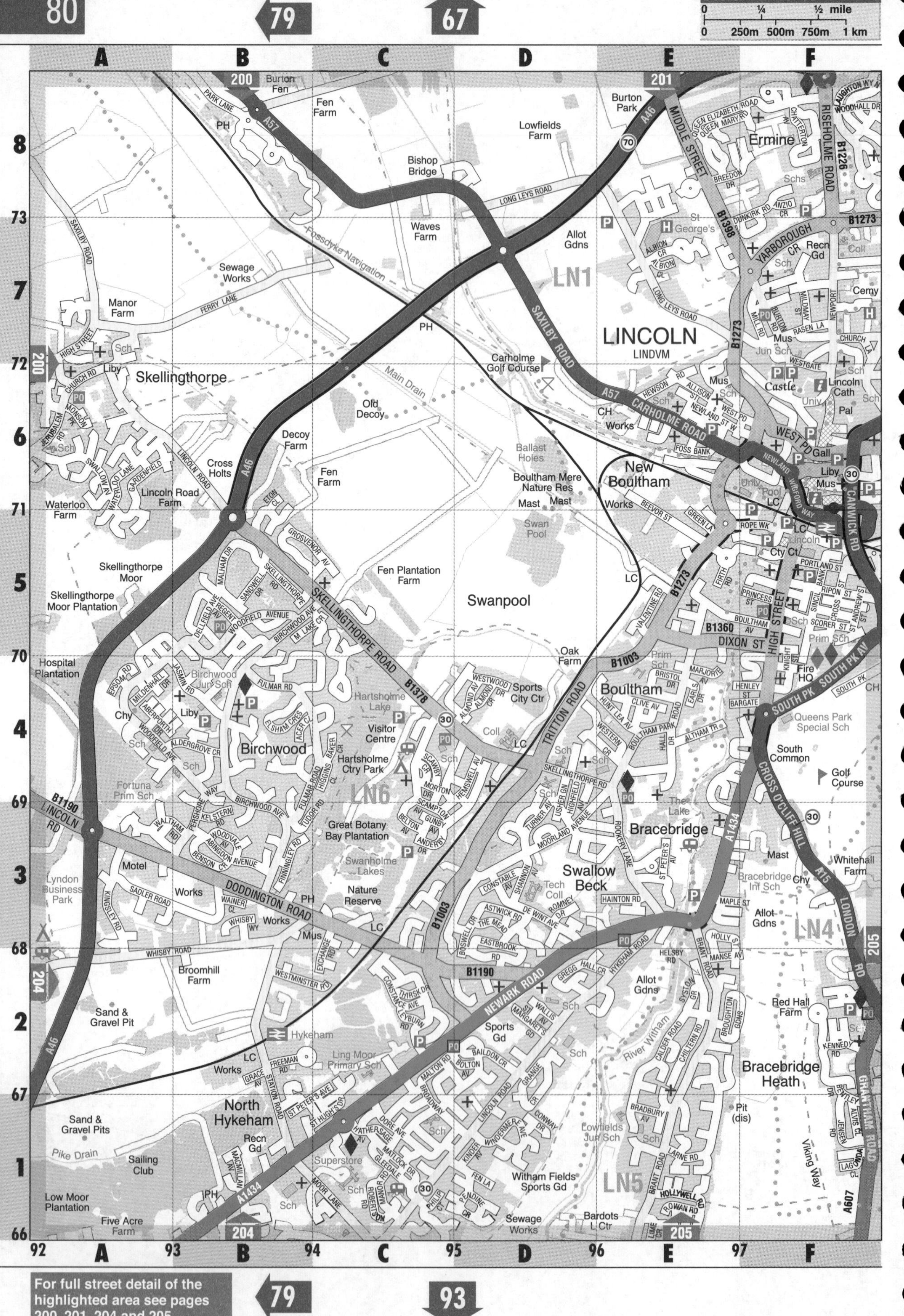

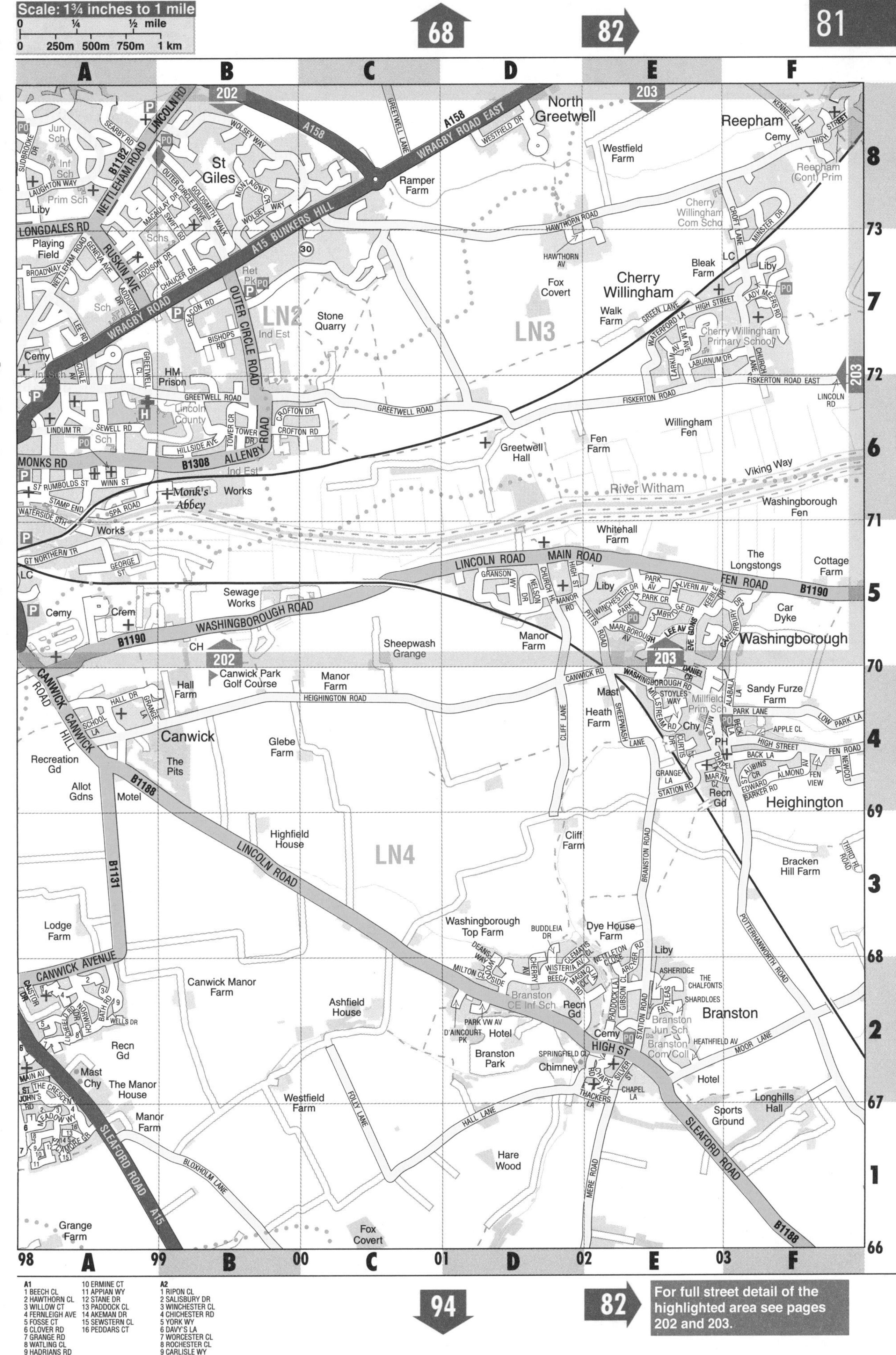

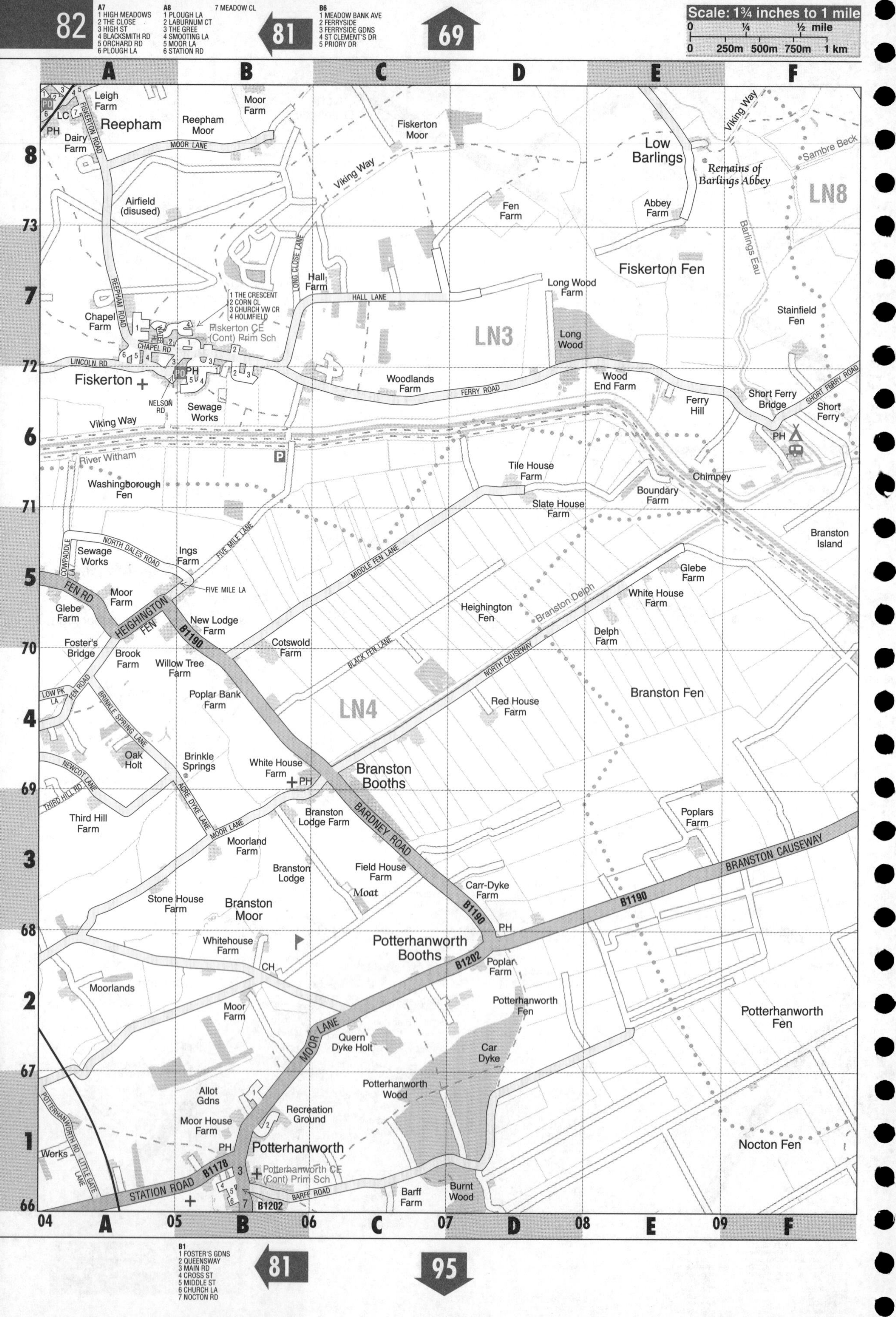

82

A7
1 HIGH MEADOWS
2 THE CLOSE
3 HIGH ST
4 BLACKSMITH'S
5 ORCHARD RD
6 PLOUGH LA

A8
1 PLOUGH LA
2 LABURNUM CT
3 THE GREE
4 SMOOTING LA
5 MOOR LA
6 STATION RD

7 MEADOW CL

B6
1 MEADOW BANK AVE
2 FERRYSIDE
3 FERRYSIDE GDNS
4 ST CLEMENT'S DR
5 PRIORY DR

81

69

Scale: 1¾ inches to 1 mile
0   ¼   ½   mile
0   250m 500m 750m 1 km

A   B   C   D   E   F

Leigh Farm
Reepham
Moor Farm
Reepham Moor
PO
LC
PH
Dairy Farm
MOOR LANE

Fiskerton Moor
Viking Way

Low Barlings
Remains of Barlings Abbey
Sambre Beck
LN8

8

Airfield (disused)
Fen Farm
Fiskerton Fen
Abbey Farm
Barlings Eau
Stainfield Fen

73

REEPHAM ROAD
LONG CLOSE LANE
Hall Farm
HALL LANE
Hall Lane

LN3
Long Wood Farm
Long Wood
Wood End Farm
Ferry Hill
Short Ferry Bridge
Short Ferry
SHORT FERRY ROAD

7

Chapel Farm
1 THE CRESCENT
2 CORN CL
3 CHURCH VW CR
4 HOLMFIELD
Fiskerton CE (Cont) Prim Sch
LINCOLN RD
CHAPEL RD
Woodlands Farm
FERRY ROAD
Ferry Road

72

Fiskerton
NELSON RD
PH
Sewage Works
Viking Way
Tile House Farm
Boundary Farm
Chimney
PH

6

River Witham
P
Slate House Farm
Branston Island

71

Washingborough Fen
NORTH DALES ROAD
Ings Farm
FIVE MILE LANE
MIDDLE FEN LANE
Heighington Fen
Branston Delph
Glebe Farm
White House Farm

5

COWPADDLE LA
Sewage Works
Moor Farm
FIVE MILE LA
New Lodge Farm
Heighington Fen
Delph Farm

FEN RD
HEIGHINGTON FEN
Glebe Farm
B1190
Cotswold Farm
BLACK FEN LANE
NORTH CAUSEWAY
Branston Fen

70

Foster's Bridge
Brook Farm
Willow Tree Farm
Poplar Bank Farm
Red House Farm

LOW PK LA
FEN ROAD
BRINKLE SPRING LANE
LN4

4

NEWCOT LANE
Oak Holt
Brinkle Springs
White House Farm PH
Branston Booths
Poplars Farm

69

THIRD HILL RD
Third Hill Farm
ACRE DYKE LANE
MOOR LANE
Branston Lodge Farm
BARDNEY ROAD
BRANSTON CAUSEWAY

3

Stone House Farm
Moorland Farm
Branston Lodge
Field House Farm
Moat
Branston Moor
Carr-Dyke Farm
PH
B1190
B1190

68

Whitehouse Farm
CH
Potterhanworth Booths
B1202
Poplar Farm

Moorlands
Moor Farm
Potterhanworth Fen
Potterhanworth Fen

2

MOOR LANE
Quern Dyke Holt
Car Dyke

Allot Gdns
Recreation Ground
Potterhanworth Wood

67

POTTERHANWORTH RD
LITTLE GATE LANE
Moor House Farm
PH
Nocton Fen

Works
B1178
Potterhanworth
Potterhanworth CE (Cont) Prim Sch
Burnt Wood

1

STATION ROAD
BARFF ROAD
Barff Farm
B1202

66

04   A   05   B   06   C   07   D   08   E   09   F

B1
1 FOSTER'S GDNS
2 QUEENSWAY
3 MAIN RD
4 CROSS ST
5 MIDDLE ST
6 CHURCH LA
7 NOCTON RD

81

95

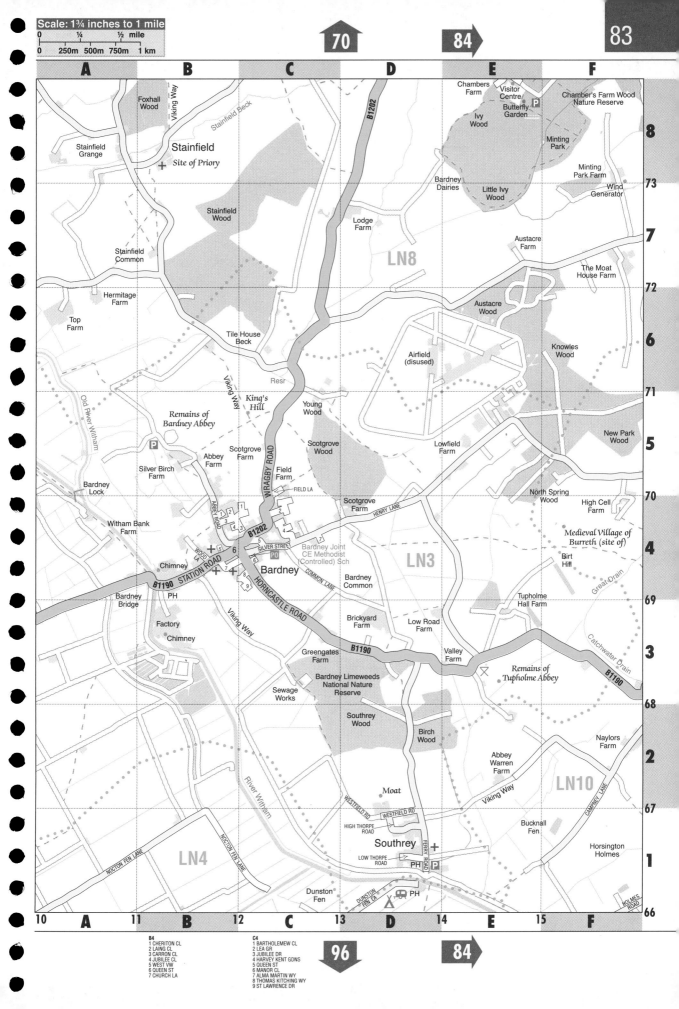

A   B   C   D   E   F

8
73
7
72
6
71
5
70
4
69
3
68
2
67
1
66

Foxhall Wood
Viking Way
Stainfield Grange
Stainfield Beck
Stainfield
+ Site of Priory
Stainfield Wood
Stainfield Common
Hermitage Farm
Top Farm
Tile House Beck
Viking Way
Resr
King's Hill
Young Wood
Remains of Bardney Abbey
Scotgrove Farm
Scotgrove Wood
Abbey Farm
Silver Birch Farm
Bardney Lock
Witham Bank Farm
Old River Witham
Chimney
WOOD
B1190   STATION ROAD
Bardney Bridge
PH
Factory
Chimney
Bardney
Viking Way
ABBEY ROAD
WRAGBY ROAD
FIELD LA
Field Farm
B1202
SILVER STREET
Bardney Joint CE Methodist (Controlled) Sch
HORNCASTLE ROAD
COMMON LANE
Scotgrove Farm
HENRY LANE
Bardney Common
Brickyard Farm
Low Road Farm
Greengates Farm
B1190
Bardney Limeweeds National Nature Reserve
Sewage Works
Southrey Wood
Birch Wood
Moat
River Witham
WESTFIELD RD
WESTFIELD RD
HIGH THORPE ROAD
Southrey
LOW THORPE ROAD
PH
FERRY ROAD
P
+
Dunston Fen
DUNSTON FEN LA
PH
NOCTON FEN LANE
NOCTON FEN LANE
LN4

B1202
LN8
Lodge Farm
Chambers Farm
Visitor Centre
P
Butterfly Garden
Chamber's Farm Wood Nature Reserve
Ivy Wood
Minting Park
Bardney Dairies
Little Ivy Wood
Minting Park Farm
Wind Generator
Austacre Farm
The Moat House Farm
Austacre Wood
Airfield (disused)
Knowles Wood
Lowfield Farm
New Park Wood
North Spring Wood
High Cell Farm
Scotgrove Farm
LN3
Medieval Village of Burreth (site of)
Birt Hill
Great Drain
Tupholme Hall Farm
Valley Farm
Remains of Tupholme Abbey
Catchwater Drain
B1190
Naylors Farm
Abbey Warren Farm
Viking Way
LN10
CAMPNEY LANE
Bucknall Fen
Horsington Holmes
Abbey Warren Farm
HOLMES ROAD

B4
1 CHERITON CL
2 LAING CL
3 CARRON CL
4 JUBILEE CL
5 WEST VW
6 QUEEN ST
7 CHURCH LA

C4
1 BARTHOLEMEW CL
2 LEA GR
3 JUBILEE DR
4 HARVEY KENT GDNS
5 QUEEN ST
6 MANOR CL
7 ALMA MARTIN WY
8 THOMAS KITCHING WY
9 ST LAWRENCE DR

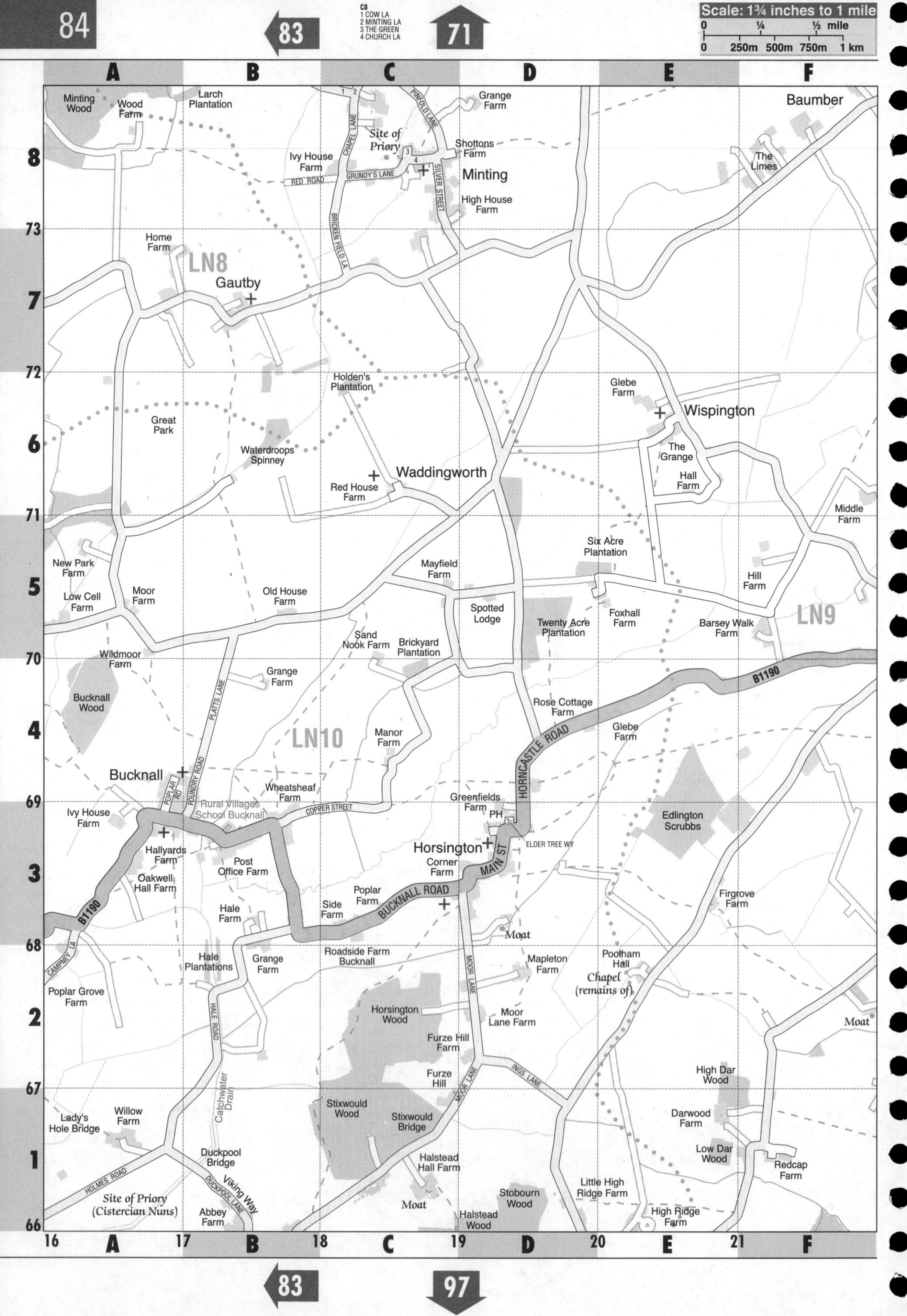
Minting Wood
Wood Farm
Larch Plantation
Ivy House Farm
Site of Priory
Grange Farm
Shottons Farm
Minting
High House Farm
Baumber
The Limes
Home Farm
LN8
Gautby
Holden's Plantation
Great Park
Waterdroops Spinney
Glebe Farm
Wispington
The Grange
Hall Farm
Red House Farm
Waddingworth
Middle Farm
New Park Farm
Low Cell Farm
Moor Farm
Old House Farm
Mayfield Farm
Six Acre Plantation
Hill Farm
Spotted Lodge
Foxhall Farm
Twenty Acre Plantation
Barsey Walk Farm
LN9
Wildmoor Farm
Sand Nook Farm
Brickyard Plantation
Bucknall Wood
Grange Farm
Rose Cottage Farm
Glebe Farm
LN10
Manor Farm
Bucknall
Wheatsheaf Farm
Greenfields Farm
Ivy House Farm
Rural Villages School Bucknall
PH
Edlington Scrubbs
Horsington
Hallyards Farm
Corner Farm
Post Office Farm
Oakwell Hall Farm
Poplar Farm
Firgrove Farm
Side Farm
Hale Farm
Moat
Roadside Farm Bucknall
Hale Plantations
Grange Farm
Mapleton Farm
Poolham Hall
Chapel (remains of)
Poplar Grove Farm
Horsington Wood
Moor Lane Farm
Moat
Furze Hill Farm
Furze Hill
High Dar Wood
Lady's Hole Bridge
Willow Farm
Stixwould Wood
Stixwould Bridge
Darwood Farm
Low Dar Wood
Duckpool Bridge
Halstead Hall Farm
Redcap Farm
Viking Way
Stobourn Wood
Little High Ridge Farm
Site of Priory (Cistercian Nuns)
Abbey Farm
Moat
Halstead Wood
High Ridge Farm
PINFOLD LANE
CHAPEL LANE
RED ROAD
GRUNDY'S LANE
SILVER STREET
BRICKEN FIELD LA
PLATTS LANE
ROUNDRY ROAD
POPLAR RD
COPPER STREET
HORNCASTLE ROAD
B1190
ELDER TREE WY
MAIN ST
BUCKNALL ROAD
CAMPNEY LA
MOOR LANE
HALE ROAD
Catchwater Drain
INGS LANE
HOLMES ROAD
DUCKPOOL LANE
A B C D E F
8 73 7 72 6 71 5 70 4 69 3 68 2 67 1 66
16 17 18 19 20 21

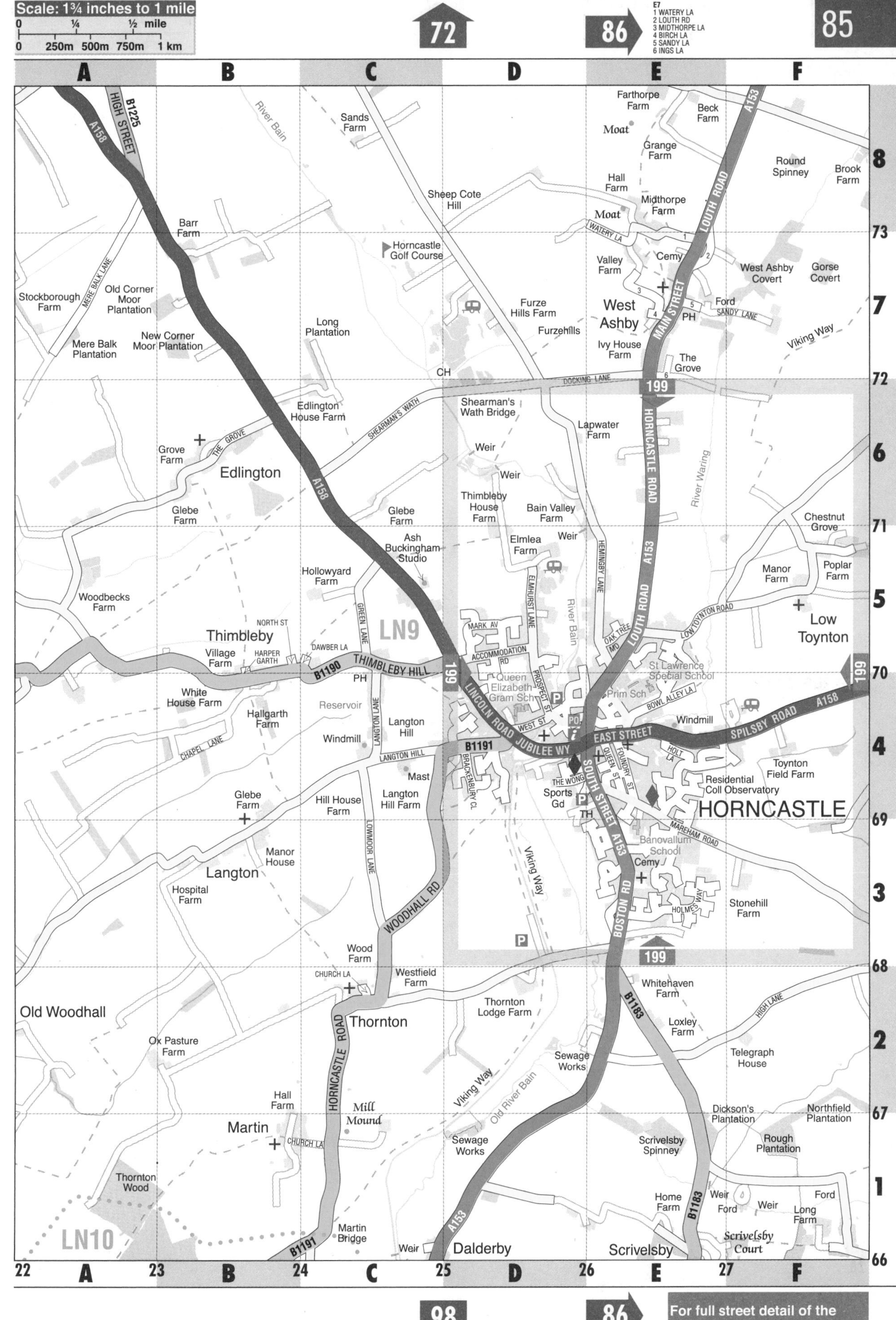

Scale: 1¾ inches to 1 mile

0   ¼   ½   mile
0 250m 500m 750m 1 km

72

86

85

E7
1 WATERY LA
2 LOUTH RD
3 MIDTHORPE LA
4 BIRCH LA
5 SANDY LA
6 INGS LA

A   B   C   D   E   F

8
73
7
72
6
71
5
70
4
69
3
68
2
67
1
66

Farthorpe Farm
Moat
Beck Farm
Grange Farm
Round Spinney
Brook Farm
Hall Farm
Midthorpe Farm
Moat
Watery La
Cemy
West Ashby Covert
Gorse Covert
Valley Farm
West Ashby
Ford
Viking Way
Furze Hills Farm
Furzehills
Ivy House Farm
The Grove
Main Street
Horncastle Road
River Waring
Chestnut Grove
Manor Farm
Poplar Farm
Low Toynton

B1225
A158 High Street

Barr Farm

Sands Farm

Sheep Cote Hill

Horncastle Golf Course

Stockborough Farm
Mere Balk Lane
Old Corner Moor Plantation
New Corner Moor Plantation
Mere Balk Plantation

Long Plantation

CH
Shearman's Wath
Docking Lane
199

Shearman's Wath Bridge
Lapwater Farm
Weir
Weir
Thimbleby House Farm
Bain Valley Farm
Weir

Edlington House Farm
The Grove
Grove Farm
Edlington
A158
Glebe Farm
Glebe Farm
Ash Buckingham Studio
Elmlea Farm
Elmhurst Lane
River Bain

Woodbecks Farm

Hollowyard Farm
LN9
Thimbleby
North St
Dawber La
Harper Garth
B1190 Thimbleby Hill
PH
Green Lane
Langton Lane
Reservoir
Langton Hill
Windmill
Langton Hill Farm
Mast
199
Lincoln Road
Accommodation Rd
Mark Av
Queen Elizabeth Gram Sch
West St
Prospect St
St Lawrence Special School
Oak Tree
Low Toynton Road
Manor Farm
Low Toynton

Village Farm
White House Farm
Hallgarth Farm
Chapel Lane
Glebe Farm
Langton
Manor House
Hill House Farm
Lowmoor Lane
Woodhall Rd
Brackenbury Cl
B1191
The Wong
Sports Gd
South Street A153
i
East Street
Jubilee Wy
PO
Foundry St
Queen St
Holt La
Spilsby Road A158
Windmill
Bowl Alley La
Prim Sch
199
A158
Toynton Field Farm
Residential Coll Observatory
HORNCASTLE

Hospital Farm
Wood Farm
Church La
Westfield Farm
Viking Way
Boston Rd
A153
Mareham Road
Banovallum School
Cemy
Stonehill Farm
Holmes Way

Old Woodhall
Ox Pasture Farm
Horncastle Road
Thornton
Thornton Lodge Farm
B1183
Whitehaven Farm
High Lane
Loxley Farm
Telegraph House

Hall Farm
Martin
Mill Mound
Church La
Viking Way
Old River Bain
Sewage Works
Sewage Works
A153
Scrivelsby Spinney
Dickson's Plantation
Rough Plantation
Northfield Plantation

Thornton Wood
LN10
Martin Bridge
B1191
Weir
Dalderby
Scrivelsby
B1183
Home Farm
Weir Ford
Weir
Ford
Long Farm
Scrivelsby Court

22   23   24   25   26   27

98

86

For full street detail of the highlighted area see page 199.

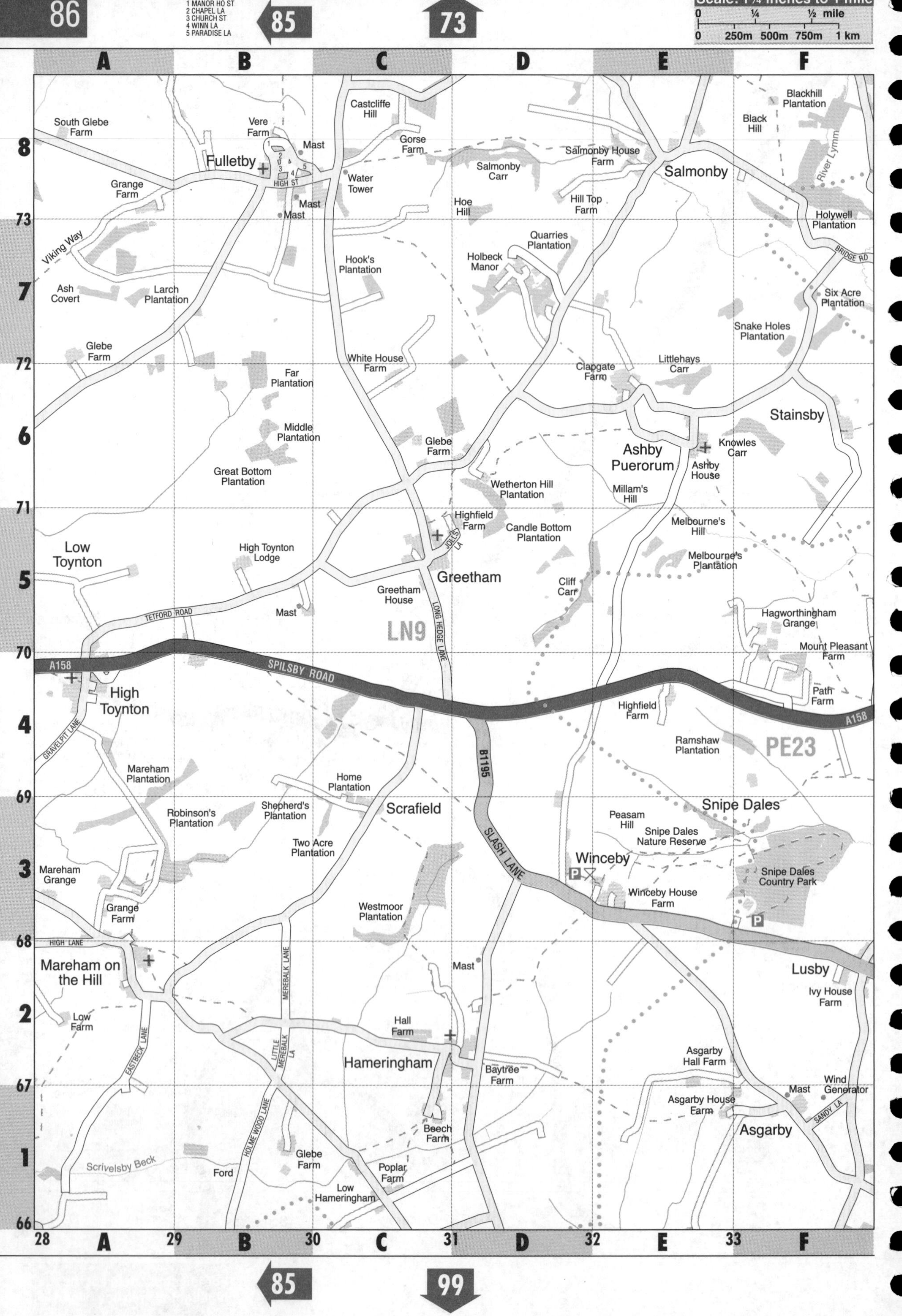

B8
1 MANOR HO ST
2 CHAPEL LA
3 CHURCH ST
4 WINN LA
5 PARADISE LA

Scale: 1¾ inches to 1 mile
0   ¼   ½   mile
0   250m 500m 750m   1 km

A B C D E F

8

South Glebe Farm
Vere Farm
Castcliffe Hill
Mast
Gorse Farm
Salmonby House Farm
Blackhill Plantation
Black Hill
River Lymm

Fulletby
Water Tower
Salmonby Carr
Salmonby

73

Grange Farm
HIGH ST
Mast
Mast
Hoe Hill
Hill Top Farm
Holywell Plantation

Viking Way

7

Ash Covert
Larch Plantation
Hook's Plantation
Holbeck Manor
Quarries Plantation
Six Acre Plantation

BRIDGE RD

72

Glebe Farm
Far Plantation
White House Farm
Clapgate Farm
Littlehays Carr
Snake Holes Plantation

Stainsby

6

Middle Plantation
Great Bottom Plantation
Glebe Farm
Wetherton Hill Plantation
Ashby Puerorum
Millam's Hill
Knowles Carr
Ashby House

71

Low Toynton
High Toynton Lodge
Highfield Farm
JOHN'S LA
Candle Bottom Plantation
Melbourne's Hill
Melbourne's Plantation

5

Greetham House
Greetham
Cliff Carr
Mast
Hagworthingham Grange

LN9

70

A158
High Toynton
TETFORD ROAD
SPILSBY ROAD
LONG HEDGE LANE
Mount Pleasant Farm
Path Farm

4

GRAVELPIT LANE
Mareham Plantation
Home Plantation
Highfield Farm
Ramshaw Plantation
A158
PE23

B1195

69

Robinson's Plantation
Shepherd's Plantation
Scrafield
Snipe Dales

3

Mareham Grange
Two Acre Plantation
Peasam Hill
Snipe Dales Nature Reserve
Winceby
Snipe Dales Country Park

Grange Farm
Westmoor Plantation
SLASH LANE
P
Winceby House Farm
P

68

HIGH LANE
Mareham on the Hill
MEREBALK LANE
Lusby

2

Low Farm
Mast
Ivy House Farm

EASTBECK LANE
LITTLE MEREBALK LA
Hall Farm
Asgarby Hall Farm
Wind Generator

67

Hameringham
Baytree Farm
Asgarby House Farm
Mast
SANDY LA

HOLME WOOD LANE
Beech Farm
Asgarby

1

Scrivelsby Beck
Ford
Glebe Farm
Poplar Farm

Low Hameringham

66

28 A 29 B 30 C 31 D 32 E 33 F

Scale: 1¾ inches to 1 mile

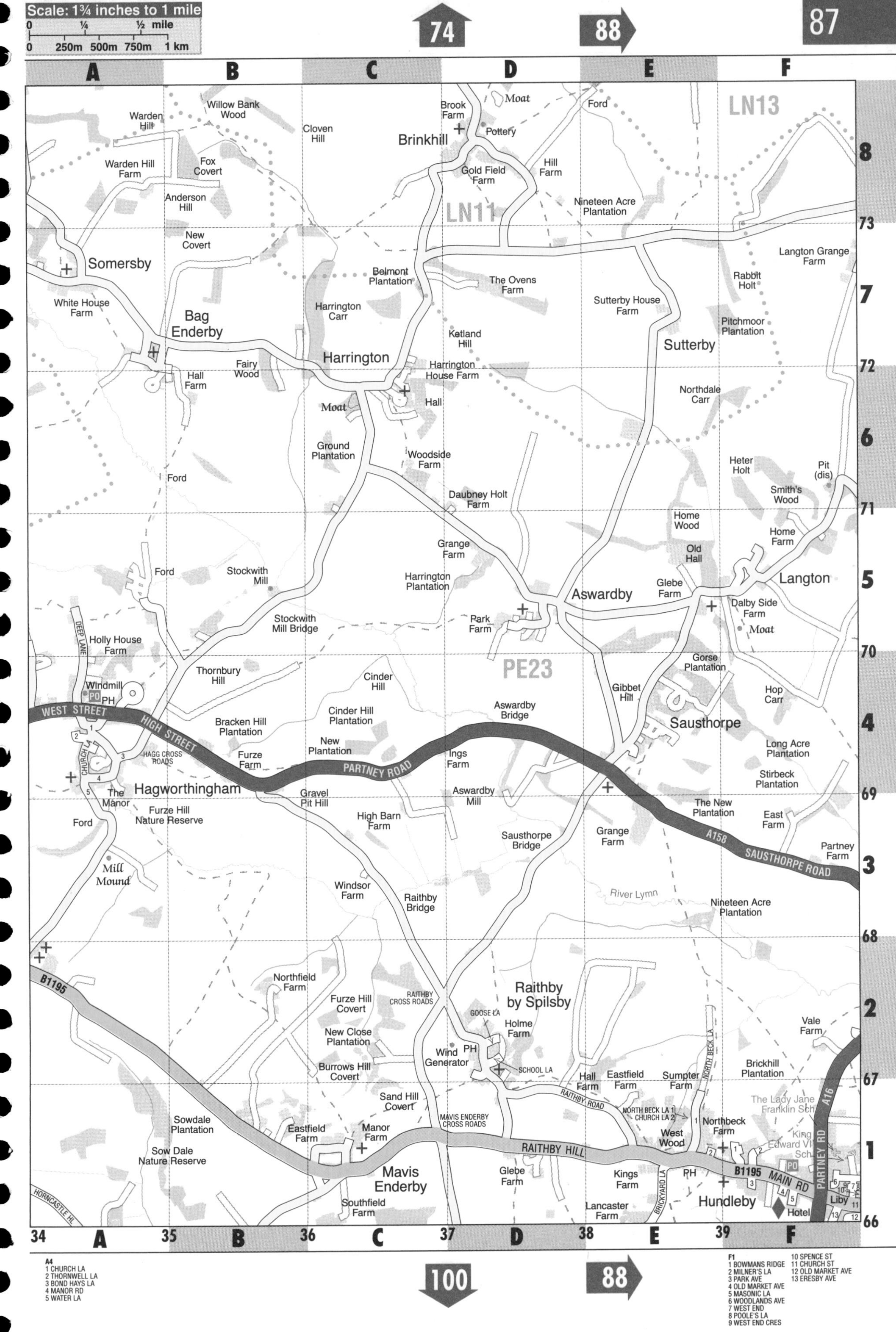

A4
1 CHURCH LA
2 THORNWELL LA
3 BOND HAYS LA
4 MANOR RD
5 WATER LA

F1
1 BOWMANS RIDGE
2 MILNER'S LA
3 PARK AVE
4 OLD MARKET AVE
5 MASONIC LA
6 WOODLANDS AVE
7 WEST END
8 POOLE'S LA
9 WEST END CRES
10 SPENCE ST
11 CHURCH ST
12 OLD MARKET AVE
13 ERESBY AVE

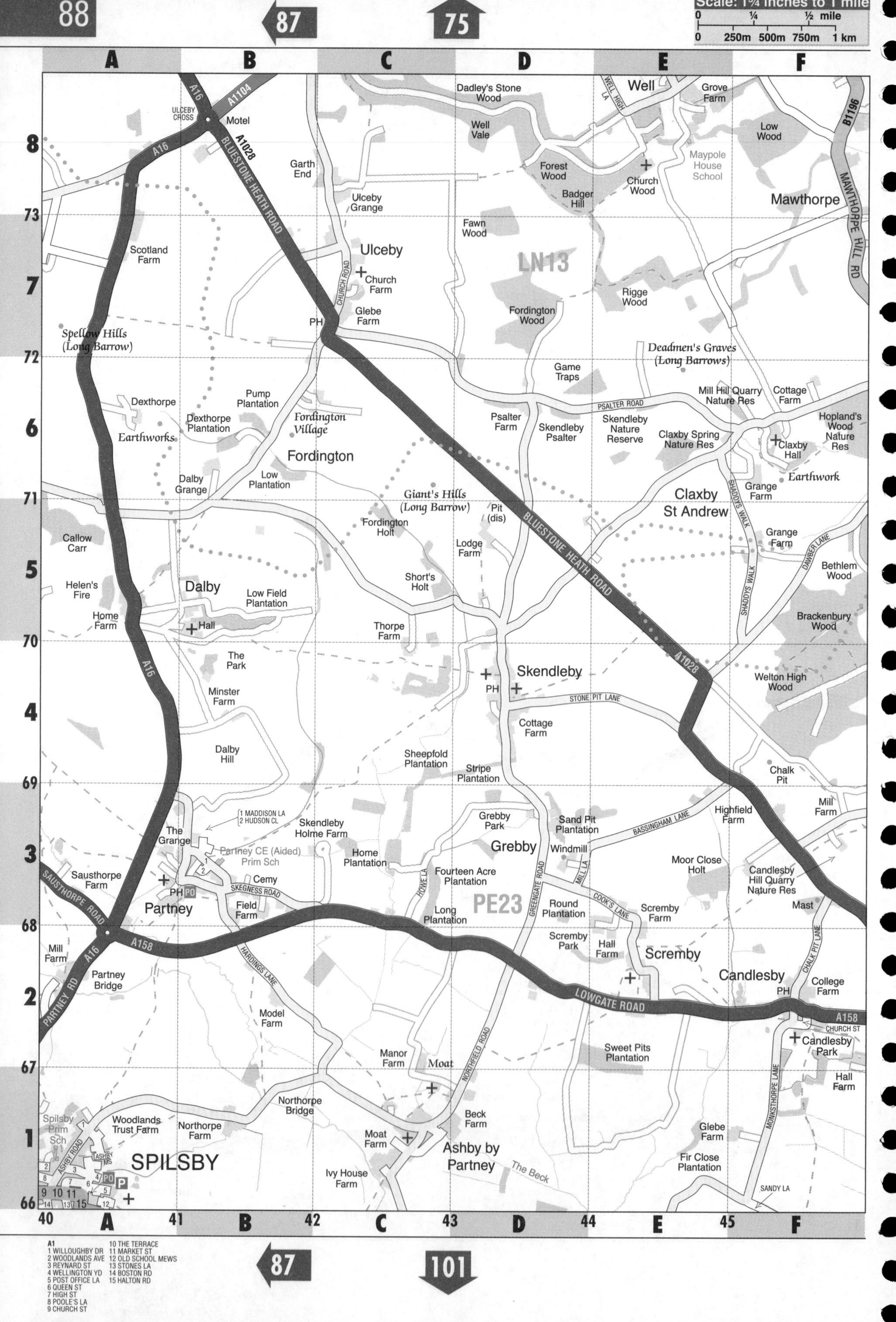

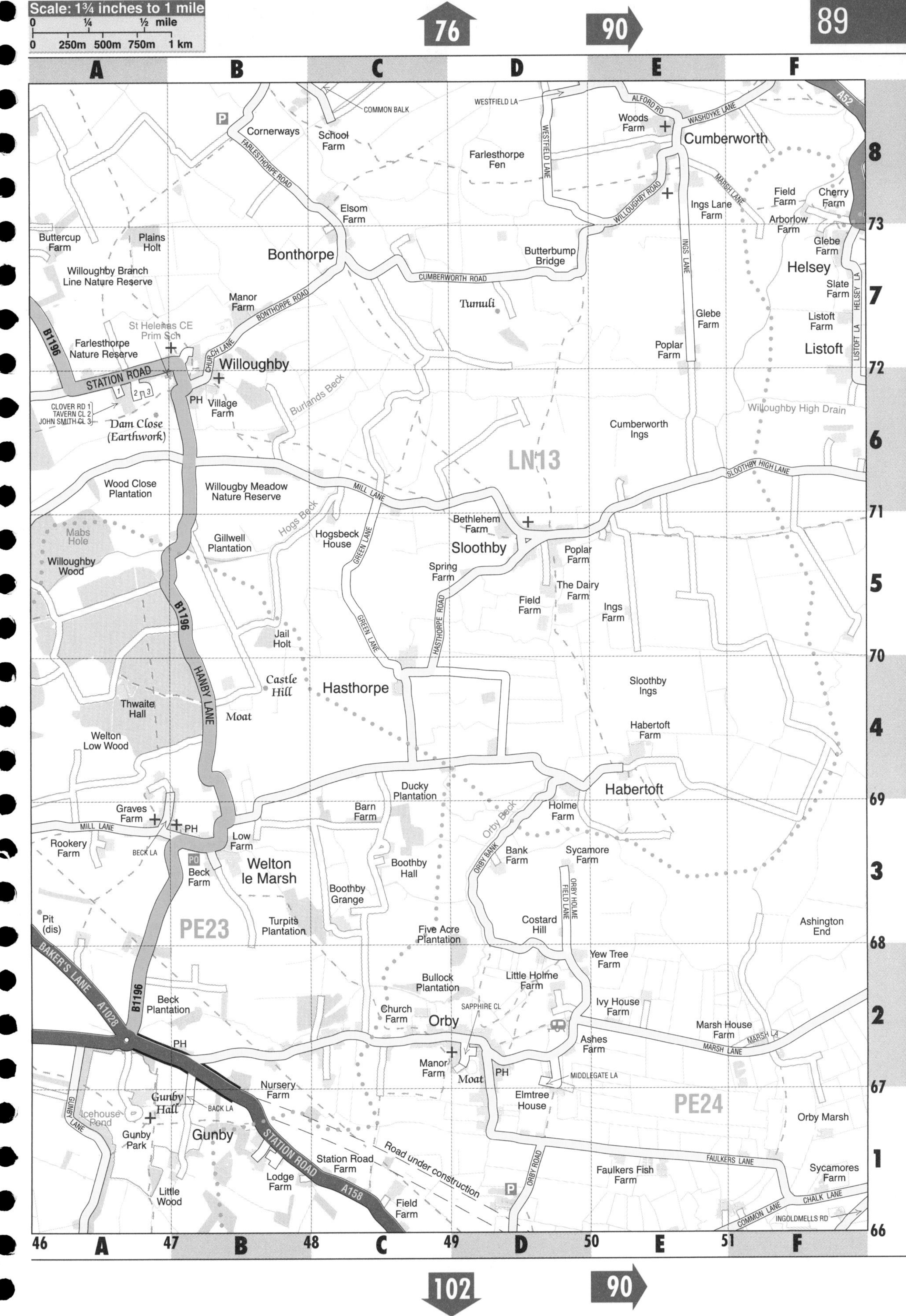

Scale: 1¾ inches to 1 mile
76
90
Cumberworth
Woods Farm
Farlesthorpe Fen
Cornerways
School Farm
Elsom Farm
Bonthorpe
Butterbump Bridge
Buttercup Farm
Plains Holt
Willoughby Branch Line Nature Reserve
Manor Farm
Tumuli
St Helenas CE Prim Sch
Farlesthorpe Nature Reserve
Willoughby
Village Farm
Dam Close (Earthwork)
Field Farm
Cherry Farm
Ings Lane Farm
Arborlow Farm
Glebe Farm
Helsey
Slate Farm
Listoft Farm
Listoft
Poplar Farm
Cumberworth Ings
Willoughby High Drain
LN13
Wood Close Plantation
Willougby Meadow Nature Reserve
Mabs Hole
Willoughby Wood
Gillwell Plantation
Hogsbeck House
Bethlehem Farm
Sloothby
Spring Farm
The Dairy Farm
Ings Farm
Jail Holt
Castle Hill
Hasthorpe
Thwaite Hall
Moat
Welton Low Wood
Sloothby Ings
Habertoft Farm
Habertoft
Ducky Plantation
Graves Farm
Rookery Farm
Barn Farm
Low Farm
Holme Farm
Bank Farm
Sycamore Farm
Beck Farm
Welton le Marsh
Boothby Hall
Boothby Grange
Pit (dis)
PE23
Turpits Plantation
Five Acre Plantation
Costard Hill
Ashington End
Yew Tree Farm
Bullock Plantation
Little Holme Farm
Beck Plantation
Church Farm
Orby
Ivy House Farm
Marsh House Farm
Ashes Farm
Manor Farm
Moat
Nursery Farm
Elmtree House
PE24
Orby Marsh
Gunby Hall
Icehouse Pond
Gunby Park
Gunby
Station Road Farm
Road under construction
Lodge Farm
Faulkers Fish Farm
Sycamores Farm
Little Wood
Field Farm

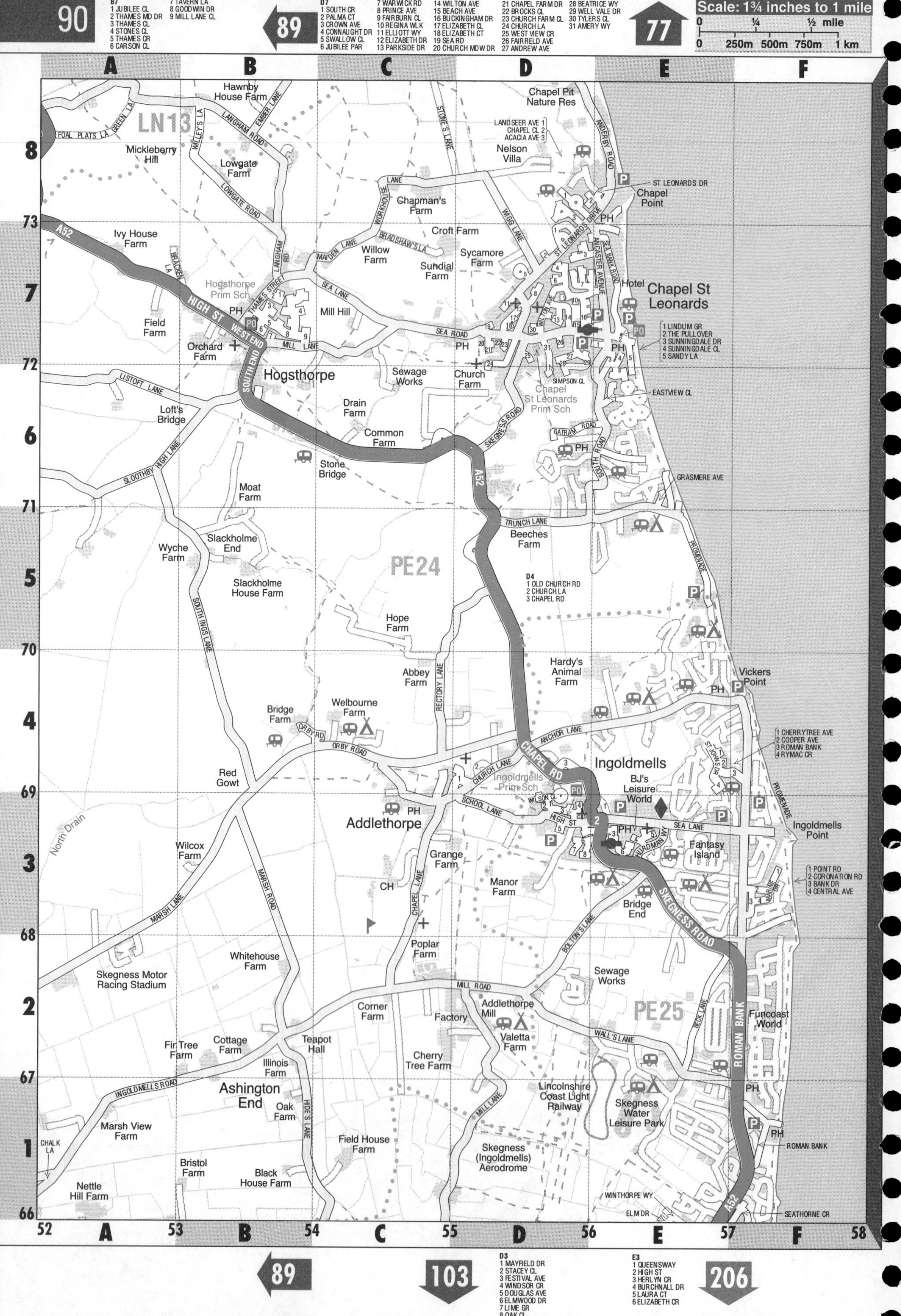
B7
1 JUBILEE CL
2 THAMES MD DR
3 THAMES CL
4 STONES CL
5 THAMES CR
6 CARSON CL
7 TAVERN LA
8 GOODWIN DR
9 MILL LANE CL
89
D7
1 SOUTH CR
2 PALMA CT
3 CROWN AVE
4 CONNAUGHT DR
5 SWALLOW CL
6 JUBILEE PAR
7 WARWICK RD
8 PRINCE AVE
9 FAIRBURN CL
10 REGINA WLK
11 ELLIOTT WY
12 ELIZABETH DR
13 PARKSIDE DR
14 WILTON AVE
15 BEACH AVE
16 BUCKINGHAM DR
17 ELIZABETH CL
18 ELIZABETH CT
19 SEA RD
20 CHURCH MDW DR
21 CHAPEL FARM DR
22 BROCKS CL
23 CHURCH FARM CL
24 CHURCH LA
25 WEST VIEW CR
26 FAIRFIELD AVE
27 ANDREW AVE
28 BEATRICE WY
29 WELL VALE DR
30 TYLERS CL
31 AMERY WY
77
Scale: 1¾ inches to 1 mile
0 ¼ ½ mile
0 250m 500m 750m 1 km
A B C D E F
8 73 7 72 6 71 5 70 4 69 3 68 2 67 1 66
LN13
FOAL PLATS LA
GREEN LA
Hawnby House Farm
WILLEY'S LA
LANGHAM ROAD
EMBER LANE
Mickleberry Hill
Lowgate Farm
LOWGATE ROAD
STONE'S LANE
Chapel Pit Nature Res
LANDSEER AVE 1
CHAPEL CL 2
ACACIA AVE 3
Nelson Villa
ANDERBY ROAD
ST LEONARDS DR
Chapel Point
WORKHOUSE LANE
Chapman's Farm
WIGG LANE
A52
Ivy House Farm
Croft Farm
BRADSHAW'S LA
ST LEONARDS DRIVE
ANCASTER AVENUE
SEA BANK ROAD
BRACKEN LA
LANGHAM RD
MAIDEN LANE
Willow Farm
Sundial Farm
Sycamore Farm
Hotel
Chapel St Leonards
Hogsthorpe Prim Sch
THAMES STREET
HIGH ST
WEST END
SEA LANE
Mill Hill
Field Farm
PH
PO
SEA ROAD
1 LINDUM GR
2 THE PULLOVER
3 SUNNINGDALE DR
4 SUNNINGDALE CL
5 SANDY LA
Orchard Farm
MILL LANE
SOUTH END
Hogsthorpe
Sewage Works
Church Farm
SIMPSON CL
LISTOFT LANE
Chapel St Leonards Prim Sch
EASTVIEW CL
Loft's Bridge
Drain Farm
SKEGNESS ROAD
GATRAM ROAD
Common Farm
SLOOTHBY HIGH LANE
Stone Bridge
GRASMERE AVE
Moat Farm
TRUNCH LANE
Beeches Farm
Wyche Farm
Slackholme End
PE24
PROMENADE
Slackholme House Farm
D4
1 OLD CHURCH RD
2 CHURCH LA
3 CHAPEL RD
SOUTH INGS LANE
Hope Farm
Hardy's Animal Farm
Abbey Farm
RECTORY LANE
Vickers Point
Bridge Farm
Welbourne Farm
ANCHOR LANE
ORBY RD
ORBY ROAD
CHAPEL RD
1 CHERRYTREE AVE
2 COOPER AVE
3 ROMAN BANK
4 RYMAC CR
Red Gowt
CHURCH LANE
Ingoldmells
Ingoldmells Prim Sch
BJ's Leisure World
North Drain
WILSON CL
Addlethorpe
SCHOOL LANE
HIGH ST
SEA LANE
Ingoldmells Point
HURDMAN WY
Fantasy Island
Wilcox Farm
Grange Farm
Manor Farm
1 POINT RD
2 CORONATION RD
3 BANK DR
4 CENTRAL AVE
CH
MARSH ROAD
MARSH LANE
CHAPEL LANE
Bridge End
SKEGNESS ROAD
Poplar Farm
BOLTON'S LANE
Whitehouse Farm
Skegness Motor Racing Stadium
Sewage Works
MILL ROAD
Corner Farm
Addlethorpe Mill
Factory
PE25
BECK LANE
ROMAN BANK
Funcoast World
Fir Tree Farm
Cottage Farm
Teapot Hall
Valetta Farm
WALL'S LANE
Illinois Farm
Cherry Tree Farm
INGOLDMELLS ROAD
Ashington End
Oak Farm
HIDE'S LANE
Lincolnshire Coast Light Railway
Skegness Water Leisure Park
Marsh View Farm
MILL LANE
CHALK LA
Field House Farm
Skegness (Ingoldmells) Aerodrome
ROMAN BANK
Bristol Farm
Black House Farm
Nettle Hill Farm
WINTHORPE WY
ELM DR
SEATHORNE CR
52 53 54 55 56 57 58
89
103
D3
1 MAYFIELD DR
2 STACEY CL
3 FESTIVAL AVE
4 WINDSOR CR
5 DOUGLAS AVE
6 ELMWOOD DR
7 LIME GR
8 OAK CL
E3
1 QUEENSWAY
2 HIGH ST
3 HERLYN CR
4 BURCHNALL DR
5 LAURA CT
6 ELIZABETH CR
206

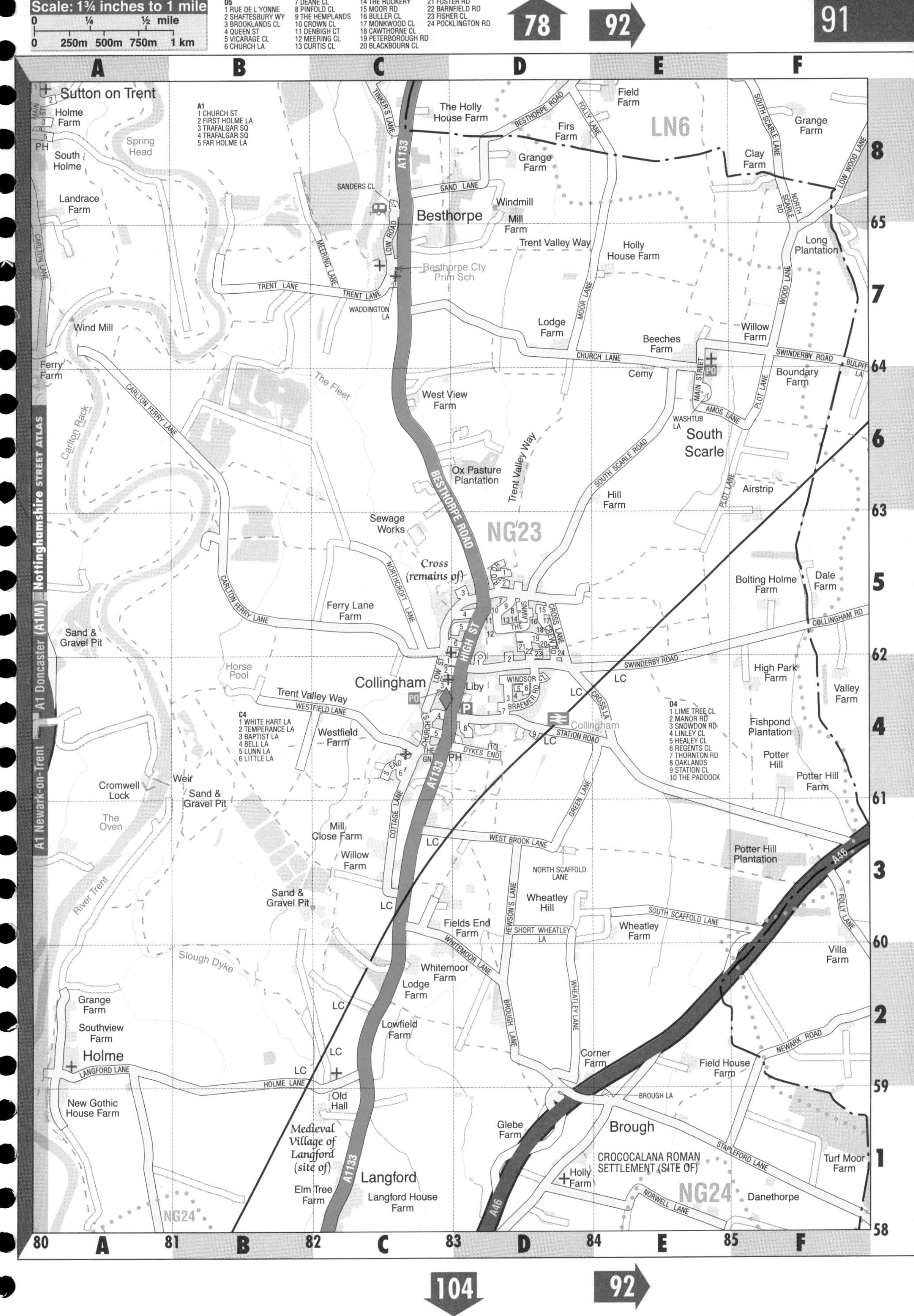
Scale: 1¾ inches to 1 mile
0 ¼ ½ mile
0 250m 500m 750m 1 km
D5
1 RUE DE L'YONNE
2 SHAFTESBURY WY
3 BROOKLANDS CL
4 QUEEN ST
5 VICARAGE CL
6 CHURCH LA
7 DEANE CL
8 PINFOLD CL
9 THE HEMPLANDS
10 CROWN CL
11 DENBIGH CT
12 MEERING CL
13 CURTIS CL
14 THE ROOKERY
15 MOOR RD
16 BULLER CL
17 MONKWOOD CL
18 CAWTHORNE CL
19 PETERBOROUGH RD
20 BLACKBOURN CL
21 FOSTER RD
22 BARNFIELD RD
23 FISHER CL
24 POCKLINGTON RD
78
92
A
B
C
D
E
F
Sutton on Trent
Holme Farm
PH
South Holme
Spring Head
A1
1 CHURCH ST
2 FIRST HOLME LA
3 TRAFALGAR SQ
4 TRAFALGAR SQ
5 FAR HOLME LA
Landrace Farm
CARLTON LANE
TINKER'S LANE
A1133
The Holly House Farm
BESTHORPE ROAD
Firs Farm
FOLLY LANE
Field Farm
LN6
SOUTH SCARLE LANE
Grange Farm
Clay Farm
LOW WOOD LANE
Grange Farm
SANDERS CL
SAND LANE
Windmill
Besthorpe
Mill Farm
NORTH SCARLE RD
LOW ROAD
MEERING LANE
Trent Valley Way
Holly House Farm
Long Plantation
Besthorpe Cty Prim Sch
TRENT LANE
WADDINGTON LA
MOOR LANE
WOOD LANE
Wind Mill
Lodge Farm
Beeches Farm
Willow Farm
CHURCH LANE
SWINDERBY ROAD
BULPIT LA
Ferry Farm
Cemy
MAIN STREET
PO
Boundary Farm
PLOT LANE
CARLTON FERRY LANE
The Fleet
West View Farm
AMOS LANE
WASHTUB LA
South Scarle
Carlton Rack
Trent Valley Way
SOUTH SCARLE ROAD
Ox Pasture Plantation
BESTHORPE ROAD
Hill Farm
Airstrip
PLOT LANE
Sewage Works
NG23
Cross (remains of)
NORTHCROFT LANE
Bolting Holme Farm
Dale Farm
CARLTON FERRY LANE
Ferry Lane Farm
COLLINGHAM RD
HIGH ST
CROSS LANE
Sand & Gravel Pit
SWINDERBY ROAD
Horse Pool
High Park Farm
Collingham
LOW ST
Liby
WINDSOR CL
BRAEMER RD
LC
Valley Farm
Trent Valley Way
WESTFIELD LANE
PO
P
Collingham
CROSS LA
C4
1 WHITE HART LA
2 TEMPERANCE LA
3 BAPTIST LA
4 BELL LA
5 LUNN LA
6 LITTLE LA
Westfield Farm
CHURCH ST
STATION ROAD
D4
1 LIME TREE CL
2 MANOR RD
3 SNOWDON RD
4 LINLEY CL
5 HEALEY CL
6 REGENTS CL
7 THORNTON RD
8 OAKLANDS
9 STATION CL
10 THE PADDOCK
Fishpond Plantation
DYKES END
PH
Potter Hill
Cromwell Lock
Weir
Sand & Gravel Pit
S END
THE GN
Potter Hill Farm
GREEN LANE
The Oven
COTTAGE LANE
Mill Close Farm
WEST BROOK LANE
LC
Willow Farm
NORTH SCAFFOLD LANE
Potter Hill Plantation
A46
River Trent
Sand & Gravel Pit
Wheatley Hill
FOLLY LANE
LC
SOUTH SCAFFOLD LANE
Fields End Farm
HEWSON'S LANE
SHORT WHEATLEY LA
Wheatley Farm
WHITEMOOR LANE
Slough Dyke
Whitemoor Farm
Villa Farm
Lodge Farm
LC
Grange Farm
BROUGH LANE
WHEATLEY LANE
Southview Farm
Lowfield Farm
Holme
NEWARK ROAD
LC
LANGFORD LANE
LC
Corner Farm
Field House Farm
HOLME LANE
Old Hall
BROUGH LA
New Gothic House Farm
Medieval Village of Langford (site of)
Glebe Farm
Brough
STAPLEFORD LANE
CROCOCALANA ROMAN SETTLEMENT (SITE OF)
Turf Moor Farm
Langford
Holly Farm
NG24
Danethorpe
Elm Tree Farm
Langford House Farm
NORWELL LANE
A46
NG24
A1 Newark-on-Trent
A1 Doncaster (A1M)
Nottinghamshire STREET ATLAS
80 81 82 83 84 85
8 65 7 64 6 63 5 62 4 61 3 60 2 59 1 58
104
92

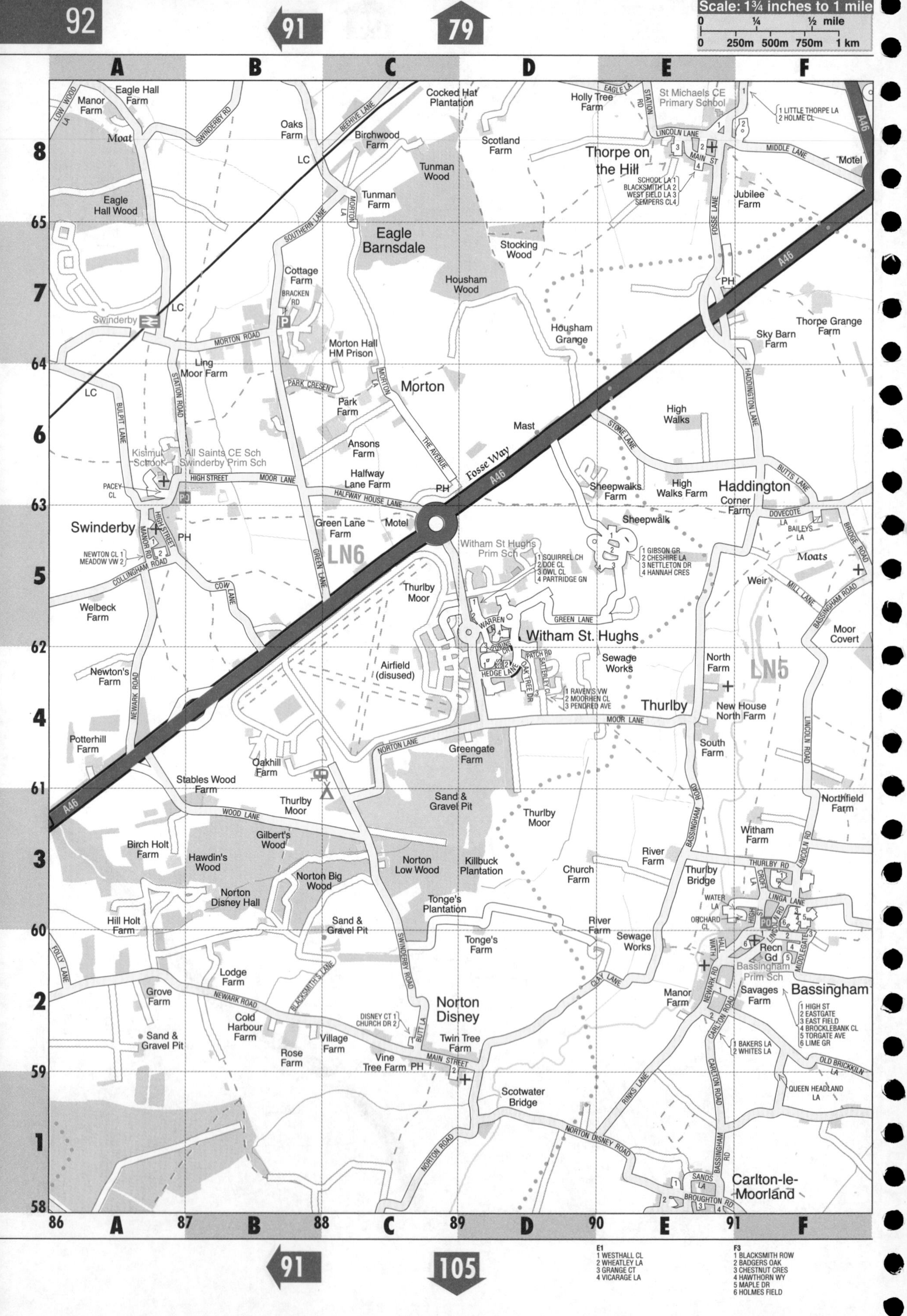
92
91
79
Scale: 1¾ inches to 1 mile
0 ¼ ½ mile
0 250m 500m 750m 1 km
A B C D E F
8 65 7 64 6 63 5 62 4 61 3 60 2 59 1 58
86 87 88 89 90 91
Manor Farm
Eagle Hall Farm
LOW WOOD LA
Moat
SWINDERBY RD
Oaks Farm
BEEHIVE LANE
Birchwood Farm
Cocked Hat Plantation
Scotland Farm
Holly Tree Farm
EAGLE LA
STATION RD
St Michaels CE Primary School
1 LITTLE THORPE LA
2 HOLME CL
A46
LINCOLN LANE
Thorpe on the Hill
MAIN ST
MIDDLE LANE
Motel
SCHOOL LA 1
BLACKSMITH LA 2
WEST FIELD LA 3
SEMPERS CL 4
LC
Tunman Wood
Tunman Farm
MORTON LA
Eagle Hall Wood
SOUTHERN LANE
Eagle Barnsdale
Stocking Wood
Jubilee Farm
FOSSE LANE
Cottage Farm
BRACKEN RD
Housham Wood
PH
Swinderby
MORTON ROAD
Morton Hall HM Prison
Housham Grange
Sky Barn Farm
Thorpe Grange Farm
Ling Moor Farm
STATION ROAD
PARK CRESENT
Morton
HADDINGTON LANE
BULPIT LANE
Park Farm
High Walks
Mast
Ansons Farm
THE AVENUE
STONE LANE
Kisimul School
All Saints CE Sch
Swinderby Prim Sch
Fosse Way
HIGH STREET
MOOR LANE
Halfway Lane Farm
PACEY CL
HALFWAY HOUSE LANE
Sheepwalks Farm
High Walks Farm
Haddington
BUTTS LANE
Corner Farm
DOVECOTE LA
BAILEYS LA
Sheepwalk
BRIDGE ROAD
Green Lane Farm
Motel
HIGH STREET
MANOR RD
NEWTON CL 1
MEADOW VW 2
COLLINGHAM ROAD
LN6
GREEN LANE
Witham St Hughs Prim Sch
1 SQUIRREL CH
2 DOE CL
3 OWL CL
4 PARTRIDGE GN
1 GIBSON GR
2 CHESHIRE LA
3 NETTLETON DR
4 HANNAH CRES
Moats
Weir
MILL LANE
BASSINGHAM ROAD
COW LANE
Welbeck Farm
Thurlby Moor
GREEN LANE
WARREN
Witham St. Hughs
Moor Covert
ROBINS CR
PATCH RD
SATTERLEY CL
HEDGE LANE
OAK TREE DR
Sewage Works
North Farm
LN5
Newton's Farm
Airfield (disused)
1 RAVEN'S VW
2 MOORHEN CL
3 PENDRED AVE
Thurlby
New House North Farm
NEWARK ROAD
MOOR LANE
LINCOLN ROAD
Potterhill Farm
NORTON LANE
Greengate Farm
South Farm
Oakhill Farm
Stables Wood Farm
Sand & Gravel Pit
Thurlby Moor
Northfield Farm
WOOD LANE
Thurlby Moor
BASSINGHAM ROAD
Gilbert's Wood
Witham Farm
Birch Holt Farm
Hawdin's Wood
Norton Low Wood
Killbuck Plantation
Church Farm
River Farm
Thurlby Bridge
THURLBY RD
CROFT LA
Norton Big Wood
Norton Disney Hall
Tonge's Plantation
WATER LA
LINGA LANE
ORCHARD CL
HIGH ST
LINCOLN RD
Hill Holt Farm
Sand & Gravel Pit
River Farm
Tonge's Farm
Sewage Works
WATH HALL
Recn Gd
MIDDLEGATE
FOLLY LANE
Lodge Farm
BLACKSMITH'S LANE
SWINDERBY ROAD
Bassingham Prim Sch
Bassingham
Grove Farm
NEWARK ROAD
Norton Disney
CLAY LANE
Manor Farm
NEWARK RD
Savages Farm
1 HIGH ST
2 EASTGATE
3 EAST FIELD
4 BROCKLEBANK CL
5 TORGATE AVE
6 LIME GR
Cold Harbour Farm
DISNEY CT 1
CHURCH DR 2
BUTT LA
CARLTON ROAD
Sand & Gravel Pit
Village Farm
Twin Tree Farm
1 BAKERS LA
2 WHITES LA
Rose Farm
Vine Tree Farm
PH
MAIN STREET
OLD BRICKKILN LA
QUEEN HEADLAND LA
Scotwater Bridge
RINKS LANE
CARLTON ROAD
NORTON ROAD
NORTON DISNEY ROAD
BASSINGHAM RD
SANDS LA
Carlton-le-Moorland
BROUGHTON RD
91
105
E1
1 WESTHALL CL
2 WHEATLEY LA
3 GRANGE CT
4 VICARAGE LA
F3
1 BLACKSMITH ROW
2 BADGERS OAK
3 CHESTNUT CRES
4 HAWTHORN WY
5 MAPLE DR
6 HOLMES FIELD

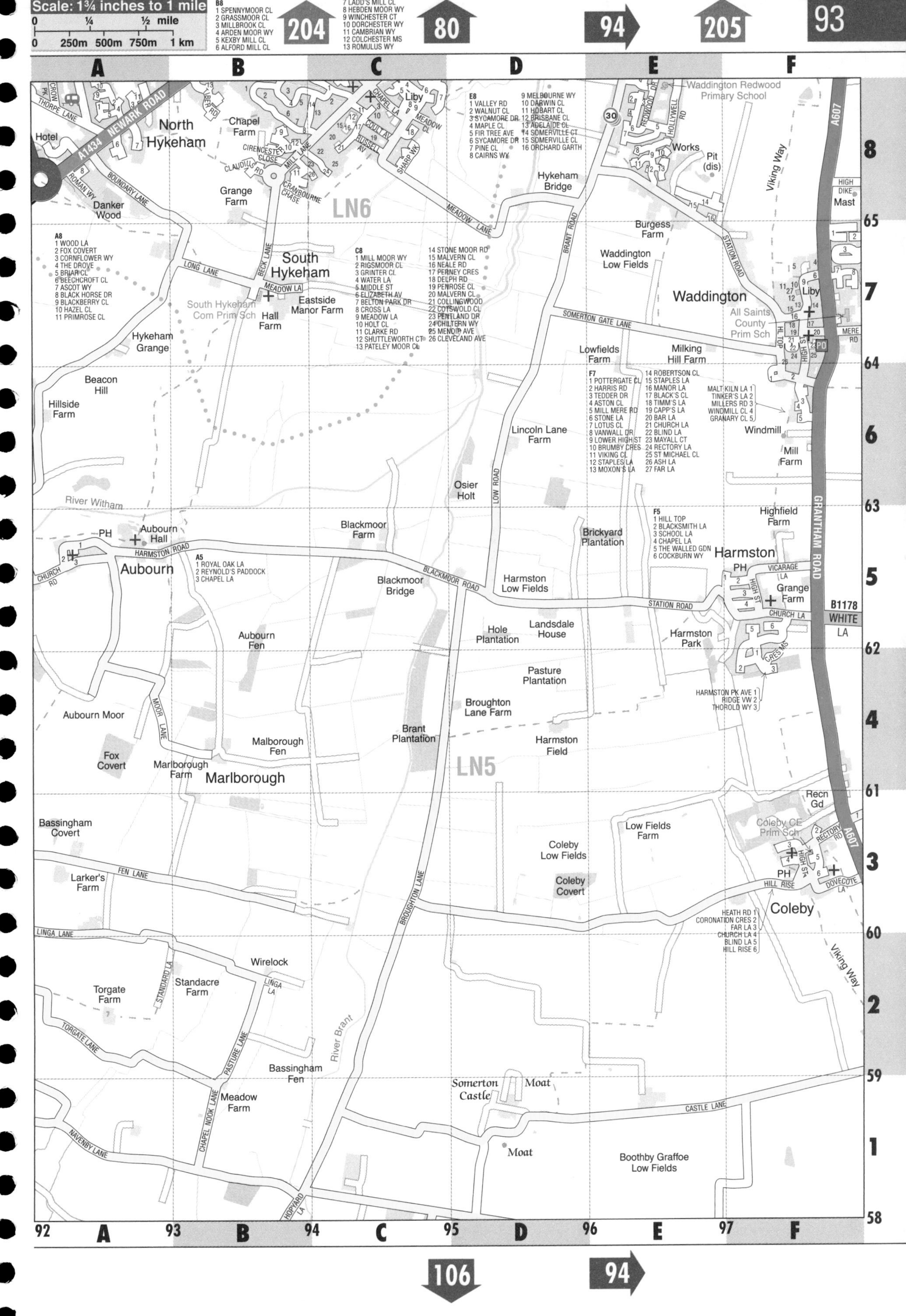

Scale: 1¾ inches to 1 mile
0 ¼ ½ mile
0 250m 500m 750m 1 km
B8
1 SPENNYMOOR CL
2 GRASSMOOR CL
3 MILLBROOK CL
4 ARDEN MOOR WY
5 KEXBY MILL CL
6 ALFORD MILL CL
7 LADD'S MILL CL
8 HEBDEN MOOR WY
9 WINCHESTER CT
10 DORCHESTER WY
11 CAMBRIAN WY
12 COLCHESTER MS
13 ROMULUS WY
204
80
94
205
93
A B C D E F
North Hykeham
Hotel
NEWARK ROAD
A1434
Chapel Farm
CIRENCESTER CLOSE
CLAUDIUS RD
MILL LANE
CRANBOURNE CHASE
CHAPEL LA
COULTAS AV
RUSSELL AV
SHARP WK
MEADOW CL
Liby
E8
1 VALLEY RD
2 WALNUT CL
3 SYCAMORE DR
4 MAPLE CL
5 FIR TREE AVE
6 SYCAMORE DR
7 PINE CL
8 CAIRNS WY
9 MELBOURNE WY
10 DARWIN CL
11 HOBART CL
12 BRISBANE CL
13 ADELAIDE CL
14 SOMERVILLE CT
15 SOMERVILLE CL
16 ORCHARD GARTH
Waddington Redwood Primary School
REDWOOD DR
HOLLYWELL RD
Works
Pit (dis)
Viking Way
A607
8
HIGH DIKE
Mast
65
THORPE LANE
CROW PK
ROMAN WY
BOUNDARY LANE
Danker Wood
Grange Farm
LN6
MEADOW LANE
Hykeham Bridge
BRANT ROAD
Burgess Farm
STATION ROAD
Waddington Low Fields
A8
1 WOOD LA
2 FOX COVERT
3 CORNFLOWER WY
4 THE DROVE
5 BRIAR CL
6 BEECHCROFT CL
7 ASCOT WY
8 BLACK HORSE DR
9 BLACKBERRY CL
10 HAZEL CL
11 PRIMROSE CL
LONG LANE
BECK LANE
MEADOW LA
South Hykeham
South Hykeham Com Prim Sch
Hall Farm
Eastside Manor Farm
C8
1 MILL MOOR WY
2 RIGSMOOR CL
3 GRINTER CL
4 WATER LA
5 MIDDLE ST
6 ELIZABETH AV
7 BELTON PARK DR
8 CROSS LA
9 MEADOW LA
10 HOLT CL
11 CLARKE RD
12 SHUTTLEWORTH CT
13 PATELEY MOOR CL
14 STONE MOOR RD
15 MALVERN CL
16 NEALE RD
17 PERNEY CRES
18 DELPH RD
19 PENROSE CL
20 MALVERN CL
21 COLLINGWOOD
22 COTSWOLD CL
23 PENTLAND DR
24 CHILTERN WY
25 MENDIP AVE
26 CLEVELAND AVE
Waddington
Liby
All Saints County Prim Sch
HL TOP
HIGH ST
MERE RD
PO
7
SOMERTON GATE LANE
Lowfields Farm
Milking Hill Farm
64
Hykeham Grange
Beacon Hill
Hillside Farm
F7
1 POTTERGATE CL
2 HARRIS RD
3 TEDDER DR
4 ASTON CL
5 MILL MERE RD
6 STONE LA
7 LOTUS CL
8 VANWALL DR
9 LOWER HIGH ST
10 BRUMBY CRES
11 VIKING CL
12 STAPLES LA
13 MOXON'S LA
14 ROBERTSON CL
15 STAPLES LA
16 MANOR LA
17 BLACK'S CL
18 TIMM'S LA
19 CAPP'S LA
20 BAR LA
21 CHURCH LA
22 BLIND LA
23 MAYALL CT
24 RECTORY LA
25 ST MICHAEL CL
26 ASH LA
27 FAR LA
MALT KILN LA 1
TINKER'S LA 2
MILLERS RD 3
WINDMILL CL 4
GRANARY CL 5
Lincoln Lane Farm
Windmill
Mill Farm
6
Osier Holt
LOW ROAD
River Witham
GRANTHAM ROAD
63
Highfield Farm
PH
Aubourn Hall
Blackmoor Farm
Brickyard Plantation
F5
1 HILL TOP
2 BLACKSMITH LA
3 SCHOOL LA
4 CHAPEL LA
5 THE WALLED GDN
6 COCKBURN WY
Harmston
HARMSTON ROAD
CHURCH RD
Aubourn
A5
1 ROYAL OAK LA
2 REYNOLD'S PADDOCK
3 CHAPEL LA
Blackmoor Bridge
BLACKMOOR ROAD
Harmston Low Fields
STATION ROAD
PH
VICARAGE LA
HIGH ST
Grange Farm
CHURCH LA
B1178
WHITE LA
5
Aubourn Fen
Hole Plantation
Landsdale House
Harmston Park
CRES MS
62
Pasture Plantation
HARMSTON PK AVE 1
RIDGE VW 2
THOROLD WY 3
MOOR LANE
Aubourn Moor
Broughton Lane Farm
Brant Plantation
Harmston Field
4
Fox Covert
Malborough Fen
Marlborough Farm
Marlborough
LN5
61
Recn Gd
Bassingham Covert
Low Fields Farm
Coleby CE Prim Sch
RECTORY RD
Coleby Low Fields
Coleby Covert
Larker's Farm
FEN LANE
PH
HIGH ST
HILL RISE
DOVECOTE LA
3
BROUGHTON LANE
Coleby
HEATH RD 1
CORONATION CRES 2
FAR LA 3
CHURCH LA 4
BLIND LA 5
HILL RISE 6
60
LINGA LANE
Wirelock
LINGA LA
STANDARD LA
Torgate Farm
Standacre Farm
Viking Way
2
TORGATE LANE
PASTURE LANE
River Brant
Bassingham Fen
59
Somerton Castle
Moat
Meadow Farm
CHAPEL NOOK LANE
CASTLE LANE
NAVENBY LANE
Moat
Boothby Graffoe Low Fields
1
HOPYARD LA
58
92 A 93 B 94 C 95 D 96 E 97 F
106
94

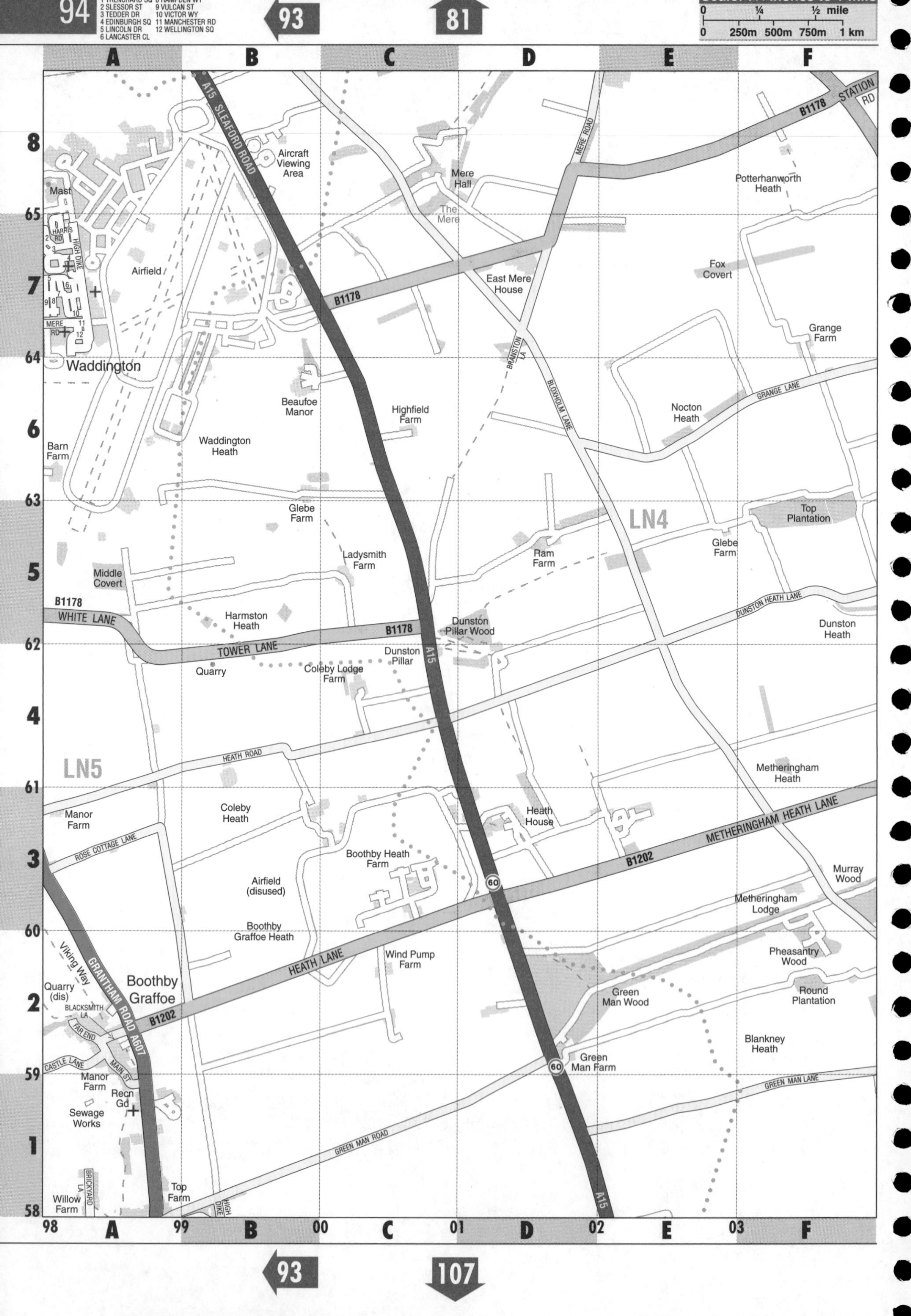

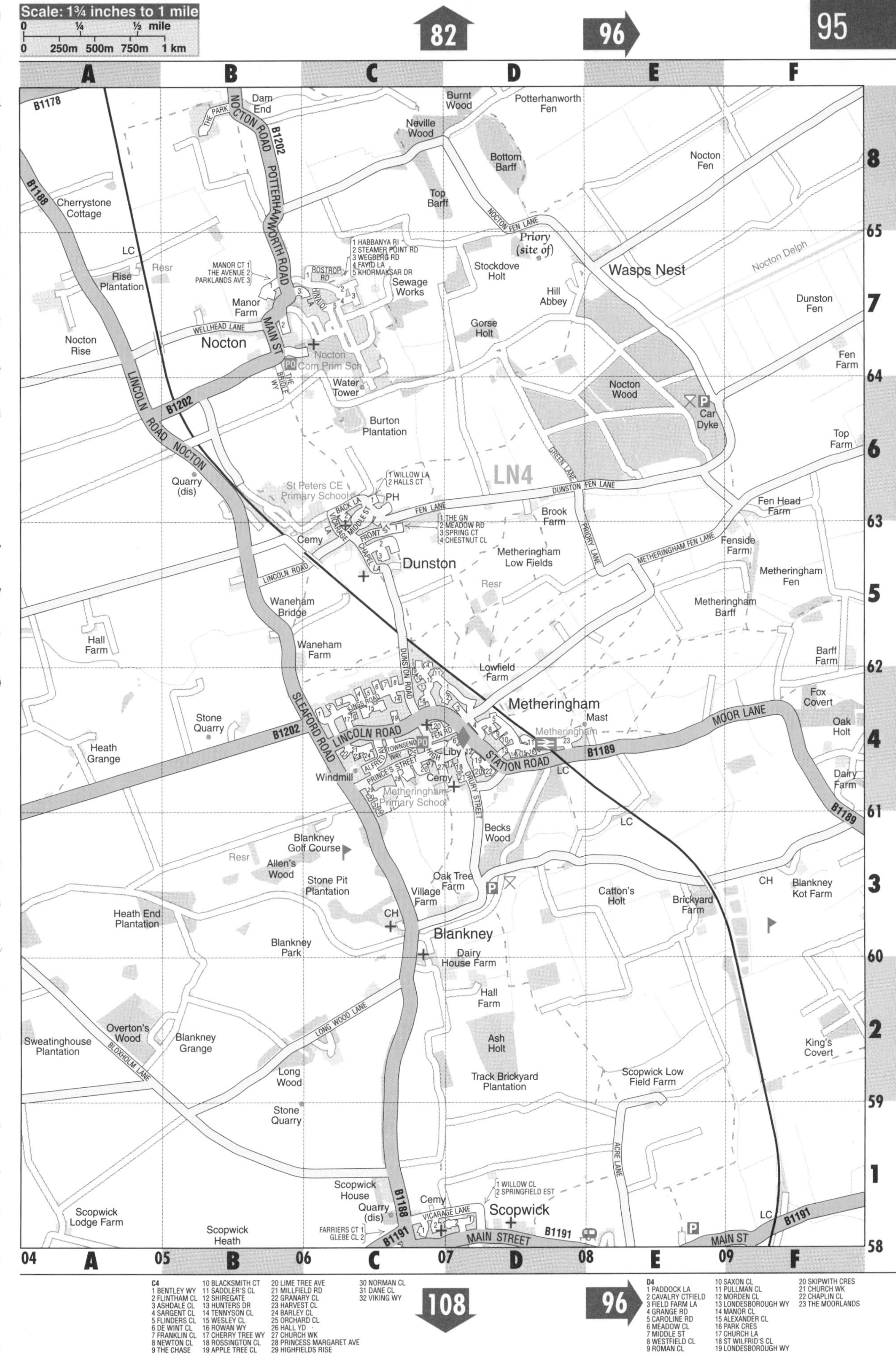

95
Scale: 1¾ inches to 1 mile
0 ¼ ½ mile
0 250m 500m 750m 1 km
82
96
A B C D E F
8 65 7 64 6 63 5 62 4 61 3 60 2 59 1 58
04 05 06 07 08 09
B1178
Dam End
THE PARK
NOCTON ROAD
B1202
POTTERHANWORTH ROAD
Burnt Wood
Potterhanworth Fen
Neville Wood
Bottom Barff
Nocton Fen
B1188
Cherrystone Cottage
Top Barff
NOCTON FEN LANE
Priory (site of)
LC
Resr
1 HABBANYA RI
2 STEAMER POINT RD
3 WEGBERG RD
4 FAYID LA
5 KHORMAKSAR DR
Stockdove Holt
Wasps Nest
Nocton Delph
Rise Plantation
MANOR CT 1
THE AVENUE 2
PARKLANDS AVE 3
ROSTROP RD
Sewage Works
Hill Abbey
Dunston Fen
Manor Farm
Nocton Rise
WELLHEAD LANE
Nocton
MAIN ST
Gorse Holt
Nocton Com Prim Sch
PO
THE BRIDLE WY
Water Tower
Fen Farm
LINCOLN ROAD
B1202
Nocton Wood
Car Dyke
Burton Plantation
NOCTON
Top Farm
GREEN LANE
LN4
Quarry (dis)
1 WILLOW LA
2 HALLS CT
St Peters CE Primary School
PH
DUNSTON FEN LANE
Fen Head Farm
BACK LA
FEN LANE
Brook Farm
1 THE GN
2 MEADOW RD
3 SPRING CT
4 CHESTNUT CL
VICARAGE LA
MIDDLE ST
FRONT ST
Cemy
CHAPEL LA
PRIORY LANE
METHERINGHAM FEN LANE
Fenside Farm
Metheringham Low Fields
Dunston
LINCOLN ROAD
Resr
Metheringham Fen
Waneham Bridge
Metheringham Barff
Hall Farm
Waneham Farm
Barff Farm
DUNSTON ROAD
Lowfield Farm
Fox Covert
KINGS ROAD
Metheringham
Stone Quarry
Mast
Oak Holt
MOOR LANE
SLEAFORD ROAD
LINCOLN ROAD
FEN RD
Metheringham
B1202
Heath Grange
PO
B1189
TOWNSEND WAY
Liby
ALFRED AV
HIGH
STATION ROAD
PRINCE'S STREET
Windmill
Cemy
DRURY STREET
Dairy Farm
LC
Metheringham Primary School
B1189
Becks Wood
LC
Blankney Golf Course
Resr
Allen's Wood
Stone Pit Plantation
Oak Tree Farm
Village Farm
P
Catton's Holt
CH
Blankney Kot Farm
Brickyard Farm
Heath End Plantation
CH
Blankney
Blankney Park
Dairy House Farm
Hall Farm
LONG WOOD LANE
Overton's Wood
Sweatinghouse Plantation
Blankney Grange
Ash Holt
King's Covert
BLOXHOLM LANE
Long Wood
Track Brickyard Plantation
Scopwick Low Field Farm
Stone Quarry
ACRE LANE
Scopwick House
1 WILLOW CL
2 SPRINGFIELD EST
Cemy
Quarry (dis)
B1188
VICARAGE LANE
Scopwick
Scopwick Lodge Farm
Scopwick Heath
FARRIERS CT 1
GLEBE CL 2
B1191
MAIN STREET
B1191
P
LC
B1191
MAIN ST
C4
1 BENTLEY WY
2 FLINTHAM CL
3 ASHDALE CL
4 SARGENT CL
5 FLINDERS CL
6 DE WINT CL
7 FRANKLIN CL
8 NEWTON CL
9 THE CHASE
10 BLACKSMITH CT
11 SADDLER'S CL
12 SHIREGATE
13 HUNTERS DR
14 TENNYSON CL
15 WESLEY CL
16 ROWAN WY
17 CHERRY TREE WY
18 ROSSINGTON CL
19 APPLE TREE CL
20 LIME TREE AVE
21 MILLFIELD RD
22 GRANARY CL
23 HARVEST CL
24 BARLEY CL
25 ORCHARD CL
26 HALL YD
27 CHURCH WK
28 PRINCESS MARGARET AVE
29 HIGHFIELDS RISE
30 NORMAN CL
31 DANE CL
32 VIKING WY
108
96
D4
1 PADDOCK LA
2 CAVALRY CTFIELD
3 FIELD FARM LA
4 GRANGE RD
5 CAROLINE RD
6 MEADOW CL
7 MIDDLE ST
8 WESTFIELD CL
9 ROMAN CL
10 SAXON CL
11 PULLMAN CL
12 MORDEN CL
13 LONDESBOROUGH WY
14 MANOR CL
15 ALEXANDER CL
16 PARK CRES
17 CHURCH LA
18 ST WILFRID'S CL
19 LONDESBOROUGH WY
20 SKIPWITH CRES
21 CHURCH WK
22 CHAPLIN CL
23 THE MOORLANDS

95 83

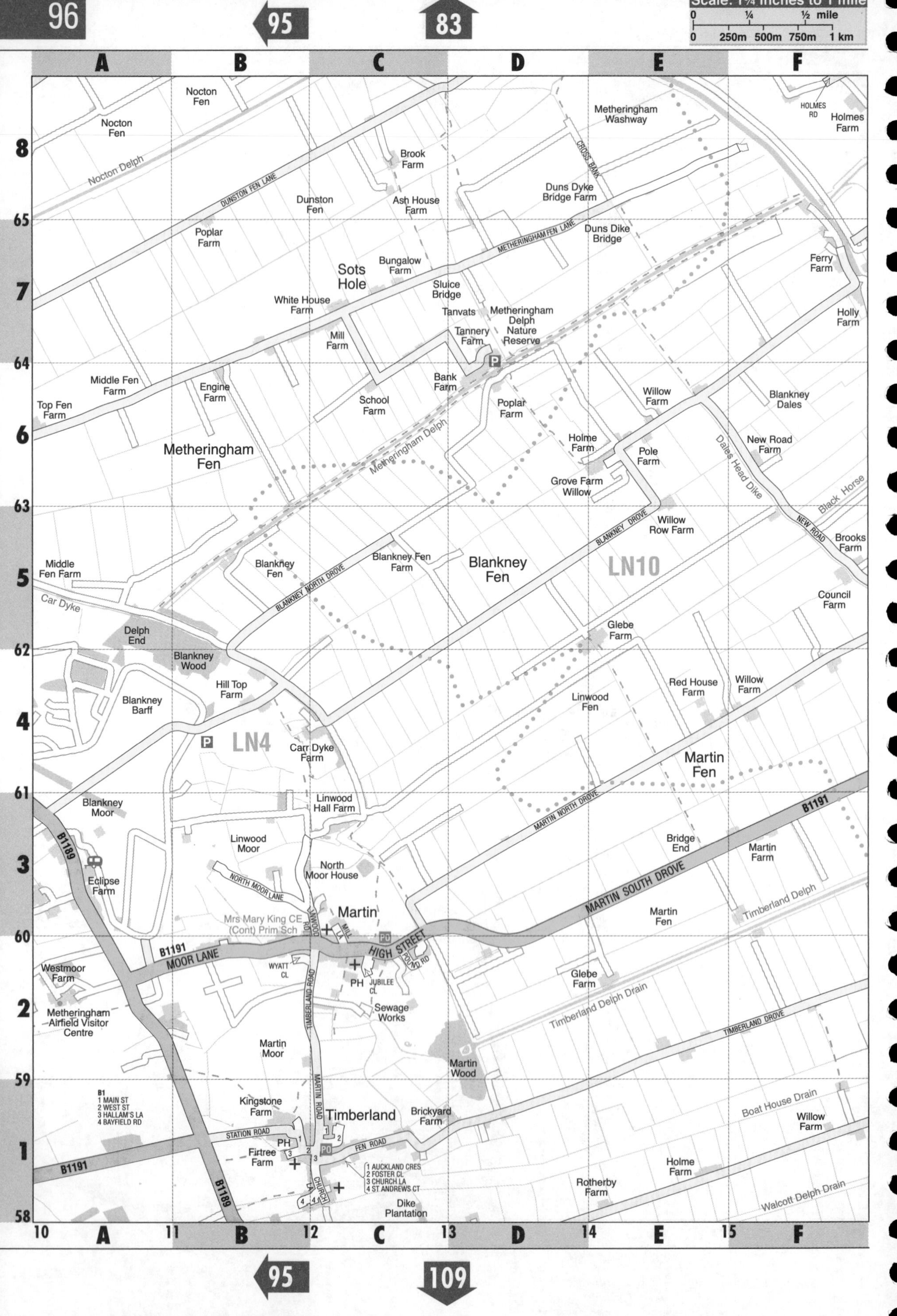
Scale: 1¾ inches to 1 mile
0 ¼ ½ mile
0 250m 500m 750m 1 km
Nocton Fen
Nocton Fen
Nocton Delph
DUNSTON FEN LANE
Metheringham Washway
HOLMES RD
Holmes Farm
CROSS BANK
Brook Farm
Ash House Farm
Dunston Fen
Duns Dyke Bridge Farm
Duns Dike Bridge
METHERINGHAM FEN LANE
Poplar Farm
Ferry Farm
Sots Hole
Bungalow Farm
Sluice Bridge
White House Farm
Tanvats
Metheringham Delph Nature Reserve
Holly Farm
Mill Farm
Tannery Farm
Middle Fen Farm
Engine Farm
Bank Farm
School Farm
Poplar Farm
Willow Farm
Blankney Dales
Top Fen Farm
Metheringham Fen
Metheringham Delph
Holme Farm
Pole Farm
New Road Farm
Dales Head Dike
Grove Farm Willow
Black Horse
Willow Row Farm
BLANKNEY DROVE
NEW ROAD
Brooks Farm
Middle Fen Farm
Blankney Fen
Blankney Fen Farm
Blankney Fen
LN10
BLANKNEY NORTH DROVE
Car Dyke
Council Farm
Delph End
Glebe Farm
Blankney Wood
Hill Top Farm
Red House Farm
Willow Farm
Blankney Barff
Linwood Fen
LN4
Carr Dyke Farm
Martin Fen
Linwood Hall Farm
MARTIN NORTH DROVE
Blankney Moor
B1191
B1189
Linwood Moor
Bridge End
Martin Farm
Eclipse Farm
North Moor House
NORTH MOOR LANE
MARTIN SOUTH DROVE
Timberland Delph
Martin
Mrs Mary King CE (Cont) Prim Sch
LINWOOD RD
MILL LA
Martin Fen
B1191 MOOR LANE
HIGH STREET
POUND RD
Westmoor Farm
WYATT CL
PH
JUBILEE CL
Glebe Farm
Metheringham Airfield Visitor Centre
TIMBERLAND ROAD
Sewage Works
Timberland Delph Drain
TIMBERLAND DROVE
Martin Moor
Martin Wood
B1 1 MAIN ST 2 WEST ST 3 HALLAM'S LA 4 BAYFIELD RD
Kingstone Farm
MARTIN ROAD
Timberland
Brickyard Farm
Boat House Drain
Willow Farm
STATION ROAD
PH
FEN ROAD
B1191
Firtree Farm
1 AUCKLAND CRES 2 FOSTER CL 3 CHURCH LA 4 ST ANDREWS CT
Holme Farm
Rotherby Farm
CHURCH LA
B1189
Dike Plantation
Walcott Delph Drain
A B C D E F
8 65 7 64 6 63 5 62 4 61 3 60 2 59 1 58
10 11 12 13 14 15

95 109

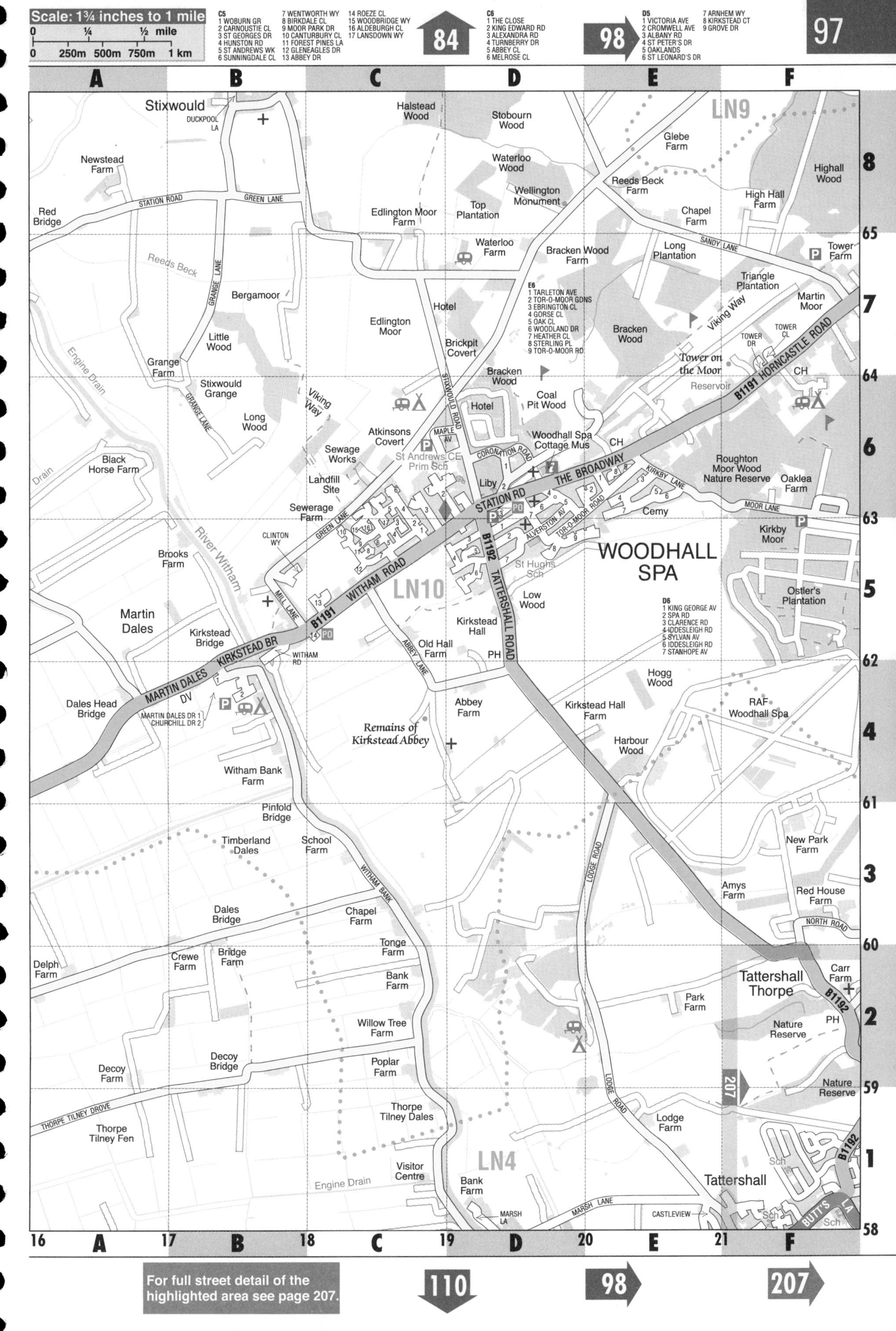

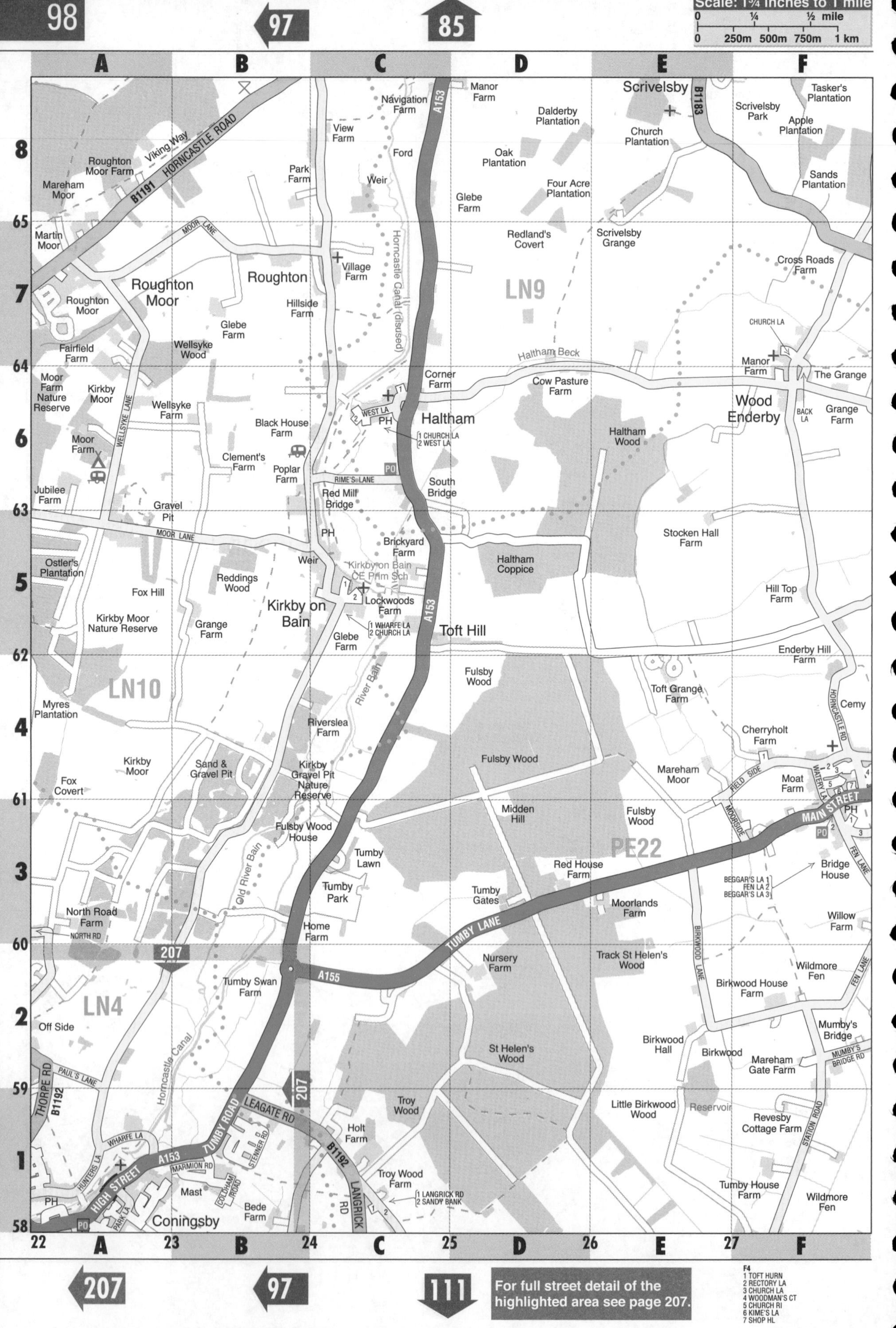

Scale: 1¾ inches to 1 mile
0   ¼   ½ mile
0   250m 500m 750m 1 km

A B C D E F

Scrivelsby

Manor Farm
Dalderby Plantation
Church Plantation
Tasker's Plantation
Scrivelsby Park
Apple Plantation

View Farm
Navigation Farm
Ford
Oak Plantation
Four Acre Plantation
Sands Plantation

8

Mareham Moor
Roughton Moor Farm
Viking Way
Park Farm
Weir
Glebe Farm
Redland's Covert
Scrivelsby Grange
Cross Roads Farm

65

Martin Moor
Roughton Moor
Roughton
Village Farm
LN9
CHURCH LA
Manor Farm
The Grange

7

Fairfield Farm
Roughton Moor
Glebe Farm
Hillside Farm
Haltham Beck
Wood Enderby

64

Moor Farm Nature Reserve
Kirkby Moor
Wellsyke Wood
Wellsyke Farm
Corner Farm
Cow Pasture Farm
BACK LA
Grange Farm

6

Moor Farm
Clement's Farm
Black House Farm
WEST LA
PH
Haltham
1 CHURCH LA
2 WEST LA
Haltham Wood

Jubilee Farm
Poplar Farm
RIME'S LANE
Red Mill Bridge
PO
South Bridge
Brickyard Farm
Haltham Coppice
Stocken Hall Farm

63

Ostler's Plantation
Gravel Pit
MOOR LANE
Weir
PH
Kirkby on Bain CE Prim Sch
Hill Top Farm

5

Fox Hill
Reddings Wood
Kirkby on Bain
Lockwoods Farm
Toft Hill
A153

Kirkby Moor Nature Reserve
Grange Farm
Glebe Farm
1 WHARFE LA
2 CHURCH LA

62

LN10
Fulsby Wood
Enderby Hill Farm

Myres Plantation
River Bain
Toft Grange Farm
Cemy

4

Kirkby Moor
Riverslea Farm
Cherryholt Farm

Fox Covert
Sand & Gravel Pit
Kirkby Gravel Pit Nature Reserve
Fulsby Wood
Mareham Moor
Moat Farm
FIELD SIDE
WATERLA

61

Fulsby Wood House
Midden Hill
Fulsby Wood
MOORSIDE
MAIN STREET
PH
PO

North Road Farm
NORTH RD
Old River Bain
Tumby Lawn
PE22
Red House Farm
BEGGAR'S LA 1
FEN LA 2
BEGGAR'S LA 3
Bridge House

3

207
Tumby Park
Tumby Gates
Moorlands Farm
Willow Farm

60

LN4
A155
Home Farm
TUMBY LANE
Nursery Farm
Track St Helen's Wood
BIRKWOOD LANE
Wildmore Fen
FEN LANE

Off Side
Tumby Swan Farm
Birkwood House Farm

2

Horncastle Canal
207
Birkwood Hall
Birkwood
Mumby's Bridge

St Helen's Wood
Mareham Gate Farm
MUMBY'S BRIDGE RD

59

THORPE RD
PAUL'S LANE
B1192
207
LEAGATE RD
Troy Wood
Little Birkwood Wood
Reservoir
Revesby Cottage Farm
STATION ROAD

Holt Farm
B1192
LANGRICK RD

1

HUNTERS LA
HIGH STREET
WHARFE LA
A153
MARMION RD
STEANER RD
TUMBY ROAD
GOODHAM ROAD
Mast
Bede Farm
Troy Wood Farm
1 LANGRICK RD
2 SANDY BANK
Tumby House Farm
Wildmore Fen

58

PH
PO
PARK LA
Coningsby

22 A 23 B 24 C 25 D 26 E 27 F

For full street detail of the highlighted area see page 207.

F4
1 TOFT HURN
2 RECTORY LA
3 CHURCH LA
4 WOODMAN'S CT
5 CHURCH RI
6 KIME'S LA
7 SHOP HL

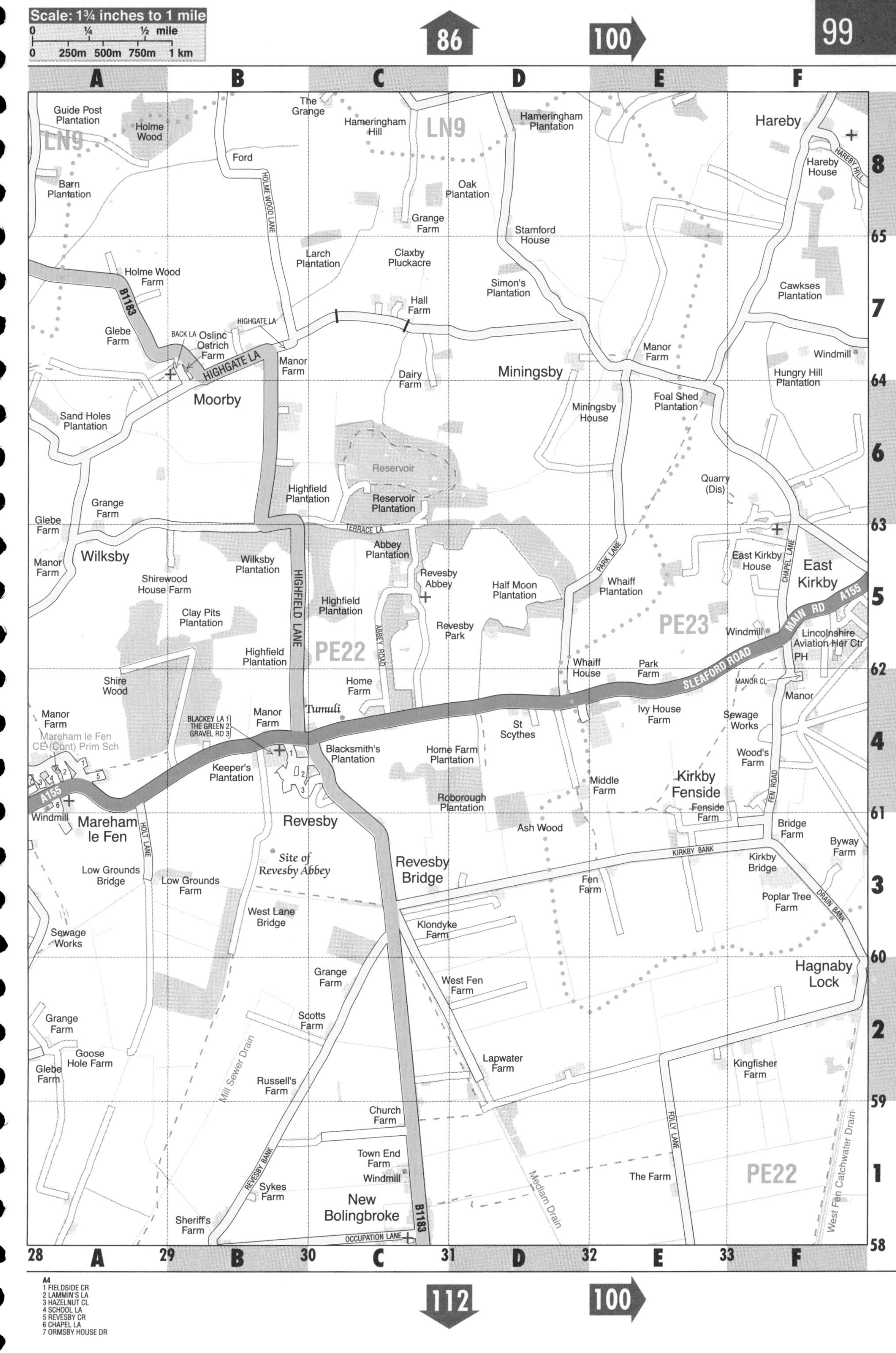

99
87

Scale: 1¾ inches to 1 mile

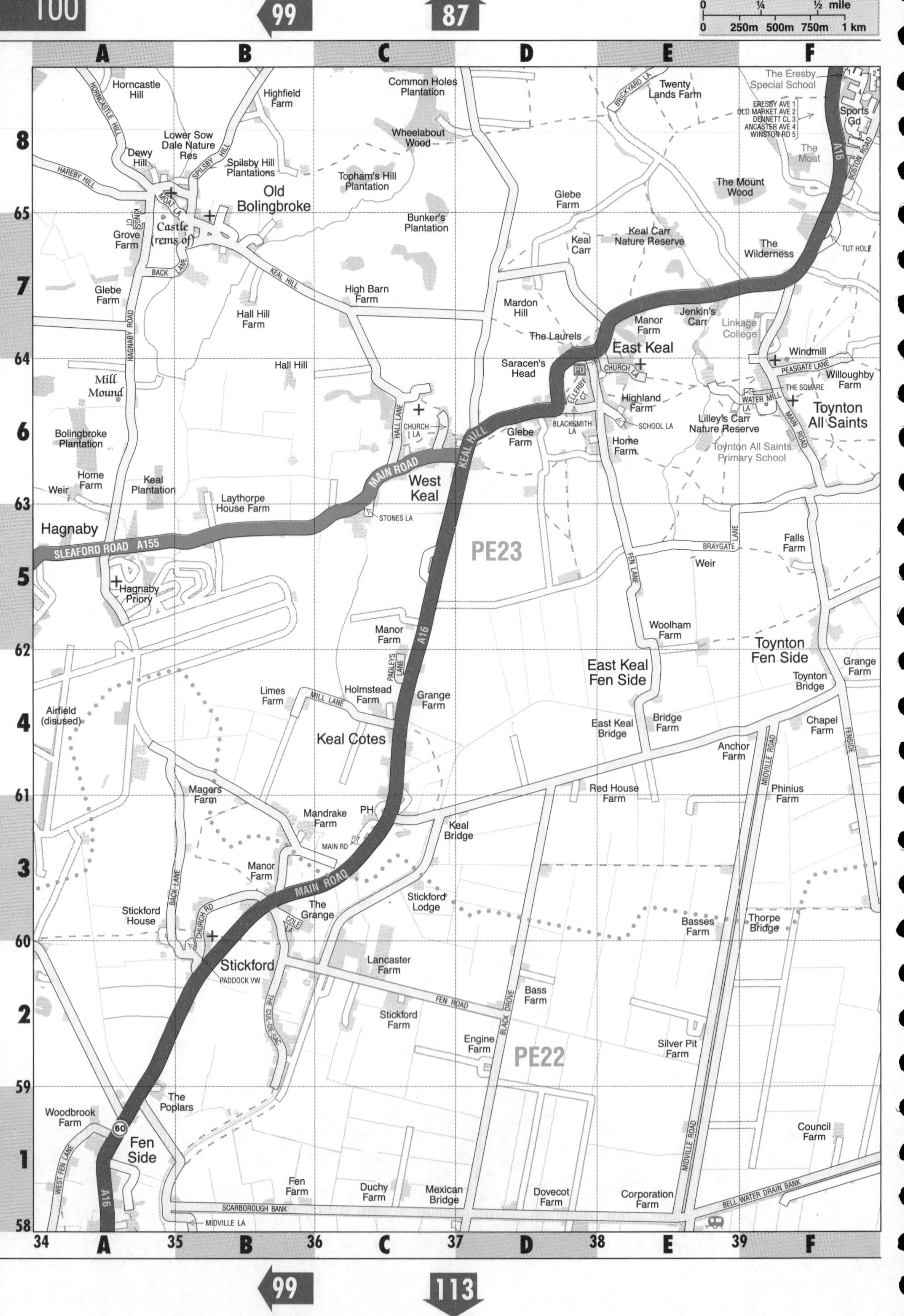

Old Bolingbroke
Horncastle Hill
Highfield Farm
Common Holes Plantation
Twenty Lands Farm
The Eresby Special School
Lower Sow Dale Nature Res
Dewy Hill
Spilsby Hill Plantations
Wheelabout Wood
Topham's Hill Plantation
Castle (rems of)
Grove Farm
Bunker's Plantation
Glebe Farm
Keal Carr
Keal Carr Nature Reserve
The Mount Wood
The Wilderness
The Moat
Sports Gd
High Barn Farm
Hall Hill Farm
Mardon Hill
Manor Farm
Jenkin's Carr
Linkage College
The Laurels
East Keal
Hall Hill
Saracen's Head
Windmill
Willoughby Farm
Mill Mound
Highland Farm
Toynton All Saints
Lilley's Carr Nature Reserve
Bolingbroke Plantation
Home Farm
Toynton All Saints Primary School
West Keal
Keal Plantation
Weir
Laythorpe House Farm
Hagnaby
PE23
Falls Farm
Hagnaby Priory
Woolham Farm
Toynton Fen Side
East Keal Fen Side
Grange Farm
Toynton Bridge
Limes Farm
Holmstead Farm
Airfield (disused)
Keal Cotes
East Keal Bridge
Bridge Farm
Chapel Farm
Anchor Farm
Magers Farm
Red House Farm
Phinius Farm
Mandrake Farm
PH
Keal Bridge
Manor Farm
Stickford Lodge
The Grange
Stickford House
Basses Farm
Thorpe Bridge
Stickford
Lancaster Farm
Bass Farm
Stickford Farm
Engine Farm
PE22
Silver Pit Farm
The Poplars
Woodbrook Farm
Fen Side
Council Farm
Fen Farm
Duchy Farm
Mexican Bridge
Dovecot Farm
Corporation Farm
SLEAFORD ROAD A155
A16
MAIN ROAD
KEAL HILL
HAGNABY ROAD
BACK LANE
MOAT LA
SPILSBY HILL
HAREBY HILL
HORNCASTLE HILL
KEAL HILL
CHURCH LA
HALL LANE
STONES LA
BRICKYARD LA
ERESBY AVE 1
OLD MARKET AVE 2
DENNETT CL 3
ANCASTER AVE 4
WINSTON RD 5
BOSTON ROAD
TUT HOLE
PEASGATE LANE
THE SQUARE
WATER MILL LA
MAIN ROAD
ELLERBY CT
BLACKSMITH LA
SCHOOL LA
BRAYGATE LANE
FEN LANE
PADLEYS LANE
MILL LANE
MIDVILLE ROAD
FENSIDE
MAIN RD
CHURCH RD
COLE LA
PADDOCK VW
THE CUL-DE-SAC
FEN ROAD
BLACK DROVE
SCARBOROUGH BANK
MIDVILLE LA
BELL WATER DRAIN BANK
WEST FEN LANE

99
113

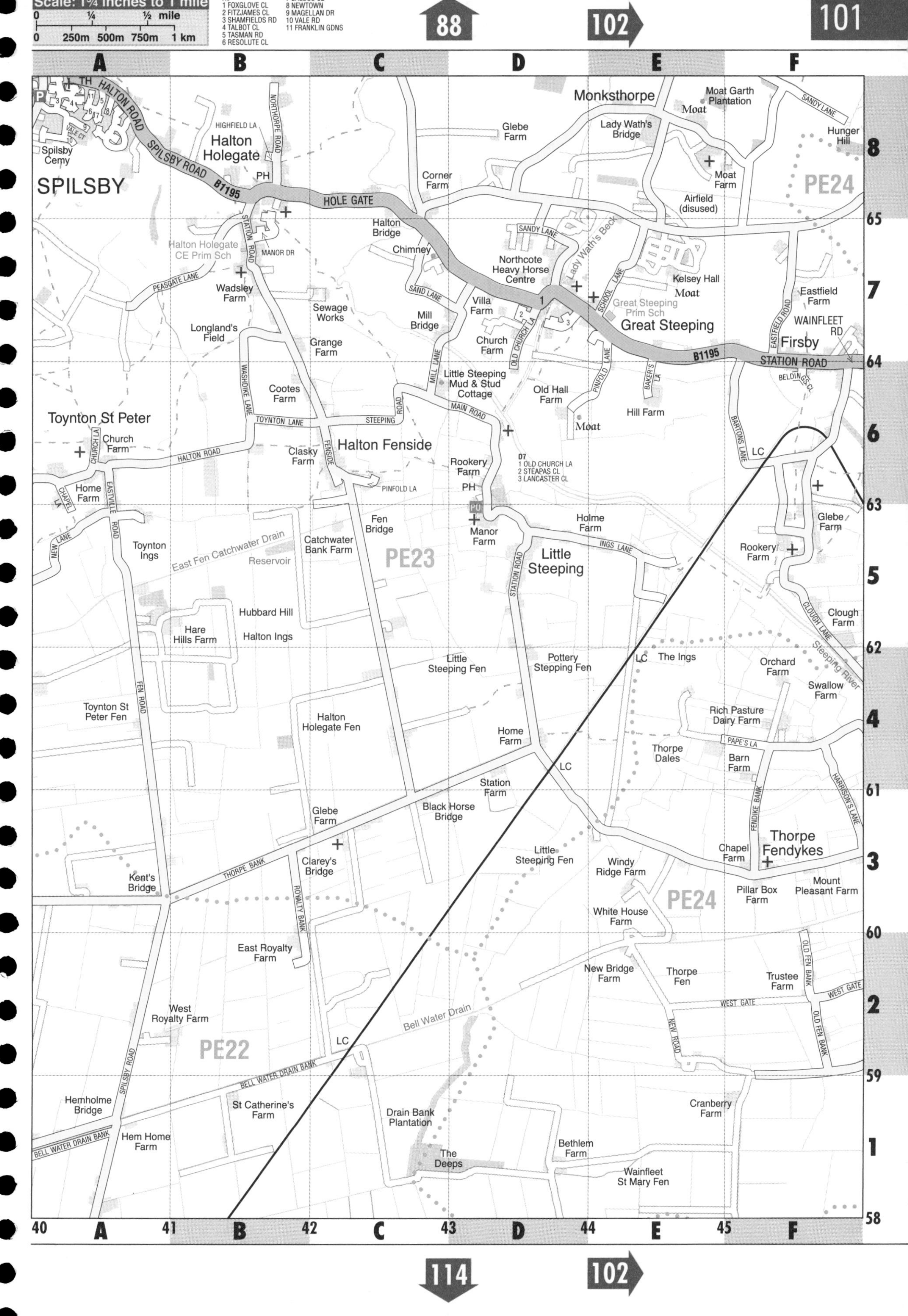
Scale: 1¾ inches to 1 mile
0 ¼ ½ mile
0 250m 500m 750m 1 km
A8
1 FOXGLOVE CL
2 FITZJAMES CL
3 SHAMFIELDS RD
4 TALBOT CL
5 TASMAN RD
6 RESOLUTE CL
7 EREBUS CL
8 NEWTOWN
9 MAGELLAN DR
10 VALE RD
11 FRANKLIN GDNS
88
102
SPILSBY
Spilsby Cemy
HALTON ROAD
SPILSBY ROAD
B1195
HOLE GATE
Halton Holegate
HIGHFIELD LA
NORTHORPE ROAD
PH
STATION ROAD
MANOR DR
Halton Holegate CE Prim Sch
PEASGATE LANE
Wadsley Farm
Longland's Field
Sewage Works
Grange Farm
Halton Bridge
Chimney
SAND LANE
Mill Bridge
Corner Farm
Glebe Farm
Monksthorpe
Lady Wath's Bridge
Moat Garth Plantation
Moat
Moat Farm
Airfield (disused)
Hunger Hill
SANDY LANE
PE24
SANDY LANE
Lady Wath's Beck
Northcote Heavy Horse Centre
Villa Farm
Church Farm
OLD CHURCH LA
SCHOOL LANE
Great Steeping Prim Sch
Great Steeping
Kelsey Hall
Eastfield Farm
EASTFIELD ROAD
WAINFLEET RD
Firsby
STATION ROAD
BELDINGS CL
PINFOLD LANE
BAKER'S LA
Old Hall Farm
Hill Farm
Little Steeping Mud & Stud Cottage
MILL LANE
MAIN ROAD
Cootes Farm
WASHDIKE LANE
TOYNTON LANE
STEEPING ROAD
Toynton St Peter
Church Farm
CHURCH LA
HALTON ROAD
Clasky Farm
FENSIDE
Halton Fenside
Rookery Farm
D7
1 OLD CHURCH LA
2 STEAPAS CL
3 LANCASTER CL
BARTONS LANE
LC
Home Farm
CHAPEL LA
EASTVILLE ROAD
PINFOLD LA
PU
Manor Farm
Fen Bridge
Holme Farm
INGS LANE
Little Steeping
Glebe Farm
Rookery Farm
NEW LANE
Toynton Ings
East Fen Catchwater Drain
Reservoir
Catchwater Bank Farm
PE23
STATION ROAD
CLOUGH LANE
Clough Farm
Hubbard Hill
Hare Hills Farm
Halton Ings
Little Steeping Fen
Pottery Stepping Fen
LC
The Ings
Orchard Farm
Steeping River
Swallow Farm
Toynton St Peter Fen
FEN ROAD
Halton Holegate Fen
Home Farm
Rich Pasture Dairy Farm
PAPE'S LA
Thorpe Dales
Barn Farm
LC
Station Farm
FENDIKE BANK
HARRISON'S LANE
Black Horse Bridge
Glebe Farm
Little Steeping Fen
Windy Ridge Farm
Chapel Farm
Thorpe Fendykes
Kent's Bridge
THORPE BANK
Clarey's Bridge
ROYALTY BANK
PE24
Pillar Box Farm
Mount Pleasant Farm
White House Farm
East Royalty Farm
New Bridge Farm
Thorpe Fen
Trustee Farm
OLD FEN BANK
WEST GATE
WEST GATE
West Royalty Farm
Bell Water Drain
NEW ROAD
PE22
LC
SPILSBY ROAD
BELL WATER DRAIN BANK
Hemholme Bridge
St Catherine's Farm
Drain Bank Plantation
Cranberry Farm
BELL WATER DRAIN BANK
Hem Home Farm
The Deeps
Bethlem Farm
Wainfleet St Mary Fen
A B C D E F
8 65 7 64 6 63 5 62 4 61 3 60 2 59 1 58
40 41 42 43 44 45
114
102

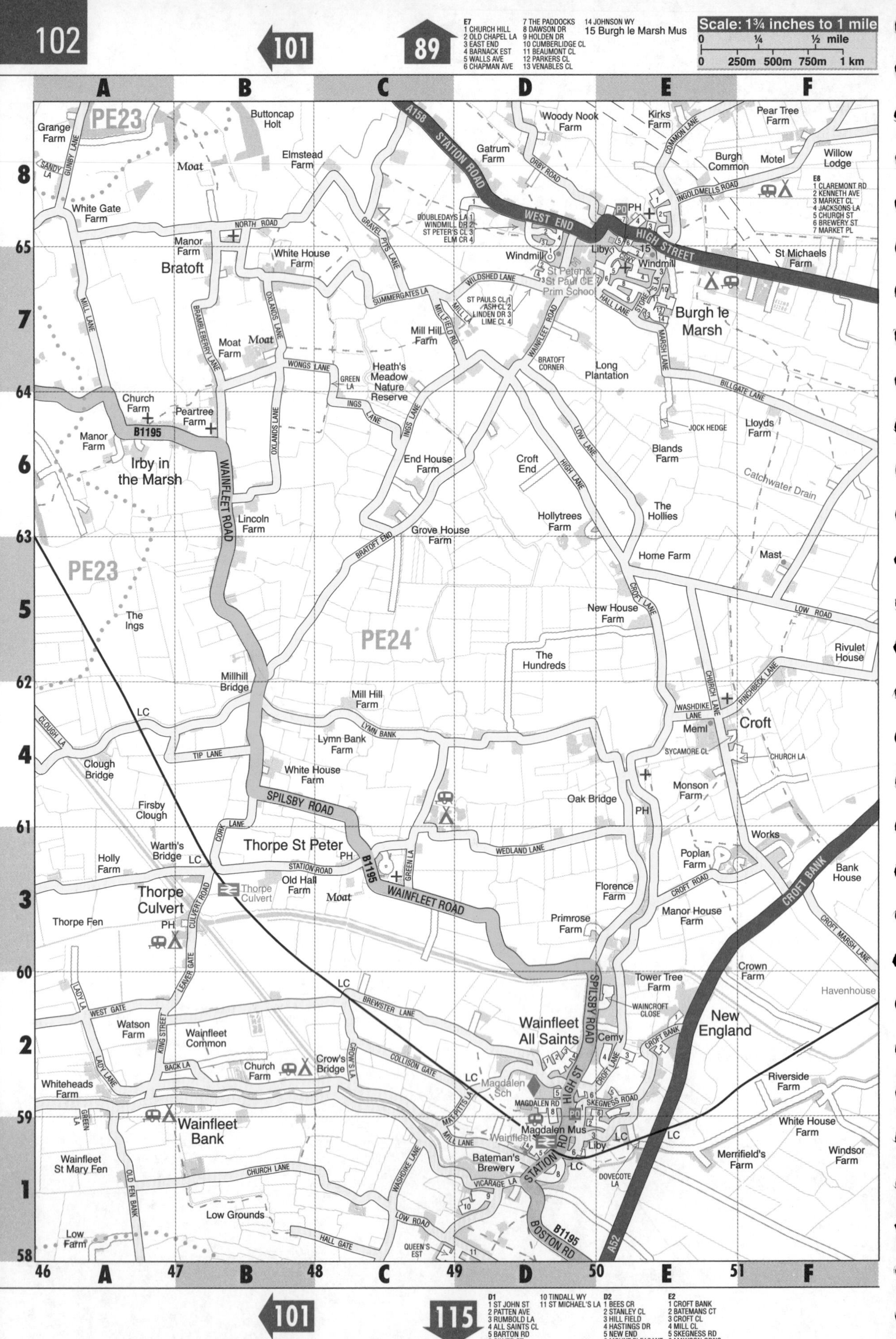
101
89
E7
1 CHURCH HILL
2 OLD CHAPEL LA
3 EAST END
4 BARNACK EST
5 WALLS AVE
6 CHAPMAN AVE
7 THE PADDOCKS
8 DAWSON DR
9 HOLDEN DR
10 CUMBERLIDGE CL
11 BEAUMONT CL
12 PARKERS CL
13 VENABLES CL
14 JOHNSON WY
15 Burgh le Marsh Mus
Scale: 1¾ inches to 1 mile
0 ¼ ½ mile
0 250m 500m 750m 1 km
A B C D E F
PE23
Grange Farm
Buttoncap Holt
Moat
Elmstead Farm
Gatrum Farm
Woody Nook Farm
Kirks Farm
Pear Tree Farm
Burgh Common
Motel
Willow Lodge
E8
1 CLAREMONT RD
2 KENNETH AVE
3 MARKET CL
4 JACKSONS LA
5 CHURCH ST
6 BREWERY ST
7 MARKET PL
White Gate Farm
NORTH ROAD
Manor Farm
Bratoft
White House Farm
DOUBLEDAYS LA 1
WINDMILL DR 2
ST PETER'S CL 3
ELM CR 4
WEST END
HIGH STREET
Windmill
Liby
Windmill
St Michaels Farm
St Peter & St Paul CE Prim School
WILDSHED LANE
SUMMERGATES LA
ST PAULS CL 1
ASH CL 2
LINDEN DR 3
LIME CL 4
Burgh le Marsh
Moat Farm
Moat
Mill Hill Farm
Heath's Meadow Nature Reserve
WONGS LANE
BRATOFT CORNER
Long Plantation
BILLGATE LANE
Church Farm
Peartree Farm
Manor Farm
B1195
Irby in the Marsh
JOCK HEDGE
Lloyds Farm
Blands Farm
End House Farm
Croft End
Catchwater Drain
The Hollies
Lincoln Farm
Hollytrees Farm
Grove House Farm
BRATOFT END
Home Farm
Mast
PE23
The Ings
PE24
New House Farm
LOW ROAD
Rivulet House
The Hundreds
Millhill Bridge
Mill Hill Farm
LYMN BANK
WASHDIKE LANE
Meml
Croft
Lymn Bank Farm
CLOUGH LA
TIP LANE
SYCAMORE CL
CHURCH LA
Clough Bridge
White House Farm
Monson Farm
Firsby Clough
SPILSBY ROAD
Oak Bridge
PH
CORK LANE
Thorpe St Peter
WEDLAND LANE
Works
Holly Farm
Warth's Bridge
LC
STATION ROAD
PH
GREEN LA
Poplar Farm
Bank House
Thorpe Culvert
Thorpe Culvert
Old Hall Farm
Moat
WAINFLEET ROAD
Florence Farm
CROFT ROAD
CROFT BANK
Thorpe Fen
Manor House Farm
Primrose Farm
CROFT MARSH LANE
CULVERT ROAD
LEAVER GATE
Crown Farm
Tower Tree Farm
Havenhouse
LADY LANE
WEST GATE
BREWSTER LANE
WAINCROFT CLOSE
Watson Farm
Wainfleet Common
Wainfleet All Saints
New England
KING STREET
BACK LA
Church Farm
Crow's Bridge
COLLISON GATE
Cemy
Whiteheads Farm
LC
Magdalen Sch
Riverside Farm
MAGDALEN RD
SKEGNESS ROAD
Wainfleet Bank
Magdalen Mus
Wainfleet
White House Farm
MILL LANE
Liby
LC
Merrifield's Farm
Windsor Farm
Wainfleet St Mary Fen
Bateman's Brewery
STATION RD
CHURCH LANE
VICARAGE LA
DOVECOTE LA
WASHDIKE LANE
Low Grounds
LOW ROAD
Low Farm
HALL GATE
QUEEN'S EST
BOSTON RD
A52
46 A 47 B 48 C 49 D 50 E 51 F
101
115
D1
1 ST JOHN ST
2 PATTEN AVE
3 RUMBOLD LA
4 ALL SAINTS CL
5 BARTON RD
6 SILVER ST
7 COLLEGE CL
8 HAVEN SIDE
9 BETHLEM CRES
10 TINDALL WY
11 ST MICHAEL'S LA
D2
1 BEES CR
2 STANLEY CL
3 HILL FIELD
4 HASTINGS DR
5 NEW END
6 MOUNT PLEASANT
7 BARKHAM ST
8 WINCHESTER RD
E2
1 CROFT BANK
2 BATEMANS CT
3 CROFT CL
4 MILL CL
5 SKEGNESS RD
6 MAWSON GDNS
7 MERRIFIELD RD

A   B   C   D   E   F

Younger's Lane
Mill Hill Farm
Ingle Side
Mill Hill
Grange Farm
HIDE'S LANE
MILL
206 Seathorne
WINTHORPE AV
CHURCH END
Cemy
PH
PH
QUEEN'S DR
P
Burgh Marsh
EVERINGTON'S LANE
CHURCH LANE
Roydene Farm
MARTIN WY
LADY MATILDA'S DR
8

GLEBE CL 1
HERON CL 2
KINGFISHER DR 3
COOTS CL 4
AYLESBURY DR 5
P
L Ctr
CH
DAVOS WAY
THE NEEDLES
Winthorpe
Recn Gd.
Sch
Sea Bank
65

KINGFISHER DR 1
MALLARD WY 2
SWAN DR 3
TEAL CL 4
BEACON PK DR
BRAMLEY WK
A52
North Shore Golf Course

MIDDLEMARSH ROAD
A158
SKEGNESS ROAD
Coronation Farm
BURGH ROAD
SKEGNESS
OLD ROMAN BANK
CH Hotel
7

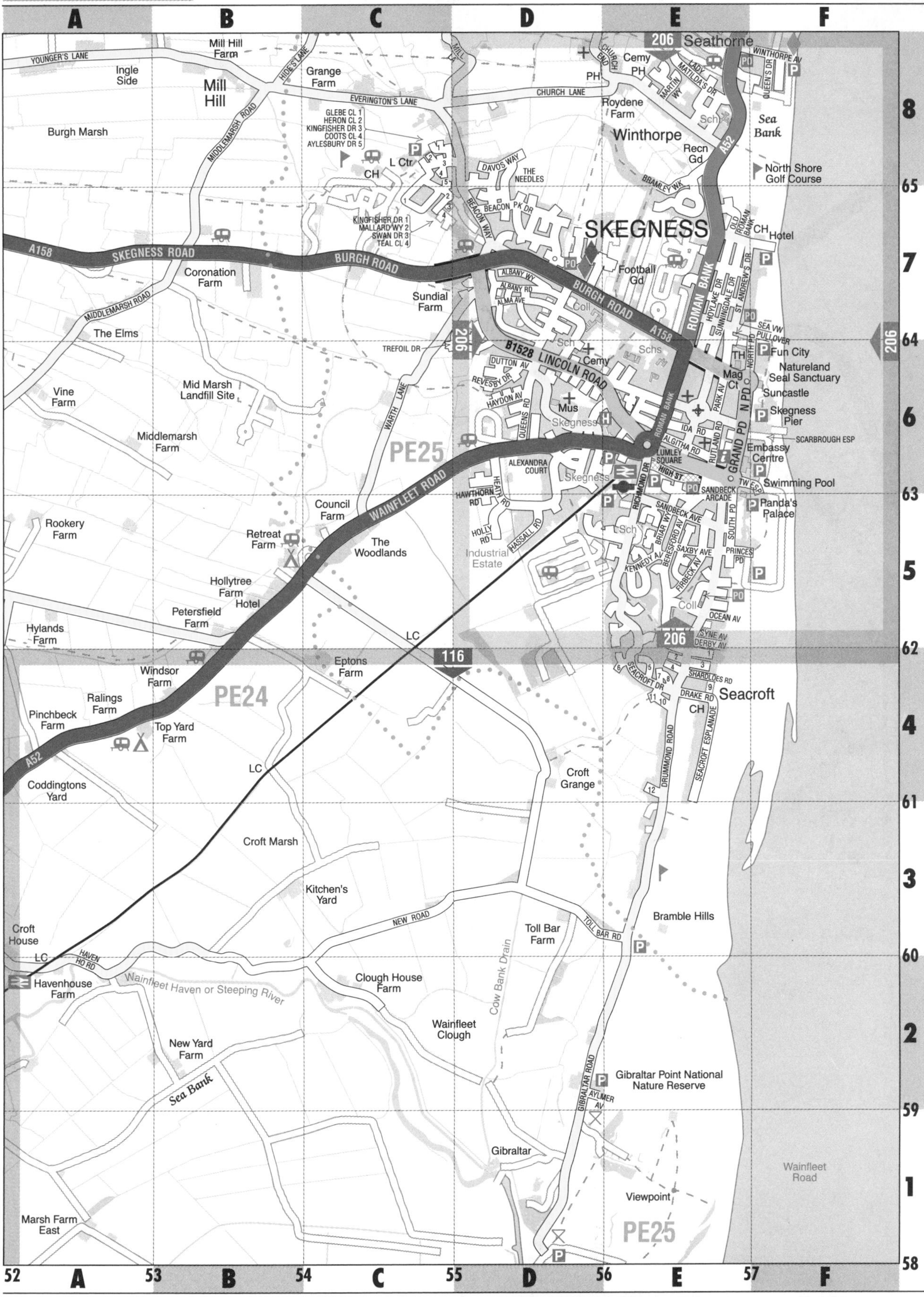

Middlemarsh Road
The Elms
Sundial Farm
ALBANY WY
ALBANY RD
ALMA AVE
Football Gd
BURGH ROAD
A158
ROMAN BANK
P
SEA VW
P
206
Fun City
64

TREFOIL DR
206
B1528
DUTTON AV
LINCOLN ROAD
Cemy
Schs
Coll
Sch
Mag Ct
TH
Natureland Seal Sanctuary
Suncastle
Vine Farm
Mid Marsh Landfill Site
WARTH LANE
REVESBY DR
HAYDON AV
QUEENS RD
Mus
Skegness
H
PARK AV
GRAND PD
N PD
IDA RD
RUTLAND RD
Skegness Pier
SCARBROUGH ESP
Embassy Centre
6

PE25
Middlemarsh Farm
WAINFLEET ROAD
HAWTHORN RD
HEATH RD
HOLLY RD
ALEXANDRA COURT
Skegness
LUMLEY SQUARE
HIGH ST
ROMAN BANK
P
P
P
Swimming Pool
63

Council Farm
Retreat Farm
The Woodlands
Industrial Estate
HASSALL RD
SANDBECK
ARCADE
SANDBECK AVE
BRIAR RD
BERESFORD RD
SAXBY AVE
KENNEDY AVE
FIRBECK AV
PRINCES
PD
SOUTH PD
P
LPO
TW
Panda's Palace
Rookery Farm
Hollytree Farm Hotel
Petersfield Farm
LC
LSch
Coll
OCEAN AV
5

Hylands Farm
Windsor Farm
Eptons Farm
116
206
SYNE AV
DERBY AV
SHARDLOES RD
DRAKE RD
Seacroft
62

PE24
Ralings Farm
Pinchbeck Farm
Top Yard Farm
SEACROFT
CH
SEACROFT ESPLANADE
4

A52
Coddingtons Yard
LC
Croft Marsh
Croft Grange
DRUMMOND ROAD
61

Croft House
LC
HAVEN HO RD
Kitchen's Yard
NEW ROAD
Bramble Hills
TOLL BAR RD
P
3

Havenhouse Farm
Wainfleet Haven or Steeping River
Toll Bar Farm
Cow Bank Drain
60

New Yard Farm
Clough House Farm
P
Gibraltar Point National Nature Reserve
GIBRALTAR ROAD
AYLMER AV
2

Sea Bank
Wainfleet Clough
59

Marsh Farm East
Gibraltar
Viewpoint
PE25
1

P
58

52   A   53   B   54   C   55   D   56   E   57   F

For full street detail of the highlighted area see page 206.

E4
1 ALBERT AVE
2 VINE RD
3 BUCKTHORN AVE
4 NORWOOD RD
5 PRECINCT CRES
6 BAYES RD
7 GREEN LA
8 LINKS CRES
9 SEA FRONT RD
10 SEACROFT SQ
11 HESKETH CRES
12 FREDERICA RD

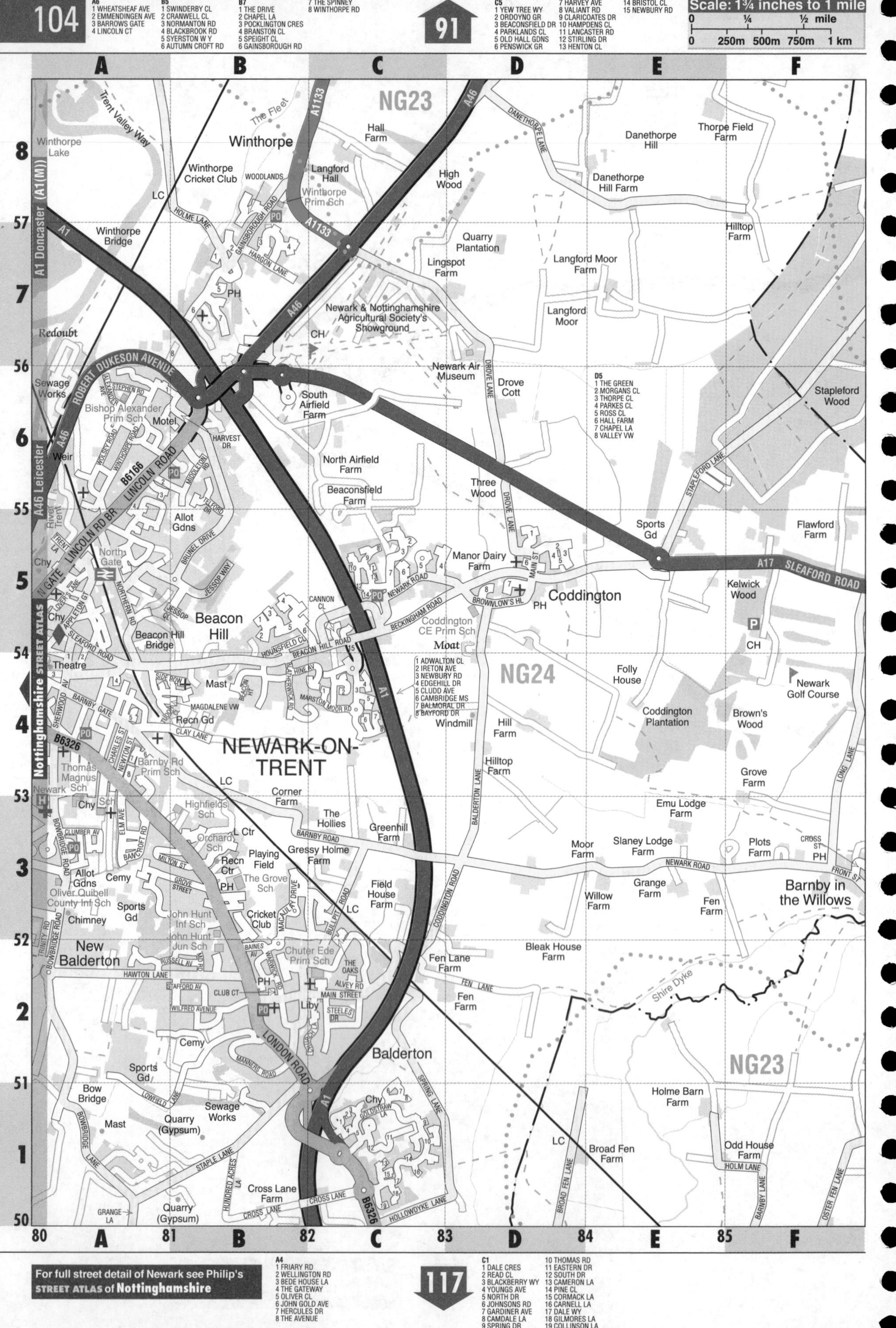
104
A6
1 WHEATSHEAF AVE
2 EMMENDINGEN AVE
3 BARROWS GATE
4 LINCOLN CT
B5
1 SWINDERBY CL
2 CRANWELL CL
3 NORMANTON RD
4 BLACKBROOK RD
5 SYERSTON W Y
6 AUTUMN CROFT RD
B7
1 THE DRIVE
2 CHAPEL LA
3 POCKLINGTON CRES
4 BRANSTON CL
5 SPEIGHT CL
6 GAINSBOROUGH RD
7 THE SPINNEY
8 WINTHORPE RD
91
C5
1 YEW TREE WY
2 ORDOYNO GR
3 BEACONSFIELD DR
4 PARKLANDS CL
5 OLD HALL GDNS
6 PENSWICK GR
7 HARVEY AVE
8 VALIANT RD
9 CLARICOATES DR
10 HAMPDENS CL
11 LANCASTER RD
12 STIRLING DR
13 HENTON CL
14 BRISTOL CL
15 NEWBURY RD
Scale: 1¾ inches to 1 mile
0 ¼ ½ mile
0 250m 500m 750m 1 km
A B C D E F
NG23
Winthorpe Lake
Trent Valley Way
The Fleet
Winthorpe
Hall Farm
Danethorpe Hill
Thorpe Field Farm
DANETHORPE LANE
Winthorpe Cricket Club
WOODLANDS
Langford Hall
Winthorpe Prim Sch
High Wood
Danethorpe Hill Farm
LC
HOLME LANE
GAINSBOROUGH ROAD
A1133
A46
A1 Doncaster (A1(M))
Winthorpe Bridge
Quarry Plantation
Hilltop Farm
HARGON LANE
Lingspot Farm
Langford Moor Farm
PH
Langford Moor
Newark & Nottinghamshire Agricultural Society's Showground
Redoubt
CH
Sewage Works
ROBERT DUKESON AVENUE
STEPHEN RD
Bishop Alexander Prim Sch
Motel
South Airfield Farm
Newark Air Museum
Drove Cott
DROVE LANE
D5
1 THE GREEN
2 MORGANS CL
3 THORPE CL
4 PARKES CL
5 ROSS CL
6 HALL FARM
7 CHAPEL LA
8 VALLEY VW
Stapleford Wood
HARVEST DR
A46 Leicester
Weir
WOLSEY ROAD
WINTHORPE ROAD
B6166
LINCOLN ROAD
MIDDLETON RD
North Airfield Farm
Three Wood
STAPLEFORD LANE
Beaconsfield Farm
TELFORD DR
River Trent
LINCOLN RD BR
Allot Gdns
BRUNEL DRIVE
Sports Gd
Flawford Farm
North Gate
Manor Dairy Farm
MAIN ST
A17 SLEAFORD ROAD
Chy
JESSOP WAY
NEWARK ROAD
Kelwick Wood
N GATE
APPLETON GT
NORTHERN RD
JESSOP CL
CANNON CL
BECKINGHAM ROAD
BROWNLOW'S HL
Coddington
PH
Beacon Hill
Coddington CE Prim Sch
P
SLEAFORD ROAD
Beacon Hill Bridge
HOUNSFIELD CL
BEACON HILL ROAD
Moat
CH
Theatre
HINE AV
1 ADWALTON CL
2 IRETON AVE
3 NEWBURY RD
4 EDGEHILL DR
5 CLUDD AVE
6 CAMBRIDGE MS
7 BALMORAL DR
8 BAYFORD DR
NG24
Folly House
Newark Golf Course
SIDE ROW
Mast
BEACON HT
MARSTON MOOR RD
A1
Coddington Plantation
Brown's Wood
SHERWOOD
BARNBY GATE
MAGDALENE VW
Recn Gd
Windmill
Hill Farm
B6326
CLAY LANE
NEWARK-ON-TRENT
Hilltop Farm
Grove Farm
CHARLES ST
NEWTON ST
Barnby Rd Prim Sch
Thomas Magnus Sch
LC
Corner Farm
LONG LANE
Nottinghamshire STREET ATLAS
Newark
Chy
Sch
Highfields Sch
Emu Lodge Farm
BOWBRIDGE ROAD
CLUMBER AV
ELM AVE
BANCROFT RD
Orchard Sch
L Ctr
The Hollies
Greenhill Farm
BALDERTON LANE
BARNBY ROAD
Moor Farm
Slaney Lodge Farm
Plots Farm
CROSS ST
PH
MILTON ST
Recn Ctr
Playing Field
Gressy Holme Farm
NEWARK ROAD
FRONT ST
Allot Gdns
Cemy
GROVE STREET
PH
The Grove Sch
Field House Farm
CODDINGTON ROAD
Grange Farm
Barnby in the Willows
Oliver Quibell County Inf Sch
Sports Gd
John Hunt Inf Sch
MACAULAY DRIVE
BULLPIT ROAD
LC
Willow Farm
Fen Farm
Chimney
Cricket Club
John Hunt Jun Sch
TRINITY RD
New Balderton
BAINES AV
RUSSELL AV
Chuter Ede Prim Sch
THE OAKS
Bleak House Farm
HAWTON LANE
Fen Lane Farm
STAFFORD AV
CLUB CT
PH
ALVEY RD
MAIN STREET
FEN LANE
Shire Dyke
Fen Farm
WILFRED AVENUE
Liby
STEELES DR
LONDON ROAD
Cemy
MANNERS ROAD
Balderton
SPRING LANE
NG23
Sports Gd
Bow Bridge
LOWFIELD LANE
Chy
GOLDSTRAW LA
Holme Barn Farm
Sewage Works
Quarry (Gypsum)
Mast
BOWBRIDGE LANE
LC
Broad Fen Farm
Odd House Farm
HOLM LANE
STAPLE LANE
HUNDRED ACRES LA
Cross Lane Farm
CROSS LANE
B6326
BROAD FEN LANE
BARNBY LANE
OSTER FEN LANE
GRANGE LA
Quarry (Gypsum)
HOLLOWDYKE LANE
8 57 7 56 6 55 5 54 4 53 3 52 2 51 1 50
80 81 82 83 84 85
For full street detail of Newark see Philip's STREET ATLAS of Nottinghamshire
A4
1 FRIARY RD
2 WELLINGTON RD
3 BEDE HOUSE LA
4 THE GATEWAY
5 OLIVER CL
6 JOHN GOLD AVE
7 HERCULES DR
8 THE AVENUE
117
C1
1 DALE CRES
2 READ CL
3 BLACKBERRY WY
4 YOUNGS AVE
5 NORTH DR
6 JOHNSONS RD
7 GARDINER AVE
8 CAMDALE LA
9 SPRING DR
10 THOMAS RD
11 EASTERN DR
12 SOUTH DR
13 CAMERON LA
14 PINE CL
15 CORMACK LA
16 CARNELL LA
17 DALE WY
18 GILMORES LA
19 COLLINSON LA

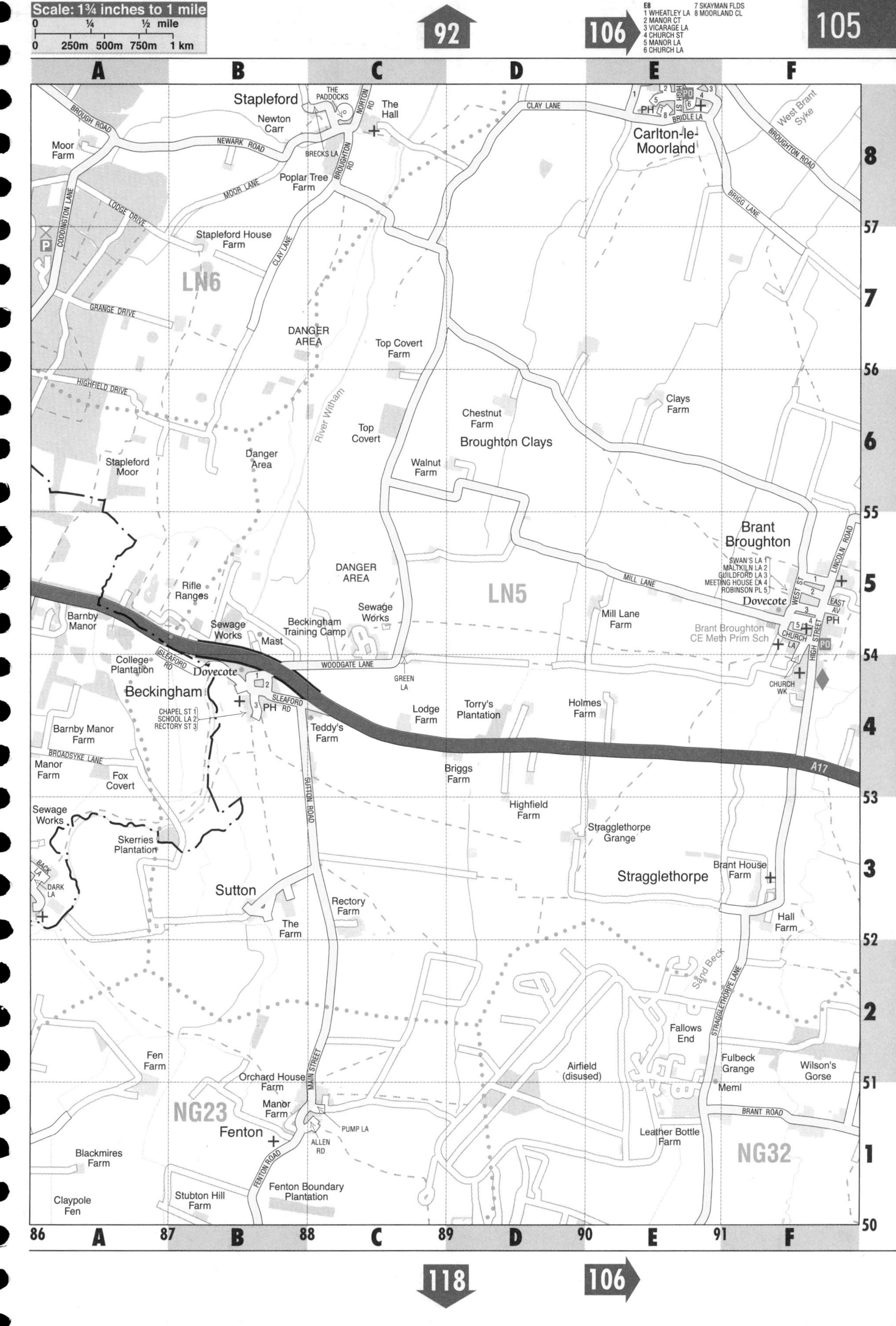

Scale: 1¾ inches to 1 mile

| 0 | ¼ | ½ | mile |
| 0 | 250m | 500m | 750m | 1 km |

92

106

105

E8
1 WHEATLEY LA
2 MANOR CT
3 VICARAGE LA
4 CHURCH ST
5 MANOR LA
6 CHURCH LA
7 SKAYMAN FLDS
8 MOORLAND CL

A B C D E F

8 57 7 56 6 55 5 54 4 53 3 52 2 51 1 50

Stapleford
Newton Carr
THE PADDOCKS
The Hall
Moor Farm
NEWARK ROAD
BROUGH ROAD
CODDINGTON LANE
LODGE DRIVE
GRANGE DRIVE
HIGHFIELD DRIVE
LN6
Stapleford House Farm
Poplar Tree Farm
MOOR LANE
BRECKS LA
CLAY LANE
BROUGHTON RD
NEWTON RD
DANGER AREA
Clay Lane
Carlton-le-Moorland
PH
West Brant Syke
BROUGHTON ROAD
BRIGG LANE
Top Covert Farm
Top Covert
River Witham
Danger Area
Stapleford Moor
Chestnut Farm
Broughton Clays
Walnut Farm
Clays Farm
DANGER AREA
LN5
Brant Broughton
SWAN'S LA 1
MALTKILN LA 2
GUILDFORD LA 3
MEETING HOUSE LA 4
ROBINSON PL 5
Dovecote
LINCOLN ROAD
WEST ST
HIGH STREET
EAST AV
PH
Rifle Ranges
Barnby Manor
Sewage Works
Mast
Beckingham Training Camp
Sewage Works
MILL LANE
Mill Lane Farm
Brant Broughton CE Meth Prim Sch
CHURCH LA
CHURCH WK
College Plantation
SLEAFORD RD
Dovecote
WOODGATE LANE
GREEN LA
Holmes Farm
Beckingham
CHAPEL ST 1
SCHOOL LA 2
RECTORY ST 3
PH
SLEAFORD RD
Teddy's Farm
Lodge Farm
Torry's Plantation
A17
Barnby Manor Farm
BROADSYKE LANE
Manor Farm
Fox Covert
Briggs Farm
Highfield Farm
Stragglethorpe Grange
Brant House Farm
Sewage Works
BACK LA
DARK LA
Skerries Plantation
SUTTON ROAD
Stragglethorpe
Hall Farm
Sutton
The Farm
Rectory Farm
SAND BECK
STRAGGLETHORPE LANE
Fallows End
Fulbeck Grange
Fen Farm
MAIN STREET
Orchard House Farm
Manor Farm
NG23
Fenton
PUMP LA
ALLEN RD
Airfield (disused)
Meml
Wilson's Gorse
BRANT ROAD
NG32
Blackmires Farm
FENTON ROAD
Stubton Hill Farm
Fenton Boundary Plantation
Leather Bottle Farm
Claypole Fen

86 A 87 B 88 C 89 D 90 E 91 F 50

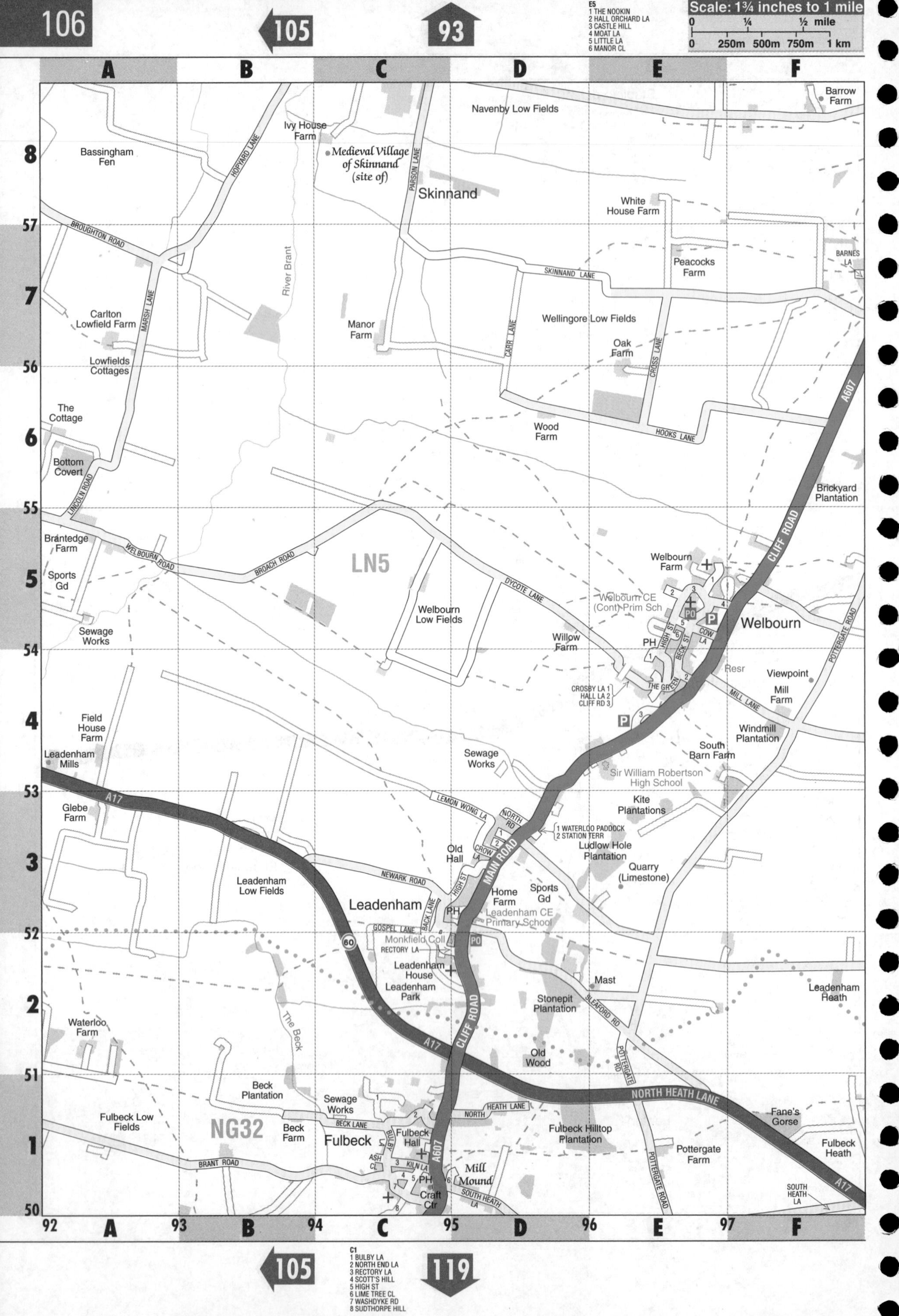

105
93

E5
1 THE NOOKIN
2 HALL ORCHARD LA
3 CASTLE HILL
4 MOAT LA
5 LITTLE LA
6 MANOR CL

Scale: 1¾ inches to 1 mile
0   ¼   ½   mile
0   250m   500m   750m   1 km

Barrow Farm

Bassingham Fen

Ivy House Farm

Medieval Village of Skinnand (site of)

Navenby Low Fields

White House Farm

BARNES LA

BROUGHTON ROAD

Skinnand

River Brant

SKINNAND LANE

Peacocks Farm

Carlton Lowfield Farm

Manor Farm

Wellingore Low Fields

CARR LANE

CRISS LANE

Oak Farm

Lowfields Cottages

A607

The Cottage

Wood Farm

HOOKS LANE

Brickyard Plantation

Bottom Covert

LINCOLN ROAD

Brantedge Farm

WELBOURN ROAD

BROACH ROAD

LN5

Welbourn Low Fields

DYCOTE LANE

Welbourn Farm

Welbourn CE (Cont) Prim Sch

PO
P

CLIFF ROAD

Welbourn

POTTERGATE ROAD

Sports Gd

Sewage Works

Willow Farm

PH

HIGH ST
BECK ST
COW LA

Resr

Viewpoint

Mill Farm

THE GREEN

MILL LANE

Field House Farm

CROSBY LA 1
HALL LA 2
CLIFF RD 3

P
3

South Barn Farm

Windmill Plantation

Leadenham Mills

Sewage Works

LEMON WONG LA

NORTH RD

Sir William Robertson High School

A17

Glebe Farm

Old Hall

CROW LA

Kite Plantations

1 WATERLOO PADDOCK
2 STATION TERR

Ludlow Hole Plantation

Quarry (Limestone)

Leadenham Low Fields

NEWARK ROAD

BACK LANE

MAIN ROAD

HIGH ST

Home Farm

Sports Gd

Leadenham CE Primary School

Leadenham

PH

GOSPEL LANE

60

Monkfield Coll
RECTORY LA

PO

Mast

Leadenham Heath

Leadenham House
Leadenham Park

Stonepit Plantation

SLEAFORD RD

Waterloo Farm

The Beck

CLIFF ROAD

A17

Old Wood

POTTERGATE RD

Beck Plantation

Sewage Works

Fulbeck Low Fields

NG32

Beck Farm

BECK LANE

Fulbeck Hall

A607

HEATH LANE

NORTH HEATH LANE

Fulbeck Hilltop Plantation

Fane's Gorse

Pottergate Farm

Fulbeck Heath

BRANT ROAD

Fulbeck

ASH CL

KILN LA

PH

Mill Mound

SOUTH HEATH LA

POTTERGATE ROAD

A17

Craft Ctr

SOUTH HEATH LA

105
119

C1
1 BULBY LA
2 NORTH END LA
3 RECTORY LA
4 SCOTT'S HILL
5 HIGH ST
6 LIME TREE CL
7 WASHDYKE RD
8 SUDTHORPE HILL

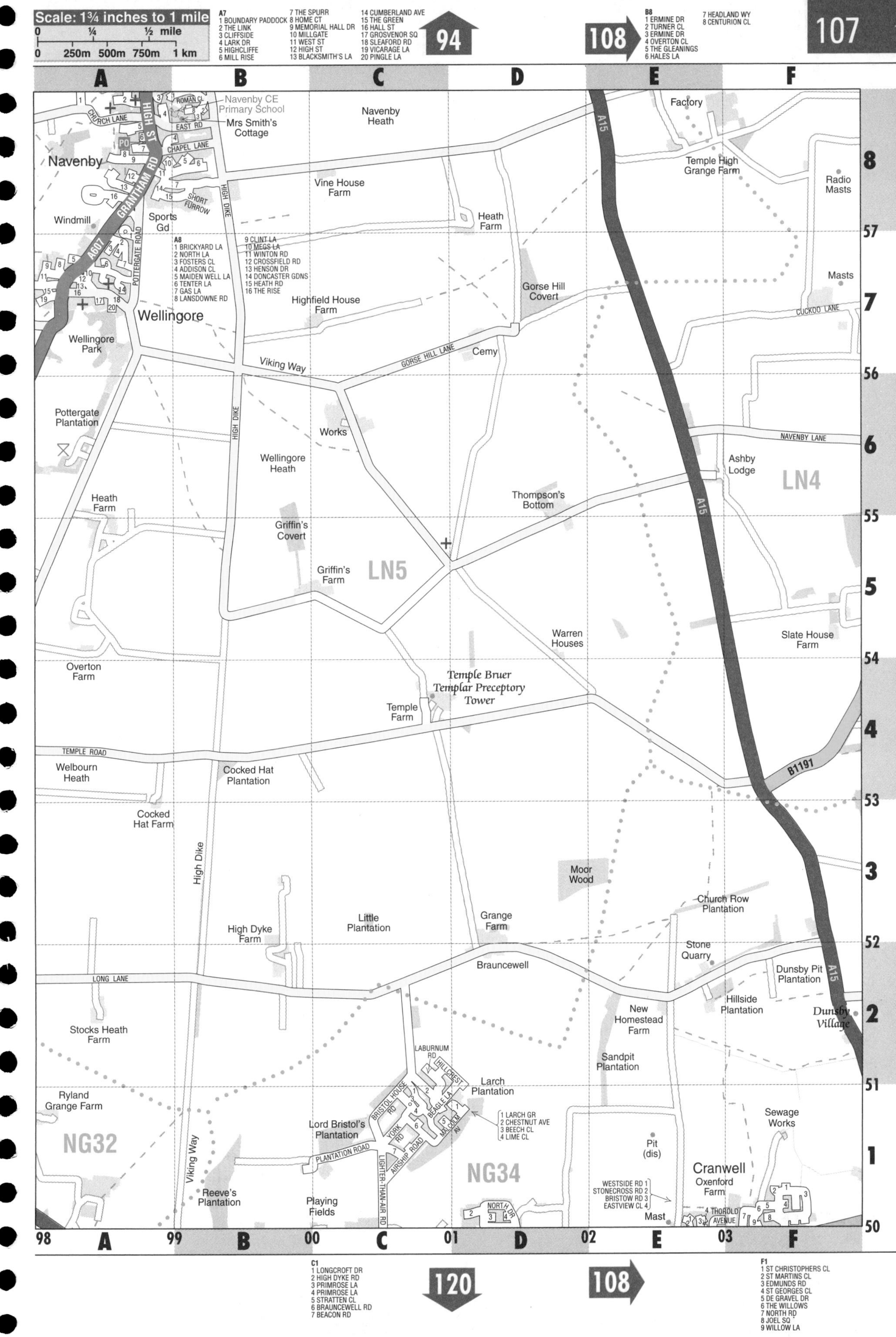

Map page with grid references and street index.

Scale: 1¾ inches to 1 mile

0   ¼   ½   mile
0   250m 500m 750m 1 km

A7
1 BOUNDARY PADDOCK
2 THE LINK
3 CLIFFSIDE
4 LARK DR
5 HIGHCLIFFE
6 MILL RISE

7 THE SPURR
8 HOME CT
9 MEMORIAL HALL DR
10 MILLGATE
11 WEST ST
12 HIGH ST
13 BLACKSMITH'S LA

14 CUMBERLAND AVE
15 THE GREEN
16 HALL ST
17 GROSVENOR SQ
18 SLEAFORD RD
19 VICARAGE LA
20 PINGLE LA

94

108

B8
1 ERMINE DR
2 TURNER CL
3 ERMINE DR
4 OVERTON CL
5 THE GLEANINGS
6 HALES LA

7 HEADLAND WY
8 CENTURION CL

107

A   B   C   D   E   F

Navenby CE Primary School

ROMAN CL

Mrs Smith's Cottage

EAST RD

CHURCH LANE

HIGH ST

GRANTHAM RD

CHAPEL LANE

Navenby

PO

SHORT FURROW

Windmill

Sports Gd

Navenby Heath

Factory

Temple High Grange Farm

Radio Masts

8

57

Vine House Farm

Heath Farm

POTTERGATE ROAD

A607

Wellingore

HIGH DIKE

A8
1 BRICKYARD LA
2 NORTH LA
3 FOSTERS CL
4 ADDISON CL
5 MAIDEN WELL LA
6 TENTER LA
7 GAS LA
8 LANSDOWNE RD

9 CLINT LA
10 MEGS LA
11 WINTON RD
12 CROSSFIELD RD
13 HENSON DR
14 DONCASTER GDNS
15 HEATH RD
16 THE RISE

Highfield House Farm

Gorse Hill Covert

Masts

CUCKOO LANE

7

Wellingore Park

Viking Way

GORSE HILL LANE

Cemy

56

Pottergate Plantation

Works

Wellingore Heath

Thompson's Bottom

NAVENBY LANE

Ashby Lodge

LN4

6

55

Heath Farm

Griffin's Covert

LN5

Griffin's Farm

A15

Warren Houses

Slate House Farm

5

54

Overton Farm

Temple Bruer Templar Preceptory Tower

Temple Farm

4

TEMPLE ROAD

Welbourn Heath

Cocked Hat Plantation

B1191

53

Cocked Hat Farm

HIGH DIKE

Moor Wood

3

High Dyke Farm

Little Plantation

Grange Farm

Church Row Plantation

Stone Quarry

52

LONG LANE

Brauncewell

Dunsby Pit Plantation

A15

2

Stocks Heath Farm

New Homestead Farm

Hillside Plantation

Dunsby Village

Ryland Grange Farm

NG32

Viking Way

LABURNUM RD

BRISTOL HOUSE RD

HILLCREST

BEAGLE LA

Larch Plantation

1 LARCH GR
2 CHESTNUT AVE
3 BEECH CL
4 LIME CL

Sandpit Plantation

Pit (dis)

Sewage Works

51

Lord Bristol's Plantation

YORK RD

AIRSHIP ROAD

PLANTATION ROAD

NG34

WESTSIDE RD 1
STONECROSS RD 2
BRISTOW RD 3
EASTVIEW CL 4

Cranwell

Oxenford Farm

THOROLD AVENUE

1

Reeve's Plantation

LIGHTER-THAN-AIR RD

Playing Fields

NORTH DR

Mast

50

98   A   99   B   00   C   01   D   02   E   03   F

C1
1 LONGCROFT DR
2 HIGH DYKE RD
3 PRIMROSE LA
4 PRIMROSE LA
5 STRATTEN CL
6 BRAUNCEWELL RD
7 BEACON RD

120

108

F1
1 ST CHRISTOPHERS CL
2 ST MARTINS CL
3 EDMUNDS RD
4 ST GEORGES CL
5 DE GRAVEL DR
6 THE WILLOWS
7 NORTH RD
8 JOEL SQ
9 WILLOW LA

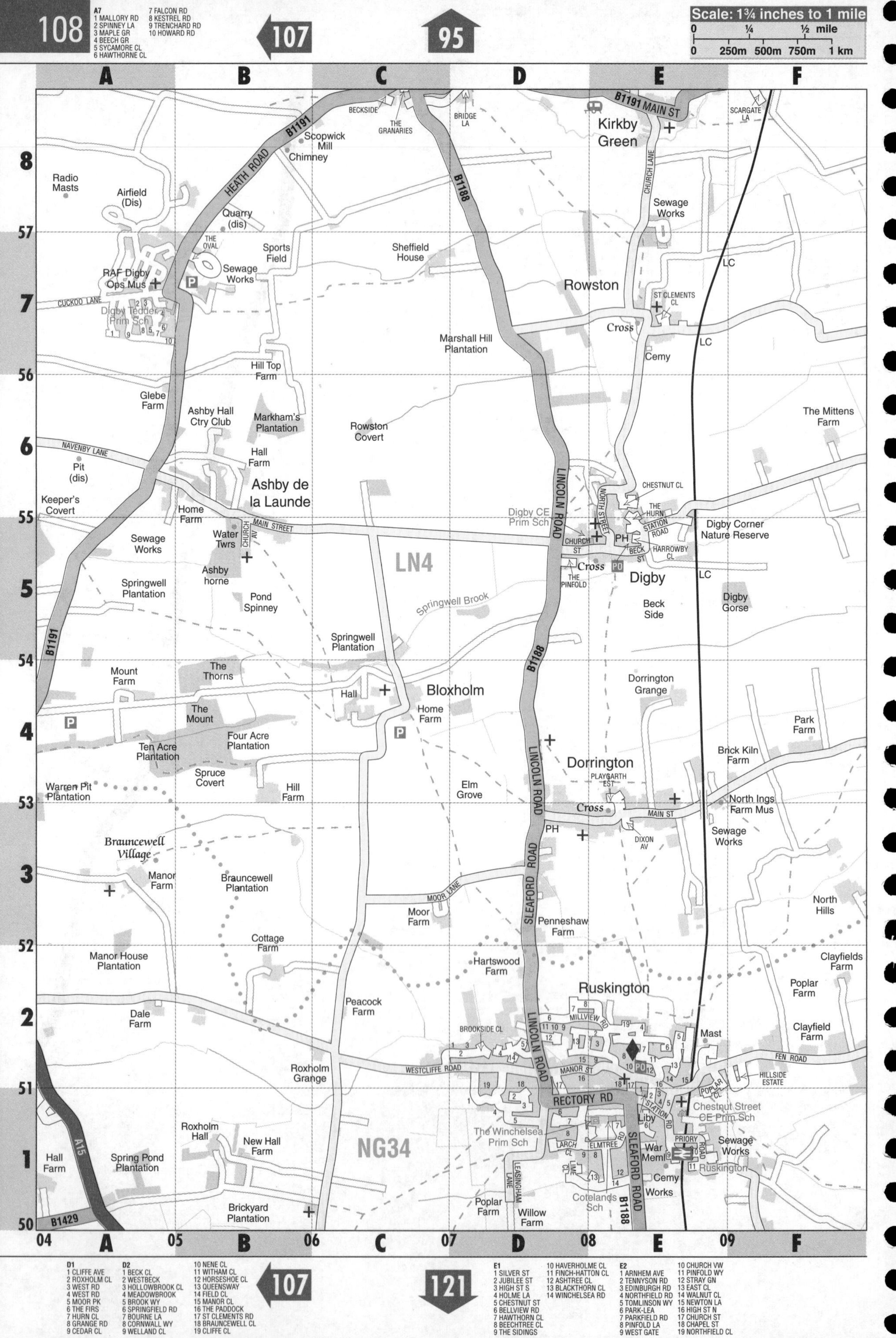

A7
1 MALLORY RD
2 SPINNEY LA
3 MAPLE GR
4 BEECH GR
5 SYCAMORE CL
6 HAWTHORNE CL
7 FALCON RD
8 KESTREL RD
9 TRENCHARD RD
10 HOWARD RD

A   B   C   D   E   F

Radio Masts

Airfield (Dis)

Quarry (dis)

THE OVAL

RAF Digby Ops Mus

Digby Tedder Prim Sch

CUCKOO LANE

Sewage Works

Sports Field

Scopwick Mill Chimney

BECKSIDE

THE GRANARIES

BRIDGE LA

Sheffield House

Marshall Hill Plantation

Kirkby Green

SCARGATE LA

MAIN ST

CHURCH LANE

Sewage Works

LC

Rowston

ST CLEMENTS CL

Cross

Cemy

LC

The Mittens Farm

Hill Top Farm

Glebe Farm

NAVENBY LANE

Pit (dis)

Keeper's Covert

Ashby Hall Ctry Club

Markham's Plantation

Hall Farm

Ashby de la Launde

Rowston Covert

LINCOLN ROAD

NORTH STREET

CHESTNUT CL

Digby CE Prim Sch

THE HURN

STATION ROAD

Digby Corner Nature Reserve

Home Farm

Sewage Works

Water Twrs

Ashby horne

Main Street

CHURCH WAY

LN4

Springwell Brook

CHURCH ST

PH

BECK ST

HARROWBY CL

Cross

THE PINFOLD

PO

Digby

Beck Side

Digby Gorse

LC

Springwell Plantation

Pond Spinney

Springwell Plantation

B1191

Mount Farm

The Thorns

Hall

Bloxholm

Home Farm

Dorrington Grange

Park Farm

P

The Mount

Four Acre Plantation

P

Brick Kiln Farm

Ten Acre Plantation

Spruce Covert

Hill Farm

Elm Grove

Dorrington

PLAYGARTH EST

Cross

MAIN ST

North Ings Farm Mus

Warren Pit Plantation

PH

DIXON AV

Sewage Works

Brauncewell Village

Manor Farm

Brauncewell Plantation

Cottage Farm

SLEAFORD ROAD

LINCOLN ROAD

MOOR LANE

Moor Farm

Penneshaw Farm

North Hills

Manor House Plantation

Peacock Farm

Hartswood Farm

Ruskington

Clayfields Farm

Poplar Farm

Dale Farm

BROOKSIDE CL

MILLVIEW RD

Mast

Clayfield Farm

Roxholm Grange

WESTCLIFFE ROAD

LINCOLN ROAD

MANOR ST

FEN ROAD

POPLAR

HILLSIDE ESTATE

NG34

Roxholm Hall

New Hall Farm

RECTORY RD

STATION RD

Chestnut Street CE Prim Sch

Libry

PRIORY ROAD

Sewage Works

A15

Hall Farm

Spring Pond Plantation

The Winchelsea Prim Sch

LESSINGHAM LANE

LARCH

ELMTREE

LIME

War Meml

Ruskington

SLEAFORD ROAD

Cemy Works

B1429

Brickyard Plantation

Poplar Farm

Willow Farm

Cotelands Sch

B1188

04   A   05   B   06   C   07   D   08   E   09   F

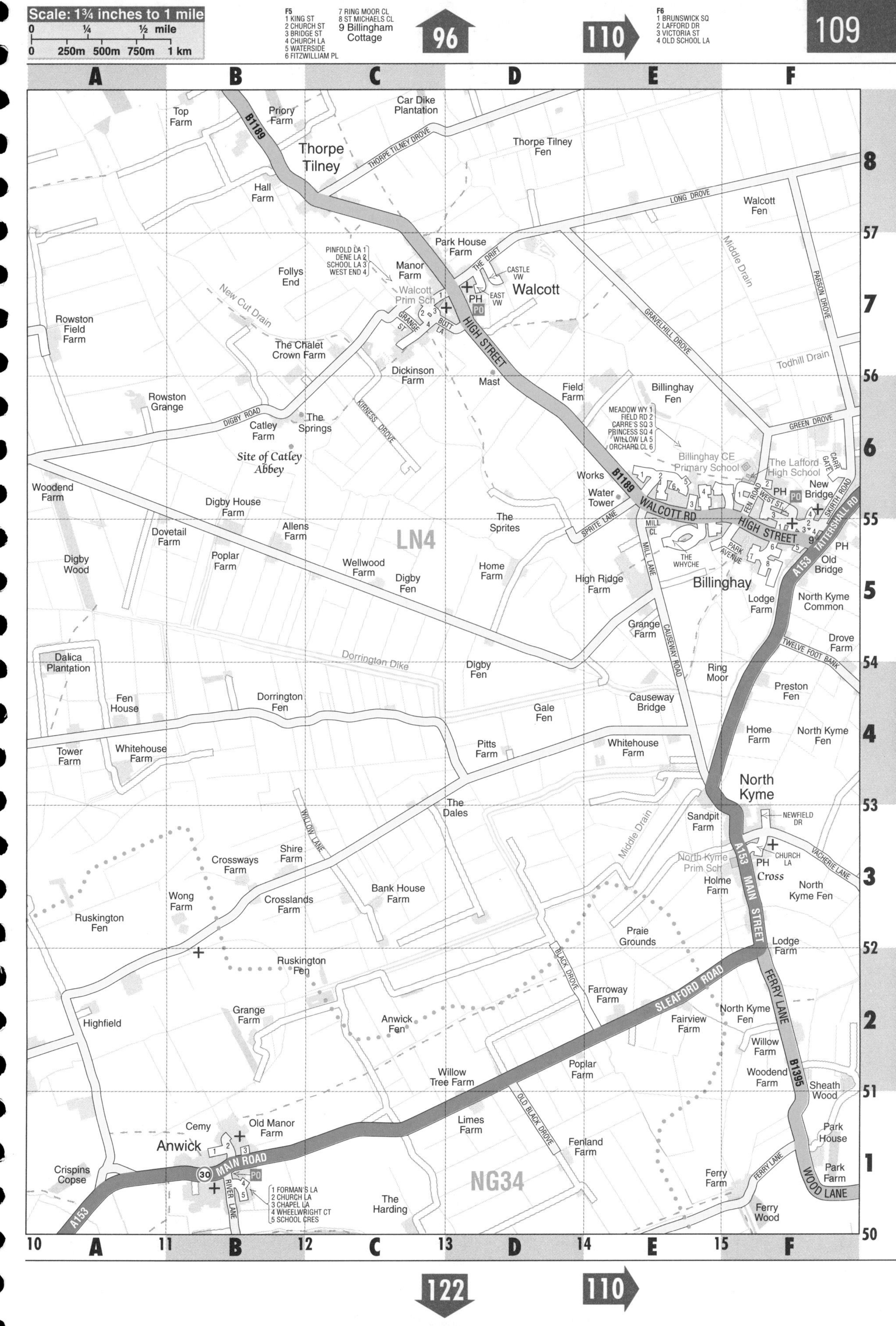

Scale: 1¾ inches to 1 mile
0 ¼ ½ mile
0 250m 500m 750m 1 km
F5
1 KING ST
2 CHURCH ST
3 BRIDGE ST
4 CHURCH LA
5 WATERSIDE
6 FITZWILLIAM PL
7 RING MOOR CL
8 ST MICHAELS CL
9 Billingham Cottage
96
110
F6
1 BRUNSWICK SQ
2 LAFFORD DR
3 VICTORIA ST
4 OLD SCHOOL LA
A
B
C
D
E
F
8
57
7
56
6
55
5
54
4
53
3
52
2
51
1
50
Top Farm
Priory Farm
B1189
Car Dike Plantation
Thorpe Tilney
THORPE TILNEY DROVE
Thorpe Tilney Fen
Hall Farm
LONG DROVE
Walcott Fen
Park House Farm
PINFOLD LA 1
DENE LA 2
SCHOOL LA 3
WEST END 4
Manor Farm
THE DRIFT
CASTLE VW
Follys End
Walcott Prim Sch
PH
PO
EAST VW
Walcott
Middle Drain
PARSON DROVE
New Cut Drain
GRANGE ST
BUTT LA
HIGH STREET
GRAVELHILL DROVE
Rowston Field Farm
The Chalet Crown Farm
Todhill Drain
Dickinson Farm
Mast
Field Farm
Billinghay Fen
Rowston Grange
DIGBY ROAD
Catley Farm
The Springs
KIRKNESS DROVE
MEADOW WY 1
FIELD RD 2
CARRE'S SQ 3
PRINCESS SQ 4
WILLOW LA 5
ORCHARD CL 6
GREEN DROVE
Site of Catley Abbey
Billinghay CE Primary School
The Lafford High School
CARR GATE
Woodend Farm
Works
Water Tower
FEN ROAD
WEST ST
New Bridge
SKIRTH ROAD
Digby House Farm
WALCOTT RD
TATTERSHALL RD
Dovetail Farm
Allens Farm
LN4
The Sprites
SPRITE LANE
MILL CL
HIGH STREET
PH
Digby Wood
Poplar Farm
Wellwood Farm
Digby Fen
Home Farm
MILL LANE
THE WHYCHE
PARK AVENUE
Old Bridge
A153
High Ridge Farm
Billinghay
Lodge Farm
North Kyme Common
Grange Farm
CAUSEWAY ROAD
Drove Farm
TWELVE FOOT BANK
Dalica Plantation
Dorrington Dike
Digby Fen
Ring Moor
Preston Fen
Fen House
Dorrington Fen
Causeway Bridge
Gale Fen
Tower Farm
Whitehouse Farm
Pitts Farm
Whitehouse Farm
Home Farm
North Kyme Fen
North Kyme
The Dales
Sandpit Farm
NEWFIELD DR
WILLOW LANE
Middle Drain
Shire Farm
CHURCH LA
VACHERIE LANE
Crossways Farm
North Kyme Prim Sch
PH
Cross
Wong Farm
Bank House Farm
Holme Farm
North Kyme Fen
Crosslands Farm
MAIN STREET
Ruskington Fen
Praie Grounds
Lodge Farm
Ruskington Fen
BLACK DROVE
SLEAFORD ROAD
Farroway Farm
FERRY LANE
Grange Farm
North Kyme Fen
Highfield
Anwick Fen
Fairview Farm
Willow Farm
Willow Tree Farm
Poplar Farm
Woodend Farm
B1395
Sheath Wood
Cemy
Old Manor Farm
Limes Farm
OLD BLACK DROVE
Park House
Anwick
Fenland Farm
MAIN ROAD
30
PO
Crispins Copse
RIVER LANE
NG34
Ferry Farm
FERRY LANE
Park Farm
WOOD LANE
1 FORMAN'S LA
2 CHURCH LA
3 CHAPEL LA
4 WHEELWRIGHT CT
5 SCHOOL CRES
The Harding
Ferry Wood
A153
10
11
12
13
14
15

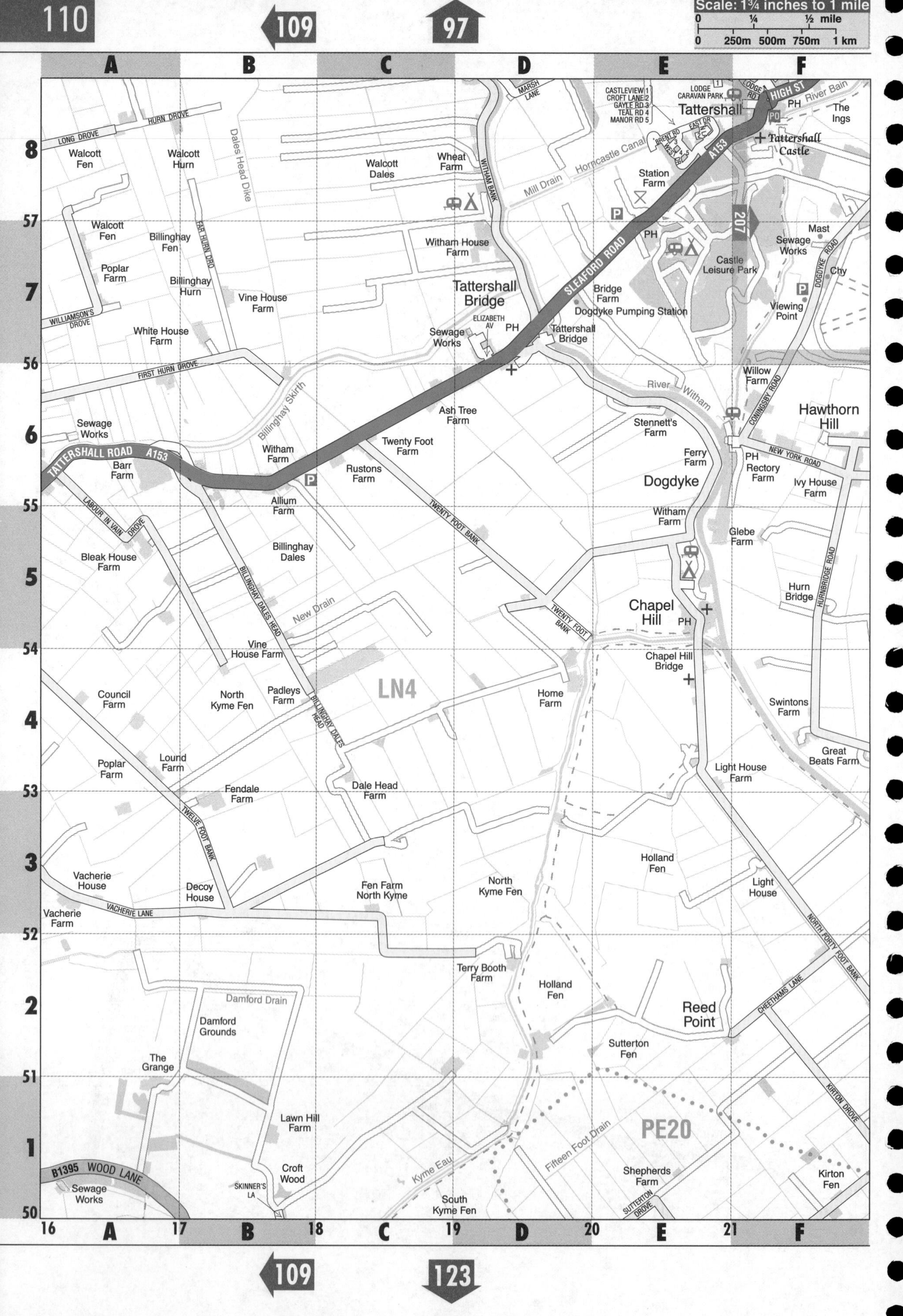
Scale: 1¾ inches to 1 mile
0 ¼ ½ mile
0 250m 500m 750m 1 km
A
B
C
D
E
F
8
57
7
56
6
55
5
54
4
53
3
52
2
51
1
50
16
17
18
19
20
21
LONG DROVE
HURN DROVE
Walcott Fen
Walcott Hurn
Dales Head Dike
Walcott Dales
Wheat Farm
MARSH LANE
WITHAM BANK
CASTLEVIEW 1
CROFT LANE 2
GAYLE RD 3
TEAL RD 4
MANOR RD 5
LODGE CARAVAN PARK
LODGE RD
HIGH ST
Tattershall
PH
PO
River Bain
The Ings
Tattershall Castle
BRENT RD
EAST DR
WEST DR
A153
Horncastle Canal
Mill Drain
Station Farm
207
FAR HURN DRO
Walcott Fen
Billinghay Fen
Poplar Farm
Billinghay Hurn
Witham House Farm
SLEAFORD ROAD
Castle Leisure Park
Mast
Sewage Works
DOGDYKE ROAD
Chy
Vine House Farm
Tattershall Bridge
ELIZABETH AV
Bridge Farm
Dogdyke Pumping Station
Viewing Point
WILLIAMSON'S DROVE
White House Farm
Sewage Works
Tattershall Bridge
FIRST HURN DROVE
Billinghay Skirth
River Witham
Willow Farm
CONINGSBY ROAD
Hawthorn Hill
Sewage Works
Ash Tree Farm
Stennett's Farm
TATTERSHALL ROAD
Barr Farm
Witham Farm
Twenty Foot Farm
NEW YORK ROAD
Ferry Farm
Rectory Farm
Ivy House Farm
Rustons Farm
Dogdyke
Allium Farm
TWENTY FOOT BANK
Witham Farm
LABOUR IN VAIN DROVE
Glebe Farm
Bleak House Farm
Billinghay Dales
HURNBRIDGE ROAD
Hurn Bridge
BILLINGHAY DALES HEAD
New Drain
Chapel Hill
TWENTY FOOT BANK
Vine House Farm
Chapel Hill Bridge
Council Farm
North Kyme Fen
Padleys Farm
LN4
Home Farm
Swintons Farm
Lound Farm
Poplar Farm
Light House Farm
Great Beats Farm
Dale Head Farm
Fendale Farm
TWELVE FOOT BANK
Holland Fen
Vacherie House
Decoy House
Fen Farm North Kyme
North Kyme Fen
Light House
Vacherie Farm
VACHERIE LANE
NORTH FORTY FOOT BANK
Terry Booth Farm
Damford Drain
Holland Fen
Damford Grounds
Reed Point
CHEETHAMS LANE
The Grange
Sutterton Fen
KIRTON DROVE
Lawn Hill Farm
PE20
Fifteen Foot Drain
B1395 WOOD LANE
Croft Wood
Kyme Eau
Shepherds Farm
Kirton Fen
Sewage Works
SKINNER'S LA
South Kyme Fen
SUTTERTON DROVE

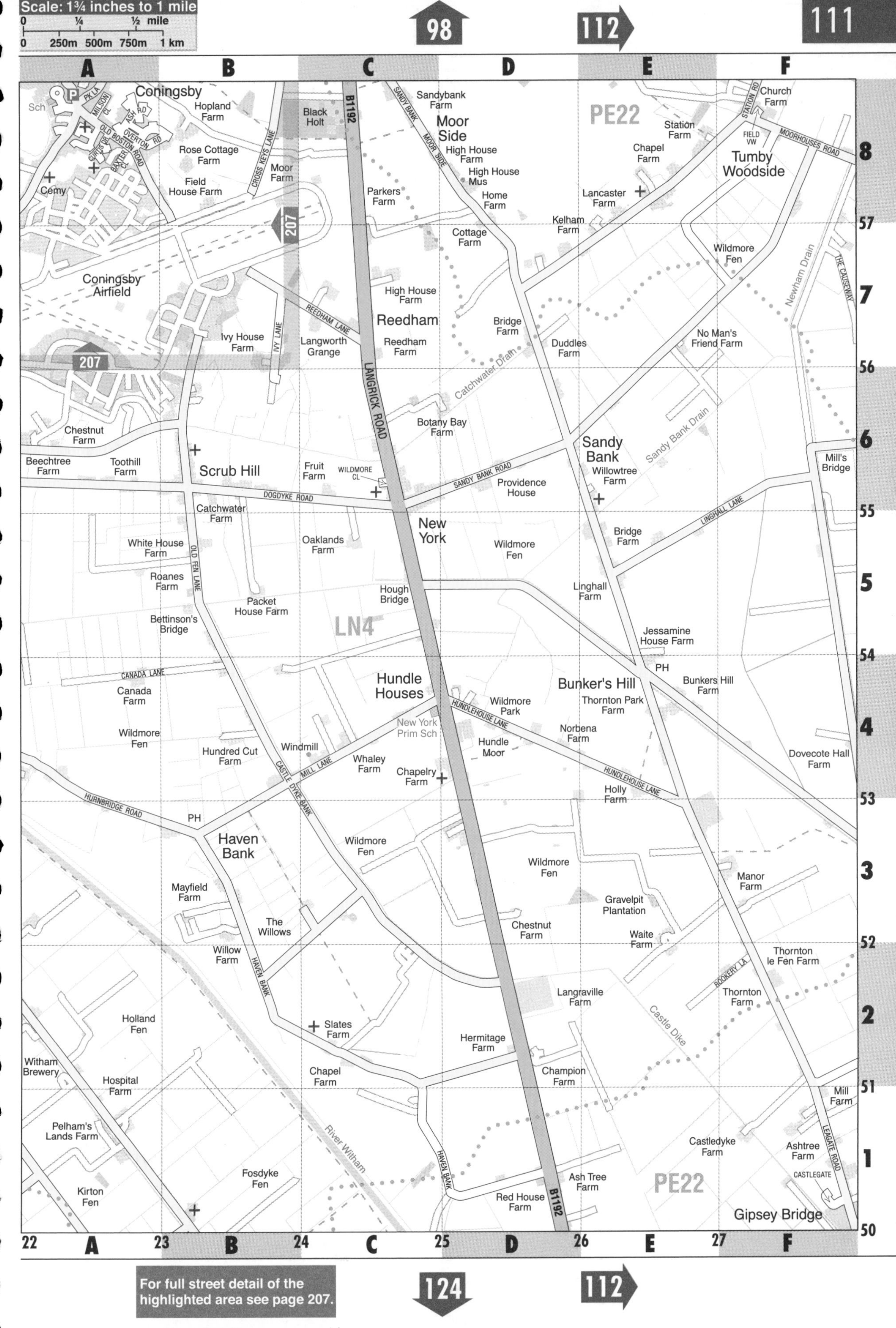

A   B   C   D   E   F

Coningsby
Sch
P
Hopland Farm
Rose Cottage Farm
Moor Farm
Field House Farm
Cemy
Coningsby Airfield
207
207
Black Holt
Sandybank Farm
Moor Side
High House Farm
High House Mus
Home Farm
Cottage Farm
Parkers Farm
PE22
Station Farm
Chapel Farm
Lancaster Farm
Kelham Farm
Tumby Woodside
Church Farm
MOORHOUSES ROAD
8
57

B1192
SANDY BANK
MOOR SIDE
High House Farm
Reedham
Reedham Farm
Bridge Farm
Duddles Farm
Wildmore Fen
No Man's Friend Farm
Newham Drain
THE CAUSEWAY
7
56

Ivy House Farm
REEDHAM LANE
IVY LANE
Langworth Grange
LANGRICK ROAD
Botany Bay Farm
Catchwater Drain
Sandy Bank
Willowtree Farm
Sandy Bank Drain
Mill's Bridge
6

Chestnut Farm
Beechtree Farm
Toothill Farm
Scrub Hill
Fruit Farm
WILDMORE CL
DOGDYKE ROAD
SANDY BANK ROAD
Providence House
Bridge Farm
LINGHALL LANE
55

Catchwater Farm
White House Farm
Roanes Farm
OLD FEN LANE
Oaklands Farm
New York
Wildmore Fen
Linghall Farm
Jessamine House Farm
5

Bettinson's Bridge
Packet House Farm
Hough Bridge
LN4
PH
54

CANADA LANE
Canada Farm
Wildmore Fen
Hundred Cut Farm
CASTLE DYKE BANK
MILL LANE
Windmill
Whaley Farm
Chapelry Farm
Hundle Houses
HUNDLEHOUSE LANE
New York Prim Sch
Wildmore Park
Hundle Moor
Bunker's Hill
Thornton Park Farm
Norbena Farm
HUNDLEHOUSE LANE
Bunkers Hill Farm
Dovecote Hall Farm
4

HURNBRIDGE ROAD
PH
Haven Bank
HAVEN BANK
Wildmore Fen
Holly Farm
53

Mayfield Farm
The Willows
Wildmore Fen
Wildmore Fen
Gravelpit Plantation
Manor Farm
3

Willow Farm
Holland Fen
Slates Farm
Chestnut Farm
Waite Farm
Langraville Farm
Castle Dike
ROOKERY LA
Thornton Farm
Thornton le Fen Farm
52

Witham Brewery
Hospital Farm
Chapel Farm
Hermitage Farm
Champion Farm
PE22
Castledyke Farm
LEGATE ROAD
Mill Farm
Ashtree Farm
CASTLEGATE
2

Pelham's Lands Farm
Kirton Fen
Fosdyke Fen
River Witham
HAVEN BANK
Ash Tree Farm
Red House Farm
B1192
Gipsey Bridge
1
51
50

22   A   23   B   24   C   25   D   26   E   27   F

For full street detail of the highlighted area see page 207.

111
99

Scale: 1¾ inches to 1 mile

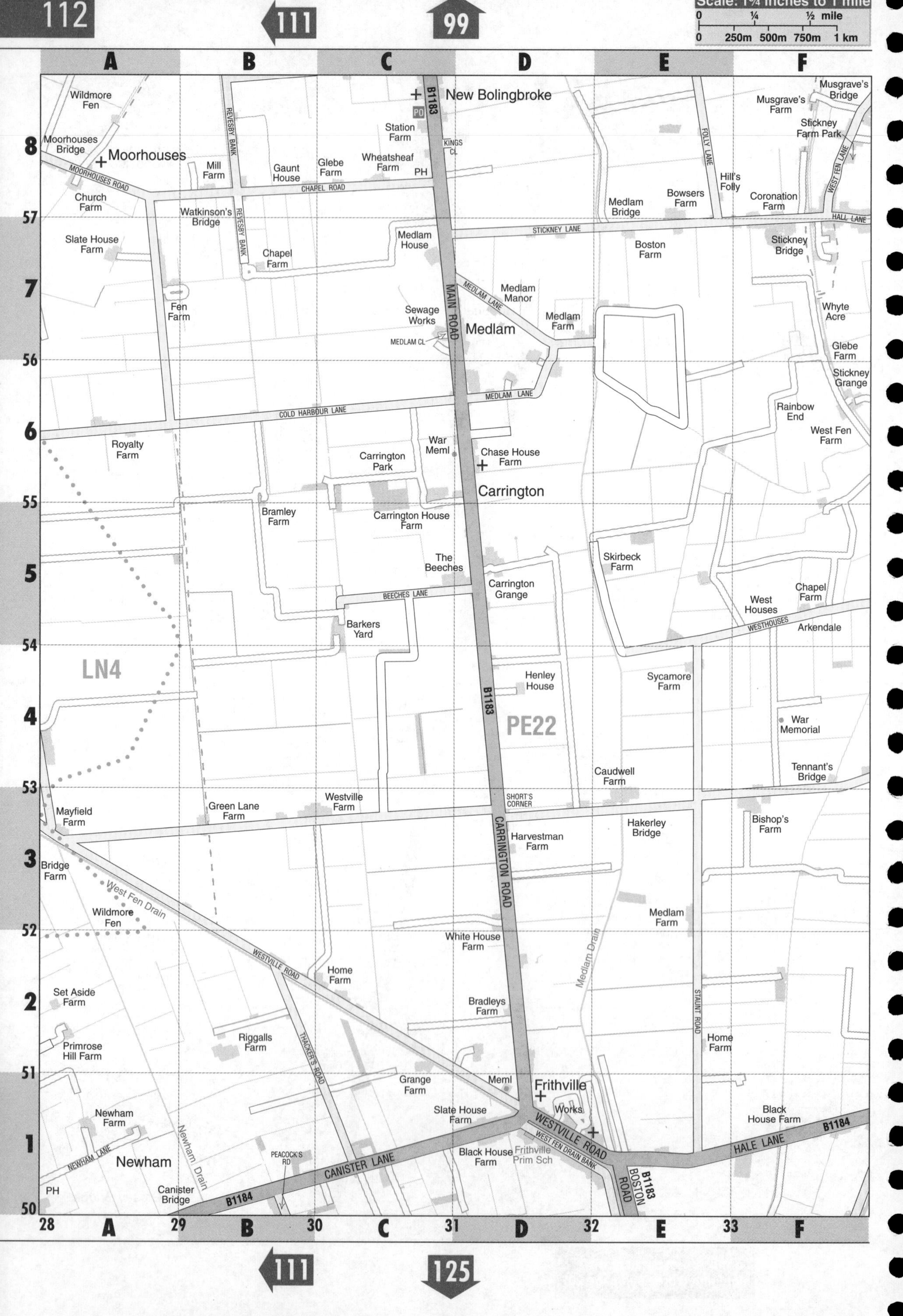
New Bolingbroke
Moorhouses
Medlam
Carrington
Frithville
Newham
LN4
PE22
Wildmore Fen
Moorhouses Bridge
Church Farm
Slate House Farm
Mill Farm
Gaunt House
Glebe Farm
Station Farm
Wheatsheaf Farm
Watkinson's Bridge
Chapel Farm
Medlam House
Fen Farm
Sewage Works
Medlam Manor
Medlam Farm
Medlam Bridge
Bowsers Farm
Hill's Folly
Coronation Farm
Musgrave's Farm
Musgrave's Bridge
Stickney Farm Park
Stickney Bridge
Boston Farm
Whyte Acre
Glebe Farm
Stickney Grange
Rainbow End
West Fen Farm
Royalty Farm
Carrington Park
War Meml
Chase House Farm
Bramley Farm
Carrington House Farm
The Beeches
Carrington Grange
Skirbeck Farm
Barkers Yard
West Houses
Chapel Farm
Arkendale
Henley House
Sycamore Farm
War Memorial
Tennant's Bridge
Caudwell Farm
Mayfield Farm
Green Lane Farm
Westville Farm
Harvestman Farm
Hakerley Bridge
Bishop's Farm
Bridge Farm
Wildmore Fen
West Fen Drain
Medlam Farm
White House Farm
Home Farm
Set Aside Farm
Bradleys Farm
Riggalls Farm
Primrose Hill Farm
Home Farm
Grange Farm
Meml
Works
Slate House Farm
Black House Farm
Newham Farm
Black House Farm
Frithville Prim Sch
Canister Bridge
Newham Drain
Medlam Drain
PH
PO
MOORHOUSES ROAD
CHAPEL ROAD
REVESBY BANK
KINGS CL
FOLLY LANE
WEST FEN LANE
HALL LANE
STICKNEY LANE
MEDLAM LANE
MEDLAM CL
MAIN ROAD
COLD HARBOUR LANE
BEECHES LANE
WESTHOUSES
SHORT'S CORNER
CARRINGTON ROAD
STAUNT ROAD
WESTVILLE ROAD
THACKER'S ROAD
WEST FEN DRAIN BANK
HALE LANE
BOSTON ROAD
CANISTER LANE
PEACOCK'S RD
NEWHAM LANE
B1183
B1184
A B C D E F
28 29 30 31 32 33
8 57 7 56 6 55 5 54 4 53 3 52 2 51 1 50

111
125

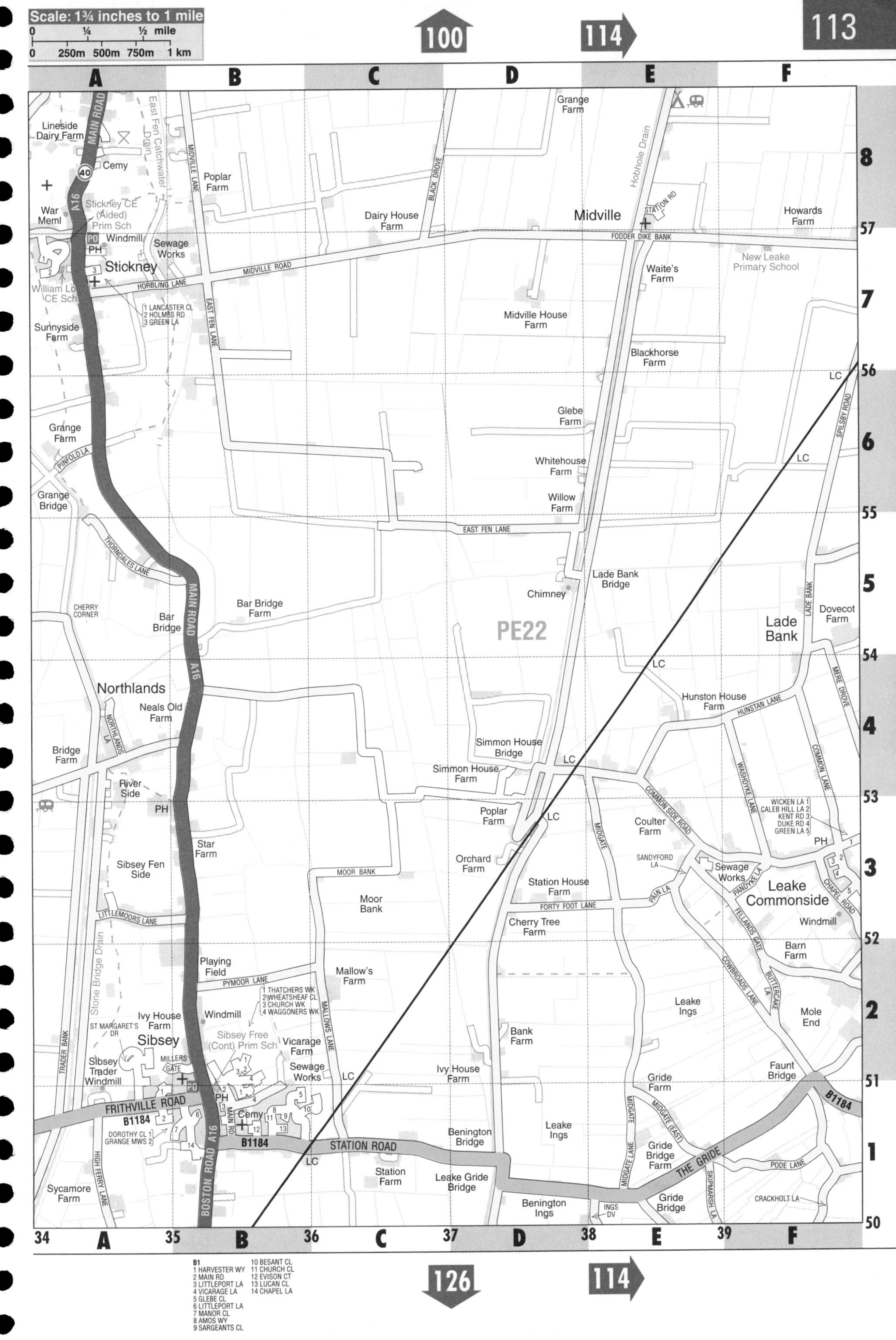
Scale: 1¾ inches to 1 mile
0 ¼ ½ mile
0 250m 500m 750m 1 km
100
114
A B C D E F
Lineside Dairy Farm
MAIN ROAD
Cemy
East Fen Catchwater Drain
MIDVILLE LANE
Poplar Farm
BLACK DROVE
Dairy House Farm
Grange Farm
Hobhole Drain
STATION RD
Midville
Howards Farm
War Meml
A16
Stickney CE (Aided) Prim Sch
PO
Windmill
PH
Sewage Works
Stickney
MIDVILLE ROAD
FODDER DIKE BANK
Waite's Farm
New Leake Primary School
William Lovell CE Sch
HORBLING LANE
1 LANCASTER CL
2 HOLMES RD
3 GREEN LA
EAST FEN LANE
Midville House Farm
Sunnyside Farm
Blackhorse Farm
LC
SPILSBY ROAD
Grange Farm
Glebe Farm
PINFOLD LA
Whitehouse Farm
Grange Bridge
Willow Farm
EAST FEN LANE
THORNDALES LANE
Lade Bank Bridge
Chimney
CHERRY CORNER
Bar Bridge
Bar Bridge Farm
PE22
Lade Bank
LADE BANK
Dovecot Farm
MERE DROVE
Northlands
Neals Old Farm
NORTHLANDS LA
Hunston House Farm
HUNSTAN LANE
Bridge Farm
Simmon House Bridge
Simmon House Farm
River Side
PH
Poplar Farm
COMMON SIDE ROAD
WASHDYKE LANE
COMMON LANE
WICKEN LA 1
CALEB HILL LA 2
KENT RD 3
DUKE RD 4
GREEN LA 5
MIDGATE
Coulter Farm
Star Farm
Orchard Farm
SANDYFORD LA
Sewage Works
PANDYKE LA
Sibsey Fen Side
MOOR BANK
Moor Bank
Station House Farm
PAIN LA
Leake Commonside
CHAPEL ROAD
LITTLEMOORS LANE
FORTY FOOT LANE
Cherry Tree Farm
FELLANDS GATE
Windmill
Barn Farm
Stone Bridge Drain
Playing Field
PYMOOR LANE
Mallow's Farm
COWBROADS LANE
BUTTERCAKE LA
1 THATCHERS WK
2 WHEATSHEAF CL
3 CHURCH WK
4 WAGGONERS WK
Leake Ings
Mole End
TRADER BANK
ST MARGARET'S DR
Ivy House Farm
Windmill
Sibsey
Sibsey Free (Cont) Prim Sch
Vicarage Farm
MALLOWS LANE
Bank Farm
Sibsey Trader Windmill
MILLERS GATE
Sewage Works
Ivy House Farm
Gride Farm
Faunt Bridge
FRITHVILLE ROAD
B1184
PH
MAIN RD
Cemy
MIDGATE (EAST)
B1184
DOROTHY CL 1
GRANGE MWS 2
BOSTON ROAD A16
B1184
STATION ROAD
Benington Bridge
Leake Ings
MIDGATE LANE
Gride Bridge Farm
THE GRIDE
PODE LANE
Sycamore Farm
HIGH FERRY LANE
Station Farm
Leake Gride Bridge
SKIPMARSH LA
Benington Ings
INGS DV
Gride Bridge
CRACKHOLT LA
8 57 7 56 6 55 5 54 4 53 3 52 2 51 1 50
34 A 35 B 36 C 37 D 38 E 39 F
B1
1 HARVESTER WY
2 MAIN RD
3 LITTLEPORT LA
4 VICARAGE LA
5 GLEBE CL
6 LITTLEPORT LA
7 MANOR CL
8 AMOS WY
9 SARGEANTS CL
10 BESANT CL
11 CHURCH CL
12 EVISON CT
13 LUCAN CL
14 CHAPEL LA
126
114

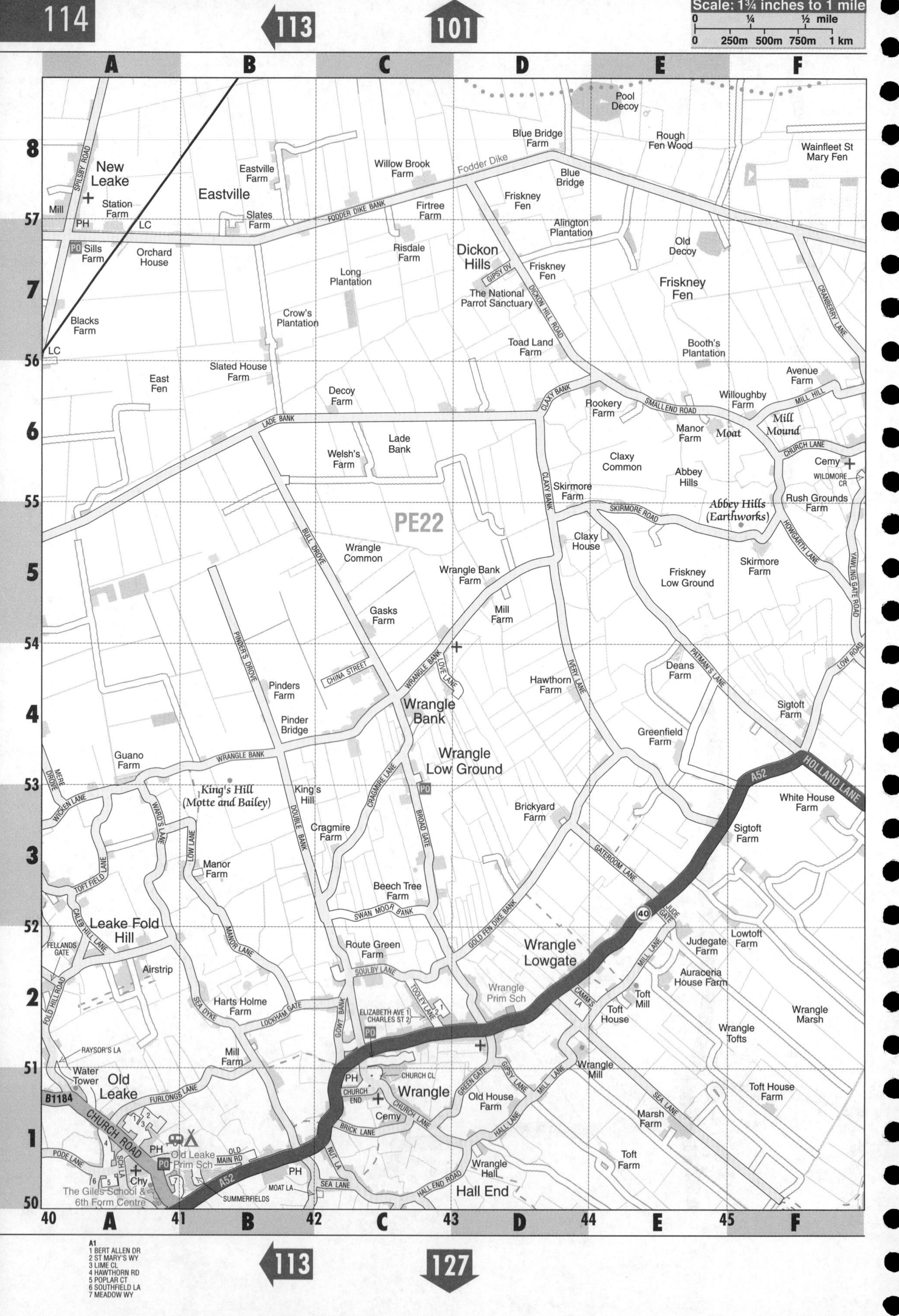
114
113
101
Scale: 1¾ inches to 1 mile
0
¼
½ mile
250m
500m
750m
1 km
A
B
C
D
E
F
8
57
7
56
6
55
5
54
4
53
3
52
2
51
1
50
40
41
42
43
44
45
Pool Decoy
Rough Fen Wood
Wainfleet St Mary Fen
Blue Bridge Farm
New Leake
Eastville Farm
Willow Brook Farm
Fodder Dike
Blue Bridge
Mill
Station Farm
Eastville
Slates Farm
FODDER DIKE BANK
Firtree Farm
Friskney Fen
Alington Plantation
SPILSBY ROAD
PH
LC
Sills Farm
Orchard House
Risdale Farm
Dickon Hills
Old Decoy
Long Plantation
GIPSY DV
Friskney Fen
The National Parrot Sanctuary
Friskney Fen
Crow's Plantation
DICKON HILL ROAD
CRANBERRY LANE
Blacks Farm
Toad Land Farm
Booth's Plantation
LC
Slated House Farm
East Fen
Decoy Farm
CLAXY BANK
Rookery Farm
SMALLEND ROAD
Willoughby Farm
Avenue Farm
MILL HILL
LADE BANK
Lade Bank
Welsh's Farm
Manor Farm
Moat
Mill Mound
CHURCH LANE
Claxy Common
Abbey Hills
Cemy
WILDMORE CR
CLAXY BANK
Skirmore Farm
SKIRMORE ROAD
Abbey Hills (Earthworks)
Rush Grounds Farm
PE22
Wrangle Common
BULL DROVE
Claxy House
HOWGARTH LANE
Wrangle Bank Farm
Friskney Low Ground
Skirmore Farm
YAWLING GATE ROAD
Gasks Farm
Mill Farm
PINDER'S DROVE
CHINA STREET
WRANGLE BANK
LOVE LANE
Hawthorn Farm
IVERY LANE
Deans Farm
PATMAN'S LANE
LOW ROAD
Pinders Farm
Wrangle Bank
Sigtoft Farm
Pinder Bridge
Wrangle Low Ground
Greenfield Farm
Guano Farm
WRANGLE BANK
MERE DROVE
King's Hill (Motte and Bailey)
King's Hill
CRAGMIRE LANE
A52
HOLLAND LANE
WICKEN LANE
WARD'S LANE
Brickyard Farm
White House Farm
LOW LANE
DOUBLE BANK
Cragmire Farm
BROAD GATE
Sigtoft Farm
Manor Farm
TOFT FIELD LANE
GATEROOM LANE
Beech Tree Farm
SWAN MOOR BANK
CALEB HILL LANE
Leake Fold Hill
GOLD FEN DIKE BANK
40
JUDE GATE
FELLANDS GATE
MANOR LANE
Route Green Farm
Wrangle Lowgate
Judegate Farm
Lowtoft Farm
Airstrip
SOULBY LANE
MILL LANE
Auraceria House Farm
FOLD HILL ROAD
SEA DYKE
Harts Holme Farm
LOCKHAM GATE
GOWT BANK
ELIZABETH AVE 1
CHARLES ST 2
TOOLEY LANE
Wrangle Prim Sch
CAMM'S LA
Toft Mill
Toft House
Wrangle Marsh
Wrangle Tofts
RAYSOR'S LA
Mill Farm
Wrangle Mill
Water Tower
Old Leake
CHURCH CL
PH
CHURCH END
Wrangle
GREEN GATE
GIPSY LANE
MILL LANE
B1184
FURLONGS LANE
Old House Farm
SEA LANE
Toft House Farm
CHURCH ROAD
Cemy
CHURCH LANE
Marsh Farm
BRICK LANE
HALL LANE
PH
Old Leake Prim Sch
OLD MAIN RD
PODE LANE
SCH LA
Chy
PH
NUT LA
Wrangle Hall
Toft Farm
The Giles School & 6th Form Centre
MOAT LA
SEA LANE
HALL END ROAD
Hall End
SUMMERFIELDS
A1
1 BERT ALLEN DR
2 ST MARY'S WY
3 LIME CL
4 HAWTHORN RD
5 POPLAR CT
6 SOUTHFIELD LA
7 MEADOW WY
113
127

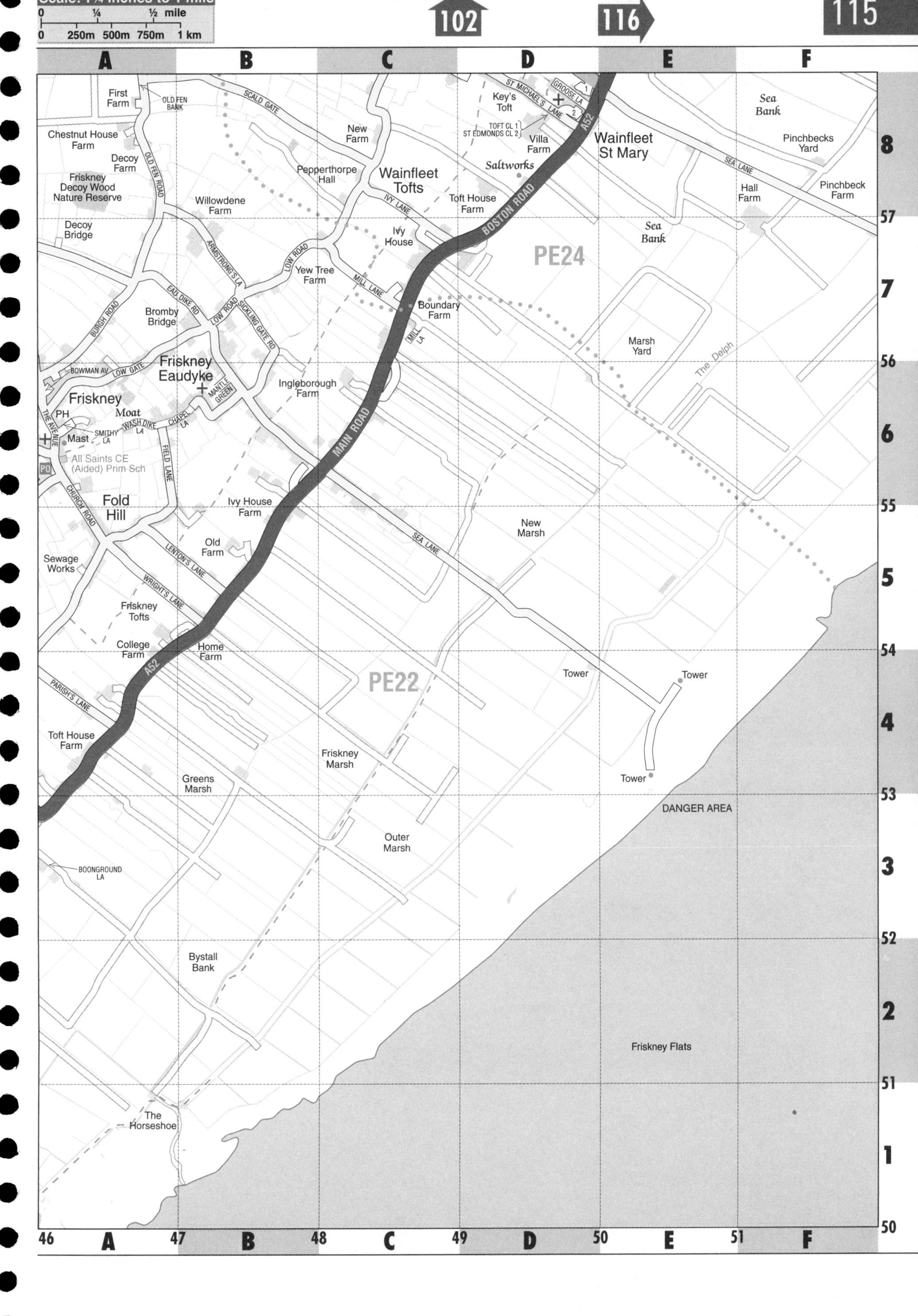

Scale: 1¾ inches to 1 mile
0 ¼ ½ mile
0 250m 500m 750m 1 km

102
116
115

A B C D E F

8
57
7
56
6
55
5
54
4
53
3
52
2
51
1
50

First Farm
Old Fen Bank
SCALD GATE
New Farm
St Michael's Lane
GROUSE LA
Key's Toft
Wainfleet St Mary
Sea Bank
Pinchbecks Yard
Chestnut House Farm
Decoy Farm
Pepperthorpe Hall
Wainfleet Tofts
Toft Gl 1
St Edmonds Cl 2
Villa Farm
Pinchbeck Farm
Friskney Decoy Wood Nature Reserve
OLD FEN ROAD
Willowdene Farm
IVY LANE
Saltworks
BOSTON ROAD
A52
Hall Farm
SEA LANE
Decoy Bridge
ARMSTRONG'S LA
Ivy House
PE24
Sea Bank
Yew Tree Farm
LOW ROAD
MILL LANE
EAU DIKE RD
Bromby Bridge
LOW ROAD
SICKLING GATE RD
Boundary Farm
MILL LA
Marsh Yard
The Delph
BURGH ROAD
BOWMAN AV LOW GATE
Friskney Eaudyke
MANTLE GREEN
Ingleborough Farm
Friskney
Moat
CHAPEL LA
MAIN ROAD
PH
WASH DIKE LA
SMITHY LA
Mast
All Saints CE (Aided) Prim Sch
FIELD LANE
Ivy House Farm
New Marsh
PO
Fold Hill
CHURCH ROAD
LENTON'S LANE
Old Farm
SEA LANE
Sewage Works
WRIGHT'S LANE
Tower
Tower
Friskney Tofts
PE22
College Farm
Home Farm
A52
PARISH'S LANE
Tower
Friskney Marsh
DANGER AREA
Toft House Farm
Greens Marsh
Outer Marsh
BOONGROUND LA
Bystall Bank
Friskney Flats
The Horseshoe

46 A 47 B 48 C 49 D 50 E 51 F 50

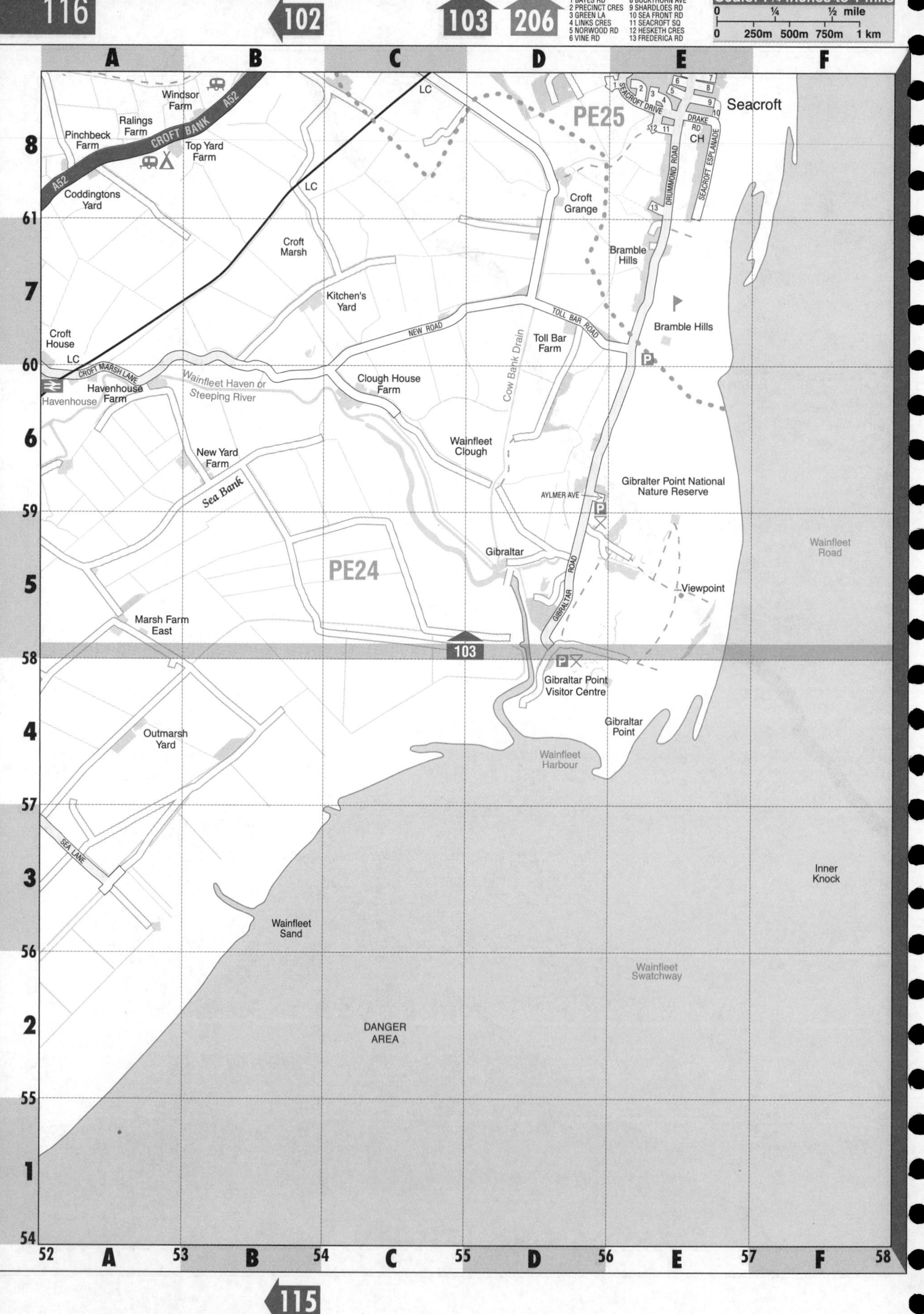

102
103 206

E8
1 BAYES RD
2 PRECINCT CRES
3 GREEN LA
4 LINKS CRES
5 NORWOOD RD
6 VINE RD
7 ALBERT AVE
8 BUCKTHORN AVE
9 SHARDLOES RD
10 SEA FRONT RD
11 SEACROFT SQ
12 HESKETH CRES
13 FREDERICA RD

Scale: 1¾ inches to 1 mile
0   ¼   ½   mile
0   250m 500m 750m 1 km

A52
Windsor Farm
Pinchbeck Farm
Ralings Farm
CROFT BANK
Top Yard Farm
Coddingtons Yard
A52
Croft Marsh
LC
LC
PE25
Seacroft
SEACROFT DRIVE
DRAKE RD
CH
DRUMMOND ROAD
SEACROFT ESPLANADE
Croft Grange
Bramble Hills
Croft Marsh
Kitchen's Yard
NEW ROAD
TOLL BAR ROAD
Bramble Hills
P
Croft House
LC
CROFT MARSH LANE
Havenhouse Farm
Havenhouse
Wainfleet Haven or Steeping River
Clough House Farm
Toll Bar Farm
Cow Bank Drain
New Yard Farm
Sea Bank
Wainfleet Clough
Gibralter Point National Nature Reserve
AYLMER AVE
P
Gibraltar
GIBRALTAR ROAD
PE24
Viewpoint
Wainfleet Road
Marsh Farm East
103
P
Gibraltar Point Visitor Centre
Gibraltar Point
Outmarsh Yard
Wainfleet Harbour
Inner Knock
SEA LANE
Wainfleet Sand
Wainfleet Swatchway
DANGER AREA

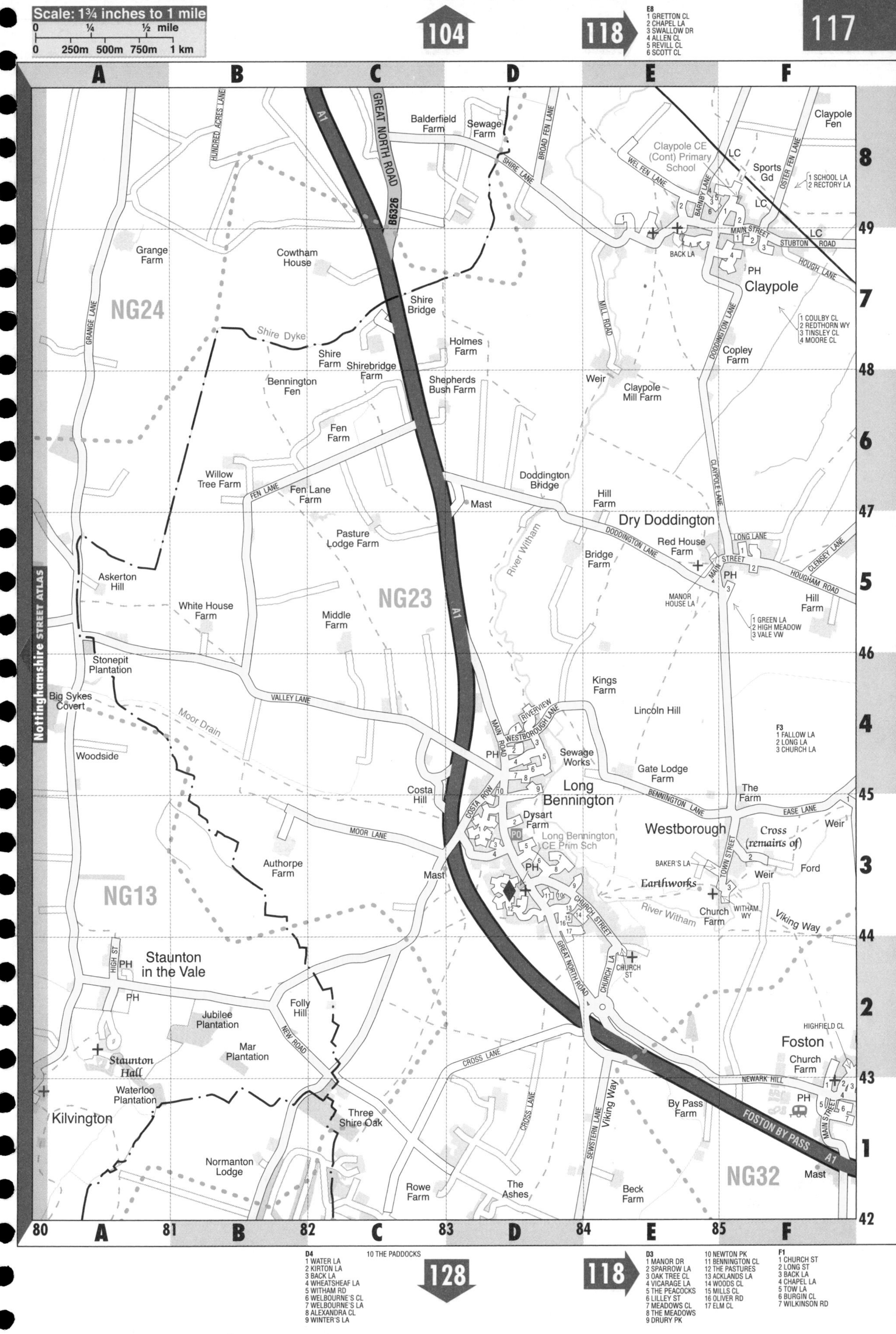

Scale: 1¾ inches to 1 mile
0 ¼ ½ mile
0 250m 500m 750m 1 km
104
118
E8
1 GRETTON CL
2 CHAPEL LA
3 SWALLOW DR
4 ALLEN CL
5 REVILL CL
6 SCOTT CL
117
A B C D E F
Nottinghamshire STREET ATLAS
A1
GREAT NORTH ROAD
B6326
HUNDRED ACRES LANE
Balderfield Farm
Sewage Farm
BROAD FEN LANE
SHIRE LANE
Claypole CE (Cont) Primary School
LC
Sports Gd
Claypole Fen
OSTER FEN LANE
1 SCHOOL LA
2 RECTORY LA
WEL FEN LANE
BARNBY LANE
MAIN STREET
STUBTON ROAD
BACK LA
HOUGH LANE
PH
Claypole
Grange Farm
Cowtham House
NG24
GRANGE LANE
Shire Bridge
Shire Dyke
Shire Farm
Shirebridge Farm
Holmes Farm
MILL ROAD
DODDINGTON LANE
1 COULBY CL
2 REDTHORN WY
3 TINSLEY CL
4 MOORE CL
Copley Farm
Bennington Fen
Shepherds Bush Farm
Weir
Claypole Mill Farm
Fen Farm
Willow Tree Farm
Fen Lane Farm
FEN LANE
Doddington Bridge
Mast
Hill Farm
CLAYPOLE LANE
Dry Doddington
Pasture Lodge Farm
LONG LANE
Red House Farm
CLENSEY LANE
Bridge Farm
River Witham
STREET
Askerton Hill
HOUGHAM ROAD
MANOR HOUSE LA
White House Farm
Middle Farm
NG23
Hill Farm
1 GREEN LA
2 HIGH MEADOW
3 VALE VW
Stonepit Plantation
Kings Farm
Big Sykes Covert
VALLEY LANE
Lincoln Hill
Moor Drain
RIVERVIEW
WESTBOROUGH LANE
MAIN ROAD
F3
1 FALLOW LA
2 LONG LA
3 CHURCH LA
Woodside
Sewage Works
Gate Lodge Farm
Costa Hill
COSTA ROW
Long Bennington
BENNINGTON LANE
The Farm
EASE LANE
Dysart Farm
Westborough
Cross (remains of)
Weir
MOOR LANE
PO
Long Bennington CE Prim Sch
Authorpe Farm
BAKER'S LA
TOWN STREET
Ford
Mast
Earthworks
Weir
NG13
CHURCH STREET
River Witham
Church Farm
WITHAM WY
Viking Way
HIGH ST
Staunton in the Vale
CHURCH LA
CHURCH ST
GREAT NORTH ROAD
Folly Hill
Jubilee Plantation
NEW ROAD
HIGHFIELD CL
Foston
Mar Plantation
Staunton Hall
CROSS LANE
Church Farm
NEWARK HILL
Waterloo Plantation
Kilvington
Three Shire Oak
Viking Way
By Pass Farm
FOSTON BY PASS
MAIN STREET
CROSS LANE
SEWSTERN LANE
Normanton Lodge
NG32
Mast
Rowe Farm
The Ashes
Beck Farm
80 81 82 83 84 85
42 43 44 45 46 47 48 49
1 2 3 4 5 6 7 8
128
118
D4
1 WATER LA
2 KIRTON LA
3 BACK LA
4 WHEATSHEAF LA
5 WITHAM RD
6 WELBOURNE'S CL
7 WELBOURNE'S LA
8 ALEXANDRA CL
9 WINTER'S LA
10 THE PADDOCKS
D3
1 MANOR DR
2 SPARROW LA
3 OAK TREE CL
4 VICARAGE LA
5 THE PEACOCKS
6 LILLEY ST
7 MEADOWS CL
8 THE MEADOWS
9 DRURY PK
10 NEWTON PK
11 BENNINGTON CL
12 THE PASTURES
13 ACKLANDS LA
14 WOODS CL
15 MILLS CL
16 OLIVER RD
17 ELM CL
F1
1 CHURCH ST
2 LONG ST
3 BACK LA
4 CHAPEL LA
5 TOW LA
6 BURGIN CL
7 WILKINSON RD

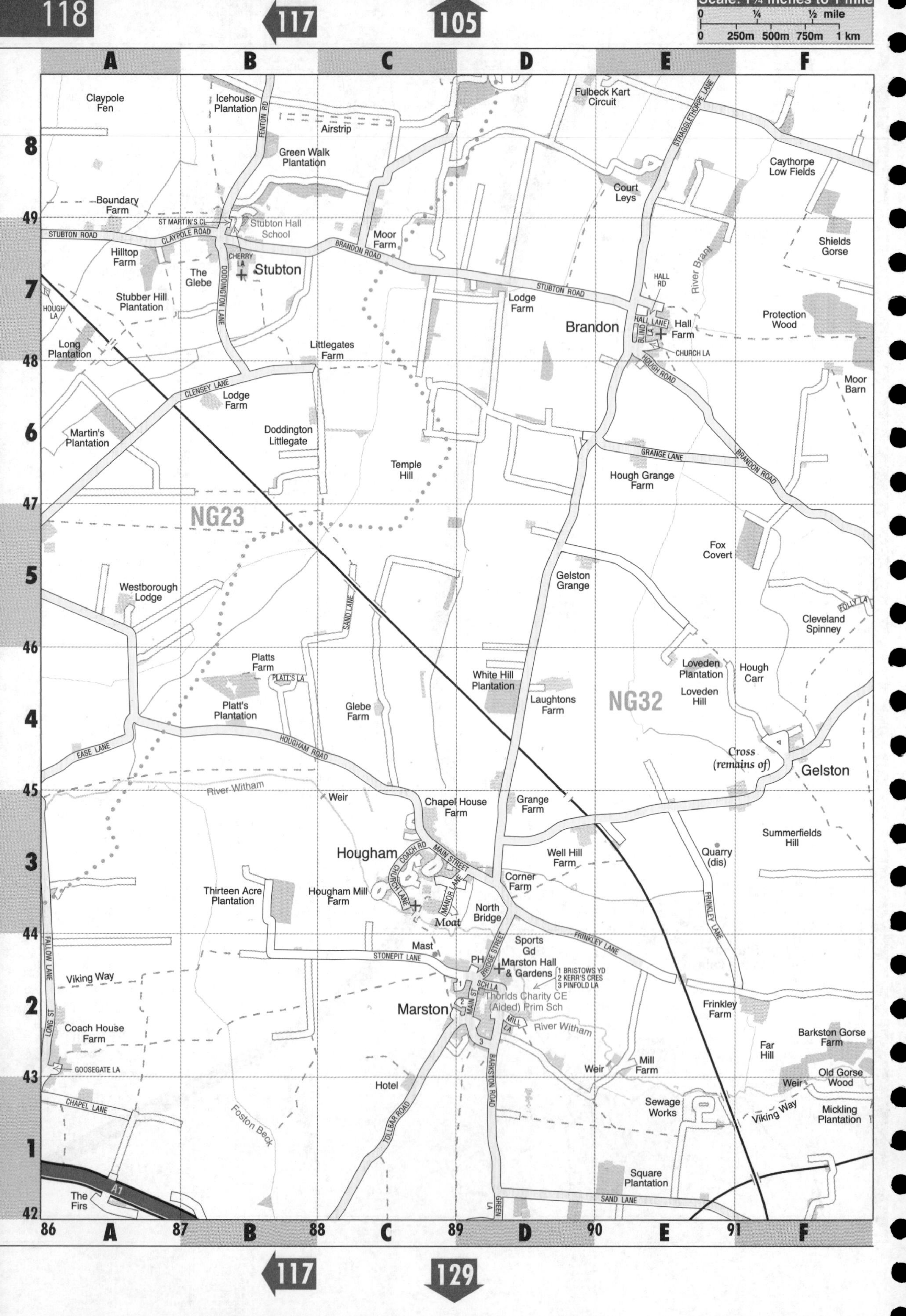

118

117

105

Scale: 1¾ inches to 1 mile

0   ¼   ½   mile
0   250m 500m 750m   1 km

A   B   C   D   E   F

8

Claypole Fen

Icehouse Plantation

Airstrip

Green Walk Plantation

Fulbeck Kart Circuit

Court Leys

Caythorpe Low Fields

49

Boundary Farm

St Martin's Cl

Stubton Hall School

Moor Farm

Stubton Road

Hall Rd

Shields Gorse

River Brant

Stubton Road

Hilltop Farm

The Glebe

Cherry La

Stubton

Brandon Road

Lodge Farm

Brandon

Hall Lane

Hall Farm

Church La

Protection Wood

7

Hough La

Stubber Hill Plantation

Littlegates Farm

Hough Road

Blind Lane

48

Long Plantation

Clensey Lane

Lodge Farm

Moor Barn

6

Martin's Plantation

Doddington Littlegate

Temple Hill

Grange Lane

Hough Grange Farm

Brandon Road

47

NG23

Fox Covert

5

Westborough Lodge

Gelston Grange

Cleveland Spinney

Folly La

46

Platts Farm

Platt's La

White Hill Plantation

Loveden Plantation

Hough Carr

Sand Lane

Loveden Hill

4

Platt's Plantation

Glebe Farm

Laughtons Farm

NG32

Ease Lane

Hougham Road

Cross (remains of)

Gelston

45

River Witham

Weir

Chapel House Farm

Grange Farm

Summerfields Hill

3

Hougham

Coach Rd

Main Street

Well Hill Farm

Quarry (dis)

Church Lane

Thirteen Acre Plantation

Hougham Mill Farm

Manor Lane

Corner Farm

Frinkley Lane

Moat

North Bridge

44

Mast

Sports Gd

Frinkley Lane

Fallow Lane

Stonepit Lane

PH

Marston Hall & Gardens

1 BRISTOWS YD
2 KERR'S CRES
3 PINFOLD LA

Frinkley Farm

2

Viking Way

Sch La

Thorlds Charity CE (Aided) Prim Sch

Mill La

Far Hill

Barkston Gorse Farm

Snots Is

Coach House Farm

Main St

Bridge Street

Marston

River Witham

Old Gorse Wood

Goosegate La

Hotel

Barkston Road

Weir

Mill Farm

Weir

Viking Way

Mickling Plantation

43

Chapel Lane

Foston Beck

Tolbar Road

Sewage Works

Square Plantation

Sand Lane

1

The Firs

A1

Green La

42

86   A   87   B   88   C   89   D   90   E   91   F

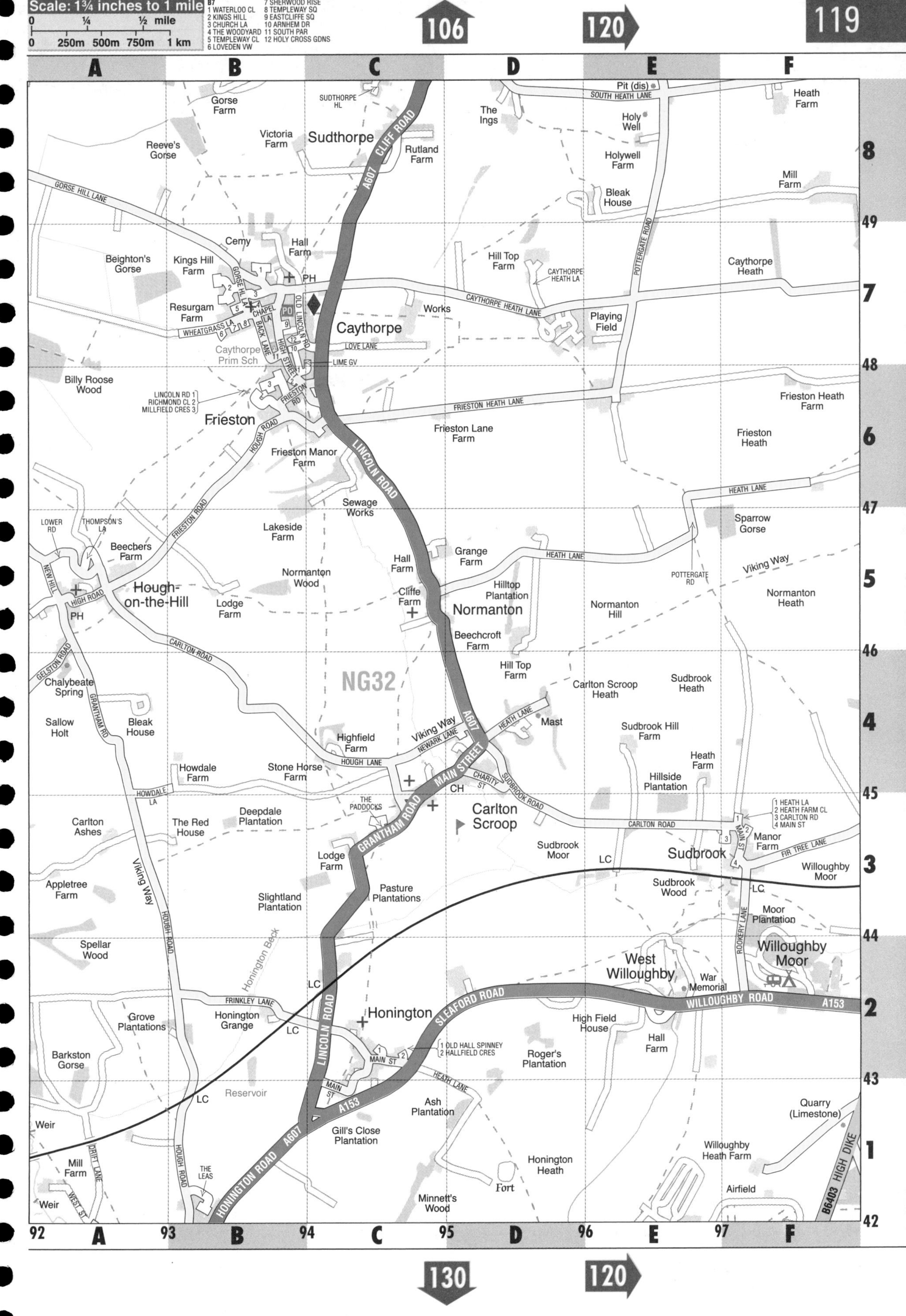
Scale: 1¾ inches to 1 mile
0 ¼ ½ mile
0 250m 500m 750m 1 km
B7
1 WATERLOO CL
2 KINGS HILL
3 CHURCH LA
4 THE WOODYARD
5 TEMPLEWAY CL
6 LOVEDEN VW
7 SHERWOOD RISE
8 TEMPLEWAY SQ
9 EASTCLIFFE SQ
10 ARNHEM DR
11 SOUTH PAR
12 HOLY CROSS GDNS
106
120
130
120
Sudthorpe
Caythorpe
Frieston
Hough-on-the-Hill
Normanton
Carlton Scroop
Sudbrook
West Willoughby
Honington
Willoughby Moor
NG32
A607 CLIFF ROAD
LINCOLN ROAD
GRANTHAM ROAD
SLEAFORD ROAD
WILLOUGHBY ROAD
A153
HONINGTON ROAD
B6403 HIGH DIKE
Viking Way
1 HEATH LA
2 HEATH FARM CL
3 CARLTON RD
4 MAIN ST
1 OLD HALL SPINNEY
2 HALLFIELD CRES
LINCOLN RD 1
RICHMOND CL 2
MILLFIELD CRES 3

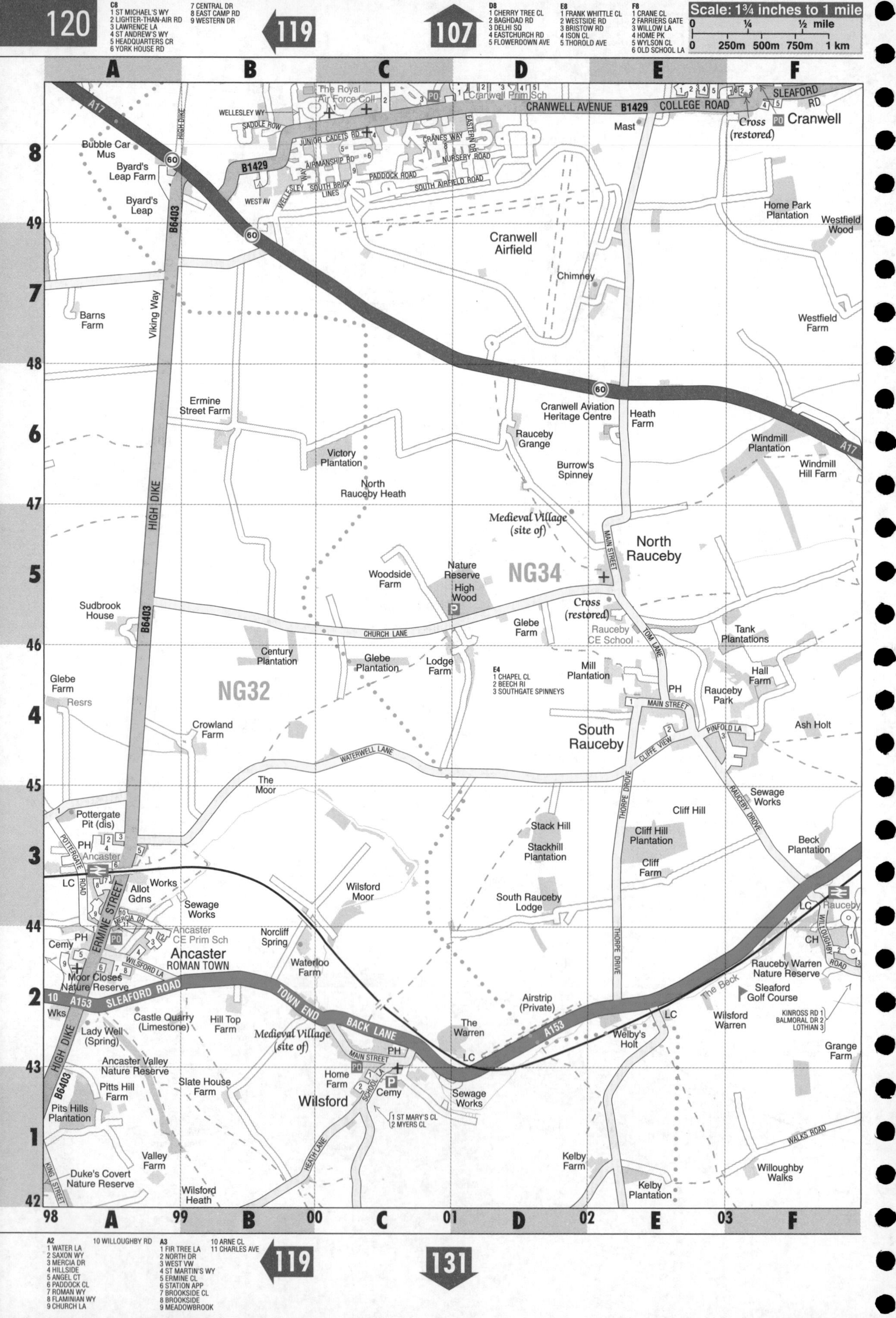

120
C8
1 ST MICHAEL'S WY
2 LIGHTER-THAN-AIR RD
3 LAWRENCE LA
4 ST ANDREW'S WY
5 HEADQUARTERS CR
6 YORK HOUSE RD
7 CENTRAL DR
8 EAST CAMP RD
9 WESTERN DR
119
107
D8
1 CHERRY TREE CL
2 BAGHDAD RD
3 DELHI SQ
4 EASTCHURCH RD
5 FLOWERDOWN AVE
E8
1 FRANK WHITTLE CL
2 WESTSIDE RD
3 BRISTOW RD
4 ISON CL
5 THOROLD AVE
F8
1 CRANE CL
2 FARRIERS GATE
3 WILLOW LA
4 HOME PK
5 WYLSON CL
6 OLD SCHOOL LA
Scale: 1¾ inches to 1 mile
0 ¼ ½ mile
0 250m 500m 750m 1 km
A B C D E F
8
49
7
48
6
47
5
46
4
45
3
44
2
43
1
42
98 99 00 01 02 03
The Royal Air Force Coll
Cranwell Prim Sch
WELLESLEY WY
SADDLE ROW
CRANWELL AVENUE B1429 COLLEGE ROAD
SLEAFORD RD
Cross (restored)
Cranwell
Mast
A17
HIGH DIKE
Bubble Car Mus
Byard's Leap Farm
Byard's Leap
B1429
JUNIOR CADETS RD
CRANES WAY
EASTERN DR
NURSERY ROAD
AIRMANSHIP RD
PADDOCK ROAD
SOUTH AIRFIELD ROAD
WELLESLEY WAY
SOUTH BRICK LINES
WEST AV
B6403
Home Park Plantation
Westfield Wood
Cranwell Airfield
Chimney
Viking Way
Barns Farm
Westfield Farm
Ermine Street Farm
Cranwell Aviation Heritage Centre
Heath Farm
Rauceby Grange
Windmill Plantation
Windmill Hill Farm
Victory Plantation
North Rauceby Heath
Burrow's Spinney
Medieval Village (site of)
North Rauceby
MAIN STREET
NG34
Woodside Farm
Nature Reserve
High Wood
Sudbrook House
Cross (restored)
CHURCH LANE
Glebe Farm
Rauceby CE School
Tank Plantations
TOM LANE
Century Plantation
Glebe Plantation
Lodge Farm
E4
1 CHAPEL CL
2 BEECH RI
3 SOUTHGATE SPINNEYS
Mill Plantation
PH
Rauceby Park
Hall Farm
Glebe Farm
Resrs
NG32
MAIN STREET
Crowland Farm
South Rauceby
CLIFFE VIEW
PINFOLD LA
Ash Holt
WATERWELL LANE
The Moor
THORPE DROVE
Sewage Works
RAUCEBY DROVE
Cliff Hill
Pottergate Pit (dis)
Stack Hill
Stackhill Plantation
Cliff Hill Plantation
Beck Plantation
PH
Ancaster
POTTERGATE ROAD
Cliff Farm
LC
Allot Gdns
Works
ERMINE STREET
Wilsford Moor
Sewage Works
South Rauceby Lodge
Rauceby
LC
MERCIA DR
Ancaster CE Prim Sch
Norcliff Spring
CH
WILLOUGHBY ROAD
Cemy
PH
Ancaster ROMAN TOWN
WILSFORD LA
Waterloo Farm
THORPE DRIVE
Rauceby Warren Nature Reserve
Moor Closes Nature Reserve
SLEAFORD ROAD
A153
TOWN END
BACK LANE
Airstrip (Private)
The Beck
Sleaford Golf Course
Wks
Castle Quarry (Limestone)
Hill Top Farm
The Warren
LC
Wilsford Warren
KINROSS RD 1
BALMORAL DR 2
LOTHIAN 3
Lady Well (Spring)
Medieval Village (site of)
Welby's Holt
Ancaster Valley Nature Reserve
MAIN STREET
PH
LC
Grange Farm
Pitts Hill Farm
Slate House Farm
Home Farm
SCHOOL LA
Cemy
Sewage Works
Pits Hills Plantation
Wilsford
1 ST MARY'S CL
2 MYERS CL
WALKS ROAD
HEATH LANE
Valley Farm
Kelby Farm
Willoughby Walks
Duke's Covert Nature Reserve
KING STREET
Wilsford Heath
Kelby Plantation
A2
1 WATER LA
2 SAXON WY
3 MERCIA DR
4 HILLSIDE
5 ANGEL CT
6 PADDOCK CL
7 ROMAN WY
8 FLAMINIAN WY
9 CHURCH LA
10 WILLOUGHBY RD
A3
1 FIR TREE LA
2 NORTH DR
3 WEST VW
4 ST MARTIN'S WY
5 ERMINE CL
6 STATION APP
7 BROOKSIDE CL
8 BROOKSIDE
9 MEADOWBROOK
10 ARNE CL
11 CHARLES AVE
119
131

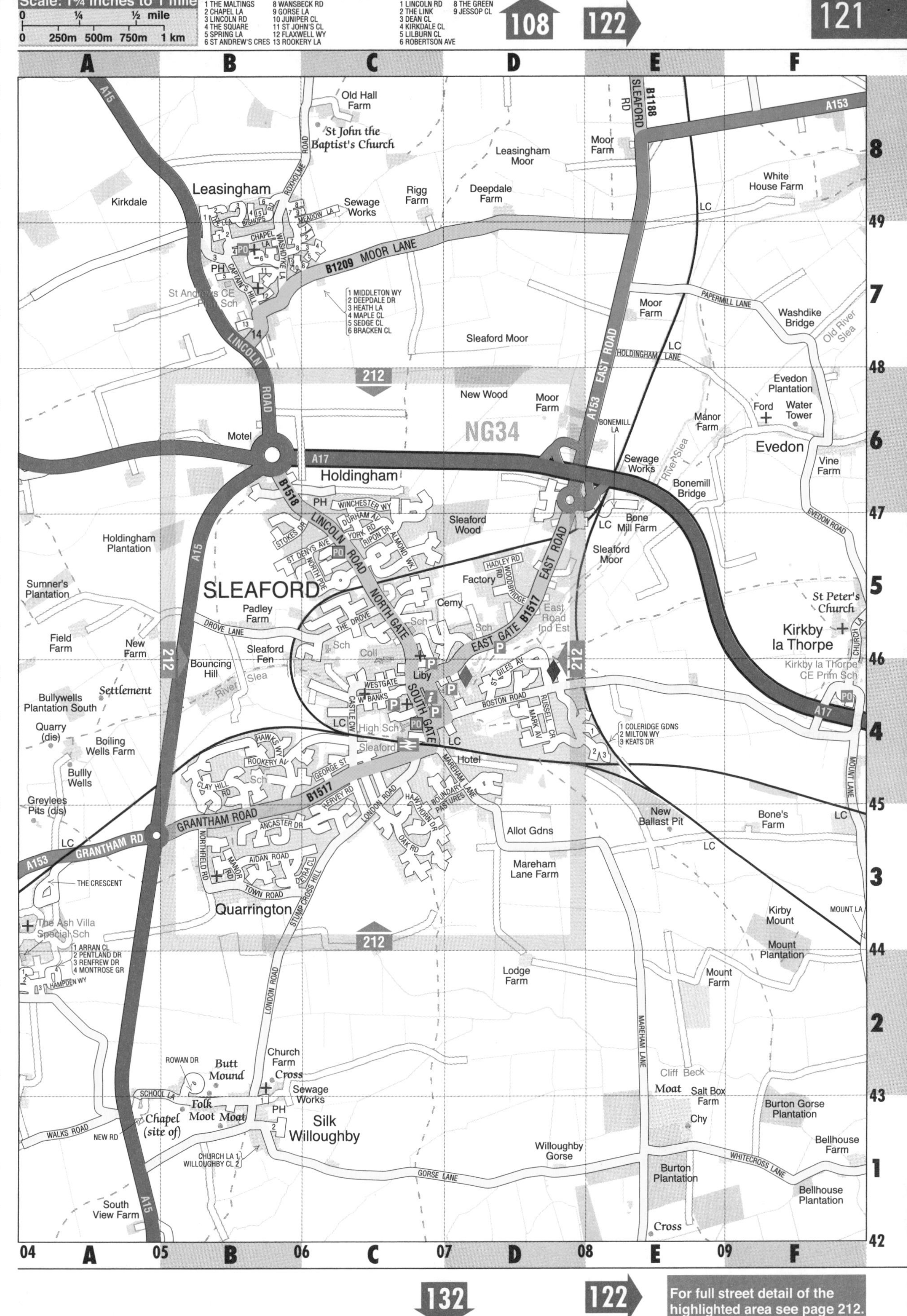

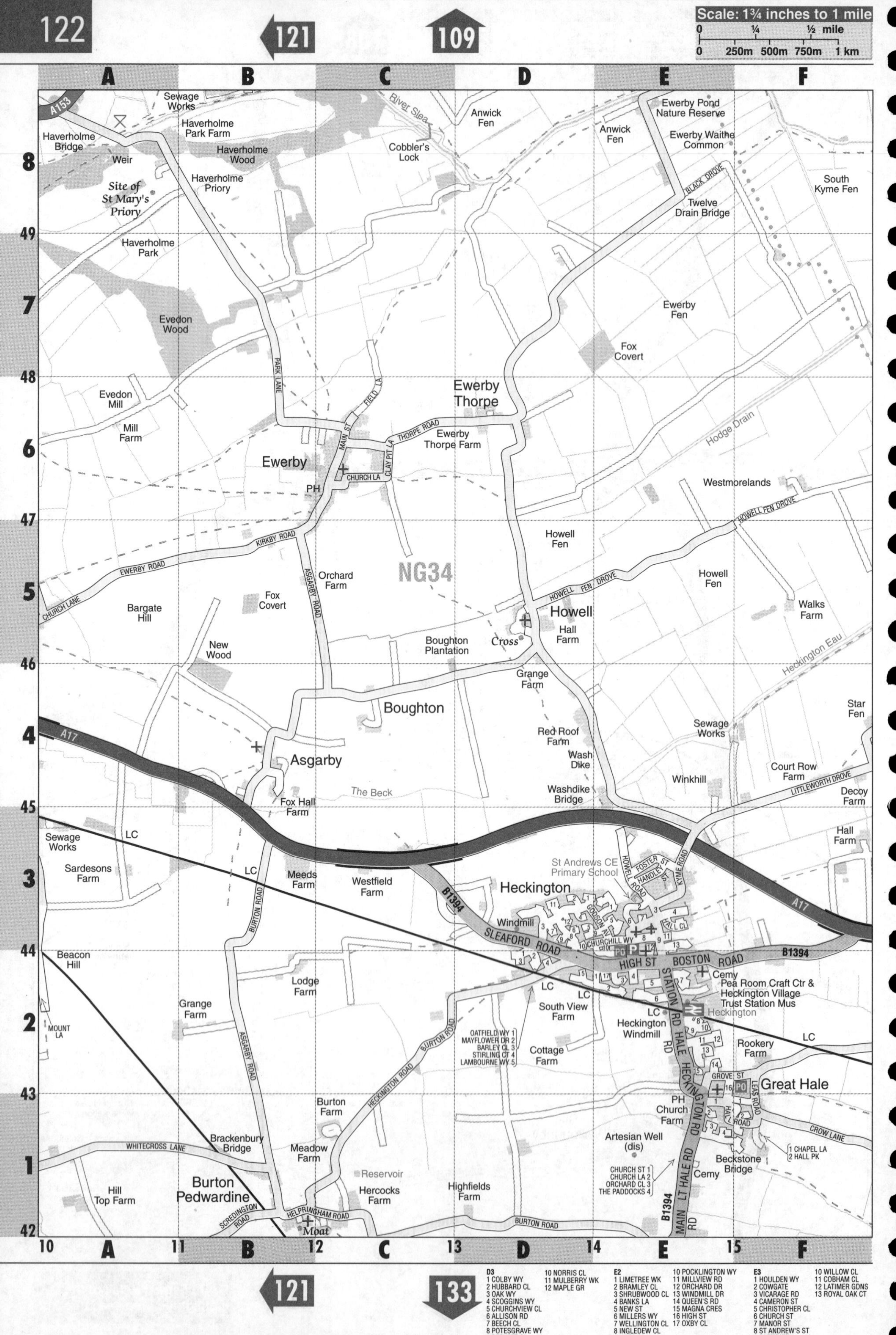
121
109
Scale: 1¾ inches to 1 mile
0 ¼ ½ mile
0 250m 500m 750m 1 km
A153
Sewage Works
Haverholme Bridge
Haverholme Park Farm
Haverholme Wood
Weir
River Slea
Cobbler's Lock
Anwick Fen
Ewerby Pond Nature Reserve
Ewerby Waithe Common
Site of St Mary's Priory
Haverholme Priory
BLACK DROVE
Twelve Drain Bridge
South Kyme Fen
Haverholme Park
Evedon Wood
Ewerby Fen
Fox Covert
Evedon Mill
PARK LANE
FIELD LA
Ewerby Thorpe
Mill Farm
MAIN ST
THORPE ROAD
Ewerby Thorpe Farm
Hodge Drain
Ewerby
CLAY PIT LA
CHURCH LA
PH
Westmorelands
HOWELL FEN DROVE
KIRKBY ROAD
Howell Fen
EWERBY ROAD
ASGARBY ROAD
Orchard Farm
NG34
Howell Fen
CHURCH LANE
Fox Covert
Bargate Hill
Howell
Walks Farm
Hall Farm
New Wood
Boughton Plantation
Cross
Heckington Eau
Grange Farm
Boughton
Star Fen
A17
Red Roof Farm
Sewage Works
Asgarby
Wash Dike
Winkhill
Court Row Farm
LITTLEWORTH DROVE
The Beck
Fox Hall Farm
Washdike Bridge
Decoy Farm
Sewage Works
LC
Hall Farm
St Andrews CE Primary School
FOSTER ST
HANDLEY ST
KYME ROAD
Sardesons Farm
Meeds Farm
Westfield Farm
B1394
Heckington
BURTON ROAD
Windmill
SLEAFORD ROAD
CHURCHILL WY
HIGH ST
BOSTON ROAD
Beacon Hill
Cemy
Pea Room Craft Ctr & Heckington Village Trust Station Mus
Lodge Farm
STATION RD
Heckington
South View Farm
Grange Farm
Heckington Windmill
MOUNT LA
OATFIELD WY 1
MAYFLOWER DR 2
BARLEY CL 3
STIRLING CT 4
LAMBOURNE WY 5
Cottage Farm
HALE RD
Rookery Farm
HECKINGTON RD
HECKINGTON ROAD
GROVE ST
Great Hale
LEAS ROAD
Burton Farm
PH
Church Farm
HALL ROAD
CROW LANE
Brackenbury Bridge
Artesian Well (dis)
1 CHAPEL LA
2 HALL PK
WHITECROSS LANE
Meadow Farm
Beckstone Bridge
CHURCH ST 1
CHURCH LA 2
ORCHARD CL 3
THE PADDOCKS 4
Cemy
Burton Pedwardine
Reservoir
Hill Top Farm
Hercocks Farm
Highfields Farm
SCREDINGTON ROAD
HELPRINGHAM ROAD
Moat
BURTON ROAD
MAIN LT HALE RD
121
133
D3
1 COLBY WY
2 HUBBARD CL
3 OAK WY
4 SCOGGINS WY
5 CHURCHVIEW CL
6 ALLISON RD
7 BEECH CL
8 POTESGRAVE WY
9 BECKETT CL
10 NORRIS CL
11 MULBERRY WK
12 MAPLE GR
E2
1 LIMETREE WK
2 BRAMLEY CL
3 SHRUBWOOD CL
4 BANKS LA
5 NEW ST
6 MILLERS WY
7 WELLINGTON CL
8 INGLEDEW CL
9 HARE CL
10 POCKLINGTON WY
11 MILLVIEW RD
12 ORCHARD DR
13 WINDMILL DR
14 QUEEN'S RD
15 MAGNA CRES
16 HIGH ST
17 OXBY CL
E3
1 HOULDEN WY
2 COWGATE
3 VICARAGE RD
4 CAMERON ST
5 CHRISTOPHER CL
6 CHURCH ST
7 MANOR ST
8 ST ANDREW'S ST
9 EASTGATE
10 WILLOW CL
11 COBHAM CL
12 LATIMER GDNS
13 ROYAL OAK CT

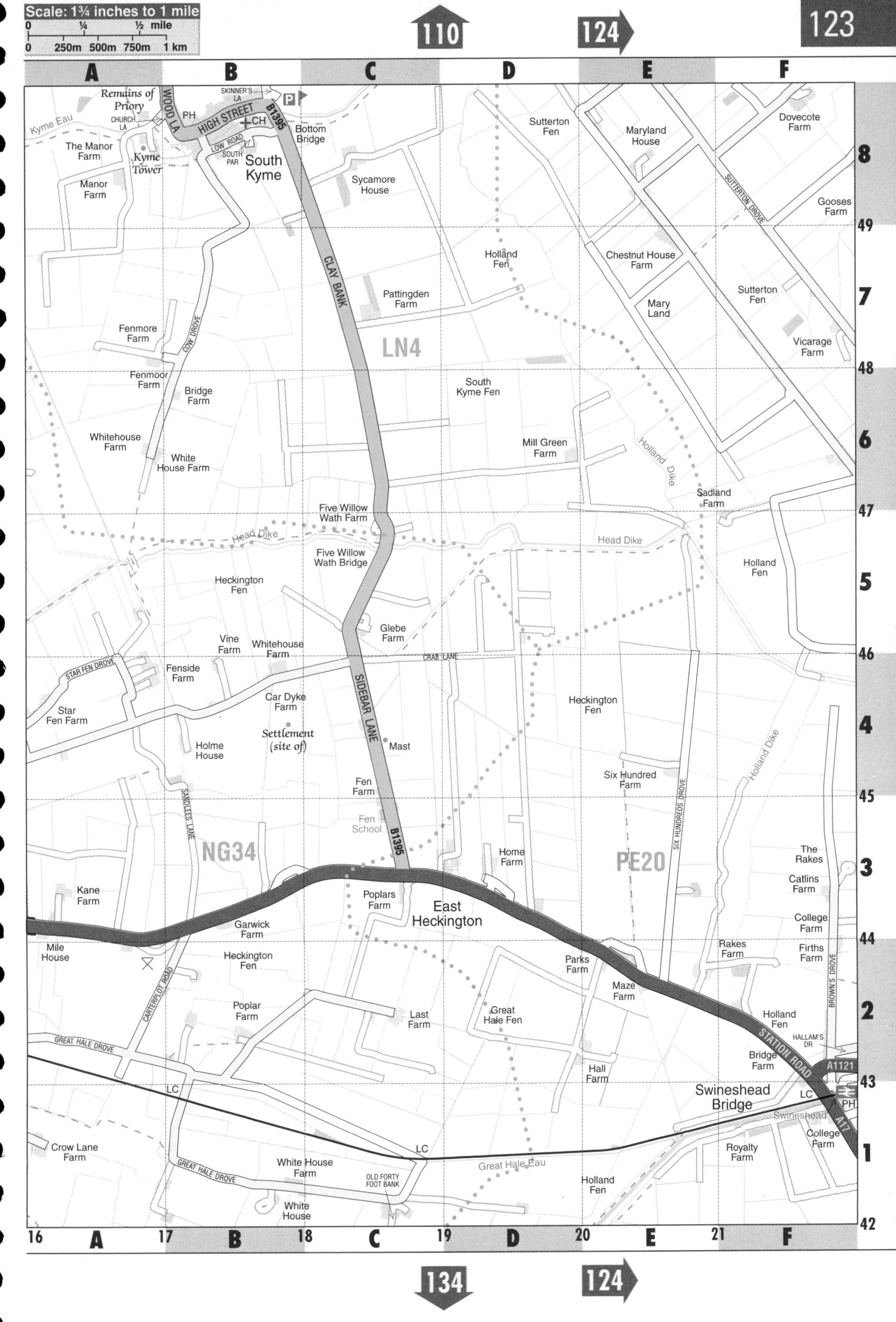
Scale: 1¾ inches to 1 mile
0 ¼ ½ mile
0 250m 500m 750m 1 km
110
124
A B C D E F
Remains of Priory
Kyme Eau
CHURCH LA
WOOD LA
PH
HIGH STREET
SKINNER'S LA
B1395
CH
Bottom Bridge
LOW ROAD
SOUTH PAR
South Kyme
The Manor Farm
Kyme Tower
Manor Farm
Sycamore House
Sutterton Fen
Maryland House
Dovecote Farm
SUTTERTON DROVE
Gooses Farm
CLAY BANK
Holland Fen
Chestnut House Farm
Pattingden Farm
Mary Land
Sutterton Fen
Fenmore Farm
COW DROVE
LN4
Vicarage Farm
Fenmoor Farm
Bridge Farm
South Kyme Fen
Whitehouse Farm
White House Farm
Mill Green Farm
Holland Dike
Sadland Farm
Five Willow Wath Farm
Head Dike
Head Dike
Five Willow Wath Bridge
Holland Fen
Heckington Fen
Glebe Farm
Vine Farm
Whitehouse Farm
CRAB LANE
STAR FEN DROVE
Fenside Farm
SIDEBAR LANE
Heckington Fen
Car Dyke Farm
Star Fen Farm
Settlement (site of)
Holme House
Mast
Holland Dike
Six Hundred Farm
Fen Farm
SANDLEES LANE
Fen School
SIX HUNDREDS DROVE
NG34
B1395
Home Farm
PE20
The Rakes
Kane Farm
Catlins Farm
Poplars Farm
East Heckington
Garwick Farm
College Farm
Mile House
Heckington Fen
Parks Farm
Rakes Farm
Firths Farm
CARTERPLOT ROAD
Maze Farm
BROWN'S DROVE
Poplar Farm
Last Farm
Great Hale Fen
Holland Fen
GREAT HALE DROVE
STATION ROAD
HALLAM'S DR
Bridge Farm
A1121
Hall Farm
LC
Swineshead Bridge
LC
PH
Swineshead
A17
Crow Lane Farm
LC
College Farm
Royalty Farm
GREAT HALE DROVE
White House Farm
OLD FORTY FOOT BANK
Great Hale Eau
Holland Fen
White House
8
49
7
48
6
47
5
46
4
45
3
44
2
43
1
42
16 A 17 B 18 C 19 D 20 E 21 F
134
124

123
111

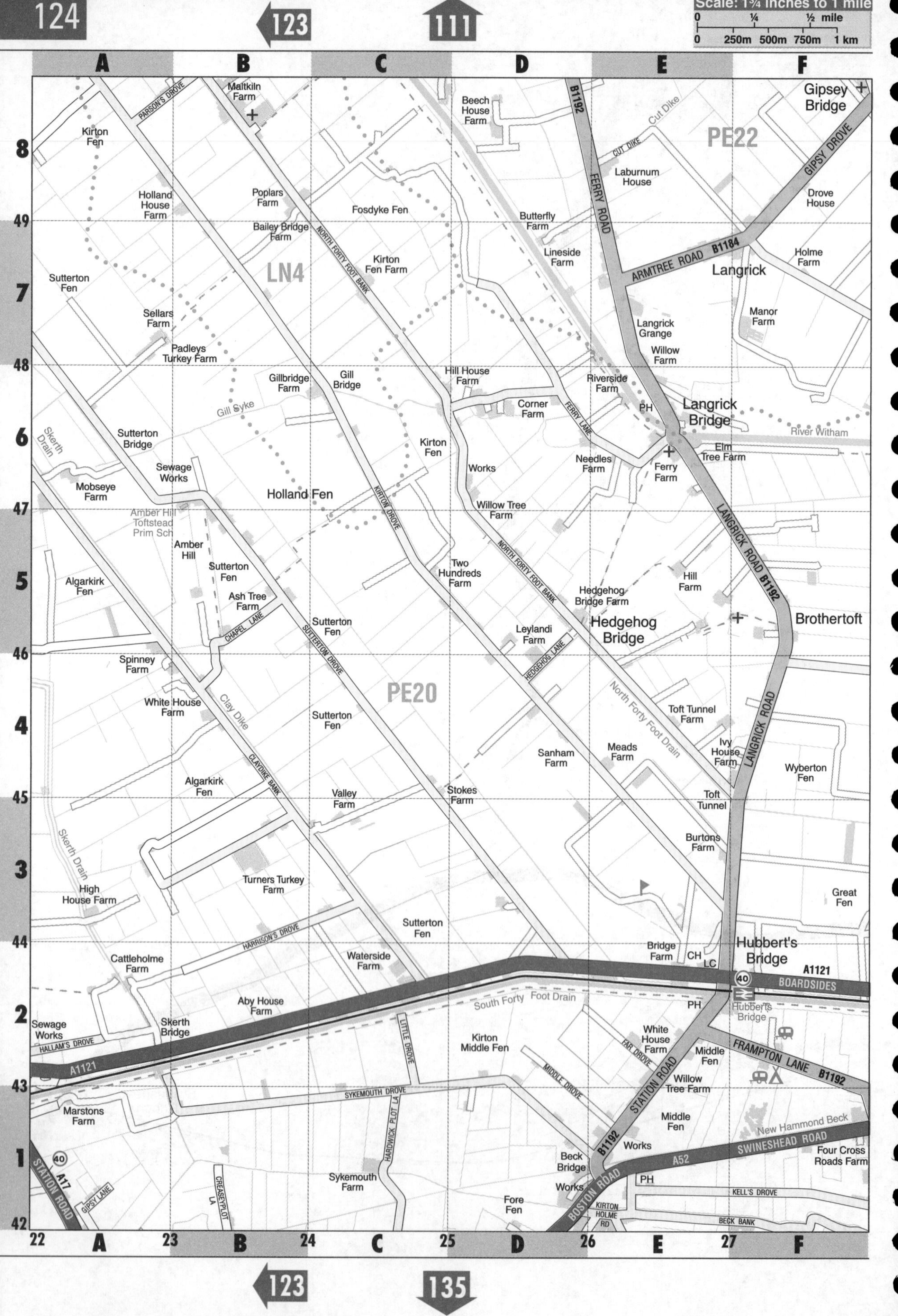
Scale: 1¾ inches to 1 mile
Gipsey Bridge
PE22
Kirton Fen
Maltkiln Farm
Beech House Farm
Cut Dike
Laburnum House
Drove House
Holland House Farm
Poplars Farm
Fosdyke Fen
Butterfly Farm
Bailey Bridge Farm
Lineside Farm
ARMTREE ROAD B1184
Langrick
Holme Farm
Sutterton Fen
LN4
Kirton Fen Farm
Manor Farm
Sellars Farm
Langrick Grange
Padleys Turkey Farm
Willow Farm
Gillbridge Farm
Gill Bridge
Hill House Farm
Riverside Farm
Corner Farm
Langrick Bridge
Gill Syke
PH
River Witham
Sutterton Bridge
Kirton Fen
Elm Tree Farm
Skerth Drain
Sewage Works
Works
Needles Farm
Ferry Farm
Mobseye Farm
Holland Fen
Amber Hill Toftstead Prim Sch
Willow Tree Farm
Amber Hill
Sutterton Fen
Two Hundreds Farm
Algarkirk Fen
Hill Farm
Ash Tree Farm
Hedgehog Bridge Farm
Hedgehog Bridge
Brothertoft
Sutterton Fen
Leylandi Farm
Spinney Farm
PE20
White House Farm
Clay Dike
North Forty Foot Drain
Toft Tunnel Farm
Sutterton Fen
Ivy House Farm
Sanham Farm
Meads Farm
Wyberton Fen
Algarkirk Fen
Valley Farm
Stokes Farm
Toft Tunnel
Burtons Farm
Turners Turkey Farm
High House Farm
Great Fen
Sutterton Fen
Cattleholme Farm
Waterside Farm
Bridge Farm
Hubbert's Bridge
A1121
BOARDSIDES
Aby House Farm
South Forty Foot Drain
Hubbert's Bridge
Sewage Works
Skerth Bridge
White House Farm
Middle Fen
Kirton Middle Fen
FRAMPTON LANE B1192
Willow Tree Farm
Marstons Farm
Middle Fen
New Hammond Beck
Works
SWINESHEAD ROAD
Four Cross Roads Farm
Beck Bridge
Sykemouth Farm
Works
Fore Fen
KELL'S DROVE
BECK BANK
STATION ROAD
BOSTON ROAD
FERRY ROAD
LANGRICK ROAD
GIPSY DROVE
NORTH FORTY FOOT BANK
KIRTON DROVE
SUTTERTON DROVE
CLAYDIKE BANK
HARRISON'S DROVE
HALLAM'S DROVE
SYKEMOUTH DROVE
LITTLE DROVE
MIDDLE DROVE
FAR DROVE
HARDWICK PLOT LA
GIPSY LANE
CHAPEL LANE
HEDGEHOG LANE
FERRY LANE
PARSON'S DROVE
KIRTON HOLME RD
A52
A17
B1192

123
135

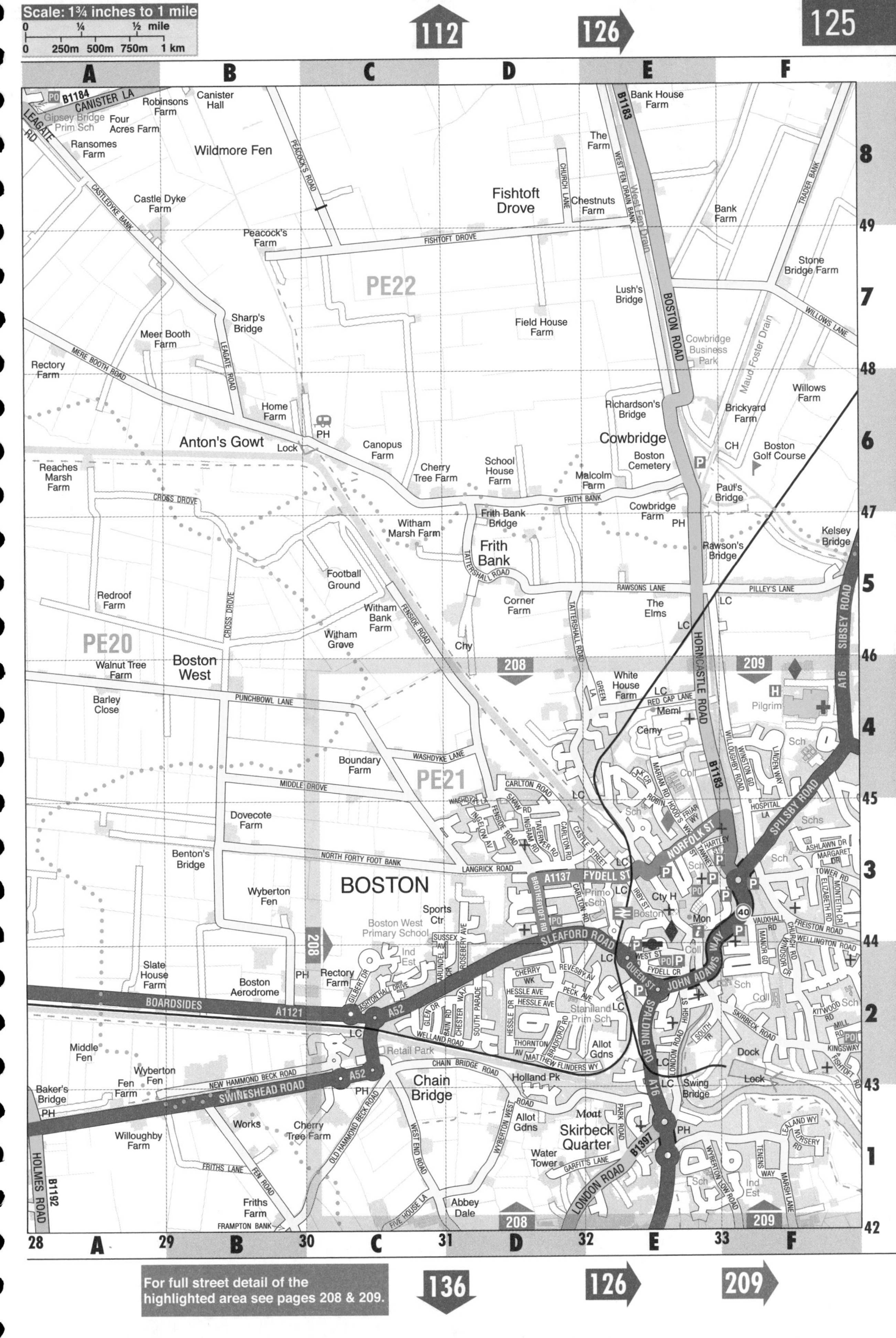

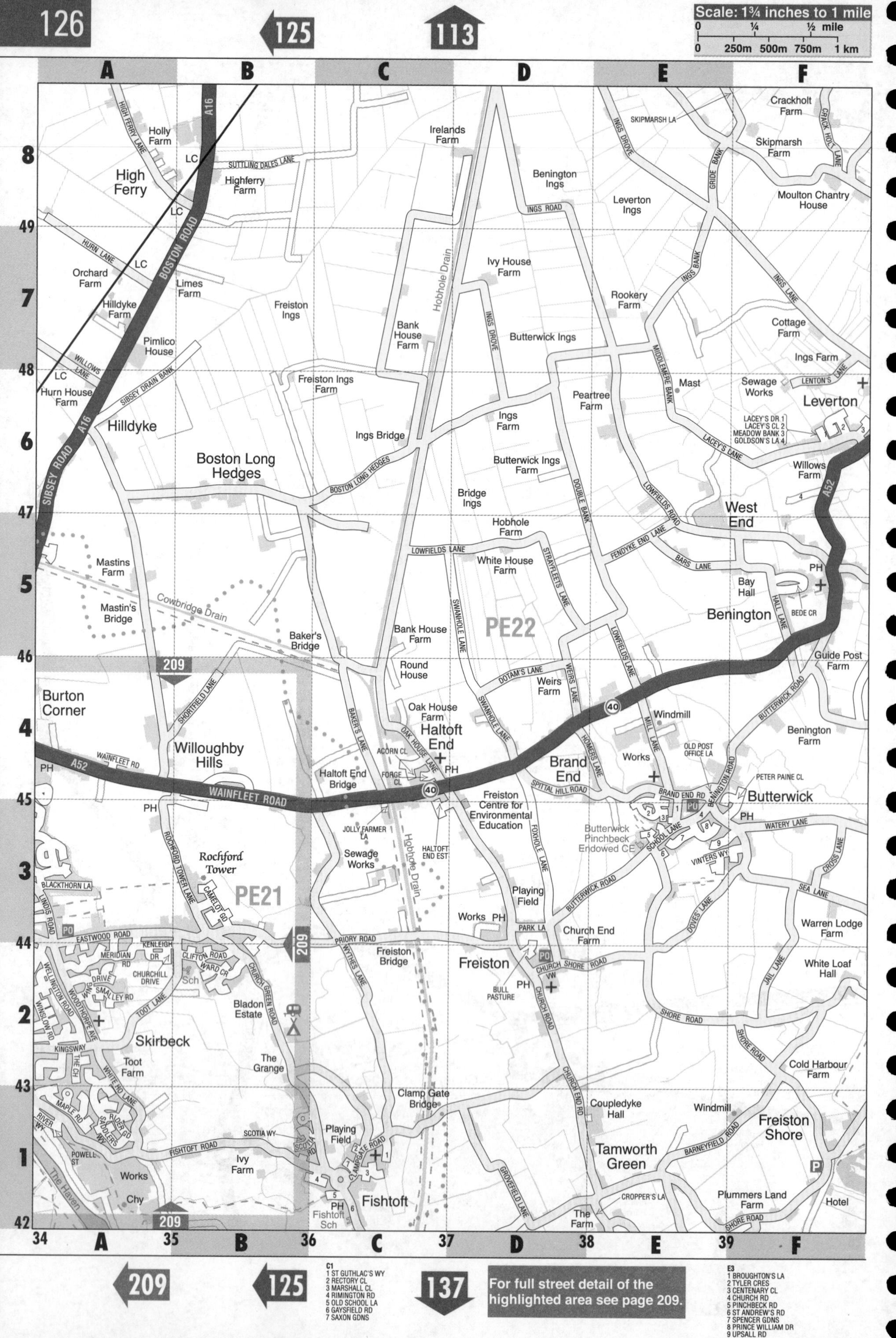

Scale: 1¾ inches to 1 mile
0   ¼   ½   mile
0   250m   500m   750m   1 km

8

49

7

48

6

5

46

4

45

3

44

2

43

1

42

A   B   C   D   E   F

34   35   36   37   38   39

High Ferry
Holly Farm
Highferry Farm
Suttling Dales Lane
LC
LC
BOSTON ROAD
A16

Orchard Farm
Hilldyke Farm
Limes Farm
Pimlico House
WILLOWS LANE
HURN LANE
LC
LC
Hurn House Farm
A16
SIBSEY ROAD

Hilldyke
SIBSEY DRAIN BANK

Boston Long Hedges
BOSTON LONG HEDGES

Freiston Ings
Freiston Ings Farm
Ings Bridge

Mastins Farm
Mastin's Bridge
Cowbridge Drain
Baker's Bridge

Burton Corner
209
SHORTFIELD LANE

Willoughby Hills
WAINFLEET RD
A52
PH
WAINFLEET ROAD
PH

Rochford Tower
ROCHFORD TOWER LANE
PE21
CARLTON RD
Sch
BAKER'S LANE

BLACKTHORN LA
LINDIS RD
PO
EASTWOOD ROAD
KENLEIGH DR
CLIFTON ROAD
WARD CR
MERIDIAN DRIVE
CHURCHILL DRIVE
SMALLEY RD
WELLINGTON RD
WINSLOW RD
WOODTHORPE AVE
TOOT LANE
CHURCH GREEN ROAD
209

Skirbeck
Toot Farm
KINGSWAY
THE CH
WHITE LOAF LANE
MAPLE RD
RIVER WY
SNOWDEN'S
POWELL ST
RIVER RD
SADLERS
FISHTOFT ROAD

Works
Chy
The Haven

Irelands Farm

Benington Ings
Leverton Ings
INGS ROAD
INGS DROVE
GRADE BANK
INGS BANK

Ivy House Farm
Bank House Farm
INGS DROVE
Hobhole Drain

Butterwick Ings
Rookery Farm

Ings Farm
Peartree Farm
MIDDLEMERE BANK
Mast

Butterwick Ings Farm
Bridge Ings
DOUBLE BANK
LOWFIELDS ROAD
FENDYKE END LANE

Hobhole Farm
White House Farm
LOWFIELDS LANE
STRANGE'S LANE
SWANNOLE LANE
PE22

Bank House Farm
Round House
DOTAM'S LANE
WEIRS LANE
Weirs Farm

Oak House Farm
Haltoft End
ACORN CL
OAK HOUSE LANE
SWANNOLE LANE
ROMER'S LANE
40
Brand End
Works
Windmill
MILL LANE
OLD POST OFFICE LA

Haltoft End Bridge
FORGE CL
40
Freiston Centre for Environmental Education
SPITTAL HILL ROAD
FOXHOLE LANE
BRAND END RD
PO
BUTTERWICK ROAD
Butterwick
PETER PAINE CL
Benington Farm

JOLLY FARMER
Sewage Works
Haltoft End Est
Butterwick Pinchbeck Endowed CE
SCHOOL LANE
PH
WATERY LANE

Playing Field
VINTERS WY
CROSS LANE
SEA LANE
Warren Lodge Farm

Works PH
PARK LA
Church End Farm
BUTTERWICK ROAD
DOVES LANE
White Loaf Hall

Freiston Bridge
PRIORY ROAD
WYTHES LANE
Freiston
PO
CHURCH SHORE ROAD
JAIL LANE
Cold Harbour Farm

Bladon Estate
The Grange
BULL PASTURE
PH
CHURCH END LANE
SHORE ROAD
Windmill
Freiston Shore

Clamp Gate Bridge
CLAMP GATE ROAD
Playing Field
SCOTIA WY
Ivy Farm
SCOTIA
Coupledyke Hall
Tamworth Green
BARNEYFIELD ROAD
P

Fishtoft
PH
Fishtoft Sch
Hobhole Drain
GROSVENOR LANE
CROPPER'S LA
The Farm
Plummers Land Farm
Hotel
SHORE ROAD

Leverton
Sewage Works
LENTON'S LANE
LACEY'S DR 1
LACEY'S CL 2
MEADOW BANK 3
GOLDSON'S LA 4
LACEY'S LANE
Willows Farm
A52

West End
PH
Bay Hall
Benington
BEDE CR
HALL LANE
BARS LANE
Guide Post Farm

Crackholt Farm
Skipmarsh Farm
Moulton Chantry House
CRACK HOLT LANE
SKIPMARSH LA
INGS LANE
Cottage Farm
Ings Farm

C1
1 ST GUTHLAC'S WY
2 RECTORY CL
3 MARSHALL CL
4 RIMINGTON RD
5 OLD SCHOOL LA
6 GAYSFIELD RD
7 SAXON GDNS

For full street detail of the highlighted area see page 209.

E3
1 BROUGHTON'S LA
2 TYLER CRES
3 CENTENARY CL
4 CHURCH RD
5 PINCHBECK RD
6 ST ANDREW'S RD
7 SPENCER GDNS
8 PRINCE WILLIAM DR
9 UPSALL RD

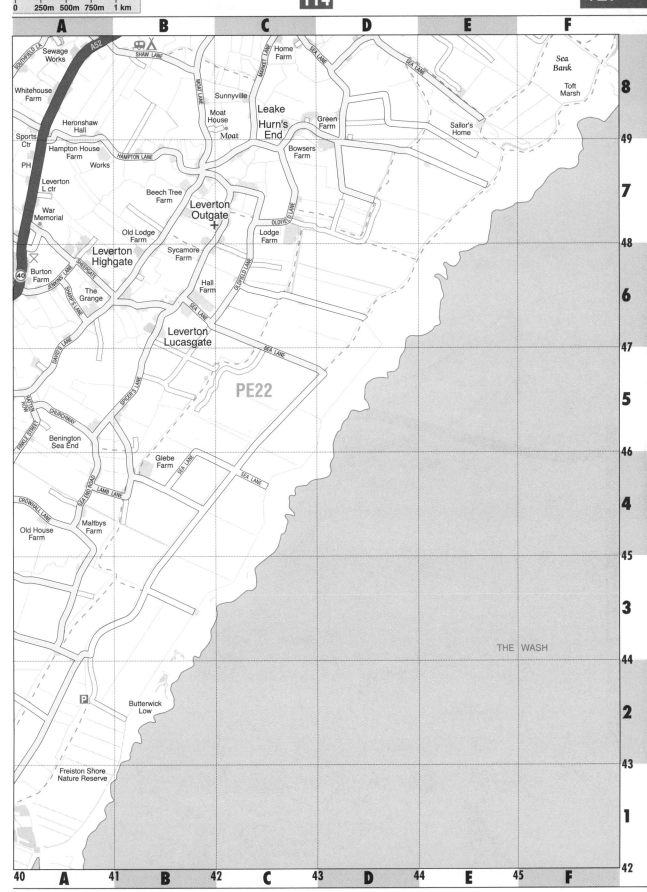

A52

SOUTHFIELD LA
Sewage Works
Whitehouse Farm
Sports Ctr
PH
Heronshaw Hall
Hampton House Farm
Works
Leverton L ctr
War Memorial
Burton Farm
40
SHEEPGATE
JENKINS LANE
SHARP'S LANE
DAVID'S LANE
Leverton Highgate
Old Lodge Farm
The Grange
BATTEN ROW
FINKLE STREET
CHURCHWAY
SPICER'S LANE
Benington Sea End
CROWHALL LANE
SEA END ROAD
LAMB LANE
Old House Farm
Maltbys Farm
Glebe Farm

SHAW LANE
MOAT LANE
HAMPTON LANE
Sunnyville
Moat House
Moat
Beech Tree Farm
Leverton Outgate
Sycamore Farm
Hall Farm
SEA LANE
Leverton Lucasgate
SEA LANE
OLDFIELD LANE
MARKET LANE
SEA LANE
Home Farm
Leake Hurn's End
Green Farm
Bowsers Farm
OLD LANE
OLDFIELD
Lodge Farm

SEA LANE
SEA LANE
SEA LANE

SEA LANE
Sailor's Home

Sea Bank
Toft Marsh

PE22

THE WASH

P
Butterwick Low

Freiston Shore Nature Reserve

8
49
7
48
6
47
5
46
4
45
3
44
2
43
1
42

40   A   41   B   42   C   43   D   44   E   45   F

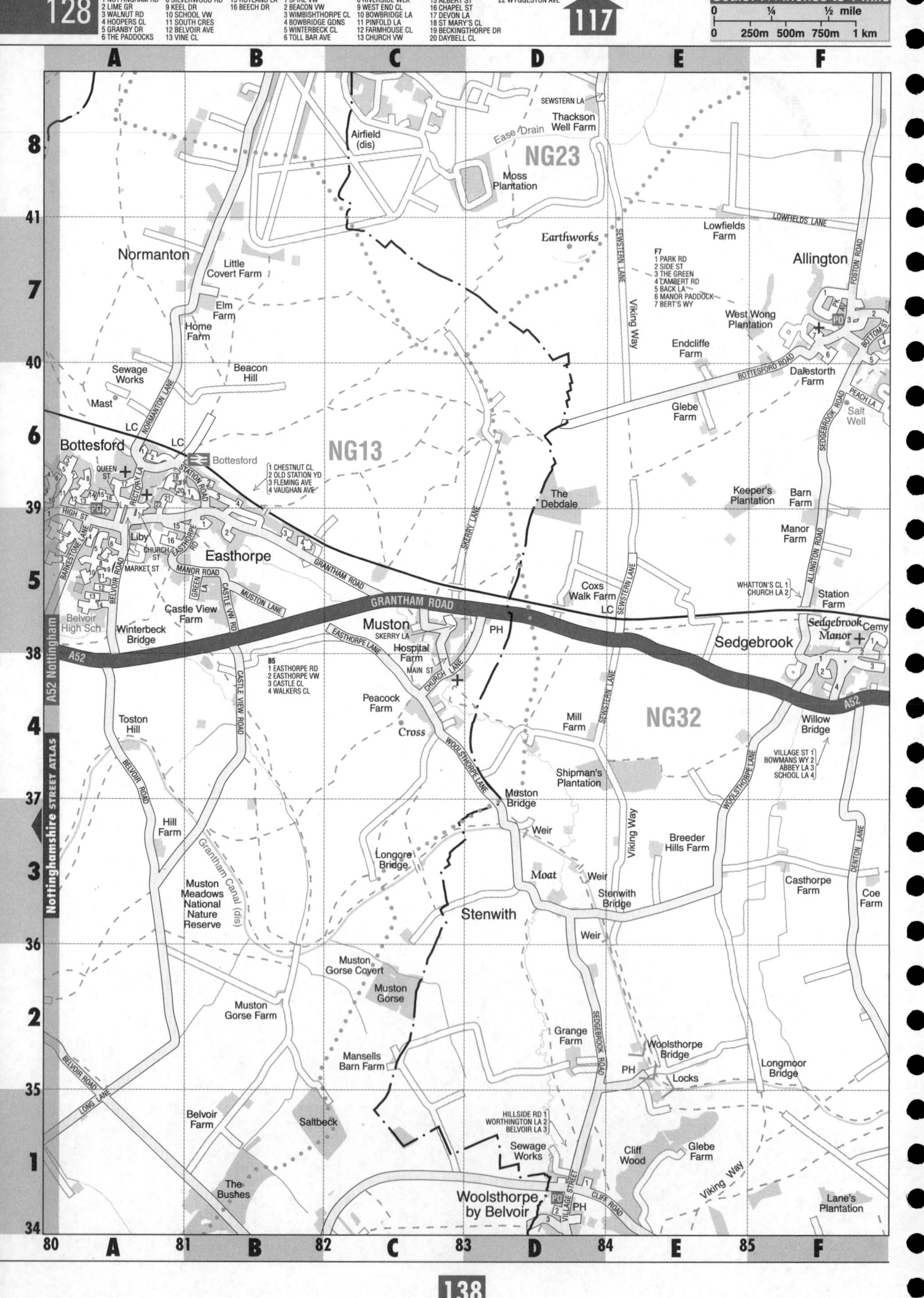

A5
1 NOTTINGHAM RD
2 LIME GR
3 WALNUT RD
4 HOOPERS CL
5 GRANBY DR
6 THE PADDOCKS

7 NORTH CRES
8 SILVERWOOD RD
9 KEEL DR
10 SCHOOL VW
11 SOUTH CRES
12 BELVOIR AVE
13 VINE CL

14 HOWITTS RD
15 RUTLAND LA
16 BEECH DR

A6
1 SPIRE VW
2 BEACON VW
3 WIMBISHTHORPE CL
4 BOWBRIDGE GDNS
5 WINTERBECK CL
6 TOLL BAR AVE

7 PINFOLD CL
8 RIVERSIDE WLK
9 WEST END CL
10 BOWBRIDGE LA
11 PINFOLD LA
12 FARMHOUSE CL
13 CHURCH VW

14 RIVERSIDE CL
15 ALBERT ST
16 CHAPEL ST
17 DEVON LA
18 ST MARY'S CL
19 BECKINGTHORPE DR
20 DAYBELL CL

21 WYGGESTON RD
22 WYGGESTON AVE

Scale: 1¾ inches to 1 mile
0   ¼   ½   mile
0   250m   500m   750m   1 km

Normanton

Little
Covert Farm

Elm
Farm

Home
Farm

Beacon
Hill

Sewage
Works

Mast

LC

Bottesford

QUEEN
ST

LC

Bottesford

1 CHESTNUT CL
2 OLD STATION YD
3 FLEMING AVE
4 VAUGHAN AVE

Liby

CHURCH
ST

Easthorpe

MARKET ST

NG13

Castle View
Farm

Winterbeck
Bridge

Belvoir
High Sch

A52 Nottingham

A52

Toston
Hill

Hill
Farm

Grantham Canal (dis)

Muston
Meadows
National
Nature
Reserve

Muston
Gorse Farm

Belvoir
Farm

Long Lane

BELVOIR ROAD

The
Bushes

Saltbeck

Airfield
(dis)

Ease Drain

Moss
Plantation

Earthworks

The
Debdale

Coxs
Walk Farm

LC

Muston

SKERRY LA

Hospital
Farm

MAIN ST

B5
1 EASTHORPE RD
2 EASTHORPE VW
3 CASTLE CL
4 WALKERS CL

Peacock
Farm

Cross

Longore
Bridge

Muston
Gorse Covert

Muston
Gorse

Mansells
Barn Farm

SEWSTERN LANE

Thackson
Well Farm

NG23

Lowfields
Farm

LOWFIELDS LANE

West Wong
Plantation

Endcliffe
Farm

Glebe
Farm

Keeper's
Plantation

Barn
Farm

Manor
Farm

WHATTON'S CL 1
CHURCH LA 2

Station
Farm

Sedgebrook

Sedgebrook
Manor
Cemy

NG32

Mill
Farm

Shipman's
Plantation

Muston
Bridge

Weir

Moat

Weir

Stenwith
Bridge

Weir

Stenwith

1 Grange
Farm

Viking Way

Breeder
Hills Farm

Woolsthorpe
Bridge

PH

Locks

HILLSIDE RD 1
WORTHINGTON LA 2
BELVOIR LA 3

Sewage
Works

Cliff
Wood

Glebe
Farm

**Woolsthorpe
by Belvoir**

PO

PH

Willow
Bridge

VILLAGE ST 1
BOWMANS WY 2
ABBEY LA 3
SCHOOL LA 4

Casthorpe
Farm

Coe
Farm

Longmoor
Bridge

Viking Way

Lane's
Plantation

F7
1 PARK RD
2 SIDE ST
3 THE GREEN
4 LAMBERT RD
5 BACK LA
6 MANOR PADDOCK
7 BERT'S WY

Allington

Dalestorth
Farm

Salt
Well

FOSTON ROAD

BOTTESFORD ROAD

Nottinghamshire STREET ATLAS

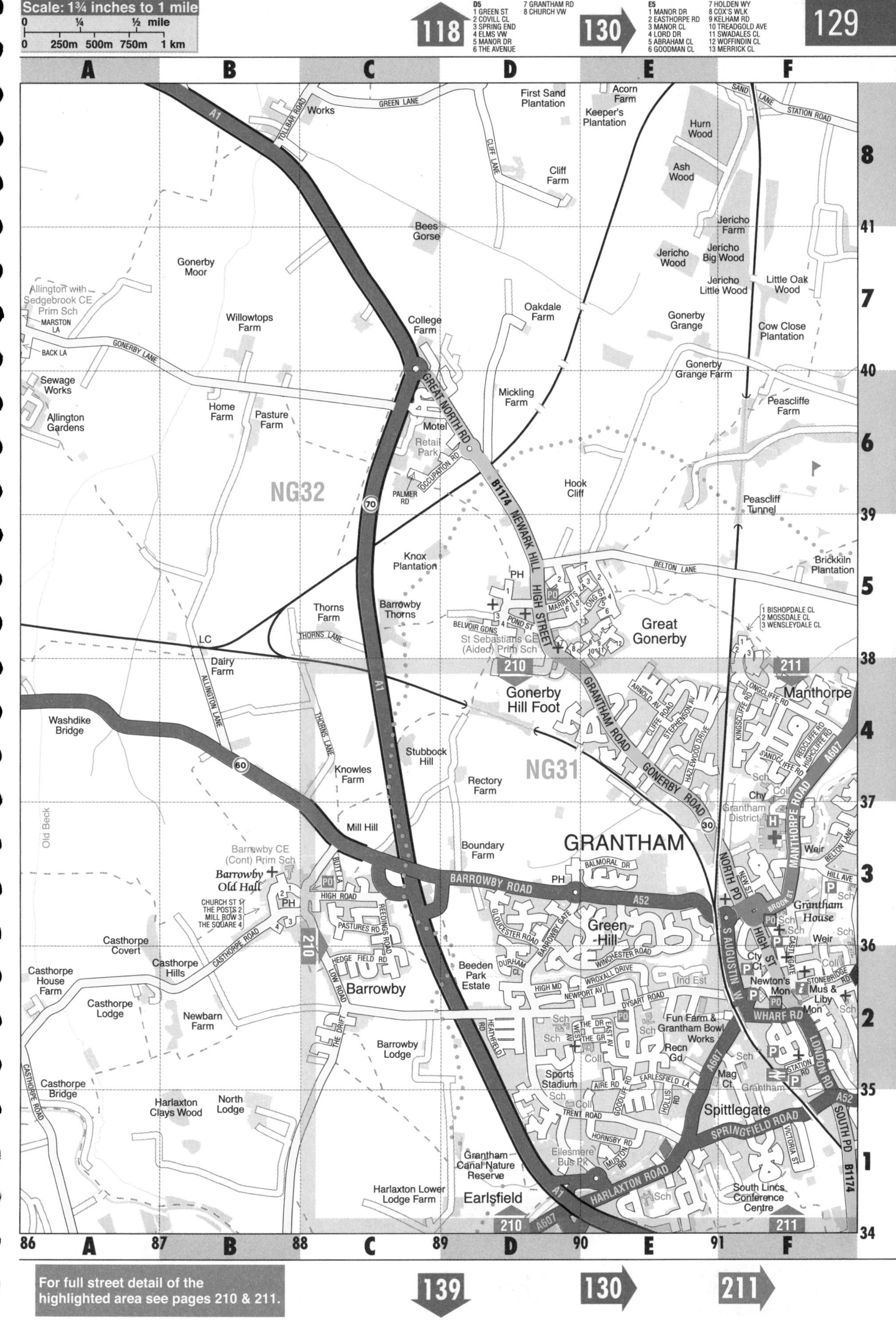

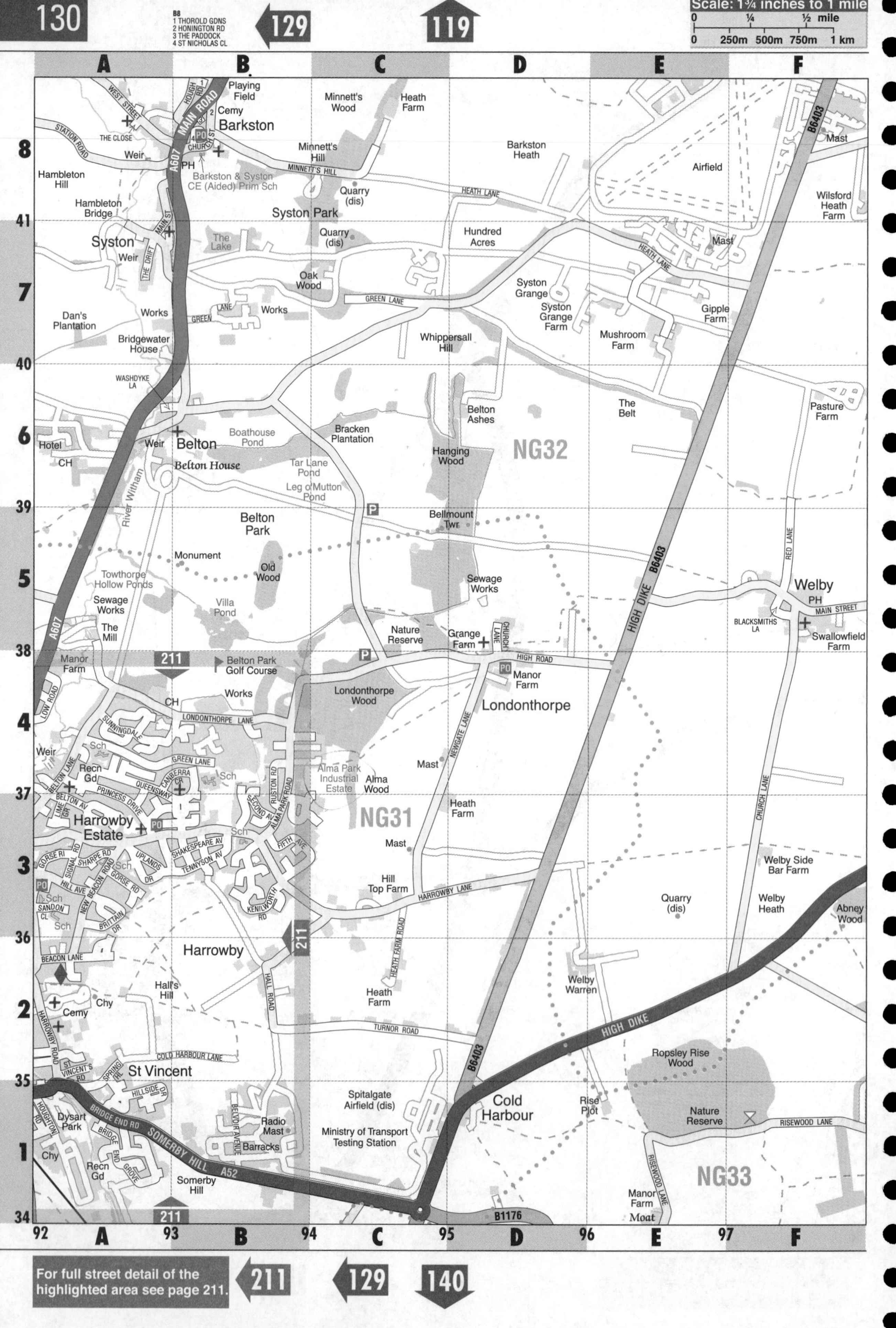

129

119

Scale: 1¾ inches to 1 mile

0   ¼   ½   mile

0   250m 500m 750m 1 km

West Street

Playing Field

Minnett's Wood

Heath Farm

Mast

B6403

The Close

Barkston

Cemy

Minnett's Hill

Barkston Heath

Wilsford Heath Farm

Station Road

A607 MAIN ROAD

HOUGH

PO ST

PH

CHURCH

Weir

Airfield

Mast

Hambleton Hill

Barkston & Syston CE (Aided) Prim Sch

Minnett's Hill

Quarry (dis)

Heath Lane

Hambleton Bridge

Syston Park

Quarry (dis)

Hundred Acres

Heath Lane

Mast

Syston

The Lake

Gipple Farm

Weir

THE DRIFT

Oak Wood

Green Lane

Syston Grange

Dan's Plantation

GREEN LANE

Works

Works

Whippersall Hill

Syston Grange Farm

Mushroom Farm

Bridgewater House

WASHDYKE LA

Belton Ashes

The Belt

Pasture Farm

Hotel

Weir

Belton

Boathouse Pond

Bracken Plantation

Hanging Wood

NG32

CH

Belton House

Tar Lane Pond

River Witham

Leg o'Mutton Pond

Bellmount Twr

B6403

Belton Park

HIGH DIKE

Red Lane

Monument

Old Wood

Welby

Towthorpe Hollow Ponds

Villa Pond

Sewage Works

PH

BLACKSMITHS LA

MAIN STREET

A607

Sewage Works

Nature Reserve

Grange Farm

CHURCH LANE

Swallowfield Farm

The Mill

Manor Farm

211

Belton Park Golf Course

PO

HIGH ROAD

Works

Londonthorpe Wood

Manor Farm

CH

LONDONTHORPE LANE

Londonthorpe

Weir

Sunningdale

Sch

Alma Park Industrial Estate

Alma Wood

Mast

NEWGATE LANE

CHURCH LANE

Recn Gd

QUEENSWAY

CANBERRA

Sch

Heath Farm

GORSE RI

GORSE RD

PRINCESS DRIVE

LIME AV

BELTON AV

RUSTON RD

SECOND AV

SCH

Mast

Welby Side Bar Farm

Harrowby Estate

PO

Hill Top Farm

HARROWBY LANE

Quarry (dis)

Welby Heath

SIGNAL RD

SHARPE RD

NEW BEACON ROAD

UPLANDS

SHAKESPEARE AV

TENNYSON AV

FIFTH AVE

Abney Wood

PO

HILL AV

KENILWORTH RD

211

Harrowby

HEATH FARM ROAD

Welby Warren

SANDON CL

Sch

BRITTAIN DR

HALL ROAD

BEACON LANE

Hall's Hill

Heath Farm

HIGH DIKE

Ropsley Rise Wood

Cemy

Chy

TURNOR ROAD

B6403

HARROWBY ROAD

COLD HARBOUR LANE

Nature Reserve

St Vincent

SPRING LA

ST VINCENT'S RD

HILLSIDE DR

Spitalgate Airfield (dis)

Cold Harbour

Rise Plot

RISEWOOD LANE

RISEWOOD LANE

Dysart Park

BRIDGE END RD

SOMERBY HILL

BELVOIR AVENUE

Radio Mast

Ministry of Transport Testing Station

NG33

HOUGHTON RD

Chy

BRIDGE END GROVE

Barracks

Manor Farm

Recn Gd

Somerby Hill

A52

Moat

211

B1176

211

129

140

92   93   94   95   96   97

A   B   C   D   E   F

34   35   36   1   2   3   37   4   5   38   6   39   7   40   41   8

Scale: 1¾ inches to 1 mile

120 132 141 132

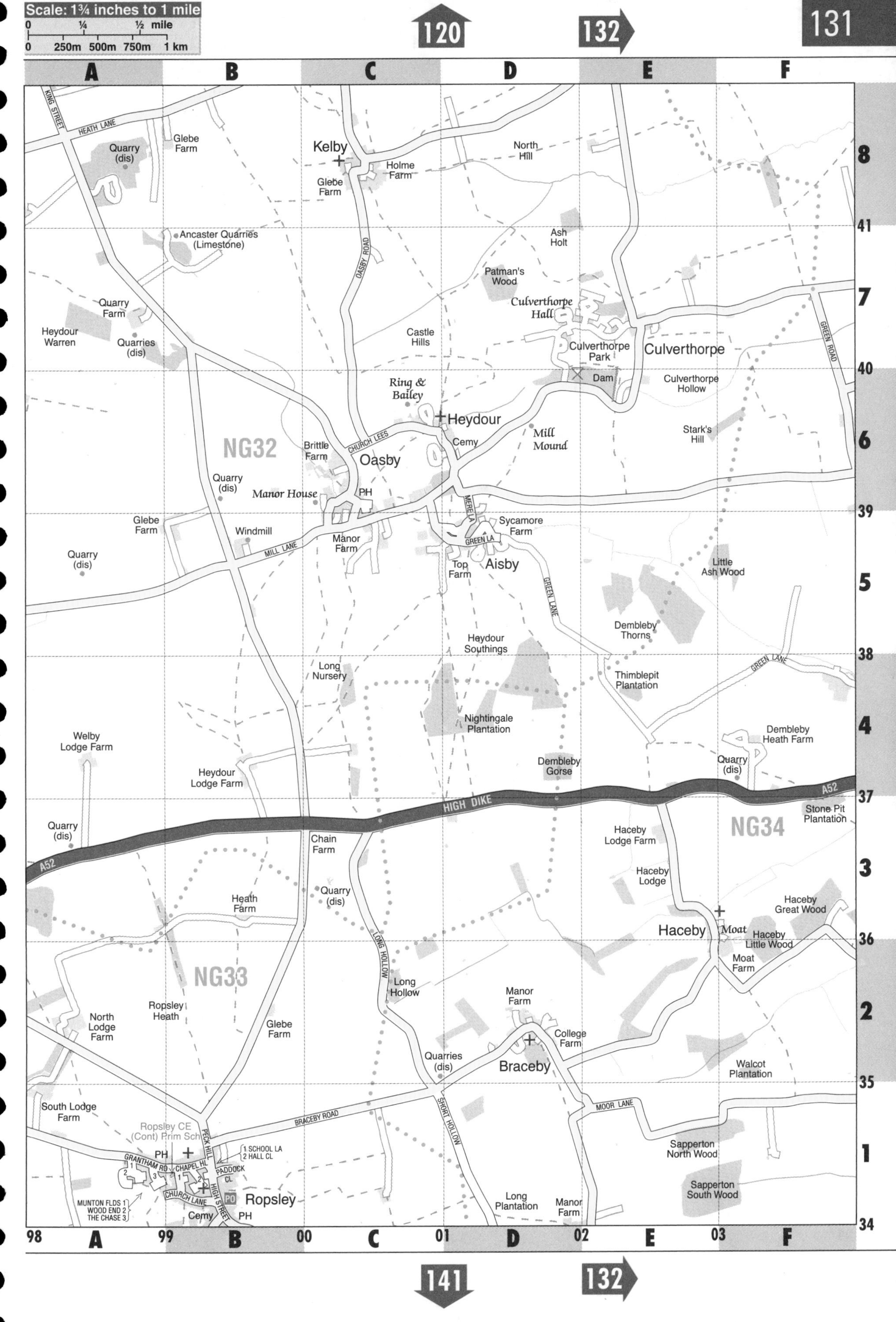

0 ¼ ½ mile
0 250m 500m 750m 1 km
Kelby
Holme Farm
Glebe Farm
North Hill
Quarry (dis)
Ancaster Quarries (Limestone)
Ash Holt
Patman's Wood
Culverthorpe Hall
Culverthorpe Park
Culverthorpe
Culverthorpe Hollow
Quarry Farm
Heydour Warren
Quarries (dis)
Castle Hills
Dam
Ring & Bailey
Heydour
Mill Mound
Stark's Hill
NG32
Brittle Farm
Oasby
Cemy
Manor House
PH
Windmill
Manor Farm
Sycamore Farm
Aisby
Top Farm
Little Ash Wood
Dembleby Thorns
Heydour Southings
Long Nursery
Thimblepit Plantation
Nightingale Plantation
Welby Lodge Farm
Heydour Lodge Farm
Dembleby Gorse
Dembleby Heath Farm
HIGH DIKE
A52
Stone Pit Plantation
NG34
Chain Farm
Haceby Lodge Farm
Haceby Lodge
Heath Farm
Haceby Great Wood
Haceby
Moat
Haceby Little Wood
Moat Farm
NG33
Long Hollow
Manor Farm
Ropsley Heath
North Lodge Farm
Glebe Farm
College Farm
Quarries (dis)
Braceby
Walcot Plantation
South Lodge Farm
Ropsley CE (Cont) Prim Sch
MOOR LANE
BRACEBY ROAD
SHORT HOLLOW
Sapperton North Wood
Sapperton South Wood
Long Plantation
Ropsley
KING STREET
HEATH LANE
OASBY ROAD
CHURCH LEES
MERE LA
GREEN LA
MILL LANE
GREEN LANE
GREEN ROAD
LONG HOLLOW
PECK HILL
GRANTHAM RD
CHAPEL HL
CHURCH LANE
HIGH STREET
PADDOCK CL
1 SCHOOL LA
2 HALL CL
MUNTON FLDS 1
WOOD END 2
THE CHASE 3
PO
A B C D E F
98 99 00 01 02 03
8 41 7 40 6 39 5 38 4 37 3 36 2 35 1 34

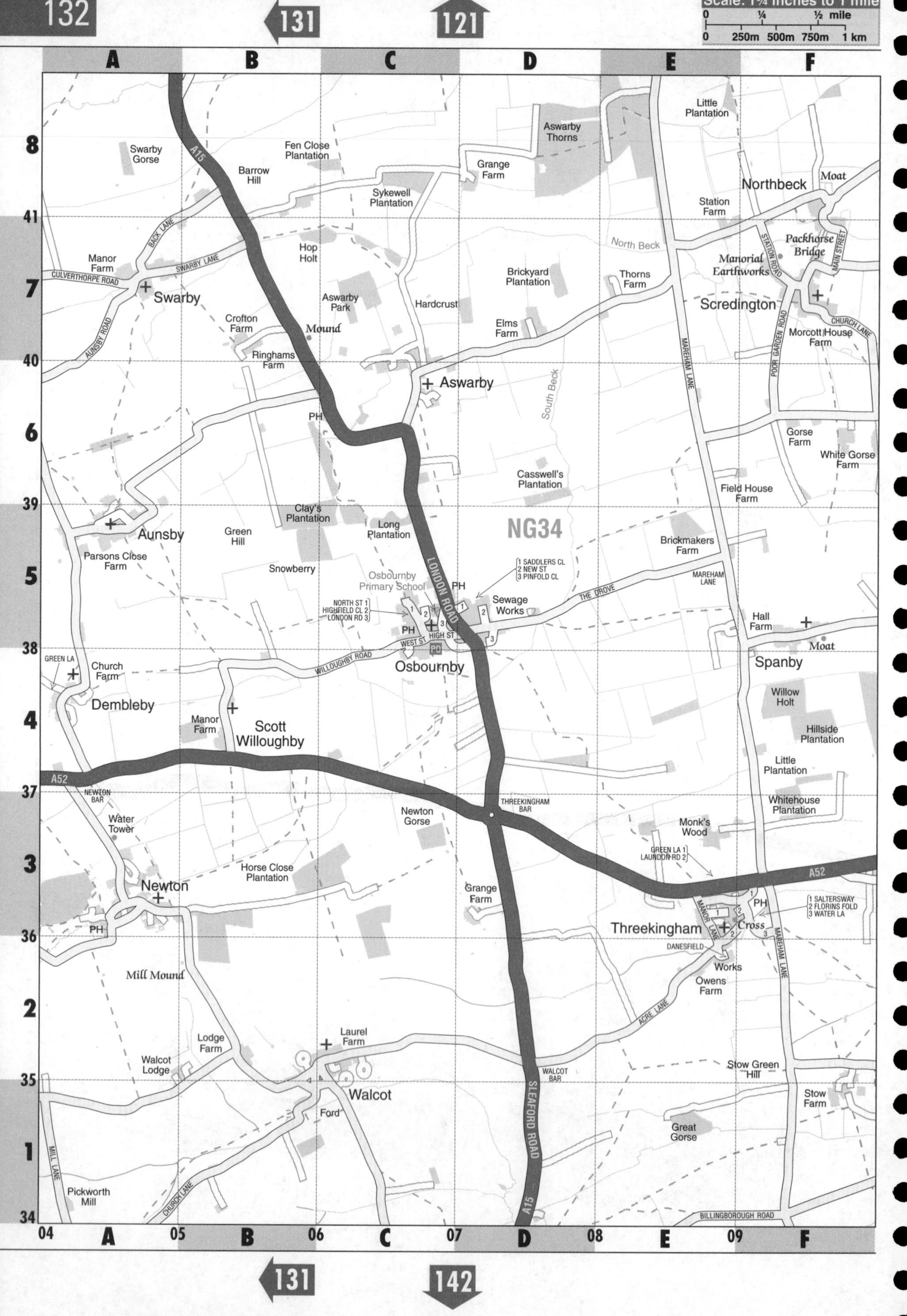
131
121
Scale: 1¾ inches to 1 mile
0 ¼ ½ mile
0 250m 500m 750m 1 km
A B C D E F
8 41 7 40 6 39 5 38 4 37 3 36 2 35 1 34
Swarby Gorse
Fen Close Plantation
Barrow Hill
Aswarby Thorns
Grange Farm
Little Plantation
Northbeck
Moat
Sykewell Plantation
Station Farm
Back Lane
Hop Holt
North Beck
Packhorse Bridge
Station Road
Main Street
Manor Farm
Culverthorpe Road
Swarby Lane
Brickyard Plantation
Thorns Farm
Manorial Earthworks
Swarby
Aswarby Park
Hardcrust
Scredington
Crofton Farm
Mound
Elms Farm
Mareham Lane
Poor Garden Road
Church Lane
Morcott House Farm
Aunsby Road
Ringhams Farm
Aswarby
South Beck
PH
Gorse Farm
White Gorse Farm
Casswell's Plantation
Field House Farm
Clay's Plantation
Long Plantation
Aunsby
Green Hill
NG34
Brickmakers Farm
Parsons Close Farm
London Road
Snowberry
1 Saddlers Cl
2 New St
3 Pinfold Cl
Osbournby Primary School
The Drove
Mareham Lane
North St 1
Highfield Cl 2
London Rd 3
Sewage Works
Hall Farm
West St
High St
PO
Willoughby Road
Green La
Church Farm
Osbournby
Spanby
Dembleby
Willow Holt
Manor Farm
Scott Willoughby
Hillside Plantation
A52
Little Plantation
Newton Bar
Threekingham Bar
Whitehouse Plantation
Water Tower
Newton Gorse
Monk's Wood
Green La 1
Laundon Rd 2
Horse Close Plantation
Newton
Grange Farm
1 Saltersway
2 Florins Fold
3 Water La
Manor Lane
Threekingham
Cross
Danesfield
Works
Owens Farm
Mill Mound
Acre Lane
Lodge Farm
Laurel Farm
Walcot Lodge
Walcot Bar
Stow Green Hill
Walcot
Sleaford Road
Stow Farm
Ford
Great Gorse
Mill Lane
Pickworth Mill
Church Lane
A15
Billingborough Road
04 05 06 07 08 09
131
142

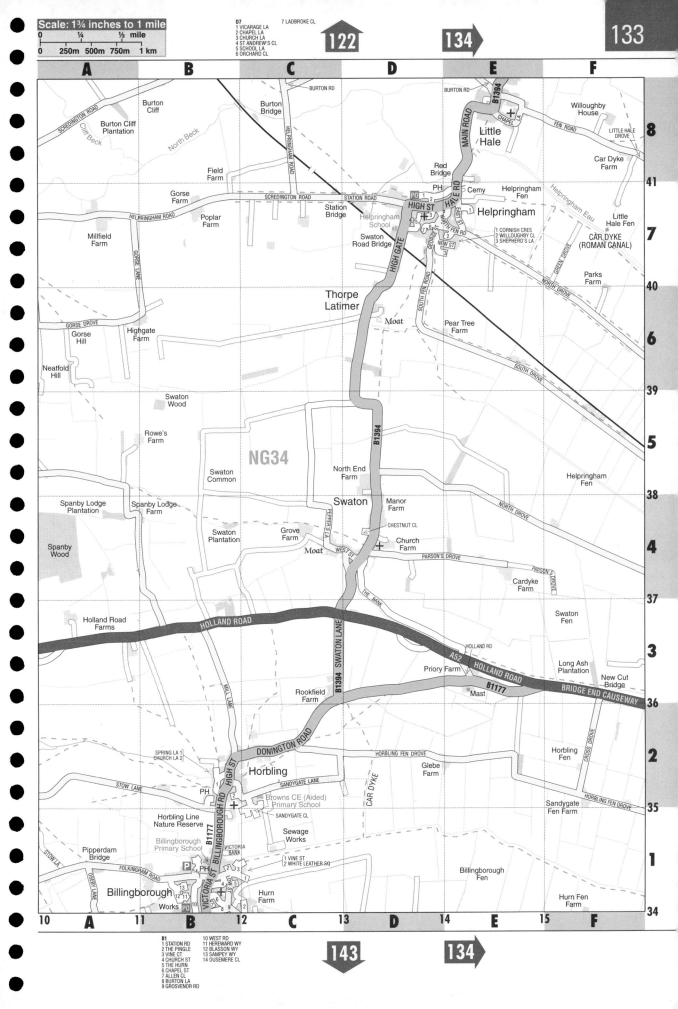

122

134

0   ¼   ½   mile
0   250m   500m   750m   1 km

D7
1 VICARAGE LA
2 CHAPEL LA
3 CHURCH LA
4 ST ANDREW'S CL
5 SCHOOL LA
6 ORCHARD CL

7 LADBROKE CL

A   B   C   D   E   F

Scredington Road
Cliff Beck
Burton Cliff
Burton Cliff Plantation
North Beck

8

Burton Bridge
BURTON RD
BURTON RD
B1394
CHAPEL
Main Road
Little Hale
Willoughby House
FEN ROAD
LITTLE HALE DROVE

Field Farm
Gorse Farm
Screddington Road
Station Road
Station Bridge
Helpringham School
Red Bridge
PH
PO
HIGH ST
HALE RD
Cemy
Helpringham Fen
HELPRINGHAM EAU
Car Dyke Farm

41
7

Helpringham Road
Poplar Farm
Swaton Road Bridge
EAST ST
NORTH FEN RD
Helpringham
1 CORNISH CRES
2 WILLOUGHBY CL
3 SHEPHERD'S LA
NEW ST
Little Hale Fen
CAR DYKE (ROMAN CANAL)

Millfield Farm
GORSE LANE
HIGH GATE
SOUTH FEN ROAD
GEORGE ST
GREEN DROVE
NORTH DROVE
Parks Farm

40

Gorse Drove
Gorse Hill
Highgate Farm
Thorpe Latimer
Moat
Pear Tree Farm
SOUTH DROVE

6

Neatfold Hill
Swaton Wood
B1394
39

Rowe's Farm
NG34
North End Farm
Helpringham Fen

5

Spanby Lodge Plantation
Spanby Lodge Farm
Swaton Common
Swaton
Manor Farm
NORTH DROVE

38

Spanby Wood
Swaton Plantation
Grove Farm
PEPPER'S LA
CHESTNUT CL
Church Farm
PARSON'S DROVE

4

Moat
WEST ST
Cardyke Farm
PARSON'S DROVE

37

Holland Road Farms
HOLLAND ROAD
SWATON LANE
THE BANK
Swaton Fen

3

A52
HOLLAND RD
HOLLAND ROAD
Long Ash Plantation
New Cut Bridge

Priory Farm
B1177
BRIDGE END CAUSEWAY

36

MILL LANE
B1394
Rookfield Farm
Mast

DONINGTON ROAD
SPRING LA 1
CHURCH LA 2
Horbling
HORBLING FEN DROVE
Glebe Farm
Horbling Fen

2

STOW LANE
HIGH ST
SANDYGATE LANE
CAR DYKE
HORBLING FEN DROVE

PH
Browns CE (Aided) Primary School
Horbling Line Nature Reserve
SANDYGATE CL
Sandygate Fen Farm

35

Billingborough Primary School
B1177
BILLINGBOROUGH RD
Sewage Works
VICTORIA BANK
1 VINE ST
2 WHITE LEATHER SQ

Pipperdam Bridge
STOW LA
OSSERY LANE
FOLKINGHAM ROAD
P
PH
VICTORIA ST
LOW ST
Billingborough Fen

1

Billingborough
Works
PO
Hurn Farm
Hurn Fen Farm

34

10   A   11   B   12   C   13   D   14   E   15   F

B1
1 STATION RD
2 THE PINGLE
3 VINE CT
4 CHURCH ST
5 THE HURN
6 CHAPEL ST
7 ALLEN CL
8 BURTON LA
9 GROSVENOR RD
10 WEST RD
11 HEREWARD WY
12 BLASSON WY
13 SAMPEY WY
14 OUSEMERE CL

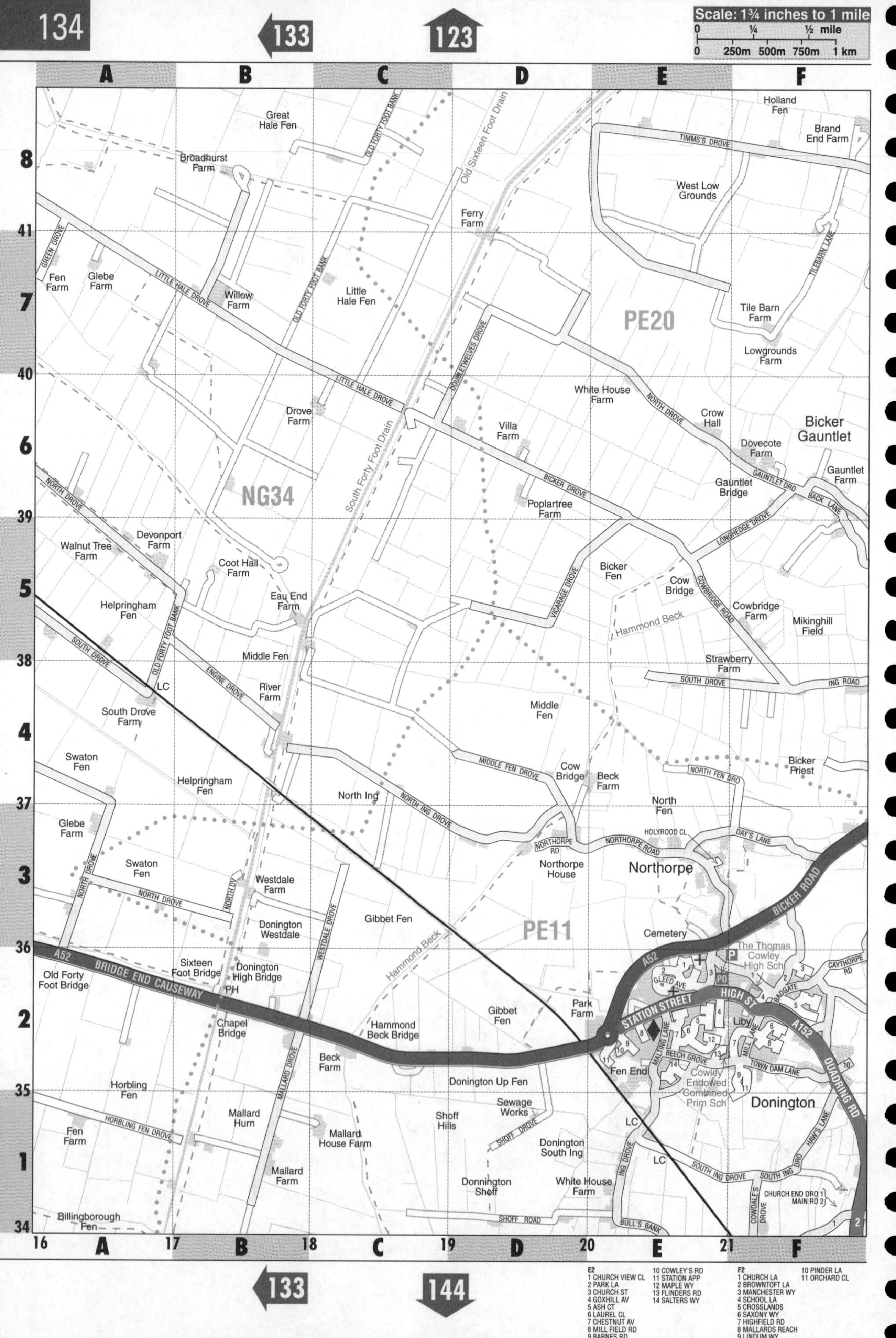

Scale: 1¾ inches to 1 mile

0   ¼   ½   mile
0 250m 500m 750m 1 km

8
41
7
40
6
39
5
38
4
37
3
36
2
35
1
34

A   B   C   D   E   F

16   17   18   19   20   21

Great
Hale Fen

Broadhurst
Farm

Old Forty Foot Bank

Old Sixteen Foot Drain

TIMMS'S DROVE

Holland
Fen

Brand
End Farm

West Low
Grounds

TILEBARN LANE

Fen Farm

Glebe
Farm

LITTLE HALE DROVE

Willow
Farm

Little
Hale Fen

Ferry
Farm

PE20

Tile Barn
Farm

Lowgrounds
Farm

GREEN DROVE

LITTLE HALE DROVE

Drove
Farm

DOUBLE TWELVES DROVE

Villa
Farm

White House
Farm

NORTH DROVE

Crow
Hall

Bicker
Gauntlet

Dovecote
Farm

GAUNTLET DRO

Gauntlet
Farm

South Forty Foot Drain

NG34

BICKER DROVE

Poplartree
Farm

Gauntlet
Bridge

Cowbridge
Farm

BACK LANE

Walnut Tree
Farm

Devonport
Farm

Coot Hall
Farm

Eau End
Farm

Bicker
Fen

LONGHEDGE DROVE

Cow
Bridge

COWBRIDGE ROAD

Mikinghill
Field

Helpringham
Fen

Middle Fen

Hammond Beck

Strawberry
Farm

NORTH DROVE

SOUTH DROVE

OLD FORTY FOOT BANK

ENGINE DROVE

River
Farm

WICKRAGE DROVE

Middle
Fen

SOUTH DROVE

Ing Road

LC

South Drove
Farm

Swaton
Fen

Helpringham
Fen

MIDDLE FEN DROVE

Cow
Bridge

Beck
Farm

NORTH FEN DRO

Bicker
Priest

North Ing

NORTH ING DROVE

North
Fen

Glebe
Farm

Swaton
Fen

NORTH DROVE

Westdale
Farm

NORTH DV

Gibbet Fen

HOLYROOD CL

DAY'S LANE

NORTHORPE
RD

NORTHORPE ROAD

Northorpe
House

Northorpe

Cemetery

BICKER ROAD

PE11

Donington
Westdale

WESTDALE DROVE

Hammond Beck

The Thomas
Cowley
High Sch

CAYTHORPE
RD

A52

Old Forty
Foot Bridge

BRIDGE END CAUSEWAY

Sixteen
Foot Bridge

Donington
High Bridge

PH

A52

P

PO

GLEED AVE

HIGH ST

BRIDGATE

A152

Chapel
Bridge

MALLARD DROVE

Hammond
Beck Bridge

Gibbet
Fen

Park
Farm

STATION STREET

MALTING LANE

Liby

MILL LANE

TOWN DAM LANE

Fen End

BEECH GROVE

Cowley
Endowed
Combined
Prim Sch

Donington

Horbling
Fen

HORBLING FEN DROVE

Mallard
Hurn

Beck
Farm

Donington Up Fen

Shoff
Hills

Sewage
Works

SHOFF DROVE

Donington
South Ing

HAWS LANE

QUADRING RD

Fen
Farm

Mallard
House Farm

Mallard
Farm

Donnington
Shoff

White House
Farm

ING DROVE

LC

LC

SOUTH ING DROVE

SOUTH ING

COWDALE'S DROVE

CHURCH END DRO 1
MAIN RD 2

Billingborough
Fen

SHOFF ROAD

BULL'S BANK

2

E2
1 CHURCH VIEW CL
2 PARK LA
3 CHURCH ST
4 GOXHILL AV
5 ASH CT
6 LAUREL CL
7 CHESTNUT AV
8 MILL FIELD RD
9 BARNES RD
10 COWLEY'S RD
11 STATION APP
12 MAPLE WY
13 FLINDERS RD
14 SALTERS WY

F2
1 CHURCH LA
2 BROWNTOFT LA
3 MANCHESTER WY
4 SCHOOL LA
5 CROSSLANDS
6 SAXONY WY
7 HIGHFIELD RD
8 MALLARDS REACH
9 LINDUM WY
10 PINDER LA
11 ORCHARD CL

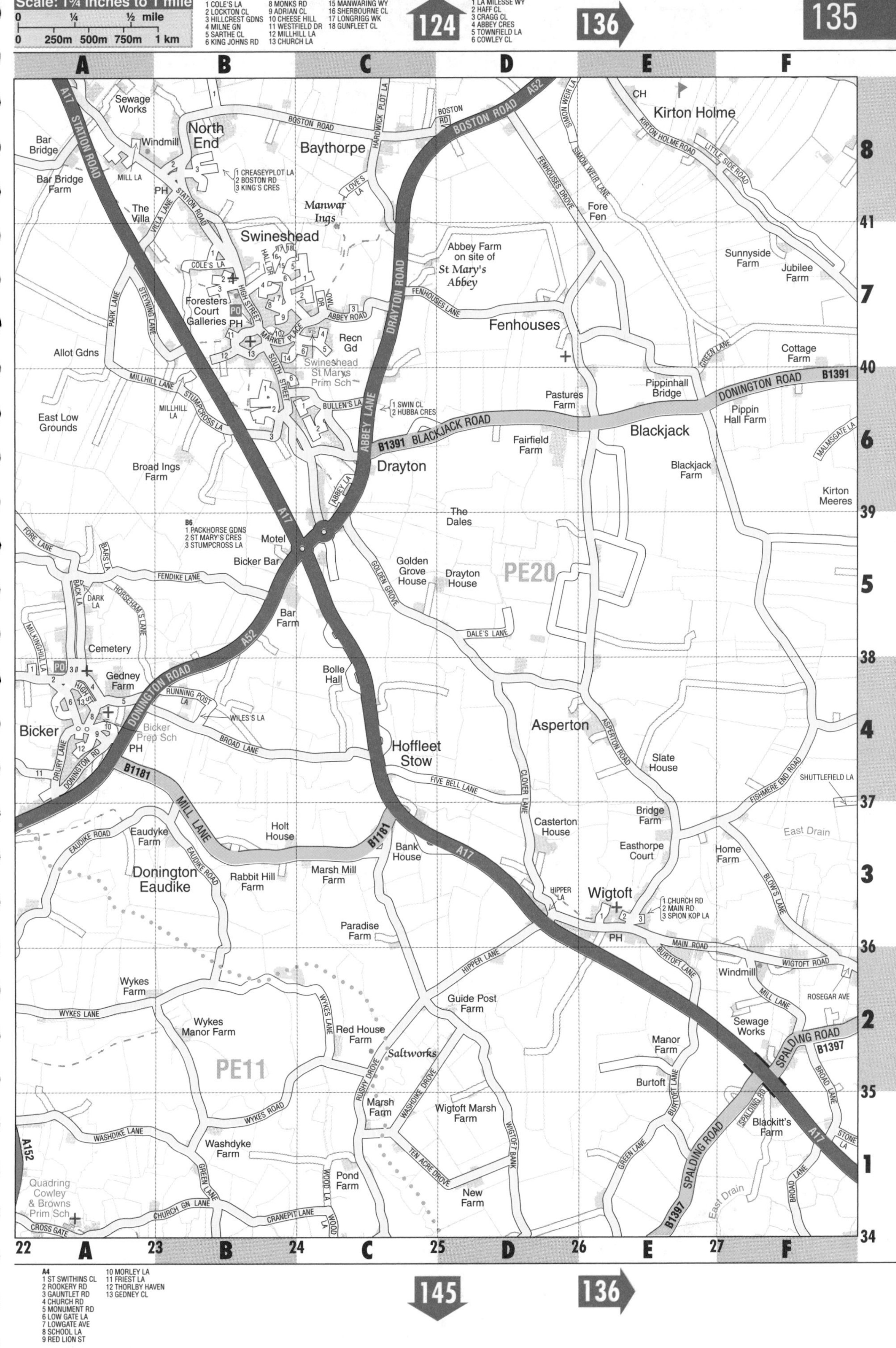

B7
1 COLE'S LA
2 LOCKTON CL
3 HILLCREST GDNS
4 SARTHE CL
5 MILNE GN
6 KING JOHNS RD

7 VIKING CL
8 MONKS RD
9 ADRIAN CL
10 CHEESE HILL
11 WESTFIELD DR
12 MILLHILL LA
13 CHURCH LA

14 BUTLER'S WY
15 MANWARING WY
16 SHERBOURNE CL
17 LONGRIGG WK
18 GUNFLEET CL

C7
1 LA MILESSE WY
2 HAFF CL
3 CRAGG CL
4 ABBEY CRES
5 TOWNFIELD LA
6 COWLEY CL

Grid labels (top): A B C D E F

Grid labels (right, top to bottom): 8 41 7 40 6 39 5 38 4 37 3 36 2 35 1 34

A17 STATION ROAD

Sewage Works
Windmill
MILL LA
North End
Baythorpe
BOSTON ROAD
BOSTON RD
BOSTON ROAD A52
HARDWICK PLOT LA
LOVE'S LA
CH
Kirton Holme
KIRTON HOLME ROAD
LITTLE SIDE LANE
SIMON WEIR LA
SIMON WEIR LA

Bar Bridge
Bar Bridge Farm
The Villa
PH
STATION ROAD
VILLA LANE
PARK LANE
STEYNING LANE
Swineshead
1 CREASEYPLOT LA
2 BOSTON RD
3 KING'S CRES
Manwar Ings
Abbey Farm on site of St Mary's Abbey
FENHOUSES DRIVE
Fore Fen
Sunnyside Farm
Jubilee Farm

COLE'S LA
HALTOFT
HIGH STREET
DRAYTON ROAD
FENHOUSES LANE
Fenhouses
GREEN LANE
Cottage Farm

Foresters Court Galleries
PO
PH
MARKET PLACE
OWL LANE
ABBEY ROAD
Recn Gd
Swineshead St Marys Prim Sch
SOUTH STREET
Pastures Farm
Pippinhall Bridge
DONINGTON ROAD
B1391
Pippin Hall Farm
MALMGATE LA

Allot Gdns
MILLHILL LANE
STUMPCROSS LA
MILLHILL LA
BULLEN'S LA
ABBEY LANE
1 SWIN CL
2 HUBBA CRES
Fairfield Farm
Blackjack
Blackjack Farm
Kirton Meeres

East Low Grounds
B1391 BLACKJACK ROAD
Drayton
The Dales
PE20

Broad Ings Farm
A17
FORE LANE
BARS LA
BACK LA
DARK LA
HORSEHAM'S LANE
FENDIKE LANE
B6
1 PACKHORSE GDNS
2 ST MARY'S CRES
3 STUMPCROSS LA
Motel
Bicker Bar
GOLDEN GROVE
Golden Grove House
Drayton House
ASPERTON ROAD

MILKINGHILL LA
PO
Cemetery
Gedney Farm
RUNNING POST LA
A52
DONINGTON ROAD
Bar Farm
DALE'S LANE
CLOVER LANE
Asperton
Slate House
SHUTTLEFIELD LA
East Drain

Bicker
HIGH ST
WILES'S LA
Bicker Prep Sch
BROAD LANE
Bolle Hall
Hoffleet Stow
FIVE BELL LANE
Casterton House
Bridge Farm
FISHMERE END ROAD

DRURY LANE
DONINGTON RD
B1181
PH
B1181
A17
Eastthorpe Court
Home Farm
BLOW'S LANE

MILL LANE
EAUDIKE ROAD
Eaudyke Farm
Holt House
Bank House
Marsh Mill Farm
Wigtoft
HIPPER LA
1 CHURCH RD
2 MAIN RD
3 SPION KOP LA
PH
MAIN ROAD
BURTOFT LANE
WIGTOFT RD
Windmill
ROSEGAR AVE

Donington Eaudike
Rabbit Hill Farm
Paradise Farm
HIPPER LANE
Guide Post Farm
Manor Farm
Sewage Works
SPALDING ROAD
B1397

WYKES LANE
Wykes Farm
WYKES LANE
Wykes Manor Farm
WYKES LANE
RUSHY DROVE
Red House Farm
Saltworks
WASHDIKE DROVE
Wigtoft Marsh Farm
WIGTOFT BANK
GREEN LANE
Burtoft
BURTOFT LANE
MILL LANE
BROAD LANE
PE11

A152
WASHDIKE LANE
Washdyke Farm
GREEN GN LANE
Marsh Farm
TEN ACRE DROVE
WOOD LA
Pond Farm
CRANEPIT LANE
WOOD LA
New Farm
WIGTOFT BANK
GREEN LANE
SPALDING ROAD
B1397
East Drain
Blackitt's Farm
SPALDING RD
STONE LA
A17

Quadring Cowley & Browns Prim Sch
CROSS GATE
CHURCH LANE

Grid labels (bottom): 22 A 23 B 24 C 25 D 26 E 27 F 34

A4
1 ST SWITHINS CL
2 ROOKERY RD
3 GAUNTLET RD
4 CHURCH RD
5 MONUMENT RD
6 LOW GATE LA
7 LOWGATE AVE
8 SCHOOL LA
9 RED LION ST

10 MORLEY LA
11 FRIEST LA
12 THORLBY HAVEN
13 GEDNEY CL

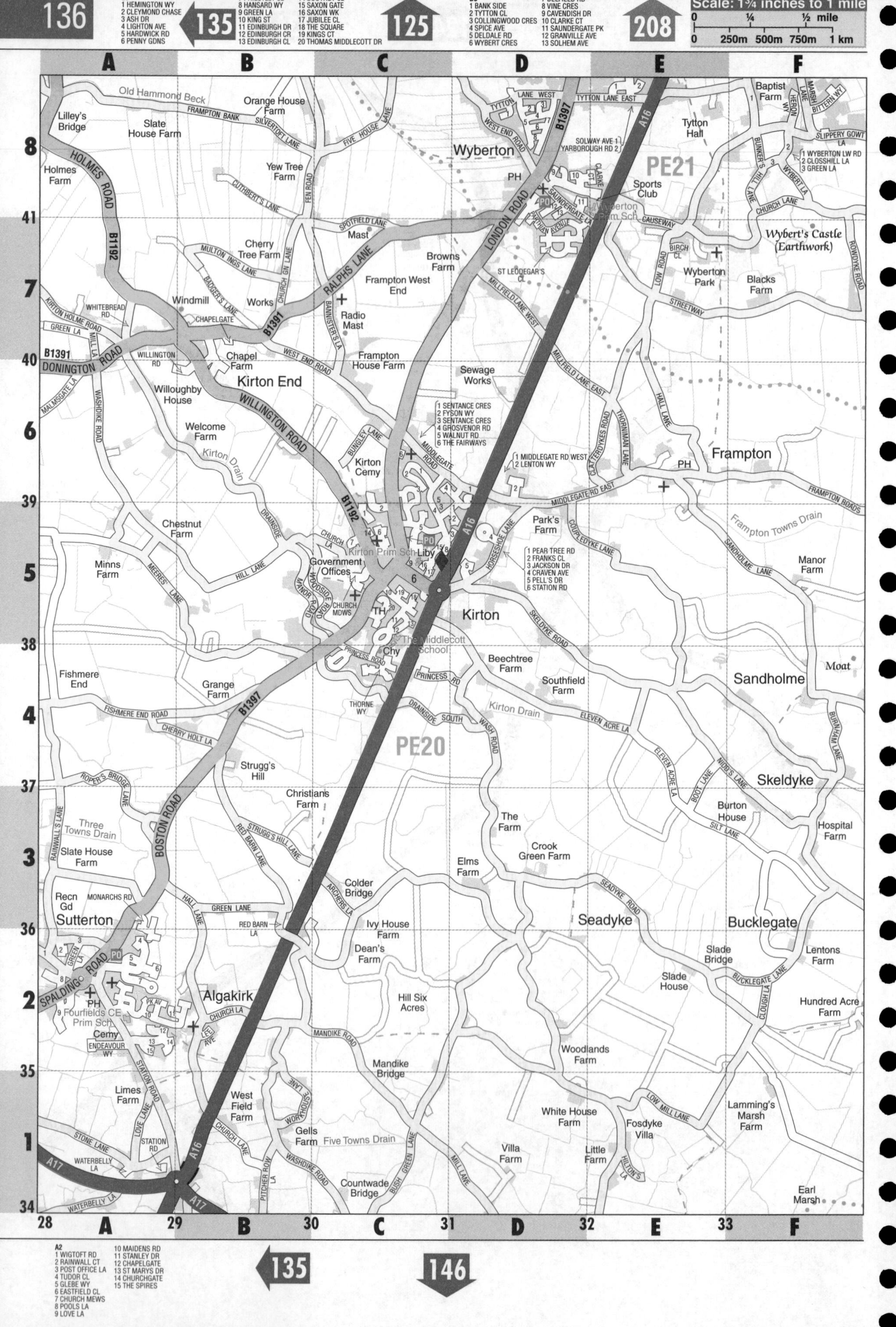
C5
1 HEMINGTON WY
2 CLEYMOND CHASE
3 ASH DR
4 LIGHTON AVE
5 HARDWICK RD
6 PENNY GDNS
7 PRIESTLEY CL
8 HANSARD WY
9 GREEN LA
10 KING ST
11 EDINBURGH DR
12 EDINBURGH CR
13 EDINBURGH CL
14 BOOTHBY CL
15 SAXON GATE
16 SAXON WK
17 JUBILEE CL
18 THE SQUARE
19 KINGS CT
20 THOMAS MIDDLECOTT DR
135
125
D8
1 BANK SIDE
2 TYTTON CL
3 COLLINGWOOD CRES
4 SPICE AVE
5 DELDALE RD
6 WYBERT CRES
7 DELFIELD RD
8 VINE CRES
9 CAVENDISH DR
10 CLARKE CT
11 SAUNDERGATE PK
12 GRANVILLE AVE
13 SOLHEM AVE
208
Scale: 1¾ inches to 1 mile
0 ¼ ½ mile
0 250m 500m 750m 1 km
A B C D E F
8 41 7 40 6 39 5 38 4 37 3 36 2 35 1 34
28 29 30 31 32 33
Old Hammond Beck
Lilley's Bridge
Slate House Farm
Orange House Farm
Holmes Farm
HOLMES ROAD
B1192
Yew Tree Farm
Cherry Tree Farm
Windmill
Works
Mast
Radio Mast
Browns Farm
Frampton West End
Wyberton
PH
PE21
Sports Club
Wyberton Prim Sch
Tytton Hall
Baptist Farm
Wybert's Castle (Earthwork)
Wyberton Park
Blacks Farm
1 WYBERTON LW RD
2 CLOSSHILL LA
3 GREEN LA
B1391
DONINGTON ROAD
Chapel Farm
Kirton End
Willoughby House
WILLINGTON ROAD
Frampton House Farm
Sewage Works
1 SENTANCE CRES
2 FYSON WY
3 SENTANCE CRES
4 GROSVENOR RD
5 WALNUT RD
6 THE FAIRWAYS
1 MIDDLEGATE RD WEST
2 LENTON WY
Welcome Farm
Kirton Drain
Kirton Cemy
Frampton
Chestnut Farm
Minns Farm
Government Offices
Kirton Prim Sch
Liby
Park's Farm
1 PEAR TREE RD
2 FRANKS CL
3 JACKSON DR
4 CRAVEN AVE
5 PELL'S DR
6 STATION RD
Frampton Towns Drain
Manor Farm
Kirton
The Middlecott School
Chy
Beechtree Farm
Southfield Farm
Fishmere End
Grange Farm
Sandholme
Moat
B1397
PE20
Strugg's Hill
Christians Farm
Skeldyke
Burton House
Hospital Farm
Three Towns Drain
Slate House Farm
The Farm
Crook Green Farm
Elms Farm
Colder Bridge
Recn Gd
Sutterton
Ivy House Farm
Seadyke
Bucklegate
Dean's Farm
Slade Bridge
Lentons Farm
Slade House
Algakirk
Hill Six Acres
Hundred Acre Farm
Fourfields CE Prim Sch
Cemy
Woodlands Farm
Mandike Bridge
Limes Farm
West Field Farm
White House Farm
Fosdyke Villa
Lamming's Marsh Farm
Gells Farm
Five Towns Drain
Villa Farm
Little Farm
Countwade Bridge
Earl Marsh
A16
A17
BOSTON ROAD
SPALDING ROAD
A2
1 WIGTOFT RD
2 RAINWALL CT
3 POST OFFICE LA
4 TUDOR CL
5 GLEBE WY
6 EASTFIELD CL
7 CHURCH MEWS
8 POOLS LA
9 LOVE LA
10 MAIDENS RD
11 STANLEY DR
12 CHAPELGATE
13 ST MARYS DR
14 CHURCHGATE
15 THE SPIRES
135
146

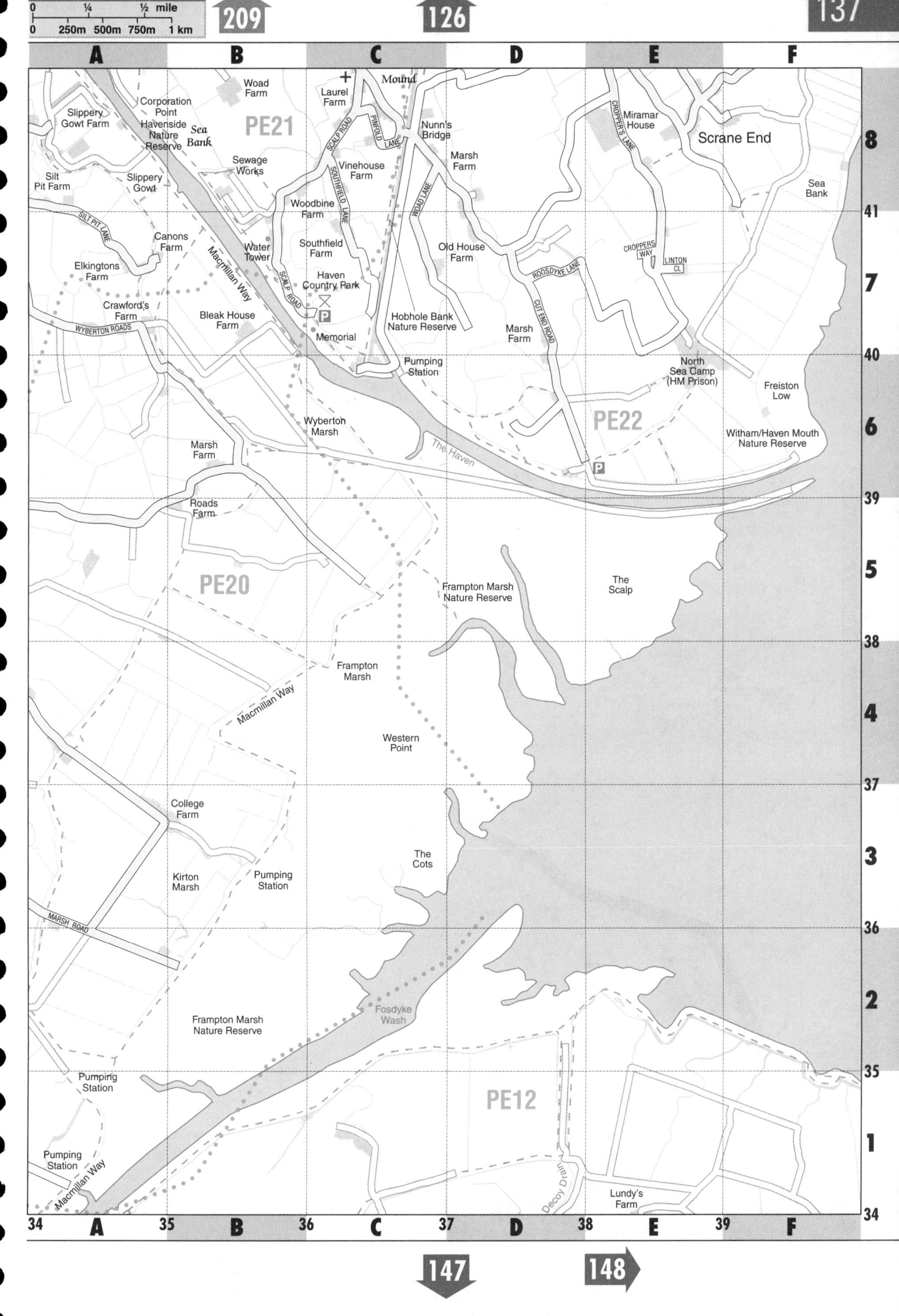
Scale: 1¾ inches to 1 mile
0 ¼ ½ mile
0 250m 500m 750m 1 km
209
126
A B C D E F
Woad Farm
Laurel Farm
Mound
Corporation Point
Slippery Gowt Farm
Havenside Nature Reserve
Sea Bank
PE21
Scalp Road
Pinfold Lane
Nunn's Bridge
Miramar House
Cropper's Lane
Scrane End
Sewage Works
Vinehouse Farm
Marsh Farm
Silt Pit Farm
Slippery Gowt
Southfield Lane
Woad Lane
Sea Bank
Woodbine Farm
Silt Pit Lane
Canons Farm
Water Tower
Southfield Farm
Old House Farm
Croppers Way
Linton Cl
Elkingtons Farm
Macmillan Way
Haven Country Park
Roosdyke Lane
Scalp Road
Crawford's Farm
Wyberton Roads
Bleak House Farm
Hobhole Bank Nature Reserve
Marsh Farm
Cut End Road
Memorial
Pumping Station
North Sea Camp (HM Prison)
Freiston Low
Wyberton Marsh
PE22
Witham/Haven Mouth Nature Reserve
Marsh Farm
The Haven
Roads Farm
The Scalp
PE20
Frampton Marsh Nature Reserve
Frampton Marsh
Macmillan Way
Western Point
College Farm
The Cots
Kirton Marsh
Pumping Station
Marsh Road
Fosdyke Wash
Frampton Marsh Nature Reserve
Pumping Station
PE12
Pumping Station
Macmillan Way
Decoy Drain
Lundy's Farm
8 41 7 40 6 39 5 38 4 37 3 36 2 35 1 34
34 35 36 37 38 39
147
148

Scale: 1¾ inches to 1 mile

0   ¼   ½ mile
0   250m 500m 750m 1 km

A   B   C   D   E   F

NG13

8

The Ash Beds

Church Thorns

West Wong

Belvoir

The Queen's Royal Lancers Museum

Woolsthorpe By Belvoir

Holy Well

Cobleas Wood

1 CHAPEL HILL
2 RECTORY LA
3 COBLEAS

France Plantation

Denton Lodge Farm

P

Belvoir Castle

Mausoleum

Belvoir Lower Lake

Kennel Wood

33

Duchess Garden

Young Oaks

Cemy

BELVOIR ROAD

Manor Farm

7

Old Park Wood

High Leys

Blackberry Hill

Knipton Pasture

Old Church Wood

Castle Farm

Sir John's Belt

Carlisle Wood

Belvoir Upper Lake

Socketwell Plantation

HARSTON ROAD

Jubilee Way

Windsor Hill

Briery Wood

The Devon

Woolsthorpe Quarries

Viking Way

32

Terrace Hills

Frog Hollow

King's Wood

The Trout Pond

DENTON LANE

Denton Park

High Leys Farm

Granby Wood

NURSERY LA 1
FINNS LA 2
CHURCH HILL 3
THE OLD HILL 4

Glebe Farm

KNIPTON LANE

Harston

Gallows Plantation

6

BELVOIR RD

Quarry (dis)

Knipton

NG32

BACK LA

Big Wood

Black Fir Plantation

A607

31

Bunkers Wood

PH

PO

CROXTON LANE

Beasley's Wood

THE DRIFT

Top Ash Plantation

5

Reservoir Wood

Nursery Plantation

Harston Wood

Hallam's Wood

Hill Top Farm

THE DRIFT

Knipton Reservoir

Cedar Hill

Croxton Banks

30

Sewage Works

Bluebell Wood

Coneygear Wood

4

Branston

PH

Memorial

Croxton Lodge Farm

MIDDLE STREET

Croxton Kerrial

Tipping's Gorse

KNIPTON ROAD

Sewage Works

PH

29

Home Farm

THE ROCK

WALTHAM ROAD

MAIN STREET

Croxton Kerrial CE Prim Sch

PO

SALTBY ROAD

MAIN STREET

House Hillside Farm

Tipping's Lodge

THE NOOK 1
HIGHFIELD CRES 2

3

Eaton Grange

MAIN STREET

Heath Farm

Bottom Farm

Lings Hill

Windmill Hill

Old Wood

28

Top Farm

GREEN LANE

Lings Farm

Kennel Plantation

Swallow Hole

Swallow Hole Farm

2

Lings Covert

Site of Abbey

Swallow Hole Covert

Saltby Lodge

MARY LANE

Croxton Park

CROXTON ROAD

Station Farm

The Moss

Lawn Hollow Plantation

27

LE14

1

STATION ROAD

A607

Croxton Race Course (dis)

Bescaby Oaks

Medieval Village of Bescaby (site of)

Dairy Farm

Joey's Wood

Cherry Tree Farm

MAIN ST

THE BUTTS

BACK ST

Saltby

Bescaby

MARY LA

Weir

PH

26

Weir

Chalybeate Spring

STONESBY ROAD

Hawthorn Farm

80   A   81   B   82   C   83   D   84   E   85   F

Leicestershire & Rutland STREET ATLAS

D4
1 CHAPEL LA
2 CHURCH LA
3 THORPES LA
4 TOP RD
5 SCHOOL LA
6 SHIRES ORCH
7 MILL LA

Scale: 1¾ inches to 1 mile

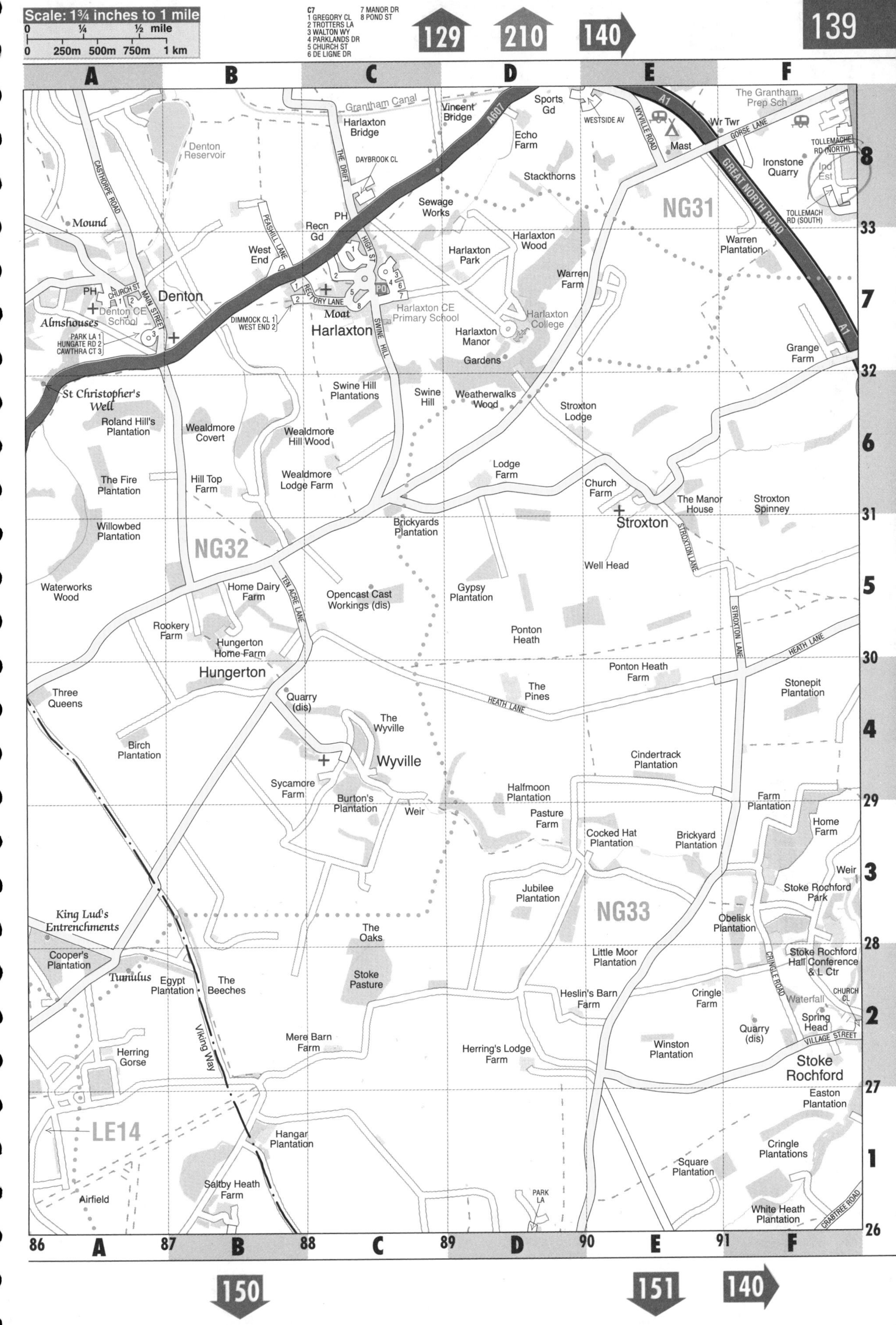

C7
1 GREGORY CL
2 TROTTERS LA
3 WALTON WY
4 PARKLANDS DR
5 CHURCH ST
6 DE LIGNE DR
7 MANOR DR
8 POND ST
129
210
140
Grantham Canal
Harlaxton Bridge
Vincent Bridge
Sports Gd
Echo Farm
Mast
Wr Twr
The Grantham Prep Sch
Ironstone Quarry
Ind Est
Denton Reservoir
Stackthorns
Sewage Works
NG31
Mound
Recn Gd
PH
West End
Harlaxton Park
Harlaxton Wood
Warren Farm
Warren Plantation
Denton
Almshouses
Denton CE School
Moat
Harlaxton
Harlaxton CE Primary School
Harlaxton Manor
Harlaxton College
Gardens
Grange Farm
St Christopher's Well
Roland Hill's Plantation
Swine Hill Plantations
Swine Hill
Weatherwalks Wood
Stroxton Lodge
Wealdmore Covert
Wealdmore Hill Wood
The Fire Plantation
Hill Top Farm
Wealdmore Lodge Farm
Lodge Farm
Church Farm
The Manor House
Stroxton
Stroxton Spinney
Willowbed Plantation
NG32
Brickyards Plantation
Well Head
Waterworks Wood
Home Dairy Farm
Opencast Cast Workings (dis)
Gypsy Plantation
Rookery Farm
Hungerton Home Farm
Hungerton
Ponton Heath
Ponton Heath Farm
Three Queens
Quarry (dis)
The Pines
Stonepit Plantation
The Wyville
Wyville
Birch Plantation
Cindertrack Plantation
Sycamore Farm
Burton's Plantation
Weir
Halfmoon Plantation
Farm Plantation
Pasture Farm
Cocked Hat Plantation
Brickyard Plantation
Home Farm
Stoke Rochford Park
Jubilee Plantation
King Lud's Entrenchments
NG33
Obelisk Plantation
The Oaks
Cooper's Plantation
Little Moor Plantation
Stoke Rochford Hall Conference & L Ctr
Tumulus
Egypt Plantation
The Beeches
Stoke Pasture
Heslin's Barn Farm
Cringle Farm
Waterfall
Spring Head
Viking Way
Mere Barn Farm
Herring's Lodge Farm
Winston Plantation
Quarry (dis)
Herring Gorse
Stoke Rochford
Easton Plantation
LE14
Hangar Plantation
Cringle Plantations
Square Plantation
Saltby Heath Farm
Airfield
White Heath Plantation
150
151
140

211 139 130

Scale: 1¾ inches to 1 mile

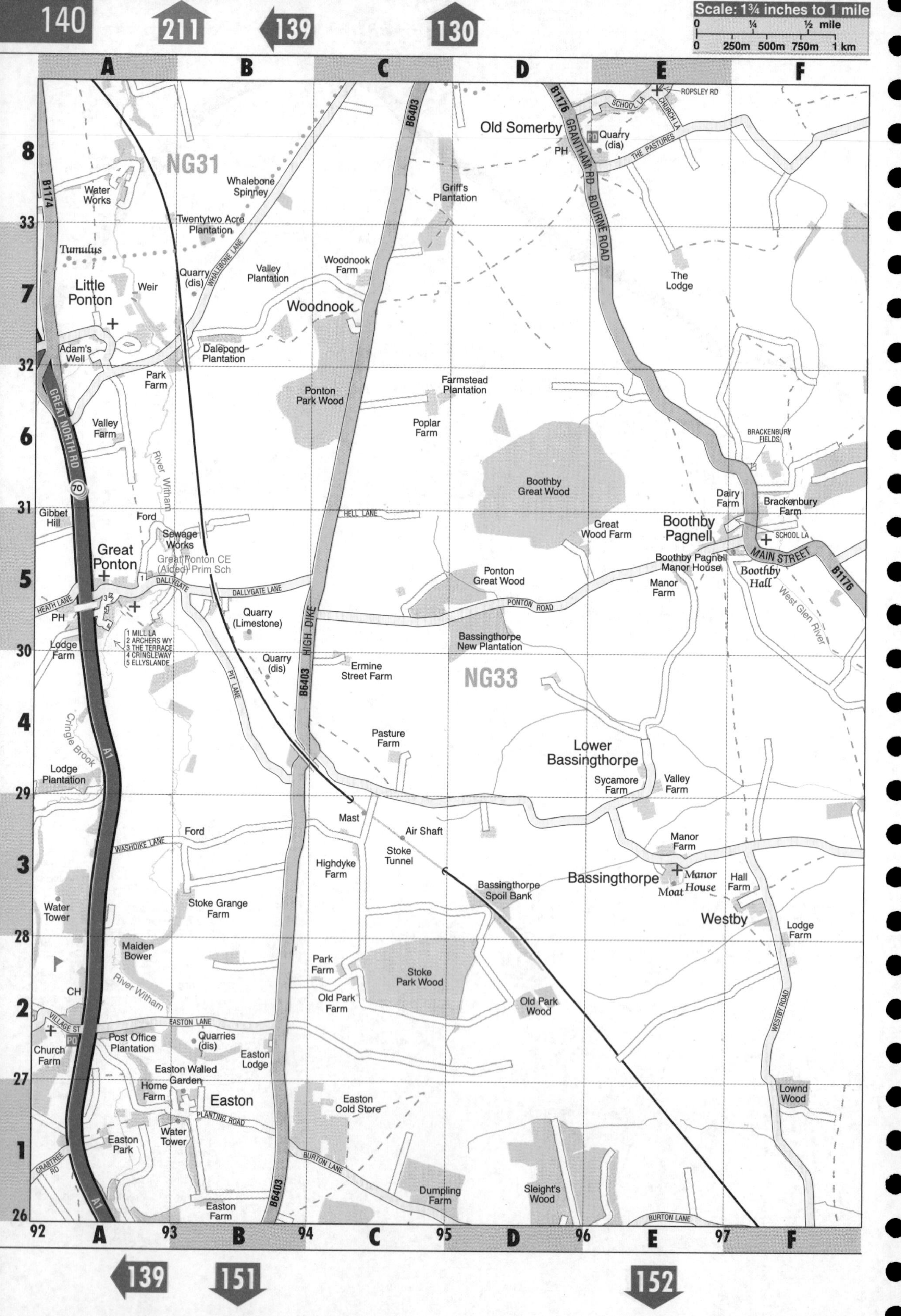

Old Somerby
NG31
Whalebone Spinney
Water Works
Twentytwo Acre Plantation
Tumulus
Little Ponton
Weir
Quarry (dis)
Valley Plantation
Woodnook Farm
Woodnook
Griff's Plantation
The Lodge
Adam's Well
Dalepond Plantation
Park Farm
Ponton Park Wood
Farmstead Plantation
Poplar Farm
Valley Farm
River Witham
Boothby Great Wood
Gibbet Hill
Ford
Sewage Works
Great Ponton
Great Ponton CE (Aided) Prim Sch
HELL LANE
Great Wood Farm
Boothby Pagnell
Dairy Farm
Brackenbury Farm
BRACKENBURY FIELDS
Boothby Pagnell Manor House
Boothby Hall
Manor Farm
Ponton Great Wood
PONTON ROAD
DALLYGATE LANE
HEATH LANE
PH
Quarry (Limestone)
1 MILL LA
2 ARCHERS WY
3 THE TERRACE
4 CRINGLEWAY
5 ELLYSLANDE
Lodge Farm
Quarry (dis)
Ermine Street Farm
Bassingthorpe New Plantation
NG33
West Glen River
HIGH DIKE
B6403
PIT LANE
Cringle Brook
Pasture Farm
Lower Bassingthorpe
Sycamore Farm
Valley Farm
Lodge Plantation
Mast
Air Shaft
Stoke Tunnel
Ford
WASHDIKE LANE
Highdyke Farm
Manor Farm
Bassingthorpe
Manor House
Moat
Hall Farm
Bassingthorpe Spoil Bank
Water Tower
Stoke Grange Farm
Westby
Lodge Farm
Maiden Bower
Park Farm
Stoke Park Wood
Old Park Farm
Old Park Wood
CH
River Witham
VILLAGE ST
EASTON LANE
Post Office Plantation
Quarries (dis)
Church Farm
Easton Lodge
Easton Walled Garden
Home Farm
Easton
Easton Cold Store
PLANTING ROAD
WESTBY ROAD
Lownd Wood
Water Tower
Easton Park
CRABTREE RD
BURTON LANE
Dumpling Farm
Sleight's Wood
Easton Farm
GREAT NORTH RD
A1
B1174
B1176
GRANTHAM RD
BOURNE ROAD
SCHOOL LA
CHURCH LA
ROPSLEY RD
THE PASTURES
MAIN STREET
SCHOOL LA
WHALEBONE LANE
DALLYGATE

139 151 152

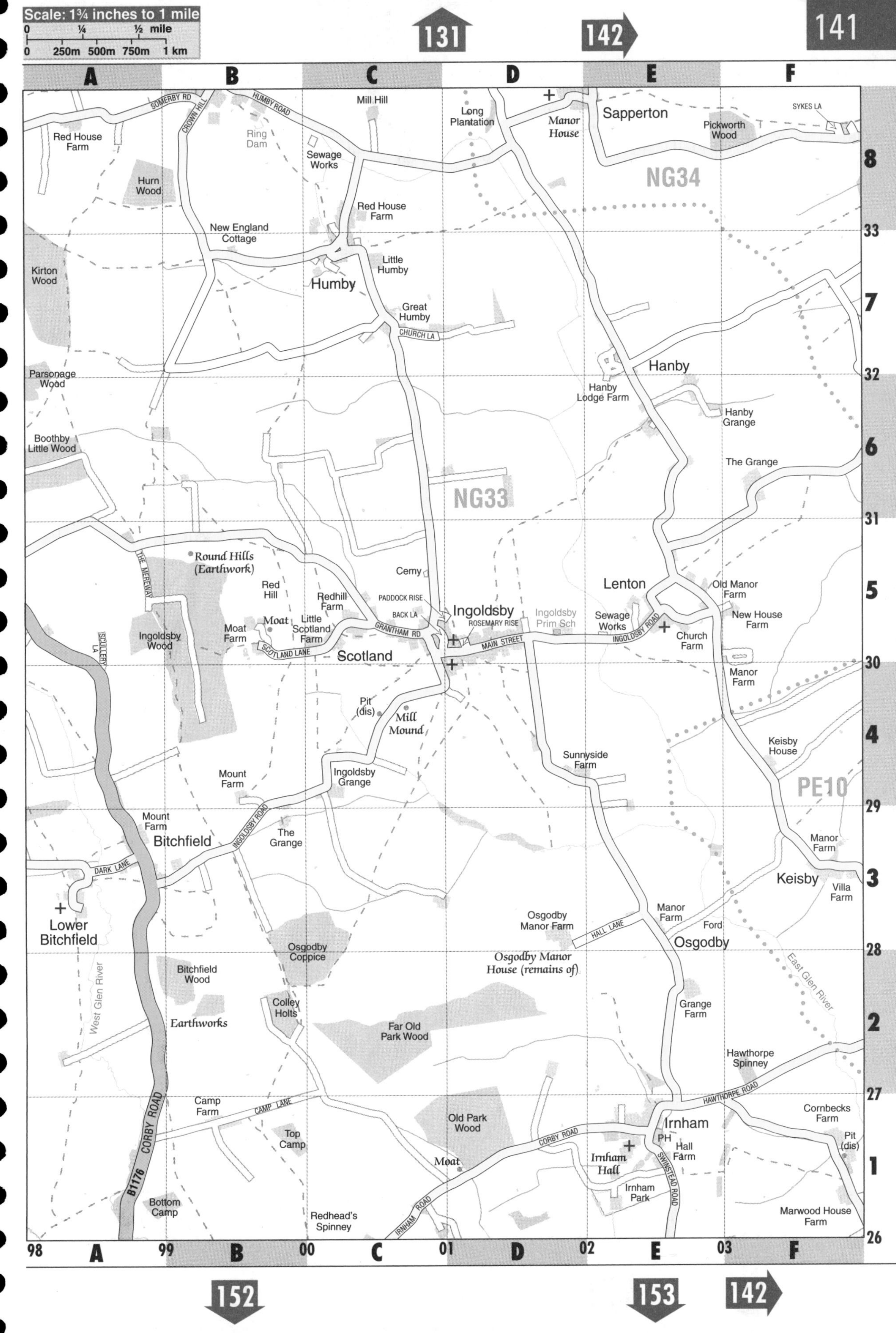

Scale: 1¾ inches to 1 mile

0   ¼   ½   mile
0   250m 500m 750m   1 km

131   142

A   B   C   D   E   F

131

SOMERBY RD

Red House Farm

Mill Hill

Long Plantation

Manor House

Sapperton

Pickworth Wood

SYKES LA

NG34

Hurn Wood

CROWN HILL

HUMBY ROAD

Ring Dam

Sewage Works

Red House Farm

New England Cottage

8

33

Kirton Wood

Little Humby

Humby

Great Humby

CHURCH LA

Hanby

Hanby Lodge Farm

7

32

Parsonage Wood

Boothby Little Wood

Hanby Grange

The Grange

6

NG33

31

THE MEREWAY

Round Hills (Earthwork)

Red Hill

Redhill Farm

PADDOCK RISE

Cemy

Lenton

Old Manor Farm

New House Farm

5

Ingoldsby Wood

Moat Farm

Moat

Little Scotland Farm

BACK LA

GRANTHAM RD

Ingoldsby

ROSEMARY RISE

Ingoldsby Prim Sch

Sewage Works

Church Farm

SCULLERY LA

SCOTLAND LANE

Scotland

MAIN STREET

INGOLDSBY ROAD

Manor Farm

30

Pit (dis)

Mill Mound

Sunnyside Farm

Keisby House

4

PE10

Mount Farm

Ingoldsby Grange

29

Mount Farm

Bitchfield

INGOLDSBY ROAD

The Grange

Manor Farm

DARK LANE

Keisby

Villa Farm

3

West Glen River

Lower Bitchfield

B1176

Osgodby Coppice

Osgodby Manor Farm

HALL LANE

Manor Farm

Ford

Osgodby

Grange Farm

28

Bitchfield Wood

Colley Holts

Far Old Park Wood

Osgodby Manor House (remains of)

East Glen River

Hawthorpe Spinney

2

Earthworks

HAWTHORPE ROAD

27

CORBY ROAD

Camp Farm

CAMP LANE

Top Camp

Old Park Wood

CORBY ROAD

Irnham

PH

Hall Farm

Cornbecks Farm

Pit (dis)

Bottom Camp

Moat

IRNHAM ROAD

Irnham Hall

SWINSTEAD ROAD

Irnham Park

Marwood House Farm

1

Redhead's Spinney

26

98   **A**   99   **B**   00   **C**   01   **D**   02   **E**   03   **F**

152   153   142

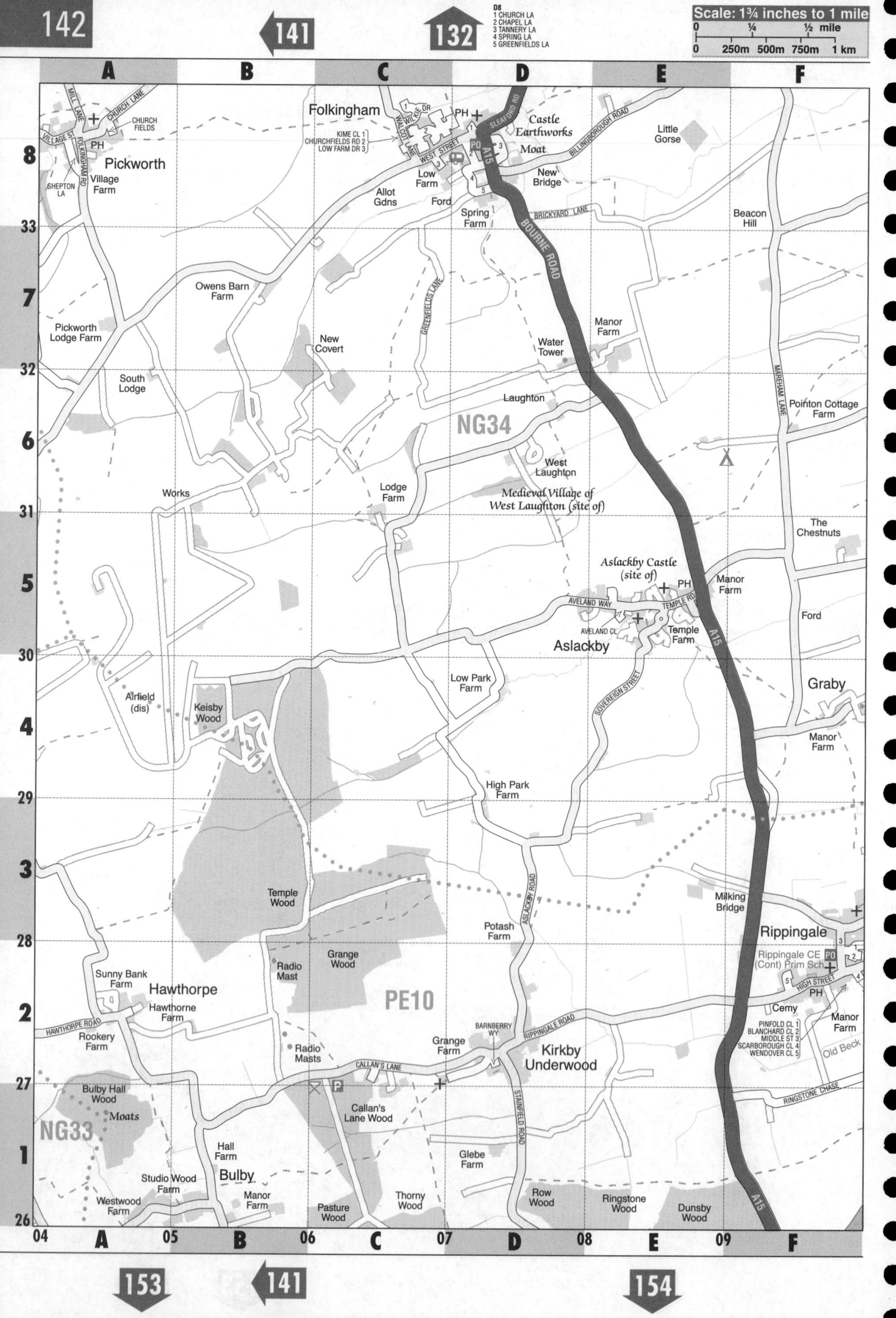

141
132

D8
1 CHURCH LA
2 CHAPEL LA
3 TANNERY LA
4 SPRING LA
5 GREENFIELDS LA

Scale: 1¾ inches to 1 mile
0   ¼   ½   mile
0   250m   500m   750m   1 km

A   **B**   **C**   **D**   **E**   **F**

8

MILL LANE
CHURCH LANE
CHURCH FIELDS
VILLAGE ST
FOLKINGHAM RD
PH
Pickworth
SHEPTON LA
Village Farm

Folkingham
WILKS DR
WALNUT LANE
KIME CL 1
CHURCHFIELDS RD 2
LOW FARM DR 3
WEST STREET
Low Farm
Allot Gdns
Ford

PH
PO
SLEAFORD RD
Castle Earthworks
Moat
New Bridge

BILLINGBROUGH ROAD

Little Gorse

33

Owens Barn Farm

Spring Farm

BRICKYARD LANE

Beacon Hill

7

Pickworth Lodge Farm

New Covert

GREENFIELDS LANE

Water Tower

Manor Farm

BOURNE ROAD

MAREHAM LANE

32

South Lodge

NG34

Laughton

West Laughton

Pointon Cottage Farm

6

Works

Lodge Farm

Medieval Village of West Laughton (site of)

The Chestnuts

31

Aslackby Castle (site of)
AVELAND WAY
AVELAND CL
PH
Manor Farm
TEMPLE RD
Temple Farm
Aslackby
A15
Ford

5

Airfield (dis)

Keisby Wood

Low Park Farm

SOVEREIGN STREET

Graby

Manor Farm

30

High Park Farm

4

Temple Wood

ASLACKBY ROAD

Milking Bridge

Rippingale

29

Potash Farm

Rippingale CE (Cont) Prim Sch
PO
HIGH STREET
3 1
PH
5

3

Sunny Bank Farm

Hawthorpe
Hawthorne Farm

Radio Mast

Grange Wood

PE10

BARNBERRY WY

Grange Farm

RIPPINGALE ROAD

Kirkby Underwood

Cemy
PINFOLD CL 1
BLANCHARD CL 2
MIDDLE ST 3
SCARBOROUGH CL 4
WENDOVER CL 5
Manor Farm
Old Beck

2

HAWTHORPE ROAD

Rookery Farm

Radio Masts

CALLAN'S LANE

P

Callan's Lane Wood

STAINFIELD ROAD

RINGSTONE CHASE

27

Bulby Hall Wood

Moats

Hall Farm

Bulby

Glebe Farm

Row Wood

Ringstone Wood

Dunsby Wood

A15

NG33

Westwood Farm

Studio Wood Farm

Manor Farm

Pasture Wood

Thorny Wood

1

26

04   **A**   **05**   **B**   **06**   **C**   **07**   **D**   **08**   **E**   **09**   **F**

153
141
154

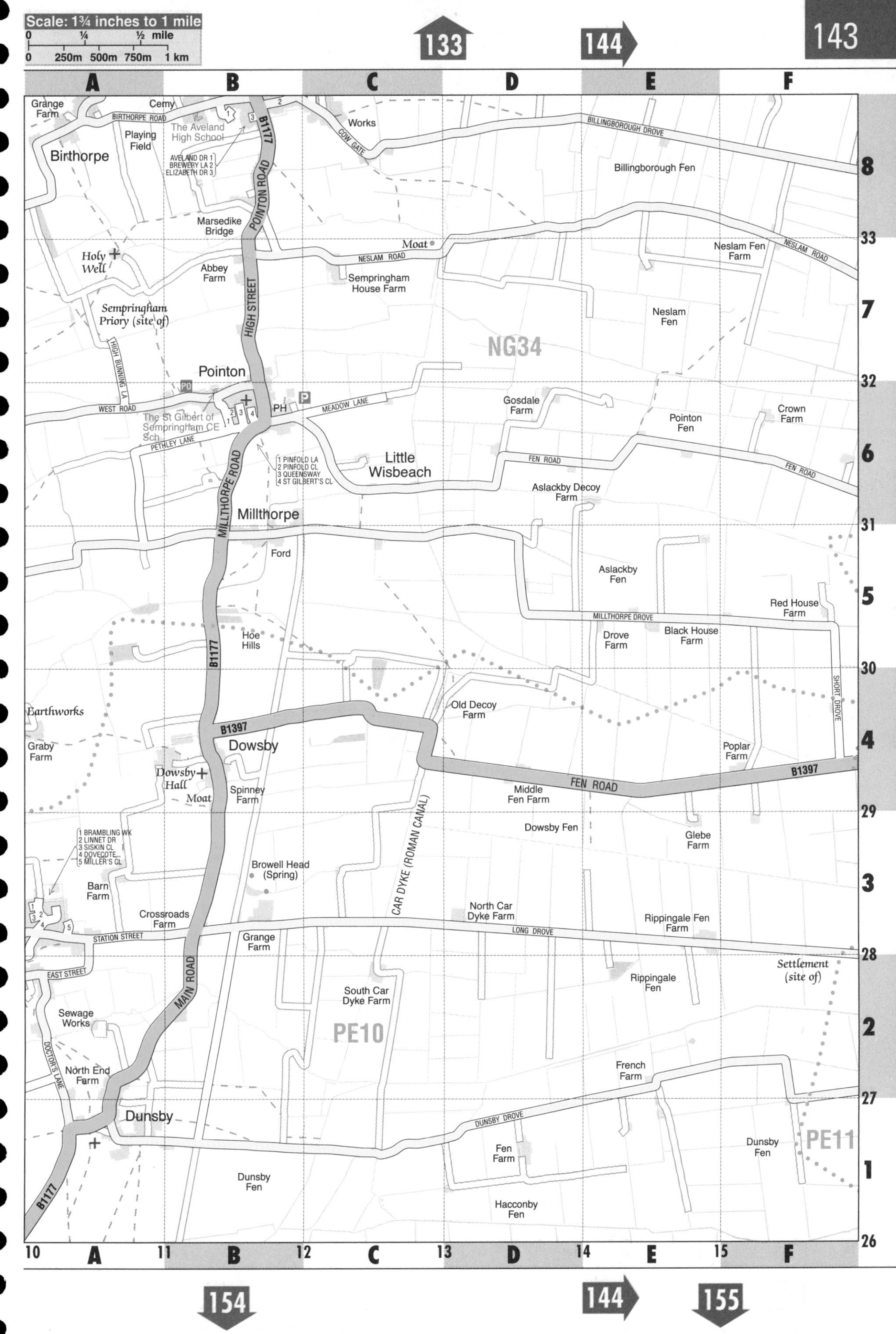
Scale: 1¾ inches to 1 mile
133
144
Birthorpe
Pointon
Millthorpe
Dowsby
Dunsby
Little Wisbeach
NG34
PE10
PE11
Billingborough Fen
Neslam Fen
Aslackby Fen
Dowsby Fen
Dunsby Fen
Hacconby Fen
Semperingham Priory (site of)
Holy Well
Dowsby Hall
Earthworks
Settlement (site of)
POINTON ROAD
HIGH STREET
MILLTHORPE ROAD
MAIN ROAD
FEN ROAD
NESLAM ROAD
BILLINGBOROUGH DROVE
MILLTHORPE DROVE
LONG DROVE
DUNSBY DROVE
CAR DYKE (ROMAN CANAL)
B1177
B1397
154
144
155

143 134

A B C D E F

Billingborough Fen

Priestly House

Crane Bridge

LC
LC
1 COWDALE'S DRO
2 CHURCH END DRO
3 TOWN DAM DRO

Far Fen Farm

Machins Farm

Bridge Farm

Bull Bridge

Shoff Farm

Sand Acre Cotts

Bank House Farm

LC

Bottom Fen Farm

Willow Tree Farm

NORTH DROVE

SOUTH DROVE

Lakeside Farm

Barholme Farm

LC

33

Hawthorn Farm

Quadring Low Fen

Sewage Works

Quadring High Fen

Corner House Farm

Sandy Gate Farm

Neslam Bridge Farm

Calf Bridge

Red Fox Farm

NESLAM ROAD

7

Low Fen

Middle Fen Farm

SOUTH DROVE

Neslam Bridge

Quadring Fen Farm

Quadring Low Fen

QUADRING BANK

GRAVECOAT LANE

LC

32

Neslam Fen

Mornington House Farm

Hundred Fen

High Fen

Vicarage Farm

COLD HURN LA

Yew Tree Farm

WESTHORPE ROAD

WINDMILL LA

Pointon Fen

LONG DROVE

Cow Bridge

BECK BANK

Osborne House

Kirkhill Farm

Westhorpe

NG34

6

FEN RD

Forty Foot Farm

Surfleet Fen Farm

Grange Farm

Swale Bank Farm

Cobbwebs Farm

CHESNULE LANE

Chespool House

Riseholme Farm

SWALE BANK

Surfleet Fen

Woodbine House

Swale Bank Farm

Seven Springs

1 SHEPPERSON'S AVE
2 SILTSIDE

31

Gosberton Fen Farm

BROAD DROVE

Dunster Farm

PE11

Willowdene Farm

SILTSIDE

RISEGATE ROAD

5

Gosberton High Fen

Five Acre Farm

BECK BANK

SHORT DROVE

Allen's Bridge

PH

PO PH

HEDGEFIELD HURN

30

Surfleet Fen Bridge

SILTSIDE

CLOUGH ROAD

Risegate

South Forty Foot Drain

Kingston's Bridge

Gosberton Fen Bridge

Gosberton Clough & Risegate Prim Sch

Charity Farm

Panton House Farm

4

FEN ROAD

B1397

HIGH FEN

FIFTH DROVE

FOURTH DROVE

THIRD DROVE

SECOND DROVE

FIRST DROVE

BECK BANK

Red Cow Farm

CHOPDIKE DROVE

Gosberton Clough

BEACH LANE

Barrowpier Hall Farm

CHEAL ROAD

29

Bottom Fen Farm

FIFTH DROVE

Beck Farm

Gosberton Fen

PE10

3

Rippingale Fen

Vicarage Farm

Benners Farm

Moat

Rigbolt House

BEACH BANK

Moats

Dunsby Fen Farm

LONG DRO

Water Works

PARSON DROVE

BECK BANK

Westfield Farm

Bridge Farm

Burtey Fen

CHEAL LANE

New Drain

28

2

Casswell's Bridge

COWBIT DROVE

Moats

COWARD'S LANE

DUNSBY DROVE

27

Dunsby Fen

Pinchbeck North Fen

SHORT DROVE

Crosslane Farm

CROSS LANE

College Farm

1 ELIZABETH CRES
2 SIX HOUSE BANK
3 RURAL AVE
4 LINDER WY

North Gate Farm

MONEY BRIDGE LA

Pear Tree Farm

1

HACCONBY DRO

STAR LODE DROVE

Woodbine Farm

Cedar Farm

Proctors Farm

PH

SMALL DROVE LA

NORTH GATE

Tofts Farm

Sewage Works

Northgate

26

16 A 17 B 18 C 19 D 20 E 21 F

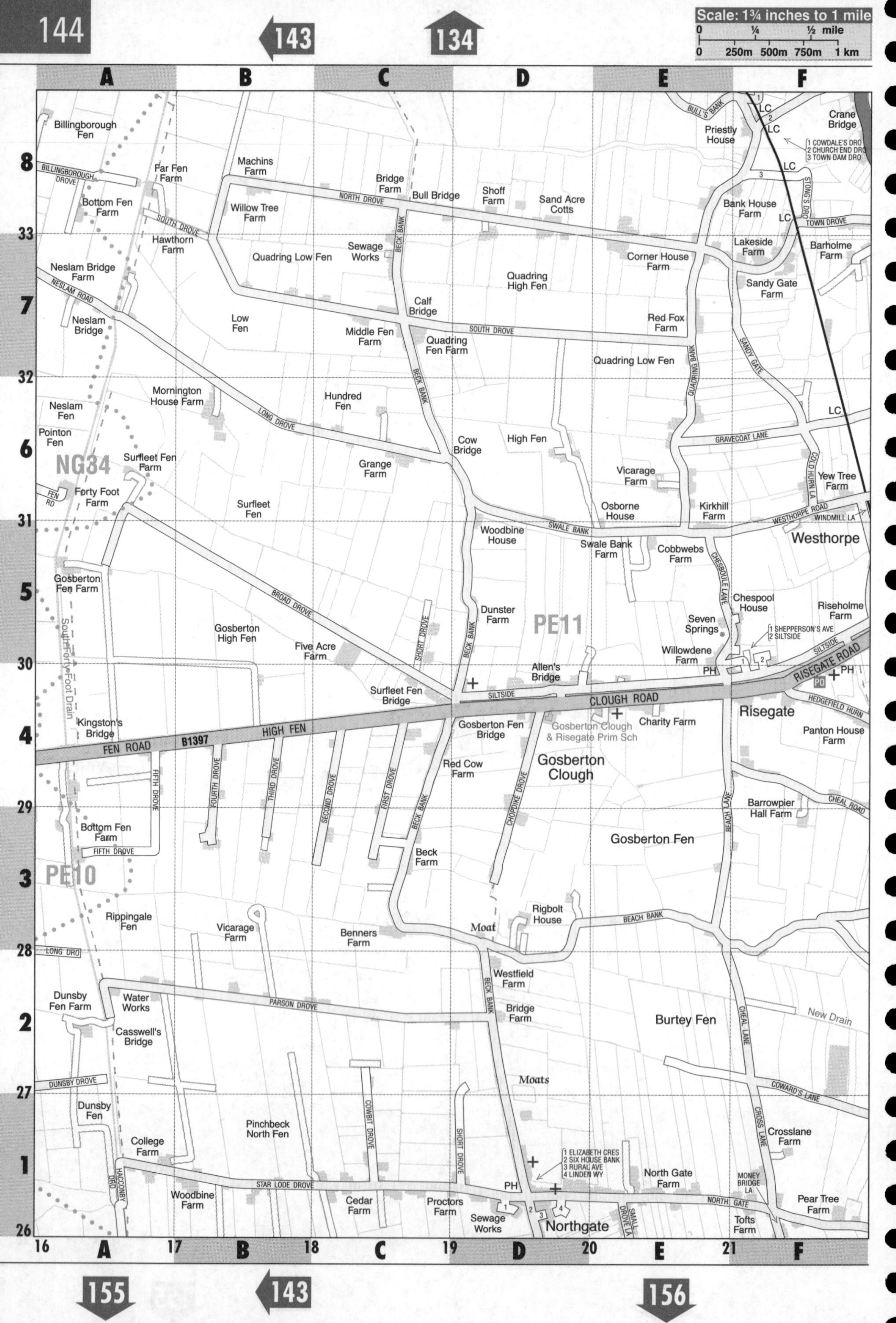

155 143 156

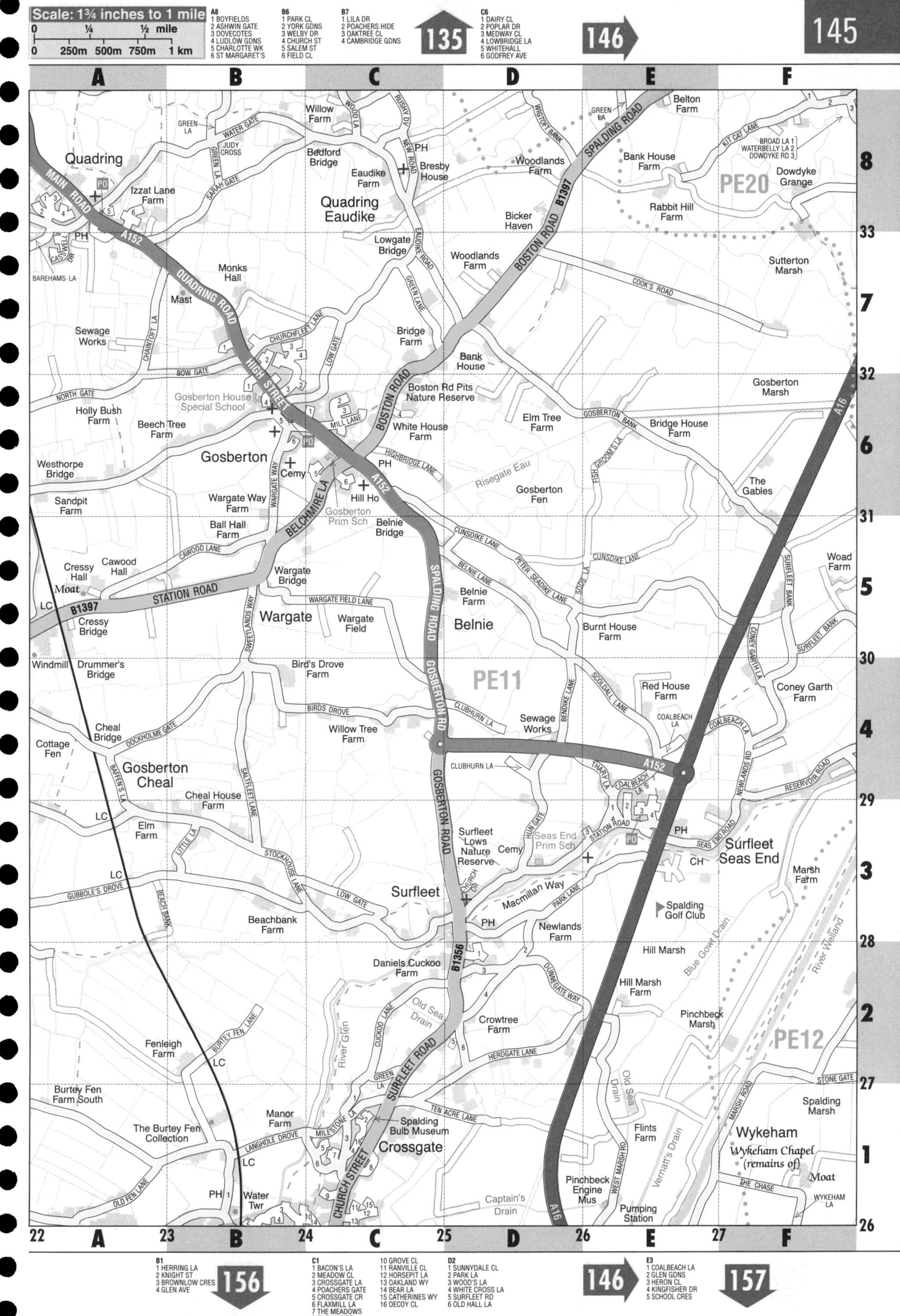
Scale: 1¾ inches to 1 mile
0 ¼ ½ mile
0 250m 500m 750m 1 km
A8
1 BOYFIELDS
2 ASHWIN GATE
3 DOVECOTES
4 LUDLOW GDNS
5 CHARLOTTE WK
6 ST MARGARET'S
B6
1 PARK CL
2 YORK GDNS
3 WELBY DR
4 CHURCH ST
5 SALEM ST
6 FIELD CL
B7
1 LILA DR
2 POACHERS HIDE
3 OAKTREE CL
4 CAMBRIDGE GDNS
135
146
C6
1 DAIRY CL
2 POPLAR DR
3 MEDWAY CL
4 LOWBRIDGE LA
5 WHITEHALL
6 GODFREY AVE
A B C D E F
Quadring
MAIN ROAD
Izzat Lane Farm
GREEN LA
WATER GATE
JUDY CROSS
GREEN LA
SARAH GATE
Willow Farm
WOOD LA
RUSHY DV
NEW ROAD
Bedford Bridge
Eaudike Farm
Bresby House
Quadring Eaudike
WIGTOFT BANK
Woodlands Farm
SPALDING ROAD
B1397
Belton Farm
KIT CAT LANE
BROAD LA 1
WATERBELLY LA 2
DOWDYKE RD 3
Bank House Farm
Dowdyke Grange
PE20
Rabbit Hill Farm
Bicker Haven
BOSTON ROAD
PH
CASSWELL DR
BAREHAMS LA
A152
Monks Hall
Mast
QUADRING ROAD
Lowgate Bridge
EAUDIKE ROAD
GREEN LANE
Woodlands Farm
COOK'S ROAD
Sutterton Marsh
Sewage Works
CHAINTOFT LA
CHURCHFLEET LANE
LOW GATE
Bridge Farm
Bank House
BOW GATE
NORTH GATE
HIGH STREET
Boston Rd Pits Nature Reserve
Gosberton Marsh
Holly Bush Farm
Gosberton House Special School
MILL LANE
White House Farm
Elm Tree Farm
GOSBERTON BANK
Bridge House Farm
A16
Beech Tree Farm
Gosberton
Westhorpe Bridge
Cemy
HIGHBRIDGE LANE
Risegate Eau
FISH GROOM'S LA
The Gables
Sandpit Farm
Wargate Way Farm
WARGATE WAY
BELCHMIRE LA
Hill Ho
Gosberton Prim Sch
Gosberton Fen
Ball Hall Farm
Belnie Bridge
CUNSDIKE LANE
CAWOOD LANE
PETER SEADIKE LANE
CUNSDIKE LANE
Woad Farm
Cressy Hall
Cawood Hall
Moat
Wargate Bridge
BELNIE LANE
SODS LA
SURFLEET BANK
STATION ROAD
Belnie Farm
LC
WARGATE FIELD LANE
B1397
SWEETLANDS WAY
Wargate
Wargate Field
SPALDING ROAD
Belnie
Burnt House Farm
CONEY GARTH LA
SURFLEET BANK
Cressy Bridge
Windmill
Drummer's Bridge
Bird's Drove Farm
GOSBERTON RD
PE11
BENDIKE LANE
SCOLDALL LANE
Red House Farm
Coney Garth Farm
BIRDS DROVE
CLUBHURN LA
Sewage Works
COALBEACH LA
COALBEACH LA
Cheal Bridge
DOCKHOLME GATE
Willow Tree Farm
Cottage Fen
Gosberton Cheal
BAFFEN'S LA
SALTFLEET LANE
CLUBHURN LA
THARY LA
A152
NEWLANDS RD
RESERVOIR ROAD
Cheal House Farm
GOSBERTON ROAD
LC
Elm Farm
LITTLE LA
Surfleet Lows Nature Reserve
HUM GATE
Seas End Prim Sch
STATION ROAD
SEAS END ROAD
PH
Surfleet Seas End
Cemy
STOCKHOUSE LANE
CH
Marsh Farm
LC
GUBBOLE'S DROVE
BEACH BANK
LOW GATE
Surfleet
CHURCH DR
Macmillan Way
PARK LANE
Spalding Golf Club
Beachbank Farm
PH
Newlands Farm
Blue Gowt Drain
River Welland
Hill Marsh
Daniels Cuckoo Farm
B1356
DUNNEGATE WAY
Hill Marsh Farm
Old Sea Drain
Crowtree Farm
Pinchbeck Marsh
CUCKOO LANE
River Glen
Fenleigh Farm
BURTEY FEN LANE
LC
SURFLEET ROAD
HERDGATE LANE
PE12
GREEN LA
Old Sea Drain
STONE GATE
Burtey Fen Farm South
Manor Farm
TEN ACRE LANE
MARSH ROAD
Spalding Marsh
Spalding Bulb Museum
MILESTONE LA
The Burtey Fen Collection
LANGHOLE DROVE
Crossgate
Flints Farm
Wykeham
Wykeham Chapel (remains of)
Vernatt's Drain
LC
CHURCH STREET
Moat
OLD FEN LANE
Pinchbeck Engine Mus
WEST MARSH RD
THE CHASE
WYKEHAM LA
PH
Water Twr
Captain's Drain
Pumping Station
A16
8 33 7 32 6 31 5 30 4 29 3 28 2 27 1 26
22 A 23 B 24 C 25 D 26 E 27 F
B1
1 HERRING LA
2 KNIGHT ST
3 BROWNLOW CRES
4 GLEN AVE
156
C1
1 BACON'S LA
2 MEADOW CL
3 CROSSGATE LA
4 POACHERS GATE
5 CROSSGATE CR
6 FLAXMILL LA
7 THE MEADOWS
8 OLDHAM DR
9 CAPTAINS BECK
10 GROVE CL
11 RANVILLE CL
12 HORSEPIT LA
13 OAKLAND WY
14 BEAR LA
15 CATHERINES WY
16 DECOY CL
D2
1 SUNNYDALE CL
2 PARK LA
3 WOOD'S LA
4 WHITE CROSS LA
5 SURFLEET RD
6 OLD HALL LA
146
E3
1 COALBEACH LA
2 GLEN GDNS
3 HERON CL
4 KINGFISHER DR
5 SCHOOL CRES
157

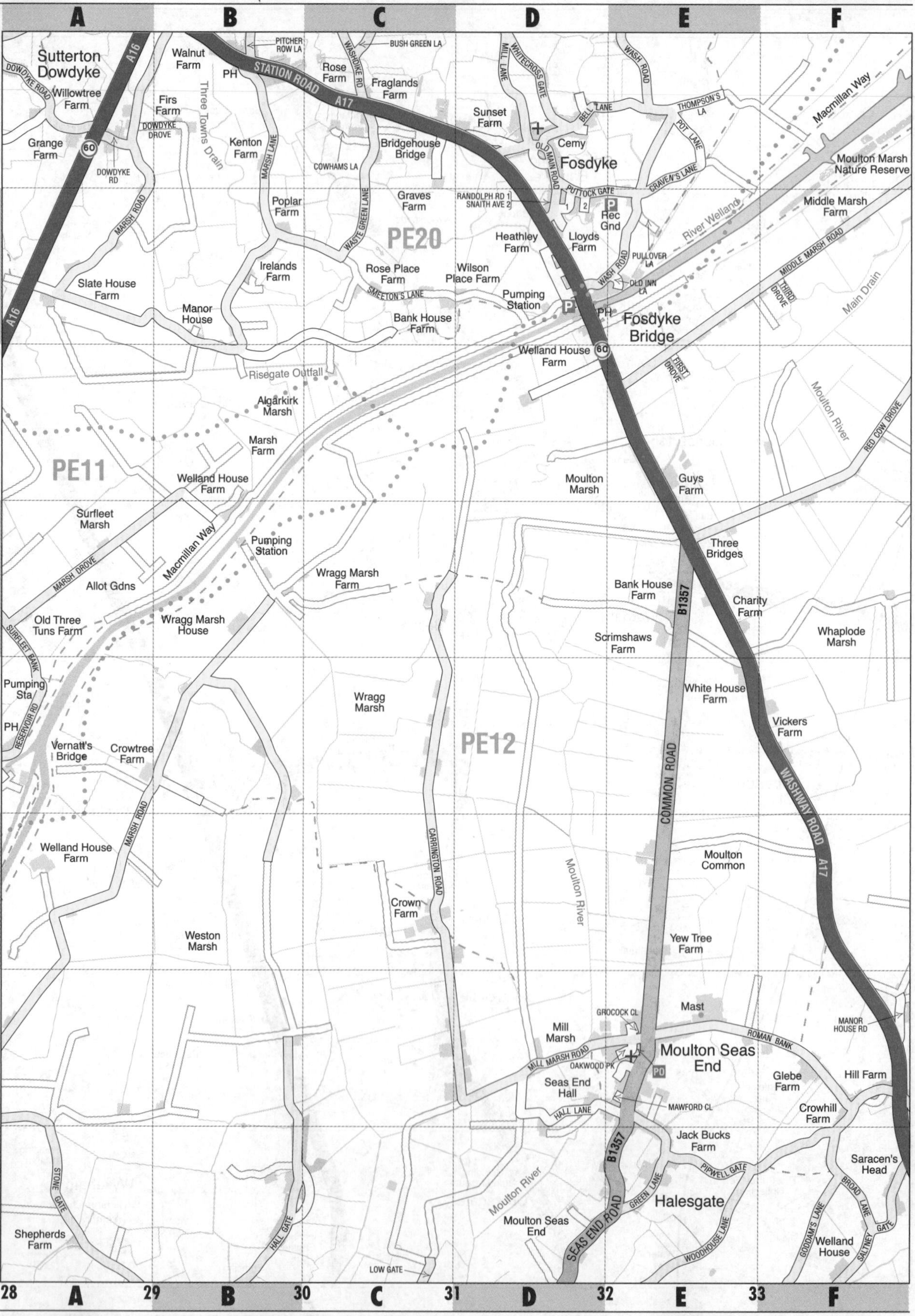

Scale: 1¾ inches to 1 mile
0   ¼   ½ mile
0 250m 500m 750m 1 km

A B C D E F

Sutterton
Dowdyke

Dowdyke Road
Willowtree Farm
Grange Farm
Dowdyke Drove
Firs Farm
Dowdyke Rd
A16

Walnut Farm
Three Towns Drain
Kenton Farm
Marsh Lane
PH
STATION ROAD
A17
Pitcher Row La
Bush Green La
Rose Farm
Washare Rd
Fraglands Farm
Bridgehouse Bridge
Cowhams La
Mill Lane
Whitecross Gate
Bell Lane
Sunset Farm
Thompson's La
Cemy
Fosdyke
Ol Main Road
Pot Lane
Craven's Lane
Puttock Gate
Macmillan Way
Moulton Marsh
Nature Reserve
Middle Marsh Farm
Wash Road

33

8

Poplar Farm
Waste Green Lane
Graves Farm
Randolph Rd 1
Snaith Ave 2
Rec Gnd
P
River Welland
Middle Marsh Road

PE20

Slate House Farm
Irelands Farm
Rose Place Farm
Smeeton's Lane
Heathley Farm
Wilson Place Farm
Lloyds Farm
Pullover La
Old Inn La
Third Drove
Main Drain

7

Manor House
Bank House Farm
Pumping Station
PH
PH
Fosdyke Bridge
60

32

Risegate Outfall
Welland House Farm
First Drove
Moulton River
Red Cow Drive

6

Algarkirk Marsh

PE11

Marsh Farm
Welland House Farm
Moulton Marsh
Guys Farm

31

Surfleet Marsh
Macmillan Way
Three Bridges
B1357
Charity Farm

5

Marsh Drove
Allot Gdns
Wragg Marsh Farm
Bank House Farm
Whaplode Marsh

Old Three Tuns Farm
Surfleet Bank
Wragg Marsh House
Scrimshaws Farm

30

Pumping Sta
PH
Reservoir Rd
Wragg Marsh
White House Farm
Vickers Farm

4

Vernatt's Bridge
Crowtree Farm
Marsh Road

PE12

Washway Road
A17
Common Road

29

Welland House Farm
Carrington Road
Moulton Common

3

Weston Marsh
Crown Farm
Moulton River
Yew Tree Farm

28

Mill Marsh
Grocock Cl
Mast
Manor House Rd
Roman Bank

2

Mill Marsh Road
Oakwood Pk
Moulton Seas End
PO
Glebe Farm
Hill Farm
Seas End Hall
Mawford Cl
Crowhill Farm

27

Stone Gate
Hall Gate
Hall Lane
Jack Bucks Farm
B1357
Pipwell Gate
Saracen's Head
Goddam's Lane
Broad Lane
Saltney Gate

1

Shepherds Farm
Low Gate
Moulton River
Moulton Seas End
Seas End Road
Green Lane
Woodhouse Lane
Halesgate
Welland House

26

28 A 29 B 30 C 31 D 32 E 33 F

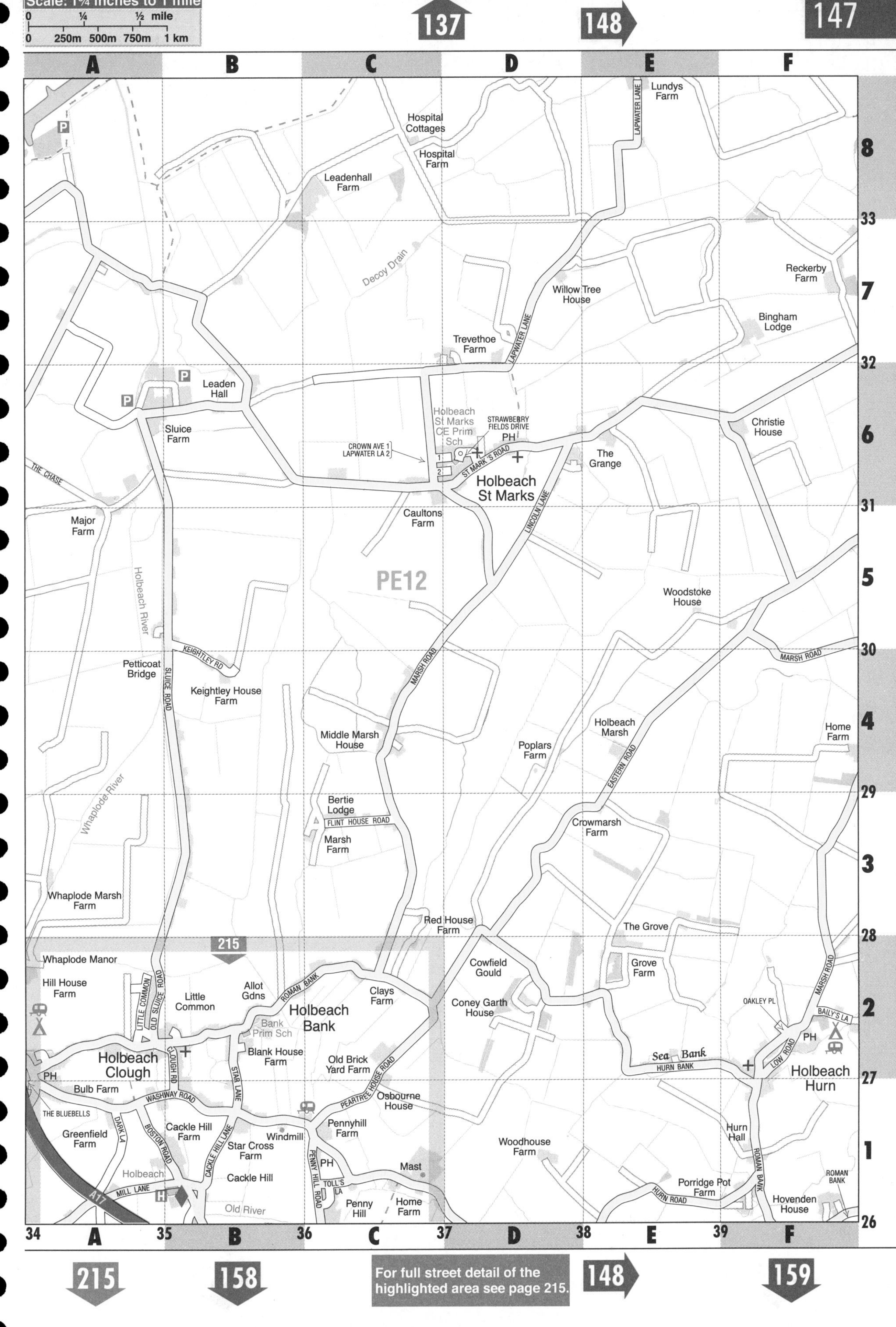

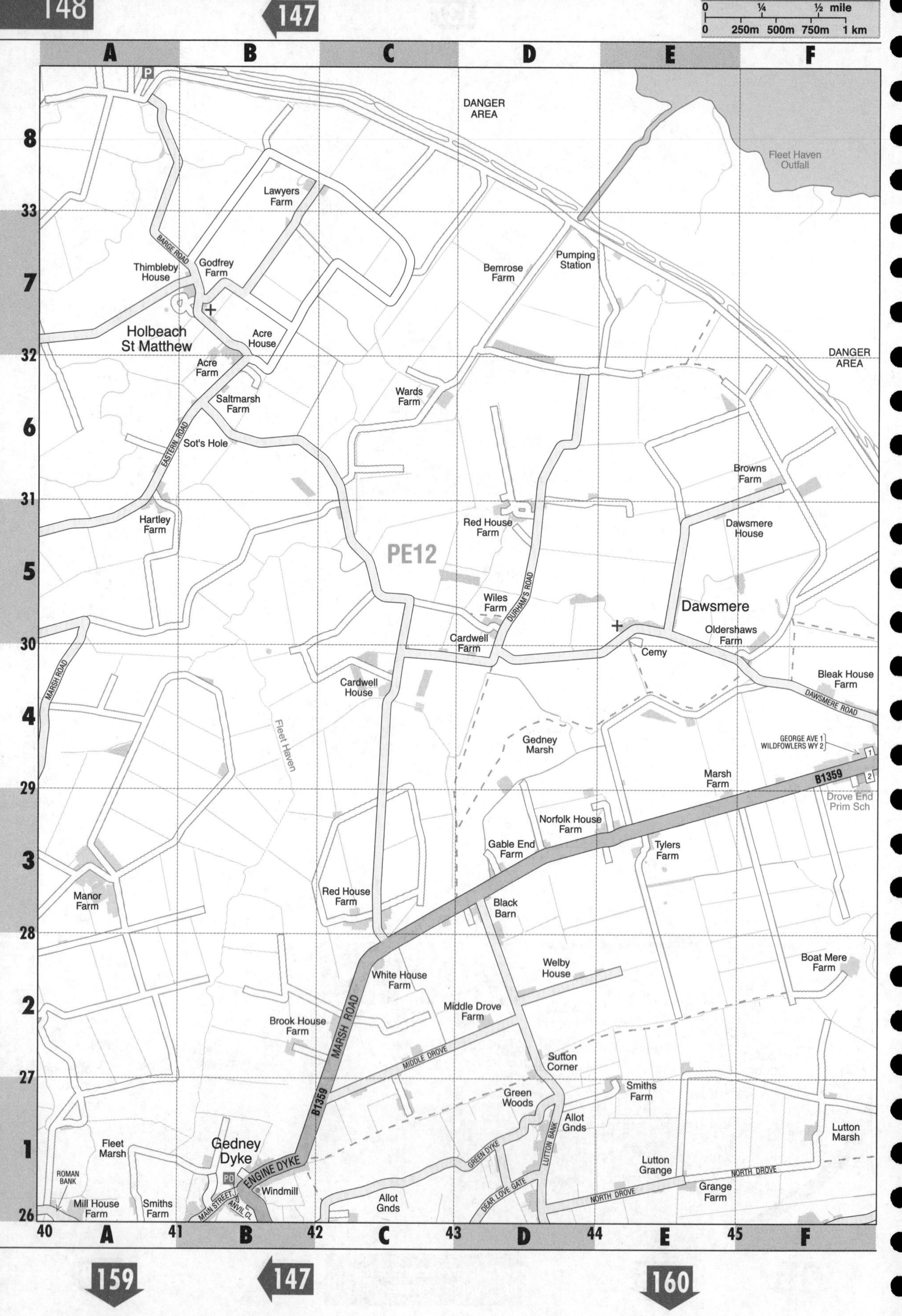
0 ¼ ½ mile
0 250m 500m 750m 1 km
A B C D E F
8 33 7 32 6 31 5 30 4 29 3 28 2 27 1 26
DANGER AREA
Fleet Haven Outfall
Lawyers Farm
BARGE ROAD
Thimbleby House
Godfrey Farm
Holbeach St Matthew
Acre House
Acre Farm
Saltmarsh Farm
EASTERN ROAD
Sot's Hole
Pumping Station
Bemrose Farm
Wards Farm
DANGER AREA
Browns Farm
Dawsmere House
Hartley Farm
Red House Farm
PE12
DURHAM'S ROAD
Wiles Farm
Dawsmere
Oldershaws Farm
Cardwell Farm
Cemy
Bleak House Farm
DAWSMERE ROAD
MARSH ROAD
Cardwell House
Fleet Haven
Gedney Marsh
GEORGE AVE 1
WILDFOWLERS WY 2
Marsh Farm
B1359
Drove End Prim Sch
Norfolk House Farm
Gable End Farm
Tylers Farm
Manor Farm
Red House Farm
Black Barn
Boat Mere Farm
White House Farm
Welby House
Middle Drove Farm
Brook House Farm
MIDDLE DROVE
Sutton Corner
Green Woods
Smiths Farm
Allot Gnds
LUTTON BANK
Lutton Marsh
Fleet Marsh
Gedney Dyke
GREEN DYKE
Lutton Grange
NORTH DROVE
ROMAN BANK
PO
ENGINE DYKE
Windmill
Allot Gnds
DEAR LOVE GATE
Grange Farm
Mill House Farm
Smiths Farm
MAIN STREET
ANVIL CL
40 41 42 43 44 45

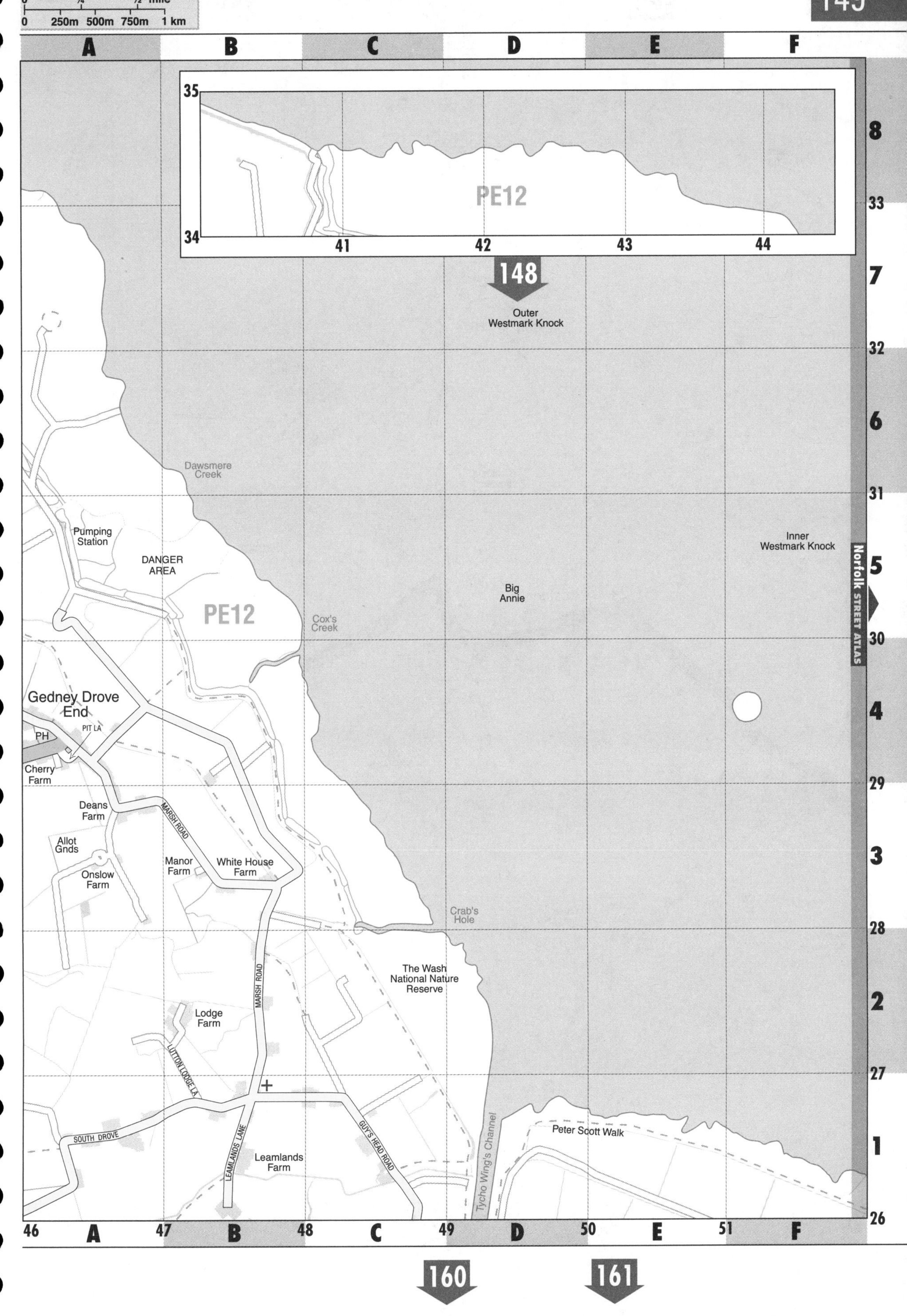

A **B** **C** **D** **E** **F**

35

34

41   42   43   44

PE12

148

Outer
Westmark Knock

Dawsmere
Creek

Pumping
Station

DANGER
AREA

PE12

Cox's
Creek

Inner
Westmark Knock

Big
Annie

Gedney Drove
End

PIT LA

PH

Cherry
Farm

Deans
Farm

MARSH ROAD

Allot
Gnds

Onslow
Farm

Manor
Farm

White House
Farm

Crab's
Hole

The Wash
National Nature
Reserve

Lodge
Farm

MARSH ROAD

LUTTON LODGE LA

LEAMLANDS LANE

GUY'S HEAD ROAD

Tycho Wing's Channel

Peter Scott Walk

SOUTH DROVE

Leamlands
Farm

46   **A**   47   **B**   48   **C**   49   **D**   50   **E**   51   **F**

8

33

7

32

6

31

5

30

4

29

3

28

2

27

1

26

Norfolk STREET ATLAS

160   161

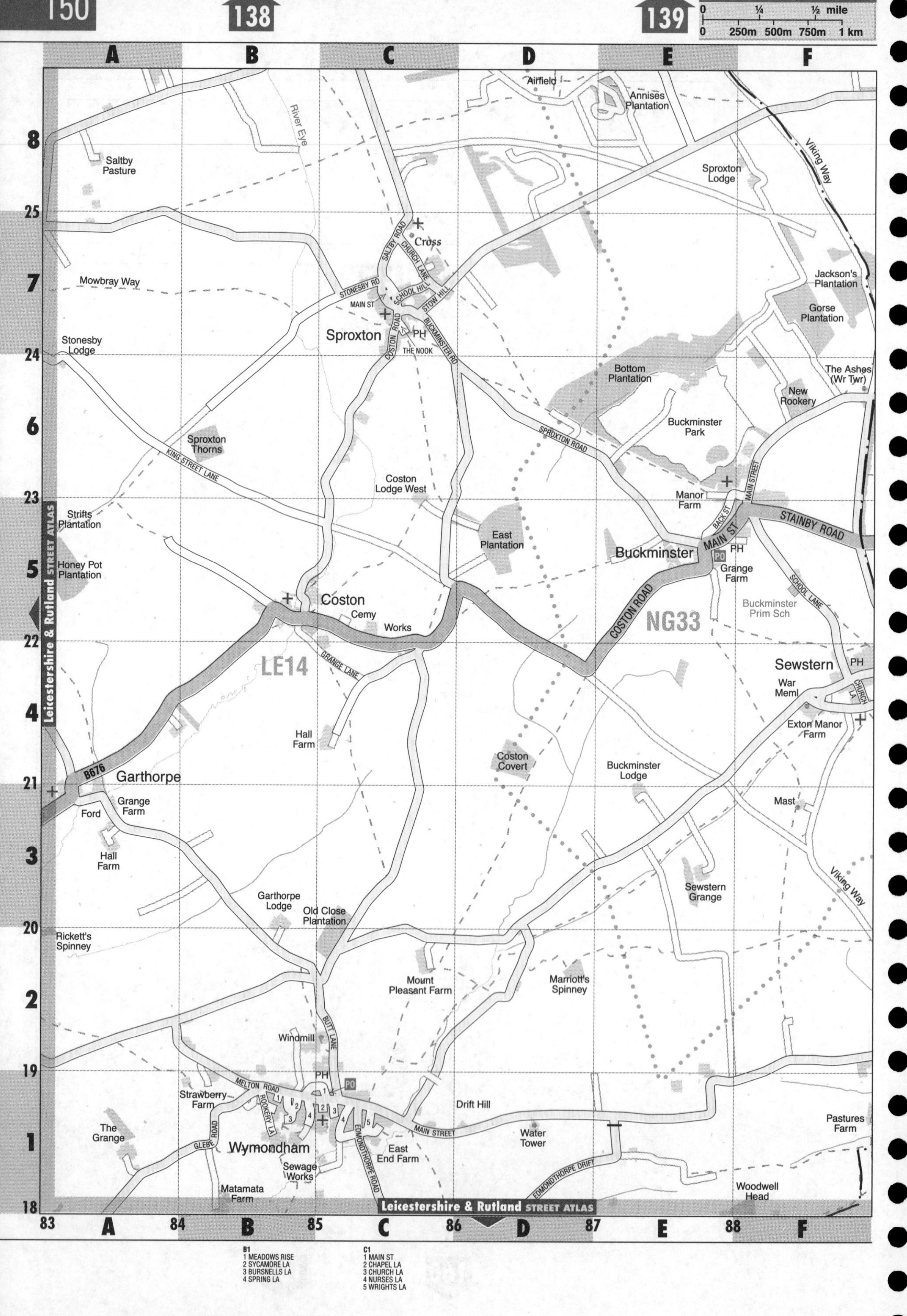

Scale: 1¾ inches to 1 mile

0   ¼   ½ mile
0 250m 500m 750m 1 km

Leicestershire & Rutland STREET ATLAS

A   B   C   D   E   F

8
25
7
24
6
23
5
22
4
21
3
20
2
19
1
18

83   A   84   B   85   C   86   D   87   E   88   F

Saltby
Pasture

River Eye

Mowbray Way

Stonesby
Lodge

Sproxton
Thorns

King Street Lane

Strifts
Plantation

Honey Pot
Plantation

Airfield

Annises
Plantation

Sproxton
Lodge

Cross

SALTBY ROAD

CHURCH LANE

STONESBY RD

SCHOOL HILL

STOW HILL

MAIN ST

Sproxton

PH

THE NOOK

COSTON ROAD

BUCKMINSTER RD

Bottom
Plantation

SPROXTON ROAD

Buckminster
Park

Jackson's
Plantation

Gorse
Plantation

The Ashes
(Wr Twr)

New
Rookery

Viking Way

Coston
Lodge West

East
Plantation

Manor
Farm

MAIN STREET

BACK ST

STAINBY ROAD

Buckminster

MAIN ST

PO

PH

Grange
Farm

SCHOOL LANE

Buckminster
Prim Sch

NG33

Coston

LE14

Cemy

Works

GRANGE LANE

COSTON ROAD

Sewstern

War
Meml

PH

CHURCH LA

Exton Manor
Farm

Hall
Farm

Coston
Covert

Buckminster
Lodge

Mast

B676

Garthorpe

Ford

Grange
Farm

Hall
Farm

Garthorpe
Lodge

Old Close
Plantation

Mount
Pleasant Farm

Marriott's
Spinney

Sewstern
Grange

Viking Way

Rickett's
Spinney

Windmill

BUTT LANE

MELTON ROAD

PH

PO

Strawberry
Farm

1 2 3

1 2 3

4

4 5

GLEBE ROAD

RECTORY LA

EDMONTHORPE ROAD

The
Grange

Wymondham

Matamata
Farm

Sewage
Works

East
End Farm

MAIN STREET

Drift Hill

Water
Tower

EDMONTHORPE DRIFT

Pastures
Farm

Woodwell
Head

B1
1 MEADOWS RISE
2 SYCAMORE LA
3 BURSNELLS LA
4 SPRING LA

C1
1 MAIN ST
2 CHAPEL LA
3 CHURCH LA
4 NURSES LA
5 WRIGHTS LA

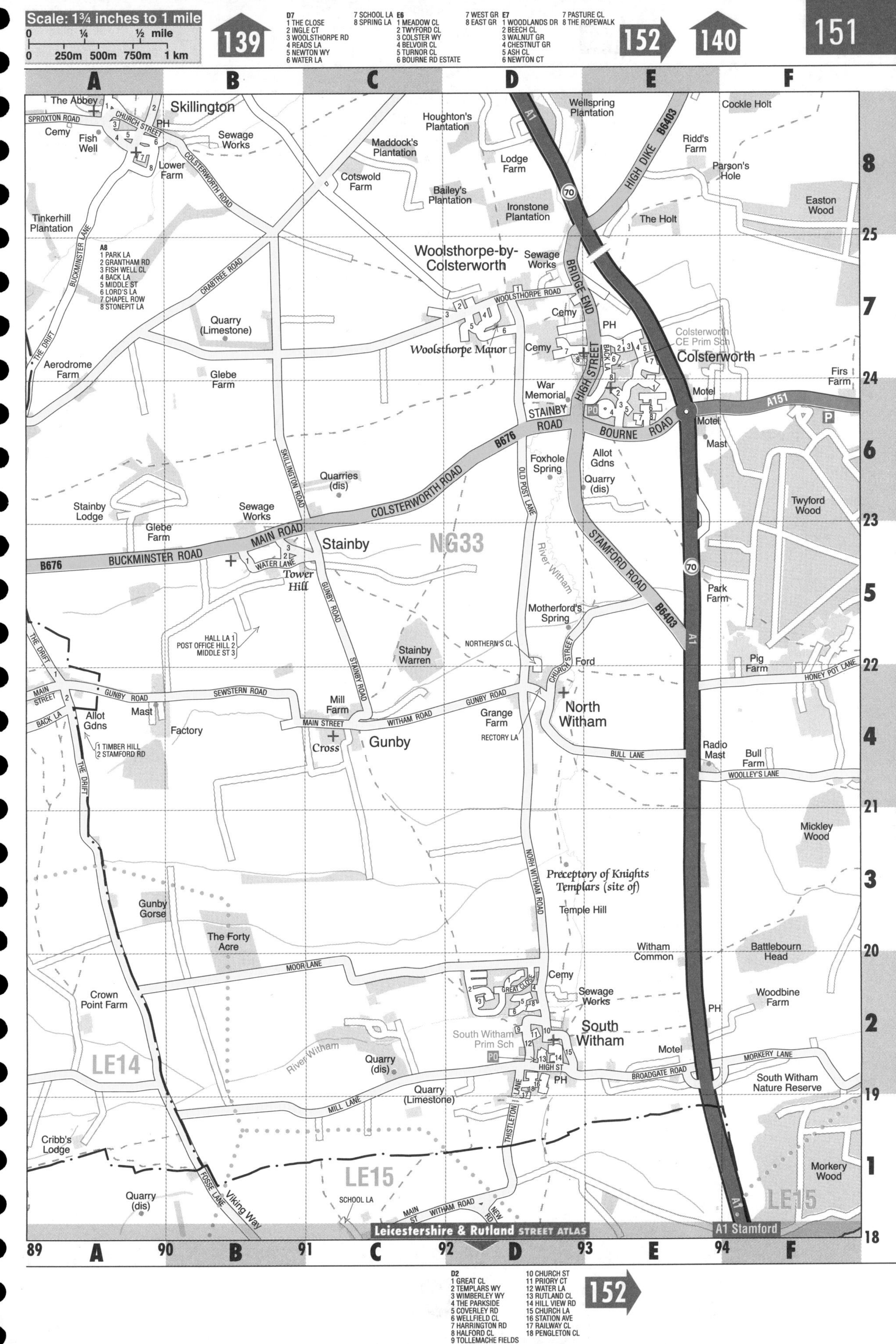

Scale: 1¾ inches to 1 mile
0 ¼ ½ mile
0 250m 500m 750m 1 km
139
D7
1 THE CLOSE
2 INGLE CT
3 WOOLSTHORPE RD
4 READS LA
5 NEWTON WY
6 WATER LA
7 SCHOOL LA
8 SPRING LA
E6
1 MEADOW CL
2 TWYFORD CL
3 COLSTER WY
4 BELVOIR CL
5 TURNOR CL
6 BOURNE RD ESTATE
7 WEST GR
8 EAST GR
E7
1 WOODLANDS DR
2 BEECH CL
3 WALNUT GR
4 CHESTNUT GR
5 ASH CL
6 NEWTON CT
7 PASTURE CL
8 THE ROPEWALK
152
140
151
A
B
C
D
E
F
The Abbey
Skillington
SPROXTON ROAD
CHURCH STREET
PH
Cemy
Fish Well
Sewage Works
Lower Farm
COLSTERWORTH ROAD
Tinkerhill Plantation
BUCKMINSTER LANE
A8
1 PARK LA
2 GRANTHAM RD
3 FISH WELL CL
4 BACK LA
5 MIDDLE ST
6 LORD'S LA
7 CHAPEL ROW
8 STONEPIT LA
CRABTREE ROAD
Quarry (Limestone)
THE DRIFT
Aerodrome Farm
Glebe Farm
Maddock's Plantation
Cotswold Farm
Houghton's Plantation
Bailey's Plantation
Lodge Farm
Ironstone Plantation
Wellspring Plantation
A1
HIGH DIKE
B6403
Cockle Holt
Ridd's Farm
Parson's Hole
Easton Wood
The Holt
Woolsthorpe-by-Colsterworth
Sewage Works
BRIDGE END
WOOLSTHORPE ROAD
Cemy
PH
Woolsthorpe Manor
Cemy
HIGH STREET
BACK LA
Colsterworth CE Prim Sch
Colsterworth
Firs Farm
Motel
A151
P
War Memorial
PO
STAINBY ROAD
BOURNE ROAD
Motel
Mast
B676
SKILLINGTON ROAD
Quarries (dis)
COLSTERWORTH ROAD
Foxhole Spring
OLD POST LANE
Allot Gdns
Quarry (dis)
Twyford Wood
Stainby Lodge
Glebe Farm
Sewage Works
MAIN ROAD
Stainby
NG33
STAMFORD ROAD
B676
BUCKMINSTER ROAD
WATER LANE
Tower Hill
GUNBY ROAD
River Witham
Park Farm
Motherford's Spring
B6403
HALL LA 1
POST OFFICE HILL 2
MIDDLE ST 3
STAINBY ROAD
Stainby Warren
NORTHERN'S CL
CHURCH STREET
Ford
Pig Farm
HONEY POT LANE
THE DRIFT
MAIN STREET
BACK LA
GUNBY ROAD
SEWSTERN ROAD
Mill Farm
GUNBY ROAD
Allot Gdns
Mast
Factory
MAIN STREET
WITHAM ROAD
Grange Farm
North Witham
1 TIMBER HILL
2 STAMFORD RD
Cross
Gunby
RECTORY LA
BULL LANE
Radio Mast
Bull Farm
WOOLLEY'S LANE
Mickley Wood
NORTH WITHAM ROAD
Preceptory of Knights Templars (site of)
Temple Hill
Gunby Gorse
The Forty Acre
Witham Common
Battlebourn Head
MOOR LANE
Cemy
GREAT CLOSE
Sewage Works
Crown Point Farm
Woodbine Farm
PH
South Witham
South Witham Prim Sch
PO
HIGH ST
PH
Motel
MORKERY LANE
BROADGATE ROAD
LE14
River Witham
Quarry (dis)
Quarry (Limestone)
MILL LANE
THISTLETON LANE
South Witham Nature Reserve
Cribb's Lodge
Morkery Wood
LE15
LE15
Quarry (dis)
FOSSE LANE
Viking Way
SCHOOL LA
MAIN ST
WITHAM ROAD
NEW RD
A1
Leicestershire & Rutland STREET ATLAS
A1 Stamford
8 25 7 24 6 23 5 22 4 21 3 20 2 19 1 18
89 90 91 92 93 94
D2
1 GREAT CL
2 TEMPLARS WY
3 WIMBERLEY WY
4 THE PARKSIDE
5 COVERLEY RD
6 WELLFIELD CL
7 HARRINGTON RD
8 HALFORD CL
9 TOLLEMACHE FIELDS
10 CHURCH ST
11 PRIORY CT
12 WATER LA
13 RUTLAND CL
14 HILL VIEW RD
15 CHURCH LA
16 STATION AVE
17 RAILWAY CL
18 PENGLETON CL
152

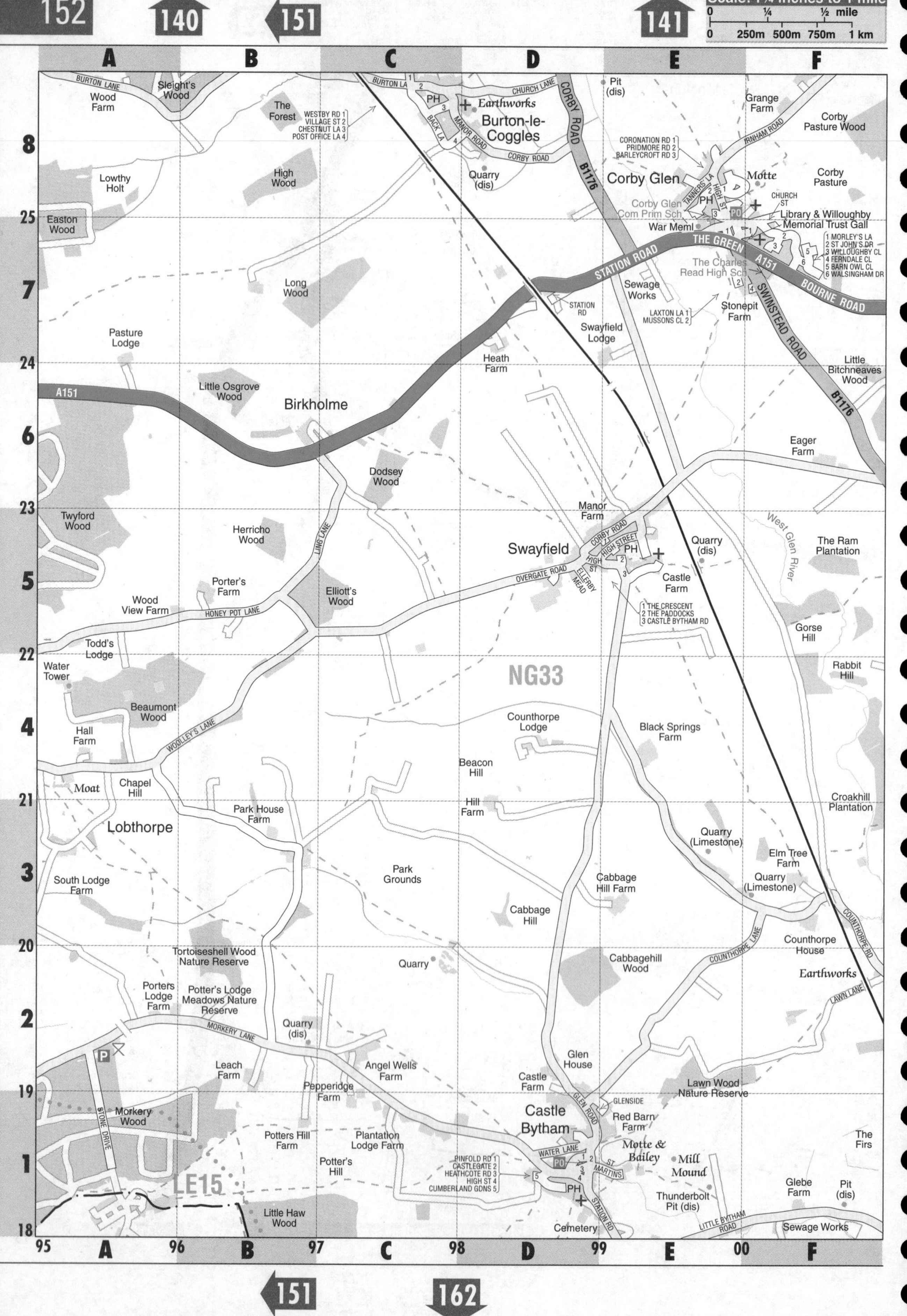

Scale: 1¾ inches to 1 mile
0   ¼   ½   mile
0   250m   500m   750m   1 km

A   B   C   D   E   F

Burton Lane
Wood Farm
Sleight's Wood
The Forest

WESTBY RD 1
VILLAGE ST 2
CHESTNUT LA 3
POST OFFICE LA 4

Burton La
BACK LA
MANOR ROAD
CHURCH LANE
PH
Earthworks
Burton-le-Coggles
Corby Road

Pit (dis)
Grange Farm

CORBY ROAD
B1176

IRNHAM ROAD
Corby Pasture Wood

8

Lowthy Holt
High Wood

Quarry (dis)
Corby Glen

CORONATION RD 1
PRIDMORE RD 2
BARLEYCROFT RD 3

Motte
Corby Pasture

25

Easton Wood

Corby Glen Com Prim Sch
War Meml

TANNERS LA
HIGH ST
PH
PO
CHURCH ST
Library & Willoughby Memorial Trust Gall

1 MORLEY'S LA
2 ST JOHN'S DR
3 WILLOUGHBY CL
4 FERNDALE CL
5 BARN OWL CL
6 WALSINGHAM DR

7

Long Wood

STATION ROAD
THE GREEN
A151
BOURNE ROAD

Pasture Lodge

Heath Farm

Sewage Works
The Charles Read High Sch

SWINSTEAD ROAD

24

Little Osgrove Wood
Birkholme

STATION RD
Swayfield Lodge

LAXTON LA 1
MUSSONS CL 2
Stonepit Farm

Little Bitchneaves Wood

B1176

A151

6

Dodsey Wood

Manor Farm

West Glen River

Eager Farm

23

Twyford Wood
Herricho Wood
LIME LANE
Swayfield

CORBY ROAD
HIGH STREET
CLIFFBY
PH

Quarry (dis)

The Ram Plantation

5

Porter's Farm
Wood View Farm
HONEY POT LANE
Elliott's Wood

OVERGATE ROAD
HIGH ST
MEAD
Castle Farm

1 THE CRESCENT
2 THE PADDOCKS
3 CASTLE BYTHAM RD

Gorse Hill

22

Water Tower
Todd's Lodge
Beaumont Wood

NG33

Rabbit Hill

4

Hall Farm
WOOLLEY'S LANE

Counthorpe Lodge
Black Springs Farm

21

Moat
Chapel Hill
Park House Farm
Beacon Hill

Hill Farm

Quarry (Limestone)

Croakhill Plantation

3

Lobthorpe
South Lodge Farm
Park Grounds
Cabbage Hill Farm

Quarry (Limestone)
Elm Tree Farm

20

Tortoiseshell Wood Nature Reserve
Quarry
Cabbage Hill

Cabbagehill Wood

Counthorpe House

COUNTHORPE LANE
COUNTHORPE RD

Earthworks

2

Porters Lodge Farm
Potter's Lodge Meadows Nature Reserve
Quarry (dis)

MORKERY LANE
Leach Farm
Angel Wells Farm

Glen House

LAWN LANE

19

P
Morkery Wood
STONE DRIVE
Pepperidge Farm

Castle Farm

GLEN ROAD
Glenside
Red Barn Farm

Lawn Wood Nature Reserve

The Firs

1

LE15
Potters Hill Farm
Plantation Lodge Farm
Potter's Hill

PINFOLD RD 1
CASTLEGATE 2
HEATHCOTE RD 3
HIGH ST 4
CUMBERLAND GDNS 5

Castle Bytham
Water Lane
PO
ST MARTINS
PH

Motte & Bailey
Mill Mound

Thunderbolt Pit (dis)

Glebe Farm

Pit (dis)

18

Little Haw Wood

STATION RD
Cemetery

LITTLE BYTHAM ROAD
Sewage Works

95   A   96   B   97   C   98   D   99   E   00   F

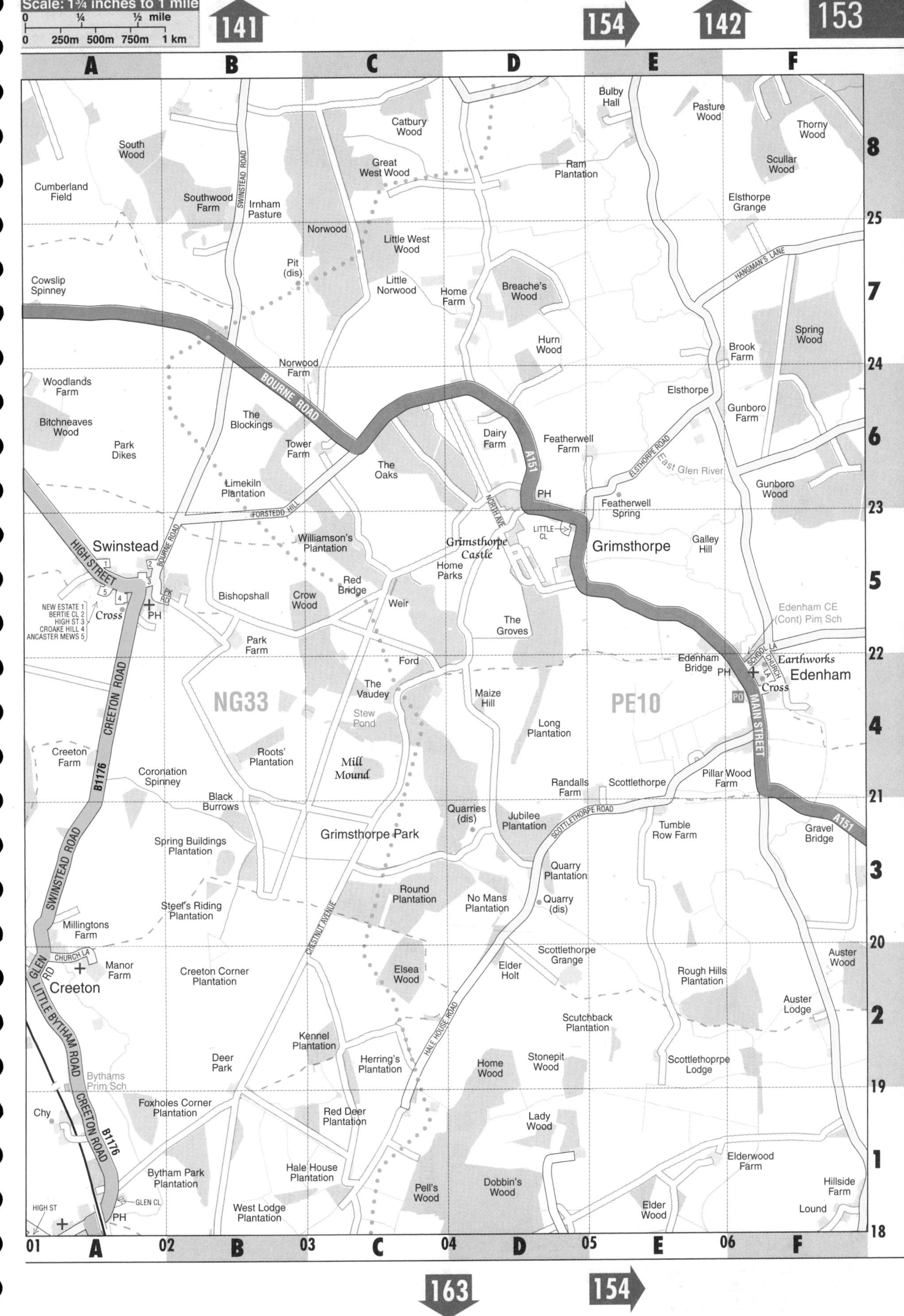

Scale: 1¾ inches to 1 mile
0 ¼ ½ mile
0 250m 500m 750m 1 km
141
154
142
A B C D E F
South Wood
Cumberland Field
Southwood Farm
Irnham Pasture
Catbury Wood
Great West Wood
Norwood
Little West Wood
Bulby Hall
Pasture Wood
Thorny Wood
Sculler Wood
Ram Plantation
Elsthorpe Grange
Cowslip Spinney
Pit (dis)
Little Norwood
Home Farm
Breache's Wood
Hurn Wood
HANGMAN'S LANE
Spring Wood
Brook Farm
Norwood Farm
Woodlands Farm
BOURNE ROAD
Elsthorpe
Gunboro Farm
Bitchneaves Wood
The Blockings
Park Dikes
Tower Farm
The Oaks
Dairy Farm
A151
Featherwell Farm
ELSTHORPE ROAD
East Glen River
Gunboro Wood
Limekiln Plantation
FORSTEDD HILL
PH
Featherwell Spring
NORTH AVE
LITTLE CL
Swinstead
HIGH STREET
BOURNE ROAD
SWINSTEAD ROAD
Williamson's Plantation
Grimsthorpe Castle
Grimsthorpe
Galley Hill
Home Parks
Red Bridge
Bishopshall
Crow Wood
Weir
PK RD
PH
Cross
NEW ESTATE 1
BERTIE CL 2
HIGH ST 3
CROAKE HILL 4
ANCASTER MEWS 5
The Groves
Edenham CE (Cont) Pim Sch
Park Farm
Ford
SCHOOL LA
CHURCH LA
Earthworks
Edenham Bridge
PH
Edenham
Cross
CREETON ROAD
NG33
The Vaudey
Stew Pond
Maize Hill
PE10
MAIN STREET
Long Plantation
Creeton Farm
Roots' Plantation
Mill Mound
B1176
Coronation Spinney
Randalls Farm
Scottlethorpe
Pillar Wood Farm
Black Burrows
Quarries (dis)
Jubilee Plantation
SCOTTLETHORPE ROAD
Tumble Row Farm
Gravel Bridge
Spring Buildings Plantation
Grimsthorpe Park
SWINSTEAD ROAD
Quarry Plantation
Round Plantation
No Mans Plantation
Quarry (dis)
Steel's Riding Plantation
CHESTNUT AVENUE
Millingtons Farm
Scottlethorpe Grange
Auster Wood
CHURCH LA
GLEN RD
Manor Farm
Creeton
Creeton Corner Plantation
Elsea Wood
Elder Holt
Rough Hills Plantation
Auster Lodge
LITTLE BYTHAM ROAD
Scutchback Plantation
HALE HOUSE ROAD
Kennel Plantation
Deer Park
Herring's Plantation
Home Wood
Stonepit Wood
Scottlethoprpe Lodge
Bythams Prim Sch
Chy
Foxholes Corner Plantation
CREETON ROAD
B1176
Red Deer Plantation
Lady Wood
Elderwood Farm
Bytham Park Plantation
Hale House Plantation
Pell's Wood
Dobbin's Wood
Hillside Farm
GLEN CL
HIGH ST
PH
West Lodge Plantation
Elder Wood
Lound
8
25
7
24
6
23
5
22
4
21
3
20
2
19
1
18
01 A 02 B 03 C 04 D 05 E 06 F
163
154

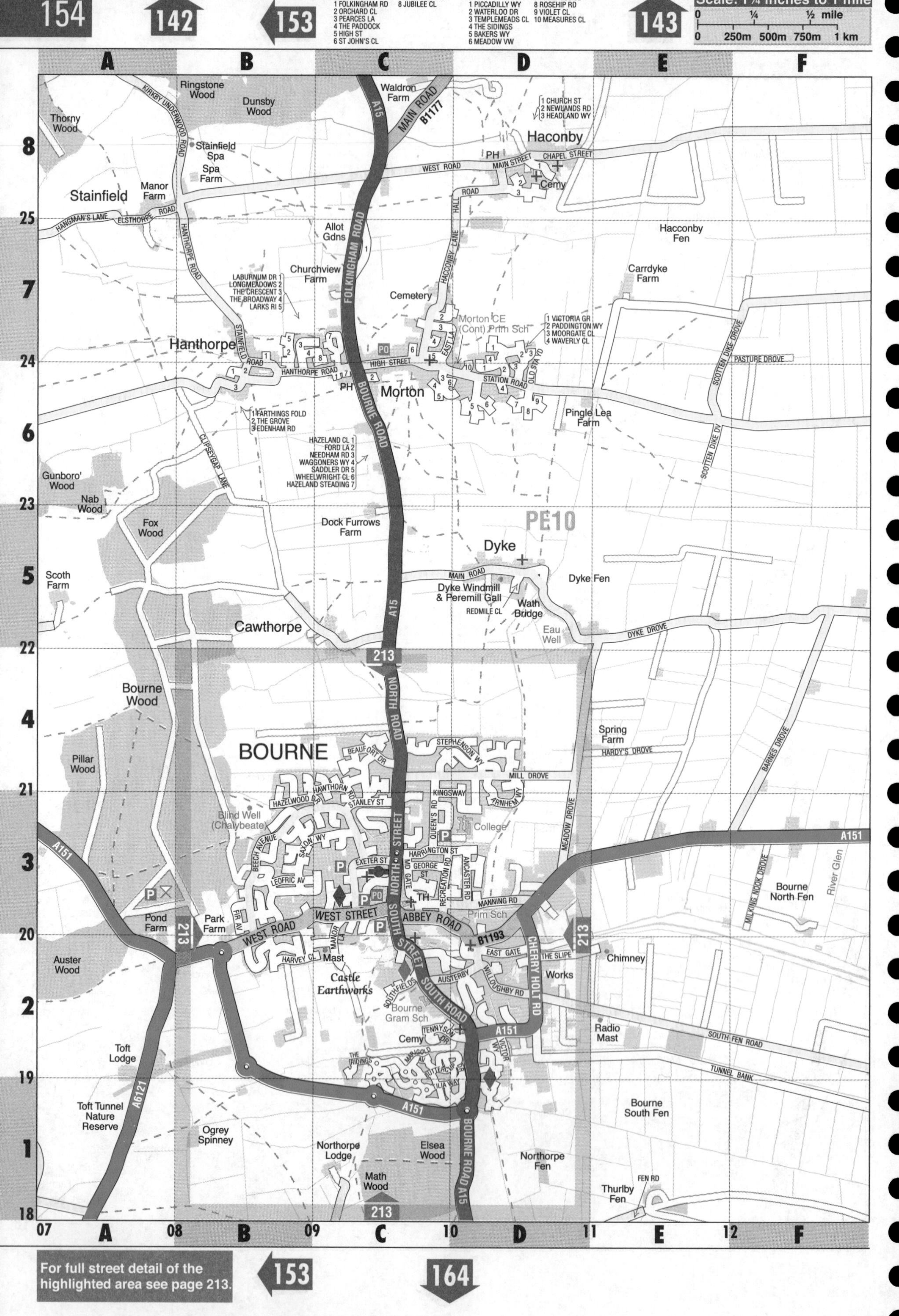

C7
1 FOLKINGHAM RD
2 ORCHARD CL
3 PEARCES LA
4 THE PADDOCK
5 HIGH ST
6 ST JOHN'S CL

7 MILLFIELD RD
8 JUBILEE CL

D6
1 PICCADILLY WY
2 WATERLOO DR
3 TEMPLEMEADS CL
4 THE SIDINGS
5 BAKERS WY
6 MEADOW VW

7 PRIMROSE CL
8 ROSEHIP RD
9 VIOLET CL
10 MEASURES CL

Scale: 1¾ inches to 1 mile

0   ¼   ½ mile
0   250m   500m   750m   1 km

Thorny Wood

Ringstone Wood

Dunsby Wood

Waldron Farm

1 CHURCH ST
2 NEWLANDS RD
3 HEADLAND WY

Haconby

PH

CHAPEL STREET

WEST ROAD

MAIN STREET

Cemy

Stainfield

Stainfield Spa
Spa Farm

Manor Farm

Allot Gdns

Churchview Farm

Cemetery

Hacconby Fen

Carrdyke Farm

LABURNUM DR 1
LONGMEADOWS 2
THE CRESCENT 3
THE BROADWAY 4
LARKS RI 5

Morton CE
(Cont) Prim Sch

1 VICTORIA GR
2 PADDINGTON WY
3 MOORGATE CL
4 WAVERLY CL

SCOTTEN DIKE DROVE

PASTURE DROVE

Hanthorpe

HANTHORPE ROAD

HIGH STREET

PO

PH

Morton

STATION ROAD

Pingle Lea Farm

1 FARTHINGS FOLD
2 THE GROVE
3 EDENHAM RD

HAZELAND CL 1
FORD LA 2
NEEDHAM RD 3
WAGGONERS WY 4
SADDLER DR 5
WHEELWRIGHT GL 6
HAZELAND STEADING 7

PE10

Gunboro' Wood

Nab Wood

Fox Wood

Dock Furrows Farm

Dyke

Dyke Fen

Scoth Farm

MAIN ROAD

Dyke Windmill
& Peremill Gall

REDMILE CL

Wath Bridge

Eau Well

DYKE DROVE

SCOTTEN DIKE DV

Cawthorpe

213

Bourne Wood

NORTH ROAD

A15

Spring Farm

HARDY'S DROVE

BARNES DROVE

Pillar Wood

BOURNE

BEAUFORT DR

STEPHENSON WY

MILL DROVE

MEADOW DROVE

HAZELWOOD CL

HAWTHORN

STANLEY ST

Kingsway

IRONHEW...

College

Blind Well
(Chalybeate)

BEECH AVENUE

SAXON WY

QUEEN'S RD

HARRINGTON ST

P

MILKING NOOK DROVE

A151

A151

Bourne North Fen

River Glen

Pond Farm

Park Farm

WEST ROAD

LEOFRIC AV

FIR AV

EXETER ST

OLD GATE

GEORGE ST

RECREATION RD

ANCASTER RD

MANNING RD

Prim Sch

Chimney

Auster Wood

213

WEST STREET

SOUTH STREET

ABBEY ROAD

B1193

EAST GATE

The Slipe

Works

HARVEY CL

Mast

MANOR

Castle Earthworks

AUSTERBY

WILLOUGHBY RD

CHERRY HOLT RD

213

Radio Mast

Toft Lodge

SOUTHFIELD RD

Bourne
Gram Sch

Cemy

THE RIDINGS

MARIGOLD

BUTTERCUP

LILIA WY

TENNYSCH...

VICTOR...

A151

SOUTH FEN ROAD

TUNNEL BANK

A6121

Toft Tunnel
Nature Reserve

Ogrey Spinney

Northorpe Lodge

Math Wood

Elsea Wood

BOURNE ROAD A15

Northorpe Fen

Bourne
South Fen

Thurlby Fen

FEN RD

213

For full street detail of the
highlighted area see page 213.

Scale: 1¾ inches to 1 mile

143 156 144

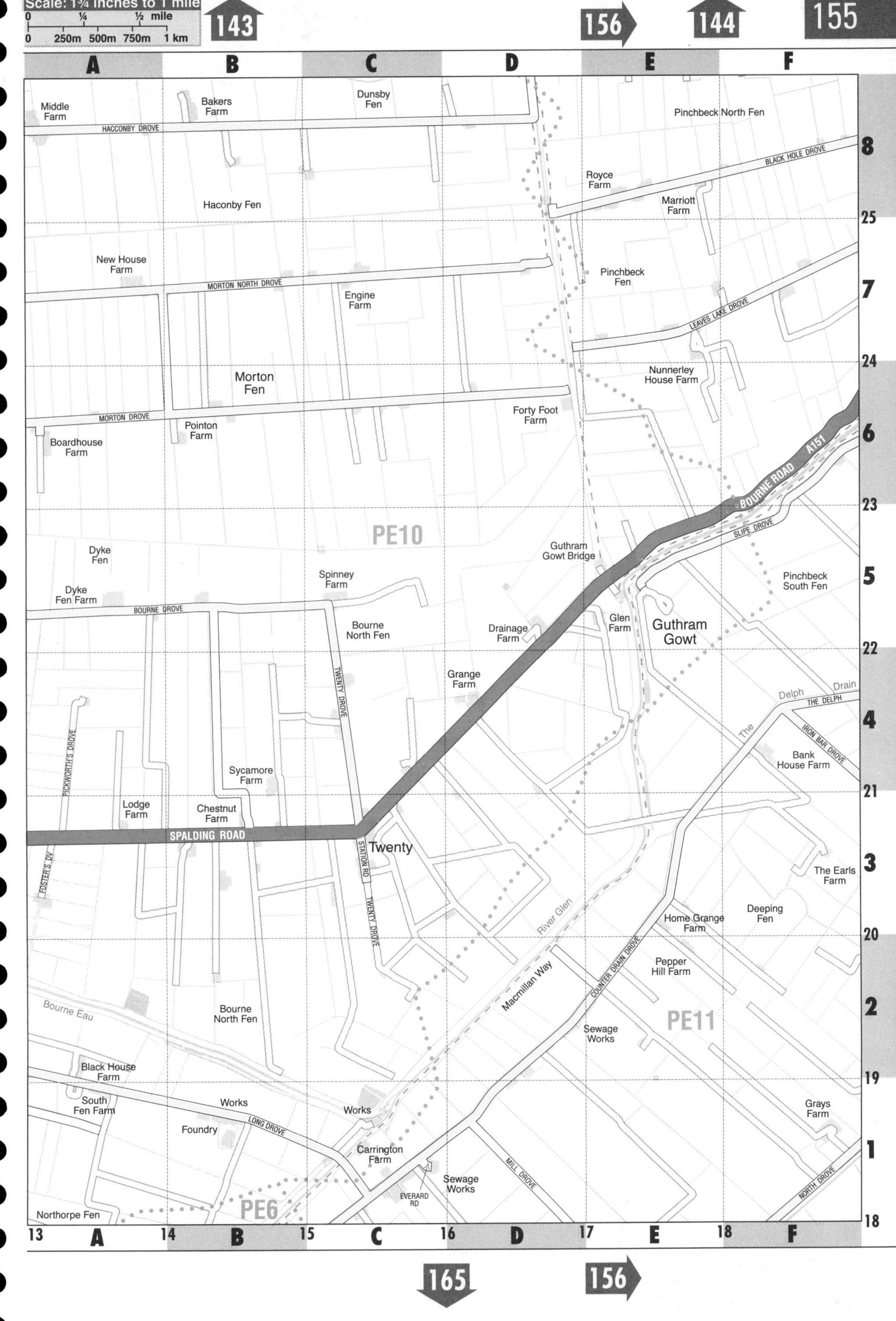

Middle Farm
Bakers Farm
Dunsby Fen
Pinchbeck North Fen
HACCONBY DROVE
BLACK HOLE DROVE
Royce Farm
Marriott Farm
Haconby Fen
New House Farm
MORTON NORTH DROVE
Pinchbeck Fen
Engine Farm
LEAVES LAKE DROVE
Morton Fen
Nunnerley House Farm
MORTON DROVE
Pointon Farm
Forty Foot Farm
Boardhouse Farm
BOURNE ROAD
A151
PE10
SLIPE DROVE
Guthram Gowt Bridge
Dyke Fen
Spinney Farm
Pinchbeck South Fen
Dyke Fen Farm
BOURNE DROVE
Bourne North Fen
Drainage Farm
Glen Farm
Guthram Gowt
Grange Farm
TWENTY DROVE
Delph
Drain
THE DELPH
The
PICKWORTH'S DROVE
IRON BAR DROVE
Bank House Farm
Sycamore Farm
Lodge Farm
Chestnut Farm
SPALDING ROAD
Twenty
STATION RD
FOSTER'S DV
The Earls Farm
Deeping Fen
Home Grange Farm
River Glen
Pepper Hill Farm
Macmillan Way
COUNTER DRAIN DROVE
Bourne Eau
Bourne North Fen
Sewage Works
PE11
Black House Farm
South Fen Farm
Works
Works
Grays Farm
LONG DROVE
Foundry
Carrington Farm
Sewage Works
MILL DROVE
EVERARD RD
NORTH DROVE
Northorpe Fen
PE6
A B C D E F
8 25 7 24 6 23 5 22 4 21 3 20 2 19 1 18
13 14 15 16 17 18

165 156

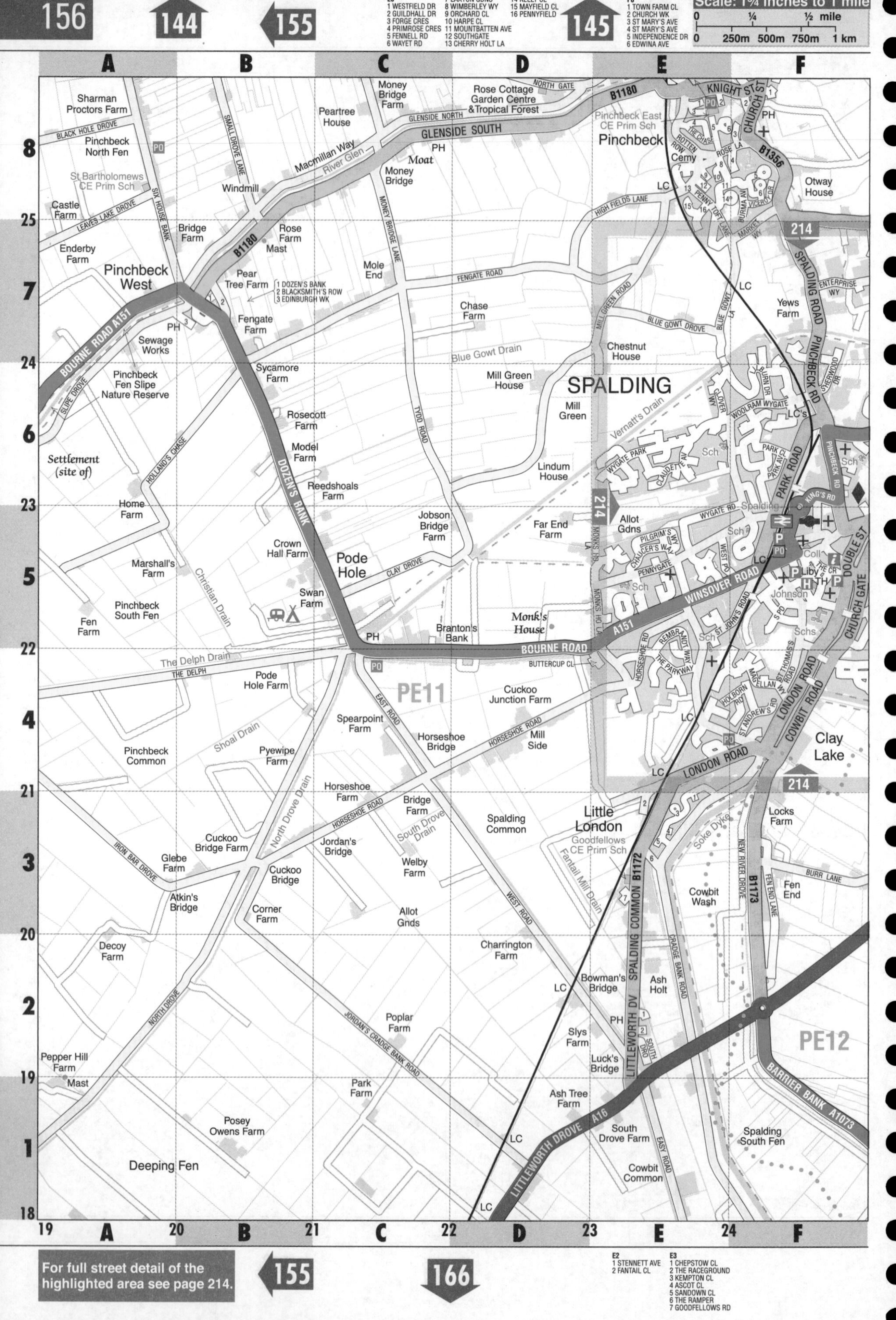

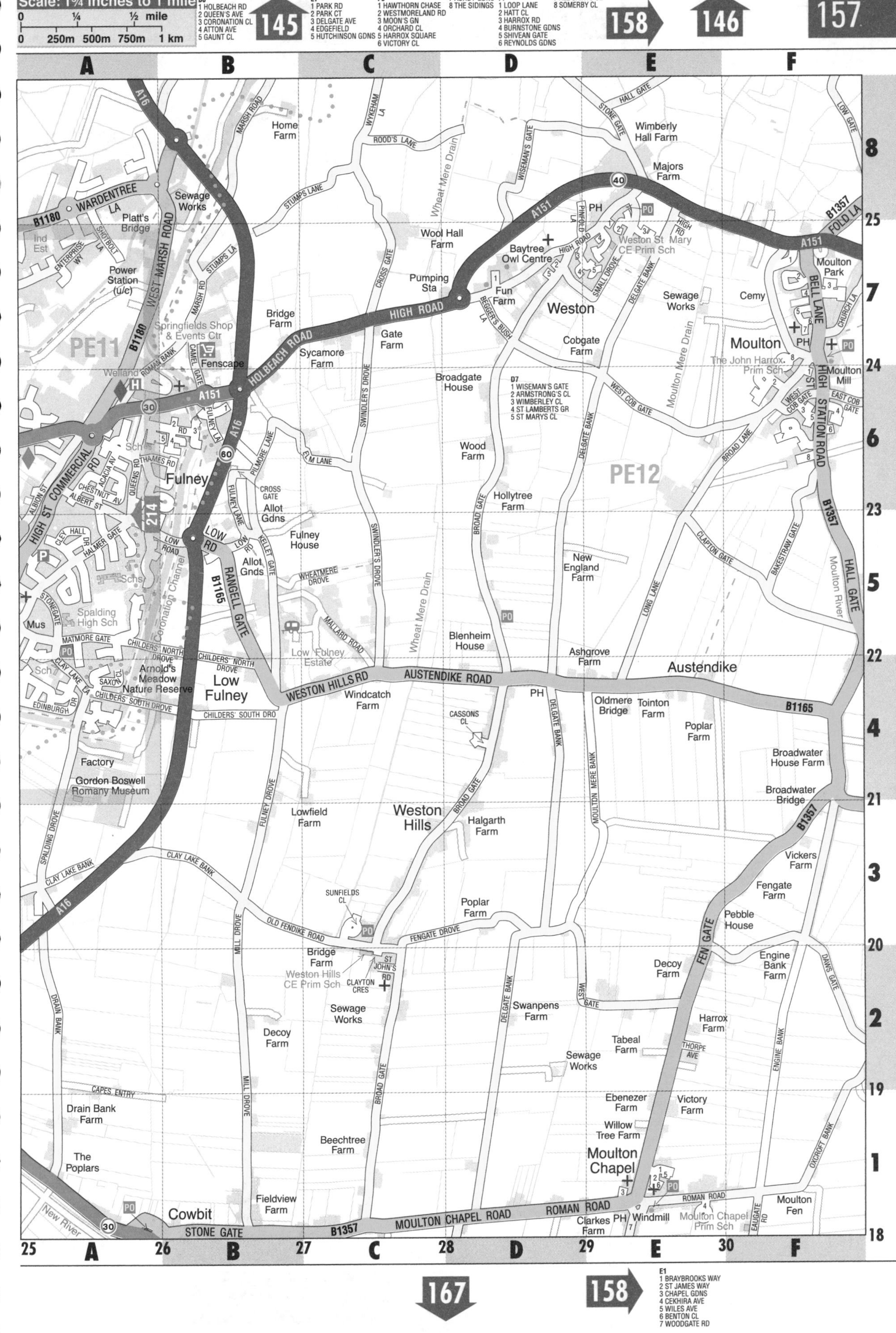

B6
1 HOLBEACH RD
2 QUEEN'S AVE
3 CORONATION CL
4 ATTON AVE
5 GAUNT CL

145

E7
1 PARK RD
2 PARK CT
3 DELGATE AVE
4 EDGEFIELD
5 HUTCHINSON GDNS

F6
1 HAWTHORN CHASE
2 WESTMORELAND RD
3 MOON'S GN
4 ORCHARD CL
5 HARROX SQUARE
6 VICTORY CL

7 ASHBY GDNS
8 THE SIDINGS

F7
1 LOOP LANE
2 HATT CL
3 HARROX RD
4 BURNSTONE GDNS
5 SHIVEAN GATE
6 REYNOLDS GDNS

7 ALL SAINTS CL
8 SOMERBY CL

158

146

A   B   C   D   E   F

PE11

Wardentree La

Home Farm

Sewage Works

Wool Hall Farm

Pumping Sta

Wimberly Hall Farm

Majors Farm

Baytree Owl Centre

Weston St Mary CE Prim Sch

Weston

Moulton Park

Moulton

Cemy

The John Harrox Prim Sch

Moulton Mill

PE12

Bridge Farm

Sycamore Farm

Gate Farm

Broadgate House

Cobgate Farm

Sewage Works

D7
1 WISEMAN'S GATE
2 ARMSTRONG'S CL
3 WIMBERLEY CL
4 ST LAMBERTS GR
5 ST MARYS CL

Wood Farm

Hollytree Farm

New England Farm

Fulney

Cross Gate

Allot Gdns

Fulney House

Allot Gnds

Low Fulney Estate

Blenheim House

Ashgrove Farm

Austendike

Spalding High Sch

Arnold's Meadow Nature Reserve

Low Fulney

Weston Hills Rd

Austendike Road

Windcatch Farm

B1165

Factory

Gordon Boswell Romany Museum

Lowfield Farm

Weston Hills

Halgarth Farm

Oldmere Bridge

Tointon Farm

Poplar Farm

Broadwater House Farm

Broadwater Bridge

Clay Lake Bank

Sunfields Cl

Poplar Farm

Vickers Farm

Fengate Farm

Pebble House

Bridge Farm

Weston Hills CE Prim Sch

Clayton Cres

Sewage Works

Old Fendike Road

Fengate Drove

Decoy Farm

Engine Bank Farm

Decoy Farm

Swanpens Farm

Harrox Farm

Tabeal Farm

Sewage Works

Capes Entry

Drain Bank Farm

The Poplars

Beechtree Farm

Ebenezer Farm

Victory Farm

Willow Tree Farm

Moulton Chapel

Cowbit

Stone Gate

Fieldview Farm

B1357

Moulton Chapel Road

Roman Road

Clarkes PH Farm

Windmill

Moulton Chapel Prim Sch

Moulton Fen

New River

E1
1 BRAYBROOKS WAY
2 ST JAMES WAY
3 CHAPEL GDNS
4 CEKHIRA AVE
5 WILES AVE
6 BENTON CL
7 WOODGATE RD

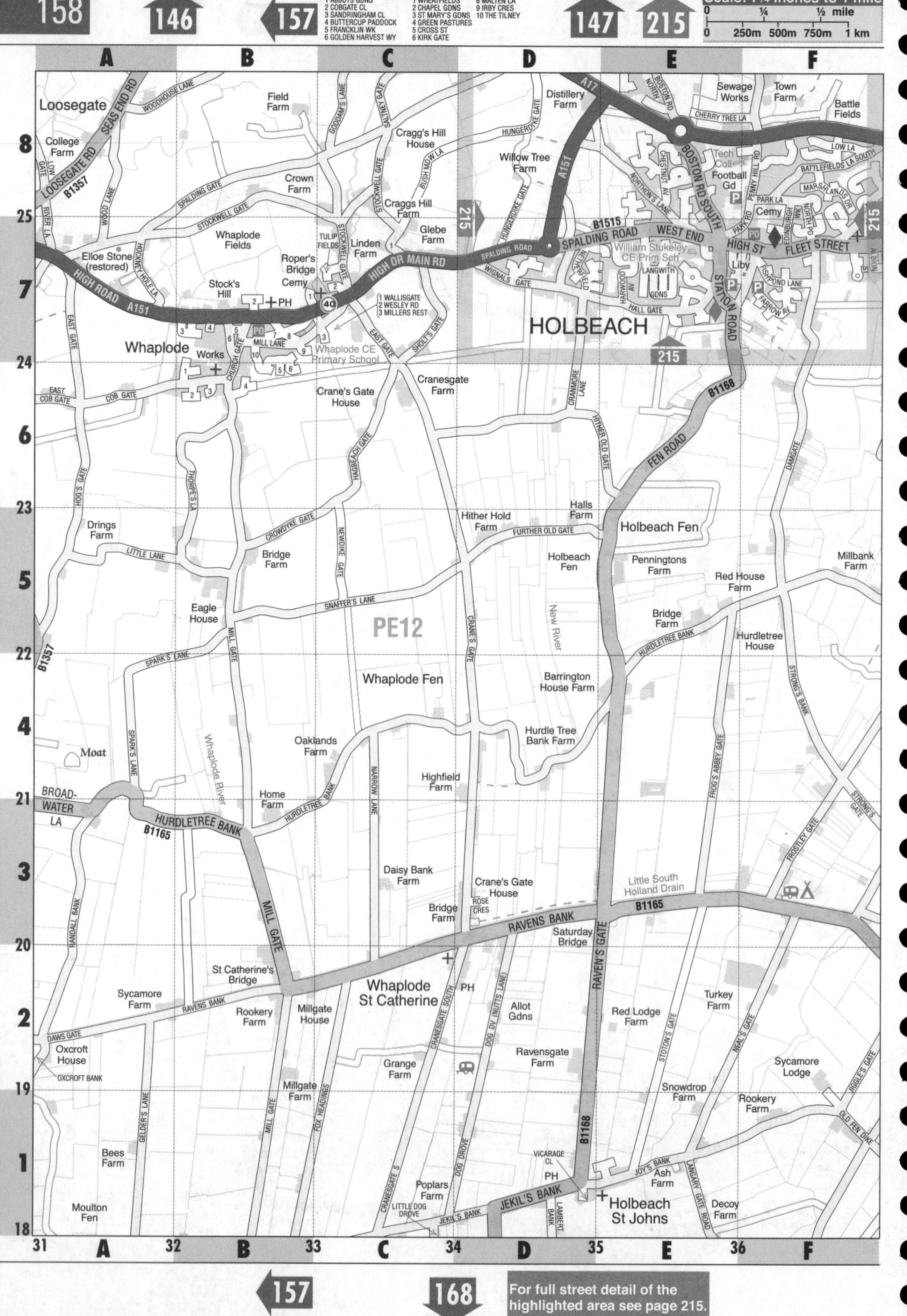

C7
1 HARGATE CL
2 PARKLANDS
3 EASTGATE GDNS
4 BURGESS DR
5 CHARLES RD
6 PROCTORS CL
7 CHERRY LA
8 BRAMLEY CL
9 HAVEN CL
10 PINSTOCK LA

D7
1 PRIESTFIELD DRO
2 ST MARY'S MDWS
3 BATEMAN'S CL
4 LEIGHTON WK
5 CHURCHGATE MEWS
6 RECTORY LA
7 BRAMLEY MEWS

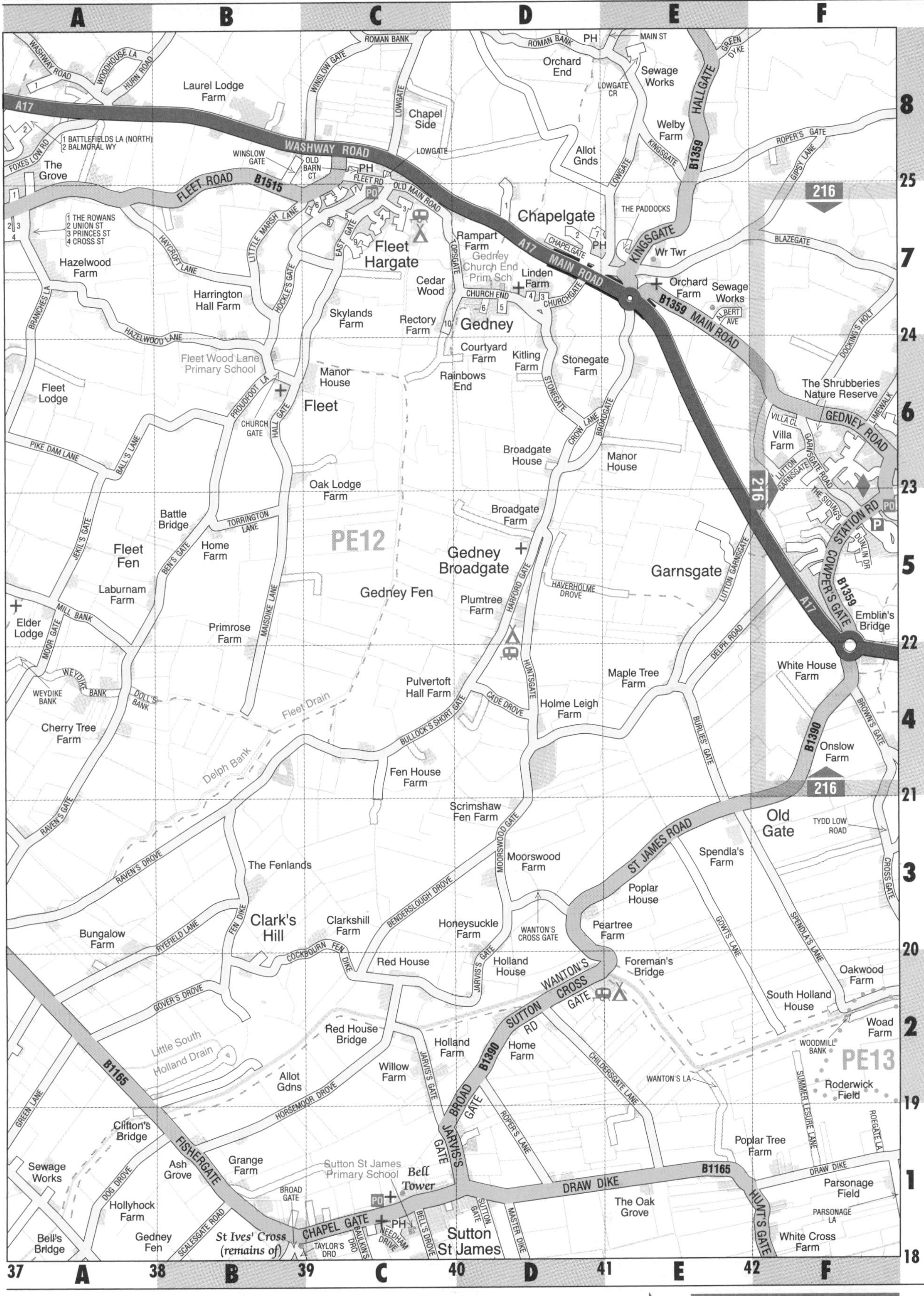

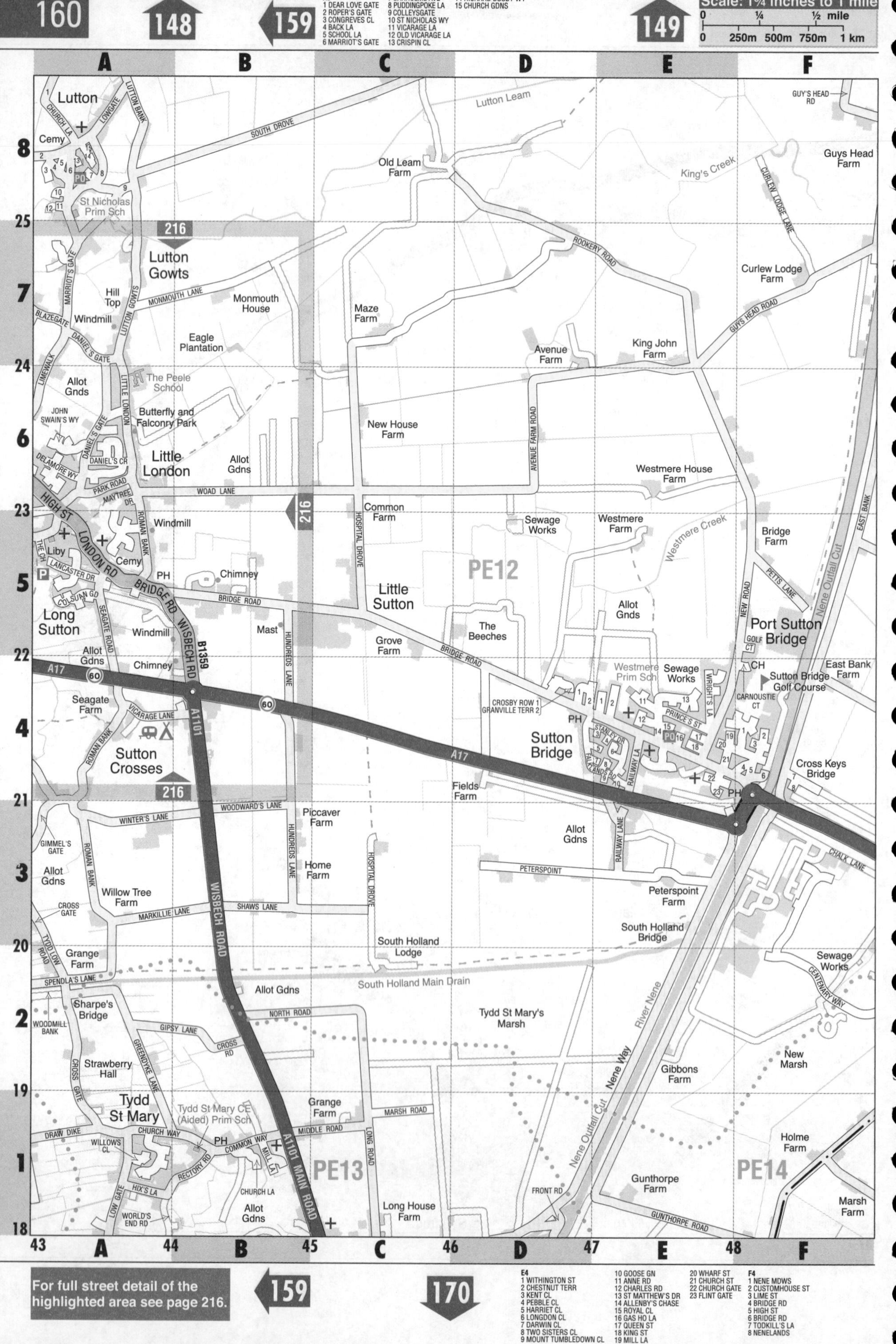

For full street detail of the highlighted area see page 216.

159 170

Scale: 1¾ inches to 1 mile

0   ¼   ½   mile
0   250m   500m   750m   1 km

A8
1 DEAR LOVE GATE
2 ROPER'S GATE
3 CONGREVES CL
4 BACK LA
5 SCHOOL LA
6 MARRIOT'S GATE

7 BARHOLME AVE
8 PUDDINGPOKE LA
9 COLLEYSGATE
10 ST NICHOLAS WY
11 VICARAGE LA
12 OLD VICARAGE LA
13 CRISPIN CL

14 RICHARD BUSBY WY
15 CHURCH GDNS

E4
1 WITHINGTON ST
2 CHESTNUT TERR
3 KENT CL
4 PEBBLE CL
5 HARRIET CL
6 LONGDON CL
7 DARWIN CL
8 TWO SISTERS CL
9 MOUNT TUMBLEDOWN CL

10 GOOSE GN
11 ANNE RD
12 CHARLES RD
13 ST MATTHEW'S DR
14 ALLENBY'S CHASE
15 ROYAL CL
16 GAS HO LA
17 QUEEN ST
18 KING ST
19 MILL LA

20 WHARF ST
21 CHURCH ST
22 CHURCH GATE
23 FLINT GATE

F4
1 NENE MDWS
2 CUSTOMHOUSE ST
3 LIME ST
4 BRIDGE RD
5 HIGH ST
6 BRIDGE RD
7 TODKILL'S LA
8 NENELANDS

Lutton
Cemy
St Nicholas Prim Sch
CHURCH LA
LONGATE
LUTTON BANK

216

Lutton Gowts
Hill Top
Windmill
Monmouth House
MARRIOT'S GATE
BLAZEGATE
SIMMS GATE
MONMOUTH LANE
LUTTON GOWTS RD

Eagle Plantation
LIMEWALK
DANIEL'S GATE
The Peele School
Butterfly and Falconry Park

JOHN SWAIN'S WY
DELAMORE WY
Allot Gnds
DANIEL'S CR
Little London
Allot Gdns
PARK ROAD
MAYTREE DR
WOAD LANE

HIGH ST
Windmill
ROMAN BANK
Chimney
THE CH
Liby
Cemy
PH
P
LANCASTER DR
COLT SUM GD

Long Sutton
Allot Gdns
Windmill
Chimney
SEAGATE ROAD
BRIDGE RD
WISBECH RD
BRIDGE ROAD
Mast
HUNDREDS LANE

A17
60
Seagate Farm
VICARAGE LANE
A1101
60
Sutton Crosses
ROMAN BANK
216

WINTER'S LANE
WOODWARD'S LANE
Piccaver Farm
Home Farm
HUNDREDS LANE
HOSPITAL DRIVE

GIMMEL'S GATE
Allot Gdns
Willow Tree Farm
CROSS GATE
MARKILLIE LANE
SHAWS LANE
WISBECH ROAD

TYDLOW ROAD
Grange Farm
SPENDLA'S LANE
Allot Gdns
South Holland Main Drain

WOODMILL BANK
Sharpe's Bridge
GIPSY LANE
NORTH ROAD
CROSS RD
Strawberry Hall
CROSS GATE
GREENDYKE LANE

Tydd St Mary
DRAW DIKE
WILLOWS CL
Tydd St Mary CE (Aided) Prim Sch
CHURCH WAY
PH
COMMON WAY
Grange Farm
MIDDLE ROAD
MARSH ROAD
LONG ROAD

LOW GATE
HIX'S LA
RECTORY RD
CHURCH LA
A1101 MAIN ROAD
PE13
Allot Gdns
WORLD'S END RD
MILL LA
Long House Farm
FRONT RD

South Drove
Lutton Leam
Old Leam Farm
King's Creek
GUY'S HEAD RD
Guys Head Farm

ROOKERY ROAD
CURLEW LODGE LANE
Curlew Lodge Farm
GUY'S HEAD ROAD

Maze Farm
Avenue Farm
King John Farm
AVENUE FARM ROAD
Westmere House Farm

New House Farm
Common Farm
HOSPITAL DRIVE
Sewage Works
Westmere Farm
Westmere Creek
Bridge Farm

PE12

Little Sutton
The Beeches
Grove Farm
Allot Gnds
BRIDGE ROAD
Westmere Prim Sch
Sewage Works
WRIGHT'S LA
NEW ROAD
PETT'S LANE
EAST BANK
Port Sutton Bridge
GOLF CT
CH
Sutton Bridge Golf Course

Crosby Row 1
Granville Terr 2
PH
STANLEY DR
RAILWAY LA
CARNOUSTIE CT
Sutton Bridge
PRINCE'S LA
PO
Fields Farm
ISLANDS RD
Cross Keys Bridge
PH
East Bank Farm

Allot Gdns
PETERSPOINT
Peterspoint Farm
South Holland Lodge
South Holland Bridge
CHALK LANE

Tydd St Mary's Marsh
River Nene
Nene Outfall Cut
Nene Way
Gibbons Farm
New Marsh
Sewage Works
CENTENARY WAY

Strawberry Hall
Gunthorpe Farm
GUNTHORPE ROAD
PE14
Holme Farm
Marsh Farm

B1359
A1101

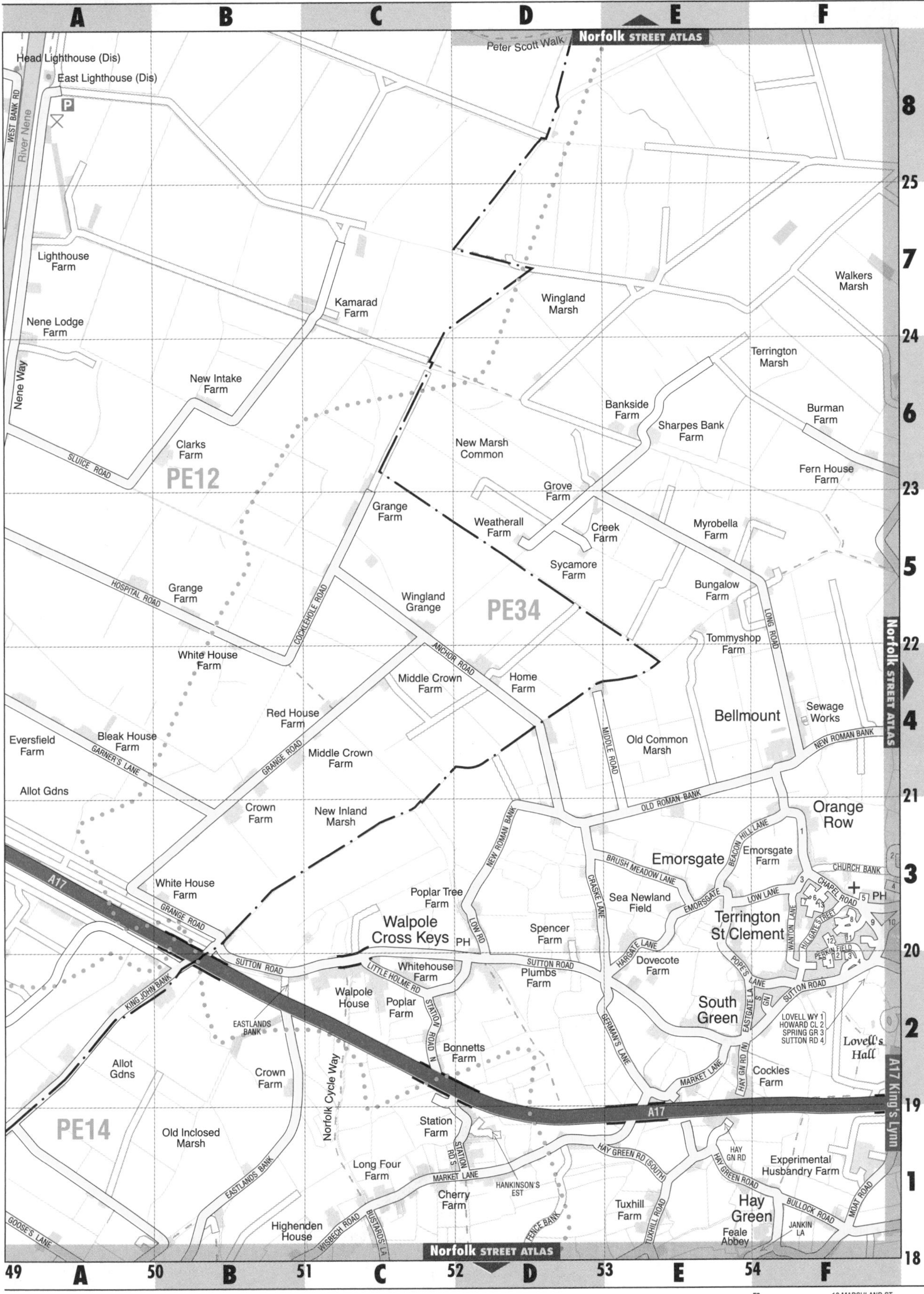

A   B   C   D   E   F

Norfolk STREET ATLAS

8
25
7
24
6
23
5
22
4
21
3
20
2
19
1
18

Norfolk STREET ATLAS

Head Lighthouse (Dis)
East Lighthouse (Dis)
P

WEST BANK RD
River Nene

Peter Scott Walk

Lighthouse Farm

Nene Lodge Farm

Nene Way

Kamarad Farm

Wingland Marsh

Walkers Marsh

New Intake Farm

Terrington Marsh

Bankside Farm

Sharpes Bank Farm

Burman Farm

Clarks Farm

PE12

New Marsh Common

Fern House Farm

SLUICE ROAD

Grange Farm

Grove Farm

Weatherall Farm

Creek Farm

Myrobella Farm

HOSPITAL ROAD

Grange Farm

Wingland Grange

PE34

Sycamore Farm

Bungalow Farm

White House Farm

COCKLE HOLE ROAD

ANCHOR ROAD

Tommyshop Farm

Bellmount

Sewage Works

NEW ROMAN BANK

Middle Crown Farm

Home Farm

Red House Farm

GRANGE ROAD

Middle Crown Farm

Eversfield Farm

Bleak House Farm

GARNER'S LANE

Old Common Marsh

MIDDLE ROAD

OLD ROMAN BANK

Orange Row

Allot Gdns

Crown Farm

New Inland Marsh

NEW ROMAN BANK

Emorsgate

BEACON HILL LANE

Emorsgate Farm

CHURCH BANK

A17

White House Farm

GRANGE ROAD

SUTTON ROAD

Poplar Tree Farm

Walpole Cross Keys   PH

BRUSH MEADOW LANE

Sea Newland Field

Emorsgate

LOW LANE

CHAPEL ROAD

Terrington St Clement

PH

LITTLE HOLME RD

Whitehouse Farm

Plumbs Farm

SUTTON ROAD

HARGATE LANE

Dovecote Farm

WALTON LANE

VILLAGE STREET

KING JOHN BANK

EASTLANDS BANK

Walpole House

Poplar Farm

STATION ROAD N

LONG RD

GERMAN'S LANE

Spencer Farm

POPE'S LANE

EASTGATE LA

South Green

LOVELL WY 1
HOWARD CL 2
SPRING GR 3
SUTTON RD 4

Lovell's Hall

Allot Gdns

Crown Farm

Norfolk Cycle Way

Bonnetts Farm

Cockles Farm

MARKET LANE

HAY GN RD W

A17 King's Lynn

PE14

Old Inclosed Marsh

EASTLANDS BANK

WISBECH BANK

RUSTLANDS LA

STATION RD S

Station Farm

MARKET LANE

HANKINSON'S EST

HAY GREEN RD (SOUTH)

Tuxhill Farm

TUXHILL ROAD

HAY GN RD

Experimental Husbandry Farm

BULLOCK ROAD

MOAT ROAD

Long Four Farm

Cherry Farm

FENCE BANK

Hay Green

Feale Abbey

JANKIN LA

GOOSE'S LANE

Highenden House

Norfolk STREET ATLAS

49   A   50   B   51   C   52   D   53   E   54   F

F3
1 ORANGE ROW RD
2 CHURCH BANK
3 ORANGE ROW
4 KING WILLIAM CL
5 WESLEY AVE
6 THE SALTINGS
7 BRELLOWS HILL
8 CAVE'S CL
9 WESLEY RD
10 MARSHLAND ST
11 WESLEY CL
12 FFOLKES DR
13 COBBS HILL

E8
1 LITTLE BYTHAM RD
2 REGAL GDNS
3 BYTHAM HEIGHTS

Scale: 1¾ inches to 1 mile

0   ¼   ½   mile
0   250m   500m   750m   1 km

| | A | B | C | D | E | F |

Stocken Park
HM Prison
Lady Wood
Little Haw Wood
Quarry (dis)
Glebe Farm
Meadows End

8

P
Chimney
Addah Wood
Clipsham Park Wood
NG33

1 HESKETH CT
2 FLEETWOOD CT
3 WILSON CT
4 STOVE CT

School Farm

17

Stretton Wood
BRADLEY LA 1
CHURCH LA 2
NEW RD 3
WEST ST 4
P
Pillowsyke Holt
Belton Firs
Lodge Farm

7

Moor Plantation
Clipsham
Clipsham Park
Quarry (dis)
New Wood
Holywell Hall

Stockton Lane Plantation
CASTLE BYTHAM ROAD
MAIN ST
The Quarries
Holywell Quarry
Holy Well

16

CLIPSHAM ROAD
STRETTON ROAD
Manor Farm
Hill Top Farm
New Quarry House
HOLYWELL ROAD
Mill Farm

PH
MANOR RD
BIDWELL LANE
New Quarry Plantation

LE15

Bidwell Farm
White's Plantation
Quarries (dis)
Infield Holt

6

Glebe Farm
Osbonall Wood
Clipsham Old Quarry (Limestone)
Holywell Wood
Pettywood Farm
Pattinson's Holt

15

Quarry (dis)
Lincolnshire Gate
Robert's Field Nature Reserve

Greetham Wood Far
Big Pits Wood
Pickworth Great Wood
The Grange
Clay Pit
Newell Wood
Castle Dike

5

Quarry (dis)

Quarry (dis)
Woolfox Wood
Church (remains of)
Pickworth

14

A1 Grantham

Airfield (dis)
Taylor's Farm
Pit (dis)

4

STREET ATLAS

The Coppice
Woolfox Depot
Turnpole Wood

13

Leicestershire & Rutland

Hardwick Wood
CH
PE9
Pickworth Plain

3

Rutland County Golf Course
Exeter Gorse

North Road Spinney
Woodhead
East Wood

12

Horn Farm
Medieval Village of Horn (site of)
Little Oaks
Warren Plantation
Woodhead Castle (site of)

2

North Brook
Bloody Oaks
Tickencote Warren
Mounts Lodge

11

Pug's Park Spinney
GREAT NORTH ROAD
PICKWORTH ROAD

Empingham Old Wood
Wing Plantations
Quarry (dis)

1

Horn Mill Spinney
LOVES LA
Tickencote Laund
A1
Quarry (dis)

10

| 95 | A | 96 | B | 97 | C | 98 | D | 99 | E | 00 | F |

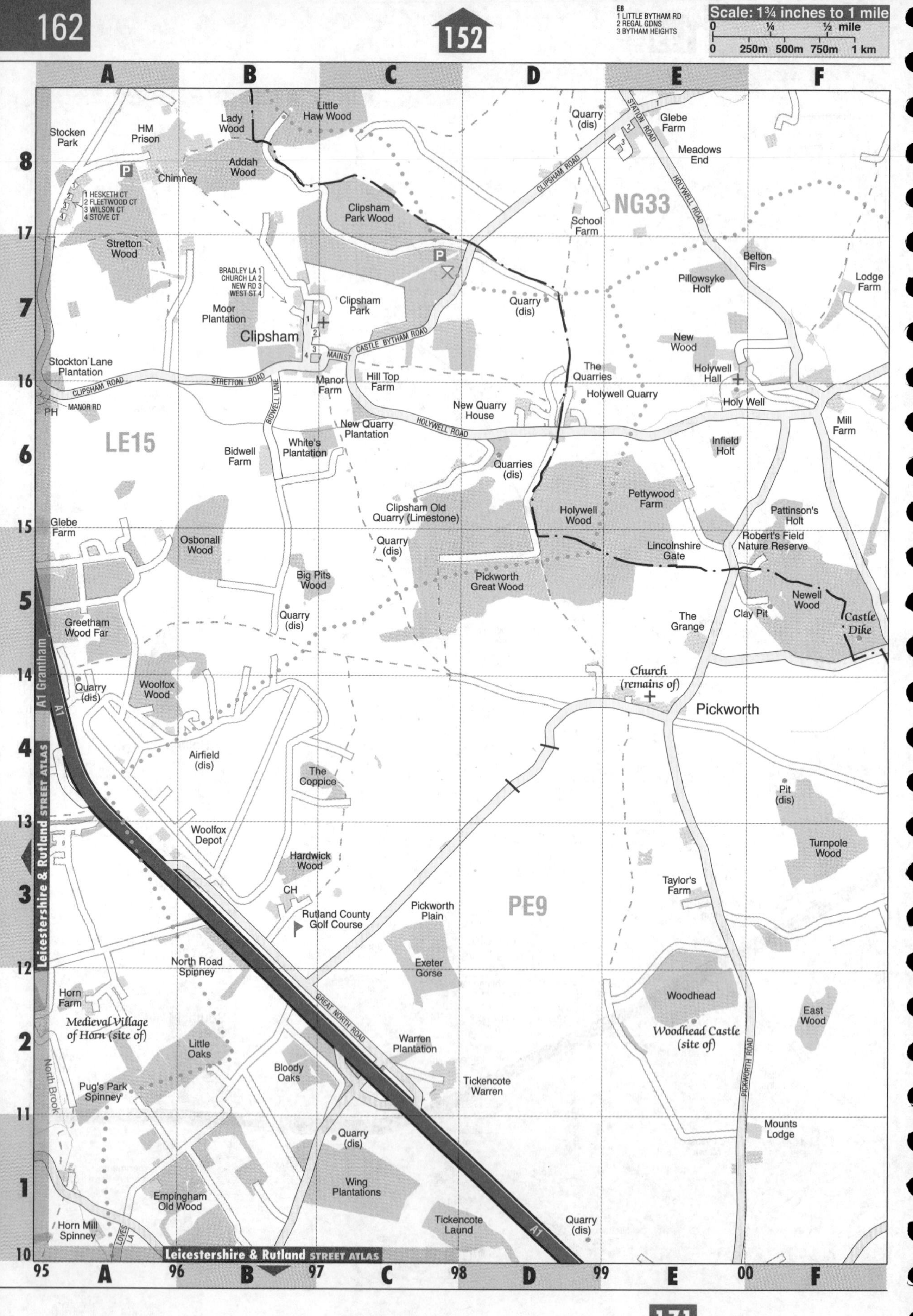

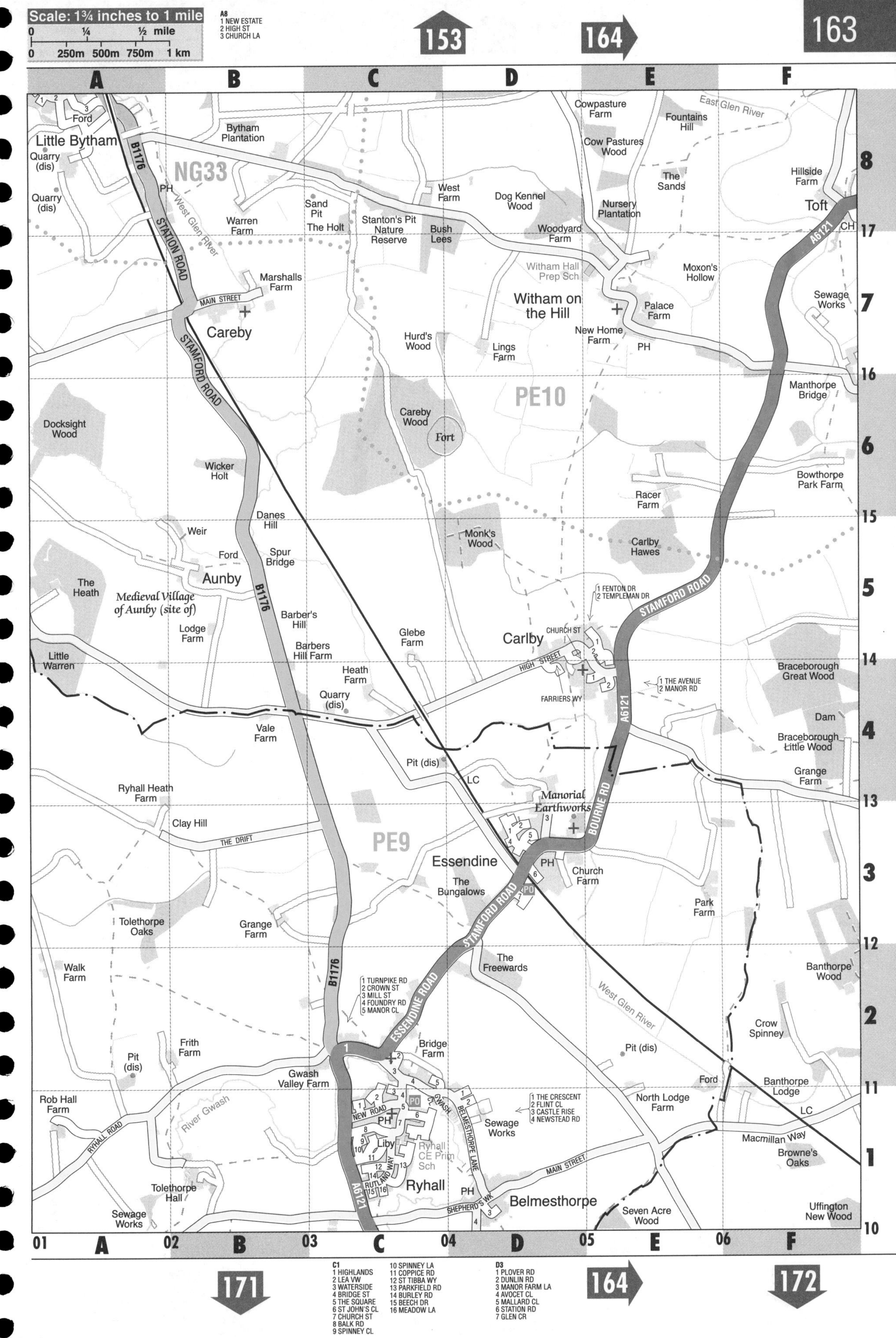

Scale: 1¾ inches to 1 mile

0   ¼   ½   mile
0 250m 500m 750m 1 km

A8
1 NEW ESTATE
2 HIGH ST
3 CHURCH LA

153
164

Little Bytham

Ford
Quarry (dis)
Quarry (dis)

NG33

B1176

West Glen River

STATION ROAD

Bytham Plantation

Sand Pit
The Holt
Warren Farm

Stanton's Pit Nature Reserve

West Farm

Dog Kennel Wood

Bush Lees

Woodyard Farm

Cowpasture Farm

Cow Pastures Wood

Fountains Hill

The Sands

Nursery Plantation

Witham Hall Prep Sch

Hillside Farm

Toft

A6121 CH

8

17

MAIN STREET

Marshalls Farm

Careby

Witham on the Hill

Moxon's Hollow

Sewage Works

7

STAMFORD ROAD

Hurd's Wood

Lings Farm

New Home Farm

Palace Farm

PH

Manthorpe Bridge

16

PE10

Docksight Wood

Wicker Holt

Careby Wood

Fort

Racer Farm

Carlby Hawes

Bowthorpe Park Farm

6

15

Danes Hill

Weir

Ford

Spur Bridge

Aunby

The Heath

Medieval Village of Aunby (site of)

Lodge Farm

Little Warren

B1176

Barber's Hill

Barbers Hill Farm

Heath Farm

Glebe Farm

Monk's Wood

1 FENTON DR
2 TEMPLEMAN DR

STAMFORD ROAD

Braceborough Great Wood

Dam

Braceborough Little Wood

Grange Farm

5

14

Quarry (dis)

Vale Farm

Pit (dis)

LC

CHURCH ST

Carlby

HIGH STREET

FARRIERS WY

1 THE AVENUE
2 MANOR RD

A6121

4

13

Ryhall Heath Farm

Clay Hill

THE DRIFT

PE9

Manorial Earthworks

3

BOURNE RD

Tolethorpe Oaks

Grange Farm

Essendine

The Bungalows

PH

Church Farm

Park Farm

3

12

Walk Farm

B1176

ESSENDINE ROAD

STAMFORD ROAD

The Freewards

West Glen River

Banthorpe Wood

2

Frith Farm

Pit (dis)

1 TURNPIKE RD
2 CROWN ST
3 MILL ST
4 FOUNDRY RD
5 MANOR CL

Bridge Farm

Crow Spinney

Rob Hall Farm

RYHALL ROAD

River Gwash

Gwash Valley Farm

1

NEW ROAD

PH

PO

GWASH WAY

Sewage Works

1 THE CRESCENT
2 FLINT CL
3 CASTLE RISE
4 NEWSTEAD RD

North Lodge Farm

Ford

Banthorpe Lodge

LC

11

Liby

Ryhall CE Prim Sch

Macmillan Way

Browne's Oaks

Tolethorpe Hall

A6121

RUTLAND WAY

BELMESTHORPE LANE

Ryhall

PH

SHEPHERD'S WK

Belmesthorpe

MAIN STREET

Seven Acre Wood

Uffington New Wood

Sewage Works

10

171
164
172

C1
1 HIGHLANDS
2 LEA VW
3 WATERSIDE
4 BRIDGE ST
5 THE SQUARE
6 ST JOHN'S CL
7 CHURCH ST
8 BALK RD
9 SPINNEY CL

10 SPINNEY LA
11 COPPICE RD
12 ST TIBBA WY
13 PARKFIELD RD
14 BURLEY RD
15 BEECH DR
16 MEADOW LA

D3
1 PLOVER RD
2 DUNLIN RD
3 MANOR FARM LA
4 AVOCET CL
5 MALLARD CL
6 STATION RD
7 GLEN CR

163 213 154

C8
1 WOODSIDE CL
2 CAPPITT DR
3 ELSEA DR
4 ELIZABETH WY
5 BECK WY
6 THE CAUSEWAY

7 VIKING WY
8 THE KIPPINGS
9 THE PINGLES
10 LAWRANCE WY
11 PINFOLD CL
12 PRIORY CL
13 MAPLE AVE

14 CROWN LA
15 PARK VW

E5
1 BRUDENELL CL
2 ST JOHNS CL
3 BEDE RD
4 MERCIA GR
5 THETFORD AVE
6 CHARIOTS WY

7 CAESAR CL
8 APPIAN WY
9 FOSSE CL
10 HADRIAN DR
11 MANOR CL
12 MANOR DR
13 CARDYKE DR

Scale: 1¾ inches to 1 mile
0   ¼   ½   mile
0   250m   500m   750m   1 km

Northorpe Fen Farm
Northorpe Fen
Northorpe
West Farm
WOOD LANE
NORTHORPE
WOODSIDE EAST
FEN ROAD
MAIN ROAD
BOURNE ROAD
Thurlby
Thurlby Com Prim Sch
WATER
THE GREEN
Mast
SWALLOW HILL
STATION ROAD
SWIFT WY
PE10
Manthorpe
Church Farm
Home Farm
TUDOR CL
HIGH ST
YH
Elm Farm
St Firmin's
ST FIRMIN'S WY
CHURCH STREET
LONG DROVE
SHORT DROVE
MANTHORPE DROVE
LAWRENCE'S DV
Thurlby Fen
Thurlby Fen Nature Reserve
BASTON FEN DROVE
Poplar Tree Farm
Red House Farm
HACK'S DROVE
Hack's Plantation
MACMILLAN WAY
Playing Field
Park Wood
Katesbridge Farm
Cross Farm
Dole Wood Nature Reserve
OBTHORPE LANE
Manor Farm
Obthorpe Lodge
Obthorpe
Thetford House Farm
Thetford
Fringes Fen
Kate's Bridge Weir
Fletland
Cemy
Works
Brook House Farm
Baston CE Prim Sch
PH
Sand & Gravel Pit
Baston
PE6
Spa Lodge Farm
EAST GLEN RIVER
Old Hall Farm
Wilsthorpe
Mill Farm
GREATFORD RD
KING STREET
Kirkstone House Sch
MAIN STREET
PO
MALTBY DR 1
FRISBY CL 2
WHATTOFF WY 3
40
DEEPING ROAD
Windmill
Middle Field
Moat
Church Farm
Manor Farm
Braceborough Great Wood
Lodge Farm
Braceborough
ELLIOTT'S WY
Church Farm
MACMILLAN WAY
Meadow Field
Truesdale Lodge
Stonehouse Farm
BOURNE ROAD
A15
EAST END
NEW ROAD
Cemy
PETERBOROUGH ROAD
PE9
Banthorpe Wood
Bottom Meadow
Middle Field
Red Inn Field
MANOR CL 1
MOSSOP DR 2
SCOTT'S CL 3
TRUESDALE GDNS 4
Langtoft Prim Sch
PO
40
Nook Field
Langtoft
WEST END
Dogkennel Plantation
MACMILLAN WAY
Greatford
GREATFORD GD
The Council Houses
Greatford Hall
PH
Glen Farm
MAIN STREET
Shillingthorpe Park
WEST GLEN RIVER
Greatford Wood
Weir
Manor Farm
Parsonage Field
Banks Farm
West Field
PH
Barholm
Old Hall
Marsh Plantation
Cank Wood
Great Maidens
Cow Pasture Plantation
Cedar Plantation
Casewick Field
Beck Field
Sand & Gravel Pit
Stowe Farm
STOWE ROAD
DICKENS CL
Bleak House Farm
KING STREET
1 WHEATFIELD
2 AQUILA WY
3 BARLEYFIELD
4 WESTFIELD WY
Middle Field
Tithe Farm
Greatford Cut
Far Field
Rectory Farm
Crown Farm
Towngate
MILLFIELD RD
Mill Field
A16

E4
1 SCHOOL LA
2 CHURCH ST
3 AVELAND WY
4 CLARE CT
5 DENSHIRE CT
6 COLTON CL
7 CHESHAM DR

F3
1 BARN OWL CL
2 LIME CL
3 DEER PK RD
4 CLOVEN ENDS
5 REEDMANS CL
6 MANOR WY
7 THE RIDES

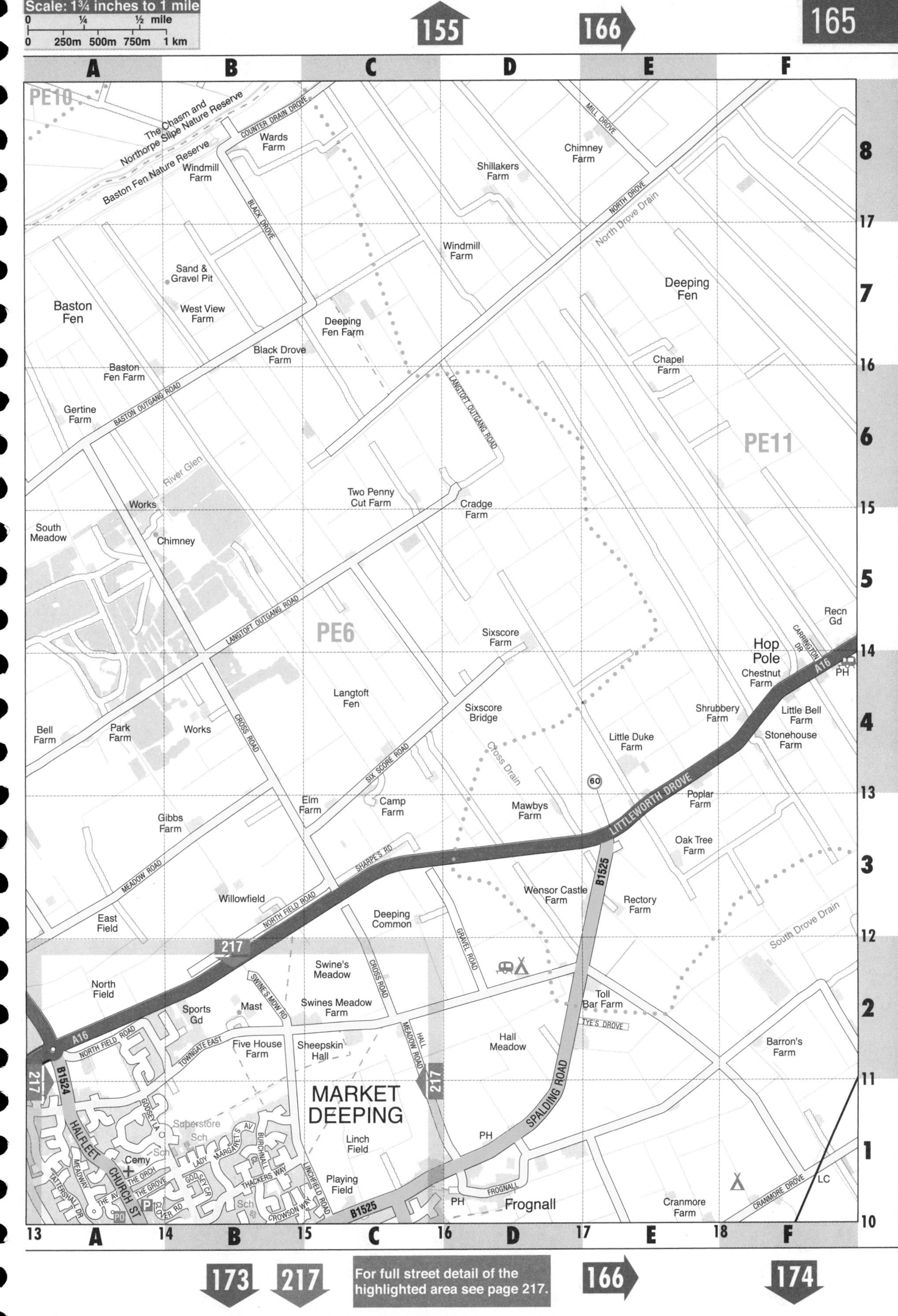

155

166

Scale: 1¾ inches to 1 mile

0   ¼   ½   mile
0   250m 500m 750m 1 km

PE10

A   B   C   D   E   F

The Chasm and
Northorpe Slipe Nature Reserve

Baston Fen Nature Reserve

Wards
Farm

COUNTER DRAIN DROVE

Windmill
Farm

Shillakers
Farm

Chimney
Farm

MILL DROVE

NORTH DROVE

8

17

Sand &
Gravel Pit

West View
Farm

Windmill
Farm

Deeping
Fen

North Drove Drain

7

Baston
Fen

BLACK DROVE

Deeping
Fen Farm

Black Drove
Farm

Chapel
Farm

PE11

16

Baston
Fen Farm

BASTON OUTGANG ROAD

Gertine
Farm

LANGTOFT OUTGANG ROAD

6

River Glen

Works

South
Meadow

Chimney

Two Penny
Cut Farm

Cradge
Farm

15

LANGTOFT OUTGANG ROAD

PE6

Sixscore
Farm

Recn
Gd

CARRINGTON DR

Hop
Pole

A16

5

Bell
Farm

Park
Farm

Works

CROSS ROAD

Langtoft
Fen

Sixscore
Bridge

Cross Drain

Little Duke
Farm

Shrubbery
Farm

Chestnut
Farm

PH

Little Bell
Farm

Stonehouse
Farm

14

4

SIX SCORE ROAD

Gibbs
Farm

Elm
Farm

Camp
Farm

Mawbys
Farm

60

LITTLEWORTH DROVE

Poplar
Farm

Oak Tree
Farm

13

MEADOW ROAD

SHARPE'S RD

Willowfield

NORTH FIELD ROAD

East
Field

Deeping
Common

GRAVEL ROAD

Wensor Castle
Farm

B1525

Rectory
Farm

South Drove Drain

3

217

Swine's
Meadow

CROSS ROAD

Toll
Bar Farm

TYE'S DROVE

12

North
Field

NORTH FIELD ROAD

Sports
Gd

Mast

SWINE'S MOW RD

Swines Meadow
Farm

Five House
Farm

Sheepskin
Hall

HALL MEADOW ROAD

217

Hall
Meadow

SPALDING ROAD

Barron's
Farm

2

A16

217

B1524

TOWNGATE EAST

MARKET
DEEPING

Linch
Field

PH

11

HALFLEET

CHURCH ST

Superstore

Sch

ST MARGARET'S AV

BIRCHNALL ROAD

LINCHFIELD ROAD

Playing
Field

Sch

B1525

PH

FROGNALL

Frognall

Cranmore
Farm

CRANMORE DROVE

LC

1

Cemy

PO

THE GROVE

CROWSON WY

10

13   A   14   B   15   C   16   D   17   E   18   F

173   217

For full street detail of the
highlighted area see page 217.

166   174

165
156
174
165
175

C6
1 WOODBANK
2 CORONATION AVE
3 CHAPPELL RD
4 BARLEY GR
5 HARVEST MEWS
6 HAYWAIN DR

7 FALLOW FIELDS
8 WHEATSHEAF CT

Scale: 1¾ inches to 1 mile

0   ¼   ½ mile

0   250 500 750   1 k

A   B   C   D   E   F

Deeping Fen

GREEN LANE

A16

Bar Farm

Willow Tree Farm

Ash Tree Farm

EAST ROAD

Lucksbridge Farm

Welland Farm

Worth's Farm

St Nicholas House

Deeping Farm

EAST RD

Spalding South Fen

CAMPAIN'S LA

Bottom Yard Farm

THE AVENUE

LC

CAMPAIN'S LA

LITTLEWORTH DRIVE

Church Farm

SOUTH DROVE DRAIN

Greenlands Farm

BELLINGHAM'S DROVE

HARROW RD

Harrow Farm

PH

Deeping St Nicholas

Deeping Fen

PE11

Porters Farm

Victoria Farm

Station Farm

The Gull

LC

WHEAT CL

Deeping St Nicholas Prim Sch

NEW ROAD

Gull House Farm

Hospital Farm

Cloot House

Blue House Farm

LC

East Reach Farm

Halfway Farm

LC

Smith's Bridge

NEW ROAD

A16

Works

WELLAND BANK

Wash Bank

Wensor Farm

NEW RIVER

CLOOT DRIVE

Law's Farm

Deeping Fen

Crowland Falls

SOUTH DROVE DRAIN

Pits (dis)

Little Lodge Farm

Common Drove Farm

RENEW'S DROVE

Willow Fall Farm

RAISIN'S DYKE

Crowland Common

SECOND DROVE

FIRST DROVE

Crowland Fodder Lots

PE6

FOREST DROVE

COMMON DROVE

ASKEW'S DROVE

Tooleys Farm

Elm Farm

Crowland Low Wash

Crowland Ponds Nature Reserve

North Bank Farm

The St Guthlac Sch

LC

PH

Fen Bridge

WEST BANK

KEMP ST

HALL ST

POSTLAND RD

B1166

CRANMORE DROVE

Stowgate Farm

Crowland Water Tower

GRAVEL CW

WEST BANK

MIDDLE RD

NORTH ST

Library

A1073

THE CHASE

Pastures Farm

B1166

Crowland

Hides Farm

WELLAND BANK

South View Com Primary School

Hotel

Abbey (remains of)

Fleet Hall

E1
1 FOREMAN WY
2 HIGH WASH DRO
3 NORTH ST
4 CLUTTON'S CL
5 THE WILLOWS
6 ST MARKS DR
7 WEST ST
8 ALBION ST
9 REFORM ST

10 TRINITY CL
11 HORSESHOE YD
12 CORPORATION BANK

F1
1 NORMANTON RD
2 GIRDLESTONE WK
3 THE GARDENS
4 EASTLANDS
5 NELSON CL
6 MILLFIELD GDNS
7 CHURCH LA
8 ST GUTHLAC'S CL
9 AMBURY GDNS

10 ABBEY WK
11 ABBEY MEWS
12 ST MARY CL
13 WYCHE AVE
14 TORFRID CL
15 CROYLAND WY
16 GODIVA CL
17 ST PEGA CL
18 ST BENEDICT CL
19 LEOFRIC CL

20 SOUTH ST
21 HEREWARD WY
22 BURGHLEY CL

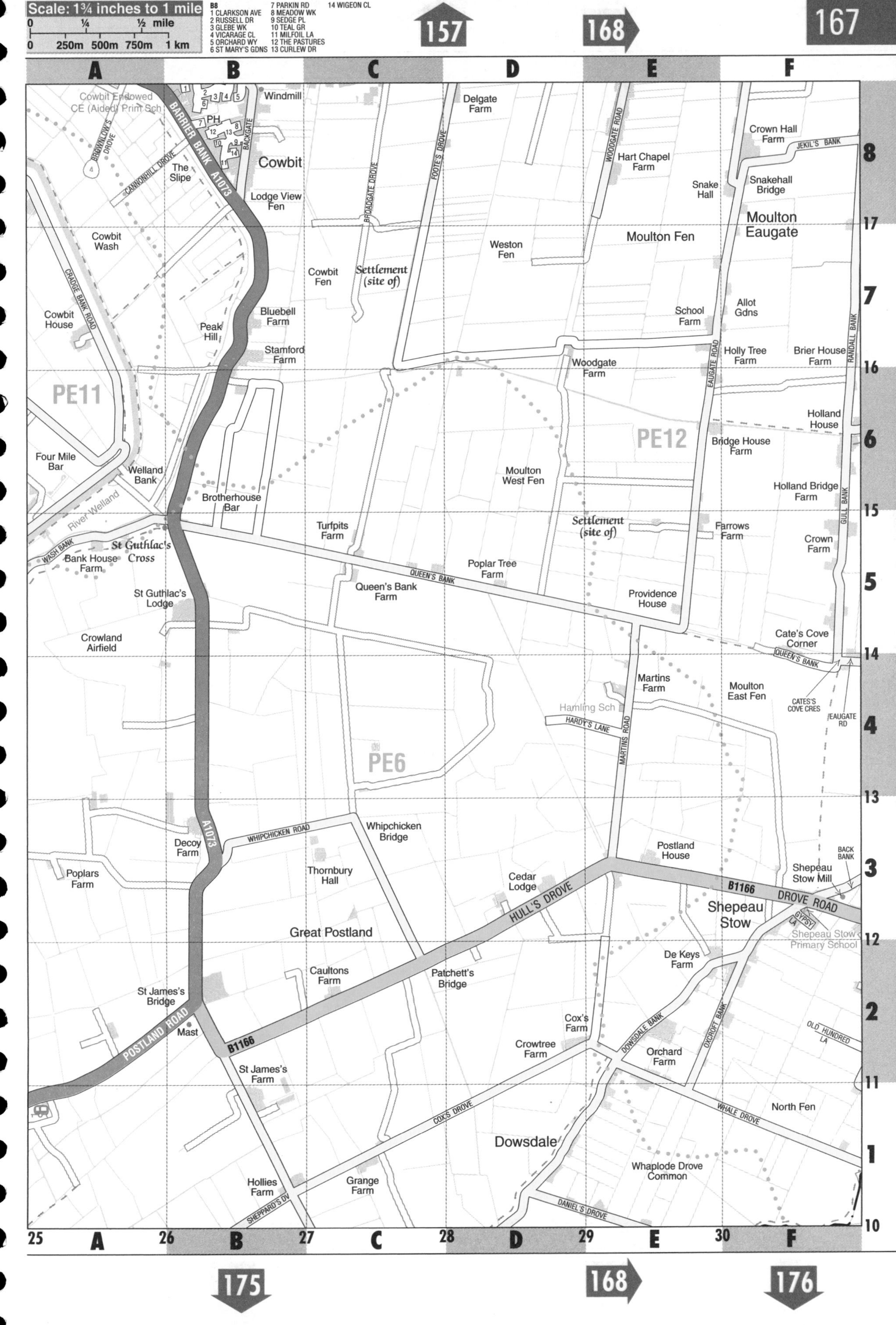
Scale: 1¾ inches to 1 mile
B8
1 CLARKSON AVE
2 RUSSELL DR
3 GLEBE WK
4 VICARAGE CL
5 ORCHARD WY
6 ST MARY'S GDNS
7 PARKIN RD
8 MEADOW WK
9 SEDGE PL
10 TEAL GR
11 MILFOIL LA
12 THE PASTURES
13 CURLEW DR
14 WIGEON CL
157
168
Cowbit
Windmill
Delgate Farm
Hart Chapel Farm
Crown Hall Farm
JEKIL'S BANK
Snake Hall
Snakehall Bridge
Moulton Eaugate
Moulton Fen
Weston Fen
Cowbit Endowed CE (Aided) Prim Sch
BARRIER BANK A1073
BROWNLOW'S DROVE
CANNONHILL DROVE
The Slipe
Lodge View Fen
BACKGATE
BROADGATE DROVE
FOOTE'S DROVE
WOODGATE ROAD
Cowbit Wash
CRADGE BANK ROAD
Cowbit House
Cowbit Fen
Settlement (site of)
Bluebell Farm
Peak Hill
Stamford Farm
School Farm
Allot Gdns
Holly Tree Farm
Brier House Farm
RANDALL BANK
Woodgate Farm
EAUGATE ROAD
PE11
PE12
Holland House
Bridge House Farm
Four Mile Bar
Welland Bank
Moulton West Fen
Brotherhouse Bar
Holland Bridge Farm
River Welland
GULL BANK
WASH BANK
St Guthlac's Cross
Bank House Farm
Turfpits Farm
Farrows Farm
Crown Farm
QUEEN'S BANK
Poplar Tree Farm
St Guthlac's Lodge
Queen's Bank Farm
Providence House
Crowland Airfield
Cate's Cove Corner
Martins Farm
Moulton East Fen
CATE'S COVE CRES
EAUGATE RD
Hamling Sch
HARDY'S LANE
MARTINS ROAD
PE6
WHIPCHICKEN ROAD
Whipchicken Bridge
A1073
Decoy Farm
Postland House
BACK BANK
Poplars Farm
Thornbury Hall
Cedar Lodge
Shepeau Stow Mill
B1166
DROVE ROAD
HULL'S DROVE
Shepeau Stow
GYPSY LA
Shepeau Stow Primary School
Great Postland
De Keys Farm
Caultons Farm
Patchett's Bridge
St James's Bridge
POSTLAND ROAD
Mast
Cox's Farm
DOWSDALE BANK
OXCROFT BANK
OLD HUNDRED LA
B1166
Crowtree Farm
Orchard Farm
St James's Farm
WHALE DROVE
North Fen
COX'S DROVE
Dowsdale
Whaplode Drove Common
Hollies Farm
Grange Farm
SHEPPARD'S DV
DANIEL'S DROVE
A B C D E F
25 26 27 28 29 30
8 17 7 16 6 15 5 14 4 13 3 12 2 11 1 10
175
168
176

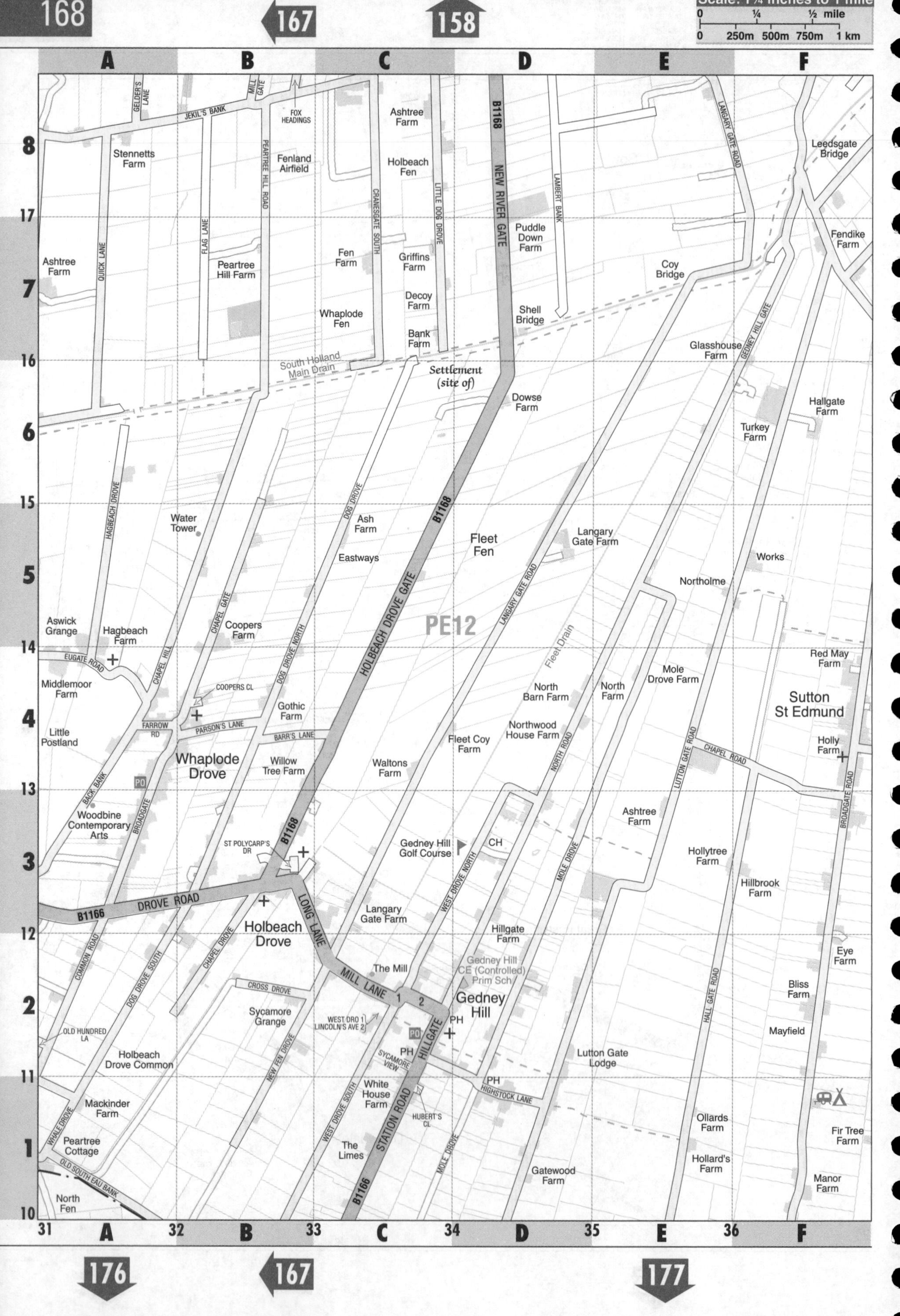

168

← 167

↑ 158

Scale: 1¾ inches to 1 mile
0   ¼   ½   mile
0   250m 500m 750m 1 km

A   B   C   D   E   F

8

17

7

16

6

15

5

14

4

13

3

12

2

11

1

10

Gelder's Lane
Jekil's Bank
Mill Gate
Fox Headings
Ashtree Farm
B1168
Langary Gate Road
Leedsgate Bridge

Stennetts Farm
Fenland Airfield
Holbeach Fen
New River Gate
Lambert Bank
Fendike Farm

Quick Lane
Peartree Hill Road
Flag Lane
Cranesgate South
Little Dog Drove
Puddle Down Farm
Coy Bridge

Ashtree Farm
Peartree Hill Farm
Fen Farm
Griffins Farm
Shell Bridge
Glasshouse Farm
Gedney Hill Gate
Hallgate Farm

Whaplode Fen
Decoy Farm
Bank Farm
Settlement (site of)
South Holland Main Drain
Dowse Farm
Turkey Farm

Hagbeach Drove
Water Tower
Dog Drove
Ash Farm
Eastways
Holbeach Drove Gate
B1168
Fleet Fen
Langary Gate Farm
Works

Aswick Grange
Hagbeach Farm
Chapel Hill
Chapel Gate
Coopers Farm
Dog Drove North
PE12
Northolme
Red May Farm

Eugate Road
Middlemoor Farm
Coopers Cl
Gothic Farm
Fleet Drain
North Barn Farm
North Farm
Mole Drove Farm
Sutton St Edmund

Farrow Rd
Parson's Lane
Barr's Lane
Fleet Coy Farm
Northwood House Farm
Chapel Road
Holly Farm

Little Postland
Back Bank
Whaplode Drove
Willow Tree Farm
Waltons Farm
Langary Gate Road
North Road
Ashtree Farm
Lutton Gate Road
Hollytree Farm

Woodbine Contemporary Arts
PO
Broadgate
St Polycarp's Dr
B1168
Gedney Hill Golf Course
CH
Hillbrook Farm
Broadgate

B1166
Drove Road
Long Lane
Langary Gate Farm
West Drove North
Hillgate Farm
Mole Drove

Holbeach Drove
Chapel Drove
Mill Lane
The Mill
Gedney Hill CE (Controlled) Prim Sch
Eye Farm

Cross Drove
Sycamore Grange
New Fen Drove
1 2
Gedney Hill
Hillgate
Hall Gate Road
Bliss Farm

Old Hundred La
Holbeach Drove Common
Dog Drove South
West Dro 1 Lincoln's Ave 2
PO
PH
Lutton Gate Lodge
Mayfield

Whale Drove
Mackinder Farm
Sycamore View
PH
Highstock Lane
PH
Ollards Farm
Fir Tree Farm

Peartree Cottage
West Drove South
White House Farm
Hubert's Cl
Mole Drove
Hollard's Farm
Manor Farm

Old South Eau Bank
North Fen
The Limes
Station Road
B1166
Gatewood Farm

31   A   32   B   33   C   34   D   35   E   36   F

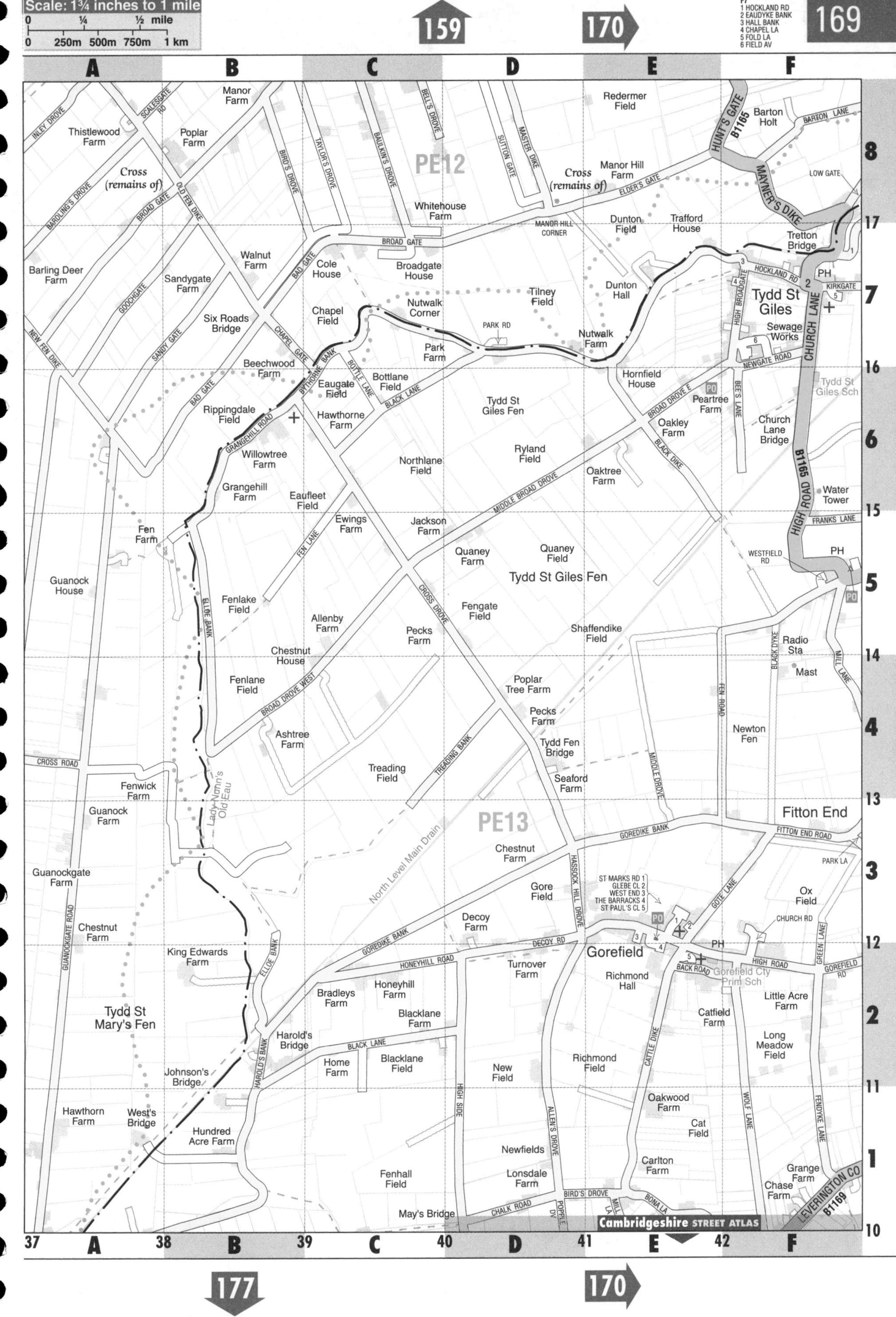

Scale: 1¾ inches to 1 mile

0   ¼   ½   mile
0 250m 500m 750m 1 km

159

170

169

F7
1 HOCKLAND RD
2 EAUDYKE BANK
3 HALL BANK
4 CHAPEL LA
5 FOLD LA
6 FIELD AV

A B C D E F

8
17
7
16
6
15
5
14
4
13
3
12
2
11
1
10

INLEY DROVE
Thistlewood Farm
Manor Farm
SCALESGATE RD
Poplar Farm
BIRD'S DROVE
TAYLOR'S DROVE
BAULKIN'S DROVE
BELL'S DROVE
SUTTON GATE
MASTER DIKE
Redermer Field
Cross (remains of)
HUNT'S GATE
Barton Holt
BARTON LANE
B1165
MAYNER'S DIKE
LOW GATE

Cross (remains of)
BROAD GATE
OLD FEN DIKE
PE12
Manor Hill Farm
ELDER'S GATE

Barling Deer Farm
GOOCHGATE
Walnut Farm
BROAD GATE
Whitehouse Farm
BROAD GATE
Broadgate House
MANOR HILL CORNER
Dunton Field
Trafford House
HOCKLAND RD
Tretton Bridge
3
PH
KIRKGATE

Sandygate Farm
Cole House
Tilney Field
Dunton Hall
4
Tydd St Giles
5

NEW FEN DIKE
SANDY GATE
Six Roads Bridge
Chapel Field
Nutwalk Corner
PARK RD
Nutwalk Farm
HIGH BROGATE
NEWGATE ROAD
CHURCH LANE
Sewage Works
6

Beechwood Farm
CHAPEL GATE
BAD GATE
BLYTHORNE BANK
Eaugate Field
Bottlane Field
BLACK LANE
Park Farm
Hornfield House
BROAD DROVE E
BEE'S LANE
Peartree Farm
Church Lane Bridge
B1165

Rippingdale Field
GRANGEHILL ROAD
Hawthorne Farm
BOTTLE LANE
Tydd St Giles Fen
Oakley Farm
PO
Tydd St Giles Sch

Willowtree Farm
Northlane Field
Ryland Field
Oaktree Farm
BLACK DIKE
HIGH ROAD
Water Tower
FRANKS LANE

Grangehill Farm
Eaufleet Field
MIDDLE BROAD DROVE
WESTFIELD RD
PH

Fen Farm
FEN LANE
Ewings Farm
Jackson Farm
Quaney Farm
Quaney Field
Tydd St Giles Fen
Shaffendike Field
PO

ELLOE BANK
Fenlake Field
Allenby Farm
Pecks Farm
Fengate Field
Radio Sta
BLACK DYKE
MILL LANE
Mast

Guanock House
CROSS DROVE
Chestnut House
Poplar Tree Farm
Pecks Farm
FEN ROAD
Newton Fen

Fenlane Field
BROAD DROVE WEST
Tydd Fen Bridge
MIDDLE DROVE

Ashtree Farm
Treading Field
TREADING BANK
Seaford Farm
Fitton End

CROSS ROAD
Fenwick Farm
North Level Main Drain
PE13
FITTON END ROAD
PARK LA

Guanock Farm
Chestnut Farm
GOREDIKE BANK
Gore Field
HASSOCK HILL DROVE
ST MARKS RD 1
GLEBE CL 2
WEST END 3
THE BARRACKS 4
ST PAUL'S CL 5
Ox Field

Guanockgate Farm
GUANOCKGATE ROAD
Chestnut Farm
ELLOE BANK
HAROLD'S BANK
GOREDIKE BANK
HONEYHILL ROAD
Decoy Farm
DECOY RD
GOTE LANE
PO
CHURCH RD
PH

King Edwards Farm
Turnover Farm
Richmond Hall
HIGH ROAD
GOREFIELD RD
GREEN LANE
BACK ROAD
Gorefield City Prim Sch
Little Acre Farm

Tydd St Mary's Fen
Bradleys Farm
Honeyhill Farm
Gorefield
Catfield Farm
Long Meadow Field

Johnson's Bridge
Harold's Bridge
BLACK LANE
Blacklane Farm
Richmond Field
CATTLE DIKE
Oakwood Farm
WOLF LANE
Cat Field
FENDYKE LANE

Hawthorn Farm
West's Bridge
Home Farm
Blacklane Field
New Field
Carlton Farm
Grange Farm
Chase Farm

Hundred Acre Farm
HIGH SIDE
ALLEN'S DROVE
Newfields
BIRD'S DROVE
MILL
BONA LA
LEVERINGTON CO
B1169

Fenhall Field
Lonsdale Farm
POPPLE DV
May's Bridge
CHALK ROAD

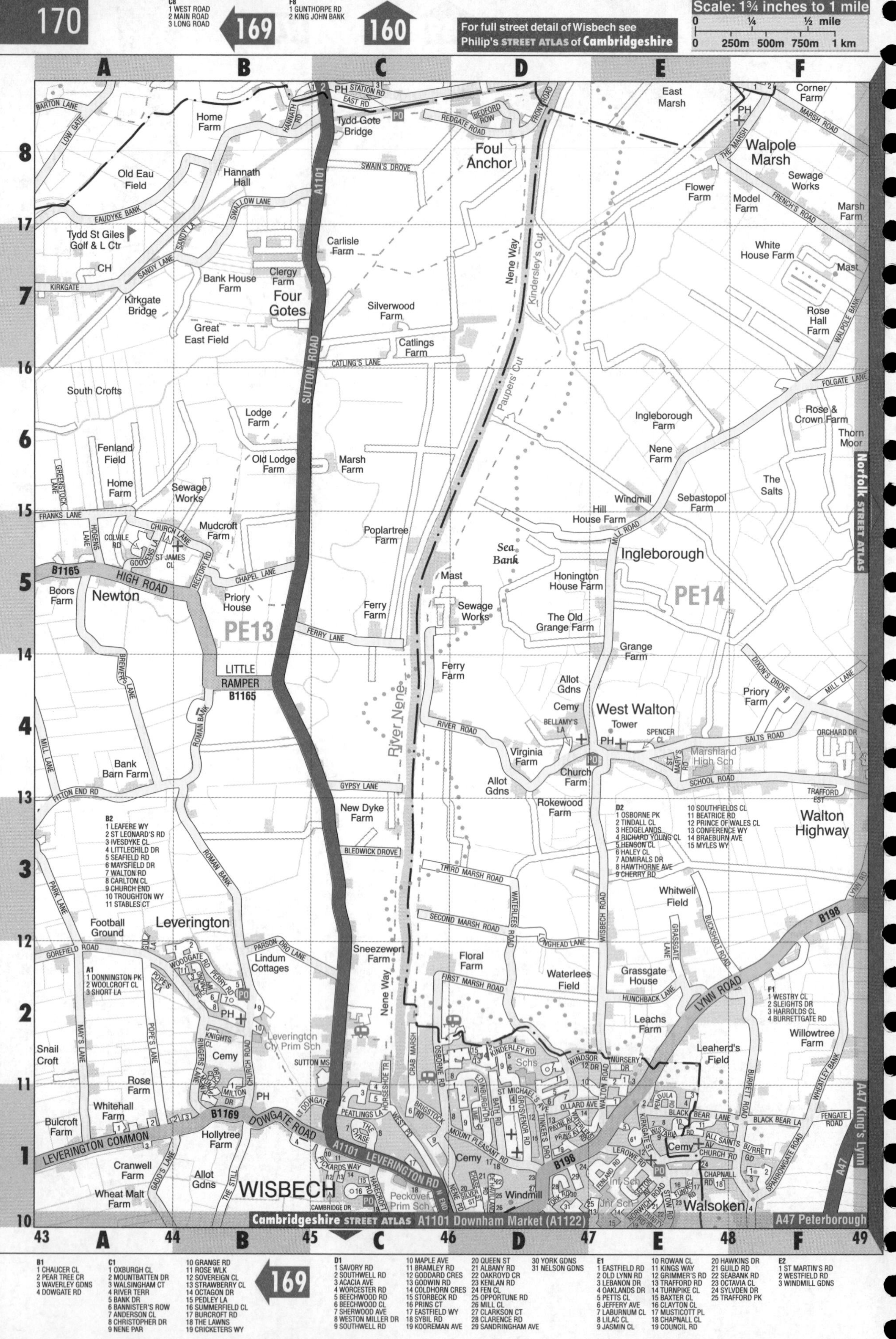
C8
1 WEST ROAD
2 MAIN ROAD
3 LONG ROAD
169
F8
1 GUNTHORPE RD
2 KING JOHN BANK
160
For full street detail of Wisbech see
Philip's STREET ATLAS of Cambridgeshire
Scale: 1¾ inches to 1 mile
0 ¼ ½ mile
0 250m 500m 750m 1 km
Home Farm
Tydd Gote Bridge
Foul Anchor
East Marsh
Corner Farm
Walpole Marsh
Old Eau Field
Hannath Hall
Sewage Works
Flower Farm
Model Farm
Marsh Farm
Tydd St Giles Golf & L Ctr
Carlisle Farm
White House Farm
Bank House Farm
Clergy Farm
Four Gotes
Kirkgate Bridge
Silverwood Farm
Nene Way
Kindersley's Cut
Rose Hall Farm
Great East Field
Catlings Farm
South Crofts
Paupers' Cut
Lodge Farm
Ingleborough Farm
Rose & Crown Farm
Fenland Field
Old Lodge Farm
Marsh Farm
Nene Farm
Thorn Moor
Home Farm
Sewage Works
The Salts
Windmill
Sebastopol Farm
Hill House Farm
Mudcroft Farm
Poplartree Farm
Sea Bank
Ingleborough
Mast
Honington House Farm
Boors Farm
Newton
Priory House
PE13
Ferry Farm
Sewage Works
The Old Grange Farm
PE14
Grange Farm
LITTLE RAMPER
B1165
Ferry Farm
Allot Gdns
West Walton
Priory Farm
Cemy
Tower
River Nene
Virginia Farm
Marshland High Sch
Bank Barn Farm
Church Farm
Allot Gdns
New Dyke Farm
Rokewood Farm
Walton Highway
B2
1 LEAFERE WY
2 ST LEONARD'S RD
3 IVESDYKE CL
4 LITTLECHILD DR
5 SEAFIELD RD
6 MAYSFIELD DR
7 WALTON RD
8 CARLTON CL
9 CHURCH END
10 TROUGHTON WY
11 STABLES CT
D2
1 OSBORNE PK
2 TINDALL CL
3 HEDGELANDS
4 RICHARD YOUNG CL
5 HENSON CL
6 HALEY CL
7 ADMIRALS DR
8 HAWTHORNE AVE
9 CHERRY RD
10 SOUTHFIELDS CL
11 BEATRICE RD
12 PRINCE OF WALES CL
13 CONFERENCE WY
14 BRAEBURN AVE
15 MYLES WY
Whitwell Field
Football Ground
Leverington
Sneezewort Farm
Floral Farm
Lindum Cottages
Waterlees Field
Grassgate House
A1
1 DONNINGTON PK
2 WOOLCROFT CL
3 SHORT LA
Leachs Farm
F1
1 WESTRY CL
2 SLEIGHTS DR
3 HARROLDS CL
4 BURRETTGATE RD
Willowtree Farm
Leverington Cty Prim Sch
Leaherd's Field
Snail Croft
Cemy
Rose Farm
Whitehall Farm
Bulcroft Farm
Hollytree Farm
Cemy
Cranwell Farm
Allot Gdns
Wheat Malt Farm
WISBECH
Peckover Prim Sch
Windmill
Walsoken
A47 King's Lynn
Norfolk STREET ATLAS
Cambridgeshire STREET ATLAS
A1101 Downham Market (A1122)
A47 Peterborough
B1
1 CHAUCER CL
2 PEAR TREE CR
3 WAVERLEY GDNS
4 DOWGATE RD
C1
1 OXBURGH CL
2 MOUNTBATTEN DR
3 WALSINGHAM CT
4 RIVER TERR
5 BANK DR
6 BANNISTER'S ROW
7 ANDERSON CL
8 CHRISTOPHER DR
9 NENE PAR
10 GRANGE RD
11 ROSE WLK
12 SOVEREIGN CL
13 STRAWBERRY CL
14 OCTAGON DR
15 PEDLEY LA
16 SUMMERFIELD CL
17 BURCROFT RD
18 THE LAWNS
19 CRICKETERS WY
169
D1
1 SAVORY RD
2 SOUTHWELL RD
3 ACACIA AVE
4 WORCESTER RD
5 BEECHWOOD RD
6 BEECHWOOD CL
7 SHERWOOD AVE
8 WESTON MILLER DR
9 SOUTHWELL RD
10 MAPLE AVE
11 BRAMLEY RD
12 GODDARD CRES
13 GODWIN RD
14 COLDHORN CRES
15 STORBECK RD
16 PRINS CT
17 EASTFIELD WY
18 SYBIL RD
19 KOOREMAN AVE
20 QUEEN ST
21 ALBANY RD
22 OAKROYD CR
23 KENLAN RD
24 FEN CL
25 OPPORTUNE RD
26 MILL CL
27 CLARKSON CT
28 CLARENCE RD
29 SANDRINGHAM AVE
30 YORK GDNS
31 NELSON GDNS
E1
1 EASTFIELD RD
2 OLD LYNN RD
3 LEBANON DR
4 OAKLANDS DR
5 PETTS CL
6 JEFFERY AVE
7 LABURNUM CL
8 LILAC CL
9 JASMIN CL
10 ROWAN CL
11 KINGS WAY
12 GRIMMER'S RD
13 TRAFFORD RD
14 TURNPIKE CL
15 BAXTER CL
16 CLAYTON CL
17 MUSTICOTT PL
18 CHAPNALL CL
19 COUNCIL RD
20 HAWKINS DR
21 GUILD RD
22 SEABANK RD
23 OCTAVIA CL
24 SYLVDEN DR
25 TRAFFORD PK
E2
1 ST MARTIN'S RD
2 WESTFIELD RD
3 WINDMILL GDNS

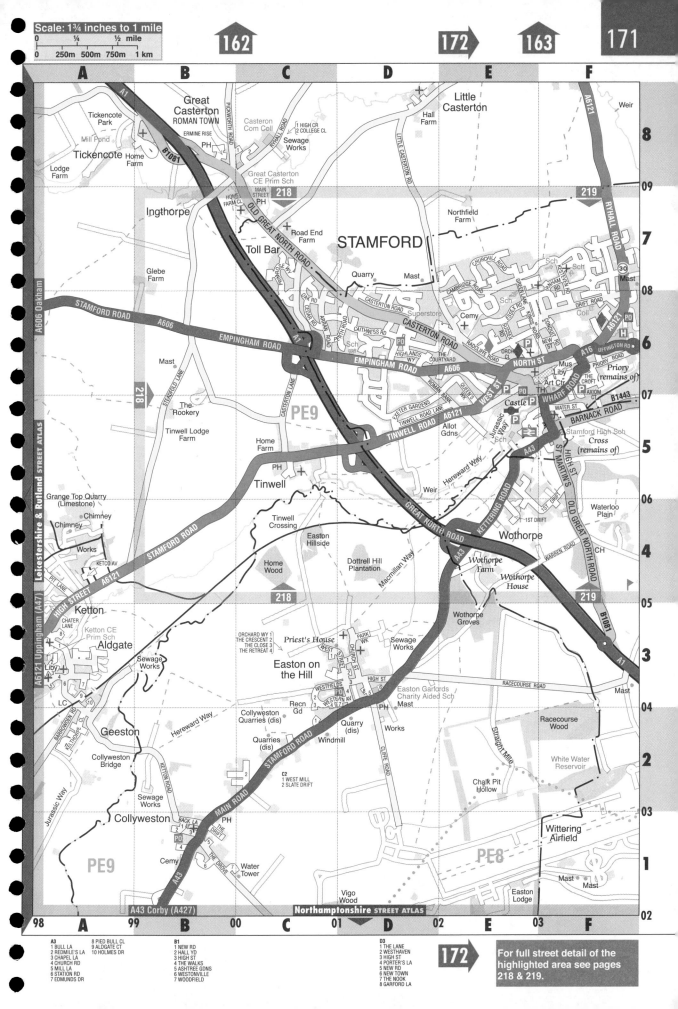

Scale: 1¾ inches to 1 mile

0   ¼   ½ mile
0 250m 500m 750m 1 km

162

172

163

171

A   B   C   D   E   F

8
09
7
08
6
07
5
06
4
05
3
04
2
03
1
02

Tickencote Park
Mill Pond
Lodge Farm
Tickencote
Home Farm

Great Casterton
ROMAN TOWN
ERMINE RISE
PH

Casterton Com Coll
1 HIGH CR
2 COLLEGE CL
Sewage Works
Great Casterton CE Prim Sch

Little Casterton
Hall Farm

Weir

Northfield Farm

STAMFORD

Ingthorpe
Glebe Farm

HOME FARM CL
MAIN STREET
PH
218

Toll Bar
Road End Farm

Churchill Road
Sch   Sch
30 Mast

Quarry
Mast

Cambridge Road
Greenlane Road
Drift Road
Coll
PO
H

219
RYHALL ROAD

A1

B1081

OLD GREAT NORTH ROAD

STAMFORD ROAD
A606
EMPINGHAM ROAD
A606

Mast

The Rookery

Tinwell Lodge Farm

PE9

Home Farm
PH

Tinwell

A6121

Grange Top Quarry (Limestone)
Chimney
Chimney
Works
KETCO AV
PIT LANE
A6121

Ketton
CHATER LANE
Ketton CE Prim Sch
Aldgate
Liby
LC

Geeston
Collyweston Bridge
KETTON ROAD
BARROWDEN RD
KELTHORPE CL

Sewage Works

Collyweston
BACK LA
PO
THE DRIFT
MAIN ROAD
THE DROVE
Cemy
A43

PE9

Jurassic Way

Water Tower

HIGH STREET
A6121 Uppingham (A47)

A606 Oakham

CASTERTON ROAD
Superstore
Cemy
PO
Sch
THE COURTYARD
HIGHLANDS WY
RADCLIFFE ROAD
ORCH CL
Essex Rd
Kings Rd
Sussex Rd
Conduit Rd
NEW ST
A16
DRIFT ROAD
UFFINGTON RD
A6121

EMPINGHAM ROAD
A606
ROMAN BANK
QUEEN'S ST
EXETER GARDENS
TINWELL ROAD LANE
A6121
North St
Mus
Liby
Art Ctr
TH
Castle
P
PO
P
P
WATER ST
WEST ST
WHARF ROAD
The Croft
AXIOM
Priory (remains of)
PRIORY ROAD
B1443
BARNACK ROAD
St Martin's
HIGH ST
Stamford High Sch
Cross (remains of)
Waterloo Plain
1ST DRIFT
WARREN ROAD

Allot Gdns
Jurassic Way
Jurassic Sch
Hereward Way
Weir

TINWELL ROAD
A6121
GREAT NORTH ROAD
KETTERING ROAD
A43
1ST DRIFT
Wothorpe
CH
OLD GREAT NORTH ROAD

Tinwell Crossing
Easton Hillside
Dottrell Hill Plantation
Macmillan Way
Home Wood

218

Wothorpe Farm
Wothorpe House
219
A1
B1081

Racecourse Wood
White Water Reservoir
Racecourse Road
Mast

Wothorpe Groves

ORCHARD WY 1
THE CRESCENT 2
THE CLOSE 3
THE RETREAT 4
WEST STREET
CHURCH ST
PARK WK
Priest's House
PH

Easton on the Hill
WESTFIELDS
WESTERN AV
HIGH ST
PO
Recn Gd
Quarry (dis)
Sewage Works

Easton Garfields Charity Aided Sch
Mast
Works

Collyweston Quarries (dis)
Quarries (dis)
Windmill
C2
1 WEST MILL
2 SLATE DRIFT

STAMFORD ROAD
CLIFFE ROAD

Hereward Way

Chalk Pit Hollow
Straight Mile

Wittering Airfield

PE8

Vigo Wood
Mast   Mast
Easton Lodge

A3
1 BULL LA
2 REDMILE'S LA
3 CHAPEL LA
4 CHURCH RD
5 MILL LA
6 STATION RD
7 EDMUNDS DR
8 PIED BULL CL
9 ALDGATE CT
10 HOLMES DR

B1
1 NEW RD
2 HALL YD
3 HIGH ST
4 THE WALKS
5 ASHTREE GDNS
6 WESTONVILLE
7 WOODFIELD

D3
1 THE LANE
2 WESTHAVEN
3 HIGH ST
4 PORTER'S LA
5 NEW RD
6 NEW TOWN
7 THE NOOK
8 GARFORD LA

For full street detail of the highlighted area see pages 218 & 219.

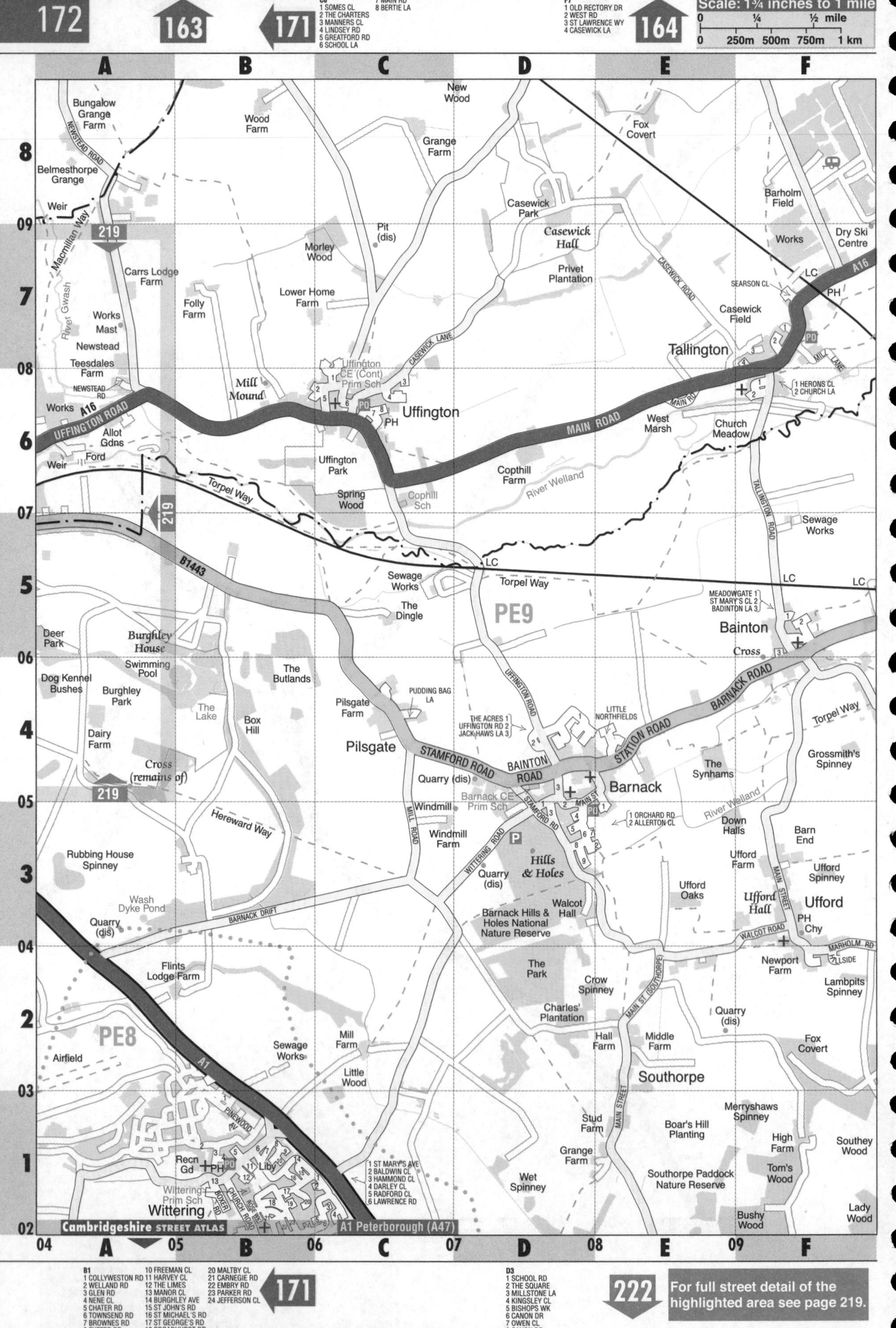

172

163

171

164

Scale: 1¾ inches to 1 mile
0   ¼   ½ mile
0   250m 500m 750m 1 km

C6
1 SOMES CL
2 THE CHARTERS
3 MANNERS CL
4 LINDSEY RD
5 GREATFORD RD
6 SCHOOL LA

7 MAIN RD
8 BERTIE LA

F7
1 OLD RECTORY DR
2 WEST RD
3 ST LAWRENCE WY
4 CASEWICK LA

171

222   For full street detail of the highlighted area see page 219.

B1
1 COLLYWESTON RD
2 WELLAND RD
3 GLEN RD
4 NENE CL
5 CHATER RD
6 TOWNSEND RD
7 BROWNES RD
8 EXETER RD
9 HOLT CL

10 FREEMAN CL
11 HARVEY CL
12 THE LIMES
13 MANOR CL
14 BURGHLEY AVE
15 ST JOHN'S RD
16 ST MICHAEL'S RD
17 ST GEORGE'S RD
18 BROADHURST RD
19 NEWMAN CL

20 MALTBY CL
21 CARNEGIE RD
22 EMBRY RD
23 PARKER RD
24 JEFFERSON CL

D3
1 SCHOOL RD
2 THE SQUARE
3 MILLSTONE LA
4 KINGSLEY CL
5 BISHOPS WK
6 CANON DR
7 OWEN CL
8 SAXON RD
9 WHITMAN CL

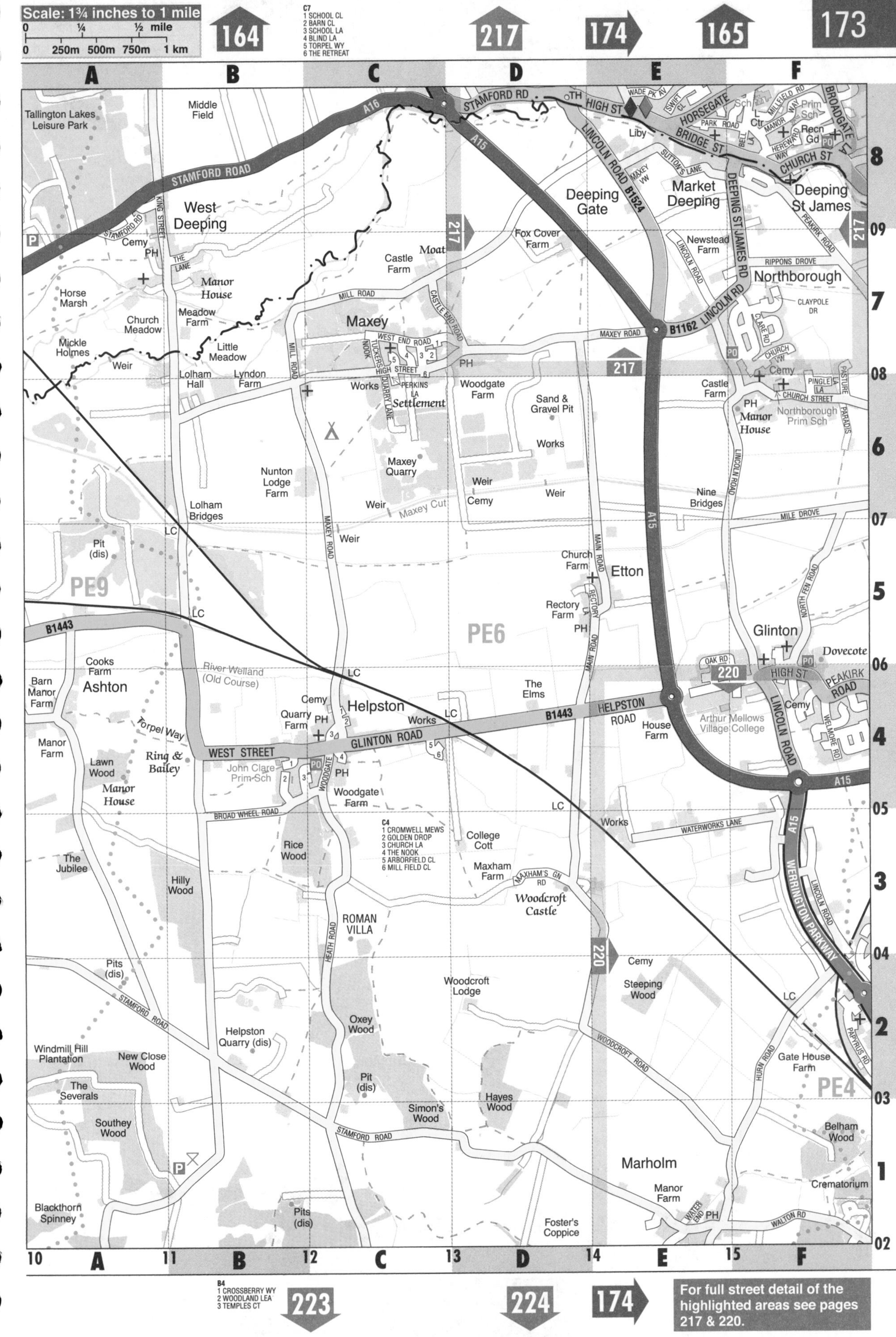

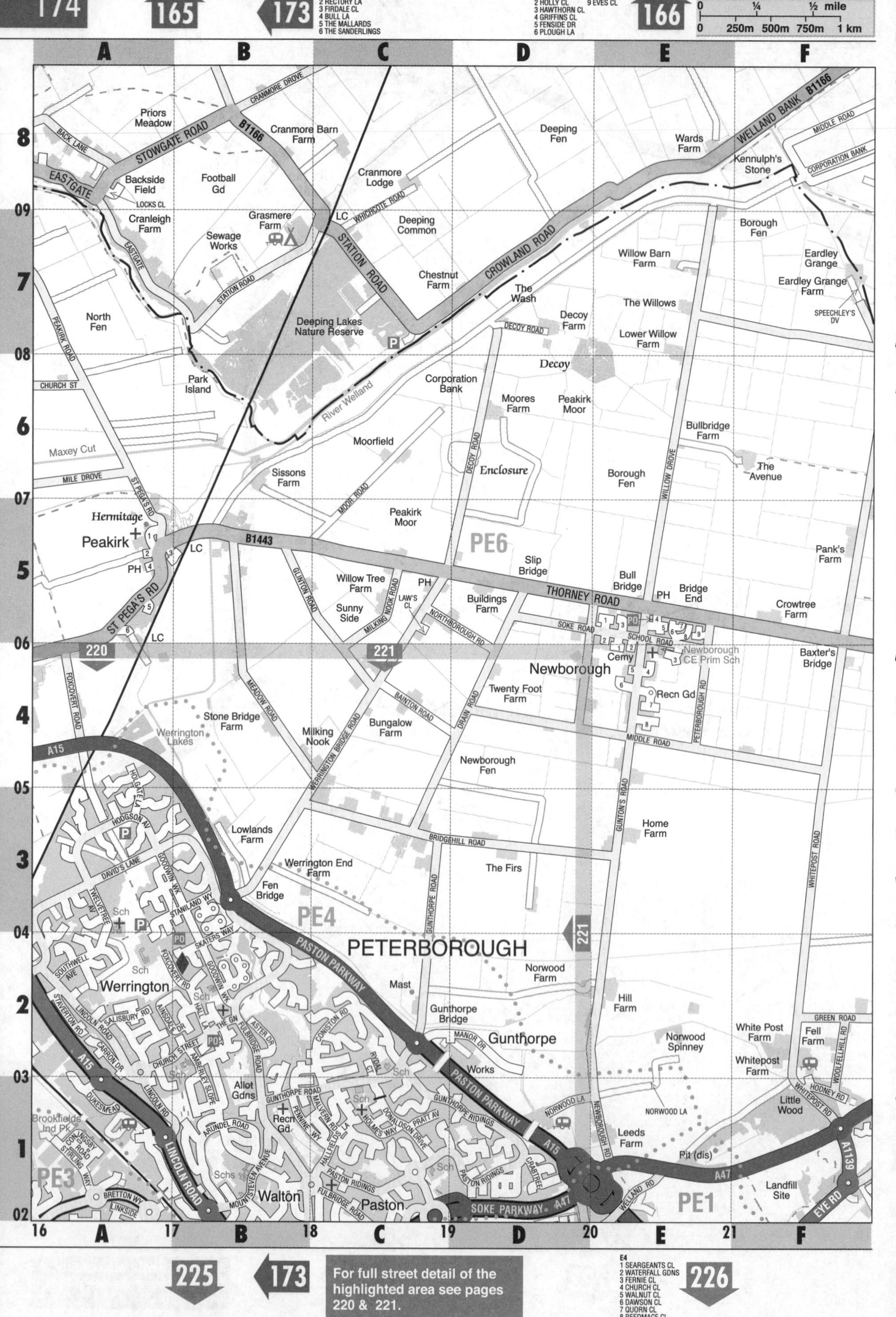
165
173
A5
1 CHESTNUT CL
2 RECTORY LA
3 FIRDALE CL
4 BULL LA
5 THE MALLARDS
6 THE SANDERLINGS
E5
1 WILLIAMS CL
2 HOLLY CL
3 HAWTHORN CL
4 GRIFFINS CL
5 FENSIDE DR
6 PLOUGH LA
7 GODFREY CL
8 WHITSED RD
9 EVES CL
166
Scale: 1¾ inches to 1 mile
0 ¼ ½ mile
0 250m 500m 750m 1 km
A B C D E F
Priors Meadow
CRANMORE DROVE
Cranmore Barn Farm
Deeping Fen
Wards Farm
WELLAND BANK B1166
MIDDLE ROAD
CORPORATION BANK
Kennulph's Stone
BACK LANE
STOWGATE ROAD
B1166
EASTGATE
Backside Field
LOCKS CL
Football Gd
Cranmore Lodge
WHITCOTE ROAD
LC
Cranleigh Farm
Grasmere Farm
Sewage Works
Deeping Common
STATION ROAD
Borough Fen
Willow Barn Farm
Eardley Grange
Eardley Grange Farm
SPEECHLEY'S DV
CROWLAND ROAD
Chestnut Farm
The Wash
The Willows
North Fen
PEAKIRK ROAD
Deeping Lakes Nature Reserve
Decoy Farm
DECOY ROAD
Lower Willow Farm
Decoy
CHURCH ST
Park Island
Corporation Bank
River Welland
Moores Farm
Peakirk Moor
Bullbridge Farm
Maxey Cut
Moorfield
DECOY ROAD
Enclosure
Borough Fen
WILLOW DROVE
The Avenue
MILE DROVE
Sissons Farm
ST PEGA'S RD
MOOR ROAD
Peakirk Moor
Hermitage
Peakirk
LC
B1443
PE6
Slip Bridge
Pank's Farm
PH
GLINTON ROAD
Willow Tree Farm
MILKING NOOK ROAD
PH
Bull Bridge
THORNEY ROAD
PH
Bridge End
Crowtree Farm
Sunny Side
LAW'S CL
Buildings Farm
NORTHBOROUGH RD
SOKE ROAD
PO
SCHOOL ROAD
ST PEGA'S RD
LC
220
221
Cemy
Newborough CE Prim Sch
Baxter's Bridge
Newborough
FOXCOVERT ROAD
MEADOW ROAD
BAINTON ROAD
Twenty Foot Farm
Recn Gd
DRAIN ROAD
PETERBOROUGH RD
Stone Bridge Farm
Werrington Lakes
Milking Nook
WERRINGTON BRIDGE ROAD
Bungalow Farm
MIDDLE ROAD
A15
HOLGATE LA
Newborough Fen
GUNTON'S ROAD
HODGSON AV
Lowlands Farm
Home Farm
WHITEPOST ROAD
BRIDGEHILL ROAD
DAVID'S LANE
GOODWIN WK
Werrington End Farm
The Firs
TWELVETREE AV
STANILAND WY
Fen Bridge
GUNTHORPE ROAD
Sch
PE4
SKATERS WAY
PASTON PARKWAY
221
PETERBOROUGH
SOUTHWELL AVE
FOXCOVERT RD
Sch
GOODWIN WK
Norwood Farm
Werrington
Mast
Hill Farm
STAVERTON RD
LINCOLN ROAD
SALISBURY RD
AINSDALE DR
HALL LA
THE GN
ASTER DR
CONISTON RD
Gunthorpe Bridge
GREEN ROAD
White Post Farm
Fell Farm
CARRON DR
CHURCH STREET
AMBERLEY SLOPE
FULBRIDGE ROAD
MANOR DR
Gunthorpe
Norwood Spinney
WOOLFELLHILL RD
RYDAL CL
Sch
Works
Whitepost Farm
A15
DUKESMEAD
LINCOLN RD
Allot Gdns
GUNTHORPE ROAD
DONALDSON DRIVE
PASTON PARKWAY
HODNEY RD
WHITEPOST RD
NORWOOD LA
NORWOOD LA
Little Wood
Brookfields Ind Pk
ARUNDEL ROAD
Recn Gd
PENNINE WY
MALVERN RD
HALLFIELDS LA
HOLMES WAY
PRATT AV
GUNTHORPE RIDINGS
Leeds Farm
A1139
CONINGSBY ROAD
STIRLING WAY
LINCOLN ROAD
Schs
MOUNTSTEVEN AVENUE
PASTON RIDINGS
Sch
PASTON RIDINGS
CRABTREE
NEWBOROUGH RD
Pit (dis)
A47
PE3
BRETTON WY
LINKSIDE
Walton
FULBRIDGE ROAD
Paston
SOKE PARKWAY A47
WELLAND RD
PE1
Landfill Site
EYE RD
16 A 17 B 18 C 19 D 20 E 21 F
8 09 7 08 6 07 5 06 4 05 3 04 2 03 1 02
225
173
For full street detail of the highlighted area see pages 220 & 221.
E4
1 SEARGEANTS CL
2 WATERFALL GDNS
3 FERNIE CL
4 CHURCH CL
5 WALNUT CL
6 DAWSON CL
7 QUORN CL
8 REEDMACE CL
226

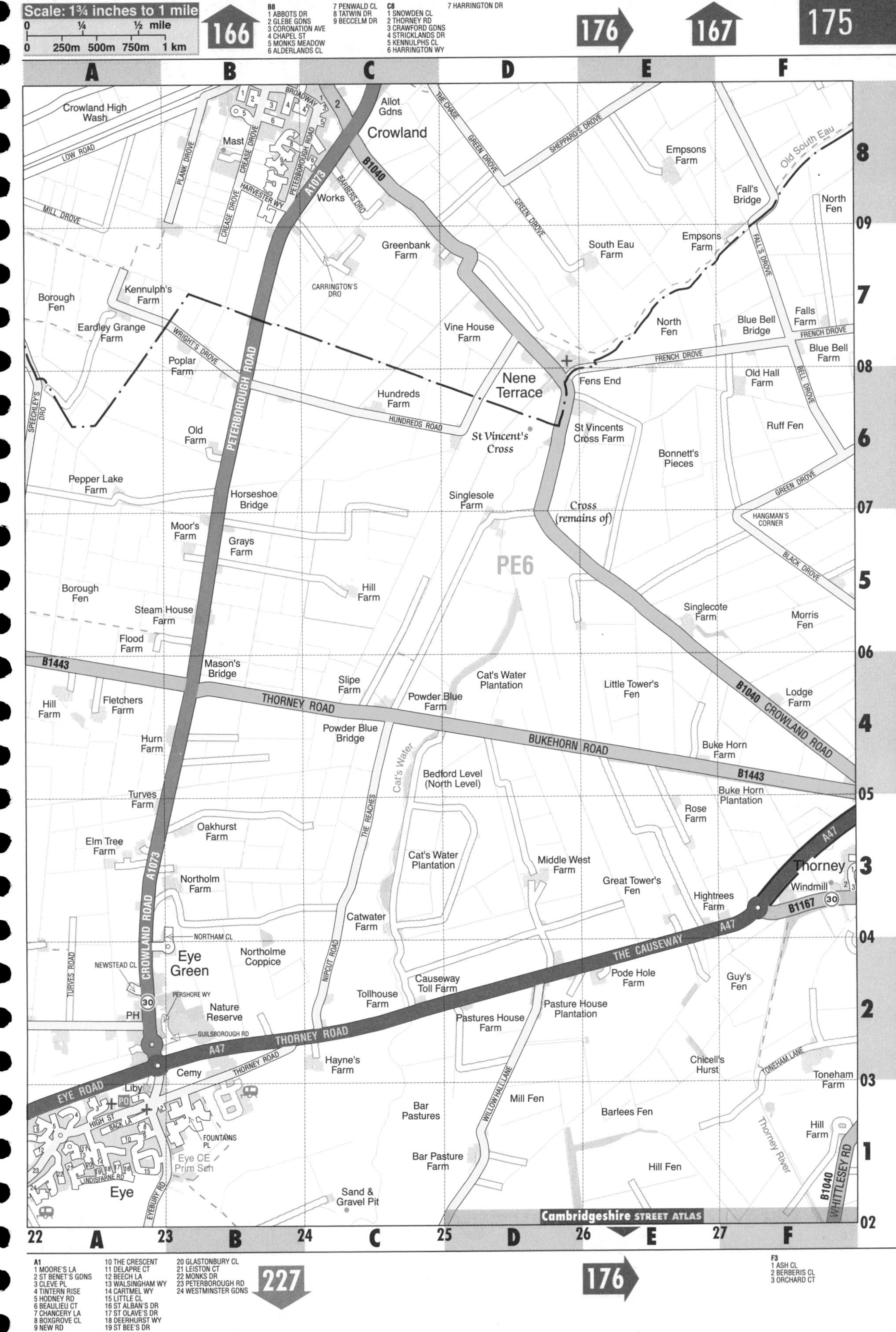

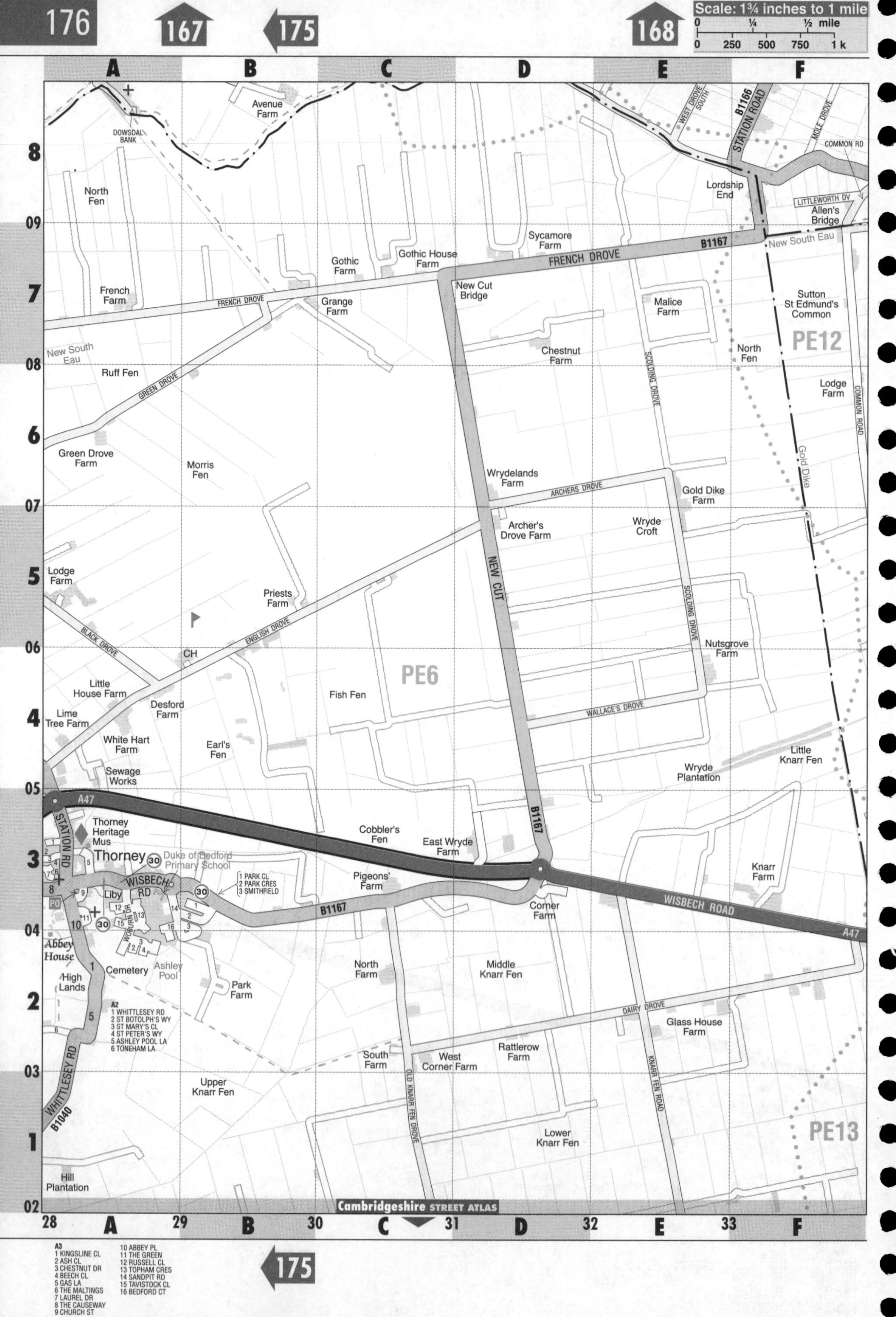
167
175
168
Scale: 1¾ inches to 1 mile
0 ¼ ½ mile
0 250 500 750 1 k
A B C D E F
8
09
7
08
6
07
5
06
4
05
3
04
2
03
1
02
28 29 30 31 32 33
DOWSDAL BANK
Avenue Farm
WEST DROVE SOUTH
B1166
STATION ROAD
MOLE DROVE
COMMON RD
North Fen
Lordship End
LITTLEWORTH DV
Allen's Bridge
Sycamore Farm
B1167
New South Eau
Gothic Farm
Gothic House Farm
FRENCH DROVE
French Farm
FRENCH DROVE
Grange Farm
New Cut Bridge
Malice Farm
Sutton St Edmund's Common
PE12
New South Eau
Ruff Fen
Chestnut Farm
North Fen
GREEN DROVE
SCOLDING DROVE
Lodge Farm
COMMON ROAD
Green Drove Farm
Morris Fen
Gold Dike
Wrydelands Farm
ARCHERS DROVE
Gold Dike Farm
Archer's Drove Farm
Wryde Croft
Lodge Farm
NEW CUT
Priests Farm
SCOLDING DROVE
BLACK DROVE
ENGLISH DROVE
Nutsgrove Farm
CH
PE6
Little House Farm
Fish Fen
Desford Farm
Lime Tree Farm
WALLACE'S DROVE
White Hart Farm
Earl's Fen
Little Knarr Fen
Sewage Works
Wryde Plantation
A47
B1167
STATION RD
Thorney Heritage Mus
Cobbler's Fen
East Wryde Farm
Thorney
Duke of Bedford Primary School
Knarr Farm
WISBECH RD
Liby
1 PARK CL
2 PARK CRES
3 SMITHFIELD
Pigeons' Farm
PO
B1167
Corner Farm
WISBECH ROAD
WOBURN DR
A47
Abbey House
North Farm
Middle Knarr Fen
Cemetery
Ashley Pool
High Lands
Park Farm
A2
1 WHITTLESEY RD
2 ST BOTOLPH'S WY
3 ST MARY'S CL
4 ST PETER'S WY
5 ASHLEY POOL LA
6 TONEHAM LA
DAIRY DROVE
Glass House Farm
South Farm
West Corner Farm
Rattlerow Farm
WHITTLESEY RD
B1040
Upper Knarr Fen
OLD KNARR FEN DROVE
KNARR FEN ROAD
Lower Knarr Fen
PE13
Hill Plantation
A3
1 KINGSLINE CL
2 ASH CL
3 CHESTNUT DR
4 BEECH CL
5 GAS LA
6 THE MALTINGS
7 LAUREL DR
8 THE CAUSEWAY
9 CHURCH ST
10 ABBEY PL
11 THE GREEN
12 RUSSELL CL
13 TOPHAM CRES
14 SANDPIT RD
15 TAVISTOCK CL
16 BEDFORD CT
175

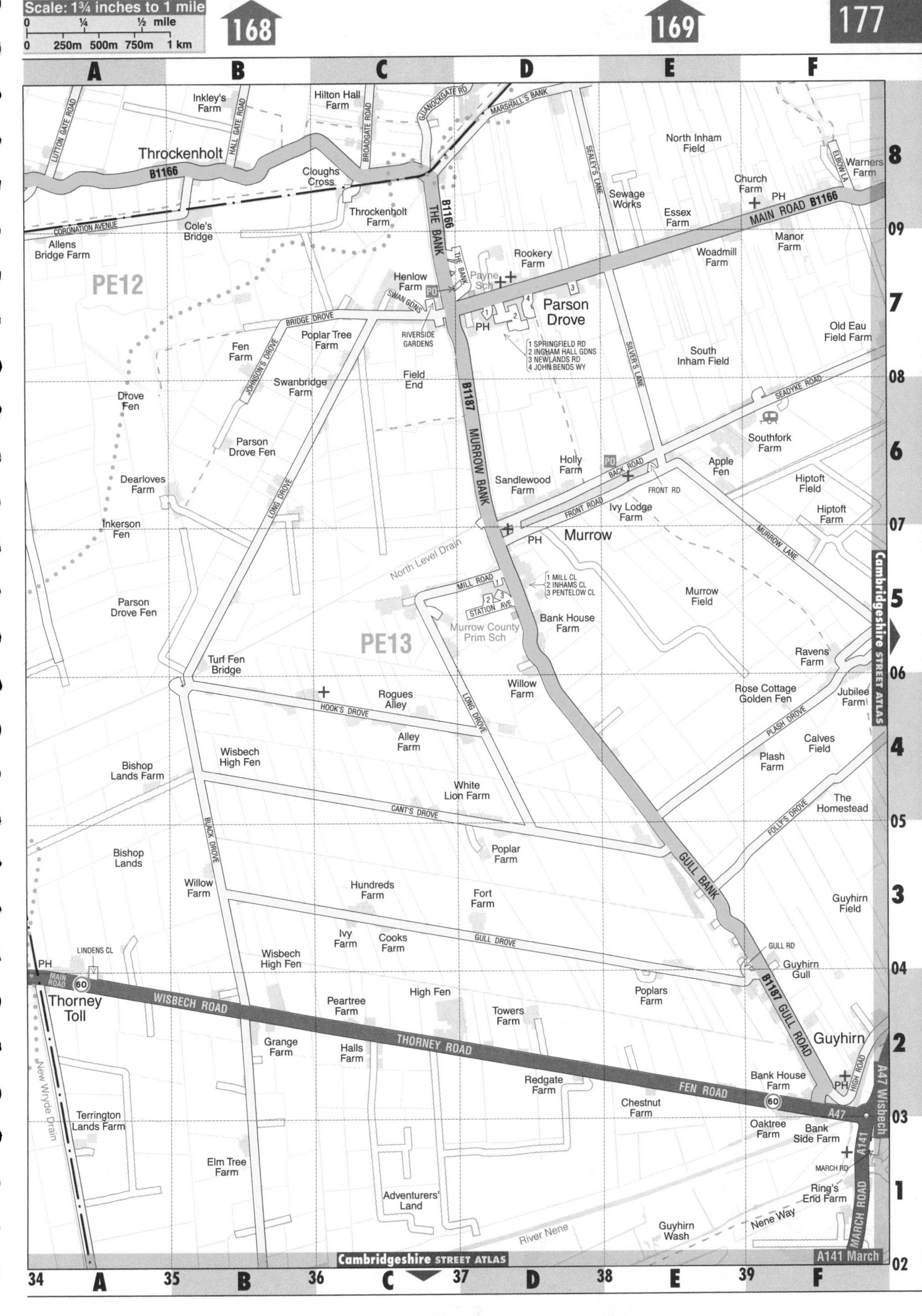
Scale: 1¾ inches to 1 mile
168
169
Throckenholt
Parson Drove
Murrow
Thorney Toll
Guyhirn
PE12
PE13
B1166
B1187
MURROW BANK
GULL BANK
GULL ROAD
WISBECH ROAD
THORNEY ROAD
FEN ROAD
MAIN ROAD
A47
A141
MARCH ROAD
A47 Wisbech
A141 March
Cambridgeshire STREET ATLAS
North Level Drain
River Nene
New Wryde Drain
Nene Way
1 SPRINGFIELD RD
2 INGHAM HALL GDNS
3 NEWLANDS RD
4 JOHN BENDS WY
1 MILL CL
2 INHAMS CL
3 PENTELOW CL

E. Yorkshire & N. Lincolnshire STREET ATLAS

E7
1 CROMWELL CT
2 WOODHILL CL
3 NORWOOD CL
4 WAULDBY CL
5 WEETON WY

E8
1 COLLYNSON CL
2 SETTERWOOD GARTH
3 OAKDALE AV

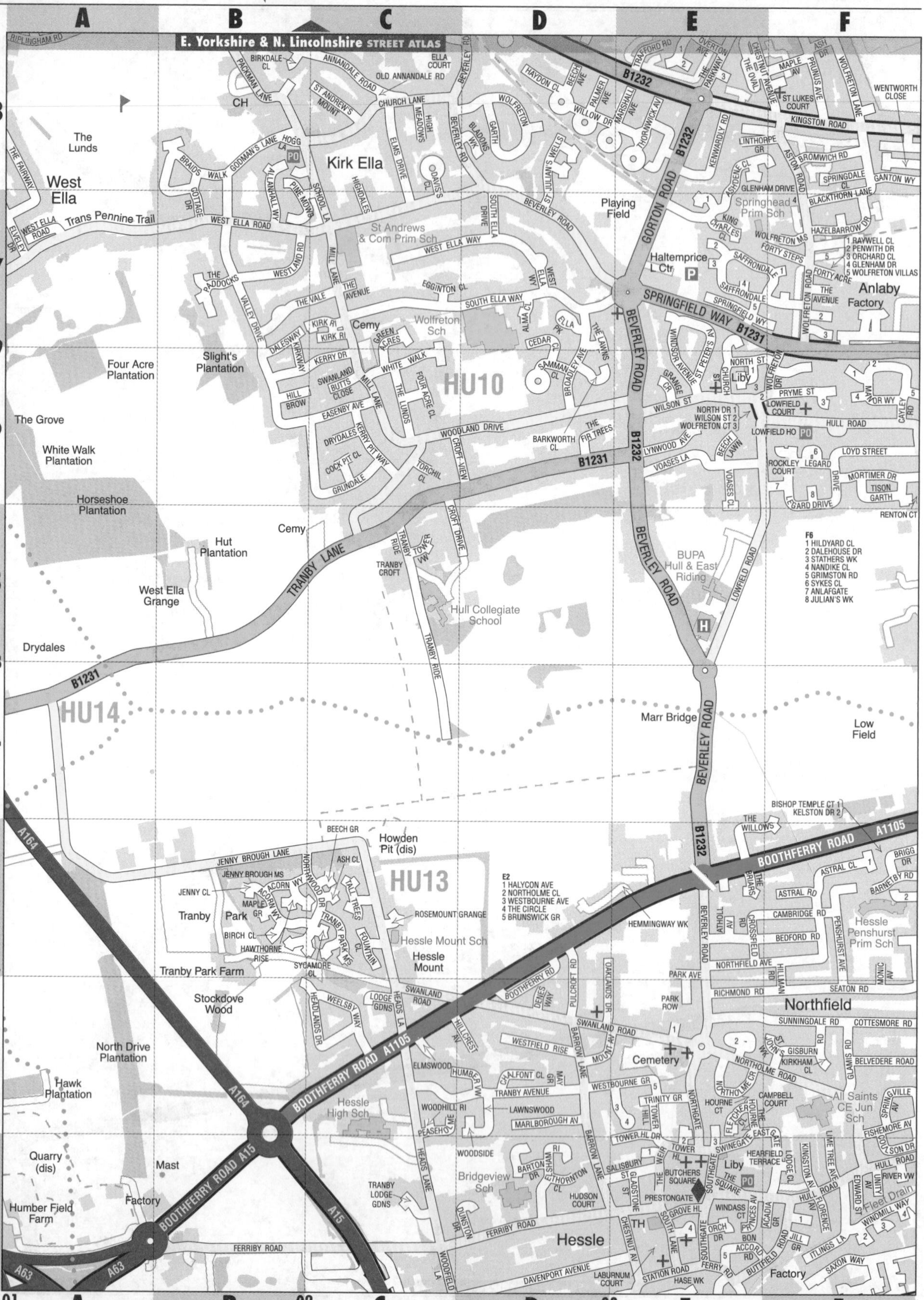

Column headers: A B C D E F

The Lunds
West Ella
The Paddocks
Trans Pennine Trail
West Ella Road
Four Acre Plantation
Slight's Plantation
The Grove
White Walk Plantation
Horseshoe Plantation
Hut Plantation
West Ella Grange
Drydales
Kirk Ella
CH
Birkdale CL
Packman Lane
Annandale Road
Old Annandale Rd
Ella Court
Church Lane
St Andrews & Com Prim Sch
West Ella Way
South Ella Way
Cemy
Wolfreton Sch
HU10
Woodland Drive
The Fir Trees
Barkworth CL
B1231
Croft View
Tranby Lane
Cemy
Hut Plantation
Hull Collegiate School
Tranby Croft
HU14
B1231
Drydales
Marr Bridge
Low Field
BUPA Hull & East Riding
Beverley Road
The Willows
Bishop Temple Ct
Kelston Dr
Boothferry Road A1105
Howden Pit (dis)
HU13
Tranby Park
Jenny Brough Lane
Rosemount Grange
Hessle Mount Sch
Hessle Mount
Tranby Park Farm
Stockdove Wood
North Drive Plantation
Hawk Plantation
Quarry (dis)
Humber Field Farm
Factory
Mast
Boothferry Road A15
A164
A15
Hessle High Sch
Swanland Road
Westfield Rise
Tranby Avenue
Lawnswood
Marlborough Av
Woodside
Bridgeview Sch
Tranby Lodge Gdns
Ferriby Road
Hessle
Ferriby Road
Davenport Avenue
Laburnum Court
Station Road
Factory
A63
A63
Springhead Prim Sch
Haltemprice L Ctr
Anlaby Factory
Beverley Road
Springfield Way B1231
B1232
Kingston Road
Wentworth Close
St Lukes Court
Northfield
Hessle Penshurst Prim Sch
Cemetery
Boothferry Road
All Saints CE Jun Sch

E2
1 HALYCON AVE
2 NORTHOLME CL
3 WESTBOURNE AVE
4 THE CIRCLE
5 BRUNSWICK GR

F6
1 HILDYARD CL
2 DALEHOUSE DR
3 STATHERS WK
4 NANDIKE CL
5 GRIMSTON RD
6 SYKES CL
7 ANLAFGATE
8 JULIAN'S WK

E1
1 SPIRE VW
2 TOWER HILL MEWS
3 VICARAGE LA
4 CLOWES CT
5 FISHWICK AVE

F1
1 MARGARET GR
2 BISHOP BLUNT CL
3 BISHOP KEMPTHORNE CL
4 BISHOP GURDON CL

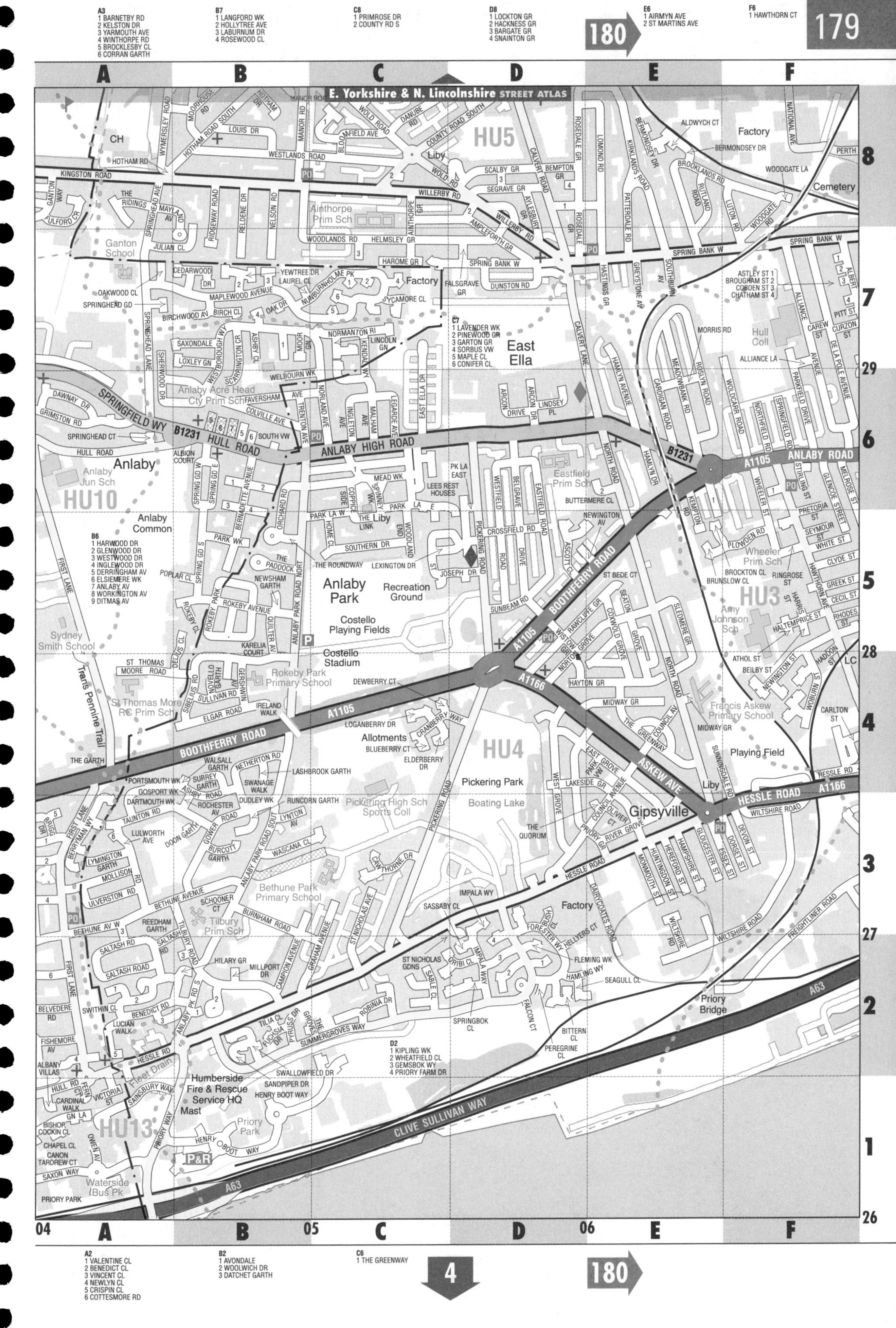

180

A3
1 BARNETBY RD
2 KELSTON DR
3 YARMOUTH AVE
4 WINTHORPE RD
5 BROCKLESBY CL
6 CORRAN GARTH

B7
1 LANGFORD WK
2 HOLLYTREE AVE
3 LABURNUM DR
4 ROSEWOOD CL

C8
1 PRIMROSE DR
2 COUNTY RD S

D8
1 LOCKTON GR
2 HACKNESS GR
3 BARGATE GR
4 SNAINTON GR

E6
1 AIRMYN AVE
2 ST MARTINS AVE

F6
1 HAWTHORN CT

E. Yorkshire & N. Lincolnshire STREET ATLAS

C7
1 LAVENDER WK
2 PINEWOOD GR
3 GARTON GR
4 SORBUS VW
5 MAPLE CL
6 CONIFER CL

B6
1 HARWOOD DR
2 GLENWOOD DR
3 WESTWOOD DR
4 INGLEWOOD DR
5 DERRINGHAM AV
6 ELSIEMERE WK
7 ANLABY AV
8 WORKINGTON AV
9 DITMAS AV

D2
1 KIPLING WK
2 WHEATFIELD CL
3 GEMSBOK WY
4 PRIORY FARM DR

A2
1 VALENTINE CL
2 BENEDICT CL
3 VINCENT CL
4 NEWLYN CL
5 CRISPIN CL
6 COTTESMORE RD

B2
1 AVONDALE
2 WOOLWICH DR
3 DATCHET GARTH

C6
1 THE GREENWAY

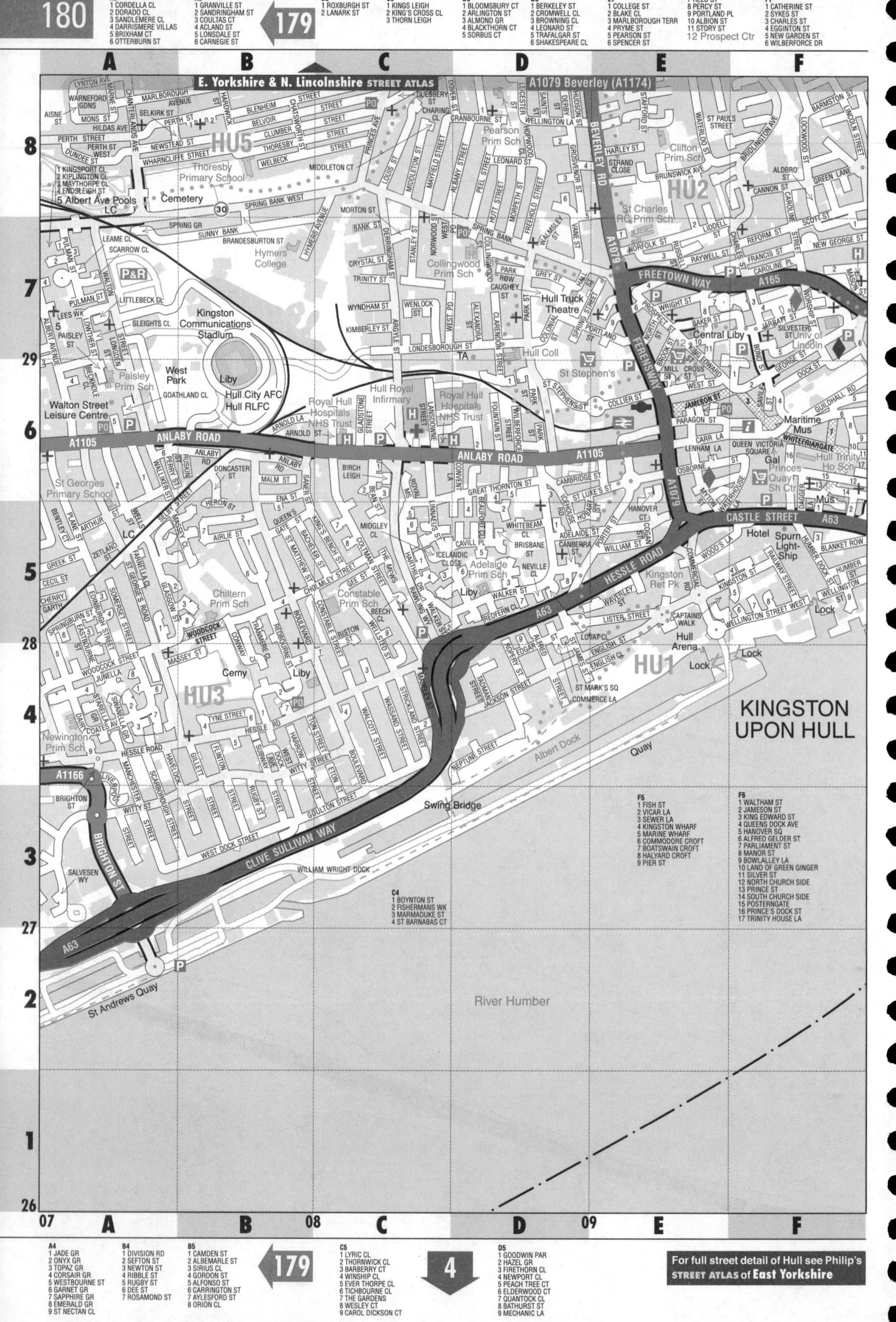

E. Yorkshire & N. Lincolnshire STREET ATLAS

179

KINGSTON UPON HULL

179

4

For full street detail of Hull see Philip's **STREET ATLAS** of **East Yorkshire**

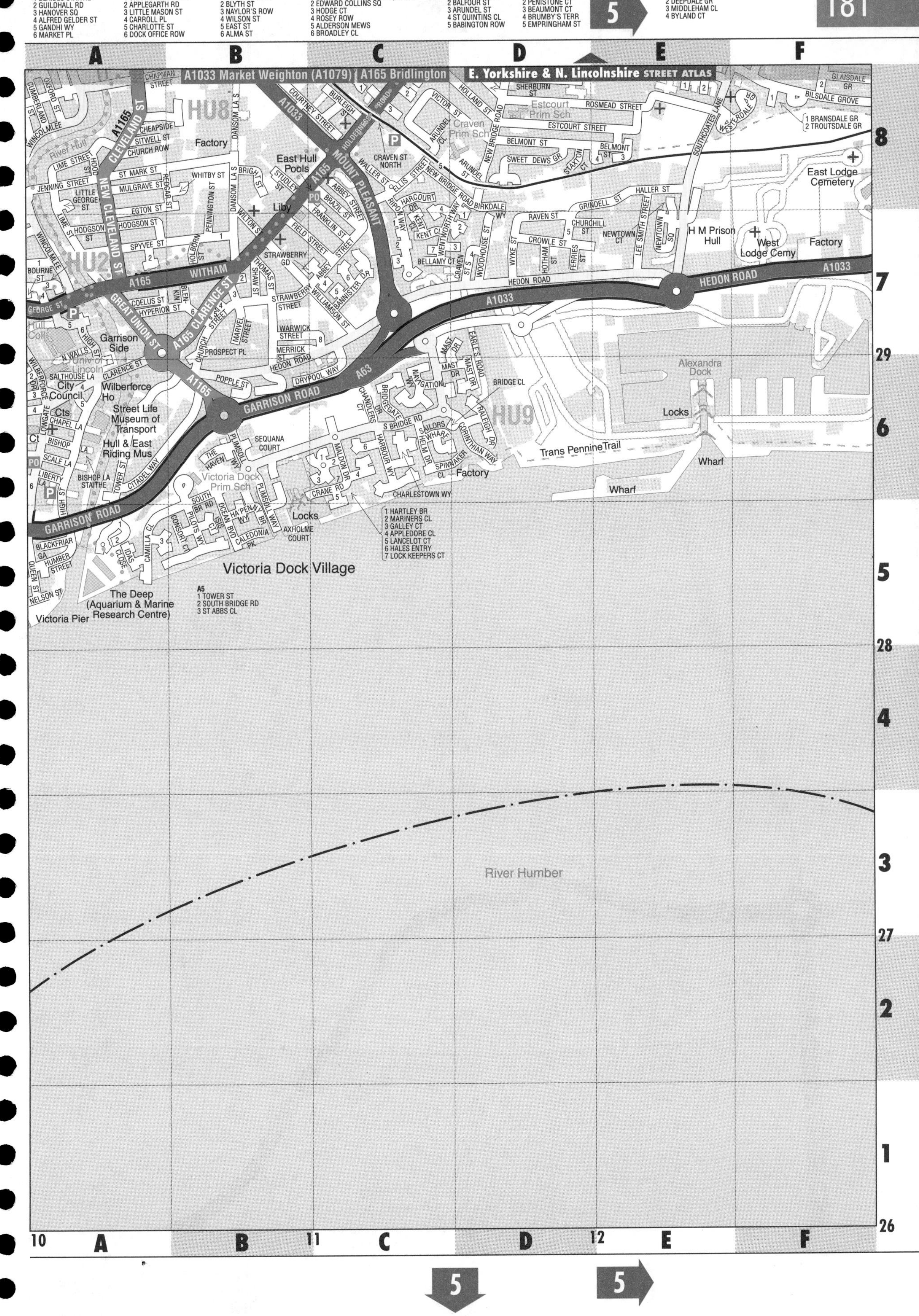

17

C5
1 ACACIA AVE
2 MAPLE AVE
3 PIPPIN CT
4 RUSSET CL

C6
1 POPPY CL
2 WOODALE CL
3 FLETCHER CL
4 COLTSFOOT CL
5 ST MARY'S CT
6 HERON CL

8

Grid columns: A B C D E F
Grid rows: 8, 7, 13, 6, 5, 12, 4, 3, 11, 2, 1, 10

River Trent, DN17, Park Ings Farm, Works, Neap House, Foxhills Plantation, Skippingdale Industrial Park, Foxhills Industrial Park, Billet La, B1216 Neap House Rd, Ferry Road West, B1216, Phoenix Parkway, A1077, DN15, Skippingdale Plantation, Allotment Gardens, Mead Garth, Poplars Mobile Homes, Atkinsons Warren Nature Reserve, Sports Ground, Foxhills Sch & Tech Coll, Portman Road, Reginald Road, Skippingdale Rd, Crosby Avenue, Buckingham Avenue, Crosby, Library, Crosby Cemy, Theodore Road, Ferry Road, Berkeley Industrial Estate, St Augustine Webster Catholic Prim Sch, Berkeley Inf & Jun Sch, Henderson Avenue Primary School, Smith St, Fox Street, Superstore, Cliff Plantation, High Ridge Sch & Adult Education Ctr, Doncaster Road, High Ridge Sports Hall, Gallagher Retail Park, A18, Glanford Park (Scunthorpe United FC), Frodingham Viaduct, Mast, M181, Coles Plantation, Kingsway Golf Course, Scunthorpe General, Church Lane, Vicarage Gardens, Brumby Common West, Viaduct Plantation, DN17, Brumby Wood Lane, Brumby Wood Nature Reserve, Cemetery, Woodlands Crematorium, Kingsway, Sports Ground, Brumby Hall, Central Park

17

B2
1 TANSLEY CT
2 ALFRETON CT
3 HATHERSAGE CT
4 GRASSMOOR CT
5 EASTWOOD CT
6 BELPER CT

B3
1 BAKEWELL CT
2 ILKESTON CT
3 DRONFIELD CT

E3
1 JACKSON RD
2 DE ASTON SQ
3 CONWAY SQ
4 TOMLINSON AVE
5 ASHDOWN AVE

E4
1 LOCKWOOD CT
2 MALLALIEU CT
3 MARY SUMNER WY

F2
1 ERYHOLME CR
2 FUCHSIA CRFT
3 PAVILION GDNS

F4
1 LONG RD
2 HENDERSON CRES
3 EDWARDS RD
4 SHEFFIELD ST
5 BUCKINGHAM ST
6 Comm Ctr

184

18

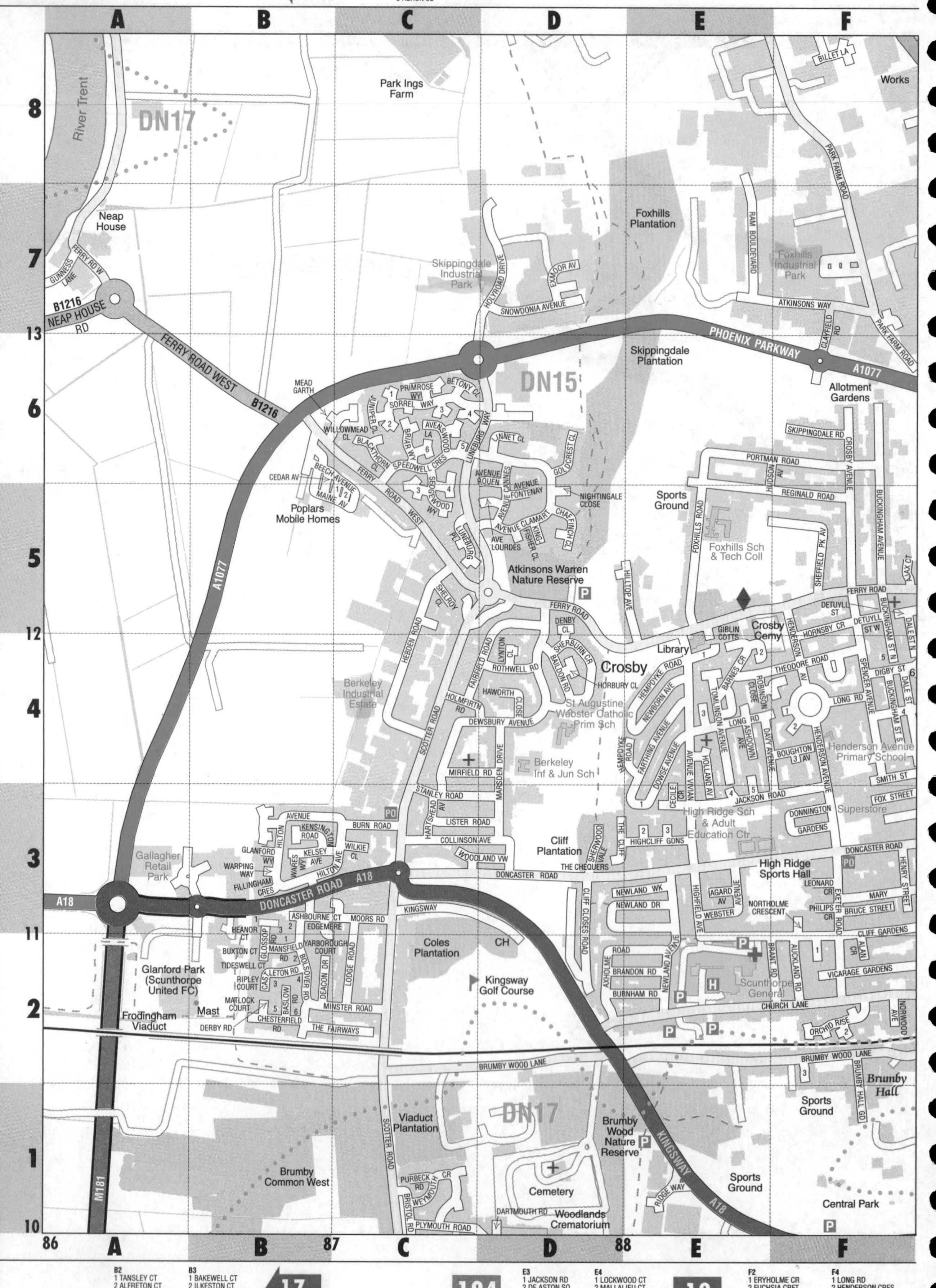

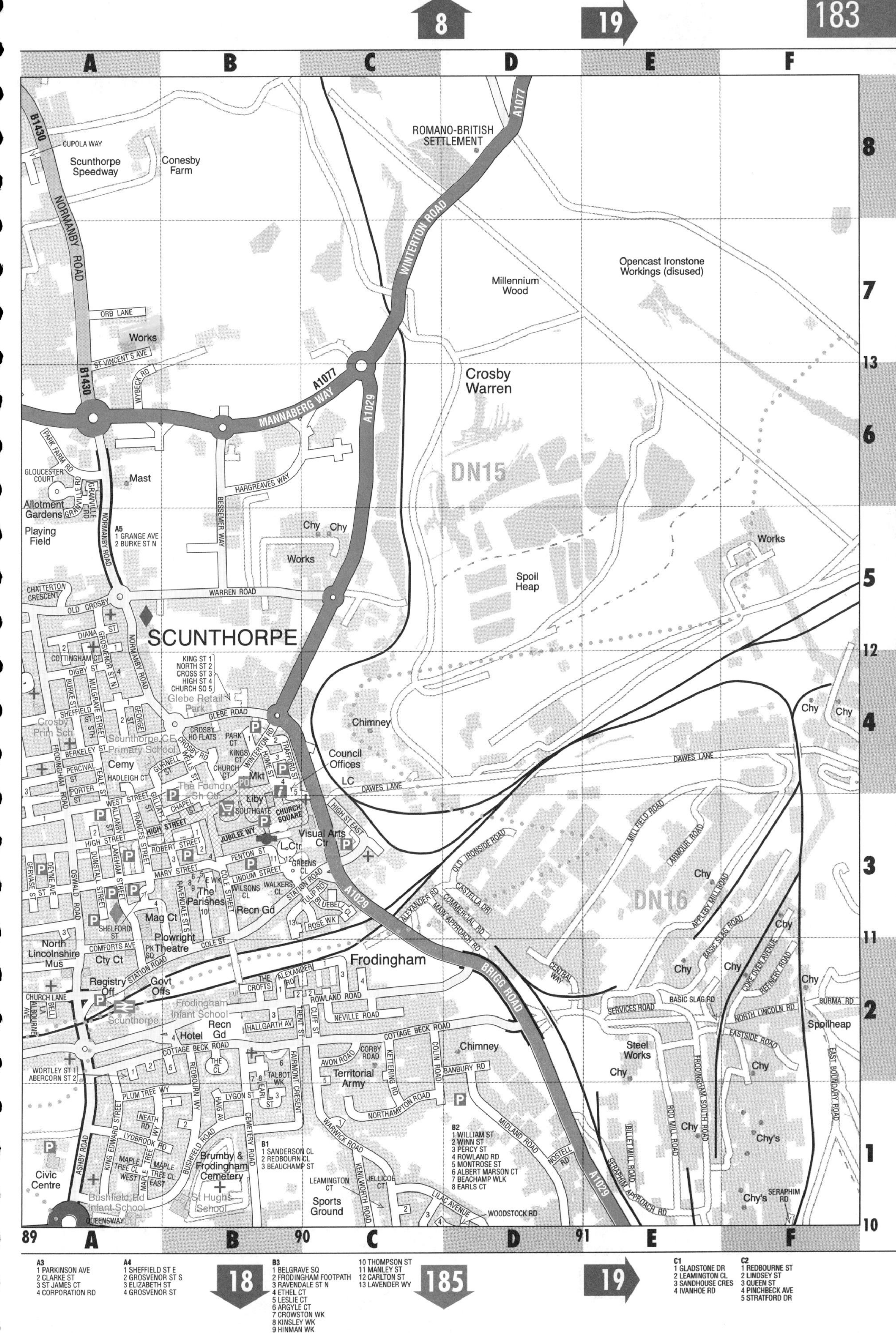

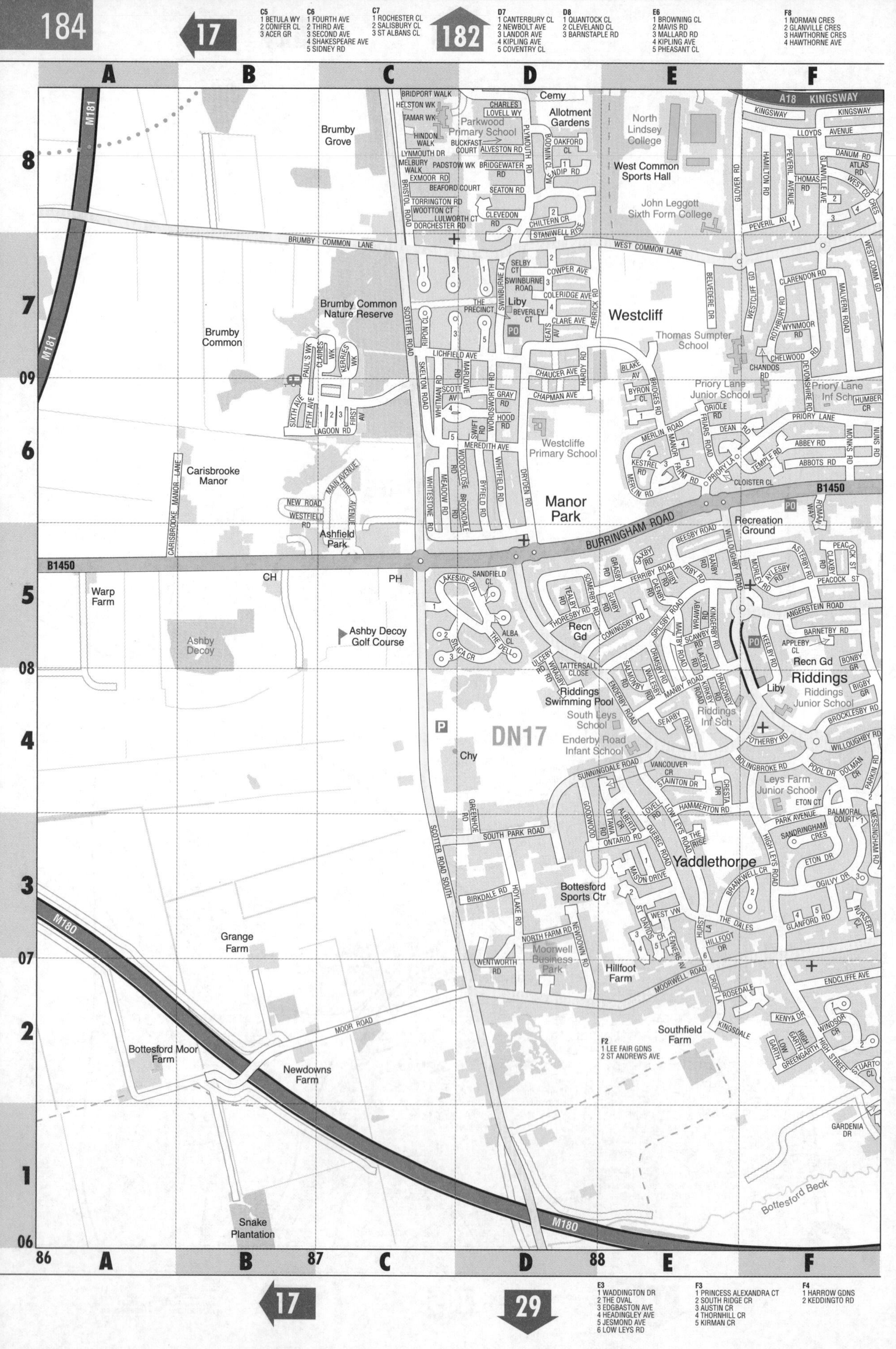

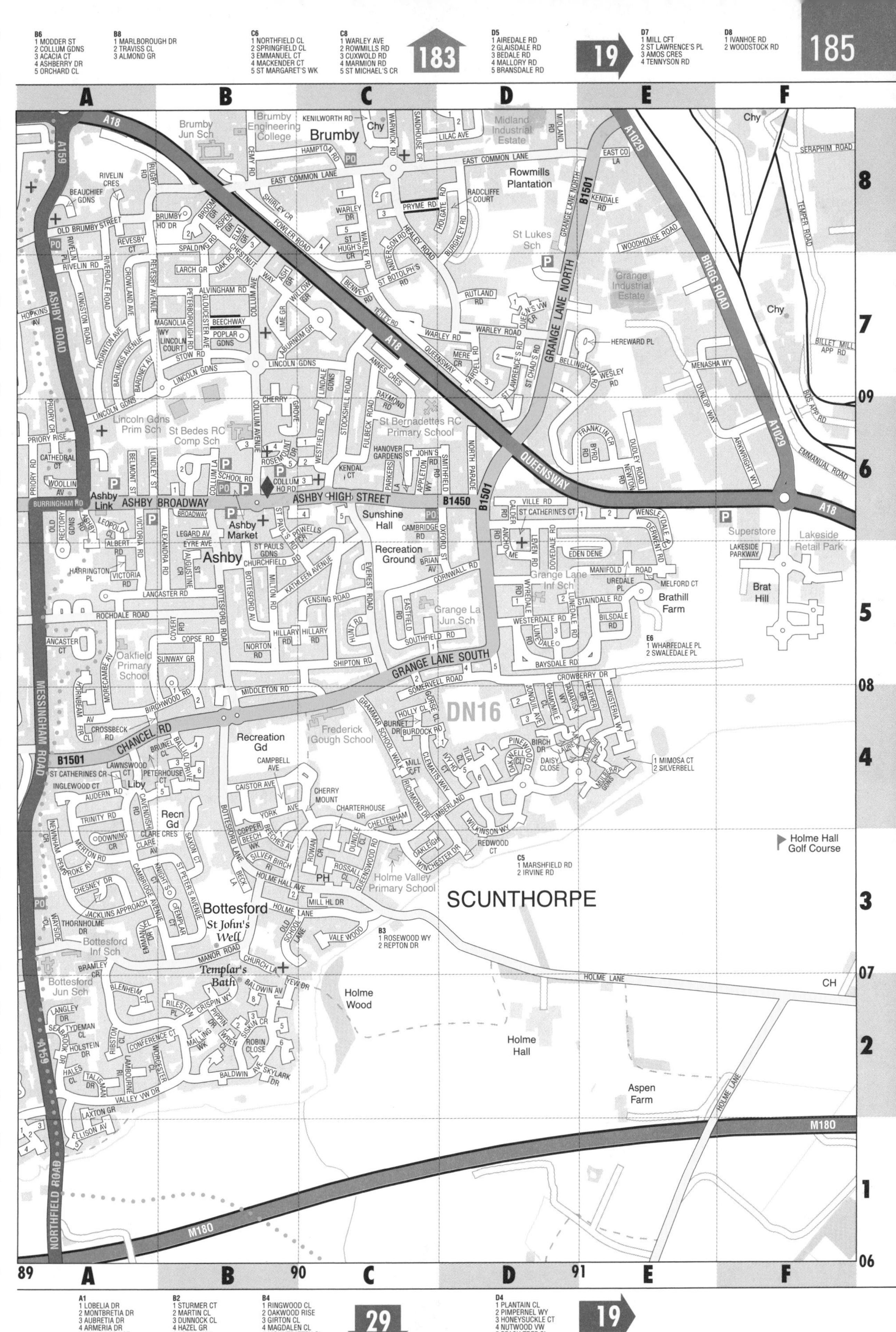

D5
1 HOYLAKE DR
2 COLLIER RD
3 BIRKDALE DR
4 SUNNINGDALE DR

A   B   C   D   E   F

8

Rosper Road
Pools Nature
Reserve

Henderson
Quay

HUMBER ROAD   A160

WEST HAVEN WY

Oil Storage
Depot

WEST RIVERSIDE

West Haven
Wy

A1173

WEST HAVEN WAY

HUMBER ROAD

LC

LC

LC

LC

Water
Tower

MINERAL QUAY ROAD

7

SOUTHERN WAY

WESTERN ACCESS ROAD

SEVEN QUAY ROAD

LOCKSIDE RD

Houlton's
Covert

16

ALEXANDRA ROAD SOUTH

ALEXANDRA
RD

ROBINSON
RD

6

MANBY ROAD

Pelham Industrial
Estate

Works

GRESLEY WAY

5

Immingham
Golf Course

STANDISH LA 1
HINKLEY DR 2
WESTON GR 3
ATWOOD CL 4

Homestead
Park
P

DN40

1 CEDAR DR
2 MAPLE GR
3 OAKLANDS RD

A1173

MIDDLEPLATT ROAD

HALL PARK RD
P

Sports
Ground

Medieval Village
of Immingham

WOODLANDS AVENUE

Football
Ground

Manby Hall
Business Park

1 HUMBERVILLE RD
2 LARCH CL
3 TRENCHARD CL

CH St ANDREWS

COPSE CL

WASHDYKE LANE

Mast

Mon

CHURCH LANE

WINSLOW DRIVE

ASH
TREE
CL

WILLOW
TREE GR

HAWTHORN AV

Stansfield
GDNS

ST ANDREWS
CT

MORTON

SPANG
CLOSE

BERB
WICK

MAYFIELD
CFT

HUMBERVILLE ROAD

CHESTNUT AV

WATERWORKS RD

15

MILL LANE

ST
ANDREWS
CT

Mon

ALLERTON DR

Allerton
Primary
School

RDS
GDNS

PARK CL

BEECHWOOD
AV

FERNDOWN DR

PELHAM ROAD

BATTERY RD

SPRING STREET

KINGS ROAD

A1173

4

VIKING
CL

PILGRIMS WAY

CLIFTON CRESCENT

BRADFORD RD

SONIA CREST

Hotel
Immingham
L Ctr
P

KENNEDY
WAY

Washdyke
Retail Park

Civic
Ctr

PAMELA
CLOSE

1 DEANE RD
2 SACKVILLE CL
3 WORSLEY CL
4 EATON RD

IMMINGHAM

Recreation
Ground

VALDA
WALK

ROYAL DRIVE

ROBERT CL

WINSLOW
CL

ALDEN
CL

Kennedy Way
Shopping Ctr

Liby

Mkt

Cannon Peter
Hall CE Prim Sch

KINGS ROAD

A1173

PELHAM ROAD

Swimming
Pool

PAMELA
RD

SACKVILLE RD

Coomb Brigg's
Prim Sch

BLUESTONE LANE

CRAKHILL
AVE

The
Immingham
School

TALBOT RD

OAKHAM
WALK

ANCHOLME AVE 1
CALDER CL 2
STEEPING DR 3
AIRE CL 4

PH

PO

The
ORCHARDS

MAYFLOWER
AVE

PRINCESS STREET

Immingham
Business
Units

BARNARD
WALK

NEWPORT WLK

LANGLEY
WALK

INGS
LANE

3

HABROUGH ROAD   B1210

HUME BRAE

HIGHLAND TARN

THORNTON PL

MARGARET STREET

CUSHMAN CR

PILGRIM AVENUE

LYDFORD RD

LULWORTH
WALK

BLAIR
WALK

HADLEIGH ROAD

KENDAL
RD

Sports
Gd

Immingham
Museum

CARISBROOKE
WALK

CORFE
WK

HARLECH
WALK

NEWARK
WALK

COLLIER RD 1
BREWSTER AV 2
THORNBURY RD 3

14

KISHORN CT 1
PERTH WY 2
TUMMEL CT 3

KIRK
WY

JASMINE WAY

Eastfield Inf
& Jun Sch

GUERNSEY GR

ALDERNEY WY

SHETLAND WY

STALLINGBOROUGH ROAD

Highfield
Farm

MULL WY

ARRAN CL

ANGLESEY DR

2

ORKNEY PL 1
FAIR ISLE RISE 2
LUNDY CT 3

DN41

A180

B1210

Mauxhall
Farm

A1173

1

KILN LANE

13

17   A   B   18   C   D   19   E   F

A4
1 MAIDEN CL
2 CLEVELAND CL
3 LYDIA CT
4 HAZEL CFT
5 MILLHOUSE ST RISE
6 JACKSON MEWS
7 ANDREWS WY
8 HELEN CRES

B3
1 BLOSSOM WY
2 CLARENCE CL
3 LINDUM AVE
4 HIGHFIELD AVE
5 MACKENZIE PL
6 HUME BRAE
7 BOWMAN WY
8 HAMISH WK
9 JAMES WY

B4
1 HOLLINGSWORTH AVE
2 HOLBECK PL
3 BALFOUR PL
4 LANSDOWN RD
5 AINSWORTH RD
6 LEYDEN CL
7 CHILTON CL
8 STAINTON DR

C3
1 PRINCESS ST
2 ROUNDWAY
3 JAPONICA HL
4 MAGNOLIA RISE
5 PADDOCK CT
6 OBAN CT

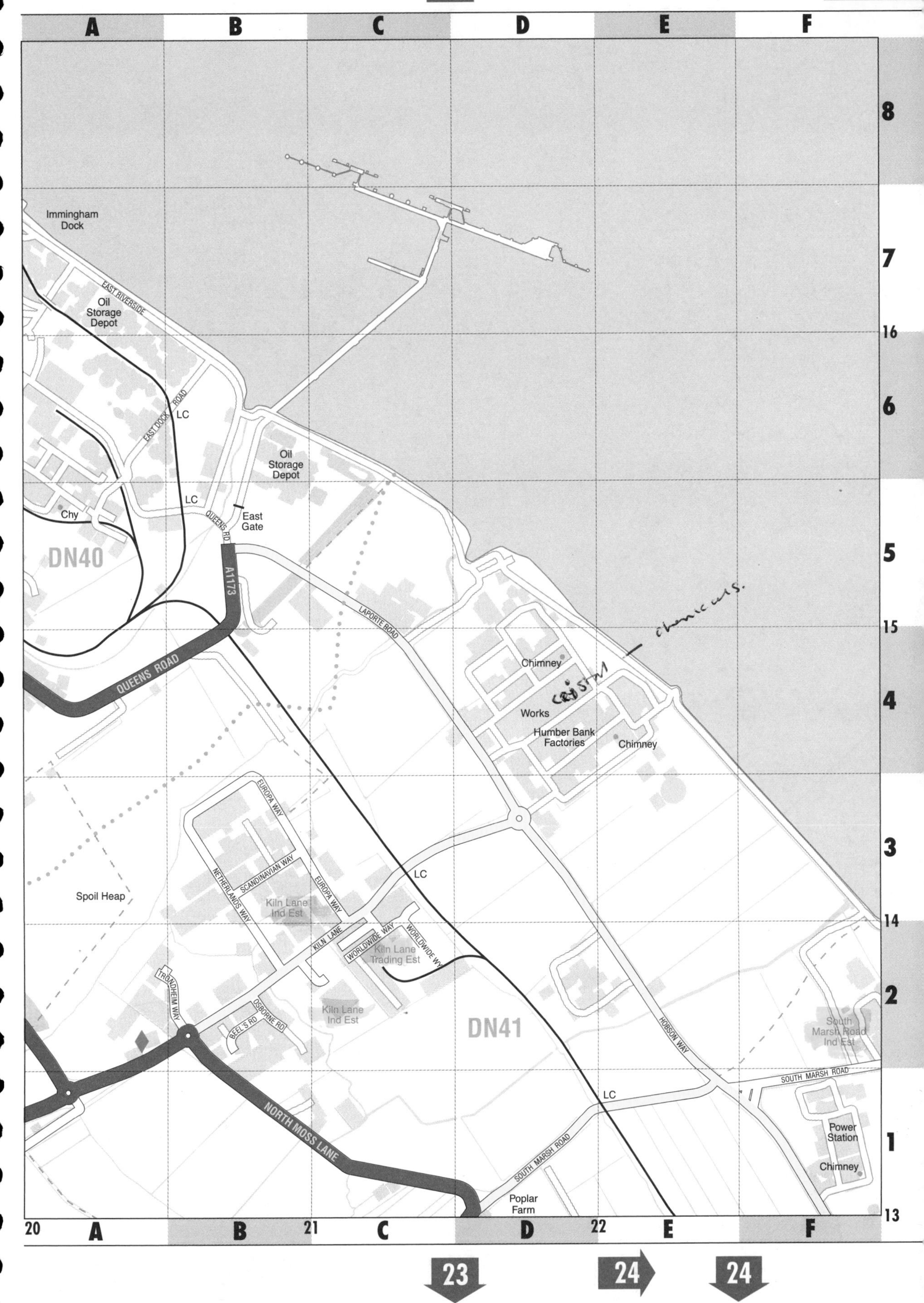

A B C D E F

8
7
16
6
5
15
4
3
14
2
1
13

Immingham
Dock

EAST RIVERSIDE

Oil
Storage
Depot

EAST DOCK ROAD

LC

QUEENS RD

A1173

LC

Chy

East
Gate

Oil
Storage
Depot

DN40

QUEENS ROAD

LAPORTE ROAD

chemicals.

C & I STM

Chimney

Works

Humber Bank
Factories

Chimney

EUROPA WAY

SCANDINAVIAN WAY

NETHERLANDS WAY

EUROPA WAY

KILN LANE

LC

Spoil Heap

Kiln Lane
Ind Est

WORLDWIDE WAY

WORLDWIDE WAY

Kiln Lane
Trading Est

TRONDHEIM WAY

BEELS RD

OSBORNE RD

Kiln Lane
Ind Est

DN41

HOBSON WAY

South
Marsh Road
Ind Est

LC

SOUTH MARSH ROAD

SOUTH MARSH ROAD

NORTH MOSS LANE

LC

Poplar
Farm

Power
Station

Chimney

20 A 21 B C 22 D E F 13

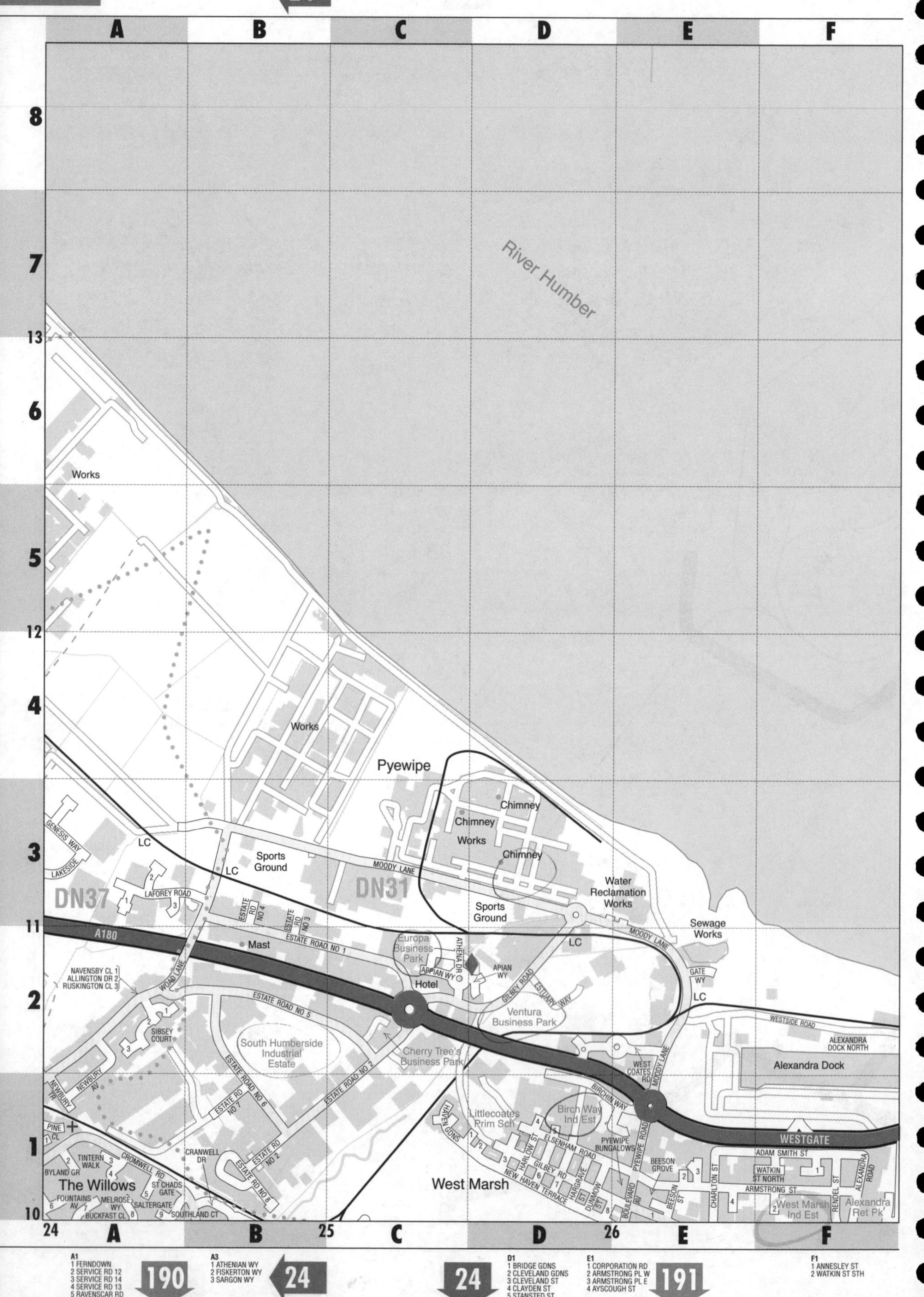

190

24

24

191

A1
1 FERNDOWN
2 SERVICE RD 12
3 SERVICE RD 14
4 SERVICE RD 13
5 RAVENSCAR RD
6 SERVICE RD 10
7 SERVICE RD 9
8 SERVICE RD 8
9 SERVICE RD 26

A3
1 ATHENIAN WY
2 FISKERTON WY
3 SARGON WY

D1
1 BRIDGE GDNS
2 CLEVELAND GDNS
3 CLEVELAND ST
4 CLAYDEN ST
5 STANSTED ST
6 CLAVERING ST
7 STORTFORD ST
8 SANDFORD ST

E1
1 CORPORATION RD
2 ARMSTRONG PL W
3 ARMSTRONG PL E
4 AYSCOUGH ST

F1
1 ANNESLEY ST
2 WATKIN ST STH

River Humber

GRIMSBY

The Dock
Tower

Mast

Piers

Locks

Locks

Royal
Dock

BROWN ST
Fish Docks
WHARNCLIFFE RD

KEMP ROAD
NORTH QUAY

DN31

D1
1 CASSWELL CL
2 RUTLAND ST
3 MANSEL ST
4 SIDNEY ST

WESTSIDE ROAD
EASTSIDE ROAD

HUTTON RD

Grimsby
Marina

FARINGDON RD
Wickham Road

Works

WICKHAM ROAD
Works

DN32

LC

LOGHILL
FLORA
DISP

AUCKLAND RD

EASTSIDE ROAD

LC

MURRAY STREET

Womersley
RD
ROBINSON LA
MURRAY ST

HUMBER BK S

HUMBER BK S

ROSS ROAD

SALTKSEN RD

MARSDEN ROAD

New Clee

DN35

RIBY SQ
ORWELL ST

TOMLINE ST
RIBY STREET

THOROLD STREET

STIRLING ST

HARRINGTON STREET

Grimsby
Docks

CLEETHORPE ROAD

The Caxton
Theatre &
Arts Ctr

KENT
Strand

Strand
Jun Sch

Strand
Inf Sch

BELPER ST

BATH ST

HOPE ST

VICTOR ST

HILDA

SPENCER
ST

MONTAGUE ST

GRANT
ST

TAYLOR ST

DAUBNEY ST

TICKTON ST

BARCROFT ST

LOVETT

Blundell
AVE

A180

High Point
Ret Pk

PRINCE
ALBERT
GARD

CHURCH ST

ALBERT
PLACE

ALBERT ST E

OXFORD STREET

Ice House

SUFFOLK CT

SUSSEX CT

GUILDFORD ST

HAMILTON STREET

GRAFTON ST

GRIMSBY ROAD

A180

Victoria
Retail Pk

NELSON
STREET

DUNCOMBE
GDNS

InShops
Ctr

East Marsh

A16 VICTORIA ST N

B1213 FREEMAN ST

RAILWAY ST

STANLEY

A
B
C
D
E
F

8
7
13
6
5
12
4
11
3
2
1
10

27
28
29

A1
1 LOWER SPRING ST
2 CRESSEY ST
3 FOTHERBY ST
4 KING EDWARD ST

B1
1 BRIDGE ST NORTH
2 THESIGER ST
3 SERVICE RD NO 1
4 SERVICE RD NO 2
5 ALBERT ST WEST
6 GARIBALDI ST
7 ALBERT CL
8 THESIGER WLK
9 FREEMAN WAY

B2
1 STUART WORTLEY ST
2 MURRAY ST
3 ROWLANDSON ST
4 RAILWAY PL

C1
1 KESGRAVE ST
2 LEVINGTON ST
3 MILFORD CT
4 MANSFIELD CT
5 WORDSWORTH CT
6 MUNSTER CT
7 WINDSOR CT
8 WESLEY CT
9 BANBURY CT

10 BEXLEY CT
11 ARNOLD CT
12 ACTON CT
13 APPLEBY CT
14 TRINITY ST
15 WEELSBY ST
16 SALACON WY
17 BRADMAN CT
18 GRAFTON ST
19 NORFOLK CT

20 SURREY CT
21 MARLBOROUGH CL
22 DUKE ST
23 DERBY CL
24 GEORGE JANNEY CT

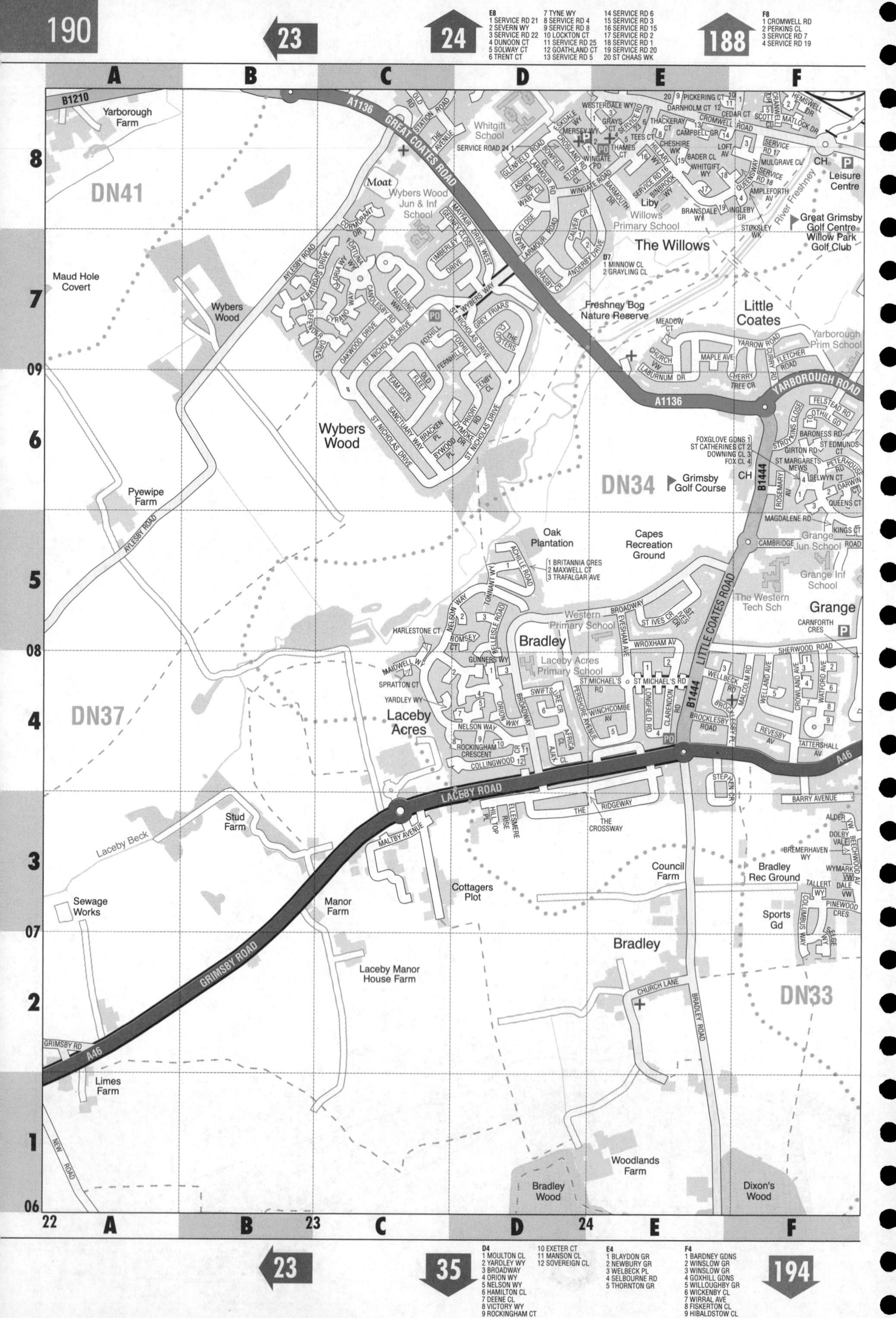
23
24
E8
1 SERVICE RD 21
2 SEVERN WY
3 SERVICE RD 22
4 DUNOON CT
5 SOLWAY CT
6 TRENT CT
7 TYNE WY
8 SERVICE RD 4
9 SERVICE RD 8
10 LOCKTON CT
11 SERVICE RD 25
12 GOATHLAND CT
13 SERVICE RD 5
14 SERVICE RD 6
15 SERVICE RD 3
16 SERVICE RD 15
17 SERVICE RD 2
18 SERVICE RD 1
19 SERVICE RD 20
20 ST CHAAS WK
188
F8
1 CROMWELL RD
2 PERKINS CL
3 SERVICE RD 7
4 SERVICE RD 19
A
B
C
D
E
F
B1210
Yarborough Farm
A1136
GREAT COATES ROAD
DN41
Moat
Wybers Wood Jun & Inf School
Whitgift School
The Willows
Liby
Willows Primary School
Leisure Centre
Great Grimsby Golf Centre
Willow Park Golf Club
River Freshney
D7
1 MINNOW CL
2 GRAYLING CL
Maud Hole Covert
Wybers Wood
Freshney Bog Nature Reserve
Little Coates
Yarborough Prim School
YARBOROUGH ROAD
A1136
Wybers Wood
DN34
Grimsby Golf Course
B1444
Pyewipe Farm
AYLESBY ROAD
Oak Plantation
Capes Recreation Ground
Grange Jun School
Grange Inf School
The Western Tech Sch
Grange
1 BRITANNIA CRES
2 MAXWELL CT
3 TRAFALGAR AVE
Western Primary School
Bradley
Laceby Acres Primary School
LITTLE COATES ROAD
DN37
Laceby Acres
LACEBY ROAD
A46
Stud Farm
Laceby Beck
Council Farm
Bradley Rec Ground
Sewage Works
Manor Farm
Cottagers Plot
Sports Gd
Bradley
GRIMSBY ROAD
Laceby Manor House Farm
DN33
CHURCH LANE
BRADLEY ROAD
GRIMSBY RD
A46
Limes Farm
NEW ROAD
Woodlands Farm
Bradley Wood
Dixon's Wood
22
23
24
23
35
D4
1 MOULTON CL
2 YARDLEY WY
3 BROADWAY
4 ORION WY
5 NELSON WY
6 HAMILTON CL
7 DEENE CL
8 VICTORY WY
9 ROCKINGHAM CT
10 EXETER CT
11 MANSON CL
12 SOVEREIGN CL
E4
1 BLAYDON GR
2 NEWBURY GR
3 WELBECK PL
4 SELBOURNE RD
5 THORNTON GR
F4
1 BARDNEY GDNS
2 WINSLOW GR
3 WINSLOW GR
4 GOXHILL GDNS
5 WILLOUGHBY GR
6 WICKENBY CL
7 WIRRAL AVE
8 FISKERTON CL
9 HIBALDSTOW CL
194

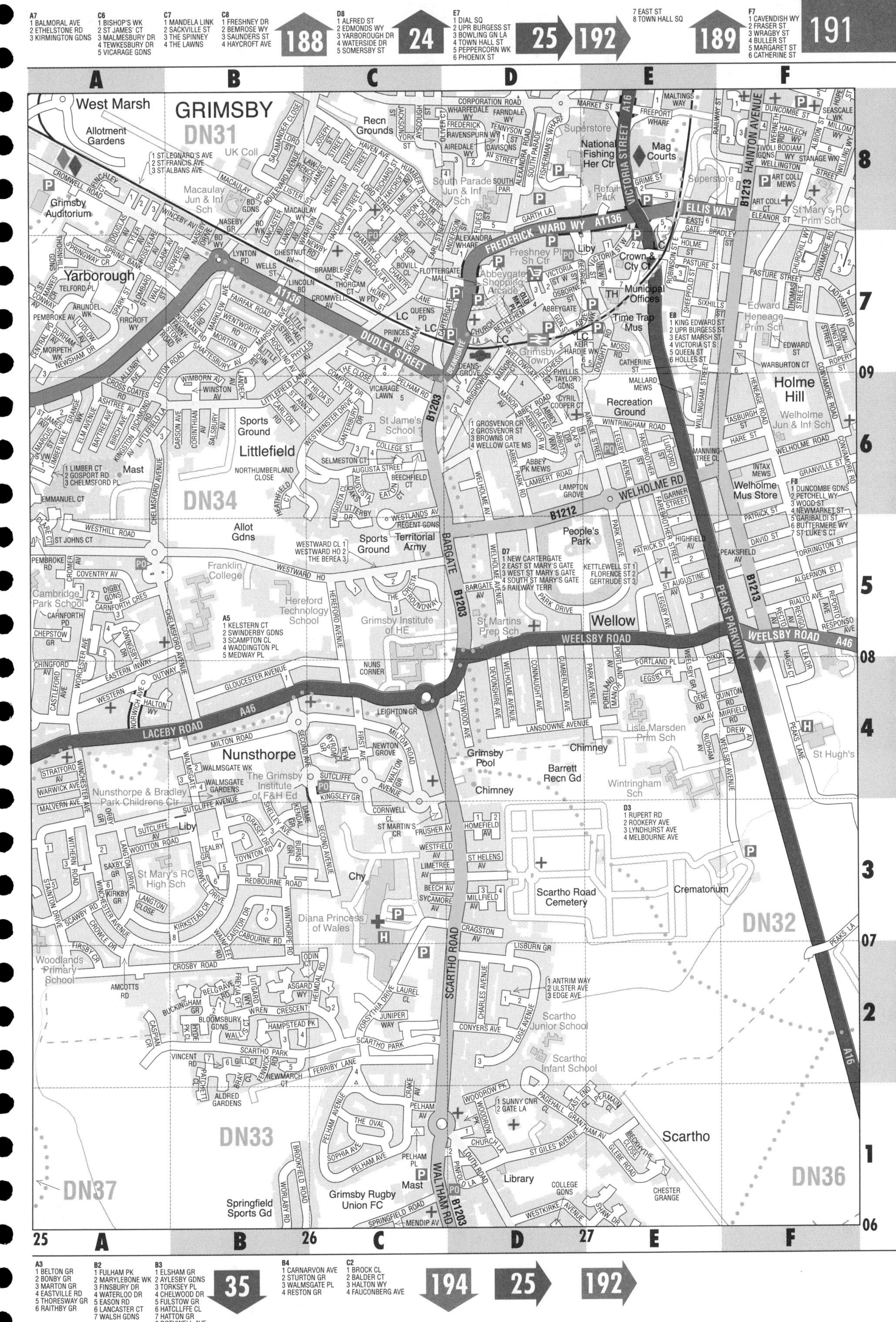
191
A7
1 BALMORAL AVE
2 ETHELSTONE RD
3 KIRMINGTON GDNS
C6
1 BISHOP'S WK
2 ST JAMES' CT
3 MALMESBURY DR
4 TEWKESBURY DR
5 VICARAGE GDNS
C7
1 MANDELA LINK
2 SACKVILLE ST
3 THE SPINNEY
4 THE LAWNS
C8
1 FRESHNEY DR
2 BEMROSE WY
3 SAUNDERS ST
4 HAYCROFT AVE
188
D8
1 ALFRED ST
2 EDMONDS WY
3 YARBOROUGH DR
4 WATERSIDE DR
5 SOMERSBY ST
24
E7
1 DIAL SQ
2 UPR BURGESS ST
3 BOWLING GN LA
4 TOWN HALL ST
5 PEPPERCORN WK
6 PHOENIX ST
25
192
7 EAST ST
8 TOWN HALL SQ
189
F7
1 CAVENDISH WY
2 FRASER ST
3 WRAGBY ST
4 BULLER ST
5 MARGARET ST
6 CATHERINE ST
A
B
C
D
E
F
8
7
09
6
5
08
4
3
07
2
1
06
25
26
27
West Marsh
GRIMSBY
DN31
Allotment Gardens
UK Coll
Grimsby Auditorium
Macaulay Jun & Inf Sch
Recn Grounds
Yarborough
South Parade Jun & Inf Sch
National Fishing Her Ctr
Mag Courts
Superstore
Retail Park
Freshney Pl Sh Ctr
Abbeygate Shopping Arcade
Liby
Crown & Cty Ct
Municipal Offices
Time Trap Mus
Grimsby Town
FREDERICK WARD WY
A1136
ELLIS WAY
DUDLEY STREET
VICTORIA STREET
A16
B1213
HAINTON AVENUE
Edward Heneage Prim Sch
St Mary's RC Prim Sch
Holme Hill
Welholme Jun & Inf Sch
Welholme Mus Store
Recreation Ground
Sports Ground
Littlefield
St James's School
DN34
Mast
Allot Gdns
Franklin College
Hereford Technology School
Territorial Army
Grimsby Institute of HE
BARGATE
B1203
B1212
WELHOLME RD
People's Park
Wellow
St Martins Prep Sch
WEELSBY ROAD
A46
PEAKS PARKWAY
Cambridge Park School
LACEBY ROAD
Nunsthorpe
The Grimsby Institute of F&H Ed
Nunsthorpe & Bradley Park Childrens Ctr
Grimsby Pool
Chimney
Barrett Recn Gd
Lisle Marsden Prim Sch
Wintringham Sch
St Hugh's
St Mary's RC High Sch
Chy
Diana Princess of Wales
Scartho Road Cemetery
Crematorium
DN32
SCARTHO ROAD
Woodlands Primary School
Scartho Junior School
Scartho Infant School
DN33
Scartho
DN36
DN37
Springfield Sports Gd
Grimsby Rugby Union FC
Library
WALTHAM RD
B4
1 CARNARVON AVE
2 STURTON GR
3 WALMSGATE PL
4 RESTON GR
C2
1 BROCK CL
2 BALDER CT
3 HALTON WY
4 FAUCONBERG AVE
A3
1 BELTON GR
2 BONBY GR
3 MARTON GR
4 EASTVILLE RD
5 THORESWAY GR
6 RAITHBY GR
B2
1 FULHAM PK
2 MARYLEBONE WK
3 FINSBURY DR
4 WATERLOO DR
5 EASON RD
6 LANCASTER CT
7 WALSH GDNS
B3
1 ELSHAM GR
2 AYLESBY GDNS
3 TORKSEY PL
4 CHELWOOD DR
5 FULSTOW GR
6 HATCLLFFE CL
7 HATTON GR
8 ROTHWELL AVE
35
194
25
192

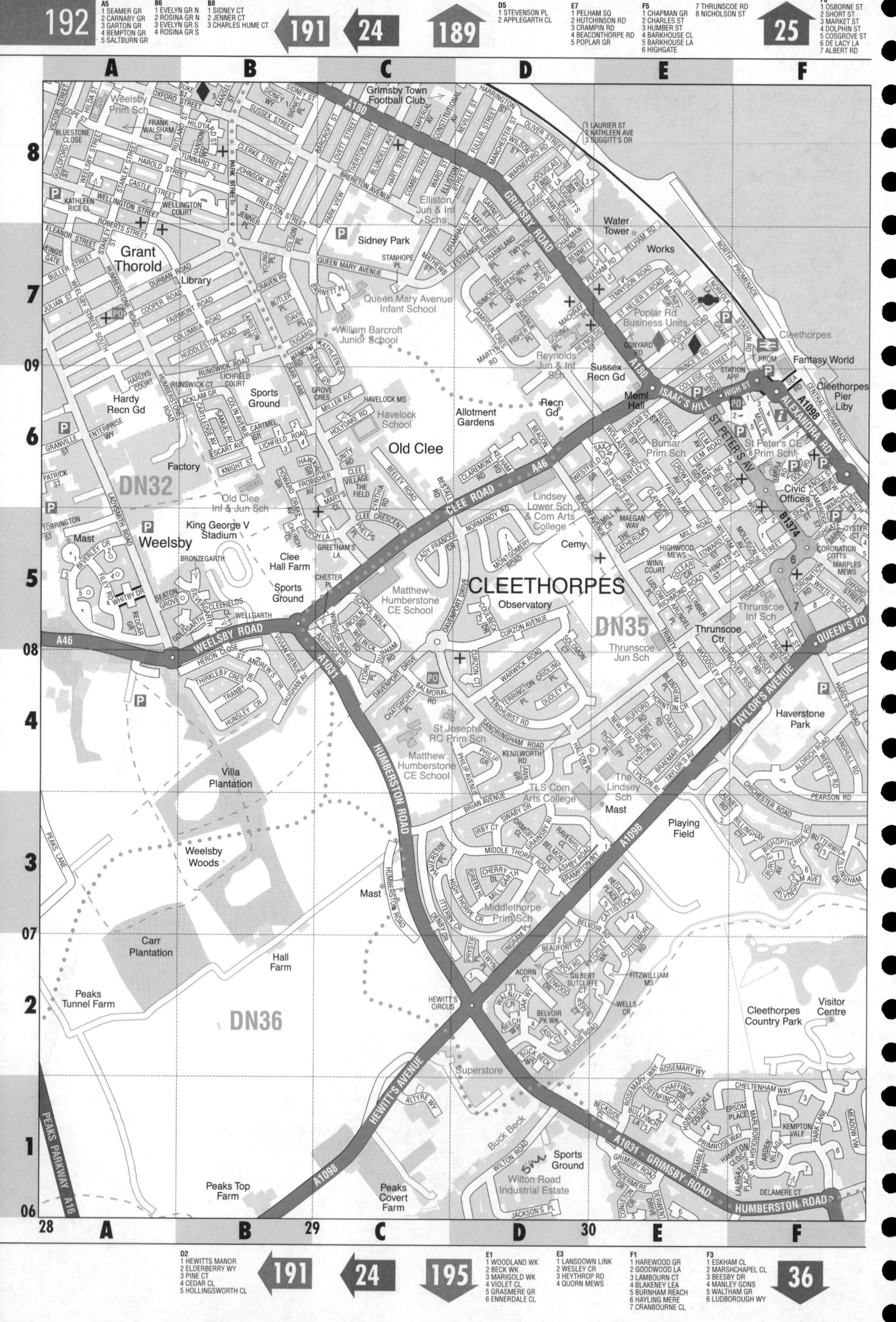

192
A5
1 SEAMER GR
2 CARNABY GR
3 GARTON GR
4 BEMPTON GR
5 SALTBURN GR
B6
1 EVELYN GR N
2 ROSINA GR N
3 EVELYN GR S
4 ROSINA GR S
B8
1 SIDNEY CT
2 JENNER CT
3 CHARLES HUME CT
191
24
189
D5
1 STEVENSON PL
2 APPLEGARTH CL
E7
1 PELHAM SQ
2 HUTCHINSON RD
3 CRAMPIN RD
4 BEACONTHORPE RD
5 POPLAR GR
F5
1 CHAPMAN GR
2 CHARLES ST
3 HUMBER ST
4 BARKHOUSE CL
5 BARKHOUSE LA
6 HIGHGATE
7 THRUNSCOE RD
8 NICHOLSON ST
25
F6
1 OSBORNE ST
2 SHORT ST
3 MARKET ST
4 DOLPHIN ST
5 COSGROVE ST
6 DE LACY LA
7 ALBERT RD
Grimsby Town Football Club
Weelsby Prim Sch
Grant Thorold
Library
Sidney Park
Elliston Jun & Inf Schs
Queen Mary Avenue Infant School
William Barcroft Junior School
Water Tower
Works
Poplar Rd Business Units
Cleethorpes
Fantasy World
Cleethorpes Pier
Liby
Reynolds Jun & Inf Sch
Sussex Recn Gd
Meml Hall
Recn Gd
Allotment Gardens
Havelock School
Old Clee
Hardy Recn Gd
Sports Ground
Factory
DN32
Old Clee Inf & Jun Sch
King George V Stadium
Weelsby
Clee Hall Farm
Sports Ground
Lindsey Lower Sch & Com Arts College
Cemy
Bursar Prim Sch
St Peter's CE Prim Sch
Civic Offices
CLEETHORPES
Observatory
Matthew Humberstone CE School
DN35
Thrunscoe Jun Sch
Thrunscoe Ctr
Thrunscoe Inf Sch
Haverstone Park
St Josephs RC Prim Sch
Matthew Humberstone CE School
TLS Com Arts College
The Lindsey Sch
Mast
Villa Plantation
Playing Field
Weelsby Woods
Mast
Middlethorpe Prim Sch
Carr Plantation
Hall Farm
Peaks Tunnel Farm
DN36
Hewitt's Circus
Cleethorpes Country Park
Visitor Centre
Superstore
Buck Beck
Sports Ground
Wilton Road Industrial Estate
Peaks Top Farm
Peaks Covert Farm
A180 GRIMSBY ROAD
A46 CLEE ROAD
WEELSBY ROAD
A1031 HUMBERSTON ROAD
A1098 TAYLOR'S AVENUE
HEWITT'S AVENUE
A1031 GRIMSBY ROAD
HUMBERSTON ROAD
PEAKS PARKWAY A16
ISAAC'S HILL
ALEXANDRA RD
QUEEN'S PD
B1374
NORTH PROMENADE
CENTRAL PROMENADE
D2
1 HEWITTS MANOR
2 ELDERBERRY WY
3 PINE CT
4 CEDAR CL
5 HOLLINGSWORTH CL
191
24
195
E1
1 WOODLAND WK
2 BECK WK
3 MARIGOLD WK
4 VIOLET CL
5 GRASMERE GR
6 ENNERDALE CL
E3
1 LANSDOWN LINK
2 WESLEY CR
3 HEYTHROP RD
4 QUORN MEWS
F1
1 HAREWOOD GR
2 GOODWOOD LA
3 LAMBOURN CT
4 BLAKENEY LEA
5 BURNHAM REACH
6 HAYLING MERE
7 CRANBOURNE CL
F3
1 ESKHAM CL
2 MARSHCHAPEL CL
3 BEESBY DR
4 MANLEY GDNS
5 WALTHAM GR
6 LUDBOROUGH WY
36

25

A5
1 SOUTH ST
2 BRIGHTON ST
3 SEGMERE ST
4 HAIGH ST

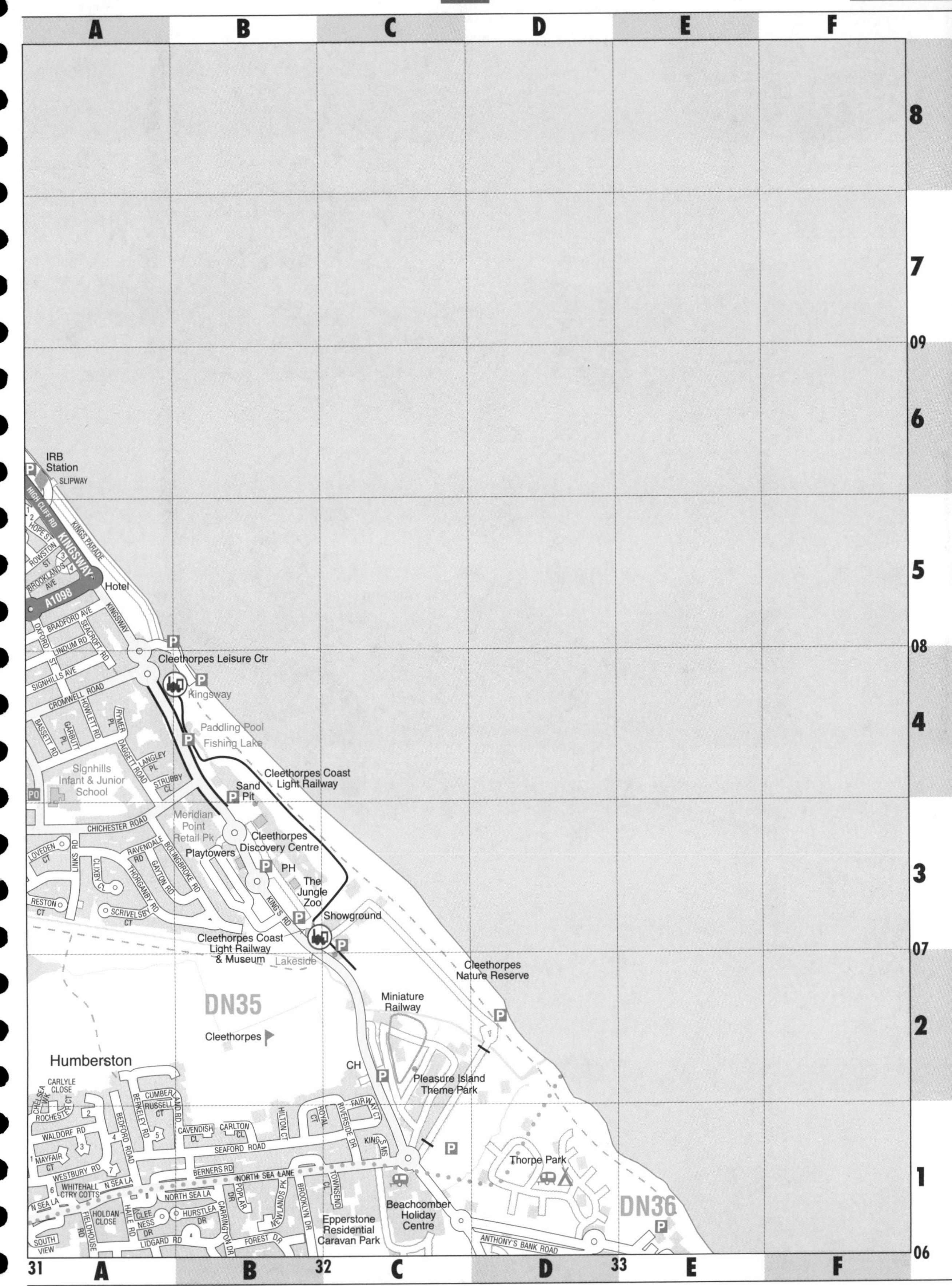

A — B — C — D — E — F

8

7

09

6

IRB
Station
SLIPWAY

5

08

BRADFORD AVE
SEACROFT RD
KINGSWAY
OXFORD
LINDUM RD
SIGNHILLS AVE
CROMWELL ROAD
BASSETT RD
GARBUTT
HOWLETT RD
RYMER
FLYMER
DAGGETT ROAD
LANGLEY PL
STRUBBY CL

Hotel

A1098

Cleethorpes Leisure Ctr

Kingsway

Paddling Pool
Fishing Lake

Cleethorpes Coast
Light Railway

Sand
Pit

Signhills
Infant & Junior
School

CHICHESTER ROAD

Meridian
Point
Retail Pk

Playtowers

Cleethorpes
Discovery Centre

PH

The
Jungle
Zoo

Showground

Cleethorpes Coast
Light Railway
& Museum

Lakeside

Cleethorpes
Nature Reserve

07

DN35

Cleethorpes

Miniature
Railway

2

Humberston

CARLYLE
CLOSE

CH

Pleasure Island
Theme Park

Thorpe Park

DN36

WALDORF RD
MAYFAIR
WESTBURY RD
WHITEHALL CTRY COTTS
N SEA LA
SOUTH VIEW

BEDFORD ROAD
BERKELEY RD
CLEE NESS DR
HURSTLEA DR
CARRINGTON DR
FOREST DR
LIDGARD RD

CAVENDISH CL
CARLTON CL
SEAFORD ROAD
BERNERS RD
NORTH SEA LANE
POPLAR DR
NEWLANDS PK
BROOKLYN DR

HILTON CT
ROYAL CT
FAIRWAY CT
RIVERSIDE DR
TOWNSEND
KING'S MS

Epperstone
Residential
Caravan Park

Beachcomber
Holiday
Centre

ANTHONY'S BANK ROAD

1

06

A1
1 WESTPORT RD
2 WESTBURY PK
3 FAIRFIELD CT
4 WEYFORD RD
5 GROVENOR CT
6 WHITEHALL RD
7 KINGSTON CL

36

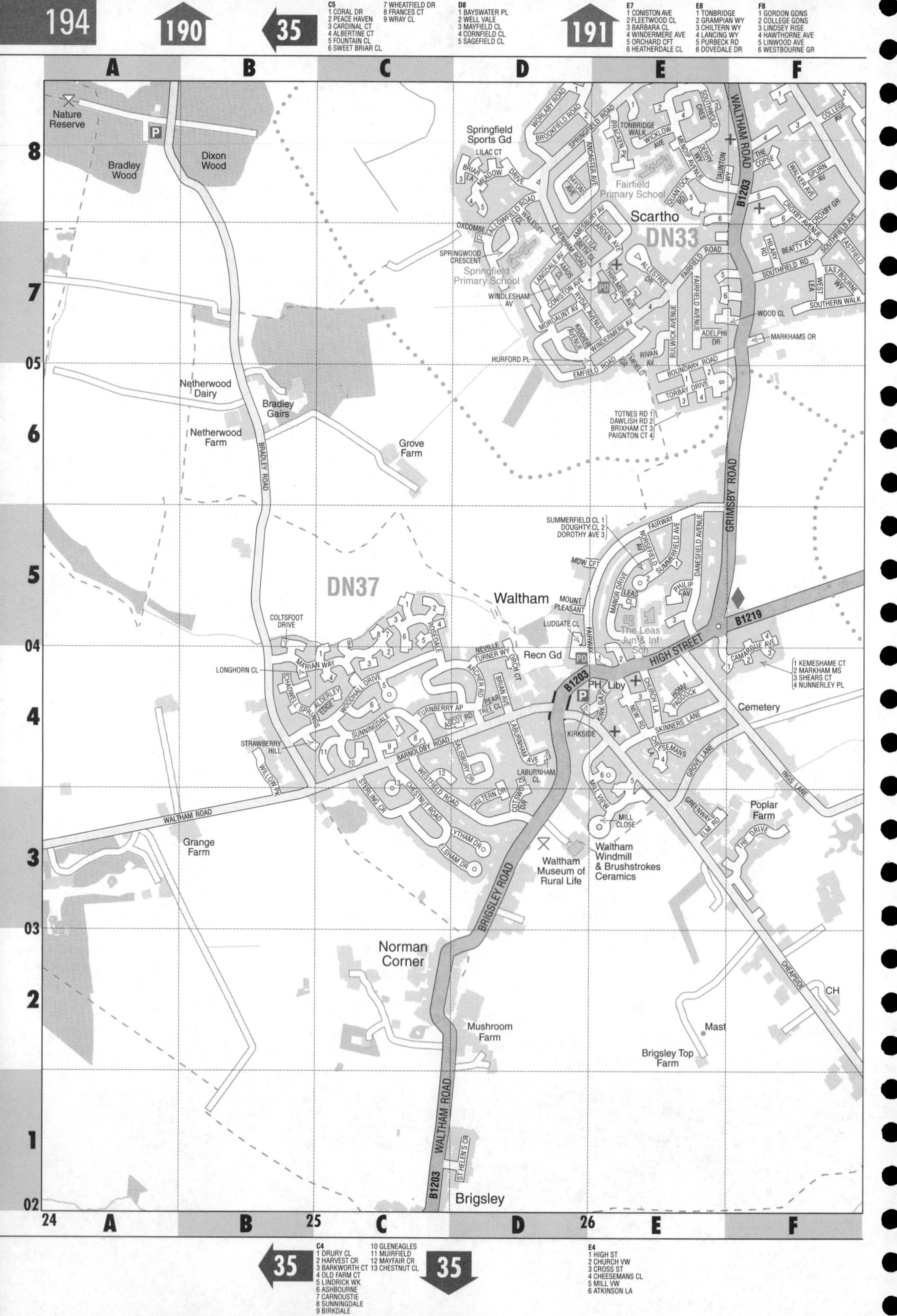
190
35
C5
1 CORAL DR
2 PEACE HAVEN
3 CARDINAL CT
4 ALBERTINE CT
5 FOUNTAIN CL
6 SWEET BRIAR CL
7 WHEATFIELD DR
8 FRANCES CT
9 WRAY CL
D8
1 BAYSWATER PL
2 WELL VALE
3 MAYFIELD CL
4 CORNFIELD CL
5 SAGEFIELD CL
191
E7
1 CONISTON AVE
2 FLEETWOOD CL
3 BARBARA CL
4 WINDERMERE AVE
5 ORCHARD CFT
6 HEATHERDALE CL
E8
1 TONBRIDGE
2 GRAMPIAN WY
3 CHILTERN WY
4 LANCING WY
5 PURBECK RD
6 DOVEDALE DR
F8
1 GORDON GDNS
2 COLLEGE GDNS
3 LINDSEY RISE
4 HAWTHORNE AVE
5 LINWOOD AVE
6 WESTBOURNE GR
A
B
C
D
E
F
Nature Reserve
Bradley Wood
Dixon Wood
Springfield Sports Gd
LILAC CT
Fairfield Primary School
Scartho
DN33
Springfield Primary School
SPRINGWOOD CRESCENT
OXCOMBE CL
WINDLESHAM AV
HURFORD PL
MARKHAMS OR
WOOD CL
TOTNES RD 1
DAWLISH RD 2
BRIXHAM CT 3
PAIGNTON CT 4
Netherwood Dairy
Bradley Gairs
Netherwood Farm
Grove Farm
BRADLEY ROAD
WALTHAM ROAD
GRIMSBY ROAD
B1203
B1219
SUMMERFIELD CL 1
DOUGHTY CL 2
DOROTHY AVE 3
MDW CFT
MOUNT PLEASANT
LUDGATE CL
DN37
Waltham
COLTSFOOT DRIVE
LONGHORN CL
STRAWBERRY HILL
The Leas Jun & Inf Sch
Recn Gd
HIGH STREET
1 KEMESHAME CT
2 MARKHAM MS
3 SHEARS CT
4 NUNNERLEY PL
Cemetery
KIRKSIDE
Poplar Farm
Grange Farm
Waltham Museum of Rural Life
Waltham Windmill & Brushstrokes Ceramics
BRIGSLEY ROAD
Norman Corner
Mushroom Farm
Mast
CH
Brigsley Top Farm
CHEAPSIDE
ST HELEN'S CR
Brigsley
8
7
05
6
5
04
4
3
03
2
1
02
24
25
26
C4
1 DRURY CL
2 HARVEST CR
3 BARKWORTH CT
4 OLD FARM CT
5 LINDRICK WK
6 ASHBOURNE
7 CARNOUSTIE
8 SUNNINGDALE
9 BIRKDALE
10 GLENEAGLES
11 MUIRFIELD
12 MAYFAIR CR
13 CHESTNUT CL
35
35
E4
1 HIGH ST
2 CHURCH VW
3 CROSS ST
4 CHEESEMANS CL
5 MILL VW
6 ATKINSON LA

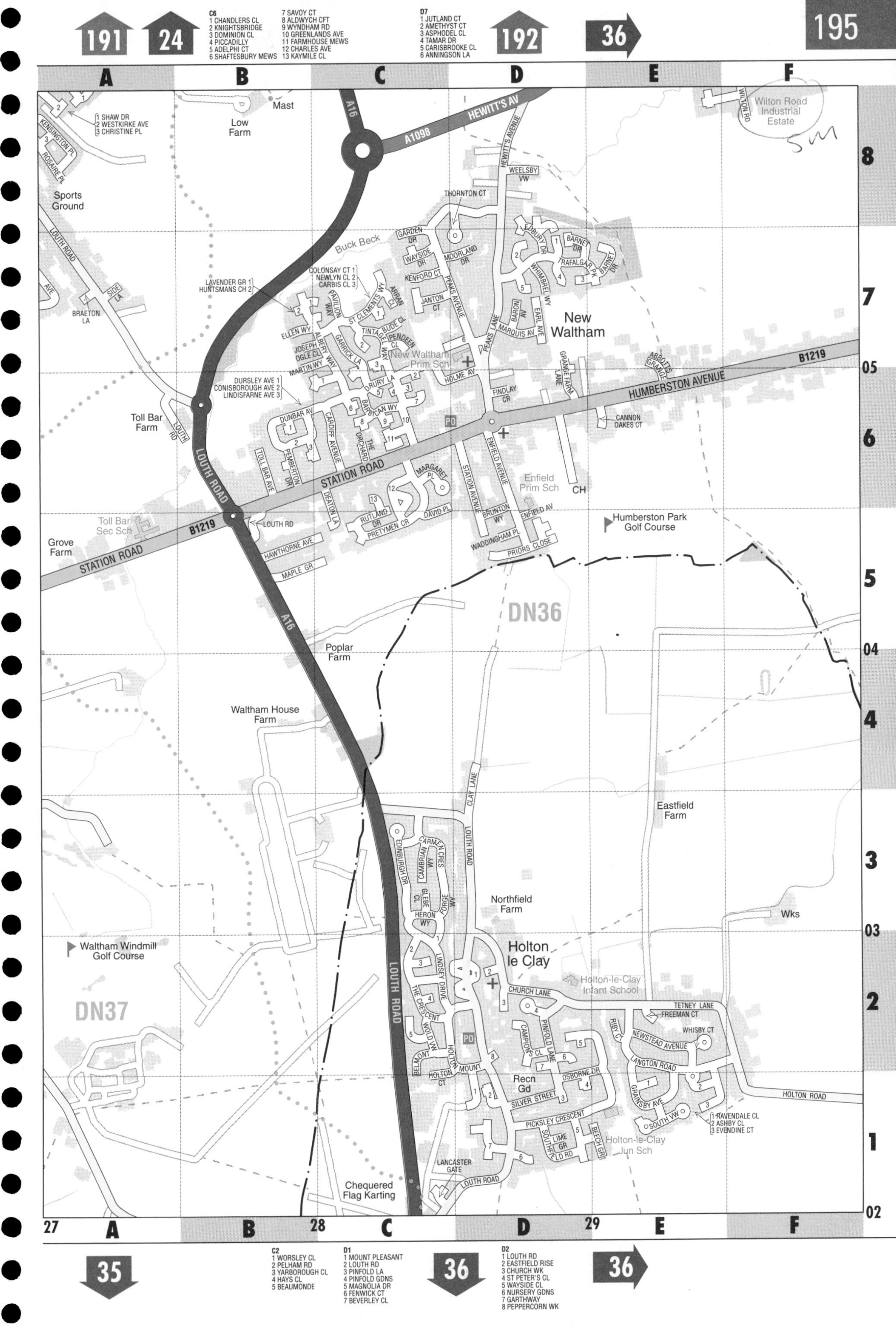
191
24
C6
1 CHANDLERS CL
2 KNIGHTSBRIDGE
3 DOMINION CL
4 PICCADILLY
5 ADELPHI CT
6 SHAFTESBURY MEWS
7 SAVOY CT
8 ALDWYCH CFT
9 WYNDHAM RD
10 GREENLANDS AVE
11 FARMHOUSE MEWS
12 CHARLES AVE
13 KAYMILE CL
D7
1 JUTLAND CT
2 AMETHYST CT
3 ASPHODEL CL
4 TAMAR DR
5 CARISBROOKE CL
6 ANNINGSON LA
192
36
1 SHAW DR
2 WESTKIRKE AVE
3 CHRISTINE PL
Low Farm
Mast
HEWITT'S AV
A1098
A16
Wilton Road Industrial Estate
WILTON RD
Sports Ground
LOUTH ROAD
New Waltham
Buck Beck
HUMBERSTON AVENUE
B1219
STATION ROAD
Toll Bar Farm
Toll Bar Sec Sch
Grove Farm
Enfield Prim Sch
New Waltham Prim Sch
Humberston Park Golf Course
DN36
Poplar Farm
Waltham House Farm
Eastfield Farm
Northfield Farm
Holton le Clay
Holton-le-Clay Infant School
Waltham Windmill Golf Course
DN37
Recn Gd
Holton-le-Clay Jun Sch
Chequered Flag Karting
Wks
HOLTON ROAD
CHURCH LANE
TETNEY LANE
LOUTH ROAD
CLAY LANE
C2
1 WORSLEY CL
2 PELHAM RD
3 YARBOROUGH CL
4 HAYS CL
5 BEAUMONDE
D1
1 MOUNT PLEASANT
2 LOUTH RD
3 PINFOLD LA
4 PINFOLD GDNS
5 MAGNOLIA DR
6 FENWICK CT
7 BEVERLEY CL
D2
1 LOUTH RD
2 EASTFIELD RISE
3 CHURCH WK
4 ST PETER'S CL
5 WAYSIDE CL
6 NURSERY GDNS
7 GARTHWAY
8 PEPPERCORN WK
35
36
36

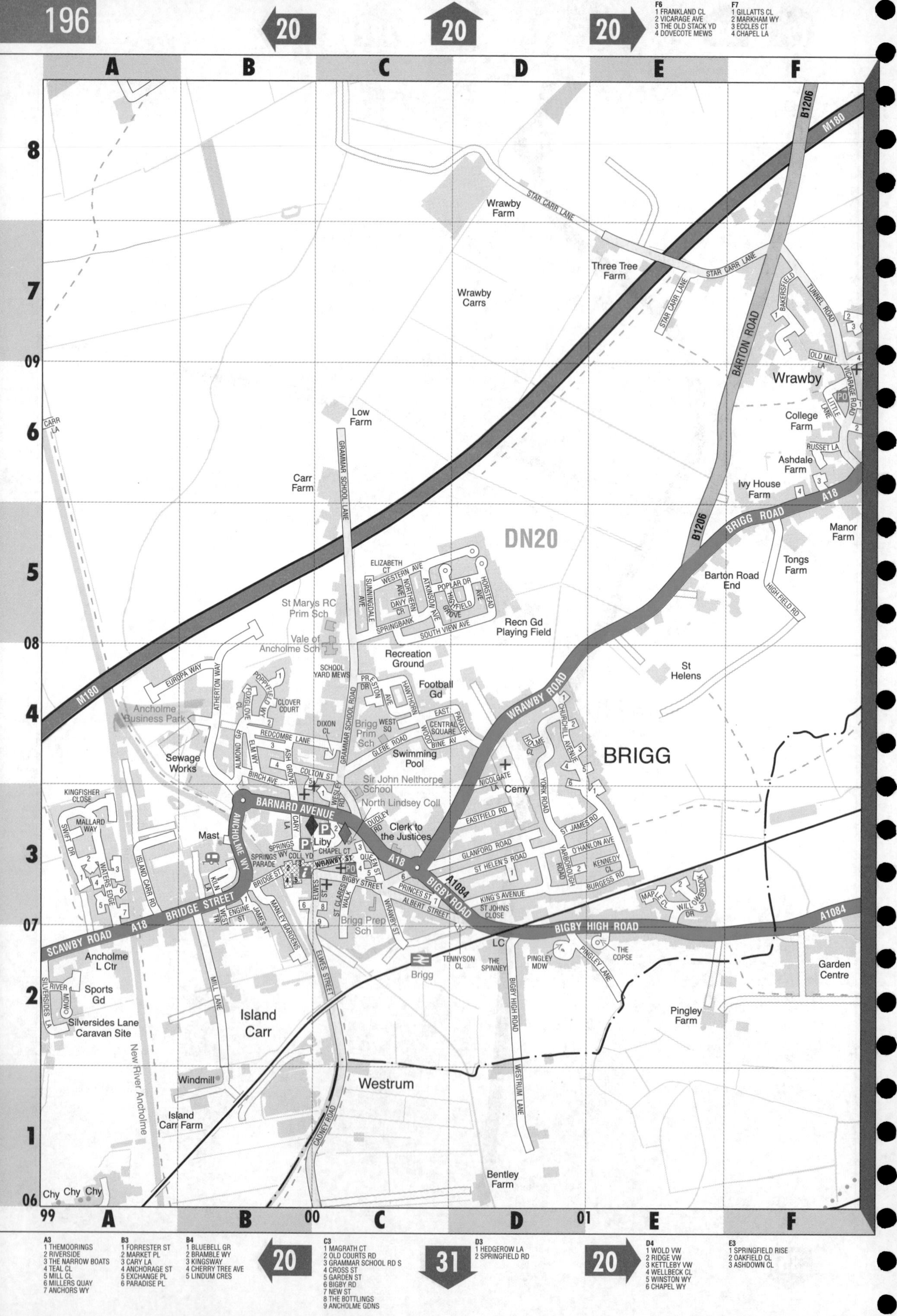

F6
1 FRANKLAND CL
2 VICARAGE AVE
3 THE OLD STACK YD
4 DOVECOTE MEWS

F7
1 GILLATTS CL
2 MARKHAM WY
3 ECCLES CT
4 CHAPEL LA

DN20

Wrawby

BRIGG

Westrum

Island Carr

A3
1 THEMOORINGS
2 RIVERSIDE
3 THE NARROW BOATS
4 TEAL CL
5 MILL CL
6 MILLERS QUAY
7 ANCHORS WY

B3
1 FORRESTER ST
2 MARKET PL
3 CARY LA
4 ANCHORAGE ST
5 EXCHANGE PL
6 PARADISE PL

B4
1 BLUEBELL GR
2 BRAMBLE WY
3 KINGSWAY
4 CHERRY TREE AVE
5 LINDUM CRES

C3
1 MAGRATH CT
2 OLD COURTS RD
3 GRAMMAR SCHOOL RD S
4 CROSS ST
5 GARDEN ST
6 BIGBY RD
7 NEW ST
8 THE BOTTLINGS
9 ANCHOLME GDNS

D3
1 HEDGEROW LA
2 SPRINGFIELD RD

D4
1 WOLD VW
2 RIDGE VW
3 KETTLEBY VW
4 WELLBECK CL
5 WINSTON WY
6 CHAPEL WY

E3
1 SPRINGFIELD RISE
2 OAKFIELD CL
3 ASHDOWN CL

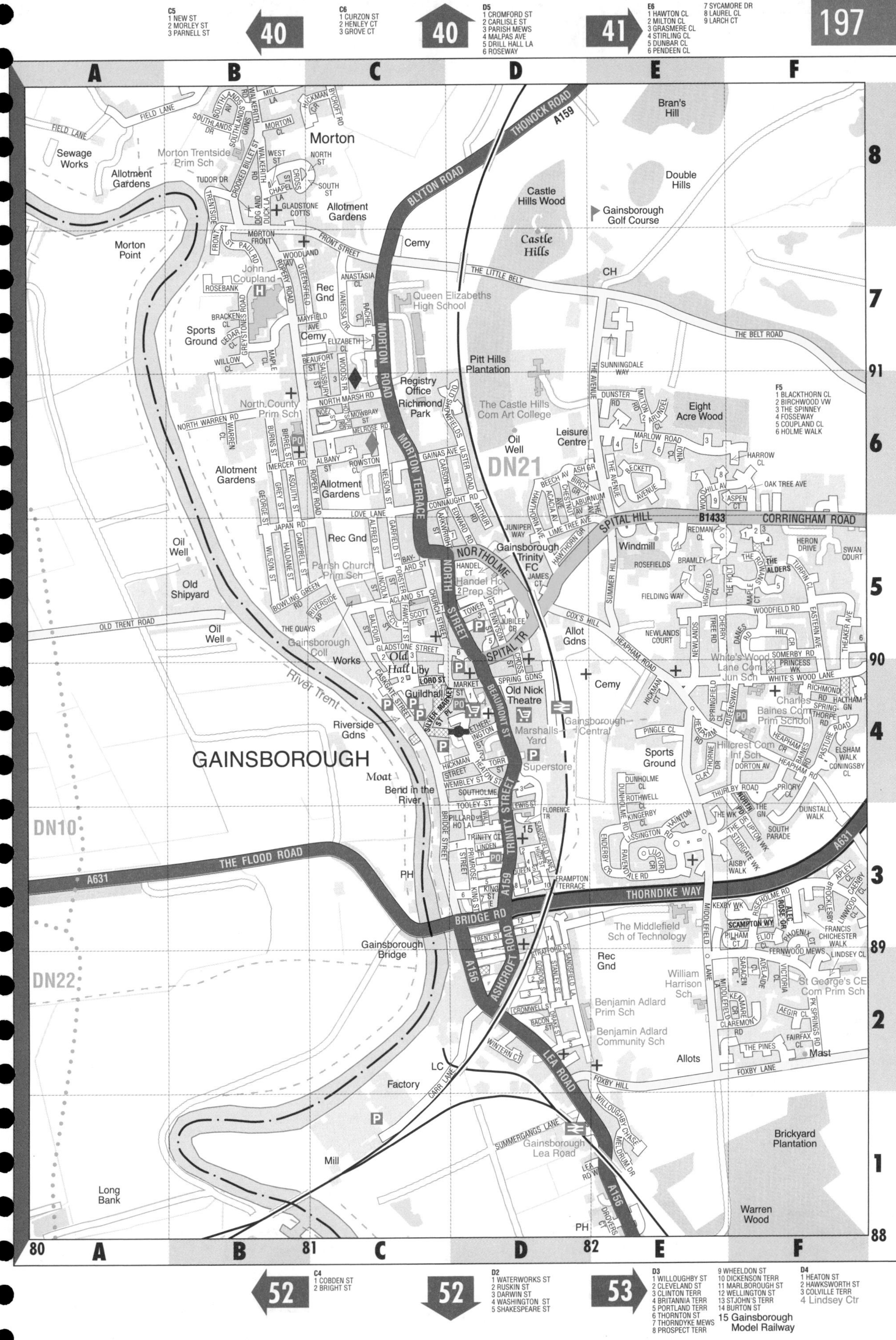
C5
1 NEW ST
2 MORLEY ST
3 PARNELL ST
40
C6
1 CURZON ST
2 HENLEY CT
3 GROVE CT
40
D5
1 CROMFORD ST
2 CARLISLE ST
3 PARISH MEWS
4 MALPAS AVE
5 DRILL HALL LA
6 ROSEWAY
41
E6
1 HAWTON CL
2 MILTON CL
3 GRASMERE CL
4 STIRLING CL
5 DUNBAR CL
6 PENDEEN CL
7 SYCAMORE DR
8 LAUREL CL
9 LARCH CT
A
B
C
D
E
F
8
7
91
6
5
90
4
3
89
2
1
88
80
81
82
Morton
Sewage Works
Allotment Gardens
Morton Trentside Prim Sch
Morton Point
John Coupland
Sports Ground
Rec Gnd
Cemy
Bran's Hill
Double Hills
Castle Hills Wood
Castle Hills
Gainsborough Golf Course
THONOCK ROAD
A159
BLYTON ROAD
FRONT STREET
THE LITTLE BELT
THE BELT ROAD
CH
Queen Elizabeths High School
MORTON ROAD
Pitt Hills Plantation
Registry Office
Richmond Park
The Castle Hills Com Art College
Oil Well
Leisure Centre
Eight Acre Wood
F5
1 BLACKTHORN CL
2 BIRCHWOOD VW
3 THE SPINNEY
4 FOSSEWAY
5 COUPLAND CL
6 HOLME WALK
North County Prim Sch
NORTH WARREN RD
MORTON TERRACE
DN21
Allotment Gardens
SPITAL HILL
B1433
CORRINGHAM ROAD
Windmill
Gainsborough Trinity FC
NORTHOLME
NORTH STREET
Parish Church Prim Sch
Handel Ho Prep Sch
Old Shipyard
OLD TRENT ROAD
Allot Gdns
Gainsborough Coll
Works
Old Hall
Liby
Guildhall
Old Nick Theatre
Cemy
Gainsborough Central
Marshalls Yard
Superstore
River Trent
Riverside Gdns
White's Wood Lane Com Jun Sch
Charles Baines Com Prim School
Hillcrest Com Inf Sch
Sports Ground
GAINSBOROUGH
Moat
Bend in the River
TRINITY STREET
DN10
THE FLOOD ROAD
A631
THORNDIKE WAY
BRIDGE RD
PH
The Middlefield Sch of Technology
Gainsborough Bridge
ASHCROFT ROAD
A156
DN22
Rec Gnd
William Harrison Sch
St George's CE Com Prim Sch
Benjamin Adlard Prim Sch
Benjamin Adlard Community Sch
Allots
Mast
LC
Factory
LEA ROAD
FOXBY HILL
FOXBY LANE
Gainsborough Lea Road
Mill
Brickyard Plantation
Long Bank
Warren Wood
PH
52
C4
1 COBDEN ST
2 BRIGHT ST
52
D2
1 WATERWORKS ST
2 RUSKIN ST
3 DARWIN ST
4 WASHINGTON ST
5 SHAKESPEARE ST
53
D3
1 WILLOUGHBY ST
2 CLEVELAND ST
3 CLINTON TERR
4 BRITANNIA TERR
5 PORTLAND TERR
6 THORNTON ST
7 THORNDYKE MEWS
8 PROSPECT TERR
9 WHEELDON ST
10 DICKENSON TERR
11 MARLBOROUGH ST
12 WELLINGTON ST
13 STJOHN'S TERR
14 BURTON ST
15 Gainsborough Model Railway
D4
1 HEATON ST
2 HAWKSWORTH ST
3 COLVILLE TERR
4 Lindsey Ctr

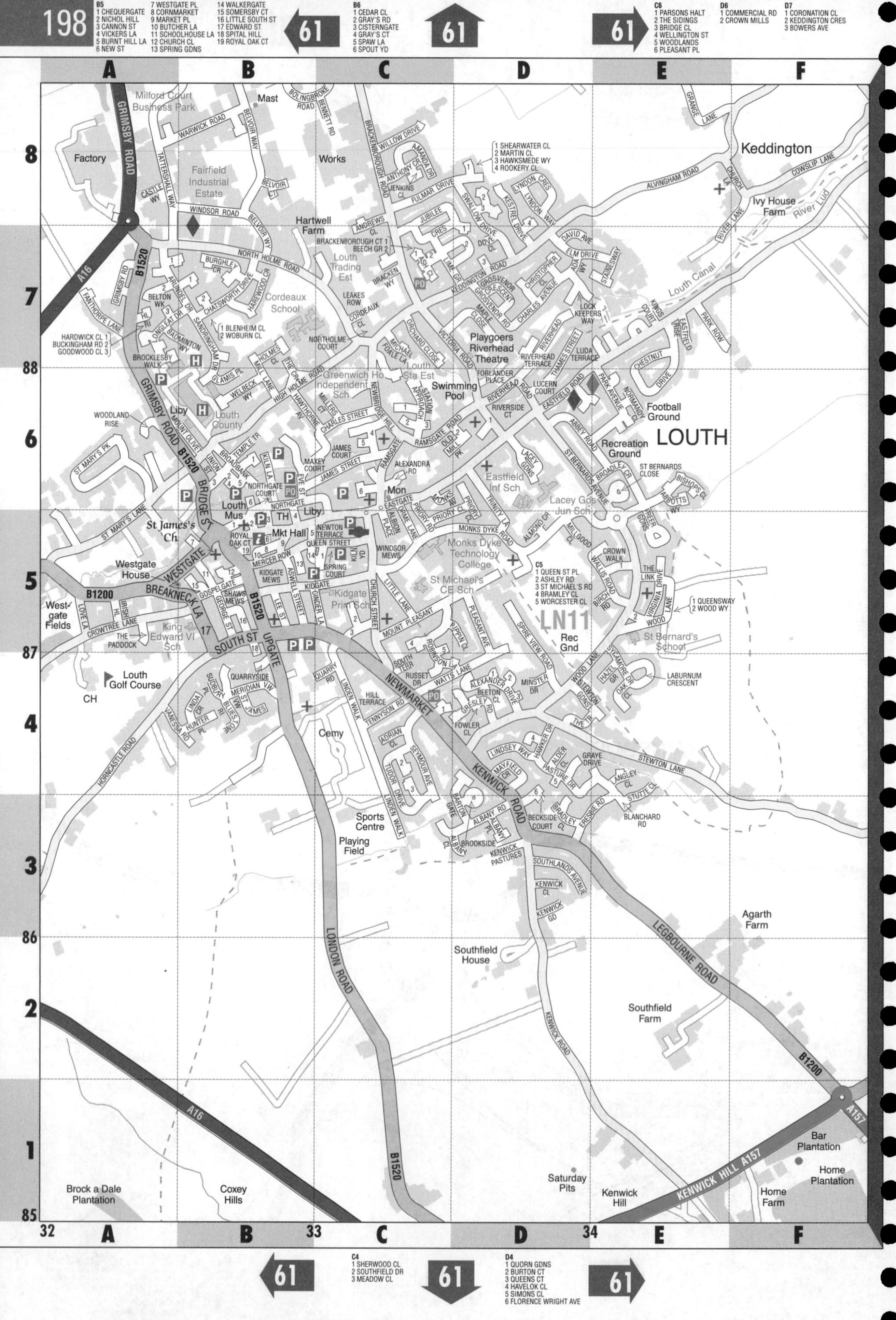
B5
1 CHEQUERGATE
2 NICHOL HILL
3 CANNON ST
4 VICKERS LA
5 BURNT HILL LA
6 NEW ST
7 WESTGATE PL
8 CORNMARKET
9 MARKET PL
10 BUTCHER LA
11 SCHOOLHOUSE LA
12 CHURCH CL
13 SPRING GDNS
14 WALKERGATE
15 SOMERSBY CT
16 LITTLE SOUTH ST
17 EDWARD ST
18 SPITAL HILL
19 ROYAL OAK CT
61
B6
1 CEDAR CL
2 GRAY'S RD
3 CISTERNGATE
4 GRAY'S CT
5 SPAW LA
6 SPOUT YD
61
61
C6
1 PARSONS HALT
2 THE SIDINGS
3 BRIDGE CL
4 WELLINGTON ST
5 WOODLANDS
6 PLEASANT PL
D6
1 COMMERCIAL RD
2 CROWN MILLS
D7
1 CORONATION CL
2 KEDDINGTON CRES
3 BOWERS AVE
A
B
C
D
E
F
8
7
88
6
5
87
4
3
86
2
1
85
32
33
34
Milford Court Business Park
Mast
Factory
Works
Fairfield Industrial Estate
GRIMSBY ROAD
WARWICK ROAD
BELVOIR WAY
BOLINGBROKE ROAD
BENNETT RD
BRACKENBOROUGH ROAD
WILLOW DRIVE
AMANDA DR
ANTHONY CRES
JENKINS CL
FULMAR DRIVE
1 SHEARWATER CL
2 MARTIN CL
3 HAWKSMEDE WY
4 ROOKERY CL
LYNDON CRES
LYNDON WAY
KESTREL DRIVE
SWALLOW DRIVE
Keddington
GRANGE LANE
ALVINGHAM ROAD
CHURCH LA
COWSLIP LANE
Ivy House Farm
River Lud
RIVER LANE
CASTLE WY
TATTERSHALL WAY
WINDSOR ROAD
BELVOIR CT
Hartwell Farm
ANDREWS CL
BRACKENBOROUGH CT 1
BEECH GR 2
JUBILEE CRES
LIME GR
ASH CL
DOVE CL
DAVID AVE
ELM DRIVE
STAINESWAY
A16
B1520
NORTH HOLME ROAD
BURGHLEY CR
HAREWOOD CR
Louth Trading Est
BRACKEN WY
PO
KEDDINGTON ROAD
GROSVENOR CRESCENT
GROSVENOR RD
CHRISTOPHER CL
CHARLES AVENUE
ADA WY
Louth Canal
KINGS COURT
GRIMSBY RD
FANTHORPE LANE
BELTON WK
ARUNDEL DR
CHATSWORTH DRIVE
Cordeaux School
LEAKES ROW
CORDEAUX CL
MAPLE CLOSE
LOCK KEEPERS WAY
EASTFIELD RISE
PARK ROW
HARDWICK CL 1
BUCKINGHAM RD 2
GOODWOOD CL 3
LONGLEAT DR
SANDRINGHAM DR
BADMINTON WY
1 BLENHEIM CL
2 WOBURN CL
NORTHOLME COURT
MICHAEL FOALE LA
ORCHARD CLOSE
VICTORIA ROAD
Playgoers Riverhead Theatre
RIVERHEAD
THAMES STREET
LUDA TERRACE
CHESTNUT DRIVE
BROCKLESBY WALK
HOLMES CL
THE CRES
GLAMIS PL
MILL LANE
HIGH HOLME ROAD
Greenwich Ho Independent Sch
Louth Sta Est
STATION APPROACH
Swimming Pool
FORLANDER PLACE
RIVERHEAD TERRACE
RIVERHEAD ROAD
LUCERN COURT
EASTFIELD ROAD
PARK AVENUE
NORMANDY CL
Football Ground
WOODLAND RISE
Liby
MOUNT OLIVET
Louth County
WELBECK WY
HAWTHORNE AV
MILLERS CT
NEWBRIDGE HILL
CHARLES STREET
RAMSGATE ROAD
RIVERSIDE CT
ABBEY ROAD
Recreation Ground
LOUTH
ST MARY'S PK
TEMPLE TR
BROADBANK
KILN LA
JAMES COURT
MAXEY COURT
JAMES STREET
RAMSGATE
ALEXANDRA RD
OLD MILL PK
LACEY GDNS
ST BERNARDS AVENUE
BROADLEY CR
ST BERNARDS CLOSE
BISHOPS CL
ABBOTTS WY
UNION ST
NORTHGATE COURT
EVE ST
Mon
Eastfield Inf Sch
Lacey Gds Jun Sch
FREER GDNS
BRIDGE ST
ST MARY'S LANE
NORTHGATE
Louth Mus
TH
Liby
EASTGATE
ALBION PLACE
ORME LANE
PRIORY RD
MONKS AV
PRIORY CL
TRINITY LA
St James's Ch
ROYAL OAK CT
Mkt Hall
NEWTON TERRACE
MONKS DYKE ROAD
ALMOND CR
MILLGOOD CL
WESTGATE
QUEEN STREET
Monks Dyke Technology College
CROWN WALK
THE LINK
Westgate House
MERCER ROW
KIDGATE MEWS
SPRING COURT
KILN YD
WINDSOR MEWS
C5
1 QUEEN ST PL
2 ASHLEY RD
3 ST MICHAEL'S RD
4 BRAMLEY CL
5 WORCESTER CL
WALLIS ROAD
VIRGINIA DRIVE
B1200
BREAKNECK LA
GOSPELGATE
SHAWS MEWS
KIDGATE
St Michael's CE Sch
BIRCH RD
WOOD LANE
1 QUEENSWAY
2 WOOD WY
West-gate Fields
LOVE LA
IRISH HL
GEORGE ST
LEE ST
ASWELL STREET
CINDER LA
Kidgate Prim Sch
CHURCH STREET
LITTLE LANE
LN11
CROWTREE LANE
THE PADDOCK
King Edward VI Sch
SOUTH ST
UPGATE
MOUNT PLEASANT
PLEASANT AVE
SPIRE VIEW ROAD
Rec Gnd
St Bernard's School
ROBINSON LA
RIPPIN CL
Louth Golf Course
CH
QUARRYSIDE
SUDBURY PL
MERIDIAN VW
BLUESTONE RI
ST JAMES VW
QUARRY RD
SOUTH TERR
RUSSET DR
WATTS LANE
ALEXANDER DRIVE
MINSTER DR
STEWTON GDNS
SYCAMORE DR
HAZEL GR
OAK DR
LABURNUM CRESCENT
HILL TERRACE
NEWMARKET
TENNYSON RD
BEETON CL
GRESLEY RD
FOWLER CL
THE RIDE
LINDA CR
HUNTER PL
VANESSA RD
LINDEN WALK
Cemy
ADRIAN CL
SEYMOUR AVE
LINDSEY WAY
HAWKER DR
ALDER CL
PASTURE DR
GRAYE DRIVE
STEWTON LANE
HORNCASTLE ROAD
KENWICK ROAD
MAYFIELD CR
LANGLEY CL
STUTTE CL
TUDOR DRIVE
BARTON GATE
BECKSIDE COURT
BRADLEY CL
ERESBIE RD
BLANCHARD RD
Sports Centre
ALBANY RD
ALBANY PL
ALBANY CL
BROOKSIDE
Playing Field
KENWICK PASTURES
SOUTHLANDS AVENUE
KENWICK CL
KENWICK GD
Agarth Farm
LEGBOURNE ROAD
LONDON ROAD
Southfield House
Southfield Farm
KENWICK ROAD
B1200
A157
Bar Plantation
KENWICK HILL A157
Home Plantation
Home Farm
Brock a Dale Plantation
Coxey Hills
Saturday Pits
Kenwick Hill
C4
1 SHERWOOD CL
2 SOUTHFIELD DR
3 MEADOW CL
61
61
D4
1 QUORN GDNS
2 BURTON CT
3 QUEENS CT
4 HAVELOK CL
5 SIMONS CL
6 FLORENCE WRIGHT AVE
61

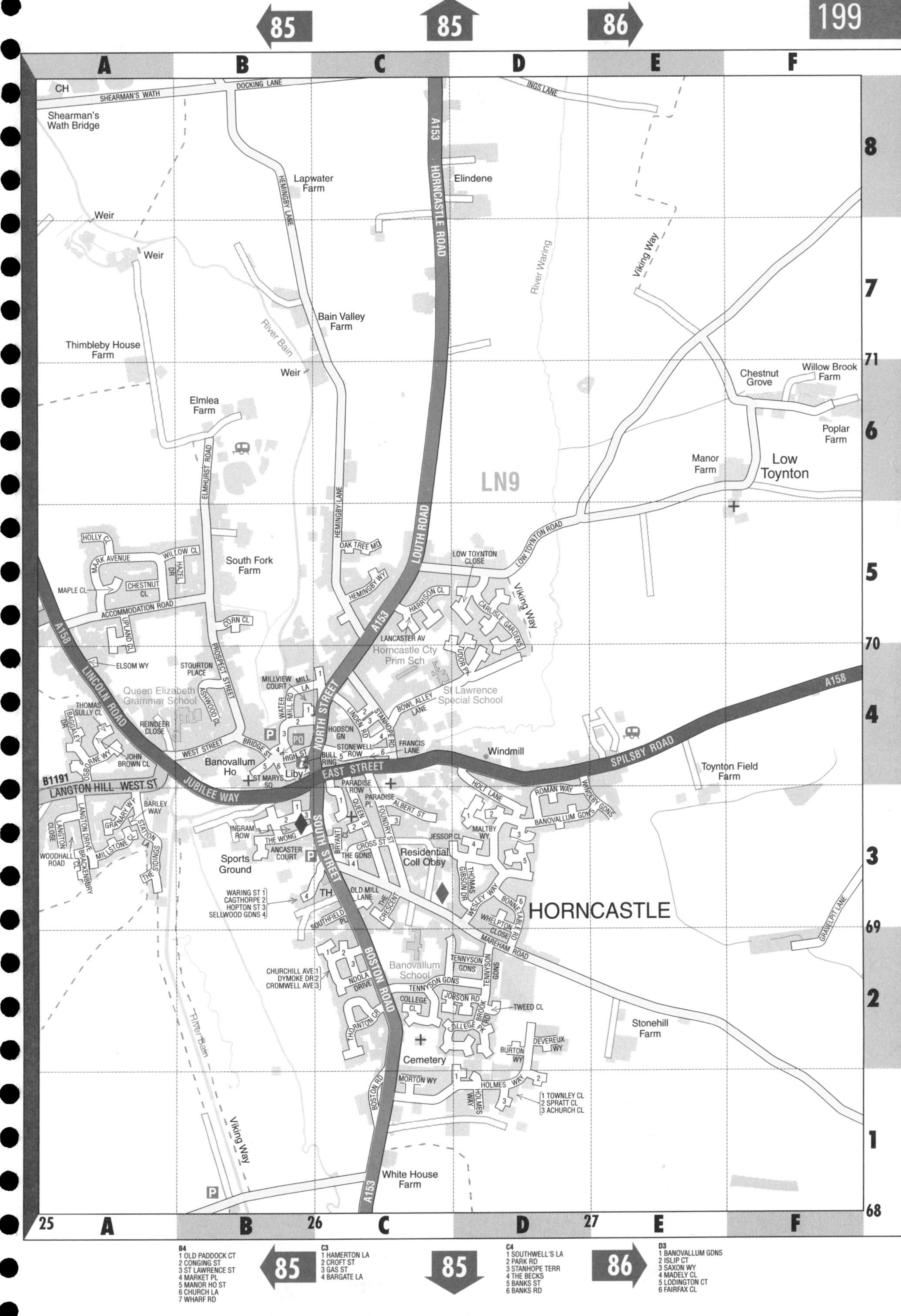

A   B   C   D   E   F

8   7   71   6   5   70   4   3   69   2   1   68

CH
SHEARMAN'S WATH
Shearman's Wath Bridge
DOCKING LANE
INGS LANE
Lapwater Farm
Elindene
Weir
HORNCASTLE ROAD
A153
River Waring
Viking Way
Weir
HEMINGBY LANE
Bain Valley Farm
River Bain
Thimbleby House Farm
Weir
Chestnut Grove
Willow Brook Farm
Elmlea Farm
Poplar Farm
LN9
Manor Farm
Low Toynton
HOLLY CL
ELMHURST ROAD
South Fork Farm
OAK TREE MT
LOUTH ROAD
Low Toynton Close
LOW TOYNTON ROAD
MARK AVENUE
WILLOW CL
HAZEL
HEMINGBY LANE
HEMINGBY WY
CHESTNUT CL
MAPLE CL
ACCOMMODATION ROAD
UPLAND CL
CORN CL
A153
HARRISON CL
CARLISLE GARDENS
Viking Way
A158
LINCOLN ROAD
A158
ELSOM WY
PROSPECT STREET
ASHWOOD CL
STOURTON PLACE
Queen Elizabeth Grammar School
MILLVIEW COURT
MILL LA
WATER MILL RD
LANCASTER AV
Horncastle Cty Prim Sch
TUDOR PK
70
THOMAS SULLY CL
BAGALEY
REINDEER CLOSE
WEST STREET
BRIDGE ST
NORTH STREET
HODSON GN
UNDER RD
STANHOPE RD
St Lawrence Special School
BOWL ALLEY LANE
Windmill
Toynton Field Farm
JANE WY
JOHN BROWN CL
Banovallum Ho
HIGH ST
PO
STONEWELL ROW
FRANCIS LANE
SPILSBY ROAD
A158
B1191
LANGTON HILL   WEST ST
St MARYS CH
Liby
EAST STREET
BULL RING
PARADISE ROW
PARADISE PL
ALBERT ST
HOLT LANE
ROMAN WAY
Toynton Field Farm
LANGTON HILL
BARLEY WAY
JUBILEE WAY
INGRAM ROW
THE WONG
QUEEN ST
FOUNDRY ST
MALTBY WY
BANOVALLUM GDNS
TWEED GDNS
GRANARY WY
STATION RD
ANCASTER COURT
BRYANT
CROSS ST
JESSOP CL
JESSEY WY
LANGTON CLOSE
BRACKENBURY
MILLSTONE CL
THE
Sports Ground
SOUTH STREET
THE GDNS
Residential Coll Obsy
THOMAS GIBSON DR
HORNCASTLE
WOODHALL ROAD
WARING ST 1
CAGTHORPE 2
HOPTON ST 3
SELLWOOD GDNS 4
TH
OLD MILL LANE
THE CRESCENT
WHELPTON RD
BONNE RD
MAREHAM ROAD
GRANGELYT LANE
SOUTHFIELD PL
BOSTON ROAD
Banovallum School
TENNYSON GDNS
BROOK RD
Stonehill Farm
CHURCHILL AVE 1
DYMOKE DR 2
CROMWELL AVE 3
NOOLA DRIVE
JOBSON RD
TENNYSON GDNS
TWEED CL
HORNTON CR
COLLEGE CL
COLLEGE
BURTON WY
DEVEREUX WY
Cemetery
MORTON WY
HOLMES WY
1 TOWNLEY CL
2 SPRATT CL
3 ACHURCH CL
River Bain
Viking Way
White House Farm
A153

B4
1 OLD PADDOCK CT
2 CONGING ST
3 ST LAWRENCE ST
4 MARKET PL
5 MANOR HO ST
6 CHURCH LA
7 WHARF RD

C3
1 HAMERTON LA
2 CROFT ST
3 GAS ST
4 BARGATE LA

C4
1 SOUTHWELL'S LA
2 PARK RD
3 STANHOPE TERR
4 THE BECKS
5 BANKS ST
6 BANKS RD

D3
1 BANOVALLUM GDNS
2 ISLIP CT
3 SAXON WY
4 MADELY CL
5 LODINGTON CT
6 FAIRFAX CL

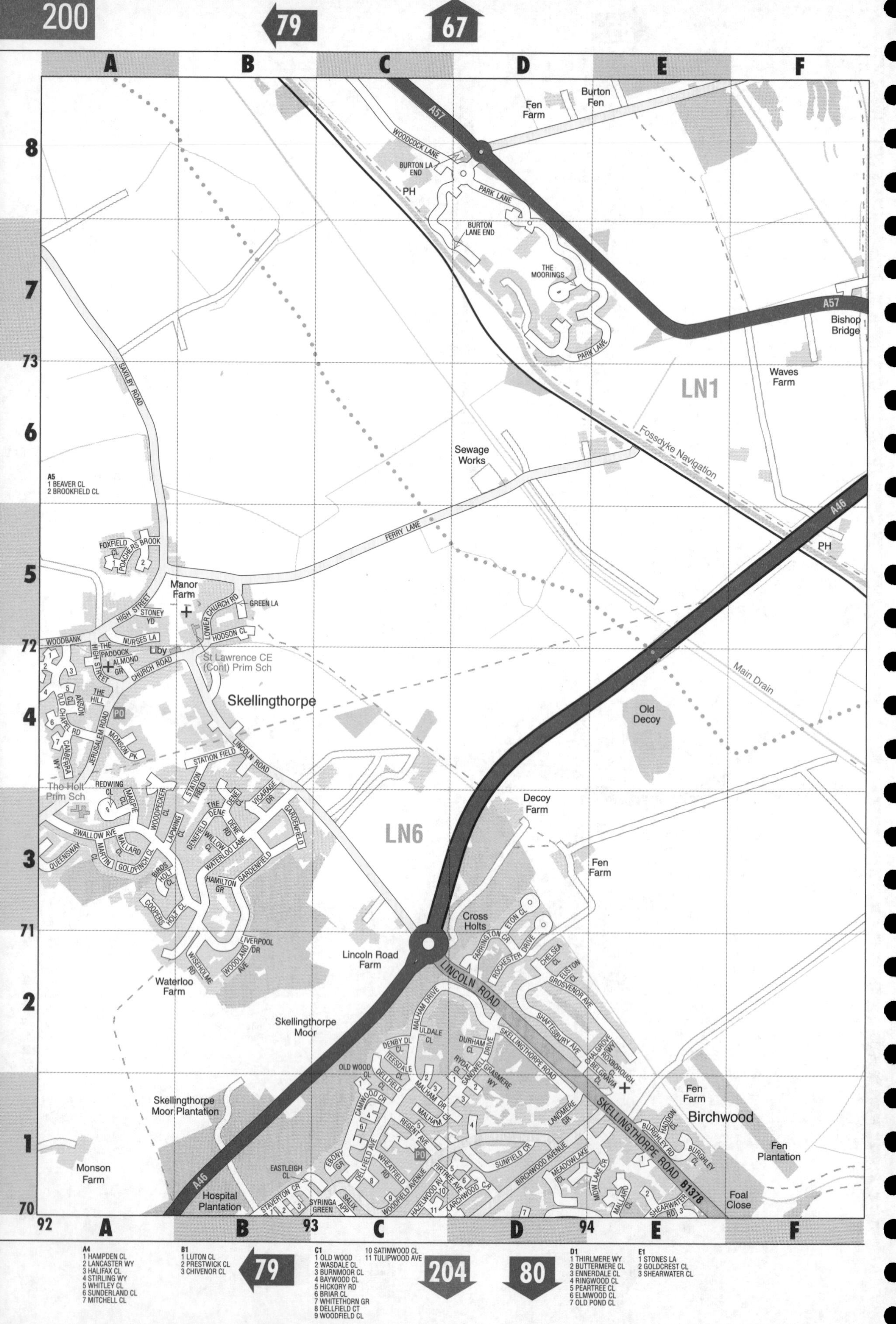

A4
1 HAMPDEN CL
2 LANCASTER WY
3 HALIFAX CL
4 STIRLING WY
5 WHITLEY CL
6 SUNDERLAND CL
7 MITCHELL CL

B1
1 LUTON CL
2 PRESTWICK CL
3 CHIVENOR CL

C1
1 OLD WOOD
2 WASDALE CL
3 BURNMOOR CL
4 BAYWOOD RD
5 HICKORY RD
6 BRIAR CL
7 WHITETHORN GR
8 DELLFIELD CT
9 WOODFIELD CL

10 SATINWOOD CL
11 TULIPWOOD AVE

D1
1 THIRLMERE WY
2 BUTTERMERE CL
3 ENNERDALE CL
4 RINGWOOD CL
5 PEARTREE CL
6 ELMWOOD CL
7 OLD POND CL

E1
1 STONES LA
2 GOLDCREST CL
3 SHEARWATER CL

A5
1 BEAVER CL
2 BROOKFIELD CL

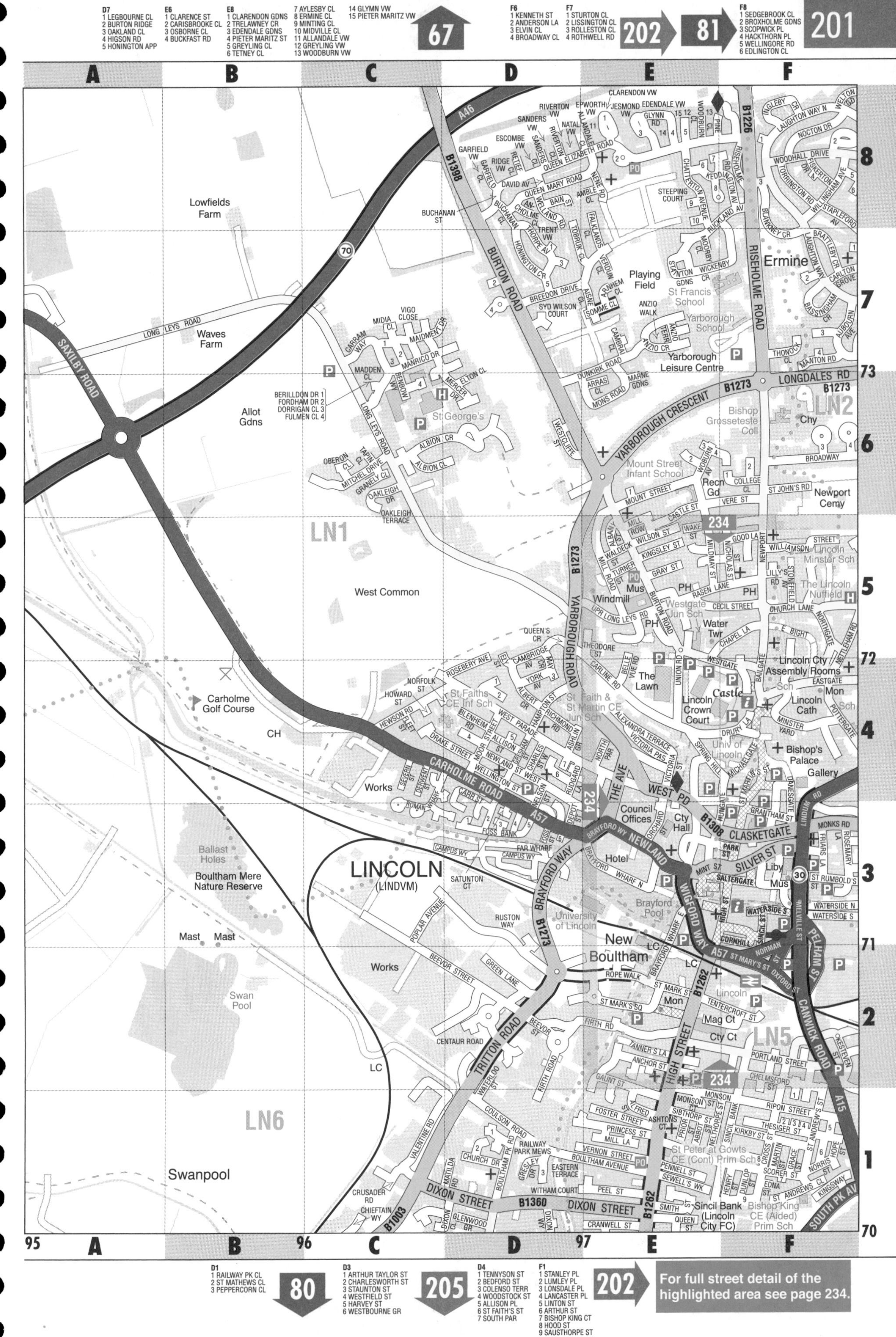
D7
1 LEGBOURNE CL
2 BURTON RIDGE
3 OAKLAND CL
4 HIGSON RD
5 HONINGTON APP
E6
1 CLARENCE ST
2 CARISBROOKE CL
3 OSBORNE CL
4 BUCKFAST RD
E8
1 CLARENDON GDNS
2 TRELAWNEY CR
3 EDENDALE GDNS
4 PIETER MARITZ ST
5 GREYLING CL
6 TETNEY CL
7 AYLESBY CL
8 ERMINE CL
9 MINTING CL
10 MIDVILLE CL
11 ALLANDALE VW
12 GREYLING VW
13 WOODBURN VW
14 GLYMN VW
15 PIETER MARITZ VW
67
F6
1 KENNETH ST
2 ANDERSON LA
3 ELVIN CL
4 BROADWAY CL
F7
1 STURTON CL
2 LISSINGTON CL
3 ROLLESTON CL
4 ROTHWELL RD
202
81
F8
1 SEDGEBROOK CL
2 BROXHOLME GDNS
3 SCOPWICK PL
4 HACKTHORN PL
5 WELLINGORE RD
6 EDLINGTON CL
A B C D E F
8 7 73 6 5 72 4 3 71 2 1 70
95 96 97
Lowfields Farm
Waves Farm
LONG LEYS ROAD
SAXILBY ROAD
A46
B1398
BURTON ROAD
Allot Gdns
LN1
West Common
Carholme Golf Course
CH
Works
Ballast Holes
Boultham Mere Nature Reserve
LINCOLN
(LINDVM)
Mast
Mast
Swan Pool
LC
LN6
Swanpool
St George's
H
P
BERILLDON DR 1
FORDHAM DR 2
DORRIGAN CL 3
FULMEN CL 4
Playing Field
St Francis School
Yarborough School
Yarborough Leisure Centre
Ermine
RISEHOLME ROAD
B1226
LONGDALES RD
B1273
YARBOROUGH CRESCENT
Bishop Grosseteste Coll
LN2
Chy
Newport Cemy
Mount Street Infant School
Recn Gd
234
YARBOROUGH ROAD
Windmill
Mus
Westgate Jun Sch
Water Twr
Lincoln Minster Sch
The Lincoln Nuffield
Lincoln Cty Assembly Rooms
The Lawn
Castle
Lincoln Crown Court
Lincoln Cath
Mon
Sch
Bishop's Palace
Gallery
Univ of Lincoln
St Faiths CE Inf Sch
St Faith & St Martin CE Jun Sch
CARHOLME ROAD
A57
THE AVE
WEST PD
Council Offices
Cty Hall
CLASKETGATE
B1308
NEWLAND
Hotel
BRAYFORD WY
Brayford Pool
University of Lincoln
New Boultham
WIGFORD WAY
SILVER ST
Liby
Mus
PELHAM ST
CANWICK ROAD
A15
B1262
HIGH STREET
Mag Ct
Cty Ct
LN5
Mon
Lincoln
B1273
TRITTON ROAD
Works
CENTAUR ROAD
St Peter at Gowts CE (Cont) Prim Sch
Sincil Bank (Lincoln City FC)
Bishop King CE (Aided) Prim Sch
DIXON STREET
B1360
B1003
SOUTH PK AV
D1
1 RAILWAY PK CL
2 ST MATHEWS CL
3 PEPPERCORN CL
80
D3
1 ARTHUR TAYLOR ST
2 CHARLESWORTH ST
3 STAUNTON ST
4 WESTFIELD ST
5 HARVEY ST
6 WESTBOURNE GR
205
D4
1 TENNYSON ST
2 BEDFORD ST
3 COLENSO TERR
4 WOODSTOCK ST
5 ALLISON PL
6 ST FAITH'S ST
7 SOUTH PAR
F1
1 STANLEY PL
2 LUMLEY PL
3 LONSDALE PL
4 LANCASTER PL
5 LINTON ST
6 ARTHUR ST
7 BISHOP KING CT
8 HOOD ST
9 SAUSTHORPE ST
202
For full street detail of the highlighted area see page 234.

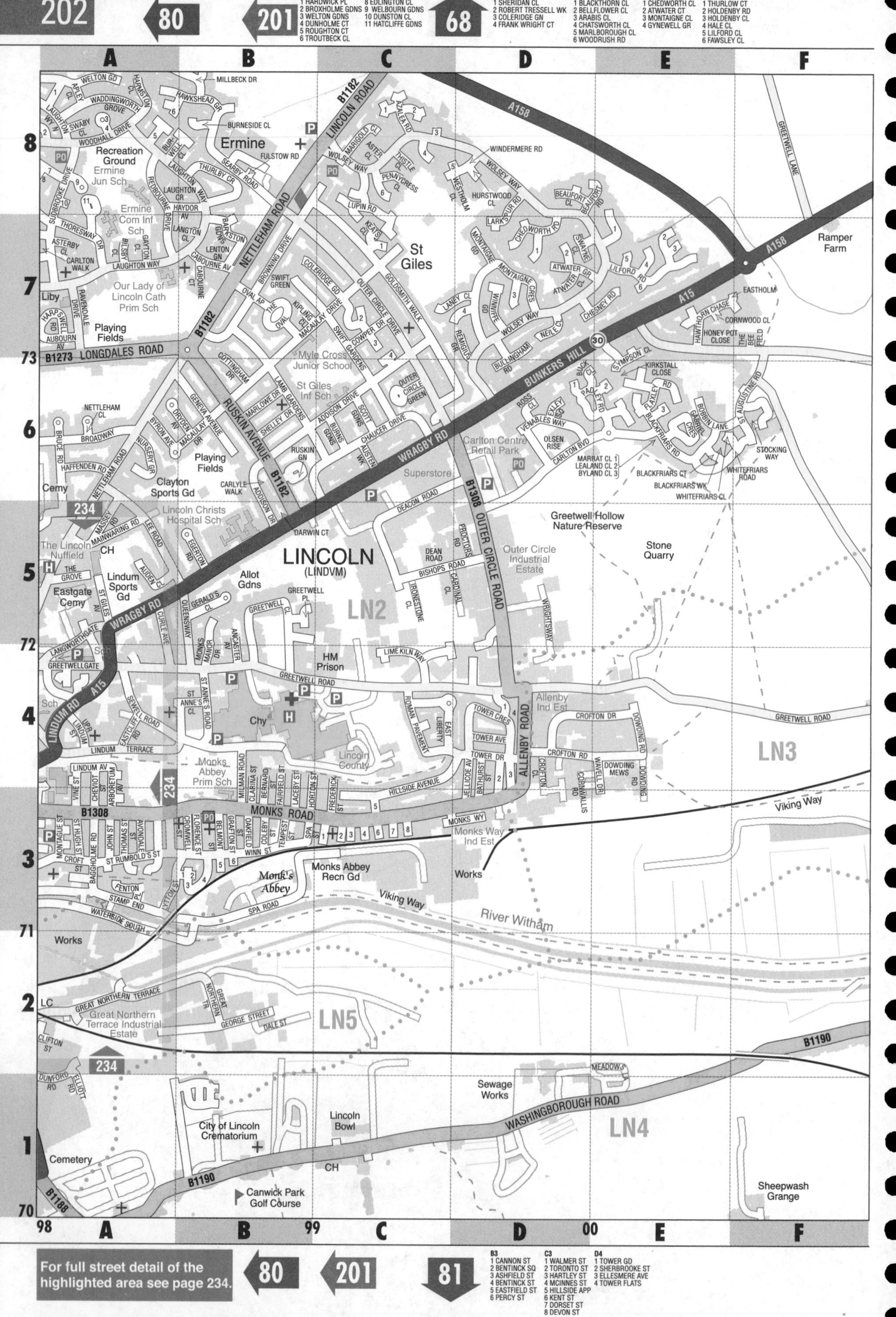
202
80
201
68
A8
1 HARDWICK PL
2 BROXHOLME GDNS
3 WELTON GDNS
4 DUNHOLME CT
5 ROUGHTON CT
6 TROUTBECK CL
7 WELLINGORE RD
8 EDLINGTON CL
9 WELBOURN GDNS
10 DUNSTON CL
11 HATCLIFFE GDNS
C7
1 SHERIDAN CL
2 ROBERT TRESSELL WK
3 COLERIDGE GN
4 FRANK WRIGHT CT
C8
1 BLACKTHORN CL
2 BELLFLOWER CL
3 ARABIS CL
4 CHATSWORTH CL
5 MARLBOROUGH CL
6 WOODRUSH RD
D7
1 CHEDWORTH CL
2 ATWATER CT
3 MONTAIGNE CL
4 GYNEWELL GR
E7
1 THURLOW CT
2 HOLDENBY RD
3 HOLDENBY CL
4 HALE CL
5 LILFORD CL
6 FAWSLEY CL
Ermine
Recreation Ground
Ermine Jun Sch
Ermine Com Inf Sch
St Giles
Ramper Farm
Our Lady of Lincoln Cath Prim Sch
Playing Fields
B1273 LONGDALES ROAD
Myle Cross Junior School
St Giles Inf Sch
NETTLEHAM ROAD
RUSKIN AVENUE
WRAGBY RD
BUNKERS HILL
Carlton Centre Retail Park
Superstore
Clayton Sports Gd
Lincoln Christs Hospital Sch
The Lincoln Nuffield
Lindum Sports Gd
Eastgate Cemy
LINCOLN
(LINDVM)
Allot Gdns
LN2
Greetwell Hollow Nature Reserve
Stone Quarry
Outer Circle Industrial Estate
OUTER CIRCLE ROAD
HM Prison
GREETWELL ROAD
Chy
Lincoln County
Allenby Ind Est
ALLENBY ROAD
LN3
Monks Abbey Prim Sch
MONKS ROAD
Monks Way Ind Est
Works
Monk's Abbey
Monks Abbey Recn Gd
Viking Way
River Witham
Works
GREAT NORTHERN TERRACE
Great Northern Terrace Industrial Estate
LN5
Sewage Works
WASHINGBOROUGH ROAD
LN4
City of Lincoln Crematorium
Lincoln Bowl
Cemetery
Canwick Park Golf Course
Sheepwash Grange
B1190
B1188
For full street detail of the highlighted area see page 234.
80
201
81
B3
1 CANNON ST
2 BENTINCK SQ
3 ASHFIELD ST
4 BENTINCK ST
5 EASTFIELD ST
6 PERCY ST
C3
1 WALMER ST
2 TORONTO ST
3 HARTLEY ST
4 MCINNES ST
5 HILLSIDE APP
6 KENT ST
7 DORSET ST
8 DEVON ST
D4
1 TOWER GD
2 SHERBROOKE ST
3 ELLESMERE AVE
4 TOWER FLATS

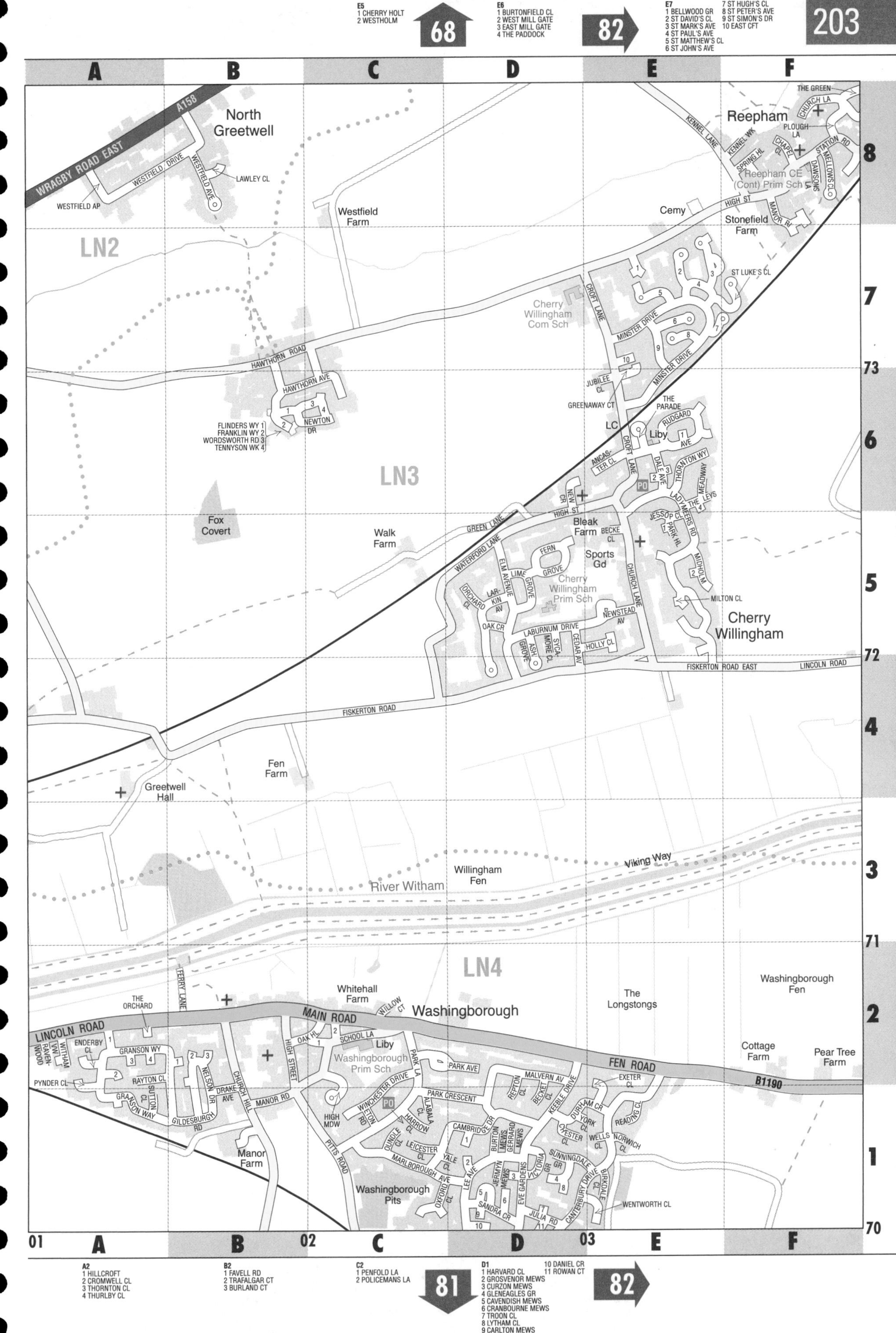

E5
1 CHERRY HOLT
2 WESTHOLM

68

E6
1 BURTONFIELD CL
2 WEST MILL GATE
3 EAST MILL GATE
4 THE PADDOCK

82

E7
1 BELLWOOD GR
2 ST DAVID'S CL
3 ST MARK'S AVE
4 ST PAUL'S AVE
5 ST MATTHEW'S CL
6 ST JOHN'S AVE

7 ST HUGH'S CL
8 ST PETER'S AVE
9 ST SIMON'S DR
10 EAST CFT

A2
1 HILLCROFT
2 CROMWELL CL
3 THORNTON CL
4 THURLBY CL

B2
1 FAVELL RD
2 TRAFALGAR CT
3 BURLAND CT

C2
1 PENFOLD LA
2 POLICEMANS LA

81

D1
1 HARVARD CL
2 GROSVENOR MEWS
3 CURZON MEWS
4 GLENEAGLES GR
5 CAVENDISH MEWS
6 CRANBOURNE MEWS
7 TROON CL
8 LYTHAM CL
9 CARLTON MEWS

10 DANIEL CR
11 ROWAN CT

82

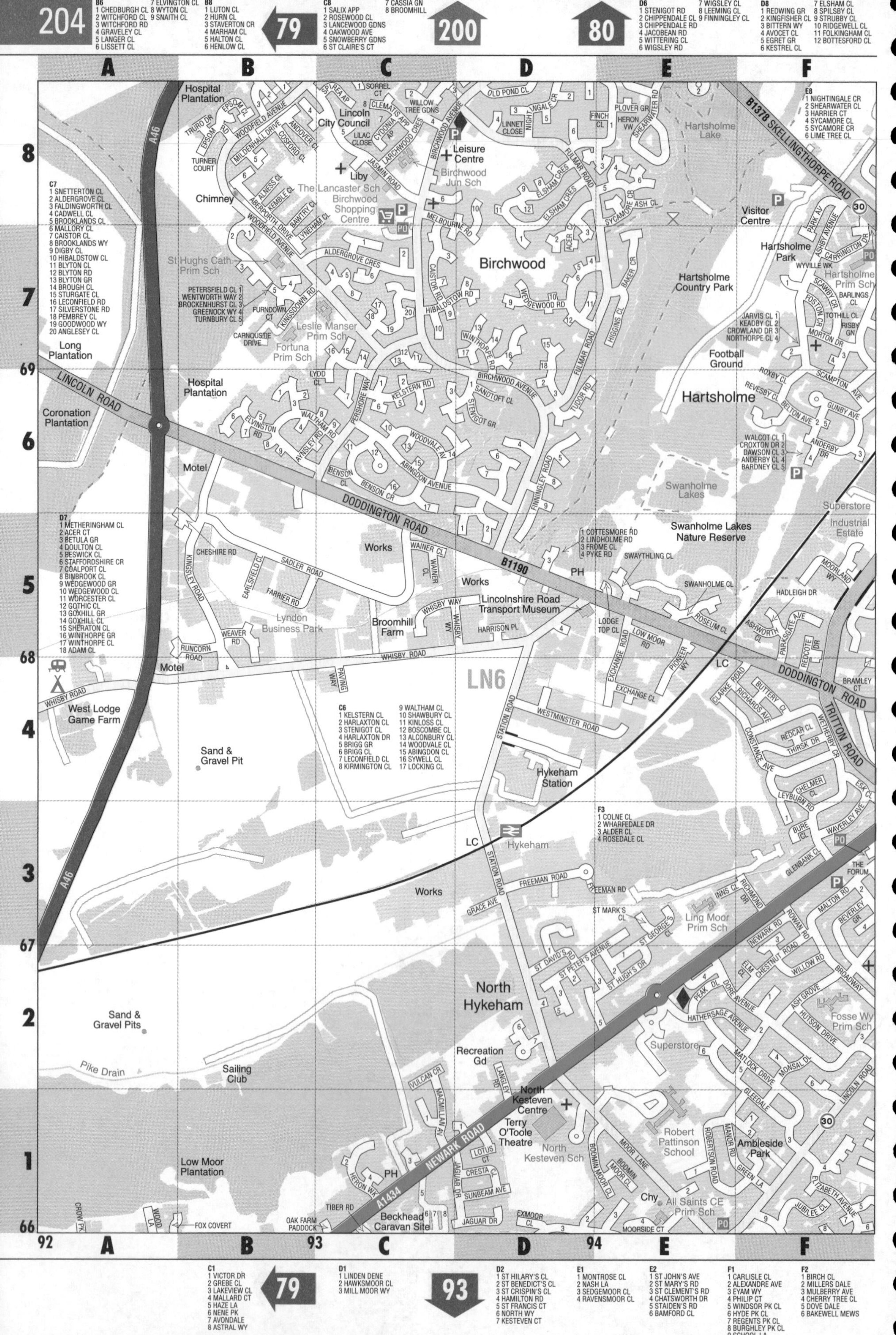
B6
1 CHEDBURGH CL
2 WITCHFORD CL
3 WITCHFORD RD
4 GRAVELEY CL
5 LANGER CL
6 LISSETT CL
7 ELVINGTON CL
8 WYTON CL
9 SNAITH CL
B8
1 LUTON CL
2 HURN CL
3 STAVERTON CR
4 MARHAM CL
5 HALTON CL
6 HENLOW CL
79
C8
1 SALIX APP
2 ROSEWOOD CL
3 LANCEWOOD GDNS
4 OAKWOOD AVE
5 SNOWBERRY GDNS
6 ST CLAIRE'S CT
7 CASSIA GN
8 BROOMHILL
200
80
D6
1 STENIGOT RD
2 CHIPPENDALE CL
3 CHIPPENDALE RD
4 JACOBEAN RD
5 WITTERING CL
6 WIGSLEY RD
7 WIGSLEY CL
8 LEEMING CL
9 FINNINGLEY CL
D8
1 REDWING GR
2 KINGFISHER CL
3 BITTERN WY
4 AVOCET CL
5 EGRET GR
6 KESTREL CL
7 ELSHAM CL
8 SPILSBY CL
9 STRUBBY CL
10 RIDGEWELL CL
11 FOLKINGHAM CL
12 BOTTESFORD CL
A
B
C
D
E
F
8
7
69
6
5
68
4
3
67
2
1
66
92
93
94
Hospital Plantation
Lincoln City Council
Leisure Centre
Birchwood Jun Sch
The Lancaster Sch
Birchwood Shopping Centre
Chimney
St Hughs Cath Prim Sch
Birchwood
Hartsholme Lake
Hartsholme Country Park
Visitor Centre
Hartsholme Park
Hartsholme Prim Sch
Leslie Manser Prim Sch
Fortuna Prim Sch
Long Plantation
Football Ground
Hartsholme
Coronation Plantation
LINCOLN ROAD
DODDINGTON ROAD
B1190
Motel
Swanholme Lakes
Swanholme Lakes Nature Reserve
Superstore
Industrial Estate
Works
Lincolnshire Road Transport Museum
Broomhill Farm
Lyndon Business Park
LN6
West Lodge Game Farm
Sand & Gravel Pit
Hykeham Station
Hykeham
Works
North Hykeham
Ling Moor Prim Sch
Fosse Wy Prim Sch
Sand & Gravel Pits
Pike Drain
Sailing Club
Recreation Gd
North Kesteven Centre
Terry O'Toole Theatre
North Kesteven Sch
Robert Pattinson School
Ambleside Park
All Saints CE Prim Sch
Low Moor Plantation
Beckhead Caravan Site
NEWARK ROAD
A1434
A46
B1378 SKELLINGTHORPE ROAD
TRITTON ROAD
C7
1 SNETTERTON CL
2 ALDERGROVE CL
3 FALDINGWORTH CL
4 CADWELL CL
5 BROOKLANDS CL
6 MALLORY CL
7 CAISTOR CL
8 BROOKLANDS WY
9 DIGBY CL
10 HIBALDSTOW CL
11 BLYTON CL
12 BLYTON RD
13 BLYTON GR
14 BROUGH CL
15 STURGATE CL
16 LECONFIELD RD
17 SILVERSTONE RD
18 PEMBREY CL
19 GOODWOOD WY
20 ANGLESEY CL
D7
1 METHERINGHAM CL
2 ACER CT
3 BETULA GR
4 DOULTON CL
5 BESWICK CL
6 STAFFORDSHIRE CR
7 COALPORT CL
8 BINBROOK CL
9 WEDGEWOOD GR
10 WEDGEWOOD CL
11 WORCESTER CL
12 GOTHIC CL
13 GOXHILL GR
14 GOXHILL CL
15 SHERATON CL
16 WINTHORPE GR
17 WINTHORPE CL
18 ADAM CL
E8
1 NIGHTINGALE CR
2 SHEARWATER CL
3 HARRIER CT
4 SYCAMORE CL
5 SYCAMORE CR
6 LIME TREE CL
C6
1 KELSTERN CL
2 HARLAXTON CL
3 STENIGOT CL
4 HARLAXTON DR
5 BRIGG GR
6 BRIGG CL
7 LECONFIELD CL
8 KIRMINGTON CL
9 WALTHAM CL
10 SHAWBURY CL
11 KINLOSS CL
12 BOSCOMBE CL
13 ALCONBURY CL
14 WOODVALE CL
15 ABINGDON CL
16 SYWELL CL
17 LOCKING CL
F3
1 COLNE CL
2 WHARFEDALE DR
3 ALDER CL
4 ROSEDALE CL
C1
1 VICTOR DR
2 GREBE CL
3 LAKEVIEW CL
4 MALLARD CT
5 HAZE LA
6 NENE PK
7 AVONDALE
8 ASTRAL WY
79
D1
1 LINDEN DENE
2 HAWKSMOOR CL
3 MILL MOOR WY
93
D2
1 ST HILARY'S CL
2 ST BENEDICT'S CL
3 ST CRISPIN'S CL
4 HAMILTON DR
5 ST FRANCIS CT
6 NORTH WY
7 KESTEVEN CT
E1
1 MONTROSE CL
2 NASH LA
3 SEDGEMOOR CL
4 RAVENSMOOR CL
E2
1 ST JOHN'S AVE
2 ST MARY'S RD
3 ST CRISPIN'S RD
4 CHATSWORTH DR
5 STAIDEN'S RD
6 BAMFORD CL
F1
1 CARLISLE CL
2 ALEXANDRE AVE
3 EYAM WY
4 PHILIP CT
5 WINDSOR PK CL
6 HYDE PK CL
7 REGENTS PK CL
8 BURGHLEY PK CL
9 SCHOOL LA
F2
1 BIRCH CL
2 MILLERS DALE
3 MULBERRY AVE
4 CHERRY TREE CL
5 DOVE DALE
6 BAKEWELL MEWS

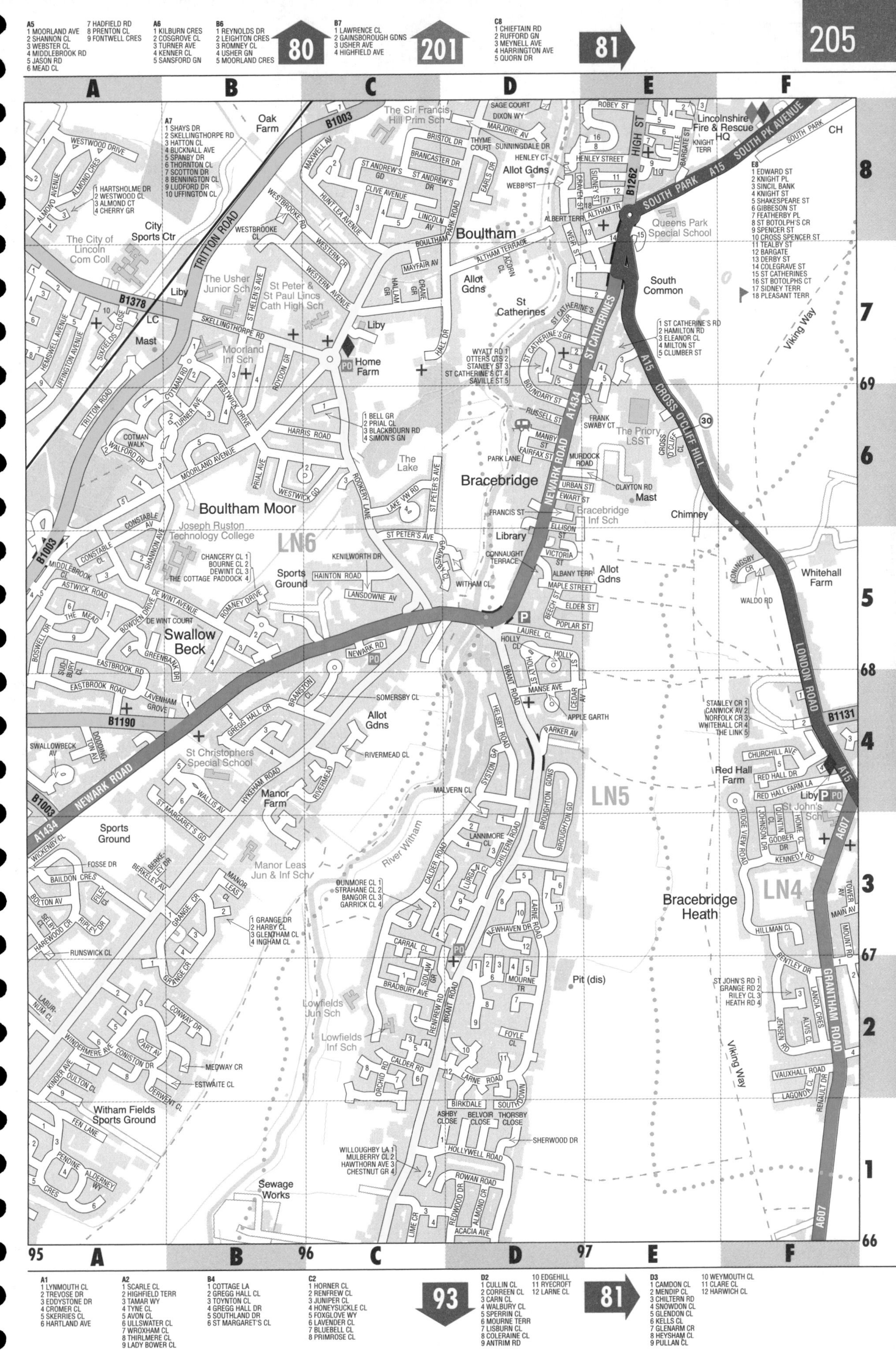
A5
1 MOORLAND AVE
2 SHANNON CL
3 WEBSTER CL
4 MIDDLEBROOK RD
5 JASON RD
6 MEAD CL
7 HADFIELD RD
8 PRENTON CL
9 FONTWELL CRES
A6
1 KILBURN CRES
2 COSGROVE CL
3 TURNER AVE
4 KENNER CL
5 SANSFORD GN
B6
1 REYNOLDS DR
2 LEIGHTON CRES
3 ROMNEY CL
4 USHER GN
5 MOORLAND CRES
80
B7
1 LAWRENCE CL
2 GAINSBOROUGH GDNS
3 USHER AVE
4 HIGHFIELD AVE
201
C8
1 CHIEFTAIN RD
2 RUFFORD GN
3 MEYNELL AVE
4 HARRINGTON AVE
5 QUORN DR
81
A
B
C
D
E
F
A7
1 SHAYS DR
2 SKELLINGTHORPE RD
3 HATTON CL
4 BUCKNALL AVE
5 SPANBY DR
6 THORNTON CL
7 SCOTTON DR
8 BENNINGTON CL
9 LUDFORD DR
10 UFFINGTON CL
1 HARTSHOLME DR
2 WESTWOOD CL
3 ALMOND CT
4 CHERRY GR
Oak Farm
B1003
The Sir Francis Hill Prim Sch
SAGE COURT
DIXON WY
MARJORIE AV
THYME COURT
SUNNINGDALE DR
BRISTOL DR
BRANCASTER DR
ST ANDREW'S GD
ST ANDREW'S DR
CLIVE AVENUE
LINCOLN AV
EARLS DR
HENLEY CT
Allot Gdns
WEBB ST
ROBEY ST
HENLEY STREET
HIGH ST
B1262
Lincolnshire Fire & Rescue HQ
KNIGHT TERR
LITTLE BARGATE ST
SOUTH PARK
A15
SOUTH PK AVENUE
CH
E8
1 EDWARD ST
2 KNIGHT PL
3 SINCIL BANK
4 KNIGHT ST
5 GIBBESON ST
6 GIBBESON ST
7 FEATHERBY PL
8 ST BOTOLPH'S CR
9 SPENCER ST
10 CROSS SPENCER ST
11 TEALBY ST
12 BARGATE
13 DERBY ST
14 COLEGRAVE ST
15 ST CATHERINES
16 ST BOTOLPHS CT
17 SIDNEY TERR
18 PLEASANT TERR
8
WESTWOOD DRIVE
ALMOND CRES
ALMOND AVENUE
City Sports Ctr
TRITTON ROAD
The City of Lincoln Com Coll
WESTBROOKE RD
WESTBROOKE CL
WESTERN CR
WESTERN AVENUE
HUNT LEA AVENUE
MAXWELL AV
Boultham
BOULTHAM PARK ROAD
ALTHAM TERRACE
MAYFAIR AV
HALLAM GR
CRANE GR
ACORN CL
ALBERT TERR
ALTHAM TR
CRAVEN ST
SIDNEY ST
WEIR ST
Queens Park Special School
South Common
The Usher Junior Sch
St Peter & St Paul Lincs Cath High Sch
Liby
B1378
LC
Mast
SKELLINGTHORPE RD
ST HELEN'S AVE
Allot Gdns
St Catherines
ST CATHERINE'S GR
ST CATHERINES
1 ST CATHERINE'S RD
2 HAMILTON RD
3 ELEANOR CL
4 MILTON ST
5 CLUMBER ST
Viking Way
7
HEMSWELL AVENUE
UFFINGTON AVENUE
SIXFIELDS CLOSE
Moorland Inf Sch
ROYDON GR
Home Farm
HALL DR
WYATT RD 1
OTTERS CTS 2
STANLEY ST 3
ST CATHERINE'S CT 4
SAVILLE ST 5
A15
CROSS O'CLIFF HILL
69
TRITTON ROAD
COTMAN RD
TURNER AVE
WESTWICK DRIVE
HARRIS ROAD
1 BELL GR
2 PRIAL CL
3 BLACKBOURN RD
4 SIMON'S GN
BOUNDARY ST
RUSSELL ST
A1434
FRANK SWABY CT
The Priory LSST
30
CROSS O'CLIFF CL
COTMAN WALK
WALFORD DR
MOORLAND AVENUE
PRIAL AVE
WESTWICK GD
The Lake
MANBY ST
FAIRFAX ST
PARK LANE
MURDOCK ROAD
CLAYTON RD
Mast
6
Bracebridge
ST PETER'S AVE
ROOKERY LANE
LAKE VW RD
Boultham Moor
CONSTABLE AV
Joseph Ruston Technology College
LN6
URBAN ST
EWART ST
NEWARK ROAD
FRANCIS ST
Bracebridge Inf Sch
ELLISON ST
Chimney
Library
B1003
CONSTABLE CL
MIDDLEBROOK RD
SHANNON AVE
CHANCERY CL 1
BOURNE CL 2
DEWINT CL 3
THE COTTAGE PADDOCK 4
Sports Ground
KENILWORTH DR
HAINTON ROAD
LANSDOWNE AV
GRANSON CL
WITHAM CL
CONNAUGHT TERRACE
VICTORIA ST
Allot Gdns
ALBANY TERR
MAPLE STREET
CONINGSBY CR
WALDO RD
Whitehall Farm
5
ASTWICK ROAD
THE MEAD
BOWDEN DRIVE
DE WINT AVENUE
ROMNEY DRIVE
DE WINT COURT
Swallow Beck
BOSWELL DR
SUDBURY CL
GREENBANK DR
EASTBROOK RD
EASTBROOK ROAD
LAVENHAM GROVE
NEWARK RD
ELDER ST
POPLAR ST
LAUREL CL
HOLLY CL
HOLLY ST
BRANT ROAD
MANSE AVE
CEDAR AV
APPLE GARTH
LONDON ROAD
68
B1190
DODDINGTON AV
SWALLOWBECK AV
GREGG HALL CR
BRANSTON CL
SOMERSBY CL
Allot Gdns
RIVERMEAD CL
HELSBY ROAD
PARKER AV
STANLEY CR 1
CANWICK AV 2
NORFOLK CR 3
WHITEHALL CR 4
THE LINK 5
B1131
CHURCHILL AVE
4
St Christophers Special School
WALLIS AV
HYKEHAM ROAD
RIVERMEAD
Manor Farm
SYSTON GR
MALVERN CL
BROUGHTON GDNS
BROUGHTON GD
LN5
Red Hall Farm
RED HALL DR
RED HALL FARM LA
Liby
St John's Sch
A15
A1434
NEWARK ROAD
B1003
Sports Ground
ST MARGARET'S GD
LANNIMORE CL
CHILTERN ROAD
RIDGE VIEW ROAD
JOHNSON DR
QUINTIN DR
HOME CL
GODBER DR
KENNEDY RD
A607
WICKENBY CL
FOSSE DR
BERKELEY DR
BERKELEY AV
Manor Leas Jun & Inf Sch
River Witham
CALDER ROAD
LURGAN CL
LARNE ROAD
BAILDON CRES
BOLTON AV
FILEY CL
SELBY CL
RIPLEY DR
HAREWOOD CR
MANOR LEAS CL
GRANGE CR
1 GRANGE DR
2 HARBY CL
3 GLENTHAM CL
4 INGHAM CL
DUNMORE CL 1
STRAHANE CL 2
BANGOR CL 3
GARRICK CL 4
NEWHAVEN DR
Bracebridge Heath
LN4
TOWER AV
MAIN AV
HILLMAN CL
3
RUNSWICK CL
CARRAL CL
SIDLAW GR
MOURNE TR
Pit (dis)
BENTLEY DR
MOUNT RD
67
LABURNUM CL
GRANGE CR
BRADBURY AVE
RENFREW RD
BRANT ROAD
ST JOHN'S RD 1
GRANGE RD 2
RILEY CL 3
HEATH RD 4
LANCIA CRES
GRANTHAM ROAD
CONWAY DR
Lowfields Jun Sch
Lowfields Inf Sch
FOYLE CL
JENSEN RD
ALVIS CL
2
WINDERMERE AVE
CONISTON DR
DART AV
MEDWAY CR
ESTWAITE CL
DERWENT CL
KINDER AVE
OULTON CL
ORCHID RD
CALDER RD
LARNE ROAD
SOUTHDOWN
VAUXHALL ROAD
LAGONDA CL
RENAULT DR
Witham Fields Sports Ground
FEN LANE
BIRKDALE
ASHBY CLOSE
BELVOIR CLOSE
THORSBY CLOSE
SHERWOOD DR
HOLLYWELL ROAD
PENDINE CRES
ALDERNEY WY
WILLOUGHBY LA 1
MULBERRY CL 2
HAWTHORN AVE 3
CHESTNUT GR 4
Viking Way
1
Sewage Works
ROWAN ROAD
REDWOOD DR
ALMOND CR
LIME CR
ACACIA AVE
A607
66
95
A
B
96
C
D
97
E
F
A1
1 LYNMOUTH CL
2 TREVOSE DR
3 EDDYSTONE DR
4 CROMER CL
5 SKERRIES CL
6 HARTLAND AVE
A2
1 SCARLE CL
2 HIGHFIELD TERR
3 TAMAR WY
4 TYNE CL
5 AVON CL
6 ULLSWATER CL
7 WROXHAM CL
8 THIRLMERE CL
9 LADY BOWER CL
B4
1 COTTAGE LA
2 GREGG HALL CL
3 TOYNTON CL
4 GREGG HALL DR
5 SOUTHLAND DR
6 ST MARGARET'S CL
C2
1 HORNER CL
2 RENFREW CL
3 JUNIPER CL
4 HONEYSUCKLE CL
5 FOXGLOVE WY
6 LAVENDER CL
7 BLUEBELL CL
8 PRIMROSE CL
93
D2
1 CULLIN CL
2 CORREEN CL
3 CARN CL
4 WALBURY CL
5 SPERRIN CL
6 MOURNE TERR
7 LISBURN CL
8 COLERAINE CL
9 ANTRIM RD
10 EDGEHILL
11 RYECROFT
12 LARNE CL
81
D3
1 CAMDON CL
2 MENDIP CL
3 CHILTERN RD
4 SNOWDON CL
5 GLENDON CL
6 KELLS CL
7 GLENARM CR
8 HEYSHAM CL
9 PULLAN CL
10 WEYMOUTH CL
11 CLARE CL
12 HARWICH CL

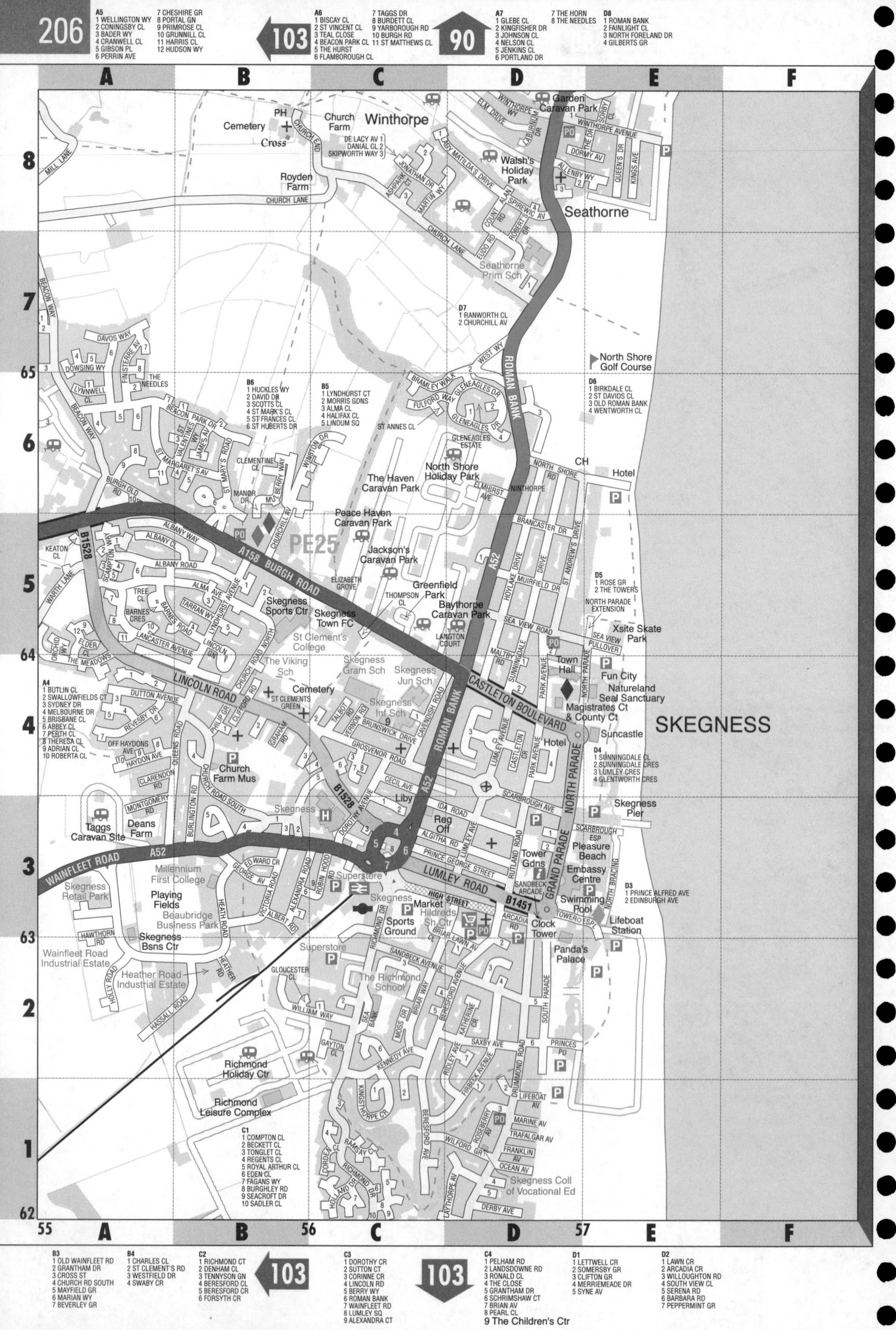

← 103

90 ↑

A5
1 WELLINGTON WY
2 CONINGSBY CL
3 BADER WY
4 CRANWELL CL
5 GIBSON PL
6 PERRIN AVE
7 CHESHIRE GR
8 PORTAL GN
9 PRIMROSE CL
10 GRUNNILL CL
11 HARRIS CL
12 HUDSON WY

A6
1 BISCAY CL
2 ST VINCENT CL
3 TEAL CLOSE
4 BEACON PARK CL
5 THE HURST
6 FLAMBOROUGH CL
7 TAGGS DR
8 BURDETT CL
9 YARBOROUGH RD
10 BURGH RD
11 ST MATTHEWS CL

A7
1 GLEBE CL
2 KINGFISHER DR
3 JOHNSON CL
4 NELSON CL
5 JENKINS CL
6 PORTLAND DR
7 THE HORN
8 THE NEEDLES

D8
1 ROMAN BANK
2 FAINLIGHT CL
3 NORTH FORELAND DR
4 GILBERTS GR

B6
1 HUCKLES WY
2 DAVID DR
3 SCOTTS CL
4 ST MARK'S CL
5 ST FRANCES CL
6 ST HUBERTS DR

B5
1 LYNDHURST CT
2 MORRIS GDNS
3 ALMA CL
4 HALIFAX CL
5 LINDUM SQ

D7
1 RANWORTH CL
2 CHURCHILL AV

D6
1 BIRKDALE CL
2 ST DAVIDS CL
3 OLD ROMAN BANK
4 WENTWORTH CL

D5
1 ROSE GR
2 THE TOWERS

D4
1 SUNNINGDALE CL
2 SUNNINGDALE CRES
3 LUMLEY CRES
4 GLENTWORTH CRES

D3
1 PRINCE ALFRED AVE
2 EDINBURGH AVE

A4
1 BUTLIN CL
2 SWALLOWFIELDS CT
3 SYDNEY DR
4 MELBOURNE DR
5 BRISBANE CL
6 ABBEY CL
7 PERTH CL
8 THERESA CL
9 ADRIAN CL
10 ROBERTA CL

C1
1 COMPTON CL
2 BECKETT CL
3 TONGLET CL
4 REGENTS CL
5 ROYAL ARTHUR CL
6 EDEN CL
7 BURGHLEY RD
8 SEACROFT DR
9 SADLER CL
10 SADLER CL

SKEGNESS

B3
1 OLD WAINFLEET RD
2 GRANTHAM DR
3 CROSS ST
4 CHURCH RD SOUTH
5 MAYFIELD GR
6 MARIAN WY
7 BEVERLEY GR

B4
1 CHARLES CL
2 ST CLEMENT'S RD
3 TENNYSON GN
4 SWABY CR

C2
1 RICHMOND CT
2 DENHAM CL
3 BERESFORD GN
4 BERESFORD CL
5 BERESFORD CR
6 FORSYTH CR

C3
1 DOROTHY CL
2 SUTTON CT
3 CORINNE CR
4 LINCOLN RD
5 BERRY WY
6 ROMAN BANK
7 WAINFLEET RD
8 LUMLEY SQ
9 ALEXANDRA CT

C4
1 PELHAM RD
2 LANSDOWNE RD
3 RONALD CL
4 THE CLOSE
5 GRANTHAM DR
6 SCHRIMSHAW CT
7 BRIAN AV
8 PEARL CL
9 THE CHILDREN'S CTR

D1
1 LETTWELL CR
2 SOMERSBY GR
3 CLIFTON CR
4 MERRIEMEADE DR
5 SYNE AV

D2
1 LAWN CR
2 ARCADIA CR
3 WILLOUGHTON RD
4 SOUTH VIEW CL
5 SERENA RD
6 BARBARA RD
7 PEPPERMINT GR

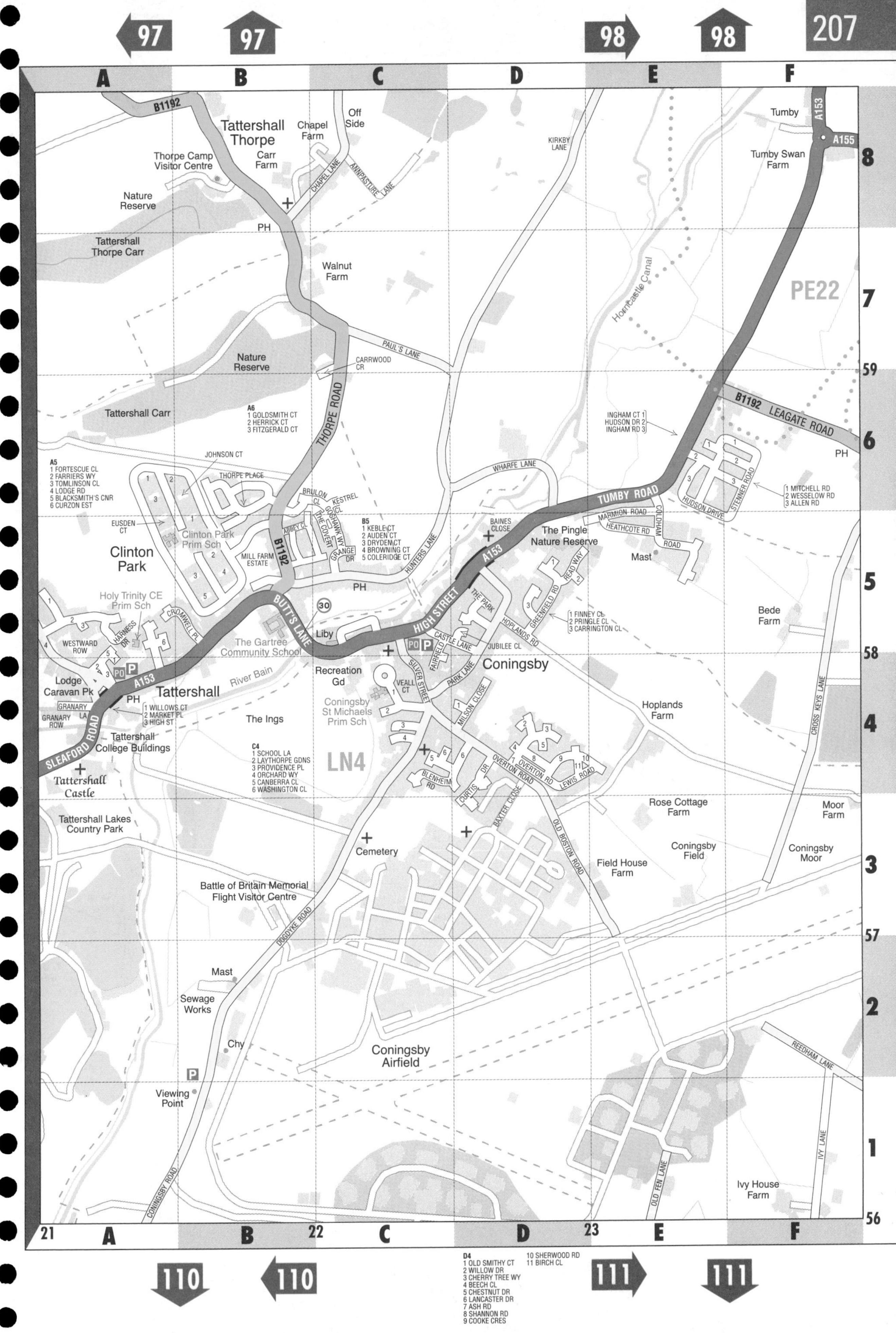

97 97 98 98

A B C D E F

B1192

Tattershall
Thorpe

Tumby

A153

A155

Chapel
Farm

Off
Side

8

Thorpe Camp
Visitor Centre

Carr
Farm

Kirkby
Lane

Tumby Swan
Farm

Nature
Reserve

PH

PE22

Tattershall
Thorpe Carr

Walnut
Farm

7

Horncastle Canal

Paul's Lane

59

Nature
Reserve

CARRWOOD
CR

A6
1 GOLDSMITH CT
2 HERRICK CT
3 FITZGERALD CT

B1192 LEAGATE ROAD

Tattershall Carr

THORPE ROAD

INGHAM CT 1
HUDSON DR 2
INGHAM RD 3

6

PH

JOHNSON CT

WHARFE LANE

TUMBY ROAD

1 MITCHELL RD
2 WESSELOW RD
3 ALLEN RD

STEMMER ROAD

A5
1 FORTESCUE CL
2 FARRIERS WY
3 TOMLINSON CL
4 LODGE RD
5 BLACKSMITH'S CNR
6 CURZON EST

THORPE PLACE

BRULON
CL

KESTREL
CL

MARMION ROAD

HUDSON DRIVE

HEATHCOTE RD

OLDHAM
ROAD

EUSDEN
CT

Clinton Park
Prim Sch

GOSHAWK WY

THE COVERT

BAINES
CLOSE

The Pingle
Nature Reserve

5

Clinton
Park

ABBEY CL

B5
1 KEBLE CT
2 AUDEN CT
3 DRYDEN CT
4 BROWNING CT
5 COLERIDGE CT

A153

Mast

Bede
Farm

Holy Trinity CE
Prim Sch

MILL FARM
ESTATE

GRANGE
DR

PH

HUNTERS LANE

BEAD WAY

GREENFIELD RD

58

WESTWARD
ROW

HARNESS
DR

CROMWELL PL

B1192

30

Liby

BUTT'S LANE

HIGH STREET

The Park

1 FINNEY CL
2 PRINGLE CL
3 CARRINGTON CL

The Gartree
Community School

River Bain

Recreation
Gd

Coningsby
St Michaels
Prim Sch

CASTLE LANE

JUBILEE CL

HOPLANDS RD

Coningsby

Bede
Farm

Lodge
Caravan Pk

A153

PH

SILVER STREET

FAIRFIELD RD

PARK LANE

Hoplands
Farm

GRANARY
ROW

GRANARY
LA

Tattershall

VEALI
CT

PA

WILSON CLOSE

4

SLEAFORD ROAD

1 WILLOWS CT
2 MARKET PL
3 HIGH ST

The Ings

CROSS KEYS LANE

Tattershall
College Buildings

C4
1 SCHOOL LA
2 LAYTHORPE GDNS
3 PROVIDENCE PL
4 ORCHARD WY
5 CANBERRA CL
6 WASHINGTON CL

LN4

OVERTON RD

OVERTON ROAD

LEWIS ROAD

Rose Cottage
Farm

Moor
Farm

Tattershall
Castle

BLENHEIM
RD

CURTIS
DR

Coningsby
Field

Coningsby
Moor

Tattershall Lakes
Country Park

BAXTER CLOSE

OLD BOSTON ROAD

3

Cemetery

Field House
Farm

Battle of Britain Memorial
Flight Visitor Centre

57

DOGDYKE ROAD

Mast

REEDHAM LANE

2

Sewage
Works

Chy

Coningsby
Airfield

IVY LANE

1

Viewing
Point

OLD FEN LANE

Ivy House
Farm

56

21 A 22 B C 23 D E F

110 110 111 111

D4
1 OLD SMITHY CT
2 WILLOW DR
3 CHERRY TREE WY
4 BEECH CL
5 CHESTNUT DR
6 LANCASTER DR
7 ASH RD
8 SHANNON RD
9 COOKE CRES
10 SHERWOOD RD
11 BIRCH CL

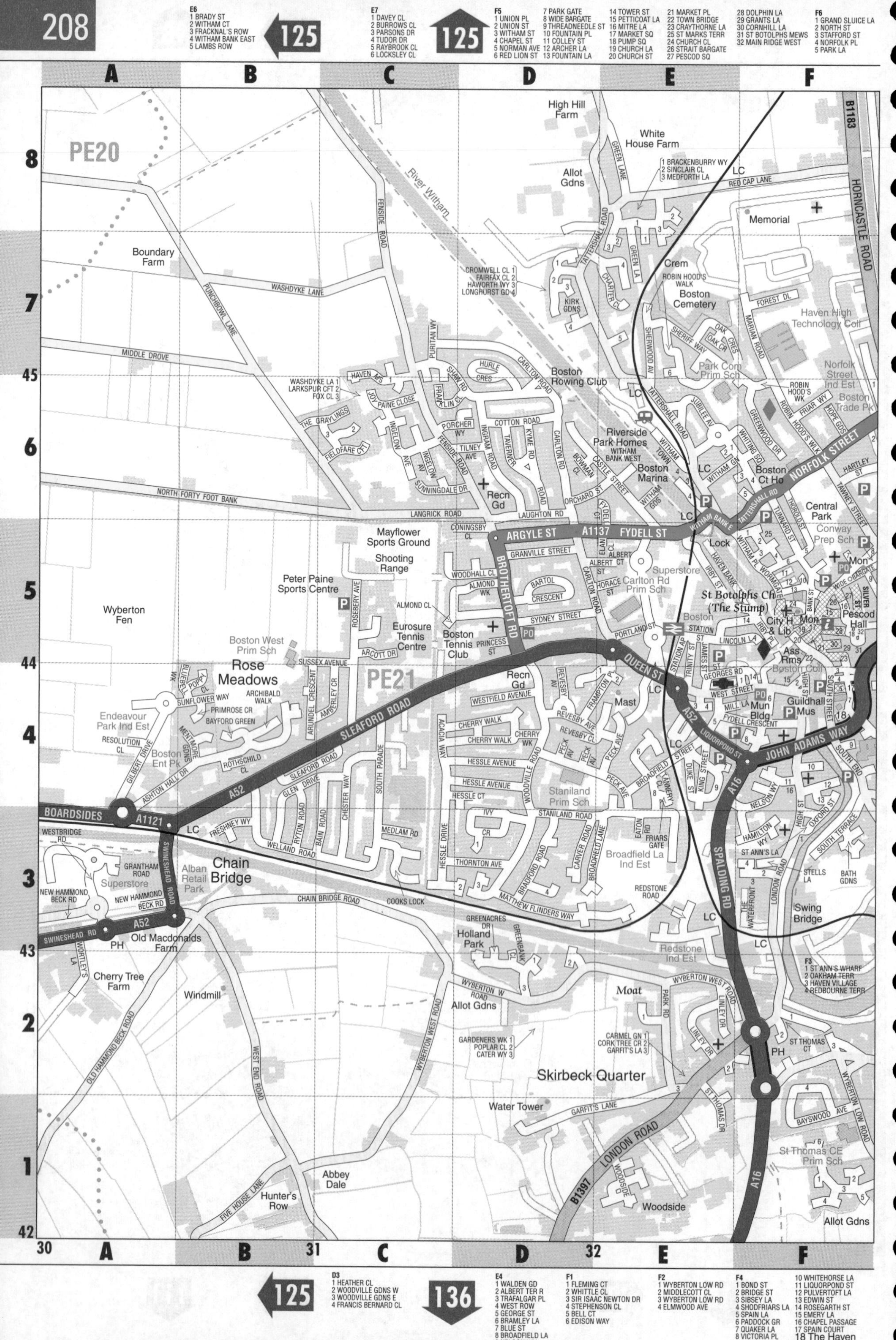

← 125

⌂ 125

E6
1 BRADY ST
2 WITHAM CT
3 FRACKNAL'S ROW
4 WITHAM BANK EAST
5 LAMBS ROW

E7
1 DAVEY CL
2 BURROWS CL
3 PARSONS DR
4 TUDOR DR
5 RAYBROOK CL
6 LOCKSLEY CL

F5
1 UNION PL
2 UNION ST
3 WITHAM ST
4 CHAPEL ST
5 NORMAN AVE
6 RED LION ST

7 PARK GATE
8 WIDE BARGATE
9 THREADNEEDLE LA
10 FOUNTAIN PL
11 COLLEY ST
12 ARCHER LA
13 FOUNTAIN LA

14 TOWER ST
15 PETTICOAT LA
16 MITRE LA
17 MARKET SQ
18 PUMP SQ
19 CHURCH LA
20 CHURCH ST

21 MARKET PL
22 TOWN BRIDGE
23 CRAYTHORNE LA
24 ST MARKS TERR
25 CHURCH CL
26 STRAIT BARGATE
27 PESCOD SQ

28 DOLPHIN LA
29 GRANTS LA
30 CORNHILL LA
31 ST BOTOLPHS MEWS
32 MAIN RIDGE WEST

F6
1 GRAND SLUICE LA
2 NORTH ST
3 STAFFORD ST
4 NORFOLK PL
5 PARK LA

PE20

Boundary Farm

River Witham

High Hill Farm

White House Farm

1 BRACKENBURRY WY
2 SINCLAIR CL
3 MEDFORTH LA

Allot Gdns

Green Lane

Red Cap Lane

LC

B1183

HORNCASTLE ROAD

Memorial

WASHDYKE LANE

PUNCHBOWL LANE

FENSIDE ROAD

Crem

ROBIN HOOD'S WALK

Boston Cemetery

FOREST DL

Haven High Technology Coll

MIDDLE DROVE

CROMWELL CL 1
FAIRFAX CL 2
HAWORTH WY 3
LONGHURST GD 4

KIRK GDNS

SHERIFF WAY

SHERWOOD AV

OAK CRES

OAK CR

Park Corn Prim Sch

ROBIN HOOD'S WK

Norfolk Street Ind Est

Boston Trade Pk

NORTH FORTY FOOT BANK

WASHDYKE LA 1
LARKSPUR CFT 2
FOX CL 3

THE GRAYLINGS

HAVEN AVE

JUDY PAINE CLOSE

FIELDFARE CT

FRANKLIN CL

SHAW RD

HURLE CRES

Boston Rowing Club

CARLTON ROAD

JUBILEE AV

TATTERSHALL RD

FRIAR WY

HOPE RD

HARTLEY ST

Rose Meadows

BLYTH FLOPPY

SUNFLOWER WAY

ARCHIBALD WALK

PRIMROSE CR

BAYFORD GREEN

ARUNDEL CRESCENT

AMBERLEY CR

SUSSEX AVENUE

ARCOTT DR

ALMOND CL

ALMOND WK

Boston West Prim Sch

PORCHER WY

INGRAM AVE

TILNEY AVE

NIGELOW AV

SUNNINGDALE DR

COTTON ROAD

KYME RD

TAVENER

BOWMAN

ORCHARD LA

CASTLE STREET

CLYDE RD

Riverside Park Homes

Witham Bank West

Boston Marina

WITHAM GDS

WITHAM ST

WITHAM EW

LC

Central Park

RAWNSLEY STREET

Boston Ct Ho

LC

NORFOLK STREET

GREENWOOD DR

PE21

Mayflower Sports Ground

Shooting Range

Peter Paine Sports Centre

ROSEBERY AVE

WOODHALL CL

CONINGSBY

Recn Gd

LAUGHTON RD

ARGYLE ST

A1137

FYDELL ST

Lock

HAVEN BANK

WITHAM PL

WORMGATE

P

P

Conway Prep Sch

Mon

P

BARTOL CRESCENT

ALBERT ST

ALBERT CT

Carlton Rd Prim Sch

HORACE ST

Superstore

St Botolphs Ch (The Stump)

Boston Station

City H & Lib

Mon

Pescod Hall

Eurosure Tennis Centre

Boston Tennis Club

PRINCESS ST

SYDNEY STREET

PORTLAND ST

LINCOLN ST

JAMES ST

TRINITY ST

Boston Coll

Ass Rms

44

RESOLUTION CL

Endeavour Park Ind Est

Boston Ent Pk

GILBERT DRIVE

MENTMORE GDNS

ROTHSCHILD CL

Wyberton Fen

ASHTON HALL DR

SLEAFORD ROAD

A52

GLEN DRIVE

SOUTH PARADE

Westfield Avenue

CHERRY WALK

CHERRY WALK

CHERRY WK

HESSLE AVENUE

HESSLE AVENUE

HESSLE CT

WOODVILLE ROAD

Staniland Prim Sch

STANILAND ROAD

REVESBY AVE

REVESBY AVE

PECK AV

PECK AV

PECK LA

CARVER ROAD

FRAMPTON LA

QUEEN ST

Mast

Recn Gd

BROTHERTOFT RD

PO

GEORGES RD

WEST STREET

PO

MILL LA

Mun Bldg

FYDELL CRESCENT

Guildhall Mus

A52

LIQUORPOND ST

JOHN ADAMS WAY

A16

DUKE ST

NELSON WY

HIGH ST

OXFORD ST

SOUTH END

SOUTH TERRACE

HAMILTON

ST ANN'S LA

STELLS LA

BATH GDNS

BOARDSIDES

A1121

LC

WESTBRIDGE RD

GRANTHAM ROAD

Alban Retail Park

Chain Bridge

FRESHNEY WY

BAIN ROAD

WELLAND ROAD

RYTON ROAD

CHESTER WAY

HESSLE DRIVE

IVY CR

THORNTON AVE

BRADFORD ROAD

BROADFIELD LANE

MATTHEW FLINDERS WAY

FRIARS GATE

EATON

TANNERY CL

CANNERY

Broadfield La Ind Est

Redstone Road

Redstone Ind Est

SPALDING RD

THE WATERFRONT

LONDON RD

Swing Bridge

LC

3

New Hammond Beck Rd

Superstore

NEW HAMMOND BECK RD

SWINESHEAD ROAD

CHAIN BRIDGE ROAD

COOKS LOCK

GREENACRES DR

Holland Park

GREENBANK

WYBERTON W ROAD

Moat

WYBERTON WEST ROAD

PARK RD

LINLEY DR

LINLEY DR

ST THOMAS DR

PH

ST THOMAS CT

F3
1 ST ANN'S WHARF
2 OAKHAM TERR
3 HAVEN VILLAGE
4 REDBOURNE TERR

43

SWINESHEAD RD

A52

PH

Old Macdonalds Farm

WORTLEY'S LA

Cherry Tree Farm

Windmill

Allot Gdns

GARDENERS WK 1
POPLAR CL 2
CATER WY 3

CARMEL GN 1
CORK TREE CR 2
GARFIT'S LA 3

Skirbeck Quarter

Water Tower

GARFIT'S LANE

Woodside

BAYSWOOD AVE

St Thomas CE Prim Sch

Allot Gdns

B1397

LONDON ROAD

WOODSIDE

A16

WYBERTON LOW ROAD

FIVE HOUSE LANE

WEST END ROAD

WYBERTON WEST ROAD

Hunter's Row

Abbey Dale

OLD HAMMOND BECK ROAD

D3
1 HEATHER CL
2 WOODVILLE GDNS W
3 WOODVILLE GDNS E
4 FRANCIS BERNARD CL

E4
1 WALDEN GD
2 ALBERT TER R
3 TRAFALGAR PL
4 WEST ROW
5 GEORGE ST
6 BRAMLEY LA
7 BLUE ST
8 BROADFIELD LA
9 NELSON WY

F1
1 FLEMING CT
2 WHITTLE CL
3 SIR ISAAC NEWTON DR
4 STEPHENSON CL
5 BELL CT
6 EDISON WAY

F2
1 WYBERTON LOW RD
2 MIDDLECOTT CL
3 WYBERTON LOW RD
4 ELMWOOD AVE

F4
1 BOND ST
2 BRIDGE ST
3 SIBSEY LA
4 SHODFRIARS LA
5 SPAIN LA
6 PADDOCK GR
7 QUAKER LA
8 VICTORIA PL
9 GREYFRIARS LA

10 WHITEHORSE LA
11 LIQUORPOND ST
12 PULVERTOFT LA
13 EDWIN ST
14 ROSEGARTH ST
15 EMERY LA
16 CHAPEL PASSAGE
17 SPAIN COURT
18 The Haven

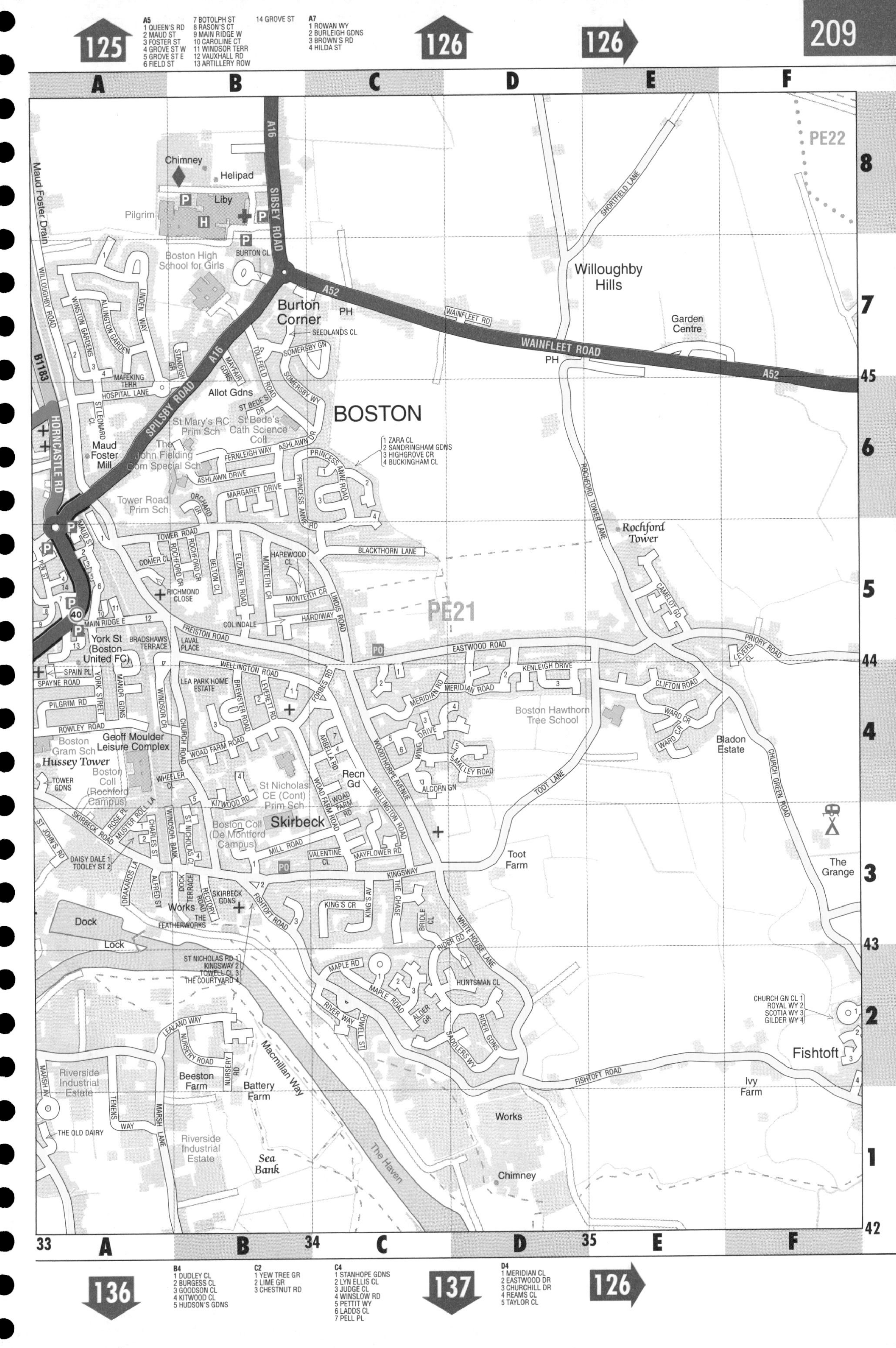

209
125
126
126
136
137
126
A5
1 QUEEN'S RD
2 MAUD ST
3 FOSTER ST
4 GROVE ST W
5 GROVE ST E
6 FIELD ST
7 BOTOLPH ST
8 RASON'S CT
9 MAIN RIDGE W
10 CAROLINE CT
11 WINDSOR TERR
12 VAUXHALL RD
13 ARTILLERY ROW
14 GROVE ST
A7
1 ROWAN WY
2 BURLEIGH GDNS
3 BROWN'S RD
4 HILDA ST
A
B
C
D
E
F
8
7
45
6
5
44
4
3
43
2
1
42
33
34
35
PE22
PE21
Chimney
Helipad
Liby
Pilgrim
Maud Foster Drain
SIBSEY ROAD
A16
BURTON CL
Boston High School for Girls
Burton Corner
PH
A52
WAINFLEET RD
WAINFLEET ROAD
SHORTFIELD LANE
Willoughby Hills
Garden Centre
SEEDLANDS CL
SOMERSBY GN
SOMERSBY WY
TOLLFIELD ROAD
MAYFAIR GDNS
STANDISH GR
WINSTON GARDENS
ALLINGTON GARDEN
LINDEN WAY
WILLOUGHBY ROAD
B1183
MAFEKING TERR
HOSPITAL LANE
Allot Gdns
SPILSBY ROAD
HORNCASTLE RD
ST LEONARD CL
BOSTON
ST BEDE'S DR
St Mary's RC Prim Sch
St Bede's Cath Science Coll
Maud Foster Mill
The John Fielding Com Special Sch
FERNLEIGH WAY
ASHLAWN DR
ASHLAWN DRIVE
MARGARET DRIVE
PRINCESS ANNE ROAD
1 ZARA CL
2 SANDRINGHAM GDNS
3 HIGHGROVE CR
4 BUCKINGHAM CL
Tower Road Prim Sch
ORCHARD GR
ROCHFORD TOWER LANE
Rochford Tower
TOWER ROAD
MAUD ST
COMER CL
ROCHFORD CR
BELTON CL
ELIZABETH ROAD
MONTEITH CR
HAREWOOD CL
BLACKTHORN LANE
RICHMOND CLOSE
MONTEITH CR
LINDIS ROAD
HARDIWAY
COLINDALE
CAMELOT GD
MAIN RIDGE E
York St (Boston United FC)
BRADSHAWS TERRACE
LAVAL PLACE
FREISTON ROAD
EASTWOOD ROAD
PRIORY ROAD
LEVERS CL
SPAIN PL
SPAYNE ROAD
WELLINGTON ROAD
LEA PARK HOME ESTATE
FORBES RD
KENLEIGH DRIVE
MERIDIAN RD
MERIDIAN ROAD
CLIFTON ROAD
PILGRIM RD
YORK STREET
MANOR GDNS
WINDSOR CR
BREWSTER ROAD
LEVERETT RD
Boston Hawthorn Tree School
WARD CR
Bladon Estate
ROWLEY ROAD
Boston Gram Sch
Geoff Moulder Leisure Complex
Hussey Tower
Boston Coll (Rochford Campus)
CHURCH ROAD
WOAD FARM ROAD
WING DRIVE
SMALLEY ROAD
ALCORN GN
TOOT LANE
CHURCH GREEN ROAD
WOODTHORPE AVENUE
TOWER GDNS
WHEELER CL
ARBELLA RD
Recn Gd
St Nicholas CE (Cont) Prim Sch
WOAD FARM RD
WOAD FARM ROAD
WELLINGTON ROAD
KITWOOD RD
SKIRBECK ROAD
ROSE PL
MUSTER ROLL LA
CHARLES ST
WINDSOR BANK
ST NICHOLAS CL
Boston Coll (De Montfort Campus)
Skirbeck
MILL ROAD
VALENTINE CL
MAYFLOWER RD
Toot Farm
ST JOHN'S RD
DAISY DALE 1
TOOLEY ST 2
KINGSWAY
The Grange
DRAKARDS LA
ALFRED ST
DOCK TERRACE
RECTORY ROAD
SKIRBECK GDNS
FISHTOFT ROAD
KING'S CR
KING'S AV
THE CHASE
BRIDLE CL
WHITE HOUSE LANE
Works
THE FEATHERWORKS
Dock
Lock
RIDER GD
ST NICHOLAS RD 1
KINGSWAY 2
TOWELL CL 3
THE COURTYARD 4
MAPLE RD
MAPLE ROAD
HUNTSMAN CL
ALDER GR
CHURCH GN CL 1
ROYAL WY 2
SCOTIA WY 3
GILDER WY 4
RIVER WAY
POWELL ST
RIDER GDNS
SADDLERS WY
Fishtoft
LEALAND WAY
NURSERY ROAD
NURSERY RD
Macmillan Way
FISHTOFT ROAD
Ivy Farm
MARSH AV
Riverside Industrial Estate
Beeston Farm
Battery Farm
TENENS WAY
MARSH LANE
Works
THE OLD DAIRY
Riverside Industrial Estate
Sea Bank
The Haven
Chimney
B4
1 DUDLEY CL
2 BURGESS CL
3 GOODSON CL
4 KITWOOD CL
5 HUDSON'S GDNS
C2
1 YEW TREE GR
2 LIME GR
3 CHESTNUT RD
C4
1 STANHOPE GDNS
2 LYN ELLIS CL
3 JUDGE CL
4 WINSLOW RD
5 PETTIT WY
6 LADDS CL
7 PELL PL
D4
1 MERIDIAN CL
2 EASTWOOD DR
3 CHURCHILL DR
4 REAMS CL
5 TAYLOR CL

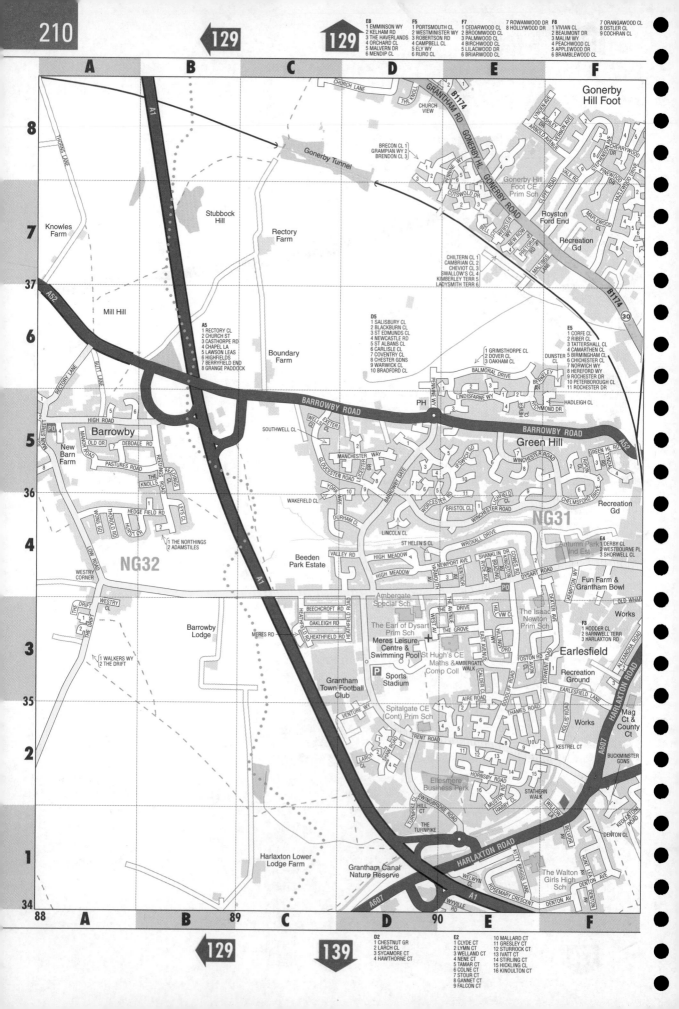

← 129

129

E8
1 EMMINSON WY
2 KELHAM RD
3 THE HAVERLANDS
4 ORCHARD CL
5 MALVERN DR
6 MENDIP CL

F5
1 PORTSMOUTH CL
2 WESTMINISTER WY
3 ROBERTSON RD
4 CAMPBELL CL
5 ELY WY
6 RURO CL

F7
1 CEDARWOOD CL
2 BROOMWOOD CL
3 PALMWOOD CL
4 BIRCHWOOD CL
5 LILACWOOD DR
6 BRIARWOOD CL

7 ROWANWOOD DR
8 HOLLYWOOD DR

F8
1 VIVIAN CL
2 BEAUMONT DR
3 MALIM WY
4 PEACHWOOD CL
5 APPLEWOOD DR
6 BRAMBLEWOOD CL

7 ORANGAWOOD CL
8 OSTLER CL
9 COCHRAN CL

Gonerby
Hill Foot

A1

THORNS LANE

Knowles
Farm

A52

Mill Hill

Stubbock
Hill

Rectory
Farm

CHURCH LANE

GRANTHAM RD

B1174

CHURCH
VIEW

THE KNOLL

Gonerby Tunnel

BRECON CL 1
GRAMPIAN WY 2
BRENDON CL 3

GONERBY HL

GONERBY ROAD

Gonerby Hill
Foot CE
Prim Sch

Royston
Ford End

Recreation
Gd

B1174

CHILTERN CL 1
CAMBRIAN CL 2
CHEVIOT CL 3
SWALLOW'S CL 4
KIMBERLEY TERR 5
LADYSMITH TERR 6

A5
1 RECTORY CL
2 CHURCH ST
3 CASTHORPE RD
4 CHAPEL LA
5 LAWSON LEAS
6 HIGHFIELDS
7 BERRYFIELD END
8 GRANGE PADDOCK

D5
1 SALISBURY CL
2 BLACKBURN CL
3 ST EDMUNDS CL
4 NEWCASTLE CL
5 ST ALBANS CL
6 CARLISLE CL
7 COVENTRY CL
8 CHESTER GDNS
9 WARWICK CL
10 BRADFORD CL

1 GRIMSTHORPE CL
2 DOVER CL
3 OAKHAM CL

E5
1 CORFE CL
2 RIBER CL
3 TATTERSHALL CL
4 CAMARTHEN CL
5 BIRMINGHAM CL
6 CHICHESTER CL
7 NORWICH WY
8 HEREFORD WY
9 ROCHESTER DR
10 PETERBOROUGH CL
11 ROCHESTER DR

Boundary
Farm

RECTORY LANE

BUTT LANE

REDDINGS ROAD

HIGH ROAD

MAIN STREET

PO

Barrowby

New
Barn
Farm

OLD OR

MANOR ROAD

DEBDALE RD

PASTURES ROAD

THE KNOLLS

BARROWBY ROAD

SOUTHWELL CL

WELLS CL

EXETER

GLOUCESTER ROAD

MANCHESTER WAY

LEICESTER GR

YORK WAY

WAKEFIELD CL

DURHAM CL

BARROWBY GATE

WORCESTER

BRISTOL CL

LINCOLN CL

PH

PENNINE WY

BALMORAL DRIVE

LINDISFARNE WY

BERKELEY

HEVER

RICHMOND DR

BARROWBY ROAD

Green Hill

WINCHESTER ROAD

IPSWICH GD

LICHFIELD CL

CHELMSFORD DRIVE

RIPON CL

GREEN HL RD

A52

NG31

Recreation
Gd

HEDGE FIELD RD

WONG RD

THOROLD RD

HURST CR

LEYS CL

1 THE NORTHINGS
2 ADAMSTILES

NG32

A1

Beeden
Park Estate

VALLEY RD

ST HELEN'S CL

HIGH MEADOW

HIGH MEADOW

NEWPORT AVE

SHANKLIN DR

VENTNOR

BRADING

RYDE AVE

WROXALL DRIVE

KINGSTON

COWES RD

DYSART ROAD

E4
1 DERBY CL
2 WESTBOURNE PL
3 SHORWELL CL

Autumn Park
Ind Est

Fun Farm &
Grantham Bowl

Works

WESTRY
CORNER

LOW ROAD

THE DRIFT

WESTRY
CL

1 WALKERS WY
2 THE DRIFT

Barrowby
Lodge

BEECHCROFT RD

OAKLEIGH RD

HEATHFIELD RD

MERES RD

HEATHFIELD RD

Ambergate
Special Sch

The Earl of Dysart
Prim Sch

Meres Leisure
Centre &
Swimming Pool

P

Sports
Stadium

Grantham
Town Football
Club

THE DRIVE

THE AVENUE

WEST AV

THE GROVE

HILLING YORD

HILL VW CL

EAST AVENUE

ST HUGH'S CE
Maths &AMBERGATE
Comp Coll

PO

The Isaac
Newton
Prim Sch

KEMPTON RD

DEXTER AV

FOSTON RD

DERWENT RD

AMBERGATE
WALK

F3
1 HODDER CL
2 BARNWELL TERR
3 HARLAXTON RD

Earlesfield

Recreation
Ground

HARLAXTON ROAD

A607

ALEXANDRA ROAD

VENTURE WY

Spitalgate CE
(Cont) Prim Sch

LARCH CL

SWAN ROAD

TRENT ROAD

HORNSBY ROAD

CALDER RD

AIRE ROAD

THAMES ROAD

GOODLIFF ROAD

HOLLIS RD

Works

KESTREL CT

MUSTON RD

HARBY CL

STATHERN WALK

WILLOW LA

Ellesmere
Business Park

SWINGBRIDGE ROAD

THE
TURNPIKE

TURNPIKE HILL

Mag
Ct &
County
Ct

BUCKMINSTER
GDNS

BELVOIR AV

KEDLESTONE ROAD

DENTON CL

Harlaxton Lower
Lodge Farm

Grantham Canal
Nature Reserve

HARLAXTON ROAD

WELWYN CL

ROSEMARY CRESCENT

A607

KITTY BRIGGS LANE

WYVILLE RD

A1

The Walton
Girls High
Sch

DENTON LA

DENTON AVE

← 129

139

D2
1 CHESTNUT GR
2 LARCH CL
3 SYCAMORE CT
4 HAWTHORNE CT

E2
1 CLYDE CT
2 LYMN CT
3 WELLAND CT
4 NENE CT
5 TAMAR CT
6 COLNE CT
7 STOUR CT
8 GANNET CT
9 FALCON CT

10 MALLARD CT
11 GRESLEY CT
12 STURROCK CT
13 IVATT CT
14 STIRLING CT
15 HICKLING CL
16 KINOULTON CT

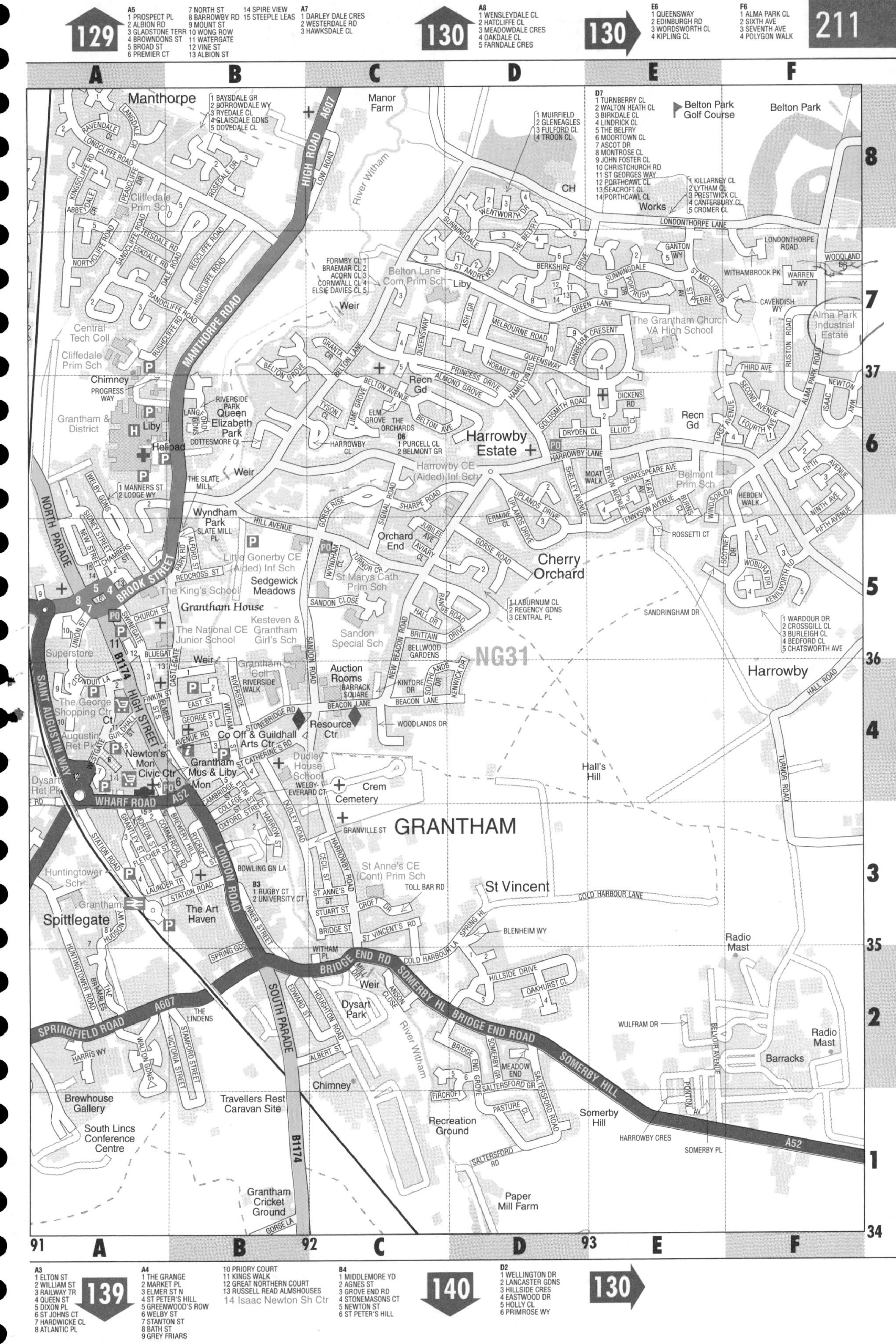

129
A5
1 PROSPECT PL
2 ALBION RD
3 GLADSTONE TERR
4 BROWNDONS ST
5 BROAD ST
6 PREMIER CT
7 NORTH ST
8 BARROWBY RD
9 MOUNT ST
10 WONG ROW
11 WATERGATE
12 VINE ST
13 ALBION ST
14 SPIRE VIEW
15 STEEPLE LEAS
A7
1 DARLEY DALE CRES
2 WESTERDALE RD
3 HAWKSDALE CL
130
A8
1 WENSLEYDALE CL
2 HATCLIFFE CL
3 MEADOWDALE CRES
4 OAKDALE CL
5 FARNDALE CRES
130
E6
1 QUEENSWAY
2 EDINBURGH RD
3 WORDSWORTH CL
4 KIPLING CL
F6
1 ALMA PARK CL
2 SIXTH AVE
3 SEVENTH AVE
4 POLYGON WALK
211
A
B
C
D
E
F
Manthorpe
1 BAYSDALE GR
2 BORROWDALE WY
3 RYEDALE CL
4 GLAISDALE GDNS
5 DOVEDALE CL
Manor Farm
D7
1 TURNBERRY CL
2 WALTON HEATH CL
3 BIRKDALE CL
4 LINDRICK CL
5 THE BELFRY
6 MOORTOWN CL
7 ASCOT DR
8 MONTROSE CL
9 JOHN FOSTER CL
10 CHRISTCHURCH RD
11 ST GEORGES WAY
12 PORTHCAWL CL
13 SEACROFT CL
14 PORTHCAWL CL
Belton Park Golf Course
Belton Park
1 MUIRFIELD
2 GLENEAGLES
3 FULFORD CL
4 TROON CL
1 KILLARNEY CL
2 LYTHAM CL
3 PRESTWICK CL
4 CANTERBURY CL
5 CROMER CL
8
HIGH ROAD
LOW ROAD
A607
River Witham
Cliffedale Prim Sch
RAVENDALE CL
LANGDALE CR
LONGCLIFFE ROAD
KINGSCLIFFE RD
PEASCLIFFE DR
ROSEDALE DR
ABBEY DALE DR
NORTHCLIFFE ROAD
TEESDALE RD
ESKDALE RD
REDCLIFFE ROAD
HIGHCLIFFE ROAD
DALE ROAD
SANDCLIFFE ROAD
RUSHCLIFFE RD
MANTHORPE ROAD
Central Tech Coll
Cliffedale Prim Sch
Chimney
PROGRESS WAY
Grantham & District
Liby
Helipad
RIVERSIDE PARK
Queen Elizabeth Park
COTTESMORE CL
THE SLATE MILL
Weir
1 MANNERS ST
2 LODGE WY
Wyndham Park
SLATE MILL PL
HILL AVENUE
Little Gonerby CE (Aided) Inf Sch
Sedgewick Meadows
REDCROSS ST
BROOK STREET
The King's School
Grantham House
NORTH PARADE
WELBY GDNS
SIDNEY STREET
NEW STREET
CHAMBERS ST
ALFORD ST
PARK RD
CHURCH ST
SWINEGATE
The National CE Junior School
Kesteven & Grantham Girl's Sch
Superstore
UNION ST
CONDUIT LA
BLUEGATE
CASTLEGATE
Weir
Grantham Coll
RIVERSIDE WALK
The George Shopping Ctr
B1174
HIGH STREET
FINKIN ST
ELMER ST S
EAST ST
WELHAM ST
RIVERSIDE
SAINT AUGUSTIN WAY
Augustin Ret Pk
GUILDHALL ST
WESTGATE
GEORGE ST
AVENUE RD
STONEBRIDGE RD
Co Off & Guildhall Arts Ctr
ST CATHERINE'S RD
Grantham Mus & Liby
Newton's Mon
Civic Ctr
Mon
Dysart Ret Pk
WHARF ROAD
A52
CAMBRIDGE ST
ETON ST
COLLEGE ST
OXFORD STREET
HARROW ST
Dudley House School
WELBY-EVERARD CT
Crem
Cemetery
DUDLEY ROAD
GRANVILLE ST
GRANTHAM
STATION ROAD
GRANTLEY ST
NORTON ST
FLETCHER ST
COMMERCIAL RD
BREWERY HILL
RYCROFT ST
LONDON ROAD
BOWLING GN LA
Huntingtower Sch
LAUNDER TR
STATION ROAD
B3
1 RUGBY CT
2 UNIVERSITY CT
Grantham
Spittlegate
HUDSON WAY
The Art Haven
INNER STREET
HUNTINGTOWER ROAD
THE BRAMBLES
SPRING GDS
SPRINGFIELD ROAD
A607
HARRIS WY
THE LINDENS
WALTON GDNS
VICTORIA STREET
STAMFORD STREET
Brewhouse Gallery
South Lincs Conference Centre
Travellers Rest Caravan Site
SOUTH PARADE
B1174
Grantham Cricket Ground
GORSE LA
SANDON ROAD
Auction Rooms
BARRACK SQUARE
BEACON LANE
Resource Ctr
WOODLANDS DR
CECIL ST
HARROWBY ROAD
ST ANNE'S ST
STUART ST
BRIDGE ST
WITHAM PL
St Anne's CE (Cont) Prim Sch
TOLL BAR RD
CROFT DR
ST VINCENT'S RD
St Vincent
COLD HARBOUR LANE
SPRING HL
BLENHEIM WY
COLD HARBOUR LA
BRIDGE END RD
MILL DR
Weir
Dysart Park
ANSON CLOSE
EDWARD ST
HOUGHTON ROAD
ALBERT ST
SOMERBY HL
BRIDGE END ROAD
HILLSIDE DRIVE
OAKHURST CL
SOMERBY HILL
River Witham
Chimney
BRIDGE END GROVE
SOMERBY GR
MEADOW END
SALTERSFORD GR
FIRCROFT
PASTURE CL
SALTERSFORD ROAD
Recreation Ground
Somerby Hill
HARROWBY CRES
SALTERSFORD RD
Paper Mill Farm
A52
SOMERBY PL
PONTON AV
WULFRAM DR
BELVOIR AVENUE
Barracks
Radio Mast
Radio Mast
TURNOR ROAD
HALL ROAD
Harrowby
Hall's Hill
NG31
1 WARDOUR DR
2 CROSSGILL CL
3 BURLEIGH CL
4 BEDFORD CL
5 CHATSWORTH AVE
SANDRINGHAM DR
WOBURN DR
KENILWORTH RD
SCOTNEY DR
ROSSETTI CT
Cherry Orchard
1 LABURNUM CL
2 REGENCY GDNS
3 CENTRAL PL
GORSE ROAD
ERMINE CL
UPLANDS DRIVE
Orchard End
JUBILEE AVE
AVIARY CL
RANGE ROAD
HALL DR
BRITTAIN DRIVE
BELLWOOD GARDENS
NEW BEACON ROAD
KINTORE DR
SOUTHLANDS DR
KENWICK DR
BEACON LANE
St Marys Cath Prim Sch
WYNDHAM CL
TURNOR CR
SANDON CLOSE
Sandon Special Sch
GORSE RISE
SIGNAL ROAD
SHARPE ROAD
Harrowby CE (Aided) Inf Sch
Harrowby Estate
D6
1 PURCELL CL
2 BELMONT GR
HARROWBY CL
ELM GROVE
THE ORCHARDS
LIME GROVE
TYSON CL
BELTON AVENUE
BELTON AVE
BELTON GROVE
GRANTA CR
BELTON LANE
Recn Gd
ALMOND GROVE
PRINCESS DRIVE
HOBART RD
QUEENSWAY
MELBOURNE ROAD
ASH GR
HAMILTON RD
CANBERRA CRESENT
GOLDSMITH ROAD
DICKENS RD
DRYDEN CL
ELLIOT
HARROWBY LANE
SHELLEY AVENUE
MOAT WALK
BYRON AVENUE
SHAKESPEARE AVE
KEATS AVE
TENNYSON AVENUE
BURNS CL
Belmont Prim Sch
WINDSOR DR
HEBDEN WALK
FIFTH AVENUE
NINTH AVE
FIFTH AVENUE
FIRST AVENUE
FOURTH AVE
SECOND AVENUE
THIRD AVE
Recn Gd
ALMA PARK ROAD
ISAAC NEWTON WAY
RUSTON ROAD
Alma Park Industrial Estate
CAVENDISH WY
WITHAMBROOK PK
WARREN WY
WOODLAND DR
LONDONTHORPE ROAD
LONDONTHORPE LANE
The Grantham Church VA High School
GANTON WY
ST MELLION DR
ST PIERRE AV
PORTRUSH DR
SUNNINGDALE
GREEN LANE
BERKSHIRE DRIVE
THE BELFRY
WENTWORTH DR
SUNNINGDALE
ST ANDREWS
CH
Works
FORMBY CL 1
BRAEMAR CL 2
ACORN CL 3
CORNWALL CL 4
ELSIE DAVIES CL 5
Belton Lane Com Prim Sch
Liby
Weir
7
37
6
5
36
4
3
35
2
1
34
91
92
93
A
B
C
D
E
F
A3
1 ELTON ST
2 WILLIAM ST
3 RAILWAY TR
4 QUEEN ST
5 DIXON PL
6 ST JOHNS CT
7 HARDWICKE CL
8 ATLANTIC PL
139
A4
1 THE GRANGE
2 MARKET PL
3 ELMER ST N
4 ST PETER'S HILL
5 GREENWOOD'S ROW
6 WELBY ST
7 STANTON ST
8 BATH ST
9 GREY FRIARS
10 PRIORY COURT
11 KINGS WALK
12 GREAT NORTHERN COURT
13 RUSSELL READ ALMSHOUSES
14 Isaac Newton Sh Ctr
B4
1 MIDDLEMORE YD
2 AGNES ST
3 GROVE END RD
4 STONEMASONS CT
5 NEWTON ST
6 ST PETER'S HILL
140
D2
1 WELLINGTON DR
2 LANCASTER GDNS
3 HILLSIDE CRES
4 EASTWOOD DR
5 HOLLY CL
6 PRIMROSE WY
130

C6
1 BARNES CL
2 LOMAX DR
3 STANNES CL
4 EXETER DR
5 ELY ST
6 ST MARYS DR

7 ST BOTOLPHS RD
8 ST MICHAELS WK
9 LINWOOD CL

C7
1 GLOUCESTER CL
2 HEREFORD CL
3 NORWICH CL
4 CANTERBURY DR
5 TRURO ST

121

D5
1 FRANKLIN CRES
2 CLAYBERG DR
3 BISHOPS CT
4 TAME CT
5 TAMSON CT
6 ROMNEY COURT

121

D6
1 BIRCHWOOD RD
2 ASHBY CT
3 SUMMERFIELD CL
4 SUMMERFIELD DR
5 RUDKIN DR
6 SMEETON CT

7 DAWSON RD
8 CHERRY CL
9 CEDAR AVE

121

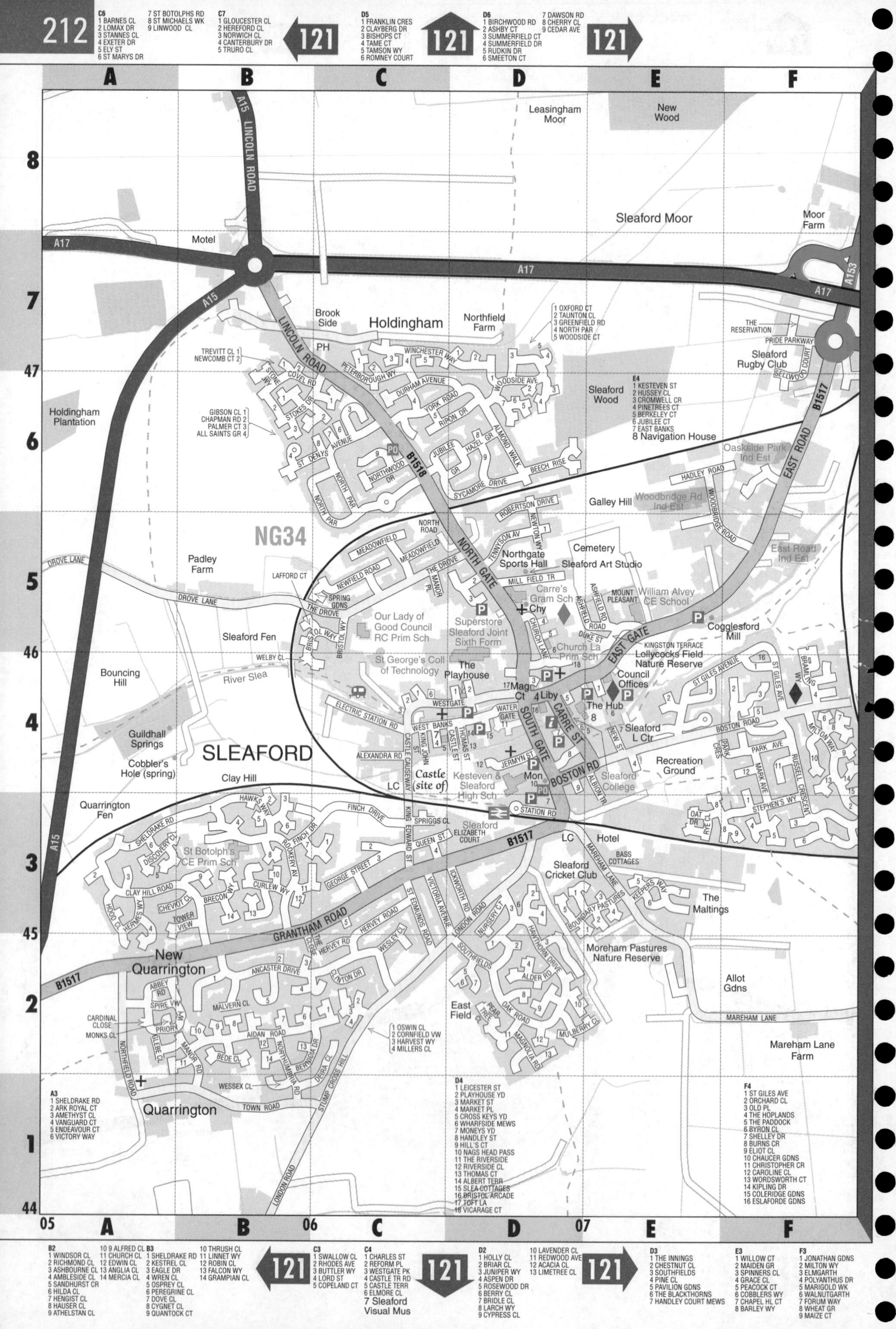

B2
1 WINDSOR CL
2 RICHMOND CL
3 ASHBOURNE CL
4 AMBLESIDE CL
5 SANDHURST CR
6 HILDA CL
7 HENGIST CL
8 HAUSER CL
9 ATHELSTAN CL

10 9 ALFRED CL
11 CHURCH CL
12 EDWIN CL
13 ANGLIA CL
14 MERCIA CL

B3
1 SHELDRAKE RD
2 KESTREL CL
3 EAGLE DR
4 WREN CL
5 OSPREY CL
6 PEREGRINE CL
7 DOVE CL
8 CYGNET CL
9 QUANTOCK CT

10 THRUSH CL
11 LINNET WY
12 ROBIN CL
13 FALCON WY
14 GRAMPIAN CL

121

C3
1 SWALLOW CL
2 RHODES AVE
3 BUTTLER WY
4 LORD ST
5 COPELAND CT

C4
1 CHARLES ST
2 REFORM PL
3 WESTGATE PK
4 CASTLE TR RD
5 CASTLE TERR
6 ELMORE CL
7 Sleaford
Visual Mus

121

D2
1 HOLLY CL
2 BRIAR CL
3 JUNIPER WY
4 ASPEN DR
5 ROSEWOOD DR
6 BERRY CL
7 BRIDLE CL
8 LARCH WY
9 CYPRESS CL

10 LAVENDER CL
11 REDWOOD AVE
12 ACACIA CL
13 LIMETREE CL

D3
1 THE INNINGS
2 CHESTNUT CL
3 SOUTHFIELDS
4 PINE CL
5 PAVILION GDNS
6 THE BLACKTHORNS
7 HANDLEY COURT MEWS

121

E3
1 WILLOW CT
2 MAIDEN GR
3 SPINNERS CL
4 GRACE CL
5 PEACOCK CT
6 COBBLERS WY
7 CHAPEL HL CT
8 BARLEY WY

F3
1 JONATHAN GDNS
2 MILTON WY
3 ELMGARTH
4 POLYANTHUS DR
5 MARIGOLD WK
6 WALNUTGARTH
7 FORUM WAY
8 WHEAT GR
9 MAIZE CT

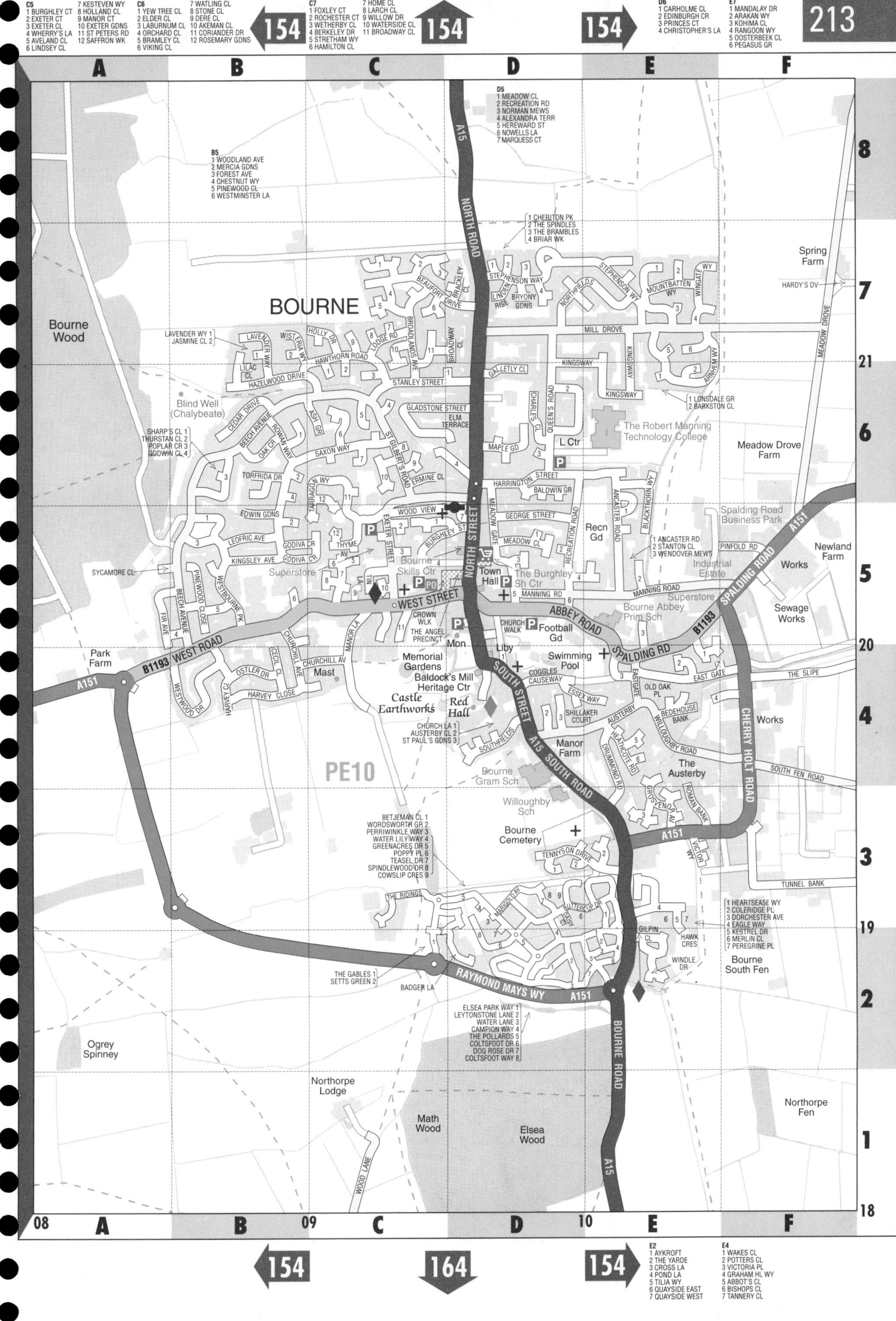

213
C5
1 BURGHLEY CT
2 EXETER CT
3 EXETER CL
4 WHERRY'S LA
5 AVELAND CL
6 LINDSEY CL
7 KESTEVEN WY
8 HOLLAND CL
9 MANOR CT
10 EXETER GDNS
11 ST PETERS RD
12 SAFFRON WK
C6
1 YEW TREE CL
2 ELDER CL
3 LABURNUM CL
4 ORCHARD CL
5 BRAMLEY CL
6 VIKING CL
7 WATLING CL
8 STONE CL
9 DERE CL
10 AKEMAN CL
11 CORIANDER DR
12 ROSEMARY GDNS
154
C7
1 FOXLEY CT
2 ROCHESTER CT
3 WETHERBY CL
4 BERKELEY DR
5 STRETHAM WY
6 HAMILTON CL
7 HOME CL
8 LARCH CL
9 WILLOW DR
10 WATERSIDE CL
11 BROADWAY CL
154
154
D6
1 CARHOLME CL
2 EDINBURGH CR
3 PRINCES CT
4 CHRISTOPHER'S LA
E7
1 MANDALAY DR
2 ARAKAN WY
3 KOHIMA CL
4 RANGOON WY
5 OOSTERBEEK CL
6 PEGASUS GR
A B C D E F
D5
1 MEADOW CL
2 RECREATION RD
3 NORMAN MEWS
4 ALEXANDRA TERR
5 HEREWARD ST
6 NOWELLS LA
7 MARQUESS CT
B5
1 WOODLAND AVE
2 MERCIA GDNS
3 FOREST AVE
4 CHESTNUT WY
5 PINEWOOD CL
6 WESTMINSTER LA
1 CHERITON PK
2 THE SPINDLES
3 THE BRAMBLES
4 BRIAR WK
BOURNE
Bourne Wood
Spring Farm
HARDY'S DV
LAVENDER WY 1
JASMINE CL 2
MILL DROVE
KINGSWAY
MEADOW DROVE
1 LONSDALE GR
2 BARKSTON CL
Blind Well (Chalybeate)
The Robert Manning Technology College
Meadow Drove Farm
SHARP'S CL 1
THURSTAN CL 2
POPLAR CR 3
GODWIN CL 4
NORTH ROAD
NORTH STREET
A15
Spalding Road Business Park
Newland Farm
1 ANCASTER RD
2 STANTON CL
3 WENDOVER MEWS
SYCAMORE CL
Superstore
Bourne Skills Ctr
Town Hall
The Burghley Sh Ctr
Recn Gd
Industrial Estate
Works
Sewage Works
WEST STREET
ABBEY ROAD
SPALDING ROAD
B1193
A151
Bourne Abbey Prim Sch
Football Gd
Swimming Pool
Park Farm
B1193 WEST ROAD
Memorial Gardens
Baldock's Mill Heritage Ctr
Mast
Castle Earthworks
Red Hall
CHURCH LA 1
AUSTERBY CL 2
ST PAUL'S GDNS 3
SOUTH STREET
Manor Farm
The Austerby
CHERRY HOLT ROAD
SOUTH FEN ROAD
PE10
Bourne Gram Sch
Willoughby Sch
SOUTH ROAD
Bourne Cemetery
BETJEMAN CL 1
WORDSWORTH GR 2
PERRIWINKLE WAY 3
WATER LILY WAY 4
GREENACRES DR 5
POPPY PL 6
TEASEL DR 7
SPINDLEWOOD DR 8
COWSLIP CRES 9
TUNNEL BANK
1 HEARTSEASE WY
2 COLERIDGE PL
3 DORCHESTER AVE
4 EAGLE WAY
5 KESTREL DR
6 MERLIN CL
7 PEREGRINE PL
Bourne South Fen
THE GABLES 1
SETTS GREEN 2
BADGER LA
RAYMOND MAYS WY
ELSEA PARK WAY 1
LEYTONSTONE LANE 2
WATER LANE 3
CAMPION WAY 4
THE POLLARDS 5
COLTSFOOT DR 6
DOG ROSE DR 7
COLTSFOOT WAY 8
BOURNE ROAD
Ogrey Spinney
Northorpe Lodge
Math Wood
Elsea Wood
Northorpe Fen
WOOD LANE
8 7 21 6 5 20 4 3 19 2 1 18
08 09 10
154
164
154
E2
1 AYKROFT
2 THE YARDE
3 CROSS LA
4 POND LA
5 TILIA WY
6 QUAYSIDE EAST
7 QUAYSIDE WEST
E4
1 WAKES CL
2 POTTERS CL
3 VICTORIA PL
4 GRAHAM HL WY
5 ABBOT'S CL
6 BISHOPS CL
7 TANNERY CL

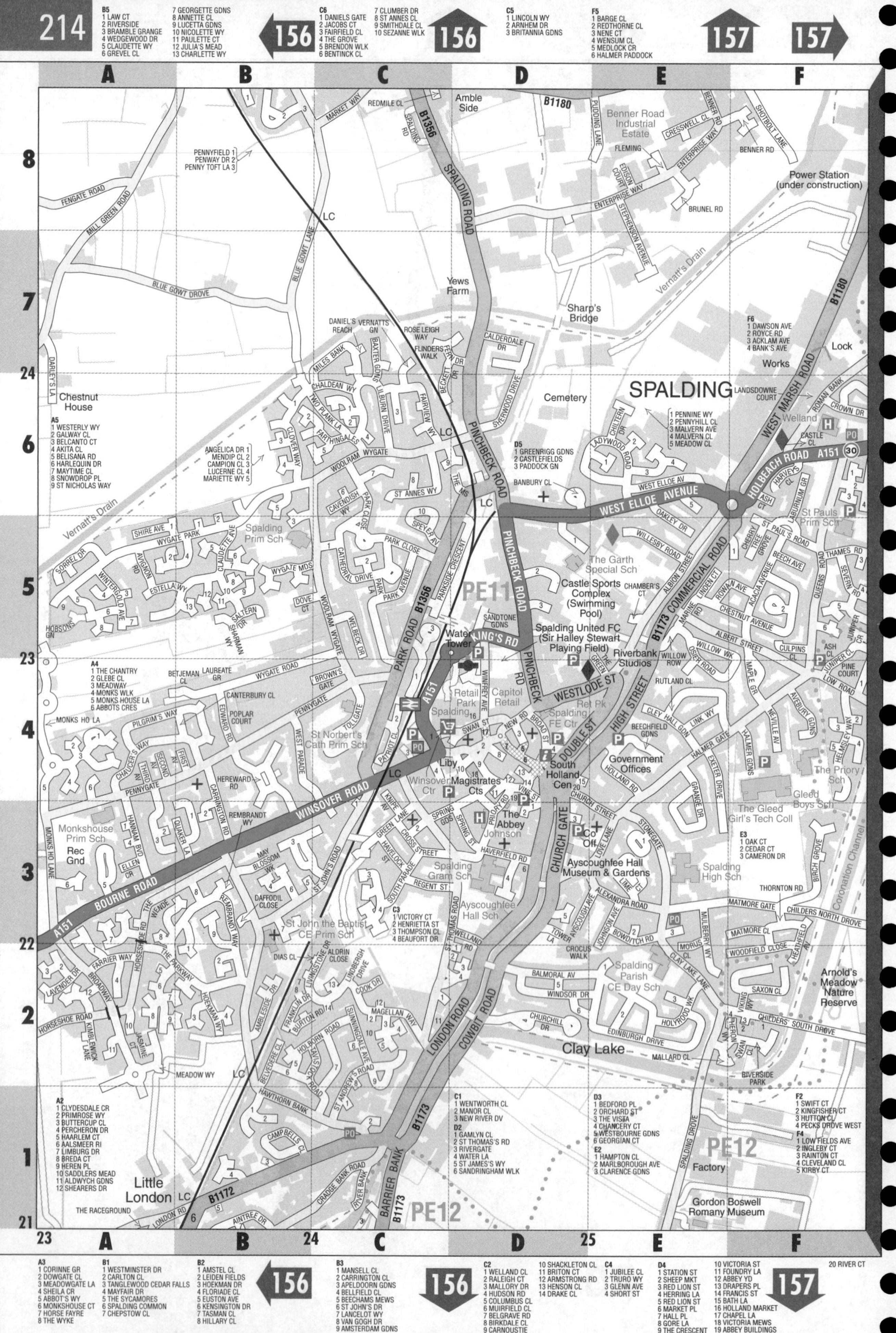
B5
1 LAW CT
2 RIVERSIDE
3 BRAMBLE GRANGE
4 WEDGEWOOD DR
5 CLAUDETTE WY
6 GREVEL CL
7 GEORGETTE GDNS
8 ANNETTE CL
9 LUCETTA GDNS
10 NICOLETTE WY
11 PAULETTE CT
12 JULIA'S MEAD
13 CHARLETTE WY
156
C6
1 DANIELS GATE
2 JACOBS CT
3 FAIRFIELD CL
4 THE GROVE
5 BRENDON WLK
6 BENTINCK CL
7 CLUMBER DR
8 ST ANNES CL
9 SMITHDALE CL
10 SEZANNE WLK
156
C5
1 LINCOLN WY
2 ARNHEM DR
3 BRITANNIA GDNS
F5
1 BARGE CL
2 REDTHORNE CL
3 NENE CT
4 WENSUM CL
5 MEDLOCK CR
6 HALMER PADDOCK
157
157
A
B
C
D
E
F
8
7
24
6
5
23
4
3
22
2
1
21
SPALDING
PE11
PE12
Amble Side
Benner Road Industrial Estate
Power Station (under construction)
Yews Farm
Sharp's Bridge
Chestnut House
Cemetery
Welland
Lock
Works
Vernatt's Drain
Spalding Prim Sch
The Garth Special Sch
Castle Sports Complex (Swimming Pool)
Spalding United FC (Sir Halley Stewart Playing Field)
Riverbank Studios
Water Tower
Retail Park
Capitol Retail
Spalding
Spalding FE Ctr
Government Offices
St Norbert's Cath Prim Sch
Winsover Ctr
Magistrates Cts
South Holland Cen
The Abbey
Johnson
Co Off
Ayscoughfee Hall Museum & Gardens
Spalding Gram Sch
Ayscoughfee Hall Sch
Spalding High Sch
St Pauls Prim Sch
The Priory Sch
Gleed Boys Sch
The Gleed Girl's Tech Coll
Monkshouse Prim Sch
Rec Gnd
St John the Baptist CE Prim Sch
Spalding Parish CE Day Sch
Arnold's Meadow Nature Reserve
Clay Lake
Little London
Factory
Gordon Boswell Romany Museum
SPALDING ROAD
PINCHBECK ROAD
WEST ELLOE AVENUE
HOLBEACH ROAD
WEST MARSH ROAD
COMMERCIAL ROAD
HIGH STREET
WINSOVER ROAD
BOURNE ROAD
PARK ROAD
LONDON ROAD
COWBIT ROAD
CHURCH GATE
BARRIER BANK
B1356
B1180
B1173
B1172
A151
A5
1 WESTERLY WY
2 GALWAY CL
3 BELCANTO CT
4 AKITA CL
5 BELISANA RD
6 HARLEQUIN DR
7 MAYTIME CL
8 SNOWDROP PL
9 ST NICHOLAS WAY
D5
1 GREENRIGG GDNS
2 CASTLEFIELDS
3 PADDOCK GN
1 PENNINE WY
2 PENNYHILL CL
3 MALVERN AVE
4 MALVERN CL
5 MEADOW CL
F6
1 DAWSON AVE
2 ROYCE RD
3 ACKLAM AVE
4 BANK'S AVE
A4
1 THE CHANTRY
2 GLEBE CL
3 MEADWAY
4 MONKS WLK
5 MONKS HOUSE LA
6 ABBOTS CRES
C3
1 VICTORY CT
2 HENRIETTA ST
3 THOMPSON CL
4 BEAUFORT DR
E3
1 OAK CT
2 CEDAR CT
3 CAMERON DR
A2
1 CLYDESDALE CR
2 PRIMROSE WY
3 BUTTERCUP CL
4 PERCHERON DR
5 HAARLEM CT
6 AALSMEER RI
7 LIMBURG DR
8 BREDA CT
9 HEREN PL
10 SADDLERS MEAD
11 ALDWYCH GDNS
12 SHEARERS DR
C1
1 WENTWORTH CL
2 MANOR CL
3 NEW RIVER DV
D2
1 GAMLYN CL
2 ST THOMAS'S RD
3 RIVERGATE
4 WATER LA
5 ST JAMES'S WY
6 SANDRINGHAM WLK
D3
1 BEDFORD PL
2 ORCHARD ST
3 THE VISTA
4 CHANCERY CT
5 WESTBOURNE GDNS
6 GEORGIAN CT
E2
1 HAMPTON CL
2 MARLBOROUGH AVE
3 CLARENCE GDNS
F2
1 SWIFT CT
2 KINGFISHER CT
3 HUTTON CL
4 PECKS DROVE WEST
F4
1 LOW FIELDS AVE
2 INGLEBY CT
3 RAINTON CT
4 CLEVELAND CL
5 KIRBY CT
23
A
B
24
C
D
25
E
F
A3
1 CORINNE GR
2 DOWGATE CL
3 MEADOWGATE LA
4 SHEILA CR
5 ABBOT'S WY
6 MONKSHOUSE CT
7 HORSE FAYRE
8 THE WYKE
B1
1 WESTMINSTER DR
2 CARLTON CL
3 TANGLEWOOD CEDAR FALLS
4 MAYFAIR DR
5 THE SYCAMORES
6 SPALDING COMMON
7 CHEPSTOW CL
B2
1 AMSTEL CL
2 LEIDEN FIELDS
3 HOEKMAN DR
4 FLORIADE CL
5 EUSTON AVE
6 KENSINGTON DR
7 TASMAN CL
8 HILLARY CL
156
B3
1 MANSELL CL
2 CARRINGTON CL
3 APELDOORN GDNS
4 BELLFIELD CL
5 BEECHAMS MEWS
6 ST JOHN'S DR
7 LANCELOT WY
8 VAN GOGH DR
9 AMSTERDAM GDNS
156
C2
1 WELLAND CL
2 RALEIGH CT
3 MALLORY DR
4 HUDSON RD
5 COLUMBUS CL
6 MUIRFIELD CL
7 BELGRAVE RD
8 BIRKDALE CL
9 CARNOUSTIE
10 SHACKLETON CL
11 BRITON CT
12 ARMSTRONG RD
13 HENSON CL
14 DRAKE CL
C4
1 JUBILEE CL
2 TRURO WY
3 GLENN AVE
4 SHORT ST
D4
1 STATION ST
2 SHEEP MKT
3 RED LION ST
4 HERRING LA
5 RED LION ST
6 MARKET PL
7 HALL PL
8 GORE LA
9 THE CRESCENT
10 VICTORIA ST
11 FOUNDRY LA
12 ABBEY YD
13 DRAPERS PL
14 FRANCIS ST
15 BATH LA
16 HOLLAND MARKET
17 CHAPEL LA
18 VICTORIA MEWS
19 ABBEY BUILDINGS
157
20 RIVER CT

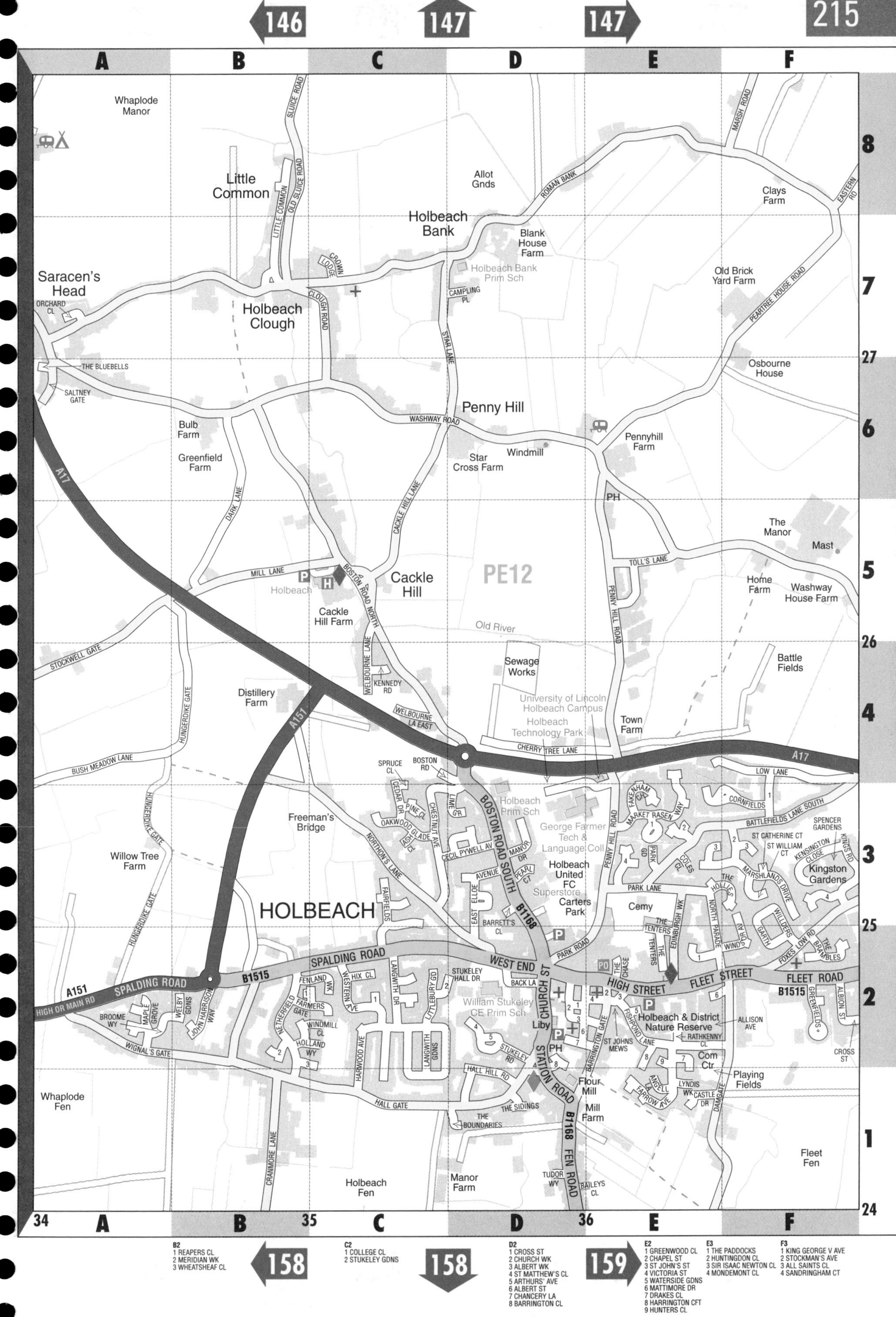
146
147
147
A
B
C
D
E
F
8
7
27
6
5
26
4
3
25
2
1
24
34
35
36
Whaplode Manor
Little Common
Allot Gnds
Holbeach Bank
Blank House Farm
Holbeach Bank Prim Sch
Clays Farm
Old Brick Yard Farm
Saracen's Head
ORCHARD CL
Holbeach Clough
CROWN LODGE
CAMPLING PL
SLUICE ROAD
OLD SLUICE ROAD
LITTLE COMMON
CLOUGH ROAD
ROMAN BANK
MARSH ROAD
EASTERN RD
PEARTREE HOUSE ROAD
STAR LANE
THE BLUEBELLS
SALTNEY GATE
Osbourne House
Penny Hill
WASHWAY ROAD
Bulb Farm
Greenfield Farm
Star Cross Farm
Windmill
Pennyhill Farm
PH
A17
DARK LANE
CACKLE HILL LANE
The Manor
Mast
TOLL'S LANE
MILL LANE
Holbeach
Cackle Hill
Cackle Hill Farm
BOSTON ROAD NORTH
PE12
Home Farm
Washway House Farm
Old River
PENNY HILL ROAD
STOCKWELL GATE
WELBOURNE LANE
KENNEDY RD
Sewage Works
Battle Fields
Distillery Farm
HUNGERDIKE GATE
A151
WELBOURNE LA EAST
University of Lincoln Holbeach Campus
Holbeach Technology Park
Town Farm
CHERRY TREE LANE
BUSH MEADOW LANE
SPRUCE CL
BOSTON RD
LOW LANE
Freeman's Bridge
CEDAR DR
PINE CL
OAKWOOD GLADE
ASH CL
CHESTNUT AVE
LIME GR
Holbeach Prim Sch
George Farmer Tech & Language Coll
FAKENHAM CH
MARKET RASEN WAY
CORNFIELDS
BATTLEFIELDS LANE SOUTH
SPENCER GARDENS
ST CATHERINE CT
ST WILLIAM CT
KENSINGTON CLOSE
KINGS RD
Willow Tree Farm
NORTHON'S LANE
CECIL PYWELL AV
BOSTON ROAD SOUTH
MANOR DR
PEARL CT
AVENUE
Holbeach United FC
Superstore
Carters Park
PARK GD
COLES CL
MARSHLANDS DRIVE
Kingston Gardens
HOLBEACH
FAIRFIELDS
EAST ELLOE
B1168
PARK LANE
Cemy
THE HOLLIES
NORTH PARADE
WILLDERS GARTH
BARRETT'S CL
THE TENTERS
EDINBURGH WK
FOXES LOW RD
THE BRAMBLES
SPALDING ROAD
WEST END
PARK ROAD
PO
THE CHASE
HIGH STREET
FLEET STREET
FLEET ROAD
B1515
A151
HIGH OR MAIN RD
SPALDING ROAD
B1515
FENLAND WK
HIX CL
WESTERN AVE
LANGWITH DR
LITTLEBURY GD
STUKELEY HALL DR
BACK LA
CHURCH ST
GREENFIELDS
ALBION ST
MAPLE GROVE
WELBY GDNS
JOHN HARRISON WAY
BROOME WY
NETHERFIELD
FARMERS GATE
WINDMILL CL
HOLLAND WY
William Stukeley CE Prim Sch
Liby
FISHPOND LANE
Holbeach & District Nature Reserve
ALLISON AVE
RATHKENNY CL
HARWOOD AVE
LANGWITH GDNS
STUKELEY RD
PH
BARRINGTON GATE
ST JOHNS MEWS
Com Ctr
CROSS ST
WIGNAL'S GATE
STATION ROAD
HALL HILL RD
Flour Mill
ANGELL LA
FARROW AVE
LYNDIS WK
CASTLE DR
DAMGATE
Playing Fields
Whaplode Fen
HALL GATE
THE SIDINGS
THE BOUNDARIES
Mill Farm
B1168 FEN ROAD
CRANMORE LANE
Holbeach Fen
Manor Farm
TUDOR WY
BAILEYS CL
Fleet Fen
B2
1 REAPERS CL
2 MERIDIAN WK
3 WHEATSHEAF CL
C2
1 COLLEGE CL
2 STUKELEY GDNS
D2
1 CROSS ST
2 CHURCH WK
3 ALBERT WK
4 ST MATTHEW'S CL
5 ARTHURS' AVE
6 ALBERT ST
7 CHANCERY LA
8 BARRINGTON CL
E2
1 GREENWOOD CL
2 CHAPEL ST
3 ST JOHN'S ST
4 VICTORIA ST
5 WATERSIDE GDNS
6 MATTIMORE DR
7 DRAKES CL
8 HARRINGTON CFT
9 HUNTERS CL
E3
1 THE PADDOCKS
2 HUNTINGDON CL
3 SIR ISAAC NEWTON CL
4 MONDEMONT CL
F3
1 KING GEORGE V AVE
2 STOCKMAN'S AVE
3 ALL SAINTS CL
4 SANDRINGHAM CT
158
158
159

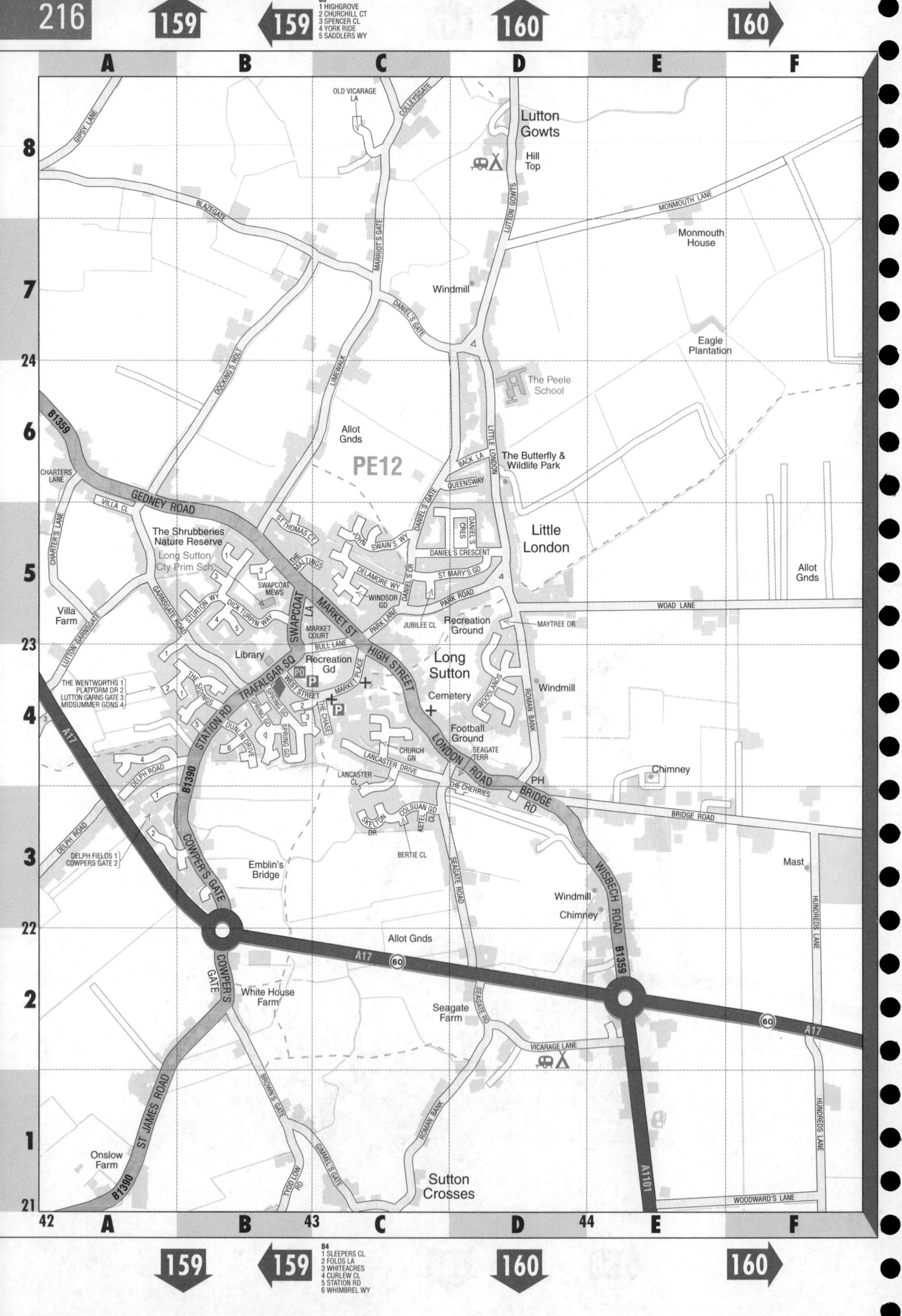
159
159
B5
1 HIGHGROVE
2 CHURCHILL CT
3 SPENCER CL
4 YORK RIDE
5 SADDLERS WY
160
160
Lutton Gowts
Hill Top
Monmouth House
Windmill
Eagle Plantation
The Peele School
Allot Gnds
PE12
The Butterfly & Wildlife Park
Little London
The Shrubberies Nature Reserve
Long Sutton Cty Prim Sch
Villa Farm
Recreation Ground
Library
Recreation Gd
Long Sutton
Cemetery
Football Ground
Windmill
Chimney
THE WENTWORTHS 1
PLATFORM DR 2
LUTTON GARNS GATE 3
MIDSUMMER GDNS 4
DELPH FIELDS 1
COWPERS GATE 2
Emblin's Bridge
Windmill
Chimney
Mast
Allot Gnds
White House Farm
Seagate Farm
Onslow Farm
Sutton Crosses
GEDNEY ROAD
MARKET ST
HIGH STREET
LONDON ROAD
BRIDGE RD
BRIDGE ROAD
WISBECH ROAD
WOAD LANE
MONMOUTH LANE
LUTTON GOWTS
LITTLE LONDON
ROMAN BANK
SEAGATE ROAD
STATION RD
TRAFALGAR SQ
COWPER'S GATE
ST JAMES ROAD
BROWN'S GATE
GIMMEL'S GATE
HUNDREDS LANE
WOODWARD'S LANE
VICARAGE LANE
BLAZEGATE
GIPSY LANE
DOCKING'S HOLT
LIMEWALK
MARRIOT'S GATE
DANIEL'S GATE
COLLEYSGATE
OLD VICARAGE LA
CHARTERS LANE
VILLA CL
LUTTON GARNSGATE
GARNSGATE ROAD
DELPH ROAD
A17
B1359
B1390
A1101
42
43
44
B4
1 SLEEPERS CL
2 FOLDS LA
3 WHITEACRES
4 CURLEW CL
5 STATION RD
6 WHIMBREL WY
159
159
160
160

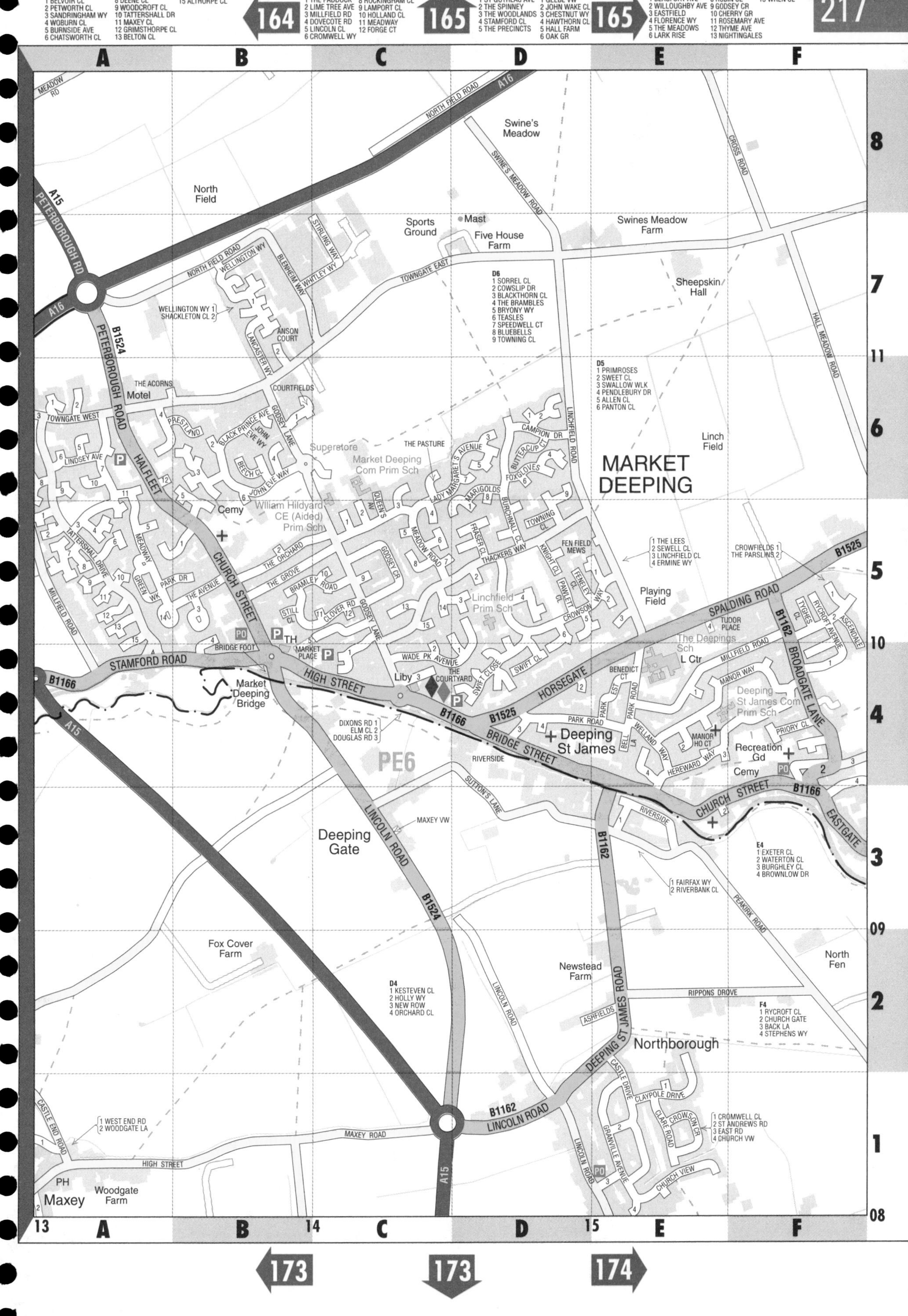

A5
1 BELVOIR CL
2 PETWORTH CL
3 SANDRINGHAM WY
4 WOBURN CL
5 BURNSIDE AVE
6 CHATSWORTH CL
7 OSBOURNE WY
8 DEENE CL
9 WOODCROFT CL
10 TATTERSHALL DR
11 MAXEY CL
12 GRIMSTHORPE CL
13 BELTON CL
14 CEDAR CL
15 ALTHORPE CL

A6
1 THE PADDOCK
2 LIME TREE AVE
3 MILLFIELD RD
4 DOVECOTE RD
5 LINCOLN CL
6 CROMWELL WY
7 KESTEVEN DR
8 ROCKINGHAM CL
9 LAMPORT CL
10 HOLLAND CL
11 MEADWAY
12 FORGE CT

B5
1 ST GUTHLAC AVE
2 THE SPINNEY
3 THE WOODLANDS
4 STAMFORD CL
5 THE PRECINCTS

B6
1 GLEBE VW
2 JOHN WAKE CL
3 CHESTNUT WY
4 HAWTHORN CL
5 HALL FARM
6 OAK GR

C5
1 BEAUFORT AVE
2 WILLOUGHBY AVE
3 EASTFIELD
4 FLORENCE WY
5 THE MEADOWS
6 LARK RISE
7 LINNET CL
8 ROBIN CL
9 GODSEY CR
10 CHERRY GR
11 ROSEMARY AVE
12 THYME AVE
13 NIGHTINGALES
14 CURLEW WLK
15 WREN CL

◄ 164

165

165 ►

Grid references and map features

D6
1 SORREL CL
2 COWSLIP DR
3 BLACKTHORN CL
4 THE BRAMBLES
5 BRYONY WY
6 TEASLES
7 SPEEDWELL CT
8 BLUEBELLS
9 TOWNING CL

D5
1 PRIMROSES
2 SWEET CL
3 SWALLOW WLK
4 PENDLEBURY DR
5 ALLEN CL
6 PANTON CL

1 THE LEES
2 SEWELL CL
3 LINCHFIELD CL
4 ERMINE WY

CROWFIELDS 1
THE PARSLINS 2

WELLINGTON WY 1
SHACKLETON CL 2

DIXONS RD 1
ELM CL 2
DOUGLAS RD 3

D4
1 KESTEVEN CL
2 HOLLY WY
3 NEW ROW
4 ORCHARD CL

1 FAIRFAX WY
2 RIVERBANK CL

E4
1 EXETER CL
2 WATERTON CL
3 BURGHLEY CL
4 BROWNLOW DR

F4
1 RYCROFT CL
2 CHURCH GATE
3 BACK LA
4 STEPHENS WY

1 WEST END RD
2 WOODGATE LA

1 CROMWELL CL
2 ST ANDREWS RD
3 EAST RD
4 CHURCH VW

MARKET DEEPING

Deeping St James

Deeping Gate

Northborough

Maxey

PE6

◄ 173

173

174 ►

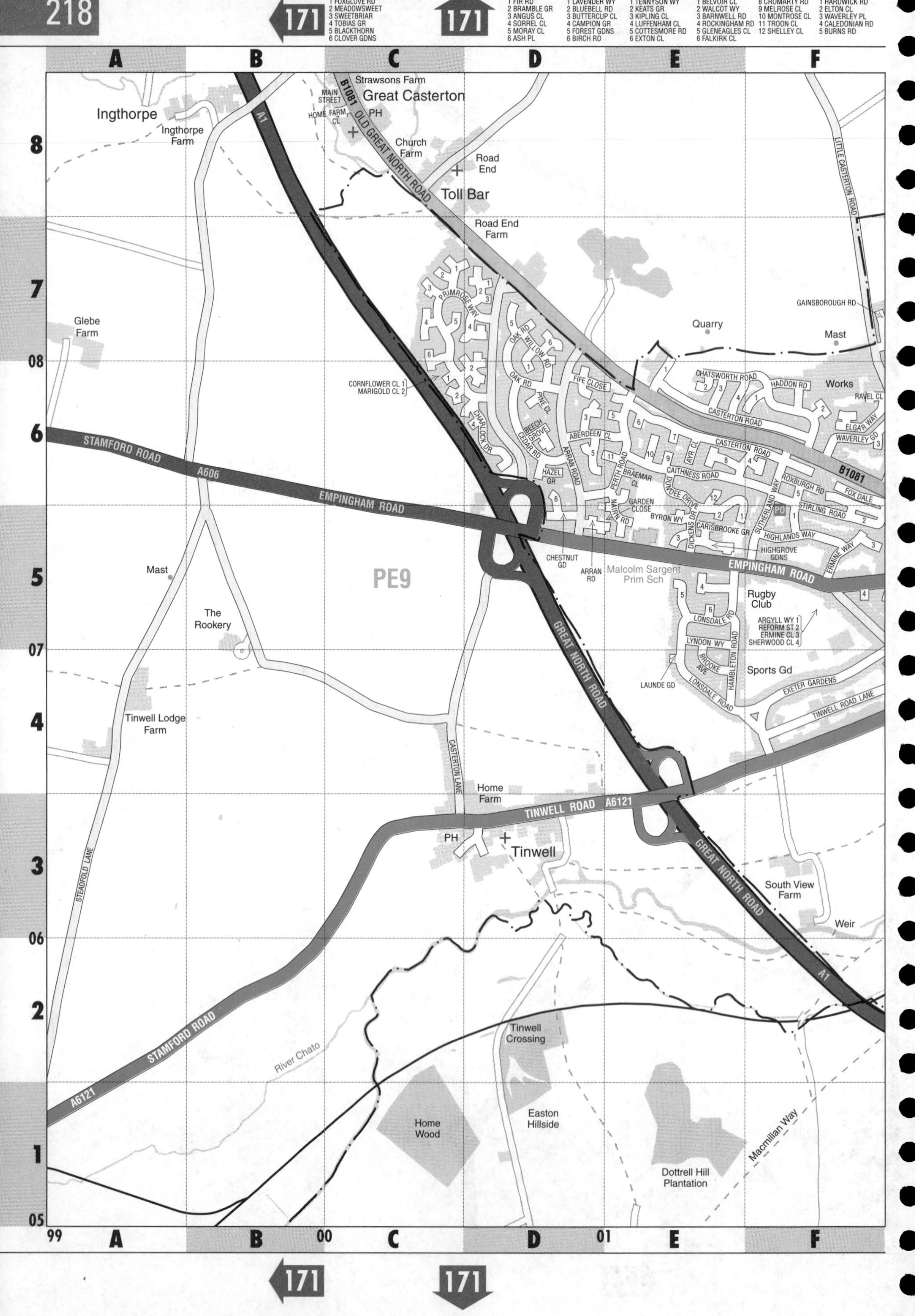
171
171
C7
1 FOXGLOVE RD
2 MEADOWSWEET
3 SWEETBRIAR
4 TOBIAS GR
5 BLACKTHORN
6 CLOVER GDNS
D6
1 FIR RD
2 BRAMBLE GR
3 ANGUS CL
4 SORREL CL
5 MORAY CL
6 ASH PL
D7
1 LAVENDER WY
2 BLUEBELL RD
3 BUTTERCUP CL
4 CAMPION GR
5 FOREST GDNS
6 BIRCH RD
E5
1 TENNYSON WY
2 KEATS GR
3 KIPLING CL
4 LUFFENHAM CL
5 COTTESMORE RD
6 EXTON CL
E6
1 BELVOIR CL
2 WALCOT WY
3 BARNWELL RD
4 ROCKINGHAM RD
5 GLENEAGLES CL
6 FALKIRK CL
7 OBAN CL
8 CROMARTY RD
9 MELROSE CL
10 MONTROSE CL
11 TROON CL
12 SHELLEY CL
F6
1 HARDWICK RD
2 ELTON CL
3 WAVERLEY PL
4 CALEDONIAN RD
5 BURNS RD
A
B
C
D
E
F
Strawsons Farm
Great Casterton
MAIN STREET
HOME FARM CL
PH
B1081
OLD GREAT NORTH ROAD
Ingthorpe
Ingthorpe Farm
Church Farm
Road End
Toll Bar
Road End Farm
A1
PRIMROSE WAY
Glebe Farm
OAK RD
WILLOW RD
Quarry
Mast
GAINSBOROUGH RD
LITTLE CASTERTON ROAD
CORNFLOWER CL 1
MARIGOLD CL 2
FIFE CLOSE
PINE CL
CHATSWORTH ROAD
HADDON RD
Works
RAVEL CL
CASTERTON ROAD
ELGAR WAY
WAVERLEY GD
STAMFORD ROAD
A606
BEECH GROVE
CEDAR RD
CHARLOCK DR
ABERDEEN CL
ARRAN ROAD
PERTH ROAD
BRAEMAR CL
AYR CL
CAITHNESS ROAD
ROXBURGH RD
FOX DALE
B1081
HAZEL GR
EMPINGHAM ROAD
GARDEN CLOSE
NAIRN RD
BYRON WY
DUNDEE DRIVE
DICKENS DR
SUTHERLAND WAY
PO
STIRLING ROAD
CARISBROOKE GR
HIGHLANDS WAY
ERMINE WAY
HIGHGROVE GDNS
CHESTNUT GD
ARRAN RD
Malcolm Sargent Prim Sch
EMPINGHAM ROAD
Mast
PE9
Rugby Club
The Rookery
LONSDALE RD
ARGYLL WY 1
REFORM ST 2
ERMINE CL 3
SHERWOOD CL 4
LYNDON WY
GREAT NORTH ROAD
BROOKE AVE
HAMBLETON ROAD
Sports Gd
LAUNDE GD
LONSDALE ROAD
EXETER GARDENS
TINWELL ROAD LANE
Tinwell Lodge Farm
CASTERTON LANE
Home Farm
TINWELL ROAD
A6121
PH
Tinwell
STEADFOLD LANE
GREAT NORTH ROAD
South View Farm
Weir
A1
STAMFORD ROAD
Tinwell Crossing
River Chater
A6121
Home Wood
Easton Hillside
Macmillan Way
Dottrell Hill Plantation
8
7
08
6
5
07
4
3
06
2
1
05
99
00
01
171
171

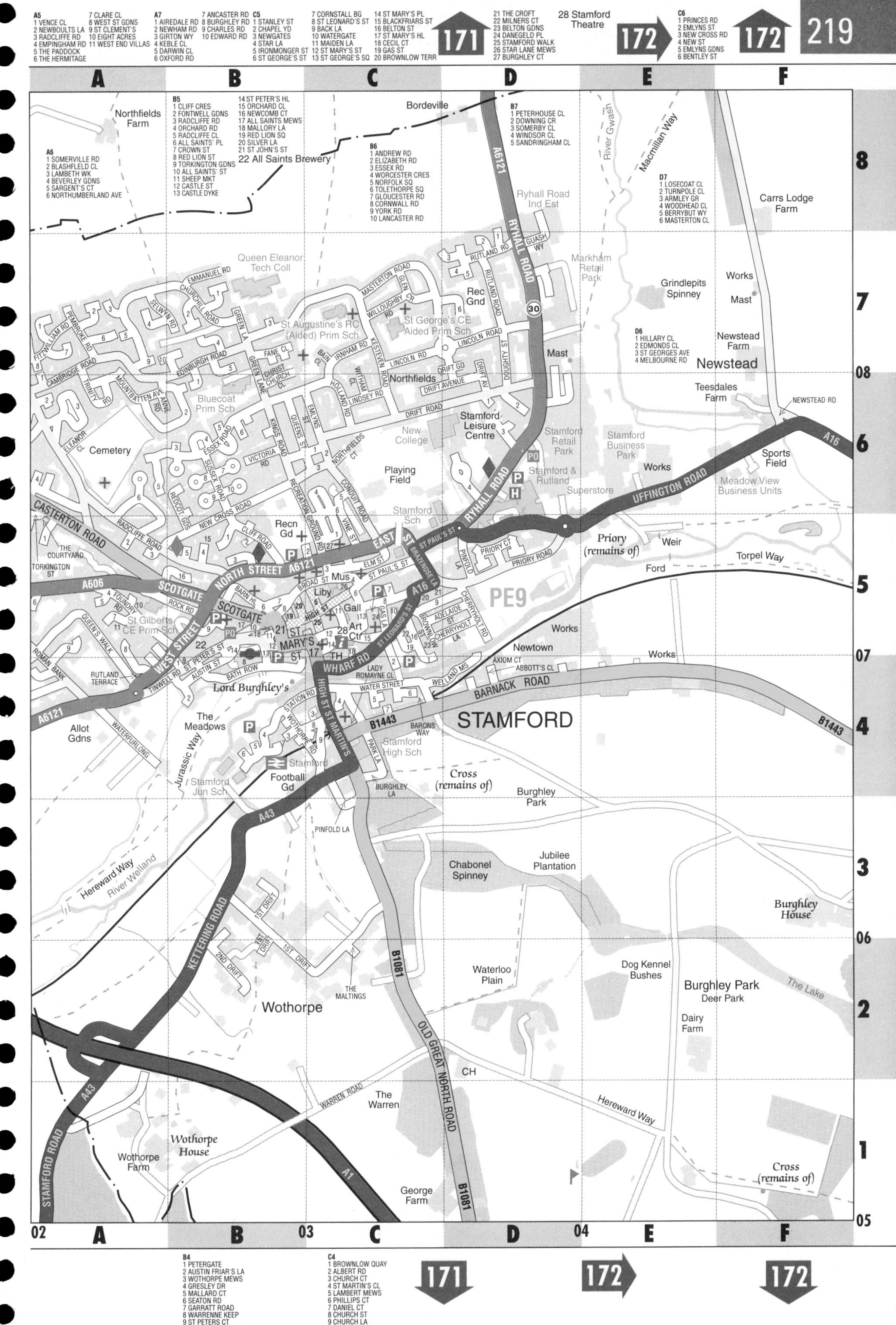
A5
1 VENCE CL
2 NEWBOULTS LA
3 RADCLIFFE RD
4 EMPINGHAM RD
5 THE PADDOCK
6 THE HERMITAGE
7 CLARE CL
8 WEST ST GDNS
9 ST CLEMENT'S
10 EIGHT ACRES
11 WEST END VILLAS
A7
1 AIREDALE RD
2 NEWHAM RD
3 GIRTON WY
4 KEBLE CL
5 DARWIN CL
6 OXFORD RD
7 ANCASTER RD
8 BURGHLEY RD
9 CHARLES RD
10 EDWARD RD
C5
1 STANLEY ST
2 CHAPEL YD
3 NEWGATES
4 STAR LA
5 IRONMONGER ST
6 ST GEORGE'S ST
7 CORNSTALL BG
8 ST LEONARD'S ST
9 BACK LA
10 WATERGATE
11 MAIDEN LA
12 ST MARY'S ST
13 ST GEORGE'S SQ
14 ST MARY'S PL
15 BLACKFRIARS ST
16 BELTON ST
17 ST MARY'S HL
18 CECIL CT
19 GAS ST
20 BROWNLOW TERR
21 THE CROFT
22 MILNERS CT
23 BELTON GDNS
24 DANEGELD PL
25 STAMFORD WALK
26 STAR LANE MEWS
27 BURGHLEY CT
28 Stamford Theatre
C6
1 PRINCES RD
2 EMLYNS ST
3 NEW CROSS RD
4 NEW ST
5 EMLYNS GDNS
6 BENTLEY ST
171
172
172
A
B
C
D
E
F
B5
1 CLIFF CRES
2 FONTWELL GDNS
3 RADCLIFFE RD
4 ORCHARD RD
5 RADCLIFFE CL
6 ALL SAINTS' PL
7 CROWN ST
8 RED LION ST
9 TORKINGTON GDNS
10 ALL SAINTS' ST
11 SHEEP MKT
12 CASTLE ST
13 CASTLE DYKE
14 ST PETER'S HL
15 ORCHARD CL
16 NEWCOMB CT
17 ALL SAINTS MEWS
18 MALLORY LA
19 RED LION SQ
20 SILVER LA
21 ST JOHN'S ST
22 All Saints Brewery
A6
1 SOMERVILLE RD
2 BLASHFIELD CL
3 LAMBETH WK
4 BEVERLEY GDNS
5 SARGENT'S CT
6 NORTHUMBERLAND AVE
B6
1 ANDREW RD
2 ELIZABETH RD
3 ESSEX RD
4 WORCESTER CRES
5 NORFOLK SQ
6 TOLETHORPE SQ
7 GLOUCESTER RD
8 CORNWALL RD
9 YORK RD
10 LANCASTER RD
B7
1 PETERHOUSE CL
2 DOWNING CR
3 SOMERBY CL
4 WINDSOR CL
5 SANDRINGHAM CL
D7
1 LOSECOAT CL
2 TURNPOLE CL
3 ARMLEY GR
4 WOODHEAD CL
5 BERRYBUT WY
6 MASTERTON CL
D6
1 HILLARY CL
2 EDMONDS CL
3 ST GEORGES AVE
4 MELBOURNE RD
Northfields Farm
Bordeville
River Gwash
Macmillan Way
Carrs Lodge Farm
Ryhall Road Ind Est
RYHALL ROAD
A6121
Queen Eleanor Tech Coll
Markham Retail Park
Grindlepits Spinney
Works
Mast
Rec Gnd
St Augustine's RC (Aided) Prim Sch
St George's CE Aided Prim Sch
Newstead Farm
Newstead
Teesdales Farm
NEWSTEAD RD
Northfields
Bluecoat Prim Sch
Stamford Leisure Centre
New College
Stamford Retail Park
Stamford Business Park
Sports Field
A16
Cemetery
Playing Field
Stamford & Rutland
Superstore
Meadow View Business Units
UFFINGTON ROAD
CASTERTON ROAD
Stamford Sch
Recn Gd
Priory (remains of)
Weir
Torpel Way
Ford
THE COURTYARD
TORKINGTON ST
A606
SCOTGATE
NORTH STREET
EAST ST
Mus
Liby
Gall
Art Ctr
PE9
St Gilberts CE Prim Sch
WEST STREET
Works
Newtown
WHARF RD
Lord Burghley's
BARNACK ROAD
B1443
RUTLAND TERRACE
STAMFORD
Allot Gdns
The Meadows
Jurassic Way
Stamford High Sch
Stamford
Football Gd
Stamford Jun Sch
Cross (remains of)
Burghley Park
A43
PINFOLD LA
Chabonel Spinney
Jubilee Plantation
Hereward Way
River Welland
Burghley House
KETTERING ROAD
B1081
Dog Kennel Bushes
Waterloo Plain
Burghley Park Deer Park
The Lake
THE MALTINGS
Wothorpe
Dairy Farm
OLD GREAT NORTH ROAD
CH
The Warren
WARREN ROAD
Hereward Way
STAMFORD ROAD
A1
Wothorpe House
Wothorpe Farm
George Farm
Cross (remains of)
8
7
08
6
5
07
4
3
06
2
1
05
02
03
04
B4
1 PETERGATE
2 AUSTIN FRIAR'S LA
3 WOTHORPE MEWS
4 GRESLEY DR
5 MALLARD CT
6 SEATON RD
7 GARRATT ROAD
8 WARRENNE KEEP
9 ST PETERS CT
C4
1 BROWNLOW QUAY
2 ALBERT RD
3 CHURCH CT
4 ST MARTIN'S CL
5 LAMBERT MEWS
6 PHILLIPS CT
7 DANIEL CT
8 CHURCH ST
9 CHURCH LA
171
172
172

173 173 174

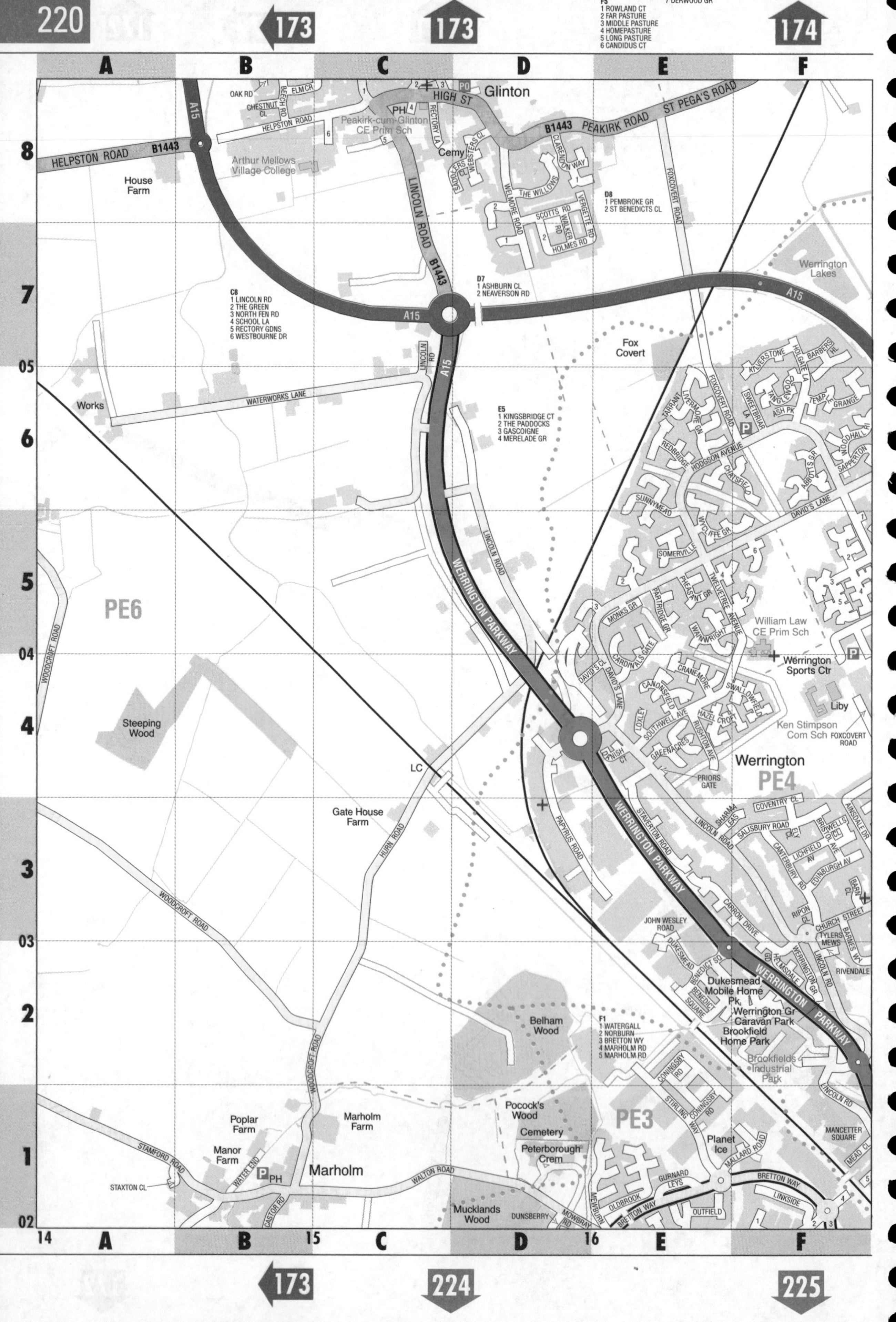
F5
1 ROWLAND CT
2 FAR PASTURE
3 MIDDLE PASTURE
4 HOMEPASTURE
5 LONG PASTURE
6 CANDIDUS CT
7 DERWOOD GR
A B C D E F
8 7 05 6 5 04 4 3 03 2 1 02
14 15 16
Glinton
HIGH ST
PO
PH
OAK RD
ELM CR
BEECH RD
CHESTNUT CL
HELPSTON ROAD
Peakirk-cum-Glinton CE Prim Sch
RECTORY LA
B1443 PEAKIRK ROAD
ST PEGA'S ROAD
HELPSTON ROAD B1443
A15
Arthur Mellows Village College
House Farm
Cemy
SADDLERS CL
WEBSTERS CL
CLARENDON WAY
THE WILLOWS
WELMORE ROAD
SCOTTS RD
WALKER RD
HOLMES RD
VERGETTE RD
LINCOLN ROAD
B1443
FOXCOVERT ROAD
D8
1 PEMBROKE GR
2 ST BENEDICTS CL
Werrington Lakes
C8
1 LINCOLN RD
2 THE GREEN
3 NORTH FEN RD
4 SCHOOL LA
5 RECTORY GDNS
6 WESTBOURNE DR
D7
1 ASHBURN CL
2 NEAVERSON RD
Fox Covert
LINCOLN RD
WATERWORKS LANE
Works
E5
1 KINGSBRIDGE CT
2 THE PADDOCKS
3 GASCOIGNE
4 MERELADE GR
KIVERSTONE
HOLGATE LA
BARBERS HL
TANGLEWOOD
TEMPLE GRANGE
ASH PK
SWEETBRIAR LA
TARRANT
LIVERMORE GN
HODGSON AVENUE
REDBRIDGE
CHATSFIELD
WOODHALL RI
ABBOTTS GR
SAPPERTON
SUNNYMEAD
WYCLIFFE GR
DAVID'S LANE
SOMERVILLE
WERRINGTON PARKWAY
PE6
WOODCROFT ROAD
PHEASANT GR
PARTRIDGE GR
TWELVETREE AVENUE
MONKS GR
CARDINALS GATE
WAINWRIGHT
William Law CE Prim Sch
Werrington Sports Ctr
DAVID'S CL
CRANEMORE
CANONSFIELD
SWALLOWFIELD
LOXLEY
SOUTHWELL AVE
HAZEL CROFT
RUSHTON AVE
GREENACRES
Liby
Ken Stimpson Com Sch
FOXCOVERT ROAD
Steeping Wood
DANISH CT
Werrington
PE4
PRIORS GATE
LC
Gate House Farm
HURN ROAD
PAPYRUS ROAD
STAVERTON ROAD
LINCOLN ROAD
SHARMA LEAS
COVENTRY CL
SALISBURY ROAD
ELY CL
BRISTOL AVE
WELLS CL
AINSDALE DR
LICHFIELD AV
CANTERBURY RD
EDINBURGH AV
BARN CL
WOODCROFT ROAD
CARRON DRIVE
JOHN WESLEY ROAD
RIPON CL
CHURCH STREET
TYLERS MEWS
BARNES WA
DUKESMEAD
BENEDICT SQ
HELMSDALE
WERRINGTON GR
LINCOLN RD
RIVENDALE
Dukesmead Mobile Home Pk.
Werrington Gr Caravan Park
Brookfield Home Park
BENEDICT SQUARE
Belham Wood
F1
1 WATERGALL
2 NORBURN
3 BRETTON WY
4 MARHOLM RD
5 MARHOLM RD
Brookfields Industrial Park
LINCOLN RD
WOODCROFT ROAD
CONINGSBY RD
STIRLING WAY
Pocock's Wood
Cemetery
Peterborough Crem
PE3
Poplar Farm
Marholm Farm
MANCETTER SQUARE
MEAD CL
Manor Farm
STAMFORD ROAD
WATER END
P PH
Marholm
WALTON ROAD
STAXTON CL
CASTOR RD
Mucklands Wood
DUNSBERRY
MOWBRAY RD
MEWBURN
OLDBROOK
GURNARD LEYS
BRETTON WAY
OUTFIELD
Planet Ice
MALLARD ROAD
BRETTON WAY
LINKSIDE

173 224 225

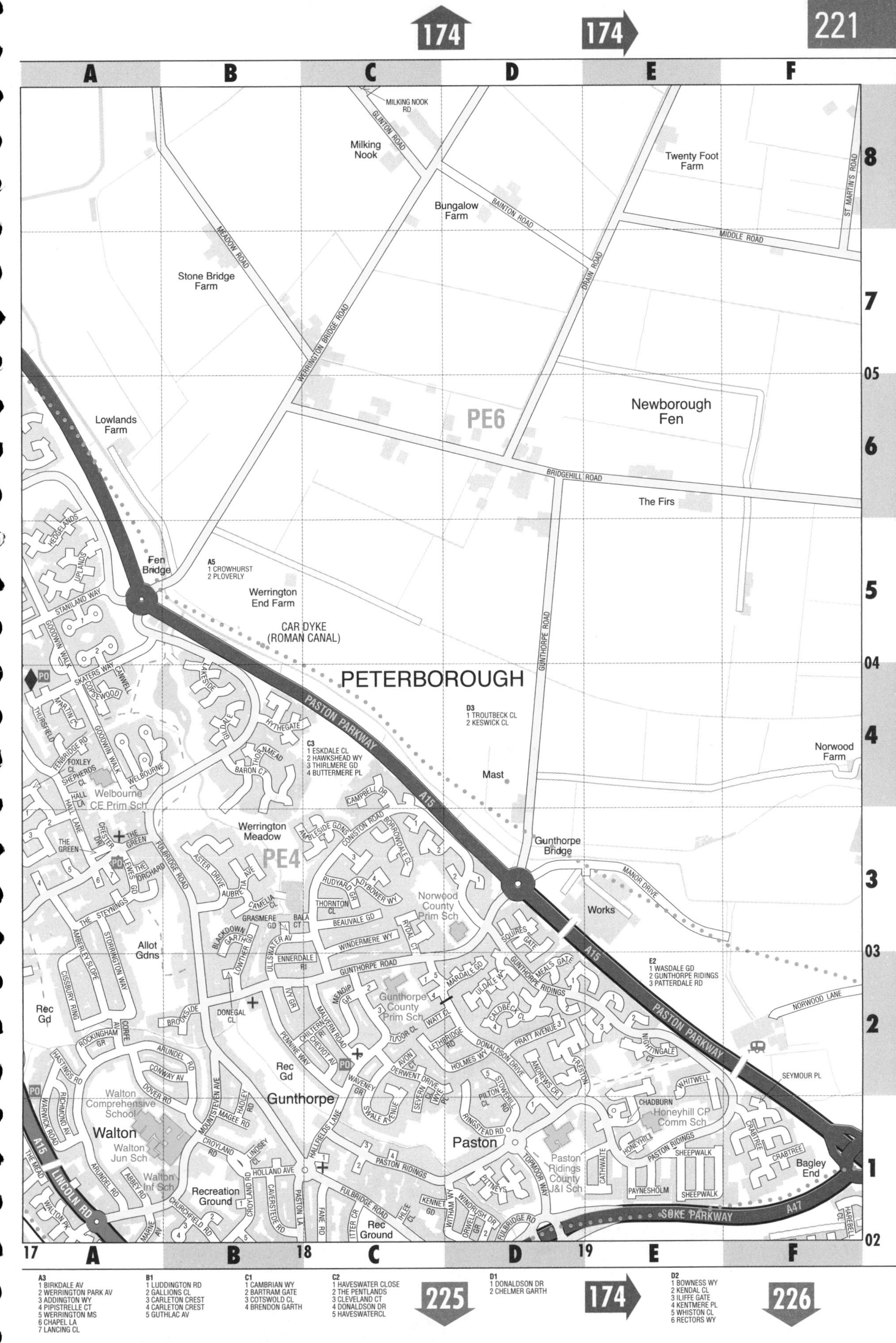

A B C D E F

8
05
7
6
5
04
4
03
3
2
03
02

Milking Nook
MILKING NOOK RD
GLINTON ROAD
MEADOW ROAD
Stone Bridge Farm
Bungalow Farm
BAINTON ROAD
Twenty Foot Farm
MIDDLE ROAD
ST MARTIN'S ROAD
WERRINGTON BRIDGE ROAD
DAMN ROAD
Lowlands Farm
PE6
Newborough Fen
BRIDGEHILL ROAD
The Firs
Fen Bridge

A5
1 CROWHURST
2 PLOVERLY

Werrington End Farm
CAR DYKE (ROMAN CANAL)
GUNTHORPE ROAD
PETERBOROUGH
HEDGELANDS
UPLANDS
PO
GOODWIN WALK
SKATERS WAY
SCOPES WAY
CANWELL
FOXWOOD
STANILAND WAY
MARTIN CL
THORSFIELD
FENBRIDGE RD
GOODWIN WALK
FOXLEY CL
SHEPHERDS CL
HALL LA
CHESTER RD
LEWIS GD
THE GREEN
THE GREEN
THE ORCHARD
FULBRIDGE ROAD
THE STEYNINGS
AMBERLEY SLOPE
CISSBURY RING
STORRINGTON WAY
ROCKINGHAM GR
HASTINGS RD
COFFE
ARUNDEL
AV
CONWAY AV
DOVER RD
MOUNT STEVEN AV
MAGEE RD
HADLEY RD
LINDSEY
STEVEN AV
CROYLAND RD
HOLLAND AVE
CAVERSTEDE RD
PASTON LA
FANE RD
Welbourne CE Prim Sch
Werrington Meadow
PE4
ASTER DRIVE
CAMELLIA AVE
TATESIDE
VALEDALE
RYTHEGATE
NINEMEAD
BARON CT

C3
1 ESKDALE CL
2 HAWKSHEAD WY
3 THIRLMERE GD
4 BUTTERMERE PL

D3
1 TROUTBECK CL
2 KESWICK CL

Mast
Norwood Farm
Norwood County Prim Sch
AMBLESIDE GDNS
CONISTON ROAD
BORROWDALE CL
CAMPBELL DR
RYDAL RD
RUDYARD CL
DYBOWER WY
THORNTON CL
BEAUVALE GD
WINDERMERE WY
BLACKDOWN
GARTHS
GRASMERE GD
BALA CT
LOWTHER
ULLSWATER AV
ENNERDALE RI
AUBREA
DONEGAL CL
BROOKSIDE
IVY GR
MENDIP
MALVERN ROAD
CATTERING RI
WAVENEY GR
AXON
DERWENT DRIVE
CHEVIOT AV
PENNINE WAY
SWALE AVE
SEVERN
RINGSTEAD RD
Gunthorpe County Prim Sch
Rec Gd
PO
Allot Gdns
Rec Gd
Gunthorpe
Gunthorpe Bridge
Works
MANOR DRIVE
SQUIRES GATE
MEALS GATE
MARDALE GD
ULDALE AV
CALDBECK CL
WATT CL
TUDOR CL
LETHBRIDGE RD
HOLMES WY
PILTON RD
PRATT AVENUE
DONALDSON DRIVE
STIXWOLD
AMDRAG CR
NIGHTINGALE
WHITWELL
CHADBURN
Honeyhill CP Comm Sch
HONEYHILL
PASTON RIDINGS
SHEEPWALK
PAYNESHOLM
SHEEPWALK
CRABTREE
CRABTREE
Bagley End
SEYMOUR PL
NORWOOD LANE
PASTON PARKWAY
A15

E2
1 WASDALE GD
2 GUNTHORPE RIDINGS
3 PATTERDALE RD

Walton Comprehensive School
Walton Jun Sch
Walton
Walton Inf Sch
WARWICK ROAD
RICHMOND AV
LINCOLN RD
THE HEAD
WALTON PL
ARUNDEL RD
ASPEC RD
MARRE RD
CHURCHFIELD RD
CROYLAND RD
Recreation Ground
PASTON RIDINGS
HALLFIELDS LANE
FULBRIDGE ROAD
ITTER CR
ILEX
Rec Ground
WITHAM
ORWELL
DERWENT GR
WINDRUSH DR
TORMORE WAY
KENNET GD
PITTEVS
FULBRIDGE RD
Paston
Paston Ridings J&I Sch
CATHWAITE
SOKE PARKWAY
A47
HARRELL CL

A15
PO

17 A B 18 C D 19 E F
02

A3
1 BIRKDALE AV
2 WERRINGTON PARK AV
3 ADDINGTON WY
4 PIPISTRELLE CT
5 WERRINGTON MS
6 CHAPEL LA
7 LANCING CL

B1
1 LUDDINGTON RD
2 GALLIONS CL
3 CARLETON CREST
4 CARLETON CREST
5 GUTHLAC AV

C1
1 CAMBRIAN WY
2 BARTRAM GATE
3 COTSWOLD CL
4 BRENDON GARTH

C2
1 HAVESWATER CLOSE
2 THE PENTLANDS
3 CLEVELAND CT
4 DONALDSON DR
5 HAVESWATERCL

D1
1 DONALDSON DR
2 CHELMER GARTH

D2
1 BOWNESS WY
2 KENDAL CL
3 ILIFFE GATE
4 KENTMERE PL
5 WHISTON CL
6 RECTORS WY

172

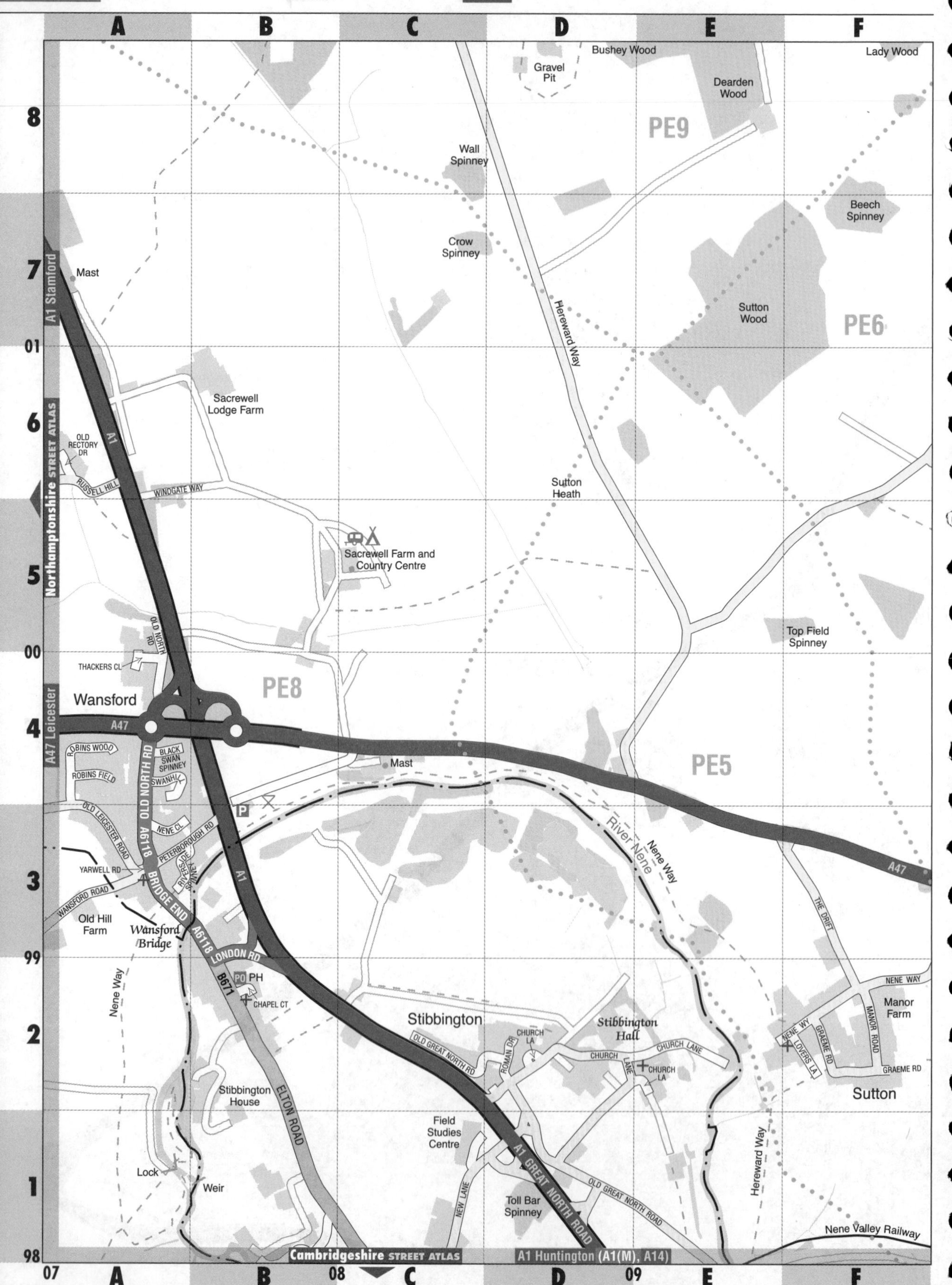

Bushey Wood
Gravel Pit
Lady Wood
Dearden Wood
PE9
Wall Spinney
Beech Spinney
Crow Spinney
Mast
A1 Stamford
Sutton Wood
PE6
Hereward Way
Sacrewell Lodge Farm
OLD RECTORY DR
RUSSELL HILL
WINDGATE WAY
Sutton Heath
Northamptonshire STREET ATLAS
Sacrewell Farm and Country Centre
OLD NORTH RD
THACKERS CL
Top Field Spinney
PE8
Wansford
A47 Leicester
A47
ROBINS WOOD
ROBINS FIELD
BLACK SWAN SPINNEY
SWANHILL
Mast
PE5
OLD NORTH RD
OLD LEICESTER ROAD
NENE CL
PETERBOROUGH RD
River Nene
Nene Way
A6118
YARWELL RD
BRIDGE END
RIVERSIDE SPINNEY
A1
A47
WANSFORD ROAD
Old Hill Farm
Wansford Bridge
A6118
LONDON RD
THE DRIFT
Nene Way
PO PH
B671
CHAPEL CT
NENE WAY
Manor Farm
Stibbington
CHURCH LA
Stibbington Hall
OLD GREAT NORTH RD
ROMAN DR
CHURCH LANE
NENE WY
LOVERS LA
GRAEME RD
MANOR ROAD
CHURCH LANE
CHURCH LA
GRAEME RD
Stibbington House
ELTON ROAD
Sutton
Field Studies Centre
A1 GREAT NORTH ROAD
Hereward Way
Lock
Weir
NEW LANE
Toll Bar Spinney
OLD GREAT NORTH ROAD
Nene Valley Railway
Cambridgeshire STREET ATLAS
A1 Huntington (A1(M), A14)

229

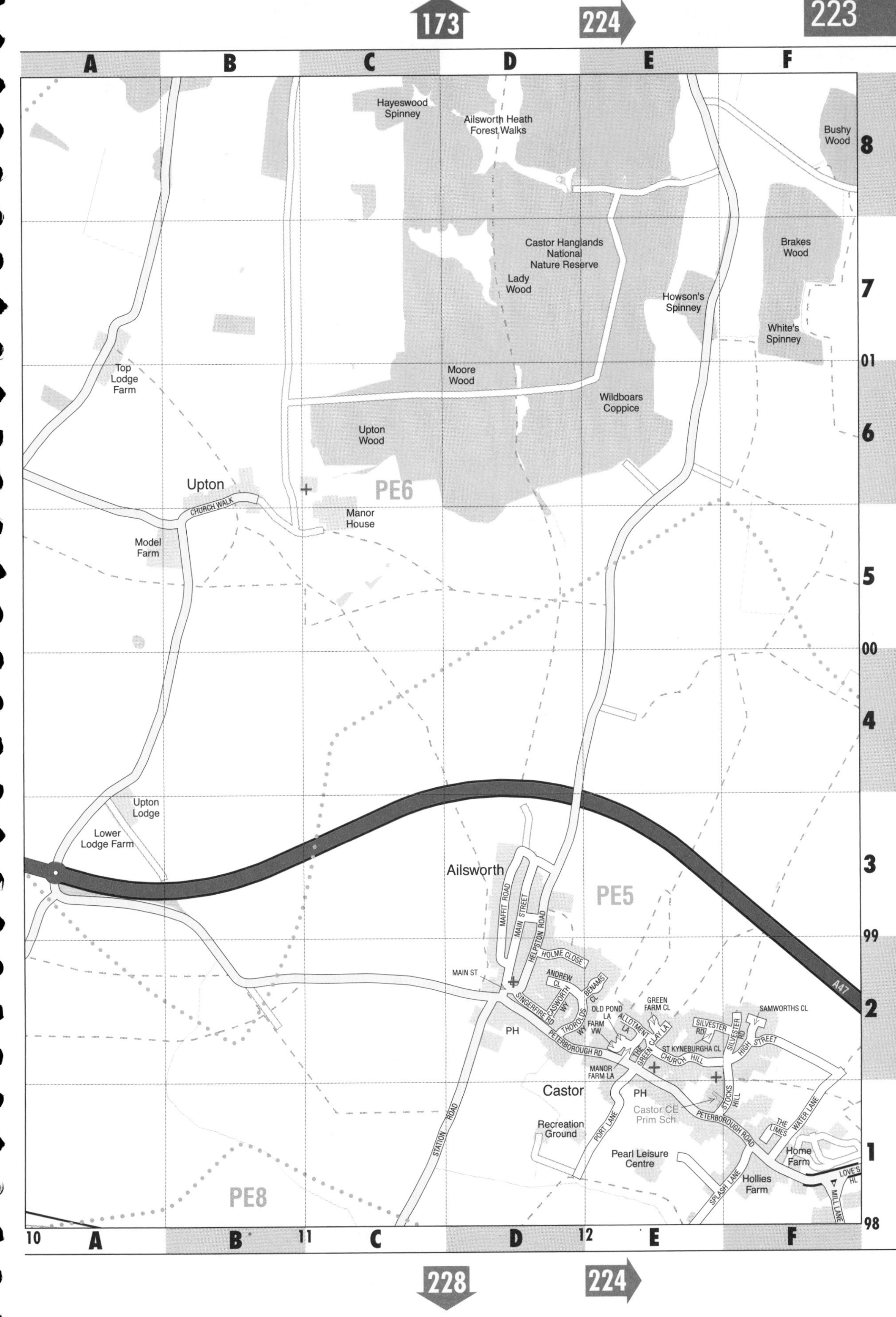

A   B   C   D   E   F

Hayeswood
Spinney

Ailsworth Heath
Forest Walks

Bushy
Wood

8

Castor Hanglands
National
Nature Reserve

Brakes
Wood

Lady
Wood

Howson's
Spinney

7

White's
Spinney

01

Moore
Wood

Wildboars
Coppice

6

Top
Lodge
Farm

Upton
Wood

Upton

PE6

5

CHURCH WALK

Manor
House

Model
Farm

00

4

Upton
Lodge

Lower
Lodge Farm

3

Ailsworth

PE5

99

A47

Castor

MAFFIT ROAD

MAIN STREET

HELPSTON ROAD

HOLME CLOSE

MAIN ST

2

ANDREW
CL

BENAMS

SINGERFIRE RD

CASWORTH
WY

THOROLDS
WY

OLD POND
LA

FARM
VW

ALLOTMENT
LA

GREEN
FARM CL

SAMWORTHS CL

SILVESTER
RD

SILVESTER
RD

HIGH STREET

PH

PETERBOROUGH RD

GREEN CLAY LA

ST KYNEBURGHA CL

CHURCH HILL

MANOR
FARM LA

PH

STOCKS
HILL

PORT LANE

Castor CE
Prim Sch

Recreation
Ground

PETERBOROUGH ROAD

THE
LIMES

WATER LANE

Home
Farm

Pearl Leisure
Centre

Hollies
Farm

LOVE'S
HL

MILL LANE

SPLASH LANE

PE8

1

98

10   A   B   11   C   12   D   E   F

173 223 220

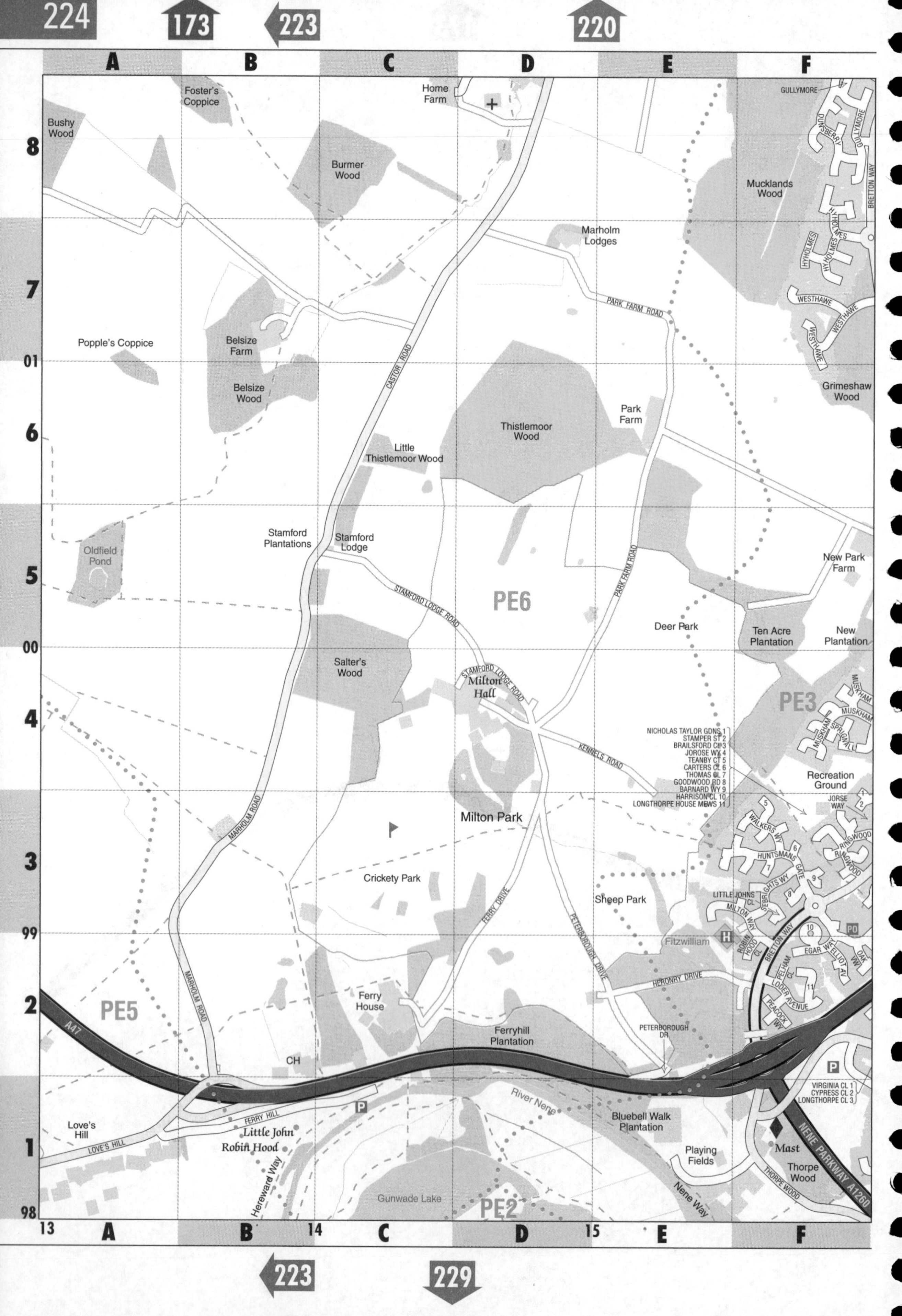
A B C D E F
Bushy Wood
Foster's Coppice
Home Farm
Burmer Wood
GULLYMORE
DUNSBERRY
Mucklands Wood
BRETTON WAY
HYHOLMES
Marholm Lodges
WESTHAWE
PARK FARM ROAD
Popple's Coppice
Belsize Farm
Belsize Wood
CASTOR ROAD
Grimeshaw Wood
Park Farm
Thistlemoor Wood
Little Thistlemoor Wood
Stamford Plantations
Stamford Lodge
Oldfield Pond
New Park Farm
STAMFORD LODGE ROAD
PE6
Deer Park
Ten Acre Plantation
New Plantation
Salter's Wood
Milton Hall
PE3
MUSKHAM
KENNELS ROAD
NICHOLAS TAYLOR GDNS 1
STAMPER ST 2
BRAILSFORD CL 3
JOROSE WY 4
TEANBY CT 5
CARTERS CL 6
THOMAS CL 7
GOODWOOD RD 8
BARNARD WY 9
HARRISON CL 10
LONGTHORPE HOUSE MEWS 11
Recreation Ground
MARHOLM ROAD
Milton Park
WALKERS WY
HUNTSMANS GATE
RINGWOOD
Crickety Park
Sheep Park
LITTLE JOHNS CL
MILTON WAY
FERRY DRIVE
PETERBOROUGH DRIVE
Fitzwilliam
ROBIN HOOD CL
BRETTON WAY
EGAR WY
ELLIOT AV
HERONRY DRIVE
PELHAM CL
LODER AVENUE
PEACOCK WY
PE5
Ferry House
A47
Ferryhill Plantation
PETERBOROUGH DR
CH
VIRGINIA CL 1
CYPRESS CL 2
LONGTHORPE CL 3
River Nene
FERRY HILL
Love's Hill
LOVE'S HILL
Little John
Robin Hood
Bluebell Walk Plantation
Playing Fields
Mast
Thorpe Wood
NENE PARKWAY A1260
THORPE WOOD
Hereward Way
Nene Way
Gunwade Lake
PE2
8 7 01 6 5 00 4 3 99 2 1 98
13 14 15

223 229

220
221
226

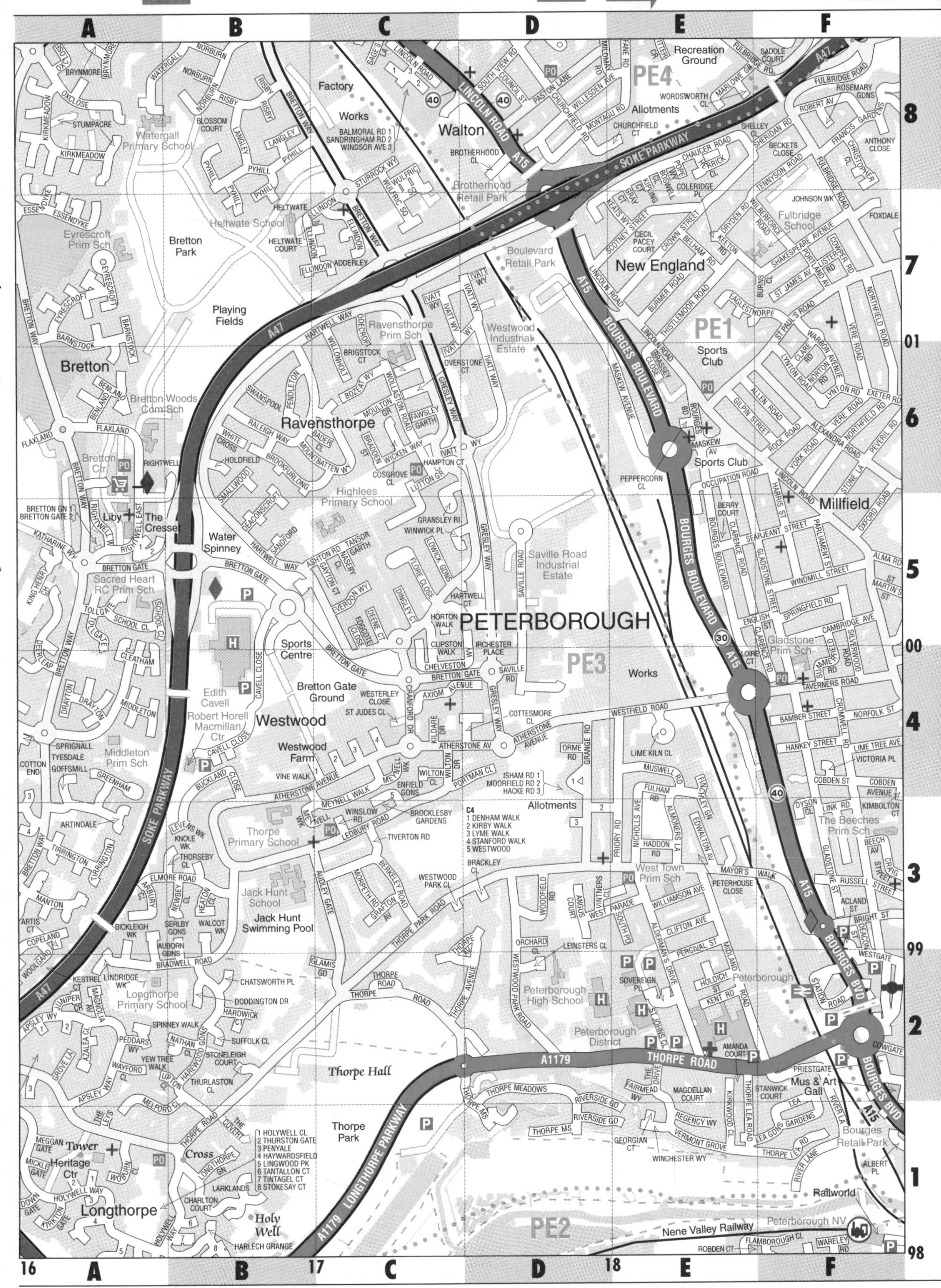
A
B
C
D
E
F
8
7
01
6
5
00
4
3
99
2
1
98
16
17
18
PETERBOROUGH
PE4
PE1
PE3
PE2
Bretton
Ravensthorpe
Westwood
Walton
New England
Millfield
Longthorpe
Westwood Farm
Recreation Ground
Factory
Works
Allotments
Brotherhood Retail Park
Boulevard Retail Park
Westwood Industrial Estate
Saville Road Industrial Estate
Bretton Park
Playing Fields
Water Spinney
Sports Centre
Bretton Gate Ground
Eyrescroft Prim Sch
Watergall Primary School
Heltwate School
Ravensthorpe Prim Sch
Highlees Primary School
Bretton Woods Com Sch
Sacred Heart RC Prim Sch
Middleton Prim Sch
Longthorpe Primary School
Thorpe Primary School
Jack Hunt School
Jack Hunt Swimming Pool
Edith Cavell
Robert Horell Macmillan Ctr
West Town Prim Sch
Peterborough High School
Peterborough District
Gladstone Prim Sch
The Beeches Prim Sch
Fulbridge School
Sports Club
Thorpe Hall
Thorpe Park
Holy Well
Tower
Heritage Ctr
Cross
Mus & Art Gall
Bourges Retail Park
Railworld
Peterborough NV
Nene Valley Railway
Peterborough
Bretton Ctr
Liby
The Cresset
SOKE PARKWAY
A47
A15
A1179
LINCOLN ROAD
BOURGES BOULEVARD
BOURGES BVD
THORPE ROAD
LONGTHORPE PARKWAY
BRETTON WAY
BRETTON GATE
HARTWELL WAY
ATHERSTONE AVENUE
WESTFIELD ROAD
THORPE PARK ROAD
BRADWELL ROAD
OCCUPATION ROAD
LINCOLN ROAD
BALMORAL RD 1
SANDRINGHAM RD 2
WINDSOR AVE 3
C4
1 DENHAM WALK
2 KIRBY WALK
3 LYME WALK
4 STANFORD WALK
5 WESTWOOD
ISHAM RD 1
MOORFIELD RD 2
HACKE RD 3
BRETTON GN 1
BRETTON GATE 2
1 HOLYWELL CL
2 THURSTON GATE
3 PENYALE
4 HAYWARDSFIELD
5 LINGWOOD PK
6 TANTALLON CT
7 TINTAGEL CT
8 STOKESAY CT

230
226

A B C D E F

PE6

225

PETERBOROUGH

PE1

PE2

Dogsthorpe

Newark

Eastfield

Fengate

A2
1 KING ST
2 QUEEN ST
3 TRINITY ST
4 PRIESTGATE
5 BROADWAY CT
6 HEREWARD CROSS
7 CATTLE MARKET WAY
8 CATTLE MARKET RD
9 MINSTER PRECINCTS

10 CATHEDRAL SQ

A3
1 BURGHLEY RD
2 BURGHLEY SQ
3 ST MARK'S CT

B2
1 FENGATE CL
2 HEREWARD CL
3 KESTEVEN WLK
4 WESTMORELAND GDNS
5 STEPHENSON CT
6 ST MARYS CT

B3
1 CRAWTHORNE ST
2 JORDAN MEWS

A1
1 WENTWORTH ST
2 BRIDGE ST
3 RIVERGATE
4 EMBANKMENT RD

A5
1 INGLEBOROUGH
2 DOGSTHORPE GR

C2
1 RUTLAND CT
2 SHROPSHIRE PL

D3
1 WETHERBY WY
2 RASEN CT
3 HEXHAM CT
4 NORTH BANK RD
5 VICARAGE FARM RD

D7
1 RATCLIFFE CT
2 ALLEXTON GDNS
3 TWYFORD GDNS
4 BUCKMINSTER PL
5 REDMILE WLK
6 DORCHESTER CRES

D8
1 MEDBOURNE GDNS
2 WALTHAM CL
3 HUNGARTON CT
4 SOMERBY GARTH

E7
1 WHETSTONE CT
2 RAGDALE CL
3 ROTHERBY GR
4 ILLSTON PL
5 REDGATE CT
6 BLANDFORD GDNS
7 WIMBORNE DR

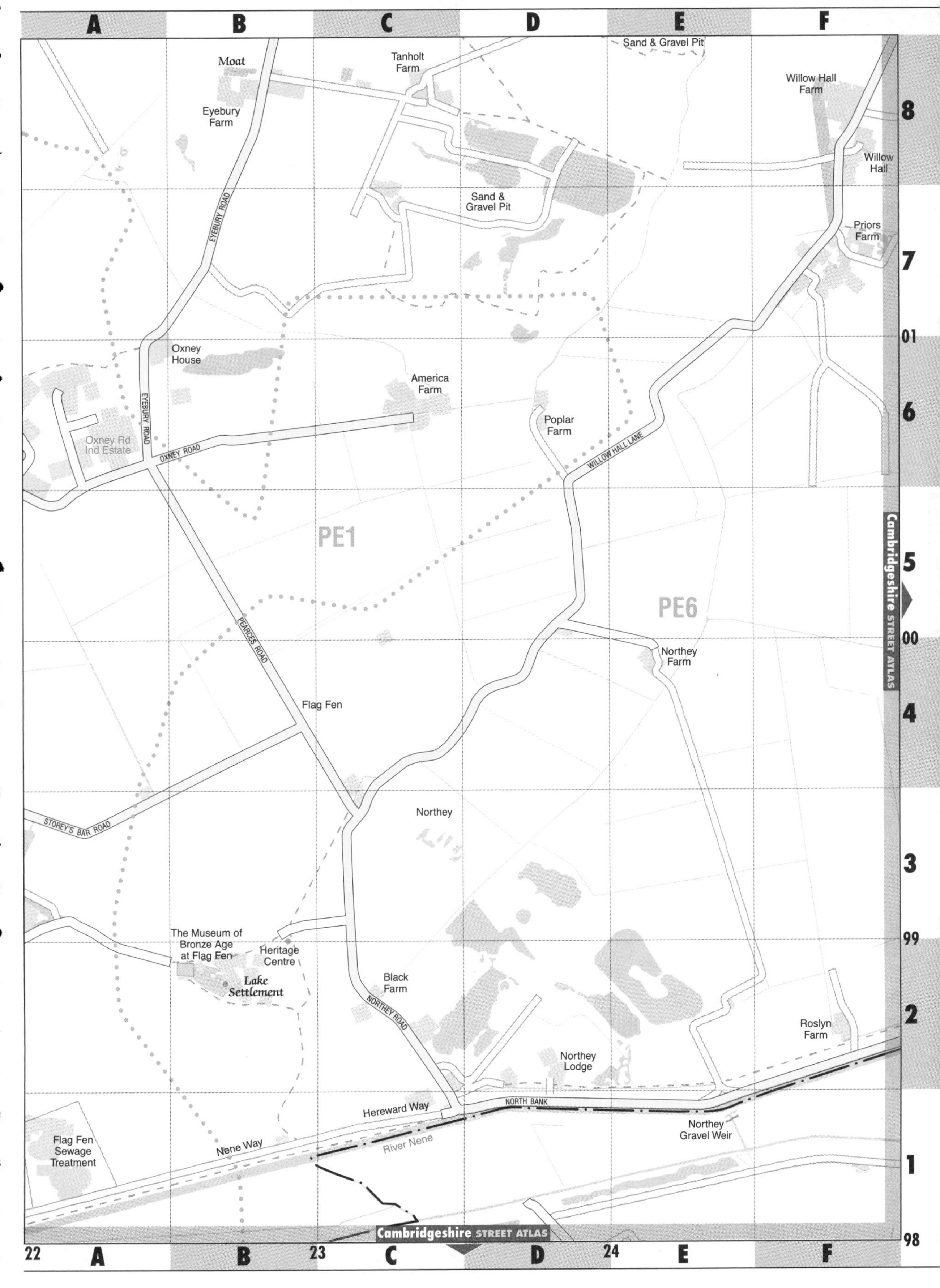
175
A
B
C
D
E
F
Moat
Tanholt Farm
Sand & Gravel Pit
Willow Hall Farm
Eyebury Farm
Willow Hall
Sand & Gravel Pit
Priors Farm
EYEBURY ROAD
Oxney House
America Farm
Oxney Rd Ind Estate
EYEBURY ROAD
OXNEY ROAD
Poplar Farm
WILLOW HALL LANE
PE1
PE6
PEARCES ROAD
Northey Farm
Flag Fen
Northey
STOREY'S BAR ROAD
The Museum of Bronze Age at Flag Fen
Heritage Centre
Lake Settlement
Black Farm
NORTHEY ROAD
Roslyn Farm
Northey Lodge
Hereward Way
NORTH BANK
Northey Gravel Weir
Flag Fen Sewage Treatment
Nene Way
River Nene
Cambridgeshire STREET ATLAS
8
7
01
6
5
00
4
3
99
2
1
98
22
23
24

223

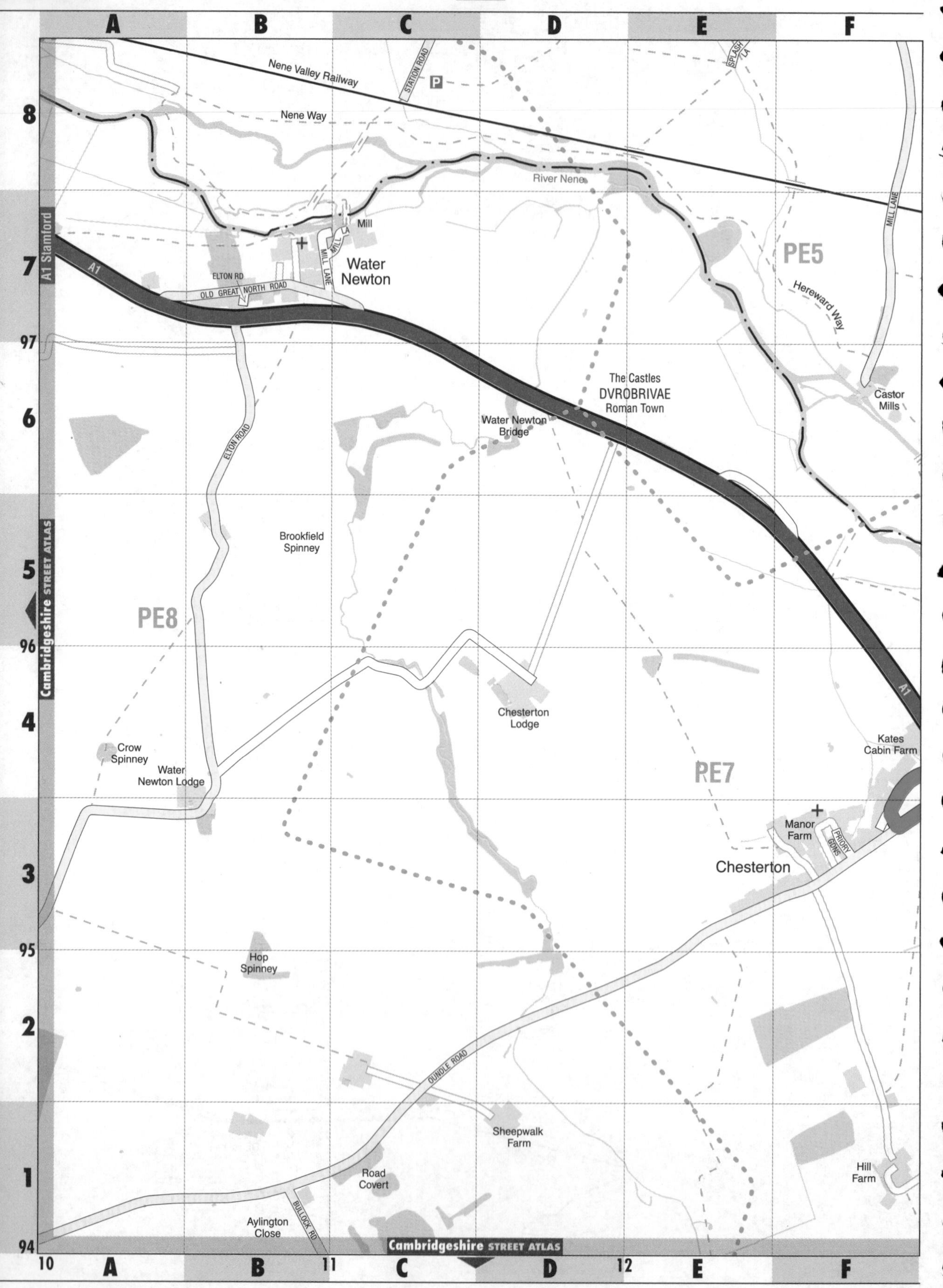
A
B
C
D
E
F
Nene Valley Railway
STATION ROAD
SPLASH LA
Nene Way
River Nene
Mill
MILL LA
MILL LANE
Water Newton
A1 Stamford
A1
ELTON RD
OLD GREAT NORTH ROAD
PE5
Hereward Way
MILL LANE
The Castles
DVROBRIVAE
Roman Town
Castor Mills
Water Newton Bridge
ELTON ROAD
Brookfield Spinney
PE8
Cambridgeshire STREET ATLAS
Chesterton Lodge
Crow Spinney
Water Newton Lodge
Kates Cabin Farm
PE7
Manor Farm
PRIORY GDNS
Chesterton
Hop Spinney
OUNDLE ROAD
Sheepwalk Farm
Road Covert
Hill Farm
Aylington Close
BULLOCK RD
8
7
97
6
5
96
4
3
95
2
1
94
10
11
12

224 230

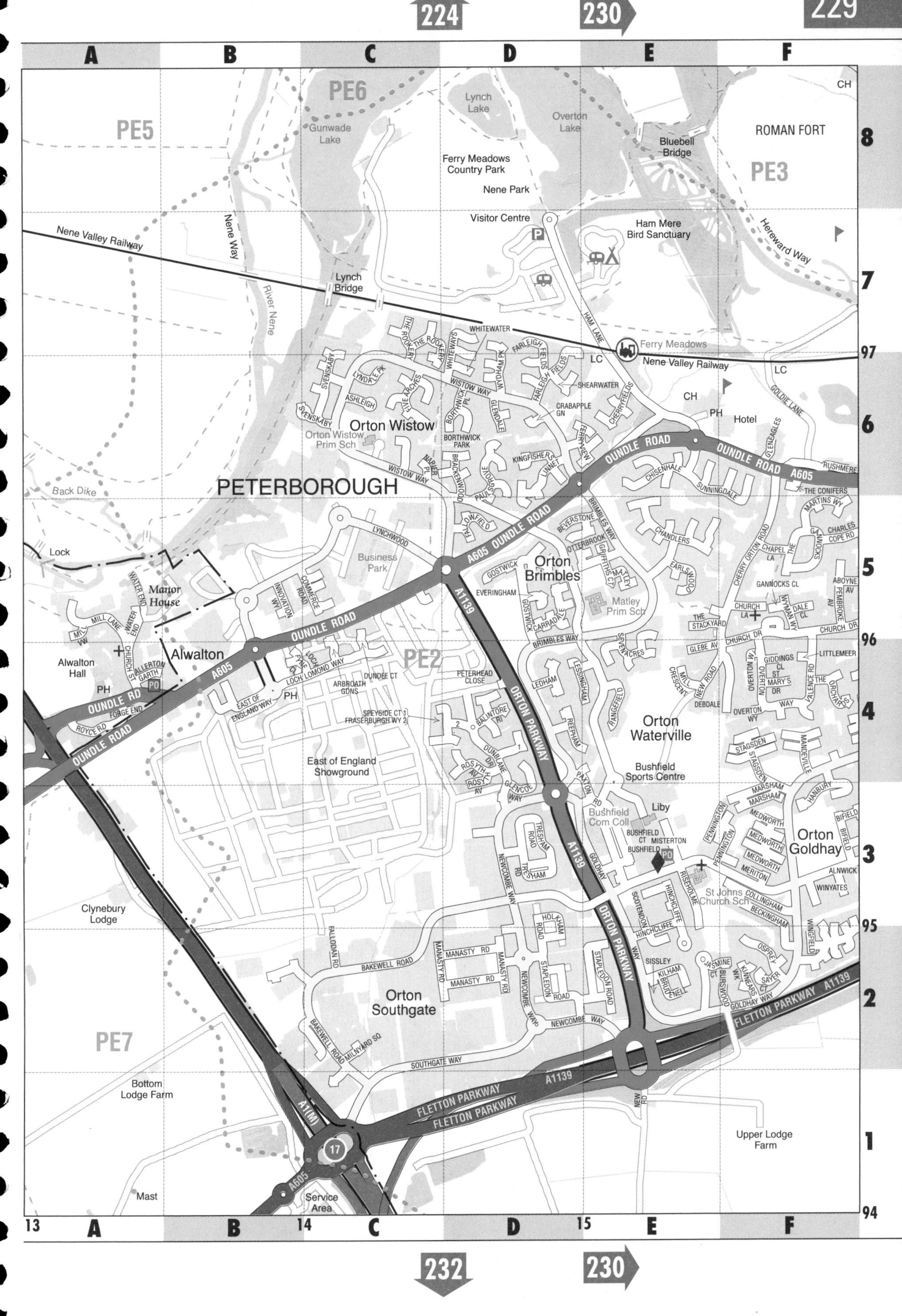
PETERBOROUGH
Orton Wistow
Orton Brimbles
Orton Waterville
Orton Goldhay
Orton Southgate
Alwalton
Ferry Meadows Country Park
Nene Park
Visitor Centre
Ham Mere Bird Sanctuary
Lynch Lake
Overton Lake
Gunwade Lake
Bluebell Bridge
ROMAN FORT
Lynch Bridge
Nene Valley Railway
Ferry Meadows
River Nene
Nene Way
Hereward Way
Back Dike
Lock
Manor House
Alwalton Hall
Business Park
East of England Showground
Bushfield Sports Centre
Bushfield Com Coll
Matley Prim Sch
Orton Wistow Prim Sch
St Johns Church Sch
Clynebury Lodge
Bottom Lodge Farm
Upper Lodge Farm
Service Area
Mast
Hotel
OUNDLE ROAD
A605
ORTON PARKWAY
A1139
FLETTON PARKWAY
A1(M)
PE2
PE3
PE5
PE6
PE7

232 230

229
225
D8
1 CRYSTAL DR
2 RUTHER CL
3 FLEMING CT

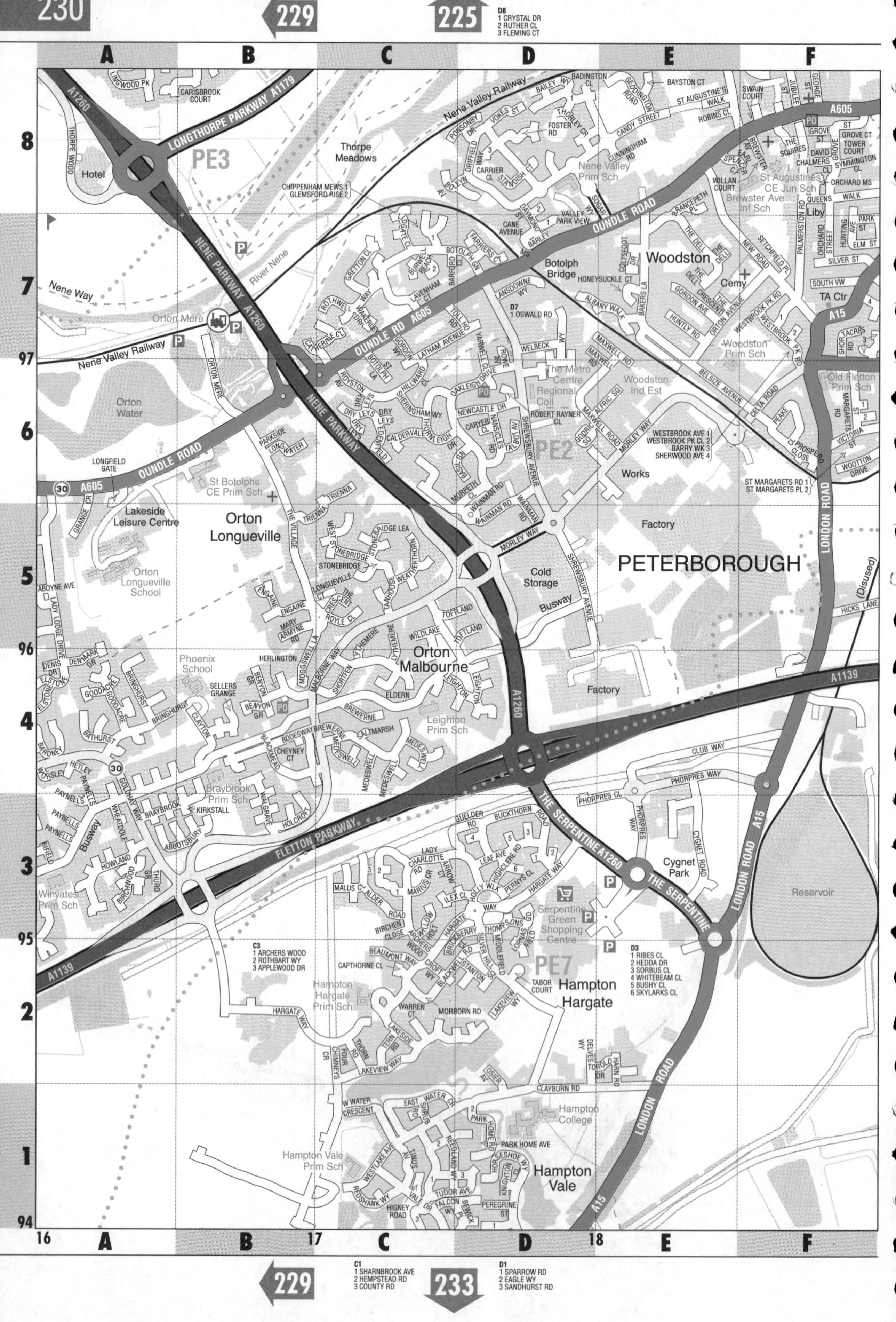
A
B
C
D
E
F
8
7
97
6
5
96
4
3
95
2
1
94
16
17
18
PE3
PE2
PE7
PETERBOROUGH
Thorpe Meadows
Hotel
Nene Valley Railway
River Nene
Nene Way
Orton Mere
Orton Water
LONGTHORPE PARKWAY A1179
NENE PARKWAY A1260
NENE PARKWAY
OUNDLE ROAD
OUNDLE RD A605
A605
A1260
A1139
FLETTON PARKWAY
THE SERPENTINE A1260
THE SERPENTINE
LONDON ROAD
LONDON ROAD A15
A15
LINGWOOD PK
CARISBROOK COURT
THORPE WOOD
CHIPPENHAM MEWS 1
GLEMSFORD RISE 2
Botolph Bridge
Woodston
Cemy
Woodston Prim Sch
Woodston Ind Est
Works
Factory
Cold Storage
Busway
The Metro Centre
Regional Coll
Nene Valley Prim Sch
St Augustines CE Jun Sch
Brewster Ave Inf Sch
Liby
TA Ctr
Old Fletton Prim Sch
D7
1 OSWALD RD
WESTBROOK AVE 1
WESTBROOK PK CL 2
BARRY WK 3
SHERWOOD AVE 4
ST MARGARETS RD 1
ST MARGARETS PL 2
HICKS LANE
(Disused)
LONGFIELD GATE
St Botolphs CE Prim Sch
Lakeside Leisure Centre
Orton Longueville
Orton Longueville School
Orton Malbourne
Leighton Prim Sch
Phoenix School
Braybrook Prim Sch
Winyates Prim Sch
Busway
CLUB WAY
PHORPRES WAY
PHORPRES CL
Cygnet Park
Reservoir
Serpentine Green Shopping Centre
Hampton Hargate
Hampton Hargate Prim Sch
HARGATE WAY
C3
1 ARCHERS WOOD
2 ROTHBART WY
3 APPLEWOOD DR
D3
1 RIBES CL
2 HEDDA DR
3 SORBUS CL
4 WHITEBEAM CL
5 BUSHY CL
6 SKYLARKS CL
CLAYBURN RD
Hampton College
Hampton Vale
Hampton Vale Prim Sch
PARK HOME AVE
PEREGRINE ST

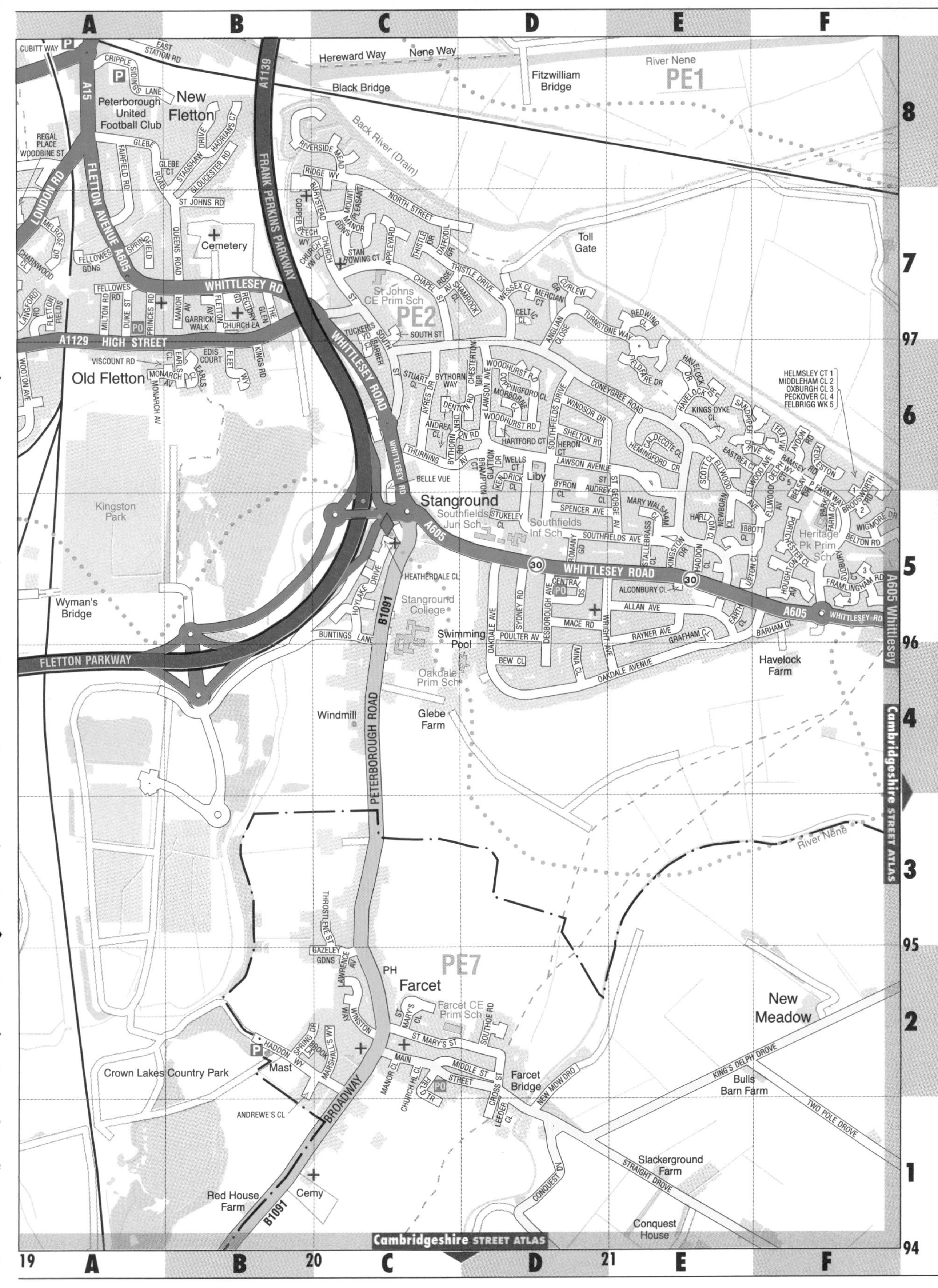
A
B
C
D
E
F
8
7
97
6
5
96
4
3
95
2
1
94
19
20
21
CUBITT WAY
EAST STATION RD
CRIPPLE SIDINGS LANE
A15
A1139
Hereward Way
Nene Way
River Nene
PE1
Fitzwilliam Bridge
Black Bridge
Peterborough United Football Club
New Fletton
REGAL PLACE
WOODBINE ST
GLEBE RD
GLEBE CT
STAGSHAW DRIVE
HADRIANS CT
GLOUCESTER RD
FAIRFIELD RD
FLETTON AVENUE
LONDON RD
FRANK PERKINS PARKWAY
Back River (Drain)
RIVERSIDE MEAD
RIDGE WY
NORTH STREET
BURYSTEAD
COPPER BEECH WY
MOUNT PLEASANT
MANOR GDNS
CHURCH WY
CHURCH VW CL
STAN BOWING CT
APPLEYARD
THISTLE DR
DAFFODIL GR
ST JOHNS RD
Cemetery
QUEENS ROAD
MELROSE DR
CHARNWOOD CL
FELLOWES GDNS
SPRINGFIELD
A605
WHITTLESEY RD
Toll Gate
THISTLE DRIVE
CHAPEL ST
ROSE AV
SHAMROCK CL
WESSEX CL
MERCIAN CT
CURLEW GR
CELTIC CL
ANGLIAN CLOSE
TURNSTONE WAY
REDWING CL
St Johns CE Prim Sch
PE2
LANGFORD RD
FLETTON FIELDS
FELLOWES RD
MILTON RD
DUKE ST
PRINCES RD
MANOR AV
GARRICK WALK
FLETTON AV
RECTORY GD
THE GLEN
CHURCH LA
TUCKERS YD
SOUTH ST
BARBER CT
A1129
HIGH STREET
WHITTLESEY ROAD
VISCOUNT RD
Old Fletton
MONARCH AV
EARLS CL
EDIS COURT
FLEET WY
KINGS RD
WOOTON AVE
STUART CL
AYRES DR
BYTHORN WAY
CHESTERTON GR
WOODHURST RD
COPPINGFORD CL
MORBORNE CL
LAWSON AVE
SOUTHFIELDS DRIVE
WINDSOR DR
CONEYGREE ROAD
FIELDFARE DR
HAVELOCK DR
KINGS DYKE CL
SANDPIPER DR
HELMSLEY CT 1
MIDDLEHAM CL 2
OXBURGH CL 3
PECKOVER CL 4
FELBRIGG WK 5
DENTON RD
ANDREA CL
HARTFORD CT
SHELTON RD
HERON CT
DECOTE CL
HEMINGFORD CR
EASTREA CT
ELLWOOD AVE
FEN VW
AYDON RD
KEDLESTON RD
RAMSEY RD
BELSAY DR
FARM WAY
BRODSWORTH RD
THURNING AV
GLATTON DR
BRAMPTON CT
WELLS CT
KENDRICK CL
Liby
LAWSON AVENUE
SCOTT CL
BELLE VUE
BYRON CL
AUDREY CL
ST GEORGE AV
MARY WALSHAM
NEWBORN CL
IBBOTT CL
PORTCHESTER CL
Heritage Pk Prim Sch
WIGMORE DR
BELTON RD
Stanground
Southfields Jun Sch
STUKELEY CL
Southfields Inf Sch
SPENCER AVE
SOUTHFIELDS AVE
STALLEBRASS CL
KINGSTON DR
HADDON CL
HARLTON CL
UPTON CL
HOUGHTON AV
FRAMLINGHAM RD
Kingston Park
HEATHERDALE CL
ROMANY GD
30
CENTRAL SQ
PO
ALCONBURY CL
A605 Whittlesey
Wyman's Bridge
HOYLAKE DRIVE
Stanground College
B1091
OAKDALE AVE
SYDNEY RD
DESBOROUGH AVE
MACE RD
ALLAN AVE
WRIGHT AVE
EARITH CL
BARHAM CL
WHITTLESEY RD
FLETTON PARKWAY
BUNTINGS LANE
Swimming Pool
POULTER AV
RAYNER AVE
GRAFHAM CL
BEW CL
MINA CL
OAKDALE AVENUE
Havelock Farm
Oakdale Prim Sch
Windmill
PETERBOROUGH ROAD
Glebe Farm
Cambridgeshire STREET ATLAS
River Nene
THROSTLENEST ST
GAZELEY GDNS
LAWRENCE AV
PH
PE7
Farcet
New Meadow
WINSTON WAY
ST MARY'S CL
Farcet CE Prim Sch
SOUTHOE RD
HADDON WY
SPRING DR
BROOK
MARSHALL'S WY
ST MARY'S ST
MAIN STREET
MIDDLE ST
Crown Lakes Country Park
Mast
MANOR CL
CHURCH HL CL
FIELD TR
CROSS ST
Farcet Bridge
NEW MDW DRO
KING'S DELPH DROVE
Bulls Barn Farm
TWO POLE DROVE
ANDREWE'S CL
BROADWAY
LEEDER CL
Slackerground Farm
STRAIGHT DROVE
CONQUEST DV
Red House Farm
Cemy
B1091
Conquest House

229

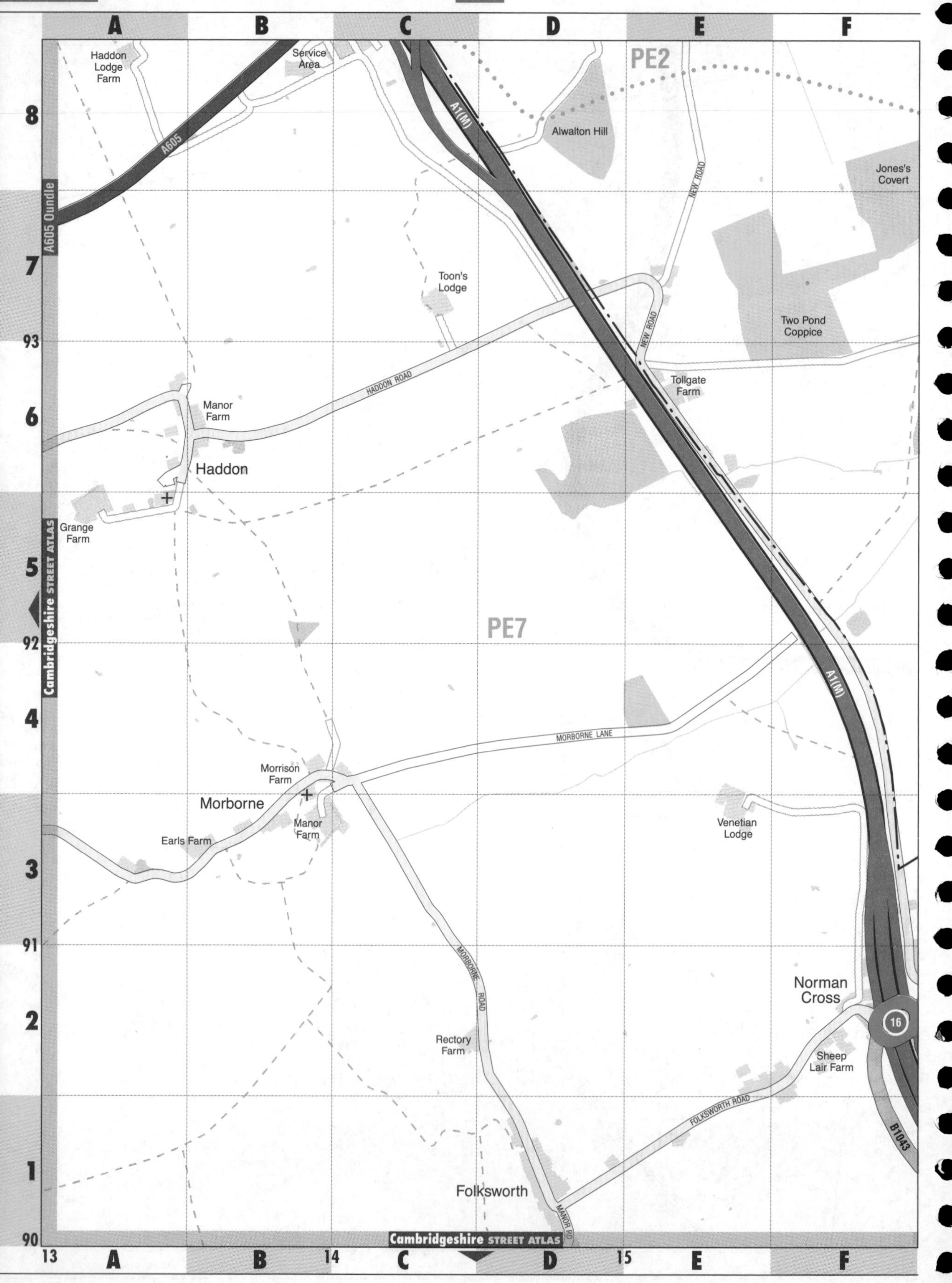

A
B
C
D
E
F
Haddon Lodge Farm
Service Area
PE2
A605
A1(M)
Alwalton Hill
NEW ROAD
Jones's Covert
A605 Oundle
Toon's Lodge
Two Pond Coppice
NEW ROAD
HADDON ROAD
Tollgate Farm
Manor Farm
Haddon
Grange Farm
PE7
Cambridgeshire STREET ATLAS
A1(M)
MORBORNE LANE
Morrison Farm
Morborne
Manor Farm
Earls Farm
Venetian Lodge
MORBORNE ROAD
Norman Cross
16
Rectory Farm
Sheep Lair Farm
FOLKSWORTH ROAD
B1043
Folksworth
MANOR RD
8
7
93
6
5
92
4
3
91
2
1
90
13
14
15

Cambridgeshire STREET ATLAS

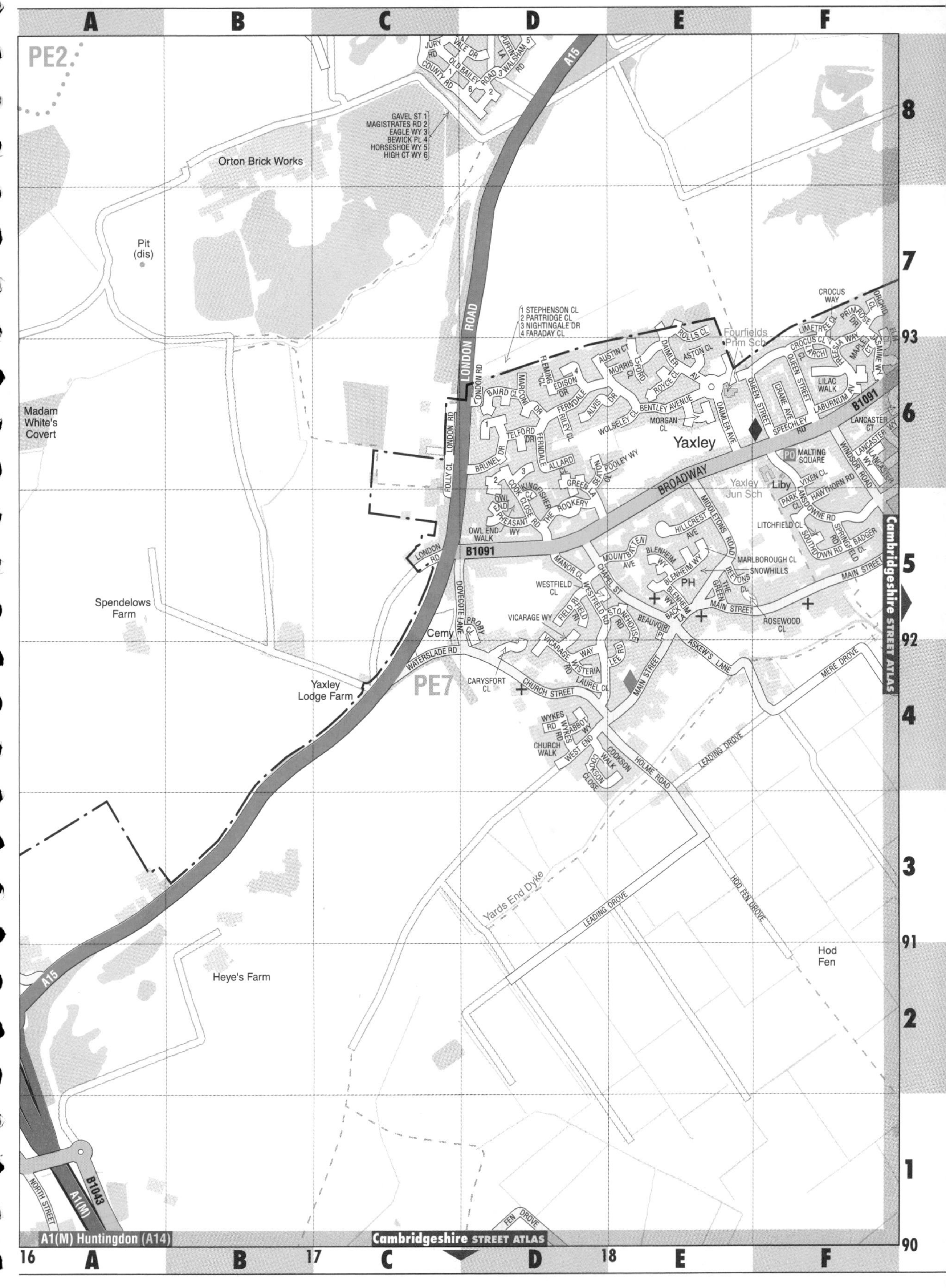

PE2

A B C D E F

8

7

93

6

5

92

4

3

91

2

1

90

Orton Brick Works

Pit
(dis)

GAVEL ST 1
MAGISTRATES RD 2
EAGLE WY 3
BEWICK PL 4
HORSESHOE WY 5
HIGH CT WY 6

JURY DR
VALE DR
OLD BAILEY
PUFFIN RD
WALSHAM RD
COUNTY RD

A15

LONDON ROAD

CROCUS
WAY

1 STEPHENSON CL
2 PARTRIDGE CL
3 NIGHTINGALE DR
4 FARADAY CL

LIMETREE CR
ORCHID
ROSEHOUSE
ELM
JASMINE WY
MAPLE
CROCUS CL
QUEEN STREET
LILAC
WALK
LABURNUM
B1091

ROLLS CL
ASTON CL
DAIMLER AV
ARCH
REESLA WY
LANCASTER
CT

Fourfields
Prim Sch

Madam
White's
Covert

LONDON RD

FOLLY CL

LONDON RD

FLEMING CL
MARCONI
EDISON DR
AUSTIN CT
MORRIS CT
ROYCE CL
ALVIS DR
WOLSELEY CL
BENTLEY AVENUE
MORGAN
CL
BAIRD CL
RILEY CL
FERNDALE
FERNDALE CL
TELFORD DR
BRUNEL DR
Yaxley
DAIMLER AVE
SPEECHLEY
CRANE AVE
QUEEN STREET

LANCASTER WY
WINDSOR ROAD
LANCASTER

PO
MALTING
SQUARE

Spendelows
Farm

COOK CLOSE
OWL
END
PHEASAN
WY
KINGFISHER
GREEN
ALLARD
THE ROOKERY
POOLEY WY
SEATON CL
Yaxley
Jun Sch
VIXEN CL
PARK
HAWTHORN RD
LANSDOWNE RD
SPRING WY
Liby

OWL END
WALK

BROADWAY

Yaxley

LITCHFIELD CL
MARLBOROUGH CL
SNOWHILLS
BADGER
SCHOFIELD WY
MAIN STREET

B1091

MANOR CL
BATTEN AVE
MOUNT
CHAPEL ST
HILLCREST
AVE
MIDDLETONS ROAD
BLENHEIM
WY
BLENHEIM
WY
BEE'ONS CL
GREEN LA
BACK LA
PH

Cemy

WESTFIELD
CL
VICARAGE WY
FIELD RD
STONEHOUSE RD
WESTFIELD RD
BEAUVOIR
ASKEW'S LANE
ROSEWOOD
CL
MAIN STREET
MERE DROVE

WATERSLADE RD

PE7

CARYSFORT
CL
VICARAGE
WAY
WISTERIA
LAUREL CL
CHURCH STREET
LEE
MAIN STREET

Yaxley
Lodge Farm

WYKES
RD
RABBOT WY
WEST END
CHURCH WALK
WEST END
COOKSON CLOSE
DOCKSON
WALK
HOLME ROAD
LEADING DROVE

HOD FEN DROVE

LEADING DROVE

Yards End Dyke

Hod
Fen

A15

Heye's Farm

FEN DROVE

B1043
A1(M)
NORTH STREET

Cambridgeshire STREET ATLAS

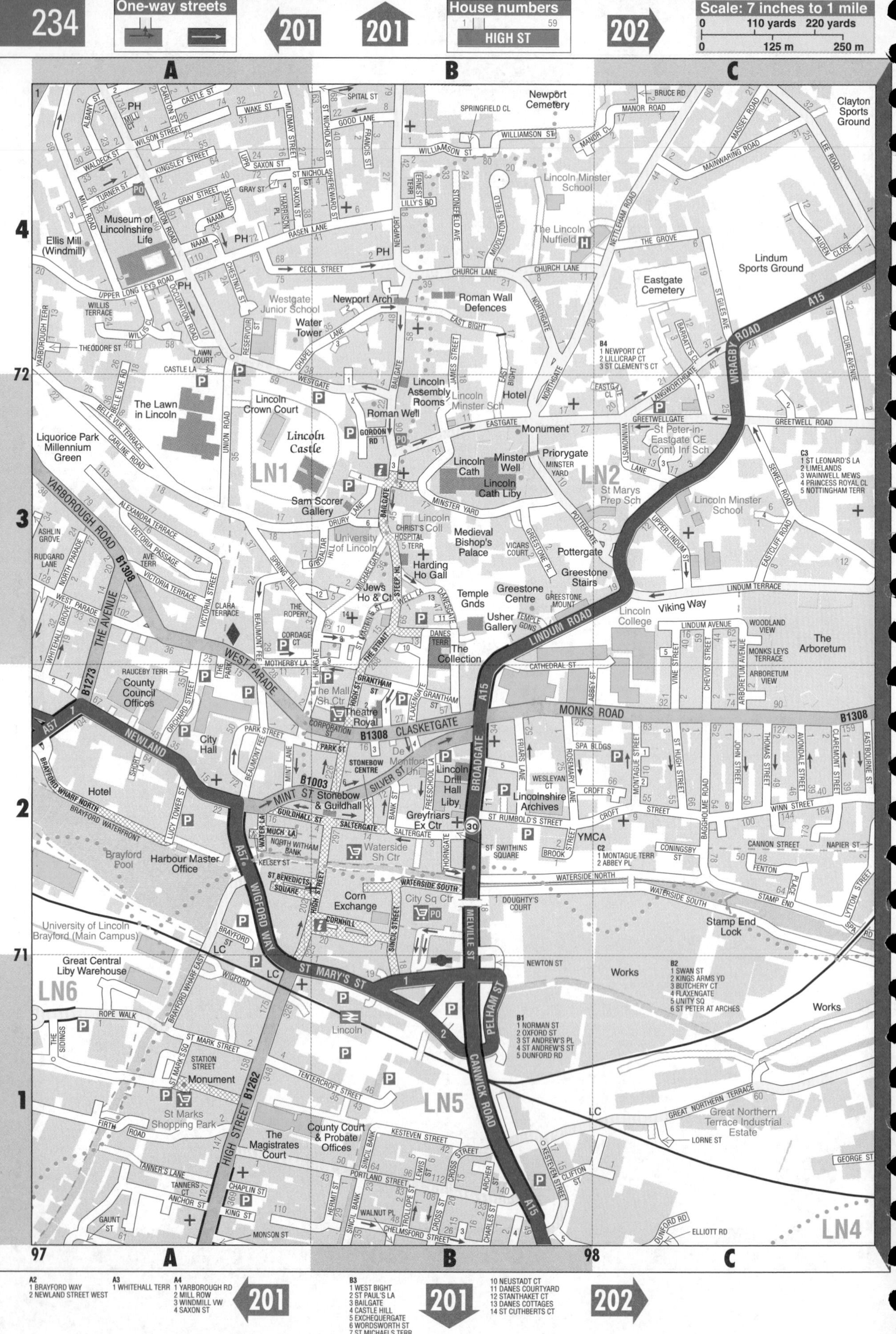

Place name May be abbreviated on the map

Location number Present when a number indicates the place's position in a crowded area of mapping

Locality, town or village Shown when more than one place has the same name

Postcode district District for the indexed place

Page and grid square Page number and grid reference for the standard mapping

Church Rd 6 Beckenham BR2..........**53** C6

Cities, towns and villages are listed in CAPITAL LETTERS

Public and commercial buildings are highlighted in magenta **Places of interest** are highlighted in blue with a star★

Abbreviations used in the index

Acad	Academy	Comm	Common	Gd	Ground	L	Leisure	Prom	Promenade
App	Approach	Cott	Cottage	Gdn	Garden	La	Lane	Rd	Road
Arc	Arcade	Cres	Crescent	Gn	Green	Liby	Library	Recn	Recreation
Ave	Avenue	Cswy	Causeway	Gr	Grove	Mdw	Meadow	Ret	Retail
Bglw	Bungalow	Ct	Court	H	Hall	Meml	Memorial	Sh	Shopping
Bldg	Building	Ctr	Centre	Ho	House	Mkt	Market	Sq	Square
Bsns, Bus	Business	Ctry	Country	Hospl	Hospital	Mus	Museum	St	Street
Bvd	Boulevard	Cty	County	HQ	Headquarters	Orch	Orchard	Sta	Station
Cath	Cathedral	Dr	Drive	Hts	Heights	Pal	Palace	Terr	Terrace
Cir	Circus	Dro	Drove	Ind	Industrial	Par	Parade	TH	Town Hall
Cl	Close	Ed	Education	Inst	Institute	Pas	Passage	Univ	University
Cnr	Corner	Emb	Embankment	Int	International	Pk	Park	Wk, Wlk	Walk
Coll	College	Est	Estate	Intc	Interchange	Pl	Place	Wr	Water
Com	Community	Ex	Exhibition	Junc	Junction	Prec	Precinct	Yd	Yard

Index of towns, villages, streets, hospitals, industrial estates, railway stations, schools, shopping centres, universities and places of interest

1st Drift PE9..........219 B2
1st Main Rd DN36........36 F8
2nd Ave DN36..........36 F8
2nd Drift PE9..........219 B2
4th Ave DN36..........36 F8
12th Ave DN36..........36 F8

A

AALPS Coll DN15..........8 F3
Aalsmeer Rise 6 PE11....214 A2
Abbey Bldgs 19 PE11....214 D4
Abbey Cl
  Coningsby LN4........207 B5
  6 Skegness PE25......206 A4
  5 Woodhall Spa LN10...97 C6
Abbey Cres 4 PE20....135 C7
Abbeydale Cres NG31....211 A8
Abbey Dr
  20 Hatfield DN7........14 D4
  13 Woodhall Spa LN10...97 C5
Abbey Dr E DN32........191 D6
Abbey Dr W DN32........191 D6
Abbeyfield Rd 1 DN7....14 C4
Abbeygate DN31........191 D7
Abbey Gdns 22 DN7......14 D4
Abbey Gr 23 DN7........14 D4
Abbey La
  Sedgebrook NG32......128 F4
  Swineshead PE20......135 C6
  Woodhall Spa LN10....97 C5
Abbey Mews 11 PE6......166 F1
Abbey Pk Mews DN32....191 D6
Abbey Pk Rd DN32......191 D6
Abbey Pl
  2 Lincoln LN2........234 C2
  10 Thorney PE6........176 A3
Abbey Rd
  Alvingham LN11........49 F2
  Bardney LN3..........83 B4
  Bourne PE10..........213 D5
  Grimsby DN32........191 D6
  Hatfield DN7..........14 D4
  Louth LN11..........198 D6
  Peterborough PE4......221 A1
  Revesby PE22..........99 C5
  Scunthorpe DN17......184 F6
  Sleaford NG34........212 A2
  Swineshead PE20......135 C7
  Ulceby DN39..........12 A1
Abbey Rise 14 DN19......11 D8

Abbey St
  Kingston upon Hull
    HU9................181 C7
  Lincoln LN2..........234 C2
Abbey Way DN7..........14 D5
Abbey Wlk
  10 Crowland PE6......166 F1
  Grimsby DN32........191 D7
Abbey Yd 12 PE11......214 D4
Abbotsbury PE2........230 A3
Abbot's Cl 5 PE10....213 E4
Abbots Cres 6 PE11....214 A4
Abbots Dr 1 PE6......175 B8
Abbots Gdns 1 PE12....158 B6
Abbotsmede Prim Com Sch
  PE1................226 C4
Abbots Rd DN17........184 F6
Abbot St LN5..........201 E1
Abbotsway DN32........191 D6
Abbot's Way 5 PE11....214 A3
Abbott Cl 10 LN8......57 B8
Abbott's Cl PE8........219 D4
Abbotts Gr PE4........220 F6
Abbotts Grange DN36....195 E7
Abbotts Way LN11......198 E6
Abbot Way PE7........233 D4
Abercorn St DN16......183 A2
Aberdeen Cl PE9......218 D6
Aberporth Dr LN6......204 B8
Abingdon Ave LN6......204 C6
Abingdon Ct 12 LN6....204 C6
Aboyne Ave PE2........229 F5
Abraham Cl 5 NG31....129 E5
ABY LN13..............75 B5
Aby CE Prim Sch LN13..75 B5
Acacia Ave
  Chapel St Leonard PE24..90 D8
  Gainsborough DN21....197 D6
  Peterborough PE1......226 B8
  Scunthorpe DN15......182 C5
  Spalding PE11........214 F5
  Waddington LN5......205 D1
  3 Wisbech PE13......170 D1
Acacia Cl 12 NG34....212 D2
Acacia Ct 3 DN16......185 B6
Acacia Way
  Boston PE21..........208 C4
  Messingham DN17......29 C7
Acadia Gr HU13........178 F1
Accommodation Rd
  LN9................199 A5
Acer Cl LN6..........204 D7
Acer Ct 2 LN6........204 D7

Acer Gr 3 DN17........184 C5
Acer Rd PE1..........226 B6
Achille Rd DN34......190 D5
Achurch Cl LN9........199 D1
Acklam Ave 3 PE11....214 F6
Acklam Gr DN32........192 B6
Acklands La 13 NG23...117 D3
Acland St
  Gainsborough DN21....197 C5
  4 Kingston upon Hull
    HU3................180 A6
  Peterborough PE1......225 F3
Acomb Comm Rd DN7....14 F4
Acorn Cl
  Freiston PE21........126 C4
  Grantham NG31........211 C7
  Lincoln LN5..........205 D7
  19 Sutton on Sea LN12..76 F8
Acorn Ct DN35........192 D2
Acorns The PE6........217 A4
Acorn Way
  5 Bottesford DN16....185 B2
  Hessle HU13..........178 B3
Acre Cl LN8..........57 D8
Acre Dyke La LN4......82 A3
Acre La
  Scopwick LN4..........95 E1
  Threekingham NG34....132 E2
Acres La DN9..........26 D7
Acres The 1 PE9......172 D4
Acton Cl 12 DN32......189 C1
Adam Cl 18 LN6........204 D7
Adam Smith St DN31....188 F1
Adamstiles 2 NG32....210 B4
Adams Way 6 DN21......65 E8
Ada Way LN11..........198 D7
Adderley PE3..........225 C7
Addington Way 3 PE4..221 A3
Addison Cl 4 LN5......107 A8
Addison Dr LN2........202 B6
Addison Pl LN1........65 E3
ADDLETHORPE PE24......90 C3
Adelaide Cl
  Gainsborough DN21....197 F2
  5 Waddington LN5......93 E8
Adelaide Prim Sch
  HU3................180 D5
Adelaide St
  Kingston upon Hull
    HU3................180 D5
  Stamford PE9........219 D5
Adelphi Ct 5 DN36....195 C6
Adelphi Dr DN33......194 E7

Adlard Gr DN36........36 C7
ADLINGFLEET DN14......7 E7
Adlingfleet Rd DN17....7 E6
Admirals Dr 7 PE13....170 D2
Admiralty Rd 19 LN12...64 B4
Adrian Cl
  Louth LN11..........198 C4
  9 Skegness PE25......206 A4
  9 Swineshead PE20....135 B7
Advent Ct 2 DN39......12 A1
Adwalton Cl NG24......104 C4
Aegir Cl DN21........197 F2
Africa Cl DN34........190 D4
Agard Ave DN15........182 E3
Agnes St 2 NG31......211 B4
Aidan Rd NG34........212 B2
AILBY LN13............75 D4
AILSWORTH PE5........223 D3
Aima Ct 2 LN2........68 C2
Ainsdale Dr PE4......220 F3
Ainslie Dr DN32......191 E6
Ainslie St DN32......191 E6
Ainsworth Rd 5 DN40...186 B4
Ainthorpe Gr HU5......179 C7
Ainthorpe Prim Sch
  HU5................179 C8
Aintree Dr PE11......214 B1
Aire Cl DN40..........186 A3
Airedale Cl
  12 Broughton DN20....19 E4
  Peterborough PE1......226 A6
Airedale Rd
  1 Scunthorpe DN16....185 D5
  1 Stamford PE9......219 A7
Airedale Way DN31....191 D8
Airfield Rd NG31......210 E3
Airlie St HU3........180 B5
Airmanship Rd NG34....120 B8
Airmyn Ave 1 HU3.....179 E6
Airship Rd NG34......107 C1
AISBY
  Heydour NG32........131 D5
  Pilham DN21..........41 D4
Aisby Wlk DN21........197 F3
Aisne Cl LN1..........201 E7
Aisne St HU5..........180 A8
AISTHORPE LN1........67 C7
Ajax Cl DN34..........190 D4
Ajax Ct DN15..........182 F5
Akeferry Rd DN9........27 C1
Akeman Cl 10 PE10....213 C6
Akeman Dr 14 LN4......81 A1
Akita Cl 4 PE11......214 A5
Alabala Cl LN4........203 C1

1st–Alb

Alabala La LN4..........81 F4
Alan Cres DN15........182 F2
Alba Cl DN17..........184 D5
Alban Ret Pk PE21....208 B3
Albany Cl
  Louth LN11..........198 D3
  Skegness PE25......206 A5
Albany Pl LN11........198 D3
Albany Rd
  Louth LN11..........198 D3
  Skegness PE25......206 A5
  21 Wisbech PE13......170 D1
  3 Woodhall Spa LN10...97 D5
Albany St
  Gainsborough DN21....197 C6
  Kingston upon Hull HU3..180 D8
  Lincoln LN1..........234 A4
Albany Terr LN5......205 D5
Albany Way PE25......206 A5
Albany Wlk PE2........230 D7
Albatross Dr DN37....190 B7
Albemarle Cl 5 HU15...2 B5
Albemarle St 2 HU3...180 B5
Alberta Cres DN17....184 E3
Albert Ave
  Kingston upon Hull
    HU3................180 A7
  Long Sutton PE12....159 F4
  1 Skegness PE25......103 E4
Albert Ave Pools HU3..180 A7
Albert Cl 17 DN32....189 B1
Albert Cres LN1......201 D4
Albert Ct PE21........208 E5
Albertine Ct 4 DN37..194 C5
Albert Marson Ct 6
  DN16................183 B2
Albert Pl
  Grimsby DN32........189 B1
  Peterborough PE3....225 F1
Albert Rd
  7 Cleethorpes DN35...192 F6
  Scunthorpe DN16......185 A5
  Skegness PE25......206 B3
  2 Stamford PE9......219 C4
Albert St E DN32......189 B1
Albert St W 5 DN32....189 B1
Albert St
  Boston PE21..........208 D5
  15 Bottesford NG13...128 A6
  Brigg DN20..........196 C3

Albert St *continued*
Grantham NG31 ..... 211 C2
6 Holbeach PE12 ..... 215 D2
Horncastle LN9 ..... 199 C3
7 New Holland DN19 ..... 4 E2
Spalding PE11 ..... 214 E5
Thorne/Moorends DN8 ..... 15 B8
Albert Terr
2 Boston PE21 ..... 208 E4
Boultham LN5 ..... 205 D8
14 Sleaford NG34 ..... 212 D4
Albert Wlk 3 PE12 ..... 215 D2
Albery Way DN36 ..... 195 C7
Albion Cl LN1 ..... 201 C6
Albion Cres LN1 ..... 201 C6
Albion Ct HU4 ..... 179 B6
Albion Hill 8 DN9 ..... 27 E6
Albion Pl LN11 ..... 198 C5
Albion Rd 2 NG31 ..... 211 A5
Albion St
8 Crowland PE6 ..... 166 E1
13 Grantham NG31 ..... 211 A5
Grimsby DN32 ..... 189 B1
Holbeach PE12 ..... 215 F2
10 Kingston upon Hull HU1 ..... 180 E7
Spalding PE11 ..... 214 E5
Albion Terr
4 Misterton DN10 ..... 40 A5
Sleaford NG34 ..... 212 E4
Albourne Ave DN15 ..... 183 A2
Alconbury Cl
13 Birchwood LN6 ..... 204 C6
Peterborough PE2 ..... 231 E5
Alcorn Gn PE21 ..... 209 C4
Aldbro' St HU2 ..... 180 F8
Aldburgh Cl 16 LN10 ..... 97 C5
Alden Cl DN40 ..... 186 C4
Alder Cl
30 Brough HU15 ..... 2 C5
3 Lincoln LN6 ..... 204 F3
Louth LN11 ..... 198 D4
Alder Gr PE21 ..... 209 C2
Aldergrove Cl 2 LN6 ..... 204 C7
Aldergrove Cres LN6 ..... 204 C7
Alderlands Cl 6 PE6 ..... 175 B8
Alderley Edge DN37 ..... 194 C4
Alderman's Dr PE3 ..... 225 E3
Alderney Way
Immingham DN40 ..... 186 C2
Lincoln LN6 ..... 205 A1
Alder Rd
Peterborough PE7 ..... 230 C3
Sleaford NG34 ..... 212 D2
Alderson Mews 5 HU9 ..... 181 C7
Alders The DN21 ..... 197 F5
Alder View DN33 ..... 190 F3
ALDGATE PE9 ..... 171 A3
Aldgate Ct 9 PE9 ..... 171 A3
Aldred Gdns DN33 ..... 191 B1
Aldrich Rd DN35 ..... 192 F4
Aldrin Cl PE11 ..... 214 C2
Aldsworth Cl 1 PE1 ..... 226 D6
Aldwych Croft 8 DN36 ..... 195 C6
Aldwych Ct HU5 ..... 179 E8
Aldwych Gdns 11 PE11 ..... 214 A2
Alec Rose Gr DN21 ..... 197 F3
Alexander Ave NG24 ..... 104 A6
Alexander Cl 15 LN4 ..... 95 D4
Alexander Dr LN11 ..... 198 D4
Alexander Rd DN16 ..... 183 C3
Alexandra Cl 8 NG23 ..... 117 D4
Alexandra Ct 9 PE25 ..... 206 C3
Alexandra Dock N DN31 ..... 188 F2
Alexandra Pk 22 LN12 ..... 64 B4
Alexandra Rd
Cleethorpes DN35 ..... 192 F6
Grantham NG31 ..... 210 F3
Grimsby DN31 ..... 188 F1
Immingham DN40 ..... 186 F6
Louth LN11 ..... 198 C6
21 Mablethorpe/Sutton on Sea LN12 ..... 64 B4
Peterborough PE1 ..... 225 F6
Scunthorpe DN16 ..... 185 B6
Skegness PE25 ..... 206 B3
Sleaford NG34 ..... 212 C4
Spalding PE11 ..... 214 E3
3 Woodhall Spa LN10 ..... 97 C6
Alexandra Rd S DN40 ..... 186 E6
Alexandra Ret Pk DN31 ..... 188 F1
Alexandra St HU3 ..... 180 D7
Alexandra Terr LN1 ..... 234 A3
Alexandra Terraces 4 PE10 ..... 213 D5
Alexandra Wharf DN31 ..... 191 D7
Alexandre Ave 2 LN6 ..... 204 F1
Alexandria Rd LN8 ..... 56 D5
Alfonso St 5 HU3 ..... 180 B5
ALFORD LN13 ..... 75 E2
Alford Mill Cl 6 LN6 ..... 93 B8
Alford Pottery* LN13 ..... 75 E3
Alford Prim Sch LN13 ..... 75 F2
Alford Rd
1 Alford LN13 ..... 75 F3
Bilsby LN13 ..... 76 A3
Mablethorpe/Sutton on Sea LN12 ..... 64 A3
Alford St NG31 ..... 211 B5
Alford War Meml Hospl LN13 ..... 75 E2
Alford Windmill* LN13 ..... 75 F3
Alfred Ave LN4 ..... 95 C4
Alfred Cl 10 NG34 ..... 212 B2
Alfred Gelder St 6 HU1 ..... 180 F6
Alfred Smith Way 5 LN11 ..... 61 F3
Alfred St
Boston PE21 ..... 209 A3
Gainsborough DN21 ..... 197 C5
Grimsby DN31 ..... 191 D8
Kingston upon Hull HU3 ..... 180 D5
Lincoln LN5 ..... 201 E1
Alfreton Ct 2 DN15 ..... 182 B2
Alfric Sq PE2 ..... 230 D6
ALGAKIRK PE20 ..... 136 B2
Algernon St DN32 ..... 191 F5
Algitha Rd PE25 ..... 206 C3
ALKBOROUGH DN15 ..... 8 C8
Alkborough La DN15 ..... 8 D7
Alkborough Prim Sch DN15 ..... 8 C8
Allan Ave PE2 ..... 231 E5
Allanby St DN15 ..... 183 A3
Allandale Cl LN1 ..... 201 D8
Allandale View 11 LN1 ..... 201 E8
Allanhall Way HU10 ..... 178 B8
Allard Cl PE7 ..... 233 D6
Allenby Ave DN34 ..... 191 A6
Allenby Cres LN11 ..... 49 A2
Allenby Ind Est LN2 ..... 202 D4
Allenby Rd LN2 ..... 202 D4
Allenby's Chase 14 PE12 ..... 160 E4
Allenby Way PE25 ..... 206 D8
Allen Cl
7 Billingborough NG34 ..... 133 B1
4 Claypole NG23 ..... 117 E8
5 Market Deeping PE6 ..... 217 D5
Allen Rd
Coningsby LN4 ..... 207 F6
Fenton NG23 ..... 105 C1
Peterborough PE1 ..... 225 E6
Allen's Dro PE13 ..... 169 D1
Allerthorpe Cres 19 HU15 ..... 2 D5
Allerton Cl PE9 ..... 172 D3
Allerton Dr DN40 ..... 186 B4
Allerton Garth PE7 ..... 229 A4
Allerton Prim Sch DN40 ..... 186 B4
Allestree Dr DN33 ..... 194 E7
Allexton Gdns 2 PE1 ..... 226 D7
Alliance Ave HU3 ..... 179 F7
Alliance La HU3 ..... 179 F7
ALLINGTON NG32 ..... 128 F7
Allington Dr DN37 ..... 188 A2
Allington Gdn PE21 ..... 209 A7
Allington La NG32 ..... 129 B4
Allington Rd NG32 ..... 128 F5
Allington with Sedgebrook CE Prim Sch NG32 ..... 129 A7
Allison Ave PE12 ..... 215 E2
Allison Cl 3 DN17 ..... 29 D7
Allison Pl 5 LN1 ..... 201 D4
Allison Rd 6 NG34 ..... 122 D3
Allison St LN1 ..... 201 D4
Allotment La PE5 ..... 223 E2
All Saints Ave PE13 ..... 170 E1
All Saints Brewery* 22 PE9 ..... 219 B5
All Saints CE (Aided) Prim Sch PE22 ..... 115 A6
All Saints CE Jun Sch
Kingston upon Hull HU13 ..... 178 F2
Peterborough PE1 ..... 226 A6
All Saints CE Prim Sch LN6 ..... 204 E1
All Saints CE Sch Swinderby Prim Sch LN6 ..... 92 B6
All Saints Cl
3 Holbeach PE12 ..... 215 F3
7 Moulton PE12 ..... 157 F7
4 Wainfleet All Saints PE24 ..... 102 D1
All Saints' Cl 17 DN19 ..... 12 A8
All Saints Cty Prim Sch LN5 ..... 93 F7
All Saints Gr 4 NG34 ..... 212 B6
All Saints La 14 LN2 ..... 68 C2
All Saints Mews 17 PE9 ..... 219 B5
All Saints' Pl 6 PE9 ..... 219 B5
All Saints' Rd PE1 ..... 226 A5
All Saints' St
Kingston upon Hull HU3 ..... 180 D8
10 Stamford PE9 ..... 219 B5
Allwood Rd 20 LN2 ..... 68 D6
Alma Ave PE25 ..... 206 B5
Alma Cl
Kingston upon Hull HU10 ..... 178 D7
3 Skegness PE25 ..... 206 B5
Alma Martin Way 7 LN3 ..... 83 C4
Alma Pk Cl 1 NG31 ..... 211 F6
Alma Pk Ind Est
Grantham NG31 ..... 211 F7
Londonthorpe & Harrowby without NG31 ..... 130 C4
Alma Pk Rd NG31 ..... 211 F6
Alma Rd PE1 ..... 225 F5
Alma St 6 HU9 ..... 181 B7
Almond Ave
Heighington LN4 ..... 81 F4
Lincoln LN6 ..... 205 A8
Almond Cl
Boston PE21 ..... 208 C5
9 Saxilby LN1 ..... 66 D2
Almond Cres
Lincoln LN6 ..... 205 A8
Louth LN11 ..... 198 D5
Waddington LN5 ..... 205 D1
Almond Ct LN6 ..... 205 A8
Almond Gr
Brigg DN20 ..... 196 B4
Grantham NG31 ..... 211 C6
3 Kingston upon Hull HU3 ..... 180 D6
3 Scunthorpe DN16 ..... 185 B8
Skellingthorpe LN6 ..... 200 A4
Stallingborough DN41 ..... 23 E6
Almond Rd PE1 ..... 226 B7
Almond Wlk
Boston PE21 ..... 208 D5
Sleaford NG34 ..... 212 D6
Almoners La PE3 ..... 225 E3
Alness Cl LN6 ..... 204 B8
Alnwick PE2 ..... 229 F3
Altham Terr LN5 ..... 205 D7
ALTHORPE DN17 ..... 17 D5
Althorpe Cl 15 PE6 ..... 217 A5
Althorpe & Keadby Prim Sch DN17 ..... 17 D5
Althorpe Sta DN17 ..... 17 D5
Altoft Cl 19 DN37 ..... 23 F1
Altyre Way DN36 ..... 192 C1
Alverston Ave LN10 ..... 97 D5
Alveston Rd DN17 ..... 184 D8
Alvey Rd NG24 ..... 104 C2
ALVINGHAM LN11 ..... 49 E2
Alvingham Ave DN35 ..... 192 F3
Alvingham Rd
Keddington LN11 ..... 198 E8
Scunthorpe DN16 ..... 185 B7
Alvis Cl LN4 ..... 205 F2
Alvis Dr PE7 ..... 233 D6
ALWALTON PE2 ..... 229 B4
Alwyn Rd 10 DN8 ..... 15 B8
Amanda Ct PE3 ..... 225 E2
Amanda Dr
Hatfield DN7 ..... 14 D4
Louth LN11 ..... 198 C8
Ambergate Specl Sch NG31 ..... 210 D3
Ambergate Wlk NG31 ..... 210 E3
Amber Hill Toftstead Prim Sch PE20 ..... 124 A5
Amberley Cres PE21 ..... 208 C4
Amberley Slope PE4 ..... 221 A3
Amble Cl LN1 ..... 201 E8
Ambleside Cl 4 NG34 ..... 212 B2
Ambleside Dr PE11 ..... 214 B2
Ambleside Gdns PE4 ..... 221 B3
Ambleside Pk LN6 ..... 204 F1
Ambrose Ave 3 DN7 ..... 14 E4
Ambury Gdns 9 PE6 ..... 166 F1
Amcott Ave DN10 ..... 40 A4
AMCOTTS DN17 ..... 7 F1
Amcotts Rd DN33 ..... 191 A2
Amelia Ct DN36 ..... 36 D8
Amery Way 31 PE24 ..... 90 D7
Amesbury Ave DN33 ..... 194 D7
Amethyst Cl 3 NG34 ..... 212 A3
Amethyst Ct 2 DN36 ..... 195 D7
Amman Sq 1 NG34 ..... 120 D8
Amos Cl DN33 ..... 194 D7
Amos Cres 3 DN16 ..... 185 D7
Amos La NG23 ..... 91 E6
Amos Way 8 PE22 ..... 113 B1
Ampleforth Ave DN32 ..... 190 F8
Ampleforth Gr HU5 ..... 179 D8
Amstel Cl 1 PE11 ..... 214 B2
Amsterdam Gdns 9 PE11 ..... 214 B3
Amwell Gn 10 DN7 ..... 14 D3
Amy Johnson Sch HU3 ..... 179 F5
Anastasia Cl DN21 ..... 197 C7
ANCASTER NG32 ..... 120 B2
Ancaster Ave
Chapel St Leonard PE24 ..... 90 D7
Grimsby DN33 ..... 194 D8
Lincoln LN2 ..... 202 B5
Spilsby PE23 ..... 100 F8
Ancaster CE Prim Sch NG32 ..... 120 A3
Ancaster Cl LN3 ..... 203 E6
Ancaster Ct
Horncastle LN9 ..... 199 B3
Scunthorpe DN16 ..... 185 A5
Ancaster Dr NG34 ..... 212 B2
Ancaster Rd
Bourne PE10 ..... 213 E5
16 Mablethorpe/Sutton on Sea LN12 ..... 64 B3
7 Stamford PE9 ..... 219 A7
Ancaster Sta NG32 ..... 120 A3
Ancaster Valley Nature Reserve* NG32 ..... 120 A2
Ancholme Ave DN40 ..... 186 A3
Ancholme Bsns Pk DN20 ..... 196 A4
Ancholme Cl LN1 ..... 201 D8
Ancholme Gdns 9 DN20 ..... 196 C3
Ancholme Leisure Ctr DN20 ..... 196 A3
Ancholme Rd DN16 ..... 185 D6
Ancholme Way DN20 ..... 196 B3
Anchorage St 4 DN20 ..... 196 B3
Anchor Cl DN8 ..... 15 A8
Anchor Ct PE4 ..... 221 D1
Anchor La PE25 ..... 90 D4
Anchor Rd
Scunthorpe DN16 ..... 19 B4
Sutton Bridge PE34 ..... 161 C4
Anchor St LN5 ..... 234 A1
Anchors Way 7 DN20 ..... 196 A3
Ancient La DN7 ..... 14 E3
ANDERBY PE24 ..... 77 A2
Anderby Cl LN6 ..... 204 F6
ANDERBY CREEK PE24 ..... 77 C3
Anderby Dr
Grimsby DN37 ..... 190 D7
Lincoln LN6 ..... 204 F6
Anderby Drainage Mus* PE24 ..... 77 C2
Anderby Rd PE24 ..... 77 D1
Anderson LN2 ..... 68 D5
Anderson Cl 7 PE13 ..... 170 C1
Anderson La 2 LN1 ..... 201 F6
Anderson Rd
2 Hemswell Cliff DN21 ..... 55 A8
Scunthorpe DN16 ..... 185 C7
Anderson St DN31 ..... 191 D7
Anderson Way DN21 ..... 52 F5
Andover Cl LN6 ..... 204 B8
Andrea Cl PE2 ..... 231 C6
Andrew Ave 27 PE24 ..... 90 D7
Andrew Cl PE5 ..... 223 D2
Andrewe's Cl PE7 ..... 231 B1
Andrew Paddock 18 DN20 ..... 30 F5
Andrew Rd
9 Humberston DN36 ..... 36 D8
1 Stamford PE9 ..... 219 B6
Andrews Cl LN11 ..... 198 C7
Andrews Cres PE4 ..... 221 D2
Andrews Rd 1 DN18 ..... 10 A7
Andrews Way 7 DN40 ..... 186 A4
Angel Ct 5 NG32 ..... 120 A2
Angelica Dr PE11 ..... 214 B6
Angell La PE12 ..... 215 E1
Angel Prec The PE10 ..... 213 C5
Angerstein Rd DN17 ..... 184 F5
Anglesey Cl 20 LN6 ..... 204 C7
Anglesey Dr DN40 ..... 186 C2
Anglia Cl 13 NG34 ..... 212 B2
Anglian Cl PE2 ..... 231 D6
Anglian Way 5 LN8 ..... 57 E8
Angus Cl 3 PE9 ..... 218 D6
Angus Ct PE3 ..... 225 D3
ANLABY HU10 ..... 179 A6
Anlaby Acre Head Cty Prim Sch HU4 ..... 179 B7
Anlaby Ave 7 HU4 ..... 179 B6
Anlaby High Rd HU4 ..... 179 C6
Anlaby Jun Sch HU4 ..... 179 A6
ANLABY PARK HU4 ..... 179 C5
Anlaby Pk Rd N HU4 ..... 179 B5
Anlaby Pk Rd S HU4 ..... 179 B2
Anlaby Rd HU3 ..... 179 F6
Anlafgate 7 HU10 ..... 178 F6
Annandale Rd HU10 ..... 178 C8
Anne Rd
Stamford PE9 ..... 219 A6
11 Sutton Bridge PE12 ..... 160 E4
Annes Cres DN16 ..... 185 C7
Annesley St 1 DN31 ..... 188 F1
Annette Cl 8 PE11 ..... 214 B5
Ann Gr DN35 ..... 192 D4
Anningson La 6 DN36 ..... 195 D7
Annpasture La LN4 ..... 207 C8
Anson Cl
Grantham NG31 ..... 211 C2
Skellingthorpe LN6 ..... 200 A4
Anson Ct PE6 ..... 217 B7
Antelope Rd DN18 ..... 4 A1
Anthony Cl PE1 ..... 225 F8
Anthony Cres LN11 ..... 198 C8
Anthony's Bank Rd DN36 ..... 193 D1
Anthony Way 3 DN41 ..... 23 D6
ANTON'S GOWT PE22 ..... 125 B6
Antrim Rd 9 LN5 ..... 205 D2
Antrim Way DN33 ..... 191 D2
Anvil Cl PE12 ..... 148 B1
Anvil Wlk 2 DN15 ..... 8 F3
ANWICK NG34 ..... 109 B1
Anzio Cres LN1 ..... 201 E7
Anzio Terr LN1 ..... 201 E7
Anzio Wlk LN1 ..... 201 E7
Apeldoorn Gdns 3 PE11 ..... 214 B3
APLEY LN8 ..... 70 A2
Apley Cl
Gainsborough DN21 ..... 197 F3
Lincoln LN2 ..... 202 A8
Appian Way
8 Baston PE6 ..... 164 E5
11 Bracebridge Heath LN4 ..... 81 A1
West Marsh DN31 ..... 188 C2
APPLEBY DN15 ..... 9 D1
Appleby Cl DN17 ..... 184 F5
Appleby Ct 17 DN32 ..... 189 C1
Appleby Gdns DN20 ..... 19 D4
Appleby La DN20 ..... 19 D4
Appleby Mill Rd DN16 ..... 183 E3
Apple Cl LN4 ..... 81 F4
Appledore Cl HU9 ..... 181 C6
Apple Garth LN5 ..... 205 D4
Applegarth Cl 2 DN35 ..... 192 D5
Applegarth Rd 2 HU8 ..... 181 A7
Appleton Gate NG24 ..... 104 A5
Appleton Way DN16 ..... 185 C6
Apple Tree Cl 19 LN4 ..... 95 C4
Apple Tree Ct 14 DN41 ..... 23 F5
Applewood Dr
5 Gonerby Hill Foot NG31 ..... 210 F8
3 Hampton Hargate PE7 ..... 230 C3
Appleyard PE2 ..... 231 C7
Appleyard Dr 33 DN18 ..... 10 E8
Apsley Way PE3 ..... 225 A2
Aqua Dr LN12 ..... 64 B2
Aquila Way PE6 ..... 164 E2
Arabis Cl 3 LN2 ..... 202 C8
Arakan Way 2 PE10 ..... 213 E7
Arbella Rd PE21 ..... 209 C4
Arboretum Ave LN2 ..... 234 C2
Arboretum The* LN2 ..... 234 C3
Arboretum View LN2 ..... 234 C2
Arborfield Cl 5 PE6 ..... 173 C4
Arbroath Gdns PE2 ..... 229 C4
Arbury Cl PE3 ..... 225 A3
Arcadia Cres 2 PE25 ..... 206 D2
Arcadia Rd PE25 ..... 206 D3
Archer La 12 PE21 ..... 208 F5
Archer Rd
Branston LN4 ..... 81 E2
Waltham DN37 ..... 194 D4
Archers Dro PE6 ..... 176 D6
Archers La PE20 ..... 136 C3
Archer St
3 Bishop Norton LN8 ..... 43 D3
Lincoln LN5 ..... 234 B1
Archers Way NG33 ..... 140 A5
Archers Wood 1 PE7 ..... 230 C3
Archibald Wlk PE21 ..... 208 B4
Archway Dr LN8 ..... 70 C4
Arcon Dr HU4 ..... 179 D6
Arcott Dr PE21 ..... 208 C5
Arden Cl 6 LN12 ..... 64 C3
Arden Moor Way 4 LN6 ..... 93 B8
Ardent Rd DN18 ..... 4 A1
Arden Village DN35 ..... 192 F1
Argyle Ct 6 DN15 ..... 183 B3
Argyle St
Boston PE21 ..... 208 D5
Kingston upon Hull HU3 ..... 180 C7
Argyll Way PE9 ..... 218 F5
Ariston St DN32 ..... 192 B7
Arkley Cl 22 HU15 ..... 2 C5
Ark Rd LN11 ..... 50 F8
Ark Royal Cl 2 NG34 ..... 212 A3
Arkwright St DN21 ..... 197 C5
Arkwright Way DN16 ..... 185 F6
Arlington Rd 4 LN8 ..... 56 D5
Arlington St 2 HU3 ..... 180 D6
Armeria Dr 4 DN17 ..... 185 A1
Armley Gr 3 PE9 ..... 219 D7
Armour Rd DN16 ..... 183 E3
Armstrong Pl E 3 DN31 ..... 188 E1
Armstrong Pl W 2 DN31 ..... 188 E1
Armstrong Rd 12 PE11 ..... 214 C2
Armstrong's Cl 2 PE12 ..... 157 D7
Armstrong's La PE22 ..... 115 B7
Armstrong St DN31 ..... 188 E1
Armthorpe La DN3 ..... 14 A3
Armtree Rd PE22 ..... 124 E7
Arne Cl 10 NG32 ..... 120 A3
Arnhem Ave 1 NG34 ..... 108 D2
Arnhem Cl LN1 ..... 201 E7
Arnhem Dr
10 Caythorpe NG32 ..... 119 B7
2 Spalding PE11 ..... 214 C5
Arnhem Way
Bourne PE10 ..... 213 E6
7 Woodhall Spa LN10 ..... 97 D5
Arnold Ave NG31 ..... 210 E8
Arnold Cl DN37 ..... 23 F2
Arnold Ct 11 DN32 ..... 189 C1
Arnold La HU3 ..... 180 B6
Arnold's Meadow Nature Reserve* PE12 ..... 214 F2
Arnold St HU3 ..... 180 B6
Arran Cl
Immingham DN40 ..... 186 D2
New Waltham DN36 ..... 195 C7
Sleaford NG34 ..... 121 A2
Arran Rd PE9 ..... 218 D5
Arras Cl LN1 ..... 201 E6
Arrow Ct PE7 ..... 230 C3
Art Coll Ct DN32 ..... 191 F8
Art Coll Mews DN32 ..... 191 F8
Art Haven The* NG31 ..... 211 B3
Arthur Mellows Village Coll PE6 ..... 220 B8
Arthur Rd DN21 ..... 197 D6
Arthurs' Ave 5 PE12 ..... 215 D2
Arthur St
Grimsby DN31 ..... 191 C8
Kingston upon Hull HU3 ..... 180 A5
6 Lincoln LN5 ..... 201 F1
Arthur Taylor St 1 LN1 ..... 201 D3
Artillery Row 13 PE21 ..... 209 A5
Artindale PE3 ..... 225 A3
Artis Ct PE3 ..... 225 A3
Arundel Cl
Gainsborough DN21 ..... 197 E6
Kingston upon Hull HU9 ..... 181 C8
Arundel Cres PE21 ..... 208 B4
Arundel Dr LN11 ..... 198 A7
Arundel Pl DN35 ..... 192 E5
Arundel Rd PE4 ..... 221 A1
Arundel St 3 HU9 ..... 181 C8
Arundel Wlk DN34 ..... 191 A7
Ascendale PE6 ..... 217 F5
Ascot Cl 4 PE11 ..... 156 E3

Ascot Dr
- 7 Grantham NG31 211 D7
- Peterborough PE1 226 B6

Ascot Rd DN37 194 D4
Ascott Cl HU4 179 D5
Ascot Way 7 LN6 93 A8
ASGARBY
- Asgarby and Howell NG34 122 B4
- Lusby with Winceby LN9 86 F1

Asgarby Rd NG34 122 B2
Asgard Way DN33 191 B2
Ash Ave 19 HU15 2 C6
Ashberry Dr
- 31 Messingham DN17 29 D7
- 4 Scunthorpe DN16 185 B6

Ashbourne 6 DN37 194 C4
Ashbourne Cl 3 NG34 212 B2
Ashbourne Ct DN15 182 B3
Ash Buckingham Studio* LN9 85 C5
Ashburn Cl 1 PE6 220 D7
Ashburnham Rd 20 DN8 15 A8
ASHBY DN16 185 B5
Ashby Ave LN6 204 F7
Ashby Broadway DN16 185 A6
ASHBY BY PARTNEY PE23 88 D1
Ashby Cl
- Bracebridge LN5 205 D1
- Grimsby DN37 190 D8
- Holton le Clay DN36 195 E1
- Kingston upon Hull HU4 179 B7

Ashby Ct 2 NG34 212 D6
ASHBY CUM FENBY DN37 35 D3
ASHBY DE LA LAUNDE LN4 108 B6
Ashby Gdns 7 PE12 157 F6
Ashby High St DN16 185 B6
Ashby Hill DN37 35 C3
ASHBY HILL DN37 35 C3
Ashby La DN37 35 D4
Ashby Mdws PE23 88 A1
ASHBY PUERORUM LN9 86 E6
Ashby Rd
- Cleethorpes DN35 192 D3
- Kingston upon Hull HU4 179 B4
- Scunthorpe DN16 183 A1
- Spilsby PE23 88 A1

Ash Cl
- Burgh le Marsh PE24 102 D7
- 5 Colsterworth NG33 151 E7
- Fulbeck NG32 106 C1
- Hessle HU13 178 C3
- Holbeach PE12 215 C3
- Langtoft PE6 164 E2
- Lincoln LN6 204 E8
- Louth LN11 198 C7
- Peterborough PE1 226 C7
- Spalding PE11 214 F5
- 1 Thorney PE6 175 F3

Ashcroft Gdns PE1 226 C5
Ashcroft Rd DN21 197 D2
Ash Ct
- Cleethorpes DN35 192 D2
- 5 Donington PE11 134 E2
- Peterborough PE1 226 C7
- Spalding PE11 214 F6

Ashdale Cl 3 LN4 95 C4
Ashdale Pk 18 HU14 3 A5
Ashdene Cl HU10 178 E7
Ashdown Ave 5 DN15 182 E3
Ashdown Cl 3 DN20 196 E3
Ashdown Way 14 DN10 39 F5
Ash Dr
- Kingston upon Hull HU10 178 F8
- 3 Kirton PE20 136 C5

Asheridge LN4 81 E2
Ashfield 2 LN1 66 D7
Ashfield Ave 2 DN8 15 A7
Ashfield Ct 20 DN17 16 D7
Ashfield Gr 1 DN7 14 C6
Ashfield Grange 5 LN1 66 C2
Ashfield Pk DN17 184 C5
Ashfield Rd
- 8 Hatfield DN7 14 C4
- Sleaford NG34 212 D5
- Thorne DN8 14 F7

Ashfields PE6 217 D2
Ashfield St 3 LN2 202 B3
Ash Gr
- Bourne PE10 213 C6
- Brigg DN20 196 B4
- Cherry Willingham/Reepham LN3 203 D5
- Gainsborough DN21 197 D6
- Grantham NG31 211 D7
- Lincoln LN6 204 F7
- 32 Messingham DN17 29 D7
- Scunthorpe DN16 185 B7

Ash Hill Cres DN7 14 D4
Ash Hill Rd DN7 14 D4
Ashing La LN2 68 F6
ASHINGTON END PE24 90 B1
Ash La 26 LN5 93 F6
Ashlawn Dr PE21 209 B6
Ashlea 3 DN10 39 F5
Ashleigh PE2 229 C6
Ashleigh Ct 3 DN41 23 F5
Ashley Cl LN12 64 C1
Ashley Dr NG31 210 E8
Ashley Pool La 5 PE6 176 A2
Ashley Rd 2 LN11 198 C5
Ashlin Gr LN1 234 A3
Ash Pk PE4 220 F6
Ash Pl 6 PE9 218 D6
Ash Rd
- 7 Coningsby LN4 207 D4
- Peterborough PE1 226 C7

Ashridge Dr DN32 192 C5
ASHTON PE9 173 A4
Ashton Hall Dr PE21 208 A1
Ashton Rd PE3 225 B5
Ashtons Ct LN5 201 E1
Ashtree Ave DN34 191 A6
Ash Tree Ave 11 LN2 68 D2
Ashtree Cl
- 1 Belton DN9 16 E2
- 12 Ruskington NG34 108 E1

Ash Tree Cl
- Immingham DN40 186 C5
- 10 Market Rasen LN8 57 D7

Ash Tree Dr 5 DN9 27 D2
Ashtree Gdns 5 PE9 171 B1
Ash Tree Rd 7 DN8 15 B7
Ash Villa Specl Sch The NG34 121 A3
Ashwell Ave 2 HU9 5 E8
Ashwin Gate 2 PE11 145 A8
Ashwood Cl LN9 199 B4
Ashwood Dr 10 DN36 36 D8
Ashworth Cl LN6 204 F5
Askew Ave HU4 179 E4
Askew's Dro PE6 166 D2
Askew's La PE7 233 E4
ASLACKBY NG34 142 D5
Aslackby Rd NG34 142 D3
Aspen Cl LN1 65 D2
Aspen Ct
- Cleethorpes DN35 192 D2
- Gainsborough DN21 197 F6

Aspen Dr 4 NG34 212 D2
Aspen Gr DN16 185 B8
Aspen Wlk 10 HU15 2 D5
ASPERTON PE20 135 D4
Asperton Rd PE20 135 E4
Asphodel Cl 3 DN36 195 D7
Asquith St DN21 197 B6
ASSERBY LN13 76 D4
ASTERBY LN11 72 E6
Asterby Cl LN2 202 A7
Asterby End LN11 72 E6
Asterby La LN11 72 E5
Asterby Rd DN17 184 F5
Aster Cl LN2 202 C8
Aster Dr PE4 221 B3
Astley Cres 15 DN21 29 C3
Astley St HU3 179 F7
Aston Cl
- 4 Waddington LN5 93 F7
- Yaxley PE7 233 E6

Aston Gn 5 DN7 14 D3
Aston Hall Dr 12 HU14 3 A5
Aston Rd HU10 178 F8
Astore Pk PE1 226 E3
Astral Cl HU13 178 F3
Astral Rd HU13 178 F3
Astral Way 8 LN6 204 C1
Astwick Rd LN6 205 A5
ASWARBY NG34 132 D6
ASWARDBY PE23 87 E5
Aswell St LN11 198 B5
Athelstan Cl 9 NG34 212 B2
Athena Dr DN31 188 C2
Athenian Way 1 DN31 188 A3
Atherstone Ave PE3 225 B4
Atherton Way DN20 196 B4
Atholl Ave HU13 178 E3
Athol St HU3 179 F4
Atkinson Ave DN20 196 C5
Atkinson Dr 24 HU15 2 C6
Atkinson La 6 DN37 194 E4
Atkinson St PE1 226 C2
Atkinsons Warren Nature Reserve* DN15 182 D5
Atkinsons Way DN15 182 F7
Atlantic Pl 8 NG31 211 A3
Atlas Rd DN17 184 F8
ATTERBY LN8 43 D3
Atterby Carr La DN21 43 F4
Atterby La LN8 43 C3
Atton Ave 4 PE11 157 B6
Atwater Cl LN2 202 D7
Atwater Ct 2 LN2 202 D7
Atwater Gr LN2 202 D7
Atwood Cl DN40 186 B5
Auborn Gdns PE3 225 B3
AUBOURN LN5 93 A5
Aubourn Ave LN2 201 F7
Aubourn Hall* LN5 93 A5
Aubretia Ave PE4 221 B3
Aubretia Dr 3 DN17 185 A1
Aubrey Parker Cl 4 LN12 64 C2
Auckland Cres 1 LN4 96 C1
Auckland Rd
- Grimsby DN31 189 B2
- Scunthorpe DN15 182 F2

Auden Cl LN2 234 C4
Auden Ct 2 LN4 207 B5
Audern Rd DN16 185 A4
Audley Gate PE3 225 C3
Augusta Cl
- Grimsby DN34 191 C5
- Peterborough PE1 226 E6

Augusta Oaks DN34 191 C6
Augusta St DN34 191 C6
Augustin Ret Pk NG31 211 A4
Augustus Dr 17 HU15 2 C5
AUNBY PE9 163 B5
AUNSBY NG34 132 A5
Aunsby Rd NG34 132 A7
AUSTENDIKE PE12 157 E4
Austendike Rd PE12 157 C4
AUSTEN FEN LN11 49 F5
Austen Wlk LN2 202 C6
Austerby PE10 213 E4
Austerby Cl PE10 213 D4
Austerby The PE10 213 E4
Austin Cres 3 DN17 184 F3
Austin Ct PE7 233 D6
Austin Friar's La 2 PE9 219 B4
Austin Garth 5 DN37 23 F1
Austin St PE9 219 B4
AUTHORPE LN11 74 F7
Autumn Croft Rd 6 NG24 104 B5
Autumn Pk Ind Est NG31 210 F4
Avebury Gdns PE11 214 F4
Aveland Cl
- Aslackby & Laughton NG34 142 E5
- 5 Bourne PE10 213 C5

Aveland Dr NG34 143 B8
Aveland High Sch The NG34 143 B8
Aveland Way
- Aslackby & Laughton NG34 142 D5
- 3 Baston PE6 164 E4

Avenswood La DN15 182 C6
Avenue A DN21 53 D5
Avenue B DN21 53 D5
Avenue Cannes DN15 182 D5
Avenue Clamart DN15 182 D5
Avenue Farm Rd PE12 160 D6
Avenue Fontenay DN15 182 D5
Avenue Lourdes DN15 182 D5
Avenue Nozay 2 DN20 19 E4
Avenue Rd NG31 211 B4
Avenue Rouen DN15 182 D6
Avenue Terr LN1 234 A3
Avenue The
- 9 Blyton DN21 41 C5
- Burton upon Stather DN15 8 B4
- Carlby PE9 163 E4
- Deeping St Nicholas PE11 166 C7
- East Ravendale DN37 35 C2
- Friskney PE22 115 A6
- Gainsborough DN21 197 E6
- Grantham NG31 210 E4
- 6 Great Gonerby NG31 129 D5
- Grimsby DN37 190 C8
- Healing DN41 23 F5
- 7 Ingham LN1 54 F2
- Kingston upon Hull HU10 178 C7
- Lincoln LN1 234 A3
- Market Deeping PE6 217 B5
- 8 Newark-on-Trent NG24 104 A4
- Nocton LN4 95 B7
- Swinderby LN6 92 C6

Avenue Vivian DN15 182 E4
Aviary Cl NG31 211 C5
Avignon Rd PE11 214 A5
Avocet Cl
- 4 Birchwood LN6 204 D8
- 4 Essendine PE9 163 D3

Avon Cl
- Grantham NG31 210 E3
- 5 Lincoln LN6 205 A2

Avon Ct PE4 221 C2
Avondale
- 1 Kingston upon Hull HU4 179 B2
- 7 Lincoln LN6 204 C1

Avondale St LN2 234 C2
Avon Rd DN16 183 C2
Axholme Ave 3 DN17 16 C7
Axholme Ct HU9 181 B5
Axholme Dr 6 DN9 27 D6
Axholme Gn 19 DN8 15 B7
Axholme Line Nature Reserve* DN9 27 C4
Axholme Rd
- Scunthorpe DN15 182 D2
- 2 Westwoodside DN9 27 A2

Axiom Ave PE3 225 C4
Axiom Ct PE9 219 D4
Ayam Cl 5 LN2 68 D6
Aydon Rd PE7 231 F6
Aykroft 1 PE10 213 E2
Aylesbury Gr HU5 179 D8
AYLESBY DN37 23 E2
Aylesby Cl 1 LN1 201 E8
Aylesby Gdns 2 DN33 191 B3
Aylesby La DN37 23 F3
Aylesby Rd
- Aylesby DN37 190 B6
- Scunthorpe DN17 184 F5

Aylesford St 7 HU3 180 B5
Aylmer Ave PE24 103 D2
Aynsley Rd LN6 204 B6
Ayots Gn 14 DN7 14 D3
Ayr Cl PE9 218 E6
Ayres Dr PE2 231 C6
Ayscough Ave
- Spalding PE11 214 D3
- 7 Stallingborough DN41 23 E6

Ayscoughfee Hall Mus & Gdns* PE11 214 D3
Ayscoughfee Hall Sch PE11 214 D3
Ayscough Gr 9 LN7 33 B4
Ayscough St 4 DN31 188 E1
Aysgarth Ave 18 DN17 29 D7
Azalea Cl PE3 225 A2
Azalea Rd LN2 202 C8

B

Babington Row HU9 181 C8
Bacheler St HU3 180 B5
Back Bank
- Crowland PE12 167 F3
- Whaplode PE12 168 A3

Back Field La DN7 14 E4
Backgate PE12 167 B8
Back La
- 5 Allington NG32 128 F7
- Aswarby & Swarby NG34 132 A7
- Barnby in the Willows NG24 105 A3
- Belvoir NG32 138 D6
- Bicker PE20 134 F6
- Bilsby LN13 76 A2
- Bolingbroke PE23 100 A7
- Buckminster NG33 151 A4
- Burton Coggles NG33 152 C8
- Cammeringham LN1 54 F1
- Candlesby with Gunby PE23 89 B1
- Caythorpe NG32 119 B7
- Claxby with Moorby PE22 99 B7
- Claypole NG23 117 E7
- Collyweston PE9 171 B1
- Colsterworth NG33 151 E7
- 3 Deeping St James PE6 217 F4
- Dunston LN4 95 C6
- Eye PE6 175 A1
- 3 Foston NG32 117 F1
- Garthorpe & Fockerby DN17 7 F6
- Heighington/Washingborough LN4 81 F4
- Holbeach PE12 215 D2
- Ingoldsby NG33 141 C5
- Leadenham LN5 106 C3
- Long Bennington NG23 128 D8
- Long Sutton PE12 216 D6
- 4 Lutton PE12 160 A8
- Market Deeping PE6 174 A8
- North Clifton NG23 78 C7
- North Cockerington LN11 50 A1
- Scothern LN2 68 F4
- 1 Searby cum Owmby DN38 32 D8
- 4 Skillington NG33 151 A8
- 4 Stainforth DN7 14 C6
- 9 Stamford PE9 219 C5
- Stickford PE22 100 A3
- Wainfleet All Saints PE24 102 A2
- Wilsford NG32 120 C2
- Winteringham DN15 2 B1
- Wood Enderby PE22 98 F6
- Yaxley PE7 233 E5

Back Rd
- Gorefield PE13 169 E2
- Murrow PE13 177 E6

Back St
- Alkborough DN15 8 C8
- Buckminster NG33 150 E5
- East Stockwith DN21 40 B5
- Saltfleetby LN11 51 C1
- South Clifton NG23 78 C5
- Sproxton LE14 138 F1

Bacon's La 1 PE11 145 C1
Bacon St DN21 197 D2
Bader Cl
- Peterborough PE3 225 B6
- The Willows DN37 190 E8

Bader Way 3 PE25 206 A5
Badgate PE11 134 F2
Bad Gate PE12 169 B6
Badger Cl PE7 233 F5
Badger La PE10 213 C2
Badger's La PE20 136 B7
Badgers Oak 2 LN5 92 F3
Badger Way 1 DN20 19 E4
Badington Cl PE2 230 D8
Badinton La PE9 172 F5
Badminton Way LN11 198 A7
Baffen's La PE11 145 A4
BAG ENDERBY PE23 87 B7
Baggaley Dr LN9 199 A4
Baggholme Rd LN2 234 C2
Baghdad Rd 1 NG34 120 D8
Bagsby Rd DN9 28 B3
Baildon Cres LN6 205 A3
Baildon Rd DN15 182 D4
Bailey La DN7 14 E6
Baileys Cl PE12 215 D1
Baileys La LN5 92 F5
Bailey Way PE2 230 D8
Bailgate 1 LN2 234 B3
Baily's La PE12 147 F2
Bain Cl PE9 219 C7
Baines Ave NG24 104 B2
Baines Cl LN4 207 D5
Baines Rd DN21 197 F4
Bain Rd PE21 208 C3
Bain Rise 3 LN8 59 A7
Bain St LN1 201 D8
BAINTON PE9 172 F5
Bainton Rd
- Barnack PE9 172 D4
- Newborough PE6 221 D8

Baird Cl PE7 233 D6
Baker Cres LN6 204 E7
Baker Dr 30 DN15 9 A5
Bakers Cl DN38 21 B5
Bakersfield DN20 196 F7
Bakers La
- Bassingham LN5 92 E2
- Peterborough PE2 230 E7

Baker's La
- Candlesby with Gunby PE23 89 A2
- Fishtoft PE21 126 C4
- Great Steeping PE23 101 E6
- Westborough & Dry Doddington NG23 117 E3

Baker St HU2 180 E7
Bakers Way 5 PE10 154 D6
Bakestraw Gate PE12 157 F5
Bakewell Ct 1 DN15 182 B3
Bakewell Mews 6 LN6 204 F2
Bakewell Rd PE2 229 C2
Bala Ct PE4 221 B3
Balder Ct 2 DN33 191 C2
BALDERTON NG24 104 C2
Balderton La NG24 104 D3
Baldock's Mill Heritage Ctr* PE10 213 D4
Baldwin Ave DN16 185 B2
Baldwin Cl PE8 172 C1
Baldwin Gr PE10 213 D6
Balfour Pl 3 DN40 186 B4
Balfour St
- Gainsborough DN21 197 C5
- 2 Kingston upon Hull HU9 181 C8

Balintore Rise PE2 229 D4
Balk Rd 8 PE9 163 C1
Balliol Dr DN16 185 B4
Ball's La PE12 159 A6
Balmoral Ave
- 1 Grimsby DN34 191 A7
- Spalding PE11 214 D2

Balmoral Cl
- 12 Mablethorpe/Sutton on Sea LN12 76 F8
- 2 Wragby LN8 70 D4

Balmoral Ct DN17 184 F4
Balmoral Dr
- Beacon Hill NG24 104 C4
- Grantham NG31 210 E6
- Sleaford NG34 120 F2

Balmoral Rd
- Cleethorpes DN35 192 C4
- 4 Hatfield DN7 14 D4
- 1 Peterborough PE4 225 C8

Balmoral Way PE12 159 A8
Bamber St PE1 225 F4
Bamford Ave 1 HU9 5 F8
Bamford Cl 6 LN6 204 E2
Banbury Cl PE11 214 D6
Banbury Ct 9 DN31 189 C1
Banbury Rd DN16 183 D2
Bancroft Rd NG24 104 A3
Bangor Cl LN5 205 C3
Bank Dr
- Ingoldmells PE25 90 F3
- 5 Wisbech PE13 170 C1

Bank End LN11 50 E8
Bank End Rd DN9 26 A3
Bank La 12 LN7 33 B4
Bank's Ave 4 PE11 214 F6
Bank Side 1 PE21 136 D8
Banks La 4 NG34 122 E2
Banks Rd 6 LN9 199 C4
Banks St 5 LN9 199 C4
Bank St
- Boston PE21 208 F5
- Kingston upon Hull HU3 180 C7
- Lincoln LN2 234 B2

Bank The
- Parson Drove PE13 177 C7
- Swaton NG34 133 D4

Bannister Dr HU9 181 C7
Bannister's La PE20 136 C7
Bannister's Row 6 PE13 170 C1
Banovallum Gdns 1 LN9 199 D3
Banovallum Sch LN9 199 C2
Baptist Chapel La 4 DN40 12 F2
Baptist La 3 NG23 91 C4
Barbara Cl 3 DN33 194 E7
Barbara Rd 6 PE25 206 D2
Barber Cl PE2 231 C7
Barberry Ct 9 HU3 180 C5
Barbers Dro PE6 175 C8
Barbers Hill PE4 220 F7
Barbican Way DN36 195 C6
Barcroft St DN35 189 E1
Bardling's Dro PE12 169 A7
BARDNEY LN3 83 C4
Bardney PE2 230 A4
Bardney Ave DN16 185 A7
Bardney Cl LN6 204 F6
Bardney Gdns 1 DN34 190 F4
Bardney Joint CE/Methodist (Controlled) Sch LN3 83 C4
Bardney Linewood National Nature Reserve* LN3 83 C3
Bardney Rd
- Branston & Mere LN4 82 C3
- Wragby LN8 70 C4

Bardots Leisure Ctr LN5 205 C1
Barehams La PE11 145 A7
Barfen La LN13 63 B3
Barff La LN8 43 F2

Barff Mdw LN8 43 E1
Barff Rd LN4 82 B1
Barfields La LN3 68 F1
Barford Cl PE2 230 C7
Bargate
  Grimsby DN34 191 C5
  12 Lincoln LN5 205 E8
Bargate Ave DN32 191 D5
Bargate Gr 3 HU5 179 D8
Bargate La 4 LN9 199 C3
Barge Cl 1 PE11 214 F5
Barge Rd PE12 148 A7
Barham Cl PE2 231 F5
BARHOLM PE9 164 C1
Barholme Ave 7 PE12 160 A8
Barkestone La NG13 128 A5
Barkham St 7 PE24 102 D2
Barkhouse Cl 4 DN35 192 F5
Barkhouse La 5 DN35 192 F5
Bark St DN35 192 F5
BARKSTON NG32 130 B8
Barkston Cl PE10 213 E6
Barkston Dr PE1 226 B6
Barkston Gdns LN2 202 B7
Barkston Rd NG32 118 D2
Barkston & Syston CE (Aided) Prim Sch NG32 130 B8
Barkwith Rd LN8 58 F1
Barkworth Cl HU10 178 D6
Barkworth Ct 3 DN37 194 C4
Bar La 20 LN5 93 F7
Barley Cl
  Heckington NG34 122 D2
  12 Hibaldstow DN20 31 A5
  24 Metheringham LN4 95 C4
Barleycroft Rd NG33 152 E8
Barleyfield PE6 164 E2
Barley Gr 4 PE11 166 C6
Barley Mews PE2 230 D7
Barley Way LN9 199 A3
BARLINGS LN3 69 D1
Barlings Ave DN16 185 A7
Barlings Cl
  1 Barlings LN3 69 C3
  Hartsholme LN6 204 F7
  7 Scotter DN21 29 C4
Barlings La LN3 69 C2
Barmouth Dr DN37 190 E8
Barmston St HU2 180 F8
BARNACK PE9 172 E4
Barnack CE Prim Sch PE9 172 D4
Barnack Drift PE9 172 B3
Barnack Est 4 PE24 102 E7
Barnack Hill & Holes National Nature Reserve* PE9 172 D3
Barnack Rd
  Bainton PE9 172 E4
  St Martin's without PE9 219 D4
Barnard Ave DN20 196 B3
Barnard Way 9 PE3 224 F3
Barnard Wlk DN40 186 D3
Barnberry Way PE10 142 D2
BARNBY DUN DN3 14 A4
Barnby Gate NG24 104 A4
BARNBY IN THE WILLOWS NG24 104 F3
Barnby La NG23 104 F1
Barnby Rd NG24 104 B3
Barnby Rd Prim Sch NG24 104 A4
Barn Cl
  2 Maxey PE6 173 C7
  Peterborough PE4 220 F3
Barnes Cl 1 NG34 212 C6
Barnes Cres
  Scunthorpe DN15 182 E4
  Skegness PE25 206 A5
Barnes Dro PE10 154 F4
Barnes Gn 2 DN21 29 C4
Barnes La LN5 106 F7
Barnes Rd
  9 Donington PE11 134 E2
  Skegness PE25 206 A5
Barnes Way PE4 220 F3
Barnetby La DN20 20 F7
BARNETBY LE WOLD DN38 21 C4
Barnetby Rd
  1 Kingston upon Hull HU13 179 A3
  Scunthorpe DN17 184 F5
Barnetby Sta DN38 21 B4
Barnet Dr DN36 195 E7
Barnet Gn 12 DN7 14 D3
Barnett Pl DN35 192 B7
Barneyfield Rd PE22 126 E1
Barnfield Rd 22 NG23 91 D5
Barn Hill PE9 219 B5
BARNOLDBY LE BECK DN37 35 B6
Barnoldby Rd DN37 194 C4
Barn Owl Cl
  Corby Glen NG33 152 F7
  1 Langtoft PE6 164 F3
Barnside 6 DN20 30 F5
Barnstaple Rd 3 DN17 184 D8
Barnstock PE3 225 A7
Barnston Way 12 DN15 8 B4
Barnswallace Ct 15 LN2 68 D7
Barnwell Rd 3 PE9 218 E6
Barnwell Terr 2 NG31 210 F3
Baron Ave DN36 195 D7
Baron Ct PE4 221 B4
Baroness Rd DN34 190 F6
Barons Way PE9 219 C4
Barrack Sq NG31 211 C4
Barracks The PE13 169 E2
Barraclough's La 1 DN18 3 E1
Barratt's Cl LN2 234 C4
Bar Rd DN10 52 B8
Bar Rd N 3 DN10 52 B8
Bar Rd S 7 DN10 52 B8
Barrett Gr 7 LN2 68 E6
Barrett's Cl PE12 215 D3
Barrick Cl 16 DN19 11 D8
Barrier Bank
  Cowbit PE12 156 F2
  Spalding PE12 214 C1
Barrington Cl 8 PE12 215 D2
Barrington Gate PE12 215 E1
Barrow Blow Wells Nature Reserve* DN19 4 D1
BARROWBY NG32 210 A5
Barrowby CE (Controlled) Prim Sch NG32 129 B3
Barrowby Gate NG31 210 D4
Barrowby Rd 8 NG31 211 A5
Barrowden Rd PE9 171 A2
Barrowfield PE1 226 E7
BARROW HANN DN19 4 E1
BARROW HAVEN DN19 4 B2
Barrow Haven Reedbed Nature Reserve* DN19 4 B2
Barrow Haven Sta DN19 4 C2
Barrow La HU13 178 D2
Barrow Rd
  Barton-upon-Humber DN18 11 A8
  New Holland DN19 4 E1
Barrows Gate
  3 Beacon Hill NG24 104 A6
  North Somercotes LN11 50 D6
BARROW UPON HUMBER DN19 11 C8
Barr's La PE12 168 B4
Barry Ave DN34 190 F3
Barry Wlk 3 PE2 230 F7
Bars La
  Benington PE22 126 E5
  Bicker PE20 135 A5
Bartholemew Cl 1 LN3 83 C4
Bartol Cres PE21 208 D5
Barton Cl
  3 Mablethorpe LN12 64 C2
  Paston PE4 221 D1
Barton Dr HU13 178 D1
Barton Gate LN11 198 D4
Barton La
  Barrow upon Humber DN19 11 C8
  Tydd St Mary PE13 169 F8
Barton-on-Humber Sta DN18 3 F1
Barton Outdoor Pursuits Ctr* DN18 3 D2
Barton Rd
  5 Wainfleet All Saints PE24 102 D1
  Wrawby DN20 196 F6
Barton St Peters CE Prim Sch DN18 3 F1
Bartons La PE23 101 F6
Barton St
  Aylesby DN37 23 D2
  Barrow upon Humber DN19 11 C8
  Fotherby LN11 49 A2
  Irby DN37 34 F7
  Keelby DN41 23 A4
  Ludborough DN36 48 C6
BARTON-UPON-HUMBER DN18 10 F7
BARTON WATERSIDE DN18 3 F2
Bartram Gate 2 PE4 221 C1
Bartrams 3 HU15 2 D6
Basic Slag Rd DN16 183 E2
Basil Gn PE2 230 D6
Baslow Rd DN15 182 B2
Bass Cotts NG34 212 E3
Bassett Cl 2 DN20 19 E3
Bassett Rd DN35 193 A4
BASSINGHAM LN5 92 F2
Bassingham Cres LN2 201 F7
Bassingham La PE23 88 E3
Bassingham Prim Sch LN5 92 F2
Bassingham Rd LN5 92 F5
BASSINGTHORPE NG33 140 E3
BASTON PE6 164 E4
Baston CE Prim Sch PE6 164 E5
Baston Edge Dro PE10 164 E7
Baston Fen Nature Reserve* PE6 165 A8
Baston Outgang Rd PE6 165 A6
Bateman's Cl 3 PE12 159 D7
Batemans Ct 2 PE24 102 E2
Bath Gdns PE21 208 F3
Bath La 15 PE11 214 D4
Bath Rd
  Bracebridge Heath LN4 81 A2
  Wisbech PE13 170 D1
Bath Row PE9 219 B4
Bath St
  8 Grantham NG31 211 A4
Bath St *continued*
  Grimsby DN32 189 C1
Bathurst PE2 230 A4
Bathurst St
  8 Kingston upon Hull HU3 180 D5
  Lincoln LN2 202 D3
Battery St DN40 186 D4
Battlefields La N PE12 159 A8
Battlefields La S PE12 215 F3
Battle Gn DN9 27 D7
Battle of Britain Meml Flight Visitor Ctr* LN4 207 B3
Baulkin's Dro PE12 159 C1
BAUMBER LN9 72 A1
Baumber Prim Sch LN9 72 A1
Bawtry Cl LN6 204 C8
Bawtry Rd DN7 14 F3
Baxter Cl
  Coningsby LN4 207 D3
  15 Wisbech PE13 170 E1
Baxter Gdns PE11 214 C7
Bayard St DN21 197 C5
Bayes Rd 6 PE25 103 E4
Bayfield Rd 4 LN4 96 B1
Bayford Dr NG24 104 C4
Bayford Gn PE21 208 B4
Bayons Ave DN33 194 D8
Baysdale Gr NG31 211 B8
Baysdale Rd DN16 185 D5
Baysgarth House Mus* DN18 10 F8
Baysgarth Leisure Ctr DN18 10 F8
Baysgarth Sch DN18 10 F8
Baysgarth View DN18 10 F7
Bayston Ct PE2 230 E8
Bayswater Pl 1 DN33 194 D8
Bayswood Ave PE21 208 F1
BAYTHORPE PE20 135 C8
Baytree Ave DN34 191 A6
Baytree Owl Ctr* PE12 157 D7
Baywood Cl 4 LN6 200 C1
Beach Ave 15 PE24 90 D7
Beach Bank
  Pinchbeck PE11 144 E3
  Surfleet PE11 145 A3
Beach Holt La DN37 23 D2
Beach La PE11 144 F3
Beachside 10 LN12 77 A8
Beacon Ave
  16 Barton-upon-Humber DN18 10 E8
  Cleethorpes DN35 192 D6
Beacon Ct DN35 192 D6
BEACON HILL NG24 104 B5
Beacon Hill La PE34 161 E3
Beacon Hill Rd
  Gringley on the Hill DN10 39 D1
  Newark-on-Trent NG24 104 B4
Beacon Hts NG24 104 B4
Beacon La NG31 211 C4
Beacon Pk Cl 4 PE25 206 A6
Beacon Pk Dr PE25 206 A6
Beacon Rd 7 NG34 107 C1
Beaconsfield Dr 3 NG24 104 C5
Beaconthorpe Rd 4 DN35 192 E7
Beacon View 2 NG13 128 A6
Beacon Way PE25 206 A6
Beaford Ct DN17 184 C8
Beagle Cl 16 DN20 19 E4
Beagle La NG34 107 C1
Bean St HU3 180 C6
Bear La 14 PE11 145 C1
Beatrice Rd 11 PE13 170 D2
Beatrice Way 28 PE24 90 D7
Beatty Ave DN33 194 F7
Beaubridge Bsns Pk PE25 206 B3
Beauchamp St 3 DN16 183 B1
Beauchamp Wlk 7 DN16 183 B2
Beauchief Gdns DN16 185 A8
Beaufort Ave 1 PE6 217 C5
Beaufort Cl
  Kingston upon Hull HU3 180 D6
  Lincoln LN2 202 D8
Beaufort Cres DN35 192 D2
Beaufort Dr
  Bourne PE10 213 C7
  4 Spalding PE11 214 C3
Beaufort Rd LN2 202 D8
Beaufort St DN21 197 B7
Beaulahland 8 DN18 10 A7
Beaulah Villas 9 DN18 10 A7
Beaulieu Ct 6 PE6 175 A1
Beaumonde 5 DN36 195 C2
Beaumont Cl 11 PE24 102 E7
Beaumont Ct 3 HU9 181 D7
Beaumont Dr 2 NG31 210 F8
Beaumont Fee LN1 234 A2
Beaumont St DN21 197 D4
Beaumont Way PE7 230 C2
Beauvale Gdns PE4 221 C3
Beauvoir Pl PE7 233 E5
Beaver Cl 1 LN6 200 A5
Beccelm Dr 9 PE6 175 B8
Beck Bank
  Gosberton PE11 144 C3
  Kirton PE20 124 E1
Beck Cl
  5 Binbrook LN8 47 C5
  13 Keelby DN41 23 A4
  1 Ruskington NG34 108 D2
Becke Cl LN3 203 E5
Becket Cl LN4 203 D1
Beckets Cl PE1 225 F8
Beckett Ave DN21 197 E6
Beckett Cl
  9 Heckington NG34 122 D3
  2 Skegness PE25 206 C1
Beckett Dr PE11 214 C6
Beckett Sch DN21 53 A8
Beckhall LN2 68 D6
Beckhead Cvn Site LN6 204 C1
Beck Hill
  6 Barton-upon-Humber DN18 10 F8
  Tealby LN8 46 C1
Beckhole Cl HU3 180 A6
Beckhythe Cl DN33 191 E1
BECKINGHAM
  Barnby in the Willows NG24 105 A4
  Beckingham DN10 40 B1
Beckingham PE2 229 F3
Beckingham Rd
  Coddington NG24 104 C5
  Walkeringham DN10 40 A2
Beckingthorpe Dr 19 NG13 128 A6
Beck La
  Appleby DN15 9 D1
  Aubourn Haddington & South Hykeham LN6 93 B7
  10 Barrow upon Humber DN19 11 D8
  7 Broughton DN20 19 E3
  Fulbeck NG32 106 C1
  Heighington/Washingborough LN4 81 F4
  Ingoldmells PE25 90 E2
  Redbourne DN21 30 F2
  Scunthorpe DN16 185 B3
  6 Welton/Dunholme LN2 68 E6
  Welton le Marsh PE23 89 A3
Beckside
  11 Brough HU15 2 D6
  Normanby by Spital LN8 55 E7
  Rothwell LN7 33 F2
  Scopwick LN4 108 C8
Beck Side 5 DN20 30 F5
Beckside Cl DN36 192 E1
Beckside Ct LN11 198 D3
Becks La DN21 29 A3
Beck St
  Digby LN4 108 E5
  Welbourn LN5 106 E4
Becks The 4 LN9 199 C4
Beck Way 5 PE10 164 C8
Beck Wlk 2 DN35 192 E1
Bedale Pl DN35 192 E3
Bedale Rd 3 DN16 185 D5
Bede Cl NG34 212 B2
Bede Cres PE22 126 F5
Bedehouse Bank PE10 213 E4
Bede House La 3 NG24 104 A4
Bede Pl PE1 226 A6
Bede Rd 3 PE6 164 E5
Bedford Cl NG31 211 F5
Bedford Ct 16 PE6 176 A3
Bedford Pl 1 PE11 214 D3
Bedford Rd
  Humberston DN35 193 A1
  Kingston upon Hull HU13 178 F3
Bedford Row PE13 170 D8
Bedford St
  Grimsby DN32 189 C1
  2 Lincoln LN1 201 D4
  Peterborough PE1 226 B4
Beechams Mews 5 PE11 214 B3
Beech Ave
  Bourne PE10 213 B5
  Gainsborough DN21 197 D6
  Grimsby DN33 191 C3
  5 Gunness DN15 17 E6
  Kingston upon Hull HU10 178 D8
  24 Nettleham LN2 68 C2
  Peterborough PE1 225 F3
  Scunthorpe DN15 182 B6
  Spalding PE11 214 F5
Beech Cl
  1 Bracebridge Heath LN4 81 A1
  5 Broughton DN20 19 D3
  2 Colsterworth NG33 151 E7
  2 Coningsby LN4 207 D4
  Dunholme LN2 68 E5
  3 Gringley on the Hill DN10 39 C1
  7 Heckington NG34 122 D3
  Kingston upon Hull HU3 180 C5
  Market Deeping PE6 217 B6
  RAF Cranwell NG34 107 D1
  9 Sudbrooke LN2 68 F2
  4 Thorney PE6 176 A3
Beech Cres 1 DN7 14 D6
Beechcroft Cl 6 LN6 93 A8
Beechcroft Rd NG31 210 C3
Beech Dr
  16 Bottesford NG13 128 A5
  6 North Ferriby HU14 3 A4
  15 Ryhall PE9 163 C1
  Welton HU14 2 F5
Beechers Way LN8 57 D7
Beeches Ave DN16 185 B4
Beeches La PE22 112 C5
Beeches Prim Sch The PE1 225 F3
Beeches The 1 LN1 66 C7
Beechfield Ct DN34 191 C6
Beechfield Rd 7 DN7 14 C4
Beech Garth 9 DN19 11 C7
Beech Gr
  Anlaby with Anlaby Common HU13 178 C3
  3 Burton upon Stather DN15 8 B5
  Donington PE11 134 E2
  Holton le Clay DN36 195 E1
  Louth LN11 198 C7
  4 Scopwick Heath LN4 108 A7
  Stamford PE9 218 D6
  4 Swanland HU14 3 C7
Beech Hill Rd HU14 3 C7
Beechings Way 10 LN13 75 E2
Beechings Way Ind Est LN13 75 E2
Beech La 12 PE6 175 A1
Beech Lawn HU10 178 E6
Beech Rd
  Branston LN4 81 D2
  6 Brough HU15 2 C6
  Glinton PE6 220 B8
Beech Rise
  Sleaford NG34 212 D6
  2 South Rauceby NG34 120 E4
Beech St LN5 205 D5
Beech Tree Ave 17 DN8 15 B7
Beechtree Cl 8 NG34 108 E1
Beechway DN16 185 B7
Beech Way DN35 192 D2
Beechwood Ave
  Grimsby DN33 190 F3
  Immingham DN40 186 C4
Beechwood Cl
  16 Kirk Sandall DN3 14 A1
  Peterborough PE1 226 C7
  6 Wisbech PE13 170 D1
Beechwood Cres 4 DN20 19 E4
Beechwood Dr
  12 Scawby DN20 30 F8
  7 Scotter DN21 29 C3
Beechwood Rd 5 PE13 170 D1
Beeden Pk Est NG31 210 C4
Bee Field The LN2 202 F7
Beehive La LN6 79 C1
Beeley Rd DN32 192 C6
BEELSBY DN37 34 E4
Beelsby Rd LN7 34 C5
Beel's Rd DN41 187 B2
BEESBY LN13 76 A7
Beesby Dr 3 DN35 192 F3
Beesby Rd
  Maltby le Marsh LN13 76 A7
  Scunthorpe DN17 184 E5
Beesby Wlk LN13 76 A6
Bees Cnr 1 PE24 102 D2
Bee's La PE13 169 F6
Beeson Gr DN31 188 E1
Beeson St DN31 188 E1
Beeston Dr PE7 231 F5
Beeton Cl LN11 198 D4
Beetons Cl PE7 233 E5
Beevor St LN6 201 C2
Beggar Hill Messingham Rd DN21 29 D4
Beggar's La PE22 98 F3
Begger's Bush La PE12 157 D7
Beilby St HU3 179 F4
Belcanto Ct 3 PE11 214 A5
BELCHFORD LN9 73 B2
Belchmire La PE11 145 B5
Beldings Cl PE23 101 F6
Belfry The 5 NG31 211 D7
Belgic Sq PE1 226 E3
Belgrave Cl 11 DN9 16 E1
Belgrave Dr HU4 179 D5
Belgrave Rd
  Grimsby DN33 191 B2
  7 Spalding PE11 214 C2
Belgrave Sq 1 DN15 183 B3
Belgravia Cl LN6 200 E1
Belham Rd PE1 225 E7
Belisana Rd 5 PE11 214 A5
Bellamy Ct HU9 181 C7
Bellamy's La PE14 170 D4
Bellbutts View DN21 29 B3
Bell Cl NG31 210 E7
Bell Ct 5 PE21 208 F1
Bell Dro PE6 175 F6
BELLEAU LN13 75 A5
Belleisle Rd DN34 190 D4
Belle Vue PE2 231 C6
Belle Vue Rd LN1 234 A3
Belle Vue Terr
  Lincoln LN1 234 A3
  21 Thorne/Moorends DN8 15 A8
Bellfield Cl 4 PE11 214 B3
Bellflower Cl 2 LN2 202 C8
Bell Gr LN6 205 C6
Bellingham Rd DN16 185 D7
Bellingham's Dro PE11 166 F7
Bell La
  4 Collingham NG23 91 C4
  Fosdyke PE20 146 D8
  Market Deeping PE6 217 E4
  Moulton PE12 157 F7
  Scunthorpe DN15 183 A2

BELLMOUNT PE34 ... 161 E4
Bell's Dro PE12 ... 159 C1
Bell's Pl PE1 ... 226 A2
Bellview Rd 6 NG34 ... 108 E1
Bellwin Dr DN15 ... 8 A1
Bellwood Cres 5 DN8 ... 15 A8
Bellwood Gdns NG31 ... 211 C5
Bellwood Grange 1
LN3 ... 203 E7
Bell Wr Drain Bank
Eastville PE22 ... 101 B1
New Leake PE22 ... 100 E1
BELMESTHORPE PE9 ... 163 D1
Belmesthorpe La PE9 ... 163 D1
Belmont DN36 ... 195 C1
Belmont Cl DN35 ... 192 D3
Belmont Gr 2 NG31 ... 211 D6
Belmont Prim Sch
NG31 ... 211 E6
Belmont St
Kingston upon Hull
HU9 ... 181 D8
Lincoln LN2 ... 202 B3
Scunthorpe DN16 ... 185 A6
BELNIE PE11 ... 145 D5
Belnie La PE11 ... 145 D5
Belper Ct
6 Crosby DN15 ... 182 B2
Grimsby DN32 ... 189 C1
Belsay Dr PE2 ... 231 F5
Belshaw La DN9 ... 16 D1
Belsize Ave PE2 ... 230 E6
Belthorn Rd 2 DN17 ... 7 F1
BELTOFT DN9 ... 17 B1
BELTON
Belton and Manthorpe
NG32 ... 130 B6
Belton DN9 ... 16 E1
Belton All Saints CE Prim
Sch DN9 ... 16 E2
Belton Ave
Grantham NG31 ... 211 C6
Lincoln LN6 ... 204 F6
Belton Cl
Boston PE21 ... 209 B5
13 Market Deeping PE6 ... 217 A5
Belton Fields 1 DN9 ... 16 D1
Belton Gdns 23 PE9 ... 219 C5
Belton Gr
Grantham NG31 ... 211 B7
1 Grimsby DN33 ... 191 A3
Belton House* NG32 ... 130 B6
Belton La
Grantham NG31 ... 211 C6
Great Gonerby NG31 ... 129 E5
Belton La Com Prim Sch
NG31 ... 211 D7
Belton Pk* NG32 ... 211 F8
Belton Pk Dr 7 LN6 ... 93 C8
Belton Rd
Belton DN9 ... 17 A1
Epworth DN9 ... 27 E7
Peterborough PE7 ... 231 F5
Sandtoft DN9 ... 16 B3
Belton St 16 PE9 ... 219 C5
Belton Wlk LN11 ... 198 A7
Belt Rd The DN21 ... 197 F7
Belvedere Cl PE11 ... 214 B2
Belvedere Dr DN17 ... 184 E7
Belvedere Rd HU13 ... 178 F2
BELVOIR NG32 ... 138 B8
Belvoir Ave
12 Bottesford NG13 ... 128 A5
Grantham NG31 ... 210 F1
Spitalgate NG31 ... 211 E2
Belvoir Castle* NG32 ... 138 B8
Belvoir Cl
Bracebridge LN5 ... 205 D1
4 Colsterworth NG33 ... 151 E6
1 Market Deeping PE6 ... 217 A5
1 Stamford PE9 ... 218 E6
Belvoir Ct LN11 ... 198 B8
Belvoir Gdns NG31 ... 129 D5
Belvoir High Sch NG13 ... 128 A5
Belvoir La NG32 ... 128 D1
Belvoir Pk Wlk DN35 ... 192 D2
Belvoir Rd
Bottesford NG13 ... 128 A4
Cleethorpes DN35 ... 192 D2
Croxton Kerrial NG32 ... 138 A6
Belvoir St HU5 ... 180 C8
Belvoir Way
Eye PE1 ... 226 D8
Louth LN11 ... 198 B8
Peterborough PE1 ... 226 C8
Belwood Dr 7 DN9 ... 16 E2
Bempton Gr
4 Grimsby DN32 ... 192 A5
Kingston upon Hull HU5 ... 179 D8
Bemrose Way 2 DN31 ... 191 C8
Benams Cl PE5 ... 223 E2
Benbow Way LN1 ... 201 C6
Benderslough Dro
PE12 ... 159 C3
Bendike La PE11 ... 145 D4
Benedict Cl 2 HU4 ... 179 A2
Benedict Ct PE6 ... 217 E5
Benedict Rd HU4 ... 179 A2
Benedict Sq PE4 ... 220 E2
BENINGTON PE22 ... 126 F5
Benington Rd PE22 ... 126 E3
Benjamin Adlard Com Sch
DN21 ... 197 E2
Benjamin Adlard Prim Sch
DN21 ... 197 E2
Benland PE3 ... 225 A6
Benner Rd PE11 ... 214 E8
Benner Rd Ind Est
PE11 ... 214 E8
Bennett Dr 28 DN15 ... 9 A5
Bennett Rd
Cleethorpes DN35 ... 192 D7
Louth LN11 ... 198 C8
Scunthorpe DN16 ... 185 C7
Bennington Cl
8 Lincoln LN6 ... 205 A7
11 Long Bennington
NG23 ... 117 D3
Bennington La NG23 ... 117 E4
BENNIWORTH LN8 ... 59 B1
Ben's Gate PE12 ... 159 B5
Benson Cl LN6 ... 204 C6
Benson Cres LN6 ... 204 C6
Benson Ct LN11 ... 48 F4
Bentinck Cl 6 PE11 ... 214 C6
Bentinck Sq 2 LN2 ... 202 B3
Bentinck St 4 LN2 ... 202 B3
Bentley Ave PE7 ... 233 E6
Bentley Ct HU3 ... 180 A5
Bentley Dr LN4 ... 205 F3
Bentley La 6 DN38 ... 32 E7
Bentley St
Cleethorpes DN35 ... 192 E6
6 Stamford PE9 ... 219 C6
Bentley Way 1 LN4 ... 95 C4
Benton Cl 6 PE12 ... 157 E1
Benyon Gr PE2 ... 230 B4
Berberis Cl 2 PE6 ... 175 F3
Berea The DN34 ... 191 C5
Beresford Ave PE25 ... 206 C2
Beresford Cl 4 PE25 ... 206 C2
Beresford Cres 5
PE25 ... 206 C2
Beresford Dr 5 LN2 ... 68 F3
Beretun Gn 7 DN18 ... 10 E8
Berilldon Dr LN1 ... 201 C7
Berkeley Ave
Green Hill NG31 ... 210 E6
Lincoln LN6 ... 205 A3
Berkeley Ct 5 NG34 ... 212 E4
Berkeley Dr
4 Bourne PE10 ... 213 C7
Lincoln LN6 ... 205 A3
Berkeley Ind Est DN15 ... 182 C4
Berkeley Inf & Jun Sch
DN15 ... 182 D4
Berkeley Rd
Humberston DN35 ... 193 A2
Peterborough PE3 ... 225 C3
Berkeley St
1 Kingston upon Hull
HU3 ... 180 D8
Scunthorpe DN15 ... 183 A4
Berkshire Dr NG31 ... 211 D7
Bermondsey Dr HU5 ... 179 E8
Bernadette Ave HU4 ... 179 B5
Bernard St LN2 ... 202 B4
Berners Rd DN35 ... 193 B1
Bernicia Dr NG34 ... 212 B2
Berrybut Way 5 PE9 ... 219 D7
Berry Cl 6 NG34 ... 212 D2
Berry Ct PE1 ... 225 E5
Berryfield End 7
NG32 ... 210 A5
Berryman Way HU13 ... 179 A3
Berry Way 5 PE25 ... 206 C3
Bert Allen Dr 1 PE22 ... 114 A1
Bertie Cl
Long Sutton PE12 ... 216 C3
Swinstead NG33 ... 153 A5
Bertie La 8 PE9 ... 172 C6
Bert's Way 7 NG32 ... 128 F7
Berwick Ct DN40 ... 186 C4
Besant Cl 10 PE22 ... 113 B1
BESCABY LE14 ... 138 B1
Bessemer Way DN15 ... 183 B6
Bestall Rd DN32 ... 192 C6
BESTHORPE NG23 ... 91 C7
Besthorpe Cty Prim Sch
NG23 ... 91 C7
Besthorpe Rd
Besthorpe NG23 ... 91 C6
North Scarle NG23 ... 78 D1
Beswick Cl 5 LN6 ... 204 D7
Bethlehem St DN32 ... 191 D7
Bethlem Cres 9 PE24 ... 102 D1
Bethune Ave HU4 ... 179 A3
Bethune Ave W HU13 ... 179 A3
Bethune Pk Prim Sch
HU4 ... 179 B3
Betjeman Cl
Bourne PE10 ... 213 D3
Spalding PE11 ... 214 B4
Betony Cl DN15 ... 182 C6
Bettesworth Rd DN21 ... 54 F8
Bettles Cl PE1 ... 226 A6
Betula Gr 3 LN6 ... 204 D7
Betula Way 1 DN17 ... 184 C5
Beverley Cl 7 DN36 ... 195 D1
Beverley Cres DN32 ... 192 A5
Beverley Ct
12 Healing DN41 ... 23 F5
Westcliffe DN17 ... 184 D7
Beverley Gdns 4 PE9 ... 219 A6
Beverley Gr
Lincoln LN6 ... 204 F3
7 Skegness PE25 ... 206 B3
Beverley Rd HU3 ... 180 D8
Beverstone PE2 ... 229 D5
Bevishall PE4 ... 221 D1
Bew Cl PE2 ... 231 D4
Bewholme Gr 3 HU9 ... 5 D8
Bewick Pl PE7 ... 233 D8
Bexley Ct 10 DN32 ... 189 C1
BICKER PE20 ... 135 A4
Bicker Dro PE20 ... 134 D6
BICKER GAUNTLET
PE20 ... 134 F6
Bicker Prep Sch PE30 ... 135 A4
Bicker Rd PE11 ... 134 F3
Bickleigh Wlk PE3 ... 225 A3
Bidwell La LE15 ... 162 B6
Biergate LN11 ... 49 F7
Bifield PE2 ... 229 F3
BIGBY DN38 ... 21 C2
Bigby Gr DN17 ... 184 F4
Bigby High Rd DN20 ... 196 D2
Bigby Hill DN38 ... 21 C1
Bigby Rd 6 DN20 ... 196 C3
Bigby St DN20 ... 196 C3
Billet La DN15 ... 182 F8
Billet Mill App Rd DN16 ... 19 A4
Billet Mill Rd DN16 ... 183 E1
Billgate La PE24 ... 102 E7
BILLINGBOROUGH
NG34 ... 133 A1
Billingborough Dro
NG34 ... 143 E8
Billingborough Prim Sch
NG34 ... 133 B1
Billingborough Rd
Billingborough NG34 ... 133 B1
Folkingham NG34 ... 132 E1
BILLINGHAY LN4 ... 109 F5
Billinghay CE Prim Sch
LN4 ... 109 F6
Billinghay Cottage* 9
LN4 ... 109 F5
Billinghay Ct DN35 ... 192 F3
Billinghay Dales Head
LN4 ... 110 B4
Billings Gate LN11 ... 50 E5
BILSBY LN13 ... 76 A3
Bilsby Cl LN2 ... 202 A7
BILSBY FIELD LN13 ... 76 A2
Bilsby Rd 2 LN13 ... 75 F3
Bilsdale Gr HU9 ... 181 F8
Bilsdale Rd DN16 ... 185 E5
BINBROOK LN8 ... 47 B4
Binbrook Cl 8 LN6 ... 204 D7
Binbrook (Controlled) Prim
Sch LN8 ... 47 B5
Binbrook La LN8 ... 47 B2
Binbrook Way DN37 ... 190 E8
Bircham Cres DN21 ... 30 C1
Birch Ave
Brigg DN20 ... 196 B4
Grimsby DN34 ... 191 A6
Birch Cl
28 Brough HU15 ... 2 C5
11 Coningsby LN4 ... 207 D4
Hessle HU13 ... 178 B3
Kingston upon Hull HU5 ... 179 B7
1 Lincoln LN6 ... 204 F2
Wyberton PE21 ... 136 E7
Birch Croft 31 HU15 ... 2 C6
Birchdale 31 DN18 ... 10 E8
Birch Dr DN17 ... 185 D4
Birchen Cl PE7 ... 230 C3
Birches The 8 DN9 ... 27 A2
Birchfield Rd 8 DN9 ... 27 D6
Birch Gr
Gainsborough DN21 ... 197 D6
Spalding PE11 ... 214 F3
Birchin Way DN31 ... 188 D1
Birch La 4 LN9 ... 85 E7
Birch Leigh HU3 ... 180 C6
Birch Rd
Louth LN11 ... 198 E5
6 Stamford PE9 ... 218 D7
Birchtree Ave PE1 ... 226 A7
Birch Tree Cl 4 DN3 ... 14 A4
Birch Way DN38 ... 21 C5
Birch Way Ind Est
DN31 ... 188 D1
BIRCHWOOD LN6 ... 204 D7
Birchwood PE2 ... 230 A3
Birchwood Ave
Birchwood LN6 ... 200 D1
Kingston upon Hull HU5 ... 179 A7
Birchwood Cl 4 NG31 ... 210 F7
Birch Wood Cl 14 DN18 ... 3 E1
Birchwood Jun Sch
LN6 ... 204 C8
Birchwood Rd
Scunthorpe DN16 ... 185 A4
1 Sleaford NG34 ... 212 D6
Birchwood Sh Ctr LN6 ... 204 C8
Birchwood View 2
DN21 ... 197 F5
Birdcroft La DN10 ... 40 A3
Birds Dro PE11 ... 145 C4
Bird's Dro
Gorefield PE13 ... 169 D1
Sutton St James PE12 ... 169 B8
Birds Holt Cl LN6 ... 200 A3
Birds Wood Nature
Reserve* DN9 ... 26 F4
Birkbeck Sch & Com Arts
Coll LN11 ... 50 E7
Birkdale
Lincoln LN5 ... 205 D1
9 Waltham DN37 ... 194 C4
Birkdale Ave 1 PE4 ... 221 A3
Birkdale Cl
3 Grantham NG31 ... 211 D7
Heighington/Washingborough
LN4 ... 203 E1
Kingston upon Hull
HU10 ... 178 B8
1 Skegness PE25 ... 206 D6
8 Spalding PE11 ... 214 C2
8 Woodhall Spa LN10 ... 97 C5
Birkdale Dr 3 DN40 ... 186 D5
Birkdale Rd DN17 ... 184 D3
Birkdale Way HU9 ... 181 D8
Birketts La LN11 ... 49 D5
BIRKHOLME NG33 ... 152 B6
Birkland La NG23 ... 78 D5
Birkwood PE22 ... 98 E2
Birkwood La PE22 ... 98 E3
Birmingham Cl 5
NG31 ... 210 E5
Birrel St DN21 ... 197 B6
BIRTHORPE NG34 ... 143 A8
Birthorpe Rd NG34 ... 143 A8
BISCATHORPE LN11 ... 59 D3
Biscay Cl 1 PE25 ... 206 A6
Bishop Alexander Prim Sch
NG24 ... 104 A6
Bishop Blunt Cl 2
HU13 ... 178 F1
BISHOPBRIDGE LN8 ... 44 C1
Bishop Burton Coll
DN20 ... 19 E3
Bishop Cockin Cl
HU13 ... 179 A1
Bishop Creighton Prim Sch
PE1 ... 226 B2
Bishopdale Cl NG31 ... 129 F5
Bishop Grosseteste Coll
LN1 ... 201 F6
Bishop Gurdon Cl 4
HU13 ... 178 F1
Bishop Kempthorne Cl 3
HU13 ... 178 F1
Bishop King CE (Aided)
Prim Sch LN5 ... 201 F1
Bishop King Ct 7 LN5 ... 201 F1
Bishop La HU1 ... 181 A6
Bishop La Staithe HU2 ... 181 A6
BISHOP NORTON LN8 ... 43 D3
Bishop Norton Rd LN8 ... 43 E1
Bishops Cl
6 Bourne PE10 ... 213 E4
Louth LN11 ... 198 E6
Peterborough PE1 ... 226 D5
Bishops Ct 3 NG34 ... 212 D5
Bishopsfield PE4 ... 221 B1
Bishop's La LN8 ... 47 D7
Bishop's Pal The* LN2 ... 234 B3
Bishop's Pl 5 LN2 ... 68 C6
Bishops Rd
Leasingham NG34 ... 121 B7
Lincoln LN2 ... 202 C5
Bishop's Rd PE1 ... 226 A1
Bishops Wlk 5 PE9 ... 172 D3
Bishop's Wlk 1 DN34 ... 191 C6
Bishop Temple Ct
HU13 ... 178 F3
Bishopthorpe Rd DN35 ... 192 F3
BITCHFIELD NG33 ... 141 B3
Bittern Cl HU4 ... 179 D2
Bittern Way
3 Birchwood LN6 ... 204 D8
Wyberton PE21 ... 136 F8
BJ's Leisure Ctr PE25 ... 90 E3
Black Bank DN17 ... 29 A6
Black Bear La PE13 ... 170 F1
Blackberry Cl 9 LN6 ... 93 A8
Blackberry Way 3
NG24 ... 104 C1
Blackbourn Cl 20 NG23 ... 91 D5
Blackbourn Rd LN6 ... 205 C6
Blackbrook Rd 4
NG24 ... 104 B5
Blackburn Ave HU15 ... 2 C5
Blackburn Cl 2 NG31 ... 210 D5
Blackburn La DN22 ... 52 D3
Black Dike PE13 ... 169 E6
Blackdown Garth PE4 ... 221 B3
Black Dro
Anwick LN4 ... 109 D2
Baston PE6 ... 165 B8
Ewerby & Evedon NG34 ... 122 E8
Midville PE22 ... 100 D2
Thorney PE6 ... 175 F5
Wisbech St Mary PE13 ... 177 B4
Black Dyke PE13 ... 169 F4
Blackdykes Rd DN9 ... 28 B4
Blackey La PE22 ... 99 B4
Black Fen La LN4 ... 82 C4
Blackfiars Ct LN2 ... 202 E6
Blackfriargate HU1 ... 181 A5
Blackfriars Rd LN2 ... 202 E6
Blackfriars St 15 PE9 ... 219 C5
Blackfriars Wlk LN2 ... 202 E6
Blackhill La LN9 ... 73 F1
Black Hole Dro PE11 ... 155 F8
Black Horse Dr 8 LN6 ... 93 A8
BLACKJACK PE20 ... 135 E6
Blackjack Rd PE20 ... 135 C6
Black La
Doddington & Whisby
LN6 ... 79 E3
Gorefield PE13 ... 169 C2
Blackmead PE2 ... 230 B4
Blackmoor Rd
Aubourn Haddington & South
Hykeham LN5 ... 93 C5
Haxey DN9 ... 27 D2
Black Prince Ave PE6 ... 217 B6
Black's Cl 17 LN5 ... 93 F7
Blacksmith Hill DN15 ... 1 E3
Blacksmith La
Boothby Graffoe LN5 ... 94 A2
East Keal PE23 ... 100 D6
2 Harmston LN5 ... 93 F5
Thorpe on the Hill LN6 ... 92 E8
Blacksmith Rd 4 LN3 ... 82 A7
Blacksmith Row 1 LN5 ... 92 F3
Blacksmiths Cl 2 DN19 ... 11 C7
Blacksmith's Cnr 5
LN4 ... 207 A5
Blacksmiths Ct 10 LN4 ... 95 C4
Blacksmiths La
North Scarle LN6 ... 78 E1
Welby NG32 ... 130 F5
Blacksmith's La
13 Navenby/Wellingore
LN5 ... 107 A7
Norton Disney LN6 ... 92 B2
Blacksmith's Row
PE11 ... 156 B7
Black Swan Spinney
PE8 ... 222 A4
Blackthorn 5 PE9 ... 218 C7
Blackthorn Cl
1 Gainsborough
DN21 ... 197 F5
1 Lincoln LN2 ... 202 C8
3 Market Deeping PE6 ... 217 D6
13 Ruskington NG34 ... 108 E1
Scunthorpe DN15 ... 182 C6
Blackthorn Ct 4 HU3 ... 180 D6
Blackthorn La
Boston PE21 ... 209 C5
Cammeringham LN1 ... 54 E1
Kingston upon Hull HU10 ... 178 F7
Blackthorns The
4 Broughton DN20 ... 19 D4
6 Sleaford NG34 ... 212 D3
Blackthorn Way PE10 ... 213 E5
Blackwell Rd PE7 ... 230 C2
Bladon Est PE21 ... 209 F4
Bladons Wlk HU10 ... 178 D8
Blaides Staithe 1
HU1 ... 181 A6
Blair Wlk DN40 ... 186 E3
Blake Ave DN17 ... 184 E7
Blake Cl 2 HU2 ... 180 E7
Blakeney Lea 4 DN35 ... 192 F1
Blanchard Cl PE10 ... 142 F2
Blanchard Rd LN11 ... 198 E3
Blandford Gdns 6
PE1 ... 226 E7
Blands Hill LN8 ... 47 D5
Blanket Row HU1 ... 180 F5
BLANKNEY LN4 ... 95 D3
Blankney Cl 4 LN1 ... 66 D2
Blankney Cres LN2 ... 201 F8
Blankney Ct 13 DN15 ... 9 A5
Blankney Dro LN10 ... 96 E5
Blankney N Dro LN4 ... 96 B5
Blashfield Cl 2 PE9 ... 219 A6
Blasson Way 12 NG34 ... 133 B1
Blatherwick Rd NG24 ... 104 B4
Blaydon Gr 1 DN34 ... 190 E4
Blazegate PE12 ... 216 B8
BLEASBY LN8 ... 58 A3
BLEASBY MOOR LN3 ... 57 F2
Bledwick Dro PE13 ... 170 C3
Blenheim Cl
17 Hatfield DN7 ... 14 D3
Louth LN11 ... 198 B7
Skellingthorpe LN6 ... 79 F6
Blenheim Ct DN16 ... 185 A2
Blenheim Pl DN35 ... 192 E4
Blenheim Rd
Coningsby LN4 ... 207 C4
Lincoln LN1 ... 201 D4
Moorland Prison DN7 ... 26 A8
Blenheim St HU5 ... 180 B8
Blenheim Way
Londonthorpe & Harrowby
without NG31 ... 211 D3
Market Deeping PE6 ... 217 B7
Yaxley PE7 ... 233 E5
Blenkin St HU9 ... 181 B7
Blind La
Coleby LN5 ... 93 F3
Hough-on-the-Hill NG32 ... 118 E7
4 Maxey PE6 ... 173 C7
22 Waddington LN5 ... 93 F7
Bloomfield Ave HU5 ... 179 C8
Bloom La DN15 ... 8 C1
Bloomsbury Ct 1 HU3 ... 180 D6
Bloomsbury Gdns
DN33 ... 191 B2
Blossom Ct PE3 ... 225 B8
Blossom Way 1 DN40 ... 186 B3
Blow Row DN9 ... 27 E6
Blow's La PE20 ... 135 F3
BLOXHOLM LN4 ... 108 C4
Bloxholm La
Blankney LN4 ... 95 A2
Bracebridge Heath LN4 ... 81 B1
Nocton LN4 ... 94 D6
Bluebell Ave PE1 ... 226 A8
Bluebell Cl
7 Lincoln LN5 ... 205 C2
Scunthorpe DN15 ... 183 C3
Bluebell Ct 23 DN41 ... 23 F5
Bluebell Gr 1 DN20 ... 196 B4
Bluebell Rd 2 PE9 ... 218 D7
Bluebells 8 PE6 ... 217 D6
Bluebells The PE12 ... 215 A6
Bluebell Wlk PE21 ... 208 B4
Blueberry Ct HU4 ... 179 C4
Bluecoat Prim Sch
PE9 ... 219 B6
Bluegate NG31 ... 211 A5
Blue Gowt Dro PE11 ... 214 A7
Blue Gowt La PE11 ... 214 B7
Blue St 7 PE21 ... 208 E4
Bluestone Cl DN32 ... 192 A8

Bluestone Heath Rd
Scamblesby LN11 73 A7
Skendleby PE23 88 D5
South Ormsby cum Ketsby LN11 74 B3
South Thoresby LN13 75 A1
Tetford LN11 73 F3
Ulceby with Fordington LN13 88 B8
Welton le Wold LN11 60 A4
Bluestone La DN40 186 B4
Bluestone Rise LN11 198 B4
Bluestone Way 24 LN12 77 A7
Blundell Ave DN35 189 E1
Blundell Pk (Grimsby Town FC) DN35 192 C8
BLYBOROUGH DN21 42 E5
Blyth Ct 28 DN18 10 F8
Blyth St 2 HU9 181 B7
Blyth Way DN37 23 E2
BLYTON DN21 41 C5
Blyton Cl 11 LN6 204 C7
Blyton cum Laughron Prim Sch DN21 41 C6
Blyton Gr 13 LN6 204 C7
Blyton Rd
12 Birchwood LN6 204 C7
Laughton DN21 41 B8
Thonock DN21 197 C8
Boardsides
Frampton PE20 124 F2
Wyberton PE21 208 A3
Boating Dyke Way 19 DN8 15 A8
Boatswain Croft 7 HU1 180 F5
Bobbin La LN2 202 E6
Bodiam Way DN32 191 F8
Bodmin Cl DN17 184 D8
Bodmin Moor Cl LN6 204 D1
Boggle La LN8 45 E5
BOLE DN22 52 C5
Boleyn Ave PE2 230 C8
Bolingbroke Castle (remains of)★ PE23 100 A7
Bolingbroke Rd
Cleethorpes DN35 193 A3
Louth LN11 198 B8
Scunthorpe DN17 184 E4
Bolsover Rd DN15 182 B2
Bolton Ave LN6 205 A3
Bolton's La PE25 90 D2
Bomber Cty Aviation Mus★ DN21 42 F1
Bon Accord Rd HU13 178 E1
Bona La PE13 169 E1
BONBY DN20 10 C2
Bonby Gr
2 Grimsby DN33 191 A3
Scunthorpe DN17 184 F5
Bonby Rd DN20 10 C1
Bond Hays La 3 PE23 87 A4
Bond St
1 Boston PE21 208 F4
Kingston upon Hull HU1 180 F7
Bonemill La NG34 121 E6
Bonnetable Rd LN9 199 D3
Bonnyhale Rd DN17 16 E6
BONTHORPE LN13 89 B7
Bonthorpe Rd LN13 89 B7
Boongate PE1 226 C3
Boonground La PE22 115 A3
Bootham Cl 6 DN7 14 D4
Bootham Cres 12 DN7 14 C6
Bootham La DN7 14 D5
Bootham Rd 11 DN7 14 C6
Boothby Cl 14 PE20 136 C5
BOOTHBY GRAFFOE LN5 94 A2
BOOTHBY PAGNELL NG33 140 E5
Boothby Pagnell Manor House★ NG33 140 E5
Boothferry Rd HU13 178 B2
Booth Nooking La DN15 2 A2
Boot La PE20 136 E3
Borman's La 7 DN36 36 B1
Borrowdale Cl PE4 221 C3
Borrowdale Way NG31 211 B8
Borthwick Pl PE2 229 D6
Bos App Rd DN16 185 F7
Boscombe Cl 12 LN6 204 C6
BOSTON PE21 209 C6
Boston Aerodrome PE21 125 B2
Boston Carlton Rd Prim Sch PE21 208 E5
Boston Coll (De Montfort Campus) PE21 209 B3
Boston Coll (Rochford Campus) PE21 209 A4
Boston Coll (Sam Newson Centre) PE21 208 F4
Boston Ent Pk PE21 208 A4
Boston Gram Sch PE21 209 A4
Boston Hawthorn Tree Sch PE21 209 D4
Boston High Sch for Girls PE21 209 B7
BOSTON LONG HEDGES PE22 126 B6
Boston Long Hedges PE22 126 C6
Boston Rd
Algarkirk PE20 136 A3
Frithville PE22 125 E7
Gosberton PE11 145 C6
Heckington NG34 122 E2
Holbeach PE12 215 C4
Horncastle LN9 199 C1
Sleaford NG34 212 D4
14 Spilsby PE23 88 A1
Swineshead PE20 124 D1
Wainfleet St Mary PE24 102 D1
Boston Rd N PE12 215 C5
Boston Rd Pits Nature Reserve★ PE11 145 C6
Boston Rd S PE12 215 D3
Boston Sta PE21 208 E5
Boston Stump (St Botolph's Ch)★ PE21 208 F5
Boston Trade Pk PE21 208 F6
BOSTON WEST PE20 125 B4
Boston W Prim Sch PE21 208 B5
Boswell Cl PE1 225 E8
Boswell Dr LN6 205 A5
Bosworth Cl 18 DN7 14 D3
Botany Bay La DN3 14 B4
Bothwell Gr 3 HU9 5 E8
Botolph Gn PE2 230 C7
Botolph St 7 PE21 209 A5
Botolph's View 1 LN11 51 C4
Botteford Jun & Inf Schools DN16 185 A2
BOTTESFORD
Bottesford NG13 128 A6
Scunthorpe DN16 185 B3
Bottesford Ave DN16 185 B5
Bottesford Cl 12 LN6 204 D8
Bottesford La DN16 185 B4
Bottesford Rd
Allington NG32 128 E6
Scunthorpe DN16 185 B5
Bottesford Sports Ctr DN17 184 C3
Bottesford Sta NG13 128 B6
Bottle La PE13 169 C7
Bottlings The 8 DN20 196 C3
Bottom St NG32 128 F7
BOUGHTON NG34 122 C4
Boughton Ave DN15 182 F4
Boulevard HU3 180 B5
Boulevard Ave DN31 188 E1
Boulevard Gdns DN31 191 B8
Boulevard Ret Pk PE1 225 D7
Boulevard The 23 LN12 64 B3
Boulevard Way DN31 191 B7
Boulevard Wlk DN31 191 B8
BOULTHAM LN5 205 D8
Boultham Ave LN5 201 D1
Boultham Mere Nature Reserve★ LN6 201 B3
BOULTHAM MOOR LN6 205 B6
Boultham Pk Rd LN6 201 D1
Boundaries The PE12 215 D1
Boundary La LN6 93 A8
Boundary Paddock 1 LN5 107 A7
Boundary Pastures NG34 212 D3
Boundary Rd DN33 194 E6
Boundary St LN5 205 D7
Boundry Wlk LN8 56 F3
Bourges Bvd PE1 225 D7
Burgess Ret Pk PE3 225 F1
BOURNE PE10 213 C7
Bourne Abbey Prim Sch PE10 213 E5
Bourne Cl LN6 205 B5
Bourne Dro PE10 155 A5
Bourne Gram Sch PE10 213 D4
Bourne La 7 NG34 108 D2
Bourne Outdoor Swimming Pool PE10 213 D4
Bourne Rd
20 Alford LN13 75 F2
Baston PE6 164 E3
Bourne PE10 213 E2
Colsterworth NG33 151 E6
Essendine PE9 163 E3
Folkingham NG34 142 D8
Morton PE10 154 C6
Old Somerby NG33 140 D8
Pinchbeck PE11 155 F5
Spalding PE11 214 A3
Swinstead NG33 153 A5
Thurlby PE10 164 D8
Bourne Rd Est 6 NG33 151 E6
Bourne Skills Ctr PE10 213 D5
Bourne St HU2 181 A7
Bourne Westfield Prim Sch PE10 213 B5
Bovill Cl DN31 191 C7
Bowbridge Gdns 4 NG13 128 A6
Bowbridge La
10 Bottesford NG13 128 A6
Hawton NG24 104 A1
Bowbridge Rd NG24 104 A2
Bowden Dr LN6 205 A5
Bowditch Rd PE11 214 E3
Bower Cl PE1 226 C5
Bowers Ave
Grimsby DN31 191 B7
3 Louth LN11 198 D7
Bowfield Cl DN37 190 D8
Bow Gate PE11 145 B6
Bowlalley La 9 HU1 180 F6
Bowl Alley La LN9 199 C4
Bowling Gn La
11 Crowle DN17 16 D8
Grantham NG31 211 B3
3 Grimsby DN32 191 E7
Bowling Gn Rd DN21 197 B5
Bowling La DN35 192 E6
Bowman Ave PE22 115 A6
Bowman Cl PE21 208 D6
Bowmandale 30 DN18 10 E8
Bowmandale Prim Sch DN18 10 E8
Bowmans Ridge 1 PE23 87 F1
Bowmans Way NG32 128 F4
Bowman Way 7 DN40 186 B3
Bowness Way 1 PE4 221 D2
Bow Rd HU15 2 E6
Boxer Rd PE8 172 B1
Boxgrove Cl 8 PE6 175 A1
Boyfields 1 PE11 145 A8
Boynton Cres 9 DN15 9 A5
Boynton St 1 HU3 180 C4
Bozeat Way PE3 225 C6
Brabbs Ave 4 DN7 14 E4
BRACEBOROUGH PE9 164 B4
BRACEBRIDGE LN5 205 D6
BRACEBRIDGE HEATH LN4 205 E3
Bracebridge Inf Sch LN5 205 E6
BRACEBY NG34 131 D2
Braceby Rd NG33 131 B1
Brackenborough Ct LN11 198 C7
Brackenborough Rd
Brackenborough with Little Grimsby LN11 49 C1
Keddington LN11 61 C8
Louth LN11 198 C8
Brackenburry Way PE21 208 E8
Brackenbury Cl LN9 199 A3
Brackenbury Fields NG33 140 F6
Bracken Cl
Gainsborough DN21 197 B7
Leasingham NG34 121 C7
Bracken Heen Cl 2 DN7 14 E4
Brackenhill Rd DN9 27 E2
Brackenholmes Rd DN15 9 A2
Bracken La PE24 90 A7
Bracken Pk DN33 194 E8
Bracken Pl DN37 190 C6
Bracken Rd LN6 92 B7
Bracken Way LN11 198 C7
Brackley Cl
Bourne PE10 213 D7
Peterborough PE3 225 D3
Brackwood PE2 229 D6
BRACON DN9 16 F2
Bracon Cl 9 DN9 16 E2
Bradbury Ave LN5 205 C2
Bradden St PE3 225 C6
Bradegate Dr PE1 226 E7
Bradford Ave DN35 193 A5
Bradford Cl 10 NG31 210 D5
Bradford Rd
Boston PE21 208 D3
Immingham DN40 186 B4
Brading Ave NG31 210 E4
BRADLEY DN37 190 E2
Bradley Cl LN11 198 D3
Bradley & Dixon Woods Nature Reserve★ DN37 194 A8
Bradley La LE15 162 B7
Bradley Rd
Bradley DN37 194 B6
Grimsby DN37 190 E2
Bradley St DN32 191 F7
Bradman Ct 17 DN32 189 C1
Bradshaw's La PE24 90 C7
Bradshaws Terr PE21 209 A5
Bradway 9 LN1 66 D7
Bradwell Cl 19 DN18 10 E8
Bradwell Rd PE3 225 A2
Brady St 1 PE21 208 E6
Braeburn Ave 14 PE13 170 D2
Braemar Cl
Grantham NG31 211 C7
1 Middle Rasen LN8 57 B8
Stamford PE9 218 E6
Braemar Rd
Cleethorpes DN35 192 E4
3 Mablethorpe/Sutton on Sea LN12 76 F8
Braemer Rd NG23 91 D4
Braeton La DN33 195 A7
Braids Wlk HU10 178 B8
Brailsford Cl 3 PE3 225 A4
BRAITHWAITE DN7 14 A7
Braithwaite La DN7 14 A8
Bramar Rd 5 DN7 14 D4
Brambleberry La PE24 102 B7
Bramble Cl
Grimsby DN31 191 C7
4 Welton/Dunholme LN2 68 D7
Bramble Ct 24 LN2 68 D2
Bramble Gr 2 PE9 218 D6
Bramble Grange 3 PE11 214 B5
Bramble Hills PE25 103 E3
Brambles The
3 Barrow upon Humber DN19 11 C8
Bourne PE10 213 D7
Grantham NG31 211 A2
Holbeach PE12 215 F2
4 Market Deeping PE6 217 D6
15 Market Rasen LN8 57 D8
Newton on Trent LN1 65 D1
Bramble Way
2 Brigg DN20 196 B4
Humberston DN36 192 E1
Bramblewood Cl 6 NG31 210 F8
Brambling Wlk PE10 143 A3
Bramhall St DN35 192 C7
Bramley Cl
1 Barton-upon-Humber DN18 3 F1
5 Bourne PE10 213 C6
8 Fleet PE12 159 C7
2 Heckington NG34 122 E2
4 Louth LN11 198 C5
Bramley Cres DN16 185 A3
Bramley Ct
Gainsborough DN21 197 F5
Lincoln LN6 204 F4
Bramley Gr 1 DN21 29 C3
Bramley La 6 PE21 208 E4
Bramley Mdws 7 PE12 159 D7
Bramley Rd
Market Deeping PE6 217 B5
11 Wisbech PE13 170 D1
Bramley Wlk PE25 206 C6
Bramling Way NG34 212 F4
BRAMPTON LN1 65 E6
Brampton Ct PE2 231 D6
Brampton Way DN35 192 D3
Bramwith La DN7 14 A6
Brancaster Dr
Lincoln LN6 205 C8
Skegness PE25 206 D5
Brancepeth Pl PE2 230 E7
Branches La PE12 159 A7
BRAND END PE22 126 D4
Brand End Rd PE22 126 E4
Brandesburton St HU3 180 B7
BRANDON NG32 118 D7
Brandon Rd
Hough-on-the-Hill NG32 118 E6
Scunthorpe DN15 182 D2
Stubton NG23 118 C7
Brandy Wharf Cider Ctr★ DN21 44 A7
Brankwell Cres DN17 184 E3
BRANSBY LN1 66 E6
Bransby Home of Rest for Horses★ LN1 66 D6
Bransdale Gr HU9 181 F8
Bransdale Rd 5 DN16 185 D5
Bransdale Way DN37 190 E8
BRANSTON
Branston and Mere LN4 81 E2
Croxton Kerrial NG32 138 A4
BRANSTON BOOTHS LN4 82 C4
Branston Causeway LN3 82 F3
Branston CE Inf Sch LN4 81 D2
Branston Cl
Lincoln LN6 205 B4
4 Winthorpe NG24 104 B7
Branston Com Coll LN4 81 E2
Branston Jun Sch LN4 81 E2
Branston La LN4 94 D7
Branston Rd LN4 81 E3
BRANT BROUGHTON LN5 105 F5
Brant Broughton CE Methodist Prim Sch LN5 105 F5
BRANTINGHAM HU15 2 C8
Brantingham Rd HU15 2 B7
Brant Rd
Fulbeck NG32 105 F1
Lincoln LN5 205 D2
Scunthorpe DN15 182 E2
Waddington LN5 93 D7
Brassey Cl PE1 225 E6
BRATOFT PE24 102 B7
Bratoft Cnr PE24 102 D7
Bratoft End PE24 102 C5
Brats La LN8 47 E5
Bratt Field Rd DN21 53 F8
BRATTLEBY LN1 67 C8
Brattleby Cres LN2 201 F7
Brauncewell Cl 18 NG34 108 D2
Brauncewell Rd 6 NG34 107 C1
Bray Ave 8 LN12 64 C2
Braybrook PE2 230 A3
Braybrook Prim Sch PE2 230 B4
Braybrooks Way 1 PE12 157 E1
Bray Cl DN33 191 B2
Brayfields 8 PE11 156 F8
Brayford St LN5 234 A2
Brayford Waterfront LN1 234 A2
Brayford Way 1 LN1 234 A2
Brayford Wharf E LN5 234 A1
Brayford Wharf N LN1 234 A2
Braygate La PE23 100 E5
Brazenose La PE9 219 C5
Brazil St HU9 181 C8
Breakneck La LN11 198 A5
Brecks La
Kirk Sandall DN3 14 A2
Stapleford LN6 105 C8
Brecon Cl NG31 210 D8
Brecon Way NG34 212 B3
Breda Ct 8 PE11 214 A2
Breedon Dr LN1 201 D7
Breezemount Ct 2 DN7 14 C6
Brellows Hill 7 PE34 161 F3
Bremerhaven Way DN33 190 F3
Brendon Cl NG31 210 D8
Brendon Garth 4 PE4 221 C1
Brendon Wlk 5 PE11 214 C6
Brent Rd LN4 110 E8
Brentwood Cl HU15 2 B6
Brereton Ave DN35 192 C8
Brethergate DN9 27 B2
BRETTON PE3 225 A6
Bretton Cl 4 DN7 14 D3
Bretton Ctr PE3 225 A5
Bretton Gate 2 PE3 225 A5
Bretton Gn 1 PE3 225 A5
Bretton Way
Bretton PE3 225 A7
3 Peterborough PE3 220 F1
Bretton Woods Com Sch PE3 225 A6
Brewerne PE2 230 B4
Brewers La PE13 170 A5
Brewery Gdns 2 DN17 16 D8
Brewery Hill NG31 211 B3
Brewery La NG34 143 B8
Brewery Rd DN17 16 D8
Brewery St 6 PE24 102 E8
Brewhouse Gall★ NG31 211 A1
Brewster Ave
Immingham DN40 186 D3
Peterborough PE2 230 F8
Brewster Ave Inf Sch PE2 230 F8
Brewster La PE24 102 C2
Brewster Rd PE21 209 B4
Breydon Ct 3 DN15 8 B4
Brian Ave
Cleethorpes DN35 192 D3
Scunthorpe DN16 185 C5
7 Skegness PE25 206 C4
Waltham DN37 194 D4
Briar Cl
6 Birchwood LN6 200 C1
5 Lincoln LN6 93 A8
Skegness PE25 206 C3
2 Sleaford NG34 212 D2
4 South Killingholme DN40 12 E3
Briar La
Grimsby DN33 194 D8
Healing DN41 23 F5
Briars La 6 DN7 14 C7
Briars The HU13 178 E3
Briar Way
Peterborough PE1 226 C5
Scunthorpe DN15 182 C6
Skegness PE25 206 C2
Briar Wlk PE10 213 D7
Briarwood Cl 6 NG31 210 F7
Brickberry Cl PE7 230 C2
Bricken Field La LN9 84 C8
Brickenhole La 7 DN10 39 F3
Brickings Way 4 DN22 52 B3
Brick La
North Killingholme DN40 12 E5
Wrangle PE22 114 C1
Brickyard La
Folkingham NG34 142 D8
Hundleby PE23 87 E1
Mablethorpe & Sutton LN12 76 E8
Melton HU14 2 F4
Navenby LN5 94 A1
Theddlethorpe St Helen LN12 63 F7
Walkeringham DN10 39 E3
Bridge Cl
Kingston upon Hull HU9 181 D6
3 Louth LN11 198 C6
Bridge Dro PE13 177 B7
Bridge End
Colsterworth NG33 151 D7
Wansford PE8 222 A3
Bridge End Causeway NG34 133 F3
Bridge End Gr NG31 211 D2
Bridge End Rd NG31 211 C2
Bridge Foot PE6 217 B4
Bridgegate Dr HU9 181 C6
Bridge Gdns 1 DN31 188 D1
Bridgehill Rd PE6 221 D6
Bridge La
Cadney DN20 31 C6
Horkstow DN18 9 F5
Scopwick LN4 108 D8
Bridge Pl 22 LN1 66 D2
Bridge Rd
Aubourn Haddington & South Hykeham LN5 92 F5
Gainsborough DN21 197 D3
Greetham with Somersby LN9 86 F7
Long Sutton PE12 216 D3
4 Sutton Bridge PE12 160 F4
Bridge St N 1 DN32 189 B1

Bridges Rd DN17......184 E7
Bridge St
3 Billinghay LN4.....109 F5
2 Boston PE21.....208 F4
Brigg DN20.........196 A3
Gainsborough DN21...197 C3
Grantham NG31.....211 C3
Horncastle LN9......199 B4
Louth LN11.........198 B6
Market Deeping PE6...217 D4
Marston NG32........118 D2
19 Nettleham LN2.....68 C2
2 Peterborough PE1...226 A1
4 Ryhall PE9........163 C1
Saxilby LN1.........66 D2
27 Thorne/Moorends
DN8.............15 A8
Bridges The 24 DN18...10 F8
Bridge View LN8......56 F8
Bridgeview Sch HU13..178 D1
Bridgewater Rd DN17..184 D8
Bridle Cl
Fishtoft PE21.......209 C3
7 Sleaford NG34....212 D2
Bridles The 11 DN19...12 A8
Bridle Way 7 DN7....70 D5
Bridle Way The LN4...95 B7
Bridlington Ave HU2...180 F8
Bridport Wlk DN17....184 C8
Brierholme Carr Rd
DN7...............14 F5
Brierholme Cl DN7.....14 F5
Brierholme Ings Rd
DN7...............14 F5
BRIGG DN20.........196 E4
Briggate Dr 19 DN17...29 D7
Brigg Cl 6 LN6......204 C6
Brigg Dr HU13.......178 F3
Brigg Gr 5 LN6.....204 C6
Brigg La LN5.........105 F8
Brigg Prep Sch DN20..196 C3
Brigg Prim Sch DN20..196 C4
Brigg Rd
Barton-upon-Humber
DN18.............10 E5
Broughton DN20.....19 E3
Cadney DN20.........31 D7
Grasby LN7..........33 A6
Hibaldstow DN20.....30 F6
North Kelsey LN7.....32 A5
Scawby DN20........30 F8
Scunthorpe DN16....183 D2
South Kelsey LN7.....32 A1
Wrawby DN20.......196 F5
Brigg Sta DN20......196 C2
Brighowgate DN32....191 D6
Brighton St
2 Cleethorpes DN35...193 A5
Kingston upon Hull HU3.180 A3
Bright St
2 Gainsborough
DN21...........197 C4
Kingston upon Hull HU8.181 B8
Peterborough PE1....225 F4
BRIGSLEY DN37......35 D4
Brigsley Rd DN37.....194 D2
Brigsley Ct PE3......225 C6
Brigstock Rd PE13....170 C1
Brimbles Way PE2....229 E5
Bringhurst PE2.......230 A4
Brinkhall Way 9 LN2..68 D7
BRINKHILL LN11......87 C8
Brinkhill Pottery* LN11.87 B8
Brinkle Spring La LN4..82 A4
Brisbane Cl
5 Skegness PE25.....206 A4
12 Waddington LN5...93 E8
Brisbane St HU3.....180 D5
Bristol Arc 16 DN34..212 D4
Bristol Ave PE4.....220 F3
Bristol Cl
14 Beacon Hill NG24..104 C5
Grantham NG31......210 E4
Bristol Dr LN6.......205 C8
Bristol House Rd NG34.107 C1
Bristol Rd
Kingston upon Hull
HU5.............179 C8
Scunthorpe DN17....182 C1
Bristol Way NG34....212 B5
Bristow Rd
3 Cranwell & Byard's Leap
NG34...........120 E8
Cranwell NG34......107 E1
Bristows Yd NG32....118 D2
Britannia Cres DN34..190 D5
Britannia Gdns 3
PE11............214 C5
Britannia Terr 4
DN21...........197 D3
Briton Ct 11 PE11....214 C4
Brittain Dr NG31.....211 C5
Britton Cl DN17.......7 D3
Brixham Ct
Grimsby DN33.......194 E6
5 Kingston upon Hull
HU3............180 A5
Broach Rd LN5......106 E1
Broadacre Pk 2 HU15..2 D5
Broadbank LN1.......198 B6
Broadbeck 7 DN21...43 D7
Broadbent Theatre*
LN3..............69 E8
Broad Cl PE1........226 D5
Broad Dale Cl 4 LN2..68 F3
Broad Dro PE11......144 B5
Broad Dro E PE13....169 E6

Broad Dro W PE13....169 B4
Broad Fen La NG23...104 D1
Broadfield La 8 PE21..208 E4
Broadfield La Ind Est
PE21............208 E3
Broadfield St PE21....208 E4
Broadgate
Gedney PE12........159 D6
Lincoln LN2.........234 B2
Whaplode PE12......168 A3
Broad Gate
Sutton St James PE12..169 A8
Weston PE12........157 C1
Wrangle PE22........114 C3
Broadgate Dro PE12..167 C8
Broadgate La PE6....217 F4
Broadgate Rd
South Witham NG33...151 E2
Sutton St Edmund PE12.168 F3
BROADHOLME LN1...66 C1
Broadholme Rd LN1...66 D1
Broadhurst Rd 18 PE8..172 B1
Broadings La DN22....65 A4
Broad La
Bicker PE20.........135 B4
Moulton PE12.......157 F6
South Leverton DN22..65 A7
Sutterton PE20......135 F1
Whaplode PE12......146 F1
Broadlands Ave PE10..213 C7
Broadlands Cl 1 DN7..14 D3
Broadlands The PE1...226 E5
Broadley Ave HU10...178 D6
Broadley Cl 6 HU9...181 C7
Broadley Cres LN11...198 E6
Broadley Croft 5 HU15.2 D5
Broadley Way 8 HU15..2 D5
Broad St
5 Grantham NG31....211 A5
Spalding PE11.......214 D4
Stamford PE9.......219 B5
Broadsyke La NG24...105 A4
Broadwater Dr 3 DN7..14 D3
Broadwater La PE12...158 A4
Broadway
Ashby DN16.........185 B6
Crowland PE6.......175 B8
Farcet PE7..........231 C1
3 Grimsby DN34....190 D4
Hatfield DN7.........14 C3
2 Keelby DN41.......23 A5
Lincoln LN2.........201 F6
Mablethorpe/Sutton on Sea
LN12...........77 A8
Peterborough PE1....226 A3
Spalding PE11.......214 A2
Yaxley PE7..........233 E5
Broadway Cl
11 Bourne PE10.....213 C7
4 Lincoln LN2.......201 F6
Broadway Ct 5 PE1...226 A2
Broadway Gdns PE1...226 B5
Broadway Nook 1 DN7.14 C3
Broadway The
Morton PE10........154 B7
Woodhall Spa LN10...97 D6
Broadway Theatre*
PE1............226 A2
Broad Wheel Rd PE6..173 B3
Brock Cl 1 DN33.....191 C2
Brockenhurst Cl LN6..204 B7
Brockenhurst Rd 9
DN7.............14 E4
Brocklebank Cl LN5...92 F2
BROCKLESBY DN41...22 E6
Brocklesby Cl
Gainsborough DN21...197 F3
6 Kingston upon Hull
HU13...........179 A3
Brocklesby Gdns PE3..225 C4
Brocklesby Pk Prim Sch
DN37............22 D4
Brocklesby Pl DN34...190 E4
Brocklesby Rd
Brocklesby DN41.....22 E5
Grimsby DN34.......190 E4
Habrough DN40......22 E8
Scunthorpe DN17....184 F4
Ulceby DN39........12 A1
Brocklesby Wlk LN11..198 A7
Brocks Cl 22 PE24...90 D7
Brockton Cl HU3.....179 F5
Brodsworth Rd PE7...231 F5
Bromwich Rd HU10...178 F8
Bronzegarth DN32....192 B5
Brookdale Rd DN17...184 D6
Brook Dr 4 LN12.....64 C3
Brooke Ave PE9......218 E4
BROOKENBY LN8.....47 B6
Brookenby Bsns Pk LN8.47 B6
Brookes Cl 34 DN21...30 B1
Brooke St DN8.......15 A8
Brookfield Ave LN2...68 D2
Brookfield Cl
2 Skellingthorpe LN6..200 A5
6 Thorne/Moorends
DN8.............15 A8
Brookfield Home Pk
PE4............220 E2
Brookfield Rd DN33...191 B1
Brookfields Ind Est
PE4............220 F2
Brookfurlong PE3....225 B6
Brook La
Farcet PE7.........231 B2
Scawby DN20........20 A1
Brooklands 1 DN20...19 E3

Brooklands Ave
Broughton DN20......19 D4
Cleethorpes DN35....193 A5
Brooklands Cl
5 Birchwood LN6....204 C7
3 Collingham NG23...91 D5
Brooklands Rd HU5...179 E8
Brooklands Way 8
LN6............204 C7
Brooklyn Dr DN36....193 B1
Brook Rd LN9.......199 D2
Brookside
8 Ancaster NG32....120 A3
4 Brough HU15......2 D6
Louth LN11.........198 D3
Peterborough PE4....221 D2
Brookside Cl
7 Ancaster NG32....120 A3
Ruskington NG34....108 D2
Brook St
Grantham NG31......211 A5
Hemswell DN21......42 D2
Kingston upon Hull HU2.180 E7
Lincoln LN2.........234 B2
Peterborough PE1....226 A2
Brook Way 5 NG34...108 D2
Broom Cl PE1........226 A8
Broome Way PE12....215 A2
BROOMFLEET HU15...1 B6
Broomfleet Sta HU15...1 B6
Broom Gr LN6.......185 B8
Broomhill 8 LN6....204 C8
Broomston La DN9...26 F1
Broomwood Cl 2
NG31...........210 F7
Brosley Ave 1 DN3...14 A4
Brotherhood Cl PE4...225 D8
Brotherhood Ret Pk
PE4............225 D8
BROTHERTOFT PE20..124 F5
Brothertoft Rd PE21..208 D5
Brotts Rd NG23......78 A3
BROUGH
Brough HU15........2 C5
Collingham NG23.....91 E1
Brougham St HU3....179 F7
Brough Cl 14 LN6....204 C7
Brough La NG23......91 D2
Brough Prim Sch HU15.2 C6
Brough Rd LN6......105 A8
Brough Sta HU15.....2 B5
BROUGHTON DN20...19 D3
BROUGHTON COMMON
DN20............19 F5
Broughton Gdns LN5..205 D3
Broughton Inf Sch
DN20............19 E3
Broughton La LN5....93 C3
Broughton Rd
Carlton-le-Moorland
LN5............92 E1
Stapleford LN6......105 C8
Broughton's La 1
PE22...........126 E3
Browndons St 4
NG31...........211 A5
Brownes Rd 7 PE8...172 B1
Browning Cl
3 Kingston upon Hull
HU3............180 D8
1 Scunthorpe DN17...184 E6
Browning Ct 4 LN4...207 B5
Browning Dr LN2....202 B7
Brown La NG23.......79 A7
Brownlow Cres 3
PE11...........145 B1
Brownlow Dr 4 PE17..217 E4
Brownlow Quay 1
PE9............219 C4
Brownlow Rd PE1....226 A6
Brownlow's Dro PE12..167 A8
Brownlow's Hill NG24..104 D5
Brownlow Terr 20 PE9.219 C5
Browns CE (Aided) Prim
Sch NG34........133 C2
Brown's Dro PE20....123 F2
Brown's Gate
Long Sutton PE12...216 B1
Spalding PE11......214 C4
Browns La 13 DN8...15 A8
Browns Orch DN21...191 D6
Brown's Rd 3 PE21..209 A7
Brown St DN31......189 C3
Browntoft La 2 PE11..134 F2
BROXHOLME LN1....66 F1
Broxholme Gdns 2
LN2............201 F8
Broxholme La 1 LN2...66 F3
Broxholme Wild at Heart
Nature Reserve & Arts
Ctr* LN1.........67 C4
Bruce Cl
7 Broughton DN20...19 D3
Lincoln LN2.........234 C4
Bruce St DN15......182 F3
Brudenell PE2.......229 E2
Brudenell Cl 1 PE6...164 E5
Brulon Cl LN4.......207 B6
BRUMBY DN16......185 C8
Brumby Comm La
DN17............184 B7
Brumby Comm Nature
Reserve* DN17.....184 C7
Brumby Cres 10 LN5..93 F7
Brumby Engineering Coll
DN16............185 B8

Brumby Hall Gdns
DN17............182 F2
Brumby House Dr
DN16............185 A8
Brumby Jun Sch DN16.185 B8
Brumby's Terr 4 HU9..181 D7
Brumby Wood La
DN15............182 C1
Brumby Wood Nature
Reserve* DN17.....182 D1
Brunel Cl DN16......185 B4
Brunel Dr
Newark NG24.......104 B5
Yaxley PE7.........233 D6
Brunel Rd PE11......214 E8
Brunslow Cl HU3.....179 E5
Brunswick Ave HU2...180 E8
Brunswick Gr 5 HU13..178 F2
Brunswick Sq 1 LN4..109 F6
Brunton Way DN36...195 D5
Brush Meadow La
PE34............161 E3
Brushtrokes Ceramics*
DN37............194 E3
Bryant Cl LN9......199 C3
Brynmore PE3.......225 A8
Bryony Gdns PE10...213 D7
Bryony Way 5 PE6...217 D6
Bubble Car Mus*
NG34...........120 A8
Buccaneer Way 21 HU15.2 C5
Buchanan Cl LN1....201 D8
Buchanan Rd DN21...54 F8
Buchanan St LN1.....201 D8
Buck Beck Way DN36..192 D2
Buck Cl LN2.........202 D6
Buckfast Cl DN17....184 D8
Buckfast Ct DN17....184 D8
Buckfast Rd 4 LN1...201 E6
Buckingham Ave DN15.182 F5
Buckingham Cl
Fishtoft PE21.......209 C6
15 Mablethorpe & Sutton
LN12...........76 F8
Buckingham Dr 16 PE24.90 D7
Buckingham Gr DN33..191 B2
Buckingham Rd LN11..198 A7
Buckingham St N
DN15............182 F5
Buckingham St S DN15.182 F4
Buckingham St 5
DN15............182 F4
Buckland Cl 2 PE25...225 B4
BUCKLEGATE PE20...136 F3
Bucklegate La PE20...136 F2
Buckle St PE1.......226 C3
BUCKMINSTER NG33..150 E5
Buckminster Gdns
NG31...........210 F2
Buckminster La NG33..151 A7
Buckminster Pl 4
PE1............226 D7
Buckminster Prim Sch
NG33............150 F5
Buckminster Rd
Gunby & Stainby NG33.151 A5
Sproxton LE14......150 C7
BUCKNALL LN10.....84 A4
Bucknall Ave 4 LN6..205 A7
Bucknall's Mdw 5 LN12.76 F8
Bucksholt Rd PE14...170 E3
Buckthorn Ave
3 Skegness PE25....103 E4
8 Skegness PE25....103 E4
Buckthorn Rd PE7....230 D3
Buddleia Cl DN41....203 D8
Buddleia Dr LN4.....81 D3
Bude Cl DN16.......195 C7
Bukehorn Rd PE6....175 D4
BULBY PE10........142 B1
Bulby La 1 NG32....106 C1
Bulham La NG23.....78 A1
Bull Bank LN1......49 D7
Bulldog Cres LN11....62 B6
Bull Dro PE22.......114 B5
Bullen's La PE20.....135 C6
Buller Cl 16 NG23....91 D5
Buller St 4 DN32....191 F7
Bullfinch La DN35....192 E1
Bullingham Rd LN2...202 D6
BULLINGTON LN8....69 E4
Bullivant Rd DN7.....14 E4
Bull La
1 Ketton PE9......171 A3
Long Sutton PE12...216 C4
North Witham NG33..151 E4
4 Peakirk PE6......174 A5
Bull Moor Rd DN7....15 A4
Bullock Rd
Terrington St Clement
PE34............161 F1
Thorney PE8........228 B1
Bullock's Short Gate
PE12............159 C4
Bull Pasture PE22....126 D2
Bullpit Rd NG24.....104 C3
Bull Ring LN9.......199 B4
Bull's Bank PE11.....144 E8
Bully Hill LN8.......46 D2
Bulpit La LN6.......91 F7
Bulwick Ave DN33...194 E7
Bungley La PE20.....136 C6
Bunkers Hill
Hemswell DN21......42 E1
Lincoln LN2........202 D6
BUNKER'S HILL LN4..111 E4

Bunkers Hill Cl 2 DN36.36 D4
Bunker's Hill La PE21..136 F8
BUPA Hull & E Riding
Hospl HU10........178 E5
Burchnall Cl PE6.....217 D6
Burchnall Dr 4 PE25..90 E3
Burcom Ave 3 DN36..36 D8
Burcott Garth HU4...179 B3
Burcroft Rd 17 PE13..170 C1
Burdett Cl 8 PE25...206 A6
Burdock Rd DN16....185 C4
Bure Cl LN6.........204 F3
Burford Way PE1....226 D6
Burgar Rd 11 DN8....15 A7
Burgate 5 DN18......10 F8
Burgess Cl 2 PE21...209 B4
Burgess Dr 4 PE21...159 C7
Burgess Rd DN20....196 E3
BURGH LE MARSH
PE24............102 E7
Burgh le Marsh Mus* **15**
PE24............102 E7
Burghley Ave 14 PE8..172 B1
Burghley Cl
Birchwood LN6.....200 E1
22 Crowland PE6....166 F1
3 Market Deeping PE6.217 E4
3 Nettleton LN7.....33 A3
Burghley Cres LN11...198 B7
Burghley Ct
1 Bourne PE10.....213 C5
27 Stamford PE9....219 C5
Burghley House* PE9.219 C3
Burghley La PE9.....219 C4
Burghley Pk Cl 8 LN6.204 F1
Burghley Rd
Birchwood LN6.....200 E1
1 Peterborough PE1..226 A3
Scunthorpe DN16....185 D7
8 Skegness PE25....206 C1
8 Stamford PE9.....219 A7
Burghley Sh Ctr The
PE10............213 D5
Burghley Sq 2 PE1...226 A3
Burghley St PE10....213 C5
Burghley Rd
Birchwood LN6.....200 E1
Burgh Old Rd PE25..206 A6
BURGH ON BAIN LN8.59 D5
Burgh Rd
Friskney PE22......115 A7
Skegness PE25.....103 C7
Burgin Cl 6 NG32...117 F1
Burgon Cres 3 DN15..9 B5
Burke St (North) 7
DN15............183 A5
Burke St DN15......183 A4
Burland Ct 3 LN4....203 B2
Burleigh Ct NG31....211 F5
Burleigh Gdns 2 PE21.209 A7
Burleigh St HU8.....181 C8
Burley Ave DN35....192 F3
Burley Cl DN37......23 F2
Burley Rd 14 PE9....163 C1
Burlies' Gate PE14...159 E4
Burlington Rd PE25..206 B3
Burma Dr HU9.......5 D8
Burma Rd DN16.....183 F2
Burmer Rd PE1......225 E7
Burneside Cl LN2....202 B8
Burnet Dr DN16.....185 C4
Burnett's Yd LN4....33 C4
BURNHAM DN18.....11 C4
Burnham La
Kirton PE20........136 F4
Thornton Curtis DN39..11 A4
Burnham Rd
Barton-upon-Humber
DN18............11 A6
Epworth DN9.......27 E6
Kingston upon Hull HU4.179 B3
Owston Ferry DN9...28 A3
Scunthorpe DN15....182 D2
Burnham Reach 5
DN35............192 F1
Burnham Sq 2 DN9..28 A3
Burnmoor Cl 3 LN6..200 C1
Burn Rd DN15......182 C3
Burns Cl
Grantham NG31.....211 E6
Peterborough PE1....225 F7
Burns Cres 8 NG34..212 F4
Burns Gdns LN2.....202 C6
Burns Gr DN33......191 B3
Burnside DN20......19 D3
Burnside Ave 5 PE6..217 A5
Burns Rd 6 PE9.....218 F6
Burns St DN21......197 B6
Burnstone Gdns 4
PE12............157 F7
Burnt Hill La 5 LN11..198 B5
Burrells Cl DN9......27 D2
Burrettgate Rd 4
PE13............170 F1
Burrett Gdns PE13...170 F1
Burrett Rd PE13......170 F2
Burrill La HU15......2 B8
BURRINGHAM DN17..17 E4
Burringham Rd
Burringham DN17....17 E5
Scunthorpe DN17....184 D5
Burr La PE12........156 F3
Burrows Cl 2 PE21...208 E2
Burrows Ct PE1......226 A5
Burrs The HU15.....2 B5
Bursar Prim Sch DN35.192 E6
Bursar St DN35......192 E6

Bursnells La 3 LE14 .... 150 B1
Burswood PE2 .... 229 F2
Burtey Fen Collection The★ PE11 .... 145 B1
Burtey Fen La PE11 .... 145 B2
Burtoft La PE20 .... 135 E2
BURTON LN1 .... 67 D1
Burton Cl PE21 .... 209 B7
BURTON CORNER PE21 .... 209 B7
Burton Ct
2 Louth LN11 .... 198 D4
Peterborough PE1 .... 226 C3
Burtonfield Cl 1 LN3 ... 203 E6
Burton Gravel Pits Nature Reserve★ LN1 .... 67 C1
Burton La
8 Billingborough NG34 .... 133 B1
Burton Coggles NG33 .... 140 E1
Burton La End LN1 ...... 200 C8
BURTON-LE-COGGLES NG33 .... 152 D8
Burton Mews LN4 .... 203 D1
Burton on Stather Prim Sch DN15 .... 8 B4
BURTON PEDWARDINE NG34 .... 122 B1
Burton Rd
Burton upon Stather DN15 .... 8 C4
Heckington NG34 .... 122 C2
Lincoln LN1 .... 234 A4
Spalding PE11 .... 214 B2
Burton Ridge 2 LN1 .... 201 D7
Burton St
14 Gainsborough DN21 .... 197 D3
Peterborough PE1 .... 226 C3
BURTON STATHER DN15 ..... 8 B5
BURTON UPON STATHER DN15 .... 8 B4
Burton Way LN9 .... 199 D2
BURWELL LN11 .... 74 B6
Burwell Cl LN2 .... 202 A8
Burwell Dr DN33 .... 191 B3
Burwell Rd LN11 .... 74 D7
Burwell Reach PE2 ...... 230 C7
Burystead PE2 .... 231 B8
Bush Cl HU4 .... 179 D3
Bushfield PE2 .... 229 E3
Bushfield Com Coll PE2 .... 229 E3
Bushfield Ct PE2 .... 229 E3
Bushfield Rd DN16 ...... 183 B1
Bushfield Rd Inf Sch DN16 .... 183 A1
Bushfield Sports Ctr PE2 .... 229 E4
Bush Gn La
Algarkirk PE20 .... 146 C8
Fosdyke PE20 .... 136 C1
Bush Meadow La PE12 . 215 A4
Bushy Cl 5 PE7 .... 230 D3
BUSLINGTHORPE LN8 ..... 57 A4
Buslingthorpe Rd LN8 .... 57 A4
Bustards' La PE14 .... 161 C1
Butcher La 10 LN11 ..... 198 B5
Butchers Sq HU13 .... 178 E1
Butchery Ct 3 LN2 ...... 234 B2
Butforth La DN19 .... 11 E8
Butler Pl DN35 .... 192 B7
Butler's Way 14 PE20 .... 135 B7
Butlin Cl 1 PE25 .... 206 A4
Buttercake La PE22 ..... 113 F2
Buttercross Cl 2 DN41 ... 23 E6
Buttercup Cl
1 Kingston upon Hull HU9 .... 181 D7
3 Spalding PE11 .... 214 A2
3 Stamford PE9 .... 218 D7
Buttercup Ct PE6 .... 217 D6
Buttercup Dr PE10 ...... 213 D3
Buttercup Paddock 4 PE12 .... 158 B6
Butterfield Cl 7 DN37 .... 23 F1
Butterfly & Wildlife Pk The★ PE12 .... 216 D6
Buttergate Hill LN9 ...... 71 F3
Buttermere Cl
2 Birchwood LN6 .... 200 D1
East Ella HU4 .... 179 E6
Buttermere Cres 2 DN36 .... 36 C8
Buttermere Pl 4 PE4 ... 221 C3
Buttermere Way 6 DN32 .... 191 F8
Butter Mkt 11 LN7 .... 33 B4
BUTTERWICK PE22 .... 126 F4
Butterwick Cl DN35 ..... 192 F3
Butterwick Pinchbeck Endowed CE Sch PE22 .... 126 E3
Butterwick Rd
Benington PE22 .... 126 F4
Messingham DN17 .... 29 A7
Buttery Cl LN6 .... 204 F4
Buttfield Rd HU13 .... 178 E1
Butt Gate LN11 .... 50 B8
Butt La
Barrowby NG32 .... 210 A6
Goulceby LN11 .... 72 D6
Laceby DN37 .... 23 F2
Norton Disney LN6 .... 92 C2
Butt La *continued*
Theddlethorpe All Saints LN12 .... 63 E7
Walcott LN4 .... 109 C7
Wymondham LE14 .... 150 C2
Buttler Way 3 NG34 .... 212 C3
Butts Hill La 5 DN15 ...... 8 C8
Butts La LN5 .... 92 F6
Butt's La LN4 .... 207 B5
Butts Rd DN18 .... 3 F1
Butts The LE14 .... 138 F1
Buxton Ct DN15 .... 182 B2
Bycroft Rd DN21 .... 197 C8
Byfield Rd DN17 .... 184 D6
Byland Cl LN2 .... 202 E6
Byland Ct 4 HU9 .... 181 E8
Byland Gr DN37 .... 188 A1
Byrd Rd DN16 .... 185 E6
Byron Ave
Grantham NG31 .... 211 E6
Lincoln LN2 .... 202 A6
Byron Cl
Peterborough PE2 .... 231 D6
Scunthorpe DN17 .... 184 E6
6 Sleaford NG34 .... 212 F4
Byron Gr DN33 .... 191 C4
Byron Rd LN12 .... 64 B4
Byron Way PE9 .... 218 E5
Bytham Hts 3 NG33 .... 162 E8
Bythams Prim Sch The NG33 .... 153 A2
Bythorne Bank PE13 .... 169 B6
Bythorn Rd PE2 .... 231 C6
Bythorn Way PE2 .... 231 C6
Bywood Pl DN37 .... 190 C6

C

CABOURNE LN7 .... 33 D4
Cabourne Ave LN2 ...... 202 B7
Cabourne Ct LN2 .... 202 B7
Cabourne Rd DN33 ...... 191 B3
CACKLE HILL PE12 .... 215 C5
Cackle Hill La PE12 ..... 215 C5
Caddle Rd 11 DN41 .... 23 A4
Cade Cl 12 LN2 .... 68 F4
Cade Dro PE12 .... 159 D4
Cade La DN21 .... 53 D6
Cades Field Rd 24 LN12 .. 77 A8
Cadman Way DN21 .... 41 A1
CADNEY DN20 .... 31 D6
Cadney Rd DN20 .... 196 C1
Cadwell Cl 4 LN6 .... 204 C7
Cadwell Pk Motor Racing Circuit★ LN11 .... 73 B8
CAENBY LN8 .... 55 F8
Caenby Cl DN21 .... 197 F3
Caenby Cnr LN8 .... 55 B8
Caenby Rd
Caenby LN8 .... 43 F1
Cleethorpes DN35 .... 192 E4
Scunthorpe DN17 .... 184 E5
Caesar Cl 7 PE6 .... 164 E5
Cagthorpe LN9 .... 199 B3
Cairns Way 8 LN5 .... 93 E8
CAISTOR LN7 .... 33 B4
Caistor Ave DN16 ...... 185 B4
Caistor By-pass LN7 ...... 33 B3
Caistor CE/Methodist Prim Sch LN7 .... 33 B3
Caistor Cl 7 LN6 .... 204 C7
Caistor Dr
Bracebridge Heath LN4 .... 81 A2
Grimsby DN33 .... 191 B3
Caistor Gram Sch LN7 .... 33 B4
Caistor La LN8 .... 46 C3
Caistor Rd
Barton-upon-Humber DN18 .... 11 A7
Birchwood LN6 .... 204 C7
Cabourne LN7 .... 33 F5
Caistor LN7 .... 32 E4
Laceby DN37 .... 23 E1
2 Market Rasen LN8 ..... 57 D8
Middle Rasen LN8 .... 45 D2
Rothwell LN7 .... 33 E2
South Kelsey LN7 .... 32 A1
Swallow LN7 .... 34 A5
Caistor Yarborough Sch LN7 .... 33 C4
Caithness Rd PE9 .... 218 E6
CALCEBY LN13 .... 74 E2
Caldbeck Cl PE4 .... 221 D2
Caldecote Cl PE2 .... 231 E6
Calder Cl
Grantham NG31 .... 210 E3
Immingham DN40 .... 186 A3
Calderdale Dr PE11 ..... 214 D7
Calder Gn 24 DN17 .... 29 D7
Calder Rd
Lincoln LN5 .... 205 C2
Scunthorpe DN16 .... 185 D6
Caldervale PE2 .... 230 C6
Caldicott Dr 8 DN21 ..... 53 A8
Caleb Hill La
Leake Commonside PE22 .... 113 F3
Old Leake PE22 .... 114 A3
Caledonian Rd 4 PE9 ... 218 F6
Caledonia Pk HU9 ...... 181 B5
Callan's La PE10 .... 142 C2
Calver Cres DN37 ...... 190 D7
Calvert La HU4 .... 179 D7
Calvert Rd HU5 .... 179 D8
Camargue Ave DN37 .... 194 F4
Camarthen Cl 4 NG31 .. 210 E5
Cambrai Cl LN1 .... 201 E7
Cambrian Cl NG31 ...... 210 E7
Cambrian Way
Holton le Clay DN36 ..... 195 C3
11 North Hykeham LN6 .... 93 B8
1 Peterborough PE4 .... 221 C1
Cambridge Ave
Lincoln LN1 .... 201 D4
Peterborough PE1 .... 225 F5
Scunthorpe DN16 .... 185 A3
Cambridge Cres 4 LN8 .. 47 B6
Cambridge Dr
Heighington/ Washingborough LN4 ... 203 D1
Wisbech PE13 .... 170 C1
Cambridge Gdns 4 PE11 .... 145 B7
Cambridge Mdws NG24 .... 104 C4
Cambridge Pk Sch DN34 .... 191 A5
Cambridge Rd
Grimsby DN34 .... 190 F5
Kingston upon Hull HU13 . 178 F3
Scunthorpe DN16 .... 185 C6
Stamford PE9 .... 219 A6
Cambridge Rd N 1 LN12 .... 64 B5
Cambridge Rd S 3 LN12 .... 64 B5
Cambridge St
Cleethorpes DN35 .... 192 F6
Grantham NG31 .... 211 B3
Kingston upon Hull HU3 .. 180 D6
Camdale La 8 NG24 .... 104 C1
Camden St 1 HU3 ...... 180 B5
Camdon Cl 1 LN5 ...... 205 D3
Camel Gate PE12 .... 157 B7
Camelia Cl PE4 .... 221 B3
Camelot Gdns
Boston PE21 .... 209 E5
11 Mablethorpe/Sutton on Sea LN12 .... 76 F8
Cameron Dr 3 PE11 .... 214 E3
Cameron La 13 NG24 ... 104 C1
Cameron St 4 NG34 .... 122 E3
Camilla Cl HU9 .... 181 A5
CAMMERINGHAM LN1 ...... 54 F1
Camm's La PE22 .... 114 D2
Campain's La PE11 ..... 166 C7
Campbell Ave DN16 ..... 185 B4
Campbell Cl 4 NG31 ... 210 F5
Campbell Ct HU13 ...... 178 E2
Campbell Dr PE4 .... 221 C4
Campbell Gr DN37 ...... 190 E8
Campbells Cl PE11 ..... 214 B1
Campbells Farm Ave 1 DN15 .... 17 E6
Campbell St DN21 ...... 197 B5
Campden Cres DN35 .... 192 D7
Campion Ave HU4 .... 179 B2
Campion Cl PE11 .... 214 B6
Campion Dr PE6 .... 217 D6
Campion Gr 4 PE9 ..... 218 D7
Campion Rd PE1 .... 226 B8
Campions Cl DN36 ...... 195 D2
Campions' La 11 DN36 .... 36 B1
Campion Way PE10 ..... 213 D2
Camp La NG33 .... 141 B1
Campling Pl PE12 .... 215 D7
Campling Way 2 LN12 ... 64 C2
Campney La LN10 .... 83 F1
Campus Way LN6 .... 201 D3
Camwood Cres LN6 ..... 200 C1
Canada La
Caistor LN7 .... 33 C4
Wildmore LN4 .... 111 A4
Canal La DN10 .... 40 B5
CANAL SIDE DN8 .... 15 A7
Canal View 12 DN8 .... 15 A7
Canberra Ave DN7 .... 26 A8
Canberra Cl 5 LN4 ..... 207 C4
Canberra Cres
11 Binbrook Tech Pk LN8 .... 47 B6
Grantham NG31 .... 211 D7
10 Manby LN11 .... 62 C6
Canberra Dr 5 LN1 ...... 67 F5
Canberra St HU3 .... 180 D5
Canberra Way LN6 ...... 200 A4
Candidus Ct 6 PE4 ..... 220 F5
Candlehouse La 9 LN13 .... 75 F3
CANDLESBY PE23 .... 88 F2
Candlesby Hill Quarry Nature Reserve★ PE23 .. 88 F2
Candlesby Rd DN37 ..... 190 C7
Candy Bank DN9 .... 26 B5
Candy St PE2 .... 230 E8
Cane Ave PE2 .... 230 D7
Canister La
Frithville PE22 .... 112 C1
Langriville PE22 .... 124 F8
Cannon Cl NG24 .... 104 C5
Cannonhill Dro PE12 .... 167 A8
Cannon Oakes Ct DN36 .... 195 E6
Cannon Peter Hall CE Prim Sch DN40 .... 186 D4
Cannon St
Kingston upon Hull HU2 .... 180 F8
1 Lincoln LN2 .... 202 B3
3 Louth LN11 .... 198 B5
Canon Dr 6 PE9 .... 172 D3
Canon Peter Hall CE Prim Sch The DN40 .... 186 D4
Canonsfield PE4 .... 220 E4
Canon Tardrew Ct HU13 .... 179 A1
Canterbury Cl
Grantham NG31 .... 211 E7
1 Scunthorpe DN17 ..... 184 D7
Spalding PE11 .... 214 B4
Canterbury Dr
Grimsby DN34 .... 191 C6
Heighington/Washingborough LN4 .... 203 D1
4 Sleaford NG34 .... 212 C7
Canterbury Rd
1 Hatfield DN7 .... 14 D4
Peterborough PE4 .... 220 F3
Cant's Dro PE13 .... 177 C4
Canturbury Cl 10 LN10 ... 97 C5
Canty Nook 5 DN38 ...... 32 E7
Canwell PE4 .... 221 A4
CANWICK LN4 .... 81 B4
Canwick Ave LN4 .... 205 F4
Canwick Hill LN4 .... 81 A4
Canwick Rd
Canwick LN5 .... 81 A4
Lincoln LN5 .... 234 B1
Washingborough LN4 ..... 81 D4
Capes Entry PE12 .... 157 A2
Capitol Pk DN8 .... 14 F8
Capper Ave 3 DN21 ...... 55 A8
Cappitt Dr 2 PE10 ...... 164 C8
Capp's La 19 LN5 .... 93 F7
Capstan Way 17 DN8 ..... 15 A8
Captains Beck 9 PE11 .. 145 C1
Captain's Hill NG34 ..... 121 B7
Captains Wlk HU1 ...... 180 E5
Capthorne Cl PE7 .... 230 C2
Caravan Pk LN6 .... 204 C1
Carbis Cl DN36 .... 195 C7
Cardiff Ave DN36 .... 195 C6
Cardigan Rd HU3 .... 179 E6
Cardinal Cl
Lincoln LN2 .... 202 D5
New Quarrington NG34 ... 212 A2
Cardinal Ct 3 DN37 .... 194 C5
Cardinals Gate PE4 ..... 220 E4
Cardinal Wlk HU13 ..... 179 A1
Cardyke Dr 13 PE6 ..... 164 E5
CAREBY PE9 .... 163 B7
Carew St HU3 .... 179 F7
Carholme Cl 1 PE10 .... 213 D6
Carholme Rd LN1 .... 201 C4
Carisbrook Ct PE3 ...... 230 B8
Carisbrooke Cl
2 Lincoln LN1 .... 201 E6
5 New Waltham DN36 .... 195 D7
Carisbrooke Gr PE9 .... 218 E5
Carisbrooke Manor La DN17 .... 184 A5
Carisbrooke Wlk DN40 . 186 D3
CARLBY PE9 .... 163 D5
Carleton Crest 3 PE4 ... 221 B1
Carline Rd LN1 .... 234 A3
Carlisle Cl
6 Grantham NG31 ...... 210 D5
1 Lincoln LN6 .... 204 F1
Carlisle Gdns LN9 ...... 199 D5
Carlisle St 2 DN21 ..... 197 D5
Carlisle Way 9 LN4 ...... 81 A2
Carlton Ave DN41 .... 23 F5
Carlton Bvd LN2 .... 202 D5
Carlton Cl
Humberston DN35 ...... 193 B1
8 Leverington PE13 ..... 170 B2
2 Spalding PE11 .... 214 B1
Carlton Ctr Ret Pk LN2 .... 202 D6
Carlton Ferry La NG23 .... 91 A6
Carlton Gr LN2 .... 201 F7
Carlton La
Broxholme LN1 .... 67 A4
Sutton-on-Trent NG23 .... 91 A7
CARLTON-LE-MOORLAND LN5 .... 105 E8
Carlton Mews 9 LN4 .... 203 D1
Carlton Pk LN11 .... 62 C5
Carlton Rd
Ancaster NG32 .... 119 E3
Bassingham LN5 .... 92 E2
Boston PE21 .... 208 D5
Grimsby DN34 .... 191 B6
9 Healing DN41 .... 23 F5
Hough-on-the-Hill NG32 .. 119 B5
Manby LN11 .... 62 C6
CARLTON SCROOP NG32 .... 119 D3
Carlton St
Kingston upon Hull HU3 .... 179 F4
Lincoln LN1 .... 234 A4
12 Scunthorpe DN15 .... 183 B3
Carlton Wlk LN2 .... 202 A7
Carlyle Cl DN35 .... 193 A2
Carlyle Wlk LN2 .... 202 B6
Carmel Gn PE21 .... 208 E2
Carmen Cres DN36 ..... 195 C3
Carnaby Gr 2 DN32 .... 192 A5
Carnarvon Ave 1 DN34 .... 191 B4
Carn Cl 3 LN5 .... 205 D2
Carnegie Rd 21 PE8 .... 172 B1
Carnegie St 6 HU3 ..... 180 A6
Carnell La 16 NG24 .... 104 C1
Carnforth Cres DN34 ... 191 A5
Carnforth Parade DN34 .... 191 A5
Carnoustie
9 Spalding PE11 .... 214 C2
7 Waltham DN37 .... 194 C4
Carnoustie Cl 2 LN10 .... 97 C5
Carnoustie Ct PE12 ..... 160 F4
Carnoustie Dr LN6 ..... 204 B7
Carol Dickson Ct 9 HU3 .... 180 C5
Caroline Cl 12 NG34 .... 212 F4
Caroline Ct 10 PE21 .... 209 A5
Caroline Pl HU2 .... 180 F7
Caroline Rd 5 LN4 ...... 95 D4
Caroline St
10 Alford LN13 .... 75 F2
Kingston upon Hull HU2 .. 180 F8
Carradale PE2 .... 229 D5
Carral Cl LN5 .... 205 C3
Carram Way LN1 .... 201 C7
Carr Dike La HU15 .... 1 C7
Carr Dyke Bank DN17 .... 28 D5
Carr Dyke Rd DN17 ...... 17 D3
Carre's Gram Sch NG34 .... 212 D5
Carre's Sq LN4 .... 109 E6
Carre St NG34 .... 212 D4
Carr Gate LN4 .... 109 F6
Carrhouse Rd DN9 .... 16 D1
Carrier Cl PE3 .... 230 D8
CARRINGTON PE22 ...... 112 D6
Carrington Cl
Coningsby LN4 .... 207 D5
2 Spalding PE11 .... 214 B3
Carrington Dr
Deeping St Nicholas PE11 .... 165 F5
8 Humberston DN36 ..... 36 D8
Lincoln LN6 .... 204 F7
Carrington Rd
Carrington PE22 .... 112 D3
Moulton PE12 .... 146 C3
Spalding PE11 .... 214 B4
Carrington's Dro PE6 ... 175 C7
Carrington St 6 HU3 ... 180 B5
Carr La
6 Alford LN13 .... 75 F2
Appleby DN15 .... 9 D2
Bishop Norton LN8 .... 43 F3
Blyton DN21 .... 41 B5
Bonby DN20 .... 10 B1
Broomfleet HU15 .... 1 B7
Broughton DN20 .... 196 A6
Burton upon Stather DN15 .. 8 D4
Doddington & Whisby LN6 .. 79 D6
Gainsborough DN21 ..... 197 C1
Garthorpe & Fockerby DN17 .... 7 E4
Grimsby DN32 .... 192 B7
Haxey DN9 .... 27 E2
Healing DN41 .... 23 F4
Hibaldstow DN20 .... 31 A6
Horkstow DN18 .... 9 F4
Kingston upon Hull HU1 .. 180 E6
Luddington & Haldenby DN17 .... 7 C1
Misterton DN10 .... 39 F5
Redbourne DN21 .... 30 F3
Skinnard LN5 .... 106 D7
Stallingborough DN41 .... 23 F7
Ulceby DN39 .... 12 B3
West Butterwick DN17 .... 28 C8
Wildsworth DN21 .... 40 F8
Winterton DN15 .... 9 D6
Worlaby DN20 .... 20 B7
Carroll Pl 4 HU1 .... 181 A7
Carron Cl 3 LN3 .... 83 B4
Carron Dr PE4 .... 220 E3
Carr Rd
Gringley on the Hill DN10 .... 39 A4
North Kelsey LN7 .... 31 E4
Peterborough PE1 .... 226 D3
Carrside DN9 .... 27 D6
Carr Side La DN7 .... 14 E2
Carr St LN1 .... 201 D4
Carrwood Cres LN4 ..... 207 C7
Carson Ave DN34 .... 191 B6
Carson Cl 6 PE24 .... 90 B7
Carson Rd DN21 .... 197 C6
Cartergate DN32 .... 191 C7
Carterplot Rd NG34 ..... 123 A2
Carters Cl 6 PE3 .... 224 F3
Carter's Garth Cl 4 LN11 .... 50 B8
Cartledge Ave DN32 .... 192 B6
Cartmel Gr DN32 .... 192 B6
Cartmel Way 14 PE6 .... 175 A1
Carver Rd
Boston PE21 .... 208 D3
Immingham DN40 .... 186 D3
Caryer Cl PE2 .... 230 D6
Cary La 3 DN20 .... 196 B3
Carysfort Cl PE7 .... 233 D4
Casewick La 4 PE9 ..... 172 F7
Casewick Rd PE9 .... 172 E7
Caskgate St DN21 ...... 197 C4
Caspian Cres DN33 ..... 191 A2
Cassbrook Dr 2 LN11 .... 49 B8
Cassia Gn 7 LN6 .... 204 C8
Cassons Cl PE12 .... 157 D4
Casson's Rd 1 DN8 ...... 15 A8
Casswell Cl 1 DN32 .... 189 D1
Casswell Cres 4 LN11 ... 49 B8
Casswell Dr PE11 .... 145 A7
Castella Dr DN16 .... 183 D3
Casterton Com Coll PE9 .... 171 C8
Casterton La PE9 .... 218 C4
Casterton Rd PE9 .... 218 E6
Casthorpe Rd
3 Barrowby NG32 ...... 210 A5
Denton NG32 .... 139 A8

CASTLE BYTHAM
NG33 . . . . .152 D1
Castle Bytham Rd
Clipsham LE15 . . . . . .162 C7
Swayfield NG33 . . . . . .152 E5
CASTLE CARLTON LN11 . . 62 C2
Castle Causeway NG34 . .212 C4
Castle Cl
3 Bottesford NG13 . . . .128 B5
Spalding PE11 . . . . . . .214 F6
Castle Ct 14 DN18 . . . . 10 F8
Castle Dr
Epworth DN9 . . . . 27 E7
Holbeach PE12 . . . . . .215 E1
Northborough PE6 . . . . .217 E2
Castle Dyke 13 PE9 . . . .219 B5
Castledyke Bank PE22 . .125 A8
Castle Dyke Bank LN4 . .111 B4
Castledyke Prim Sch
DN18 . . . . .3 E1
Castledyke S 13 DN18 . . 10 F8
Castledyke W 7 DN18 . . . 3 E1
Castle End Rd PE6 . . . . .217 A1
Castlefields 2 PE11 . . . .214 D5
Castleford Ave DN34 . . .191 A4
Castlegate
Castle Bytham NG33 . . . .152 D1
Grantham NG31 . . . . . .211 B4
Thornton le Fen PE22 . . .111 F1
Castle Hill
15 Caistor LN7 . . . . 33 B4
4 Lincoln LN1 . . . . . . .234 B3
3 Welbourn LN5 . . . . . .106 E5
Castle Hills Com Art Coll
DN21 . . . . .197 D7
Castle Keep DN20 . . . . . 30 F6
Castle La
Boothby Graffoe LN5 . . . 93 E1
Coningsby LN4 . . . . . . .207 C5
Lincoln LN1 . . . . .234 A4
Castle Rise PE9 . . . . . .163 D1
Castle Sports Complex
PE11 . . . . .214 E5
Castle St
Boston PE21 . . . . .208 D6
Grimsby DN32 . . . . . . .192 A8
Kingston upon Hull HU1 . .180 E6
Lincoln LN1 . . . . .234 A4
Sleaford NG34 . . . . . . .212 D4
12 Stamford PE9 . . . . . .219 B5
Castle Terr 5 NG34 . . . .212 C4
Castle Terr Rd 4
NG34 . . . . .212 C4
CASTLETHORPE DN20 . . 20 A1
Castleton Bvd PE25 . . . .206 D4
Castleton Cres PE25 . . . .206 D4
Castleton Rd DN15 . . . .182 B2
Castleview
Coningsby LN4 . . . . . . .110 E8
Tattershall LN4 . . . . 97 E1
Castle View LN4 . . . . . .109 D7
Castle View Rd NG13 . . .128 B4
Castle Way LN11 . . . . . .198 A8
CASTOR PE5 . . . . .223 D1
Castor CE Sch PE5 . . . .223 E2
Castor Hanglands National
Nature Reserve*
PE6 . . . . .223 D7
Castor Rd
Marholm PE6 . . . . .220 B1
Peterborough PE6 . . . . .224 C6
Casworth Way PE5 . . . . .223 D2
Cater La LN7 . . . . 44 F7
Cater Way PE21 . . . . . .208 D2
Cates's Cove Cnr PE6 . . .167 F4
Cathedral Ct
13 Hatfield DN7 . . . . . . 14 C2
Scunthorpe DN17 . . . . .185 A6
Cathedral Dr PE11 . . . . .214 C5
Cathedral Sq 10 PE1 . . .226 A2
Cathedral St LN2 . . . . . .234 B2
Catherine Cl PE2 . . . . . .230 B7
Catherine Gr 6 DN20 . . 19 E3
Catherine St
6 Grimsby DN32 . . . . . .191 F7
1 Kingston upon Hull
HU2 . . . . .180 F7
Catherines Way 15
PE11 . . . . .145 C1
Cathwaite PE4 . . . . . . .221 E1
Catkin Rd 6 DN16 . . . . .185 B2
Catley PE4 . . . . .221 E1
Catling's La PE13 . . . . . .170 C7
Catskin La LN8 . . . . 46 A3
Cattistock Rd DN35 . . . .192 E3
Cattle Dike PE13 . . . . . .169 E2
Cattle Mkt Rd 8 PE1 . . .226 A2
Cattle Mkt Way 7 PE1 . .226 A1
Cattle Rd DN10 . . . . . . 39 B5
Caughey St HU3 . . . . . .180 D7
Causeway
Burgh le Marsh PE24 . . .102 E7
Wyberton PE21 . . . . . . .136 E7
Causeway Bank La LN13 . 63 F1
Causeway La 3 DN21 . . 52 F6
Causeway Rd LN4 . . . . .109 E5
Causeway The
6 Northorpe PE10 . . . . .164 C8
Revesby PE22 . . . . .111 F7
Thorney PE6 . . . . .175 E2
Cavalry Ct 2 LN4 . . . . . . 95 C4
Cavell Cl PE3 . . . . .225 B4
Cavendish Cl DN35 . . . .193 B1
Cavendish Dr
9 Boston PE21 . . . . . . .136 D8
Gainsborough DN21 . . . . 52 F5
Cavendish Mews 5
LN4 . . . . .203 D1

Cavendish Pk 10 HU15 . . . 2 C5
Cavendish Rd
Scunthorpe DN16 . . . . .185 A4
Skegness PE25 . . . . . . .206 C4
Cavendish St PE1 . . . . . .226 B3
Cavendish Way
1 Grimsby DN32 . . . . . .191 F7
Harrowby Est NG31 . . . .211 F7
Spalding PE11 . . . . . . .214 C6
Cave Rd HU15 . . . . 2 B6
Caverstede Rd PE4 . . . . .221 B1
Cave's Cl 8 PE34 . . . . . .161 F3
Cave's La DN10 . . . . 39 E3
Cavill Pl HU3 . . . . .180 D5
CAWKWELL LN11 . . . . . . 73 A6
Cawkwell Cl 25 LN12 . . . 77 A7
Cawkwell Hill LN11 . . . . . 73 A6
Cawood La PE11 . . . . . .145 B5
Cawthorne Cl 18 NG23 . . 91 D5
Cawthorne Dr HU4 . . . . .179 C3
CAWTHORPE PE10 . . . . .154 B5
Cawthra Ct NG32 . . . . . .139 A7
Caxton Theatre & Arts Ctr
The* DN32 . . . . .189 B1
Cayley Rd HU10 . . . . . . .178 F6
CAYTHORPE NG32 . . . . .119 C7
Caythorpe Heath La
NG32 . . . . .119 D7
Caythorpe Prim Sch
NG32 . . . . .119 B7
Caythorpe Rd PE11 . . . . .134 F2
Cecil Ave PE25 . . . . . . .206 C4
Cecil Cl
Bourne PE10 . . . . .213 B4
16 Scotter DN21 . . . . . . 29 C3
Cecil Ct 18 PE9 . . . . . . .219 C5
Cecile Cres DN35 . . . . . .182 E3
Cecil Pacey Ct PE3 . . . . .225 E7
Cecil Pywell Ave PE12 . . .215 C3
Cecil Rd PE1 . . . . .226 A6
Cecil St
Gainsborough DN21 . . . .197 C5
Grantham NG31 . . . . . .211 C3
Kingston upon Hull HU3 . .179 F5
Lincoln LN1 . . . . .234 A4
Cedar Ave
Cherry Willingham/Reepham
LN3 . . . . .203 D5
Lincoln LN5 . . . . .205 D4
Scunthorpe DN15 . . . . .182 B6
5 Sleaford NG34 . . . . . .212 D6
2 Stainforth DN7 . . . . . 14 D6
Cedar Cl
4 Cleethorpes DN35 . . . .192 D2
Gainsborough DN21 . . . .197 B7
Kingston upon Hull
HU10 . . . . .178 D7
1 Louth LN11 . . . . . . .198 B6
14 Market Deeping PE6 . .217 A5
6 Market Rasen LN8 . . . 57 D7
6 Ruskington NG34 . . . .108 D1
6 Scawby DN20 . . . . . . 30 F8
2 Scotter DN21 . . . . . . 29 C3
13 Sudbrooke LN2 . . . . . 68 F2
Cedar Ct
2 Spalding PE11 . . . . . .214 E3
The Willows DN37 . . . . .190 E8
Cedar Dr
2 Spalding PE11 . . . . . .214 E3
2 The Willows DN37 . . . .190 E8
Cedar Gr PE1 . . . . .226 B8
Cedar Rd PE9 . . . . .218 D6
Cedarwood Cl 1 NG31 . .210 F7
Cedarwood Dr HU5 . . . . .179 B7
Cedric Rd 10 DN3 . . . . . 14 A1
Cekhira Ave 4 PE12 . . . .157 E1
Celta Rd PE2 . . . . .230 F6
Celtic Cl PE2 . . . . .231 D7
Cemetery Cres 10 DN37 . . 23 F1
Cemetery La LN7 . . . . . . 32 A5
Cemetery Rd
Hatfield DN7 . . . . 14 F4
16 Laceby DN37 . . . . . . 23 F1
North Somercotes LN11 . . 50 E8
Scunthorpe DN16 . . . . .185 B8
Winterton DN15 . . . . 9 B5
4 Wragby LN8 . . . . 70 D4
Centaur Rd LN6 . . . . . . .201 D2
Centenary Cl 8 PE22 . . .126 E3
Centenary Way PE12 . . . .160 F2
Central Ave
Ingoldmells PE25 . . . . . 90 F3
Peterborough PE1 . . . . .226 C7
Central Dr 7 NG34 . . . . .120 C8
Central Parade DN34 . . .191 A7
Central Pl NG31 . . . . . . .211 D5
Central Prom DN35 . . . . .192 F6
Central Sq
Brigg DN20 . . . . .196 C4
Peterborough PE2 . . . . .231 D5
Central Tech Coll
NG31 . . . . .211 A7
Central Way DN16 . . . . .183 D2
Centurion Cl 8 LN5 . . . .107 B8
Centurion Way 12 HU15 . . 2 C5
Century La 1 LN1 . . . . . 66 D3
Cerris Rd PE1 . . . . .226 B7
Ceylon St 9 HU9 . . . . 5 D8
Chadburn PE4 . . . . .221 E1
Chadwell Springs
DN37 . . . . .194 B4
Chaffinch Cl DN15 . . . . .182 D5
Chaffinch Dr DN35 . . . . .192 E1
CHAIN BRIDGE PE21 . . . .208 B3
Chain Bridge Rd PE21 . . .208 B3
Chain Cl PE1 . . . . .226 B6
Chaintoft La PE11 . . . . . .145 A7

Chaldean Way PE11 . . . .214 B6
Chalfont Ave LN12 . . . . . 64 A5
Chalfont Cl HU13 . . . . . .178 D2
Chalfonts The LN4 . . . . . 81 E2
Chalgrove Way LN6 . . . .200 E2
Chalk La
Burgh le Marsh PE24 . . . 89 F1
Sutton Bridge PE12 . . . .160 F3
Withern with Stain LN13 . . 63 A1
Chalk Pit La PE23 . . . . . . 88 F2
Chalk Rd PE13 . . . . .169 D1
Chamber's Ct PE11 . . . . .214 E5
Chamber's Farm Wood
Nature Reserve* LN8 . . . 83 F8
Chambers St NG31 . . . . .211 A5
Chamomile Cl DN16 . . . .185 D5
Champion Way LN12 . . . . 64 B2
Chancel Rd DN16 . . . . . .185 A4
Chancel Wlk 13 DN20 . . . 19 E3
Chancery Cl LN6 . . . . . .205 B5
Chancery Ct 4 PE11 . . . .214 D3
Chancery La
3 Crowle DN17 . . . . 16 D7
7 Eye PE6 . . . . .175 A1
7 Holbeach PE12 . . . . . .215 D2
Chanctonbury Cl 20
LN12 . . . . 77 A8
Chanctonbury Way 19
LN12 . . . . 77 A8
Chandlers PE2 . . . . .229 E5
Chandlers Cl 1 DN36 . . .195 C6
Chandlers Ct HU9 . . . . . .181 C6
Chandos Rd DN17 . . . . . .184 F7
Chanterlands Ave HU5 . . .180 A8
Chantreys Dr 16 HU15 . . . 2 C6
Chantry Cl
Grimsby DN31 . . . . . . .191 C7
Peterborough PE1 . . . . .226 A5
Chantry La DN31 . . . . . .191 C7
Chantry The 1 PE11 . . . .214 A4
Chantry Way 16 HU14 . . . . 3 B7
Chantry Way E 14 HU14 . . . 3 B7
Chapel Baulk DN9 . . . . . 26 E1
Chapel Cl
Barrow upon Humber
DN19 . . . . 11 D7
Chapel St Leonard PE24 . . 90 D8
Cherry Willingham/Reepham
LN3 . . . . .203 F8
9 Misterton DN10 . . . . . 39 F5
Northfield HU13 . . . . . .179 A1
1 South Rauceby NG34 . .120 E4
2 Westwoodside DN9 . . . 27 B2
Chapel Ct
6 Alkborough DN15 . . . . . 8 C8
Brigg DN20 . . . . .196 C3
17 Hibaldstow DN20 . . . 30 F5
Scunthorpe DN15 . . . . .183 B4
Wansford PE8 . . . . . . .222 B2
Chapel Dro PE12 . . . . . .168 B2
Chapel Farm Dr 21
PE24 . . . . 90 D7
Chapelfield Rd DN19 . . . . 5 C1
Chapel Garth
Broomfleet HU15 . . . . . . 1 B5
16 Tetney DN36 . . . . . . 36 C4
Chapelgate PE12 . . . . . .159 D2
CHAPELGATE PE12 . . . . .159 D2
Chapelgate
Kirton End PE20 . . . . . .136 B7
12 Sutterton PE20 . . . . .136 A2
Chapel Gate
Sutton St James PE12 . . .159 B1
Whaplode PE12 . . . . . . .168 B5
Chapel Gdns
3 Moulton PE12 . . . . . .157 E1
2 Whaplode PE12 . . . . .158 B7
Chapel Hill HU15 . . . . . . 2 D6
CHAPEL HILL LN4 . . . . . .110 E5
Chapel Hill
Ropsley NG33 . . . . . . .131 B1
Whaplode PE12 . . . . . . .168 A4
Woolsthorpe by Belvoir
NG32 . . . . .138 D8
Chapel Hill Ct 7 NG34 . .212 B4
Chapel Hill La HU15 . . . . 2 E6
Chapel La
Addlethorpe PE24 . . . . . 90 C3
Amber Hill PE20 . . . . . .124 B5
Anwick NG34 . . . . .109 B1
Ashby cum Fenby DN37 . . 35 B8
3 Aubourn Haddington &
South Hykeham LN5 . . . . 93 A5
3 Barnetby le Beck DN37 . 35 B6
4 Barrowby NG32 . . . . .210 A5
1 Barton-upon-Humber
DN18 . . . . 10 F8
Belchford LN9 . . . . 73 B2
1 Holbeach PE12 . . . . . .215 E2
1 Market Rasen LN8 . . . 57 D7
7 North Kelsey LN7 . . . . 32 A4
Peterborough PE1 . . . . .226 B2
18 Ruskington NG34 . . . .108 C2
Scunthorpe DN15 . . . . .183 B3
Yaxley PE7 . . . . .233 D6

Chapel La continued
Heighington/Washingborough
LN4 . . . . 81 E4
2 Helpringham NG34 . . .133 D7
Hemingby LN9 . . . . 72 B1
Horkstow DN18 . . . . . . 10 A5
Keadby with Althorpe
DN17 . . . . 17 C6
6 Ketton PE9 . . . . .171 A3
Kingston upon Hull HU1 . .181 A6
2 Leasingham NG34 . . . .121 B7
6 Legbourne LN11 . . . . . 61 F3
Lincoln LN1 . . . . .234 A4
Little Hale NG34 . . . . . .133 E8
Ludborough DN36 . . . . . 48 E6
Ludford LN8 . . . . 59 A8
Manby LN11 . . . . 62 C6
6 Mareham le Fen PE22 . . 99 A4
Messingham DN17 . . . . . 29 D7
Minting LN9 . . . . 84 C8
4 Misterton DN10 . . . . . 39 F5
Navenby/Wellingore
LN5 . . . . .107 A8
13 Nettleham LN2 . . . . . 68 C2
7 Newark-on-Trent
NG24 . . . . .104 D5
Newton PE13 . . . . .170 B5
Normanby by Spital LN8 . . 55 F7
North Cockerington LN11 . 49 F1
Northorpe PE10 . . . . . .164 C8
North Scarle LN6 . . . . . . 78 E2
Peterborough PE2 . . . . .229 F5
1 Peterborough PE4 . . . .221 A3
Scamblesby LN11 . . . . . 73 A5
10 Scawby DN20 . . . . . . 30 E8
14 Sibsey PE22 . . . . . . .113 B1
Snitterby DN21 . . . . . . 43 D5
South Cockerington LN11 . 62 A8
17 Spalding PE11 . . . . . .214 D4
Spalford NG23 . . . . 78 D4
Springthorpe DN21 . . . . 53 E8
Swallow LN7 . . . . 34 B5
Tattershall Thorpe LN4 . . .207 C8
Thimbleby LN9 . . . . 85 B4
14 Thorne/Moorends
DN8 . . . . 15 A4
Toynton St Peter PE23 . . .101 A6
Utterby LN11 . . . . 48 F4
Welton/Dunholme LN2 . . 68 C6
West/East Butterwick
DN17 . . . . 17 D1
Whitton DN15 . . . . 1 E3
16 Winterton DN15 . . . . . 9 A5
2 Winthorpe NG24 . . . .104 B7
5 Wrawby DN20 . . . . . . 20 E4
2 Wymondham LE14 . . .150 C1
Chapel Lodge Dr LN8 . . . 55 F7
Chapel Mews 3 HU15 . . . 2 C6
Chapel Nook La LN5 . . . . 93 B1
Chapel Pas 16 PE21 . . . .208 F4
Chapel Pit Nature
Reserve* PE24 . . . . . . 90 D8
Chapel Rd
Branston LN4 . . . . 81 E2
4 Broughton DN20 . . . . 19 E3
Carrington PE22 . . . . . .112 B8
Fillingham DN21 . . . . . . 54 F4
4 Habrough DN40 . . . . . 22 E8
Ingoldmells PE25 . . . . . 90 D4
Leake Commonside PE22 . .113 F3
Sutton St Edmund PE12 . .168 E4
Terrington St Clement
PE34 . . . . .161 F3
Chapel Row
Baumber LN9 . . . . 72 A1
7 Skillington NG33 . . . . .151 A8
CHAPEL ST LEONARDS
PE24 . . . . 90 E7
Chapel St Leonards Prim
Sch
Chapel St Leonard PE24 . . 90 D6
Collingham NG23 . . . . . . 91 D4
Chapel St
10 Alford LN13 . . . . 75 F3
3 Amcotts DN17 . . . . . . .7 F1
Beckingham LN5 . . . . . .105 B4
5 Billingborough NG34 . .133 B1
4 Boston PE21 . . . . . . .208 F5
4 Bottesford NG13 . . . .128 A6
13 Caistor LN7 . . . . 33 B4
4 Crowland PE6 . . . . . .175 B8
10 Crowle DN17 . . . . . . 16 D8
6 Epworth DN9 . . . . . . 27 E6
Goxhill DN19 . . . . 12 A8
Haconby PE10 . . . . . . .154 D8
7 Holbeach PE12 . . . . . .215 E2
1 Market Rasen LN8 . . . 57 D7
7 North Kelsey LN7 . . . . 32 A4
Peterborough PE1 . . . . .226 B2
18 Ruskington NG34 . . . .108 C2
Scunthorpe DN15 . . . . .183 B3
Yaxley PE7 . . . . .233 D6
Chapel Way 6 DN20 . . . .196 D3
Chapel Yd 2 PE9 . . . . . .219 C5
Chaplin Cl 22 LN4 . . . . . 95 D4
Chaplin St LN5 . . . . . . .234 A1
Chapman Ave
6 Burgh le Marsh
PE24 . . . . .102 E7
Scunthorpe DN17 . . . . .184 D6
Chapman Cres 4 DN36 . . 36 D8
Chapman Gr 1 DN35 . . .192 F5
Chapman Rd
Cleethorpes DN35 . . . . .192 D7
5 Sleaford NG34 . . . . . .212 B6

Chapman St
Kingston upon Hull
HU8 . . . . .181 A8
3 Market Rasen LN8 . . . 57 E7
Chapnall Cl 18 PE13 . . . .170 E1
Chapnall Rd PE13 . . . . . .170 E1
Chappell Rd 3 PE11 . . . .166 C6
Chapter Cl LN2 . . . . 68 C7
Chapter Wk 12 DN20 . . . 19 E3
Charing Cl HU3 . . . . . . .180 C8
Chariots Way 6 PE6 . . . .164 C5
Charity St NG32 . . . . . . .119 D4
Charles Ave
11 Ancaster NG32 . . . . .120 A2
Grimsby DN33 . . . . . . .191 D2
3 Laceby DN37 . . . . . . 23 E1
Louth LN11 . . . . .198 D7
12 New Waltham DN36 . .195 C6
18 Scotter DN21 . . . . . . 29 C3
Charles Baines Com Prim
Sch DN21 . . . . .197 F4
Charles Cl
Bourne PE10 . . . . .213 D6
1 Skegness PE25 . . . . . .206 B4
Charles Cope Rd PE2 . . . .229 F5
Charles Gate LN11 . . . . . 63 A8
Charles Hume Ct 3
DN32 . . . . .192 B8
Charles Lovell Way
DN17 . . . . .184 D8
Charles Rd
5 Fleet Hargate PE12 . . .159 C7
2 Stamford PE9 . . . . . .219 A7
6 Sutton Bridge PE12 . . .160 E4
Charles Read High Sch The
NG33 . . . . .152 F7
Charles St W LN1 . . . . . .201 D4
Charles St
Boston PE21 . . . . .209 A3
2 Cleethorpes DN35 . . . .192 F5
3 Kingston upon Hull
HU2 . . . . .180 F7
Lincoln LN5 . . . . .234 B1
Louth LN11 . . . . .198 C6
Newark-on-Trent NG24 . .104 A4
Peterborough PE1 . . . . .226 B3
1 Sleaford NG34 . . . . . .212 C4
Wrange PE22 . . . . .114 C2
Charlestown Way HU9 . . .181 C6
Charlesworth St 2
LN1 . . . . .201 D3
Charles Wright Cl 15
LN12 . . . . 64 B4
Charlette Way 13 PE11 . .214 B5
Charlock Dr PE9 . . . . . . .218 D6
Charlotte Cl 4 LN8 . . . . . 57 E7
Charlotte St 5 HU1 . . . . .181 A7
Charlotte Wlk 5 PE11 . . .145 A8
Charlton Ct PE3 . . . . . . .225 B1
Charlton St DN31 . . . . . .188 E1
Charnwood Cl PE2 . . . . . .231 A7
Charter Cl PE21 . . . . . . .208 E7
Charterhouse Dr DN16 . . .185 C4
Charterhouse La 1
HU2 . . . . .181 A7
Charters La PE12 . . . . . .216 A6
Charter's La PE12 . . . . . .216 A5
Charters The 2 PE9 . . . .172 C6
Chase Hill Rd DN40 . . . . 12 C5
Chase St PE13 . . . . .170 D1
Chase The
Boston PE21 . . . . .209 C3
Crowland PE6 . . . . . . .166 F1
Holbeach PE12 . . . . . . .215 E2
Long Sutton PE12 . . . . .216 C4
9 Metheringham LN4 . . . 95 C4
Pinchbeck PE11 . . . . . .156 E8
Ropsley NG33 . . . . . . .131 A1
Weston PE12 . . . . .145 F1
Whaplode PE12 . . . . . . .147 A6
Wisbech PE13 . . . . . . .170 C1
Chasm & Northorpe Slipe
Nature Reserve The*
PE10 . . . . .165 B8
Chater La PE9 . . . . .171 A3
Chater Rd 5 PE8 . . . . . .172 B1
Chatham St HU3 . . . . . . .179 F7
Chatsfield PE4 . . . . .220 B3
Chatsworth Ave NG31 . . .211 F5
Chatsworth Cl
4 Lincoln LN2 . . . . . . .202 C8
6 Market Deeping PE6 . .217 A5
Chatsworth Dr
4 Lincoln LN6 . . . . . . .204 C2
Louth LN11 . . . . .198 B7
Chatsworth Pl
Cleethorpes DN35 . . . . .192 C4
Peterborough PE3 . . . . .225 B2
Chatsworth Rd PE9 . . . . .218 C6
Chatsworth St HU5 . . . . .180 B8
Chatsworth Way 12
DN9 . . . . 27 D2
Chatterton Ave LN1 . . . . .201 E8
Chatterton Cres DN15 . . .183 C4
Chaucer Ave
12 Mablethorpe/Sutton on
Sea LN12 . . . . 64 B4
Scunthorpe DN17 . . . . .184 D7
Chaucer Cl 1 PE13 . . . . .170 B1
Chaucer Dr LN2 . . . . . . .202 C6
Chaucer Gdns 10 NG34 . .212 F4
Chaucer Rd PE1 . . . . . . .225 C4
Chaucer's Way PE11 . . . .214 A4
Chauntry Rd 19 LN13 . . . 75 F2
Cheal La PE11 . . . . .144 F2

Cheal Rd PE11 . . . . **144** F4
Cheapside
　Kingston upon Hull
　　HU8 . . . . **181** A8
　Waltham DN37 . . . . **194** F2
Cheapside Rd DN36 . . . . . . **36** A4
Chedburgh Cl 1 LN6 . . . . **204** B6
Chedworth Cl 1 LN2 . . . . **202** D7
Chedworth Rd LN2 . . . . . . **202** D7
Cheese Hill 10 PE20 . . . . **135** B7
Cheesemans Cl 4
　DN37 . . . . **194** E4
Cheesemans La DN37 . . . . **194** E4
Cheethams La LN4 . . . . . . **110** F2
Chelmer Cl LN6 . . . . **204** F4
Chelmer Garth 2 PE4 . . **221** D1
Chelmsford Ave DN34 . . . **191** A5
Chelmsford Dr NG31 . . . . **210** F4
Chelmsford Pl DN34 . . . . **191** A6
Chelmsford St LN5 . . . . . . **234** B1
Chelsea Cl LN6 . . . . **200** D2
Chelsea Wlk DN35 . . . . . . **193** A1
Cheltenham Cl
　Peterborough PE2 . . . . . . **226** B6
　Scunthorpe DN16 . . . . . . **185** C4
Cheltenham Way
　Humberston DN35 . . . . . . **192** F1
　7 Mablethorpe/Sutton on Sea
　　LN12 . . . . **64** A3
Chelveston Way PE3 . . . . **225** C4
Chelwood Dr DN33 . . . . . . **191** B3
Chelwood Rd DN17 . . . . . . **184** F7
Chepstow Cl 1 PE11 . . . **156** E3
Chepstow Gr DN34 . . . . . . **191** A5
Chequered Flag Karting★
　DN36 . . . . **195** C1
Chequergate 1 LN11 . . . **198** B5
Chequers La DN22 . . . . **65** A2
Chequers The DN15 . . . . . **182** D3
Cheriton Cl 1 LN3 . . . . **83** B4
Cheriton Pk PE10 . . . . **213** D7
Cherries The PE12 . . . . . . **216** D4
Cherry Ave LN4 . . . . **81** D2
Cherry Cl
　Humberston DN36 . . . . **36** D8
　8 Sleaford NG34 . . . . . . **212** D6
Cherry Cnr PE22 . . . . **113** A5
Cherry Cobb Sands Rd
　HU12 . . . . **13** F8
Cherry Dale DN35 . . . . . . **192** D3
Cherryfields PE2 . . . . **229** E6
Cherry Garth HU3 . . . . **180** A5
Cherry Gr
　10 Belton DN9 . . . . **16** E1
　Lincoln LN6 . . . . **205** A8
　10 Market Deeping PE6 . . **217** C5
　Scunthorpe DN16 . . . . . . **185** B6
Cherry Holt 1 LN3 . . . . **203** E5
Cherryholt La PE9 . . . . . . **219** D5
Cherry Holt La
　13 Pinchbeck PE11 . . . . **156** E8
　Sutterton PE20 . . . . **136** A4
Cherryholt Rd PE9 . . . . . . **219** D5
Cherry Holt Rd PE10 . . . **213** F4
Cherry La
　Barrow upon Humber
　　DN19 . . . . **11** D8
　7 Fleet PE12 . . . . **159** C7
　Stubton NG23 . . . . **118** B7
　Wootton DN39 . . . . **11** E2
Cherry Mount DN16 . . . . **185** C4
Cherry Orch
　21 Epworth DN9 . . . . **27** E6
　Grantham NG31 . . . . **211** D5
Cherry Orton Rd PE2 . . . **229** F5
Cherry Rd 9 PE13 . . . . . . **170** D2
Cherrytree Ave PE25 . . . . . **90** E4
Cherry Tree Ave 4
　DN20 . . . . **196** B4
Cherry Tree Cl 4 LN6 . . **204** F2
Cherry Tree Cres DN34 . . **190** F6
Cherry Tree Dr 5 DN7 . . **14** D5
Cherrytree Gr PE1 . . . . . **226** C6
Cherry Tree Gr
　2 Hatfield DN7 . . . . **14** D5
　Spalding PE11 . . . . **214** F5
Cherry Tree La
　Holbeach PE12 . . . . **215** D4
　23 Nettleham LN2 . . . . . . **68** C2
Cherry Tree Rd DN21 . . . **197** E5
Cherry Tree Rise DN21 . . . **29** C4
Cherry Tree's Bsns Pk
　DN31 . . . . **188** C2
Cherry Tree Way
　3 Coningsby LN4 . . . . . . **207** D4
　17 Metheringham LN4 . . . . **95** C4
Cherry Way 34 DN17 . . . . **29** D7
CHERRY WILLINGHAM
　LN3 . . . . **203** E5
Cherry Willingham Com
　Sch LN3 . . . . **203** D7
Cherry Willingham Prim
　Sch LN3 . . . . **203** D5
Cherry Wlk PE21 . . . . . . **208** D4
Cherrywood Dr NG31 . . . **210** F8
Chesboule La PE11 . . . . . **144** E5
Chesham Dr 7 PE6 . . . . . **164** E4
Cheshire Gr 7 PE25 . . . . **206** A5
Cheshire La LN6 . . . . **92** E5
Cheshire Rd LN6 . . . . **204** B5
Cheshire Wlk DN37 . . . . . **190** E8
Chesney Dr DN16 . . . . . . **185** A3
Chesney Rd LN2 . . . . **202** D7
Chesnut Cl 11 LN2 . . . . . . **68** F2
Chesnut Dr 12 LN2 . . . . . . **68** F2

Chesnut Way 4 DN19 . . . . **12** A8
Chesswick Ave DN17 . . . . . **17** D5
Chester Cl LN4 . . . . **203** D1
Chesterfield Rd DN15 . . . **182** B2
Chester Gdns 8 NG31 . . **210** D5
Chester Grange DN33 . . . **191** E1
Chester Pl DN32 . . . . **192** C5
Chester Rd PE1 . . . . **226** C3
CHESTERTON PE7 . . . . . **228** F3
Chesterton Gr PE2 . . . . . **231** D6
Chester Way PE21 . . . . . . **208** C3
Chestnut Ave
　7 Donington PE11 . . . . . . **134** E2
　Edenham PE10 . . . . **153** C2
　Gainsborough DN21 . . . . **197** D6
　Grimsby DN31 . . . . **191** B7
　Holbeach PE12 . . . . **215** C3
　Immingham DN40 . . . . . . **186** E5
　Kingston upon Hull
　　HU3 . . . . **178** C1
　Peterborough PE1 . . . . . . **226** B7
　RAF Cranwell NG34 . . . . **107** D1
　Spalding PE11 . . . . **214** E5
　3 Stainforth DN7 . . . . **14** D6
　7 Thorne/Moorends
　　DN8 . . . . **15** B7
Chestnut Cl
　Bottesford NG13 . . . . **128** B6
　Digby LN4 . . . . **108** E6
　Glinton PE6 . . . . **220** B8
　Horncastle LN9 . . . . **199** A5
　4 Metheringham LN4 . . . . **95** C4
　1 Peakirk PE6 . . . . **174** A5
　4 Scotter DN21 . . . . **29** C3
　2 Sleaford NG34 . . . . . . **212** D3
　Swaton NG34 . . . . **133** D4
　13 Waltham DN37 . . . . . . **194** C4
Chestnut Cres 3 LN5 . . . . **92** F3
Chestnut Dr
　5 Coningsby LN4 . . . . . . **207** D4
　Louth LN11 . . . . **198** E6
　38 Messingham DN17 . . . . **29** D7
　2 Thorney PE6 . . . . **176** A3
Chestnut Gdns PE9 . . . . . **218** D5
Chestnut Gr
　11 Barnetby le Wold
　　DN38 . . . . **21** A8
　3 Broughton DN20 . . . . . . **19** E4
　4 Colsterworth NG33 . . . **151** E7
　1 Grantham NG31 . . . . . **210** D2
　Waddington LN5 . . . . **205** C1
Chestnut La NG33 . . . . . . **152** C8
Chestnut Rd
　3 Boston PE21 . . . . **209** C2
　Lincoln LN6 . . . . **204** F2
　Waltham DN37 . . . . **194** C4
Chestnut Rise 1 DN19 . . . . **11** C8
Chestnut St CE Prim Sch
　NG34 . . . . **108** F1
Chestnut St
　Lincoln LN1 . . . . **234** A4
　5 Ruskington NG34 . . . . **108** E1
Chestnuts The 7 LN2 . . . . **68** C2
Chestnut Terr 2 PE12 . . **160** E4
Chestnut Way
　6 Binbrook LN8 . . . . **47** C5
　4 Bourne PE10 . . . . **213** B5
　3 Market Deeping PE6 . . **217** B6
　Scunthorpe DN16 . . . . . . **185** B8
Chestnut Wlk 5 DN41 . . . . **24** A5
Cheviot Ave PE4 . . . . **221** C2
Cheviot Cl
　Gonerby Hill Foot
　　NG31 . . . . **210** E7
　Sleaford NG34 . . . . **212** A3
　6 Thorne/Moorends
　　DN8 . . . . **15** A7
Cheviot St LN2 . . . . **234** C2
Chichester Cl 6 NG31 . . **210** E5
Chichester Dr 20 LN7 . . . **33** B4
Chichester Rd
　6 Binbrook Tech Pk
　　LN8 . . . . **47** C5
　4 Bracebridge Heath
　　LN4 . . . . **81** A4
　Cleethorpes DN35 . . . . . **192** F4
Chieftain Rd 1 LN6 . . . . **205** C8
Chieftain Way 1 LN6 . . . **205** C8
Childersgate La PE12 . . . **159** D2
Childers' N Dro
　Cowbit PE12 . . . . **157** B5
　Spalding PE11 . . . . **214** F3
Childers' S Dro
　Cowbit PE12 . . . . **157** B4
　Pinchbeck PE11 . . . . **214** F2
Chiltern Cl NG31 . . . . **210** E7
Chiltern Cres DN17 . . . . . **184** D8
Chiltern Dr
　Spalding PE11 . . . . **214** E6
　Waltham DN37 . . . . **194** D3
Chiltern Prim Sch HU3 . . **180** B5
Chiltern Rd 3 LN5 . . . . . **205** D3
Chiltern Rise PE4 . . . . . . **221** B2
Chiltern Way
　3 Grimsby DN33 . . . . . . **194** E8
　24 North Hykeham LN6 . . . **93** C8
Chilton Cl 7 DN40 . . . . . **186** B4
China St PE22 . . . . **114** C4
Chingford Ave DN34 . . . . **191** A4
Chippendale Cl
　2 Birchwood LN6 . . . . . . **204** D6
　2 Humberston DN36 . . . . . **36** D8
Chippendale Rd 3
　LN6 . . . . **204** D6
Chippenham Mews 1
　PE2 . . . . **230** C7
Chisenhale PE2 . . . . **229** E6
Chivenor Cl 3 LN6 . . . . . **200** B1

Cholmley St HU3 . . . . **180** B5
Chopdike Dro PE11 . . . . . **144** D3
Christ Church Cl PE9 . . . **219** B7
Christchurch Rd 10
　NG31 . . . . **211** D7
Christine Pl DN33 . . . . . . **195** A8
Christopher Cl
　5 Heckington NG34 . . . . **122** E3
　Louth LN11 . . . . **198** D7
　3 Manby LN11 . . . . **62** C6
　Peterborough PE1 . . . . . . **225** F8
Christopher Cres 11
　NG34 . . . . **212** F4
Christopher Dr 8
　PE13 . . . . **170** C1
Christopher Rd 6 LN13 . . . **75** C2
Christopher's La 4
　PE10 . . . . **213** D6
Christ's Hospl Terr
　LN2 . . . . **234** B3
Church Ave
　Ashby de la Launde &
　　Bloxholm LN4 . . . . **108** B5
　Humberston DN36 . . . . . . **36** C8
　7 North Ferriby HU14 . . . . **3** A4
Church Balk DN8 . . . . **15** B8
Church Bank 2 PE34 . . . **161** F3
Church Cl
　2 Bonby DN20 . . . . **10** C2
　24 Boston PE21 . . . . **208** F5
　Donington on Bain LN11 . . **59** E2
　Grimsby DN32 . . . . **192** B5
　12 Louth LN11 . . . . **198** B5
　16 Mablethorpe/Sutton on Sea
　　LN12 . . . . **77** A8
　4 Newborough PE6 . . . . **174** E4
　11 Sibsey PE22 . . . . **113** B1
　11 Sleaford NG34 . . . . . **212** B4
　Stoke Rochford NG33 . . . **139** F2
　3 Thorne/Moorends
　　DN8 . . . . **15** B8
　Wrangle PE22 . . . . **114** C1
Church Cres 4 DN9 . . . . . **28** A3
Church Ct
　Scunthorpe DN15 . . . . . . **183** B4
　3 Stamford PE9 . . . . **219** C4
Church Dr
　Lincoln LN6 . . . . **201** D1
　Misterton DN10 . . . . **39** F5
　Norton Disney LN6 . . . . . . **92** C1
　Peterborough PE2 . . . . . . **229** F4
　Surfleet PE11 . . . . **145** D3
Church End
　Gedney PE12 . . . . **159** D7
　9 Leverington PE13 . . . . **170** B2
CHURCH END LN11 . . . . . **50** F6
Church End
　Skegness PE25 . . . . **206** B8
　Wrangle PE22 . . . . **114** C1
Church End Dro PE11 . . . **134** F1
Church Farm Cl 23
　PE24 . . . . **90** D7
Church Farm Mus★
　PE25 . . . . **206** B4
Churchfield Ct PE4 . . . . . **225** E8
Churchfield Rd
　Peterborough PE4 . . . . . . **221** B1
　Scunthorpe DN16 . . . . . . **185** B5
Church Fields
　Pickworth NG34 . . . . **142** A8
　Winterton DN15 . . . . **9** A5
Churchfields Rd DN34 . . . **142** C6
Churchfleet La PE11 . . . . **145** B7
Churchgate
　Gedney PE12 . . . . **159** D7
　4 Sutterton PE20 . . . . . . **136** A2
Church Gate
　Fleet PE12 . . . . **159** B6
　2 Market Deeping PE6 . . **217** F4
　Spalding PE11 . . . . **214** D3
　2 Sutton Bridge PE12 . . **160** E4
　Whaplode PE12 . . . . **158** B6
Churchgate Mews 5
　PE12 . . . . **159** D7
Church Gdns 15 PE12 . . **160** A8
Church Gn PE12 . . . . **216** C4
Church Gn Cl PE21 . . . . . **209** F2
Church Gn La
　Frampton PE20 . . . . **136** B7
　Quadring PE11 . . . . **135** A1
Church Gn Rd PE21 . . . . **209** F4
Church Hill
　Belvoir NG32 . . . . **138** C6
　1 Burgh le Marsh PE24 . . **102** E7
　Castor PE5 . . . . **223** E2
　2 Grasby DN38 . . . . **32** E7
　Heighington/Washingborough
　　LN4 . . . . **203** B2
　Ingham LN1 . . . . **55** A2
　Riby DN37 . . . . **23** C2
　Spridlington LN8 . . . . **55** F3
　Whitton DN15 . . . . **1** E3
Church Hill Cl PE7 . . . . . **231** C1
Churchill Ave
　Bourne PE10 . . . . **213** B4
　Bracebridge Heath LN4 . . **205** F4
　Brigg DN20 . . . . **196** D4
　2 Hatfield DN7 . . . . **14** F4
　Horncastle LN9 . . . . **199** C2
　4 Keelby DN41 . . . . **23** A5
　4 Market Rasen LN8 . . . . **57** D7
　4 Skegness PE25 . . . . . . **206** D7
Churchill Cl 6 LN11 . . . . **50** F7
Churchill Ct 2 PE12 . . . . **216** B5
Churchill Dr
　3 Boston PE21 . . . . **209** D4
　2 Martin LN10 . . . . **97** B4
　Spalding PE11 . . . . **214** D2

Churchill La LN12 . . . . **63** E8
Churchill Rd
　Gorefield PE13 . . . . **169** F3
　North Somercotes LN11 . . **50** F7
　Stamford PE9 . . . . **219** B7
Churchill St HU9 . . . . **181** D7
Churchill Way
　Grimsby DN32 . . . . **191** F7
　Heckington NG34 . . . . . . **122** D3
　5 Lea DN21 . . . . **52** F6
Church La
　Addlethorpe PE24 . . . . **90** D4
　Algarkirk PE20 . . . . **136** B2
　Alvingham LN11 . . . . **49** F2
　Appleby DN15 . . . . **9** D1
　9 Ancaster NG32 . . . . . . **120** A2
　Aylesby DN37 . . . . **23** E2
　Balderton NG24 . . . . **104** C2
　7 Bardney LN3 . . . . **83** B4
　Baumber LN9 . . . . **72** B1
　Benniworth LN8 . . . . **71** E8
　Besthorpe NG23 . . . . **91** D7
　4 Billinghay LN4 . . . . . . **109** F5
　Blyton DN21 . . . . **41** C5
　Bonby DN20 . . . . **10** C2
　19 Boston PE21 . . . . **208** F5
　Bottesford NG13 . . . . . . **128** C4
　Bourne PE10 . . . . **213** D4
　Brant Broughton LN5 . . . **105** F5
　Brigsley DN37 . . . . **35** D4
　4 Brough HU15 . . . . **2** C7
　5 Broughton DN20 . . . . . . **19** E3
　Buckminster NG33 . . . . . **150** F4
　Burton Coggles NG33 . . **152** D8
　Cadney DN20 . . . . **31** D6
　6 Carlton-le-Moorland
　　LN5 . . . . **105** E8
　3 Caythorpe NG32 . . . . . **119** B7
　24 Chapel St Leonard
　　PE24 . . . . **90** D7
　Cherry Willingham/Reepham
　　LN3 . . . . **203** E5
　Clipsham LE15 . . . . **162** B7
　Coleby LN5 . . . . **93** F3
　6 Collingham NG23 . . . . . **91** D5
　Corringham DN21 . . . . **41** E2
　Counthorpe & Creeton
　　NG33 . . . . **153** A2
　Croft PE24 . . . . **102** E5
　7 Crowland PE6 . . . . **166** F1
　Croxton Kerrial
　　NG32 . . . . **138** D4
　1 Donington DN21 . . . . . . **39** F5
　Eagle & Swinethorpe LN6 . . **79** B2
　East Keal PE23 . . . . **100** E6
　Edenham PE10 . . . . **153** F4
　Elkington LN11 . . . . **60** E7
　Ewerby & Evedon NG34 . . **122** C6
　5 Fishlake DN7 . . . . **14** D8
　3 Folkingham NG34 . . . . **142** D8
　Fotherby LN11 . . . . **49** A2
　Friesthorpe LN3 . . . . **57** A2
　Friskney PE22 . . . . **114** F6
　Frithville PE22 . . . . **125** D8
　5 Glentham LN8 . . . . **43** F1
　Goulceby LN11 . . . . **72** D6
　Grainthorpe LN11 . . . . **50** B7
　Great Gonerby NG31 . . . **210** C8
　Great Limber DN37 . . . . . **22** D3
　Grimsby DN37 . . . . **190** E2
　1 Hagworthingham PE23 . . **87** A4
　Harmston LN5 . . . . **93** F5
　Haxey DN9 . . . . **27** C2
　Heckington NG34 . . . . . . **122** E1
　3 Helpringham NG34 . . . **133** D4
　3 Helpston PE6 . . . . **173** C4
　Holton le Clay DN36 . . . **195** D4
　Horbling NG34 . . . . **133** B4
　3 Horncastle LN9 . . . . . . **199** B4
　Hougham NG32 . . . . **118** C3
　Humberston DN36 . . . . . . **36** B8
　Huttoft LN13 . . . . **76** E3
　Immingham DN40 . . . . . . **186** B5
　3 Ingham LN1 . . . . **54** F2
　Ingoldmells PE25 . . . . . . **206** C8
　7 Keadby with Althorpe
　　DN17 . . . . **17** D4
　Keddington LN11 . . . . . . **198** E8
　3 Keelby DN41 . . . . **23** A4
　Kingston upon Hull
　　HU10 . . . . **178** C8
　Kirkby la Thorpe NG34 . . **121** F4
　Kirkby on Bain LN10 . . . . **98** C5
　Kirton PE20 . . . . **136** C5
　12 Laceby DN37 . . . . **23** F1
　2 Legbourne LN11 . . . . . . **61** F3
　Lincoln LN4 . . . . **234** B4
　3 Little Bytham NG33 . . **163** A8
　Londonthorpe & Harrowby
　　without NG31 . . . . **130** D5
　Long Bennington NG23 . . **117** E2
　Luddington & Haldenby
　　DN17 . . . . **7** D4
　Lutton PE12 . . . . **160** C4
　14 Mablethorpe/Sutton on Sea
　　LN12 . . . . **77** A8
　3 Mareham le Fen PE22 . . **98** F4
　Marshchapel DN36 . . . . . **37** B1
　17 Metheringham LN4 . . . . **95** D4
　Minting LN9 . . . . **84** C8
　5 Misterton DN10 . . . . . . **39** F5
　Misterton LN13 . . . . **89** B6
　Moulton PE12 . . . . **157** F7
　Navenby LN5 . . . . **107** A8
　Newton PE13 . . . . **170** A5
　North Carlton LN1 . . . . . . **67** C4
　10 North Kelsey LN7 . . . . **32** A4
　North Kyme LN4 . . . . **109** F3

Church La continued
　North Rauceby NG32 . . . **120** C5
　North Scarle LN6 . . . . **78** E1
　North Somercotes LN11 . . **50** E6
　Old Somerby NG33 . . . . **140** E8
　Owersby LN8 . . . . **44** F5
　5 Owmby LN8 . . . . **55** F6
　Peterborough PE2 . . . . . . **229** F5
　Pickworth NG34 . . . . **132** A1
　6 Potterhanworth LN4 . . . **82** B1
　Rand LN8 . . . . **70** A5
　Ropsley & Humby NG33 . . **131** B1
　Roughton LN9 . . . . **85** B1
　Saltfleetby LN12 . . . . **63** B7
　Saxby All Saints DN20 . . . **10** B3
　Saxilby with Ingleby LN1 . . **66** C3
　Scambleby LN11 . . . . **72** F5
　Scawby DN20 . . . . **20** A1
　Scopwick LN4 . . . . **108** E8
　6 Scotter DN21 . . . . **29** C3
　Scredington NG34 . . . . . . **132** F7
　Scunthorpe DN15 . . . . . . **182** E2
　Sedgebrook NG32 . . . . . **128** F4
　Silk Willoughby NG34 . . . **121** B1
　Skegness PE25 . . . . **206** B8
　Skidbrooke with Saltfleet
　　Haven LN11 . . . . **51** B4
　Sleaford NG34 . . . . **212** D5
　Snitterby DN21 . . . . **43** D5
　South Clifton NG23 . . . . . **78** C6
　South Kyme LN4 . . . . **123** A8
　15 South Witham NG33 . . **151** D2
　Spilsby PE23 . . . . **87** E1
　Springthorpe DN21 . . . . . **53** E8
　Sproxton LE14 . . . . **150** C7
　Stallingborough DN41 . . . **23** D6
　9 Stamford PE9 . . . . **219** C4
　Sudbrooke LN2 . . . . **68** F3
　Swaby LN13 . . . . **74** E3
　13 Swineshead PE20 . . . **135** B7
　Tallington PE9 . . . . **172** F6
　Tealby LN8 . . . . **46** C1
　Tetford LN9 . . . . **73** F1
　Tetney DN36 . . . . **36** D3
　3 Timberland LN4 . . . . . . **96** C1
　Torksey LN1 . . . . **65** D5
　Toynton St Peter PE23 . . . **101** A6
　Twin Rivers DN14 . . . . **7** A8
　Tydd St Giles PE13 . . . . . **169** F7
　Tydd St Mary PE13 . . . . **160** B1
　2 Ulceby DN39 . . . . **12** A1
　Utterby LN11 . . . . **48** F3
　Waddington DN21 . . . . . . **43** D7
　21 Waddington LN5 . . . . . **93** F7
　Wainfleet St Mary PE24 . . **102** B1
　Waithe DN36 . . . . **36** A3
　Waltham DN37 . . . . **194** E4
　Wansford PE8 . . . . **222** D2
　Welby NG32 . . . . **130** F3
　2 Welton/Dunholme
　　LN2 . . . . **68** D6
　3 Westborough & Dry
　　Doddington NG23 . . . . . **117** F3
　West Keal PE23 . . . . **100** C6
　Withern with Stain LN13 . . **62** F1
　Wood Enderby LN9 . . . . . **98** F7
　Wrangle PE22 . . . . **114** C1
　Wyberton PE21 . . . . **136** F8
　Wymondham LE14 . . . . . **150** C1
CHURCH LANEHAM
　DN22 . . . . **65** B3
Church La Prim Sch
　NG34 . . . . **212** D5
Church Lees NG32 . . . . . **131** C6
Church Mdws PE20 . . . . **136** C5
Church Meadow Dr 20
　PE24 . . . . **90** D7
Church Mews 7 PE20 . . **136** A2
Church Pk 17 LN12 . . . . . . **77** A8
Church Rd
　Auburn Haddington & South
　　Hykeham LN5 . . . . **93** A5
　4 Bicker PE20 . . . . **135** A4
　Boston PE21 . . . . **209** B4
　4 Butterwick PE22 . . . . . **126** E3
　Friskney PE22 . . . . **115** A6
　Harby NG23 . . . . **79** B5
　4 Ketton PE9 . . . . **171** A3
　Laughton DN21 . . . . **41** C8
　Leverington PE13 . . . . . . **170** E1
　3 Mablethorpe/Sutton on Sea
　　LN12 . . . . **64** A3
　North Ferriby HU14 . . . . . . **3** A4
　Old Leake PE22 . . . . **114** A1
　Saxilby LN1 . . . . **66** D2
　Skellingthorpe LN6 . . . . . **200** A4
　Stainforth DN7 . . . . **14** C6
　Stickford PE22 . . . . **100** B3
　1 Stow LN1 . . . . **66** C8
　Ulceby with Fordington
　　LN13 . . . . **88** C7
　Upton DN21 . . . . **53** D5
　Wigtoft PE20 . . . . **135** E3
　Wisbech PE13 . . . . **170** B1
　Wittering PE8 . . . . **172** B4
Church Rd N PE25 . . . . . **206** B4
Church Rd S 4 PE25 . . . **206** B3
Church Rise 5 PE22 . . . . **98** F4
Church Row HU8 . . . . **181** A8
Church Side
　3 Alkborough DN15 . . . . . **8** C8
　Appleby DN15 . . . . **9** D1
　19 Goxhill DN19 . . . . **12** A8
　3 Grasby DN38 . . . . **32** E7
　3 West Halton DN15 . . . . . **8** E7
　14 Winterton DN15 . . . . . . **9** A5
Church Sq DN15 . . . . **183** B3

Church St
4 Alford LN13 75 F3
Amcotts DN17 7 F1
Barkston NG32 130 B8
2 Barrowby NG32 210 A5
2 Baston PE6 164 E4
Beckingham DN10 40 A1
4 Billingborough NG34 133 B1
2 Billinghay LN4 109 F5
20 Boston PE21 208 F5
Bottesford NG13 128 A5
7 Brough HU15 2 C7
5 Burgh le Marsh PE24 102 E8
14 Caistor LN7 33 B4
Candlesby PE23 88 F2
Carlby PE9 163 D5
4 Carlton-le-Moorland LN5 105 E8
Collingham NG23 91 C4
Corby Glen NG33 152 F8
2 Crowle DN17 16 D7
Denton NG32 139 A7
Digby LN4 108 D5
3 Donington PE11 134 E2
Easton on the Hill PE9 171 D3
Elsham DN20 20 F7
1 Epworth DN9 27 E6
6 Fishlake DN7 14 D8
1 Foston NG32 117 F1
3 Fulletby LN9 86 B8
Gainsborough DN21 197 C5
Glentworth DN21 54 F6
4 Gosberton PE11 145 B6
16 Goxhill DN19 12 A8
Grantham NG31 211 A5
Grimsby DN32 189 B1
1 Haconby PE10 154 D8
5 Harlaxton NG32 139 C7
Haxey DN9 27 C2
6 Heckington NG34 122 E3
Hemswell DN21 42 D1
7 Hibaldstow DN20 30 F5
Holbeach PE12 215 D2
Kingston upon Hull HU10 178 E6
7 Kirton in Lindsey DN21 30 B1
Long Bennington NG23 117 D3
Louth LN11 198 C5
Market Deeping PE6 217 B5
6 Market Rasen LN8 57 D8
Messingham DN17 29 D7
7 Middle Rasen LN8 57 B8
Misterton DN10 39 F5
20 Nettleham LN2 68 C2
Nettleton LN7 33 B3
Northborough PE6 173 F6
12 North Kelsey LN7 32 A4
North Witham NG33 151 D4
Owston Ferry DN9 28 A3
Peterborough PE2 231 C7
Peterborough PE4 220 F3
Peterborough PE7 229 A4
Pinchbeck PE11 145 C1
17 Ruskington NG34 108 E2
7 Ryhall PE9 163 C1
9 Scawby DN20 30 E8
10 Scothern LN2 68 F4
Skillington NG33 151 A8
10 South Witham NG33 151 D2
Spalding PE11 214 D4
11 Spilsby PE23 87 F1
8 Stamford PE9 219 C4
Sturton le Steeple DN22 52 B2
21 Sutton Bridge PE12 160 E4
1 Sutton on Trent NG23 91 A8
26 Thorne/Moorends DN8 15 A8
9 Thorney PE6 176 A3
Thurlby PE10 164 D7
Willoughton DN21 42 E4
1 Wragby LN8 70 D4
Yaxley PE7 233 D4
Churchthorpe 1 LN11 49 B8
Churchtown 9 DN9 16 E1
CHURCH TOWN DN9 16 E1
Church View
2 Alkborough DN15 8 C8
11 Barton-upon-Humber DN18 10 F8
1 Beckingham DN10 40 A1
13 Bottesford NG13 128 A6
9 Brough HU15 2 C7
Freiston PE22 126 D2
3 Gainsborough DN21 53 A5
8 Great Gonerby NG31 129 D5
Grimsby DN34 190 E7
Northborough PE6 217 E1
10 Ruskington NG34 108 E2
2 Waltham DN37 194 E4
Churchview Cl 5 NG34 122 D3
Church View Cl
3 Belton DN9 16 E1
1 Donington PE11 134 E2
Peterborough PE2 231 B7
Church View Cres LN3 82 B7
Churchway PE22 127 A5
Church Way PE13 160 A1
Church Wlk
Bourne PE10 213 D5
Brant Broughton & Stragglethorpe LN5 105 F4
1 Dunham-on-Trent NG22 65 B1
2 Holbeach PE12 215 D2
3 Holton le Clay DN36 195 D2
1 Legbourne LN11 61 F3
1 Manby LN11 62 C6
Church Wlk *continued*
21 Metheringham LN4 95 D4
1 Owston Ferry DN9 28 A3
Peterborough PE1 226 A3
2 Pinchbeck PE11 156 F8
Sibsey PE22 113 B2
Upton PE6 223 B5
Yaxley PE7 233 D4
Chuter Ede Prim Sch NG24 104 C2
Cinder La LN11 198 B5
Circle The 4 HU13 178 E2
Cirencester Cl LN6 93 B8
Cissbury Cl 12 LN12 77 A8
Cissbury Ring PE4 221 A2
Cissplatt La DN41 23 A5
Cisterngate 3 LN11 198 B6
Citadel Way HU9 181 A6
City of Lincoln Com Coll The LN6 205 A8
City Rd PE1 226 A2
City Sports Ctr LN6 205 A8
City Sq Ctr LN1 234 B2
Claires Wlk DN17 184 C7
Clampgate Rd PE21 126 C1
Clapgate Pits Nature Reserve* DN15 19 E5
Clapton Gate PE12 157 E5
Clara Terr LN1 234 A3
Clare Ave DN17 184 D7
Clare Cl
11 Lincoln LN5 205 D3
7 Stamford PE9 219 A5
Clare Cres DN16 185 A3
Clare Ct
4 Baston PE6 164 E4
Grimsby DN34 191 A5
Claremont Rd
1 Burgh le Marsh PE24 102 E8
Gainsborough DN21 197 E2
Grimsby DN32 192 D6
Claremont St LN2 234 C2
Clarence Cl 2 DN40 186 B3
Clarence Gdns 3 PE11 214 E2
Clarence Rd
Peterborough PE1 225 E5
28 Wisbech PE13 170 D1
3 Woodhall Spa LN10 97 D6
Clarence St
Kingston upon Hull HU1 181 A6
1 Lincoln LN1 201 E6
Clarendon Gdns 1 LN1 201 E8
Clarendon Rd
Grimsby DN34 190 E4
Scunthorpe DN17 184 F7
Skegness PE25 206 A4
Clarendon St HU3 180 D7
Clarendon View LN1 201 E8
Clarendon Way PE6 220 D8
Clare Rd
Northborough PE6 217 E1
Peterborough PE1 225 F6
Claricoates Dr 9 NG24 104 C8
Clarina St LN2 202 B4
Clark Ave DN31 191 A7
Clarke Ct 10 PE21 136 D8
Clarke Rd 11 LN6 93 C8
Clarkes Rd 3 DN40 12 E4
Clarke St 2 DN15 183 A3
CLARK'S HILL PE12 159 B3
Clarkson Ave 1 PE12 167 B8
Clarkson Ct 27 PE13 170 D1
Clarkson Infants Sch The PE13 170 E1
Clarksons Dr 3 DN41 23 E6
Clasketgate LN2 234 B2
Clatterdykes Rd PE20 136 E6
Claudette Ave PE11 214 B5
Claudette Way 5 PE11 214 B5
Claudius Rd LN6 93 B8
Clavering St 6 DN31 188 D1
CLAXBY LN8 45 D5
Claxby Rd DN17 184 F5
CLAXBY ST ANDREW LN13 88 E6
Claxby Springs Nature Reserve* LN13 88 E6
Claxy Bank PE22 114 D6
Clay Bank LN4 123 C7
Clay Bank Rd DN8 15 C6
Clayberg Dr 2 NG34 212 D5
Clayburn Rd PE7 230 D1
Clayden St 4 DN31 188 D1
Claydike Bank PE20 124 B4
Clay Dro PE11 156 C5
Clayfield Rd DN15 182 F6
Clay Hill Rd NG34 212 A3
Clayhough La DN22 65 B3
Clay La
Carlton-le-Moorland LN5 105 D8
Castor PE5 223 E2
Fenton LN1 65 E4
Gate Burton DN21 53 B1
Harby NG23 79 C5
Holton le Clay DN36 195 D3
Kirton in Lindsey DN21 30 A1
Newark NG24 104 B4
Norton Disney LN5 92 D2
Scotter DN21 29 C4
Stapleford LN6 105 B7
Tetford LN9 73 F2
Clay La *continued*
Toft Newton LN8 56 C7
Waddingham DN21 43 D7
CLAY LAKE PE11 214 E2
Clay Lake Bank PE12 157 A3
Clay Lake La PE11 214 E2
Claymore Cl DN35 192 E6
Clay Pit La NG34 122 C6
Claypole NG23 117 F7
Claypole CE (Controlled) Prim Sch NG23 117 F8
Claypole Dr PE6 217 E1
Claypole La NG23 117 E6
Claypole Rd NG23 118 A7
Claythorne Dr DN21 197 E4
CLAYTHORPE LN13 75 B6
Claythorpe Wr Mill* LN13 75 B5
Clayton PE2 230 B4
Clayton Cl 16 PE13 170 E1
Clayton Cres PE12 157 C2
Clayton Rd LN5 205 E6
Clayworth Rd 6 DN10 39 C1
CLEATHAM DN21 30 B3
Cleatham PE3 225 A4
Cleatham Rd DN21 30 B3
Clee Cres DN32 192 C5
Cleefields Cl DN32 192 B5
Clee Ness Dr DN36 193 A1
Clee Rd DN35 192 C5
Cleethorpe Rd DN32 189 B1
CLEETHORPES DN35 192 D5
Cleethorpes Coast Light Rly & Mus* DN35 193 B3
Cleethorpes Ctry Pk* DN35 192 F2
Cleethorpes Discovery Ctr* DN35 193 B3
Cleethorpes Leisure Ctr DN35 193 A4
Cleethorpes Nature Reserve* DN35 193 D2
Cleethorpes Showground* DN35 193 C3
Cleethorpes Sta DN35 192 F7
Clee Village DN32 192 C6
Clematis App LN6 204 C8
Clematis Ave 7 DN41 23 F5
Clematis Cl LN4 81 D2
Clematis Way DN16 185 C4
Clementine Cl PE25 206 B6
Clensey La NG23 117 F5
Clerke St DN35 192 B8
Clevedon Rd DN17 184 D8
Cleveland Ave 26 LN6 93 C8
Cleveland Cl
2 Immingham DN40 186 A4
2 Scunthorpe DN17 184 D8
4 Spalding PE11 214 F4
Cleveland Ct 3 PE4 221 C2
Cleveland Gdns 2 DN31 188 D1
Cleveland St
2 Gainsborough DN21 197 D3
3 Grimsby DN31 188 D1
Kingston upon Hull HU8 181 A8
Cleveland Way 27 DN7 14 D4
Cleve Pl 3 PE6 175 A1
Cley Hall Gdns PE11 214 E4
Cleymond Chase 2 PE20 136 C5
Cliff Ave
22 Nettleham LN2 68 C2
Winterton DN15 8 F5
Cliff Closes Rd DN15 182 D3
Cliff Cres 1 PE9 219 B5
Cliff Dr
Burton upon Stather DN15 8 B5
3 Kingston upon Hull HU13 3 E4
Cliffe Ave 1 NG34 108 D1
Cliffe Cl 19 NG34 108 D2
Cliffedale Prim Sch NG31 211 A8
Cliffe Rd
Easton on the Hill PE9 171 D2
Gonerby Hill Foot NG31 210 E7
Cliffe View NG34 120 E4
Cliff Gdns DN15 182 F2
Cliff Gr 9 DN18 10 E8
Cliff La
Marston NG32 129 D8
Waddingham DN21 43 C6
Washingborough LN4 81 D4
Clifford Rd PE25 206 B4
Cliff Rd
Fulbeck NG32 119 C8
Hessle HU13 3 E4
Leadenham LN5 106 D2
Snitterby DN21 43 C5
Spridlington LN8 55 F3
Stamford PE9 219 B5
Welbourn LN5 106 E4
Welton LN2 68 C6
Winteringham DN15 9 A8
Woolsthorpe by Belvoir NG32 128 D1
Cliffside 3 LN5 107 A7
Cliff St DN16 183 C2
Cliff The DN15 182 D3
Cliff Top La 2 HU13 3 E4
Clifton Ave PE3 225 E3
Clifton Ct 2 DN8 15 A8
Clifton Gr 3 PE25 206 D1
Clifton Prim Sch HU2 180 E8
Clifton Rd
Boston PE21 209 E4
Grimsby DN34 191 A6
Clifton St LN5 234 B1
Clint La 9 LN5 107 A8
Clinton Dr NG34 212 C2
CLINTON PARK LN4 207 A5
Clinton Pk Prim Sch LN4 207 A5
Clinton Terr 3 DN21 197 D3
Clinton Way LN10 97 B5
Clipseygap La PE10 154 B6
CLIPSHAM LE15 162 B7
Clipsham Rd PE9 162 D8
Clipston Wlk PE3 225 C5
Clive Ave LN6 205 C8
Clive Sullivan Way
Barton-upon-Humber DN19 4 A4
Kingston upon Hull HU4 179 C1
CLIXBY DN38 33 A7
Clixby Cl DN35 193 A3
Clixby La DN38 32 E7
Cloddy Gate LN11 50 F5
Cloister Cl DN17 184 E6
Cloisters The
Grimsby DN37 190 D7
17 Humberston DN36 36 D8
Welton LN2 68 C7
Cloister Wk 14 DN20 19 E3
Cloot Dro PE6 166 F2
Close The
Barkston NG32 130 A8
1 Colsterworth NG33 151 D7
Easton on the Hill PE9 171 C3
2 Fiskerton LN3 82 A7
2 Goxhill DN19 5 A1
Grimsby DN34 191 C7
Scunthorpe DN16 183 B2
4 Skegness PE25 206 C4
Sleaford NG34 212 B2
5 Sturton by Stow LN1 66 D7
1 Woodhall Spa LN10 97 C6
Closshill La PE21 136 F8
Clouds La
Belton DN9 17 B1
West Butterwick DN17 28 C8
Clough La
Firsby PE23 101 F5
Kirton PE20 136 F2
Clough Rd
Gosberton PE11 144 D4
Holbeach PE12 215 B7
Cloven Ends 4 PE6 164 F3
Clover Ct DN20 196 B4
Cloverfields Prim Sch DN36 36 C8
Clover Gdns 6 PE9 218 C7
Clover La PE20 135 D4
Clover Rd
6 Bracebridge Heath LN4 81 A1
Market Deeping PE6 217 C5
Misterton LN13 89 A6
Clover Way PE11 214 B6
Clowes Ct 4 HU13 178 E1
Club Ct NG24 104 B2
Clubhurn La PE11 145 D4
Club Way PE7 230 E4
Cludd Ave NG24 104 C4
Clumber Ave NG24 104 A3
Clumber Dr 7 PE11 214 C6
Clumber Pl DN35 192 E5
Clumber St
Kingston upon Hull HU5 180 C8
Lincoln LN5 205 E7
Clutton's Cl 4 PE6 166 E1
Clyde Ct 1 NG31 210 E2
Clydesdale Cres 1 PE11 214 A2
Clyde St HU3 179 F5
Clyfton Cres DN40 186 B4
Coach House Gdns 8 DN20 30 E8
Coachings The HU13 3 E4
Coach Rd NG32 118 C3
Coachroad Hill DN21 54 F7
Coalbeach La 1 PE11 145 E3
Coalbeach La S PE11 145 E4
Coalport Cl 7 LN6 204 D7
Coal Shore La LN11 37 D1
Coal Yd La NG23 78 C4
COATES
North Leverton with Habblesthorpe DN22 65 B8
Stow LN1 54 C2
Coates Ave 27 DN15 9 A5
Coates Rd DN22 65 B8
Cobbet Pl PE1 226 B3
Cobblers Way 6 NG34 212 E3
Cobbs Hill 13 PE34 161 F3
Cobden Ave PE1 225 F4
Cobden St
1 Gainsborough DN21 197 C4
Kingston upon Hull HU3 179 F7
Peterborough PE1 225 F4
Cob Gate PE12 158 A6
Cobgate Cl 2 PE12 158 B6
Cobham Cl 11 NG34 122 E3
Cobleas NG32 138 D8
Cochran Cl 9 NG31 210 F8
Cockbourn Fen Dike PE12 159 B2
Cockburn Way 6 LN5 93 F5
Cockerels Roost LN1 65 D1
Cocketts La 10 DN20 30 F5
Cocklehole Rd PE34 161 B5
Cock Pit Cl HU10 178 C6
Cockthorne La DN15 9 C7
CODDINGTON NG24 104 D5
Coddington CE Prim Sch NG24 104 D5
Coddington La LN6 105 A7
Coddington Rd NG24 104 C3
Coelus St HU9 181 A7
Cogan St HU1 180 E5
Coggles Causeway PE10 213 D4
Cogglesford Mill* NG34 212 F5
Coggles Way LN11 61 E3
Cohort Cl 13 HU15 2 C5
Coke Oven Ave DN16 183 F2
Colchester Mews 12 LN6 93 B8
Coldham Rd LN4 207 E6
COLD HANWORTH LN2 56 C2
COLD HARBOUR NG33 130 D1
Cold Harbour La
Carrington PE22 112 B6
Covenham St Mary LN11 49 D5
Grantham NG31 211 C2
Coldhorn Cres 14 PE13 170 D1
Cold Hurn La PE11 144 F6
COLEBY
Coleby LN5 93 F3
West Halton DN15 8 E6
Coleby CE Prim Sch LN5 93 F3
Coleby Rd DN15 8 E7
Coleby St LN2 202 B3
Colegrave St 14 LN5 205 E8
Cole La PE22 100 B3
Colenso Terr 3 LN1 201 D4
Coleraine Cl 8 LN5 205 D2
Coleridge Ave DN17 184 D7
Coleridge Ct 5 LN4 207 B5
Coleridge Gdns
Lincoln LN2 202 B7
15 Sleaford NG34 212 F4
Coleridge Gn 3 LN2 202 C7
Coleridge Pl
Bourne PE10 213 E3
Peterborough PE1 225 E8
Coles Ave LN13 75 E2
Coles Cl PE12 215 E3
Cole's La 1 PE20 135 B7
Cole St DN15 183 B3
Colin Ave DN32 192 B6
Colindale PE21 209 B5
Colin Rd DN16 183 C2
Colins Wy 4 DN21 29 C4
College Ave DN33 194 F8
College Cl
7 Alkborough DN15 8 C8
1 Holbeach PE12 215 C2
Horncastle LN9 199 C2
Lincoln LN1 201 F6
Stamford PE9 171 C8
7 Wainfleet All Saints PE24 102 D1
College Gdns 2 DN33 194 F8
College Pk
Horncastle LN9 199 C2
Peterborough PE1 226 C5
College Rd
Barrow upon Humber DN19 11 E7
Cranwell & Byard's Leap NG34 120 E8
Thornton Curtis DN39 12 B6
College St
Cleethorpes DN35 192 E6
Grantham NG31 211 B3
Grimsby DN34 191 C6
1 Kingston upon Hull HU2 180 E7
College Yd DN20 196 B3
Colleysgate PE12 216 C8
Colley St 11 PE21 208 F5
Colleywell Cl 5 DN9 27 A2
Collier Cl 11 HU14 3 A4
Collier Rd 2 DN40 186 D5
Collier St HU1 180 E6
COLLINGHAM NG23 91 C4
Collingham PE2 229 F3
Collingham Rd LN6 91 F5
Collingham Sta NG23 91 D4
Collingwood 21 LN6 93 C8
Collingwood Cres
3 Boston PE21 136 D8
Grimsby DN34 190 D4
Collingwood Prim Sch HU3 180 C7
Collingwood St HU3 180 D7
Collinson Ave DN15 182 C3
Collinson La
19 Balderton NG24 104 C1
Newport HU15 1 A8
Collison Gate PE24 102 C2
Collum Ave DN16 185 B6
Collum Gdns 2 DN16 185 B6
Collum House Rd DN16 185 B6
Collum La DN16 185 B6
Collynson Cl 1 HU10 178 E8
COLLYWESTON PE9 171 B1
Collyweston Rd 1 PE8 172 B1
Colne Cl 1 LN6 204 F3
Colne Ct 6 NG31 210 E2

Colne Valley Visitor Ctr★ PE6 .... 227 B2
Colonial St HU2 .... 180 D7
Colonsay Ct DN36 .... 195 C7
Colson Pl DN35 .... 192 B7
Colster Way 3 NG33 .... 151 E6
COLSTERWORTH NG33 .... 151 E7
Colsterworth CE Prim Sch NG33 .... 151 E7
Colsterworth Rd NG33 .... 151 C6
Colsuan Gdns PE12 .... 216 C3
Coltman St HU3 .... 180 C5
Colton Cl 6 PE6 .... 164 E4
Colton St
Brigg DN20 .... 196 B4
2 Misterton DN10 .... 39 F5
Coltsfoot Cl 4 DN15 .... 182 C6
Coltsfoot Dr
Bourne PE10 .... 213 D2
Bradley DN37 .... 194 B5
Peterborough PE2 .... 230 E7
Coltsfoot Way PE10 .... 213 D2
Columbia Rd DN32 .... 192 A7
Columbus Cl 5 PE11 .... 214 C2
Columbus Way DN33 .... 190 F3
Colvile Rd PE13 .... 170 A5
Colville Ave HU4 .... 179 B6
Colville Terr 3 DN21 .... 197 D4
Colwyn Ave PE1 .... 226 E6
Comber Pl DN32 .... 189 B1
Combe St DN35 .... 192 C8
Comer Cl PE21 .... 209 A5
Comforts Ave DN15 .... 183 A2
Commerce La HU1 .... 180 D4
Commerce Rd PE2 .... 229 C5
Commercial Rd
2 Alford LN13 .... 75 F2
Grantham NG31 .... 211 A3
Kingston upon Hull HU1 .... 180 E5
1 Louth LN11 .... 198 D6
Scunthorpe DN16 .... 183 D3
Spalding PE11 .... 214 E5
Commodore Croft 6 HU1 .... 180 F5
Common Balk LN13 .... 76 C1
Common Dro PE6 .... 166 C3
Common La
Bardney LN3 .... 83 C4
Barnby Dun with Kirk Sandall DN3 .... 14 B4
Burgh le Marsh PE24 .... 89 F1
Heapham DN21 .... 53 F7
North Somercotes LN11 .... 50 F8
Old Leake PE22 .... 113 F4
Sturton le Steeple DN22 .... 52 C3
Twin Rivers DN14 .... 7 B6
Welton HU15 .... 2 D4
Woodside DN9 .... 26 E6
Common Mid Rd DN17 .... 16 C8
Common Rd
Broughton DN20 .... 19 E4
Gedney Hill PE12 .... 176 F8
Moulton PE12 .... 146 E3
Parson Drove PE12 .... 176 F6
South Cave HU15 .... 1 C7
Waddingham DN21 .... 43 D6
Whaplode PE12 .... 168 A2
Wrangle PE22 .... 114 B4
Commonside
2 Crowle DN17 .... 16 C8
Westwoodside DN9 .... 27 A2
Common Side Rd PE22 .... 113 E4
Common Way PE13 .... 160 B1
Comper Swift Cl 1 LN12 .... 77 A7
Compton Cl 1 PE25 .... 206 C1
Compton Dr DN34 .... 191 C7
Concast Rd DN16 .... 19 A3
Conduit La NG31 .... 211 A4
Conduit Rd PE9 .... 219 C6
Coney Garth La PE11 .... 145 F5
Coneygree Rd PE2 .... 231 D6
Conference Ct DN16 .... 185 A2
Conference Way 13 PE13 .... 170 D2
Conging St 2 LN9 .... 199 B4
Congreves Cl 3 PE12 .... 160 A8
Conifer Cl
6 Kingston upon Hull HU5 .... 179 C7
2 Scunthorpe DN17 .... 184 C5
Conifers The PE2 .... 229 F6
CONINGSBY LN4 .... 207 D4
Coningsby Airfield LN4 .... 207 C2
Coningsby Cl
Boston PE21 .... 208 D5
Gainsborough DN21 .... 197 F4
2 Skegness PE25 .... 206 A5
Coningsby Cres LN4 .... 205 F5
Coningsby Dr DN34 .... 191 A5
Coningsby Rd
Coningsby LN4 .... 207 A1
Peterborough PE3 .... 220 E1
Scunthorpe DN17 .... 184 D5
Coningsby St Michaels Prim Sch LN4 .... 207 C4
Coningsby St LN2 .... 234 C2
Conisborough Ave DN36 .... 195 B6
Conisborough Mews 22 HU15 .... 2 D5
CONISHOLME LN11 .... 50 D6
Conisholme Rd LN11 .... 50 B7
Coniston Ave 1 DN33 .... 194 E7
Coniston Cres DN36 .... 192 E1
Coniston Dr LN6 .... 205 A2
Coniston Rd PE4 .... 221 C3
Connaught Ave DN32 .... 191 D4
Connaught Dr
4 Chapel St Leonard PE24 .... 90 D7
6 Kirk Sandall DN3 .... 14 A2
Connaught Rd DN21 .... 197 C6
Connaught Terr LN5 .... 205 D5
Conquest Dro PE7 .... 231 D1
Consort Ct HU9 .... 181 B5
Constable Ave LN6 .... 205 A6
Constable Cl LN6 .... 205 A5
Constable Prim Sch HU3 .... 180 C5
Constable St HU3 .... 180 C5
Constable Way 23 HU15 .... 2 D5
Constance Ave LN6 .... 204 F4
Constitutional Ave DN35 .... 192 C8
Convamore Rd DN32 .... 191 F6
Convent La HU3 .... 180 D6
Conway Ave
Grimsby DN34 .... 191 A7
Peterborough PE4 .... 221 A2
Conway Cl HU3 .... 180 B5
Conway Dr LN6 .... 205 B2
Conway Prep Sch PE21 .... 208 F5
Conway Sq 3 DN15 .... 182 E3
Conworth Cl PE1 .... 226 D5
Conyard Rd DN35 .... 192 E7
Conyers Ave DN33 .... 191 D2
Cook Cl Rd PE7 .... 233 D6
Cook Dr PE11 .... 214 C2
Cooke Cres 9 LN4 .... 207 D4
Cookridge Dr 31 DN7 .... 14 D4
Cooks La
Grimsby DN37 .... 24 B5
4 Nettleton LN7 .... 33 A3
Cook's La PE23 .... 88 E3
Cooks Lock PE21 .... 208 C3
Cookson Cl PE7 .... 233 D4
Cookson Wlk PE7 .... 233 E4
Cook's Rd PE11 .... 145 E7
Coomb Brigg's Prim Sch DN40 .... 186 A3
Cooper Ave PE25 .... 90 E4
Cooper La DN37 .... 23 E1
Cooper Rd DN32 .... 192 A7
Coopers Cl PE12 .... 168 B4
Coopers Holt Cl LN6 .... 200 A3
Coots Cl PE25 .... 103 C8
Coots La LN13 .... 76 E1
Copeland PE3 .... 225 A3
Copeland Ct 5 NG34 .... 212 C3
Cope St DN32 .... 192 A8
Copper Beech Cl
1 Gainsborough DN21 .... 52 F6
6 Swanland HU14 .... 3 B6
Copper Beech Way PE2 .... 231 B7
Copper Beech Wlk DN16 .... 185 B3
Copper St LN10 .... 84 B3
Coppice Ave 13 DN7 .... 14 D3
Coppice La 2 DN7 .... 14 D3
Coppice Rd 11 PE9 .... 163 C1
Coppice Side HU4 .... 179 C6
Coppingford Cl PE2 .... 231 D6
Copse Cl DN40 .... 186 C5
Copse Rd DN16 .... 185 B5
Copse The
Brigg DN20 .... 196 E2
Grimsby DN33 .... 194 F8
16 Mablethorpe/Sutton on Sea LN12 .... 77 A7
Copsewood PE4 .... 221 A4
Copthill Sch PE9 .... 172 C6
Coral Dr 1 DN37 .... 194 C5
CORBY GLEN NG33 .... 152 E8
Corby Glen Com Prim Sch NG33 .... 152 E8
Corby Pk HU14 .... 3 A5
Corby Rd
Burton Coggles NG33 .... 141 A1
Scunthorpe DN16 .... 183 C2
Swayfield NG33 .... 152 D5
Cordage Ct LN1 .... 234 A3
Cordeaux Cl
Louth LN11 .... 198 C7
8 Scotter DN21 .... 29 C4
Cordeaux Sch LN11 .... 198 B7
Cordella Cl 1 HU3 .... 180 A5
Corden Cl PE25 .... 206 C1
Corfe Ave PE4 .... 221 A2
Corfe Cl 1 NG31 .... 210 E5
Corfe Wlk DN40 .... 186 D3
Coriander Dr 11 PE10 .... 213 C6
Corinne Cres 3 PE25 .... 206 C3
Corinne Gr 1 PE11 .... 214 A3
Corinthian Ave DN34 .... 191 B6
Corinthian Way HU9 .... 181 D6
Cork La PE24 .... 102 B3
Cork Tree Cres PE21 .... 208 E2
Cormack La 15 NG24 .... 104 C1
Cormorant Dr DN37 .... 190 C8
Corn Cl
Fiskerton LN3 .... 82 B7
Horncastle LN9 .... 199 B5
Cornfield Cl 4 DN33 .... 194 D8
Cornfields PE12 .... 215 F3
Cornfield View 2 NG34 .... 212 C2
Cornflower Cl
18 Healing DN41 .... 23 F5
Stamford PE9 .... 218 C6
Cornflower Way 3 LN6 .... 93 A8
Cornhill LN5 .... 234 B2
Cornhill Dr DN18 .... 11 A8
Cornhill La 30 PE21 .... 208 F5
Cornish Cres NG34 .... 133 E7
Cornley Rd DN10 .... 39 C7
Cornmarket 8 LN11 .... 198 B5
Cornstall Bldgs 7 PE9 .... 219 C5
Cornwall Cl
Grantham NG31 .... 211 C7
12 Scampton LN1 .... 67 E5
Cornwallis Rd LN2 .... 202 D4
Cornwall Rd
5 Keadby DN17 .... 17 D6
Scunthorpe DN16 .... 185 C5
8 Stamford PE9 .... 219 B6
Cornwall St 21 DN21 .... 30 B1
Cornwall Way 8 NG34 .... 108 D2
Cornwell Cl DN33 .... 191 C3
Corona Dr 3 DN8 .... 15 A8
Coronation Ave
3 Crowland PE6 .... 175 B8
2 Deeping St Nicholas PE11 .... 166 C6
Parson Drove PE12 .... 177 A7
Coronation Cl
1 Louth LN11 .... 198 D7
3 Spalding PE11 .... 157 B6
Coronation Cotts DN35 .... 192 F5
Coronation Cres
Coleby LN5 .... 93 F3
3 Epworth DN9 .... 27 D6
Coronation Rd
Cleethorpes DN35 .... 192 F5
Corby Glen NG33 .... 152 E8
Ingoldmells PE25 .... 90 F3
3 Market Rasen LN8 .... 57 D7
9 Stainforth DN7 .... 14 C6
5 Ulceby DN39 .... 12 A1
Woodhall Spa LN10 .... 97 D6
Corporation Bank 12 PE6 .... 166 E1
Corporation Rd
1 Grimsby DN31 .... 188 E1
Grimsby DN31 .... 191 D8
10 Kingston upon Hull HU9 .... 5 D8
4 Scunthorpe DN15 .... 183 A3
Corran Garth 6 HU4 .... 179 A3
Correen Cl 2 LN5 .... 205 D2
CORRINGHAM DN21 .... 41 E2
Corringham CE Prim Sch DN21 .... 41 E2
Corringham Rd DN21 .... 197 F5
Corringham Rd Ind Est DN21 .... 41 A1
Corsair Gr 4 HU3 .... 180 A4
Corwood Cl LN2 .... 202 E7
Cosford Cl LN6 .... 204 B8
Cosgrove Cl
2 Lincoln LN6 .... 205 A6
Peterborough PE3 .... 225 C6
Cosgrove St 5 DN35 .... 192 F6
Costa Row NG23 .... 117 D3
Costello Stadium★ HU4 .... 179 C4
COSTON LE14 .... 150 C5
Coston Rd NG33 .... 150 E5
Cotelands Sch NG34 .... 108 E1
Cot Garth La DN21 .... 53 E3
Cotham Gdns 22 DN41 .... 23 A4
Cotman Rd LN6 .... 205 B6
Cotman Wlk LN6 .... 205 A6
Cotswold Cl
22 Lincoln LN6 .... 93 C8
3 Peterborough PE4 .... 221 C1
Cotswold Dr
Great Gonerby NG31 .... 210 E7
Waltham DN37 .... 194 D4
Cotswold Rd 5 DN8 .... 15 A7
Cottage Beck Rd DN16 .... 183 B2
Cottage Cl 2 DN20 .... 30 F5
Cottage Dr HU10 .... 178 B8
Cottage La
Collingham NG23 .... 91 C3
1 Lincoln LN6 .... 205 B4
North Clifton NG23 .... 78 D7
Cottage Paddock The LN6 .... 205 B5
Cottage Yd La DN36 .... 36 C7
COTTAM DN22 .... 65 C7
Cottesmore Cl
Grantham NG31 .... 211 B6
Peterborough PE3 .... 225 D4
Cottesmore Rd
Birchwood LN6 .... 204 D5
Cleethorpes DN35 .... 192 E2
Kingston upon Hull HU13 .... 178 F2
5 Stamford PE9 .... 218 E5
Cottingham Ct DN15 .... 183 A4
Cottingham Dr LN2 .... 202 B7
Cotton End PE3 .... 225 A4
Cotton Rd PE21 .... 208 D6
Cotton Smith Way 1 LN2 .... 68 C2
Coulam Pl 11 DN36 .... 36 D8
Coulbeck Dr DN35 .... 192 D5
Coulby Cl NG23 .... 117 F7
Coulman Rd DN8 .... 15 B8
Coulman St DN8 .... 15 B8
Coulson Cl 13 DN20 .... 31 A5
Coulson Dr HU13 .... 178 F2
Coulson Rd LN6 .... 201 D1
Coultas Ct 3 HU3 .... 180 A6
Coult Ave LN6 .... 93 C8
Council Ave HU4 .... 179 E3
Council Rd 19 PE13 .... 170 E1
Council St PE4 .... 225 D8
Council Terr 6 DN18 .... 3 E1
Count Alan Rd PE25 .... 206 D8
Counter Drain Dro PE11 .... 155 E2
Counthorpe La NG33 .... 152 E2
Counthorpe Rd NG33 .... 152 F3
County Rd
3 Hampton Vale PE7 .... 230 C1
Yaxley PE7 .... 233 C8
County Rd S 2 HU5 .... 179 C8
Coupland Cl 5 DN21 .... 197 F5
Coupledyke La PE20 .... 136 D5
Courtfield Cl 10 LN2 .... 68 F2
Courtfields PE6 .... 217 B6
Courtney St HU8 .... 181 B8
Court The PE24 .... 77 C3
Courtyard The
Boston PE21 .... 209 B3
Market Deeping PE6 .... 217 C4
Stamford PE9 .... 219 A5
Covel Rd NG34 .... 212 B6
COVENHAM ST BARTHOLOMEW LN11 .... 49 C5
COVENHAM ST MARY LN11 .... 49 C5
Coventry Ave DN34 .... 191 A5
Coventry Cl
7 Grantham NG31 .... 210 D5
Peterborough PE4 .... 220 F3
5 Scunthorpe DN17 .... 184 D7
Coventry Rd 7 DN8 .... 15 B8
Cove Rd DN9 .... 26 F3
Coverley Rd 5 NG33 .... 151 D2
Covert Rd DN16 .... 185 B5
Covert The
Clinton Park LN4 .... 207 C5
Peterborough PE3 .... 225 B1
Covill Cl 2 NG31 .... 129 D5
Covington 29 HU15 .... 2 C6
Covin's La LN11 .... 49 C8
Coward's La PE11 .... 144 F2
COWBIT PE12 .... 157 B1
Cowbit Dro PE11 .... 144 C1
Cowbit Endowed CE (Aided) Prim Sch PE12 .... 167 A8
Cowbit Rd PE12 .... 214 D2
COWBRIDGE PE22 .... 125 E6
Cowbridge Bsns Pk PE22 .... 125 E7
Cowbridge Rd PE20 .... 134 E5
Cowbroads La PE22 .... 113 E2
Cowdale La LN1 .... 66 B6
Cow Dale La DN10 .... 39 C3
Cowdale's Dro PE11 .... 134 F1
Cow Dro LN4 .... 123 B7
Cowes Rd NG31 .... 210 E4
Cowgate
Brough HU15 .... 2 D6
2 Heckington NG34 .... 122 E3
Peterborough PE1 .... 225 F2
Cow Gate NG34 .... 143 C8
Cowhams La PE20 .... 146 C8
Cow La
Minting LN8 .... 71 B1
Swinderby LN6 .... 92 B5
Tealby LN8 .... 46 C1
Twin Rivers DN17 .... 7 C6
Upton DN21 .... 53 F6
Welbourn LN5 .... 106 E5
Cowle La 1 LN11 .... 62 A3
Cowley Cl 6 PE20 .... 135 C7
Cowley Endowed (Combined) Prim Sch PE11 .... 134 E2
Cowley's Rd 10 PE11 .... 134 E2
Cow Marsh La DN36 .... 36 E5
Cowpaddle La LN4 .... 82 A5
Cowpasture La DN22 .... 52 D3
Cow Pasture La DN22 .... 65 A7
Cowper Ave DN17 .... 184 D7
Cowper Dr LN2 .... 202 C7
Cowper Rd PE1 .... 225 F7
Cowpers Gate PE12 .... 216 A3
Cowslip Cres PE10 .... 213 D3
Cowslip Dr 2 PE6 .... 217 D6
Cowslip La LN11 .... 198 F8
Cox La 7 DN17 .... 16 D8
Cox's Ct 7 DN20 .... 31 A5
Cox's Dro PE6 .... 167 C1
Cox's Hill DN21 .... 197 D5
Cox's Wlk 8 NG31 .... 129 E5
Coxwold Gr HU4 .... 179 E5
Crabapple Gn PE2 .... 229 D6
Crab La PE20 .... 123 C4
Crabley La HU15 .... 1 E7
Crab Marsh PE13 .... 170 C2
Crabtree PE4 .... 221 F1
Crabtree La
Beckingham DN10 .... 52 A8
Mablethorpe & Sutton LN12 .... 77 A7
Saltfleetby LN12 .... 51 D1
Crabtree Rd
Colsterworth NG33 .... 151 B7
Easton NG33 .... 140 A1
8 Hatfield DN7 .... 14 C5
Skillington NG33 .... 139 F1
Crack Holt La PE22 .... 126 F8
Crackle Hill 6 DN9 .... 27 B2
Cradge Bank Rd
Deeping St Nicholas PE11 .... 167 A7
Spalding PE11 .... 214 C1
Cragg Cl 3 PE20 .... 135 C7
Cragmire La PE22 .... 114 C3
Cragston Ave DN33 .... 191 D3
Craig Cl 3 DN20 .... 19 D3
Craig St PE1 .... 225 F3
Craikbank La DN22 .... 65 A8
Craikhill Ave DN40 .... 186 C4
Craithie Rd DN35 .... 192 E4
Crake Ave DN33 .... 191 C1
Crakedale Rd 9 DN15 .... 9 B5
Crampin Rd 3 DN35 .... 192 E7
Cranberry La PE22 .... 114 F7
Cranberry Way HU4 .... 179 C4
Cranbourne Chase LN6 .... 93 B8
Cranbourne Cl 7 DN35 .... 192 F1
Cranbourne Mews 6 LN4 .... 203 D1
Cranbourne St HU3 .... 180 C8
Crane Ave PE7 .... 233 F6
Crane Cl 1 NG34 .... 120 F8
Crane Gr LN6 .... 205 C7
Cranemore PE4 .... 220 E4
Cranepit La PE11 .... 135 B1
Crane Rd HU9 .... 181 C6
Crane's Gate PE12 .... 158 C1
Cranesgate S PE12 .... 168 C8
Cranford Dr PE3 .... 225 C4
Cranidge Cl 8 DN17 .... 16 D8
Cranmore Dro PE6 .... 165 F1
Cranmore La PE12 .... 215 B1
CRANWELL NG34 .... 120 F8
Cranwell Airfield NG34 .... 120 D7
Cranwell Ave NG34 .... 120 D8
Cranwell Aviation Heritage Centre★ NG34 .... 120 D6
Cranwell Cl
2 Beacon Hill NG24 .... 104 B5
6 Kirton in Lindsey DN21 .... 42 F8
4 Skegness PE25 .... 206 A5
Cranwell Dr DN37 .... 190 F8
Cranwell Prim Sch NG34 .... 120 D8
Cranwell St LN5 .... 201 E1
Crapple La DN21 .... 29 C2
Craske La PE34 .... 161 D3
Craven Ave 4 PE20 .... 136 D5
Craven Prim Sch HU9 .... 181 C8
Craven Rd
Cleethorpes DN35 .... 192 B7
4 Hatfield DN7 .... 14 C4
Craven St N HU9 .... 181 C8
Craven St S HU9 .... 181 D7
Craven's La PE20 .... 146 E7
Craven St LN5 .... 205 D8
Crawcroft La LN13 .... 76 E5
Crawford Gdns 3 PE6 .... 175 C8
Crawthorne Rd PE1 .... 226 A3
Crawthorne St 1 PE1 .... 226 B3
Craycroft Rd 3 DN9 .... 27 B2
Craypool La 7 LN2 .... 68 F4
Craythorne La 23 PE21 .... 208 F5
Creampoke Cres 8 DN21 .... 55 A8
Crease Dro PE6 .... 175 B7
Creaseyplot La PE20 .... 124 B1
CREETON NG33 .... 153 A2
Creeton Rd NG33 .... 153 A1
Crescent Cl 7 LN2 .... 68 D2
Crescent Mews LN5 .... 93 F4
Crescent St DN31 .... 191 C7
Crescent The
Beckingham DN10 .... 40 B1
Bracebridge Heath LN4 .... 81 A2
15 Brough HU15 .... 2 D6
Easton on the Hill PE9 .... 171 C3
10 Eye PE6 .... 175 A1
Fiskerton LN3 .... 82 B7
Gainsborough DN21 .... 52 F5
Hatfield DN7 .... 14 C5
Holton le Clay DN36 .... 195 C2
Horncastle LN9 .... 199 C3
9 Kirk Sandall DN3 .... 14 A1
Louth LN11 .... 198 B7
13 Mablethorpe/Sutton on Sea LN12 .... 77 A7
Morton PE10 .... 154 B7
12 Nettleham LN2 .... 68 C2
Peterborough PE2 .... 230 C5
Ryhall PE9 .... 163 D1
Sleaford NG34 .... 121 A3
9 Spalding PE11 .... 214 D4
Swayfield NG33 .... 152 E5
Cresent The 3 LN8 .... 70 D4
Cresset The★ PE3 .... 225 A5
Cressey St 2 DN31 .... 189 A1
Cresswell Cl PE11 .... 214 E8
Cresta Cl LN6 .... 204 D1
Cresta Dr DN17 .... 184 E4
Cresta The DN34 .... 191 C5
Crester Dr PE4 .... 221 A3
Crew Rd NG23 .... 91 D5
Creyke La 12 HU15 .... 2 D6
Cricketers Way 19 PE13 .... 170 C1
Cridling Pl DN35 .... 192 D4
Cringle Rd NG33 .... 139 F2
Cringleway NG33 .... 140 A5
Cripple Sidings La PE2 .... 231 A8
Crispin Cl
5 Kingston upon Hull HU4 .... 179 A2
13 Lutton PE12 .... 160 A8
Crispin Way DN16 .... 185 B2
Croake Hill NG33 .... 153 A5
Crocus Cl PE7 .... 233 F6
Crocus Gr PE1 .... 226 A8
Crocus Wlk PE11 .... 214 D2
CROFT PE24 .... 102 F4
Croft Bank 1 PE24 .... 102 E2
Croft Cl 3 PE24 .... 102 E2

Croft Dr
Grantham NG31 ... 211 C3
Kingston upon Hull HU10 ... 178 C6
Croft La
Bassingham LN5 ... 92 F3
Cherry Willingham LN3 ... 203 E7
Coningsby LN4 ... 110 E8
Croft PE24 ... 102 E2
Scunthorpe DN17 ... 184 E2
Croft Lodge 1 DN9 ... 16 E1
Croft Marsh La PE24 ... 102 F3
Crofton Cl LN2 ... 202 D4
Crofton Dr LN2 ... 202 D4
Crofton Rd LN2 ... 202 D4
Croft Pk 4 HU14 ... 3 A5
Croft Rd
Croft PE24 ... 102 E3
Finningley DN10 ... 26 A1
Crofts La DN7 ... 14 B6
Croft's La DN9 ... 28 B3
Croft St
2 Horncastle LN9 ... 199 C3
Lincoln LN2 ... 234 B2
Crofts The
7 Humberston DN36 ... 36 C8
Scunthorpe DN16 ... 183 B2
Croft The
6 Beckingham DN10 ... 52 B8
10 Nettleham LN2 ... 68 D2
21 Stamford PE9 ... 219 C5
23 Thorne/Moorends DN8 ... 15 B7
2 West/East Butterwick DN17 ... 28 D8
Croft View HU10 ... 178 C6
Croft Way PE7 ... 230 C2
Cromarty Rd 8 PE9 ... 218 E6
Cromer Ave
Grimsby DN34 ... 191 A5
Mablethorpe/Sutton on Sea LN12 ... 64 D1
Cromer Cl
Harrowby Est NG31 ... 211 E7
4 Lincoln LN6 ... 205 A1
Cromford St 1 DN21 ... 197 D5
Cromwell Ave
6 Gainsborough DN21 ... 52 F6
Grimsby DN31 ... 191 C7
Horncastle LN9 ... 199 C2
2 Woodhall Spa LN10 ... 97 D5
Cromwell Cl
Boston PE21 ... 208 D7
2 Heighington/Washingborough LN4 ... 203 A2
2 Kingston upon Hull HU3 ... 180 D8
Northborough PE6 ... 217 E1
Cromwell Cres 3 NG34 ... 212 E4
Cromwell Ct 1 HU10 ... 178 E7
Cromwell Mews 1 PE6 ... 173 C4
Cromwell Pl LN4 ... 207 A5
Cromwell Rd
Cleethorpes DN35 ... 193 A4
Grimsby DN37 ... 188 A1
Peterborough PE1 ... 225 F4
Cromwell St
Gainsborough DN21 ... 197 D2
Lincoln LN2 ... 202 B3
Cromwell View 21 LN7 ... 33 B4
Cromwell Way 6 PE6 ... 217 A6
Crook Bank LN12 ... 63 F6
Crooked Billet St DN21 ... 197 B8
Crookes Broom Ave 32 DN7 ... 14 D4
Crookes Broom La DN7 ... 14 D4
Crook Hill HU15 ... 2 C8
Crook Mill Rd DN40 ... 12 C4
Crook Tree La DN7 ... 14 F5
Cropper's La PE22 ... 126 F1
Croppers Way PE22 ... 137 E7
Cropston Rd PE1 ... 226 E7
CROSBY DN15 ... 182 D4
Crosby Ave DN15 ... 182 F6
Crosby House Flats DN15 ... 183 B4
Crosby La 1 LN5 ... 106 E4
Crosby Prim Sch DN15 ... 183 A4
Crosby Rd
Grimsby DN33 ... 191 B2
Scunthorpe DN15 ... 183 B4
Crosby Row PE12 ... 160 D4
CROSBY WARREN DN15 ... 183 D6
Crosland Rd DN37 ... 190 D8
Cross Bank LN4 ... 96 D8
Crossbeck Rd DN16 ... 185 A4
Crossberry Way 1 PE6 ... 173 B4
Cross Carr Rd DN20 ... 31 B5
Crosscliff Hill LN11 ... 60 A8
Cross Coates Rd DN34 ... 191 A6
Cross Comm La DN22 ... 52 D3
Cross Dro
Fleet PE12 ... 168 B2
Holland Fen with Brothertoft PE20 ... 125 B5
Horbling NG34 ... 133 F2
Tydd St Giles PE13 ... 169 C5
Crossfield Rd
Kingston upon Hull HU13 ... 178 E3
12 Navenby/Wellingore LN5 ... 107 A8
CROSSGATE PE11 ... 145 C1
Cross Gate
Long Sutton PE12 ... 159 F3
Quadring PE11 ... 135 A1
Spalding PE12 ... 157 B6
Tydd St Mary PE13 ... 160 A2
Weston PE12 ... 157 C7
Crossgate Cres 5 PE11 ... 145 C1
Crossgate La 3 PE11 ... 145 C1
Crossgill Cl NG31 ... 211 F5
Cross Hill
Gringley on the Hill DN10 ... 39 C1
Haxey DN9 ... 27 C3
Cross Keys La LN4 ... 207 F4
Cross Keys Yd 5 NG34 ... 212 D4
Cross La
4 Alkborough DN15 ... 8 C8
4 Amcotts DN17 ... 7 F1
Balderton NG24 ... 104 B1
3 Bourne PE10 ... 213 E2
Butterwick PE22 ... 126 F3
Collingham NG23 ... 91 D5
Flixborough DN15 ... 8 B1
Glentham LN8 ... 44 A2
Gringley on the Hill DN10 ... 39 A5
Harby NG23 ... 79 B5
8 Lincoln LN6 ... 93 C8
Long Bennington NG23 ... 117 D1
North Kelsey LN7 ... 32 B5
Pinchbeck PE11 ... 144 F1
Wellingore LN5 ... 106 E6
Crosslands 5 PE11 ... 134 F2
Crossmoor Bank DN14 ... 6 C5
Cross O'Cliff Cl LN5 ... 205 E6
Cross O'Cliff Hill LN5 ... 205 E6
Cross Rd
Hatfield DN7 ... 15 B4
Langtoft PE6 ... 165 B4
Market Deeping PE6 ... 217 F8
Sutton St Edmund PE12 ... 169 A4
Tydd St Mary PE13 ... 160 B2
Ulceby DN39 ... 12 B3
Cross Slack 5 DN17 ... 16 D8
Cross Spencer St 10 LN5 ... 205 E8
Cross St
Barnby in the Willows NG24 ... 104 F3
8 Barrow upon Humber DN19 ... 11 D8
4 Brigg DN20 ... 196 C3
Cleethorpes DN35 ... 192 E6
13 Crowle DN17 ... 16 D8
Gainsborough DN21 ... 197 B8
Garthorpe & Fockerby DN17 ... 7 E6
Grimsby DN31 ... 189 B2
1 Holbeach PE12 ... 215 D2
Horncastle LN9 ... 199 C3
Kingston upon Hull HU1 ... 180 E6
Lincoln LN5 ... 234 B1
11 Nettleham LN2 ... 68 C2
Peterborough PE1 ... 226 A2
4 Potter Hanworth LN4 ... 82 B1
Scunthorpe DN15 ... 183 B4
3 Skegness PE25 ... 206 B3
Spalding PE11 ... 214 C3
Sturton le Steeple DN22 ... 52 B3
3 Waltham DN37 ... 194 E4
2 West Halton DN15 ... 8 E8
5 Whaplode PE12 ... 158 B7
Cross Tree Rd 21 DN17 ... 29 D7
Crossways 8 DN7 ... 14 C6
Crossway The DN34 ... 190 E3
Crowberry Dr DN16 ... 185 D5
Crowdyke Gate PE12 ... 158 B5
Crowfields PE6 ... 217 F5
Crowhall La PE22 ... 127 A4
Crow Hill Ave DN35 ... 192 E6
Crowhurst 1 PE4 ... 221 A5
Crow La
Gedney PE12 ... 159 D6
Great Hale NG34 ... 122 F1
Leadenham LN5 ... 106 D3
CROWLAND PE6 ... 166 E1
Crowland Ave
Grimsby DN34 ... 190 F4
Scunthorpe DN16 ... 185 A7
Crowland Dr LN6 ... 204 F7
Crowland Ponds Nature Reserve* PE6 ... 166 D2
Crowland Rd
14 Crowle DN17 ... 16 D7
Deeping St James PE6 ... 174 D7
Eye PE6 ... 175 A3
CROWLE DN17 ... 16 D7
Crowle Bank Rd DN17 ... 17 C4
Crowle Dr DN33 ... 191 A3
Crowle Moor Nature Reserve* DN17 ... 6 B1
Crowle Prim Sch DN17 ... 16 C7
Crowle Rd DN17 ... 6 F2
Crowle St HU9 ... 181 D7
Crowle Sta DN17 ... 16 E5
Crown Ave
3 Chapel St Leonard PE24 ... 90 D7
Holbeach PE12 ... 147 C6
Crown Cl 10 NG23 ... 91 D5
Crown Ct 3 DN22 ... 52 B3
Crown Dr PE11 ... 214 F6
Crown Gdns 22 DN21 ... 29 C3
Crown Hill NG33 ... 141 B8
Crown La 14 PE10 ... 164 C8
Crown Lakes Ctry Pk* PE7 ... 231 B2
Crown Lodge PE12 ... 215 C7
Crown Mills 2 LN11 ... 198 D6
Crown St
Peterborough PE1 ... 225 E7
Ryhall PE9 ... 163 C2
7 Stamford PE9 ... 219 B5
Crown Wlk
Bourne PE10 ... 213 C5
Louth LN11 ... 198 E5
Crow Pk LN6 ... 204 A1
Crow's La PE24 ... 102 C2
Crowson Cres PE6 ... 217 E1
Crowson Way PE6 ... 217 D5
Crowston Wlk 7 DN15 ... 183 B3
Crowther Way 8 HU14 ... 3 B7
Crow Tree Bank DN8 ... 15 D4
Crowtree La LN11 ... 198 A5
CROXBY DN37 ... 34 D1
Croxby Ave DN33 ... 194 F8
Croxby Gr DN33 ... 194 F7
CROXTON DN39 ... 21 F7
Croxton Dr LN6 ... 204 F6
CROXTON KERRIAL NG32 ... 138 D4
Croxton Kerrial CE Prim Sch NG32 ... 138 D4
Croxton La NG32 ... 138 D5
Croxton Rd
Croxton DN39 ... 21 F7
Kirmington DN39 ... 22 A5
Sproxton LE14 ... 138 E2
Croyland Rd PE4 ... 221 B1
Croyland Way 15 PE6 ... 166 F1
Crusader Rd LN6 ... 201 C1
Crystal Dr 1 PE2 ... 230 D8
Crystal St HU3 ... 180 C7
Cubitt Way PE2 ... 231 A8
Cuckoo La
Ashby de la Launde & Bloxholm LN4 ... 107 F7
Hatfield DN7 ... 14 E6
Pinchbeck PE11 ... 145 C2
Cul-de-sac The PE22 ... 100 B2
Cullin Cl 1 LN5 ... 205 D2
Culpins Cl PE11 ... 214 F5
CULVERTHORPE NG32 ... 131 E7
Culverthorpe Hall* NG32 ... 131 D7
Culverthorpe Rd NG34 ... 132 A7
Culvert Rd PE24 ... 102 B3
Cumberland Ave
Grimsby DN32 ... 191 D5
14 Navenby/Wellingore LN5 ... 107 A7
Cumberland Gdns NG33 ... 152 D1
Cumberland Rd DN35 ... 193 A2
Cumberland St HU2 ... 181 A8
Cumberland Terr 12 LN8 ... 47 B6
Cumberland Way 17 LN1 ... 67 E5
Cumberlidge Cl 10 PE24 ... 102 E7
CUMBERWORTH LN13 ... 89 F8
Cumberworth La 2 LN13 ... 76 F1
Cumberworth Rd LN13 ... 89 C7
Cunningham Rd
1 Moorland Prison DN7 ... 26 A8
Woodston PE2 ... 230 E8
Cunsdike La PE11 ... 145 D5
Cupola Way DN15 ... 183 A8
Curle Ave LN2 ... 234 C4
Curlew Cl 4 PE12 ... 216 B4
Curlew Dr 8 PE12 ... 167 B8
Curlew Gr PE2 ... 231 D7
Curlew Lodge La PE12 ... 160 F8
Curlew Way NG34 ... 212 B3
Curlew Wlk 14 PE6 ... 217 C5
Curry Rd DN34 ... 190 F7
Curtis Cl 13 NG23 ... 91 D5
Curtis Dr
Coningsby LN4 ... 207 D4
Heighington LN4 ... 81 E4
Curzen Cres 8 DN3 ... 14 A2
Curzon Ave DN35 ... 192 D5
Curzon Ct DN35 ... 192 D5
Curzon Est 6 LN4 ... 207 A5
Curzon Mews 3 LN4 ... 203 D1
Curzon St
1 Gainsborough DN21 ... 197 C6
Kingston upon Hull HU3 ... 179 F7
Cushman Cres DN40 ... 186 C3
Customhouse St 2 PE12 ... 160 F4
Cut Dike PE22 ... 124 D8
Cut End Rd PE22 ... 137 D7
Cuthbert Ave 6 DN38 ... 21 B4
Cuthbert's La PE20 ... 136 B8
CUXWOLD LN7 ... 34 B4
Cuxwold Rd
3 Scunthorpe DN16 ... 185 C8
Swallow LN7 ... 34 B5
Cydonia App LN6 ... 204 C8
Cygnet Cl 8 NG34 ... 212 B3
Cygnet Pk PE7 ... 230 E3
Cygnet Rd PE7 ... 230 E3
Cynthia Rd DN32 ... 192 C5
Cypress Cl
2 Peterborough PE3 ... 225 A2
9 Sleaford NG34 ... 212 D2
Cyprus St 5 HU9 ... 5 D8
Cyrano Way DN37 ... 190 C7
Cyril Cooper Ct DN32 ... 191 D6

D

Daffodil Cl PE11 ... 214 B3
Daffodil Gr PE2 ... 231 C7
Dagger La HU1 ... 180 F6
Daggett Rd DN35 ... 193 A4
Daimler Ave PE7 ... 233 E6
D'aincourt Pk LN4 ... 81 D2
Dairy Cl
1 Gosberton PE11 ... 145 C6
Normanby DN15 ... 8 C3
Dairycoates Ave HU3 ... 180 A4
Dairycoates Rd HU4 ... 179 E3
Dairy Dro PE6 ... 176 E2
Daisy Cl DN16 ... 185 D4
Daisy Ct PE10 ... 213 D3
Daisy Dale PE21 ... 209 A3
DALBY PE23 ... 88 B5
Dalby Ct PE1 ... 226 C8
DALDERBY LN9 ... 85 D1
Dalderby Cres 16 LN2 ... 68 C2
Dale Ave LN3 ... 203 E6
Dale Cl
Peterborough PE2 ... 229 F5
10 Swanland HU14 ... 3 B7
Dale Cres 1 NG24 ... 104 C1
Dalehouse Dr 2 HU10 ... 178 F6
Dale Pit Rd 8 DN7 ... 14 F3
Dale Pk Ave DN15 ... 9 A5
Dale Rd
6 Brough HU15 ... 2 C7
Grantham NG31 ... 211 A7
Swanland HU14 ... 3 B7
Welton HU15 ... 2 E6
Dale St N DN15 ... 182 F5
Dales La DN10 ... 39 A6
Dale's La PE20 ... 135 D5
Dale St
Lincoln LN5 ... 202 B2
Scunthorpe DN15 ... 182 F4
Dales The
25 Nettleham LN2 ... 68 C2
Scunthorpe DN17 ... 184 E3
Dalesway HU10 ... 178 B6
Dale View DN33 ... 190 F3
Dale Way 17 NG24 ... 104 C1
Dallisons Rd 5 DN20 ... 31 A5
Dallygate NG33 ... 140 A5
Dallygate La NG33 ... 140 B5
Dalmatian Way 14 DN20 ... 19 E4
Dame Kendal Gr DN33 ... 191 B3
Damgate PE12 ... 215 E1
Dam Gn La 5 HU15 ... 2 C7
Dam La DN39 ... 11 E5
Dam Rd DN18 ... 3 D1
Dams La LN9 ... 73 B2
Danby Rd 16 DN17 ... 29 D7
Dane Cl
15 Broughton DN20 ... 19 E4
31 Metheringham LN4 ... 95 C4
Danegeld Pl 24 PE9 ... 219 C5
Danes Cl PE1 ... 226 C4
Danes Cotts 13 LN2 ... 234 B3
Danes Ctyd 11 LN2 ... 234 B3
Danesfield NG34 ... 132 E2
Danesfield Ave DN37 ... 194 E5
Danesgate
Lincoln LN2 ... 234 B3
11 New Holland DN19 ... 4 E2
Danes Rd DN21 ... 197 F5
Danes Terr LN2 ... 234 B3
Danethorpe La NG24 ... 104 D8
Danial Cl PE25 ... 206 C8
Daniel Cres 10 LN4 ... 203 D1
Daniel Ct 7 PE9 ... 219 C4
Daniel's Cres PE12 ... 216 C5
Daniel's Dro PE6 ... 167 D1
Daniels Gate 1 PE11 ... 214 C6
Daniel's Gate PE12 ... 216 C7
Daniel's Reach PE11 ... 214 C7
Danish Ct PE4 ... 220 E4
Dansom La S HU8 ... 181 B8
Danson Cl 19 DN18 ... 10 F8
Danube Rd HU5 ... 179 C8
Danum Cl 11 DN8 ... 15 B8
Danum Rd
6 Hatfield DN7 ... 14 D3
Scunthorpe DN17 ... 184 F8
Dar Beck Rd DN21 ... 29 C4
Darby Rd DN15 ... 8 B4
Darbyshire Cl NG23 ... 79 B5
Dark La
Amcotts DN17 ... 7 F1
Barnby in the Willows NG24 ... 105 A3
Bicker PE20 ... 135 A5
Bitchfield & Bassingthorpe NG33 ... 141 A3
Burwell LN11 ... 74 C6
Holbeach PE12 ... 215 B5
Darley Cl PE8 ... 172 C1
Darley Dale Cres 1 NG31 ... 211 A7
Darley's La PE11 ... 214 A6
Darnholm Ct DN37 ... 190 E8
Darnholme Cres
Epworth DN9 ... 28 A8
15 Messingham DN17 ... 29 D7
Darrismere Villas 4 HU3 ... 180 A5
Dart Ave LN6 ... 205 A2
Dartmouth Rd DN17 ... 182 D1
Dartmouth Wlk HU4 ... 179 A3
Darwin Cl
5 Stamford PE9 ... 219 A7
7 Sutton Bridge PE12 ... 160 E4
10 Waddington LN5 ... 93 E8
Darwin Ct
Lincoln LN2 ... 202 B5
Little Coates DN34 ... 190 F6
Darwin St
3 Gainsborough DN21 ... 197 D2
6 Kirton in Lindsey DN21 ... 30 B1
Dashwood Rd 7 LN13 ... 75 E2
Datchet Garth 3 HU4 ... 179 B2
Daubeney Ave LN1 ... 66 D2
Daubney St DN35 ... 189 E1
Davenport Ave HU13 ... 178 D1
Davenport Dr DN35 ... 192 C4
Davey Cl 1 PE21 ... 208 E7
David Ave
Lincoln LN1 ... 201 D8
Louth LN11 ... 198 D7
David Chalmers Cl PE2 ... 230 F8
David Dr PE25 ... 206 B6
David Pl DN36 ... 195 C5
David's Cl PE4 ... 220 D4
David's La
Benington PE22 ... 127 A5
Peterborough PE4 ... 220 F5
David St DN32 ... 191 F5
Davie Pl DN35 ... 192 B7
Davisons Ave DN31 ... 191 D8
Davis's Cl HU10 ... 178 C8
Davos Way PE25 ... 206 A7
Davy Ave DN15 ... 182 E4
Davy Cl 3 LN11 ... 61 F3
Davy Cres DN20 ... 196 C5
Davy's La 6 LN4 ... 81 A2
Dawber La
Claxby St Andrew LN13 ... 88 F5
Thimbleby LN9 ... 85 C5
Dawes La DN16 ... 183 D4
Dawlish Rd DN33 ... 194 E6
Dawnay Dr HU10 ... 179 A6
Dawnhill La DN21 ... 42 E2
Daws Gate
Moulton PE12 ... 157 F2
Whaplode PE12 ... 158 A2
DAWSMERE PE12 ... 148 E5
Dawsmere Rd PE12 ... 148 F4
Dawson Ave 1 PE11 ... 214 F6
Dawson City Claypits Nature Reserve* DN19 ... 5 C4
Dawson Cl
Lincoln LN6 ... 204 F6
6 Newborough PE6 ... 174 E4
Dawson Dr 8 PE24 ... 102 E7
Dawson Rd 7 NG34 ... 212 D6
Dawsons La LN3 ... 203 F8
Daybell Cl 20 NG13 ... 128 A6
Daybrook Cl NG32 ... 139 C8
Day Cl
6 Keadby DN17 ... 17 D6
Wrawby DN20 ... 20 E4
Daymond St PE2 ... 230 D8
Day's La PE20 ... 134 F3
Deacon Dr DN15 ... 182 B2
Deacon Rd LN2 ... 202 C5
Deaconscroft PE3 ... 225 B5
Deacons Sch PE1 ... 226 B5
Deacon St PE1 ... 225 F3
Dealtry Cl DN21 ... 53 D5
Dean Cl 3 NG34 ... 121 B8
Deane Cl 7 NG23 ... 91 D5
Deane Rd DN40 ... 186 D4
Dean Rd
Lincoln LN2 ... 202 C5
Scunthorpe DN17 ... 184 E6
Deans Cl 6 DN10 ... 39 F5
Deansgate DN32 ... 191 C6
Deansgrove DN32 ... 191 D7
Deansway LN4 ... 81 D3
Dear Love Gate
1 Gedney PE12 ... 160 A8
Lutton PE12 ... 148 D1
Dearne Ct 9 HU15 ... 2 D5
Dear St 11 LN8 ... 57 D8
De Aston Sch LN8 ... 57 E7
De Aston Sq 2 DN15 ... 182 E3
Deaton La DN36 ... 195 C6
Debdale PE2 ... 229 E4
Debdale Rd NG32 ... 210 A5
Debdhill Rd DN10 ... 39 F6
De Bec Cl PE1 ... 226 C3
Decoy Cl 16 PE11 ... 145 C1
Decoy Rd
Borough Fen PE6 ... 174 D6
Gorefield PE13 ... 169 D2
Deene Cl
7 Grimsby DN34 ... 190 D4
8 Market Deeping PE6 ... 217 A5
Deene Ct PE3 ... 225 C5
Deep (Aquarium & Marine Research Centre) The* HU1 ... 181 A5
Deepdale Dr NG34 ... 121 C7
Deepdale Gr 2 HU9 ... 181 E8
Deepdale La LN2 ... 68 C2
DEEPING GATE PE6 ... 217 C3
Deeping Lakes Nature Reserve* PE6 ... 174 C7
Deeping Rd PE6 ... 164 E4
DEEPING ST JAMES PE6 ... 217 D4
Deeping St James Com Prim Sch PE6 ... 217 F4
Deeping St James Rd PE6 ... 217 D2
DEEPING ST NICHOLAS PE11 ... 166 C6

Deeping St Nicholas Prim
Sch PE11 . . . . 166 B6
Deepings Leisure Ctr
PE6 . . . . 217 E4
Deepings Sch The PE6 . 217 E5
Deep La PE23 . . . . 87 A5
Deerhurst Way 18 PE6. . 175 A1
Deerleap PE3 . . . . 225 A5
Deer Pk Rd 3 PE6 . . . . 164 F3
Dee St 6 HU3 . . . . 180 B4
Defender Dr DN37 . . . . 190 B7
De Gravel Dr 5 NG34 . . 107 F1
De Havilland Rd PE13 . . 170 D1
Deira Cl NG34 . . . . 212 C1
De la Bere Ave 25 LN12. . 77 A8
De Lacy Ave PE25 . . . . 206 C8
De Lacy La 6 DN35 . . . 192 F6
De Lacy Way DN15 . . . . . . 9 A5
Delamere Cl PE1 . . . . . 226 C5
Delamere Ct DN36 . . . . 192 F1
Delamore Way PE12 . . . 216 C5
De la Pole Ave LN6 . . . 179 F7
Delapre Ct 11 PE6. . . . . 175 A1
Deldale Rd PE21 . . . . . 136 D8
Delfield Rd PE21. . . . . . 136 D8
Delgate Ave 3 PE2 . . . 157 E7
Delgate Bank PE12. . . . 157 D2
Delhi Sq 3 NG34 . . . . . 120 D8
Delhi St 7 HU9. . . . . 5 D8
De Ligne Dr 6 NG32 . . 139 C7
Delius Cl HU4. . . . . 179 B4
Dellfield Ave LN6 . . . . . 200 C1
Dellfield Cl LN6. . . . . . 200 C2
Dellfield Ct 8 LN6. . . . 200 C1
Dell The
16 Broughton DN20 . . . . 19 E3
Peterborough PE2 . . . . 230 E7
Scunthorpe DN17 . . . . 184 D5
Delph Ct PE2 . . . . 231 F6
Delph Fields PE12. . . . . 216 A3
Delph Rd
18 Lincoln LN6. . . . . . . 93 C8
Long Sutton PE12 . . . . 216 A3
Delph The PE11. . . . . . 155 F4
Delves Way PE7 . . . . . . 230 D2
DEMBLEBY NG34 . . . . 132 A4
De Montfort Univ LN2. . 234 B2
Denbigh Ct 11 NG23 . . . 91 D5
Denby Cl DN15. . . . . . . 182 D5
Denby Dale Cl LN6 . . . . 200 C2
Denby Dr DN35 . . . . . . 192 C3
Dene Cl LN6 . . . . 200 B3
Denefield LN6 . . . . 200 B3
Denehall Rd 14 DN3. . . . 14 A2
Dene La LN4. . . . . 109 C7
Dene Rd
Grimsby DN32 . . . . . . 191 E4
Skellingthorpe LN6 . . . 200 B3
Denesway HU13 . . . . . . 178 D2
Dene The
6 Nettleham LN2 . . . . . 68 C2
Skellingthorpe LN6 . . . 200 B3
Denham Cl 2 PE25 . . . 206 C2
Denham Wlk 1 PE3. . . . 225 C4
Denis Dr PE2 . . . . 230 A4
Denmark Ct 7 HU9 . . . 181 C7
Denmark Dr PE2 . . . . . 230 A4
Dennett Cl PE23 . . . . . 100 F8
Dennor Cl 15 LN12 . . . . . 77 A8
Denshire Ct 5 PE6 . . . 164 E4
DENTON NG32. . . . . . . 139 B7
Denton Ave NG31 . . . . 210 F1
Denton CE Sch NG32 . . 139 A7
Denton Cl NG31. . . . . . 210 F1
Denton La
Barrowby NG32 . . . . . 128 F3
Belvoir NG32 . . . . 138 E6
Denton Rd PE2 . . . . . . 231 C6
Denton's Way 11 DN20 . 31 A5
Depot St LN1 . . . . 201 D3
Derby Ave PE25 . . . . . . 206 D1
Derby Cl
1 Grantham NG31 . . . . 210 E4
23 Grimsby DN32 . . . . . 189 C1
Derby Dr PE1 . . . . 226 C5
Derby Rd DN15 . . . . . . 182 B2
Derby St
Kingston upon Hull
HU3. . . . . 180 D8
19 Lincoln LN5. . . . . . . 205 E8
Dere Cl 9 PE10. . . . . . 213 C6
Derringham Ave 5
HU4. . . . . 179 B6
Derringham St HU3 . . . 180 C7
DERRYTHORPE DN17. . . 17 C3
Derrythorpe Rd DN17. . . 17 D4
Derry Way DN33 . . . . . 194 E8
Derwent Ave 18 HU14 . . . 3 A4
Derwent Cl LN6. . . . . . 205 A2
Derwent Dr
1 Humberston DN36 . . 36 C8
Peterborough PE4 . . . . 221 C2
Derwent Rd
Grantham NG31. . . . . . 210 F3
Scunthorpe DN16 . . . . 185 E6
Derwent St LN1. . . . . . 201 C4
Derwood Gr 7 PE4 . . . 220 F5
Desborough Ave PE2. . . 231 D5
Detuyll St S DN15 . . . . 182 F5
Detuyll St DN15. . . . . . 182 F5
Devereux Way LN9. . . . 199 D2
Devon La 17 NG13. . . . . 128 A6
Devonshire Ave DN32 . . 191 D4

Devonshire Rd
2 Scampton Airfield
LN1 . . . . 67 E5
Scunthorpe DN17 . . . . 184 F6
Devon St
Kingston upon Hull
HU4. . . . . 179 F3
8 Lincoln LN2. . . . . . . 202 C3
Dewberry Ct HU4 . . . . . 179 C4
De Wint Ave LN6. . . . . 205 A5
De Wint Cl
Lincoln LN6 . . . . 205 B5
6 Metheringham LN4. . . 95 C4
De Wint Ct LN6 . . . . . . 205 A5
Dewsbury Ave DN15. . . 182 C4
Dexter Ave NG31 . . . . . 210 F3
Deyne Ave DN15 . . . . . 183 A3
Dial Sq 2 LN5 . . . . . . 191 F7
Diana Princess of Wales
Hospl DN33. . . . . 191 C3
Diana St DN15 . . . . . . 183 A5
Dias CI PE11. . . . . 214 B2
Dickens Beck La LN11. . . 49 D5
Dickens Cl PE6 . . . . . . 164 E2
Dickens Dr PE9 . . . . . . 218 E5
Dickenson Terr 10
DN21 . . . . 197 D3
Dickens Rd NG31 . . . . . 211 E6
Dickens St PE1 . . . . . . 226 B3
Dickinson Cl 11 DN20 . . 30 F5
Dickinson's La 6 DN36. . 36 B1
Dickon Hill Rd PE22. . . 114 D7
DICKON HILLS PE22. . . 114 D7
Dick Turpin Way PE12. . 216 B5
DIGBY LN4 . . . . 108 C5
Digby CE Prim Sch
LN4 . . . . 108 D6
Digby CI 9 LN6. . . . . . 204 C7
Digby Cnr Nature
Reserve★ LN4 . . . . . . 108 F5
Digby Gdns DN34 . . . . 191 A5
Digby Rd LN4. . . . . . . 109 B6
Digby St DN15 . . . . . . 182 F4
Digby Tedder Prim Sch
LN4 . . . . 108 B7
Dimmock Cl NG32 . . . . 139 B7
Dingley Ct PE3. . . . . . . 225 C5
Dirty La 4 DN7 . . . . 14 D8
Discovery Ct DN34 . . . . 212 A3
Disney Ct LN6 . . . . 92 C2
Ditmas Ave 9 HU4. . . . 179 B6
Division Rd 1 HU3. . . . 180 B4
Dixon Ave
14 Broughton DN20 . . . . 19 D3
Dorrington LN4 . . . . . . 108 E3
Grimsby DN32 . . . . . . 191 E4
Dixon Cl
Brigg DN20 . . . . 196 C4
Lincoln LN6 . . . . 201 D1
12 Tetney DN36 . . . . . . 36 C4
Dixon Dr LN13 . . . . 75 E2
Dixon Pl 5 NG31 . . . . . 211 A3
Dixon's Dro PE14 . . . . . 170 F4
Dixons Rd PE6 . . . . . . 217 C4
Dixon St LN5 . . . . 201 D1
Dixon Way LN6 . . . . . . 201 D1
Dockholme Gate PE11. . 145 A4
Docking La LN9. . . . . . 199 B8
Docking's Holt PE12 . . . 216 B6
Dock Office Row 6
HU1. . . . . 181 A7
Dock St HU1. . . . . 180 F6
Dock Terr PE21. . . . . . . 209 B3
Dock Twr PN 2 DN31. . . 189 B3
Doctor's La PE10. . . . . 143 A2
DODDINGTON LN6 . . . . 79 E5
Doddington Ave LN6 . . 205 A4
Doddington Dr PE3 . . . 225 B2
Doddington Hall & Gdns★
LN6. . . . . 79 D5
Doddington La
Claypole NG23 . . . . . . 117 E7
Stubton NG23 . . . . . . 118 B7
Westborough & Dry
Doddington NG23 . . . 117 E5
Doddington Rd
Birchwood LN6 . . . . . . 204 C6
Doddington & Whisby LN6 . . 79 E3
Lincoln LN6 . . . . 204 F4
Dodswell Gr HU9 . . . . . . 5 F8
Doe Cl LN6. . . . . 92 C5
Dog and Duck La
DN21 . . . . 197 B8
Dog Dro
Holbeach PE12 . . . . . . 158 C5
Sutton St James PE12 . . 159 A1
Dog Dro N PE12. . . . . . 168 B4
Dog Dro (Nutts Lane)
PE12 . . . . 158 D2
Dog Dro S PE12. . . . . . 168 A2
DOGDYKE LN4. . . . . . . 110 E6
Dogdyke Ppg Sta★
LN4 . . . . 110 D7
Dogdyke Rd
Coningsby LN4 . . . . . . 207 B2
Wildmore LN4 . . . . . . 111 B6
Dog Holes La DN22 . . . . 52 A1
Dog Kennel Rd DN21. . . 55 A8
Dog Rose Dr PE10. . . . . 213 D2
DOGSTHORPE PE1. . . . 226 C7
Dogsthorpe Gr 2 PE1. . 226 A5
Dogsthorpe Jun Sch
PE1. . . . . 226 B7
Dogsthorpe Rd PE1. . . 226 A5
Dolby Vale DN33. . . . . . 190 F3
Dole Rd DN17. . . . . 6 B1
Dole Wood Nature
Reserve★ PE10. . . . . . 164 C7

Doll La 1 DN20. . . . . . . 20 F7
Doll's Bank PE12. . . . . 159 A4
Dolman Cres DN17. . . . 184 F4
Dolphin La 28 PE21 . . . 208 F5
Dolphin St 4 DN35 . . . 192 F6
Dominion Cl 3 DN36. . . 195 C6
Donaldson Dr 4 PE4. . . 221 C2
Doncaster Gdns 14
LN5 . . . . 107 A8
Doncaster Rd
Gunness DN15. . . . . . . 17 E6
Hatfield DN7 . . . . 14 C3
Haxey DN9. . . . . 26 F2
Scunthorpe DN15 . . . . 182 B3
Stainforth DN7. . . . . . . 14 B6
Doncaster St HU3 . . . . 180 B6
Donegal Cl PE4 . . . . . . 221 B2
DONINGTON PE11. . . . . 134 F1
DONINGTON EAUDIKE
PE20 . . . . 135 A3
DONINGTON ON BAIN
LN11 . . . . 59 F1
Donington on Bain Prim
Sch LN11. . . . . 59 E1
Donington Rd
Bicker PE20 . . . . 135 A4
Horbling NG34. . . . . . 133 C2
Kirton PE20 . . . . 135 F6
DONNA NOOK LN11 . . . 38 D2
Donna Nook National
Nature Reserve★
Donna Nook LN11 . . . 38 C2
North Somercotes LN11 . . 51 B7
Donnington Gdns
DN15. . . . . 182 F3
Donnington Pk 1
PE13 . . . . 170 A1
Donnington Rd LN8 . . . . 59 B2
Donnington St DN32 . . 191 F7
Donville Rd DN17 . . . . . . 7 A2
Dooks Cl DN21 . . . . 29 C1
Doon Garth HU4 . . . . . 179 A3
Dorado Cl 2 HU3. . . . . 180 A5
Dorchester Ave PE10 . . 213 E3
Dorchester Cres 6
PE1 . . . . 226 D7
Dorchester Rd DN17 . . 184 C4
Dorchester Way 10 LN6 . . 93 B8
Dore Ave LN6. . . . . 204 E2
Dormy Way PE25 . . . . . 206 D8
Dorothy Ave
Skegness PE25 . . . . . . 206 C3
Waltham DN37 . . . . . . 194 E5
Dorothy Cl PE22 . . . . . 113 A1
Dorothy Cres 1 PE25 . . 206 C3
Dorrigan Cl LN1 . . . . . . 201 C7
DORRINGTON LN4 . . . . 108 E4
Dorset Cl E 6 DN15. . . . . 8 B4
Dorset Cl W 5 DN15. . . . . 8 B4
Dorset Pl 8 LN1. . . . . . . 67 E5
Dorset St
Kingston upon Hull
HU4. . . . . 179 F3
7 Lincoln LN2. . . . . . . 202 C3
Dorton Ave DN21 . . . . . 197 F4
Dotam's La PE22 . . . . . 126 D4
Double Bank PE22 . . . . 126 D6
Double Bridges Rd DN8 . . 15 B6
Doubledays La PE24. . . 102 D8
Double St PE11. . . . . . 214 C4
Doubletwelves Dro
PE20 . . . . 134 D6
Doughty Cl DN37. . . . . 194 E5
Doughty Rd DN32 . . . . 191 E7
Doughty's Ct LN5 . . . . 234 B2
Doughty St PE9 . . . . . . 219 D6
Douglas Ave
Grimsby DN31 . . . . . . 191 A8
5 Ingoldmells PE25. . . . 90 D3
Douglas Rd
Cleethorpes DN35. . . . 192 D8
Market Deeping PE6 . . 217 C4
Waltham DN37 . . . . . . 194 F3
Doulton Cl 4 LN6. . . . . 204 D7
Dove Cl
Louth LN11 . . . . 198 D7
7 Sleaford NG34 . . . . 212 B3
Dovecote
4 Middle Rasen LN8 . . . 57 B8
Rippingale PE10. . . . . 143 A3
Dovecote Cl PE1 . . . . . 226 B7
Dovecote La
Aubourn Haddington & South
Hykeham LN5 . . . . . . 92 F5
Coleby LN5. . . . . 93 F3
Wainfleet St Mary PE24 . . 102 E1
Yaxley PE7. . . . . 233 C5
Dovecote Mews 4
DN20. . . . . 196 F6
Dovecote Rd 8 PE6. . . 217 A6
Dovecotes 3 PE11. . . . 145 A8
Dove Ct PE11 . . . . 214 B5
Dove Dale 5 LN6 . . . . 204 F2
Dovedale Cl
Grantham NG31. . . . . . 211 B8
2 Winterton DN15. . . . . . 9 A6
Dovedale Dr 8 DN15 . . 194 E8
Dovedale Gr 1 HU9. . . 181 E8
Dovedale Rd DN16 . . . . 185 D5
DOVENDALE LN11. . . . . 60 F1
Dover Cl NG31 . . . . . . 210 E6
Dover Rd PE4. . . . . 221 C4
Dover St
Grimsby DN31 . . . . . . 191 C8
Kingston upon Hull HU3 . 180 C8
Doves' La PE22 . . . . . . 126 E3
Dowding Mews LN2. . . 202 E4
Dowding Rd LN2. . . . . 202 E4
Dowdyke Dro PE20. . . . 146 B8

Dowdyke Rd PE20. . . . . 145 F8
Dower Rise 11 HU14. . . . 3 B7
Dowgate Cl 2 PE11. . . 214 A3
Dowgate Rd 4 PE13 . . 170 B1
Dowlands Bsns Pk LN11. . 62 C5
Down Gate PE3 . . . . . . 225 A1
Downing Cl DN34 . . . . 190 F6
Downing Cres
Scunthorpe DN16 . . . . 185 A3
2 Stamford PE9 . . . . . 219 B7
DOWSBY PE10. . . . . . . 143 B4
DOWSDALE PE6 . . . . . 167 D1
Dowsdale Bank
Thorney PE6 . . . . 176 A8
Whaplode PE12. . . . . . 167 E2
Dowse Ave DN32 . . . . . 182 E3
Dowsing Way PE25 . . . 206 A6
Dozen's Bank PE11 . . . 156 B6
DRAGONBY DN15. . . . . . 8 E1
Dragonby Rd DN17 . . . 184 E4
Drain Bank
Cowbit PE12 . . . . 157 A2
East Kirkby PE23 . . . . . 99 F3
Newport HU15. . . . . 1 B8
Drain Rd PE6 . . . . 221 E7
Drainside PE20 . . . . . . 136 B5
Drainside S PE20 . . . . 136 C4
Drakards La PE20 . . . . 209 A3
Drake Ave
Grimsby DN32 . . . . . . 192 B6
Heighington/Washingborough
LN4. . . . . 203 B1
Drake Cl 14 PE11. . . . . 214 C2
Drake Rd PE25 . . . . . . 103 C4
Drakes Cl
7 Holbeach PE12. . . . . 215 E2
19 Mablethorpe & Sutton
LN12. . . . . 77 A7
Drakes Mdw LN8. . . . . . 55 F4
Drake St
Gainsborough DN21 . . . 197 D2
Lincoln LN1 . . . . 201 C4
Drapers Pl 18 PE11. . . 214 D4
Draw Dike PE12. . . . . . 159 D1
Drax Ct 6 LN8. . . . . 57 B8
Draycot 5 LN7 . . . . 33 A3
Drayton PE3. . . . . 225 A4
DRAYTON PE20. . . . . . 135 C6
Drayton Rd PE20. . . . . 135 C7
Drew Ave DN32 . . . . . . 191 F4
Drewry La 10 DN9. . . . . 27 A2
Driffield Way PE2 . . . . . 230 D8
Driffil Way 29 DN15 . . . . 9 A5
Drift Ave PE9 . . . . 219 C6
Drift Gdns PE9. . . . . . . 219 C6
Drift La NG32 . . . . 119 A1
Drift Rd PE9 . . . . 219 C6
Drift The
Barrowby NG32 . . . . . 210 A3
Belvoir NG32 . . . . 138 F5
Buckminster NG33. . . . 151 A4
Collyweston PE9 . . . . . 171 B1
Croxton Kerrial NG32. . 138 F5
Harlaxton NG32. . . . . . 139 C8
Ryhall PE9 . . . . 163 B3
Skillington NG33 . . . . 151 A7
Syston NG32. . . . . 130 A7
Walcott LN4. . . . . 109 D7
Wansford PE5 . . . . . . 222 F3
Drigh Rd 17 LN8. . . . . . 47 B6
Drill Hall La 5 DN21. . . 197 D5
Dring La DN21 . . . . 41 D7
Drinsey Nook La NG23 . . 66 B1
Drive The
Gainsborough DN21 . . . 197 E3
Grantham NG31. . . . . . 210 D3
Ingoldmells PE25. . . . . 206 E8
7 Kirk Sandall DN3 . . . . 14 A1
2 Mablethorpe/Sutton on Sea
LN12. . . . . 64 A4
Peterborough PE3 . . . . 225 C2
Waltham DN37 . . . . . . 194 F3
1 Winthorpe NG24. . . . 104 B7
Dronfield Ct 3 DN15. . . 182 B4
Drove End Prim Sch
PE12. . . . . 148 F3
Drove La
Coddington NG24. . . . . 104 D7
Sleaford NG34 . . . . . . 212 A5
Drove Rd
Crowland PE12 . . . . . . 167 F3
Whaplode PE12 . . . . . 168 A3
Drovers Ct DN21 . . . . . 197 E1
Drovers Rise 1 HU15 . . . 2 C6
Drove The
4 Aubourn Haddington &
South Hykeham LN6. . . 93 A8
Collyweston PE9 . . . . . 171 B1
Osbournby NG34. . . . . 132 D5
Sleaford NG34 . . . . . . 212 B5
Drummond Rd
Bourne PE10 . . . . 213 D4
Skegness PE25 . . . . . . 206 D1
Drury Cl 1 DN37. . . . . 194 C4
Drury La
Bicker PE20 . . . . 135 A4
Lincoln LN1 . . . . 234 B3
New Waltham DN36. . . 195 C6
Drury Pk 9 NG23. . . . . 117 D3
Drury St LN4. . . . . 95 D4
Drydales HU10. . . . . . . 178 C6
Dryden Ave LN2 . . . . . 202 B6
Dryden Cl NG31. . . . . . 211 D6
Dryden Ct 3 LN4 . . . . . 207 B5
Dryden Rd
Peterborough PE1. . . . 225 E7
Scunthorpe DN17 . . . . 184 D6

DRY DODDINGTON
NG23 . . . . 117 E5
Dry Leys PE2 . . . . 230 C6
Drypool Way HU9 . . . . . 181 B6
Duchess St DN32. . . . . 191 D6
Ducie La DN22 . . . . 52 C5
Duckpool La LN10. . . . . 84 B1
Duckthorpe La DN36 . . . 37 B2
Dudley Cl 1 PE21. . . . . 209 B4
Dudley House Sch
NG31. . . . . 211 B4
Dudley Pl DN35 . . . . . . 192 D4
Dudley Rd
Brigg DN20 . . . . 196 C3
Grantham NG31. . . . . . 211 B4
Scunthorpe DN16 . . . . 185 E6
Dudley St DN31 . . . . . . 191 C7
Dudley Wlk HU4 . . . . . 179 B3
Duesbery St HU3 . . . . . 180 C8
Dugard Rd DN32 . . . . . 192 B7
Duke of Bedford Prim Sch
PE6 . . . . 176 A3
Duke Rd PE22 . . . . 113 F3
Duke's Covert Nature
Reserve★ NG32. . . . . 120 A1
Dukesmead PE4 . . . . . 220 E2
Dukesmead Mobile Home
Pk PE4. . . . . 220 E2
Duke St
Boston PE21 . . . . 208 E4
22 Grimsby DN32 . . . . 189 C1
Grimsby DN32 . . . . . . 192 B8
Peterborough PE2 . . . . 231 A7
Sleaford NG34. . . . . . . 212 C5
14 Stainforth DN7 . . . . . 14 C6
Dunbar Ave DN36 . . . . 195 B6
Dunbar Cl 5 DN21. . . . 197 E6
Dunblane Dr PE2 . . . . . 229 D4
Duncombe Gdns 1
DN32 . . . . 191 F8
Duncombe St DN32 . . . 191 F8
Dundee Ct PE2 . . . . . . 229 C4
Dundee Dr PE9 . . . . . . 218 E6
Dundee St HU5 . . . . . . 180 A8
Dunes Family
Entertainment Ctr The★
LN12. . . . . 64 C4
Dunford Rd 5 LN5. . . . 234 B1
Dunham Cl LN1 . . . . 65 D1
DUNHAM ON TRENT
NG22. . . . . 65 A1
Dunham on Trent Prim Sch
NG22. . . . . 65 A1
Dunham Rd DN22 . . . . . 65 A3
DUNHOLME LN2 . . . . . . 68 E3
Dunholme Cl
Gainsborough DN21 . . . 197 E4
11 Welton/Dunholme
LN2 . . . . 68 D6
Dunholme Ct 4 LN2 . . 202 A8
Dunholme Rd
Gainsborough DN21 . . . 197 E4
9 Welton/Dunholme
LN2 . . . . 68 D6
Dunholme St Chads CE
Prim Sch LN2 . . . . 68 E6
Dunkirk Rd LN1 . . . . . 201 D6
Dunlin Dr PE12 . . . . . . 216 B4
Dunlin Rd 2 PE9 . . . . . 163 D3
Dunlop St LN5 . . . . . . 201 F1
Dunlop Way DN16. . . . . 185 E7
Dunmires La DN14 . . . . . 6 E8
Dunmore Cl LN5 . . . . . 205 C3
Dunmow St DN31 . . . . 188 C1
Dunnegate Way PE11. . 145 D2
Dunnock Cl 3 DN16 . . 185 B2
Dunns Paddock 3
DN20 . . . . 20 F7
Dunoon Ct 4 DN37. . . 190 E8
Dunsberry
Marholm PE6 . . . . . . 220 D1
Peterborough PE3 . . . . 224 F8
DUNSBY PE10 . . . . . . 143 A1
Dunsby Dro PE10 . . . . 143 B3
DUNSCROFT DN7 . . . . . 14 C4
Dunstall St DN15. . . . . 183 A4
Dunstall Wlk DN21 . . . 197 F3
Dunstan Dr DN8 . . . . . . 15 A8
Dunstan Hill 26 DN21. . . 30 B1
Dunstan Villas 29 DN21. . 30 B1
Dunster Cl NG31 . . . . . 210 F6
Dunster Rd DN21 . . . . . 197 E6
DUNSTON LN4. . . . . 95 C5
Dunston Cl 10 LN2 . . . 202 A8
Dunston Dr HU13 . . . . 178 D1
Dunston Fen La LN4. . . . 83 D1
Dunston Heath La LN4 . . 94 C1
Dunston Rd
Kingston upon Hull
HU5. . . . . 179 D7
Metheringham LN4 . . . . 95 C5
DUNSVILLE DN7 . . . . . . 14 C3
Durban Rd DN32 . . . . . 192 A7
Durham Ave
Grimsby DN34 . . . . . . 191 A7
Sleaford NG34 . . . . . . 212 C6
Thorne/Moorends DN8 . . 15 A8
Durham Cl
Birchwood LN6 . . . . . . 200 D2
Grantham NG31. . . . . . 210 C4
Durham Cres LN4 . . . . 203 D1
Durham Rd
Cleethorpes DN35 . . . . 192 C4
Hatfield DN7 . . . . 14 D4
Peterborough PE1 . . . . 226 C4
Durham's Rd LN12 . . . 148 D5
Dursley Ave DN36. . . . . 195 B6
Dutton Ave PE25 . . . . . 206 A4

Dycote La LN5 . . . . 106 D5
DYKE PE10 . . . . 154 D5
Dyke Dro PE10 . . . . 154 E5
Dyke Rd 5 DN36 . . . . 37 C5
Dykes End NG23 . . . . 91 D4
Dyke Windmill & Peremill Galery★ PE10 . . . . 154 D5
Dymoke Cl 3 LN12 . . . . . . 64 C3
Dymoke Dr
Grimsby DN37 . . . . 190 C6
Horncastle LN9 . . . . 199 C2
Dymoke Rd 5 LN12 . . . . . 64 C3
Dysart Rd NG31 . . . . 210 E4
Dysart Ret Pk NG31 . . . . . 211 A4
Dyson Cl PE1 . . . . 225 F3

E

EAGLE LN6 . . . . 79 C2
EAGLE BARNSDALE LN6 . . . 92 C7
Eagle Cl 7 LN12 . . . . 64 A4
Eagle Com Prim Sch LN6 . . . . 79 B2
Eagle Dr
3 Sleaford NG34 . . . . 212 B3
8 Welton/Dunholme LN2 . . . . 68 D7
Eagle La LN6 . . . . 79 D1
EAGLE MOOR LN6 . . . . 79 C2
Eagle Moor LN6 . . . . 79 C3
Eagle Rd
Doddington & Whisby LN6 . . . . 79 D3
North Scarle LN6 . . . . 78 F2
Spalford NG23 . . . . 78 D4
Eaglesthorpe PE1 . . . . 225 E7
Eagle Way
Bourne PE10 . . . . 213 E3
2 Hampton Vale PE7 . . . . 230 D1
Yaxley PE7 . . . . 233 D8
EALAND DN17 . . . . 16 E6
Ealand Rd 3 DN17 . . . . 17 C6
Eames Gdns PE1 . . . . 226 E6
Earl Ave DN36 . . . . 195 D7
EARLESFIELD NG31 . . . . . . 210 F3
Earlesfield La NG31 . . . . . 210 F3
Earle's Rd HU9 . . . . 181 D7
Earl of Dysart Prim Sch The NG31 . . . . 210 D3
Earls Cl PE2 . . . . 231 B6
Earls Dr LN5 . . . . 205 D8
Earlsfield Cl LN6 . . . . 204 B5
Earlsgate Gdns 3 DN15 . . . . 8 F5
Earlsgate Rd DN15 . . . . 8 F5
Earl Spencer Ct PE2 . . . . . 230 E8
Earl St
Grimsby DN31 . . . . 191 C7
Scunthorpe DN16 . . . . 183 B1
Earls Wlk 8 DN16 . . . . . . 183 B2
Earlswood PE2 . . . . 229 E5
Earth Cl PE2 . . . . 231 E5
Ease La NG23 . . . . 117 F3
Easenby Ave HU10 . . . . . . 178 C6
Easenby Cl 2 HU14 . . . . 3 C7
Eason Rd 5 DN33 . . . . 191 B2
East Acridge 15 DN18 . . . . . . 3 F1
East Ave
Brant Broughton LN5 . . . . 105 F5
Grantham NG31 . . . . 210 E3
1 Stainforth DN7 . . . . 14 C5
East Bank
2 Stainforth DN7 . . . . 14 C7
Sutton Bridge PE12 . . . . . 160 F5
East Banks 7 NG34 . . . . . . 212 E4
EAST BARKWITH LN8 . . . . . . 71 A8
Eastbeck La LN9 . . . . 86 A2
East Bight LN2 . . . . 234 B3
East Boundary Rd DN16 . . . . 183 F2
Eastbourne St
Kingston upon Hull HU3 . . . . 180 A5
Lincoln LN2 . . . . 234 C2
Eastbourne Way DN33 . . . 194 F7
Eastbrook Rd LN6 . . . . 205 A5
EAST BUTTERWICK DN17 . . . . 28 E8
East Camp Rd 8 NG34 . . 120 C8
Eastchurch Rd 4 NG34 . . . . 120 D8
East Cl 13 NG34 . . . . 108 E2
Eastcliffe Sq 9 NG32 . . . 119 B7
Eastcliff Rd LN2 . . . . 234 C3
East Cob Gate PE12 . . . . . 157 F6
East Comm La DN16 . . . . . 185 B8
Eastcroft 5 LN1 . . . . 66 D3
East Croft 10 LN3 . . . . 203 E7
East Cross St 25 DN21 . . . . 30 B1
East Dale Dr 3 DN21 . . . . . 30 B2
East Dale Rd HU14 . . . . 2 E5
East Dr LN4 . . . . 110 E8
EAST ELLA HU5 . . . . 179 D7
East Ella Dr HU4 . . . . 179 C6
East Elloe Ave PE12 . . . . . 215 D3
East End
3 Burgh le Marsh PE24 . . . . 102 E7
Humberside Airport DN39 . . 22 A6
Langtoft PE6 . . . . 164 F3
East End Cl DN33 . . . . 191 D1
Eastern Ave
Gainsborough DN21 . . . . . 197 F5
Peterborough PE1 . . . . 226 C8
Eastern Cl PE1 . . . . 226 D7
Eastern Dr
11 Balderton NG24 . . . . . . 104 C1
RAF Cranwell NG34 . . . . . . 120 D8
Eastern Ind Est PE1 . . . . . 226 E3
Eastern Inway DN34 . . . . . 191 A4
Eastern Rd PE12 . . . . 215 F8
Eastern Terr LN5 . . . . 201 D1
East Fen La PE22 . . . . 113 B7
EAST FERRY DN21 . . . . 28 B2
East Ferry Rd
East Ferry DN21 . . . . 28 E3
Laughton DN21 . . . . 41 B8
Wildsworth DN21 . . . . 40 D8
Eastfield
14 Humberston DN36 . . . . . 36 D8
3 Market Deeping PE6 . . . 217 C5
EASTFIELD PE1 . . . . 226 D4
Eastfield 11 LN1 . . . . 66 D7
East Field LN5 . . . . 92 F2
Eastfield Ave DN33 . . . . . . 195 A7
Eastfield Cl
1 Dunholme LN2 . . . . 68 E6
6 Sutterton PE20 . . . . 136 A2
Eastfield Gr PE1 . . . . 226 B4
Eastfield Inf & Jun Sch DN40 . . . . 186 C2
Eastfield Inf Sch LN11 . . . 198 D6
Eastfield La
Manby LN11 . . . . 62 C7
Welton LN2 . . . . 68 E7
Eastfield N Ind Est DN40 . . . . 12 F3
Eastfield Prim Sch HU4 . . . . 179 D6
Eastfield Rd
Barton-upon-Humber DN18 . . . . 10 F7
Brigg DN20 . . . . 196 D3
Epworth DN9 . . . . 27 E6
Firsby PE23 . . . . 101 F7
Immingham DN40 . . . . 12 F3
3 Keelby DN41 . . . . 23 A5
Kingston upon Hull HU4 . . 179 D6
Louth LN11 . . . . 198 D6
40 Messingham DN17 . . . . . 29 D7
North Killingholme DN40 . . . 12 E5
Peterborough PE1 . . . . 226 C4
Scunthorpe DN16 . . . . 185 C5
1 Wisbech PE13 . . . . 170 E1
East Field Rd DN7 . . . . 14 C8
Eastfield Rise
2 Holton le Clay DN36 . . . . 195 D2
Louth LN11 . . . . 198 E7
Eastfields 2 LN8 . . . . 43 D3
Eastfield S Ind Est DN40 . . 12 F3
Eastfield St 5 LN2 . . . . . . 202 B3
Eastfield Way 17 PE13 . . . 170 D1
EAST FIRSBY LN8 . . . . 55 F4
Eastgate
Bassingham LN5 . . . . 92 F2
Bourne PE10 . . . . 213 E4
Grimsby DN32 . . . . 191 E8
Heckington NG34 . . . . 122 E3
Kingston upon Hull HU13 . . . . 178 E2
Lincoln LN2 . . . . 234 B3
Louth LN11 . . . . 198 C6
Market Deeping PE6 . . . . . 217 F3
Peterborough PE1 . . . . 226 B2
EASTGATE PE1 . . . . 226 B2
Eastgate DN21 . . . . 29 C2
East Gate
Bourne PE10 . . . . 213 E4
Fleet PE12 . . . . 159 C7
Moulton PE12 . . . . 158 A7
Sleaford NG34 . . . . 212 E4
Whaplode PE12 . . . . 158 C7
Eastgate Cl LN2 . . . . 234 C3
Eastgate Gdns 3 PE12 . . . 159 C7
Eastgate La PE34 . . . . 161 E2
East Gn 30 DN17 . . . . 29 D7
East Gr
12 Barton-upon-Humber DN18 . . . . 3 F1
8 Colsterworth NG33 . . . . 151 E6
Kingston upon Hull HU4 . . 179 D4
Easthall Rd LN7 . . . . 32 B4
EAST HALTON DN40 . . . . 12 E6
East Halton Prim Sch DN40 . . . . 12 D6
East Halton Rd DN40 . . . . . . 12 E3
East Hann La DN19 . . . . 4 E1
EAST HECKINGTON PE20 . . . . 123 D3
Eastholm LN2 . . . . 202 E7
Eastholm Cl PE1 . . . . 226 C3
Eastholme Gdns 10 DN15 . . . 8 B4
EASTHORPE NG13 . . . . 128 B5
Easthorpe La NG13 . . . . . . 128 C5
Easthorpe Rd
1 Bottesford NG13 . . . . . . 128 B5
2 Great Gonerby NG31 . . 129 E5
Easthorpe View 2 NG13 . . . . 128 B5
East Hull Pools★ HU9 . . . 181 C8
EAST KEAL PE23 . . . . 100 E7
EAST KEAL FEN SIDE PE23 . . . . 100 E4
EAST KIRKBY PE23 . . . . 99 F5
East La
Corringham DN21 . . . . 41 E2
Morton PE10 . . . . 154 C7
Stainforth DN7 . . . . 14 C6
Eastlands 4 PE6 . . . . 166 F1
Eastlands Bank PE14 . . . . 161 B1
Eastleigh Cl LN6 . . . . 200 B1
Eastleigh Rd PE1 . . . . 226 C3
East Liberty LN2 . . . . 202 C4
EAST LOUND DN9 . . . . 27 E2
East Lound Rd
Haxey DN9 . . . . 27 D2
Owston Ferry DN9 . . . . 28 A3
EAST MARSH DN32 . . . . . . 189 B1
East Marsh Rd DN19 . . . . . . 5 C3
East Marsh St 3 DN31 . . . 191 E8
East Mid Mere Rd DN40 . . . 12 F4
East Mill Gate 3 LN3 . . . . 203 E6
Eastmoor Villas DN9 . . . . . 27 D3
East Mount 12 HU14 . . . . . . 3 A4
East of England Showground★ PE2 . . . . . 229 C4
East of England Way PE2 . . . . 229 B4
EASTOFT DN17 . . . . 7 A3
Eastoft CE Prim Sch DN17 . . . . 7 A3
Eastoft Rd
Crowle DN17 . . . . 16 D8
Luddington & Haldenby DN17 . . . . 7 C3
EASTON NG33 . . . . 140 B1
Easton Garfords Charity Aided Sch PE9 . . . . 171 D3
Easton La NG33 . . . . 140 A2
EASTON ON THE HILL PE9 . . . . 171 C3
Easton Walled Gdn★ NG33 . . . . 140 B2
East Parade DN20 . . . . 196 C4
EAST RAVENDALE DN37 . . . 35 C2
East Ravendale CE Prim Sch DN37 . . . . 35 C2
East Rd
Deeping St Nicholas PE11 . . . . 156 C4
4 Keadby with Althorpe DN17 . . . . 17 C6
Navenby/Wellingore LN5 . . . . 107 B8
Northborough PE6 . . . . 217 E1
Sleaford NG34 . . . . 212 F6
Tetford LN9 . . . . 73 F1
Tydd St Mary PE13 . . . . . . 170 C8
East Rd Ind Est NG34 . . . . 212 F5
Eastrea Ct PE2 . . . . 231 E6
East Row LN11 . . . . 50 E4
East St Mary's Gate 2 DN31 . . . . 191 D7
Eastside Rd
Grimsby DN31 . . . . 189 B1
Scunthorpe DN16 . . . . 183 F2
East St
Alford LN13 . . . . 75 F4
Bole DN22 . . . . 52 C6
Crowland PE6 . . . . 166 E1
Grantham NG31 . . . . 211 B4
Grimsby DN32 . . . . 191 E7
Helpringham NG34 . . . . . . 133 E7
13 Hibaldstow DN20 . . . . . . 30 F5
Horncastle LN9 . . . . 199 C4
5 Kingston upon Hull HU9 . . . . 181 B7
Nettleham LN2 . . . . 68 C2
Rippingale PE10 . . . . 143 A2
Roxby cum Risby DN15 . . . . . 9 A3
Stamford PE9 . . . . 219 C5
East Sta Rd PE2 . . . . 231 B8
EAST STOCKWITH DN21 . . . 40 C5
EAST TORRINGTON LN8 . . . 58 C2
East View LN4 . . . . 109 D7
Eastview Cl
Chapel St Leonard PE24 . . . 90 E6
Cranwell NG34 . . . . 107 E1
EASTVILLE PE22 . . . . 114 B8
Eastville Rd
4 Grimsby DN33 . . . . 191 A3
Toynton St Peter PE23 . . . . 101 A6
Eastway 19 LN2 . . . . 68 D2
East Wlk DN15 . . . . 183 B3
East Wold CE Prim Sch LN11 . . . . 62 A3
Eastwood Ave DN32 . . . . . 191 D4
Eastwood Ct 5 DN15 . . . . 182 B2
Eastwood Dr
2 Boston PE21 . . . . 209 D4
10 Broughton DN20 . . . . 19 E4
4 Grantham NG31 . . . . 211 D2
Eastwood Rd PE21 . . . . . . 209 D5
East Wr Cres PE7 . . . . 230 C1
Easy Rd PE11 . . . . 156 E1
Eathwaite Gn PE4 . . . . 221 C1
Eaton Ct DN34 . . . . 191 C6
Eaton Rd
Boston PE21 . . . . 208 E3
Immingham DN40 . . . . 186 D4
Eau Bank LN11 . . . . 50 D7
Eaudike Rd
Donington PE20 . . . . 135 A3
Quadring PE11 . . . . 145 C8
Eau Dike Rd PE22 . . . . 115 A7
Eaudyke Bank 1 PE13 . . . 169 F7
Eaugate Rd PE12 . . . . 157 F1
Ebony Gr LN6 . . . . 200 C1
Ebrington Cl 3 LN10 . . . . . 97 E6
Eccles Ct 3 DN20 . . . . 196 F7
Eccleston Rd 15 DN3 . . . . . 14 A3
Eddystone Dr 3 LN6 . . . . . 205 A1
Eden Cl 6 PE25 . . . . 206 C1
Edendale Gdns 3 LN1 . . . 201 E8
Edendale View LN1 . . . . . 201 E8
Eden Dene DN16 . . . . 185 D5
Edenfield PE2 . . . . 230 C6
Eden Field Rd 4 DN3 . . . . . 14 A1
Eden Gr Rd 8 DN3 . . . . 14 A1
EDENHAM PE10 . . . . 153 F4
Edenham CE (Controlled) Prim Sch PE10 . . . . 153 F5
Edenham Rd PE10 . . . . . . 154 B6
EDENTHORPE DN3 . . . . 14 A1
Edenthorpe Hall Prim Sch DN3 . . . . 14 A1
Edgar Cl 10 DN21 . . . . 29 C4
Edgar St HU3 . . . . 180 D5
Edgbaston Ave 3 DN17 . . . . 184 E3
Edgcote Cl PE3 . . . . 225 C5
Edge Ave DN33 . . . . 191 D2
Edgefield 4 PE12 . . . . 157 E7
Edgehill 10 LN5 . . . . 205 D2
Edgehill Dr NG24 . . . . 104 C4
Edgemere DN15 . . . . 182 B3
Edgerley Drain Rd PE1 . . . 226 F5
Edinburgh Ave
Peterborough PE4 . . . . 220 F3
2 Skegness PE25 . . . . 206 D3
Edinburgh Cl 13 PE20 . . . 136 C5
Edinburgh Cres
2 Bourne PE10 . . . . 213 D6
12 Kirton PE20 . . . . 136 C5
Edinburgh Dr
Holton le Clay DN36 . . . . . 195 C3
11 Kirton PE20 . . . . 136 C5
Spalding PE11 . . . . 214 E2
Wisbech PE13 . . . . 170 D2
Edinburgh Rd
16 Binbrook Tech Pk LN8 . . . . 47 B6
2 Grantham NG31 . . . . . . 211 E6
3 Ruskington NG34 . . . . . 108 E2
Stamford PE9 . . . . 219 B6
Edinburgh Sq 4 LN5 . . . . . 94 A7
Edinburgh St HU3 . . . . 180 A5
Edinburgh Wlk
Holbeach PE12 . . . . 215 E2
Pinchbeck PE11 . . . . 156 B7
Edington Ct 3 DN21 . . . . . 53 A8
Edis Ct PE2 . . . . 231 B6
Edison Dr PE7 . . . . 233 D6
Edison Way 6 PE21 . . . . . 208 F1
Edith Cavell Hosp PE3 . . 225 B4
EDLINGTON LN9 . . . . 85 B6
Edlington Cl 6 LN2 . . . . . 201 F8
Edmonds Cl 2 PE9 . . . . . 219 D6
Edmonds Way 2 DN31 . . . . 191 D8
Edmondthorpe Drift LE14 . . . . 150 D1
Edmondthorpe Rd LE14 . . . . 150 C1
Edmund Cl DN21 . . . . 41 D2
Edmunds Dr 7 PE9 . . . . . 171 A3
Edmunds Rd 3 NG34 . . . . 107 F1
Edna St LN5 . . . . 201 F1
Edwalton Ave
9 Mablethorpe/Sutton on Sea LN12 . . . . 77 A8
Peterborough PE3 . . . . 225 E3
Edward Barker Rd LN4 . . . 81 F4
Edward Collins Sq 2 HU9 . . . . 181 C7
Edward Cres PE25 . . . . . . 206 B3
Edward Heneage Prim Sch DN32 . . . . 191 F7
Edward Rd
Gainsborough DN21 . . . . . 197 D6
Spalding PE11 . . . . 214 B4
10 Stamford PE9 . . . . 219 A7
Edward Richardson Prim Sch The LN9 . . . . 73 F1
Edwards Rd 3 DN15 . . . . 182 F4
Edward St
Cleethorpes DN35 . . . . 192 E5
Grantham NG31 . . . . 211 B2
Grimsby DN32 . . . . 191 F7
Kingston upon Hull HU13 . 178 F1
1 Lincoln LN5 . . . . 205 E8
17 Louth LN11 . . . . 198 B5
Edwina Ave 6 PE11 . . . . . 156 F8
Edwin Cl 12 NG34 . . . . 212 B2
Edwin Gdns PE10 . . . . 213 B5
Edwin St 13 PE21 . . . . 208 F4
Egar Way PE3 . . . . 224 F2
Egerton Rd LN2 . . . . 202 B5
Egginton Cl HU10 . . . . 178 C7
Egginton St 4 HU2 . . . . . . 180 F7
Egret Gr 5 LN6 . . . . 204 D8
Egton Ave 17 DN17 . . . . 29 D7
Egton St HU8 . . . . 181 A8
Eider Cl 42 DN18 . . . . 10 E8
Eight Acres 10 PE9 . . . . . . 219 A5
Eighth Ave DN15 . . . . 8 A1
Elan Cl PE21 . . . . 208 E5
Elba St 6 HU9 . . . . 5 E8
Elbow La PE13 . . . . 177 F8
Elderberry Dr HU4 . . . . . . 179 C4
Elderberry Way 2 DN35 . . . . 192 D2
Elder Cl
2 Bourne PE10 . . . . 213 C6
Skegness PE25 . . . . 206 A5
Eldern PE2 . . . . 230 C4
Elder's Gate PE12 . . . . 169 E8
Elder St LN5 . . . . 205 D5
Elder Tree Way LN10 . . . . . 84 D3
Elderwood Ct 6 HU3 . . . . 180 D5
Eleanor Cl
Lincoln LN5 . . . . 205 E7
Stamford PE9 . . . . 219 A6
Eleanor St DN32 . . . . 191 F8
Electric Sta Rd NG34 . . . . 212 C4
Eleven Acre La PE20 . . . . 136 D4
Elgar Rd HU4 . . . . 179 B4
Elgar Way PE9 . . . . 218 F6
Eliot Cl
Gainsborough DN21 . . . . . 197 F3
Eliot Cl *continued*
9 Sleaford NG34 . . . . 212 F4
Elizabeth Ave
Dogdyke LN4 . . . . 110 D7
11 Kirk Sandall DN3 . . . . . . 14 A2
6 Lincoln LN6 . . . . 93 C8
Lincoln LN6 . . . . 204 F1
Wrange PE22 . . . . 114 C2
Elizabeth Cl
17 Chapel St Leonard PE24 . . . . 90 D7
23 Crowe DN17 . . . . 16 D7
Gainsborough DN21 . . . . . 197 C7
Glentworth DN21 . . . . 54 F6
Grimsby DN33 . . . . 194 D7
1 Scotter DN21 . . . . 29 C4
Elizabeth Cres
6 Ingoldmells PE25 . . . . . . 90 E3
Pinchbeck PE11 . . . . 144 D1
Elizabeth Ct
Brigg DN20 . . . . 196 C5
18 Chapel St Leonard PE24 . . . . 90 D7
Dogsthorpe PE1 . . . . 226 A5
Sleaford NG34 . . . . 212 D3
Elizabeth Dr
Billingborough NG34 . . . . . 143 B8
12 Chapel St Leonard PE24 . . . . 90 D7
Elizabeth Gr PE25 . . . . 206 C5
Elizabeth Rd
Boston PE21 . . . . 209 B5
2 Stamford PE9 . . . . 219 B6
Elizabeth St 3 DN15 . . . . 183 A4
Elizabeth Way 4 PE10 . . . 164 C8
Ella Ct HU10 . . . . 178 C8
Ella Pk HU10 . . . . 178 D7
Ellen Cres PE11 . . . . 214 A3
Ellen Way DN36 . . . . 195 B7
Ellerby Ct PE23 . . . . 100 D6
Ellerby Mead NG33 . . . . . . 152 D5
ELLERKER HU15 . . . . 2 A8
Ellesmere Ave 3 LN2 . . . 202 D4
Ellesmere Bsns Pk NG31 . . . . 210 E2
Ellesmere Gr 4 DN7 . . . . . . 14 D6
Ellesmere Rise DN34 . . . . 190 D3
Ellicar La DN10 . . . . 39 A3
Ellindon PE3 . . . . 225 B7
Elliot Ave PE3 . . . . 224 F2
Elliot Cl NG31 . . . . 211 E6
Elliott Rd LN5 . . . . 234 C1
Elliott's Way PE9 . . . . 164 B4
Elliott Way 11 PE24 . . . . . . 90 D7
Ellis Mill★ LN1 . . . . 234 A4
Ellison Ave DN16 . . . . 185 A1
Ellison Boulters CE (Con) Prim Sch LN2 . . . . 68 F4
Ellison Cl 5 LN2 . . . . 68 F2
Ellison St
Lincoln LN5 . . . . 205 D5
Thorne/Moorends DN8 . . . . 15 A7
Ellis St HU9 . . . . 181 C8
Elliston Jun & Inf Schs DN35 . . . . 192 C8
Elliston St DN35 . . . . 192 C8
Ellis Way DN32 . . . . 191 E8
Ellmore La LN7 . . . . 32 C3
Elloe Bank PE13 . . . . 169 B2
ELLOUGHTON HU15 . . . . 2 B6
Elloughton Cty Prim Sch HU15 . . . . 2 B7
Elloughton Dale HU15 . . . . . 2 D8
Elloughton Rd HU15 . . . . . . 2 C6
Elloughtonthorpe Way 15 HU15 . . . . 2 D5
Ellwood Ave PE2 . . . . 231 E5
Ellyslande NG33 . . . . 140 A5
Elm Ave
18 Brough HU15 . . . . 2 C6
Cherry Willingham/Reepham LN3 . . . . 203 D5
Cleethorpes DN35 . . . . 192 E6
Grimsby DN34 . . . . 191 A6
13 Mablethorpe/Sutton on Sea LN12 . . . . 64 B3
Newark-on-Trent NG24 . . . 104 A3
Elm Cl
Lincoln LN6 . . . . 204 F2
17 Long Bennington NG23 . . . . 117 D3
Market Deeping PE6 . . . . . 217 C4
13 Saxilby LN1 . . . . 66 D2
Yaxley PE7 . . . . 233 F7
Elm Cres
Burgh le Marsh PE24 . . . . . 102 D8
Glinton PE6 . . . . 220 B8
Elmdale 29 DN18 . . . . 10 E8
Elmdene 5 LN2 . . . . 68 F4
Elm Dr
Ingoldmells PE25 . . . . 206 D8
Louth LN11 . . . . 198 D7
Skegness PE25 . . . . 90 E1
3 Sudbrooke LN2 . . . . 68 F2
Elmer St N 3 NG31 . . . . . . 211 A4
Elmer St S NG31 . . . . 211 A4
Elmfield Rd PE1 . . . . 226 A7
Elmgarth 3 NG34 . . . . 212 F3
Elm Gdns DN35 . . . . 192 E6
Elm Gr
Grantham NG31 . . . . 211 C6
8 Healing DN41 . . . . 24 A5
Scunthorpe DN16 . . . . 185 B8
Elmhirst Ave PE25 . . . . 206 D6
Elmhirst Rd 5 DN8 . . . . 15 B8

Elmhurst La LN9 . . . 199 B6
Elm La
Goxhill DN19 . . . 5 A1
7 Laceby DN37 . . . 23 E1
Low Fulney PE12 . . . 157 C6
Elmore Cl 6 NG34 . . . 212 C4
Elmore Rd PE3 . . . 225 A3
Elm Rd
Cleethorpes DN35 . . . 192 E6
Waltham DN37 . . . 194 E3
Elms Dr HU10 . . . 178 C8
Elm St
Peterborough PE2 . . . 230 F7
Stamford PE9 . . . 219 C5
Elms View 4 NG31 . . . 129 D5
Elmswood HU13 . . . 178 C2
Elm Terr PE10 . . . 213 B6
Elmtree Ave 10 HU14 . . . 3 A4
Elm Tree Cl 11 LN8 . . . 57 D7
Elm Tree Gr 8 DN8 . . . 15 B7
Elmtree Rd NG34 . . . 108 D1
Elm Way
Brigg DN20 . . . 196 B4
Messingham DN17 . . . 29 C7
Elmwood Ave 4 PE21 . . . 208 F2
Elmwood Cl 6 LN6 . . . 200 D1
Elmwood Dr 6 PE25 . . . 90 D3
Elsea Dr 3 PE10 . . . 164 C8
Elsea Pk Way PE10 . . . 213 D2
Elsenham Rd DN31 . . . 188 D1
ELSHAM DN20 . . . 20 F7
Elsham Cl 7 LN6 . . . 204 D8
Elsham Cres LN6 . . . 204 D8
Elsham Dr DN37 . . . 194 C3
Elsham Gr 1 DN33 . . . 191 B3
Elsham Hall Ctry & Wildlife Pk* DN20 . . . 20 F6
Elsham Rd DN20 . . . 20 D7
Elsham Rise HU13 . . . 178 D1
Elsham Wlk DN21 . . . 197 F4
Elsham Wold Ind Est DN20 . . . 21 A8
Elsie Davies Cl NG31 . . . 211 C7
Elsiemere Wlk 6 HU4 . . . 179 B6
Elsom Way LN9 . . . 199 A4
Elsthorpe Rd
Edenham PE10 . . . 153 E6
Haconby PE10 . . . 154 A7
Elstone PE2 . . . 230 A4
Elter Wlk PE4 . . . 221 C3
Elton Cl
Ermine LN1 . . . 201 D6
2 Stamford PE9 . . . 218 F6
Elton Rd
Thorney PE8 . . . 228 B6
Wansford PE8 . . . 222 B2
Elton St 1 NG31 . . . 211 A3
Elveley Dr HU10 . . . 178 A7
Elvin Cl 3 LN2 . . . 201 F6
Elvington Cl 7 LN6 . . . 204 B6
Elvington Rd LN6 . . . 204 B6
Elwes St DN20 . . . 196 C2
Elwyn Pl DN35 . . . 192 D2
Ely Cl PE4 . . . 220 F3
Ely St
Lincoln LN1 . . . 201 D4
5 Sleaford NG34 . . . 212 C6
Ely Way 5 NG31 . . . 210 F5
Embankment Rd 4 PE1 . . . 226 A1
Embassy Ctr* PE25 . . . 206 E3
Ember La
Chapel St Leonard PE24 . . . 77 B1
Hogsthorpe PE24 . . . 90 B8
Embry Rd 22 PE8 . . . 172 B1
Emerald Gr 8 HU3 . . . 180 A4
Emerson Ave DN7 . . . 14 C5
Emery La 15 PE21 . . . 208 F4
Emfield Gr DN33 . . . 194 E7
Emfield Rd DN33 . . . 194 D6
Emily St 8 HU9 . . . 181 C7
Eminson Cl 6 DN21 . . . 29 C4
Emlyns Gdns 5 PE9 . . . 219 C6
Emlyns St 2 PE9 . . . 219 C6
Emmanual Rd DN16 . . . 185 F6
Emmanuel Ct
3 Scunthorpe DN16 . . . 185 C6
Yarborough DN34 . . . 191 A6
Emmanuel Dr DN16 . . . 185 A3
Emmanuel Rd PE9 . . . 219 B7
Emmendingen Ave 2 NG24 . . . 104 A6
Emmery Cl 2 DN20 . . . 19 D4
Emminson Way 1 NG31 . . . 210 E8
Emorsgate PE34 . . . 161 E3
EMORSGATE PE34 . . . 161 E3
Empingham Rd
4 Stamford PE9 . . . 219 A5
Tinwell PE9 . . . 218 B6
Empringham St 5 HU9 . . . 181 D7
Empson Rd PE1 . . . 226 F5
Ena St HU3 . . . 180 B6
Endcliffe Ave DN17 . . . 184 F2
Endeavour Cres 1 HU9 . . . 5 D8
Endeavour Ct 5 NG34 . . . 212 A3
Endeavour Pk Ind Est PE21 . . . 208 A4
Endeavour Way PE20 . . . 136 A2
Endell Dr 35 DN21 . . . 30 B1
Enderby Cl LN4 . . . 203 A2
Enderby Cres DN21 . . . 197 E3
Enderby Rd DN17 . . . 184 E4
Enderby Rd Inf Sch DN17 . . . 184 D4
Endsleigh St HU3 . . . 180 A7
Enfield Ave DN36 . . . 195 D5
Enfield Gdns PE3 . . . 225 C4
Enfield Prim Sch DN36 . . . 195 D6
Enfield Rd 8 LN11 . . . 59 E1
Engaine PE2 . . . 230 B5
Engine Bank PE12 . . . 157 F2
Engine Dro NG34 . . . 134 B4
Engine Dyke PE12 . . . 148 B1
Engine St DN20 . . . 196 B3
English Cl HU3 . . . 180 E4
English Rd PE6 . . . 176 B5
English St
Kingston upon Hull HU3 . . . 180 E4
Peterborough PE1 . . . 225 E5
Ennerdale Cl
3 Birchwood LN6 . . . 200 D1
6 Humberston DN36 . . . 192 E1
Ennerdale Rise PE4 . . . 221 B2
Enterprise Rd
Caistor LN7 . . . 33 A4
Mablethorpe/Sutton on Sea LN12 . . . 64 A4
Enterprise Way
Grimsby DN32 . . . 192 A6
Pinchbeck PE11 . . . 214 E8
4 Winterton DN15 . . . 8 F5
Ephams La DN41 . . . 23 E7
Epperstone Residential Cvn Pk DN36 . . . 193 C1
Epsom Cl LN6 . . . 204 B8
Epsom Pl DN35 . . . 192 F1
Epsom Rd LN6 . . . 204 B8
EPWORTH DN9 . . . 27 E7
Epworth Cty Prim Sch DN9 . . . 27 D6
Epworth Leisure Ctr DN9 . . . 27 D6
Epworth Rd
Hatfield DN7 . . . 14 F4
Haxey DN9 . . . 27 D3
Owston Ferry DN9 . . . 28 A4
Epworth Rd (West) 10 DN7 . . . 14 E4
EPWORTH TURBARY DN9 . . . 27 C6
Epworth Turbary Nature Reserve* DN9 . . . 27 B6
Epworth View LN1 . . . 201 E8
Erebus Cl 7 PE23 . . . 101 A8
Eresbie Rd LN11 . . . 198 D3
Eresby Ave 13 PE23 . . . 87 F1
Eresby Specl Sch The PE23 . . . 100 F8
ERMINE LN2 . . . 202 B8
Ermine Cl
5 Ancaster NG32 . . . 120 A3
Bourne PE10 . . . 213 C6
Grantham NG31 . . . 211 D5
8 Lincoln LN1 . . . 201 E8
Stamford PE9 . . . 218 F5
Ermine Com Inf Sch LN2 . . . 202 A7
Ermine Ct 10 LN4 . . . 81 A1
Ermine Dr 3 LN5 . . . 107 B8
Ermine Jun Sch LN2 . . . 202 A8
Ermine Rise PE9 . . . 171 B8
Ermine St
Ancaster NG32 . . . 120 A2
Appleby DN15 . . . 9 C1
Winteringham DN15 . . . 9 B8
Ermine Way
Market Deeping PE6 . . . 217 E5
Stamford PE9 . . . 218 F5
Ernest Terr LN2 . . . 234 B4
Eryholme Cres 1 DN15 . . . 182 F2
Escart Ave DN32 . . . 192 B6
Escombe View LN1 . . . 201 D8
Eshings The LN2 . . . 68 D7
Esk Cl LN6 . . . 204 F4
Eskdale Cl 1 PE4 . . . 221 C3
Eskdale Rd NG31 . . . 211 A7
Eskdale Way DN37 . . . 190 D8
ESKHAM DN36 . . . 37 C1
Eskham Cl 1 DN35 . . . 192 F3
Eslaforde Gdns 16 NG34 . . . 212 F4
ESSENDINE PE9 . . . 163 D3
Essendine Rd PE9 . . . 163 C2
Essendyke PE3 . . . 225 A7
Essex Dr 9 DN15 . . . 8 B4
Essex Rd 3 PE9 . . . 219 B6
Essex St HU4 . . . 179 E3
Essex Way PE10 . . . 213 D4
Estate Ave DN20 . . . 19 D3
Estate Rd No 1 DN31 . . . 188 B2
Estate Rd No 2 DN31 . . . 188 B1
Estate Rd No 3 DN31 . . . 188 B3
Estate Rd No 4 DN31 . . . 188 B3
Estate Rd No 5 DN31 . . . 188 B2
Estate Rd No 6 DN31 . . . 188 B2
Estate Rd No 7 DN31 . . . 188 B1
Estate Rd No 8 DN31 . . . 188 B1
Estcourt Prim Sch HU9 . . . 181 D8
Estcourt St HU9 . . . 181 D8
Estella Way PE11 . . . 214 A5
Estuary Way DN31 . . . 188 D2
Estwaite Cl LN6 . . . 205 B2
Ethel Ct 4 DN15 . . . 183 B3
Ethelstone Rd 2 DN34 . . . 191 A7
Etherington St DN21 . . . 197 D4
Eton Cl LN6 . . . 200 D3
Eton Ct DN17 . . . 184 F4
Eton Dr DN17 . . . 184 F3
Eton Rd
Heighington/Washingborough LN4 . . . 203 C1
9 Mablethorpe/Sutton on Sea LN12 . . . 64 C2
Eton St
Grantham NG31 . . . 211 B4
Kingston upon Hull HU3 . . . 180 C4
ETTON PE6 . . . 173 E5
Eudo Rd PE25 . . . 206 D7
Eugate Rd PE6 . . . 167 F4
Europa Bsns Pk DN31 . . . 188 C2
Europarc Innovation Ctr DN37 . . . 24 B6
Europa Way
Brigg DN20 . . . 196 A4
Immingham DN41 . . . 187 B3
Eusden Ct LN4 . . . 207 A5
Euston Ave 5 PE11 . . . 214 B2
Euston Cl LN6 . . . 200 D2
EVEDON NG34 . . . 121 F6
Evedon Rd NG34 . . . 121 F5
Eve Gdns LN4 . . . 203 D1
Evelyn Gr N 1 DN32 . . . 192 B6
Evelyn Gr S 3 DN32 . . . 192 B6
Evendine Ct DN36 . . . 195 E1
Everard Rd PE11 . . . 155 C1
Everdon Way PE3 . . . 225 C5
Everest Rd DN16 . . . 185 D5
Everingham PE2 . . . 229 D5
Everington's La PE25 . . . 103 C8
Everthorpe Cl 16 HU15 . . . 2 D5
Ever Thorpe Cl 5 HU3 . . . 180 C5
Eves Cl 9 PE6 . . . 174 E5
Evesham Ave DN34 . . . 190 E5
Eve St LN11 . . . 198 B6
Evison Cres 2 LN13 . . . 75 E3
Evison Ct 12 PE22 . . . 113 B1
Evison Way LN11 . . . 50 E7
Ewart St LN5 . . . 205 D6
EWERBY NG34 . . . 122 B6
Ewerby Pond Nature Reserve* NG34 . . . 122 E8
Ewerby Rd NG34 . . . 122 A5
EWERBY THORPE NG34 . . . 122 D6
Exchange Cl LN6 . . . 204 E4
Exchange Pl 5 DN20 . . . 196 B3
Exchange Rd LN6 . . . 204 E4
Exchange St PE1 . . . 226 A2
Exchequergate 5 LN2 . . . 234 B3
Exeter Cl
3 Bourne PE10 . . . 213 C5
Grantham NG31 . . . 210 C5
Heighington/Washingborough LN4 . . . 203 E2
1 Market Deeping PE6 . . . 217 E4
Exeter Ct
2 Bourne PE10 . . . 213 C5
10 Grimsby DN34 . . . 190 D4
Exeter Dr
4 Sleaford NG34 . . . 212 C6
Spalding PE11 . . . 214 E4
Exeter Gdns
10 Bourne PE10 . . . 213 C5
Stamford PE9 . . . 218 F4
Exeter Rd
Peterborough PE1 . . . 225 F6
Scunthorpe DN15 . . . 182 F3
8 Wittering PE8 . . . 172 B1
Exeter St PE10 . . . 213 C5
Exley Sq LN2 . . . 202 D6
Exmoor Ave DN15 . . . 182 D7
Exmoor Cl LN6 . . . 204 D1
Exmoor Rd DN17 . . . 184 C8
Exton Cl 6 PE9 . . . 218 E5
Eyam Way 3 LN6 . . . 204 F1
EYE PE6 . . . 175 A1
Eyebury Rd
Eye PE6 . . . 175 A1
Peterborough PE6 . . . 227 A6
Eye CE Prim Sch PE6 . . . 175 B1
EYE GREEN PE6 . . . 175 B2
Eye Rd PE1 . . . 174 F1
Eyre Ave DN16 . . . 185 B5
Eyrescroft PE3 . . . 225 A7
Eyrescroft Prim Sch PE3 . . . 225 A7
Eyre's La LN6 . . . 78 F1

F

Fagans Way 7 PE25 . . . 206 C1
Fainlight Cl 2 PE25 . . . 206 D8
Fairburn Cl 9 PE24 . . . 90 D7
Fairchild Way PE1 . . . 226 A7
Fairfax Cl
Boston PE21 . . . 208 D7
Gainsborough DN21 . . . 197 F2
6 Horncastle LN9 . . . 199 D3
2 Toft Newton LN8 . . . 56 D5
Fairfax Rd DN31 . . . 191 B7
Fairfax St LN5 . . . 205 D6
Fairfax Way PE6 . . . 217 E3
Fairfield LN4 . . . 207 C4
Fairfield Ave
26 Chapel St Leonard PE24 . . . 90 D7
Grimsby DN33 . . . 194 E7
Fairfield Cl
8 Broughton DN20 . . . 19 E3
3 Spalding PE11 . . . 214 C6
Fairfield Croft 6 DN9 . . . 27 E6
Fairfield Ct 3 DN35 . . . 193 A1
Fairfield Dr
29 Barton-upon-Humber DN18 . . . 10 F8
39 Messingham DN17 . . . 29 D7
Fairfield Ind Est LN11 . . . 198 B8
Fairfield Pit Nature Reserve* DN19 . . . 4 D3
Fairfield Prim Sch DN33 . . . 194 E8
Fairfield Rd
Grimsby DN33 . . . 194 E7
Peterborough PE2 . . . 231 A8
Scunthorpe DN15 . . . 182 C4
Fairfields
Holbeach PE12 . . . 215 C3
33 Kirton in Lindsey DN21 . . . 30 B1
Fairfield St LN2 . . . 202 B4
Fairfield View 11 HU15 . . . 2 D5
Fair Isle Rise DN40 . . . 186 C2
Fairleas LN4 . . . 81 E2
Fairmead Way PE3 . . . 225 E2
Fairmont Cres DN16 . . . 183 B2
Fairmont Rd DN32 . . . 192 A7
Fairtree Wlk 24 DN8 . . . 15 A8
Fair View Ave DN35 . . . 192 E6
Fairview Way PE11 . . . 214 C6
Fairway DN37 . . . 194 D5
Fairway Ct DN35 . . . 193 C1
Fairways PE10 . . . 164 A8
Fairways The
Kirton PE20 . . . 136 C6
Scunthorpe DN15 . . . 182 B2
Fairway The
Kingston upon Hull HU10 . . . 178 A8
1 Mablethorpe/Sutton on Sea LN12 . . . 64 A4
Fairweather Ct PE1 . . . 226 E3
Fakenham Chase PE12 . . . 215 E3
Falcon Cl LN6 . . . 79 B2
Falcon Ct
9 Grantham NG31 . . . 210 E2
Kingston upon Hull HU4 . . . 179 D2
Falconers The DN21 . . . 30 F2
Falcon Rd 7 LN4 . . . 108 A7
Falcon Way
Hampton Vale PE2 . . . 230 C1
13 Sleaford NG34 . . . 212 B3
FALDINGWORTH LN8 . . . 56 F3
Faldingworth Cl 3 LN6 . . . 204 C7
Faldingworth Com Prim Sch LN8 . . . 56 F3
Faldingworth Rd LN8 . . . 55 F3
Faldos Way 3 LN12 . . . 64 A4
Falkirk Cl 6 PE9 . . . 218 E6
Falkland Rd 4 HU9 . . . 5 F8
Falklands Cl LN1 . . . 201 E8
Falklands Rd PE12 . . . 160 D4
Falkland Way DN18 . . . 3 F1
Fallodan Rd PE2 . . . 229 C3
Fallowfield PE2 . . . 229 D5
Fallowfield Rd DN33 . . . 194 D7
Fallow Fields 7 PE11 . . . 166 C6
Fallow La
Foston NG32 . . . 118 A2
1 Westborough & Dry Doddington NG23 . . . 117 F3
Fall's Dro PE6 . . . 175 F7
Falsgrave Gr HU5 . . . 179 D7
Fane Cl PE9 . . . 219 B7
Fane Rd PE4 . . . 221 C1
Fanny Hands La 1 LN8 . . . 59 A7
Fannystone Rd DN34 . . . 191 B7
Fantail Cl 2 PE11 . . . 156 E2
Fantasy Island* PE25 . . . 90 E3
Fantasy World* DN35 . . . 192 F7
Fanthorpe La LN11 . . . 198 A7
Faraday Cl PE7 . . . 233 D6
FAR BANK DN7 . . . 14 C8
Far Bank La DN7 . . . 14 C8
FARCET PE7 . . . 231 C2
Farcet CE Prim Sch PE7 . . . 231 C2
Far Comm Rd DN7 . . . 15 A3
Fardell Rd DN16 . . . 185 D7
Far Dro PE20 . . . 124 E2
Farebrother St DN32 . . . 191 E6
Far End LN5 . . . 94 A2
Far Field Rd 22 DN3 . . . 14 A2
FARFORTH LN11 . . . 73 D5
Far Holme La 5 NG23 . . . 91 A8
Far Hurn Dro LN4 . . . 110 B7
Faringdon Rd DN31 . . . 189 C2
Far Ings La DN18 . . . 3 C1
Far Ings Nature Reserve* DN18 . . . 3 D2
Far Ings Rd DN18 . . . 3 D1
Far La
Coleby LN5 . . . 93 F3
27 Waddington LN5 . . . 93 F7
Farleigh Fields PE2 . . . 229 D6
FARLESTHORPE LN13 . . . 76 B1
Farlesthorpe Nature Reserve* LN13 . . . 89 A7
Farlesthorpe Rd
Alford LN13 . . . 75 F2
Bilsby LN13 . . . 76 A2
Willoughby with Sloothby LN13 . . . 89 B8
Farm Cl
2 Gunness DN15 . . . 17 E6
12 Kirk Sandall DN3 . . . 14 A1
Farmers Gate PE12 . . . 215 B2
Farmhouse Cl 12 NG13 . . . 128 A6
Farmhouse Mews 11 DN36 . . . 195 C6
Farm La 1 DN17 . . . 28 D8
Farm View
Castor PE5 . . . 223 E2
18 Welton LN2 . . . 68 D7
Farndale Cres 5 NG31 . . . 211 A8
Farndale Way
Grimsby DN31 . . . 191 D8
1 Winterton DN15 . . . 9 A5
Farnella Cl HU3 . . . 180 A5
Far Pasture 2 PE4 . . . 220 F5
Farrier Rd LN6 . . . 204 B5
Farriers Ct
Peterborough PE2 . . . 230 D7
Scopwick LN4 . . . 95 C1
Farriers Fold 13 DN9 . . . 27 D2
Farriers Gate 2 NG34 . . . 120 F8
Farriers Way
Carlby PE9 . . . 163 D4
8 Market Rasen LN8 . . . 57 E7
2 Tattershall LN4 . . . 207 A5
Farrier Way PE11 . . . 214 A2
Farringdon Cl 2 PE1 . . . 226 D6
Farrington Cres LN6 . . . 200 D2
Farrishes La DN18 . . . 10 A8
Farrow Ave PE12 . . . 215 E1
Farrow Rd PE12 . . . 168 A4
Farrows Pond 3 DN19 . . . 5 A1
Farthingales PE11 . . . 214 C6
Farthing Ave DN15 . . . 182 E4
Farthings Fold PE10 . . . 154 B6
Far Wharf LN6 . . . 201 D3
Fauconberg Ave 4 DN33 . . . 191 C2
Faulding La DN40 . . . 12 F2
Faulding Way DN37 . . . 190 C7
Faulkers La PE24 . . . 89 E1
Favell Rd 1 LN4 . . . 203 B2
Faversham Ave HU4 . . . 179 B6
Fawcett St DN21 . . . 197 C5
Fawsley Cl 6 LN2 . . . 202 E7
Fawsley Garth PE3 . . . 225 C6
FAXFLEET DN14 . . . 1 A2
Faxfleet La DN14 . . . 1 A3
Fayid La LN4 . . . 95 C7
Feale Abbey PE34 . . . 161 E1
Featherby Pl 7 LN5 . . . 205 E8
Feather La 8 DN19 . . . 11 C7
Featherworks The* PE21 . . . 209 B3
Felbrigg Wlk PE2 . . . 231 F6
Fellands Gate PE22 . . . 113 F3
Fellowes Gdns PE2 . . . 231 A7
Fellowes Rd PE2 . . . 231 A7
Felstead Rd DN34 . . . 190 F6
Fenbridge Rd PE4 . . . 221 A4
Fenby Cl DN37 . . . 190 D6
Fence Bank PE34 . . . 161 D1
Fen Cl 24 PE13 . . . 170 D1
Fen Ct 1 DN3 . . . 14 A1
Fen Dike PE12 . . . 159 B3
Fendike Bank PE24 . . . 101 F3
Fendike La PE20 . . . 135 B5
Fen Dro PE7 . . . 233 D1
Fendyke End La PE22 . . . 126 E5
Fendyke La PE13 . . . 169 F1
Feneley Cl PE6 . . . 217 D5
Fen End La PE12 . . . 156 F3
Fen Field Mews PE6 . . . 217 D5
Fengate PE1 . . . 226 D1
FENGATE PE1 . . . 226 D2
Fen Gate PE12 . . . 157 E2
Fengate Cl 1 PE1 . . . 226 B2
Fengate Dro PE12 . . . 157 C3
Fengate Mobile Home Pk PE1 . . . 226 D1
Fengate Rd
Pinchbeck PE11 . . . 214 A8
Walsoken PE14 . . . 170 F1
Fengate Trad Est PE1 . . . 226 D2
FENHOUSES PE20 . . . 135 D7
Fenhouses Dro PE20 . . . 135 D8
Fenhouses La PE20 . . . 135 C7
Fen La
Balderton NG24 . . . 104 D2
Bassingham LN5 . . . 93 A3
Beesby with Saleby LN13 . . . 76 A7
Conisholme LN11 . . . 50 C5
Dunston LN4 . . . 95 C6
East Keal PE23 . . . 100 E5
Grainthorpe LN11 . . . 49 F5
Lincoln LN6 . . . 205 A1
Long Bennington NG23 . . . 117 B6
Mablethorpe & Sutton LN12 . . . 64 A1
Maltby le Marsh LN13 . . . 63 E1
Mareham le Fen PE22 . . . 98 F2
North Somercotes LN11 . . . 50 D6
North Thoresby DN36 . . . 36 C1
South Carlton LN1 . . . 67 C2
Tydd St Giles PE13 . . . 169 B5
Fenland Airfield PE12 . . . 168 B8
Fenland Rd
13 Thorne/Moorends DN8 . . . 15 B7
Wisbech PE13 . . . 170 E1
Fenland Wlk PE12 . . . 215 B2
Fennell Rd 5 PE11 . . . 156 E8
Fenners Ave DN17 . . . 184 E3
Fen Rd
Billinghay LN4 . . . 109 F6
Dowsby PE10 . . . 143 D4
East Kirkby PE23 . . . 99 F4
Frampton PE20 . . . 125 B1
Gosberton PE11 . . . 144 A4
Heighington LN4 . . . 82 A4
Heighington/Washingborough LN4 . . . 203 E2
Holbeach PE12 . . . 215 D1

Fen Rd *continued*
Little Hale NG34 133 F8
Metheringham LN4 95 C4
Newton PE13 169 E4
Owmby LN8 55 F6
Pointon & Sempringham NG34 143 D6
Ruskington NG34 108 F2
Stickford PE22 100 C2
Thurlby PE10 154 E1
Timberland LN4 96 C1
Toynton St Peter PE23 101 A4
Wisbech St Mary PE13 177 E2
Fenscape* PE12 157 B7
Fen Sch NG34 123 C3
Fenside
Halton Holegate PE23 101 C6
Toynton All Saints PE23 100 F4
FEN SIDE PE22 100 A1
Fenside Dr 5 PE6 174 E5
Fenside Rd
Boston PE21 208 C6
Holland Fen with Brothertoft PE21 125 C5
FENTON
Fenton LN1 65 E3
Fenton NG23 105 B1
Fenton Dr PE9 163 E5
Fenton La DN22 52 C1
Fenton Pl LN2 234 C2
Fenton Rd
Fenton NG23 105 B1
Stubton NG23 118 B8
Fenton St DN15 183 B3
Fen View
Heighington LN4 81 F4
Peterborough PE2 231 F6
Fenwick Ct 6 DN36 195 D1
Fenwick Rd DN33 191 B2
Fen Wlk DN36 37 C5
Ferens Art Gall* HU2 180 F6
Ferensway HU2 180 E7
Fernbank 2 DN9 27 D7
Fern Croft 10 DN9 27 E6
Fern Ct HU13 179 A1
Ferndale PE7 233 D6
Ferndale Cl NG33 152 F7
Ferndown 1 DN37 188 A1
Ferndown Dr DN40 186 D4
Fern Dr
Market Rasen LN8 57 D8
Pinchbeck PE11 214 C7
Ferneries La 3 DN38 21 B4
Fern Gr LN3 203 D5
Fernhall Cl 15 DN3 14 A2
Fernhill DN37 190 C7
Fernie Cl 3 PE6 174 E4
Fernland Cl 18 HU15 2 C5
Fernleigh Ave 4 LN4 81 A1
Fernleigh Way PE21 209 B6
Fernwood Mews DN21 197 F2
Ferriby High Rd HU14 3 B5
Ferriby La DN33 191 C2
Ferriby Rd
Barton-upon-Humber DN18 10 E8
Hessle HU13 178 B1
Scunthorpe DN17 184 E5
FERRIBY SLUICE DN18 9 F7
Ferriby Sta HU14 3 A3
Ferries St HU9 181 D7
Ferry Dr PE6 224 D3
Ferry Hill PE5 224 B1
Ferry La
Holland Fen with Brothertoft PE20 124 D6
Newton PE13 170 B5
North Kyme LN4 109 F2
Skellingthorpe LN6 200 C5
South Kyme LN4 109 F1
Sturton le Steeple DN22 52 D3
Washingborough LN4 203 B2
Winteringham DN15 2 B1
Ferry Mdws Ctry Pk* PE2 229 D8
Ferry Mdws Sta PE2 229 E7
Ferry Rd
Bardney LN3 83 D1
Barrow upon Humber DN19 4 C1
Fiskerton LN3 82 D6
Haxey DN9 27 D1
2 Keadby with Althorpe DN17 17 D4
Kingston upon Hull HU13 178 E1
Langriville PE22 124 D8
Scunthorpe DN15 182 E5
Ferry Rd W DN15 182 A6
Ferryside 2 LN3 82 B6
Ferryside Gdns 3 LN3 82 B6
Ferryview PE2 229 E6
Festival Ave 3 PE25 90 D3
Feyzin Dr 40 DN18 10 E8
Ffolkes Dr 12 PE34 161 F3
Field Ave 6 PE13 169 F7
Field Cl
6 Gosberton PE11 145 B6
13 Laceby DN37 23 F1
23 Nettleham LN2 68 D2
14 Ruskington NG34 108 D2
1 Welton LN2 68 D7
Fieldfare Cl 8 DN16 185 B2
Fieldfare Croft PE21 208 C6
Fieldfare Dr PE2 231 E6
Field Farm La 3 LN4 95 D4
Field Head 5 DN37 23 E1
Fieldhouse Rd DN36 193 A1
Fielding Way DN21 197 E5
Field La
Bardney LN3 83 C5
Eastoft DN17 7 A3
Ewerby & Evedon NG34 122 C6
Friskney PE22 115 A6
Morton DN21 197 A8
2 Normanby by Spital LN8 55 F6
Strubby with Woodthorpe LN13 63 C1
Wroot DN9 26 D5
Field Rd
Billinghay LN4 109 E6
Crowle DN17 16 D7
Stainforth DN7 14 C6
Thorne/Moorends DN8 15 A8
Field Rise PE7 233 D5
Fields Cl 3 DN9 27 D7
Fields End DN39 12 B2
Fieldside
6 Blyton DN21 41 C5
11 Crowle DN17 16 D7
Epworth DN9 27 D6
Field Side
Mareham le Fen PE22 98 F4
Thorne DN8 15 A8
Fieldside Cres 1 PE22 99 A4
Fields Rd DN9 27 E2
Field St
6 Boston PE21 209 A5
Kingston upon Hull HU9 181 B7
Field Terr PE7 231 C2
Field The DN32 192 C6
Field View PE22 111 F8
Field Wlk PE1 226 B2
Fife Cl PE9 218 D6
Fifth Ave
Fixborough Ind Est DN15 8 A1
Grantham NG31 211 F6
Scunthorpe DN17 184 B6
Fifth Dro PE11 144 A4
Fiftyeights Rd DN10 26 B2
Figtree Wlk PE1 226 A7
Fildes St DN31 191 D7
Filey Cl LN6 205 A3
Filey Rd DN32 192 A5
FILLINGHAM DN21 54 F4
Fillingham Cres
Cleethorpes DN35 192 F3
Scunthorpe DN15 182 B3
Fillingham La DN21 53 F3
Finch Cl LN6 204 D8
Finch Dr NG34 212 B3
Finchfield PE1 226 F7
Finchley Ct DN31 191 A8
Finchley Gn PE3 225 E4
Findlay Cres DN36 195 D6
Fingle St 3 DN22 52 B1
Finisterre Ave PE25 206 A6
Finkell St DN10 39 C1
Finkin St NG31 211 A4
Finkle La 11 DN18 3 F1
Finkle St
Benington PE22 127 A5
Stainforth DN7 14 C7
Finney Cl LN4 207 D5
Finningley Cl 9 LN6 204 D6
Finningley Rd LN6 204 D6
Finns La NG32 138 C6
Finsbury Dr 3 DN33 191 B2
Finsbury St 13 LN13 75 F2
Fir Ave PE10 213 A5
Firbeck Ave PE25 206 D1
Fir Cl DN16 185 A4
Fircroft NG31 211 C1
Firdale Cl 3 PE6 174 A5
Firebeacon La
Grainthorpe LN11 49 E8
Marshchapel LN11 37 D1
Firethorn Cl 3 HU3 180 D5
Fir Hill Quarry Nature Reserve* LN11 61 E1
Fir Rd 1 PE9 218 D6
FIRSBY PE23 101 F7
Firsby Cres DN33 191 A2
First Ave
1 Fixborough Ind Est DN15 7 F1
Grantham NG31 211 E6
Grimsby DN33 191 C4
6 Scampton Airfield LN1 67 E5
Scunthorpe DN17 184 C6
Spalding PE11 214 B4
First Dro
Crowland PE6 166 E2
Gosberton PE11 144 C3
Moulton PE12 146 E6
Peterborough PE1 226 D1
Firs The 6 NG34 108 D1
First Holme La 2 NG23 91 A8
First Hurn Dro LN4 110 A6
First La HU10 179 A5
First Marsh Rd PE13 170 C2
Firth Field Rd DN7 14 F4
Firth La DN9 26 D6
Firth Rd LN6 234 A1
Firtree Ave LN6 200 C1
Fir Tree Ave 5 LN5 93 E8
Fir Tree Cl 4 LN2 68 F2
Firtree Dr 6 DN20 20 F7
Fir Tree La NG32 119 F3
Fir Trees The HU10 178 D6
Fish Dock Rd DN31 189 B2
Fishemore Ave HU13 178 F2
Fisher Cl 23 NG23 91 D5
Fishergate PE12 159 B1
Fisherman's Wharf DN31 191 D8
Fishermans Wlk 2 HU3 180 C4
Fisher Pl DN35 192 D7
Fish Groom's La PE11 145 E6
FISHLAKE DN7 14 D8
Fishlake Nab DN7 14 C7
Fishmere End Rd
Sutterton PE20 136 A4
Wigtoft PE20 135 F3
Fishmere Gate Rd LN11 51 B1
Fishpond La PE12 215 E2
Fish St 1 HU1 180 F5
FISHTOFT PE21 126 C1
Fishtoft Dro PE22 125 C7
FISHTOFT DROVE PE22 125 D8
Fishtoft Rd PE21 209 B3
Fishtoft Sch PE21 126 C1
Fish Well Cl 3 NG33 151 A8
Fishwick Ave 5 HU13 178 E1
FISKERTON LN3 82 A6
Fiskerton CE (Controlled) Prim Sch LN3 82 B7
Fiskerton Cl 8 DN34 190 F4
Fiskerton Dr LN2 201 F8
Fiskerton Rd
Cherry Willingham LN3 203 C4
Cherry Willingham/Reepham LN3 82 A8
Fiskerton Rd E LN3 203 E4
Fiskerton Way 2 DN31 188 A3
Fitties La 2 DN36 37 C5
FITTON END PE13 169 F3
Fitton End Rd PE13 169 F3
Fitzgerald Ct 3 LN4 207 A6
Fitzjames Cl 2 PE23 101 A8
Fitzwilliam Hospl PE6 224 E2
Fitzwilliam Mews DN35 192 E2
Fitzwilliam Pl 6 LN4 109 F5
Fitzwilliam Rd PE9 219 A7
Fitzwilliam St
10 Mablethorpe/Sutton on Sea LN12 64 B4
Peterborough PE1 226 A3
Five Arches PE2 229 C6
Five Bell La PE20 135 C4
Five House La
Frampton PE20 136 C8
Wyberton PE21 208 B1
Five La Ends NG23 79 C8
Five Mile La LN4 82 B5
Flag Bsns Exchange PE1 226 E3
Flag Fen Bronze Age Mus* PE6 227 B3
Flag Fen Rd PE1 226 C4
Flag La PE12 168 B7
Flamborough Cl
Peterborough PE2 225 E1
6 Skegness PE25 206 A6
Flaminian Way 8 NG32 120 A2
Flarepath The DN20 21 A8
Flaxengate 4 LN2 234 B2
Flaxland PE3 225 A6
Flaxley Rd LN2 202 E6
Flaxmill La 6 PE11 145 C1
Flaxwell Way 12 NG34 121 B7
FLEDBOROUGH NG22 78 A7
FLEET PE12 159 C6
Fleetgate 8 DN18 3 E1
FLEET HARGATE PE12 159 C7
Fleet Rd
Fleet PE12 159 B7
Holbeach PE12 215 F2
Fleets La LN1 54 A1
Fleets Rd LN1 66 D7
Fleet St
Holbeach PE12 215 E2
Lincoln LN1 201 C4
Fleetway DN36 37 A3
Fleet Way PE2 231 B6
Fleetwood Cl 2 DN33 194 E7
Fleetwood Ct LE15 162 A8
Fleet Wood La Prim Sch PE12 159 B6
Fleming Ave NG13 128 B6
Fleming Cl PE7 233 D6
Fleming Ct
1 Boston PE21 208 F1
3 Woodston PE2 230 D8
Fleming Rd PE11 214 E8
Fleming Wlk HU4 179 D2
Fletcher Cl
Kingston upon Hull HU13 178 E2
3 Scunthorpe DN15 182 C6
Fletcher Rd DN34 190 F7
Fletcher St NG31 211 A3
Fletton Ave PE2 231 A8
Fletton Fields PE2 231 A7
Fletton Parkway PE2 229 F2
Flinders Cl 5 LN4 95 C4
Flinders Rd 13 PE11 134 E2
Flinders Way LN3 203 B6
Flinders Wlk PE11 214 C7
Flint Cl PE9 163 D1
Flint Gate 23 PE12 160 E4
Flintham Cl 2 LN4 95 C4
Flint House Rd PE12 147 C3
Flinton St HU3 180 B3
FLIXBOROUGH DN15 8 B1
Flixborough Rd DN15 8 B4
FLIXBOROUGH STATHER DN15 8 A1
Flood Rd The DN21 197 B3
Flore Cl PE3 225 C5
Florence Ave HU13 178 F1
Florence St
Grimsby DN32 191 E5
Lincoln LN2 202 B3
Florence Way 4 PE6 217 C5
Florence Wright Ave 6 LN11 198 D4
Floriade Cl 4 PE11 214 B2
Florins Fold NG34 132 F3
Floss La DN22 65 B6
Flottergate Mall DN31 191 D7
Flour Sq DN31 189 A1
Flowerdown Ave 5 NG34 120 D8
Foal Plats La LN13 90 A8
FOCKERBY DN17 7 E5
Fodder Dike Bank
Eastville PE22 114 C7
Midville PE22 113 E7
FOLD HILL PE22 115 A6
Fold Hill Rd PE22 114 A2
Fold La
Moulton PE12 157 F7
5 Tydd St Giles PE13 169 F7
Folds La 2 PE12 216 B4
Folgate La PE14 170 F6
FOLKINGHAM NG34 142 C8
Folkingham Cl 11 LN6 204 D8
Folkingham Rd
Billingborough NG34 133 A1
1 Morton PE10 154 C7
Pickworth NG34 142 A8
FOLKSWORTH PE7 232 D1
Folksworth Rd PE7 232 E1
Folly Cl PE7 233 C5
Folly La
Branston & Mere LN4 81 C2
Hough-on-the-Hill NG32 118 F5
North Kelsey LN7 32 C5
North Scarle NG23 91 D8
West Fen PE22 99 E1
Folly's Dro PE13 177 F3
Fontwell Cres 9 LN6 205 A5
Fontwell Gdns 2 PE9 219 B5
Foote's Dro PE12 167 C8
Forbes Rd PE21 209 C4
Ford Cl PE7 233 E6
Fordham Dr LN1 201 C7
FORDINGTON LN13 88 C6
Ford La
8 Hibaldstow DN20 30 F5
Morton PE10 154 C6
Ford's Ave 17 DN41 23 F5
Ford Way LN11 72 D6
Foredyke Prim Sch HU9 5 D8
Fore La PE20 135 A5
Foreman Way 1 PE6 166 E1
Forest Ave 3 PE10 213 B5
Forest CE Prim Sch PE7 231 C2
Forest Dale PE21 208 F7
Forest Dr DN36 193 B1
Forest Dro PE6 166 C2
Foresters Ct Galleries* PE20 135 B7
Forester Way HU4 179 D3
Forest Gdns 5 PE9 218 D7
Forest Pines La 11 LN10 97 C5
Forest Way 7 DN36 36 D8
Forge Cl
Freiston PE22 126 C4
South Kelsey LN7 32 A1
Forge Cres
3 Pinchbeck PE11 156 E8
Ulceby DN39 12 A1
Forge Ct 12 PE6 217 A6
Forge End PE7 229 A4
Forge La LN8 56 F8
Forge Way DN36 195 C3
Forkedale DN18 10 E8
Forlander Pl LN11 198 D6
Forman's La NG34 109 B1
Formby Cl NG31 211 C7
Forrester St 1 DN20 196 B3
Forrington Pl LN1 66 E2
Forstedd Hill NG33 153 B5
Forster St DN21 197 C5
Forsyth Cres 6 PE25 206 C2
Forsythia Ave 25 DN41 23 F5
Forsythia Dr DN33 191 C2
Fortescue Cl 1 LN4 207 A5
Fortuna Prim Sch LN6 204 B7
Fortuna Way DN37 190 C7
Forty Acre HU10 178 F7
Forty Acre Rd PE1 226 D2
Forty Foot La
Humberside Airport DN39 21 F6
Old Leake PE22 113 D3
Forty Stps HU10 178 F7
Forum The LN6 204 F3
Forum Way 7 NG34 212 F3
FOSDYKE PE20 146 D8
FOSDYKE BRIDGE PE12 146 E7
Foss Bank LN1 201 D3
Fossdyke Gdns 18 LN1 66 D2
Fosse Cl 9 PE6 164 E5
Fosse Ct 5 LN4 81 A1
Fosse Dr LN6 205 A3
Fosse La
Thistleton LE15 151 B1
Thorpe on the Hill LN6 92 E7
Fosseway 4 DN21 197 F5
Fosse Way Prim Sch LN6 204 F2
Foss St LN1 201 D3
Foster Cl 2 LN4 96 C1
Foster Rd
21 Collingham NG23 91 D5
7 Thorne/Moorends DN8 15 A8
Woodston PE2 230 D8
Fosters Cl 3 LN5 107 A8
Foster's Dro PE10 155 A3
Foster's Gdns 1 LN4 82 B1
Foster St
3 Boston PE21 209 A5
Heckington NG34 122 E3
Lincoln LN5 201 E1
FOSTON NG32 117 F2
Foston by Pass NG32 117 F1
Foston Cres LN6 204 F7
Foston La NG32 128 F7
Foston Rd NG31 210 E3
FOTHERBY LN11 49 A3
Fotherby Rd DN17 184 F4
Fotherby St 3 DN31 189 A1
Fothergill Dr 17 DN3 14 A2
FOUL ANCHOR PE13 170 D8
Foundry La
11 Spalding PE11 214 D4
12 Thorne/Moorends DN8 15 A8
Foundry Rd
Bucknall LN10 84 B3
Ryhall PE9 163 C2
Stamford PE9 219 A5
Foundry Sh Ctr The DN15 183 B4
Foundry St LN9 199 C4
Fountain Cl
Kingston upon Hull HU13 178 C3
5 Waltham DN37 194 C5
Fountain Hill DN10 39 E3
Fountain Hill Rd DN10 39 E4
Fountain La 13 PE21 208 F5
Fountain Pl 10 PE21 208 F5
Fountains Ave DN37 188 A1
Fountains Pl PE6 175 B1
Fountain St
22 Caistor LN7 33 B4
Kingston upon Hull HU3 180 D6
Four Acre Cl HU10 178 C6
Four Chimneys Cres PE7 230 C2
Fourfields CE Prim Sch PE20 136 A2
Fourfields Com Prim Sch PE7 233 E6
FOUR GOTES PE13 170 B7
Fourth Ave
2 Fixborough Ind Est DN15 8 A1
Grantham NG31 211 F6
3 Scampton Airfield LN1 67 E5
1 Scunthorpe DN17 184 C6
Fourth Dro
Gosberton PE11 144 B4
Peterborough PE1 226 F3
Fourways 6 DN36 36 D4
Fowler Cl LN11 198 D4
Fowler Rd DN16 185 B8
Foxby Hill DN21 197 E2
Foxby La DN21 197 F2
Fox Cl
Boston PE21 208 C6
Little Coates DN34 190 F6
Fox Covert
2 Aubourn Haddington & South Hykeham LN6 93 A8
North Hykeham LN6 204 B1
Sudbrooke LN2 69 A2
Fox Covert La DN10 40 A4
Foxcovert Rd PE6 220 E8
Fox Ct 1 DN17 16 D8
Foxdale PE1 225 F7
Fox Dale PE9 218 F6
Foxe End 19 LN12 64 B3
Foxendale Hill LN9 72 F1
Foxes Low Rd PE12 215 F2
Foxfield Cl LN6 200 A5
Foxglove Cl
Brigg DN20 196 B4
1 Spilsby PE23 101 A8
Foxglove Gdns DN34 190 F6
Foxglove Rd
16 Market Rasen LN8 57 D8
1 Stamford PE9 218 C7
Foxgloves PE6 217 D6
Foxglove Way 5 LN5 205 C2
Fox Headings PE12 158 C1
Foxhill DN37 190 C7
Foxhill Rd DN8 15 B7
Foxhills Ind Pk DN15 182 F7
Foxhills Rd DN15 182 E5
Foxhills Sch & Tech Coll DN15 182 E5
Foxhole La PE22 126 D3
Foxley Cl PE4 221 A4
Foxley Ct 1 PE10 213 C7
Fox St DN15 182 F3
Foyle Cl LN5 205 D2
Fracknal's Row 3 PE21 208 E6
Framlingham Rd PE7 231 F5
FRAMPTON PE20 136 F6
Frampton Bank PE20 136 B8
Frampton La PE20 124 E2

Frampton Marsh Nature Reserve★ PE20 ... 137 D5
Frampton Pl PE21 ... 208 D4
Frampton Roads PE20 ... 136 F6
Frances Askew Prim Sch HU4 ... 179 F4
Frances Ct 8 DN37 ... 194 C5
Frances St DN15 ... 183 A3
Francis Bernard Cl 4 PE21 ... 208 D3
Francis Chichester Wlk DN21 ... 197 F3
Francis Gdns PE1 ... 225 F8
Francis La LN9 ... 199 C4
Francis St
  Kingston upon Hull HU2 ... 180 F7
  Lincoln LN1 ... 234 B4
  14 Spalding PE11 ... 214 D4
Francklin Wlk 5 PE12 ... 158 B6
Frankland Cl 1 DN20 ... 196 F6
Frankland Pl DN35 ... 192 D7
Franklin Ave PE25 ... 206 D1
Franklin Cl
  Boston PE21 ... 208 C6
  7 Metheringham LN4 ... 95 C4
Franklin Coll DN34 ... 191 B5
Franklin Cres
  Peterborough PE1 ... 226 E6
  Scunthorpe DN16 ... 185 E6
  1 Sleaford NG34 ... 212 D5
Franklin Dr PE11 ... 214 B2
Franklin Gdns 11 PE23 ... 101 A8
Franklin Rd 3 DN21 ... 29 C4
Franklin St HU9 ... 181 C8
Franklin Way
  Humberside Airport DN38 ... 21 F5
  North Greetwell LN3 ... 203 B6
Frank Perkins Parkway PE1 ... 226 E6
Frank Perkins Way PE1 ... 226 D3
Franks Cl 2 PE20 ... 136 D5
Franks La PE13 ... 169 F5
Frank Swaby Ct LN5 ... 205 E6
Frank Walsham Ct DN32 ... 192 A8
Frank Whittle Cl 1 NG34 ... 120 E8
Frank Wright Ct 4 LN2 ... 202 C7
Fraserburgh Way 2 PE2 ... 229 D4
Fraser Cl PE6 ... 217 D5
Fraser St 2 DN32 ... 191 F7
Frederica Rd 12 PE25 ... 103 E4
Frederick Gough Sch DN16 ... 185 C4
Frederick St
  Cleethorpes DN35 ... 192 E6
  Grimsby DN31 ... 191 D8
  Lincoln LN2 ... 202 C3
Frederick Ward Way DN31 ... 191 D7
Freehold St HU3 ... 180 D7
Freeman Ave 4 HU15 ... 2 C5
Freeman Cl 10 PE8 ... 172 B1
Freeman Ct DN36 ... 195 E2
Freeman Rd LN6 ... 204 D3
Freemans La 6 DN20 ... 10 C2
Freeman's La DN22 ... 52 A2
Freeman St DN32 ... 189 B1
Freeman Way 9 DN32 ... 189 B1
Freeport Wharf DN31 ... 191 E8
Freer Gdns LN11 ... 198 E6
Freeschool La LN2 ... 234 B2
Freesia Way PE7 ... 233 F6
Freeston St DN35 ... 192 B8
Freetown Way HU2 ... 180 E7
Freightliner Rd HU3 ... 179 F2
FREISTON PE22 ... 126 D2
Freiston Ctr for Environmental Ed★ PE22 ... 126 D3
Freiston Rd PE21 ... 209 B5
FREISTON SHORE PE22 ... 126 F1
French Dro PE6 ... 175 E7
French's Rd PE14 ... 170 F8
Fresh Fields 14 HU15 ... 2 C5
Freshney Bog Nature Reserve★ DN37 ... 190 E7
Freshney Dr 1 DN31 ... 191 C8
Freshney Pl Sh Ctr DN32 ... 191 D7
Freshney Way PE21 ... 208 B3
Freston PE4 ... 221 D2
Freyja Croft DN33 ... 191 B2
Friars Gate PE21 ... 208 E4
Friars La LN2 ... 234 B2
Friars Rd DN17 ... 184 E6
Friar Way PE21 ... 208 F6
Friary Rd 1 NG24 ... 104 A4
FRIESTHORPE LN3 ... 57 A2
Friest La 11 PE20 ... 135 A4
FRIESTON NG32 ... 119 B6
Frieston Heath La NG32 ... 119 D6
Frieston Rd NG32 ... 119 B6
Frieston Shore Nature Reserve★ PE22 ... 127 A1
Frinkley La
  Honington NG32 ... 119 B2
  Hougham NG32 ... 118 D2
Frisby Cl PE6 ... 164 D4
FRISKNEY PE22 ... 115 A6
Friskney Decoy Wood Nature Reserve★ PE22 ... 115 A8
FRISKNEY EAUDYKE PE22 ... 115 B7
FRITH BANK PE21 ... 125 D5
Frith Bank PE22 ... 125 D6
Friths La PE20 ... 125 B1
FRITHVILLE PE22 ... 112 D1
Frithville Prim Sch PE22 ... 112 D1
Frithville Rd PE22 ... 113 A1
Frobisher Ave DN32 ... 192 B6
FRODINGHAM DN16 ... 183 C2
Frodingham Footpath 2 DN15 ... 183 B3
Frodingham Inf Sch DN16 ... 183 B2
Frodingham Rd DN15 ... 183 A4
Frodingham S Rd DN16 ... 183 E2
Frodsham St 8 HU9 ... 5 D8
FROGNALL PE6 ... 165 D1
Frognall PE6 ... 165 D1
Frog's Abbey Gate PE12 ... 158 E4
Frome Cl LN6 ... 204 D5
Front Rd
  Tydd St Mary PE13 ... 160 D1
  Wisbech St Mary PE13 ... 177 D6
Front St
  Alkborough DN15 ... 8 C8
  Barnby in the Willows NG24 ... 104 F3
  Dunston LN4 ... 95 C5
  East Stockwith DN21 ... 40 B5
  Elsham DN20 ... 20 F7
  Gainsborough DN21 ... 197 B7
  4 Grasby DN38 ... 32 E7
  Normanby by Spital LN8 ... 55 E7
  South Clifton NG23 ... 78 C5
  Tealby LN8 ... 46 C1
  Ulceby DN39 ... 12 A1
Frost Cl DN15 ... 2 A1
Frostley Gate PE12 ... 158 F3
Frusher Ave DN33 ... 191 C3
Fryston 28 HU15 ... 2 C6
Fuchsia Croft 2 DN15 ... 182 F2
Fuchsia Dr HU4 ... 179 B2
FULBECK NG32 ... 106 C1
Fulbeck Rd DN16 ... 185 C6
Fulbridge Rd PE4 ... 221 A3
Fulbridge Sch PE1 ... 225 F7
Fulford Cl NG31 ... 211 D8
Fulford Cres
  Kingston upon Hull HU10 ... 179 A8
  3 New Holland DN19 ... 4 E2
Fulford Way PE25 ... 206 C6
Fulham Pk 1 DN33 ... 191 B2
Fulham Rd PE3 ... 225 E4
Fuller St DN35 ... 192 D8
FULLETBY LN9 ... 86 B8
Fulmar Dr LN11 ... 198 C8
Fulmar Rd LN6 ... 204 D8
Fulmen Cl LN1 ... 201 C7
FULNETBY LN8 ... 69 F6
FULNEY PE11 ... 157 B6
Fulney Dro PE12 ... 157 B3
Fulney La PE12 ... 157 B6
FULSTOW LN11 ... 49 B8
Fulstow Gr 5 DN33 ... 191 B3
Fulstow Prim Sch LN11 ... 49 B8
Fulstow Rd LN2 ... 202 B8
Fundrey Rd PE13 ... 170 E1
Fun Farm★ PE12 ... 157 D7
Furlongs La
  Belchford LN9 ... 73 B1
  Old Leake PE22 ... 114 A1
Furlongs Rd LN12 ... 77 A8
Furlongs The 17 LN8 ... 57 D8
Furndown Ct LN6 ... 204 B7
Furniss Ct 2 DN18 ... 10 E8
Furrow Cl 16 LN2 ... 68 D6
Further Old Gate PE12 ... 158 D5
Fury Ave LN11 ... 62 B6
Furze Hill Nature Reserve★ PE23 ... 87 A3
Furze La LN11 ... 62 A5
Furze Ride PE1 ... 226 B8
Fussey Gdns DN20 ... 10 C1
Fydell Cres PE21 ... 208 E4
Fydell Ct PE21 ... 208 E6
Fydell St PE21 ... 208 E5
Fyson Way PE20 ... 136 C6

G

Gables The PE10 ... 213 C2
Gabriel Cres LN2 ... 202 E6
Gadd's La PE13 ... 170 A1
Gainas Ave DN21 ... 197 C6
GAINSBOROUGH DN21 ... 197 B4
Gainsborough Central Sta DN21 ... 197 E4
Gainsborough Coll DN21 ... 197 C5
Gainsborough Gdns 2 LN6 ... 205 B7
Gainsborough La DN20 ... 30 F8
Gainsborough Lea Rd Sta DN21 ... 197 D1
Gainsborough Leisure Ctr DN21 ... 197 D6
Gainsborough Model Railway★ 15 DN21 ... 197 D3
Gainsborough Old Hall★ DN21 ... 197 C5
Gainsborough Rd
  Blyton DN21 ... 41 B4
  Bole DN22 ... 52 A6
  Girton NG23 ... 78 C2
  32 Kirton in Lindsey DN21 ... 30 B1
  Kirton in Lindsey DN21 ... 42 D8
  Little Casterton PE9 ... 218 F7
  Middle Rasen LN8 ... 57 B7
  Saundby DN22 ... 52 B7
  Saxilby with Ingleby LN1 ... 66 D2
  Scotter DN21 ... 29 B3
  Sturton le Steeple DN22 ... 52 B3
  West Rasen LN8 ... 57 A7
  Willingham DN21 ... 53 E4
  6 Winthorpe NG24 ... 104 B7
  Wiseton DN10 ... 39 A1
Gainsthorpe Rd E DN21 ... 30 D4
Gainsthorpe Rd W DN21 ... 30 C4
Gallagher Ret Pk DN15 ... 182 A3
Gallamore Ct 5 LN8 ... 57 C8
Gallamore La 6 LN8 ... 57 C8
Gallands Cl 19 HU14 ... 3 B7
Galletly Cl PE10 ... 213 D6
Galley Ct HU9 ... 181 C6
GALLEY HILL LN13 ... 75 E6
Gallions Cl 2 PE4 ... 221 B1
Galway Cl 2 PE11 ... 214 A5
Gamlyn Cl 1 PE11 ... 214 D2
Gannet Ct 8 NG31 ... 210 E2
Gannocks Cl PE2 ... 229 F5
Gannocks The PE2 ... 229 F5
Ganton Sch HU10 ... 179 A7
Ganton Way
  Harrowby Est NG31 ... 211 E7
  Kingston upon Hull HU10 ... 178 F8
Garbutt Pl DN35 ... 193 A4
Garden Cl PE9 ... 218 E6
Garden Dr DN36 ... 195 C7
Garden End Rd PE1 ... 226 B6
Gardeners Wlk PE21 ... 208 D2
Gardenfield LN6 ... 200 B3
Gardenia Dr DN17 ... 184 F1
Garden St
  5 Brigg DN20 ... 196 C3
  Grimsby DN31 ... 191 D7
Gardens The
  3 Crowland PE6 ... 166 F1
  Horncastle LN9 ... 199 C3
Gardiner Ave 7 NG24 ... 104 C1
Garfield Cl LN1 ... 201 D8
Garfield St DN21 ... 197 C5
Garfield View LN1 ... 201 D8
Garfit's La PE21 ... 208 D1
Garford La 8 PE9 ... 171 D3
Garibaldi St 6 DN32 ... 189 B1
Garmston St 8 LN1 ... 234 B3
Garner's La PE34 ... 161 A4
Garner St DN32 ... 191 E6
Garnet Gr 6 HU3 ... 180 A4
Garnett St DN35 ... 192 D8
GARNSGATE PE12 ... 159 E5
Garnsgate Rd PE12 ... 216 A5
Garratt Rd 7 PE9 ... 219 B4
Garrick Cl LN5 ... 205 C3
Garrick La DN36 ... 195 C7
Garrick Wlk PE2 ... 231 B7
Garrison Rd HU9 ... 181 C6
Garth La DN31 ... 191 D8
GARTHORPE
  Garthorpe and Fockerby DN17 ... 7 F6
  Garthorpe LE14 ... 150 A4
Garthorpe Rd DN17 ... 7 C4
Garth Specl Sch The PE11 ... 214 E5
Garth The HU10 ... 179 A4
Garthway 7 DN36 ... 195 D2
Garton Gr
  3 Grimsby DN32 ... 192 A5
  3 Kingston upon Hull HU5 ... 179 C7
Garton St PE1 ... 226 A5
Gartree Com Sch The LN4 ... 207 B5
Gascoigne 3 PE4 ... 220 E5
Gashouse La 3 DN9 ... 28 A3
Gas House La 16 PE12 ... 160 E4
Gas La
  7 Navenby/Wellingore LN5 ... 107 A8
  Stamford PE9 ... 219 C5
  5 Thorney PE6 ... 176 A3
Gas St
  3 Horncastle LN9 ... 199 C3
  19 Stamford PE9 ... 219 C5
GATE BURTON DN21 ... 53 B2
Gatehouse Rd DN19 ... 11 F7
Gate La DN33 ... 191 D1
Gateroom La PE22 ... 114 E3
Gate Way DN31 ... 188 E2
Gateway The 4 NG24 ... 104 A4
Gatewood La DN7 ... 14 E1
Gatherums The DN35 ... 192 E5
Gatram Rd PE24 ... 90 D6
Gaunt Cl 5 PE12 ... 157 B6
Gauntlet Dro PE20 ... 134 F6
Gauntlet Rd
  3 Bicker PE20 ... 135 A4
  Grimoldby LN11 ... 62 B6
Gaunt St LN5 ... 234 A1
GAUTBY LN8 ... 84 B7
Gautry La DN9 ... 28 B4
Gavel St PE7 ... 233 C8
Gayle Rd LN4 ... 110 E8
Gaysfield Rd 6 PE21 ... 126 C1
Gayton Cl
  Lincoln LN2 ... 202 A7
  Skegness PE25 ... 206 C2
Gayton Ct PE3 ... 225 C5
GAYTON ENGINE LN12 ... 63 C6
GAYTON LE MARSH LN13 ... 62 F3
GAYTON LE WOLD LN11 ... 59 E4
Gayton Rd DN35 ... 193 A3
Gazeley Gdns PE7 ... 231 B2
Geddington Rd PE2 ... 230 E8
GEDNEY PE12 ... 159 D7
GEDNEY BROADGATE PE12 ... 159 D5
Gedney Church End Prim Sch PE12 ... 159 D7
Gedney Cl
  13 Bicker PE20 ... 135 A4
  Grimsby DN37 ... 190 C8
GEDNEY DROVE END PE12 ... 149 A4
GEDNEY DYKE PE12 ... 148 B1
GEDNEY HILL PE12 ... 168 D2
Gedney Hill CE (Controlled) Prim Sch PE12 ... 168 D2
Gedney Hill Gate PE12 ... 168 F7
Gedney Rd PE12 ... 216 A6
Gee St HU3 ... 180 C5
GEESTON PE9 ... 171 A2
Gelder Beck Rd DN17 ... 29 D6
Gelder's La PE12 ... 158 A1
GELSTON NG32 ... 118 F4
Gelston Rd NG32 ... 119 A4
Gemsbok Cl 3 HU4 ... 179 D2
Genesis Way
  Great Coates DN37 ... 24 B6
  Pyewipe DN37 ... 188 A3
Geneva Ave LN2 ... 202 B6
Geneva St PE1 ... 226 A3
Geoff Moulder Leisure Complex★ PE21 ... 209 A4
George Ave
  Gedney PE12 ... 148 F4
  4 Keadby DN17 ... 17 D5
  Skegness PE25 ... 206 B3
George Butler Cl 23 DN37 ... 23 F1
George Farmer Tech & Language Coll PE12 ... 215 D3
George Janney Ct 24 DN32 ... 189 C1
George Mews 2 LN7 ... 33 B4
George Sh Ctr The NG31 ... 211 A4
George St
  2 Barton-upon-Humber DN18 ... 10 F8
  5 Boston PE21 ... 208 E4
  Bourne PE10 ... 213 D5
  Broughton DN20 ... 19 D3
  Cleethorpes DN35 ... 192 F5
  Gainsborough DN21 ... 197 B6
  Grantham NG31 ... 211 B4
  Grimsby DN31 ... 191 D7
  Helpringham NG34 ... 133 D7
  5 Keadby DN17 ... 17 D5
  Kingston upon Hull HU1 ... 180 F6
  11 Kirton in Lindsey DN21 ... 30 B1
  Lincoln LN5 ... 234 C1
  Louth LN11 ... 198 B5
  Mablethorpe/Sutton on Sea LN12 ... 64 B3
  7 Market Rasen LN8 ... 57 D8
  Peterborough PE2 ... 230 F8
  Scunthorpe DN15 ... 183 A4
  Sleaford NG34 ... 212 C3
Georgette Gdns 7 PE11 ... 214 B5
George Yd 5 HU1 ... 181 A6
Georgian Ct
  Peterborough PE3 ... 225 E1
  6 Spalding PE11 ... 214 D3
Georgina Ct 27 DN18 ... 10 E8
Gerald's Cl LN2 ... 202 B5
German's La PE34 ... 161 D2
Gerrard Mews LN4 ... 203 D1
Gershwin Ave HU4 ... 179 B4
Gertrude St DN32 ... 191 E5
Gervase St DN15 ... 183 A3
Gibbeson St 6 LN5 ... 205 E8
Gibbet La LN8 ... 57 A5
Giblin Cotts DN15 ... 182 E5
Gibraltar Hill LN1 ... 234 A3
Gibraltar La 2 DN37 ... 23 F1
Gibraltar Point National Nature Reserve★ PE24 ... 103 E2
Gibraltar Point Visitor Ctr★ PE24 ... 116 D4
Gibraltar Rd
  Croft PE24 ... 103 D1
  5 Hemswell Cliff DN21 ... 55 A8
  Mablethorpe/Sutton on Sea LN12 ... 64 B4
  Seacroft PE24 ... 116 D5
Gibson Cl
  Branston LN4 ... 81 E2
  1 Sleaford NG34 ... 212 B6
Gibson Gn LN6 ... 92 E5
Gibson La HU14 ... 2 E4
Gibson Pl 5 PE25 ... 206 A5
Gibson Rd 2 DN7 ... 26 A8
Gibsons Gdn 2 LN11 ... 50 F7
Giddings Cl PE2 ... 229 F4
Gilbert Dr PE21 ... 208 A1
Gilberts Gr 4 PE25 ... 206 D8
Gilbert Sutcliffe Ct DN35 ... 192 A2
Gilbey Rd DN31 ... 188 D1
Gildale PE4 ... 221 B4
Gildenburgh Ave PE1 ... 226 D5
Gilder Way PE21 ... 209 F2
Gildesburgh Rd LN4 ... 203 B1
Giles Sch & 6th Form Ctr The PE22 ... 114 A1
Giles St DN35 ... 192 E6
Gillatts Cl 1 DN20 ... 196 F7
Gill Ct DN33 ... 191 B2
Gillett St HU3 ... 180 B4
Gilliatt St DN15 ... 183 A4
Gilmores La 18 NG24 ... 104 C1
Gilmorton Dr PE1 ... 226 D7
Gilpin Cl PE10 ... 213 E2
Gilpin St PE1 ... 225 E6
Gimmel's Gate PE12 ... 216 C1
GIPSEY BRIDGE PE22 ... 124 F8
Gipsey Bridge Prim Sch PE22 ... 125 A8
Gipsy Dro
  Friskney PE22 ... 114 D7
  Langriville PE22 ... 124 F8
Gipsy La
  Gedney PE12 ... 216 A8
  Holton le Moor LN7 ... 32 C1
  Osgodby LN8 ... 45 D3
  Owersby LN7 ... 44 F8
  Owston Ferry DN9 ... 40 C8
  South Kelsey LN7 ... 32 C1
  Swineshead PE20 ... 124 A1
  Tydd St Mary PE13 ... 160 A2
  Wrangle PE22 ... 114 D2
GIPSYVILLE HU4 ... 179 E3
Girdlestone Wlk 2 PE6 ... 166 F1
GIRSBY LN8 ... 59 C6
Girsby La LN8 ... 59 B6
GIRTON NG23 ... 78 C1
Girton Cl 3 DN16 ... 185 B4
Girton La NG23 ... 78 D1
Girton Rd DN37 ... 190 F6
Girton Way 3 PE9 ... 219 A7
Gisburn Rd HU13 ... 178 F2
Glade The 8 LN12 ... 77 A7
Gladiator Rd LN11 ... 62 B6
Gladstone Cotts DN21 ... 197 B8
Gladstone Dr 1 DN16 ... 183 C1
Gladstone Prim Sch PE1 ... 225 F5
Gladstone St
  Bourne PE10 ... 213 C6
  Gainsborough DN21 ... 197 C5
  Kingston upon Hull HU3 ... 180 C6
  Peterborough PE1 ... 225 F3
Gladstone Terr 3 NG31 ... 211 A5
Glaisdale Gdns NG31 ... 211 B8
Glaisdale Gr HU9 ... 181 F8
Glaisdale Rd 2 DN16 ... 185 D5
Glamis Gdns PE3 ... 225 B2
Glamis Pl LN11 ... 198 B6
Glamis Rd HU13 ... 178 F2
Glanford Gr 12 DN19 ... 11 D8
Glanford Pk (Scunthorpe United FC) DN15 ... 182 A2
Glanford Rd
  Brigg DN20 ... 196 D3
  Scunthorpe DN17 ... 184 F3
Glanford Way DN15 ... 182 B3
Glanville Ave DN17 ... 184 F8
Glanville Cres 2 DN17 ... 184 F8
Glasgow St HU3 ... 180 A5
Glastonbury Cl 20 PE6 ... 175 A1
Glatton Dr PE2 ... 231 D6
Gleanings The 5 LN5 ... 107 B8
Glebe Ave PE2 ... 229 E4
Glebe Cl
  Burton upon Stather DN15 ... 8 A5
  3 Donington on Bain LN11 ... 59 E1
  Gorefield PE13 ... 169 E3
  Holton le Clay DN36 ... 195 C3
  Humberston DN36 ... 36 C8
  5 Ingham LN1 ... 54 F2
  Scopwick LN4 ... 95 C1
  5 Sibsey PE22 ... 113 B1
  1 Skegness PE25 ... 206 A7
  Sleaford NG34 ... 212 A2
  2 Spalding PE11 ... 214 A4
Glebe Ct PE2 ... 231 B8
Glebe Gdns 2 PE6 ... 175 B8
Glebe Rd
  Brigg DN20 ... 196 C4
  Cleethorpes DN35 ... 192 E6
  Grimsby DN33 ... 191 E1
  Humberston DN36 ... 36 C7
  Peterborough PE2 ... 231 A8
  Scunthorpe DN15 ... 183 B4
  Thorne/Moorends DN8 ... 15 B8
  Wymondham LE14 ... 150 B1
Glebe Ret Pk DN15 ... 183 B4
Glebe The
  Sturton by Stow LN1 ... 66 D8
  Upton DN21 ... 53 D5
Glebe View 1 PE6 ... 217 B6
Glebe Way
  Barton-upon-Humber DN18 ... 11 A8
  5 Sutterton PE20 ... 136 A2
Glebe Wlk 3 PE12 ... 167 B8
Gleedale LN6 ... 204 F1
Gleed Ave PE11 ... 134 E2
Gleed Boys Sch PE11 ... 214 F4

Gleeds Girl's Tech Coll The PE11 214 F3
Glemsford Rise 2 PE2 230 C7
Glenarm Cres 7 LN5 205 D3
Glen Ave 4 LN12 145 B1
Glenbank Cl LN6 204 F3
Glen Cl NG33 153 A1
Glencoe Cl 2 DN7 14 D4
Glencoe St HU3 179 F6
Glencoe Way PE2 229 D3
Glen Cres
  7 Essendine PE9 163 D3
  Stamford PE9 219 C7
Glendale PE2 229 D6
Glendon Cl 5 LN5 205 D3
Glen Dr PE21 208 B4
Gleneagles
  Grantham NG31 211 D8
  Peterborough PE2 229 F6
  10 Waltham DN37 194 C4
Gleneagles Cl 5 PE9 218 E6
Gleneagles Cres 6 DN19 4 E2
Gleneagles Dr
  Skegness PE25 206 D6
  12 Woodhall Spa LN10 97 C5
GLENEAGLES ESTATE PE25 206 D6
Gleneagles Gr 4 LN4 203 D1
Glenfield Rd DN37 190 D8
Glen Gdns 2 PE11 145 E3
Glen Hall Rise 10 DN19 11 C8
Glenham Dr HU10 178 F7
Glenn Ave 3 PE11 214 C4
Glen Rd
  Castle Bytham NG33 152 D1
  Counthorpe & Creeton NG33 153 A2
  3 Wittering PE8 172 B1
Glenrock Pk HU15 2 B6
Glenside NG33 152 E1
Glenside N PE11 156 C8
Glenside S PE11 156 C8
GLENTHAM LN8 43 E1
Glentham Cl LN6 205 B3
Glentham Ct 6 LN8 43 F1
Glentham Rd
  Bishop Norton LN8 43 D3
  5 Gainsborough DN21 53 A8
Glen The PE2 231 B7
Glenton St PE1 226 C2
GLENTWORTH DN21 54 E7
Glentworth Cres 4 PE25 206 D4
Glentworth Rd DN21 53 F4
Glenwood Dr 2 HU4 179 B6
Glenwood Gr LN6 201 D1
GLINTON PE6 220 D8
Glinton Rd
  Helpston PE6 173 C4
  Newborough PE6 221 C8
Global Ctr Ind Est PE1 226 E4
Gloria Way DN37 190 C7
Glossop Rd DN15 182 B2
Gloucester Ave
  Grimsby DN34 191 B4
  Scunthorpe DN16 185 B7
Gloucester Cl
  Skegness PE25 206 B2
  1 Sleaford NG34 212 C7
Gloucester Ct DN15 183 A6
Gloucester Rd
  Grantham NG31 210 C5
  Peterborough PE2 231 B7
  7 Stamford PE9 219 B6
Gloucester St HU4 179 E3
Glover Rd DN17 184 E8
Glovers Ave 8 DN17 17 D4
Glynn Rd LN1 201 E8
Glynn View 14 LN1 201 E8
Goathland Cl HU3 180 A6
Goathland Ct 12 DN37 190 E8
Godber Dr LN4 205 F3
Goddam's La PE12 146 F1
Goddard Cl 37 DN18 10 E8
Goddard Cres 12 PE13 170 D1
Godfrey Ave 6 PE11 145 C6
Godfrey Cl 7 PE6 174 E5
Godfrey Rd 11 DN8 15 A8
Godiva Cl 16 PE6 166 F1
Godiva Cres PE10 213 B5
Godman's La HU10 178 B8
Godnow Rd DN17 16 C6
Godric Sq PE2 230 D6
Godsey Cres 9 PE6 217 C5
Godsey's La PE6 217 B6
Godson Ave 1 NG34 122 D3
Godwin Cl PE10 213 B6
Godwin Rd 13 PE13 170 D1
Goffsmill PE3 225 A4
Goldcrest Cl
  2 Birchwood LN6 200 E1
  Scunthorpe DN15 182 D6
Golden Drop 2 PE6 173 C4
Golden Gr PE20 135 C5
Golden Harvest Way 6 PE12 158 B6
Goldenholme La 4 DN22 65 A5
Gold Fen Dike Bank PE22 114 D2
Goldfinch Cl LN6 200 A3
Goldgarth DN32 192 A5
Goldhay Way PE2 229 F2
Goldie La PE2 229 F6
Goldings The 10 DN9 27 D2
Gold La LN13 63 A1
Goldsmith Ct 1 LN4 207 A6
Goldsmith Rd NG31 211 D6
Goldsmith Wlk LN2 202 C7
Goldson's La PE22 126 F6
Golf Ct PE17 160 F5
Golf Links Dr HU15 2 B6
Golf Rd 4 LN12 64 A4
Gollands La DN9 27 B2
Gonerby Hill NG31 210 E8
GONERBY HILL FOOT NG31 210 F8
Gonerby Hill Foot CE Prim Sch NG31 210 E8
Gonerby La NG32 129 A7
Gonerby Rd NG31 210 E8
Goochgate PE12 169 A7
Goodacre PE2 230 A4
Goodens La PE13 170 A5
Goodfellows CE Prim Sch PE11 156 E3
Goodfellows Rd 7 PE11 156 E3
Goodhand Cl DN18 11 A8
Good La LN1 234 B4
Goodliff Rd NG31 210 E2
Goodman Cl 6 NG31 129 E5
Goodson Cl 3 PE21 209 B4
Goodwin Dr 8 PE24 90 B7
Goodwin Parade 1 HU3 180 D5
Goodwin Wlk PE4 221 A4
Goodwood DN17 184 D4
Goodwood Cl LN11 198 A7
Goodwood La 2 DN35 192 F1
Goodwood Rd 8 PE3 224 F3
Goodwood Way 19 LN6 204 C7
Goole Rd DN14 6 C8
Gooseacre 33 DN17 29 D7
Goosegate La NG32 118 A2
Goose Gn 10 PE12 160 E4
Goose La PE23 87 D2
Goose's La PE14 161 A1
Gordon Ave PE2 230 E7
Gordon Boswell Romany Mus★ PE12 214 E1
Gordon Fendick Sch The PE13 170 D2
Gordon Field 8 LN8 57 D7
Gordon Gdns 1 DN33 194 F8
Gordon Rd LN1 234 B3
Gordon St
  Gainsborough DN21 197 D2
  4 Kingston upon Hull HU3 180 B5
Gordon Way PE2 230 C7
Goredike Bank PE13 169 C2
GOREFIELD PE13 169 E2
Gorefield Cty Prim Sch PE13 169 F2
Gorefield Rd PE13 169 F2
Gorehall Dr 10 LN2 68 D7
Gore La 8 PE11 214 D4
Goring Pl DN35 192 D7
Gorse Cl
  Bottesford DN16 185 C4
  5 Hatfield DN7 14 C3
  4 Woodhall Spa LN10 97 E6
Gorse Dro NG34 133 A6
Gorse Gn PE1 226 B8
Gorse Hill La
  Caythorpe NG32 119 A8
  Wellingore LN5 107 C7
Gorse La
  Gonerby Hill Foot NG31 211 B1
  Great Ponton NG31 139 F8
  9 Leasingham NG34 121 B7
  Scredington NG34 133 A7
  Silk Willoughby NG34 121 C1
Gorse Rd NG31 211 D5
Gorse Rise NG31 211 C5
Gorton Rd HU10 178 E7
Gorton St DN31 189 B2
Gorwick La LN1 66 B6
GOSBERTON PE11 145 B6
Gosberton Bank PE11 145 E6
GOSBERTON CHEAL PE11 145 A4
GOSBERTON CLOUGH PE11 144 D4
Gosberton Clough & Risegate Prim Sch PE11 144 D4
Gosberton House Specl Sch PE11 145 B6
Gosberton Prim Sch PE11 145 B6
Gosberton Rd PE11 145 C4
Goshawk Way LN4 207 C6
Goslings Cnr Wood Nature Reserve★ LN8 70 E2
Gospelgate LN11 198 B5
Gospel La LN5 106 C3
Gosport Rd DN34 191 A6
Gosport Wlk HU4 179 A4
Gostwick PE2 229 D5
Gote La PE13 169 E3
Gothic Cl 12 LN6 204 D7
GOULCEBY LN11 72 D6
Gouldeby La LN11 72 D6
Goulton St HU3 180 B3
Gover's Dro PE12 159 A2
Gower Rd HU4 179 B3
Gowt Bank PE22 114 C2
Gowts La PE12 159 E3
GOXHILL DN19 12 A8
Goxhill Ave 4 PE11 134 E2
Goxhill Cl 14 LN6 204 D7
Goxhill Gdns 4 DN34 190 F4
Goxhill Gr 13 LN6 204 D7
Goxhill Prim Sch DN19 12 A8
Goxhill Rd DN19 11 E8
Goxhill Sta DN19 11 F8
GRABY NG34 142 F4
Grace Ave LN6 204 D3
Grace Cl 4 NG34 212 E3
Grace Cres PE24 77 C3
Gracefield La NG23 78 A4
Grace St LN5 201 F1
Graeme Rd PE5 222 F2
Grafham Cl PE2 231 E4
Grafton Ave PE3 225 C3
Grafton St
  Grimsby DN32 189 C1
  Lincoln LN2 202 B3
Graham Ave HU4 179 C2
Graham Hill Way 4 PE10 213 E4
Graham Rd PE25 206 B4
GRAINSBY DN36 35 F2
Grainsby Ave
  Cleethorpes DN35 192 D3
  Holton le Clay DN36 195 E1
Grainsby Cl LN6 205 C5
Grainsby La DN36 35 E1
Grains Gate LN11 37 E1
GRAINTHORPE LN11 50 B8
Grainthorpe Sch LN11 50 B7
GRAISELOUND DN9 27 C1
Graizelound Fields Rd DN9 27 D1
Grammar Sch La DN20 196 C6
Grammar Sch Rd DN20 196 C4
Grammar Sch Rd S 3 DN20 196 C3
Grammar Sch Wlk DN16 185 C4
Grampian Cl 14 NG34 212 B3
Grampian Way
  Gonerby Hill Foot NG31 210 D8
  2 Grimsby DN33 194 E8
  Thorne/Moorends DN8 15 A7
Granaries The LN4 108 C8
Granary Cl
  22 Metheringham LN4 95 C4
  5 Waddington LN5 93 F6
Granary Croft 7 DN9 27 D2
Granary La LN4 207 A4
Granary Row LN4 207 A4
Granary The DN21 29 C4
Granary Way LN9 199 A3
Granby Dr 5 NG13 128 A5
Granby Rd LN8 47 B5
Granby St PE1 226 B2
Grand Parade PE25 206 D3
Grand Sluice La 1 PE21 208 F6
Granely Cl LN1 201 C6
GRANGE DN34 191 F5
Grange Ave
  13 Barton-upon-Humber DN18 10 E8
  Hatfield DN7 14 D4
  24 Laceby DN37 23 F1
  Misterton DN10 40 A4
  Peterborough PE1 226 A6
  1 Scunthorpe DN15 183 A5
Grange Cl
  17 Hatfield DN7 14 D4
  1 Ingham LN1 54 F2
  5 Misterton DN10 40 A5
Grange Cres
  Kingston upon Hull HU10 178 E6
  Lincoln LN6 205 B3
  Peterborough PE2 230 A5
Grange Ct 3 LN5 92 E1
Grange Dr
  Clinton Park LN4 207 C5
  Lincoln LN6 205 B3
  Misterton DN10 40 A4
  Spalding PE11 214 E4
  Stapleford LN6 105 A7
Grange Farm La DN36 195 D6
Grange Field DN20 20 D8
Grangehill Rd PE12 169 B6
Grange Ind Est DN16 185 E7
Grange Inf & Jun Sch DN34 190 F5
Grange La
  Balderton NG24 104 A1
  Canwick LN4 81 A4
  Covenham St Bartholomew LN11 49 D6
  Garthorpe LE14 150 C4
  Heighington LN4 81 E4
  Hough-on-the-Hill NG32 118 E6
  2 Ingham LN1 54 F2
  Keddington LN11 198 E8
  8 Manby LN11 62 C6
  Nocton LN4 94 F6
  North Cockerington LN11 50 A1
  North Kelsey LN7 32 A3
  Stixwould & Woodhall LN10 97 B6
  Utterby LN11 49 A4
  3 Willingham by Stow DN21 53 E3
Grange La Inf Sch DN16 185 D5
Grange La Jun Sch DN16 185 D5
Grange La N DN16 185 D7
Grange La S DN16 185 C5
Grange Mdws PE22 113 A1
Grange Paddock 8 NG32 210 A5
Grange Pk
  2 Brough HU15 2 C5
  17 Kirk Sandall DN3 14 A3
  Morton DN21 40 D3
  8 Swanland HU14 3 B6
Grange Rd
  Bracebridge Heath LN4 205 F2
  Gainsborough DN21 41 A1
  Garthorpe & Fockerby DN14 7 E8
  14 Mablethorpe/Sutton on Sea LN12 77 A7
  4 Metheringham LN4 95 D4
  Peterborough PE3 225 D4
  8 Ruskington NG34 108 D1
  Sutton Bridge PE34 161 B4
  10 Wisbech PE13 170 C1
Grange St LN4 109 C7
Grange The 1 NG31 211 A4
Grange Wlk
  Grimsby DN34 191 A6
  6 Misterton DN10 40 A5
Gransley Rise PE3 225 C5
Granson Way LN4 203 A2
Granta Cres NG31 211 C7
GRANTHAM NG31 211 C3
Grantham Ave DN33 191 D1
Grantham Canal Nature Reserve★ NG31 210 D1
Grantham Church VA High Sch The NG31 211 E7
Grantham Coll NG31 211 B4
Grantham Cricket Gd NG31 211 B1
Grantham District Hospl NG31 211 A6
Grantham Dr 2 PE25 206 B3
Grantham Fun Farm The★ NG31 210 F4
Grantham House★ NG31 211 B5
Grantham Mus★ NG31 211 B4
Grantham Prep Sch The NG31 139 F8
Grantham Rd
  Boothby Graffoe LN5 94 A2
  Boston PE21 208 A3
  Bottesford NG13 128 B5
  Bracebridge Heath LN4 205 F2
  Carlton Scroop NG32 119 C3
  7 Great Gonerby NG31 129 D5
  Great Gonerby NG31 210 D8
  Harmston LN5 93 F6
  Hough-on-the-Hill NG32 119 A4
  Ingoldsby NG33 141 C5
  Navenby/Wellingore LN5 107 A8
  Old Somerby NG33 140 D8
  Ropsley & Humby NG33 131 A1
  2 Skillington NG33 151 A8
  Sleaford NG34 212 B2
Grantham St LN2 234 B2
Grantham Sta NG31 211 A3
Granthams The 12 LN2 68 E6
Grantham Town FC NG31 210 D3
Grantley St NG31 211 A3
Grants La 29 PE21 208 F5
Grant St
  Cleethorpes DN35 192 E7
  Grimsby DN31 189 D1
GRANT THOROLD DN32 192 A7
Granville Ave
  12 Boston PE21 136 D8
  Northborough PE6 217 E1
Granville Rd DN15 183 A6
Granville St
  Boston PE21 208 D5
  Grantham NG31 211 C3
  Grimsby DN32 191 F6
  1 Kingston upon Hull HU3 180 A6
  Peterborough PE1 226 A4
Granville Terr PE12 160 D4
GRASBY DN38 32 F7
Grasby All Saints CE Prim Sch DN38 32 E7
Grasby Cl 4 DN21 53 A8
Grasby Cres DN37 190 D7
Grasby Rd
  Great Limber DN37 22 C3
  North Kelsey LN7 32 D5
  Scunthorpe DN17 184 E5
Grasby Wold La DN38 21 F1
Grasmere Ave PE24 90 E6
Grasmere Cl 3 DN21 197 E6
Grasmere Gdns PE4 221 B3
Grasmere Gr 5 DN36 192 E1
Grasmere Way LN6 200 D1
Grassdale Pk 2 HU15 2 B5
Grassgate La PE14 170 E3
Grassmoor Cl 2 LN6 93 B8
Grassmoor Ct 4 DN15 182 B2
Gravecoat La PE11 144 E6
Gravel Causeway PE6 166 D1
Graveley Cl 4 LN6 204 B6
Gravelhill Dro LN4 109 E7
Gravelholes La DN10 39 F5
Gravel Pit Hill DN20 31 D6
Gravelpit La LN9 199 F2
Gravel Pit La 1 DN39 22 A6
Gravel Pit Rd
  Barton-upon-Humber DN18 3 D1
Gravel Pit Rd *continued*
  Scotter DN21 29 C4
Gravel Pits La PE24 102 C8
Gravel Rd
  Market Deeping PE6 165 D3
  Revesby PE22 99 B4
Gravel Wlk PE1 226 A2
Gray Ct PE1 225 E8
Graye Dr LN11 198 D4
GRAYINGHAM DN21 42 D7
Grayingham Rd DN21 42 E7
Grayling Cl 2 DN37 190 D7
Graylings The PE21 208 B6
Gray Rd DN17 184 D6
Grays Ct DN37 190 E8
Gray's Ct 4 LN11 198 B6
Gray's Rd 2 LN11 198 B6
Gray St LN1 234 A4
GREAT CARLTON LN11 62 E4
GREAT CASTERTON PE9 171 B8
Great Casterton CE Prim Sch PE9 171 C8
Great Cl 1 NG33 151 D2
GREAT COATES DN37 24 B5
Great Coates Prim Sch DN37 190 E8
Great Coates Rd
  Grimsby DN37 190 C8
  Healing DN41 23 F5
Great Coates Sta DN37 24 B5
Great Field La 1 HU9 5 E8
GREATFORD PE9 164 B3
Greatford Gdns PE9 164 B3
Greatford Rd
  Baston PE6 164 D4
  5 Uffington PE9 172 C6
GREAT GONERBY NG31 129 E5
GREAT HALE NG34 122 F2
Great Hale Dro NG34 123 A2
GREAT LIMBER DN37 22 D3
Great Northern Ct 12 NG31 211 A4
Great Northern Terr LN5 234 C1
Great Northern Terr Ind Est LN5 234 C1
Great N Rd
  Balderton NG24 117 C8
  Empingham PE9 162 B2
  Great Gonerby NG32 129 C6
  Long Bennington NG23 117 D2
  Tinwell PE9 218 D5
  Wansford PE8 222 D1
GREAT PONTON NG33 140 A5
Great Ponton CE (Aided) Prim Sch NG33 140 A5
GREAT STEEPING PE23 101 E7
Great Steeping Prim Sch PE23 101 E7
GREAT STURTON LN9 71 F3
Great Thornton St HU3 180 D6
GREAT TOWS LN8 47 D1
Great Union St HU9 181 A7
GREBBY PE23 88 D3
Grebe Cl 2 LN6 204 C1
Greek St HU3 179 F5
Greenacre Cl 7 DN7 14 C2
Greenacres
  6 Donington on Bain LN11 59 E1
  Peterborough PE4 220 E4
  5 Swanland HU14 3 C7
Green Acres HU10 178 C6
Greenacres Dr
  Boston PE21 208 D3
  Bourne PE10 213 D3
Greenaway Ct LN3 203 E6
Green Bank DN8 15 D6
Greenbank Cl PE21 208 D3
Greenbank Dr LN6 205 A5
Green Dro
  Billinghay LN4 109 F6
  Crowland PE6 175 D8
  Helpringham NG34 133 F7
  Little Hale NG34 134 A7
  Thorney PE6 175 F6
Green Dyke PE12 148 D1
Greendyke La PE13 160 A2
Green Farm Cl PE5 223 E2
Greenfield Cl 13 DN3 14 A3
Greenfield Dr 9 DN20 31 A5
Greenfield La LN13 75 D4
Greenfield Rd
  Coningsby LN4 207 D5
  3 Sleaford NG34 212 D7
Greenfields
  3 Glentham LN8 43 F1
  Holbeach PE12 215 F2
  22 Nettleham LN2 68 D2
Greenfields La 5 NG34 142 D8
Greenfinch Dr DN35 192 E1
Greengarth DN17 184 F2
Greengate 11 DN9 27 E6
Green Gate PE22 114 D1
Greengate Ct PE1 226 C4
Greengate La 14 DN19 12 A8
Greengate Rd PE23 88 D3
Greenham PE3 225 A4
Greenhill 8 DN20 19 D3
Green Hill DN35 192 D3

GREEN HILL NG31......**210** E5
Greenhill Dr **1** LN8.....**43** D3
Greenhill Rd DN9.....**27** C2
Green Hill Rd NG31....**210** F5
Greenhoe Rd DN17......**184** D3
Green La
  Algarkirk PE20.......**136** B3
  Aunsby & Dembleby
   NG34............**132** A4
  10 Barton-upon-Humber
   DN18............**10** F8
  Beckingham LN5.......**105** C4
  Belton DN9.........**16** D2
  Belton & Manthorpe
   NG32...........**130** B7
  Boston PE21........**208** E7
  Bottesford NG13......**128** B5
  Bratoft PE24.......**102** C7
  Brigsley DN37.......**35** D4
  5 Broughton DN20....**19** E3
  Cherry Willingham LN3..**203** D5
  Collingham NG23......**91** D3
  Deeping St Nicholas
   PE11...........**166** C8
  Dunham-on-Trent NG22...**65** B1
  Dunston LN4........**95** D6
  Eagle & Swinethorpe LN6..**79** C2
  Eaton NG32.........**138** A2
  Gedney PE12........**159** A1
  Girton NG23........**78** C1
  Gosberton PE11......**145** C7
  Grantham NG31.......**211** D7
  Hatfield DN7.......**14** E1
  Hemingby LN9.......**72** C3
  Heydour NG32.......**131** D5
  Hogsthorpe LN13......**90** A8
  Kingston upon Hull
   HU13...........**179** A1
  Kirton PE20........**135** E6
  Lea DN21..........**52** F5
  Leake Commonside PE22.**113** F3
  Leverington PE13.....**169** F2
  Lincoln LN6........**201** D2
  Mablethorpe & Sutton
   LN12...........**63** F4
  Marston NG32.......**118** D1
  Middle Rasen LN8.....**57** C7
  Moulton PE12.......**146** E1
  13 North Kelsey LN7....**32** A4
  North Somercotes LN11..**50** F7
  Peterborough PE1.....**226** A4
  Pilham DN21........**41** D4
  Pinchbeck PE11......**145** C2
  3 Skegness PE25.....**103** E4
  Skellingthorpe LN6....**200** B5
  Spalding PE11.......**214** C3
  Stamford PE9.......**219** B7
  Stickney PE22.......**113** A7
  Stixwould & Woodhall
   LN10...........**97** B8
  Strubby with Woodthorpe
   LN13...........**63** B1
  Sutterton PE20......**136** A2
  Swinderby LN6.......**92** B5
  Thimbleby LN9.......**85** C5
  Threekingham NG34....**132** E3
  Wainfleet St Mary PE24..**102** A1
  18 Welton/Dunholme....**68** D6
  Westborough & Dry
   Doddington NG23....**117** F5
  Wigtoft PE20.......**135** E1
  Willoughby with Sloothby
   LN13...........**89** C5
  Witham St Hughs LN6...**92** D5
  Woodhall Spa LN10....**97** C5
  Wyberton PE21.......**136** F8
  Yaxley PE7.........**233** D6
Green La Mid Sch DN8..**15** B7
Greenlands Ave **10**
 DN36............**195** C6
Green Man La LN4.....**94** F1
Green Man Rd LN5.....**94** C1
Greenock Way LN6.....**204** B7
Green Pastures **4**
 PE12............**158** B7
Green Rd
  Aswarby & Swarby
   NG34...........**131** F7
  Newborough PE6......**174** F2
Greenrigg Gdns **1**
 PE11............**214** D5
Greens Cl DN15......**183** B3
Green's Rd **4** DN7....**14** C3
Green St **1** NG31....**129** D5
Greenstiles La HU14...**3** C7
Greenstock La PE13....**170** A6
Green The
  3 Allington NG32....**128** F7
  8 Brough HU15.....**2** C6
  Castor PE5.........**223** E2
  Cherry Willingham/Reepham
   LN3............**203** F8
  1 Coddington NG24...**104** D5
  Collingham NG23.....**91** C4
  Corby Glen NG33.....**152** E7
  Dunston LN4........**95** C5
  Gainsborough DN21....**197** F4
  2 Glinton PE6......**220** C8
  8 Leasingham NG34...**142** E6
  6 Mablethorpe/Sutton on Sea
   LN12...........**64** A4
  3 Minting LN9......**84** C8
  15 Navenby/Wellingore
   LN5............**107** A7
  Peterborough PE4.....**221** A3

Green The *continued*
  3 Reepham LN3......**82** A8
  Revesby PE22.......**99** B4
  6 Scothern LN2.....**68** F4
  Scotter DN21.......**29** C3
  Spalding PE11.......**214** C5
  4 Swanland HU14....**3** B7
  23 Thorne/Moorends
   DN8............**15** A8
  11 Thorney PE6.....**176** A3
  Thurlby PE10.......**164** C7
  Welbourn LN5.......**106** C4
  Yaxley PE7.........**233** E5
Greenway
  7 Barton-upon-Humber
   DN18...........**3** F1
  Waltham DN37.......**194** E3
  2 Welton/Dunholme LN2..**68** C7
Greenways **1** HU14...**3** A5
Greenway The **1** HU4..**179** C6
Greenwich House Ind Sch
 LN11............**198** C6
Greenwich House Sch
 LN11............**198** C6
Green Wlk PE6.......**217** A5
Greenwood Cl **1** PE12..**215** E2
Greenwood Dr PE21....**208** F6
Greenwood's Row **5**
 NG31............**211** A4
Greestone Mount LN2...**234** B3
Greestone Pl **2** LN2...**234** B3
Greestone Strs★ LN2...**234** B3
GREETHAM LN9.......**86** D5
Greetham's La DN32....**192** C5
GREETWELL DN20......**30** C7
Greetwell Cl LN2.....**202** B5
Greetwellgate LN2....**234** C3
Greetwell Hollow Nature
 Reserve★ LN2.......**202** D5
Greetwell La LN2.....**202** F8
Greetwell Pl LN2.....**202** B5
Greetwell Rd LN2.....**234** C3
Gregg Hall Cl **2** LN6..**205** B4
Gregg Hall Cres LN6...**205** B4
Gregg Hall Dr **4** LN6..**205** B4
Gregory **1** NG32.....**139** C7
Gresham St LN1......**201** D4
Gresley Ct **11** NG31...**210** E2
Gresley Dr
  Lincoln LN6........**201** D1
  4 Stamford PE9.....**219** B4
Gresley Rd LN11......**198** D1
Gresley Way
  Immingham DN40.....**186** F5
  Peterborough PE3.....**225** C6
Gretton Cl
  1 Claypole NG23....**117** E8
  Peterborough PE2.....**230** C7
Grevel Cl **6** PE11....**214** B5
Greyfleet Bank **7** LN11..**51** C4
Grey Friars
  9 Grantham NG31....**211** A4
  Grimsby DN37.......**190** D7
Greyfriars La **9** PE21..**208** F4
Greyfriars Rd **11** DN20..**19** E3
GREY GREEN DN9......**16** E2
Greyling Cl **5** LN1...**201** E8
Greyling View **12** LN1..**201** E8
Grey St
  Gainsborough DN21....**197** B6
  Kingston upon Hull HU2..**180** D7
Greystone Ave HU5....**179** E7
Greystones Rd DN21...**197** B7
Gride Bank PE22......**126** E8
Gride The PE22.......**113** E1
Griffins Cl **4** PE6...**174** E5
Griffiths Ct PE2.....**229** E5
Grime St DN31.......**191** E8
Grimmer's Rd PE13....**170** E1
GRIMOLDBY LN11......**62** B7
Grimoldby Prim Sch
 LN11............**62** C7
GRIMSBY DN31.......**191** B8
Grimsby Auditorium
 DN34............**190** F8
Grimsby Docks Sta
 DN31............**189** A1
Grimsby Institue of Further
 & Higher Ed DN34....**191** C4
Grimsby Inst of Higher Ed
 (Nunsthorne Com
 Campus) The DN33....**191** B4
Grimsby Leisure Ctr
 DN34............**190** F8
Grimsby Maternity Hospl
 DN33............**191** C3
Grimsby Pool DN33....**191** D4
Grimsby Rd
  2 Binbrook LN8.....**47** C5
  Brackenborough with Little
   Grimsby LN11.......**61** A8
  Cleethorpes DN35.....**192** D8
  Fotherby LN11.......**49** A1
  Grimsby DN32.......**189** D1
  Humberston DN36.....**192** E1
  Laceby DN37........**190** A2
  Louth LN11.........**198** A6
  Swallow LN7........**34** B6
  Waltham DN37.......**194** F5
Grimsby Town Sta
 DN32............**191** D7
Grimshaw Rd PE1.....**226** B6
GRIMSTHORPE PE10....**153** E5
Grimsthorpe Castle★
 PE10............**153** D5
Grimsthorpe Cl
  Grantham NG31......**210** E6
  12 Market Deeping PE6..**217** A5

Grimston Rd **5** HU10...**178** F6
Grindell St HU9.....**181** D8
GRINGLEY ON THE HILL
 DN10............**39** C1
Gringley Rd DN10.....**39** E4
Grinter Cl **3** LN6....**93** C8
Grocock Cl PE12.....**146** E2
Groose La PE24......**115** D8
Grosvenor Ave
  Birchwood LN6......**200** D2
  Bourne PE10........**213** E4
Grosvenor Cres
  Grimsby DN32.......**191** D6
  Louth LN11.........**198** D7
Grosvenor Ct **3** DN7...**14** D8
Grosvenor Mews **2**
 LN4.............**203** D1
Grosvenor Rd
  9 Billingborough
   NG34...........**133** B1
  Kirton PE20........**136** C6
  Louth LN11.........**198** C6
  Skegness PE25......**206** C4
  Wisbech PE13.......**170** D1
Grosvenor St N DN15...**183** A5
Grosvenor St (South) **2**
 DN15............**183** A4
Grosvenor Sq **17** LN5..**107** A7
Grosvenor St
  Grimsby DN32.......**191** D6
  Kingston upon Hull HU3..**180** D8
  4 Scunthorpe DN15...**183** A4
Grove Cl LN11.......**145** C1
Grove Cres DN32.....**192** C6
Grove Ct
  3 Gainsborough
   DN21...........**197** C6
  Woodston PE2.......**230** F8
Grove Dr **9** LN10....**97** D5
Grove End Rd **3** NG31..**211** B4
Grovefield La PE22....**126** D1
Grove Hill HU13......**178** E1
Grove La
  Peterborough PE3.....**225** A2
  Waltham DN37.......**194** E4
Grove Leisure Ctr
 NG24............**104** B3
Grovenor Ct **5** DN35..**193** A1
Grove Pk DN10.......**39** F5
Grove Rd
  1 Fishlake DN7.....**14** D8
  Mablethorpe/Sutton on Sea
   LN12...........**64** C1
  Theddlethorpe All Saints
   LN12...........**63** D6
Grove St E **5** PE21...**209** A5
Grove St W **4** PE21...**209** A5
Grove Sch The NG24...**104** B3
Grove St
  14 Boston PE21.....**209** A5
  Heckington NG34.....**122** E2
  5 Kirton in Lindsey DN21..**30** B1
  Newark-on-Trent NG24...**104** B3
  Peterborough PE2.....**230** F8
Groves The HU4......**179** B2
Grove The
  13 Barrow upon Humber
   DN19...........**11** C8
  4 Beckingham DN10...**40** A1
  Edlington with Wispington
   LN9............**85** B6
  6 Gainsborough DN21...**53** A5
  Grantham NG31......**210** E3
  Lincoln LN2........**234** C4
  Market Deeping PE6...**217** B5
  Morton DN10........**154** B6
  Newton on Trent LN1...**65** D1
  4 Spalding PE11.....**214** C6
  4 Welton/Dunholme
   LN2............**68** D6
Grove Wood Rd DN10...**39** F5
Grove Wood Terr **16**
 DN10............**39** F5
Grundale HU10......**178** C6
Grundy La LN3.......**57** D2
Grundy's La LN9.....**84** C8
Grunnill Cl **10** PE25..**206** A5
Guanockgate Rd PE12...**169** A2
Guash Way PE9.......**219** D7
Gubbole's Dro PE11....**145** A3
Guelder Rd PE7......**230** D3
Guernsey Gr DN40....**186** C2
Guildford Cl **11** NG31..**210** E5
Guildford La LN5.....**105** F5
Guildford St DN32....**192** A8
Guildhall Dr **2** PE1..**156** E8
Guildhall Mus★ PE21..**208** F4
Guildhall Rd HU1....**180** F6
Guildhall St
  Grantham NG31......**211** A4
  Lincoln LN1........**234** A2
Guild Rd PE13.......**170** E1
Guilicarr La LN7.....**31** F4
Guilsborough Rd PE6...**175** B2
Guisefield Rd **9** DN9...**27** D6
Gulham Rd LN8......**44** D5
Gull Bank
  Whaplode PE12......**167** F5
  Wisbech St Mary PE13..**177** E3
Gull Dro PE13.......**177** D3
Gull La PE13........**170** A2
Gull Rd PE13........**177** F2
Gullymore PE3.......**224** F8
GUNBY
  Candlesby with Gunby
   PE23...........**89** B1
  Gunby and Stainby NG33..**151** C4
Gunby Ave LN6......**204** F6

Gunby Hall★ PE23.....**89** A1
Gunby La PE23.......**89** A1
Gunby Pl DN35.......**192** E4
Gunby Rd
  Gunby & Stainby NG33..**151** A4
  Scunthorpe DN17.....**184** E5
Gunfleet Cl **18** PE20..**135** B7
GUNNERBY DN37......**34** F2
Gunners Way DN34....**190** D4
GUNNESS DN15.......**17** E6
Gunness & Burringham CE
 Prim Sch DN17......**17** E5
Gunness La
  Amcotts DN17.......**17** F8
  Flixborough DN15....**182** A7
GUNTHORPE
  Owston Ferry DN9....**40** D7
  Peterborough PE4.....**221** B1
Gunthorpe Prim Sch
 PE4.............**221** C2
Gunthorpe Rd
  Newborough PE6......**221** D4
  Owston Ferry DN9....**40** C8
  Peterborough PE4.....**221** C2
  Sutton Bridge PE14...**160** E1
  1 Walpole PE14.....**170** F8
Gunthorpe Ridings **2**
 PE4.............**221** E2
Gunton's Rd PE6.....**174** E3
Gurnard Leys PE3....**220** E1
Gurnell St DN15.....**183** A4
Gurth Ave **6** DN3...**14** A1
Guthlac Ave **5** PE4..**221** B1
GUTHRAM GOWT PE11..**155** E5
GUYHIRN PE13.......**177** F2
Guys Head Rd PE12....**160** E7
Guy's Head Rd
  Lutton PE12........**149** C1
  Sutton Bridge PE12...**160** F8
Gwash Cl PE12.......**163** C1
Gynewell Gr **4** LN2...**202** D7
Gypsy La
  Newton PE13........**170** C4
  Whaplode PE12......**167** F3

H

Haalam Bank LN12.....**63** C4
Haarlem Ct **5** PE11...**214** A2
Habbanya Rise LN4....**95** C7
Habblesthorpe Cl DN22..**52** C1
Habblesthorpe Rd DN22..**52** C1
HABERTOFT PE24......**89** E4
HABROUGH DN40......**22** E8
Habrough La DN39....**22** B6
Habrough Rd
  Immingham DN40.....**186** A3
  South Killingholme DN40..**12** C2
Habrough Sta DN40....**22** E8
Hacconby Dro
  Dunsby PE10........**144** A1
  Haconby PE10.......**155** A8
Hacconby La PE10.....**154** C7
HACEBY NG34........**131** E3
Hacke Rd **3** PE3.....**225** D3
Hackness Gr **2** HU5...**179** D8
Hack's Dro PE6......**164** F6
HACKTHORN LN2......**55** E1
Hackthorn CE (Controlled)
 Prim Sch LN2.......**55** F1
Hackthorn Pl **4** LN2..**201** F8
Hackthorn Rd LN2....**68** D8
HACONBY PE10.......**154** B8
HADDINGTON LN5.....**92** F6
Haddington La LN6....**92** F6
HADDON DN7........**232** B6
Haddon Cl
  Birchwood LN6......**200** E1
  Peterborough PE2.....**231** C5
Haddon Rd
  Peterborough PE3.....**225** C3
  Peterborough PE7.....**232** C6
  Stamford PE9.......**218** F6
Haddon St HU3.......**179** F4
Haddon Way PE7......**231** B2
Hadfield Rd **7** LN6...**205** A5
Hadleigh Cl NG31.....**210** F5
Hadleigh Ct DN15....**183** A4
Hadleigh Dr LN6.....**204** F5
Hadleigh Rd **3** DN17...**17** D4
Hadleigh Rd DN40....**186** D3
Hadley Rd
  Peterborough PE4.....**221** B1
  Sleaford NG34.......**212** E6
Hadrian Dr **10** PE6...**164** E5
Hadrians Ct PE2.....**231** B8
Hadrians Rd **9** LN4...**81** A1
Haff Cl **2** PE20.....**135** C7
Haffenden Rd LN2....**202** A6
Hagbeach Dro PE12....**168** A5
Hagbeach Gate PE12...**158** C6
Hagg Cross Roads PE23..**87** A4
Hagg La **1** DN17.....**16** E3
HAGNABY
  East Kirkby PE23.....**100** A5
  Hannah cum Hagnaby
   LN13...........**76** C6
Hagnaby Abbey LN13...**76** C6
HAGNABY LOCK PE22...**99** F2
Hagnaby Rd PE23.....**100** A6
HAGWORTHINGHAM
 PE23............**87** A4
Haig Ave DN16......**183** B1
Haigh Ct DN32.......**191** F5
Haigh St **4** DN35....**193** A5
Haile Rd DN36.......**193** A1
HAINTON LN8........**58** F3

Hainton Ave DN32.....**191** F8
Hainton Cl DN21.....**197** E3
Hainton Rd
  Hainton LN8........**58** F3
  Lincoln LN6........**205** C5
Haith's La **4** DN36...**36** B1
Haldane St DN35.....**197** B5
Hale Cl **4** LN2......**202** E7
Hale Hill La DN7.....**14** E2
Hale House Rd PE10...**153** C2
Hale La PE22........**112** F1
Hale Rd
  Heckington NG34.....**122** E2
  Helpringham NG34....**133** E7
  Horsington LN10.....**84** B2
Hales Cl DN16.......**185** A2
Hales Entry HU9.....**181** C6
HALESGATE PE12......**146** E1
Hales La LN5........**107** B8
Haley Cl **6** PE13....**170** D2
Half Acre Wood **3**
 DN17............**17** D4
Halfleet PE6........**217** A6
Halford Cl **8** NG33...**151** D2
Halfpenny Cl **19** LN2..**68** D7
Halfway House La LN6..**92** C6
Halfway Houses LN6...**92** D5
Halifax App DN20.....**21** A8
Halifax Cl
  4 Skegness PE25....**206** B5
  3 Skellingthorpe LN6..**200** A4
Halkon Cl DN17......**7** D3
Hallam Cl
  3 Alford LN13......**75** E2
  Barrow upon Humber
   DN19...........**11** D8
Hallam Gr LN6......**205** C7
Hallam's Dro PE20....**123** F2
Hallam's La **3** LN4...**96** B1
Hallaton Rd PE1.....**226** D8
Hall Bank **3** PE13...**169** F7
Hallbrook Ct **5** DN16..**185** A1
Hall Cl
  Heckington NG34.....**122** E3
  Ropsley NG33.......**131** B3
Hallcroft **6** DN39....**12** A1
Hallcroft Rd **1** DN9...**27** D2
Hall Ct DN17........**7** A3
Hall Dr
  Canwick LN4........**81** A4
  Grantham NG31......**211** C5
  Lincoln LN6........**205** C7
  Swineshead PE20....**135** B7
HALL END PE22.......**114** D1
Hall End Rd PE22....**114** C1
Haller St HU9.......**181** E8
Hall Farm
  5 Market Deeping
   PE6............**217** B6
  6 Newark-on-Trent
   NG24...........**104** D5
Hall Farm Pk★ LN7....**44** D8
Hallfield Cres NG32...**119** C2
Hallfields La PE4.....**221** C1
Hallgarth DN36......**37** B2
Hallgarth Ave DN16...**183** B2
Hallgate PE12.......**159** E8
Hall Gate
  Fleet PE12.........**159** B6
  Holbeach PE12......**215** C1
  Moulton PE12.......**157** F5
  Wainfleet St Mary PE24..**102** C1
  Weston PE12........**146** B1
Hall Gate Rd PE12....**168** E2
Hall Gdns **8** DN15....**9** B5
Hall Hill Rd PE12....**215** D4
HALLINGTON LN11.....**60** F4
Halliwell Cl **5** HU9...**5** F8
Hall La
  Algarkirk PE20......**136** B3
  Benington PE22.....**126** F5
  Branston & Mere LN4...**81** D1
  Burgh le Marsh PE24..**102** B3
  Elsham DN20........**20** F7
  Fiskerton LN3.......**82** C7
  Frampton PE20......**136** E6
  Gunby & Stainby NG33..**151** B5
  Hough-on-the-Hill NG32..**118** E7
  Lenton Keisby & Osgodby
   NG33...........**141** E3
  Moulton PE12.......**146** D2
  Nettleham LN2......**68** B2
  Peterborough PE4.....**221** A4
  Stainforth DN7......**14** A6
  Stenigot LN11.......**72** D7
  Stickney PE22.......**112** F7
  Welbourn LN5.......**106** C4
  West Keal PE23......**100** C6
  Wrangle PE22.......**114** C1
Hall Leas Dr **1** LN12..**64** C1
Hall Mdw **1** DN20....**10** C2
Hall Meadow Rd PE6...**217** F7
Hall Orch La **2** LN5..**106** E5
Hall Pk
  Heckington NG34.....**122** F1
  Swanland HU14......**3** C7
Hall Pk Rd DN40.....**186** D5
Hall Pl **7** PE11.....**214** D4
Hall Rd
  Haconby PE10.......**154** D8
  Heckington NG34.....**122** F1
  Hough-on-the-Hill NG32..**118** E7
  Londonthorpe & Harrowby
   NG31...........**211** F4
Hall Rise **7** DN17....**29** D7
Halls Ct LN4........**95** C6
Halls Hill LN11......**72** D6

Halls La
6 Keelby DN41 . . . . 23 A4
9 North Kelsey LN7 . . . . 32 A4
Hall's Rd DN10 . . . . 39 D2
Hall St
Crowland PE6 . . . . 166 F1
Kingston upon Hull HU2 . . 180 D7
16 Navenby/Wellingore LN5 . . . . 107 A7
Hall Wath LN5 . . . . 92 E2
Hall Way DN38 . . . . 21 F5
Hall Wlk 1 HU15 . . . . 2 D6
Hall Yd
2 Collyweston PE9 . . . . . 171 B1
26 Metheringham LN4 . . . . . 95 C4
Halmer Gate PE11 . . . . . . 214 E4
Halmer Gdns PE11 . . . . . . 214 F4
Halmer Paddock 6 PE11 . . . . 214 F5
Haltemprice Leisure Ctr HU10 . . . . 178 E7
Haltemprice St HU3 . . . . . 179 F5
HALTHAM LN9 . . . . 98 C6
Haltham Gn DN21 . . . . 197 F4
HALTOFT END PE22 . . . . . . 126 C4
Haltoft End Est PE22 . . . . 126 C3
Halton Cl
5 Birchwood LN6 . . . . 204 B8
4 Kirton in Lindsey DN21 . 42 F8
HALTON FENSIDE PE23 . . . . 101 C6
HALTON HOLEGATE PE23 . . . . 101 B8
Halton Holegate CE Prim Sch PE23 . . . . 101 B7
Halton Pl DN35 . . . . 192 D4
Halton Rd PE23 . . . . 101 A8
Halton Way 3 DN33 . . . . . 191 C2
Halyard Croft 8 HU1 . . . . 180 F5
Halycon Ave 1 HU13 . . . . . 178 E2
Hambleton La LN8 . . . . 57 E8
Hambleton Rd PE9 . . . . . . 218 E4
HAMERINGHAM LN9 . . . . 86 C2
Hamerton La 1 LN9 . . . . 199 C3
Hamilton Cl
6 Bourne PE10 . . . . 213 C7
6 Grimsby DN34 . . . . 190 D4
Hamilton Gr LN6 . . . . 200 B3
Hamilton Rd
Alford LN13 . . . . 75 F2
Grantham NG31 . . . . 211 D6
4 Lincoln LN6 . . . . 204 D2
Scunthorpe DN17 . . . . 184 F8
Hamilton St DN32 . . . . 189 D1
Hamilton Way PE21 . . . . . . 208 F3
Hamish Wlk 8 DN40 . . . . . 186 B3
Ham La PE2 . . . . 229 E7
Hamling Sch PE6 . . . . 167 E4
Hamling Way HU4 . . . . . . 179 D2
Hamlyn Ave HU4 . . . . 179 E7
Hamlyn Dr HU4 . . . . 179 E6
Ham Mere Bird Sanctuary★ PE2 . . . . 229 E7
Hammerton Rd DN17 . . . . . 184 E4
Hammond Cl PE8 . . . . 172 C1
Hammond Ct LN12 . . . . 64 B3
Hamont Rd DN32 . . . . 192 B7
Hampden Cl 1 LN6 . . . . . 200 A4
Hampden Cres 3 DN7 . . . 26 A8
Hampdens Cl 10 NG24 . . . 104 C5
Hampden Way
Sleaford NG34 . . . . 121 A2
8 Waddington LN5 . . . . 94 A7
Hampshire St HU4 . . . . . . 179 E3
Hampson Gdns 18 DN3 . . . 14 A2
Hampstead Pk DN33 . . . . 191 B2
Hampton Cl
Humberston DN35 . . . . 192 F1
1 Spalding PE11 . . . . 214 E2
Hampton Coll PE7 . . . . 230 D1
Hampton Ct PE3 . . . . 225 C6
HAMPTON HARGATE PE7 . . . . 230 D2
Hampton Hargate Prim Sch PE7 . . . . 230 C2
Hampton La PE22 . . . . 127 B7
Hampton Rd
2 Hatfield DN7 . . . . 14 C4
Scunthorpe DN16 . . . . 185 C8
Hampton St LN1 . . . . 201 D4
HAMPTON VALE PE7 . . . . . 230 D1
Hampton Vale Prim Sch PE7 . . . . 230 C1
Hanbury PE2 . . . . 229 F3
HANBY NG33 . . . . 141 E7
Hanby La
11 Alford LN13 . . . . 75 F2
Welton le Marsh PE23 . . . . . 89 B4
Handel Ct DN21 . . . . 197 D5
Handel House Prep Sch DN21 . . . . 197 D5
Handley Ct Mews 7 NG34 . . . . 212 D3
Handley St
Heckington NG34 . . . . 122 E3
8 Sleaford NG34 . . . . 212 D4
Hands on History Mus★ HU1 . . . . 180 F6
Hangman's Cnr PE6 . . . . . . 175 F5
Hangman's La
Edenham PE10 . . . . 153 F7
Haconby PE10 . . . . 154 A7
Hankey St PE1 . . . . 225 F4
Hankinson's Est PE34 . . . . 161 D1
HANNAH LN13 . . . . 76 E6
Hannah Cres LN6 . . . . 92 E5
Hannam Bvd PE11 . . . . . . 214 A3
Hannath Rd PE13 . . . . 170 B8
Hanover Ct HU1 . . . . 180 E6
Hanover Dr 26 HU15 . . . . 2 C5
Hanover Gdns DN16 . . . . . . 185 C6
Hanover Hill DN21 . . . . 54 F6
Hanover Sq 5 HU1 . . . . . . 180 F6
Hansard Cres 3 LN7 . . . . . 33 B4
Hansards Dr 2 LN8 . . . . . . 70 D5
Hansard Way 8 PE20 . . . . 136 C5
Hanson Dr 2 LN12 . . . . 76 F8
Hanson Way DN32 . . . . . . 192 B8
HANTHORPE PE10 . . . . 154 B7
Hanthorpe Rd PE10 . . . . . 154 B7
Ha'penny Bridge Way HU9 . . . . 181 B5
Harbour Way HU9 . . . . 181 C6
HARBY NG23 . . . . 79 C5
Harby Cl
Grantham NG31 . . . . 210 E1
Lincoln LN6 . . . . 205 B3
Harcourt Dr HU9 . . . . 181 C8
Harden's La LN9 . . . . 73 F1
Harding Cl
9 Mablethorpe & Sutton LN12 . . . . 64 C1
6 Mablethorpe/Sutton on Sea LN12 . . . . 76 F8
Harding House Gall★ LN2 . . . . 234 B3
Hardings La PE23 . . . . 88 B2
Hardings The 20 LN2 . . . . . 68 D7
Hardiway PE21 . . . . 209 B5
HARDWICK LN1 . . . . 66 A2
Hardwick Cl
Louth LN11 . . . . 198 A7
3 Saxilby with Ingleby LN1 . . . . 66 C2
Hardwick Ct PE3 . . . . 225 B2
Hardwicke Cl 7 NG31 . . . . 211 A3
Hardwick Pl 1 LN2 . . . . . . 202 A8
Hardwick Plot La PE20 . . 124 C1
Hardwick Rd
5 Kirton PE20 . . . . 136 C5
1 Stamford PE9 . . . . 218 F6
Hardwick St HU5 . . . . 180 B8
Hardy Rd DN17 . . . . 184 D6
Hardy's Animal Farm★ PE25 . . . . 90 E5
Hardys Ct DN32 . . . . 192 A6
Hardy's Dro PE10 . . . . 213 F7
Hardy's La PE6 . . . . 167 D4
Hardy's Rd DN35 . . . . 192 F4
Harebell Cl PE1 . . . . 221 F1
HAREBY PE23 . . . . 99 F8
Hareby Hill PE23 . . . . 100 A8
Hare Cl 9 NG34 . . . . 122 E2
Harecroft Rd PE13 . . . . . . 170 C1
Hare St DN32 . . . . 191 F6
Harewood Ave 7 DN3 . . . . . 14 A2
Harewood Cl PE21 . . . . 209 B5
Harewood Cres
Lincoln LN6 . . . . 205 A3
Louth LN11 . . . . 198 B7
Harewood Gdns PE3 . . . . 225 B2
Harewood Gr 1 DN35 . . . . 192 F1
Harford Gate PE12 . . . . . . 159 D5
Hargate Cl 1 PE12 . . . . . . 159 C7
Hargate La PE34 . . . . 161 E2
Hargate Way PE7 . . . . 230 D3
Hargon La NG24 . . . . 104 B7
Hargrave St DN31 . . . . 188 D1
Hargreaves Way DN15 . . . 183 B6
Harland Rd 9 HU15 . . . . 2 C6
HARLAXTON NG32 . . . . 139 C7
Harlaxton CE Prim Sch NG32 . . . . 139 C7
Harlaxton Cl 2 LN6 . . . . . 204 C6
Harlaxton College NG32 . . . . 139 D7
Harlaxton Dr 4 LN6 . . . . . 204 C6
Harlaxton Manor & Gdns★ NG32 . . . . 139 D7
Harlaxton Rd 3 NG31 . . . . 210 F3
Harlech Grange PE3 . . . . 225 B1
Harlech Way DN32 . . . . . . 191 F8
Harlech Wlk DN40 . . . . . . 186 D3
Harlequin Dr
10 Mablethorpe/Sutton on Sea LN12 . . . . 64 B3
6 Spalding PE11 . . . . 214 A5
Harlestone Ct DN34 . . . . . 190 C4
Harley St HU2 . . . . 180 E8
Harlow St DN31 . . . . 188 D1
Harlton Cl PE2 . . . . 231 E5
HARMSTON LN5 . . . . 93 F5
Harmston Cl LN2 . . . . 202 A8
Harmston Pk Ave LN5 . . . . 93 F4
Harmston Rd LN5 . . . . 93 A5
Harneis Cres DN37 . . . . 23 F2
Harness Dr LN4 . . . . 207 A5
Harn Rd PE7 . . . . 230 E2
Harold's Bank PE13 . . . . . 169 B2
Harold St DN32 . . . . 192 A8
Harome Gr HU5 . . . . 179 C7
Harpe Cl 10 PE11 . . . . 156 E8
Harpenden Cl 15 DN7 . . . . 14 D3
Harpendon Dr 16 DN7 . . . . 14 D3
Harper Garth LN9 . . . . 85 B5
Harpham Rd
Gate Burton DN21 . . . . 53 A1
Marshchapel DN36 . . . . 37 B2
Marton DN21 . . . . 65 D8
HARPSWELL DN21 . . . . 54 E8
Harpswell Cl 7 DN21 . . . . . 53 A8
Harpswell La DN21 . . . . 42 C1
Harpswell Rd LN2 . . . . 202 A7
Harrier Ct 3 LN6 . . . . 204 E8
Harrier Rd 3 DN18 . . . . 3 F1
Harriet Cl 5 PE12 . . . . 160 E4
HARRINGTON PE23 . . . . 87 C7
Harrington Ave 4 LN6 . . 205 C8
Harrington Croft 8 PE12 . . . . 215 E2
Harrington Dr 7 PE6 . . . 175 C8
Harrington Pl DN16 . . . . . 185 A5
Harrington Rd 7 NG33 . . . . 151 D2
Harrington St
Bourne PE10 . . . . 213 D6
Cleethorpes DN35 . . . . 189 D1
Harrington Way 6 PE6 . . . . 175 C8
Harris Bvd 12 LN12 . . . . . . 64 B3
Harris Cl 11 PE25 . . . . 206 A5
Harrison Cl
Horncastle LN9 . . . . 199 C5
10 Peterborough PE3 . . . . 224 F3
Winteringham DN15 . . . . 9 A8
Harrison Pl
Lincoln LN1 . . . . 234 A4
North Hykeham LN6 . . . . . 204 D5
Harrison's Dro PE20 . . . . . 124 B2
Harrison's La PE24 . . . . . . 101 F4
Harrison St DN31 . . . . 191 C7
Harris Rd LN6 . . . . 205 B6
Harris St
Kingston upon Hull HU3 . . . . 179 F5
Peterborough PE1 . . . . 225 F6
Harris Way NG31 . . . . 211 A2
Harrolds Cl 3 PE13 . . . . . 170 F1
HARROWBY NG31 . . . . 211 F4
Harrowby CE (Aided) Inf Sch NG31 . . . . 211 C6
Harrowby Cl
Digby LN4 . . . . 108 E5
Grantham NG31 . . . . 211 C6
Harrowby Cres NG31 . . . . 211 E1
Harrowby Est NG31 . . . . . 211 D6
Harrowby La
Grantham NG31 . . . . 211 D6
Londonthorpe & Harrowby without NG31 . . . . 130 C3
Harrowby Rd NG31 . . . . . . 211 C3
Harrow Cl
Gainsborough DN21 . . . . . 197 F6
Heighington/Washingborough LN4 . . . . 203 C1
Harrowdyke 6 DN18 . . . . . 10 E8
Harrow Gdns DN17 . . . . . . 184 F4
Harrow Rd
Deeping St Nicholas PE11 . . . . 166 C7
6 Mablethorpe/Sutton on Sea LN12 . . . . 64 B4
Harrow St
Grantham NG31 . . . . 211 B3
Kingston upon Hull HU3 . . 180 B4
Harrows The 15 LN2 . . . . . 68 D6
Harrox Rd 3 PE12 . . . . . . 157 F7
Harrox Sq 5 PE12 . . . . . . 157 F6
Harrys Dream 3 DN20 . . . 19 E3
HARSTON NG32 . . . . 138 E6
Harston Rd NG32 . . . . 138 F7
Hartford Ct PE2 . . . . 231 D6
Harthill Dr HU3 . . . . 180 C5
Hart La DN15 . . . . 9 B5
Hartland Ave 6 LN6 . . . . . 205 A1
Hartley Bridge HU9 . . . . . 181 C6
Hartley St
Boston PE21 . . . . 208 F6
3 Lincoln LN2 . . . . 202 C3
Hartshead Ave DN15 . . . . 182 C3
HARTSHOLME LN6 . . . . 204 E6
Hartsholme Dr LN6 . . . . . . 205 A8
Hartsholme Pk LN6 . . . . . 204 F7
Hartsholme Prim Sch LN6 . . . . 204 F7
Hart St DN35 . . . . 192 C8
Hartwell Ct PE3 . . . . 225 D5
Hartwell Way PE3 . . . . 225 B5
Harvard Cl 1 LN4 . . . . 203 D1
Harvest Ave 34 DN18 . . . . . 10 E8
Harvest Cl
21 Kirk Sandall DN3 . . . . . . 14 A2
23 Metheringham LN4 . . . . . 95 C4
Harvest Cres 2 DN37 . . . 194 C4
Harvest Dr NG24 . . . . 104 B6
Harvester Cl 19 DN9 . . . . . 27 E6
Harvester Way
Crowland PE6 . . . . 175 B8
Peterborough PE1 . . . . 226 C1
1 Sibsey PE22 . . . . 113 B1
Harvest Mews 5 PE11 . . . 166 C6
Harvest Rise 2 DN19 . . . . . 11 C8
Harvest Way 3 NG34 . . . . 212 C2
Harvey Ave 7 NG24 . . . . . 104 C5
Harvey Cl
Bourne PE10 . . . . 213 B4
11 Wittering PE8 . . . . 172 B1
Harvey Kent Gdns 4 LN3 . . . . 83 C4
Harveys Cl PE11 . . . . 214 F6
Harvey St 5 LN1 . . . . 201 D3
Harwich Cl 12 LN5 . . . . . . 205 D3
Harwood Ave PE12 . . . . . . 215 C1
Harwood Dr 1 HU4 . . . . . 179 B6
Hase Wlk HU13 . . . . 178 E1
Hassall Rd PE25 . . . . 206 A2
Hassock Hill Dro PE13 . . . 169 D3
HASTHORPE LN13 . . . . 89 C4
Hasthorpe Rd LN13 . . . . . . 89 C5
Hastings Dr 4 PE24 . . . . . 102 D2
Hastings Gr HU5 . . . . 179 E7
Hastings Rd PE4 . . . . 221 A2
HATCLIFFE DN37 . . . . 34 F3
Hatcliffe Cl 2 NG31 . . . . . 211 A8
Hatcliffe Gdns 11 LN2 . . . 202 A8
Hatcllffe Cl 6 DN33 . . . . . 191 B3
HATFIELD DN7 . . . . 14 D5
Hatfield Crookesbroom Prim Sch DN7 . . . . 14 C4
Hatfield High Sch DN7 . . . 14 D3
Hatfield La DN3 . . . . 14 A4
Hatfield Manor CE Jun Sch DN7 . . . . 14 E5
Hatfield Rd
Hatfield DN7 . . . . 14 F6
Thorne/Moorends DN8 . . . . 15 A7
Hatfield & Stainforth Sta DN7 . . . . 14 C5
HATFIELD WOODHOUSE DN7 . . . . 15 A3
Hatfield Wr Pk★ DN7 . . . . 14 E5
Hathersage Ave LN6 . . . . 204 E2
Hathersage Ct 3 DN15 . . . . 182 B2
Hatt Cl 2 PE12 . . . . 157 F7
HATTON LN8 . . . . 71 B3
Hatton Cl 3 LN6 . . . . 205 A7
Hatton Gr 7 DN33 . . . . . . 191 B3
Hatton Mdws Nature Reserve★ LN8 . . . . 71 A2
HAUGH LN13 . . . . 75 B2
HAUGHAM LN11 . . . . 73 F8
Haugham Pastures LN11 . . . . 61 E2
Haugh La LN13 . . . . 75 A3
Hauser Cl 8 NG34 . . . . 212 B2
Havelock Dr PE2 . . . . 231 E6
Havelock Mews DN32 . . . . 192 C6
Havelock Sch DN32 . . . . . 192 C6
Havelock St
Kingston upon Hull HU3 . . . . 180 A4
Spalding PE11 . . . . 214 C3
Havelok Cl 4 LN11 . . . . . . 198 D4
Haven Ave
Brough HU15 . . . . 2 B6
Grimsby DN31 . . . . 191 C8
Haven Bank
Boston PE21 . . . . 208 E5
6 Skidbrooke with Saltfleet Haven LN11 . . . . 51 C4
Wildmore LN4 . . . . 111 B2
HAVEN BANK LN4 . . . . 111 B3
Haven Cl
7 Blyton DN21 . . . . 41 C5
9 Fleet PE12 . . . . 159 C7
Haven Ctry Pk★ PE21 . . . 137 C7
Haven Garth 1 HU15 . . . . 2 B5
Haven Gdns DN31 . . . . 188 C1
Haven High Tech Coll The PE21 . . . . 208 F7
Haven House Rd PE24 . . . . 102 F3
Havenhouse Sta PE24 . . . . 102 F2
Haven Mdws PE21 . . . . . . 208 C7
Haven Rd
4 Barton-upon-Humber DN18 . . . . 3 E1
North Killingholme DN40 . . . 13 A6
Haven Side 8 PE24 . . . . . . 102 D1
Havenside Nature Reserve★ PE21 . . . . 137 A8
Haven The★ PE21 . . . . 208 F4
Haven The HU9 . . . . 181 B6
Haven Village 3 PE21 . . . . 208 F3
Haverfield Rd PE11 . . . . . 214 D3
Haverholme Cl 10 NG34 . . . . 108 E1
Haverholme Dro PE12 . . . 159 D5
Haverlands The 3 NG31 . . . . 210 E8
Haverstoe Pl DN35 . . . . . . 192 C3
Haveswater Cl 1 PE4 . . . . 221 C2
Hawerby Rd 3 DN37 . . . . . 23 F1
Hawker Dr LN11 . . . . 198 D4
Hawkins Dr 20 PE13 . . . . . 170 E1
Hawkins Gr DN32 . . . . 192 B6
Hawkins Way 7 DN40 . . . . 12 E3
Hawksdale Cl 3 NG31 . . . 211 A7
Hawkshead Gr LN2 . . . . . . 202 A8
Hawkshead Way 2 PE4 . . . . 221 C3
Hawksmede Way LN11 . . . 198 D8
Hawksmoor Cl 2 LN6 . . . . 204 D1
Hawks Way NG34 . . . . 212 B3
Hawksworth St 2 DN21 . . . . 197 D4
Haworth Cl DN15 . . . . 182 D4
Haworth Way PE21 . . . . . . 208 D7
Haw's La PE11 . . . . 134 F1
Hawthorn Ave
Brigg DN20 . . . . 196 C4
Cherry Willingham LN3 . . . 203 B6
Gainsborough DN21 . . . . . 197 D6
Immingham DN40 . . . . 186 E5
Kingston upon Hull HU3 . . 179 F5
Waddington LN5 . . . . 205 C1
Hawthorn Bank PE11 . . . . 214 B1
Hawthorn Chase
Lincoln LN2 . . . . 202 E7
1 Moulton PE12 . . . . 157 F6
Hawthorn Cl
Beckingham DN10 . . . . 52 A8
Healing DN41 . . . . 23 F6
4 Market Deeping PE6 . . . 217 B6
3 Newborough PE6 . . . . . . 174 E5
7 Ruskington NG34 . . . . . 108 E1
Hawthorn Ct 1 HU3 . . . . 179 F6
Hawthorn Dr
1 Mablethorpe LN12 . . . . . 64 B3
Sleaford NG34 . . . . 212 D3
Hawthorne Ave
Cleethorpes DN35 . . . . 192 D8
Hawthorne Ave *continued*
4 Grimsby DN33 . . . . 194 F8
9 Hatfield DN7 . . . . 14 C2
Louth LN11 . . . . 198 B6
New Waltham DN36 . . . . . . 195 B5
4 Scunthorpe DN17 . . . . . 184 F8
8 Wisbech PE13 . . . . 170 D2
Hawthorne Cl
2 Bracebridge Heath LN4 . . . . 81 A1
5 Manby LN11 . . . . 62 C6
6 Scopwick Heath LN4 . . 108 A7
20 Winterton DN15 . . . . 9 A5
Wootton DN39 . . . . 11 E2
Hawthorne Cres 3 DN17 . . . . 184 F8
Hawthorne Ct 4 NG31 . . 210 D2
Hawthorne Gdns 8 DN19 . . . . 12 A8
Hawthorne Rise HU13 . . . 178 B3
Hawthorn Gate 26 DN18 . . . 10 F8
Hawthorn Gr DN21 . . . . . . 197 D5
HAWTHORN HILL LN4 . . . . 110 F6
Hawthorn Rd
Bourne PE10 . . . . 213 C6
Cherry Willingham LN3 . . . 203 B7
4 Old Leake PE22 . . . . . . 114 A1
Peterborough PE1 . . . . 226 C6
Skegness PE25 . . . . 206 A2
Yaxley PE7 . . . . 233 F5
Hawthorn Rise 4 DN19 . . . 11 C8
Hawthorns The 14 LN2 . . . 68 D2
Hawthorn Way 4 LN5 . . . . 92 F3
Hawthorn Wlk 1 LN1 . . . . . 66 D7
HAWTHORPE PE10 . . . . 142 A2
Hawthorpe Rd NG33 . . . . 141 E1
Hawton Cl 1 DN21 . . . . . . 197 E6
Hawton La NG24 . . . . 104 A2
HAXEY DN9 . . . . 27 C2
HAXEY CARR DN9 . . . . 27 B4
Haxey CE Prim Sch DN9 . . 27 D3
Haxey Gate Rd DN10 . . . . . 39 F7
Haxey Grange 9 DN9 . . . . . 27 D2
Haxey La DN9 . . . . 27 D1
Haxey Rd DN10 . . . . 39 F6
Haxey Turbary Nature Reserve★ DN9 . . . . 27 A4
Haycroft Ave 4 DN31 . . . 191 C8
Haycroft La PE12 . . . . 159 B7
Haycroft St DN31 . . . . 191 C7
Haydon Ave PE25 . . . . 206 A4
Haydon Cl HU10 . . . . 178 D8
Haydor Ave LN2 . . . . 202 A8
Hayes Yd 4 LN1 . . . . 54 F2
Hayfield Cl
7 Barnby Dun DN3 . . . . 14 A4
6 Haxey DN9 . . . . 27 D2
Hay Gn Rd PE34 . . . . 161 E1
Hay Gn Rd (North) PE34 . . . . 161 E2
Hay Gn Rd (South) PE34 . . . . 161 D1
HAY GREEN PE34 . . . . 161 E1
Hayling Mere 4 DN35 . . . . 192 F1
Haynes Cl 3 DN8 . . . . 15 B7
Haynes Gdns 13 DN8 . . . . . 15 B8
Haynes Gn 6 DN8 . . . . 15 B8
Haynes Gr 1 DN8 . . . . 15 B7
Haynes Rd DN8 . . . . 15 B8
Hays Cl 4 DN36 . . . . 195 C2
Hayton Cl 2 DN15 . . . . 9 B5
Hayton Gr HU4 . . . . 179 D4
Haytons La 2 DN15 . . . . 9 D1
Haywain Dr 6 PE11 . . . . . 166 C6
Haywardsfield 4 PE3 . . . . 225 A1
Haze La 5 LN6 . . . . 204 C1
Hazeland Cl PE10 . . . . 154 C6
Hazeland Steading PE10 . . . . 154 C6
Hazelbarrow Dr HU10 . . . 178 F7
Hazel Cl
Messingham DN17 . . . . 29 C7
10 North Hykeham LN6 . . . . 93 A8
Hazel Croft
4 Immingham DN40 . . . . . . 186 A4
Peterborough PE4 . . . . 220 E4
Hazel Ct 29 HU15 . . . . 2 C5
Hazel Dr LN9 . . . . 199 B5
Hazel Gr
4 Bottesford DN16 . . . . . . 185 B2
2 Kingston upon Hull HU3 . . . . 180 D5
Louth LN11 . . . . 198 E4
Sleaford NG34 . . . . 212 D6
Stamford PE9 . . . . 218 D6
Welton/Dunholme LN2 . . . . . 68 C6
Hazelnut Cl 3 PE22 . . . . . . 99 A4
Hazel Rd 6 DN7 . . . . 14 C5
Hazelwood Ave LN6 . . . . . 204 C8
Hazelwood Dr PE10 . . . . . 213 B6
Hazelwood La PE12 . . . . . 159 A7
Hazlewood Dr NG31 . . . . . 210 F7
Headingley Ave 4 DN17 . . . . 184 E3
Headlands Dr HU13 . . . . . 178 C2
Headland Way
3 Haconby PE10 . . . . 154 D8
7 Navenby LN5 . . . . 107 B8
Headquarters Cres 5 NG34 . . . . 120 C8
Heads La HU13 . . . . 178 C1
Headstead Bank DN22 . . . . 65 B7
Healey Cl 5 NG23 . . . . 91 D4
Healey La LN12 . . . . 63 C4
Healey Rd DN16 . . . . 185 C8

HEALING DN41 23 F5
Healing Moated Settlement★ DN4 23 F5
Healing Prim Sch DN41 23 F5
Healing Rd 5 DN41 23 D6
Healing Sch DN41 23 F5
Healing Sta DN41 23 F6
Heanor Ct DN15 182 B3
HEAPHAM DN21 53 E7
Heapham Cres DN21 197 F4
Heapham La DN21 53 F7
Heapham Rd DN21 197 E5
Hearfield Terr HU13 178 E1
Heartsease Way PE10 213 E3
Heath Cl 4 LN2 68 C7
Heathcote Rd
Bourne PE10 213 E4
Castle Bytham NG33 152 D1
Coningsby LN4 207 E5
Heather Ave PE1 226 A8
Heather Cl
1 Boston PE21 208 D3
7 Woodhall Spa LN10 97 E6
Heatherdale Cl
6 Grimsby DN33 194 E7
Peterborough PE7 231 C5
Heather Gr DN16 185 E5
Heather Rd PE25 206 B2
Heather Rd Ind Est PE25 206 B2
Heath Farm Cl NG32 119 F3
Heath Farm Rd NG31 130 C2
Heathfield Ave
Branston LN4 81 E2
Spalding PE11 214 F2
Heathfield Cl 9 DN3 14 A3
Heathfield Ct DN34 191 B6
Heathfield Rd NG31 210 C3
Heath La
Ancaster NG32 119 F3
Boothby Graffoe LN5 94 B2
Carlton Scroop NG32 119 D4
Great Ponton NG33 139 D4
Honington NG32 119 C2
Leasingham NG34 121 C7
Normanton NG32 119 F6
Syston NG32 130 D8
Welton LN1 67 F6
Wilsford NG32 120 B1
Heathlea 11 LN2 68 F4
Heath Rd
Bracebridge Heath LN4 205 F2
Coleby LN5 93 F3
Helpston PE6 173 C2
15 Navenby LN5 107 A8
5 Nettleham LN2 68 C2
Scopwick LN4 108 B8
Scothern LN2 68 D4
Skegness PE25 206 B3
Heath's Meadow Nature Reserve★ PE24 102 C7
Heaton Cl PE3 225 B3
Heaton St 1 DN21 197 D4
Hebden Moor Way 8 LN6 93 B8
Hebden Rd DN15 182 C4
Hebden Wlk NG31 211 F6
HECKDYKE DN10 40 C7
Heckdyke La DN10 40 C7
HECKINGTON NG34 122 D3
Heckington Rd NG34 122 C1
Heckington Sta NG34 122 E2
Heckington Windmill★ NG34 122 E2
Hedda Dr 2 PE7 230 D3
Hedgefield Hurn PE11 144 F4
Hedge Field Rd NG32 210 A4
HEDGEHOG BRIDGE PE20 124 E5
Hedgehog La PE20 124 D4
Hedge La LN6 92 D4
Hedgelands
Peterborough PE4 221 A5
3 Wisbech PE13 170 D2
Hedgerow Cl 5 DN19 11 C8
Hedgerow La 1 DN20 196 D3
Hedon Rd HU9 181 B6
HEIGHINGTON LN4 81 F4
Heighington Fen LN4 82 A5
Heighington Rd LN4 81 C4
Heimdal Rd DN33 191 C2
Helen Cres 8 DN40 186 A4
Helene Gr DN32 192 B7
Helenship La DN22 65 A4
Hell La NG33 140 C5
Hellyers Ct HU4 179 D2
Helm Dr HU9 181 C6
Helmsdale Gdns PE4 220 F2
Helmsley Ct 1 PE7 231 F5
Helmsley Gr HU5 179 C7
Helmsley Way PE11 214 F4
HELPRINGHAM NG34 133 E7
Helpringham Rd
Burton Pedwardine NG34 122 B1
Helpringham NG34 133 C8
Helpringham Sch NG34 133 D7
HELPSTON PE6 173 C4
Helpston Rd
Castor PE5 223 D2
Etton PE6 220 A8
Helsby Rd LN5 205 D4
HELSEY PE24 89 F7
Helsey La PE24 89 F7
Helston Wlk DN17 184 C8
Heltwate PE3 225 B7
Heltwate Ct PE3 225 B7
Heltwate Sch PE3 225 B7
HEMINGBY LN9 72 B1
Hemingby La LN9 199 C6
Hemingby Way LN9 199 C5
Hemingford Cres PE2 231 E6
Hemington Way 1 PE20 136 C5
Hemmingway Wlk HU13 178 E3
Hempdyke Rd DN15 182 E4
Hemplands The 9 NG23 91 D5
Hempstead Rd 2 PE7 230 C1
HEMSWELL DN21 42 D1
Hemswell Ave
4 Kingston upon Hull HU9 5 E8
Lincoln LN6 205 A7
HEMSWELL CLIFF LN8 55 A8
Hemswell Cliff Prim Sch LN8 43 A1
Hemswell Dr DN31 190 F8
Hemswell La DN21 42 D1
Henderson Ave DN15 182 F4
Henderson Ave Prim Sch DN15 182 F4
Henderson Cres 2 DN15 182 F4
Henderson Way DN15 9 A5
Heneage Rd DN32 191 F6
Hengist Cl 7 NG34 212 B2
Henley Ct
2 Gainsborough DN21 197 C6
Lincoln LN5 205 D8
Henley St LN5 205 D8
Henlow Cl
6 Birchwood LN6 204 B8
3 Kirton in Lindsey DN21 42 F8
Henrietta St 2 PE11 214 C3
Henry Boot Way HU4 179 B1
Henry La LN3 83 D4
Henry St
Grimsby DN31 191 C8
Lincoln LN5 201 F1
Peterborough PE1 226 A4
Scunthorpe DN15 182 F3
Henshaw PE1 226 E6
Henshaw Ave 2 LN12 77 A7
Henson Cl
13 Spalding PE11 214 C2
5 Wisbech PE13 170 D2
Henson Dr 13 LN5 107 A8
Henton Cl 13 NG24 104 C5
Hercules Dr 7 NG24 104 A4
Herdgate La PE11 145 D2
Hereford Ave DN34 191 C5
Hereford Cl 2 NG34 212 C7
Hereford St HU4 179 E3
Hereford Tech Sch DN34 191 B5
Hereford Way 8 NG31 210 E5
Heren Pl 9 PE11 214 A2
Hereward Cl 2 PE1 226 B2
Hereward Cross 6 PE1 226 A2
Hereward Pl DN16 185 E7
Hereward Rd
Peterborough PE1 226 B2
Spalding PE11 214 B4
Hereward St
5 Bourne PE10 213 D5
Lincoln LN1 234 B4
Hereward Way
11 Billingborough NG34 133 B1
21 Crowland PE6 166 E1
Market Deeping PE6 217 E4
Herewood Com Coll PE1 226 D5
Herewood Cross Sh Ctr PE1 226 A3
Heritage Pk Prim Sch PE7 231 F5
Herlington PE2 230 B4
Herlyn Cres 3 PE25 90 E3
Hermes Way NG34 212 A3
Hermitage The 6 PE9 219 A5
Hermit St LN5 234 B1
Heron Cl
Grimsby DN32 192 B4
6 Scunthorpe DN15 182 C6
Skegness PE25 103 C8
3 Surfleet PE11 145 E3
Heron Ct PE2 231 D6
Heron Dr DN21 197 F5
Heron Holt 3 DN20 19 D4
Heron Pk PE1 226 F6
Heronry Dr PE6 224 E2
Herons Cl PE9 172 F6
Heron St HU3 180 B5
Heron View LN6 204 E8
Heron Way
43 Barton-upon-Humber DN18 10 E8
Holton le Clay DN36 195 C3
Spalding PE11 214 F2
Wyberton PE21 136 F8
Heron Wlk LN6 204 C1
Herrick Cl PE1 225 E8
Herrick Ct 2 LN4 207 A6
Herrick Rd DN17 184 D7
Herring La
1 Pinchbeck PE11 145 B1
4 Spalding PE11 214 D4
Herrington Ave 3 LN2 68 C2
Hersey Rd 16 LN7 33 B4
Hervey Rd NG34 212 C2
Hesketh Cres 11 PE25 103 E4
Hesketh Ct LE15 162 A8
Hesketh Dr 3 DN3 14 A2
HESSLE HU13 178 D1
Hessle Ave PE21 208 D4
Hessle Ct PE21 208 C4
Hessle Dr PE21 208 C3
Hessle High Sch HU13 178 C2
Hessle Mount Sch HU13 178 C3
Hessle Penshurst Prim Sch HU13 178 F3
Hessle Rd HU4 179 D3
Hessle Sta HU13 3 E4
Hessle View 4 DN18 10 E8
Hetley PE2 230 A4
Hever Cl NG31 210 E5
Hewde La DN15 2 A1
Hewitt's Ave
Humberston DN36 192 C1
New Waltham DN36 195 D8
Hewitt's Cir DN36 192 C2
Hewitts Manor 1 DN35 192 D2
Hewitt's Windmill★ DN21 53 E7
Hewson Rd
5 Humberston DN36 36 D8
Lincoln LN1 201 C4
Hewson's La NG23 91 D3
Hewson St 23 DN17 29 D7
Hexham Ct 3 PE1 226 D3
HEYDOUR NG32 131 D6
Heyford Ct PE4 221 D2
Heynings Cl DN21 53 B4
Heysham Cl 8 LN5 205 D3
Hey St DN35 192 F5
Heythrop Rd 3 DN35 192 E3
HIBALDSTOW DN20 31 A5
Hibaldstow Cl
10 Birchwood LN6 204 C7
9 Grimsby DN34 190 F4
Hibaldstow Prim Sch DN20 31 A5
Hibaldstow Rd LN6 204 C7
Hickling Cl 15 NG31 210 E2
Hickling Wlk PE4 221 C3
Hickman Cres DN21 197 C8
Hickman Ct DN21 197 E4
Hickman Gr 2 DN21 41 B5
Hickman St DN21 197 C4
Hickory Rd 5 LN6 200 C1
Hicks La PE7 230 F5
Hide's La
Addlethorpe PE24 90 B1
Skegness PE25 103 B8
Higgins Cl LN6 204 E7
Higgins Rd 5 LN13 75 E2
Higham Way 1 HU15 2 D5
Highbridge La PE11 145 C6
Highbridge Rd LN11 49 F2
High Bridge Rd DN8 15 C7
High Broadgate PE13 169 F7
High Bunning La NG34 143 A7
High Burgage DN15 2 B1
Highbury St PE1 226 A5
Highclere Rd PE7 230 D3
Highcliffe 5 LN5 107 A7
Highcliffe Rd NG31 211 B7
Highcliff Gdns DN15 182 E3
High Cliff Rd DN35 193 A6
High Cres PE9 171 C8
High Ct Way PE7 233 D8
Highdales HU10 178 C8
High Dike
Cranwell & Byard's Leap NG34 120 B8
Easton NG33 151 E8
Great Ponton NG33 140 C4
Navenby/Wellingore LN5 94 B1
North Rauceby NG32 120 A5
Old Somerby NG33 130 E2
Waddington LN5 93 F8
Welby NG31 130 E5
Wellingore LN5 107 B6
Wilsford NG32 119 F1
High Dyke Rd 2 NG34 107 C1
High Fen PE11 144 B4
HIGH FERRY PE22 126 A8
High Ferry La PE22 113 A1
Highfield Ave
4 Immingham DN40 186 B3
4 Lincoln LN6 205 B7
4 Mablethorpe/Sutton on Sea LN12 64 C1
Scunthorpe DN15 182 E3
Wellow DN32 191 E5
Highfield Cl
8 Barnby Dun DN3 14 A4
Foston NG32 117 F2
Gainsborough DN21 197 E5
8 North Thoresby DN36 36 B1
Osbournby NG34 132 C5
Highfield Cres
17 Barton-upon-Humber DN18 10 F8
Croxton Kerrial NG32 138 D3
4 Westwoodside DN9 27 B2
Highfield Dr
2 Kirton in Lindsey DN21 30 B1
Stapleford LN6 105 A6
Highfield Gr DN20 196 C5
Highfield La
Halton Holegate PE23 101 B8
Revesby PE22 99 B5
Highfield Rd
7 Donington PE11 134 F2
North Thoresby DN36 36 B1
14 Saxilby LN1 66 D2
High Field Rd DN20 196 F5
Highfields
6 Barrowby NG32 210 A5
1 Barrow upon Humber DN19 11 C7
17 Crowle DN17 16 D8
2 Nettleham LN2 68 D2
High Fields La PE11 156 E8
Highfields Rise 29 LN4 95 C4
Highfields Sch NG24 104 B3
Highfield Terr
4 Glentham LN8 43 F1
2 Lincoln LN6 205 A2
High Garth DN17 184 F2
Highgate 6 DN35 192 F5
High Gate
Helpringham NG34 133 D7
Mablethorpe & Sutton LN12 64 C1
Theddlethorpe St Helen LN12 63 D5
Highgate Cl 3 LN12 64 C1
Highgate La
Claxby with Moorby PE22 99 B6
Normanby by Spital LN8 56 B7
Owmby LN8 55 F6
Highgrove
1 Long Sutton PE12 216 B5
4 Messingham DN17 29 D7
Highgrove Cres PE21 209 C6
Highgrove Gdns PE9 218 E5
High Holme Rd LN11 198 B6
High Horse Mus★ PE22 111 D8
High House Rd DN22 52 A2
High La
Croft PE24 102 D6
Mareham on the Hill LN9 85 F2
Highlands 1 PE9 163 C1
Highlands Way PE9 218 F5
Highland Tarn DN40 186 B3
High Leas 1 LN2 68 D2
Highlees Prim Sch PE3 225 C6
High Levels Bank DN8 15 F5
High Leys Rd DN17 184 F3
HIGH MARNHAM NG23 78 B5
High Mdw
Grantham NG31 210 D4
Heighington/Washingborough LN4 203 C1
Westborough & Dry Doddington NG23 117 F5
High Mdws
1 Fiskerton LN3 82 A7
Kingston upon Hull HU10 178 C8
High or Main Rd PE12 215 A2
High Point Ret Pk DN31 189 A1
High Rd
Barrowby NG32 210 A5
Elloughton-cum-Brough HU15 2 D7
Gorefield PE13 169 F2
Grantham NG31 211 C8
Hough-on-the-Hill NG32 119 A5
Londonthorpe & Harrowby without NG31 130 D4
Moulton PE12 158 A7
Newton PE13 169 F5
Weston PE12 157 C7
Wisbech St Mary PE13 177 F2
High Ridge Comp Sch DN15 182 E3
High Ridge Sch & High Ridge Adult Ed Ctr DN15 182 E3
High Ridge Sports Hall DN15 182 E3
HIGH RISBY DN15 9 A1
High St E DN15 183 C3
High St N 16 NG34 108 E2
High St S 3 NG34 108 E1
High St St Martin's PE9 219 C3
High St W DN21 29 B4
High Side PE13 169 D2
High St
8 Alford LN13 75 F3
Alvingham LN11 49 F2
Barrow upon Humber DN19 11 D8
Barton-upon-Humber DN18 3 E1
Bassingham LN5 92 F2
Baumber LN9 85 A8
1 Beckingham DN10 52 B8
Belton DN9 16 E1
Benniworth LN8 71 F8
Bicker PE20 135 A4
Binbrook LN8 47 C4
Blyton DN21 41 C5
Boston PE21 208 F3
Bottesford NG13 128 A5
Branston LN4 81 E2
Brant Broughton LN5 105 F4
Broughton DN20 19 D3
Burgh le Marsh PE24 102 E8
Burringham DN17 17 D4
High St *continued*
Caistor LN7 33 B4
Carlby PE9 163 D4
Carlton-le-Moorland LN5 105 E8
Castle Bytham NG33 152 D1
Castor PE5 223 F2
Caythorpe NG32 119 B7
Cherry Willingham/Reepham LN3 203 D5
Cleethorpes DN35 192 E6
Collingham NG23 91 D4
3 Collyweston PE9 171 B1
Colsterworth NG33 151 D6
Coningsby LN4 207 A4
Corby Glen NG33 152 E8
Corringham DN21 41 E1
9 Crowle DN17 16 D7
Donington PE11 134 E2
Eagle & Swinethorpe LN6 79 B2
East Ferry DN21 28 B2
Eastoft DN17 7 A3
3 Easton on the Hill PE9 171 D3
Elkington LN11 60 E7
Epworth DN9 27 D7
Eye PE6 175 A1
Faldingworth LN8 56 F3
Fillingham DN21 54 F4
3 Fiskerton LN3 82 A7
Flixborough DN15 8 B2
5 Fulbeck NG32 106 C1
Fulletby LN9 86 B8
Gainsborough DN21 197 D3
Garthorpe & Fockerby DN17 7 E5
Gate Burton DN21 53 A1
Girton NG23 78 C1
Glentham LN8 43 F1
Glinton PE6 220 C8
Gosberton PE11 145 B6
Grainthorpe LN11 50 B8
Grantham NG31 211 A4
Great Gonerby NG31 129 D5
Great Limber DN37 22 D3
Gringley on the Hill DN10 39 C1
Hagworthingham PE23 87 A4
Harby NG23 79 C5
Harlaxton NG32 139 C7
Harmston LN5 93 F5
Hatfield DN7 14 C2
Haxey DN9 27 C2
16 Heckington NG34 122 E2
Heighington/Washingborough LN4 203 B2
Helpringham NG34 133 D7
Hogsthorpe PE24 90 B7
Holbeach PE12 215 E2
Horbling NG34 133 B2
Horncastle LN9 199 B4
Humberside Airport DN39 22 A6
Ingham LN1 54 F2
2 Ingoldmells PE25 90 E3
Ketton PE9 171 A3
Kexby DN21 53 E5
Kingston upon Hull HU1 181 A5
18 Kirton in Lindsey DN21 30 B1
Laceby DN37 23 F1
Leadenham LN5 106 D3
Lincoln LN5 234 A1
2 Little Bytham NG33 163 A8
Long Sutton PE12 216 C4
Luddington & Haldenby DN17 7 C4
18 Mablethorpe/Sutton on Sea LN12 64 B4
Market Deeping PE6 217 B4
Market Stainton LN8 72 A6
Martin LN4 96 C2
Marton DN21 65 D8
Maxey PE6 217 A1
Messingham DN17 29 D7
Metheringham LN4 95 C4
Misterton DN10 39 F5
5 Morton PE10 154 C7
Moulton PE12 157 F6
12 Navenby/Wellingore LN5 107 A7
Nettleham LN2 68 C2
Nettleton LN7 33 C2
Newton on Trent LN1 65 D1
North Ferriby HU14 3 A5
8 North Kelsey LN7 32 A4
Northorpe PE10 164 C7
North Scarle LN6 78 E1
North Thoresby DN36 36 A1
Osbournby NG34 132 C5
Owston Ferry DN9 28 B3
Peterborough PE2 231 A6
Pointon & Sempringham NG34 143 B7
Redbourne DN21 30 F2
Reepham LN3 203 F8
Rippingale PE10 142 F2
Ropsley NG33 131 B1
Roxby cum Risby DN15 8 E1
Saxilby LN1 66 D2
Scampton LN1 67 C6
Scotton DN21 29 C1
Scunthorpe DN15 183 A3
Sixhills LN8 59 A7
Skegness PE25 206 C3
Skellingthorpe LN6 200 A5
Snitterby DN21 43 D5
South Clifton NG23 78 C5
South Ferriby DN18 10 A7
South Kyme LN4 123 B8
South Witham NG33 151 D2
Spalding PE11 214 E4

High St *continued*
7 Spilsby PE23 88 A1
Stamford PE9 219 C5
Staunton NG13 117 A2
Sturton by Stow LN1 66 C7
5 Sutton Bridge PE12 160 F4
Swayfield NG33 152 D5
Swinderby LN6 92 A5
Swineshead PE20 135 B7
Swinstead NG33 153 A5
Upton DN21 53 D5
Waddingham DN21 43 D7
Waddington LN5 93 F7
Wainfleet All Saints PE24 102 D1
Walcott LN4 109 D7
Walesby LN8 46 B5
Walkeringham DN10 39 F3
1 Waltham DN37 194 E4
Welbourn LN5 106 E5
West/East Butterwick DN17 17 D1
Willingham by Stow DN21 53 E3
11 Winterton DN15 9 A5
Wootton DN39 11 E2
Wroot DN9 26 D6
Highstock La PE12 168 D1
High Thorpe Cres DN35 192 D3
High Thorpe Rd LN3 83 D1
HIGH TOYNTON LN9 86 A4
High Wash Dro 2 PE6 166 E1
Highwood Mews DN35 192 E5
Higney Rd PE7 230 C1
Higson Rd 4 LN1 201 D7
Hilary Gr HU4 179 B2
Hilary Rd DN33 194 F7
Hilda Cl 6 NG34 212 B2
Hildas Ave HU5 180 A8
Hilda St
4 Boston PE21 209 A7
Grimsby DN32 189 C1
Hildreds Sh Ctr PE25 206 D3
Hildyard Cl 1 HU10 178 F6
Hildyard St DN32 192 B8
Hiles Ave 6 DN15 9 A5
Hill Abbey LN4 95 D7
Hillary Cl
8 Spalding PE11 214 B2
1 Stamford PE9 219 D6
Hillary Rd DN16 185 B5
Hillary Way DN37 190 E8
Hill Ave NG31 211 B5
Hill Brow HU10 178 B6
Hill Cl PE1 226 D5
Hill Cres DN21 197 F5
Hillcrest NG34 107 C2
Hillcrest Ave
Kingston upon Hull HU13 178 C2
Yaxley PE7 233 E5
Hillcrest Com Inf Sch DN21 197 F4
Hillcrest Dr 2 DN15 8 A4
Hillcrest Gdns 3 PE20 135 B7
Hillcroft 1 LN4 203 A2
Hill Ct NG31 210 D2
HILLDYKE PE22 126 A6
Hill Field 3 PE24 102 D2
Hillfoot Dr DN17 184 E3
Hillgate PE12 168 C2
Hillgate St PE34 161 F3
Hillingford Way NG31 210 E3
Hill La PE20 136 B5
Hillman Cl LN4 205 F3
Hillman Rd HU13 178 F3
Hill Rd DN21 41 E1
Hill Rise
8 Brough HU15 2 C6
Coleby LN5 93 F3
Louth LN11 198 A7
Hill's Ct 9 NG34 212 D4
Hills Dr 14 DN36 36 D4
Hillside
4 Ancaster NG32 120 A2
3 Marton DN21 65 E8
Hillside App 5 LN2 202 C3
Hillside Ave
Lincoln LN2 202 C3
7 Mablethorpe/Sutton on Sea LN12 77 A8
Hillside Cl PE9 172 F2
Hillside Cres
Barnetby le Wold DN38 21 B5
3 Grantham NG31 211 D2
Hillside Dr
5 Barton-upon-Humber DN18 10 E8
Grantham NG31 211 D2
Hillside Est NG34 108 F2
Hillside Rd
6 Broughton DN20 19 E4
Glentworth DN21 54 F7
Woolsthorpe by Belvoir NG32 128 D1
Hillstead Cl 13 DN36 36 D4
Hillsyde Ave 11 DN10 39 F5
Hill Terr LN11 198 C4
Hill The
4 Saltfleet LN11 51 C4
Skellingthorpe LN6 200 A4
Worlaby DN20 10 E1
Hill Top 1 LN5 93 E5
Hilltop Ave DN15 182 D5
Hilltop Cl LN6 79 B2
Hilltop Gdns DN17 29 C7
Hill Top La 1 DN21 41 B5
Hill Top Pl DN34 190 D3
Hill View Cl NG31 210 E3
Hill View Rd 14 NG33 151 D2
Hillward Cl PE2 230 C6
Hilton Ave DN15 182 B3
Hilton Cl 2 DN9 16 E2
Hilton Ct DN35 193 B1
Hilton's La PE20 136 E1
Hinaidi La LN4 95 C7
Hinchcliffe PE2 229 E2
Hindon Wlk DN17 184 C8
Hine Ave NG24 104 B4
Hinkler St DN35 192 E5
Hinkley Dr DN40 186 B5
Hinman Wlk 9 DN15 183 B3
Hipper La PE20 135 D2
Hither Old Gate PE12 158 D6
Hives La LN6 78 E2
Hix Cl PE12 215 C2
Hix's La PE13 160 A1
Hobart Cl 11 LN5 93 E8
Hobart Rd NG31 211 D7
Hobart St HU3 180 D5
Hobb La 4 DN21 29 C3
Hobhole Bank Nature Reserve★ PE21 137 C7
Hobson Rd 7 HU15 2 C6
Hobsons Gn PE11 214 A5
Hobson Way DN41 187 E2
Hockland Rd 2 PE13 169 F7
Hockle's Gate PE12 159 B7
Hockney Hole La PE12 158 A7
Hodder Cl 1 NG31 210 F3
Hoddesdon Cres 20 DN7 14 D3
Hod Fen Dro PE7 233 F2
Hodge Ct 3 HU9 181 C7
Hodgetoft La LN13 63 E1
Hodgson Ave PE4 220 E6
Hodgson St HU8 181 A7
Hodgson Way 3 LN12 77 A8
Hodney Rd 5 PE6 175 A1
Hodson Cl LN6 200 B5
Hodson Gn LN9 199 C4
Hoe Dr 19 LN8 57 D8
Hoekman Dr 3 PE11 214 B2
Hoekman Way PE11 214 B2
HOFFLEET STOW PE20 135 C4
Hogens La PE13 170 A5
Hoggard La DN14 7 E8
Hogg La HU10 178 B8
Hog's Gate PE12 158 A6
HOGSTHORPE PE24 90 B6
Hogsthorpe Prim Sch PE24 90 B7
Hogsthorpe Rd LN13 76 F1
HOLBEACH PE12 215 C3
HOLBEACH BANK PE12 215 C7
Holbeach Bank Prim Sch PE12 215 D7
HOLBEACH CLOUGH PE12 215 B7
Holbeach & District Nature Reserve★ PE12 215 E2
Holbeach Dro Gate PE12 168 C4
HOLBEACH DROVE PE12 168 B3
Holbeach Hospl PE12 215 B5
HOLBEACH HURN PE12 147 F2
Holbeach Prim Sch PE12 215 D3
Holbeach Rd
Spalding PE11 214 F6
1 Spalding PE12 157 B6
HOLBEACH ST JOHNS PE12 158 E1
HOLBEACH ST MARKS PE12 147 D6
Holbeach St Marks CE Prim Sch PE12 147 D6
HOLBEACH ST MATTHEW PE12 148 A7
Holbeach Tecnology Pk PE12 215 B4
Holbeck Pl 2 DN40 186 B4
Holborn Rd PE11 214 B2
Holborn St HU8 181 B7
Holcroft PE2 230 B3
Holdan Cl DN36 193 A1
Holdenby Cl 3 LN2 202 E7
Holden Dr 9 PE24 102 E7
Holden Way 7 NG31 129 E5
Holderness Rd HU9 181 C8
Holdfield PE3 225 B6
Holdich St PE3 225 E2
HOLDINGHAM NG34 212 C7
Holdingham La NG34 121 E7
Hole Gate PE23 101 C8
Holgate La PE4 220 F7
Holgate Pl 13 HU14 3 B7
Holgate Rd DN16 185 D8
Holkham Rd PE2 229 D3
Holland Ave
18 Crowle DN17 16 D8
Peterborough PE4 221 B1
Scunthorpe DN15 182 E4
Holland Cl
8 Bourne PE10 213 C5
10 Market Deeping PE6 217 A6
Holland Dr PE25 206 C1
Holland La PE22 114 F4
Holland Mkt 16 PE11 214 D4
Holland Rd
Horbling NG34 133 B3
Spalding PE11 214 E4
Stamford PE9 219 C6
Holland Rd *continued*
Swaton NG34 133 E3
Holland's Chase PE11 156 A6
Holland St HU9 181 D8
Holland Way PE12 215 B2
Hollengs La 1 LN11 59 E1
Holles St 6 DN32 191 E8
Hollies The PE12 215 E3
Hollin Bridge La DN7 15 A3
Hollingsworth Ave 1 DN40 186 B4
Hollingsworth Cl 5 DN35 192 D2
Hollingsworth La DN9 27 E6
Hollis' Rd NG31 210 F2
Hollowbrook Cl 3 NG34 108 D2
Hollowdyke La NG24 104 C1
Hollowgate Hill DN21 42 E4
Hollowgate La NG23 78 A5
Hollows The 4 LN11 61 F3
Holly Cl
Cherry Willingham/Reepham LN3 203 E5
5 Grantham NG31 211 D2
Horncastle LN9 199 A5
Lincoln LN5 205 D5
2 Newborough PE6 174 E5
Scunthorpe DN16 185 C4
1 Sleaford NG34 212 D2
6 Stallingborough DN41 23 E6
Holly Dr PE10 213 C7
Holly Hill 1 HU15 2 E6
Holly Rd PE25 206 A2
Holly St LN5 205 D5
Hollytree Ave 2 HU5 179 B7
Holly Tree Cl 9 LN8 57 D7
Holly Way 2 PE6 217 D4
Hollywell Rd LN5 205 D1
Hollywell Rd (The Rookery) 23 LN13 75 F2
Holly Wlk PE7 230 D3
Hollywood Dr 8 NG31 210 F7
HOLME
Holme DN16 19 A1
Holme NG23 91 A2
Holme Ave DN36 195 C6
Holme Cl
Brigg DN20 196 D4
Castor PE5 223 D2
Thorpe on the Hill LN6 92 F8
Holme Dene 1 DN9 27 C2
Holme Dr
Burton upon Stather DN15 8 B5
Sudbrooke LN2 68 F2
Holme Gdns 7 DN7 14 C7
Holme Hall Ave DN16 185 B3
HOLME HILL DN32 191 F6
Holme La
Grassthorpe NG23 78 A2
Holme DN16 185 E2
Marnham NG23 78 A4
Messingham DN17 29 E8
4 Ruskington NG34 108 E1
Scunthorpe DN16 185 B3
Winthorpe NG24 104 B8
Holme Rd PE7 233 E4
Holmes Cl
Louth LN11 198 B7
2 Skidbrooke with Saltfleet Haven LN11 51 C4
Holmes Dr 10 PE9 171 A3
Holmes Field 6 LN5 92 F3
Holmes La
North Somercotes LN11 38 A1
Roxby cum Risby DN15 9 D5
2 Welton/Dunholme LN2 68 E6
Holmes Rd
Frampton PE20 124 F1
Glinton PE6 220 D7
Horsington LN10 83 F1
Kirton PE20 136 A8
Stickney PE22 113 A7
Stixwould & Woodhall LN10 84 A1
Holme St DN32 191 E7
Holmes Way
Horncastle LN9 199 D1
Peterborough PE4 221 D2
Wragby LN8 70 C5
Holme Valley Prim Sch DN16 185 C3
Holme Wlk 6 DN21 197 F5
Holme Wood Ct 5 DN3 14 A1
Holme Wood La
Claxby with Moorby LN9 99 B8
Hameringham LN9 86 B1
Holmfield LN3 82 B7
Holmfirth Rd DN15 182 C4
Holm La NG23 104 F1
Holm Rd DN9 27 B2
Holmshaw Cl 24 DN3 14 A2
Holstein Dr DN16 185 A2
Holt Cl
10 Lincoln LN6 93 C8
9 Wittering PE8 172 B1
Holt La
Horncastle LN9 199 D4
Mareham le Fen PE22 99 A3
Holton Ct DN36 195 C1
HOLTON CUM BECKERING LN8 70 C8
HOLTON LE CLAY DN36 195 D2
Holton-le-Clay Inf Sch DN36 195 D2
Holton le Clay Jun Sch DN36 195 E1
HOLTON LE MOOR LN7 45 A8
Holton Mount DN36 195 C2
Holton Rd
Nettleton LN7 33 A2
South Kelsey LN7 32 D1
Tetney DN36 195 F1
Holt Prim Sch The LN6 200 A3
Holt The DN21 197 F5
Holy Cross Gdns 12 NG32 119 B7
Holydyke DN18 10 E8
Holy Family Prim Sch DN7 14 D7
Holyoake Rd DN32 192 C6
Holyroad Dr DN15 182 D7
Holyrood Cl PE20 134 E3
Holyrood Wlk PE11 214 E2
Holy Trinity CE Prim Sch LN4 207 A5
Holywell Cl 1 PE3 225 A1
Holy Well La LN11 49 A4
Holywell Rd PE9 162 E8
Holywell Way PE3 224 F2
Home Beat Dr DN20 19 C3
Home Cl
7 Bourne PE10 213 C7
Bracebridge Heath LN4 205 F3
Kingston upon Hull HU4 179 C5
Home Ct 8 LN5 107 A7
Home Farm Cl
Great Casterton PE9 218 C8
Laughterton LN1 65 D2
Homefarm La NG23 79 A7
Homefield Ave DN33 191 D3
Home Paddock DN37 194 E4
Home Pasture 4 PE4 220 F5
Home Pk 4 NG34 120 F8
Homers La PE22 126 D4
Home St DN15 183 B4
Homestead Garth 11 DN7 14 D4
Honeyhill PE4 221 E1
Honeyhill Com Prim Sch PE4 221 E1
Honeyhill Rd PE13 169 C2
Honeyholes La LN2 68 D6
Honey Pot Cl LN2 202 E7
Honey Pot La NG33 151 F4
Honeysuckle Cl
4 Lincoln LN5 205 C2
14 Mablethorpe & Sutton LN12 76 F8
18 Sutton on Sea Ln11 76 F8
Honeysuckle Ct
Humberston DN35 192 E1
Peterborough PE2 230 D7
3 Scunthorpe DN16 185 D4
Honeysuckle Pl 19 HU15 2 C5
HONINGTON NG32 119 C2
Honington App 5 LN1 201 D7
Honington Cres LN1 201 D7
Honington Rd 2 NG32 130 B8
Hood Cl NG34 212 A3
Hood Rd DN17 184 D6
Hood St
Kingston upon Hull HU8 181 A8
8 Lincoln LN5 201 F1
Hook's Dro PE13 177 C4
Hooks La LN5 106 E6
Hoop End DN36 36 D4
Hoopers Cl 4 NG13 128 A5
Hoop La LN8 70 E2
Hope Gdns PE21 208 F6
Hope St
Cleethorpes DN35 193 A5
Grimsby DN32 191 F8
Lincoln LN5 201 F1
Hopfield DN20 31 A5
Hopgardens 1 DN21 53 E3
Hopgarth 11 DN9 27 D2
Hop Hills La DN7 14 D5
Hopkins Ave DN17 185 A7
Hoplands Rd LN4 207 D5
Hoplands The 4 NG34 212 F4
Hopland's Wood Nature Reserve★ LN13 88 F6
HOP POLE PE11 165 F5
Hopton St LN9 199 B3
Hopwood Cl HU3 180 D8
Hopyard La
Bassingham LN5 93 B1
Normanton on Trent NG23 78 A3
Horace St PE21 208 E5
HORBLING NG34 133 C2
Horbling Fen Dro NG34 133 D2
Horbling La PE22 113 A7
Horbling Line Nature Reserve★ NG34 133 B1
Horbury Cl DN15 182 D4
HORKSTOW DN18 10 A5
Horkstow Rd DN18 10 E7
Hornbeam Ave DN16 185 A5
Hornby Dr 20 LN12 77 A7
HORNCASTLE LN9 199 D3
Horncastle Cty Prim Sch LN9 199 C4
Horncastle Hill PE23 87 A1
Horncastle La
Dunholme LN2 68 B5
Grange de Lings LN1 67 F5
Horncastle Rd
Bardney LN3 83 C4
Horncastle Rd *continued*
Boston PE21 208 F8
Fishtoft PE21 125 E5
Goulceby LN9 72 D5
Horsington LN10 84 D4
Louth LN11 198 A4
Mareham le Fen PE22 98 F4
Raithby cum Maltby LN11 60 F2
Roughton LN9 85 C2
Tathwell LN11 73 A8
West Ashby LN9 199 C8
Woodhall Spa LN10 97 F6
Wragby LN8 70 D4
Horne La 3 NG22 65 B1
Horner Cl 1 LN5 205 C2
Hornsby Cres DN15 182 F4
Hornsby Rd NG31 210 E2
Hornsea Parade 4 HU9 181 C8
Hornsey Hill Rd DN21 28 D1
Horn The 7 PE25 206 A7
Horse Fair Gn 25 DN8 15 A8
Horse Fayre 7 PE11 214 A3
Horsegate PE6 217 D4
Horsegate Field Rd DN19 5 B2
Horseham's La PE20 135 A5
Horse Mkt 24 LN7 33 B4
Horsemoor Dro PE12 159 B1
Horsemoor La LN9 72 C2
Horse Pasture La DN22 65 C7
Horsepit La 12 PE11 145 C1
Horseshoe Cl 12 NG34 108 D2
Horseshoe La PE20 136 D5
Horseshoe Rd PE11 214 A2
Horseshoe Terr PE13 170 C1
Horseshoe Way
Hampton Vale PE7 230 D1
Yaxley PE7 233 D8
Horseshoe Yd 11 PE6 166 E1
Horsewells St 1 DN10 39 C1
HORSINGTON LN10 84 C3
Horstead Ave DN20 196 D5
Horton St LN2 202 C3
Horton Wlk PE3 225 C5
Hospital Dro PE12 160 C3
Hospital La PE21 209 A6
Hospital Rd PE12 161 A5
Hotchkin Ave LN1 66 E2
Hotham Dr HU5 179 B8
Hotham Rd HU5 179 A8
Hotham Rd S HU5 179 B8
Hotham St HU9 181 D7
Hotspur Rd DN21 197 C6
HOUGHAM NG32 118 C3
Hougham Rd
Hougham NG32 118 B4
Westborough & Dry Doddington NG23 117 F5
Hough La
Carlton Scroop NG32 119 C4
Claypole NG23 117 F7
HOUGH-ON-THE-HILL NG32 119 A5
Hough Rd
Barkston NG32 130 B8
Carlton Scroop NG32 119 A3
Hough-on-the-Hill NG32 118 E7
Houghton Ave PE2 231 F5
Houghton Rd NG31 211 C2
Houlden Way 1 NG34 122 E3
Hounsfield Cl NG24 104 B5
Houps Rd 8 DN8 15 B8
Hourne Ct HU13 178 E2
Hourne The HU13 178 E2
House Ct DN16 185 D4
Househams La LN11 61 F3
Howard Cl PE34 161 F2
Howard Gr DN32 192 B6
Howard Rd 10 LN4 108 A7
Howard St LN1 201 C4
Howdale La NG32 119 A3
Howden Croft Hill HU15 2 A8
Howe La
Ashby with Scremby PE23 88 C3
Goxhill DN19 11 F8
HOWELL NG34 122 D5
Howell Fen Dro NG34 122 D5
Howell Rd NG34 122 E3
Howgarth La PE22 114 F5
Howitts Rd 14 NG13 128 A5
Howland PE2 230 A3
Howlett Rd DN35 193 A4
HOWSHAM LN7 32 A6
Howsham La 2 DN38 32 D8
Howville Ave 2 DN7 14 F3
Howville Rd 1 DN7 14 F3
Hoylake Dr
1 Immingham DN40 186 D5
Peterborough PE7 231 C5
Skegness PE25 206 D5
Hoylake Rd DN17 184 D3
Hubba Cres PE20 135 C6
Hubbard Cl 2 NG34 122 D3
HUBBERT'S BRIDGE PE20 124 F2
Hubberts Bridge Sta PE20 124 E2
Hubert's Cl PE12 168 C1
Hub The★ NG34 212 E4
Huckles Way PE25 206 B6
Huddleston Rd DN32 192 B7
Hudson Ave DN15 182 E5
Hudson Cl PE23 88 B3
Hudson Ct HU13 178 D1

Hudson Dr LN4 207 E6
Hudson Rd 4 PE11 214 C2
Hudson's Gdns 5 PE21 209 B4
Hudson St HU3 180 D8
Hudson Way
Grantham NG31 211 A3
12 Skegness PE25 206 A5
Huggin Carr Rd DN7 14 F1
Hughes Ford Way 20 LN1 66 D2
Hugh Hill La DN7 14 D6
Hughson Wlk 3 LN2 68 E6
Hulberry Cl 10 DN41 23 A4
Hull Arena* HU1 180 E4
Hull Coll
Kingston upon Hull HU1 181 A7
Kingston upon Hull HU2 180 D7
Kingston upon Hull HU3 179 F7
Hull Collegiate HU10 178 D5
Hull & E Riding Mus* HU9 181 A6
Hull Maritime Mus* HU1 180 F6
Hull Rd HU13 178 F1
Hull Royal Infmy HU3 180 C6
Hull's Dro PE6 167 D3
Hull Sta HU1 180 E6
Hull Trinity House Sch HU1 180 F6
Hull Truck Theatre* HU2 180 D7
Humber Bank Factories DN41 187 D4
Humber Bank S DN31 189 C2
Humber Bridge Rd DN31 189 C1
Humber Cres
6 Brough HU15 2 C5
Scunthorpe DN17 184 F6
Humberdale Cl 5 HU14 3 B6
Humberdale Dr HU14 3 C5
Humber Dock St HU1 180 F5
Humber Rd
Barton-upon-Humber DN18 3 E1
Immingham DN40 186 A8
North Ferriby HU14 3 A4
Humberside Int Airport DN38 21 F5
Humber St
3 Cleethorpes DN35 192 F5
Grimsby DN31 189 C1
Kingston upon Hull HU1 180 F5
HUMBERSTON DN35 193 A2
Humberston Ave DN36 195 E6
Humberston CE Prim Sch DN36 36 D8
Humberston Comp Sch DN36 36 C8
Humberstone Holt 1 LN11 50 F7
Humberstone Rd DN32 192 A6
Humberston Fitties* Dn36 36 F8
Humberston Pk Specl Sch DN36 36 C8
Humberston Rd
Cleethorpes DN36 192 C3
Tetney DN36 36 C6
Humber Terr DN31 191 C8
Humber View
3 Barton-upon-Humber DN18 10 E8
Kingston upon Hull HU13 178 C2
4 Swanland HU14 3 B6
Humberville Rd DN40 186 D4
HUMBY NG33 141 C7
Humby Rd NG33 141 B8
Hume Brae 6 DN40 186 B3
Hume St 5 DN31 191 C7
Hunchback La PE13 170 E2
HUNDLEBY PE23 87 F1
Hundlehouse La LN4 111 D4
HUNDLE HOUSES LN4 111 C4
Hundle Houses La LN4 111 D4
Hund Oak Dr 9 DN7 14 D4
Hundred Acres La NG24 104 B1
Hundreds La
Gringley on the Hill DN10 39 A5
Little Sutton PE12 216 F1
Hundreds Rd PE6 175 C6
Hungarton Ct 3 PE1 226 D8
Hungate LN1 234 B2
Hun Gate PE11 145 D3
Hungate Rd NG32 139 A7
Hungerdike Gate PE12 215 A2
HUNGERTON NG32 139 B4
Hungry Hill La LN11 62 C5
Hunsley Cres DN32 192 B4
Hunsley Dr 5 DN41 23 E6
Hunstan La PE22 113 F4
Hunston Rd 4 LN10 97 C5
Huntcliff Sch DN21 30 C1
Hunter Ave LN11 62 C6
Hunter Pl LN11 198 B4
Hunter Rd
Brookenby LN8 47 A6
Brough HU15 2 C6
Hunters Cl 9 PE12 215 E2
Hunter's Croft 1 DN9 27 D3
Hunters Dr 13 LN4 95 C4
Hunter's Dr 5 DN10 39 C1
Hunters La
Baumber LN9 72 A1
Tattershall LN4 207 C5
Hunting Ave PE2 230 F7
Huntingdon Cl 2 PE12 215 E3
Huntingdon Cres 8 DN15 8 B4
Huntingdon St HU4 179 E3
Huntingtower Com Prim Sch NG31 211 A3
Huntingtower Rd NG31 211 A3
Hunt Lea Ave
Grantham NG31 210 F1
Lincoln LN6 205 C8
Huntly Gr PE1 226 A4
Huntly Rd PE2 230 E7
Hunt Rd DN16 185 C5
Hunts Cl 7 DN20 19 E4
Huntsgate PE12 159 D4
Hunt's Gate PE12 159 E1
Hunts La 4 DN20 30 F5
Huntsman Cl PE21 209 D2
Huntsmans Chase DN36 195 B7
Huntsmans Gate PE3 224 F3
Hurdletree Bank PE12 158 E4
Hurdman Way PE25 90 E3
Hurd's Farm DN20 20 D8
Hurford Pl DN37 194 D7
Hurle Cres PE21 208 D6
Hurlstone Cl 25 DN3 14 A2
Hurn Bank PE12 147 E2
Hurnbridge Rd LN4 111 A4
Hurn Cl
2 Birchwood LN6 204 B8
7 Ruskington NG34 108 D1
Hurn Dro LN4 110 A8
Hurn La PE22 126 A7
Hurn Rd
Holbeach PE12 147 E1
Marholm PE6 220 C3
HURN'S END PE22 127 C8
Hurn The
5 Billingborough NG34 133 B1
Digby LN4 108 E6
Hurst Cres NG32 210 A4
Hurst La DN17 184 E3
Hurstlea Dr DN36 193 B1
Hurst The 5 PE25 206 A6
Hurstwood Cl LN2 202 D8
Hurton's La LN11 49 C6
Hussey Cl 2 NG34 212 E4
Hussey Twr* PE21 209 A4
Husthwaite Rd 18 HU15 2 D5
Hutchinson Gdns 5 PE12 157 E7
Hutchinson Rd 2 DN35 192 E7
Huteson La DN15 8 C8
Hutson Dr LN6 204 F2
HUTTOFT LN13 76 E3
Huttoft Bank Pit nature Reserve* LN13 77 B6
Huttoft Prim Sch LN13 76 F3
Huttoft Rd 17 LN12 76 F8
Hutton Cl 3 PE11 214 F2
Hutton Rd DN31 189 B2
Hutt St HU3 180 D7
Hyde Gdns PE6 164 F3
Hyde Pk Cl
6 Lincoln LN6 204 F1
Nunsthorpe DN33 191 B2
Hyholmes PE3 224 F7
Hykeham Rd LN6 205 B4
Hykeham Sta LN6 204 D3
Hymers Ave HU3 180 B7
Hymers Coll HU3 180 B7
Hyperion St HU9 181 A7
Hythegate PE4 221 B4

I

Ibbott Cl PE2 231 E5
Icehouse Rd HU3 180 D6
Icelandic Cl HU3 180 C5
Ickworth Rd NG34 212 D3
Ida Rd PE25 206 C3
Idas Cl HU9 181 A5
Iddesleigh Rd 4 LN10 97 D6
Idle Bank
Epworth DN9 15 F1
Haxey DN9 26 E2
Ihlee Cl PE4 221 C1
Ilex Cl PE7 230 C3
Iliffe Gate 3 PE4 221 D2
Ilkeston Ct 2 DN15 182 B3
Illston Pl 4 PE1 226 F7
IMMINGHAM DN40 186 E4
Immingham Bsns Units DN40 186 D3
Immingham Leisure Ctr DN40 186 C4
Immingham Mus* DN40 186 C3
Immingham Sch The DN40 186 C4
Impala Way HU4 179 D2
Imperial Ave DN35 192 C8
Independence Dr 5 PE11 156 F8
Ingamells Dr LN1 66 E2
Ingelow Ave PE21 208 C6
INGHAM LN1 54 F2
Ingham Cl LN6 205 B3
Ingham Ct LN4 207 E6
Ingham Hall Gdns PE13 177 D7
Ingham La LN1 55 B1
Ingham Prim Sch LN1 54 F2
Ingham Rd
Coningsby LN4 207 E6
3 Stow LN1 66 C8
Inghams La 1 DN36 36 D4
Inghams Rd 3 DN36 36 D4
Ingleborough 1 PE1 226 A5
INGLEBOROUGH PE14 170 E5
INGLEBY LN1 66 C4
Ingleby Cres LN2 201 F8
Ingleby Ct 2 PE11 214 F4
Ingleby Gr DN37 190 F8
Ingleby Rd 14 DN17 29 D7
Ingle Ct 2 NG33 151 D7
Ingledew Cl 8 NG34 122 E2
Inglenook Dr 2 DN8 15 B8
Ingleton Ave HU4 179 C6
Inglewood Ct DN16 185 A4
Inglewood Dr 4 HU4 179 B5
Ingmires 7 HU15 2 D6
INGOLDMELLS PE25 90 E4
Ingoldmells Prim Sch PE25 90 D4
Ingoldmells Rd PE24 102 E8
INGOLDSBY NG33 141 D5
Ingoldsby Prim Sch NG33 141 D5
Ingoldsby Rd NG33 141 B3
Ingram Cres 9 DN7 14 C4
Ingram Gdns 11 DN20 30 E8
Ingram Gr 10 DN7 14 C4
Ingram La NG23 78 A1
Ingram Pl DN35 192 D2
Ingram Rd
Boston PE21 208 D6
Hatfield DN7 14 C3
Ingram Row LN9 199 B3
Ing Rd PE20 134 F4
Ings Bank PE22 126 E7
Ings Dro
Butterwick PE22 126 D7
Leverton PE22 113 E1
Ings La
Belchford LN9 73 B2
Brackenborough with Little Grimsby LN11 49 B4
Bratoft PE24 102 C6
Brough HU15 2 C5
Cumberworth LN13 89 E7
Ellerker HU15 1 F8
2 Hibaldstow DN20 31 A5
Horsington LN10 84 D2
Immingham DN40 186 E3
1 Kirk Bramwith DN7 14 C7
Leverton PE22 126 F7
Little Steeping PE23 101 E5
North Coates DN36 37 A3
North Ferriby HU14 3 A4
Saltfleetby LN11 62 F8
Scamblesby LN11 73 A4
Skidbrooke with Saltfleet Haven LN11 51 A3
South Cave HU15 1 E7
South Somercotes LN11 50 E3
Walkerith DN21 40 C3
Waltham DN37 194 F4
6 West Ashby LN9 85 E7
West Ashby LN9 199 D8
West Stockwith DN10 40 C6
Winterton DN15 9 D7
Ings Rd
Benington PE22 126 D8
Gringley on the Hill DN10 39 B3
Kirton in Lindsey DN21 29 F1
Mablethorpe & Sutton LN12 76 E7
INGTHORPE PE9 218 A8
Inhams Cl PE13 177 D5
Inley Dro PE12 169 A8
Inner St NG31 211 B3
Innings The 1 NG34 212 D3
Innovation Way
Alwalton PE2 229 B5
Great Coates DN37 24 B6
Inns Cl LN6 204 E3
Inshops Ctr DN32 189 B1
Intax Mews DN32 191 F6
Inverness Rd 14 DN7 14 D4
Iona Cl DN21 197 E6
Iona Dr DN36 36 D8
Ipswich Gdns NG31 210 E5
Irby Cres 9 PE12 158 B7
Irby Ct DN35 192 D3
IRBY IN THE MARSH PE24 102 B6
Irby Pl PE21 208 F5
Irby Rd DN17 184 E5
Irby St PE21 208 E5
IRBY UPON HUMBER DN37 34 D7
Irchester Pl PE3 225 D5
Ireland Wlk HU4 179 B4
Ireton Ave NG24 104 C4
Irish Hill LN11 198 A5
IRNHAM NG33 141 E1
Irnham Rd
Corby Glen NG33 141 C1
Stamford PE9 219 C7
Iron Bar Dro PE11 155 F4
Ironestone Cl LN2 202 C5
Ironmonger St 5 PE9 219 C5
Irvine Rd 2 DN16 185 C5
Irwin Rd DN21 41 C6
Isaac Newton Prim Sch The NG31 210 F3
Isaac Newton Way NG31 211 F6
Isaac's Hill DN35 192 E6
Isaan Newton Ctr 14 NG31 211 A4
Isham Rd 1 PE3 225 D4
Isis Ct HU9 181 B5
ISLAND CARR DN20 196 B2
Island Carr Rd DN20 196 A3
Island Rd DN17 7 E6
Isle Cl 3 DN17 16 D8
Islip Ct 2 LN9 199 D3
Ison Cl 4 NG34 120 E8
Itlings La HU13 178 F1
Itterby Cres DN35 192 C3
Itter Cres PE4 221 C1
Ivanhoe Rd 4 DN16 183 C1
Ivatt Ct 13 NG31 210 E2
Ivatt Way PE3 225 C6
Ivel Cl 6 LN12 64 B5
Ivel Gr 4 LN12 64 B5
Ivery La PE22 114 D4
Ivesdyke Cl 3 PE13 170 B2
Ivy Cl DN7 14 E4
Ivy Cres PE21 208 D3
Ivy Farm Ct 20 DN41 23 F5
Ivy Gr PE4 221 B2
Ivy La
Coningsby LN4 207 F1
Grainthorpe LN11 37 E1
Wainfleet St Mary PE24 115 C8

J

Jack Haws La 3 PE9 172 D4
Jack Hunt Sch PE3 225 B3
Jack Hunt Swimming Pool PE3 225 B3
Jacklin Cl 5 LN11 50 B8
Jacklin Cres LN12 64 A4
Jacklin Dr 3 LN11 51 C4
Jacklin La DN17 7 C3
Jacklins App DN16 185 A3
Jack Row La DN7 14 B8
Jackson Dr 3 PE20 136 C5
Jackson Mews 6 DN40 186 A4
Jackson Rd 1 DN15 182 E3
Jackson's Field LN8 57 B7
Jacksons La 4 PE24 102 E8
Jackson's Pl DN36 192 D1
Jackson St
Grimsby DN31 191 C8
Kingston upon Hull HU3 180 D4
Jacobean Rd 4 LN6 204 D6
Jacobs Ct 2 PE11 214 C6
Jade Gr 1 HU3 180 A4
Jaguar Dr LN6 204 D1
Jail La PE22 126 F2
James Ave
6 Mablethorpe/Sutton on Sea LN12 64 C2
Skegness PE25 206 B6
James Ct
Gainsborough DN21 197 D5
Louth LN11 198 C6
Jameson Bridge St 8 LN8 57 D8
Jameson St 2 HU1 180 F6
James Pl DN39 12 B1
James Rd 1 DN21 55 A8
James St
Boston PE21 208 E5
Brigg DN20 196 B3
Grimsby DN31 191 C8
Lincoln LN2 234 B3
Louth LN11 198 C6
James Way 9 DN40 186 B3
Jankin La PE34 161 F1
Janton Ct DN36 195 C7
Japan Rd DN21 197 B5
Japonica Hill 3 DN40 186 C3
Jaque's Bank DN8 16 A5
Jarratt Hill La HU15 1 D8
Jarratt St HU1 180 F7
Jarvis Cl LN6 204 F7
Jarvis's Gate PE12 159 C1
Jasmin Cl 9 PE13 170 E1
Jasmine Cl PE10 213 B7
Jasmine Ct
2 Goxhill DN19 12 A8
Peterborough PE2 229 E2
Spalding PE11 214 A2
Jasmine Way
Immingham DN40 186 C3
Yaxley PE7 233 F6
Jasmin Rd LN6 204 C8
Jason Rd 5 LN6 205 A5
Javelin Ave 8 LN8 47 B6
Javelin Rd 12 LN11 62 C6
Jefferson Cl 24 PE8 172 B1
Jefferson Dr 23 HU15 2 C6
Jeffery Ave 6 PE13 170 E1
Jeffrey La DN9 16 E1
Jekil's Bank
Holbeach PE12 158 C1
Moulton PE12 167 F8
Whaplode PE12 168 B8
Jekil's Gate PE12 159 A5
Jellicoe Ave LN2 202 D3
Jellicoe Ct DN16 183 C1
Jellings Pl PE1 226 A4
Jenkins Cl
Louth LN11 198 C8
5 Skegness PE25 206 A7
Jenkins' La PE22 127 A6
Jenner Ct 2 DN35 192 B8
Jenner Pl DN35 192 B8
Jenning St HU8 181 A8
Jenny Brough La HU13 178 B3
Jenny Brough Mdws HU13 178 B3
Jenny Cl HU13 178 B3
Jensen Rd LN4 205 F2
Jericho La DN40 12 D7
Jermyn Mews LN4 203 D1
Jermyn St NG34 212 D4
Jerusalem LN6 79 F5
Jerusalem Rd LN6 200 A4
Jesmond Ave 5 DN17 184 E3
Jesmond View LN1 201 E8
Jessop Cl
Beacon Hill NG24 104 B5
Cherry Willingham/Reepham LN3 203 E5
Horncastle LN9 199 C3
9 Leasingham NG34 121 B8
Jessop Way NG24 104 B5
Jiggle's Gate PE12 158 F1
Jill Gr HU13 178 F1
Job's La LN6 79 C1
Jobson Rd LN9 199 D2
Jock Hedge PE24 102 E6
Joel Sq 8 NG34 107 F1
John Adams Way PE21 208 F4
John Brown Cl LN9 199 A4
John Clare Prim Sch PE6 173 B4
John Coupland Hospl DN21 197 B7
John Eve Way PE6 217 B6
John Fielding Com Specl Sch PE21 209 A6
John Foster Cl 9 NG31 211 D7
John Gold Ave 6 NG24 104 A4
John Harrison CE Prim Sch DN19 11 C8
John Harrison's Cl 3 DN19 11 D8
John Harrison Way PE12 215 B2
John Harrox Prim Sch The PE12 157 F7
John Hunt Infants Sch NG24 104 B3
John Hunt Jun Sch The NG24 104 B2
John Leggott Sixth Form Coll DN17 184 E8
John Mansfield Sch PE1 226 B8
John Smith Cl LN13 89 A6
Johnson Ave PE11 214 E2
Johnson Cl
8 Belton DN9 16 E2
3 Skegness PE25 206 A7
Johnson Ct LN4 207 B6
Johnson Dr
Bracebridge Heath LN4 205 F4
9 Scotter DN21 29 C4
Johnson Hospl PE11 214 D3
Johnson's Dro PE13 177 B6
Johnson's La 7 DN17 16 D7
Johnsons Rd 6 NG24 104 C1
Johnson St DN35 192 B8
Johnson Way 14 PE24 102 E7
Johnson Wlk PE1 225 F7
John Spendluffe Tech Coll LN13 75 F2
John St
Lincoln LN2 234 C2
13 Market Rasen LN8 57 D8
Johnston's Rd DN7 14 E7
John Swain's Way PE12 216 C5
John Wake Cl 2 PE6 217 B6
John Wesley Rd PE4 220 E3
Jolls La LN9 86 C5
Jolly Comm La LN13 77 A3
Jolly Farmer La PE21 126 C3
Jonathan Dr PE25 206 C8
Jonathan Gdns 1 NG34 212 F3
Jonquil Ave DN16 185 D5
Jordan Mews 2 PE1 226 B3
Jordan's Cradge Bank Rd PE11 156 C2
Jorose St 4 PE3 225 A3
Jorose Way PE3 224 F3
Joseph Ogle Cl DN36 195 B7
Joseph Ruston Tech Coll LN6 205 B5
Joseph St DN31 191 C8
Joshua Way 4 DN21 43 D7
Joy Paine Cl PE21 208 C6
Joy's Bank PE12 158 E1
Jubilee Ave
Boston PE21 208 E6
Faldingworth LN8 56 F3
Grantham NG31 211 C5
Jubilee Cl
4 Bardney LN3 83 B4
Cherry Willingham/Reepham LN3 203 E6
Coningsby LN4 207 D5
1 Hogsthorpe PE24 90 B7
17 Kirton PE20 136 C5
Lincoln LN6 204 F1
Long Sutton PE12 216 C5
Martin LN4 96 C2

Jubilee Cl *continued*
8 Morton PE10 ... 154 C7
Scotter DN21 ... 29 B3
1 Spalding PE11 ... 214 C4
Jubilee Cres
Gainsborough DN21 ... 197 D5
Louth LN11 ... 198 C8
Jubilee Ct 6 NG34 ... 212 E4
Jubilee Dr
3 Bardney LN3 ... 83 C4
10 Wragby LN8 ... 70 D4
Jubilee Gr NG34 ... 212 C6
Jubilee Parade 6 PE24 ... 90 D7
Jubilee Rd LN11 ... 50 E7
Jubilee St
Peterborough PE2 ... 230 F8
2 Ruskington NG34 ... 108 E1
Jubilee Way
Crowland PE6 ... 166 F1
Horncastle LN9 ... 199 B4
Scunthorpe DN15 ... 183 B3
Jude Gate PE22 ... 114 E3
Judge Cl 3 PE21 ... 209 C4
Judy Cross PE11 ... 145 B8
Julian Cl HU5 ... 179 A7
Julian St DN32 ... 192 A7
Julian's Wlk 3 HU10 ... 178 F6
Julia Rd LN4 ... 203 D1
Julia's Mead 12 PE11 ... 214 B5
Junction Rd 10 DN7 ... 14 C6
Junella Cl HU3 ... 180 A4
Jungle Zoo The* DN35 ... 193 B3
Junior Cadets Rd NG34 ... 120 B8
Juniper Cl
Flixborough DN15 ... 182 C6
10 Leasingham NG34 ... 121 B7
3 Lincoln LN5 ... 205 C2
Spalding PE11 ... 214 F4
Juniper Cres
Peterborough PE3 ... 225 A2
Spalding PE11 ... 214 F5
Juniper Dr 13 LN2 ... 68 F4
Juniper Way
Gainsborough DN21 ... 197 D5
Grimsby DN33 ... 191 C2
3 Sleaford NG34 ... 212 D2
Jury Rd PE7 ... 233 C8
Justice Hall La 10 DN17 ... 16 D8
Justice La DN14 ... 7 B8
Jutland Ct 1 DN36 ... 195 D7

K

Karelia Ct HU4 ... 179 B5
Karen Ave 12 DN41 ... 23 A4
Karsons Way LN2 ... 68 D7
Katherine Cres PE25 ... 206 D2
Kathleen Ave
Cleethorpes DN35 ... 192 D8
Scunthorpe DN16 ... 185 B5
Kathleen Gr DN32 ... 192 C7
Kathleen Rice Cl DN35 ... 192 A8
Kaymile Cl 13 DN36 ... 195 C6
KEADBY DN17 ... 17 D7
Keadby Cl LN6 ... 204 F7
Keal Carr Nature Reserve* PE23 ... 100 E7
KEAL COTES PE23 ... 100 C4
Keal Hill PE23 ... 100 B7
Kealholme Rd DN17 ... 29 D7
Keaton Cl PE25 ... 206 A5
Keats Ave
Grantham NG31 ... 211 E6
Scunthorpe DN17 ... 184 D7
Keats Cl
Lincoln LN2 ... 202 C7
17 Mablethorpe/Sutton on Sea LN12 ... 77 A7
Keats Dr NG34 ... 121 E4
Keats Gr 2 PE9 ... 218 E5
Keats Way PE1 ... 225 D7
Keb La DN15 ... 9 D2
Keble Cl 4 PE9 ... 219 A7
Keble Ct 1 LN4 ... 207 B5
KEDDINGTON LN11 ... 198 F8
Keddington Ave LN1 ... 201 E8
Keddington Cres 2 LN11 ... 198 D7
Keddington Rd
Louth LN11 ... 198 C7
Scunthorpe DN17 ... 184 F4
Kedlestone Rd NG31 ... 210 F1
Kedleston Rd PE7 ... 231 F6
Keeble Dr LN4 ... 203 D1
KEELBY DN41 ... 23 A5
Keelby Prim Sch DN41 ... 23 A5
Keelby Rd
6 Gainsborough DN21 ... 53 A8
Scunthorpe DN17 ... 184 F5
Stallingborough DN41 ... 23 C6
Keel Dr 9 NG13 ... 128 A5
Keeling St 7 LN11 ... 50 F7
Keepers Cl 2 LN2 ... 68 D7
Keepers Way NG34 ... 212 E3
Keeper's Way 6 DN9 ... 16 E1
Keeton Rd PE1 ... 225 E7
Keightley Rd PE12 ... 147 B5
Keir Hardie Wlk DN32 ... 191 D7
KEISBY PE10 ... 141 F3
Keith Cres 15 DN37 ... 23 F1
KELBY NG32 ... 131 C8
KELFIELD DN9 ... 28 C4
Kelham Rd
9 Great Gonerby NG31 ... 129 E5

Kelham Rd *continued*
2 Great Gonerby NG31 ... 210 E8
Grimsby DN32 ... 192 D6
Kellet Gate PE12 ... 157 B5
Kells Cl 6 LN5 ... 205 D3
Kell's Dro PE20 ... 124 E1
Kelly Cl 14 PE11 ... 156 E8
Kelsey Ave DN15 ... 182 B3
Kelsey La 1 DN17 ... 17 D4
Kelsey Rd LN7 ... 32 C2
Kelsey St LN1 ... 234 A2
Kelso Ct PE4 ... 221 A1
KELSTERN LN11 ... 48 A1
Kelstern Cl 1 LN6 ... 204 C6
Kelstern Ct 1 DN34 ... 191 A5
Kelstern Rd LN6 ... 204 C6
Kelston Dr 2 HU13 ... 179 A3
Kelthorpe Cl PE9 ... 171 A2
Kemble Cl LN6 ... 204 B8
Kemeshame Ct DN37 ... 194 F4
Kemp Rd
Grimsby DN31 ... 189 C3
3 Swanland HU14 ... 3 B6
Kemp St PE6 ... 166 E1
Kempton Cl 3 PE11 ... 156 E3
Kempton Dr 4 DN7 ... 14 C2
Kempton Rd HU3 ... 179 E6
Kempton Vale DN35 ... 192 F1
Kempton Way NG31 ... 210 F4
Kendal Cl 2 PE4 ... 221 D2
Kendal Ct DN16 ... 185 C6
Kendale Rd DN16 ... 185 E8
Kendal Rd DN40 ... 186 E3
Kendal Way HU5 ... 179 C7
Kendon Gdns DN8 ... 15 B8
Kendrick Cl PE2 ... 231 D6
Kenford Ct DN36 ... 195 C7
Kenilworth Cl 3 LN1 ... 66 D2
Kenilworth Dr LN6 ... 205 C5
Kenilworth Rd
Cleethorpes DN35 ... 192 D4
Grantham NG31 ... 211 F5
Scunthorpe DN16 ... 183 C1
Kenlan Rd 23 PE13 ... 170 D1
Kenleigh Dr PE21 ... 209 D4
Kenmare Cres DN21 ... 197 F2
Kenmar Rd 20 DN37 ... 23 F1
Kennedy Ave
21 Alford LN13 ... 75 F2
Skegness PE25 ... 206 C2
Kennedy Cl DN20 ... 196 E3
Kennedy Rd
Bracebridge Heath LN4 ... 205 F3
Holbeach PE12 ... 215 C4
Kennedy Way DN40 ... 186 C4
Kennedy Way Sh Ctr DN40 ... 186 C4
Kennel La
Doddington & Whisby LN6 ... 79 E5
Reepham LN3 ... 203 E8
Kennels Rd PE6 ... 224 D4
Kennel Wlk LN3 ... 203 F8
Kenner Cl 4 LN6 ... 205 A6
Kennet Gdns PE4 ... 221 C1
Kenneth Ave
2 Burgh le Marsh PE24 ... 102 E8
8 Hatfield DN7 ... 14 C2
5 Stainforth DN7 ... 14 C6
Kenneth Campbell Rd 4 DN36 ... 37 C5
Kenneth St 1 LN1 ... 201 F6
Kennington Cl LN2 ... 68 E5
Kennulphs Cl 5 PE6 ... 175 C8
Kensington Cl PE12 ... 215 F3
Kensington Dr 6 PE11 ... 214 B2
Kensington Gdns 7 LN12 ... 64 B3
Kensington Pl DN33 ... 195 A8
Kensington Rd DN15 ... 182 B3
Ken Stimpson Com Sch PE4 ... 220 F4
Kent Ave LN12 ... 63 F5
Kent Cl
Kingston upon Hull HU9 ... 181 C7
3 Sutton Bridge PE12 ... 160 E4
Kent Dr 4 DN20 ... 31 A5
Kentmere Pl 4 PE4 ... 221 D2
Kent Rd
9 Binbrook Tech Pk LN8 ... 47 B6
Leake Commonside PE22 ... 113 F3
Peterborough PE3 ... 225 E2
Kent St
Grimsby DN32 ... 189 B1
6 Lincoln LN2 ... 202 C3
Kenwardly Rd HU10 ... 178 E8
Kenwick Cl LN11 ... 198 D3
Kenwick Dr NG31 ... 211 D4
Kenwick Gdns LN11 ... 198 D3
Kenwick Hill
Legbourne LN11 ... 198 E1
Raithby cum Maltby LN11 ... 61 C3
Kenwick Pastures LN11 ... 198 D3
Kenwick Rd LN11 ... 198 D2
Kenya Dr DN17 ... 184 F2
Kenyon Cl 8 DN8 ... 15 A8
Kerries Wlk DN17 ... 184 C7
Kerrison View 5 LN2 ... 68 D2
Kerr's Cres NG32 ... 118 D2
Kerry Dr HU10 ... 178 C6
Kerry Pit Way HU10 ... 178 C6
Kesgrave St 1 DN31 ... 189 C1
Kesteven Cl 1 PE6 ... 217 D4

Kesteven Ct
3 Habrough DN40 ... 22 E8
7 Lincoln LN6 ... 204 D2
Kesteven Dr 7 PE6 ... 217 A6
Kesteven Gr 19 DN17 ... 16 D8
Kesteven & Grantham Girl's Sch NG31 ... 211 B5
Kesteven Rd PE9 ... 219 C7
Kesteven & Sleaford Girl's High Sch NG34 ... 212 D4
Kesteven St
Lincoln LN5 ... 234 B1
1 Sleaford NG34 ... 212 E4
Kesteven Way 7 PE10 ... 213 C5
Kesteven Wlk 3 PE1 ... 226 B2
Kestrel Cl
6 Birchwood LN6 ... 204 D8
Clinton Park LN4 ... 207 C6
2 Sleaford NG34 ... 212 B3
Kestrel Ct
Grantham NG31 ... 210 F2
Longthorpe PE3 ... 225 A2
Kestrel Dr
Bourne PE10 ... 213 E3
Louth LN11 ... 198 D8
Kestrel Rd
8 Scopwick Heath LN4 ... 108 A7
Scunthorpe DN17 ... 184 E6
Kestrel Rise LN6 ... 79 B1
Keswick Cl 2 PE4 ... 221 D3
Ketco Ave PE9 ... 171 A4
Ketel Cl PE12 ... 216 C3
Ketlock Hill La 1 DN22 ... 52 B1
KETSBY LN11 ... 74 D3
Kettering Rd
Scunthorpe DN16 ... 183 C2
Wothorpe PE9 ... 219 B2
Kettlebridge La DN40 ... 12 E6
Kettleby La DN20 ... 20 E3
Kettleby View 3 DN20 ... 196 D4
KETTLETHORPE LN1 ... 65 F2
Kettlethorpe Dr 17 HU15 ... 2 D5
Kettlethorpe Rd LN1 ... 65 E3
Kettlewell St DN32 ... 191 E5
KETTON PE9 ... 171 A3
Ketton CE Prim Sch PE9 ... 171 A3
Ketton Rd PE9 ... 171 B2
Kew Rd DN35 ... 192 E6
KEXBY DN21 ... 53 E5
Kexby La DN21 ... 53 C4
Kexby Mill Cl 5 LN6 ... 93 B8
Kexby Rd DN21 ... 54 D6
Kexby Wlk DN21 ... 197 F3
Keyholme La DN36 ... 37 D2
Key Theatre* PE1 ... 226 B1
Keyworth Dr 10 LN7 ... 33 B4
Khormaksar Dr LN4 ... 95 C7
Kiddier Ave DN37 ... 194 D7
Kidd La HU15 ... 2 D6
Kidgate LN11 ... 198 B5
Kidgate Mews LN11 ... 198 B5
Kidgate Prim Sch LN11 ... 198 C5
Kilburn Cres 1 LN6 ... 205 A6
Kildare Dr PE3 ... 225 C4
Kilham PE2 ... 229 E2
Killarney Cl NG31 ... 211 E7
Killingholme Haven Pits Nature Reserve* DN40 ... 13 A6
Killingholme Prim Sch DN40 ... 12 E3
Killingholme Rd DN40 ... 12 F2
Kiln Hill 4 LN8 ... 59 A7
Kiln La
Brigg DN20 ... 196 B3
Fulbeck NG32 ... 106 C1
Immingham DN41 ... 187 C2
Louth LN11 ... 198 B6
Stallingborough DN41 ... 186 F1
Kiln La Ind Est DN41 ... 187 B3
Kiln La Trading Est DN41 ... 187 C2
Kilnwell Rd 12 LN8 ... 57 D8
Kiln Yd LN11 ... 198 C5
Kilverstone PE4 ... 220 F6
KILVINGTON NG13 ... 117 A1
Kimberley St HU3 ... 180 C7
Kimberley Terr NG31 ... 210 E7
Kimblewick La PE11 ... 214 A2
Kimbolton Ct PE1 ... 225 F3
Kime Cl NG34 ... 142 C8
Kime's La 6 PE22 ... 98 F4
Kinder Ave LN6 ... 205 A2
Kinderley Rd PE13 ... 170 D2
King Charles Cl HU10 ... 178 E7
King Edward Fst Sch DN8 ... 15 B8
King Edward Rd
Thorne/Moorends DN8 ... 15 A8
2 Woodhall Spa LN10 ... 97 C6
King Edward St
Belton DN9 ... 16 E2
4 Grimsby DN31 ... 189 A1
3 Kingston upon Hull HU1 ... 180 F6
Kirton in Lindsey DN21 ... 30 B1
Scunthorpe DN16 ... 183 A1
Sleaford NG34 ... 212 C3
King Edwards Terr 4 HU15 ... 2 B5
King Edward VI Sch
Louth LN11 ... 198 A5
Splisby PE23 ... 87 F1
KINGERBY LN8 ... 44 E3

Kingerby Beck Mdws Nature Reserve* LN8 ... 44 E5
Kingerby Cl DN21 ... 197 E3
Kingerby Rd DN17 ... 184 E5
Kingfisher Cl
2 Birchwood LN6 ... 204 D8
Brigg DN20 ... 196 A3
Scunthorpe DN15 ... 182 D5
Yaxley PE7 ... 233 D5
Kingfisher Ct 2 PE11 ... 214 F2
Kingfisher Dr
2 Skegness PE25 ... 206 A7
4 Surfleet PE11 ... 145 E3
Kingfishers PE2 ... 229 D6
King George Ave 1 LN10 ... 97 D6
King Georges Ct 3 DN7 ... 14 C5
King George V Ave 1 PE12 ... 215 F3
King George V Stadium DN32 ... 192 B5
King Henry Chase PE3 ... 225 A5
King John Bank
2 Sutton Bridge PE14 ... 170 F8
Walpole PE14 ... 161 A2
King Johns Rd 6 PE20 ... 135 B7
King John St NG34 ... 212 C4
King St E DN21 ... 197 D3
King St La LE14 ... 150 A6
Kings Arms Yd 2 LN2 ... 234 B2
Kings Ave PE25 ... 206 E8
King's Ave
Boston PE21 ... 209 C3
Brigg DN20 ... 196 D3
King's Bench St HU3 ... 180 B5
Kingsbridge Ct 1 PE4 ... 220 E5
King's Causeway DN14 ... 6 E8
Kings Cl PE22 ... 112 C8
King's Cl 15 DN7 ... 14 D4
Kingscliffe Rd NG31 ... 211 A8
King's Cres
Boston PE21 ... 209 C3
Swineshead PE20 ... 135 B8
Kings Croft 1 DN17 ... 16 E6
King's Cross Cl 2 HU3 ... 180 C6
Kings Ct
19 Kirton PE20 ... 136 C5
Louth LN11 ... 198 E7
Old Bolingbroke PE23 ... 100 A7
9 Scawby DN20 ... 30 F8
Scunthorpe DN15 ... 183 B4
Kingsdale DN17 ... 184 E2
King's Delph Dro PE7 ... 231 E2
Kingsdown Rd LN6 ... 204 B7
Kings Dyke Cl PE2 ... 231 E6
Kingsgate PE12 ... 159 E7
Kings Gate DN32 ... 192 A7
King's Gdns PE1 ... 226 A5
Kings Hill 2 NG32 ... 119 B7
Kings Leigh 1 HU3 ... 180 C6
Kingsley Ave PE10 ... 213 B5
Kingsley Cl
4 Barnack PE9 ... 172 D3
6 Brough HU15 ... 2 B5
Kingsley Gr DN33 ... 191 C4
Kingsley Rd
14 Mablethorpe/Sutton on Sea LN12 ... 64 B4
North Hykeham LN6 ... 204 B5
Peterborough PE1 ... 226 C4
Kingsley St LN1 ... 234 A4
Kingsline Cl 1 PE6 ... 176 A3
Kings Mews DN35 ... 193 C1
Kings Parade DN35 ... 193 A5
Kingsport Cl HU3 ... 180 A7
Kings Rd
Holbeach PE12 ... 215 F3
Immingham DN40 ... 186 E5
Metheringham LN4 ... 95 C4
Peterborough PE2 ... 231 B6
Stamford PE9 ... 219 B6
King's Rd
Barnetby le Wold DN38 ... 21 B5
Humberston DN35 ... 193 B3
Spalding PE11 ... 214 D5
Kings Sch PE1 ... 226 A4
Kings Sch The NG31 ... 211 B5
King St
1 Billinghay LN4 ... 109 F5
Boston PE21 ... 208 E4
East Halton DN40 ... 12 D7
Gainsborough DN21 ... 197 D3
15 Goxhill DN19 ... 12 A8
2 Keelby DN41 ... 23 A4
10 Kirton PE20 ... 136 C5
Lincoln LN5 ... 234 A1
14 Mablethorpe/Sutton on Sea LN12 ... 64 B3
Market Rasen LN8 ... 57 D8
1 Peterborough PE1 ... 226 A2
Scunthorpe DN15 ... 183 B4
18 Sutton Bridge PE12 ... 160 E4
Thorne/Moorends DN8 ... 15 A8
Wainfleet All Saints PE24 ... 102 A2
West Deeping PE6 ... 173 A8
Wilsford NG32 ... 120 A1
Winterton DN15 ... 9 A5
Yarburgh LN11 ... 49 E4
Kingsthorpe Cres PE25 ... 206 C1
Kingston Ave
Grantham NG31 ... 210 E4
Grimsby DN34 ... 191 A6
Kingston upon Hull HU13 ... 178 F1
Kingston Cl 7 DN35 ... 193 A1

Kingston Communications Stadium (Hull City AFC Hull RLFC)* HU3 ... 180 B7
Kingston Dr PE2 ... 231 E5
Kingston Rd
Kingston upon Hull HU10 ... 178 F8
Scunthorpe DN16 ... 185 A7
Kingston Ret Pk HU1 ... 180 E5
Kingston St HU1 ... 180 E5
Kingston Terr NG34 ... 212 E5
KINGSTON UPON HULL HU1 ... 180 F4
Kingston View 20 DN18 ... 10 F8
Kingston Wharf 4 HU1 ... 180 F5
Kingsway
Boston PE21 ... 209 B3
Bourne PE10 ... 213 D6
3 Brigg DN20 ... 196 B4
Cleethorpes DN35 ... 193 A5
11 Leverington PE13 ... 170 E1
Lincoln LN5 ... 201 F1
Nettleham LN2 ... 68 C2
Scunthorpe DN15 ... 182 C3
Stainforth DN7 ... 14 C6
Tealby LN8 ... 46 C1
Kings Way LN2 ... 68 C7
Kingsway Sta DN35 ... 193 B4
Kings Wlk 11 NG31 ... 211 A4
KINGTHORPE LN8 ... 70 C2
King William Cl 4 PE34 ... 161 F3
Kinloch Way DN40 ... 186 B2
Kinloss Cl 11 LN6 ... 204 C6
Kinnears Wlk PE2 ... 229 F2
Kinoulton Ct 16 NG31 ... 210 E2
Kinross Rd NG34 ... 120 F2
Kinsbourne Gn 40 DN7 ... 14 D4
Kinsley Wlk 8 DN15 ... 183 B3
Kintore Dr NG31 ... 211 C4
Kipling Ave 4 DN17 ... 184 D7
Kipling Cl
4 Grantham NG31 ... 211 E6
3 Stamford PE9 ... 218 E5
St Giles LN2 ... 202 B7
Kipling Ct PE1 ... 225 E8
Kipling Dr
4 Mablethorpe/Sutton on Sea LN12 ... 77 A7
14 Sleaford NG34 ... 212 F4
Kiplington Cl HU3 ... 180 A7
Kipling Wlk 1 HU4 ... 179 D2
Kippings The 8 PE10 ... 164 C8
Kirby Ct 5 PE11 ... 214 F4
Kirby Wlk 2 PE3 ... 225 C4
KIRK BRAMWITH DN7 ... 14 A6
KIRKBY LN8 ... 44 F3
Kirkby Bank PE23 ... 99 E3
KIRKBY FENSIDE PE23 ... 99 E4
Kirkby Gr DN33 ... 191 A3
Kirkby Gravel Pit Nature Reserve* LN4 ... 207 A8
KIRKBY GREEN LN4 ... 108 E8
Kirkby La
Coningsby LN4 ... 207 D8
Woodhall Spa LN10 ... 97 E6
KIRKBY LA THORPE NG34 ... 121 F5
Kirkby la Thorpe CE Prim Sch NG34 ... 121 F4
Kirkby Moor Nature Reserve* LN10 ... 98 A5
KIRKBY ON BAIN LN10 ... 98 B5
Kirkby on Bain CE Prim Sch LN10 ... 98 C5
Kirkby Rd
Ewerby & Evedon NG34 ... 122 B5
Scunthorpe DN17 ... 184 E4
Kirkby St LN5 ... 201 F1
KIRKBY UNDERWOOD PE10 ... 142 D2
Kirkby Underwood Rd PE10 ... 154 A8
Kirkdale Cl 4 NG34 ... 121 B8
Kirkden Paddocks DN9 ... 16 C2
KIRK ELLA HU10 ... 178 C8
Kirkgate PE13 ... 169 F7
Kirk Gate
Waltham DN37 ... 194 E4
6 Whaplode PE12 ... 158 B7
Kirkgate St PE13 ... 170 E1
Kirk Gdns PE21 ... 208 D7
Kirkham Cl HU13 ... 178 F2
Kirkhouse Gn Rd DN7 ... 14 A8
Kirklands Rd HU5 ... 179 E8
Kirkmeadow PE3 ... 225 A8
Kirk Rise HU10 ... 178 C7
Kirkside DN37 ... 194 D4
Kirkstall PE2 ... 230 B3
Kirkstall Cl LN2 ... 202 E6
Kirkstead Bridge LN10 ... 97 B4
Kirkstead Cres DN33 ... 191 B3
Kirkstead Ct 8 LN10 ... 97 D5
Kirkstone House Sch PE6 ... 164 E4
Kirkton Gate PE3 ... 225 A1
Kirkway HU10 ... 178 B7
Kirkwood Cl PE3 ... 225 E2
Kirman Cres 5 DN17 ... 184 F3
KIRMINGTON DN39 ... 22 A6
Kirmington CE Prim Sch DN39 ... 22 A6
Kirmington Cl 8 LN6 ... 204 C6

Kirmington Gdns 3 DN34 191 A7
KIRMOND LE MIRE LN8 46 F3
Kirmond Rd LN8 47 A4
Kirness Dro LN4 109 C6
KIRTON PE20 136 D5
Kirton Dro LN4 110 F1
KIRTON END PE20 136 B6
KIRTON HOLME PE20 135 E8
Kirton Holme Rd PE20 124 D1
KIRTON IN LINDSEY DN21 30 C2
Kirton La
Hatfield DN8 14 E7
2 Long Bennington NG23 117 D4
Stainforth DN7 14 D6
Kirton Lindsey Prim Sch DN21 30 B1
Kirton Lindsey Sta DN21 30 B2
Kirton Prim Sch PE20 136 C5
Kirton Rd
Blyton DN21 41 D6
Holme DN16 19 B2
Manton DN21 30 A3
Messingham DN17 29 E6
Scawby DN20 30 C8
Scotter DN21 29 D3
Waddingham DN21 43 B7
Kisgate 10 LN1 66 D7
Kishorn Ct DN40 186 B2
Kisimul Sch LN6 92 A6
Kit Cat La PE20 145 F8
Kitty Briggs La NG31 210 E1
Kitwood Cl 4 PE21 209 B4
Kitwood Rd PE21 209 B4
KNAITH DN21 53 A3
Knaith Hall La DN22 52 E3
Knaith Hill DN21 53 A3
KNAITH PARK DN21 53 B4
Knapton Ct LN7 33 B4
Knarr Fen Rd PE6 176 E2
Kneeland 24 LN2 68 D6
Knight Cl PE6 217 D5
Knighton Cl PE7 230 D1
Knight Pl 2 LN5 205 E8
Knightsbridge 2 DN36 195 C6
Knightsbridge Rd 41 DN17 29 D7
Knights Cl
5 Belton DN9 16 E2
18 Laceby DN37 23 F1
Leverington PE13 170 B2
Knight's Ct DN16 185 A3
Knight St
Grimsby DN32 192 B6
4 Lincoln LN5 205 E8
2 Pinchbeck PE11 145 B1
Knight Terr LN5 205 E8
Knipe Ave PE11 214 C3
KNIPTON NG32 138 C6
Knipton La NG32 138 D6
Knipton Rd NG32 138 B4
Knole Wlk PE3 225 B3
Knoll St DN35 192 F6
Knolls The NG32 210 B5
Knoll The NG31 210 D8
Knowle St 20 LN12 64 B3
Kohima Cl 3 PE10 213 E7
Kooreman Ave 19 PE13 170 D1
Kyme Rd
Boston PE21 208 D6
Heckington NG34 122 E3

L

Labour in Vain Dro LN4 110 A6
Labrador Dr 11 DN20 19 E4
Laburnham Ave DN37 194 D4
Laburnham Cl DN37 194 D4
Laburnum Ave
Gainsborough DN21 197 D6
4 Gunness DN15 17 E6
Yaxley PE7 233 F6
Laburnum Cl
3 Bourne PE10 213 C6
Grantham NG31 211 D5
Lincoln LN6 205 A2
7 Wisbech PE13 170 E1
Laburnum Cres LN11 198 E4
Laburnum Ct
2 Cherry Willingham/Reepham LN3 82 A8
Hessle HU13 178 E1
Laburnum Dr
Cherry Willingham/Reepham LN3 203 D5
Grimsby DN34 190 E7
Ingoldmells PE25 206 D8
3 Kingston upon Hull HU5 179 B7
Morton PE10 154 B7
Laburnum Gr
8 Burton upon Stather DN15 8 B5
16 Crowle DN17 16 D7
Peterborough PE1 226 B8
Scunthorpe DN16 185 B7
Spalding PE11 214 F5
Laburnum Rd NG34 107 C2
LACEBY DN37 23 E1
LACEBY ACRES DN34 190 C4
Laceby Acres Prim Sch DN34 190 D5
Laceby Rd
Grimsby DN34 191 A4
Laceby DN37 190 C3
Scunthorpe DN17 184 E5
Laceby St LN2 202 B3
Lacey Gdns LN11 198 D6
Lacey Gdns Jun Sch LN11 198 D6
Lacey's Cl PE22 126 F6
Lacey's Dr PE22 126 F6
Lacey's La PE22 126 E6
Lacy Cl 21 LN2 68 D2
Ladbroke Cl 7 NG34 133 D7
Ladds Cl 6 PE21 209 C4
Ladd's Mill Cl 7 LN6 93 B8
LADE BANK PE22 113 F5
Lade Bank
Old Leake PE22 113 F5
Wrangle PE22 114 B6
Lady Bower Cl 9 LN6 205 A2
Ladybower Way PE4 221 C3
Lady Charlotte Rd PE7 230 C3
Lady Fen La LN13 76 B1
Lady Frances Cres DN35 192 C5
Lady Frances Dr 1 LN8 57 D8
Lady Jane Franklin Sch The PE23 87 F1
Lady La PE24 102 A2
Lady Lodge Dr PE2 230 A5
Lady Margaret's Ave PE6 217 C5
Lady Matilda's Dr PE25 206 C8
Lady Meers Rd LN3 203 E6
Lady Romayne Cl PE9 219 C4
Ladysmith Rd DN32 191 F7
Ladysmith Terr NG31 210 E7
Ladywell Gate 4 HU15 2 E6
Ladywood Rd PE11 214 E6
Lafford Ct NG34 212 B5
Lafford Dr 2 LN4 109 F6
Lafford High Sch The LN4 109 F6
Laforey Rd DN31 188 A3
Lagonda Cl LN4 205 F1
Lagoon Rd DN17 184 B6
Laing Cl 2 LN3 83 B4
Lakeside
Anderby PE24 77 C3
Great Coates DN37 24 B6
Peterborough PE4 221 B5
Peterborough PE7 230 C2
Pyewipe DN37 188 A3
Lakeside Dr DN17 184 C5
Lakeside Gr HU4 179 D4
Lakeside Leisure Ctr PE2 230 A5
Lakeside Parkway DN16 185 F5
Lakeside Ret Pk DN16 185 F6
Lakeside Sta DN35 193 B2
Lakeview Cl 3 LN6 204 C1
Lake View Rd LN6 205 C6
Lakeview Way PE7 230 C2
Lalrgate Pl DN35 192 F1
Lambert Ave 12 HU15 2 C6
Lambert Bank
Fleet PE12 158 D1
Holbeach PE12 168 D8
Lambert Mews 5 PE9 219 C4
Lambert Rd
4 Allington NG32 128 F7
Grimsby DN32 191 D6
Lambeth Wlk 3 PE9 219 A6
Lamb Gdns LN2 202 B6
Lamb La
Benington PE22 127 A4
Newport HU15 1 B8
Lambourn Ct 3 DN35 192 F1
Lambourne Rise DN16 185 A2
Lambourne Way 5 NG34 122 D2
Lambs Row 5 PE21 208 E6
La Milesse Way 1 PE20 135 C7
Lammas Leas Rd 4 LN8 57 E7
Lammas Rd PE1 226 A7
Lammin's La 2 PE22 99 A4
Lamport Cl 9 PE6 217 A6
Lampton Gr DN32 191 D6
Lanark St 2 HU5 180 B8
Lancaster App DN40 12 D4
Lancaster Ave
Grimsby DN31 191 B7
Horncastle LN9 199 C5
Skegness PE25 206 A5
Lancaster Cl
3 Great Steeping PE23 101 D7
Long Sutton PE12 216 C4
Stickney PE22 113 A7
6 Waddington LN5 94 A7
Lancaster Ct
6 Nunsthorpe DN33 191 B2
14 Welton/Dunholme LN2 68 D7
Yaxley PE7 233 F6
Lancaster Dr
6 Coningsby LN4 207 D4
Long Sutton PE12 216 C4
Moorland Prison DN7 26 A8
6 Scampton Airfield LN1 67 F5
Lancaster Dr *continued*
10 South Killingholme DN40 12 E3
Lancaster Gate DN36 195 C1
Lancaster Gdns 2 NG31 211 D2
Lancaster Gn DN21 54 F8
Lancaster Pl 4 LN5 201 F1
Lancaster Rd
11 Beacon Hill NG24 104 C5
3 Binbrook Tech Pk LN8 47 B6
Gringley on the Hill DN10 39 D1
Scunthorpe DN16 185 A5
10 Stamford PE9 219 B6
Lancaster Sch The LN6 204 C8
Lancaster Way
25 Brough HU15 2 C5
Market Deeping PE6 217 B7
2 Skellingthorpe LN6 200 A4
Yaxley PE7 233 F6
Lancelot Ct HU9 181 C6
Lancelot Way 7 PE11 214 B3
Lancewood Gdns 3 LN6 204 C8
Lancia Cres LN4 205 F2
Lancing Cl 7 PE4 221 A3
Lancing Way 4 DN33 194 E8
Land Dike LN11 37 A1
Landeck Ave DN34 191 B6
Landing La HU15 1 A7
Landmere Gr LN6 200 D1
Land of Gn Ginger 10 HU1 180 F6
Landor Ave 3 DN17 184 D7
Landsdowne Cl 22 LN12 77 A8
Landsdowne Ct PE11 214 F6
Landsdowne Rd 2 PE25 206 C4
Landseer Ave PE24 90 D8
LANEHAM DN22 65 A3
Laneham Rd NG22 65 A1
Laneham St
Rampton DN22 65 A5
Scunthorpe DN15 183 A3
Lanes The 10 DN36 36 D4
Lane The
1 Easton on the Hill PE9 171 D3
West Deeping PE6 173 B7
Laney Cl LN2 202 C7
Langary Gate Rd PE12 158 E1
Langdale Ave DN33 194 D7
Langdale Cres NG31 211 A8
Langdyke PE1 226 F6
Langer Cl 5 LN6 204 B6
LANGFORD NG23 91 C1
Langford Gdns NG31 211 B6
Langford La NG23 91 A2
Langford Rd PE2 231 A7
Langford Wlk 1 HU4 179 B7
Langham Rd PE24 90 B7
Langhole Dro PE11 145 B1
LANGHOLME DN9 39 E8
Langholme La DN9 27 B1
Langholme Wood Nature Reserve* DN9 39 D8
Langley PE3 225 B8
Langley Cl LN11 198 E4
Langley Dr DN16 185 A2
Langley Pl DN35 193 A4
Langley Rd LN6 204 D2
Langley Wlk DN40 186 D3
LANGRICK PE22 124 E7
LANGRICK BRIDGE PE22 124 E6
Langrick Rd
Boston PE21 208 C6
Coningsby LN4 98 C1
Holland Fen with Brothertoft PE20 124 E4
Langthwaite Cl 20 HU15 2 D5
LANGTOFT PE6 164 F3
Langtoft Outgang Rd PE11 165 D6
Langtoft Prim Sch PE6 164 F3
LANGTON
Langton by Spilsby PE23 87 F5
Langton LN9 85 B3
LANGTON BY WRAGBY LN8 70 F3
Langton Cl
Grimsby DN33 191 A3
Horncastle LN9 199 A3
Lincoln LN2 202 B7
Langton Ct PE25 206 C5
Langton Dr
Grimsby DN33 191 A3
Horncastle LN9 199 A3
Langton Hill LN9 199 A3
Langton La LN9 85 C4
Langton Rd
Holton le Clay DN36 195 E2
Peterborough PE1 226 D7
Langwith Dr PE12 215 C2
Langwith Gdns PE12 215 C1
LANGWORTH LN3 69 B3
Langworthgate LN2 234 C3
Langworth Rd LN2 69 B4
Lannimore Cl LN5 205 D3
Lansdall Ave 4 DN21 52 F6
Lansdowne Ave
Grimsby DN32 191 D4
Lincoln LN6 205 C5
Lansdowne Dr 21 LN12 77 A8
Lansdowne Rd
8 Navenby/Wellingore LN5 107 A8
Lansdowne Rd *continued*
Yaxley PE7 233 F6
Lansdowne St HU3 180 C6
Lansdowne Way PE2 230 D7
Lansdown Link 1 DN35 192 E3
Lansdown Rd 4 DN40 186 B4
Lansdown Way 17 LN10 97 C5
Laporte Rd DN40 187 C5
Lapwater La PE12 147 C6
Lapwing Cl LN6 200 A3
Larch Ave 16 LN2 68 D2
Larch Cl
8 Bourne PE10 213 C7
2 Grantham NG31 210 D2
Immingham DN40 186 E5
Ruskington NG34 108 D1
Yaxley PE7 233 F6
Larch Ct 9 DN21 197 F6
Larch Gn NG34 107 D1
Larch Gr
Peterborough PE1 226 C6
8 Scawby DN20 30 F8
Scunthorpe DN16 185 B7
Larchmont Cl 10 HU15 2 C6
Larch Rd DN35 192 D2
Larch Way 8 NG34 212 D2
Larchwood Cres LN6 200 D1
Larden Ave DN33 194 E8
Lark Cl 13 LN8 70 D4
Lark Dr 4 LN5 107 A7
Larkin Ave LN3 203 D5
Larklands PE3 225 B1
Lark Rise
6 Market Deeping PE6 217 C5
Scotter DN21 29 B3
Larkspur Ave 6 DN41 23 F5
Larkspur Croft PE21 208 C6
Larkspur Rd LN2 202 D7
Larkspur Wlk PE4 221 B3
Larks Rise PE10 154 B7
Larmour Rd DN37 190 D7
Larne Cl 12 LN5 205 C2
Larne Rd LN5 205 D2
Larners Fields 6 LN1 66 C7
Lashbrook Garth HU4 179 B4
Lastingham 30 HU15 2 C6
Latham Ave PE2 230 C7
Latimer Gdns 12 NG34 122 E3
LAUGHTERTON LN1 65 D2
LAUGHTON DN21 41 C8
Laughton Cres LN2 202 A8
Laughton Endowed CE Sch DN21 41 C8
Laughton Rd
Blyton DN21 40 F5
Boston PE21 208 D6
Laughton Way LN2 201 F7
Laughton Way N LN2 201 F8
Launde Gdns PE9 218 E4
Launder Terr NG31 211 A3
Laundon Rd NG34 132 E3
Laura Ct 5 PE25 90 E3
Laureate Gr PE11 214 B4
Laurel Cl
6 Donington PE11 134 E2
8 Gainsborough DN21 197 E6
Grimsby DN33 191 C2
Kingston upon Hull HU5 179 B7
Lincoln LN5 205 D5
Yaxley PE7 233 D4
Laurel Dr 7 PE6 176 A3
Laurels Cl 1 DN40 22 E8
Laurel Way DN16 185 D4
Lauridston Cl 9 DN37 23 E1
Laurier St DN35 192 D8
Laurold Ave 1 DN7 15 A3
Laval Pl PE21 209 B5
Lavender Cl
6 Lincoln LN5 205 C2
10 Sleaford NG34 212 D2
Lavender Cres PE1 226 B8
Lavender Dr PE11 214 A2
Lavender Gr DN36 195 B7
Lavender Way
Bourne PE10 213 B7
13 Scunthorpe DN15 183 B3
1 Stamford PE9 218 D7
Lavender Wlk 1 HU5 179 C7
Lavenham Ct PE2 230 C7
Lavenham Gr LN6 205 A4
Lavenham Rd DN33 194 D7
Lavington Grange PE1 226 E6
Law Ct 1 PE11 214 B5
Lawley Cl LN2 203 B8
Lawn Ave
Peterborough PE1 226 A7
Skegness PE25 206 D2
Lawn Cres 1 PE25 206 D2
Lawn Ct LN1 234 A4
Lawn in Lincoln The* LN1 234 A3
Lawn La NG33 152 F2
Lawns The
Collingham NG23 91 D5
4 Grimsby DN31 191 C7
Kingston upon Hull HU10 178 D7
18 Wisbech PE13 170 C1
Lawnswood HU13 178 D2
Lawnswood Ct DN16 185 A4
Lawn Wood Nature Reserve* NG33 152 E2
Lawrance Way 10 PE10 164 C8
Lawrence Ave PE7 231 C2
Lawrence Cl 1 LN6 205 B7
Lawrence La 3 NG34 120 C8
Lawrence Rd PE8 172 C1
Lawrence's Dro PE10 164 F8
Lawrence St DN31 191 C8
Law's Cl PE6 174 C5
Lawson Ave
Grimsby DN31 191 B7
Peterborough PE2 231 D6
Lawson Ct 15 LN2 68 E6
Lawson Leas 5 NG32 210 A5
Laxton Gdns 7 PE11 156 E8
Laxton Gr DN16 185 A2
Laxton La NG33 152 E7
Laycock Ave 2 DN10 39 C1
Laythorpe Ave PE25 206 D1
Laythorpe Gdns 2 LN4 207 C4
LEA DN21 52 F5
Leaburn Rd DN17 29 D7
LEADENHAM LN5 106 C3
Leadenham CE Prim Sch LN5 106 D3
Leading Dro PE7 233 D3
Lea Dr DN33 191 F5
Leaf Ave PE7 230 D3
Leafere Way 1 PE13 170 B2
Lea Frances Olive Anderson Prim Sch DN21 53 A5
Lea Garth 6 DN17 29 D7
Leagate Rd
Coningsby LN4 207 F6
Langriville PE22 124 F8
Thornton le Fen PE22 111 F1
Lea Gdns PE3 225 F1
Lea Gr 2 LN3 83 C4
LEAKE PE22 127 C8
LEAKE COMMONSIDE PE22 113 F3
LEAKE FOLD HILL PE22 114 A2
Leakes Row LN11 198 C7
Lealand Cl LN2 202 E6
Lealand Way PE21 209 A2
Leame Cl HU3 180 A7
Leamington Cl 2 DN16 183 C1
Leamington Ct DN16 183 C1
Leamlands La PE12 149 B1
Lea Pk Home Est PE21 209 B4
Lea Rd DN21 197 D2
Lea Rd W DN21 197 D1
Leas Cl DN37 194 E5
Lease La DN40 12 D6
LEASINGHAM NG34 121 B8
Leasingham La NG34 108 D1
Leas Jun & Inf Sch The DN37 194 E5
Leas Rd NG34 122 F2
Leas The NG32 119 B1
Lea The NG34 121 B8
Leaver Gate PE24 102 B2
Leaves Lake Dro PE11 155 E7
Lea View 2 PE9 163 C1
Lebanon Dr 3 PE13 170 E1
Lechler Cl LN2 68 D3
Leconfield Cl 7 LN6 204 C6
Leconfield Rd 16 LN6 204 C7
Ledbury Dr DN36 195 D7
Ledbury Rd PE3 225 C3
Ledham PE2 229 D4
Lee Ave
Heighington/Washingborough LN4 203 D1
Sutterton PE20 136 B2
Leeder Cl PE7 231 D1
Lee Fair Gdns 1 DN17 184 F2
Leek Hill 18 DN15 9 A5
Leeming Cl 8 LN6 204 D6
Lee Rd
Lincoln LN2 234 C4
Yaxley PE7 233 E4
Lee Smith St HU9 181 E7
Lees Rest Houses HU4 179 C6
Lee St LN11 198 B5
Lees The PE6 217 E5
Lees Wlk HU3 180 A7
Legard Ave DN16 185 B6
Legard Dr HU10 178 F6
Legarde Ave HU4 179 C6
LEGBOURNE LN11 61 F3
Legbourne Abbey LN11 61 F3
Legbourne Cl 1 LN1 201 D7
Legbourne Rd LN11 198 E3
Legbourne Wood Nature Reserve* LN11 61 F2
Leggott Way 8 DN41 23 E6
Legion Cl 8 HU15 2 C5
LEGSBY LN8 58 A4
Legsby Ave DN32 191 E5
Legsby Pl DN32 191 E4
Legsby Prim Sch LN8 58 A4
Legsby Rd LN8 57 E7
Leicester Cl LN4 203 C1
Leicester Gr NG31 210 D5
Leicester St
Kingston upon Hull HU3 180 D8
1 Sleaford NG34 212 D4
Leiden Fields 2 PE11 214 B2
Leighton PE2 230 C4
Leighton Cres 2 LN6 205 B6
Leighton Gr DN33 191 C4
Leighton Prim Sch PE2 230 C4
Leighton Wlk 4 PE12 159 D7
Leinsters Cl PE3 225 D3
Leiston Ct 21 PE6 175 A1

Lemon Wong La LN5 106 C3
Lenham La HU1 180 E6
LENTON NG33 141 E5
Lenton Gn LN2 202 B7
Lenton's La
Friskney PE22 115 A5
Leverton PE22 126 F6
Lenton Way 2 PE20 136 D6
Leofric Ave PE10 213 B5
Leofric Cl 19 PE6 166 F1
Leofric Sq PE1 226 E3
Leonard Cres DN15 182 F3
Leonard St 4 HU3 180 D8
Leopold Cl DN16 185 A6
Lerowe Rd PE13 170 E1
Leslie Ct 5 DN15 183 B3
Leslie Manser Prim Sch LN6 204 B7
Lessingham PE2 229 D4
Lestrange St DN35 192 C7
Lethbridge Rd PE4 221 D2
Lettwell Cres 1 PE25 206 D1
Levels La
Blaxton DN9 26 A4
Misson DN10 39 A7
Leven Rd DN16 185 D6
Levens Wlk PE3 225 B3
Leverett Rd PE21 209 B4
LEVERINGTON PE13 170 B3
Leverington Comm PE13 169 F1
Leverington Cty Prim Sch PE13 170 B2
Leverington Rd PE13 170 C1
Levers Cl PE21 209 F5
Leverstock Gn 38 DN7 14 D4
LEVERTON PE22 126 F6
LEVERTON HIGHGATE PE22 127 A6
Leverton Leisure Ctr PE22 127 A7
LEVERTON LUCASGATE PE22 127 B6
LEVERTON OUTGATE PE22 127 B7
Leverton Rd DN22 52 B1
Levington St 2 DN31 189 C1
Lewes Gdns PE4 221 A3
Lewis Ave 13 LN12 77 A8
Lewis Rd
Cleethorpes DN35 192 D8
Coningsby LN4 207 D4
Lewis St
Gainsborough DN21 197 D3
Lincoln LN5 234 B1
Lexington Dr HU4 179 C5
Leyburn Rd LN6 204 F4
Leyden Cl 6 DN40 186 B4
Leyland Ave DN7 14 E4
Leys Cl NG32 210 B4
Leys Farm Jun Sch DN17 184 F4
Leys La DN15 9 B6
Leys The
Cherry Willingham LN3 203 E6
Peterborough PE3 225 A1
Leytonstone La PE10 213 D2
Liberty La HU1 181 A6
Lichfield Ave
Peterborough PE4 220 F3
Scunthorpe DN17 184 C7
Lichfield Cl NG31 210 E4
Lichfield Ct DN32 192 B6
Lichfield Rd
Bracebridge Heath LN4 81 A2
Grimsby DN32 192 B6
12 Hatfield DN7 14 D4
Liddell St HU2 180 E7
Lidgard Rd DN36 193 A1
Lidgate Cl PE2 230 C7
Lidgett Cl 10 DN20 30 F8
Lidgett The 7 DN9 27 D6
Lifeboat Ave PE25 206 D1
Lighter-than-Air Rd NG34 107 C1
Lighton Ave 4 PE20 136 C5
Lilac Ave DN16 183 C1
Lilac Cl
Birchwood LN6 204 C8
Bourne PE10 213 B6
Wisbech PE13 170 E1
Lilac Ct DN33 194 D8
Lilac Rd
9 Elloughton-cum-Brough HU15 2 C5
Peterborough PE1 226 C7
Lilac Wlk PE7 233 F6
Lilacwood Dr 5 NG31 210 F7
Lila Dr 1 PE11 145 B7
Lilburn Cl 5 NG34 121 B8
Lilburn Dr PE11 214 C6
Lilford Cl 5 LN2 202 E7
Lilford Rd LN2 202 E7
Lilley St 6 NG23 117 D3
Lillicrap Ct 2 LN1 234 B4
Lilly's Carr Nature Reserve★ PE23 100 E6
Lilly's Rd LN2 234 B4
Lilywood Rd 12 DN20 19 D3
Limber Cl 2 DN21 53 A7
Limber Ct DN34 191 A6
Limber Hill LN8 47 D4
Limber Rd
Humberside Airport DN39 22 A6
Swallow LN7 34 A7
Limber Vale DN34 191 A6
Limburg Dr 7 PE11 214 A2
Lime Ave
Scunthorpe DN16 19 A3
Wisbech PE13 170 D1
Lime Cl
Burgh le Marsh PE24 102 D7
2 Langtoft PE6 164 F3
3 Old Leake PE22 114 A1
RAF Cranwell NG34 107 D1
Ruskington NG34 108 D1
Lime Cres LN5 205 C1
Lime Ct PE11 214 E3
Limedale View 2 DN3 14 A3
Lime Gr
Bassingham LN5 92 F2
2 Boston PE21 209 C2
2 Bottesford NG13 128 A5
Caythorpe NG32 119 C7
Cherry Willingham/Reepham LN3 203 D5
9 Goxhill DN19 12 A8
Grantham NG31 211 C6
Holbeach PE12 215 D3
Holton le Clay DN36 195 D1
Humberston DN36 36 C7
7 Ingoldmells PE25 90 D3
Louth LN11 198 C7
Scunthorpe DN16 185 B7
Lime Kiln Cl PE3 225 E4
Lime Kiln Way LN2 202 C4
Limelands 2 LN2 234 C3
Lime St
Grimsby DN31 191 C8
Kingston upon Hull HU8 181 A8
3 Sutton Bridge PE12 160 F4
Limes The
7 Beckingham DN10 40 A1
Castor PE5 223 F1
4 Stallingborough DN41 23 D6
12 Wittering PE8 172 B1
Limetree Ave DN33 191 C3
Lime Tree Ave
Gainsborough DN21 197 D5
Kingston upon Hull HU13 178 F2
2 Market Deeping PE6 217 A6
20 Metheringham LN4 95 C4
Peterborough PE1 225 F4
Limetree Cl
13 Sleaford NG34 212 D2
Yaxley PE7 233 F7
Lime Tree Cl
1 Collingham NG23 91 D4
6 Fulbeck NG32 106 C1
6 Lincoln LN6 204 E8
Lime Tree Gr 4 DN8 15 A8
Lime Tree Paddock 2 LN2 68 F4
Limetree Wlk 1 NG34 122 E2
Limewalk PE12 216 C6
Linchfield Cl PE6 217 E5
Linchfield Prim Sch PE6 217 D5
Linchfield Rd PE6 217 D6
LINCOLN LN5 234 C2
Lincoln Ass Rm★ LN2 234 B3
Lincoln Ave LN6 205 C8
Lincoln Bvd DN31 191 B7
Lincoln Castle★ LN1 234 A3
Lincoln Castle Way DN19 4 D2
Lincoln Cath★ LN2 234 B3
Lincoln Christs Hospl Sch LN2 202 B6
Lincoln Cl
4 Crowle DN17 16 D7
Grantham NG31 210 D4
5 Market Deeping PE6 217 A6
Lincoln Coll
Lincoln LN1 234 B3
Lincoln LN2 234 C3
Lincoln Cres 2 DN21 42 F8
Lincoln Ct
4 Beacon Hill NG24 104 A6
Brumby DN16 185 B7
Lincoln Cty Hospl LN2 202 C4
Lincoln Dr
27 Barton-upon-Humber DN18 10 F8
30 Caistor LN7 33 B4
3 Scampton Airfield LN1 67 F5
5 Waddington LN5 94 A7
24 Winterton DN15 9 A5
Lincoln Drill Hall★ LN1 234 B2
Lincoln Gate DN36 48 D5
Lincoln Gdns DN16 185 A6
Lincoln Gdns Prim Sch DN16 185 A6
Lincoln Gn
Kingston upon Hull HU4 179 C7
Skegness PE25 206 B5
Lincoln La
Boston PE21 208 E5
Holbeach PE12 147 D5
Kettlethorpe LN1 65 F3
Osgodby LN8 44 F2
Thorpe on the Hill LN6 92 E8
Lincoln Minst Sch
Lincoln LN2 234 B4
Lincoln LN2 234 C3
Lincoln Nuffield Hospl The LN2 234 B4
Lincoln Rd
Bassingham LN5 92 F2
10 Binbrook Tech Pk LN8 47 B6
Brant Broughton LN5 105 F5
Brant Broughton & Stragglethorpe LN5 106 A5
Canwick LN4 81 B3
Lincoln Rd *continued*
Caythorpe NG32 119 B6
Cleethorpes DN35 192 C5
Deeping Gate PE6 217 C3
Digby LN4 108 D6
Doddington & Whisby LN6 204 A6
Dunholme LN2 68 D6
Dunston LN4 95 B5
Faldingworth LN8 56 F3
Fenton LN1 65 E3
Fiskerton LN3 203 F4
1 Glinton PE6 220 C8
Heighington/Washingborough LN4 203 A2
Holton cum Beckering LN8 70 B7
Honington NG32 119 C2
Horncastle LN9 199 A4
Ingham LN1 54 F2
1 Leasingham NG34 121 B8
Lincoln LN6 204 F1
Louth LN11 61 B8
Metheringham LN4 95 C4
Middle Rasen LN8 57 B7
Moorland Prison DN7 26 A8
Nettleham LN2 68 B1
Newark-on-Trent NG24 104 A6
Northborough PE6 217 D1
Peterborough PE6 220 D5
Ruskington NG34 108 D2
Saxilby with Ingleby LN1 66 E1
4 Skegness PE25 206 C3
Skellingthorpe LN6 200 B4
Sleaford NG34 212 B7
Stamford PE9 219 C7
West Barkwith LN8 71 A7
Lincoln Rd Bridge NG24 104 A5
Lincoln Rd Nocton LN4 95 A7
Lincoln's Ave PE12 168 C2
Lincolnshire Archives★ LN1 234 B3
Lincolnshire Aviation Heritage Ctr★ PE23 99 F5
Lincolnshire Coast Light Rly★ PE25 90 D1
Lincolnshire Rare Breeds Poultry★ LN11 61 F8
Lincolnshire Rd Transport Mus★ LN6 204 D5
Lincolnshire Showground★ LN1 67 E4
Lincolnshire Wolds Rly★ DN36 48 F6
Lincoln St
Gainsborough DN21 197 C5
Kingston upon Hull HU2 180 F8
Lincoln Sta LN5 234 B1
Lincoln Way 1 PE11 214 C5
Linda Cres LN11 198 B4
Lindale Gdns DN16 185 C7
Lindbergh Dr PE11 214 C2
Linden Cl 16 DN7 14 D4
Linden Ct PE11 214 E5
Linden Dene 1 LN6 204 D1
Linden Dr PE24 102 D7
Linden Rd LN9 199 C4
Linden Rise PE10 213 D7
Lindens Cl PE13 177 A3
Lindens The NG31 211 B2
Linden Terr DN21 197 D3
Linden Way
Boston PE21 209 A7
Pinchbeck PE11 144 D1
Linden Wlk LN11 198 C4
Lindholme 5 DN21 29 C3
Lindholme Bank Rd DN7 15 B1
Lindholme Rd LN6 204 D5
Lindisfarne Ave DN36 195 B6
Lindisfarne Rd PE6 175 A1
Lindisfarne Way NG31 210 E5
Lindis Rd PE21 209 C5
Lindley St DN16 185 A6
Lindrick Cl 4 NG31 211 D7
Lindrick Rd 6 DN7 14 F3
Lindrick Wlk 5 DN37 194 C4
Lindridge Wlk PE3 225 A2
Lindsey Ave PE6 217 A6
Lindsey Cl
6 Bourne PE10 213 C5
Gainsborough DN21 197 F2
Peterborough PE4 221 B1
Lindsey Ct 12 DN9 27 E6
Lindsey Ctr 4 DN21 197 D4
Lindsey Dr
Crowle DN17 16 D8
6 Healing DN41 24 A5
Holton le Clay DN36 195 C2
Lindsey Lower Sch & Com Arts Coll DN35 192 D6
Lindsey Pl HU4 179 D6
Lindsey Rd
Cleethorpes DN35 192 F4
Stamford PE9 219 C6
4 Uffington PE9 172 C6
Lindsey Rise 3 DN33 194 F8
Lindsey Sch The DN35 192 E4
Lindsey St 2 DN16 183 C2
Lindsey Way LN11 198 D4
Lindum Ave
3 Immingham DN40 186 B3
Lincoln LN2 234 C3
Lindum Cotts PE13 170 B2
Lindum Cres 5 DN20 196 B4
Lindum Gr
Chapel St Leonard PE24 90 E7
2 Crowle DN17 16 C7
Lindum Rd
Cleethorpes DN35 193 A4
Lincoln LN2 234 B3
Lindum Sq 5 PE25 206 B5
Lindum St DN15 183 B3
Lindum Terr LN2 234 C3
Lindum Way 9 PE11 134 F2
Lindum Wlk 1 LN7 32 A4
Linecroft La DN10 40 B4
Linga La LN5 93 A3
Lingfield Cl 6 LN1 66 D3
Ling Garth PE1 226 B8
Linghall La LN4 111 E5
Ling House La DN7 14 A5
Ling La NG33 152 C5
Ling Moor Prim Sch LN6 204 E3
Lings La DN7 14 D3
Lingwood Pk 5 PE3 225 A1
Linkage Coll PE23 100 F7
Link Rd PE1 225 F3
Links Ave 2 LN12 64 B5
Links Cres 4 PE25 103 E4
Linkside PE3 220 F1
Links Rd DN35 193 A3
Link The
Bracebridge Heath LN4 205 F4
Kingston upon Hull HU4 179 C5
2 Leasingham NG34 121 B8
Louth LN11 198 E5
2 Navenby/Wellingore LN5 107 A7
Linkway 7 DN7 14 F3
Link Way PE11 214 E4
Linley Cl 4 NG23 91 D4
Linley Dr PE21 208 E2
Linnaeus St HU3 180 C6
Linnet PE2 229 D6
Linnet Cl
Birchwood LN6 204 D8
7 Market Deeping PE6 217 C5
Scunthorpe DN15 182 D6
Linnet Dr PE10 143 A3
Linnet Way 11 NG34 212 B3
Linthorpe Gr HU10 178 E8
Linton 21 HU15 2 C6
Linton Cl
Freiston PE22 137 E7
Westwoodside DN9 27 A2
Linton Rise 3 DN15 8 A4
Linton St 5 LN5 201 F1
LINWOOD LN8 57 D5
Linwood Ave 5 DN33 194 F8
Linwood Cl
Gainsborough DN21 197 F3
9 Sleaford NG34 212 C6
Linwood Rd
Lissington LN8 57 D3
Martin LN4 96 B3
Linwood Warren Nature Reserve★ LN8 58 A6
Liquorpond St 11 PE21 208 F4
Lisburn Cl 7 LN5 205 D2
Lisburn Gr DN33 191 D2
Lisle Marsden Prim Sch DN32 191 E4
Lissett Cl 6 LN6 204 B6
LISSINGTON LN3 57 E2
Lissington Cl 2 LN2 201 F7
Lissington Rd
Gainsborough DN21 197 E3
Wickenby LN3 57 C1
Lister Rd
Peterborough PE1 225 F7
Scunthorpe DN15 182 C3
Lister St
Grimsby DN31 191 B8
Kingston upon Hull HU1 180 E5
LISTOFT PE24 89 F7
Listoft La PE24 89 F7
Litchfield Cl PE7 233 F5
Little Bargate St LN5 205 E8
Littlebeck Cl HU3 180 A7
Littlebeck Rd 3 DN36 36 C8
Little Belt The DN21 197 D7
LITTLEBOROUGH DN22 52 F1
Littleborough La DN21 53 A1
Littleborough Rd DN22 52 C2
Littlebury Gdns PE12 215 C2
LITTLE BYTHAM NG33 163 A8
Little Bytham Rd
Castle Bytham NG33 152 E1
Counthorpe & Creeton NG33 153 A2
LITTLE CARLTON LN11 62 C4
LITTLE CASTERTON PE9 171 E8
Little Casterton Rd PE9 218 F8
LITTLE CAWTHORPE LN11 61 E2
Littlechild Dr 4 PE13 170 B2
Little Cl
Edenham PE10 153 D5
15 Eye PE6 175 A1
LITTLE COATES DN34 190 F7
Littlecoates Prim Sch DN31 188 D1
Little Coates Rd DN34 190 E4
Little Comm PE12 215 B7
LITTLE COMMON PE12 215 B8
Little Dog Dro PE12 158 C1
Little Dowgate PE13 170 B1
Little Dro PE20 124 C2
Littlefair Rd 6 HU9 5 D8
LITTLEFIELD DN34 191 B6
Littlefield La
Grimsby DN34 191 A6
Marshchapel DN36 37 B2
Little Gate La LN4 82 A1
Little George St HU8 181 A8
Little Gonerby CE (Aided) Infant's Sch NG31 211 B5
LITTLE GRIMSBY LN11 49 B2
Little Grimsby La LN11 49 A1
LITTLE HALE NG34 133 E8
Little Hale Dro NG34 133 F8
Little Hale Rd NG34 122 E1
Little Holme Rd PE34 161 C2
Little Johns Cl PE3 224 F3
Little John St DN34 191 B7
Little La
Broomfleet HU15 1 C6
6 Collingham NG23 91 C4
Gringley on the Hill DN10 39 C1
Louth LN11 198 C5
Surfleet PE11 145 B3
5 Welbourn LN5 106 E5
Whaplode PE12 158 A5
Wrawby DN20 196 F6
LITTLE LIMBER DN37 22 C5
LITTLE LONDON
Legsby LN8 58 A5
Long Sutton PE12 216 D5
Little London PE12 216 D6
LITTLE LONDON
Spalding PE11 214 A1
Tetford LN9 73 F2
Little Marsh La PE12 159 B7
Little Mason St 3 HU1 181 A7
Littlemeer PE2 229 F4
Little Merebalk La LN9 86 B2
Little Michael St DN31 191 B7
Littlemoors La 6 PE22 113 A3
Little Northfields PE9 172 E4
LITTLE PONTON NG31 140 A7
Littleport La 3 PE22 113 B1
Little Ramper PE13 170 B4
Little Scrubs Wood Nature Reserve★ LN8 70 E1
Little Side Rd PE20 135 E8
Little S St 16 LN11 198 B5
LITTLE STEEPING PE23 101 D5
Little Steeping Mud & Stud Cottage★ PE23 101 D6
LITTLE SUTTON PE12 160 C5
Little Thorpe La LN6 79 F1
LITTLE WELTON LN11 60 F6
LITTLE WISBEACH NG34 143 C6
Little Wlk DN21 40 B5
Littlewood Rd DN8 15 B8
Littleworth Dro
Deeping St Nicholas PE11 156 D1
Heckington NG34 122 F4
Spalding PE11 156 E2
Sutton St Edmund PE12 176 F8
Livermore Gn PE4 220 E6
Liverpool Dr LN6 200 B2
Liverpool St HU3 180 A3
Livesey Rd DN36 48 E6
Livingstone Dr PE11 214 B2
Lloyd Pl 10 DN21 55 A8
Lloyds Ave DN17 184 F8
Lobelia Dr 1 DN17 185 A1
LOBTHORPE NG33 152 A3
Loch Fyne Cl PE2 229 B4
Loch Lomond Way PE2 229 C4
Lockham Gate PE22 114 B2
Lockhill DN31 189 A2
Lock Hill 30 DN8 15 A8
Locking Cl 17 LN6 204 C6
Locking Garth LN11 49 D5
Lock Keepers Ct HU9 181 C6
Lock Keepers Way LN11 198 D7
Lock La DN8 15 A8
Lock Rd
Alvingham LN11 49 F2
North Coates DN36 37 A3
Locks Cl PE6 174 A8
Locksley Christian Sch LN11 62 C6
Locksley Cl
6 Boston PE21 208 E7
4 North Somercotes LN11 50 F7
Locksley Way 5 LN11 50 F7
Lockton Cl 2 PE20 135 B7
Lockton Ct 10 DN37 190 E8
Lockton Gr 1 HU5 179 D8
Lockwood Bank DN9 27 E6
Lockwood Cl 12 DN8 15 B8
Lockwood Ct 1 DN15 182 E4
Lockwood St HU2 180 F8
Loder Ave PE3 224 F2
Lodge Ave 22 DN18 10 F8
Lodge Cl
10 Brough HU15 2 C7
Kingston upon Hull HU13 178 F1
6 Welton/Dunholme LN2 68 D7
Lodge Ct 37 DN7 14 D4
Lodge Cvn Pk LN4 207 A4
Lodge Dr LN6 105 A8
Lodge Gdns HU13 178 C2

Lodge La
Flixborough DN15 . . . . 8 B2
Kirk Bramwith DN7 . . . . . . 14 A8
Nettleham LN2. . . . . 68 D1
Upton DN21 . . . . 53 D5
Lodge Rd
Bourne PE10 . . . . 213 C7
4 Coningsby LN4 . . . . . . 207 A5
Scunthorpe DN15 . . . . 182 C2
Tattershall Thorpe LN10 . . . 97 E3
Lodge Top Cl LN6 . . . . . . 204 E5
Lodge Way NG31 . . . . 211 A6
Lodington Ct 5 LN9 . . . 199 D3
Loft Ave DN37 . . . . 190 E8
Loganberry Dr HU4 . . . . 179 C4
Loire Ct PE3 . . . . 225 E4
Lomax Dr 2 NG34 . . . . . 212 C6
Lombard St DN34 . . . . . 191 A7
Lombardy Dr PE1 . . . . . . 226 B8
Lomond Gr DN36 . . . . . . 36 C8
Lomond Rd HU5 . . . . 179 E8
Londesborough St
HU3 . . . . 180 C7
Londesborough Way 13
LN4 . . . . 95 D4
London Rd
Boston PE21 . . . . 208 E1
Bracebridge Heath LN4 . . . 205 F5
Frampton PE20 . . . . 136 D7
Grantham NG31 . . . . 211 B3
Haugham LN11 . . . . 74 A7
Long Sutton PE12 . . . . 216 C4
Louth LN11 . . . . 198 C3
Newark-on-Trent NG24 . . . . 104 B2
Osbournby NG34 . . . . 132 C5
Peterborough PE2 . . . . 226 A1
Sleaford NG34 . . . . 212 B1
Spalding PE11 . . . . 214 C2
Tathwell LN11 . . . . 61 C2
Wansford PE8 . . . . 222 B2
Yaxley PE7 . . . . 233 C5
LONDONTHORPE
NG31 . . . . 130 D4
Londonthorpe La
NG31 . . . . 211 E8
Londonthorpe Rd
NG31 . . . . 211 F7
Long Acre 1 LN12 . . . . . . 64 B4
LONG BENNINGTON
NG23 . . . . 117 D3
Long Bennington CE Prim
Sch NG23 . . . . 117 D3
Long Causeway PE1. . . . 226 A2
Longcliffe Rd NG31 . . . . 211 A8
Long Cl La LN5 . . . . 82 B7
Longcroft Dr 1 NG34 . . . 107 C1
Longdales Rd LN2. . . . . . 201 F6
Longden St HU3 . . . . 180 A7
Longdon Cl 6 PE12 . . . . 160 E4
Long Dro
Bourne PE10 . . . . 155 B1
Gosberton PE11 . . . . 144 B6
Rippingale PE10. . . . . 143 D3
Thurlby PE10 . . . . 164 E7
Walcott LN4. . . . . 109 E8
Wisbech St Mary PE13 . . . 177 D4
Long Farm La DN22 . . . . . 52 E2
Long Field Dr 2 DN3 . . . . 14 A1
Longfield Gate PE2 . . . . 230 A6
Longfield Rd DN34 . . . . . 190 E4
Long Field Rd 23 DN3 . . . 14 A2
Long Gates LN11. . . . . 51 A1
Longhead La PE14 . . . . . 170 D3
Longhedge Dro PE20. . . . 134 E5
Long Hedge La
Greetham with Somersby
LN9 . . . . 86 C5
Swaby LN13. . . . . 74 E4
Long Hollow NG33 . . . . . 131 C3
Longhorn Cl DN37 . . . . . 194 B4
Longhurst Gdns PE21 . . . 208 D7
Long La
Aubourn Haddington & South
Hykeham LN6 . . . . 93 B7
Barnby in the Willows
NG24. . . . . 104 F4
Fleet PE12 . . . . 168 B3
Ingham LN1 . . . . 54 E2
Leadenham LN5. . . . . 107 A2
Moulton PE12 . . . . 157 E5
Mumby LN13 . . . . 76 E2
Redmile NG32 . . . . 128 A1
2 Westborough & Dry
Doddington NG23 . . . . . 117 F3
Willoughton LN8 . . . . 42 E3
Longlands LN13. . . . . 63 D3
Longleat Dr LN11 . . . . . . 198 A4
Long Leys Rd LN1 . . . . . . 201 C6
Longmeadow Rise 18
DN41 . . . . 23 A4
Longmeadows PE10. . . . . 154 B7
Longmeadows Dr DN37 . . 23 F2
Long Pasture 5 PE4 . . . . 220 F5
Long Rd
1 Scunthorpe DN15 . . . . . 182 F4
Terrington St Clement
PE34. . . . . 161 F5
3 Tydd St Mary PE13 . . . . 170 C8
Longrigg Wlk 17 PE20 . . . 135 B7
Long St
2 Foston NG32 . . . . 117 F1
Great Gonerby NG31. . . . . 129 E5
LONG SUTTON PE12. . . . 216 C4
Long Sutton Butterfly Pk★
PE12. . . . . 216 D6

Long Sutton Cty Prim Sch
PE12. . . . . 216 B5
LONGTHORPE PE3 . . . . . 225 A1
Longthorpe Cl 3 PE3 . . . 225 A2
Longthorpe Gn PE3 . . . . 225 B1
Longthorpe House Mews
11 PE3 . . . . 224 F2
Longthorpe Parkway
PE3 . . . . 225 C1
Longthorpe Prim Sch
PE3 . . . . 225 A2
Longton Rd 4 DN3 . . . . . . 14 A2
Longueville Ct PE2. . . . . . 230 B5
Longwater PE2 . . . . 230 B6
Long Wood La LN4. . . . . . . 95 C2
Long Wood Rd DN21 . . . . . 41 A1
Lonsdale Cl 20 DN36 . . . . . 36 D8
Lonsdale Gr PE10 . . . . . . 213 E6
Lonsdale Pl 4 LN5. . . . . . 201 F1
Lonsdale Rd PE9. . . . . . . 218 E5
Lonsdale St 5 HU3 . . . . . 180 A6
Loop La 1 PE12 . . . . 157 F7
LOOSEGATE PE12. . . . . . 158 A8
Loosegate Rd PE12 . . . . 158 A8
Lopham La DN37. . . . . 34 F8
Lord Dr 4 NG31 . . . . 129 E5
Lords La 19 DN19 . . . . 11 D8
Lord's La 6 NG33. . . . . . 151 A8
Lord St
Gainsborough DN21 . . . . . 197 C4
Grimsby DN31 . . . . 191 B8
4 Sleaford NG34 . . . . . . 212 C3
17 Stainforth DN7 . . . . . . 14 C6
Lornas Field PE7. . . . . . . 230 D4
Lorne St LN5 . . . . 234 C1
Losecoat Cl 1 PE9 . . . . . 219 D7
Lothian LN4. . . . . 120 F2
Lotus Cl 7 LN5. . . . . 93 F7
Lotus Ct LN6. . . . . 204 D1
**Loughborough Univ of
Peterborough** PE1. . . . 226 A3
Lough Rd LN9 . . . . 72 F1
Louisberg Rd DN21 . . . . . . 54 F8
Louis Dr HU5 . . . . 179 B8
Louis St HU3 . . . . 180 C8
LOUTH LN11 . . . . 198 E6
Louth City Hospl LN11 . . . 198 B6
Louth Mus★ LN11. . . . . . . 198 B5
**Louth Playgoers Riverhead
Theatre**★ LN11 . . . . . . 198 D7
Louth Rd
East Barkwith LN8. . . . . 58 E1
Fotherby LN11 . . . . 49 A3
Grimsby DN31 . . . . 191 D1
1 Holton le Clay DN36 . . . 195 D2
Horncastle LN9 . . . . 199 C5
New Waltham DN36. . . . . . 195 B5
Skidbrooke with Saltfleet
Haven LN11 . . . . 51 C4
2 West Ashby LN9. . . . . . . 85 E7
Wragby LN8 . . . . 70 D5
Louth Sta Est (Ind)
LN11 . . . . 198 C6
Louth Trading Est
LN11 . . . . 198 C2
Lovat Cl HU3 . . . . 180 D5
Loveden Ct DN35 . . . . . . 193 A3
Loveden View 6 NG32 . . . 119 B7
Love La
Caythorpe NG32 . . . . 119 C2
Gainsborough DN21 . . . . . 197 C6
Louth LN11 . . . . 198 A5
Spalding PE11 . . . . 214 E3
9 Sutterton PE20. . . . . . . 136 A2
Wrangle PE22 . . . . 114 C4
Lovell Rd DN17 . . . . 184 E3
Lovell Way PE34 . . . . 161 F2
Lovers La PE5 . . . . 222 F2
Love's Hill
Castor PE5. . . . . 223 F1
Peterborough PE5. . . . . . . 224 A1
Loves La LE15 . . . . 162 A1
Love's La PE20. . . . . 135 C8
Lovett St DN35. . . . . 189 E1
LOW BARLINGS LN3. . . . . 82 E8
Lowbridge La 4 PE11. . . . 145 C6
Low Burgage DN15. . . . . . . 2 B1
LOW BURNHAM DN9 . . . . . 27 E5
Low Church Rd 2 LN8 . . . . 57 C8
Low Comm La HU15. . . . . . . 2 D4
Lowcroft Ave 3 DN9 . . . . . 27 D2
Lowcroft Cl 4 DN9 . . . . . . 27 D2
Low Cross St 6 DN17 . . . . 16 D8
Low Deeps La DN10. . . . . . 26 C1
LOWER BASSINGTHORPE
NG33 . . . . 140 E4
LOWER BITCHFIELD
NG33 . . . . 141 A3
Lower Church Rd LN6. . . . 200 B5
Lowerdale 27 HU15 . . . . . . 2 D6
Lower High St 9 LN5 . . . . . 93 F7
Lower Kenyon St 10
DN8 . . . . 15 A8
Lower Rd NG32 . . . . 119 A5
**Lower Sow Dale Nature
Reserve**★ PE23. . . . . . 100 B8
Lower Spring St 1
DN31 . . . . 189 A1
Low Farm Dr NG34 . . . . . 142 C4
Lowfield Cl
4 Barnby Dun DN3 . . . . . . 14 A3
31 Kirton in Lindsey DN21 . 30 B1
Lowfield Ct HU10 . . . . . . 178 F6
Lowfield House HU10 . . . 178 F6
Lowfield La
Balderton NG24. . . . . 104 A1
Belchford LN9 . . . . 73 C2
Low Field La HU15 . . . . 2 E5

Lowfield Rd HU10 . . . . . . 178 E5
Low Fields Ave 1
PE11 . . . . 214 F4
Lowfields Inf Sch LN5. . . . 205 C2
Lowfields Jun Sch
LN5 . . . . 205 C2
Lowfields La
Allington NG32. . . . . 128 F7
Butterwick PE22 . . . . 126 E5
Lowfields Rd PE22 . . . . . 126 E6
LOW FULNEY PE12. . . . . . 157 B4
Low Fulney Est PE12. . . . 157 C5
Low Garth DN17 . . . . 184 F2
Lowgate
Fleet PE12 . . . . 159 C8
Kingston upon Hull HU1. . . 181 A6
Lutton PE12 . . . . 160 A8
Low Gate
Friskney PE22 . . . . 115 A6
Gosberton PE11 . . . . 145 C3
Marshchapel DN36 . . . . . . 37 C1
Moulton PE12 . . . . 146 C1
Surfleet PE11. . . . . 145 C3
Tydd St Mary PE13 . . . . . . 160 A1
Lowgate Ave 7 PE20. . . . . 135 A4
Lowgate Cres PE12 . . . . . 159 E8
Low Gate La 6 PE20 . . . . 135 A4
Lowgate Rd
Ashby with Scremby
PE23. . . . . 88 D2
Conisholme LN11. . . . . 50 C5
Hogsthorpe PE24. . . . . 90 B8
Low Holland La DN22 . . . . 52 C2
Lowick Gdns PE3 . . . . . . 225 C5
Low La
Croft PE24 . . . . 102 D6
Holbeach PE12 . . . . 215 F4
Kirk Bramwith DN7 . . . . . . 14 A6
Middle Rasen LN8 . . . . 45 C1
Terrington St Clement
PE34. . . . . 161 E3
Wrangle PE22 . . . . 114 B3
Low Levels Bank DN8 . . . . 15 D4
Low Leys Rd 6 DN17 . . . . 184 E3
LOW MARNHAM NG23. . . . . 78 A4
Low Mill La PE20. . . . . . . 136 E1
Lowmoor La LN5. . . . . 85 C3
Low Moor Rd LN6 . . . . . . 204 C6
Low Pk La LN4 . . . . 81 F4
Low Rd
Barrowby NG32. . . . . 210 A4
Besthorpe NG23 . . . . 91 C7
Blyborough DN21 . . . . 42 E6
Croft PE24 . . . . 102 F5
Crowland PE6 . . . . 175 A8
Friskney PE22 . . . . 114 F4
Grantham NG31 . . . . 211 C8
Harmston LN5 . . . . 93 D6
Healing DN41 . . . . 23 F5
Holbeach PE12 . . . . 147 F2
Marshchapel DN36 . . . . . . 37 A1
Osgodby LN8 . . . . 45 B3
South Kyme LN4 . . . . 123 B8
Spalding PE11 . . . . 214 F4
Wainfleet St Mary PE24 . . . 102 C1
LOW RISBY DN15. . . . . 9 A2
Low St
Beckingham DN10 . . . . 40 A1
Billingborough NG34 . . . . . 133 B1
Collingham NG23. . . . . 91 C4
Dunham-on-Trent NG22. . . . 65 A1
Harby NG23. . . . . 79 B5
Haxey DN9. . . . . 27 D2
North Ferriby HU14. . . . . 3 A4
5 South Ferriby DN18 . . . . 10 A7
Winterton DN15. . . . . 9 A5
Lowther Gdns PE4 . . . . . 221 B2
Lowther St DN35 . . . . . . 180 A7
Low Thorpe Rd LN3 . . . . . 83 D1
LOW TOYNTON LN9 . . . . . 199 F6
Low Toynton Cl LN9. . . . . 199 D5
Low Toynton Rd LN9 . . . . 199 D5
Low Wood La LN6. . . . . 91 F8
Loxley PE4 . . . . 220 E4
Loxley Gn HU4 . . . . 179 B7
Loxley Way 6 HU15 . . . . . . 2 D5
Loyalty La DN18. . . . . 3 E2
Loyd St HU10 . . . . 178 E6
Lucan Ct 4 DN41 . . . . 23 F5
Lucas Ct 4 DN41 . . . . 23 F5
Lucern Ct LN11 . . . . 198 D6
Lucerne Cl PE11 . . . . 214 E5
Lucetta Gdns 9 PE11 . . . 214 E5
Lucian Wlk HU4. . . . . 179 A1
Lucy Twr St LN1 . . . . 234 A2
Luda Terr LN11 . . . . 198 D7
LUDBOROUGH DN36 . . . . . 48 D6
Ludborough Pk DN36 . . . . 48 E6
Ludborough Rd
13 North Thoresby
DN36. . . . . 36 B1
North Thoresby DN36. . . . . 48 D8
Ludborough Sta DN36. . . . 48 F6
Ludborough Way 6
DN35 . . . . 192 F3
LUDDINGTON DN17 . . . . . . 7 D3
**Luddington & Garthorpe
Prim Sch** DN17 . . . . 7 C3
Luddington Rd
Garthorpe & Fockerby
DN17. . . . . 7 E5
1 Peterborough PE4 . . . . 221 B1
LUDFORD LN8. . . . . 59 A8
Ludford CE Sch LN8. . . . . . 59 B8

Ludford Cres DN21 . . . . . 197 E3
Ludford Dr 9 LN6 . . . . . . 205 A7
Ludford Rd LN8. . . . . 47 C4
Ludford St DN32 . . . . 191 E6
Ludgate Cl DN37 . . . . 194 D4
Ludlow Ave DN34 . . . . . . 191 A7
Ludlow Gdns 4 PE11 . . . . 145 A8
Ludlow Pl DN35. . . . . 192 E5
LUDNEY LN11 . . . . 50 C6
Ludney La LN11 . . . . 50 C6
Luffenham Cl 4 PE9 . . . . 218 E5
Lulworth Ave HU4. . . . . . 179 A3
Lulworth Ct DN17 . . . . . . 184 C8
Lulworth Wlk DN40 . . . . . 186 D3
Lumley Ave PE25. . . . . . . 206 D3
Lumley Cres 3 PE25 . . . . 206 D4
Lumley Pl 2 LN5 . . . . 201 F1
Lumley Rd PE25 . . . . 206 C3
Lumley Sq 8 PE25 . . . . . 206 C3
Lunds The HU10 . . . . 178 C6
Lundy Cl DN40 . . . . 186 C2
Luneburg Pl DN15. . . . . . 182 C5
Luneburg Way DN15. . . . 182 C6
Lunedale Rd DN16 . . . . . 185 D5
Lunn La 5 NG23 . . . . 91 C4
Lunn's Cres 21 DN18. . . . . 10 E8
Lupin Rd LN2 . . . . 202 C8
Lurgan Cl LN5 . . . . 205 D3
LUSBY PE23. . . . . 86 F2
Lusher Way DN21 . . . . 41 A1
Luton Cl 1 LN6. . . . . 200 B1
Luton Rd HU5. . . . . 179 F8
LUTTON PE12 . . . . 160 A8
Lutton Bank PE12 . . . . . . 148 D1
Lutton Garnsgate
PE12 . . . . 216 A4
Lutton Gate Rd PE12 . . . 168 E4
Lutton Gowts PE12. . . . . 216 D7
LUTTON GOWTS PE12 . . . 216 D8
Lutton Gr PE3 . . . . 225 C6
Lutton Lodge La PE12. . . 149 B2
Lych Gate 10 DN20 . . . . . . 19 D3
Lydbrook Rd DN16 . . . . . 183 A1
Lydd Cl LN6 . . . . 204 C6
Lydford Rd DN40 . . . . . . 186 D3
Lydia Ct 3 DN40 . . . . 186 A4
Lygon St DN16 . . . . 183 B1
Lyle Cl 5 LN12 . . . . 64 A4
Lyme Wlk 3 PE3 . . . . 225 C4
Lymington Garth HU4 . . . 179 A3
Lymn Bank PE24 . . . . 102 C4
Lymn Ct 2 NG31 . . . . 210 E2
Lynchwood PE2. . . . . 229 C5
Lyndale Ave 17 DN3 . . . . . 14 A1
Lyndale Pk PE2 . . . . 229 C6
Lynden Ave NG31 . . . . . . 210 E8
Lyndhurst Ave
3 Grimsby DN33 . . . . . . 191 D3
Skegness PE25 . . . . 206 B5
Lyndhurst Ct 1 PE25 . . . . 206 B4
Lyndis Wlk LN12 . . . . 215 E1
Lyndon Bsns Pk LN6 . . . . 204 B5
Lyndon Cres LN11. . . . . . 198 D8
Lyndon Way
Louth LN11 . . . . 198 D8
Stamford PE9. . . . . 218 E5
Lyneham Cl LN6 . . . . 204 B7
Lyn Ellis Cl 2 PE21 . . . . . 209 C4
Lynmouth Cl 1 LN6. . . . . 205 A1
Lynmouth Dr DN17 . . . . . 184 C8
Lynn Rd
Walpole Cross Keys
PE34. . . . . 161 C3
Walsoken PE13 . . . . 170 E2
Lynnwell Cl PE25 . . . . . . 206 A6
Lynton Ave HU4. . . . . 179 B3
Lynton Cl DN15 . . . . 182 D4
Lynton Parade DN31 . . . . 191 B7
Lynton Prep Sch DN15 . . 183 A4
Lynton Rd PE1. . . . . 225 F6
Lynton Rise DN35 . . . . . . 192 E4
Lynwood Ave HU10. . . . . 178 E6
Lyric Cl 1 HU3 . . . . 180 C5
Lysaghts Way DN15. . . . . . 8 C1
Lytham Cl
8 Heighington/
Washingborough LN4 . . 203 D1
Londonthorpe & Harrowby
without NG31 . . . . 211 E7
Lytham Dr DN37 . . . . 194 C3
Lythemere PE2 . . . . 230 C4
Lytton St LN2 . . . . 234 C2
Lyvelly Gdns PE1. . . . . . . 226 E6

M

MABLETHORPE LN12 . . . . 64 C3
**Mablethorpe Com Prim
Sch** LN12 . . . . 64 A4
Mablethorpe Rd
North Coates DN36 . . . . . . 37 A3
Theddlethorpe St Helen
LN12. . . . . 63 F5
MacAulay Dr
Lincoln LN2 . . . . 202 B6
Newark-on-Trent NG24 . . . . 104 B3
Macaulay Jun & Inf Sch
DN31. . . . . 191 B8
MacAulay St DN31. . . . . . 191 B8
MacAulay Way DN31. . . . 191 C8
Mace Rd PE2 . . . . 231 D5
Machray Pl DN35. . . . . . . 192 D7
McInnes St 1 LN2 . . . . . . 202 C3
Mackender Ct 4
DN16 . . . . 185 C6
Mackenzie Pl 5 DN40. . . . 186 B3
Maclure St DN31 . . . . . . 189 B2

Macmillan Ave LN6 . . . . . 204 C2
MacPhail Cres LN1. . . . . . . 66 E2
McVeigh Ct 13 DN41 . . . . . 23 F5
Maddison La PE23. . . . . . . 88 B3
Madeley St HU3. . . . . 180 C4
Madely Cl 4 LN9 . . . . 199 D3
Maegan Way DN35. . . . . . 192 E5
Mafeking Terr PE21. . . . . 209 A7
Maffit Rd PE5. . . . . 223 D3
Magdalen Cl 4 DN16 . . . . 185 B4
Magdalene Rd DN34 . . . . 190 F5
Magdalene View NG24 . . . 104 B4
Magdalen Mus★ PE24. . . . 102 D1
Magdalen Rd PE24. . . . . . 102 D2
Magdalen Sch PE24. . . . . . 102 D2
Magdellan Ct PE3. . . . . . . 225 E2
Magee Rd PE4 . . . . 221 B1
Magellan Dr 9 PE23 . . . . 101 A8
Magellan Way PE11 . . . . . 214 C2
Magistrates Rd PE7 . . . . . 233 D8
Magna Cres 15 NG34 . . . . 122 E2
Magna Mile LN8 . . . . 59 B8
Magnolia Ave PE3 . . . . . . 225 A2
Magnolia Cl LN4 . . . . 81 D2
Magnolia Dr 6 DN36. . . . . 195 D1
Magnolia Rd NG34 . . . . . 212 D2
Magnolia Rise 4
DN40 . . . . 186 C3
Magnolia Way DN16. . . . . 185 B7
Magpie Cl LN6. . . . . 200 A3
Magpie La DN22 . . . . 52 C1
Magrath Ct 1 DN20. . . . . 196 C3
Maiden Cl 1 DN40. . . . . . 186 A4
Maiden Ct 19 LN1 . . . . 66 D2
Maiden Gr 2 NG34 . . . . . 212 E3
Maiden La
Hogsthorpe PE24. . . . . 90 B7
11 Stamford PE9. . . . . . . 219 C5
Maidens Rd 10 PE20. . . . . 136 A2
MAIDENWELL LN11 . . . . . . 73 E6
Maidenwell La 11 LN7. . . . 32 A4
Maiden Well La 5
LN5 . . . . 107 A8
Maidment Dr LN1. . . . . . . 201 C7
Maidwell Way DN34 . . . . . 190 C4
Main App Rd DN16. . . . . . 183 C3
Main Ave
Bracebridge Heath
LN4 . . . . 205 F3
Scunthorpe DN17 . . . . 184 C6
Maine Ave DN15 . . . . 182 B5
Main Rd
Anwick NG34. . . . . 109 B1
Ashby cum Fenby DN37. . . . 35 D3
Barkston NG32 . . . . 130 B8
Belchford LN9 . . . . 73 A2
Benniworth LN8. . . . . 59 B1
Bourne PE10 . . . . 154 C5
Carrington PE22 . . . . 112 C7
Collyweston PE9 . . . . 171 D7
2 Donington on Bain
LN11. . . . . 59 E1
Dunsby PE10 . . . . 143 B2
East Kirkby PE23 . . . . 99 F5
Etton PE6. . . . . 173 E5
Friskney Eaudike PE22 . . . . 115 C6
Gedney PE12 . . . . 159 D7
Goulceby LN11. . . . . 72 D6
Gunby & Stainby NG33 . . . 151 B5
Haconby PE10 . . . . 154 C8
Heighington/Washingborough
LN4 . . . . 203 B2
Leadenham LN5. . . . . 106 D3
Little Hale NG34 . . . . 122 E1
Little Steeping PE23 . . . . . 101 D6
Long Bennington NG23 . . . 117 D3
Nocton LN4 . . . . 95 B7
North Willingham LN8 . . . . 58 D7
Parson Drove PE13 . . . . . . 177 F8
3 Potterhanworth LN4. . . . 82 B1
Quadring PE11 . . . . 134 F1
Saltfleet LN11 . . . . 51 C4
2 Sibsey PE22 . . . . 113 B1
Spilsby PE23 . . . . 87 F1
Stickford PE22. . . . . 100 B3
Stickney PE22 . . . . 113 B5
Tallington PE9 . . . . 172 E6
Thurlby PE10 . . . . 164 D8
Toynton All Saints PE23. . . 100 F6
2 Tydd St Mary PE13 . . . . 170 C8
7 Uffington PE9. . . . . 172 C6
Utterby LN11. . . . . 48 F5
West Keal PE23 . . . . 100 C3
Wigtoft PE20. . . . . 135 E3
Wisbech St Mary PE13 . . . 177 A2
Withern with Stain LN11. . . 62 E1
Main Ridge E PE21 . . . . . 209 A5
Main Ridge W 9 PE21 . . . 209 A5
Main St (Southorpe)
PE9 . . . . 172 E2
Main St
Ailsworth PE5 . . . . 223 D2
Ancaster NG32 . . . . 119 F3
Ashby de la Launde & Bloxholm
LN4 . . . . 108 B5
Barlings LN3 . . . . 69 C3
Barnack PE9 . . . . 172 D3
Barrowby NG32. . . . . 210 A5
Baston PE6 . . . . 164 E4
4 Bishop Norton LN8. . . . . 43 D3
Bonby DN20. . . . . 10 C2
Boothby Graffoe LN5. . . . . 94 A2
Boothby Pagnell NG33. . . . 140 F5
Bottesford NG13 . . . . 128 C4
Broomfleet HU15. . . . . 1 C6
Brough HU15 . . . . 2 C6
Buckminster NG33. . . . . . . 150 E5
Cadney DN20. . . . . 31 E6

Main St continued
Careby Aunby & Holywell PE9 163 B7
Carlton Scroop NG32 119 C4
Castor PE5 223 D3
Claypole NG23 117 F7
Clipsham LE15 162 C7
Crowle DN17 16 E6
Croxton Kerrial NG32 138 D3
Denton NG32 139 A7
Doddington & Whisby LN6 79 D5
Dorrington LN4 108 E3
Dunham-on-Trent NG22 65 B1
East/West Stockwith DN10 40 C5
Edenham PE10 153 F4
Ellerker HU15 2 A8
Ewerby & Evedon NG34 122 C6
Farcet PE7 231 C2
Fenton NG23 105 C1
Fishlake DN7 14 D8
Foston NG32 117 F1
Fulstow LN11 49 B8
Gedney PE12 148 B1
Graiselound DN9 27 D1
1 Grasby DN38 32 E7
Great Casterton PE9 218 C8
Greatford PE9 164 C2
Gunby & Stainby NG33 151 B4
Hackthorn LN2 55 E1
Haconby PE10 154 D8
Hatfield DN7 14 F3
Honington NG32 119 C1
Horkstow DN18 10 A5
Horsington LN10 84 D3
Hougham NG32 118 C3
Ingoldsby NG33 141 D5
Laneham DN22 65 A3
Mablethorpe & Sutton LN12 64 B1
Mareham le Fen PE22 98 F3
Marston NG32 118 D2
Newark-on-Trent NG24 104 C2
Normanby by Spital LN8 55 F7
North Kyme LN4 109 F3
North Leverton with Habblesthorpe DN22 52 B1
North Rauceby NG34 120 E5
Norton Disney LN6 92 C2
Osgodby LN8 45 A3
RAF Cranwell NG34 120 C8
Ryhall PE9 163 D1
Scawby DN20 30 F7
Scopwick LN4 95 D1
Scothern LN2 68 F4
Scredington NG34 132 F7
Southorpe PE9 172 E1
South Rauceby NG34 120 E4
South Scarle NG23 91 E6
Sproxton LE14 138 F1
Sutton on Trent NG23 91 A8
Swanland HU14 3 B7
Syston NG32 130 A7
Thistleton LE15 151 C1
Thorney NG23 78 F7
Thornton Curtis DN39 11 E5
Thorpe on the Hill LN6 92 E8
1 Timberland LN4 96 B1
Torksey LN1 65 D6
Ufford PE9 172 F3
Upton DN21 53 D5
Welby NG32 130 F5
West Ashby LN9 85 E7
Westborough & Dry Doddington NG23 117 E5
Whitton DN15 1 E3
Wilsford NG32 120 C2
Worlaby DN20 20 D8
1 Wymondham LE14 150 C1
Yaxley PE7 233 E5
Mainwaring Cl 5 LN2 68 E6
Mainwaring Rd LN2 234 C4
Maisdike La PE12 159 B5
Maize Ct 9 NG34 212 F3
Malborne Way PE2 230 B4
Malborough Dr 4 LN12 64 A3
Malcolm Ave NG34 107 C1
Malcolm Rd DN34 190 F4
Malcolm Sargent Prim Sch PE9 218 E5
Maldon Dr HU9 181 C6
Malham Ave HU4 179 C6
Malham Cl LN6 200 C1
Malham Dr LN6 200 C1
Malim Way 3 NG31 210 F8
Malkinson Cl
4 West Halton DN15 8 E7
12 Winterton DN15 9 A5
Mallalieu Ct 2 DN15 182 E4
Mallard Ave 6 DN3 14 A4
Mallard Cl
Birchwood LN6 200 E1
5 Essendine PE9 163 D3
19 Healing DN41 23 F5
Skellingthorpe LN6 200 A3
Spalding PE11 214 E2
Mallard Ct
10 Grantham NG31 210 E2
4 North Hykeham LN6 204 C1
5 Stamford PE9 219 B4
Mallard Dr 6 LN7 33 B4
Mallard Dro PE11 134 B1
Mallard Mews DN32 191 E6
Mallard Rd
Low Fulney PE12 157 C5
Peterborough PE3 220 E1
3 Scunthorpe DN17 184 E6
Mallards Reach 8 PE11 134 F2
Mallards The 5 PE6 174 A5
Mallard Way
Brigg DN20 196 A3
Skegness PE25 103 C7
Malling Wlk DN16 185 B2
Mallory Cl 6 LN6 204 C7
Mallory Dr 3 PE11 214 C2
Mallory La 18 PE9 219 B5
Mallory Rd
1 Ashby de la Launde & Bloxholm LN4 108 A7
Peterborough PE1 226 C2
4 Scunthorpe DN16 185 D5
Mallowfield 2 LN8 57 B8
Mallows La PE22 113 C2
Mall Sh Ctr The LN1 234 B2
Malmesbury Dr 3 DN34 191 C6
Malmsgate La PE20 135 F6
Malm St HU3 180 B6
Malpas Ave 4 DN21 197 D5
MALTBY LN11 60 F3
Maltby Ave DN37 190 C3
Maltby Cl 20 PE8 172 B1
Maltby Dr PE6 164 D4
Maltby La 12 DN18 3 E1
MALTBY LE MARSH LN13 76 A8
Maltby Rd
Scunthorpe DN17 184 E5
Skegness PE25 206 D5
Maltby Way LN9 199 D3
Malten La 8 PE12 158 B7
Malting La PE11 134 E2
Maltings La NG31 210 E7
Malting Sq PE7 233 F6
Maltings The
5 Alford LN13 75 F3
1 Leasingham NG34 121 B7
Long Sutton PE12 216 B5
6 Thorney PE6 176 A3
Wothorpe PE9 219 C2
Maltings Way DN32 191 E8
Maltkiln La
Brant Broughton LN5 105 F5
2 Elsham DN20 20 F7
Malt Kiln La 1 LN5 93 F6
Maltkiln Rd
Barton-upon-Humber DN18 3 F1
Fenton LN1 65 E3
Malton Rd LN6 204 F3
Malus Cl PE7 230 C3
Malvern Ave
Grimsby DN33 191 A3
Heighington/Washingborough LN4 203 D2
Spalding PE11 214 E6
Malvern Cl
Lincoln LN5 205 D4
15 Lincoln LN6 93 C8
20 Lincoln LN6 93 C8
Sleaford NG34 212 B2
Spalding PE11 214 E6
4 Thorne/Moorends DN8 15 A7
Malvern Dr 5 NG31 210 E8
Malvern Rd
5 Mablethorpe/Sutton on Sea LN12 64 B4
Peterborough PE4 221 C2
Scunthorpe DN17 184 F7
Manasty Rd PE2 229 C2
MANBY LN11 62 D6
Manby Hall Bsns Pk DN40 186 D5
Manby Middlegate LN11 62 D7
Manby Rd
Immingham DN40 186 C6
Legbourne LN11 61 E4
Scunthorpe DN17 184 E4
Manby Rd by Pass DN40 186 D6
Manby St LN5 205 D6
Mancetter Sq PE4 220 F1
Manchester Rd 11 LN5 94 A7
Manchester St
Cleethorpes DN35 192 D8
Kingston upon Hull HU3 180 A4
Manchester Way
3 Donington PE11 134 F2
Grantham NG31 210 C5
Mandalay Dr 1 PE10 213 E7
Mandela Link 1 DN31 191 C7
Mandeville PE2 229 F4
Mandike Rd PE20 136 C2
Manifold Rd DN16 185 E5
Manlake Ave DN15 9 A5
Manley Ct 1 DN9 27 D6
Manley Gdns
Brigg DN20 196 B3
11 Cleethorpes DN35 192 F3
Manley St 4 DN15 183 B3
Mannaberg Way DN15 183 B6
Manners Cl 3 PE9 172 C6
Manners Rd NG24 104 B2
Manners St NG31 211 A6
Manning Rd PE10 213 D5
Manningtree Cl DN32 191 E6
Mann La DN9 16 D2
Manor Ave
Grimsby DN32 191 D6
Peterborough PE2 231 B7
Manor Cl
6 Bardney LN3 83 C4
Manor Cl continued
11 Baston PE6 164 E5
East Kirkby PE23 99 F4
Farcet PE7 231 C2
3 Great Gonerby NG31 129 E5
11 Keelby DN41 23 A5
Langtoft PE6 164 E3
7 Leasingham NG34 121 B7
Lincoln LN2 234 B4
14 Metheringham LN4 95 D4
15 Ruskington NG34 108 D2
Ryhall PE9 163 C2
7 Sibsey PE22 113 B1
2 Spalding PE11 214 C1
6 Welbourn LN5 106 E5
13 Wittering PE8 172 B1
Yaxley PE7 233 D5
Manor Cliff 1 LN8 55 F6
Manor Ct
9 Bourne PE10 213 C5
2 Carlton-le-Moorland LN5 105 E8
Grimsby DN32 191 D7
17 Nettleham LN2 68 C2
Nocton LN4 95 B7
1 Stallingborough DN41 23 E6
2 Sudbrooke LN2 68 F3
Manor Ct Rd 7 DN9 27 E6
Manor Dr
12 Baston PE6 164 E5
2 Binbrook LN8 47 C4
3 Bonby DN20 10 C2
4 Brough HU15 2 C6
5 Great Gonerby NG31 129 D5
1 Great Gonerby NG31 129 E5
Halton Holegate PE23 101 B7
7 Harlaxton NG32 139 C7
Holbeach PE12 215 D3
1 Long Bennington NG23 117 D3
Peterborough PE6 221 E3
3 Scawby DN20 30 E8
Skegness PE25 206 B5
2 Sudbrooke LN2 68 F2
Waltham DN37 194 E5
7 Wragby LN8 70 D4
Manor Farm Cl 43 DN17 29 D6
Manor Farm Dr 3 LN1 66 D7
Manor Farm La
Castor PE5 223 E2
3 Essendine PE9 163 D3
Manor Farm Rd DN17 184 E6
Manor Gdns
Boston PE21 209 A4
8 Hatfield DN7 14 E4
Peterborough PE2 231 C7
Manor Hill LN11 60 A1
Manor Hill Cnr PE12 169 D7
Manor House Ct PE6 217 E4
Manor House La NG23 117 E5
Manor House Mus★ LN13 75 F3
Manor House Rd PE12 146 F2
Manor House St
1 Fulletby LN9 86 B8
5 Horncastle LN9 199 B4
Peterborough PE1 226 A3
Manor La
Aisthorpe LN1 67 C7
4 Barrow upon Humber DN19 11 D8
Bourne PE10 213 C4
Broadholme LN6 66 D1
5 Carlton-le-Moorland LN5 105 E8
Goxhill DN19 11 F8
Hougham NG32 118 C3
Threekingham NG34 132 E3
16 Waddington LN5 93 F7
1 Welton/Dunholme LN2 68 D6
Wrangle PE22 114 B2
Manor Leas Cl LN6 205 B3
Manor Leas Inf Sch LN6 205 B3
Manor Leas Jun Sch LN6 205 B3
Manor Paddock 6 NG32 128 F7
MANOR PARK DN17 184 D6
Manor Pk 7 LN11 61 F3
Manor Pl NG34 212 C5
Manor Rd
Barrowby NG32 210 A5
Bottesford NG13 128 A5
Burton Coggles NG33 152 C8
Carlby PE9 163 E4
2 Collingham NG23 91 D4
Coningsby LN4 110 E8
1 Crowle DN17 16 D7
East Ella HU5 179 B8
Folksworth PE7 232 D1
4 Hagworthingham PE23 87 A4
Hatfield DN7 14 E4
Heighington/Washingborough LN4 203 B1
Kingston upon Hull HU5 179 B8
Kirton PE20 136 B5
Lincoln LN2 234 C4
Northorpe DN21 42 A8
Saxilby LN1 66 D2
Scunthorpe DN16 185 B3
Sleaford NG34 212 B2
5 Stainforth DN7 14 C7
Stretton LE15 162 A6
Swanland HU14 3 B6
Swinderby LN6 92 A5
Twin Rivers DN14 7 E7
Manor Rd continued
Wansford PE5 222 F2
Manor Rise LN3 203 F8
Manor St
7 Heckington NG34 122 E3
Keelby DN41 23 A5
8 Kingston upon Hull HU1 180 F6
Ruskington NG34 108 D2
Manor Stables Craft Ctr★ NG32 106 C1
Manor Way
Kingston upon Hull HU10 178 F6
6 Langtoft PE6 164 F3
Market Deeping PE6 217 E4
Manrico Dr LN1 201 C7
Manse Ave LN5 205 D4
Mansell Cl 1 PE11 214 B3
Mansel St 3 DN32 189 D1
Mansfield Ct
4 Grimsby DN32 189 C1
Peterborough PE1 226 C5
Mansfield Rd DN15 182 B2
Mansgate Hill LN7 33 B3
Mansion Ct Gdns DN8 15 A8
Manson Cl 11 DN34 190 D4
MANTHORPE
Grantham NG31 211 A8
Toft with Lound and Manthorpe PE10 164 A7
Manthorpe Dro PE10 164 F8
Manthorpe Rd NG31 211 B7
Mantle Gn PE22 115 B6
MANTON DN21 30 B5
Manton PE3 225 A3
Manton Ct DN20 30 F6
Manton La DN20 30 E6
Manton Rd
Lincoln LN2 201 F7
Manton DN21 30 B4
MANTON WARREN DN16 30 B8
Mantree Cross DN21 41 A8
Manwaring Way 15 PE20 135 B7
Maple Ave
15 Crowle DN17 16 D7
Grimsby DN34 190 E7
Keelby DN41 23 A4
Kingston upon Hull HU10 178 F8
13 Northorpe PE10 164 C8
2 Scunthorpe DN15 182 C5
10 Wisbech PE13 170 D1
Woodhall Spa LN10 97 C6
Maple Cl
Brigg DN20 196 E3
Gainsborough DN21 197 B7
9 Keelby DN41 23 A4
5 Kingston upon Hull HU5 179 C7
Leasingham NG34 121 C7
Louth LN11 198 D7
42 Messingham DN17 29 D7
Thimbleby LN9 199 A5
4 Waddington LN5 93 E8
Maple Ct
Gainsborough DN21 197 F5
Yaxley PE7 233 F6
Maple Dr
5 Bassingham LN5 92 F3
1 Sudbrooke LN2 68 F2
Maple Gdns PE10 213 D6
Maple Gr
22 Healing DN41 23 F5
12 Heckington NG34 122 D3
Holbeach PE12 215 A2
Immingham DN40 186 C5
New Waltham DN36 195 B5
Peterborough PE1 226 C7
3 Scopwick Heath LN4 108 A7
Spalding PE11 214 F4
Maple Rd PE21 209 C2
Maple St LN5 205 D5
Maples The PE1 226 F5
Maple Tree Cl E DN16 183 A1
Maple Tree Cl W DN16 183 A1
Maple Tree Way DN16 183 A1
Maple Way 12 PE11 134 E2
Maple Wlk PE7 230 C2
Maplewood Ave HU5 179 B7
Maplewood Cl NG31 210 F7
March Rd PE13 177 F1
March St 13 DN21 30 B1
Marconi Dr PE7 233 D6
Marcus St DN34 191 A6
Mardale Gdns PE4 221 D2
Mareham La
Aswarby & Swarby NG34 132 E7
Pointon & Sempringham NG34 142 F7
Sleaford NG34 212 F2
Threekingham NG34 132 F3
MAREHAM LE FEN PE22 99 A3
Mareham le Fen CE (Controlled) Prim Sch PE22 99 A4
MAREHAM ON THE HILL LN9 86 A2
Mareham Rd LN9 199 D2
MARFLEET HU9 5 E8
Marfleet Ave 4 HU9 5 D8
Marfleet Cnr 9 DN36 36 B1
Marfleet La HU9 5 E8
Marfleet Prim Sch HU9 5 E8
Margaret Ave 1 DN17 17 D5
Margaret Dr PE21 209 B6
Margaret Gr 1 HU13 178 F1
Margaret Pl DN36 195 C6
Margaret St
5 Grimsby DN32 191 F7
Immingham DN40 186 C3
Margrave La
Garthorpe & Fockerby DN17 7 E5
Reedness DN14 6 E7
Marham Cl 4 LN6 204 B8
MARHOLM PE6 220 C1
Marholm Rd
4 Peterborough PE3 220 F1
Peterborough PE6 224 B3
Ufford PE9 172 F2
Marian Ave 22 LN12 64 B3
Marian Rd PE21 208 F7
Marian Way
6 Skegness PE25 206 B3
Waltham DN37 194 B4
Mariette Way PE11 214 B6
Marigold Ave PE10 213 D3
Marigold Cl
Lincoln LN2 202 C8
Stamford PE9 218 C6
Marigolds PE6 217 D5
Marigold Wlk
3 Humberston DN35 192 E1
5 Sleaford NG34 212 F3
Marina Rd 15 LN12 64 B3
Marina View 8 DN8 15 A7
Marine Ave
11 Mablethorpe LN12 64 B3
8 Mablethorpe/Sutton on Sea LN12 64 C1
North Ferriby HU14 3 A4
Skegness PE25 206 D1
Marine Ave W 8 LN12 76 F8
Marine Rd PE11 214 E5
Mariners Arms Flats 2 DN17 17 D6
Mariners Cl HU9 181 C6
Marine Wharf 5 HU1 180 F5
Marisco Ct 2 LN12 77 A8
Marjorie Ave LN6 205 D8
Mark Ave
Horncastle LN9 199 A5
Sleaford NG34 212 F4
MARKBY LN13 76 C5
Market Cl 3 PE24 102 E8
Market Ct
8 Crowle DN17 16 D7
Long Sutton PE12 216 C5
MARKET DEEPING PE6 217 E6
Market Deeping Com Prim Sch PE6 217 C6
Market Hall★ LN11 198 B5
Market Hill
Scunthorpe DN15 183 B4
Winteringham DN15 2 B1
Market La
Old Leake PE22 127 C8
Terrington St Clement PE34 161 E2
Market Pl
3 Alford LN13 75 F2
1 Binbrook LN8 47 C4
21 Boston PE21 208 F5
2 Brigg DN20 196 B3
Coningsby LN4 207 A4
2 Epworth DN9 27 E6
Gainsborough DN21 197 C4
2 Grantham NG31 211 A4
4 Horncastle LN9 199 B4
6 Kingston upon Hull HU1 181 A6
36 Kirkby in Lindsey DN21 30 B1
Long Sutton PE12 216 C4
9 Louth LN11 198 B5
Market Deeping PE6 217 B4
10 Market Rasen LN8 57 D8
Owston Ferry DN9 28 B3
4 Sleaford NG34 212 D4
6 Spalding PE11 214 D4
Swineshead PE20 135 B7
4 Wragby LN8 70 D5
MARKET RASEN LN8 57 E8
Market Rasen CE Prim Sch LN8 57 D7
Market Rasen Race Course LN8 57 F7
Market Rasen Rd
Dunholme LN2 68 E6
Holton cum Beckering LN8 70 B8
Lissington LN3 57 E1
Snarford LN8 56 E1
Welton/Dunholme LN2 68 E6
Market Rasen Sta LN8 57 D7
Market Rasen Way PE12 215 E3
Market Sq 17 PE21 208 F5
Market St
Bottesford NG13 128 A5
3 Cleethorpes DN35 192 F6
Gainsborough DN21 197 D4
Grimsby DN31 191 D8
Long Sutton PE12 216 C5
3 Sleaford NG34 212 D4
11 Spilsby PE23 88 A1
31 Winterton DN15 9 A5
MARKET STAINTON LN8 72 B6
Market Way PE11 214 C8
Markham Mews DN32 194 F4
Markham Ret Pk PE9 219 E7
Markhams Orch DN33 194 F7

Markham Way 2 DN20 196 F7
Markillie La PE12 160 A3
Marklew Ave DN34 191 B7
Mark Rise 1 DN21 41 C5
MARLBOROUGH LN5 93 B4
Marlborough Ave
- 2 Haxey DN9 27 D2
- Heighington/Washingborough LN4 203 C1
- Kingston upon Hull HU13 178 D2
- 2 Spalding PE11 214 E2

Marlborough Cl
- 21 Grimsby DN32 189 C1
- 5 Lincoln LN2 202 C8
- Yaxley PE7 233 E5

Marlborough Dr 1 DN16 185 B8
Marlborough Rd 11 DN8 15 B7
Marlborough St 11 DN21 197 D3
Marlborough Terr 3 HU2 180 E7
Marlborough Way DN35 192 F1
Marlowe Dr LN2 202 B6
Marlowe Gr PE4 225 E8
Marlowe Rd DN17 184 D7
Marlow Rd DN21 197 E6
Marmaduke St 3 HU3 180 C4
Marmion Dr 7 DN15 9 A5
Marmion Rd
- Coningsby LN4 207 E5
- 4 Scunthorpe DN16 185 C8

Marne Ave PE4 221 A1
Marne Gdns LN1 201 E6
Marne St HU5 180 A8
Marples Mews DN35 192 F5
Marquess Ct 7 PE10 213 D5
Marquis Ave DN36 195 D7
Marrat Cl LN2 202 E6
Marratts La NG31 129 D5
Marriot's Gate 6 PE12 160 A8
Marriott Ct PE1 226 E5
Marris Dr 11 DN15 9 B5
Marr La HU15 1 A7
Marsden Dr DN15 182 D3
Marsden Rd DN31 189 D1
Marshall Ave
- Grimsby DN34 191 B7
- Kingston upon Hull HU10 178 E8

Marshall Cl
- 3 Fishtoft PE21 126 C1
- 8 Laceby DN37 23 E1

Marshall's Bank PE13 177 D8
Marshall's Way PE7 231 C2
Marshalls Yard DN21 197 D4
Marshall Way 2 DN21 53 A8
Marsham PE2 229 F3
Marsh Ave PE21 209 A2
MARSHCHAPEL DN36 37 B2
Marshchapel Cl 2 DN35 192 F3
Marshchapel Prim Sch DN36 37 B2
Marsh Dro PE11 146 A5
Marshfield Rd 1 DN16 185 C5
Marshfields Sch PE1 226 D7
Marsh La
- Algarkirk PE20 146 B8
- Barnetby le Wold DN38 21 B4
- Barrow upon Humber DN19 4 C2
- Barton-upon-Humber DN18 3 F1
- Boston PE21 209 A1
- Burgh le Marsh PE24 102 E7
- Carlton-le-Moorland LN5 106 A7
- Dunham-on-Trent NG22 65 B1
- Grainthorpe LN11 50 C7
- Kettlethorpe LN1 65 C2
- Middle Rasen LN8 57 B8
- Misterton DN10 40 A5
- New Holland DN19 4 D2
- North Leverton with Habblesthorpe DN22 52 E1
- North Somercotes LN11 38 C1
- Orby PE24 89 E2
- Saundby DN22 52 B7
- Skidbrooke with Saltfleet Haven LN11 51 C5
- South Cockerington LN11 62 B8
- South Killingholme DN40 13 B4
- Tattershall LN4 97 D1
- Winteringham DN15 2 A1
- Wyberton PE21 136 F8

Marshland High Sch PE14 170 E4
Marshlands Dr PE12 215 F3
Marshland St 10 PE34 161 F3
Marsh Rd
- 3 Crowle DN17 16 C8
- Gedney PE12 148 C2
- Holbeach PE12 215 F8
- Kirton PE20 137 A3
- Orby PE24 90 B3
- Spalding PE12 157 B7
- Sutterton PE20 146 A7
- Tydd St Mary PE13 160 C1
- Walkeringham DN10 40 B3
- Walpole PE14 170 F8
- Weston PE12 145 F1

Marsh The PE14 170 E8
Marsh Way 3 DN36 37 C5
MARSTON NG32 118 C2
Marston Hall & Gdns★ NG32 118 D2
Marston La NG32 129 A7
Marston Moor Rd NG24 104 C4
MARTIN
- Martin LN4 96 C3
- Roughton LN9 85 B1

Martin Cl
- 2 Bottesford DN16 185 B2
- Heighington/Washingborough LN4 81 E4
- Louth LN11 198 D8
- Skellingthorpe LN6 200 A3

Martin Ct PE4 221 A4
Martin Dales Dro 1 LN10 97 B4
Martin N Dro LN4 96 D3
Martin Rd LN4 96 C2
Martinsbridge PE1 226 F7
Martin's Cl 5 DN19 11 D8
Martin S Dro LN4 96 D3
Martins Rd
- Crowland PE6 167 E4
- Ulceby DN39 12 B1

Martin St LN5 201 F1
Martins Way PE2 229 F5
Martins Wlk 11 LN12 77 A8
Martin Way
- Ingoldmells PE25 206 C8
- New Waltham DN36 195 B6

MARTON DN21 65 D8
Marton Gr
- 3 Grimsby DN33 191 A3
- 35 Hatfield DN7 14 D4

Marton Prim Sch DN21 65 E8
Marton Rd
- Sturton by Stow LN1 66 B7
- Willingham DN21 53 E2

Martyn Rd DN35 192 D7
Marvel St HU9 181 B7
Marvis Cres PE7 230 C3
Mary Armyne Rd PE2 230 B5
Mary La LE14 138 B1
Marylebone Wlk 2 DN33 191 B2
Mary St DN15 182 F3
Mary Sumner Way 3 DN15 182 E4
Mary Walsham Cl PE2 231 E5
Masefield Dr 10 LN12 77 A7
Maskew Ave PE1 225 E6
Mason Dr DN17 184 E3
Masonic La 5 PE23 87 F1
Masons Ct 25 DN18 10 E8
Mason St HU2 180 F7
Massey Cl
- 11 Epworth DN9 27 D6
- Kingston upon Hull HU3 180 A5

Massey Rd LN2 234 C4
Massey St HU3 180 A4
Mast Dr HU9 181 C6
Master Dike PE12 159 D1
Masterton Cl 6 PE9 219 D7
Masterton Rd PE9 219 C7
Mathews St DN35 192 C7
Matilda Rd LN6 201 D1
Matley PE2 229 E5
Matley Prim Sch PE2 229 E5
Matlock Ct DN15 182 B2
Matlock Dr
- Grimsby DN37 190 F8
- Lincoln LN6 204 E2

Matmore Cl PE11 214 F3
Matmore Gate PE11 214 F3
Mat Pitts La PE24 102 C1
Matthew Flinders Way PE21 208 D3
Matthew Humberstone CE Sch DN35 192 C4
Mattimore Dr 6 PE12 215 E2
Maud Foster Mill★ PE21 209 A6
Maud St 2 PE21 209 A5
MAVIS ENDERBY PE23 87 C1
Mavis Enderby Cross Roads PE23 87 D1
Mavis Rd 2 DN17 184 E6
Mawford Cl PE12 146 E2
Mawson Gdns 6 PE24 102 E2
MAWTHORPE LN13 88 F8
Mawthorpe Hill Rd LN13 88 F8
MAXEY PE6 173 C7
Maxey Cl 11 PE6 217 A5
Maxey Ct LN11 198 B6
Maxey Rd
- Maxey PE6 173 C6
- Northborough PE6 217 C1

Maxey View PE6 217 C3
Maxham's Gn Rd PE6 173 D3
Maxwell Ave LN6 205 C8
Maxwell Ct DN34 190 D5
Maxwell Dr 1 LN12 64 B3
Maxwell Rd PE2 230 D6
Mayall Ct 23 LN5 93 F7
May Blossom Wlk PE11 214 B3
May Cres LN1 201 D4
Mayfair Ave LN6 205 C7
Mayfair Cres 12 DN37 194 C4
Mayfair Ct DN35 193 A1
Mayfair Dr 4 PE11 214 B1
Mayfair Dr W DN37 190 C8
Mayfair Gdns PE21 209 B7
Mayfield Ave
- Gainsborough DN21 197 B7
- 3 South Killingholme DN40 12 F2
- 6 Stainforth DN7 14 D6

Mayfield Cl
- 3 Grimsby DN33 194 D8
- 15 Pinchbeck PE11 156 E8

Mayfield Cres
- Louth LN11 198 D4
- 3 Middle Rasen LN8 57 C8

Mayfield Dr 1 PE25 90 D3
Mayfield Gr 5 PE25 206 B3
Mayfield Rd PE1 226 A6
Mayfield St HU3 180 C8
Mayflower Ave DN40 186 C3
Mayflower Cl
- 2 Gainsborough DN21 52 F6
- 6 South Killingholme DN40 12 E3

Mayflower Dr NG34 122 D2
Mayflower Rd PE21 209 C3
Mayflower Way 2 LN12 64 B3
May Gr HU13 178 D2
Mayland Ave HU5 179 A8
Mayner's Dike PE12 169 F8
Mayor's Wlk PE3 225 E3
Maypole House Sch LN13 88 E8
Maypole St DN21 42 D2
Maysfield Ct 10 DN20 31 A5
Maysfield Dr 6 PE13 170 B2
Mays La LN1 66 E2
May's La PE13 170 A2
May St DN35 192 D8
Maythorpe Cl HU3 180 A7
Maytime Cl 7 PE11 214 A5
Maytree Dr PE12 216 D5
Mead Cl
- 6 Lincoln LN6 205 A5
- Peterborough PE3 220 F1

Meadenvale PE1 226 F5
Mead Garth DN15 182 B6
Meadow Ave DN39 12 A2
Meadowbank 5 DN9 16 E1
Meadow Bank PE22 126 F6
Meadow Bank Ave 1 LN3 82 B6
Meadowbank Rd HU3 179 E7
Meadowbrook
- 9 Ancaster NG32 120 A3
- 4 Ruskington NG34 108 D2

Meadow Cl
- 1 Bourne PE10 213 D5
- 7 Cherry Willingham/Reepham LN3 82 A8
- 1 Colsterworth NG33 151 E6
- 5 Goxhill DN19 5 A1
- Lincoln LN6 93 C8
- 3 Louth LN11 198 C4
- 2 Manby LN11 62 C6
- 6 Metheringham LN4 95 D4
- 2 Pinchbeck PE11 145 C1
- 4 Scothern LN2 68 F4
- Spalding PE11 214 E6

Meadowcroft 7 LN11 59 E1
Meadow Croft
- 3 Kirk Sandall DN3 14 A1
- Waltham DN37 194 E5

Meadow Ct
- Grimsby DN34 190 E7
- 15 Hibaldstow DN20 30 F5

Meadowdale Cres 3 NG31 211 A8
Meadow Dr
- Barton-upon-Humber DN18 10 F8
- 4 Binbrook LN8 47 C5
- Grimsby DN33 194 D8
- 2 Healing DN41 24 A5
- 13 Misterton DN10 39 F5

Meadow Dro PE10 213 F7
Meadow End NG31 211 D2
Meadowfield
- 4 Middle Rasen LN8 57 C8
- Sleaford NG34 212 C5

Meadow Field Rd 6 DN3 14 A3
Meadowgate PE9 172 F5
Meadow Gate PE10 213 D6
Meadowgate La 3 PE11 214 A3
Meadow La
- Aubourn Haddington & South Hykeham LN6 93 B7
- Benniworth LN8 59 B1
- Girton NG23 78 C2
- Leasingham NG34 121 B7
- 9 Lincoln LN6 93 C8
- Normanton on Trent NG23 78 B3
- North Cockerington LN11 50 A1
- North Hykeham LN6 93 C8
- North Scarle LN6 78 F1
- Pointon & Sempringham NG34 143 C6
- 16 Ryhall PE9 163 C1

Meadowlake Cl LN6 200 D1
Meadow Rd
- Dunston LN4 95 C5
- Langtoft PE6 217 A8
- Newark-on-Trent NG24 104 B2
- Newborough PE6 221 B8
- Scunthorpe DN17 184 C6

Meadow Rise
- 5 Barnby Dun DN3 14 A4
- Blyton DN21 41 C6
- 1 Gainsborough DN21 53 A5
- 7 Saxilby LN1 66 D2

Meadows Cl 7 NG23 117 D3
Meadows La
- Lincoln LN4 202 E2
- Reepham LN3 69 A1

Meadows Rise 1 LE14 150 B1
Meadows The
- 2 Beckingham DN10 52 B8
- Burringham DN17 17 D4
- 8 Long Bennington NG23 117 D3
- Mablethorpe/Sutton on Sea LN12 64 C2
- 5 Market Deeping PE6 217 C5
- Messingham DN17 29 D8
- 7 Pinchbeck PE11 145 C1
- Skegness PE25 206 A4
- Westwoodside DN9 27 A2

Meadowsweet 2 PE9 218 C7
Meadow The 29 LN7 33 B4
Meadow Vale 4 DN20 30 F8
Meadow View
- Humberston DN35 192 F1
- 6 Morton PE10 154 D6
- Swinderby LN6 92 A5

Meadow View Bsns Units PE9 219 F6
Meadow Way
- Billinghay LN4 109 E6
- Bracebridge Heath LN4 81 A1
- 7 Old Leake PE22 114 A1
- Spalding PE11 214 A2
- 6 Welton/Dunholme LN2 68 D6

Meadow Wlk
- 19 Kirk Sandall DN3 14 A2
- 6 Swanland HU14 3 B7

Mead The
- 11 Laceby DN37 23 F1
- Lincoln LN6 205 A5
- Peterborough PE4 221 A1

Meadway
- Cherry Willingham/Reepham LN3 203 E6
- 11 Market Deeping PE6 217 A6
- 3 Spalding PE11 214 A4

Mead Wlk HU4 179 C6
Meakers Way LN13 76 F3
Meals Gate PE4 221 D2
Measham Dr 4 DN7 14 D7
Measures Cl 10 PE10 154 D6
Mechanic La 9 HU3 180 D5
Medbourne Gdns 1 PE1 226 D8
Meden Ave 12 HU15 2 D5
Medeswell PE2 230 C3
Medforth La PE21 208 E8
Medieval Village of Gainsthorpe★ DN21 30 D4
Medina Gdns LN12 64 B2
Medium Section Rd DN16 19 A4
MEDLAM PE22 112 D7
Medlam Cl PE22 112 C7
Medlam La PE22 112 D7
Medlam Rd PE21 208 C3
Medlar Dr 4 HU15 2 D5
Medlock Cres 5 PE11 214 F5
Medway 7 LN1 66 D7
Medway Cl 3 PE11 145 C6
Medway Cres LN6 205 B2
Medway Pl 5 DN34 191 A5
Medworth PE2 229 F3
Meeres' La PE20 136 A5
Meering Cl 12 NG23 91 D5
Meering La NG23 91 C7
Meers Bank LN12 64 A6
Meeting House La LN5 105 F5
Meggan Gate PE3 225 A1
Meggitt La DN15 2 A1
Megs La 10 LN5 107 A8
Melbourne Ave 4 DN33 191 D3
Melbourne Dr 4 PE25 206 A4
Melbourne Rd
- Birchwood LN6 204 C8
- Grantham NG31 211 D7
- 4 Stamford PE9 219 D6

Melbourne Way 9 LN5 93 E8
Melbury Wlk DN17 184 C8
Meldrum Dr DN21 197 E1
Melford Cl PE3 225 A2
Melford Ct DN16 185 E5
Melholme La LN11 50 A2
Mellows Cl
- Cherry Willingham/Reepham LN3 203 F8
- Peterborough PE1 226 C3

Mellwood View DN9 28 A3
Melrose Cl
- 9 Stamford PE9 218 E6
- 6 Woodhall Spa LN10 97 C6

Melrose Dr PE2 231 A7
Melrose Rd DN21 197 C6
Melrose St HU3 179 F6
Melrose Way DN37 188 A1
MELTON HU14 2 F5
Melton Bottom HU14 2 F6
Melton Fields HU14 2 F5
Melton Old Rd HU14 2 E5
Melton Rd
- North Ferriby HU14 3 A5
- Wrawby DN20 20 F4
- Wymondham LE14 150 B1

MELTON ROSS DN38 21 D5
Melville St LN5 234 B2
Melwood Cl DN9 27 F6
Melwood Hill DN9 27 F6
Melwood View 18 DN9 27 E6
Memorial Hall Dr 9 LN5 107 A7
Menasha Way DN16 185 E7
Mendip Ave
- Grimsby DN33 191 C1
- 25 Lincoln LN6 93 C8

Mendip Cl
- 6 Gonerby Hill Foot NG31 210 E8
- 2 Lincoln LN5 205 D3
- Spalding PE11 214 B6

Mendip Gr PE4 221 C2
Mendip Rd DN17 184 D8
Menson Dr DN7 14 D4
Mentmore Gdns PE21 208 B4
Mercer Dr LN1 201 D6
Mercer Rd DN21 197 B6
Mercer Row LN11 198 B5
Mercia Cl 14 NG34 212 B2
Mercia Dr 3 NG32 120 A2
Mercia Gdns 2 PE10 213 B5
Mercia Gr 4 PE6 164 E5
Mercian Ct PE2 231 D7
Merebalk La LN9 86 B2
Mere Balk La LN9 85 A7
Mere Booth Rd PE22 125 A7
Mere Cres DN16 185 D7
Meredith Ave DN17 184 D6
Mere Dro
- Old Leake PE22 113 F4
- Yaxley PE7 233 F4

Meredyke Rd DN17 7 D3
Mere La
- Edenthorpe DN3 14 A1
- Heydour NG32 131 D6
- Winterton DN15 9 A7

Merelade Gr 4 PE4 220 E5
Mere Rd
- Branston & Mere LN4 81 E1
- Waddington LN5 93 F7

Meres Leisure Ctr & Swimming Pool NG31 210 D3
Meres Rd NG31 210 C3
Mereway The NG33 141 A5
Meridian Cl 1 PE21 209 D4
MERIDIAN POINT DN35 193 B3
Meridian Point Ret Pk DN35 193 B3
Meridian Rd PE21 209 C4
Meridian View LN11 198 B4
Meridian Wlk 2 PE12 215 B2
Meriton PE2 229 F3
Merleswen LN2 68 D6
Merlin Cl PE10 213 E3
Merlin Dr 2 DN20 21 A8
Merlin Rd
- 14 Binbrook Tech Pk LN8 47 B6
- Scunthorpe DN17 184 E6

Merrick Cl 13 NG31 129 E5
Merrick St HU9 181 B7
Merriemeade Dr 4 PE25 206 D1
Merrifield Rd 7 PE24 102 E2
Merryweather Ct 7 DN16 185 B2
Mersey Way DN37 190 D8
Merton Rd DN16 185 A3
MESSINGHAM DN17 29 D7
Messingham La DN20 30 D8
Messingham Nature Reserve★ DN17 29 F6
Messingham Prim Sch DN17 29 D7
Messingham Rd
- East Butterwick DN17 28 D8
- Scotter DN21 29 C4
- Scunthorpe DN17 184 F4

Meteor Rd LN11 62 C6
METHERINGHAM LN4 95 D4
Metheringham Airfield Visitor Ctr★ LN4 96 A2
Metheringham Cl 1 LN6 204 D7
Metheringham Delph Nature Reserve★ LN4 96 D7
Metheringham Fen La LN4 95 E5
Metheringham Heath La LN4 94 E3
Metheringham Prim Sch LN4 95 C4
Metheringham Sta LN4 95 D4
Metro Ctr The PE2 230 D6
Mewburn PE3 220 E1
Mew Gull Dr 27 LN12 77 A7
Mews The HU3 180 C5
Meynell Ave 3 LN6 205 C8
Meynell St DN21 40 D8
Meynell Wlk PE3 225 B3
Michael Foale La LN11 198 C7
Michaelgate LN2 234 B3
Mickle Gate PE3 225 A1
Middle Barn Hill DN20 10 D1
Middlebridge Rd DN10 39 B3
Middle Broad Dro PE13 169 D5
Middlebrook Cl LN6 205 A5
Middlebrook La 1 DN8 15 A7
Middlebrook Rd 4 LN6 205 A5
Middlecott Cl 2 PE21 208 F2
Middlecott Sch The PE20 136 C5
Middle Dro
- Gedney PE12 148 C2

Middle Dro *continued*
Holland Fen with Brothertoft PE21 ... 208 A7
Kirton PE20 ... 124 D2
Newton PE13 ... 169 E4
Middle Fen Dro PE20 ... 134 D4
Middle Fen La LN4 ... 82 C5
Middlefield PE7 ... 230 D3
Middlefield La
Gainsborough DN21 ... 197 E2
1 Glentham LN8 ... 43 F1
Middlefield Sch of Tech The DN21 ... 197 E3
Middlegate LN5 ... 92 F2
Middlegate Cl 12 DN19 ... 11 C8
Middlegate La
Bonby DN20 ... 10 C3
Elsham DN20 ... 21 A7
Orby PE24 ... 89 D2
South Ferriby DN18 ... 10 B7
Middlegate Rd PE20 ... 136 C6
Middlegate Rd E PE20 ... 136 D5
Middlegate Rd (West) 1 PE20 ... 136 D6
Middleham Cl
3 Kingston upon Hull HU9 ... 181 E8
2 Peterborough PE7 ... 231 F5
Middle Holme La 3 NG23 ... 91 A8
Middle La
Amcotts DN17 ... 7 E1
Sturton le Steeple DN22 ... 52 E3
Thorpe on the Hill LN6 ... 92 F8
Middlemarsh Rd PE24 ... 103 A7
Middle Marsh Rd PE12 ... 146 F7
Middlemere Bank PE22 ... 126 E7
Middlemore Yd 1 NG31 ... 211 B4
Middle Pasture 3 PE4 ... 220 F5
Middleplatt Rd DN40 ... 186 E5
MIDDLE RASEN LN8 ... 57 B8
Middle Rasen Prim Sch LN8 ... 57 B8
Middle Rd
Crowland PE6 ... 166 E1
Newborough PE6 ... 221 E7
Terrington St Clement PE34 ... 161 D4
Tydd St Mary PE13 ... 160 B1
7 Whaplode PE12 ... 158 B7
Middle St
Aisthorpe LN1 ... 67 D7
Cammeringham LN1 ... 55 A1
Corringham DN21 ... 41 E2
Croxton Kerrial NG32 ... 138 D4
Dunston LN4 ... 95 C5
Farcet PE7 ... 231 C2
Fillingham DN21 ... 55 A5
Gunby & Stainby NG33 ... 151 B5
5 Lincoln LN6 ... 93 C8
7 Metheringham LN4 ... 95 D4
14 North Kelsey LN7 ... 32 A4
5 Potterhanworth LN4 ... 82 B1
Rippingale PE10 ... 142 F2
Scampton LN1 ... 67 D6
Scotton DN21 ... 29 C1
5 Skillington NG33 ... 151 A8
South Carlton LN1 ... 67 D3
Willoughton DN21 ... 42 E3
Middlesykes La LN11 ... 62 C7
Middlethorpe Prim Sch DN35 ... 192 D3
Middle Thorpe Rd DN35 ... 192 D3
Middleton PE3 ... 225 A4
Middleton Cl 9 DN17 ... 29 D7
Middleton Ct HU5 ... 180 B8
Middleton Prim Sch PE3 ... 225 A4
Middleton Rd
Newark NG24 ... 104 B6
Scunthorpe DN16 ... 185 B4
Middleton's Field LN2 ... 234 B4
Middletons Rd PE7 ... 233 E5
Middleton St HU3 ... 180 C8
Middleton Way NG34 ... 121 C7
Midfield Pl 16 DN36 ... 36 D8
Midfield Rd DN36 ... 36 D8
Midfield Way 14 DN41 ... 23 A4
Midgate PE1 ... 226 A2
Mid Gate PE22 ... 113 E3
Midgate (East) PE22 ... 113 E1
Midgate La PE22 ... 113 E1
Midgley Cl HU3 ... 180 C5
Midholm LN3 ... 203 E5
Midia Cl LN1 ... 201 C7
Midland Ind Est DN16 ... 185 D8
Midland Rd
Peterborough PE3 ... 225 E3
Scunthorpe DN16 ... 183 D1
Midsummer Gdns PE12 ... 216 A4
Midthorpe La 3 LN9 ... 85 E7
MIDVILLE PE22 ... 113 E8
Midville Cl 10 LN1 ... 201 E8
Midville La PE22 ... 100 B1
Midville Rd
Midville PE22 ... 113 B7
Toynton All Saints PE23 ... 100 F4
Midway Cl 9 LN2 ... 68 D2
Midway Gr HU4 ... 179 E4
Milcroft Cres DN7 ... 14 D4
Mildenhall Dr LN6 ... 204 B8
Mildmay Rd PE4 ... 225 D8
Mildmay St LN1 ... 234 A4
Mile Dro PE6 ... 173 F5
Mile End Ave 19 DN7 ... 14 D3
Mile La LN12 ... 64 A2
Miles Bank PE11 ... 214 C7
Miles Cross Hill LN13 ... 75 D1
Miles Hawk Cl 26 LN12 ... 77 A7
Milestone La PE11 ... 145 C1
Milfoil La 11 PE12 ... 167 B8
Milford Ct 3 DN32 ... 189 C1
Milford Ct Bsns Pk LN11 ... 198 A8
Milkinghill La PE20 ... 135 A5
Milking Nook Dro PE10 ... 154 F3
Milking Nook Rd PE6 ... 221 C8
Millard Ave DN7 ... 14 D4
Millard Nook 30 DN7 ... 14 D4
Mill Bank PE12 ... 159 A5
Mill Baulk Rd 3 DN10 ... 39 F3
Millbeck Bank HU15 ... 1 E8
Millbeck Dr LN2 ... 202 B8
Millbrook Cl 3 LN6 ... 93 B8
Millbrook La LN8 ... 70 C4
Millbrook Sch DN16 ... 185 B6
Millbrook Way 30 DN18 ... 10 F8
Mill Cl
7 Alford LN13 ... 75 F3
Billinghay LN4 ... 109 E5
5 Brigg DN20 ... 196 A3
4 Croft PE24 ... 102 E2
5 Marshchapel DN36 ... 37 C2
Murrow PE13 ... 177 D5
2 North Leverton with Habblesthorpe DN22 ... 52 B1
Waltham DN37 ... 194 E3
26 Wisbech PE13 ... 170 D1
Mill Cres
Peterborough PE2 ... 229 E4
20 Scotter DN21 ... 29 C3
Mill Croft
3 Scawby DN20 ... 30 F8
1 Scunthorpe DN16 ... 185 D7
Mill Ct
Lincoln LN1 ... 234 A4
1 Waddingham DN21 ... 43 D7
Mill Dr NG31 ... 211 C2
Mill Dro
Bourne PE10 ... 213 E7
Cowbit PE12 ... 157 B2
Crowland PE6 ... 175 A8
Deeping St Nicholas PE11 ... 155 D1
Millennium Fst Coll PE25 ... 206 B3
Miller Ave DN32 ... 192 C6
Miller Cl 12 DN8 ... 15 B7
Miller La DN8 ... 15 B7
Miller Rd DN21 ... 41 A1
Millers Brook DN9 ... 16 E1
Millers Cl
Heighington/Washingborough LN4 ... 81 E4
4 Sleaford NG34 ... 212 C2
Miller's Cl PE10 ... 143 A3
Millers Ct LN11 ... 198 C6
Millers Dale 2 LN6 ... 204 F2
Millers' Gate PE22 ... 113 A2
Millers Quay 6 DN20 ... 196 A3
Millers Rd LN5 ... 93 F6
Millers Rest PE12 ... 158 C7
Millers Way
6 Alford LN13 ... 75 F3
6 Heckington NG34 ... 122 E2
Mill Farm Est LN4 ... 207 B5
MILLFIELD PE1 ... 225 F5
Mill Field 1 LN12 ... 64 C2
Millfield Ave
Grimsby DN33 ... 191 D3
8 Saxilby LN1 ... 66 D2
Mill Field Cl 6 PE6 ... 173 C4
Millfield Cres NG32 ... 119 B6
Mill Field Ct 11 DN3 ... 14 A3
Millfield Gdns 6 PE6 ... 166 F1
Millfield La E PE20 ... 136 D7
Millfield La W PE20 ... 136 D7
Millfield Prim Sch LN4 ... 81 F4
Millfield Rd
Bratoft PE24 ... 102 C7
3 Market Deeping PE6 ... 217 A6
21 Metheringham LN4 ... 95 C4
7 Morton PE10 ... 154 C7
South Somercotes LN11 ... 50 F5
Thorne/Moorends DN8 ... 15 A8
Mill Field Rd
8 Donington PE11 ... 134 E2
Fishlake DN7 ... 14 C8
Scunthorpe DN16 ... 183 E3
Millfields
22 Barton-upon-Humber DN18 ... 10 E8
18 Caistor LN7 ... 33 B4
Millfields Way 9 DN19 ... 11 C8
Mill Field Terr NG34 ... 212 D5
Millfield The 1 DN20 ... 31 A5
Mill Garth DN35 ... 192 D3
Millgate 10 LN5 ... 107 A7
Mill Gate PE12 ... 158 B1
Mill Gn Rd PE11 ... 214 A7
Millgood Cl LN11 ... 198 D5
MILL HILL PE24 ... 103 B8
Mill Hill
Ellerker HU15 ... 2 A8
Friskney PE22 ... 114 F6
Gringley on the Hill DN10 ... 39 B1
Nettleham LN2 ... 68 C2
Mill Hill Cres DN35 ... 192 E5
Mill Hill Dr DN16 ... 185 C3
Millhill La 12 PE20 ... 135 B7
Mill Hill Rd DN7 ... 14 E3
Mill Hill Way LN11 ... 62 A8
Mill House La 1 DN15 ... 9 B5
Millhouse St Rise 5 DN40 ... 186 A4
Mill House Windmill★ DN17 ... 7 C4
Mill La
Addlethorpe PE25 ... 90 D1
Ashby with Scremby PE23 ... 88 D3
Aubourn Haddington & South Hykeham LN5 ... 92 F5
8 Barrow upon Humber DN19 ... 11 C8
Beesby with Saleby LN13 ... 75 F5
Bicker PE20 ... 135 B4
Billinghay LN4 ... 109 E5
Boston PE21 ... 208 E4
Brant Broughton & Stragglethorpe LN5 ... 105 E5
Bratoft PE24 ... 102 C7
Brigg DN20 ... 196 B2
Brough HU15 ... 2 C6
9 Broughton DN20 ... 19 E3
Burgh on Bain LN8 ... 59 D5
Butterwick PE22 ... 126 E4
Caistor LN7 ... 33 C4
Castor PE5 ... 223 F1
7 Croxton Kerrial NG32 ... 138 D4
Donington PE11 ... 134 F2
Eagle & Swinethorpe LN6 ... 79 C2
East Halton DN40 ... 12 D6
Firsby PE24 ... 102 A7
Fleet PE12 ... 168 C2
Fosdyke PE20 ... 136 D1
Friskney PE22 ... 115 C7
Gainsborough DN21 ... 197 B8
Gorefield PE13 ... 169 E1
Gosberton PE11 ... 145 C6
4 Goxhill DN19 ... 5 A1
Grainthorpe LN11 ... 50 B8
Great Ponton NG33 ... 140 A5
Hackthorn LN2 ... 56 B1
Haxey DN9 ... 27 B2
Heighington/Washingborough LN4 ... 81 E4
Hemingby LN9 ... 72 B1
Heydour NG32 ... 131 B5
Hogsthorpe PE24 ... 90 B7
Holbeach PE12 ... 215 B5
Holton le Clay DN36 ... 36 B4
Horbling NG34 ... 133 B3
Horncastle LN9 ... 199 B4
Huttoft LN13 ... 76 E4
Immingham DN40 ... 186 A4
8 Keelby DN41 ... 23 A4
5 Ketton PE9 ... 171 A3
Kingston upon Hull HU10 ... 178 C6
Kirton in Lindsey DN21 ... 30 C1
Kirton PE20 ... 136 A7
Legbourne LN11 ... 61 F3
Lincoln LN5 ... 201 E1
Little Steeping PE23 ... 101 C6
Louth LN11 ... 198 D7
Maltby le Marsh LN13 ... 75 F8
Manby LN11 ... 62 C7
4 Marshchapel DN36 ... 37 C2
Marston NG32 ... 118 D2
Martin LN4 ... 96 C3
Middle Rasen LN8 ... 57 C7
Minting LN8 ... 71 B2
Mumby LN13 ... 76 F1
Newton PE13 ... 169 F5
North Clifton NG23 ... 78 C7
3 North Kelsey LN7 ... 32 A4
Osgodby LN8 ... 45 A3
Owmby LN8 ... 55 E6
Peterborough PE5 ... 228 F7
Pickworth NG34 ... 132 A1
Saltfleetby LN11 ... 51 C1
Saxilby LN1 ... 66 D2
Scamblesby LN11 ... 72 F5
Scawby DN20 ... 30 F8
Skegness PE25 ... 206 A8
Skidbrooke with Saltfleet Haven LN11 ... 51 C4
10 South Ferriby DN18 ... 10 A7
South Somercotes LN11 ... 50 D4
South Witham NG33 ... 151 C1
Sturton by Stow LN1 ... 66 C6
Sutterton PE20 ... 135 F2
19 Sutton Bridge PE12 ... 160 E4
Swineshead PE20 ... 135 A8
Tallington PE9 ... 172 F7
Tetford LN9 ... 73 E1
Thorney PE8 ... 228 B7
Tydd St Mary PE13 ... 160 B1
Wainfleet All Saints PE24 ... 102 C1
Walkeringham DN10 ... 39 F3
Welbourn LN5 ... 106 F4
Welton le Marsh PE23 ... 89 A3
Welton LN2 ... 68 E8
West Keal PE23 ... 100 B4
West Walton PE14 ... 170 F4
Whaplode PE12 ... 158 B7
Wigsley NG23 ... 78 F4
Wildmore LN4 ... 111 C4
Willoughby with Sloothby LN13 ... 89 C6
Woodhall Spa LN10 ... 97 B5
Wrangle PE22 ... 114 D1
Wrawby DN20 ... 20 E3
Mill La Cl PE24 ... 90 B7
Mill La W HU15 ... 2 B6
Mill Marsh Rd PE12 ... 146 D2
Mill Mere Rd
Corringham DN21 ... 41 D2
5 Waddington LN5 ... 93 F7
Mill Moor Way 3 LN6 ... 204 D1
Millom Way DN32 ... 191 F8
Mill Pl DN35 ... 192 F6
Millport Dr HU4 ... 179 B2
Mill Race DN36 ... 36 E4
Mill Rd
Addlethorpe PE24 ... 90 D2
Boston PE21 ... 209 B3
Claypole NG23 ... 117 E7
Cleethorpes DN35 ... 192 E5
Crowle DN17 ... 16 D8
Donington on Bain LN11 ... 59 E2
Hibaldstow DN20 ... 30 E4
2 Keadby DN17 ... 17 D5
Lincoln LN1 ... 234 A4
Luddington & Haldenby DN17 ... 7 C4
Market Rasen LN8 ... 57 D7
Maxey PE6 ... 173 C7
Pilsgate PE9 ... 172 C3
Swanland HU14 ... 3 A6
Walpole PE14 ... 170 F6
Wisbech St Mary PE13 ... 177 D5
Mill Rise
6 Navenby/Wellingore LN5 ... 107 A7
14 Scothern LN2 ... 68 F4
Swanland HU14 ... 3 A6
Mill Row
Barrowby NG32 ... 129 B3
2 Lincoln LN1 ... 234 A4
Mills Cl 15 NG23 ... 117 D3
Mills Dr DN7 ... 26 A8
Mills Service Rd DN16 ... 19 A4
Mill St
Kingston upon Hull HU1 ... 180 E6
Ryhall PE9 ... 163 C2
Scamblesby LN11 ... 73 A4
Millstone Cl LN9 ... 199 A3
Millstone La 3 PE9 ... 172 D3
Millstream Rd LN4 ... 81 E4
MILLTHORPE NG34 ... 143 B6
Millthorpe Dro NG34 ... 143 E5
Millthorpe Rd NG34 ... 143 B5
Mill View
Peterborough PE7 ... 229 A5
5 Waltham DN37 ... 194 E4
Mill View Cl DN9 ... 27 D7
Millview Ct LN9 ... 199 B4
Mill View Ct 12 LN8 ... 70 D4
Millview Gdns 3 DN20 ... 20 E3
Millview Rd
11 Heckington NG34 ... 122 E2
Ruskington NG34 ... 108 D2
Mill View Rd 9 LN8 ... 70 D4
Milman Rd LN2 ... 202 B4
Milne Gn 4 PE20 ... 135 B7
Milners Ct 22 PE9 ... 219 C5
Milner's La 2 PE23 ... 87 F1
Milnyard Sq PE2 ... 229 C2
Milson Cl
18 Barton-upon-Humber DN18 ... 10 E8
7 Broughton DN20 ... 19 D4
Coningsby LN4 ... 207 D4
Milson Rd 17 DN41 ... 23 A4
Milton Cl
Branston LN4 ... 81 D2
Cherry Willingham LN3 ... 203 E5
2 Gainsborough DN21 ... 197 E6
Milton Dr PE13 ... 170 B1
Milton Rd
Gainsborough DN21 ... 197 E6
Grimsby DN34 ... 191 B4
Peterborough PE2 ... 231 A7
Scunthorpe DN16 ... 185 B5
Milton St
Lincoln LN5 ... 205 E7
Newark-on-Trent NG24 ... 104 A3
Milton Way
Kirkby la Thorpe NG34 ... 121 E4
Peterborough PE3 ... 224 E3
2 Sleaford NG34 ... 212 F3
Mimosa Ct DN16 ... 185 E4
Mina Cl PE2 ... 231 D4
Minden Pl 4 DN21 ... 55 A8
MININGSBY PE22 ... 99 D7
Minnett's Hill NG32 ... 130 B8
Minnow Cl 1 DN37 ... 190 D7
Minshull Rd DN35 ... 192 F4
Minster Dr
Cherry Willingham/Reepham LN3 ... 203 E7
Louth LN11 ... 198 D4
Minster Precincts 9 PE1 ... 226 A2
Minster Rd
15 Misterton DN10 ... 39 F5
Scunthorpe DN15 ... 182 B2
Minster Yd LN2 ... 234 B3
MINTING LN9 ... 84 D8
Minting Cl 9 LN1 ... 201 E8
Minting La LN9 ... 71 D1
Mint La LN1 ... 234 A2
Mint St LN1 ... 234 A2
Mirfield Rd
Grimsby DN32 ... 191 F4
Scunthorpe DN15 ... 182 C4
Misson Bank DN9 ... 26 C3
MISTERTON DN10 ... 39 F5
Misterton PE2 ... 229 E3
Misterton Cty Prim Sch DN10 ... 39 F4
Mitchell Cl
Eastgate PE1 ... 226 C2
3 Hatfield DN7 ... 14 D5
7 Skellingthorpe LN6 ... 200 A4
Mitchell Dr LN1 ... 201 C6
Mitchell Rd LN4 ... 207 F6
Mitre La 16 PE21 ... 208 F5
Moat House Rd 22 DN21 ... 30 B1
Moat La
Bolingbroke PE23 ... 100 A8
Old Leake PE22 ... 114 B1
3 South Killingholme DN40 ... 12 E3
4 Welbourn LN5 ... 106 E5
Moat Rd
Scunthorpe DN15 ... 8 C1
Terrington St Clement PE34 ... 161 F1
Moat Wlk NG31 ... 211 E6
Modder St 1 DN16 ... 185 B6
Moggswell La PE2 ... 230 B4
Moira Cl 5 DN7 ... 14 D7
Mole Dro PE12 ... 168 C1
Mollison Ave DN35 ... 192 F5
Mollison Rd HU4 ... 179 A3
Monarch Ave PE2 ... 231 A6
Monarchs Rd PE20 ... 136 A3
Monce Cl LN2 ... 68 C7
Monckton Way LN2 ... 68 D5
Mondemont Cl 4 PE12 ... 215 E3
Money Bridge La PE11 ... 144 F1
Moneys Yd 7 NG34 ... 212 D4
Monic Ave HU13 ... 178 F2
Monkfield Coll LN5 ... 106 C2
Monkhouse Ct 6 PE11 ... 214 A3
Monks Abbey Prim Sch LN2 ... 202 B4
Monks Ave LN11 ... 198 C6
Monks Cl
4 Hatfield DN7 ... 14 D5
New Quarrington NG34 ... 212 A2
Monks Dr 22 PE6 ... 175 A1
Monks Dyke Rd LN11 ... 198 D5
Monks Dyke Tech Coll LN11 ... 198 D5
Monks Gr PE4 ... 220 E5
Monks House La 5 PE11 ... 214 A4
Monkshouse Prim Sch PE11 ... 214 A3
Monks Leys Terr LN2 ... 234 C3
Monks Manor Ct LN2 ... 202 B5
Monks Manor Dr LN2 ... 202 B4
Monks Mdw 5 PE6 ... 175 B8
Monks Rd
Lincoln LN2 ... 234 B2
Scunthorpe DN17 ... 184 F6
8 Swineshead PE20 ... 135 B7
MONKSTHORPE PE23 ... 101 E8
Monksthorpe La PE23 ... 88 F1
Monks Way LN2 ... 202 C3
Monks Way Ind Est LN2 ... 202 D3
Monks Wlk 4 PE11 ... 214 A4
Monkton 2 HU15 ... 2 D6
Monkwood Cl 17 NG23 ... 91 D5
Monmouth La PE12 ... 216 E8
Monmouth St HU4 ... 179 E3
Monsal Dale LN6 ... 204 F2
Monson Ct LN5 ... 201 E1
Monson Pk LN6 ... 200 A4
Monson Rd DN21 ... 42 A8
Monson St LN5 ... 234 A1
Mons Rd LN1 ... 201 E6
Mons St HU5 ... 180 A8
Montague St
Cleethorpes DN35 ... 189 D1
Lincoln LN2 ... 234 C2
Montague Terr 1 LN2 ... 234 C2
Montagu Rd PE4 ... 225 D8
Montaigne Cl 3 LN2 ... 202 D7
Montaigne Cres LN2 ... 202 D7
Montaigne Gdn LN2 ... 202 D7
Montbretia Dr 2 DN17 ... 185 A1
Monteith Cres PE21 ... 209 B5
Montgomery Rd
Cleethorpes DN35 ... 192 D5
Skegness PE25 ... 206 A3
Montrose Cl
8 Grantham NG31 ... 211 D7
1 Lincoln LN6 ... 204 E1
10 Stamford PE9 ... 218 E6
Montrose Gr NG34 ... 121 A2
Montrose St 5 DN16 ... 183 B2
Monument Rd 5 PE20 ... 135 A4
Monument St PE1 ... 226 A3
Moody La DN31 ... 188 C3
Moon's Gn 3 PE12 ... 157 F6
Moor Bank PE22 ... 113 C3
MOORBY PE22 ... 99 B6
Moorby Cl LN1 ... 201 E7
Moor Closes Nature Reserve★ NG32 ... 120 A2
Moor Dike Rd DN7 ... 26 A8
Moore Cl NG23 ... 117 F7
Moor Edges Rd DN8 ... 15 B8
Moore's La 1 PE6 ... 175 A1
Moor Farm Nature Reserve★ LN10 ... 98 A6
Moorfield Rd 2 PE3 ... 225 D3
Moorfields La DN14 ... 6 F7
Moor Gate PE12 ... 159 A4

Moorgate Cl PE10 . . . . . . 154 D7
Moor Gn HU4 . . . . 179 B7
Moorhen Cl LN6 . . . . 92 C6
Moorhouse Rd HU5 . . . . . 179 B8
MOORHOUSES PE22 . . . . . . 112 A8
Moorhouses Rd PE22 . . . 111 F8
Moorings The
  Broughton DN20 . . . . . . 196 A3
  Burton LN1 . . . . 200 D7
Moor La
  Ashby de la Launde &
    Bloxholm LN4 . . . . . . 108 C3
  Besthorpe NG23 . . . . 91 D7
  Blankney LN4 . . . . 95 E4
  Braceby & Sapperton
    NG34 . . . . 131 E1
  Branston & Mere LN4 . . . 81 F2
  Caistor LN7 . . . . 33 A5
  5 Cherry Willingham/
    Reepham LN3 . . . . 82 A8
  Hatfield DN8 . . . . 15 D3
  Horsington LN10 . . . . . . 84 D2
  Kirkby on Bain LN10 . . . 97 F6
  Laneham DN22 . . . . 65 A3
  Leasingham NG34 . . . . . 121 C7
  Lincoln LN6 . . . . 204 E1
  Long Bennington NG23 . . 117 C3
  Marlborough LN5 . . . . . . 93 A4
  Martin LN4 . . . . 96 A2
  North Clifton NG23 . . . . . 78 D6
  Potter Hanworth LN4 . . . 82 B2
  Reepham LN3 . . . . 69 B1
  Roughton LN10 . . . . 98 B7
  South Clifton NG23 . . . . . 78 E5
  South Witham NG33 . . . . 151 B2
  Stapleford LN6 . . . . 105 B8
  Thorpe on the Hill LN6 . . 79 E1
  Thurlby LN6 . . . . 92 E4
  Wroot DN9 . . . . 26 C6
Moorland Ave
  1 Lincoln LN6 . . . . 205 A5
  4 Walkeringham DN10 . . 39 F3
Moorland Cl
  8 Carlton-le-Moorland
    LN5 . . . . 105 E8
  5 Walkeringham DN10 . . 39 F3
Moorland Cres 5 LN6 . . 205 B6
Moorland Dr DN36 . . . . . 195 C7
Moorland Inf Sch LN6 . . 205 B7
Moorlands 9 DN9 . . . . . . 27 A2
Moorlands The 23 LN4 . . 95 D4
Moorland Way
  5 Epworth DN9 . . . . . . 27 E6
  Lincoln LN6 . . . . 204 F5
Moor Owners Rd DN8 . . 15 D8
Moor Pk 5 NG34 . . . . . . 108 C1
Moor Pk Dr 9 LN10 . . . . 97 C5
Moor Rd
  Bottesford DN17 . . . . . . 184 C2
  15 Collingham NG23 . . . 91 D5
  Crowle DN17 . . . . 16 C8
  Newborough PE6 . . . . . 174 C5
  Owersby LN8 . . . . 45 A5
  Snitterby DN21 . . . . 43 D5
  Thorne DN8 . . . . 15 C7
  Walesby LN8 . . . . 45 E3
Moorside PE22 . . . . 98 E3
Moor Side PE22 . . . . 111 C8
MOOR SIDE PE22 . . . . . . 111 D8
Moorside Ct LN6 . . . . . . 204 E1
Moors Rd DN15 . . . . 182 C3
Moor St LN1 . . . . 201 D4
Moorswood Gate PE12 . . 159 D3
MOORTOWN LN7 . . . . 32 C2
Moortown Cl 6 NG31 . . . 211 D7
Moortown Rd LN7 . . . . . . 33 A3
Moorwell Bsns Pk
  DN17 . . . . 184 D3
Moorwell Rd DN17 . . . . . 184 E2
Moray Cl 5 PE9 . . . . 218 D6
MORBORNE PE7 . . . . 232 B3
Morborne Cl PE2 . . . . . . 231 D6
Morborne La PE7 . . . . . . 232 D4
Morborne Rd PE7 . . . . . . 232 C2
Morborn Rd PE7 . . . . . . 230 C2
Mordaunt Ave DN33 . . . . 194 D7
Morden Cl 12 LN4 . . . . . . 95 D4
Morecambe Ave DN16 . . . 185 A4
Moreland Ave 1 LN12 . . . 77 A8
Morfield Gr 5 DN9 . . . . . 27 D6
Morgan Cl PE7 . . . . 233 E6
Morgans Cl 2 NG24 . . . . 104 D5
Morgan Way 5 DN19 . . . . 4 E2
Morkery La
  Castle Bytham NG33 . . . . 152 B2
  North Witham NG33 . . . . 151 F2
Morley La 10 PE20 . . . . . 135 A4
Morley Rd DN17 . . . . 184 F5
Morley's La NG31 . . . . . . 152 F7
Morley St 2 DN21 . . . . . . 197 C5
Morley Way PE2 . . . . . . 230 D5
Morpeth Cl PE2 . . . . 230 C6
Morpeth Rd PE3 . . . . . . 225 C3
Morpeth St HU3 . . . . 180 D7
Morpeth Wlk DN34 . . . . . 191 A7
Morris Cl 21 LN2 . . . . 68 D6
Morris Ct PE7 . . . . 233 E6
Morris Gdns 2 PE25 . . . . 206 B5
Morrison Cl 10 LN12 . . . . 76 F8
Morris Rd HU3 . . . . 179 E7
Morris St PE1 . . . . 226 B3
Mortal Ash Hill DN16 . . . 19 C2
Mortimer Dr HU10 . . . . . 178 F6
MORTON
  Morton DN21 . . . . 197 C8

MORTON continued
  Morton PE10 . . . . 154 C6
  Thorpe on the Hill LN6 . . 92 C6
Morton CE (Controlled)
  Prim Sch PE10 . . . . . . 154 D7
Morton Cl
  Gainsborough DN21 . . . . 197 B8
  Immingham DN40 . . . . . 186 B5
Morton Dr LN6 . . . . 204 F7
Morton Dro PE10 . . . . . . 155 A6
Morton La LN6 . . . . 92 C6
Morton N Dro PE10 . . . . . 155 B7
Morton Rd
  Gainsborough DN21 . . . . 197 C7
  Grimsby DN34 . . . . 191 B7
  Laughton LN6 . . . . 41 B8
  Swinderby LN6 . . . . 92 B7
Morton St HU3 . . . . 180 C8
Morton Terr DN21 . . . . . . 197 C6
Morton Trentside Prim Sch
  DN21 . . . . 197 B8
Morton Way LN9 . . . . 199 C1
Morus Cl PE11 . . . . 214 E2
Mosscroft La DN7 . . . . . . 14 F3
Mossdale Cl NG31 . . . . . 129 F5
Moss Dr PE25 . . . . 206 C2
Mossop Dr PE6 . . . . 164 E3
Moss Rd
  Grimsby DN32 . . . . 191 E7
  Kirk Bramwith DN7 . . . . 14 A8
Motherby La LN1 . . . . . . 234 A2
MOULTON PE12 . . . . 157 F7
MOULTON CHAPEL
  PE12 . . . . 157 E1
Moulton Chapel Prim Sch
  PE12 . . . . 157 F1
Moulton Chapel Rd
  PE12 . . . . 157 C1
Moulton Cl 1 DN34 . . . . . 190 F4
MOULTON EAUGATE
  PE12 . . . . 167 F8
Moulton Gr PE3 . . . . 225 C6
Moulton Marsh Nature
  Reserve★ PE12 . . . . . . 146 F8
Moulton Mere Bank
  PE12 . . . . 157 E3
MOULTON SEAS END
  PE12 . . . . 146 E2
Mount Ave
  14 Barton-upon-Humber
    DN18 . . . . 10 E8
  Kingston upon Hull
    HU13 . . . . 178 D2
  10 Winterton DN15 . . . . . 9 B5
Mountbatten Ave
  11 Pinchbeck PE11 . . . . 156 E8
  Stamford PE9 . . . . 219 A6
  Yaxley PE7 . . . . 233 D5
Mountbatten Cl 5
  DN16 . . . . 185 B4
Mountbatten Dr 2
  PE13 . . . . 170 C1
Mountbatten Way
  Bourne PE10 . . . . 213 E2
  Peterborough PE3 . . . . . 225 B6
Mount La
  Burton Pedwardine
    NG34 . . . . 122 A2
  Kirkby la Thorpe NG34 . . 121 F3
  Legsby LN8 . . . . 58 A3
Mount Olivet LN11 . . . . . 198 A6
Mount Pleasant
  2 Alford LN13 . . . . 75 F2
  Binbrook LN8 . . . . 47 B4
  1 Holton le Clay DN36 . . 195 D1
  Kingston upon Hull HU9 . . 181 C8
  Louth LN11 . . . . 198 C5
  8 New Holland DN19 . . . 4 E2
  Peterborough PE2 . . . . . 231 D4
  Sleaford NG34 . . . . 212 C4
  6 Wainfleet All Saints
    PE24 . . . . 102 D2
  Waltham DN37 . . . . 194 D5
Mount Pleasant Cl
  DN21 . . . . 53 B1
Mount Pleasant Rd
  PE13 . . . . 170 D1
Mount Pleasant Windmill★
  DN21 . . . . 30 B2
Mount Rd HU4 . . . . 205 F3
Mount Royale Cl DN39 . . . 12 A1
Mount St Inf Sch LN1 . . . 201 E6
Mount St
  9 Grantham NG31 . . . . 211 A5
  Lincoln LN1 . . . . 201 E6
Mountsteven Ave PE4 . . . 221 B1
Mount The 15 DN3 . . . . . 14 A1
Mount Tumbledown Cl 9
  PE12 . . . . 160 E4
Mount View 5 HU14 . . . . . 3 A5
Mourne Terr 6 LN5 . . . . . 205 D2
Mowbray Cl 3 DN9 . . . . . 27 D3
Mowbray Ct 23 DN9 . . . . . 27 E6
Mowbray Rd
  Bretton PE3 . . . . 220 D1
  14 Thorne/Moorends
    DN8 . . . . 15 B7
Mowbray St
  Epworth DN9 . . . . 27 E6
  Gainsborough DN21 . . . . 197 C6
Moxon's La 18 LN5 . . . . . 93 F7
Mrs Mary Kings CE
  (Controlled) Prim Sch
  LN4 . . . . 96 B3
Mrs Smith's Cottage★
  LN5 . . . . 107 B8
Much La LN1 . . . . 234 A2

MUCKTON LN11 . . . . 74 D8
Muckton Wood Nature
  Reserve★ LN11 . . . . . . 74 E8
Muirfield
  Grantham NG31 . . . . . . 211 D8
  11 Waltham DN37 . . . . . 194 C4
Muirfield Cl 6 PE11 . . . . 214 C2
Muirfield Croft DN40 . . . 186 C4
Muirfield Dr DN25 . . . . . 206 D5
Mulberry Ave 3 LN6 . . . . 204 F2
Mulberry Cl
  5 North Thoresby
    DN36 . . . . 36 B1
  Sleaford NG34 . . . . 212 D2
  Waddington LN5 . . . . . . 205 C1
Mulberry Ct 6 PE20 . . . . 135 B6
Mulberry Dr 21 DN17 . . . . 16 D7
Mulberry Gdns
  Bottesford DN16 . . . . . . 185 E4
  Paston PE4 . . . . 221 C1
Mulberry Rd LN8 . . . . . . 45 E5
Mulberry Way
  Skegness PE25 . . . . 206 B6
  Spalding PE11 . . . . 214 E3
Mulberry Wlk 11 NG34 . . 122 D3
Mulgrave Cl DN37 . . . . . 190 F8
Mulgrave St S DN15 . . . . 183 A4
Mulgrave St HU8 . . . . . . 181 A8
Mull Way DN40 . . . . 186 C2
Multon Ings La PE20 . . . 136 B7
MUMBY LN13 . . . . 76 F1
Mumby Cl 12 DN36 . . . . . 36 B1
Mumby Mdws LN13 . . . . . 76 F1
Mumby Rd LN13 . . . . 76 F2
Mumby's Bridge Rd
  PE22 . . . . 98 F2
Munday Way PE13 . . . . . 170 B2
Munster Ct 6 DN31 . . . . 189 C1
Munton Fields NG33 . . . . 131 A1
Murdock Rd LN5 . . . . 205 E6
Murray St 2 DN31 . . . . . 189 B2
MURROW PE13 . . . . 177 D5
Murrow Bank PE13 . . . . . 177 D6
Murrow Cty Prim Sch
  PE13 . . . . 177 D5
Murrow La PE13 . . . . . . 177 F5
Museum of Lincolnshire
  Life★ LN1 . . . . 234 A4
Musgraves Orch LN2 . . . . 68 C7
Muskham PE3 . . . . 224 F4
Mussons Cl NG33 . . . . . 152 E7
Muster Roll La PE21 . . . 209 A3
Musticott Pl 17 PE13 . . . 170 E1
MUSTON NG13 . . . . 128 C5
Muston La NG13 . . . . . . 128 B5
Muston Meadows National
  Nature Reserve★
  NG13 . . . . 128 B3
Muston Rd NG31 . . . . . . 210 E2
Muswell Rd PE3 . . . . . . 225 E4
Mutton La DN10 . . . . 39 F1
Myers Cl NG32 . . . . 120 C1
Myle Cross Jun Sch
  LN2 . . . . 202 C6
Myles Way 15 PE13 . . . . 170 D2
Myrtle Ave PE1 . . . . . . 226 C7
Myrtle Cl PE1 . . . . 226 C7
Myrtle Gr PE1 . . . . 226 C7
Myrtle House Cvn Pk
  PE1 . . . . 226 F5
Myrtle Rd 5 DN7 . . . . . . 14 C4
Myrtle Way 16 HU15 . . . . . 2 C5
Myton St HU1 . . . . 180 E6

N

Naam Gr LN1 . . . . 234 A4
Naam Pl LN1 . . . . 234 A4
Nab La DN7 . . . . 14 C8
Nags Head Pas 10
  NG34 . . . . 212 D4
Nairn Rd PE9 . . . . 218 E6
Nandike Cl 4 HU10 . . . . . 178 F6
Nan Sampson Bank
  DN9 . . . . 26 A4
Nansicles Rd PE2 . . . . . 230 D6
Napier Pl PE2 . . . . 229 C6
Napier St LN2 . . . . 234 C2
Narrow Boats The 3
  DN20 . . . . 196 A3
Narrow La
  Belchford LN9 . . . . 73 B2
  Twin Rivers DN14 . . . . . 7 C8
  Whaplode PE12 . . . . . . 158 C4
Naseby Cl
  21 Hatfield DN7 . . . . . . 14 D3
  Peterborough PE3 . . . . . 225 C5
Naseby Dr DN31 . . . . . . 191 B8
Naseby Gr DN31 . . . . . . 191 B7
Nash La 2 LN6 . . . . 204 E1
Natal View LN1 . . . . 201 D8
Nathan Cl PE3 . . . . 225 B2
National Ave HU5 . . . . . 179 F8
National CE Jun Sch The
  NG31 . . . . 211 B5
National Fishing Heritage
  Ctr★ DN31 . . . . 191 E8
National Parrot Sanctuary
  The★ PE22 . . . . 114 D7
Natural World Ctr★ LN6 . . 79 F1
Natureland Seal
  Sanctuary★
  PE25 . . . . 206 E4
NAVENBY LN5 . . . . 107 A8
Navenby CE Prim Sch
  LN5 . . . . 107 B8

Navenby La
  Ashby de la Launde &
    Bloxholm LN4 . . . . . . 107 F6
  Bassingham LN5 . . . . . . 93 A1
Navensby Cl DN31 . . . . . 188 A2
Navigation House★ **8**
  NG34 . . . . 212 E4
Navigation La 28 LN7 . . . 33 B4
Navigation Way HU9 . . . 181 C6
Naylors Dr 5 LN8 . . . . . . 57 B8
Naylor's Row 3 HU9 . . . . 181 B7
Ndola Gr LN2 . . . . 199 C2
Neale Rd 16 LN6 . . . . 93 C8
Neal's Gate PE12 . . . . . . 158 E2
Neap House Rd
  Flixborough DN15 . . . . . 182 A7
  Gunness DN15 . . . . 17 E6
Neatgangs La DN19 . . . . . 5 A3
Neath Rd DN16 . . . . 183 A1
Neaverson Rd 2 PE6 . . . 220 D7
Needham Dr PE12 . . . . . 159 C1
Needham Rd PE10 . . . . . 154 C6
Needhams Mdw LN13 . . . . 76 B3
Needles The 8 PE25 . . . . 206 A7
Neile Cl LN2 . . . . 202 D7
Nelson Cl
  5 Crowland PE6 . . . . . 166 F1
  4 Skegness PE25 . . . . 206 A7
Nelson Dr LN4 . . . . 203 B2
Nelson Gdns 31 PE13 . . . 170 D1
Nelson Rd
  Fiskerton LN3 . . . . 82 A6
  Kingston upon Hull HU5 . 179 B7
  4 Mablethorpe/Sutton on Sea
    LN12 . . . . 64 B3
Nelson St
  Gainsborough DN21 . . . . 197 C6
  Grimsby DN32 . . . . 189 B1
  Kingston upon Hull HU1 . . 181 A5
  Lincoln LN1 . . . . 201 D3
Nelson Way
  9 Boston PE21 . . . . . . 208 E4
  2 Grimsby DN34 . . . . . 190 D4
Nelthorpe Cl 9 DN39 . . . . 12 A1
Nelthorpe St LN5 . . . . . . 201 E1
Nene Cl
  10 Ruskington NG34 . . . 108 D2
  Wansford PE8 . . . . 222 A3
  4 Wittering PE8 . . . . . 172 B1
Nene Ct
  4 Grantham NG31 . . . . 210 E2
  3 Spalding PE11 . . . . . 214 F5
Nenelands 2 PE21 . . . . . 160 F4
Nene Mdws 1 PE12 . . . . 160 F4
Nene Parade 9 PE13 . . . 170 C1
Nene Parkway PE3 . . . . . 224 F1
Nene Pk 6 LN6 . . . . 204 C1
Nene Rd LN1 . . . . 201 E8
Nene St PE1 . . . . 226 B2
NENE TERRACE PE6 . . . . . 175 D6
Nene Valley Prim Sch
  PE2 . . . . 230 D8
Nene Way PE5 . . . . 222 F2
Neptune St
  Cleethorpes DN35 . . . . . 192 E7
  Kingston upon Hull HU1 . . 180 D4
Neslam Rd NG34 . . . . . . 143 C7
Ness La DN17 . . . . 7 E6
Netherfield PE12 . . . . . . 215 B2
Nethergate DN9 . . . . 27 B2
Netherlands Way
  DN41 . . . . 187 B3
Netherton Rd HU4 . . . . . 179 B4
NETTLEHAM LN2 . . . . 68 D2
Nettleham CE (Aided) Jun
  Sch LN2 . . . . 68 C2
Nettleham Cl LN2 . . . . . 202 A6
Nettleham Inf Sch LN2 . . . 68 C2
Nettleham Rd
  Lincoln LN2 . . . . 234 C4
  Scothern LN2 . . . . 68 E3
Nettleholme 10 DN7 . . . . 14 D4
NETTLETON LN7 . . . . 33 A3
Nettleton Cl LN6 . . . . . . 81 E2
Nettleton Dr LN6 . . . . . . 92 E5
Nettleton Prim Sch LN7 . . 33 A3
Nettleton Rd LN7 . . . . . . 33 B3
Neustadt Ct 10 LN2 . . . . . 234 B3
Neville Ave PE11 . . . . . . 214 F4
Neville Cl
  5 Keadby with Althorpe
    DN17 . . . . 17 D4
  Kingston upon Hull HU3 . 180 D5
Neville Cres 5 DN15 . . . . 9 A5
Neville La DN7 . . . . 14 A8
Neville Rd DN16 . . . . . . 183 C2
Neville St DN35 . . . . 192 D8
Neville Turner Way
  DN37 . . . . 194 D4
NEWARK PE1 . . . . 226 E6
Newark Air Mus★
  NG24 . . . . 104 D6
Newark Ave PE1 . . . . . . 226 C6
Newark Hill
  Foston NG23 . . . . 117 F1
  Great Gonerby NG31 . . . 129 D6
Newark Hill Prim Sch
  PE1 . . . . 226 D6
Newark Hospl NG24 . . . . 104 A4
Newark La NG32 . . . . . . 119 C4
Newark N Gate Sta
  NG24 . . . . 104 A6
Newark & Nottinghamshire
  Agricultural Society's
  Showground★ NG24 . . 104 C7
NEWARK-ON-TRENT
  NG24 . . . . 104 B4

Newark Rd
  Barnby in the Willows
    NG24 . . . . 104 E3
  Bassingham LN5 . . . . . . 92 E2
  Fenton LN1 . . . . 65 D4
  Leadenham LN5 . . . . . . 106 C3
  Lincoln LN6 . . . . 204 F3
  Newark-on-Trent NG24 . . 104 C5
  Norton Disney LN6 . . . . 91 F2
  Peterborough PE1 . . . . . 226 E2
  Stapleford LN6 . . . . 105 B8
  Swinderby LN6 . . . . 92 A4
Newark Rd Ind Est
  PE1 . . . . 226 E4
Newark Wlk DN40 . . . . . 186 D3
NEW BALDERTON
  NG24 . . . . 104 A2
NEWBALL LN3 . . . . 69 D3
NEW BARNETBY DN38 . . . 21 D5
New Beacon Rd NG31 . . . 211 C4
Newbey Cl PE3 . . . . 225 B3
Newbigg
  1 Crowle DN17 . . . . . . 16 C8
  Westwoodside DN9 . . . . 27 B2
NEW BOLINGBROKE
  PE22 . . . . 112 D8
Newbolt Ave 2 DN17 . . . 184 D7
Newbolt Cl 1 LN7 . . . . . . 33 A3
Newborn Ave DN15 . . . . 182 E4
Newborn Cl PE2 . . . . . . 231 E5
NEWBOROUGH PE6 . . . . . 174 E4
Newborough CE Prim Sch
  PE6 . . . . 174 E4
Newborough Rd PE4 . . . . 174 E1
Newboults La 2 PE9 . . . . 219 A5
Newbridge Hill LN11 . . . . 198 C6
Newbridge La LN11 . . . . . 49 E5
New Bridge Rd HU9 . . . . 181 C8
Newbury Ave DN37 . . . . 188 A1
Newbury Gr 2 DN34 . . . . 190 E4
Newbury Rd 15 NG24 . . . 104 C5
Newbury Terr DN37 . . . . 188 A1
Newby Rd DN31 . . . . . . 191 C7
New Cartergate 1
  DN31 . . . . 191 D7
Newcastle Dr PE2 . . . . . 230 D6
Newcastle Rd 4 NG31 . . . 210 D5
New Chapel La 8 DN37 . . . 23 F1
New Cl DN33 . . . . 191 C4
New Clee Sta DN31 . . . . 189 D1
New Cleveland St HU8 . . 181 A8
New Coll LN2 . . . . 219 C6
Newcomb Ct
  2 Sleaford NG34 . . . . . 212 B7
  16 Stamford PE9 . . . . . 219 B5
Newcombe Way PE2 . . . . 229 D2
Newcot La LN4 . . . . 81 F4
New Cres LN3 . . . . 203 D6
New Cross Rd 3 PE9 . . . 219 C6
New Cut PE6 . . . . 176 D5
Newdike Gate PE12 . . . . 158 C5
Newdown Rd DN17 . . . . . 184 D3
New End
  Hemingby LN9 . . . . 72 B1
  5 Wainfleet All Saints
    PE24 . . . . 102 D2
NEW ENGLAND
  Croft PE24 . . . . 102 E2
  Peterborough PE1 . . . . . 225 E7
New Est
  1 Little Bytham NG33 . . 163 A8
  Swinstead NG33 . . . . . . 153 A5
New Fen Dike PE12 . . . . 169 A7
New Fen Dro PE12 . . . . . 168 B1
Newfield Cl 10 DN3 . . . . . 14 A4
Newfield Dr LN4 . . . . . . 109 F3
Newfield Rd NG34 . . . . . 212 C5
Newfields PE13 . . . . 169 D1
NEW FLETTON PE2 . . . . . 231 B8
Newgate La NG31 . . . . . 130 D4
Newgate Rd PE13 . . . . . 169 F6
Newgates 3 PE9 . . . . . . 219 C5
New Gdn St 5 HU1 . . . . . 180 F7
New George St HU2 . . . . 180 F7
New Green 3 DN7 . . . . . . 14 C6
Newhall Rd
  10 Kirk Sandall DN3 . . . 14 A2
  13 Kirk Sandall DN3 . . . 14 A2
NEWHAM PE22 . . . . 112 A1
Newham La PE22 . . . . . . 112 A1
New Hammond Beck Rd
  PE21 . . . . 208 A3
Newham Rd 2 PE9 . . . . . 219 A7
Newhaven Dr LN5 . . . . . 205 D5
New Haven Terr DN31 . . . 188 D1
New Hill NG32 . . . . 119 A5
NEW HOLLAND DN19 . . . . .4 E2
New Holland CE Methodist
  Prim Sch DN19 . . . . . . 4 E2
New Holland Rd DN19 . . . . 4 E1
New Holland Sta DN19 . . . 4 E3
New Ings La DN22 . . . . . 52 E3
Newington Ave HU4 . . . . 179 E5
Newington Prim Sch
  HU3 . . . . 180 A4
Newington St HU3 . . . . . 179 F4
New Inn La 3 DN7 . . . . . 14 C7
New La
  Girton NG23 . . . . 78 D2
  Great Carlton LN11 . . . . 62 E3
  Reedness DN14 . . . . 6 E8
  Tathwell LN11 . . . . 61 A1
  Toynton St Peter PE23 . . 101 A5
  Wansford PE8 . . . . 222 C1
Newland LN1 . . . . 234 A2
Newland Ave DN15 . . . . 182 E2
Newland Dr DN15 . . . . . 182 D3
Newlands DN21 . . . . 197 E5

Newland St W 2 LN1 . . . 234 A2
Newlands Ct DN21 . . . . . . 197 E5
Newlands Pk DN36 . . . . . . 193 B1
Newlands Rd
2 Haconby PE10 . . . . 154 D8
Parson Drove PE13 . . . . . . 177 D7
Surfleet PE11 . . . . 145 F4
Newland View 17 DN9 . . . . 27 E6
Newland Wlk DN15 . . . . . . 182 E3
NEW LEAKE PE22 . . . . 114 A8
New Leake Prim Sch
PE22 . . . . 113 F7
Newlyn Cl
4 Kingston upon Hull
HU13 . . . . 179 A2
New Waltham DN36 . . . . . . 195 C7
Newman Cl 19 PE8 . . . . . . 172 B1
Newmarch Ct DN33 . . . . . . 191 B2
Newmarket LN11 . . . . 198 C4
Newmarket Cl PE1 . . . . . . 226 B6
Newmarket St 4 DN32 . . 191 F8
NEW MEADOW PE7 . . . . . . 231 F2
New Meadow Dro PE7 . . 231 D1
New Mill Field Rd DN7 . . . 14 E3
Newnham Cres DN16 . . . . 185 A4
New Options Barton Sch
DN18 . . . . 11 A8
New Pk Est 1 DN7 . . . . 14 D7
Newport LN2 . . . . 234 B4
Newport Ave NG31 . . . . . . 210 D4
Newport Cl 4 HU3 . . . . . . 180 D5
Newport Cres 2 LN5 . . . . . 93 F7
Newport Ct 1 LN1 . . . . . . 234 B4
Newport Dr DN15 . . . . 9 A6
Newport St 8 DN18 . . . . 3 F1
Newport Wlk DN40 . . . . . . 186 D3
NEW QUARRINGTON
NG34 . . . . 212 A2
New Rd
Blankney LN10 . . . . 96 F5
Brantingham HU15 . . . . 2 C8
Cleethorpes DN35 . . . . 192 F6
Clipsham LE15 . . . . 162 B7
1 Collyweston PE9 . . . . . . 171 B1
Croft PE24 . . . . 103 C3
Deeping St Nicholas PE6 . . 166 D5
5 Easton on the Hill
PE9 . . . . 171 D3
9 Eye PE6 . . . . 175 A1
Folksworth PE7 . . . . 232 E6
Laceby DN37 . . . . 35 A8
Langtoft PE6 . . . . 164 F3
Peterborough PE1 . . . . 226 B2
Quadring PE11 . . . . 145 C8
Ryhall PE9 . . . . 163 C1
Scunthorpe DN17 . . . . 184 B6
Silk Willoughby NG34 . . . . 121 A1
Spalding PE11 . . . . 214 D4
Staunton NG13 . . . . 117 B2
Sutton Bridge PE12 . . . . . . 160 F5
Swinefleet DN14 . . . . 6 C4
Thistleton LE15 . . . . 151 D1
Wainfleet All Saints
PE24 . . . . 101 E2
Waltham DN37 . . . . 194 E4
Worlaby DN20 . . . . 10 D1
New River Dro
Cowbit PE12 . . . . 156 F3
3 Spalding PE12 . . . . 214 C1
New River Gate PE12 . . . . 168 D8
New Roman Bank
PE34 . . . . 161 D3
New Row
Gonerby Hill Foot
NG31 . . . . 210 E7
3 Market Deeping PE6 . . 217 D4
8 Messingham DN17 . . . . . 29 D7
Newsham Dr DN34 . . . . . . 191 A7
Newsham Garth HU4 . . . . 179 B5
Newsham La DN39 . . . . 22 D8
New St
Aby with Greenfield
LN13 . . . . 75 B5
7 Brigg DN20 . . . . 196 C3
Elsham DN20 . . . . 20 E7
1 Gainsborough DN21 . . . 197 C5
Grantham NG31 . . . . 211 A5
Grimsby DN31 . . . . 191 E7
5 Heckington NG34 . . . . . 122 E2
Helpringham NG34 . . . . . . 133 D7
6 Louth LN11 . . . . 198 B5
Osbournby NG34 . . . . 132 D5
Sleaford NG34 . . . . 212 E4
4 Stamford PE9 . . . . 219 C6
Newstead Ave
Cherry Willingham/Reepham
LN3 . . . . 203 E5
Holton le Clay DN36 . . . . . 195 E2
Newstead Cl PE6 . . . . 175 A2
Newstead Rd
Cleethorpes DN35 . . . . 192 E4
2 Mablethorpe/Sutton on Sea
LN12 . . . . 64 C3
Newstead PE9 . . . . 219 F6
Ryhall PE9 . . . . 163 D1
Newstead St HU5 . . . . 180 A8
NEWTOFT LN8 . . . . 56 E5
NEWTON
Newton and Haceby
NG34 . . . . 132 A3
Newton PE13 . . . . 170 A5
Newton Bar NG34 . . . . 132 A3
NEWTON BY TOFT LN8 . . . . 56 E6
Newton Cl
8 Metheringham LN4 . . . . . 95 C4
Swinderby LN6 . . . . 92 A5
5 Wragby LN8 . . . . 70 D4
Newton Ct 6 NG33 . . . . . 151 E7
Newton Dr LN3 . . . . 203 C6
Newton Gr DN33 . . . . 191 C4
Newton La
Binbrook LN8 . . . . 47 D5
15 Ruskington NG34 . . . . . 108 E2
Newton Marsh La DN36 . . 36 F6
NEWTON ON TRENT
LN1 . . . . 65 D1
Newton-on-Trent CE Prim
Sch LN1 . . . . 65 C1
Newton Pk 10 NG23 . . . . . 117 D3
Newton Rd DN16 . . . . 185 E6
Newton St
5 Grantham NG31 . . . . . . 211 B4
3 Kingston upon Hull
HU3 . . . . 180 B4
Lincoln LN5 . . . . 234 B1
Newark-on-Trent NG24 . . . 104 A4
Newton Terr LN11 . . . . . . 198 C5
Newton Way
5 Colsterworth NG33 . . . 151 D7
Sleaford NG34 . . . . 212 D5
Newtown
8 Spilsby PE23 . . . . 101 A8
Stamford PE9 . . . . 219 D5
New Town 6 PE9 . . . . 171 D3
Newtown Ct HU9 . . . . 181 E7
Newtown Sq HU9 . . . . 181 E7
New Trent St DN17 . . . . 16 E6
NEW WALTHAM DN36 . . . . 195 D7
New Waltham Prim Sch
DN36 . . . . 195 C7
New Wlk HU14 . . . . 3 A4
NEW YORK LN4 . . . . 111 C5
New York Prim Sch
LN4 . . . . 111 C4
New York Rd LN4 . . . . 110 F6
Nicholas Ct 26 DN18 . . . . . 10 E8
Nicholas Taylor Gdns 1
PE3 . . . . 224 F3
Nicholas Way DN21 . . . . . . 41 E2
Nichol Hill 2 LN11 . . . . . . 198 B5
Nicholls Ave PE3 . . . . 225 E3
Nicholson Rd
3 Healing DN41 . . . . 24 A5
Immingham DN40 . . . . 12 E4
Nicholson St 8 DN35 . . . 192 F5
Nicholson Way 7 DN9 . . . 27 D7
Nicolette Way 10 PE11 . . 214 B5
Nicolgate La DN20 . . . . . . 196 D4
Nicolson Dr 18 DN18 . . . . . 10 F8
Nidd's La PE20 . . . . 136 E4
Nightingale Cl DN15 . . . . 182 D5
Nightingale Cres 1
LN6 . . . . 204 E8
Nightingale Ct PE4 . . . . . 221 E2
Nightingale Dr PE7 . . . . . 233 D6
Nightingales 13 PE6 . . . . . 217 C5
Nightleys Rd DN22 . . . . 65 B5
Ninescores La DN9 . . . . 26 B4
Ninth Ave
3 Fixborough Ind Est
DN15 . . . . 8 A1
Grantham NG31 . . . . 211 F5
NINTHORPE PE25 . . . . 206 D6
Nipcut Rd PE6 . . . . 175 C2
NOCTON LN4 . . . . 95 B7
Nocton Com Prim Sch
LN4 . . . . 95 C7
Nocton Dr LN2 . . . . 201 F8
Nocton Fen La LN4 . . . . 83 A1
Nocton Rd
7 Potterhanworth LN4 . . . . 82 B1
Potter Hanworth LN4 . . . . . 95 B8
Noel St DN21 . . . . 197 C6
Nooking La DN37 . . . . 23 D2
Nookings Dr 3 DN20 . . . . . 31 A5
Nooking The DN9 . . . . 27 C3
Nookin The 1 LN5 . . . . . . 106 E5
Nook The
Croxton Kerrial NG32 . . . . 138 D3
7 Easton on the Hill
PE9 . . . . 171 D3
4 Helpston PE6 . . . . 173 C4
Sproxton LE14 . . . . 150 C7
Norbeck La LN2 . . . . 68 C6
Norburn
2 Peterborough PE3 . . . . 220 F1
Peterborough PE3 . . . . 225 B8
Norfolk Ave DN15 . . . . 8 B4
Norfolk Bank La HU15 . . . . . . 1 F8
Norfolk Cl 1 LN8 . . . . 47 B6
Norfolk Cres
Bracebridge Heath
LN4 . . . . 205 F4
1 Scampton Airfield LN1 . . 67 E5
Norfolk Ct 19 DN32 . . . . . 189 C1
Norfolk La DN35 . . . . 192 E7
Norfolk Pl 4 PE21 . . . . . . 208 F6
Norfolk St Ind Est
PE21 . . . . 208 F7
Norfolk Sq 5 PE9 . . . . 219 B6
Norfolk St
Boston PE21 . . . . 208 F6
Kingston upon Hull HU2 . . 180 E7
Lincoln LN1 . . . . 201 C4
Peterborough PE1 . . . . 225 F4
Norland Ave HU4 . . . . 179 C6
Norman Ave 5 PE21 . . . . 208 F5
NORMANBY DN15 . . . . 8 C3
NORMANBY-BY-SPITAL
LN8 . . . . 55 E7
NORMANBY BY STOW
DN21 . . . . 53 E1
Normanby Cliff Rd LN8 . . . 55 D7
Normanby Hall Ctry Pk*
DN15 . . . . 8 C3
NORMANBY LE WOLD
LN7 . . . . 45 F5
Normanby Pk Farming
Mus* DN15 . . . . 8 C3
Normanby Prim Sch
LN8 . . . . 55 E7
Normanby Rd
Burton upon Stather
DN15 . . . . 8 C3
Nettleton LN7 . . . . 33 B2
3 Owmby LN8 . . . . 55 F6
Scunthorpe DN15 . . . . 183 A5
Stow DN21 . . . . 53 F1
Normanby Rise LN8 . . . . . . 45 E5
Norman Cl
9 Barton-upon-Humber
DN18 . . . . 10 F8
30 Metheringham LN4 . . . . 95 C4
NORMAN CORNER
DN37 . . . . 194 C2
Norman Cres 1 DN17 . . . . 184 F8
NORMAN CROSS PE7 . . . . 232 F2
Norman Dr 7 DN7 . . . . 14 D3
Normandy Cl LN11 . . . . . . 198 E6
Normandy Rd DN35 . . . . . 192 D5
Norman Mews 3
PE10 . . . . 213 D5
Norman Rd
Grimsby DN34 . . . . 191 B7
Hatfield DN7 . . . . 14 D3
Peterborough PE1 . . . . 226 C4
Norman St 1 LN5 . . . . 234 B1
NORMANTON
Bottesford NG13 . . . . 128 A7
Normanton NG32 . . . . 119 D5
Normanton La NG13 . . . . . 128 A6
Normanton Rd
3 Beacon Hill NG24 . . . . . 104 B5
1 Crowland PE6 . . . . 166 F1
Peterborough PE1 . . . . 226 D7
Normanton Rise HU4 . . . . 179 C7
Nornabell St 1 HU8 . . . . . 181 C8
Norris Cl 10 NG34 . . . . . . 122 D3
Norris St LN5 . . . . 201 F1
Norsefield Ave DN37 . . . . . 194 E5
Nortcote Heavy Horse Ctr*
PE23 . . . . 101 D7
Northam Cl PE6 . . . . 175 B3
Northampton Rd DN16 . . 183 C1
North Ave PE10 . . . . 153 D6
North Axholme Comp Sch
DN17 . . . . 16 D7
North Bank
Crowland PE6 . . . . 166 E1
Thorney PE6 . . . . 227 D1
North Bank Rd 4 PE1 . . . 226 D3
NORTHBECK NG34 . . . . . . 132 F8
North Beck La PE23 . . . . . . 87 E1
NORTHBOROUGH PE6 . . . . 217 E2
Northborough Prim Sch
PE6 . . . . 173 F6
Northborough Rd PE6 . . . 174 C5
North Bracing PE25 . . . . . 206 E3
NORTH CARLTON LN1 . . . . . 67 C4
NORTH CARR DN9 . . . . 27 C3
North Carr La DN20 . . . . 9 F3
North Carr Rd
Misterton DN10 . . . . 39 F7
Scotter DN17 . . . . 28 E5
West Stockwith DN10 . . . . . 40 B6
North Causeway LN4 . . . . . 82 D4
North Church Side 12
HU1 . . . . 180 F6
Northcliffe Rd NG31 . . . . . 211 A7
North Cliff Rd DN21 . . . . . . 30 C2
NORTH CLIFTON NG23 . . . . . 78 C7
North Clifton Prim Sch
NG23 . . . . 78 C6
North Coates Rd DN36 . . . 37 A4
NORTH COCKERINGTON
LN11 . . . . 50 A1
North Cockerington CE
Prim Sch LN11 . . . . 50 A1
Northcote Heavy Horse
Ctr* PE23 . . . . 101 D7
NORTH COTES DN36 . . . . . . 37 A3
North Cotes CE
(Controlled) Prim Sch
DN36 . . . . 37 B3
North County Prim Sch
DN21 . . . . 197 B6
North Court 10 LN2 . . . . . . 68 C2
North Cres 7 NG13 . . . . . 128 A5
Northcroft 4 LN1 . . . . 66 D3
Northcroft La NG23 . . . . 91 C5
North-dale Ct 4 DN21 . . . . 30 B2
Northdale Pk 1 HU14 . . . . . . 3 B7
North Dales Rd LN4 . . . . . . 82 A5
North Dr
2 Ancaster NG32 . . . . 120 A3
5 Balderton NG24 . . . . . . 104 C1
Kingston upon Hull
HU10 . . . . 178 E6
RAF Cranwell NG34 . . . . . 107 D1
Swanland HU14 . . . . 3 B7
North Dro
Bicker PE20 . . . . 134 E6
Deeping St Nicholas
PE11 . . . . 155 F1
Helpringham NG34 . . . . . . 133 E7
Lutton PE12 . . . . 148 D1
Quadring PE11 . . . . 144 C8
Swaton NG34 . . . . 133 E4
North Eastern Rd DN8 . . . . 15 A8
NORTH ELKINGTON
LN11 . . . . 48 D1
North Elkington La
LN11 . . . . 48 E1
NORTH END LN11 . . . . 49 E3
North End 5 DN19 . . . . 12 A8
NORTH END LN11 . . . . 62 F8
North End DN18 . . . . 10 A8
NORTH END PE20 . . . . 135 B8
North End PE13 . . . . 170 C1
North End Cres 9
DN36 . . . . 36 D4
North End La
2 Fulbeck NG32 . . . . 106 C1
Saltfleetby LN11 . . . . 62 F8
South Cockerington LN11 . . 50 F1
South Kelsey LN7 . . . . 32 A2
Sturton le Steeple DN22 . . . 52 E4
North End Rd 7 DN36 . . . . 36 D4
Northern Ave DN20 . . . . . . 196 C5
Northern Rd NG24 . . . . 104 A5
Northern's Cl NG33 . . . . . . 151 D5
Northey Rd PE6 . . . . 227 C2
North Farm Rd DN17 . . . . 184 D3
Northfeild Rd DN21 . . . . 41 B8
North Fen Dro PE20 . . . . . 134 E4
North Fen Rd
3 Glinton PE6 . . . . 220 C8
Helpringham NG34 . . . . . . 133 D7
NORTH FERRIBY HU14 . . . . 3 B4
North Ferriby CE Prim Sch
HU14 . . . . 3 A5
Northferry La 2 DN9 . . . . . 16 D1
NORTHFIELD HU13 . . . . 178 F2
Northfield HU14 . . . . 3 B7
Northfield Ave
Kingston upon Hull
HU13 . . . . 178 E3
3 Sudbrooke LN2 . . . . 68 F3
Northfield Cl
19 Ruskington NG34 . . . . . 108 E2
1 Scunthorpe DN16 . . . . . 185 C6
11 Tetney DN36 . . . . 36 D4
West Butterwick DN17 . . . . 17 D1
Northfield La
Amcotts DN17 . . . . 7 E2
North Clifton NG23 . . . . 78 D7
Thornton Curtis DN39 . . . . . 11 D5
Willoughton DN21 . . . . 42 C4
Northfield Rd
Ashby with Scremby
PE23 . . . . 88 D1
Kingston upon Hull HU3 . . 179 F6
Messingham DN17 . . . . 185 A1
North Leverton with
Habblesthorpe DN22 . . . . 52 D1
Peterborough PE1 . . . . 225 F7
4 Ruskington NG34 . . . . . 108 E2
Sleaford NG34 . . . . 212 A2
Welton LN2 . . . . 68 D7
North Field Rd PE6 . . . . . . 217 B7
Northfield Rise 1 LN1 . . . . 66 C2
Northfields
Bourne PE10 . . . . 213 D7
Stamford PE9 . . . . 219 C6
Northfields Ct PE9 . . . . . . 219 C6
North Foreland Dr 3
PE25 . . . . 206 D8
North Forty Foot Bank
PE21 . . . . 208 A6
Northgate
Kingston upon Hull
HU13 . . . . 178 E2
Lincoln LN2 . . . . 234 B4
Louth LN11 . . . . 198 B5
NORTHGATE PE11 . . . . 144 D1
North Gate
Gosberton PE11 . . . . 145 A6
Newark-on-Trent NG24 . . . 104 A5
Pinchbeck PE11 . . . . 144 E1
Sleaford NG34 . . . . 212 D5
Northgate Ct LN11 . . . . . . 198 B6
Northgate La LN11 . . . . 62 B7
Northgate Sports Hall
NG34 . . . . 212 D5
NORTH GREETWELL
LN2 . . . . 203 B8
North Halls 1 LN8 . . . . 47 C5
NORTH HARBY NG23 . . . . . . 79 C7
North Heath La NG32 . . . . 106 D1
North Holme 8 DN36 . . . . . 36 D4
North Holme Rd LN11 . . . 198 B7
NORTH HYKEHAM
LN6 . . . . 204 D2
North Ing Dro PE11 . . . . . 134 C4
Northing La NG23 . . . . 68 F5
North Ings La LN13 . . . . 77 A5
North Ings Rd DN7 . . . . 14 E5
Northings The 1
NG32 . . . . 210 B4
North Intake La DN9 . . . . . 40 C8
NORTH KELSEY LN7 . . . . 32 A4
NORTH KELSEY MOOR
LN7 . . . . 32 D4
North Kelsey Prim Sch
LN7 . . . . 32 A4
North Kelsey Rd LN7 . . . . . 33 A4
North Kesteven Ctr*
LN6 . . . . 204 D1
North Kesteven Sch
LN6 . . . . 204 D1
NORTH KILLINGHOLME
DN40 . . . . 12 D3
NORTH KYME LN4 . . . . 109 F4
North Kyme Cty Prim Sch
LN4 . . . . 109 E3
North La
Coningsby LN4 . . . . 110 E8
Marshchapel DN36 . . . . 37 C2
2 Navenby/Wellingore
LN5 . . . . 107 A8
Reepham LN3 . . . . 68 F1
North La continued
Swaby LN13 . . . . 74 E4
NORTHLANDS PE22 . . . . . . 113 A4
Northlands Ave 3 DN15 . . . 9 A5
Northlands La PE22 . . . . . 113 A4
Northlands Rd
Glentworth DN21 . . . . 54 E6
Winterton DN15 . . . . 9 A6
Northlands Rd S 10 DN15 . . 9 A5
North Leverton CE Sch
DN22 . . . . 52 B1
NORTH LEVERTON WITH
HABBLESTHORPE
DN22 . . . . 52 B1
North Leys Rd DN22 . . . . . . 52 E1
North Lincoln Rd DN16 . . 183 F2
North Lincolnshire Mus*
DN15 . . . . 183 A2
North Lindsey Coll
DN17 . . . . 184 E8
North Marsh Rd DN21 . . . 197 C6
Northminster PE1 . . . . 226 A3
North Moor Dr 2 DN10 . . 39 F3
North Moor La
Martin LN4 . . . . 96 B3
Messingham DN17 . . . . 29 B8
Northmoor Rd DN17 . . . . . . 6 C1
North Moor Rd
Scotter DN17 . . . . 29 C5
Walkeringham DN10 . . . . . . 39 F3
North Moss La DN41 . . . . 187 B1
Northolme
Gainsborough DN21 . . . . . 197 D5
Sutton St Edmund PE12 . . . 168 E5
Northolme Circ 2
HU13 . . . . 178 E2
Northolme Cres
Kingston upon Hull
HU13 . . . . 178 E2
Scunthorpe DN15 . . . . 182 F3
Northolme Ct LN11 . . . . . . 198 C7
Northolme Rd HU13 . . . . . 178 E2
Northon's La PE12 . . . . . . 215 C3
NORTH ORMSBY LN11 . . . . . 48 E4
NORTHORPE
Donington PE20 . . . . 134 E3
Northorpe DN21 . . . . 42 A8
Thurlby PE10 . . . . 164 C8
Northorpe Cl LN6 . . . . 204 F7
Northorpe La PE10 . . . . . . 164 C8
Northorpe Rd
Donington PE11 . . . . 134 D3
Halton Holegate PE23 . . . . 101 B8
Scotton DN21 . . . . 29 D1
NORTH OWERSBY LN8 . . . . . 44 E5
North Parade
Gainsborough DN21 . . . . . 197 F4
Grantham NG31 . . . . 211 A6
Holbeach PE12 . . . . 215 E3
Lincoln LN1 . . . . 234 A3
Scunthorpe DN16 . . . . 185 D6
Skegness PE25 . . . . 206 D3
4 Sleaford NG34 . . . . 212 D7
North Parade Extension
PE25 . . . . 206 E5
North Prom DN35 . . . . 192 E7
North Quay DN31 . . . . 189 C3
North Ramper DN21 . . . . . . 44 A7
NORTH RAUCEBY
NG34 . . . . 120 E5
North Rd
Bourne PE10 . . . . 213 D8
Bratoft PE24 . . . . 102 B8
7 Cranwell NG34 . . . . 107 F1
Gedney Hill PE12 . . . . 168 D4
1 Keadby with Althorpe
DN17 . . . . 17 C6
Kingston upon Hull HU4 . . 179 E4
Leadenham LN5 . . . . 106 D3
Mablethorpe & Sutton
LN12 . . . . 64 B1
Sleaford NG34 . . . . 212 C5
Sturton le Steeple DN22 . . . 52 B4
Tattershall Thorpe LN4 . . . . 97 F3
Tetford LN9 . . . . 73 F1
Tydd St Mary PE13 . . . . . . 160 B2
NORTH RESTON LN11 . . . . . 62 B2
North Scaffold La NG23 . . 91 D3
NORTH SCARLE LN6 . . . . . . 78 F2
North Scarle Miniature
Railway* LN6 . . . . 78 F1
North Scarle Prim Sch
LN6 . . . . 78 E2
North Scarle Rd NG23 . . . . 91 F8
North Sea La DN35 . . . . . . 193 A1
North Shore Rd PE25 . . . . 206 D6
Northside 2 DN9 . . . . 27 C2
Northside La DN22 . . . . 52 C1
North's La DN37 . . . . 34 D8
NORTH SOMERCOTES
LN11 . . . . 50 F8
North Somercotes CE
(Controlled) Prim Sch
LN11 . . . . 50 F7
North St
1 Barrow upon Humber
DN19 . . . . 11 D8
2 Boston PE21 . . . . 208 F6
Bourne PE10 . . . . 213 D5
Caistor LN7 . . . . 33 B4
Cleethorpes DN35 . . . . 192 F6
3 Crowland PE6 . . . . 166 E1
9 Crowle DN17 . . . . 16 D8
Digby LN4 . . . . 108 E6
Folksworth PE7 . . . . 233 A1

North St *continued*
Gainsborough DN21 197 C5
7 Grantham NG31 211 A5
Horncastle LN9 199 C4
Kingston upon Hull HU10 178 E6
Middle Rasen LN8 57 B8
Morton DN21 197 C8
8 Nettleham LN2 68 C2
Osbournby NG34 132 C5
Owston Ferry DN9 28 B3
Peterborough PE1 226 A2
Roxby cum Risby DN15 9 A4
Scunthorpe DN15 183 B4
Stamford PE9 219 B5
Sturton le Steeple DN22 52 B3
Thimbleby LN9 85 B5
West Butterwick DN17 17 D1
West/East Butterwick DN17 28 D8
Winterton DN15 9 B6
North Terr PE1 226 E7
NORTH THORESBY DN36 36 B1
North Thoresby Prim Sch DN36 36 A1
Northumberland Ave
13 Scampton Airfield LN1 67 E5
6 Stamford PE9 219 A6
Northumberland Cl DN34 191 B6
Northumbria Rd NG34 212 B2
North Walls HU1 181 A6
North Warren Rd DN21 197 B6
Northway 3 LN11 49 B8
North Way
6 Lincoln LN6 204 D2
Marshchapel DN36 37 B2
NORTH WILLINGHAM LN8 58 D7
NORTH WITHAM NG33 151 D4
North Witham Bank LN1 234 A2
North Witham Rd NG33 151 D3
Northwood Dr
Hessle HU13 178 B3
Sleaford NG34 212 C6
NORTON DISNEY LN6 92 C2
Norton Disney Rd LN5 92 D1
Norton Gr HU4 179 D4
Norton La
Bishop Norton LN8 43 C2
Thurlby LN6 92 C4
Norton Rd
Peterborough PE1 225 F6
Scunthorpe DN16 185 B5
Stapleford LN6 105 C8
Norton St NG31 211 A3
Norwell La NG23 91 E1
Norwich Ave DN34 191 A4
Norwich Cl
Heighington/Washingborough LN4 203 E1
3 Sleaford NG34 212 C7
Norwich Dr LN4 81 A2
Norwich Rd PE13 170 E1
Norwich Way 7 NG31 210 E5
Norwood Ave DN15 182 F2
Norwood Cl 3 HU10 178 E7
Norwood La
Borough Fen PE6 174 E1
Peterborough PE4 221 F2
Norwood Prim Sch PE4 221 C3
Norwood Rd
7 Hatfield DN7 14 C5
4 Skegness PE25 103 E4
Norwood St HU3 180 C7
Nostell Rd DN16 183 D1
Nottingham Rd 1 NG13 128 A5
Nottingham Terr 5 LN2 234 C3
Nottingham Way PE1 226 C6
Novello Garth HU4 179 B4
Nowells La 6 PE10 213 D5
Nuffield Cl 6 DN16 185 B4
Nunburnholme Ave 5 HU14 3 A4
Nunburnholme Pk HU5 179 B7
Nunnerley Pl DN37 194 F5
Nuns Cnr DN33 191 C4
Nuns Rd DN17 184 F6
NUNSTHORPE DN33 191 B4
Nunsthorpe & Bradley Pk Children's Ctr DN33 191 A4
Nunthorpe Cl 36 DN7 14 D4
Nursery Cl
4 Barton-upon-Humber DN18 3 F1
14 Dunholme LN2 68 E6
Peterborough PE1 226 A4
10 Saxilby LN1 66 D2
Scunthorpe DN17 184 F3
Nursery Ct
15 Brough HU15 2 C5
Sleaford NG34 212 D2
Nursery Dr PE13 170 E2
Nursery Gdns
25 Alford LN13 75 F2
6 Holton le Clay DN36 195 D2
Nursery Gr LN2 202 A6
Nursery La
Belvoir NG32 138 C6
Morton DN21 40 D3
Peterborough PE1 226 D2
Nursery Rd
Boston PE21 209 B2
Cranwell & Byard's Leap NG34 120 C8
Nursery St 2 LN8 57 D7
Nurses La
Skellingthorpe LN6 200 A5
4 Wymondham LE14 150 C1
Nutfields Gr 7 DN7 14 C6
Nut La PE22 114 C1
Nutwood View 4 DN16 185 D4

O

Oak Ave
13 Brough HU15 2 C6
Grimsby DN32 191 E4
5 Scawby DN20 30 F8
11 Welton/Dunholme LN2 68 E6
Oak Cl
8 Ingoldmells PE25 90 D3
Louth LN11 198 E4
14 Sudbrooke LN2 68 F2
5 Woodhall Spa LN10 97 E6
Oak Cres
Boston PE21 208 E7
Bourne PE10 213 B6
Cherry Willingham/Reepham LN3 203 D5
Oak Ct 1 PE11 214 E3
Oakdale Ave
3 Kingston upon Hull HU10 178 E8
Peterborough PE2 231 D4
Oakdale Cl 4 NG31 211 A8
Oakdale Prim Sch PE7 231 C4
Oak Dr HU5 179 B7
Oak Farm Paddock LN6 204 C1
Oakfield 16 LN1 66 D2
Oakfield Cl 2 DN20 196 E3
Oakfield Prim Sch DN16 185 A5
Oakfield St LN2 202 B3
Oakford Cl DN17 184 D8
Oak Gr
13 Barnetby le Wold DN38 21 B4
3 Barrow upon Humber DN19 11 C7
6 Market Deeping PE6 217 B6
Oakham Ave 5 LN12 64 A3
Oakham Cl NG31 210 E6
Oakham Terr 2 PE21 208 F3
Oakham Wlk DN40 186 E3
Oak Hill LN4 203 B2
Oak House La PE22 126 C4
Oakhurst Cl NG31 211 D2
Oakland Ave 39 DN7 14 D4
Oakland Cl 3 LN1 201 D7
Oaklands
3 Beckingham DN10 40 A1
8 Collingham NG23 91 D4
Eastfield PE1 226 B4
5 Woodhall Spa LN10 97 D5
Oaklands Dr
Kingston upon Hull HU13 178 D3
4 Wisbech PE13 170 E1
Oaklands Rd DN40 186 C5
Oaklands The 6 LN8 70 D4
Oakland Way 13 PE11 145 C1
Oakleaf Rd PE1 226 C6
Oakleigh DN16 185 C3
Oakleigh Dr
Canwick LN1 201 C6
Peterborough PE2 230 C6
Oakleigh Rd NG31 210 C3
Oakleigh Terr LN1 201 C6
Oakley Dr PE11 214 E6
Oakley Pl PE12 147 F2
Oak Rd
Glinton PE6 220 B8
1 Healing DN41 24 A5
Scunthorpe DN16 185 B7
Sleaford NG34 212 D2
Stamford PE9 218 D7
Oakroyd Cres 22 PE13 170 D1
Oakside Pk Ind Est NG34 212 F6
Oaks La DN10 39 F2
Oaks The
Balderton NG24 104 C2
15 Nettleham LN2 68 D2
1 Scothern LN2 68 F3
Oak Tree Ave DN21 197 F6
Oaktree Cl 3 PE11 145 B7
Oak Tree Cl
3 Long Bennington NG23 117 D3
7 Market Rasen LN8 57 D7
Oak Tree Dr LN6 92 D4
Oak Tree Mdw LN9 199 C5
Oak Tree Wlk 25 DN17 16 D7
Oak View
13 Dunholme LN2 68 E6
Peterborough PE3 224 F2
Oak Way
Cleethorpes DN35 192 D2
3 Heckington NG34 122 D3
Oakwell Cl DN16 185 D4
Oakwood Ave 4 LN6 204 C8
Oakwood Cl HU10 179 A7
Oakwood Dr DN37 190 C7
Oakwood Glade PE12 215 C3
Oakwood Pk PE12 146 E2
Oakwood Rise 2 DN16 185 B4
OASBY NG32 131 C6
Oasby Rd NG32 131 C7
Oat Dr NG34 212 E3
Oatfield Way NG34 122 D2
Oban Cl 7 PE9 218 E6
Oban Ct 6 DN40 186 C3
Oberon Cl LN1 201 C6
OBTHORPE PE10 164 C6
Obthorpe La PE10 164 C7
Occupation La
Anderby PE24 77 C3
Carrington PE22 99 C1
6 North Kelsey LN7 32 A4
Swanland HU14 3 B8
Occupation Rd
Great Gonerby NG32 129 C6
Lincoln LN1 234 A4
Peterborough PE1 225 E6
Ocean Ave PE25 206 D1
Ocean Bvd HU9 181 B6
Octagon Dr 14 PE13 170 C1
Octavia Cl 23 PE13 170 E1
Odecroft PE3 225 C7
Odin Ct DN33 191 B2
Off Haydons Ave PE25 206 A4
Ogilvy Dr DN17 184 F3
Ogrey PE10 164 C7
O'Hanlon Ave DN20 196 D3
Old Annandale Rd HU10 178 C8
Old Bailey Rd PE7 233 C8
Old Barn Ct
Fleet Hargate PE12 159 C8
Ludford LN8 59 A7
Old Barracks The NG31 211 C4
Old Black Dro NG34 109 D1
OLD BOLINGBROKE PE23 100 B8
Old Boston Rd LN4 207 D3
Old Bowling Gn 4 LN13 75 F2
Old Brickkiln La LN5 92 F2
Oldbrook PE3 220 E1
Old Brumby St DN16 185 A8
Old Carpenter's Yd 1 DN7 14 B6
Old Chapel Ct 2 DN21 43 D7
Old Chapel La
2 Burgh le Marsh PE24 102 E7
9 Laceby DN37 23 F1
Old Chapel Rd LN6 200 A4
Old Church La 1 PE23 101 D7
Old Church Rd PE24 90 D4
OLD CLEE DN32 192 C6
Old Clee Infants & Jun Sch DN32 192 B6
Old Courts Rd 2 DN20 196 C3
Old Courtyard The 1 DN21 65 D6
Old Crosby DN15 183 A5
Old Dairy 11 DN19 11 D8
Old Dairy The PE21 209 A1
Olde Curiosity Mus★ LN12 64 C3
Old Epworth Rd (East) 1 DN7 14 F4
Old Farm Ct 4 DN37 194 C4
Old Fen Bank
Wainfleet All Saints PE24 101 F2
Wainfleet St Mary PE24 102 A1
Old Fen Dike
Gedney PE12 158 F1
Sutton St James PE12 169 B8
Old Fendike Rd PE12 157 B3
Old Fen La
Coningsby LN4 207 E1
Pinchbeck PE11 145 A1
Old Fen Rd PE22 115 A8
Oldfield Cl
9 Barnby Dun DN3 14 A4
1 Stainforth DN7 14 B6
Oldfield Cres 16 DN7 14 C6
Oldfield La PE22 127 C6
Old Field La DN7 14 A5
Oldfield Rd 20 DN8 15 B7
Old Fleet DN37 190 C6
OLD FLETTON PE2 231 A6
Old Fletton Prim Sch PE2 230 F6
Old Forge Rd 7 DN10 39 F5
Old Forty Foot Bank NG34 123 C1
OLD GATE PE12 159 F3
Old Great N Rd
Stamford PE9 218 C8
Thorney PE8 228 B7
Wansford PE8 222 C2
Wothorpe PE9 219 C2
Old Hall Gdns 5 NG24 104 C5
Old Hall La 6 PE11 145 D2
Old Hall Spinney NG32 119 C2
Oldham Dr 8 PE11 145 C1
Old Hammond Beck Rd PE21 208 A2
Old Haxey Rd DN10 39 F6
Old Hill The NG32 138 C6
Old Hundred La PE12 167 F2
Old Inn La PE12 146 E7
Old Ironside Rd DN16 183 D3
Old Knarr Fen Dro PE6 176 C2
Old Lane DN14 6 F7
Oldlane Gate DN14 6 D4
OLD LEAKE PE22 114 A1
Old Leake Prim Sch PE22 114 A1
Old Leicester Rd PE8 222 A3
Old Leys La DN21 43 A3
Old Lincoln Rd NG32 119 B7
Old Lynn Rd 2 PE13 170 E1
Old Main Rd
2 Barnetby le Beck DN37 35 B6
Fleet Hargate PE12 159 C7
Fosdyke PE20 146 D8
Irby DN37 34 D7
Old Leake PE22 114 B1
Scamblesby LN11 72 F5
Old Market Ave
4 Hundleby PE23 87 F1
12 Spilsby PE23 87 F1
Spilsby PE23 100 F8
Old Market Pl DN31 191 D7
Old Mill La
10 Broughton DN20 19 E3
Grimoldby LN11 62 B6
Horncastle LN9 199 C3
Whitton DN15 1 E3
Wrawby DN20 196 F7
Old Mill Pk LN11 198 C6
Old Nick Theatre DN21 197 D4
Old North Rd PE8 222 A3
Old Oak Pl PE10 213 E4
Old Orchard NG32 210 A5
Old Paddock Ct 1 LN9 199 B4
Old Place 3 NG34 212 F4
Old Plumtree La 3 DN36 36 B1
Old Pond Cl 7 LN6 200 D1
Old Pond La PE5 223 E2
Old Pond Pl 20 HU14 3 A4
Old Post La NG33 151 D6
Old Post Office La
8 Barnetby le Wold DN38 21 B4
Butterwick PE22 126 E4
4 South Ferriby DN18 10 A7
Old Rectory Dr
1 Tallington PE9 172 F7
Wansford PE8 222 A6
Old Rectory Gdns DN16 185 A6
Old Rectory The★ DN9 27 E6
Old Road
Grimsby DN37 190 C8
Healing DN37 24 B5
Old Roman Bank
3 Skegness PE25 206 D6
Terrington St Clement PE34 161 E3
Old School Dr 14 DN20 30 F5
Old School La
4 Billinghay LN4 109 F6
6 Cranwell NG34 120 F8
Donington on Bain LN11 59 E2
5 Fishtoft PE21 126 C1
2 North Kelsey LN7 32 A4
Scunthorpe DN16 185 B3
Old School Mews 12 PE23 88 A1
Old School Yd 17 DN21 30 B1
Old Showfields DN21 197 D6
Old Sluice Rd PE12 215 B8
Old Smithy Ct 1 LN4 207 D4
Old Smithy & Heritage Ctr The★ DN9 23 B3
OLD SOMERBY NG33 140 D8
Old South Eau Bank PE12 168 A1
Old Stack Yd The 3 DN20 196 F6
Old Station Yd
Bottesford NG13 128 B6
Morton PE10 154 D6
Old Thorne Rd DN7 14 E4
Old Trent Rd DN21 197 A5
Old Upper Ings La DN22 52 D3
Old Vicarage La
12 Lutton PE12 160 A8
Lutton PE12 216 C8
Old Vicarage Pk 2 DN20 30 E8
Old Village St DN15 17 E6
Old Wainfleet Rd 1 PE25 206 B3
Old Warp La 11 DN18 10 A7
Old Wharf Rd 9 NG31 211 A4
Old Wood 1 LN6 200 C1
Old Wood Cl LN6 200 C1
OLD WOODHALL LN9 85 A2
Oliver Cl 5 NG24 104 A4
Oliver Ct DN31 191 D8
Olive Rd PE1 226 C7
Oliver Quibell Cty Infants Sch NG24 104 A3
Oliver Rd 16 NG23 117 D3
Oliver St DN35 192 D8
Olivier Ct HU4 179 E3
Ollard Ave PE13 170 D1
Olsen Rise LN2 202 D6
Omega Bvd DN8 14 F8
On Hill 17 HU14 3 B7
Ontario Rd DN17 184 E3
Onyx Gr 2 HU3 180 A4
Oole Rd DN35 192 F6
Oosterbeek Cl 5 PE10 213 E7
Opportune Rd 25 PE13 170 D1
Orangewood Cl 7 NG31 210 F8
Orange Row 3 PE34 161 F3
ORANGE ROW PE34 161 F3
Orange Row Rd 1 PE34 161 F3
Orb La DN15 183 A7
ORBY PE24 89 C2
Orby Bank PE24 89 D3
Orby Gr DN33 191 A3
Orby Holme Field La PE24 89 D3
Orby Rd
Addlethorpe PE24 90 B4
Burgh le Marsh PE24 89 D1
Orchard Ave 8 DN21 29 C3
Orchard Cl
4 Barrow upon Humber DN19 11 C7
23 Barton-upon-Humber DN18 10 F8
Bassingham LN5 92 F3
Billinghay LN4 109 E6
4 Blyton DN21 41 C5
4 Bourne PE10 213 C6
6 Burringham DN17 17 D4
9 Burton upon Stather DN15 8 B5
Cherry Willingham/Reepham LN3 203 D5
11 Donington PE11 134 F2
4 Gonerby Hill Foot NG31 210 E8
Great Hale NG34 122 E1
2 Hatfield DN7 14 C3
6 Helpringham NG34 133 D7
Kingston upon Hull HU10 178 F7
1 Kirton in Lindsey DN21 30 B2
Leverington PE13 170 B2
Louth LN11 198 C7
2 Mablethorpe/Sutton on Sea LN12 64 A3
4 Market Deeping PE6 217 D4
12 Messingham DN17 29 D7
25 Metheringham LN4 95 C4
2 Morton PE10 154 C7
4 Moulton PE12 157 F6
Peterborough PE3 225 D3
9 Pinchbeck PE11 156 E8
8 Scothern LN2 68 F4
5 Scunthorpe DN16 185 B6
2 Sleaford NG34 212 F4
15 Stamford PE9 219 B5
7 Welton/Dunholme LN2 68 D6
Whaplode PE12 215 A7
Orchard Croft
4 Epworth DN9 27 D7
5 Grimsby DN33 194 E7
Orchard Ct
3 Thorney PE6 175 F3
Waltham DN37 194 D4
Orchard Dr
7 Burton upon Stather DN15 8 B5
3 Gunness DN15 17 E6
3 Hatfield DN7 14 C3
12 Heckington NG34 122 E2
Kingston upon Hull HU13 178 E1
2 Rampton DN22 65 A5
Walton Highway PE14 170 F4
Winteringham DN15 2 B1
Orchard Garth 16 LN5 93 E8
Orchard Gr
Boston PE21 209 B6
1 Hatfield DN7 14 D5
Misterton DN10 40 A4
Orchard La 12 LN1 66 D2
Orchard Mews PE2 230 F8
Orchard Pk 4 LN11 62 C6
Orchard Rd
Barnack PE9 172 E3
5 Fiskerton LN3 82 A7
Kingston upon Hull HU4 179 B5
4 Stamford PE9 219 B5
Orchard Sch NG24 104 B3
Orchard St
Boston PE21 208 D6
Lincoln LN1 234 A2
Peterborough PE2 230 F7
2 Spalding PE11 214 D3
22 Thorne/Moorends DN8 15 A8
Orchards The
Harrowby Est NG31 211 C6
Immingham DN40 186 B3
8 Middle Rasen LN8 57 B8
Peterborough PE2 229 F4
Orchard The
Market Deeping PE6 217 B5
New Waltham DN36 195 C6
Peterborough PE4 221 A3
Washingborough LN4 203 A2
Orchard Way
4 Coningsby LN4 207 C4
5 Cowbit PE12 167 B8
Easton on the Hill PE9 171 C3
1 Mablethorpe/Sutton on Sea LN12 64 A3
3 Market Rasen LN8 57 E8
6 Nettleham LN2 68 D2
Orchid Cl PE7 233 F7
Orchid Rd LN5 205 C2
Orchid Rise DN15 182 F2
Orchid Way PE25 206 A4

Ordoyno Gr 2 NG24 . . . . . . 104 C5
Ore Blending Rd DN16 . . . . 19 A4
Orford Rd LN8 . . . . 47 B5
Oribi Cl HU4 . . . . 179 C2
Oriole Rd DN17 . . . . 184 E6
Orion Cl 8 HU3 . . . . 180 B5
Orion Way 4 DN34 . . . . . . 190 D4
Orkney Pl DN40 . . . . 186 C2
Orme La LN11 . . . . 198 C6
Orme Rd PE3 . . . . 225 D4
Ormsby Cl DN35 . . . . 192 D3
Ormsby House Dr 7
 PE22 . . . . 99 A4
Ormsby Rd DN17 . . . . 184 E5
Ormsby Ring LN11 . . . . 74 C1
Orton Ave PE2 . . . . 230 E7
Orton Brick Works
 PE7 . . . . 233 B8
ORTON BRIMBLES
 PE2 . . . . 229 D5
ORTON GOLDHAY PE2 . . . 229 F3
ORTON LONGUEVILLE
 PE2 . . . . 230 B5
Orton Longueville Sch
 PE2 . . . . 230 A5
ORTON MALBOURNE
 PE2 . . . . 230 C4
Orton Mere PE2 . . . . 230 B7
Orton Parkway PE2 . . . . . . 229 C4
ORTON SOUTHGATE
 PE2 . . . . 229 C2
ORTON WATERVILLE
 PE2 . . . . 229 E4
ORTON WISTOW PE2 . . . . 229 C6
Orton Wistow Prim Sch
 PE2 . . . . 229 C6
Orwell Gr PE4 . . . . 221 D1
Orwell St DN31 . . . . 189 C1
Osborne Cl 3 LN1 . . . . . . 201 E6
Osborne Dr DN36 . . . . 195 D1
Osborne Pk 1 PE13 . . . . . 170 C2
Osborne Rd
 Immingham DN41 . . . . . 187 B2
 Wisbech PE13 . . . . 170 C2
Osborne St
 1 Cleethorpes DN35 . . . 192 F6
 Grimsby DN31 . . . . 191 D7
 Kingston upon Hull HU1 . 180 E6
Osborne Way LN9 . . . . 199 A4
Osborn Way 9 NG34 . . . . . 122 D4
OSBOURNBY NG34 . . . . . . 132 C4
Osbournby Prim Sch
 NG34 . . . . 132 C5
Osbourne Cl PE4 . . . . 221 D1
Osbourne Way 7 PE6 . . . . 217 A5
Ose 3 PE25 . . . . 206 B6
Oseby La NG34 . . . . 133 C4
OSGODBY
 Lenton Keisby and Osgodby
 NG33 . . . . 141 E3
 Osgodby LN8 . . . . 45 A3
Osgodby Prim Sch LN8 . . . 45 A3
Osgodby Rd LN8 . . . . 44 E5
Osier Ave PE7 . . . . 230 D2
Osier Rd PE11 . . . . 214 C5
Oslear Cres DN35 . . . . 192 E5
Oslear's La LN11 . . . . 73 D5
Oslinc Ostrich Farm ★
 PE22 . . . . 99 B7
Osprey PE2 . . . . 229 F2
Osprey Cl 5 NG34 . . . . . . 212 B3
Osric Ct PE1 . . . . 226 C5
Oster Fen La NG34 . . . . . . 104 F1
Ostler Cl 8 NG31 . . . . 210 F8
Ostler Dr PE10 . . . . 213 B4
Ostler's La DN18 . . . . 10 A5
Oswald Rd
 Scunthorpe DN15 . . . . . . 183 A3
 1 Woodston PE2 . . . . . . 230 D7
Oswin Cl 1 NG34 . . . . 212 C2
OTBY LN8 . . . . 46 A4
Otby La LN8 . . . . 46 A3
Ottawa Rd DN17 . . . . 184 E4
Otter Ave 11 LN1 . . . . 66 D2
Otterbrook PE2 . . . . 229 D5
Otterburn St 6 HU3 . . . . . 180 A5
Otters Cotts LN5 . . . . 205 D7
Oulton Cl LN6 . . . . 205 A2
Oundle Cl
 Heighington/
 Washingborough LN4 . . . 203 C1
 Scunthorpe DN16 . . . . . 185 C3
Oundle Rd
 5 Mablethorpe/Sutton on
 Sea LN12 . . . . 64 C1
 Peterborough PE2 . . . . . 229 E6
Our Lady of Lincoln Cath
 Prim Sch LN2 . . . . 202 A7
Ousemere Cl 14 NG34 . . . 133 B1
Outer Circ Dr LN2 . . . . . . 202 C7
Outer Circ Gn LN2 . . . . . . 202 C6
Outer Circ Ind Est LN2 . . . 202 D5
Outer Circ Rd LN2 . . . . . . 202 D5
Outfield PE3 . . . . 220 E1
Outgang La LN2 . . . . 65 A6
Outgang The HU15 . . . . 2 B7
Outgate DN17 . . . . 16 E7
Out Holme La DN36 . . . . . . 36 E3
Oval App LN2 . . . . 202 B7
Oval The
 5 Brough HU15 . . . . 2 C5
 Grimsby DN32 . . . . 191 C1
 5 Hatfield DN7 . . . . 14 C5
 Kingston upon Hull
 HU10 . . . . 178 E8
 Lincoln LN2 . . . . 202 B7
 Scopwick LN4 . . . . 108 B7
 2 Scunthorpe DN17 . . . 184 E3

Overcoat La DN22 . . . . 65 B7
Overgate Rd NG33 . . . . . . 152 D5
Overstone Ct PE3 . . . . 225 D6
Overstone Ave HU10 . . . . . 178 E8
Overton Cl 4 LN5 . . . . 107 B8
Overton Cl 9 DN18 . . . . 3 E1
Overton Rd LN4 . . . . 207 D4
Overton Way PE2 . . . . 229 F4
Owen Ave HU13 . . . . 179 A1
Owen Cl 7 PE9 . . . . 172 D3
Owe's La LN11 . . . . 51 A5
Owl Cl LN6 . . . . 92 D5
Owl Dr PE20 . . . . 135 B7
Owl End PE7 . . . . 233 D5
Owl End Wlk PE7 . . . . 233 D5
OWMBY DN38 . . . . 32 D7
OWMBY-BY-SPITAL
 LN8 . . . . 55 F6
Owmby Cliff Rd LN8 . . . . . 55 C5
Owmby Hill DN38 . . . . 32 D8
Owmby La LN7 . . . . 32 C5
Owmby Rd
 4 Searby cum Owmby
 DN38 . . . . 32 D8
 Spridlington LN8 . . . . . . 55 F3
Owmby Wold La DN38 . . . . 21 E1
OWSTON FERRY DN9 . . . . 28 B3
Owston Ferry Rd DN9 . . . . 27 F1
Owston Rd DN10 . . . . 40 B6
Oxburgh Cl
 3 Peterborough PE7 . . . 231 F5
 1 Wisbech PE13 . . . . . 170 C1
Oxby Cl 17 NG34 . . . . 122 E2
Oxclose PE3 . . . . 225 A8
OXCOMBE LN9 . . . . 73 D4
Oxcombe Cl DN33 . . . . . . 194 D7
Oxcroft Bank
 Moulton PE12 . . . . 157 F1
 Whaplode PE12 . . . . . . 158 A2
Oxeney Dr 2 LN3 . . . . 69 C3
Oxford Cl LN4 . . . . 203 C1
Oxford Ct 1 NG34 . . . . . . 212 D4
Oxford Rd
 Peterborough PE1 . . . . . 225 F5
 6 Stamford PE9 . . . . . . 219 A7
Oxford St
 Boston PE21 . . . . 208 F3
 Cleethorpes DN35 . . . . . 192 F5
 Grantham NG31 . . . . . . 211 B3
 Grimsby DN32 . . . . 189 B1
 Kingston upon Hull HU2 . 181 A8
 2 Lincoln LN5 . . . . 234 B1
 Market Rasen LN8 . . . . . 57 D8
 Scunthorpe DN16 . . . . . 185 D6
Oxlands La PE24 . . . . 102 B7
Oxmarsh La DN19 . . . . 4 E2
Oxney Rd PE1 . . . . 226 D5
Oxney Rd Ind Est PE1 . . . 227 A6
Oyster Ct DN35 . . . . 192 F5

P

Pacey Cl LN6 . . . . 92 A6
Packhorse Gdns PE20 . . . . 135 B6
Packman La HU10 . . . . 178 B8
Paddington Way PE10 . . . . 154 D7
Paddock Cl
 6 Ancaster NG32 . . . . . 120 A2
 13 Bracebridge Heath
 Ln4 . . . . 81 A1
 Ropsley NG33 . . . . 131 B1
Paddock Cl 5 DN40 . . . . . 186 C3
Paddock Gn 5 PE11 . . . . . 214 D5
Paddock Gr 6 PE21 . . . . . 208 F4
Paddock La
 5 Blyton DN21 . . . . 41 C5
 1 Metheringham LN4 . . . 95 D4
 West Butterwick DN17 . . 17 C1
Paddock Rd NG34 . . . . . . 120 C8
Paddock Rise
 11 Barrow upon Humber
 DN19 . . . . 11 C8
 Ingoldsby NG33 . . . . . . 141 C5
Paddocks The
 1 Barnetby le Beck
 DN37 . . . . 35 B6
 5 Beckingham DN10 . . . 40 A1
 6 Bottesford NG13 . . . . 128 A5
 7 Burgh le Marsh PE24 . . 102 E7
 Carlton Scroop NG32 . . . 119 C3
 12 Crowle DN17 . . . . . . 16 D7
 Gedney PE12 . . . . 159 E7
 Great Hale NG34 . . . . . . 122 E1
 1 Holbeach PE12 . . . . . 215 E3
 Kingston upon Hull
 HU10 . . . . 178 B7
 10 Long Bennington
 NG23 . . . . 117 D4
 Newton on Trent LN1 . . . 65 C1
 2 Peterborough PE4 . . . 220 E5
 Stapleford LN6 . . . . 105 C8
 Swayfield NG33 . . . . . . 152 E5
 4 Willingham DN21 . . . . 53 E3
Paddock The
 3 Barkston NG32 . . . . . 130 B8
 2 Burton upon Stather
 DN15 . . . . 8 B4
 4 Cherry Willingham
 LN3 . . . . 203 E6
 10 Collingham NG23 . . . 91 D4
 Kingston upon Hull HU4 . 179 B5
 Louth LN11 . . . . 198 A5
 Manby LN11 . . . . 62 C5
 1 Market Deeping PE6 . . 217 A6
 2 Marton DN21 . . . . . . 65 D8
 2 Morton PE10 . . . . . . 154 C7
 2 North Ferriby HU14 . . . 3 A5

Paddock The continued
 16 Ruskington NG34 . . . 108 D2
 Skellingthorpe LN6 . . . . 200 A4
 5 Sleaford NG34 . . . . . 212 F4
 5 Stamford PE9 . . . . . . 219 A5
 16 Sudbrooke LN2 . . . . . 68 F2
 3 Swanland HU14 . . . . . . 3 C7
Paddock View PE22 . . . . . 100 B2
Pademoor Terr DN17 . . . . . 7 A2
Padholme Rd PE1 . . . . 226 C3
Padholme Rd E PE1 . . . . . 226 D3
Padley Rd LN2 . . . . 202 E6
Padleys La PE23 . . . . 100 C4
Padmoor La DN21 . . . . 53 C5
Pado La LN13 . . . . 74 E4
Padstow Wlk DN17 . . . . . . 184 C8
Pagehall Cl DN33 . . . . 191 D1
Paignton Ct DN33 . . . . . . 194 E6
Pain La PE22 . . . . 113 E3
Painshall Cl 11 LN2 . . . . . . 68 D7
Painters Way 20 LN12 . . . . 76 F8
Paisley Prim Sch HU3 . . . . 180 A6
Paisley St HU3 . . . . 180 A7
Palace Theatre ★
 NG24 . . . . 104 A4
Palma Ct 2 PE24 . . . . 90 D7
Palm Ct PE1 . . . . 226 B8
Palmer Ave HU10 . . . . 178 D8
Palmer Ct 3 NG34 . . . . . . 212 B6
Palmer La 15 DN19 . . . . . . 11 D8
Palmer Rd NG32 . . . . 129 C6
Palmers Rd PE1 . . . . 226 F5
Palmerston Rd 2 PE7 . . . . 230 F7
Palmwood Cl 3 NG31 . . . . 210 F7
Pamela Cl DN40 . . . . 186 D4
Pamela Rd DN40 . . . . 186 D4
Pandyke La PE22 . . . . 113 F3
PANTON LN8 . . . . 71 B5
Panton Cl 6 PE6 . . . . 217 D5
Panton Rd LN8 . . . . 71 B8
Papermill La
 Ewerby & Evedon
 NG34 . . . . 121 E7
 Tealby LN8 . . . . 46 D2
Pape's La PE24 . . . . 101 F4
Papyrus Rd PE4 . . . . 220 D3
Parade The LN3 . . . . 203 E6
Paradise La
 5 Fulletby LN9 . . . . 86 B8
 Northborough PE6 . . . . . 173 F6
Paradise Pl
 6 Brigg DN20 . . . . 196 B3
 Horncastle LN9 . . . . 199 C3
Paradise Row LN9 . . . . . . 199 C4
Paragon St HU1 . . . . 180 E6
Parish Church Prim Sch
 DN21 . . . . 197 C5
Parishes Sh Ctr The
 DN15 . . . . 183 B3
Parish Mews 3 DN21 . . . 197 D5
Parish's La PE22 . . . . 115 A4
Park Ave
 Allington NG32 . . . . 128 F7
 15 Barton-upon-Humber
 DN18 . . . . 10 E8
 Billinghay LN4 . . . . 109 F5
 17 Crowle DN17 . . . . . . 16 D7
 Grimsby DN32 . . . . 191 E4
 Heighington/Washingborough
 LN4 . . . . 203 D2
 Kingston upon Hull
 HU13 . . . . 178 E3
 Lincoln LN6 . . . . 204 F7
 Louth LN11 . . . . 198 E6
 21 Mablethorpe/Sutton on Sea
 LN12 . . . . 64 B3
 Misterton DN10 . . . . . . 39 E6
 Scunthorpe DN17 . . . . . 184 F3
 Skegness PE25 . . . . 206 D4
 Sleaford NG34 . . . . 212 F4
 Spalding PE11 . . . . 214 C5
 3 Spilsby PE23 . . . . . . 87 F1
 Sutterton PE20 . . . . 136 A2
Park Cl
 1 Gosberton PE11 . . . . . 145 B6
 Immingham DN40 . . . . . 186 C4
 Lea DN21 . . . . 52 F5
 Spalding PE11 . . . . 214 C5
 8 Sudbrooke LN2 . . . . . 68 F2
 Thorney PE6 . . . . 176 B3
 7 Westwoodside DN9 . . . 27 A2
 Yaxley PE7 . . . . 233 F5
Park Cres
 Heighington/
 Washingborough LN4 . . 203 D1
 16 Metheringham LN4 . . . 95 D4
 Peterborough PE1 . . . . . 226 B5
 Sleaford NG34 . . . . 212 F4
 Swinderby LN6 . . . . 92 B6
 Thorne/Moorends DN8 . . 15 A7
 Thorney PE6 . . . . 176 B3
Park Ct
 Scunthorpe DN15 . . . . . 183 B4
 2 Weston PE12 . . . . . . 157 E7
Park Dr
 Grimsby DN32 . . . . 191 E5
 Market Deeping PE6 . . . 217 A5
 6 Westwoodside DN9 . . . 27 A2
Parker Ave LN5 . . . . 205 D4
Parker Cl DN37 . . . . 23 E2
Parker Rd
 Humberston DN36 . . . . . 36 D8
 23 Wittering PE8 . . . . . 172 B1
Parkers Cl 12 PE24 . . . . . 102 E7
Parkers La DN16 . . . . 185 C6
Parker St DN35 . . . . 192 F5
Parkes Cl 4 NG24 . . . . . . 104 D5
Park Est PE6 . . . . 217 E4

Park Farm Cres PE7 . . . . . 231 F5
Park Farm Rd
 Peterborough PE6 . . . . . 224 E5
 Scunthorpe DN15 . . . . . 182 F7
Park Farm Way PE7 . . . . . 231 F6
Parkfield Ave 14 HU14 . . . . 3 A4
Parkfield Dr HU3 . . . . 179 F6
Parkfield Rd
 7 Ruskington NG34 . . . 108 E2
 23 Ryhall PE9 . . . . 163 C1
Park Gate 7 PE21 . . . . . . 208 F5
Park Gdns PE12 . . . . 215 E3
Park Hill
 Cherry Willingham/Reepham
 LN3 . . . . 203 E5
 28 Kirton in Lindsey DN21 . 30 B1
Parkhill Cres 3 DN3 . . . . . 14 A4
Parkhill Rd 2 DN3 . . . . . . 14 A4
Parkhill Rise 7 DN15 . . . . 9 B5
Park Home Ave PE7 . . . . . 230 D1
Park Home Rd PE7 . . . . . . 230 D1
Parkin Rd
 7 Cowbit PE12 . . . . . . 167 B8
 Scunthorpe DN17 . . . . . 184 F4
Parkinson Ave 1
 DN15 . . . . 183 A3
Parkinson's Way 5
 LN12 . . . . 64 C2
Park La
 12 Alford LN13 . . . . 75 F3
 Billinghay LN4 . . . . 109 F5
 5 Boston PE21 . . . . . . 208 F6
 Bracebridge LN5 . . . . . 205 D6
 Burton LN1 . . . . 200 D7
 Coningsby LN4 . . . . 207 C4
 Denton NG32 . . . . 139 A7
 2 Donington PE11 . . . . 134 E2
 East Kirkby PE23 . . . . . 99 E5
 Ewerby & Evedon NG34 . . 122 B7
 Freiston PE22 . . . . 126 D3
 Gorefield PE13 . . . . 169 F3
 Heighington/Washingborough
 LN4 . . . . 203 C2
 Holbeach PE12 . . . . . . 215 E3
 Humberston DN35 . . . . . 192 F1
 Leverington PE13 . . . . . 170 A3
 Long Sutton PE12 . . . . . 216 C5
 Manby LN11 . . . . 62 C5
 Peterborough PE1 . . . . . 226 C4
 Pinchbeck PE11 . . . . . . 145 D3
 Redbourne DN21 . . . . . . 30 F3
 Saxby All Saints DN20 . . . 10 A3
 1 Scawby DN20 . . . . . . 30 F8
 1 Skillington NG33 . . . . 151 A8
 Spalding PE11 . . . . 214 C5
 Stamford PE9 . . . . 219 C4
 2 Surfleet PE11 . . . . . . 145 D2
 Swineshead PE20 . . . . . 135 A7
 Westwoodside DN9 . . . . 27 A2
 Wigsley NG23 . . . . 78 F5
Park La Cl 6 DN7 . . . . 14 C2
Park La E HU4 . . . . 179 C6
Parklands
 2 Fleet Hargate PE12 . . 159 C7
 Mablethorpe/Sutton on Sea
 LN12 . . . . 64 B3
 1 Mumby LN13 . . . . . . 76 F1
 4 West/East Butterwick
 DN17 . . . . 28 D8
Parklands Ave LN6 . . . . . . 204 F7
Parklands Cl 4 NG24 . . . . 104 C5
Parklands Cres 11 HU14 . . 3 A5
Parklands Dr
 4 Harlaxton NG32 . . . . 139 C7
 10 North Ferriby HU14 . . . 3 A5
Parkland Way LN8 . . . . 70 C4
Park La Rd DN7 . . . . 14 C2
Park La W HU4 . . . . 179 C5
Park-lea 6 NG34 . . . . 108 E2
Park Rd
 11 Alford LN13 . . . . 75 F3
 1 Allington NG32 . . . . . 128 F7
 Boston PE21 . . . . 208 E4
 5 Brough HU15 . . . . 2 E6
 Claxby LN8 . . . . 45 E4
 Grantham NG31 . . . . . . 211 B5
 Holbeach PE12 . . . . . . 215 D4
 2 Horncastle LN9 . . . . . 199 C4
 Long Sutton PE12 . . . . . 216 C5
 Mablethorpe/Sutton on Sea
 LN12 . . . . 64 C1
 Market Deeping PE6 . . . 217 D1
 Peterborough PE1 . . . . . 226 A3
 Spalding PE11 . . . . 214 C4
 Sutton St James PE12 . . 169 D7
 Swinstead NG33 . . . . . . 153 A5
 1 Weston PE12 . . . . . . 157 E7
 5 Willingham DN21 . . . . 53 E3
Park Rd E LN12 . . . . 64 D1
Park Rd W LN12 . . . . 64 C1
Park Row
 Kingston upon Hull
 HU3 . . . . 180 D7
 Louth LN11 . . . . 198 E7
 Northfield HU13 . . . . . . 178 E2
Parks Cl 4 DN39 . . . . 12 A1
Parksgate Ave LN6 . . . . . . 204 F5
Parkside
 17 Nettleham LN2 . . . . . 68 D2
 Peterborough PE2 . . . . . 230 B6
Parkside Cres PE11 . . . . . 214 C5
Parkside Dr 13 PE24 . . . . 90 D7
Parkside The 4 NG33 . . . . 151 D2
Park Springs Rd DN21 . . . 197 F2
Parks Rd 3 DN7 . . . . 14 C4
Park St
 Cleethorpes DN35 . . . . . 189 D1

Park St continued
 Grimsby DN32 . . . . 192 B8
 Kingston upon Hull HU3 . 180 D6
 Lincoln LN1 . . . . 234 A2
 11 Messingham DN17 . . . 29 D7
 Peterborough PE2 . . . . . 230 F7
 Swinefleet DN14 . . . . . . 6 D8
 Winterton DN15 . . . . 9 B5
Parkstone Gr 28 DN7 . . . . 14 C4
Park Terr PE1 . . . . 226 A6
Park The
 Coningsby LN4 . . . . 207 D5
 Lincoln LN1 . . . . 234 A2
 Potter Hanworth LN4 . . . 95 B8
Park View
 25 Barton-upon-Humber
 DN18 . . . . 10 F8
 Cleethorpes DN35 . . . . . 192 C8
 Crowle DN17 . . . . 16 D6
 Kingston upon Hull HU4 . 179 E4
 Mablethorpe/Sutton on Sea
 LN12 . . . . 64 C1
 10 Messingham DN17 . . . 29 D7
 15 Northorpe PE10 . . . . 164 C8
 13 Thorne/Moorends
 DN8 . . . . 15 A7
Park View Ave LN4 . . . . . . 81 D2
Park View Cl 7 DN19 . . . . 11 C7
Park View Terr DN17 . . . . . 28 C8
Parkway The
 Kingston upon Hull
 HU10 . . . . 178 E8
 Spalding PE11 . . . . 214 A2
Park Wlk
 Easton on the Hill PE9 . . . 171 D3
 Kingston upon Hull HU4 . 179 B5
Parkwood Prim Sch
 DN17 . . . . 184 D8
Parkwood Rise 14 DN3 . . . 14 A3
Parliament St
 5 Brough HU15 . . . . 2 D6
 7 Kingston upon Hull
 HU1 . . . . 180 F6
 Peterborough PE1 . . . . . 225 F5
Parnell St 3 DN21 . . . . . . 197 C5
Parnwell Prim Sch
 PE1 . . . . 226 F7
Parnwell Way 2 PE1 . . . . . 226 F6
Parris Pl DN35 . . . . 192 C7
Parry Rd 22 LN12 . . . . 64 B3
Parslins The PE6 . . . . 217 F5
Parsonage La PE12 . . . . . 159 F1
Parson Dro
 Billinghay LN4 . . . . 109 F7
 Pinchbeck PE11 . . . . . . 144 B2
Parson Dro La PE13 . . . . . 170 B2
PARSON DROVE PE13 . . . . 177 D7
Parson La LN5 . . . . 106 C8
Parsons Dr 3 PE21 . . . . . 208 E7
Parson's Dro
 Holland Fen with Brothertoft
 PE20 . . . . 124 A2
 Swaton NG34 . . . . 133 D4
Parsons Halt 1 LN11 . . . . 198 C6
Parsons La 18 LN13 . . . . . 75 F2
Parson's La PE12 . . . . 168 B4
Parthian Ave PE21 . . . . . . 136 D8
Partney CE (Aided) Prim
 Sch PE23 . . . . 88 B3
Partney Rd PE23 . . . . 87 C4
Partridge Cl
 4 Caistor LN7 . . . . 33 B4
 4 Scunthorpe DN17 . . . 184 E6
 Yaxley PE7 . . . . 233 D6
Partridge Dr LN7 . . . . 33 F2
Partridge Gn LN6 . . . . 92 D5
Partridge Gr PE4 . . . . 220 E5
Pashley Rd DN8 . . . . 15 B7
PASTON PE4 . . . . 221 D1
Paston Farm Adventure
 Ctr ★ PE4 . . . . 221 E2
Paston La PE4 . . . . 221 D1
Paston Parkway PE4 . . . . . 221 C4
Paston Ridings PE4 . . . . . 221 C1
Paston Ridings Prim Sch
 PE4 . . . . 221 D1
Pasture Ave 9 DN17 . . . . . 17 D4
Pasture Cl
 7 Colsterworth NG33 . . 151 E2
 Grantham NG31 . . . . . . 211 D1
Pasture Dr LN11 . . . . 198 D4
Pasture Dro PE10 . . . . . . 154 F7
Pasture La
 Amcotts DN17 . . . . 7 D1
 Bassingham LN5 . . . . . . 93 B2
 Belvoir NG32 . . . . 138 C2
 Garthorpe & Fockerby
 DN17 . . . . 7 D6
 Market Rasen LN8 . . . . . 57 E8
 Northborough PE6 . . . . . 173 F6
Pasture Rd DN21 . . . . 197 F4
Pasture Rd N DN18 . . . . . . 3 F1
Pasture Rd S DN18 . . . . . . 4 A1
Pastures Ct 36 DN17 . . . . . 29 D7
Pastures Rd NG32 . . . . . . 210 A5
Pasture St DN32 . . . . 191 E7
Pastures The
 12 Cowbit PE12 . . . . . 167 B8
 12 Long Bennington
 NG23 . . . . 117 D3
 Old Somerby NG33 . . . . 140 E8
 1 Rampton DN22 . . . . . 65 A5
 12 Welton LN2 . . . . . . 68 D6
Pasture The PE6 . . . . 217 C6

Pasture Wharf Nature Reserve★ DN18 4 A2
Patchett Cl DN33 191 B2
Patch Rd LN6 92 D4
Pateley Moor Cl 13 LN6 93 C8
Patman's La PE22 114 E4
Patricks Cl 5 LN7 32 A4
Patrick St DN32 191 E5
Patriot Cl PE11 214 C4
Patten Ave 2 PE24 102 D1
Patterdale Rd
Kingston upon Hull HU5 179 E8
3 Peterborough PE4 221 E2
Paul Cres 4 DN36 36 C8
Paulette Ct 11 PE11 214 B5
Paul La 1 DN15 9 D1
Paulsgrove PE2 229 D5
Paul's La LN4 207 C7
Paul's Wlk DN17 184 B7
Pavilion Gdns
3 Scunthorpe DN17 182 F2
5 Sleaford NG34 212 D3
Pavilion Way DN36 195 C7
Paving Way LN6 204 C4
Pawlett Cl PE6 217 D5
Paxton Rd PE2 229 D4
Payne Ave PE13 170 D1
Paynell 23 LN2 68 D6
Paynells PE2 230 A3
Payne Sch PE13 177 D7
Paynesholm PE4 221 E1
Peace Haven 2 DN37 194 C5
Peach La NG32 128 F6
Peach Tree Cl 5 DN16 185 D4
Peach Tree Ct 5 HU3 180 D5
Peachwood Cl 4 NG31 210 F8
Peacock Ct 5 NG34 212 E3
Peacock's Rd PE22 112 B1
Peacock St DN17 184 F5
Peacocks The 5 NG23 117 D3
Peacock Way PE3 224 F2
Peak Dale LN6 204 E2
Peake Cl PE2 230 F6
PEAKIRK PE6 174 A5
Peakirk-cum-Glinton CE Prim Sch PE6 220 C8
Peakirk Rd
Deeping Gate PE6 217 F3
Glinton PE6 220 D8
Northborough PE6 174 A7
Peaks Ave DN36 195 C7
Peaksfield Ave DN32 191 F5
Peaks La
Grimsby DN36 191 F2
New Waltham DN36 195 D7
Peaks Parkway
Grimsby DN32 191 E5
New Waltham DN36 192 A1
Pearces La 3 PE10 154 C7
Pearces Rd PE6 227 B5
Pearl Cl 8 PE25 206 C4
Pearl Ct PE12 215 D3
Pearl Leisure Ctr PE5 223 E1
Pea Rm Craft Ctr & Heckington Village Trust Sta Mus★ NG34 122 F2
Pearson Prim Sch HU3 180 D8
Pearson Rd DN35 192 F3
Pearson St 5 HU2 180 E7
Peartree Cl 5 LN6 200 D1
Pear Tree Cl
4 Epworth DN9 27 D6
Sleaford NG34 212 D2
Waltham DN37 194 D4
Pear Tree Cres 2 PE13 170 B1
Peartree Hill Rd PE12 168 B8
Peartree House Rd PE12 215 F7
Pear Tree La
Covenham St Bartholomew LN11 49 B6
Kirk Bramwith DN7 14 A8
Utterby DN36 48 E5
Pear Tree Rd PE20 136 D5
Peascliffe Dr NG31 211 A8
Peaseholme HU13 178 C1
Peasgate La
Toynton All Saints PE23 100 F6
Toynton St Peter PE23 101 A7
Peashill La NG32 139 B8
Peat Carr Bank DN9 26 C3
Peatlings La PE13 170 C1
Pebble Cl 4 PE12 160 E4
Peck Ave PE21 208 D4
Peck Hill NG33 131 B1
Peckover Cl 4 PE7 231 F5
Peckover Prim Sch PE13 170 C1
Pecks Dro W 4 PE11 214 F2
Peddars Ct 16 LN4 81 A1
Peddars Way PE3 225 A2
Pedlar La LN11 62 A7
Pedley La 15 PE13 170 C1
Peel Castle Rd 10 DN8 15 B7
Peele Sch The PE12 216 D6
Peel Hill Rd 9 DN8 15 B7
Peel St
Kingston upon Hull HU3 180 D8
Peel St *continued*
Lincoln LN5 201 E1
Pegasus Gr 6 PE10 213 E7
Pegasus Rd DN20 21 A8
Pelham Ave DN33 191 C1
Pelham Cl
20 Barton-upon-Humber DN18 10 E8
Peterborough PE3 224 F2
7 Sudbrooke LN2 68 F2
Pelham Cres 1 DN41 23 A4
Pelham Dr 1 HU9 181 C7
Pelham Ind Est DN40 186 D6
Pelham Pl DN33 191 C1
Pelham Rd
Claxby LN8 45 D6
Cleethorpes DN35 192 D7
Grimsby DN31 191 C7
2 Holton le Clay DN36 195 C2
Immingham DN40 186 B3
1 Skegness PE25 206 C4
Pelham Sq 1 DN35 192 E7
Pelham St LN5 234 B1
Pelham View 3 DN20 30 F5
Pell Pl 7 PE21 209 C4
Pell's Dr 5 PE20 136 D5
Pemberton Dr DN36 195 B6
Pemberton St 1 HU8 181 B7
Pembrey Cl 18 LN6 204 C7
Pembroke Ave
Peterborough PE2 229 F5
Scunthorpe DN16 185 A3
Yarborough DN34 191 A7
Pembroke Gr 1 PE6 220 D8
Pembroke Rd
Grimsby DN34 191 A5
Stamford PE9 219 A7
Pendeen Cl
6 Gainsborough DN21 197 E6
New Waltham DN36 195 C7
Pendine Cres LN6 205 A1
Pendlebury Dr 4 PE6 217 D5
Pendleton PE3 225 B6
Pendred Ave LN6 92 D4
Pendreth Pl DN35 192 D7
Pendula Rd PE13 170 E1
Penfold La 1 LN4 203 C2
Pengleton Cl 18 NG33 151 D2
Penistone Ct 2 HU9 181 D7
Pennell St LN5 201 E1
Pennine Rd 7 DN8 15 A7
Pennine Way
Gonerby Hill Foot NG31 210 E7
Peterborough PE4 221 B2
Spalding PE11 214 E6
Pennington PE2 229 E3
Pennington St HU8 181 B7
Pennycress Cl LN2 202 C8
Pennyfield 16 PE11 156 E8
Pennygate PE11 214 A4
Penny Gdns 6 PE20 136 C5
PENNY HILL PE12 215 D6
Pennyhill Cl PE11 214 E6
Penny Hill Rd PE12 215 E3
Penny Toft La PE11 214 B8
Penrose Cl 19 LN6 93 C8
Penshurst Ave HU13 178 F3
Penshurst Rd DN35 192 D4
Pen St PE21 209 A5
Penswick Gr 6 NG24 104 C5
Pentelow Cl PE13 177 D5
Pentland Dr
23 North Hykeham LN6 93 C8
Sleaford NG34 121 A2
Pentlands The 2 PE4 221 C2
Penwald Cl 7 PE6 175 B8
Penway Dr PE11 214 B8
Penwith Dr HU10 178 F7
Penyale 3 PE3 225 A1
Peploe Cres 10 DN19 4 E2
Peploe La 9 DN19 4 E2
Peppercorn Cl
3 Lincoln LN6 201 D1
Peterborough PE1 225 E6
Peppercorn Wlk
5 Grimsby DN32 191 E7
8 Holton le Clay DN36 195 D2
Peppermint Gr 7 PE25 206 D2
Pepper's La NG34 133 C4
Peppin La LN11 49 A2
Percheron Dr 4 PE11 214 A2
Percival St
Peterborough PE3 225 E2
Scunthorpe DN15 183 A4
Percy St
8 Kingston upon Hull HU2 180 E7
6 Lincoln LN2 202 B3
3 Scunthorpe DN16 183 B2
Peregrine Cl
Kingston upon Hull HU4 179 D2
6 Sleaford NG34 212 B3
Peregrine Pl PE10 213 E3
Peregrine St PE7 230 D1
Perkin Field PE34 161 F2
Perkins Cl 2 DN37 190 F8
Perkins La PE6 173 C6
Permain Cl DN33 191 E1
Perney Cres 17 LN6 93 C8
Pernys Cl PE7 230 D3
Perrin Ave 6 PE25 206 A5
Perriwinkle Way PE10 213 D3
Perry Rd PE13 170 B2
Perry St HU3 180 A6
Pershore Ave DN34 190 D4
Pershore Way
Birchwood LN6 204 C6
Eye PE6 175 B2
Perth Cl 7 PE25 206 A4
Perth Rd PE9 218 E6
Perth St W HU5 180 A8
Perth St HU5 179 F8
Perth Way DN40 186 B2
Pescod Sq 27 PE21 208 F5
Petchell Way 2 DN32 191 F8
PETERBOROUGH PE3 225 D5
Peterborough Cath★ PE1 226 A2
Peterborough Cl 10 NG31 210 E5
Peterborough Coll of Adult Ed PE1 226 B3
Peterborough District PE3 225 E2
Peterborough Dr PE6 224 E2
Peterborough Her Ctr★ PE3 225 A1
Peterborough High Sch PE3 225 D2
Peterborough Mus & Art Gall★ PE3 225 A2
Peterborough NV Sta PE2 225 F1
Peterborough Rd
Castor PE5 223 E1
19 Collingham NG23 91 D5
23 Eye PE6 175 A1
Langtoft PE6 217 A8
Newborough PE6 174 E4
Peterborough PE7 231 C3
Scunthorpe DN16 185 B7
Wansford PE8 222 A3
Peterborough Regional Coll PE1 226 B5
Peterborough Sta PE3 225 F2
Peterborough Way NG34 212 C7
Petergate 1 PE9 219 B4
Peterhead Cl PE2 229 D4
Peterhouse Cl
Peterborough PE3 225 E3
1 Stamford PE9 219 B7
Peterhouse Ct DN16 185 A4
Peterhouse Rd DN34 190 F6
Peter Paine Cl PE22 126 F4
Peter Paine Sports Ctr PE21 208 B5
Peter Seadike La PE11 145 D5
Petersfield Cl LN6 204 B7
Peter's La LN13 63 B2
Peterspoint PE12 160 D3
Pethley La NG34 143 A6
Petticoat La 15 PE21 208 F5
Pettit Way 5 PE21 209 C4
Petts Cl 5 PE13 170 E1
Petts La PE12 160 F5
Petuaria Cl HU15 2 B6
Petworth Cl 2 PE6 217 A5
Peveril Ave DN17 184 F8
Peveril Rd PE1 225 F6
Pheasant Cl 5 DN17 184 E6
Pheasant Ct 5 LN7 33 B4
Pheasant Gr PE4 220 E5
Pheasant Way PE7 233 D5
Phelps Pl DN32 192 C5
Phelps St DN35 189 D1
Philip Ave
Cleethorpes DN35 192 D4
Waltham DN37 194 E5
Philip Ct 4 LN6 204 F1
Philip Gr
Cleethorpes DN35 192 D4
Skegness PE25 206 B4
Philips Cres DN15 182 F3
Phillips Ct 6 PE9 219 C4
Phillips La 6 DN37 23 F1
Phoenix Clayton Sch PE2 230 B4
Phoenix Ct DN21 197 F3
Phoenix Parkway DN15 182 E7
Phoenix St 6 DN32 191 D7
Phorpres Cl PE7 230 D3
Phorpres Way PE7 230 E3
Phyllis Ave DN34 191 B7
Phyllis Taylor Gdns DN32 191 D7
Piccadilly 4 DN36 195 C6
Piccadilly Way 1 PE10 154 D6
Pickards Way PE13 170 C1
Pickathorpe La LN11 50 E6
Pickering Ct DN37 190 E8
Pickering Gr 15 DN8 15 A7
Pickering High Sch Sports Coll HU4 179 C4
Pickering Rd HU4 179 C3
Pickering's Meadow Nature Reserve★ LN2 68 F6
Pickerings The 19 HU14 3 A4
Pick Hill La
Grimoldby LN11 62 C8
South Cockerington LN11 50 C1
Picksley Cres DN36 195 D1
PICKWORTH
Pickworth NG34 142 A8
Pickworth PE9 162 E4
Pickworth Rd PE9 162 F2
Pickworth's Dro PE10 155 A3
Pidgeon Cote La 20 DN19 12 A8
Pied Bull Cl 8 PE9 171 A3
Pier St 9 HU1 180 F5
Pietermaritz St 4 LN1 201 E8
Pieter Maritz View 15 LN1 201 E8
Pike Dam La PE12 159 A6
Pilgrim Ave DN40 186 D3
Pilgrim Hospl PE21 209 A8
Pilgrim Rd PE21 209 A4
Pilgrim's Cl 5 DN40 12 E3
Pilgrims Way DN40 186 A4
Pilgrim's Way PE11 214 A4
PILHAM DN21 41 D4
Pilham Ct DN21 197 F3
Pilham La DN21 41 C4
Pilley's La PE21 125 F5
Pilmore La PE12 157 B6
Pilots View DN18 3 E2
Pilots Way HU9 181 B5
PILSGATE PE9 172 C4
Pilton Cl PE4 221 D1
Pimpernel Way 2 DN16 185 D4
PINCHBECK PE11 156 E8
Pinchbeck Ave 4 DN16 183 C2
Pinchbeck E CE Prim Sch PE11 156 E8
Pinchbeck Engine Mus★ PE11 145 E1
Pinchbeck Fen Slipe Nature Reserve★ PE11 156 A6
Pinchbeck La PE24 102 F4
Pinchbeck Rd
5 Butterwick PE22 126 E3
Spalding PE11 214 D5
PINCHBECK WEST PE11 156 A7
Pinder La 10 PE11 134 F2
Pinder's Dro PE22 114 B5
Pine Cl
14 Balderton NG24 104 C1
Grimsby DN37 188 A1
Holbeach PE12 215 C3
Lincoln LN1 201 E8
4 Sleaford NG34 212 D3
Stamford PE9 218 D6
7 Waddington LN5 93 E8
Pine Ct
3 Cleethorpes DN35 192 D2
Spalding PE11 214 F4
Pinefield Ave 7 DN3 14 A3
Pinefield Rd 3 DN3 14 A3
Pine Hall Rd DN3 14 A3
Pine Mdws HU10 178 B8
Pines The DN21 197 F2
Pinetree Ave 11 DN21 29 C3
Pinetree Cl 5 DN20 19 E4
Pine Tree Cl PE1 226 B8
Pinetrees Ct 4 NG34 212 E4
Pine Wlk
5 Brough HU15 2 C6
4 Healing DN41 24 A5
Pinewood Ave PE8 172 B1
Pinewood Cl
Bottesford DN16 185 A4
5 Bourne PE10 213 B5
Pinewood Cres DN33 190 F3
Pinewood Dr NG31 210 F8
Pinewood Gr 2 HU5 179 C7
Pinfold 15 DN9 27 E6
Pinfold Cl
7 Bottesford NG13 128 A6
8 Collingham NG23 91 D5
11 Northorpe PE10 164 C8
Osbournby NG34 132 D5
Pointon & Sempringham NG34 143 B6
Rippingale PE10 142 F2
Pinfold Gdns 4 DN36 195 D1
Pinfold La
11 Bottesford NG13 128 A6
Fishlake DN7 14 D8
Fishtoft PE21 137 C8
Great Steeping PE23 101 E6
Grimsby DN33 191 D1
Halton Holegate PE23 101 C6
3 Holton le Clay DN36 195 D1
Legbourne LN11 61 E3
Marston NG32 118 D2
Minting LN9 71 C1
1 Misterton DN10 39 F5
Pointon & Sempringham NG34 143 B6
8 Ruskington NG34 108 E2
South Rauceby NG34 120 E4
2 Stallingborough DN41 23 D6
Stamford PE9 219 C3
Stickney PE22 113 A6
Swaby LN13 74 E4
Walcott LN4 109 C7
Weston PE12 157 D8
Pinfold Rd
Bourne PE10 213 F5
Castle Bytham NG33 152 D1
Pinfold The LN4 108 D5
Pinfold Way 11 NG34 108 E2
Pingle Cl DN21 197 E4
Pingle La
Bishop Norton LN8 43 D3
Northborough PE6 173 F6
20 Wellingore LN5 107 A7
Pingle Nature Reserve The★ LN4 207 D5
Pingles The 9 PE10 164 C8
Pingle The 2 NG34 133 B1
Pingley La DN20 196 D2
Pingley Mdw DN20 196 D2
Pinney's Ct 21 DN41 23 F5
Pinnings La DN21 43 D6
Pinstock La 10 PE12 159 C7
Pioneer Way LN6 204 E4
Pipistrelle Ct 4 PE4 221 A3
Pippin Cl LN11 198 C5
Pippin Ct 3 DN15 182 C5
Pippin Dr DN16 185 B2
Pipwell Gate PE12 146 E1
Pitcher Row La PE20 136 B1
Pit La
Gedney PE12 149 A4
Great Ponton NG33 140 B4
Ketton PE9 171 A4
Pitman Ave 23 DN18 10 E8
Pitmoor La 8 DN39 12 A1
Pitt La DN10 39 C2
Pittneys PE4 221 D1
Pitts Rd LN4 203 C1
Pitt St HU3 179 F7
Pk Com Prim Sch PE21 208 E7
Plains La DN8 15 F3
Plane St HU3 180 A5
Planet Ice PE3 220 E1
Plank Dro PE6 175 B8
Plantain Cl 1 DN16 185 D4
Plantation Dr HU14 2 F5
Plantation Rd
Cranwell & Byard's Leap NG34 107 C1
29 Thorne/Moorends DN8 15 A8
Planting Rd NG33 140 B1
Plash Dro PE13 177 F4
Plassey Rd 6 DN21 55 A8
Platform Dr PE12 216 A4
Platts La
Bucknall LN10 84 B4
Tetford LN9 73 E1
Platt's La NG32 118 B4
Playgarth Est LN4 108 E4
Playhouse The★ NG34 212 D4
Playhouse Yd 2 NG34 212 D4
Playing Field La 2 LN8 59 A7
Playtowers★ DN35 193 B3
Pleasance Way LN11 62 C6
Pleasant Ave LN11 198 D5
Pleasant Pl 6 LN11 198 C6
Pleasant Terr 18 LN5 205 E8
Pleasure Island Theme Pk★ DN35 193 C2
Plimsoll Way HU9 181 B6
Plot La NG23 91 E6
Plough Dr 18 LN8 57 D8
Plough Hill 23 LN7 33 B4
Plough La
1 Cherry Willingham/Reepham LN3 82 A8
6 Fiskerton LN3 82 A7
6 Newborough PE6 174 E5
Plover Ct 18 Dn18 3 E1
Plover Dr 15 HU15 2 C6
Plover Gr LN6 204 E8
Ploverly 2 PE4 221 A5
Plover Rd 1 PE9 163 D3
Plover Sq 7 LN7 33 B4
Plowden Rd HU3 179 F5
Plowright Theatre★ DN15 183 A2
Plum Tree Dr 3 DN36 37 C2
Plumtree Hill Rd DN7 14 C7
Plumtree La 2 DN36 36 B1
Plum Tree Way DN16 183 A1
Plymouth Cl 23 DN15 9 A5
Plymouth Rd DN17 182 C1
Poachers Brook LN6 200 A5
Poacher's Croft 8 DN9 16 E1
Poachers Ct 23 LN1 66 D2
Poachers Gate 4 PE11 145 C1
Poachers Hide 2 PE11 145 B7
Poachers La LN2 68 F3
Poachers Mdw 20 LN2 68 D2
Poachers Rest 3 LN2 68 D7
Pocklington Cres 3 NG24 104 B7
Pocklington Rd 24 NG23 91 D5
Pocklington Way 10 NG34 122 E2
PODE HOLE PE11 156 C5
Pode La PE22 113 F1
Poffinder Wood Rd DN7 14 E7
POINTON NG34 143 B7
Pointon Rd NG34 143 B8
Point Rd PE25 90 F3
Poles Bank DN9 26 E6
Policemans La 2 LN4 203 C2
Pollards The PE10 213 D2
Pollyplatt La LN1 67 E5
Pollyplatt Prim Sch LN1 67 F5
Polton Cl 3 DN7 14 D7
Polton Toft 2 DN7 14 D7
Polyanthus Dr 4 NG34 212 F3
Polygon Wlk 4 NG31 211 F6
Pond Cl 19 LN2 68 D6
Pond La 4 PE10 213 E2
Pond Side DN39 11 E3
Pond St
Great Gonerby NG31 129 D5
8 Harlaxton NG32 139 C7
Ponds Way 10 DN18 3 E1
Ponsonby Dr PE2 230 D8
Ponton Ave NG31 211 E2
Ponton Rd NG33 140 D5
Poolbank La HU15 2 E5

Pool Dr DN17 . . . . 184 F4
Poole's La 𝟠 PE23 . . . . 87 F1
Pooley Way PE7 . . . . 233 D6
Pools La 𝟠 PE20 . . . . 136 A2
Poor Gdn Rd NG34 . . . . . . 132 F6
Poor Plat La LN13 . . . . 62 F3
Pope's La
  Leverington PE13 . . . . 170 A2
  Terrington St Clement
    PE34 . . . . 161 E2
Pope Way PE1 . . . . 225 E8
Poplar Ave
  Lincoln LN6 . . . . 201 C3
  Mablethorpe/Sutton on Sea
    LN12 . . . . 64 A5
  Peterborough PE1 . . . . . . 226 C8
Poplar Cl
  Anlaby with Anlaby Common
    HU4 . . . . 179 A5
  Boston PE21 . . . . 208 D2
  Ruskington NG34 . . . . . . 108 C2
Poplar Cres PE10 . . . . 213 B6
Poplar Ct
  𝟝 Old Leake PE22 . . . . . . 114 A1
  Spalding PE11 . . . . 214 B4
Poplar Dr
  Brigg DN20 . . . . 196 C5
  𝟞 Broughton DN20 . . . . . . 19 D3
  𝟤 Gosberton PE11 . . . . . . 145 C6
  Humberston DN36 . . . . . 193 B1
Poplar Gdns DN16 . . . . . . 185 B7
Poplar Gr
  𝟝 Cleethorpes DN35 . . . . . 192 E7
  𝟥 Scotter DN21 . . . . 29 C3
Poplar La DN21 . . . . 41 D2
Poplar Rd
  Bucknall LN10 . . . . 84 A3
  Cleethorpes DN35 . . . . . . 192 E7
  𝟞 Hatfield DN7 . . . . 14 C4
  𝟦 Healing NG41 . . . . 23 F5
Poplar Rd Bsns Units
  DN35 . . . . 192 E7
Poplars Mobile Homes
  DN15 . . . . 182 B5
Poplar St LN5 . . . . 205 D6
Popple Dro PE13 . . . . 169 D1
Popple St HU9 . . . . 181 B6
Popplewell Cl 𝟥 DN9 . . . . . 16 E2
Popplewell Terr 𝟙𝟥 DN9 . . . 27 E6
Poppy Cl
  Boston PE21 . . . . 208 B4
  𝟙 Scunthorpe DN15 . . . . . 182 C6
Poppyfield Way DN20 . . . . 196 B4
Poppy Pl PE10 . . . . 213 D3
Porcher Way PE21 . . . . . . 208 C6
Portal Gn 𝟠 PE25 . . . . 206 A5
Portchester Cl PE2 . . . . . . 231 F5
Porter's La 𝟦 PE9 . . . . 171 D3
Porter St
  Kingston upon Hull
    HU3 . . . . 180 E5
  Scunthorpe DN15 . . . . . . 183 A4
Porthcawl Cl 𝟙𝟤 NG31 . . . 211 D7
Port La PE5 . . . . 223 E7
Portland Ave
  Grimsby DN32 . . . . 191 E4
  Peterborough PE1 . . . . . . 225 F7
Portland Dr 𝟞 DN35 . . . . . 206 A4
Portland Manor DN32 . . . 191 E4
Portland Pl
  Grimsby DN32 . . . . 191 E4
  𝟫 Kingston upon Hull
    HU2 . . . . 180 E7
Portland St
  Boston PE21 . . . . 208 E5
  Kingston upon Hull HU2 . 180 D7
  Lincoln LN5 . . . . 234 B1
Portland Terr 𝟝 DN21 . . . 197 D3
Portman Cl PE3 . . . . 225 C4
Portman Rd DN15 . . . . . . 182 E6
Portsmouth Cl 𝟙
  NG31 . . . . 210 F5
Portsmouth Wlk HU4 . . . . 179 B4
PORT SUTTON BRIDGE
  PE12 . . . . 160 F4
Posterngate HU1 . . . . 180 F6
Postland Rd PE6 . . . . 166 F1
Post Office Hill NG33 . . . . 151 B5
Post Office La
  Ashby cum Fenby DN37 . . . 35 D3
  Burton Coggles NG33 . . . 152 C8
  𝟤 Humberside Airport
    DN39 . . . . 22 A6
  𝟝 Spilsby PE23 . . . . 88 A1
  𝟥 Sutterton PE20 . . . . . . 136 A2
  Whitton DN15 . . . . 1 E3
Posts The NG32 . . . . 129 B3
Potesgrave Way 𝟠
  NG34 . . . . 122 D3
Pot La PE20 . . . . 146 E8
Pottergate LN2 . . . . 234 B3
Pottergate Cl 𝟙 LN5 . . . . . 93 F7
Pottergate Rd
  Ancaster NG32 . . . . 120 A3
  Caythorpe NG32 . . . . . . 119 E7
  Fulbeck NG32 . . . . 106 E1
  Normanton NG32 . . . . . . 119 C5
  Welbourn LN5 . . . . 106 F4
POTTERHANWORTH
  LN4 . . . . 82 B1
POTTERHANWORTH
  BOOTHS LN4 . . . . 82 C2
Potterhanworth CE
  (Controlled) Prim Sch
    LN4 . . . . 82 B1
Potterhanworth Rd
  Branston & Mere LN4 . . . . 82 A1
  Heighington LN4 . . . . 81 F3

Potterhanworth Rd continued
  Potter Hanworth LN4 . . . . 95 B8
Potters Cl 𝟤 PE10 . . . . . . 213 E4
Potter's Lodge Meadows
  Nature Reserve★
    NG33 . . . . 152 B2
Potters Way PE1 . . . . 226 B1
Pottinger Gdns 𝟞 LN7 . . . 33 A3
Potts La DN17 . . . . 16 D7
Poulter Ave PE2 . . . . 231 D5
Pound Rd LN4 . . . . 96 C2
Poverty La LN11 . . . . 61 B2
Powells Cres DN16 . . . . . . 185 B6
Powell St PE21 . . . . 209 C2
Pratt Ave PE4 . . . . 221 D2
Prebend La LN2 . . . . 68 C7
Precinct Cres
  𝟤 Skegness PE25 . . . . . . 103 E4
  𝟝 Skegness PE25 . . . . . . 103 E4
Precincts The 𝟝 PE6 . . . . . 217 B5
Precinct The DN17 . . . . . . 184 D7
Premier Ct 𝟞 NG31 . . . . . 211 A5
Prenton Cl 𝟠 LN6 . . . . 205 A5
Prescott Ave 𝟙𝟙 HU15 . . . . . 2 C5
Prescott Gr 𝟥 DN7 . . . . 14 D4
Prestland PE6 . . . . 217 A6
Preston Dr DN20 . . . . 196 C4
Prestongate HU13 . . . . . . 178 E1
Preston La 𝟙𝟝 DN18 . . . . . . 10 F8
Prestwick Cl
  𝟤 Birchwood LN6 . . . . . . 200 B1
  Londonthorpe & Harrowby
    without NG31 . . . . 211 E7
Pretoria Rd NG31 . . . . . . 210 E7
Pretoria St HU3 . . . . 179 F5
Pretymen Cres DN36 . . . . 195 C5
Prial Ave LN6 . . . . 205 B6
Prial Cl LN6 . . . . 205 C6
Pride Parkway NG34 . . . . 212 F7
Pridmore Rd NG33 . . . . . . 152 E8
Priestfield Dro 𝟙
  PE12 . . . . 159 D7
Priestgate
  𝟥 Barton-upon-Humber
    DN18 . . . . 10 F8
  𝟦 Peterborough PE1 . . . . . 226 A2
Priestley Ct 𝟤 PE10 . . . . . 136 C5
Priest's House★ PE9 . . . . 171 C3
Primitive Chapel La 𝟙
  DN40 . . . . 12 F2
Primrose Cl
  𝟠 Healing DN41 . . . . 23 F5
  𝟠 Lincoln LN5 . . . . 205 C2
  𝟕 Morton PE10 . . . . 154 D6
  𝟙𝟙 North Hykeham LN6 . . 93 A8
  Peterborough PE1 . . . . . . 226 A8
  𝟫 Skegness PE25 . . . . . . 206 A5
Primrose Cres
  Boston PE21 . . . . 208 B4
  𝟦 Pinchbeck PE11 . . . . . 156 E8
Primrose Dr
  𝟙 Kingston upon Hull
    HU5 . . . . 179 C8
  Yaxley PE7 . . . . 233 F7
Primrose La 𝟦 NG34 . . . . 107 C1
Primroses 𝟙 PE6 . . . . 217 D5
Primrose St DN21 . . . . . . 197 D3
Primrose Way
  𝟞 Grantham NG31 . . . . . 211 D2
  Humberston DN35 . . . . . 192 E1
  Scunthorpe DN15 . . . . . . 182 C6
  𝟤 Spalding PE11 . . . . . . 214 A2
  Stamford PE9 . . . . 218 C7
Prince Albert Gdns 𝟤
  DN32 . . . . 189 A1
Prince Alfred Ave 𝟙
  PE25 . . . . 206 D3
Prince Ave 𝟠 PE24 . . . . . . 90 D7
Prince Charles Ave 𝟙𝟙
  LN8 . . . . 70 D4
Prince Charles Dr 𝟥𝟤
  DN18 . . . . 10 F8
Prince George St PE25 . . 206 C3
Prince of Wales Cl 𝟙𝟤
  PE13 . . . . 170 D2
Prince Philip Dr DN18 . . . . 10 F7
Princes Ave
  Grimsby DN31 . . . . 191 C7
  Kingston upon Hull
    HU13 . . . . 178 E1
Princes Ct 𝟥 PE10 . . . . . . 213 D6
Prince's Dock St 𝟙𝟞
  HU1 . . . . 180 F6
Princes Gate PE1 . . . . 226 B4
Princes Gdns PE1 . . . . . . 226 B4
Princes Parade 𝟞 PE25 . . 206 D2
Princes Quay Sh Ctr
  HU1 . . . . 180 F6
Princes Rd
  Peterborough PE2 . . . . . . 231 A7
  𝟙 Stamford PE9 . . . . 219 C4
Prince's Rd DN35 . . . . 192 E6
Princess Alexandra Ct 𝟙
  DN17 . . . . 184 F3
Princess Anne Rd
  PE21 . . . . 209 C6
Princess Ave DN7 . . . . 14 C6
Princess Dr
  𝟥𝟦 Barton-upon-Humber
    DN18 . . . . 10 F8
  Grantham NG31 . . . . . . 211 D7
Princess Margaret Ave 𝟤𝟠
  LN4 . . . . 95 C4
Princess Rd PE20 . . . . . . 136 C4
Princess Royal Cl 𝟦
  LN2 . . . . 234 C3
Princess Sq LN4 . . . . 109 E6

Princess St
  Boston PE21 . . . . 208 D5
  𝟙 Immingham DN40 . . . . 186 C3
  Lincoln LN5 . . . . 201 E1
Princes St
  Brigg DN20 . . . . 196 C3
  Holbeach PE12 . . . . 159 A7
Prince's St
  Metheringham LN4 . . . . . . 95 C4
  Peterborough PE1 . . . . . . 226 A4
  Sutton Bridge PE12 . . . . 160 E4
Princess Wlk DN21 . . . . . 197 F4
Prince St 𝟙𝟥 HU1 . . . . 180 F6
Prince William Dr 𝟠
  PE22 . . . . 126 E3
Prince William Rd 𝟥
  LN8 . . . . 56 D5
Pringle Cl LN4 . . . . 207 D5
Prins Ave PE25 . . . . 103 E4
Prins Ct 𝟙𝟞 PE13 . . . . . . 170 D1
Printing Office La 𝟙𝟦
  DN17 . . . . 16 D8
Priors Cl DN36 . . . . 195 D5
Priors Gate PE4 . . . . 220 E4
Prior St LN5 . . . . 201 E1
Priory Cl
  Gainsborough DN21 . . . . 197 F3
  Louth LN11 . . . . 198 C5
  Market Deeping PE6 . . . . 217 F4
  𝟙𝟤 Northorpe PE10 . . . . 164 C8
  𝟙𝟙 Ruskington NG34 . . . 108 C1
  𝟙𝟤 Swanland HU14 . . . . . 3 B7
Priory Cres
  Scunthorpe DN17 . . . . . . 185 A6
  Ulceby DN39 . . . . 12 A2
Priory Ct
  𝟙𝟢 Grantham NG31 . . . . 211 A4
  𝟙𝟙 South Witham NG33 . 151 D2
  Stamford PE9 . . . . 219 D5
Priory Dr 𝟝 LN3 . . . . 82 B6
Priory Farm Dr 𝟦
  HU4 . . . . 179 D2
Priory Gdns PE7 . . . . 228 F3
Priory Gr HU4 . . . . 179 D3
Priory La
  𝟞 Barrow upon Humber
    DN19 . . . . 11 D8
  Dunston LN4 . . . . 95 D5
  Manby LN11 . . . . 62 C6
  Scunthorpe DN17 . . . . . . 184 F6
Priory La Inf Sch DN17 . . . 184 F6
  DN17 . . . . 184 E6
Priory La Jun Sch
Priory LSST The LN5 . . . . 205 E6
Priory Pk HU4 . . . . 179 B1
Priory Rd
  Boston PE21 . . . . 209 F5
  Fishtoft PE21 . . . . 126 C2
  Grimsby DN37 . . . . 190 D6
  Louth LN11 . . . . 198 C6
  Peterborough PE3 . . . . . . 225 E3
  Ruskington NG34 . . . . . . 108 C1
  Scunthorpe DN17 . . . . . . 185 A6
  Spalding PE11 . . . . 214 D3
  Stamford PE9 . . . . 219 D5
Priory Sch The PE11 . . . . 214 E4
Priory Way
  𝟤 Gainsborough DN21 . . . 53 A5
  Kingston upon Hull HU4 . 179 A1
  Sleaford NG34 . . . . 212 A2
Private La LN8 . . . . 55 F1
Proby Cl PE7 . . . . 233 D5
Procters Dr NG23 . . . . 78 C1
Proctors Cl 𝟞 PE12 . . . . . 159 C7
Proctors Rd LN2 . . . . 202 D5
Proctor's Way 𝟞 DN20 . . . 31 A5
Progress Way NG31 . . . . . 211 A6
Promenade
  Chapel St Leonard PE24 . . 90 E5
  Cleethorpes DN35 . . . . . . 192 E4
  Mablethorpe/Sutton on Sea
    LN12 . . . . 64 D1
Prospect Ctr 𝟙𝟤 HU2 . . . 180 E7
Prospect Pl
  𝟙 Grantham NG31 . . . . . 211 A5
  Kingston upon Hull HU9 . 181 B7
  𝟤 Market Rasen LN8 . . . . 57 E7
Prospect St
  Horncastle LN9 . . . . 199 B5
  Kingston upon Hull HU2 . 180 E7
Prospect Terr 𝟠 DN21 . . . 197 D3
Prospero Cl PE2 . . . . 230 F4
Proudfoot La PE20 . . . . . . 159 B6
Providence Cres 𝟙𝟕
  DN18 . . . . 10 E8
Providence Pl 𝟙𝟦 LN4 . . . 207 C4
Provost Rd 𝟙𝟙 LN11 . . . . . 62 C4
Prunus Ave HU10 . . . . . . 178 F4
Pryme Rd DN16 . . . . 185 C6
Pryme St HU10 . . . . 178 F6
Prystie Pl DN35 . . . . 192 D2
Psalter Rd LN13 . . . . 88 E6
Puddiners La DN14 . . . . 6 E7
Pudding and Dip La 𝟠
  DN7 . . . . 14 D4
Pudding Bag La PE9 . . . . 172 C4
Pudding La PE11 . . . . 214 E8
Puddingpoke La 𝟠
  PE12 . . . . 160 A8
Puffin La PE7 . . . . 233 D8
Pulcroft Rd HU13 . . . . . . 178 D2
Pullan Cl 𝟫 LN5 . . . . 205 D3
Pullman Cl 𝟙𝟙 LN4 . . . . . . 95 D4
Pullover La PE20 . . . . 146 E2
Pullover The PE24 . . . . 90 C7
Pulman St HU3 . . . . 180 A7
Pulvertoft La 𝟙𝟤 PE21 . . . 208 F4
Pump Hill LN4 . . . . 31 D6

Pump La
  Fenton NG23 . . . . 105 C1
  𝟕 Skidbrooke with Saltfleet
    Haven LN11 . . . . 51 C4
Pump Sq 𝟙𝟠 PE21 . . . . . . 208 F5
Punchbowl La
  Boston PE21 . . . . 208 B7
  Holland Fen with Brotherтoft
    PE20 . . . . 125 B4
Purbeck Rd
  𝟝 Grimsby DN33 . . . . . . 194 E8
  Scunthorpe DN17 . . . . . . 182 C1
Purcell Cl 𝟙 NG31 . . . . . . 211 D6
Puritan Way PE21 . . . . . . 208 C7
Puttock Gate PE20 . . . . . . 146 D7
Pyecroft PE1 . . . . 226 B6
PYEWIPE DN31 . . . . 188 C4
Pyewipe Bglws DN31 . . . . 188 E1
Pyewipe Rd DN31 . . . . . . 188 E1
Pyhill PE3 . . . . 225 B7
Pyke Rd LN6 . . . . 204 D5
Pymoor La PE22 . . . . 113 B2
Pynder Cl LN4 . . . . 203 A2
Pyruss Dr HU4 . . . . 179 B2
Pytchley Wlk DN35 . . . . . 192 E2

Q

QUADRING PE11 . . . . 145 A8
Quadring Bank PE11 . . . . 144 E6
Quadring Cowley & Browns
  Prim Sch PE11 . . . . 135 A1
QUADRING EAUDIKE
  PE11 . . . . 145 C8
Quadring Rd
  Donington PE11 . . . . 134 F2
  Quadring PE11 . . . . 145 B7
Quaker La
  𝟕 Boston PE21 . . . . 208 F4
  Spalding PE11 . . . . 214 A3
Quantock La
  𝟕 Kingston upon Hull
    HU3 . . . . 180 D5
  𝟙 Scunthorpe DN17 . . . . 184 D8
  𝟥 Thorne/Moorends
    DN8 . . . . 15 A7
Quantock Ct 𝟫 NG34 . . . . 212 B3
Quantock Rd DN33 . . . . . 194 E8
QUARRINGTON NG34 . . . 212 B1
Quarry La PE6 . . . . 173 C7
Quarry Rd LN11 . . . . 198 C4
Quarryside LN11 . . . . 198 B4
Quart La DN17 . . . . 6 D6
Quay La DN14 . . . . 6 C7
Quayside Ctr★ NG34 . . . . 212 E4
Quayside E 𝟞 PE10 . . . . . 213 E2
Quayside W 𝟕 PE10 . . . . . 213 E2
Quays The DN21 . . . . 197 B5
Quebec Rd
  Mablethorpe/Sutton on Sea
    LN12 . . . . 64 B4
  Scunthorpe DN17 . . . . . . 184 E3
Queen Eleanor Prim Sch
  NG23 . . . . 79 B6
Queen Eleanor Tech Coll
  PE9 . . . . 219 B7
Queen Elizabeth Ave 𝟥
  DN18 . . . . 10 A7
Queen Elizabeth Gram Sch
  LN9 . . . . 199 A4
Queen Elizabeth Rd
  𝟞 Humberston DN36 . . . . 36 C8
  Lincoln LN1 . . . . 201 D8
Queen Elizabeth's Gram
  Sch LN13 . . . . 75 E2
Queen Elizabeths High Sch
  DN21 . . . . 197 C5
Queen Elizabeth St 𝟙
  LN8 . . . . 70 D5
Queen Elizabeth Way 𝟥𝟥
  DN18 . . . . 10 F8
Queen Headland La LN5 . . 92 F1
Queen Mary Ave DN35 . . 192 C7
Queen Mary Ave Inf Sch
  DN32 . . . . 192 C7
Queen Mary Rd LN1 . . . . 201 D8
Queen St Pl 𝟙 LN11 . . . . . 198 C5
Queen's Ave
  𝟝 Barton-upon-Humber
    DN18 . . . . 3 F1
  Market Deeping PE6 . . . . 217 C6
  𝟤 Spalding PE11 . . . . . . 157 B6
Queen's Bank PE12 . . . . . 167 C5
Queensbury Way 𝟤
  HU4 . . . . 3 B6
Queens Cres DN17 . . . . . . 17 D6
Queen's Cres
  Lincoln LN1 . . . . 201 D5
  𝟙𝟝 Stainforth DN7 . . . . . 14 C6
Queens Ct 𝟥 LN11 . . . . . . 198 D4
Queen's Ct 𝟙𝟠 DN8 . . . . . 15 A8
Queens Dock Ave 𝟦
  HU1 . . . . 180 F6
Queens Dr PE25 . . . . 206 E8
Queen's Dr Inf Sch PE1 . . 226 A5
Queen's Dr W PE1 . . . . . . 226 A5
Queen's Est PE24 . . . . . . 102 C1
Queensfield
  Gainsborough DN21 . . . . 197 B7
  South Kelsey LN7 . . . . . . 32 A1
Queensgate Ctr PE1 . . . . 226 A2
Queen's Gate St LN8 . . . . 180 B5
Queens Gdns PE1 . . . . . . 226 A5
Queens Parade DN17 . . . 191 C7
Queen's Parade DN35 . . . 192 F5
Queens Pk Cl 𝟙 LN12 . . . . 64 C3

Poo–Rai 271

Queens Pk Specl Sch
  LN5 . . . . 205 E8
Queens Rd
  Immingham DN40 . . . . . 187 A4
  𝟠 Mablethorpe/Sutton on Sea
    LN12 . . . . 77 A8
  Peterborough PE2 . . . . . . 231 B7
  Skegness PE25 . . . . 206 B4
  Spalding PE11 . . . . 214 F5
Queen's Rd
  𝟫 Barnetby le Wold
    DN38 . . . . 21 B4
  𝟙 Boston PE21 . . . . 209 A5
  Bourne PE10 . . . . 213 D6
  𝟙𝟦 Heckington NG34 . . . 122 E2
  Newark-on-Trent NG24 . . 104 A5
Queen's Royal Lancers Mus
  The★ NG32 . . . . 138 C8
Queens St PE9 . . . . 219 B6
Queen St
  𝟞 Bardney LN3 . . . . 83 B4
  𝟝 Bardney LN3 . . . . 83 C4
  Barton-upon-Humber DN18 . 3 F1
  Boston PE21 . . . . 208 E5
  Bottesford NG13 . . . . . . 128 A6
  Brigg DN20 . . . . 196 C3
  𝟦 Collingham NG23 . . . . 91 D5
  Epworth DN9 . . . . 27 E6
  Gainsborough DN21 . . . . 197 D3
  𝟦 Grantham NG31 . . . . . 211 A3
  𝟝 Grimsby DN32 . . . . . . 191 E8
  Horncastle LN9 . . . . 199 C3
  Kingston upon Hull HU1 . 181 A5
  Kirton in Lindsey DN21 . . 30 B1
  Lincoln LN5 . . . . 201 E1
  Louth LN11 . . . . 198 B5
  𝟫 Market Rasen LN8 . . . . 57 D8
  𝟤 Peterborough PE1 . . . . 226 A2
  𝟥 Scunthorpe DN16 . . . . 183 C2
  Sleaford NG34 . . . . 212 C3
  𝟝 Spilsby PE23 . . . . 88 A1
  𝟙𝟕 Sutton Bridge PE12 . . 160 E4
  Thorne/Moorends DN8 . . 15 A8
  𝟙𝟝 Winterton DN15 . . . . . 9 A5
  𝟤𝟢 Wisbech PE13 . . . . . 170 D1
  Yaxley PE7 . . . . 233 F6
Queen's View Cres
  DN16 . . . . 185 D7
Queensway
  Gainsborough DN21 . . . . 197 F4
  𝟙 Grantham NG31 . . . . . 211 E6
  Grimsby DN37 . . . . 190 F8
  𝟙 Ingoldmells PE25 . . . . . 90 E3
  Lincoln LN2 . . . . 202 B5
  Long Sutton PE12 . . . . . 216 C6
  Louth LN11 . . . . 198 E5
  𝟠 Mablethorpe/Sutton on Sea
    LN12 . . . . 64 A5
  Pointon & Sempringham
    NG34 . . . . 143 B6
  𝟤 Potterhanworth LN4 . . . 82 B1
  𝟙𝟥 Ruskington NG34 . . . 108 D2
  𝟤𝟙 Saxilby LN1 . . . . 66 D2
  Scunthorpe DN16 . . . . . . 185 C7
  Skellingthorpe LN6 . . . . . 200 A3
  Sturton by Stow LN1 . . . . 66 C6
Queens Wlk PE2 . . . . 230 F8
Queen's Wlk PE9 . . . . 219 A5
Queenswood Rd DN35 . . . 185 C3
Queen Victoria Sq
  HU1 . . . . 180 F6
Quick La PE12 . . . . 168 A7
Quilter Ave HU4 . . . . 179 B5
Quintin Cl LN4 . . . . 205 F3
Quinton Rd DN32 . . . . . . 191 E4
Quorn Cl 𝟕 PE6 . . . . 174 E4
Quorn Dr 𝟝 LN6 . . . . 205 C8
Quorn Gdns 𝟙 LN11 . . . . 198 D4
Quorn Mews 𝟦 DN35 . . . . 192 E3
Quorum The HU4 . . . . . . 179 D3

R

Rabbithill La NG23 . . . . . . 78 D3
Racecourse Rd PE9 . . . . . 171 E3
Raceground The
  Bourne PE11 . . . . 214 A1
  𝟤 Spalding PE11 . . . . . . 156 E3
Race La DN39 . . . . 11 C3
Rachel Cl DN21 . . . . 197 C7
Radcliffe Cl 𝟝 PE9 . . . . . . 219 B5
Radcliffe Ct DN16 . . . . . . 185 D8
Radcliffe Rd
  𝟕 Healing DN41 . . . . 24 A5
  𝟥 Stamford PE9 . . . . 219 B5
Radford Cl PE8 . . . . 172 C1
RAF Digby Ops Mus★
  LN4 . . . . 108 A3
Ragdale Cl 𝟤 PE1 . . . . . . 226 E7
RAGNALL NG22 . . . . 78 A8
Railway Cl 𝟙𝟕 NG33 . . . . 151 D1
Railway La PE12 . . . . 160 E3
Railway Pk Cl 𝟙 LN6 . . . . 201 D1
Railway Pk Mews LN6 . . . 201 D1
Railway Pl 𝟦 DN31 . . . . . 189 B2
Railway St
  Barnetby le Wold DN38 . . 21 B4
  Grimsby DN32 . . . . 189 B1
  Kingston upon Hull HU1 . 180 F5
Railway Terr
  𝟥 Grantham NG31 . . . . . 211 A3
  𝟝 Grimsby DN32 . . . . . . 191 D7
Railworld★ PE3 . . . . 225 D1
Rainsbutt Rd DN17 . . . . 6 C1

Rainton Ct 3 PE11 214 F4
Rainwall Ct 2 PE20 136 A2
Rainwall's La PE20 136 A3
RAITHBY LN11 60 F3
Raithby Ave 20 DN41 23 A4
RAITHBY BY SPILSBY
PE23 87 D2
Raithby Cross Roads
PE23 87 C2
Raithby Gr 6 DN33 191 A3
Raithby Hill PE23 87 D1
Raithby Rd PE23 87 D1
Rake Bridge Bank DN7 14 D2
Raleigh Ct 2 PE11 214 C2
Raleigh Dr HU9 181 D6
Raleigh Way PE3 225 B6
Ralphs La PE20 136 C7
Ram Bvd DN15 182 E7
Ramper La LN1 65 E4
Ramper Rd DN22 52 B7
Ramper The 6 PE11 156 E3
RAMPTON DN22 65 A4
Rampton Rd DN22 65 A4
Ramsay Cl PE25 206 C1
Ramsden Ave 8 DN18 10 E8
Ramsey Way PE2 231 F6
Ramsgate LN11 198 C6
Ramsgate Rd LN11 198 C6
Ramskir La DN7 14 C7
RANBY LN8 72 B5
Ranby Rd DN17 184 E5
RAND LN8 70 A5
Randall Bank PE12 158 A2
Rand Farm Pk★ LN8 70 A5
Randolph Rd PE20 146 D7
Randsfield Ave 20 HU15 2 C5
Rangefield PE2 229 E4
Rangell Gate PE12 157 B5
Range Rd NG31 211 C5
Rangoon Way 4 PE10 213 E7
Ransom Ct 4 DN39 22 A6
Ransome Way 17 HU15 2 C6
Ranters Row 8 LN13 75 F2
Ranville Cl 11 PE11 145 C1
Ranworth Cl 1 PE25 206 D7
Ranyard La LN11 72 E5
Rase La 5 LN8 57 D8
Rasen Cl 3 LN8 57 B8
Rasen Ct 2 PE1 226 D3
Rasen La LN1 234 A4
Rasen Rd
Tealby LN8 46 B1
Walesby LN8 45 F1
Rason's Ct 8 PE21 209 A5
Rasper Rd Pools Nature
Reserve★ DN40 186 A8
Rat Abbey DN15 9 C4
Ratcliffe Ct 1 PE1 226 D7
Rathkenny Cl PE12 215 E2
Rats Pen La LN11 62 C1
Ratten Row PE22 127 A5
Rauceby CE Sch NG34 120 E5
Rauceby Dro NG34 120 F3
Rauceby Sta NG34 120 F3
Rauceby Terr LN1 234 A2
Rauceby Warren Nature
Reserve★ NG34 120 F2
Ravel Cl PE9 218 F6
Raven Cl 1 DN20 19 D4
Ravencroft La 6 DN10 40 A1
Ravendale 31 DN18 10 F8
Ravendale Cl
Gonerby Hill Foot
NG31 211 A8
Holton le Clay DN36 195 E1
Ravendale Dr LN2 202 A7
Ravendale Rd
Cleethorpes DN35 193 A3
Gainsborough DN21 197 E3
Ravendale St N 3
DN15 183 B3
Ravendale St S DN15 183 B3
Ravenhill Cl DN35 192 D3
Ravens Bank PE12 158 B2
Ravenscar Rd 5 DN37 188 A1
Raven's Dro PE12 159 A3
Ravensfleet Rd DN21 40 C6
Raven's Gate
Fleet PE12 159 A3
Holbeach PE12 158 E2
Ravensmoor Cl 4 LN6 204 E1
Ravenspurn Way DN31 191 D8
Raven St HU9 181 D7
RAVENSTHORPE PE3 225 C6
Ravensthorpe Prim Sch
PE3 225 C7
Ravens View LN6 92 D4
Ravenwood LN4 203 A2
Rawcliffe Gr HU4 179 D5
Rawling Way HU3 180 C5
Rawlinson Ave 27 LN7 33 B3
Rawnsley Cl 15 LN13 75 F2
Rawsons La PE21 125 E5
Raybrook Cl 5 PE21 208 E7
Raymond Mays Way
PE10 213 D2
Raymond Rd DN16 185 C7
Rayner Ave PE2 231 E5
Raysor's La PE22 114 A2
Rayton Cl LN4 203 A2
Raywell Cl HU10 178 F7
Raywell St HU2 180 E7
Reaches The PE6 175 C3
Read Cl 2 NG24 104 C1
Reading Cl LN4 203 E1
Reading Gate DN14 6 C4
Reading Rm Yd 2 HU14 3 A4
Reads La 4 NG33 151 D7
Read Way LN4 207 D5
Reams Cl 4 PE21 209 D4
Reapers Cl 1 PE12 215 B2
Reaper's Rise 20 DN9 27 E6
Reaper's Way 8 DN9 27 D2
REASBY LN3 69 C6
Recreation Gd Rd PE9 219 B6
Recreation Rd 2 PE10 213 D5
Recto Ave DN32 191 F5
Rectors Way 6 PE4 221 D2
Rectory Cl
1 Barrowby NG32 210 A5
7 Binbrook LN8 47 C5
2 Fishtoft PE21 126 C1
Rectory Gdns
2 Beckingham DN10 40 A1
5 Glinton PE6 220 C8
Peterborough PE2 231 B7
Rectory La
Addlethorpe PE24 90 C4
Barrowby NG32 210 A5
Bottesford NG13 128 A6
Claypole NG23 117 F8
Etton PE6 173 D5
3 Fulbeck NG32 106 C1
Gainsborough DN21 52 F5
6 Gedney PE12 159 D7
Glinton PE6 220 C8
Harlaxton NG32 139 C7
Leadenham LN5 106 C2
2 Mareham le Fen PE22 98 F4
North Witham NG33 151 D4
4 Owmby LN8 55 F6
2 Peakirk PE6 174 A5
24 Waddington LN5 93 F7
Woolsthorpe by Belvoir
NG32 138 D8
Rectory Lea DN21 54 F4
Rectory Rd
Anderby PE24 76 F2
Boston PE21 209 B3
Coleby LN5 93 F3
Newton PE13 170 B5
Ruskington NG34 108 D1
Tydd St Mary PE13 160 B1
Rectory St
Beckingham LN5 105 B4
Epworth DN9 27 E6
Red Barn La PE20 136 B3
Redbourn Cl 2 DN16 183 B1
REDBOURNE DN21 30 F3
Redbourne Dr LN2 202 A8
Redbourne Mere DN21 30 E2
Redbourne Rd
Grimsby DN33 191 B3
Hibaldstow DN20 30 F4
Waddingham DN21 43 C7
Redbourn E Rd DN16 19 A6
Redbourne St
Kingston upon Hull
HU3 180 B5
1 Scunthorpe DN16 183 C2
Redbourne Terr 4
PE21 208 F3
Redbourn Way DN16 183 B2
Redbridge PE4 220 E6
Red Cap La PE21 208 E8
Redcar Cl LN6 204 F4
Redcar Gr DN32 192 A5
Redcar St HU8 181 A8
Redcliff Dr 22 HU14 3 A4
Redcliffe Rd NG31 211 B7
Redcombe La DN20 196 B4
Redcote Dr LN6 204 F4
Redcot Gdns PE9 219 B6
Red Cow Dro PE12 146 F6
Redcross St NG31 211 B5
Redfern Cl HU3 180 D5
Redgate Ct 5 PE1 226 E7
Redgate Rd PE13 170 C8
Red Hall★ PE10 213 D4
Redhall Cl 9 DN3 14 A2
Red Hall Dr LN4 205 F4
Red Hall Farm La LN4 205 F4
Redhill La LN8 59 A8
Red Hill Nature Reserve★
LN11 72 E7
Red La
South Ferriby DN18 9 F7
Welby NG32 130 F5
Redland Cres 1 DN8 15 B8
Red Leas La LN11 62 A8
Red Lion Sq 19 PE9 219 B5
Red Lion St
9 Bicker PE20 135 A4
6 Boston PE21 208 F5
3 Spalding PE11 214 D4
8 Stamford PE9 219 B5
Redman Cl DN21 197 E5
Redmile Cl
Bourne PE10 154 D5
Pinchbeck PE11 214 C8
Redmile's La 2 PE9 171 A3
Redmile Wlk 5 PE1 226 D7
Red Rd LN8 84 B8
Redshank Way PE7 230 C1
Redstone Ind Est PE21 208 E3
Redstone Rd PE21 208 E3
Redthorne Cl 2 PE11 214 F5
Redthorn Way NG23 117 F7
Redwing Cl
Peterborough PE2 231 E7
Skellingthorpe LN6 200 A3
Redwing Gr 1 LN6 204 D8
Redwood Ave 11 NG34 212 D2
Redwood Ct DN16 185 D3
Redwood Dr
Cleethorpes DN35 192 D2
Waddington LN5 205 D1
REEDHAM LN4 111 C7
Reedham Garth HU4 179 A3
Reedham La LN4 207 F2
Reedings Cl NG32 210 B5
Reedings Rd NG32 210 B5
Reedland Way PE7 230 C1
Reedmace Cl 8 PE6 174 E4
Reedmans Cl 5 PE6 164 F3
REED POINT LN4 110 E2
Reed St 7 HU2 180 E7
Reepham PE2 229 D4
REEPHAM LN3 203 F8
Reepham CE (Controlled)
Prim Sch LN3 203 F8
Reepham Rd LN3 82 A7
Reet 2 DN31 189 B1
Reeves Way PE1 226 D5
Refinery Rd DN16 183 F2
Reform Pl 2 NG34 212 C4
Reform St
9 Crowland PE6 166 E1
Kingston upon Hull HU2 180 F7
Stamford PE9 218 F5
Regal Gdns 2 NG33 162 E8
Regal Pl PE2 231 A8
Regency Ct 13 DN18 3 E1
Regency Gdns NG31 211 D5
Regency Way PE3 225 E1
Regent Ave LN6 200 C1
Regent Dr 18 DN17 16 D7
Regent Gdns DN31 191 C5
Regent Rd LN12 64 B4
Regent St Sh Arc
DN32 191 D7
Regents Cl
6 Collingham NG23 91 D4
4 Skegness PE25 206 C1
Regents Pk Cl 7 LN6 204 F1
Regent St PE11 214 C3
Reginald Rd DN15 182 F5
Regina Wlk 10 PE24 90 D7
Regional Coll PE2 230 D6
Reindeer Ct LN9 199 A4
Rein The DN9 27 A2
Reldene Dr HU5 179 B7
Rembrandt Way PE11 214 B3
Remigius Gr LN2 202 C7
Remple Ave 2 DN7 15 A3
Remple Comm Rd DN7 14 F2
Remple La 3 DN7 15 A3
Renault Dr LN4 205 F1
Rendel St DN31 188 F1
Renew's Dro PE6 166 D3
Renfrew Cl 2 LN5 205 C2
Renfrew Dr NG34 121 A2
Renfrew Rd LN5 205 C2
Renton Ct HU10 178 F5
Reporto Ave DN32 191 F5
Repton Cl LN4 203 D1
Repton Dr 2 DN16 185 B3
Repton Rd 7 LN12 64 B4
Reservation The NG34 212 F7
Reservoir Rd PE11 145 F4
Reservoir St LN1 234 A4
Resolute Cl 6 PE23 101 A8
Resolution Cl PE21 208 A4
Responso Ave DN32 191 F5
Reston Ct DN35 193 A3
Reston Gr 4 DN33 191 B4
Retief Cl LN1 201 D8
Retief View LN1 201 D8
Retreat The
Easton on the Hill PE9 171 C3
6 Maxey PE6 173 C6
REVESBY PE22 99 C3
Revesby Abbey PE22 99 C5
Revesby Ave
Boston PE21 208 D4
Grimsby DN34 190 F4
Scunthorpe DN16 185 A7
Revesby Bank
Carrington PE22 99 B1
Revesby PE22 112 B8
REVESBY BRIDGE PE22 99 C3
Revesby Cl
Boston PE21 208 D4
Lincoln LN6 204 F6
Revesby Cnr 5 PE22 99 A4
Revesby Ct DN16 185 A8
Revesby Dr PE25 206 A4
Revigo Ave DN32 191 F5
Revill Cl
5 Claypole NG23 117 E8
17 Scotter DN21 29 C3
Reynard Ct DN21 53 E3
Reynard St 3 PE23 88 A1
Reynolds Cl HU14 2 F5
Reynolds Dr 1 LN6 205 B6
Reynolds Gdns 6
PE12 157 F7
Reynolds Jun & Inf Sch
DN35 192 D7
Reynold's Paddock 2
LN5 93 A5
Reynolds St DN35 192 D7
Rhodes Ave 2 NG34 212 C3
Rhodes St HU3 179 F5
Rialto Ave DN32 191 F5
Ribble St 4 HU3 180 B4
Riber Cl 2 NG31 210 E5
Ribes Cl 1 PE7 230 D3
Ribston Cl DN16 185 A2
RIBY DN37 23 C2
Riby Cl 3 DN21 53 A7
Riby Cross Roads DN37 23 C3
Riby Ct DN36 195 E2
Riby Rd
Cabourne LN7 33 D6
Keelby DN41 23 A4
Scunthorpe DN17 184 E5
Stallingborough DN41 23 C4
Swallow LN7 34 A7
Riby Sq DN31 189 B1
Riby St DN31 189 B1
Richard Busby Way 14
PE12 160 A8
Richards Ave LN6 204 F4
Richardson Cl 18 DN36 36 D8
Richard St DN31 191 C8
Richard Young Cl 4
PE13 170 D2
Richdale Ave 1 DN21 30 B2
Richmond Ave PE4 221 A2
Richmond Cl
Boston PE21 209 A5
Caythorpe NG32 119 B6
2 Sleaford NG34 212 B2
Richmond Ct 1 PE25 206 C2
Richmond Dr
Green Hill NG31 210 E5
Lincoln LN6 204 F3
Scunthorpe DN16 185 C4
Skegness PE25 206 C1
Richmond Leisure Complex
PE25 206 B1
Richmond Rd
Cleethorpes DN35 192 E5
Gainsborough DN21 197 F4
Grimsby DN34 191 A6
Kingston upon Hull
HU13 178 E2
Lincoln LN1 201 D4
Richmond Sch The
PE25 206 C2
Richmond Way PE13 170 B2
RIDDINGS DN17 184 F4
Riddings Inf Sch DN17 184 E4
Riddings Jun Sch
DN17 184 F4
Rider Gdns PE21 209 D2
Rides The 7 PE6 164 F3
Ridge Cl 14 LN2 68 D6
Ridge View
2 Brigg DN20 196 D4
Ermine LN1 201 D8
Fillingham DN21 54 F4
Harmston LN5 93 F4
Ridge View Rd LN4 205 F4
Ridgeway 13 LN2 68 D2
Ridge Way
Peterborough PE2 231 B8
Scunthorpe DN17 182 E1
Ridgeway Rd HU5 179 B7
Ridgeway The DN34 190 D3
Ridgewell Cl 10 LN6 204 D8
Ridgewood Ave 14 DN3 14 A1
Ridgewood Dr 5 DN15 8 A4
Ridings The
Bourne PE10 213 C3
Kingston upon Hull HU5 179 A8
Market Rasen LN8 57 E7
17 North Ferriby HU14 3 A4
Ridley Ave PE25 206 D2
Rightwell PE3 225 A6
Rightwell E PE3 225 A5
Rightwell W PE3 225 A5
RIGSBY LN13 75 D2
Rigsby Wood Nature
Reserve★ LN13 75 C3
Rigsmoor Cl 2 LN6 93 C8
Rileston Pl DN16 185 B2
Riley Cl
Bracebridge Heath
LN4 205 F2
Yaxley PE7 233 D6
Rimac Rd LN11 51 D2
Rimes La DN22 65 A7
Rime's La LN10 98 C6
Rimington Rd 4 PE21 126 C1
Ring Beck La HU15 2 A8
Ringers La PE13 170 B2
Ring Moor Cl 7 LN4 109 F5
Ringrose St HU3 179 F5
Ringstead Rd PE4 221 D1
Ringstone Chase PE10 142 F1
Ringwood PE3 224 F3
Ringwood Cl
4 Birchwood LN6 200 D1
1 Scunthorpe DN16 185 B4
Rinks La LN5 92 E1
Rio Dr NG23 91 D5
Ripley Ct DN15 182 B2
Ripley Dr LN6 205 A3
Riplingham Rd HU10 178 A8
Ripon Cl
1 Bracebridge Heath
LN4 81 A2
Grantham NG31 210 F5
Peterborough PE4 220 F3
Scunthorpe DN17 184 C7
Ripon Dr NG34 212 C6
Ripon Pl 17 LN12 64 B3
Ripon St
Grimsby DN31 191 C8
Lincoln LN5 201 F1
Ripon Way HU9 181 C8
RIPPINGALE PE10 142 F3
Rippingale CE (Controlled)
Prim Sch PE10 142 F2
Rippingale Rd PE10 142 D2
Rippons Dro PE6 217 E2
Risby PE3 225 B8
RISBY LN8 46 B3
Risby Gn LN6 204 F7
Risby Rd DN15 9 A1
Risedale 26 LN7 33 B4
RISEGATE PE11 144 F4
Risegate Rd PE11 144 F4
Riseholme PE2 229 E3
RISEHOLME LN2 68 A2
Riseholme La LN2 67 F2
Riseholme Rd
Gainsborough DN21 197 F3
Lincoln LN2 201 F7
Rise The
16 Navenby/Wellingore
LN5 107 A8
8 North Ferriby HU14 3 A5
Scunthorpe DN17 184 E3
South Ferriby DN18 10 A8
Risewood La NG33 130 F1
Riston St HU3 180 C5
Rivan Ave DN33 194 E7
Rivehall Ave 7 LN2 68 D7
Rivelin Cres DN16 185 A8
Rivelin Pl DN16 185 A8
Rivelin Rd DN16 185 A7
Rivendale PE4 220 F2
River Bank PE12 214 C1
Riverbank Cl PE6 217 E3
Riverbank Rise 17 DN18 3 E1
Riverbank Studios★
PE11 214 E4
River Ct 20 PE11 214 D4
Riverdale 8 LN2 68 D2
Riverdale Rd DN16 185 A7
Rivergate
3 Peterborough PE1 226 A1
3 Spalding PE11 214 D2
Rivergate Sh Ctr PE1 226 A1
River Gr HU4 179 E3
Riverhead LN11 198 D7
Riverhead Rd LN11 198 D6
Riverhead Terr LN11 198 D7
River La
Anwick NG34 109 B1
Keddington LN11 198 E7
Moulton PE12 158 A8
Peterborough PE3 225 F2
River Mdw DN20 196 A2
Rivermead LN6 205 C4
Rivermead Cl LN6 205 C4
River Rd
West Burton DN22 52 D4
West Walton PE14 170 C4
Riverside
2 Brigg DN20 196 A3
Grantham NG31 211 B4
Market Deeping PE6 217 D4
5 Scotter DN21 29 C4
2 Spalding PE11 214 B5
Riverside App DN21 197 C5
Riverside Cl
14 Bottesford NG13 128 A6
12 Sleaford NG34 212 D4
Riverside Ct
Louth LN11 198 D6
South Field HU13 3 E4
Riverside Dr DN35 193 C2
Riverside Gdns
Parson Drove PE13 177 C7
Peterborough PE3 225 D1
Riverside Ind Est PE21 209 A2
Riverside Mead PE2 231 B8
Riverside Pk
Grantham NG31 211 B6
Spalding PE11 214 E2
Riverside Pk Homes
PE21 208 E6
Riverside Spinney PE8 222 A3
Riverside The 11 NG34 212 D4
Riverside Wlk
8 Bottesford NG13 128 A6
Grantham NG31 211 B4
River Terr 4 PE13 170 C1
Riverton Cl LN1 201 D8
Riverton View LN1 201 D8
Riverview NG23 117 D4
River View
21 Barton-upon-Humber
DN18 10 F8
Northfield HU13 178 F1
Riverview Ave HU14 3 A4
River Way PE21 209 C2
Roadwood La NG23 78 F8
Robden Ct PE2 225 E1
Roberta Cl 10 PE25 206 A4
Robert Ave PE1 225 F8
Robert Cl DN40 186 B4
Robert Dukeson Ave
NG24 104 A6
Robert Manning Tech Coll
The PE10 213 E6
Robert Pattinson Sch
LN6 204 E2
Robert Rayner Cl PE2 230 D6
Robert's Field Nature
Reserve★ PE9 162 F5
Robert's Gr PE25 206 D7
Robertson Ave 6
NG34 121 B8
Robertson Cl 14 LN5 93 F7
Robertson Dr NG34 212 D5
Robertson Rd
3 Grantham NG31 210 F5
Lincoln LN6 204 E1
Roberts St DN32 192 A8
Robert St DN15 183 A3
Robert Tressell Wlk 2
LN2 202 C7

Robey St LN5 ... 205 E8
Robin Cl
Bottesford DN16 ... 185 B2
8 Market Deeping PE6 .. 217 C5
12 Sleaford NG34 ... 212 B3
Robin Hood Cl PE3 ... 224 F2
Robin Hood Cres 13 DN3 ... 14 A1
Robin Hood Rd
11 Kirk Sandall DN3 ... 14 A1
Skegness PE25 ... 206 C3
Robin Hood's Wlak PE21 ... 208 E7
Robin Hood's Wlk PE21 ... 208 F6
Robinia Dr HU4 ... 179 C2
Robins Cl PE2 ... 230 E8
Robins Cres LN6 ... 92 D5
Robins Field PE8 ... 222 A4
Robinson Ave 4 LN13 ... 75 E2
Robinson Cl DN15 ... 182 E4
Robinson La
Grimsby DN31 ... 189 C2
Louth LN11 ... 198 C5
Robinson Pl LN5 ... 105 F5
Robinson Rd DN40 ... 186 F6
Robinson St E DN32 ... 191 E7
Robinson's Gr 8 DN20 ... 31 A5
Robinson's La 1 DN36 ... 36 B1
Robins Wood PE8 ... 222 A4
Robson Rd DN35 ... 192 D7
Rochdale Rd DN16 ... 185 A5
Rochester Ave HU4 ... 179 B3
Rochester Cl
8 Bracebridge Heath LN4 ... 81 A2
1 Scunthorpe DN17 ... 184 C7
Rochester Ct
2 Bourne PE10 ... 213 C7
Humberston DN35 ... 193 A1
Rochester Dr
Birchwood LN6 ... 200 D2
9 Grantham NG31 ... 210 E5
Rochford Cres PE21 ... 209 B5
Rochford Twr★ PE21 ... 209 E5
Rochford Twr La PE21 ... 209 D6
Rockingham Cl 8 PE6 .. 217 A6
Rockingham Cres DN34 ... 190 D4
Rockingham Ct 9 DN34 ... 190 D4
Rockingham Gr PE4 ... 221 A2
Rockingham Rd 4 PE9 ... 218 E6
Rockley Ct HU10 ... 178 F6
Rock Rd
Peterborough PE1 ... 225 F6
Stamford PE9 ... 219 B5
Rock The NG32 ... 138 B4
Rod Mill Rd DN16 ... 183 E1
Roegate La PE12 ... 159 F1
Roeze Cl 14 LN10 ... 97 C5
Rogues Alley PE13 ... 177 C4
Rokeby Ave HU4 ... 179 B5
Rokeby Cl HU4 ... 179 B5
Rokeby Pk HU4 ... 179 B5
Rokeby Pk Prim Sch HU4 ... 179 B4
Rolleston Cl 3 LN2 ... 201 F7
Rolleston Garth PE1 ... 226 C8
Rolls Cl PE7 ... 233 E7
Roman Bank
Bourne PE10 ... 213 E4
Holbeach PE12 ... 215 D8
Huttoft PE24 ... 77 C4
1 Ingoldmells PE25 ... 206 D8
Moulton PE12 ... 146 E2
Newton PE13 ... 170 B4
6 Skegness PE25 ... 206 C3
Spalding PE11 ... 214 F6
Stamford PE9 ... 219 A5
Roman Cl
9 Metheringham LN4 ... 95 D4
Navenby LN5 ... 107 B8
Roman Dr PE8 ... 222 D2
Roman Pavement LN2 ... 202 C4
Roman Rd
Moulton PE12 ... 157 D1
Scawby DN20 ... 30 D8
Roman Way
7 Ancaster NG32 ... 120 A2
Aubourn Haddington & South Hykeham LN6 ... 93 A8
Horncastle LN9 ... 199 D3
Riddings DN17 ... 184 F6
Roman Wharf LN1 ... 201 C3
Romany Gdns PE2 ... 231 D5
Romney Cl 3 LN6 ... 205 B6
Romney Ct 6 NG34 ... 212 D5
Romney Dr LN6 ... 205 B5
Romsey Ct DN34 ... 190 D5
Romulus Way 13 LN6 ... 93 B8
Ronald Cl 3 PE25 ... 206 C4
Rood's La PE12 ... 157 C8
Rookery Ave
2 Grimsby DN33 ... 191 D3
Sleaford NG34 ... 212 B3
Rookery Cl LN11 ... 198 D8
Rookery Croft 14 DN9 ... 27 E6
Rookery La
Ancaster NG32 ... 119 F2
13 Leasingham NG34 ... 121 B7
Lincoln LN6 ... 205 C6
Wildmore LN4 ... 111 E2
Wymondham LE14 ... 150 B1
Rookery Rd
2 Bicker PE20 ... 135 A4
16 Healing DN41 ... 23 F5
Rookery Rd *continued*
Sutton Bridge PE12 ... 160 D7
Rookery The
14 Collingham NG23 ... 91 D5
Peterborough PE2 ... 229 C7
2 Scawby DN20 ... 30 F8
Yaxley PE7 ... 233 D5
Rooklands 10 DN21 ... 29 C3
Rook's La DN10 ... 39 F6
Roosdyke La PE22 ... 137 D7
Roper's Bridge La PE20 ... 136 A4
Roper's Gate
Gedney PE12 ... 159 F8
2 Lutton PE12 ... 160 A8
Roper's La PE12 ... 159 D1
Ropery La 2 DN18 ... 3 E1
Ropery Rd DN21 ... 197 B7
Ropery St
Grimsby DN32 ... 191 F7
Kingston upon Hull HU3 .. 180 D4
Ropery The LN1 ... 234 A3
Ropewalk 6 LN8 ... 70 D5
Ropewalk Gall★ DN18 ... 3 F1
Ropewalk The
1 Caistor LN7 ... 33 B4
8 Colsterworth NG33 ... 151 E6
Rope Wlk
Lincoln LN6 ... 234 A1
15 Thorne/Moorends DN8 ... 15 A8
ROPSLEY NG33 ... 131 B1
Ropsley CE (Controlled) Prim Sch NG33 ... 131 A1
Ropsley Rd NG33 ... 140 E8
Rosaire Pl DN33 ... 195 A8
Rosalind Ave DN34 ... 191 B7
Rosamond St 7 HU3 ... 180 B4
Rose Ave PE2 ... 231 C7
Rosebank DN21 ... 197 B7
Roseberry Ave
26 Hatfield DN7 ... 14 D4
Skegness PE25 ... 206 D1
Rosebery Ave
Boston PE21 ... 208 C5
Lincoln LN1 ... 201 D4
Rose Cottage Gdn Ctr & Tropical Forest★ PE11 ... 156 D8
Rose Cottage La LN5 ... 94 A3
Rose Cres PE12 ... 158 D3
Rosedale
Scunthorpe DN17 ... 184 E2
Waltham DN37 ... 194 C5
Rosedale Cl 4 LN6 ... 204 F3
Rosedale Dr NG31 ... 211 B8
Rosedale Gr HU5 ... 179 D7
Rosefields DN21 ... 197 E5
Rosegar Ave PE20 ... 135 F2
Rosegarth St 14 PE21 ... 208 F4
Rose Gdns DN40 ... 186 C4
Rose Gr 11 PE25 ... 206 D5
Rosehill Cl 6 LN1 ... 66 D2
Rosehip Rd 8 PE10 ... 154 D6
Rose La
Beesby with Saleby LN13 ... 75 F5
Pinchbeck PE11 ... 156 E8
Roselea Ave 8 LN2 ... 68 D6
Rose Leigh Way PE11 ... 214 C7
Rosemary Ave
Grimsby DN34 ... 190 F6
11 Market Deeping PE6 .. 217 C5
Rosemary Cres NG31 ... 210 E1
Rosemary Gdns
12 Bourne PE10 ... 213 C6
Peterborough PE1 ... 225 F8
Rosemary La LN2 ... 234 B2
Rosemary Rise NG33 ... 141 D5
Rosemary Way DN35 ... 192 E1
Rose Mdws ... 208 B4
Rosemount Dr DN16 ... 185 B6
Rosemount Grange HU13 ... 178 C3
Rosemount La 5 DN21 ... 43 D7
Rose Pl PE21 ... 209 A3
Roseum Cl LN6 ... 204 E5
Roseveare Ave DN31 ... 191 A7
Roseway 6 DN21 ... 197 D5
Rose Wlk
Scunthorpe DN15 ... 183 C3
11 Wisbech PE13 ... 170 C1
Wittering PE9 ... 172 B1
Rosewood Cl
2 Birchwood LN6 ... 204 C8
4 Kingston upon Hull HU5 ... 179 B7
Rosewood Dr 5 NG34 ... 212 D2
Rosewood Way 1 DN16 ... 185 B3
Rosey Row 4 HU9 ... 181 C7
Rosina Gr N 2 DN32 ... 192 B6
Rosina Gr S 4 DN32 ... 192 B6
Roslyn Rd HU3 ... 179 E7
Rosmead St HU9 ... 181 D8
Rosper Rd DN40 ... 186 A8
Rosper Road Pools Nature Reserve★ DN40 ... 186 A8
Rossall Cl
9 Mablethorpe/Sutton on Sea LN12 ... 77 A7
Scunthorpe DN16 ... 185 C3
Rossa Rd LN13 ... 76 D7
Ross Cl
5 Coddington NG24 ... 104 D5
St Giles LN2 ... 202 D6
Rossetti Ct NG31 ... 211 E5
Rossington Cl 18 LN4 ... 95 C4
Ross La 6 DN15 ... 9 B5
Ross Rd DN31 ... 189 D1
Rostrop Rd LN4 ... 95 C7
Rosyth Ave PE2 ... 229 D3
Rothbart Way 2 PE7 ... 230 C3
Rothbury Rd DN17 ... 184 F7
Rotherby Gr 3 PE1 ... 226 E7
Rothschild Cl PE21 ... 208 B4
ROTHWELL LN7 ... 33 F2
Rothwell Ave 8 DN33 ... 191 B3
Rothwell Cl DN21 ... 197 E4
Rothwell Rd
Cabourne LN7 ... 33 C3
4 Lincoln LN2 ... 201 F7
Scunthorpe DN15 ... 182 D4
Rothwell Way PE2 ... 230 C7
Rotten Row
Pinchbeck PE11 ... 156 E8
Theddlethorpe St Helen LN12 ... 63 E5
Rotton Sykes La DN15 ... 1 F2
ROUGHTON LN10 ... 98 B7
Roughton Ct 5 LN2 ... 202 A8
ROUGHTON MOOR LN10 ... 98 A7
Roughton Moor Wood Nature Reserve★ LN10 ... 97 F6
Roundhouse Cl PE1 ... 226 D3
Roundway
Grimsby DN34 ... 191 C5
2 Immingham DN40 ... 186 C3
Roundway The HU4 ... 179 C5
Routland Cl 8 LN8 ... 70 D4
Roval Dr DN40 ... 186 A4
Rowan Ave
Peterborough PE1 ... 226 C6
Spalding PE11 ... 214 E5
Rowan Cl
6 Barrow upon Humber DN19 ... 11 C8
16 Keelby DN41 ... 23 A4
10 Wisbech PE13 ... 170 E1
Rowan Cres DN16 ... 185 C3
Rowan Ct
3 Goxhill DN19 ... 12 A8
11 Heighington/Washingborough LN4 ... 203 D1
Rowan Dr
5 Healing DN41 ... 23 F5
Silk Willoughby NG34 ... 121 B2
Rowan Rd
Lincoln LN6 ... 204 F3
Waddington LN5 ... 205 D1
Rowans The
Gainsborough DN21 ... 197 F5
Holbeach PE12 ... 159 A7
9 Nettleham LN2 ... 68 C2
4 Westwoodside DN9 ... 27 A2
Rowan Way
1 Boston PE21 ... 209 A7
Bourne PE10 ... 213 B6
16 Metheringham LN4 ... 95 C4
Rowanwood Dr 7 NG31 ... 210 F7
Rowdyke Rd PE21 ... 136 F7
Rowe Ave PE2 ... 230 D7
Rowgate Rd LN11 ... 73 A5
Rowland Ct 1 PE4 ... 220 F5
Rowland Rd 4 DN16 ... 183 B2
Rowlandson St 3 DN31 ... 189 B2
Rowley Rd PE21 ... 209 A4
Rowmills Rd 2 DN16 ... 185 C8
ROWSTON LN4 ... 108 E7
Rowston Cl DN21 ... 197 C6
Rowston St DN35 ... 193 A5
Roxborough Cl LN6 ... 200 E2
Roxburgh Rd PE9 ... 218 F6
Roxburgh St 1 HU5 ... 180 B8
ROXBY DN15 ... 9 A3
Roxby Causeway DN15 ... 9 C4
Roxby Cl LN6 ... 204 F6
Roxby Rd DN15 ... 8 F4
Roxholm Cl 2 NG34 ... 108 D1
Roxholme Rd NG34 ... 121 B8
Roxton Ave DN41 ... 23 A5
Roxton Hall Dr 15 HU14 ... 3 A5
Royal Air Force Coll The NG34 ... 120 B8
Royal Arthur Cl 5 PE25 ... 206 C1
Royal Cl 15 PE12 ... 160 E4
Royal Ct DN35 ... 193 B1
Royal Hull Hospitals NHS Trust HU3 ... 180 C6
Royal Mews HU3 ... 180 C6
Royal Oak Ct
13 Heckington NG34 ... 122 E3
19 Louth LN11 ... 198 B5
Royal Oak La 1 LN5 ... 93 A5
Royal St DN31 ... 189 A2
Royalty Bank PE22 ... 101 B3
Royal Way PE21 ... 209 F2
Royce Cl PE7 ... 233 E6
Royce Rd
Peterborough PE1 ... 226 D3
2 Spalding PE11 ... 214 F6
Roydon Gr LN6 ... 205 B6
Royle Cl PE2 ... 230 C5
Royston Ave PE2 ... 230 C6
Ruards La DN19 ... 5 A1
RUCKLAND LN11 ... 73 F5
Ruckland Ave LN1 ... 201 E7
Rudgard Ave LN3 ... 203 E6
Rudgard La LN1 ... 234 A3
Rudham Ave DN32 ... 191 E4
Rudkin Dr 5 NG34 ... 212 D6
Rudyard Cl 7 LN12 ... 77 A7
Rudyard Gr PE4 ... 221 C3
Rue de L'yonne 1 NG23 ... 91 D5
Rue de Nozay 3 DN20 ... 19 E4
Rufford Gn 2 LN6 ... 205 C8
Rufford Rd DN35 ... 192 E4
Rugby Ct 1 NG31 ... 211 B3
Rugby Rd
4 Mablethorpe/Sutton on Sea LN12 ... 64 B4
Scunthorpe DN16 ... 185 A8
Rugby St 5 HU3 ... 180 B4
Rumbold La 3 PE24 ... 102 D1
Runcorn Garth HU4 ... 179 B3
Runcorn Rd LN6 ... 204 B5
Running Post La PE20 ... 135 B4
Runswick Cl LN6 ... 205 A3
Runswick Ct DN32 ... 192 B6
Runswick Rd DN32 ... 192 B6
Rupert Rd 1 DN33 ... 191 D3
Rural Ave PE11 ... 144 D1
Rural Villages Sch Bucknall LN10 ... 84 B3
Rushcarr La DN17 ... 17 C1
Rushcliffe Rd NG31 ... 211 A7
Rush Furlong Nature Reserve★ DN9 ... 27 E3
Rushmere PE2 ... 229 F6
Rushmore Ctry Pk★ LN11 ... 61 F8
Rushton Ave PE4 ... 220 E4
Rushtons Way 12 DN20 ... 30 F5
Rushy Dro PE11 ... 145 C8
Ruskin Ave LN2 ... 202 B6
Ruskin Gn LN2 ... 202 B6
RUSKINGTON NG34 ... 108 E2
Ruskington Cl DN37 ... 188 A2
Ruskington Sta NG34 ... 108 E1
Ruskin Rd 13 LN12 ... 64 B4
Ruskin St
2 Gainsborough DN21 ... 197 D2
Kingston upon Hull HU3 .. 180 B6
Russell Ave
Lincoln LN6 ... 93 C8
Newark-on-Trent NG24 ... 104 A2
Russell Cl 12 PE6 ... 176 A3
Russell Cres NG34 ... 212 F4
Russell Ct DN35 ... 193 A1
Russell Dr 2 PE12 ... 167 B8
Russell Hill PE8 ... 222 A6
Russell Rd 7 NG34 ... 121 B8
Russell Read Almshouses 13 NG31 ... 211 A4
Russell St
Kingston upon Hull HU2 ... 180 E7
Lincoln LN5 ... 205 D6
Peterborough PE1 ... 225 F3
Russell Wlk 2 DN17 ... 29 D7
Russet Cl 4 DN15 ... 182 C5
Russet Dr LN11 ... 198 C4
Russet La DN20 ... 196 F6
Rustic La DN21 ... 41 C6
Ruston Rd NG31 ... 211 F7
Ruston Way LN6 ... 201 D3
Ruther Cl 2 PE2 ... 230 D8
Rutland Cl 13 NG33 ... 151 D2
Rutland Dr DN36 ... 195 C5
Rutland La 15 NG13 ... 128 A5
Rutland Rd
Kingston upon Hull HU5 ... 179 E8
Scunthorpe DN16 ... 185 D7
Skegness PE25 ... 206 D3
Stamford PE9 ... 219 D7
Rutland St 2 DN32 ... 189 D1
Rutland Terr PE9 ... 219 A4
Rutland Way
Ryhall PE9 ... 163 C1
15 Scampton Airfield LN1 .. 67 E5
Rycroft Ave PE6 ... 217 F5
Rycroft Cl 1 PE6 ... 217 F4
Rycroft St NG31 ... 211 B3
Rydal Ave DN33 ... 194 D7
Rydal Cl LN6 ... 200 D2
Rydal Ct PE4 ... 221 C3
Ryde Ave NG31 ... 210 E4
Rye Cl NG34 ... 212 E3
Rye Cres 3 HU15 ... 2 D5
Ryecroft 11 LN5 ... 205 D2
Ryedale 6 HU15 ... 2 D6
Ryedale Ave 1 DN15 ... 9 A6
Ryedale Cl NG31 ... 211 B8
Ryefield La PE12 ... 159 B3
Rye La LN13 ... 75 D5
RYHALL PE9 ... 163 C1
Ryhall CE Prim Sch PE9 ... 163 C1
Ryhall Rd
Great Casterton PE9 ... 171 C8
Stamford PE9 ... 219 D5
Ryhall Rd Ind Est PE9 ... 219 D8
Ryland Bridge LN2 ... 68 E6
Ryland Gdns 10 LN2 ... 68 D6
Ryland Rd LN2 ... 68 D6
Rymac Cres PE25 ... 90 E4
Rymer Pl DN35 ... 193 A4
Ryton Rd PE21 ... 208 B3

S

Sable Cl HU4 ... 179 C2
Sabre Way PE1 ... 226 F4
Sackville Cl DN40 ... 186 D4
Sackville Rd DN40 ... 186 D4
Sackville St 2 DN31 ... 191 C7
Sacred Heart RC Prim Sch PE3 ... 225 A5
Sacrewell Farm & Ctry Ctr★ PE8 ... 222 C5
Saddleback Rd
Skidbrooke with Saltfleet Haven LN11 ... 51 A3
South Cockerington LN11 .. 50 E1
Saddle Ct PE4 ... 225 E8
Saddler Dr PE10 ... 154 C6
Saddle Row NG34 ... 120 B8
Saddlers Cl
Glinton PE6 ... 220 D8
Osbournby NG34 ... 132 D5
Saddler's Cl 11 LN4 ... 95 C4
Saddlers Mead 10 PE11 ... 214 A2
Saddlers Way
Fishtoft PE21 ... 209 C2
5 Long Sutton PE12 ... 216 B5
9 Middle Rasen LN8 ... 57 E7
Saddler's Way 2 DN9 ... 27 D3
Sadler Cl 9 PE25 ... 206 C1
Sadler Rd LN6 ... 204 B5
Saffrondale HU10 ... 178 E7
Saffron Wlk 12 PE10 ... 213 C5
Sage Ct LN6 ... 205 D8
Sagefield Cl 5 DN33 ... 194 D8
Sage's La PE4 ... 225 C8
Sailors Wharf HU9 ... 181 C6
Sainsbury Way HU4 ... 179 A1
St Abbs Cl 8 HU9 ... 181 A5
St Aiden's Rd 5 LN6 ... 204 E2
St Albans Ave DN31 ... 191 A8
St Albans Cl
5 Grantham NG31 ... 210 D5
16 Hibaldstow DN20 ... 30 F5
3 Scunthorpe DN17 ... 184 C7
St Alban's Dr 16 PE6 ... 175 A1
St Andrews NG31 ... 211 D7
St Andrews Ave 2 DN17 ... 184 F2
St Andrews CE Prim Sch
Heckington NG34 ... 122 E3
Leasingham NG34 ... 121 B7
Woodhall Spa LN10 ... 97 C6
St Andrews Cl LN5 ... 201 F1
St Andrew's Cl
4 Helpringham NG34 ... 133 D7
Redbourne DN21 ... 30 F3
St Andrews Com Prim Sch HU10 ... 178 C7
St Andrew's Cres 6 NG34 ... 121 B7
St Andrews Ct
Immingham DN40 ... 186 A4
4 Timberland LN4 ... 96 C1
St Andrews Dr 6 LN1 ... 66 C2
St Andrew's Dr
1 Burton upon Stather DN15 ... 8 B4
Grimsby DN32 ... 192 B4
Lincoln LN6 ... 205 C8
Skegness PE25 ... 206 D5
St Andrew's Gdns LN6 ... 205 C8
St Andrews Gr 33 DN7 ... 14 D4
St Andrews La DN40 ... 186 B5
St Andrew's Mount HU10 ... 178 C8
St Andrew's Pl 3 LN5 ... 234 B1
St Andrews Rd
2 Mablethorpe/Sutton on Sea LN12 ... 64 B4
Northborough PE6 ... 217 E1
St Andrew's Rd
6 Butterwick PE22 ... 126 E3
Spalding PE11 ... 214 C1
St Andrew's St
8 Heckington NG34 ... 122 E3
16 Kirton in Lindsey DN21 . 30 B1
4 Lincoln LN5 ... 234 B1
St Andrew's Way
8 Barnby Dun DN3 ... 14 A3
Epworth DN9 ... 27 E7
4 RAF Cranwell NG34 ... 120 C8
St Andrews Wlk 5 LN10 ... 97 C5
St Annes Ave 8 LN11 ... 50 F7
St Anne's CE (Cont) Prim Sch NG31 ... 211 C3
St Annes Cl
Lincoln LN2 ... 202 B4
Skegness PE25 ... 206 C6
3 Sleaford NG34 ... 212 C6
8 Spalding PE11 ... 214 C6
St Anne's Rd
9 Keelby DN41 ... 23 A5
Lincoln LN2 ... 202 B4
St Anne's Specl Sch HU15 ... 2 E5
St Anne's St NG31 ... 211 C3
St Annes Way PE11 ... 214 C6
St Anne's Wlk 13 HU15 ... 2 D6
St Ann's Ave DN34 ... 191 B6
St Ann's La PE21 ... 208 F3
St Anns Wharf 1 PE21 ... 208 F3
St Aubins Cres LN4 ... 81 F4
St Audrey Cl PE2 ... 231 D6
St Augustine Ave DN32 ... 191 E5
St Augustine Cres DN16 ... 185 B5
St Augustine Rd LN2 ... 202 F6

St Augustines CE Jun Sch
PE2 . . . . **230** F8
St Augustine's CE Sch
PE13 . . . . **170** D2
St Augustine's RC (Aided)
Prim Sch PE9 . . . . **219** C7
St Augustine's Wlk
PE2 . . . . **230** E8
St Augustine Webster Cath
Prim Sch DN15 . . . . **182** D4
St Augustin Way NG31 . . **211** A4
St Barbara's Cres 7
DN15 . . . . **8** B4
St Barnabas CE Prim Sch
DN38 . . . . **21** B4
St Barnabas Ct 4 HU3 . . **180** C4
St Barnabas Dr 1 HU14 . . **3** C7
St Barnabas Rd DN38 . . . **21** B4
St Bartholomews CE Prim
Sch PE11 . . . . **156** A8
St Bartholomew's Cl 4
DN41 . . . . **23** A4
St Bede Ct HU4 . . . . **179** E5
St Bedes Cath Science Coll
PE21 . . . . **209** B6
St Bedes RC Comp Sch
DN16 . . . . **185** B6
St Bee's Dr 19 PE6 . . . . **175** A1
St Benedict Cl 18 PE6 . . **166** F1
St Benedicts Ct 2 PE6 . . **220** D8
St Benedict's Cl 2
LN6 . . . . **204** D2
St Benedicts Sq LN5 . . . **234** A2
St Benet's Gdns 2
PE6 . . . . **175** A1
St Bernadettes RC Prim
Sch DN16 . . . . **185** C6
St Bernards Ave LN11 . . **198** D6
St Bernards Cl LN11 . . . . **198** E6
St Bernard's Cl 13 DN20 . . **19** E4
St Bernard's Sch LN11 . . **198** E5
St Botolph La PE2 . . . . . **230** C6
St Botolphs CE Prim Sch
Peterborough PE2 . . . . . . **230** B6
Sleaford NG34 . . . . **212** B3
St Botolphs Cl 2 LN1 . . . . **66** D3
St Botolph's Cres 8
LN5 . . . . **205** E8
St Botolphs Ct 16 LN5 . . **205** E8
St Botolphs Gate LN1 . . . **66** D3
St Botolphs Infants Sch
LN5 . . . . **205** D8
St Botolphs Mews 31
PE21 . . . . **208** F5
St Botolphs Rd 7
NG34 . . . . **212** C6
St Botolph's Rd DN16 . . **185** C7
St Botolph's Way PE6 . . **176** A2
St Catherine Ct PE12 . . **215** F3
St Catherines 15 LN5 . . **205** E8
St Catherines Cres
DN16 . . . . **185** A4
St Catherines Ct
Ashby DN16 . . . . **185** D6
Grimsby DN34 . . . . **190** F6
St Catherine's Ct LN5 . . **205** D7
St Catherine's Dr 3
DN7 . . . . **14** C2
St Catherine's Ct LN5 . . **205** D7
St Catherine's Rd
Grantham NG31 . . . . **211** B4
Lincoln LN5 . . . . **205** E7
St Chads Ct 8 LN2 . . . . . . **68** E6
St Chads Gate DN37 . . . **188** A1
St Chad's Rd DN16 . . . . **185** D7
St Chads Wlk S 20
DN37 . . . . **190** E8
St Charles RC Prim Sch
HU2 . . . . **180** E8
St Christophers Cl 1
NG34 . . . . **107** F1
St Christopher's Rd 11
DN36 . . . . **36** C8
St Christophers Specl Sch
LN6 . . . . **205** B4
St Claire's Ct 6 LN6 . . . . **204** C8
St Clares Wlk DN20 . . . . **196** C5
St Clement's 9 PE25 . . . **219** A5
St Clements Cl LN4 . . . . **108** E7
St Clements Coll PE25 . . **206** C5
St Clement's Ct 3 LN1 . . **234** B4
St Clement's Dr 4 LN3 . . **82** B6
St Clements Gn PE25 . . **206** B4
St Clements Rd 17
NG34 . . . . **108** D2
St Clement's Rd
1 Lincoln LN6 . . . . **204** C8
2 Skegness PE25 . . . . . **206** B4
St Clements Way
DN36 . . . . **195** C7
St Crispins Cl 2 DN40 . . **12** E4
St Crispin's Cl 3 LN3 . . . **203** D2
St Cuthberts Ct 14 LN1 . . **234** B3
St Davids Cl 2 PE25 . . . **206** D6
St David's Cl 2 LN3 . . . . **203** E7
St Davids Cres DN17 . . **184** E3
St David's Rd LN6 . . . . . **204** D2
St David's Sq PE1 . . . . . **226** D1
St David's St 13 LN8 . . . . **47** B6
St Denys Ave NG34 . . . **212** B6
St Deny's Cl 2 DN40 . . . . **12** E3
St Edith Gate 6 LN11 . . . **62** C6
St Edmonds Cl PE24 . . . **115** D8
St Edmunds Cl 3
NG31 . . . . **210** D5

St Edmunds Ct DN34 . . . **190** F6
St Edmunds Rd NG34 . . **212** C3
St Edward's Dr 15 LN2 . . **68** F2
St Edwins Cl 18 DN7 . . . . **14** D4
St Edwins Dr 19 DN7 . . . . **14** D4
St Faith & St Martin CE Jun
Sch LN1 . . . . **201** D4
St Faiths CE Inf Sch
LN1 . . . . **201** D4
St Faith's St 6 LN1 . . . . **201** D4
St Firmin's Way PE10 . . **164** D7
St Frances Cl PE25 . . . . **206** B6
St Francis Ave DN31 . . . **191** A8
St Francis Cl LN6 . . . . . **204** D2
St Francis Gdns 23
LN12 . . . . **77** A7
St Francis Gr 1 DN37 . . . **23** E1
St Francis Sch LN1 . . . . **201** E7
St George Ave PE2 . . . . **231** E6
St Georges Ave 3
PE9 . . . . **219** D6
St George's Ave 5 DN7 . . **14** C2
St George's CE Aided Prim
Sch PE9 . . . . **219** C7
St George's CE Com Prim
Sch DN21 . . . . **197** F2
St Georges Cl
4 Cranwell NG34 . . . . . **107** F1
22 Thorne/Moorends
DN8 . . . . **15** B7
St George's Cl LN6 . . . . **204** E2
St Georges Coll of Tech
NG34 . . . . **212** C4
St George's Ct DN21 . . . . **30** F3
St Georges Dr 3 LN10 . . **97** C5
St George's Hill DN21 . . **54** F7
St Georges Hospl LN1 . . **201** C6
St Georges La LN2 . . . . . **67** F1
St Georges Prim Sch
HU3 . . . . **180** A6
St Georges Rd 21 DN8 . . **15** B7
St George's Rd
Kingston upon Hull
HU3 . . . . **180** A5
17 Wittering PE8 . . . . . **172** B1
St George's Sq 13 PE9 . . **219** C5
St Georges St 6 PE9 . . . **219** C5
St Georges Way 11
NG31 . . . . **211** D7
St Gilbert of Sempringham
CE Prim Sch NG34 . . . . . **143** B7
St Gilberts CE Prim Sch
PE9 . . . . **219** A5
St Gilbert's Cl NG34 . . . **143** B6
St Gilbert's Rd PE10 . . . **213** C6
St GILES LN2 . . . . **202** C7
St Giles Ave
Lincoln LN2 . . . . **234** C4
1 Sleaford NG34 . . . . . **212** F4
St Giles' Ave DN33 . . . . **191** D1
St Giles Inf Sch LN2 . . . **202** B6
St Guthlac Ave 1 PE6 . . **217** B5
St Guthlac Sch PE6 . . . . **166** F1
St Guthlac's Cl 6 PE6 . . **166** F1
St Guthlac's Way 1
PE21 . . . . **126** C1
St Helenas CE Prim Sch
LN13 . . . . **89** A7
St Helens Ave DN33 . . . **191** D3
St Helen's Ave LN6 . . . . **205** B7
St Helen's Cl NG31 . . . . **210** D4
St Helen's Cres DN37 . . **194** D1
St Helen's Dr 14 HU15 . . **2** D6
St Helen's Rd DN20 . . . **196** D3
St Helens Way DN21 . . . **42** E2
St Helier Rd DN35 . . . . . **192** E7
St Hilary's Cl 1 LN6 . . . . **204** D2
St Hilda's Ave DN34 . . . **191** B6
St Huberts Dr PE25 . . . . **206** B6
St Hugh Cl PE1 . . . . **226** C4
St Hugh's Ave DN35 . . . **192** E6
St Hughs Cath Prim Sch
LN6 . . . . **204** B4
St Hugh's Cl 7 LN3 . . . . **203** E7
St Hugh's Cres DN16 . . **185** C8
St Hugh's Dr
3 Barlings LN3 . . . . **69** C3
Lincoln LN6 . . . . **204** E2
St Hugh's Hospl LN2 . . . **191** F4
St Hugh's Maths & Comp
Sch NG31 . . . . **210** E3
St Hughs Sch
Scunthorpe DN16 . . . . . . **183** B1
Woodhall Spa LN10 . . . . . **97** D5
St Hugh St LN2 . . . . **234** C2
St Hugh's Terr 3 LN1 . . . **66** C7
St Hybald's Gr 2 DN20 . . **30** F7
St Ives Cres DN34 . . . . . **190** E5
St James Ave
Grimsby DN34 . . . . **191** A6
7 Hatfield DN7 . . . . **14** C4
Peterborough PE1 . . . . . **225** F7
St James Cl
19 Crowle DN17 . . . . **16** D7
Newton PE13 . . . . **170** A5
St James Ct 3 DN15 . . . **183** A3
St James' Ct 2 DN34 . . **191** C6
St James Rd
Brigg DN20 . . . . **196** D3
Long Sutton PE12 . . . . . . **216** A1
Welton HU14 . . . . **2** F5
St Jame's Rd LN6 . . . . . **204** D2
St James's Rd 6 DN20 . . **30** E8
St James St DN16 . . . . . **183** D5
St James's Way 5
PE11 . . . . **214** D2
St James View LN11 . . . **198** B4
St James Way 2 PE12 . . **157** E1

St Joan's Dr 5 DN20 . . . . **30** E8
St John Fisher RC Sch
PE1 . . . . **226** C4
St John's Ave
6 Cherry Willingham/
Reepham LN3 . . . . **203** E7
1 Lincoln LN6 . . . . **204** E2
St Johns CE Prim Sch
PE2 . . . . **231** C7
St Johns Church Sch
PE2 . . . . **229** F3
St Johns Cl
2 Baston PE6 . . . . **164** E5
Brigg DN20 . . . . **196** D3
21 Goxhill DN19 . . . . **12** A8
Scampton LN1 . . . . **67** C6
St John's Cl
11 Leasingham NG34 . . **121** B7
6 Morton NG34 . . . . **154** C7
Ryhall PE9 . . . . **163** C1
St Johns Ct
Grange DN34 . . . . **191** A5
6 Grantham NG31 . . . . . **211** A3
St John's Dr
Corby Glen NG33 . . . . . . **152** F7
Ingoldmells PE25 . . . . **90** E4
6 Spalding PE11 . . . . . . **214** B3
St Johns Mews PE12 . . **215** E2
St Johns Rd PE2 . . . . . . **231** B7
St John's Rd
Boston PE21 . . . . **209** A3
Bracebridge Heath LN4 . . **205** F2
9 Humberston DN36 . . . **36** C8
Lincoln LN2 . . . . **201** F6
Scunthorpe DN16 . . . . . . **185** C6
Spalding PE11 . . . . **214** C3
Weston PE12 . . . . **157** C2
15 Wittering PE8 . . . . . . **172** B1
St John's Sch LN4 . . . . **205** F4
St John's St
3 Holbeach PE12 . . . . . **215** E2
Peterborough PE1 . . . . . **226** B2
21 Stamford PE9 . . . . . **219** B5
St John St 1 PE24 . . . . **102** D1
St John's Terr 13
DN21 . . . . **197** D3
St John's Wlk HU13 . . . . **178** F2
St John the Baptist CE
Prim Sch PE11 . . . . **214** C2
St Joseph Dr HU4 . . . . . **179** C5
St Josephs RC Prim Sch
DN35 . . . . **192** D4
St Judes Cl PE3 . . . . . . **225** C4
St Julian's Wells HU10 . . **178** D7
St Kyneburgha Cl PE5 . . **223** E2
St Lamberts Gr 4
PE2 . . . . **157** D7
St Lawrence CE
(Controlled) Prim Sch
LN6 . . . . **200** B4
St Lawrence Dr 9 LN3 . . **83** C4
St Lawrence Rd DN7 . . . . **14** C4
St Lawrence Specl Sch
LN9 . . . . **199** D4
St Lawrence's Pl 2
PE6 . . . . **185** D7
St Lawrence's Rd
DN16 . . . . **185** D6
St Lawrence St 3 LN9 . . **199** B4
St Lawrence Way 3
PE9 . . . . **172** F7
St Leodegar's Cl PE20 . . **136** D7
St Leonard Cl PE21 . . . . **209** A6
St Leonard's Ave DN31 . . **191** A8
St Leonards Dr PE24 . . . . **90** D7
St Leonard's Dr 6 LN10 . . **97** D5
St Leonard's La
Lincoln LN2 . . . . **234** C3
South Cockerington LN11 . . **62** B7
St Leonard's Rd 2
PE13 . . . . **170** B2
St Leonard's St 8 PE9 . . **219** C5
St Luke's Cl
Cherry Willingham/Reepham
LN3 . . . . **203** D2
1 Hatfield DN7 . . . . **14** C2
St Luke's Cres 8 DN36 . . **36** C8
St Lukes Ct 7 DN32 . . . . **191** F8
St Lukes Sch DN16 . . . . **185** D8
St Luke's St HU3 . . . . . . **180** D6
St Margaret's 6 PE11 . . **145** A8
St Margaret's Ave
PE25 . . . . **206** A6
St Margarets CE
(Controlled) Prim Sch
LN13 . . . . **63** A1
St Margaret's Cl
17 Laceby DN37 . . . . **23** F1
6 Lincoln LN6 . . . . **205** B4
St Margaret's Cres 6
DN40 . . . . **22** E8
St Margaret's Dr PE22 . . **113** A2
St Margaret's Gdns
LN6 . . . . **205** A4
St Margarets Mews
DN34 . . . . **190** F6
St Margarets Pl 2
PE2 . . . . **230** F6
St Margarets Rd 1
PE2 . . . . **230** F6
St Margaret's Wlk 5
DN16 . . . . **185** C6
St Mark's Ave 3 LN3 . . . **203** E7
St Mark's Cl
North Hykeham LN6 . . . . **204** E3
Skegness PE25 . . . . **206** B6
St Mark's Ct 3 PE1 . . . . **226** A3

St Marks Dr 6 PE6 . . . . **166** E1
St Marks Rd PE13 . . . . . **169** E3
St Mark's Rd
Holbeach PE12 . . . . **147** D6
10 Humberston DN36 . . . **36** C8
St Marks Sh Ctr LN5 . . . **234** A1
St Mark's Sq
Kingston upon Hull
HU3 . . . . **180** D4
Lincoln LN5 . . . . **234** A1
St Marks St PE1 . . . . . . **226** A3
St Mark St
Kingston upon Hull
HU8 . . . . **181** A8
Lincoln LN5 . . . . **234** A1
St Marks Terr 25 PE21 . . **208** F5
St Martins Ave 2 HU4 . . **179** E6
St Martins CE Prim Sch
DN9 . . . . **28** A3
St Martins Cl 2 NG34 . . **107** F1
St Martin's Cl
8 Blyton DN21 . . . . **41** C5
4 Stamford PE9 . . . . **219** C4
Stubton NG23 . . . . **118** B7
St Martin's Cres
Grimsby DN33 . . . . **191** C3
7 Scawby DN20 . . . . **30** E8
St Martin's La LN1 . . . . **234** B3
St Martin's Pl 5 DN41 . . . **23** A4
St Martins Prep Sch
DN32 . . . . **191** D5
St Martin's Rd
Newborough PE6 . . . . **221** F8
4 Scawby DN20 . . . . **30** E8
1 Wisbech PE13 . . . . . . **170** E2
St Martin's St
Lincoln LN2 . . . . **234** B3
Peterborough PE1 . . . . . **225** F5
St Martin's Way 4
NG32 . . . . **120** A3
St Mary Cl 12 PE6 . . . . . **166** F1
St Mary's Abbey✱
PE20 . . . . **135** C7
St Mary's Ave
4 Barnetby le Wold
DN38 . . . . **21** B4
4 Pinchbeck PE11 . . . . . **156** E8
12 Welton/Dunholme
LN2 . . . . **68** D7
Wittering PE8 . . . . **172** C1
St Mary's Cath Prim Sch
NG31 . . . . **211** C5
St Marys CE (Controlled)
Prim Sch LN2 . . . . **68** C6
St Marys Cl
South Field HU13 . . . . **3** E4
5 Weston PE12 . . . . **157** D7
St Mary's Cl
Bainton PE9 . . . . **172** F5
18 Bottesford NG13 . . . **128** A6
2 Brough HU15 . . . . **2** C7
Farcet PE7 . . . . **231** C2
Grimsby DN32 . . . . **192** C6
Peterborough PE1 . . . . . **226** B4
Thorney PE6 . . . . **176** A2
Wilsford NG32 . . . . **120** C1
St Mary's Cres
9 Manby LN11 . . . . **62** C6
1 Stow LN1 . . . . **66** C8
Swineshead PE20 . . . . . . **135** B6
St Marys Ct 6 PE1 . . . . **226** B2
St Mary's Ct 5 DN15 . . . **182** C6
St Marys Dr
6 Sleaford NG34 . . . . . . **212** C6
13 Sutterton PE20 . . . . **136** A2
St Mary's Dr
2 Hatfield DN7 . . . . **14** C2
Peterborough PE2 . . . . . **229** F4
St Mary's Gdns
6 Cowbit PE12 . . . . **167** B8
Long Sutton PE12 . . . . . . **216** C5
3 Whaplode PE12 . . . . . **158** B7
St Mary's Hill 17 PE9 . . **219** C5
St Mary's La
4 Barton-upon-Humber
DN18 . . . . **10** F8
Binbrook LN8 . . . . **47** C4
Claxby LN8 . . . . **45** E5
Louth LN11 . . . . **198** A5
St Mary's Mdws 2
PE12 . . . . **159** D7
St Mary's Pk LN11 . . . . **198** A6
St Mary's Pl 14 PE9 . . . **219** C5
St Mary's RC (Aided)
Prim Sch PE21 . . . . **209** B6
St Mary's RC High Sch
DN33 . . . . **191** A4
St Marys RC Prim Sch
DN20 . . . . **196** C5
St Mary's RC Prim Sch
DN32 . . . . **191** F8
St Mary's Rd
Hatfield DN7 . . . . **14** C3
2 Lincoln LN6 . . . . **204** D2
Skegness PE25 . . . . **206** B6
West Walton PE14 . . . . . **170** E4
St Marys Sch LN2 . . . . . **234** C3
St Marys Sq LN9 . . . . . . **199** B4
St Mary's St
Farcet PE7 . . . . **231** C2
Lincoln LN5 . . . . **234** A1
12 Stamford PE9 . . . . . **219** C5
St Mary's Way 2 PE22 . . **114** A1
St Mathews Cl 2 LN6 . . **201** D1
St Matthews Cl 11
PE25 . . . . **206** A6

St Matthew's Cl
5 Cherry Willingham/
Reepham LN3 . . . . **203** E7
4 Holbeach PE12 . . . . . **215** D2
St Matthew's Dr 13
PE12 . . . . **160** E4
St Matthew's Rd 12
DN36 . . . . **36** C8
St Matthew St HU3 . . . . **180** B5
St Mawes Cres DN34 . . **191** A7
St Mellion Dr NG31 . . . . **211** E7
St Michael Cl 2 LN5 . . . . **93** F7
St Michael's Ave PE13 . . **170** D1
St Michaels CE Prim Sch
LN6 . . . . **92** E8
St Michael's CE Prim Sch
LN6 . . . . **92** E8
St Michael's CE Sch
LN11 . . . . **198** D5
St Michaels Cl 8 LN4 . . **109** F5
St Michael's Cl 16 DN8 . . **15** B7
St Michael's Cres 5
DN16 . . . . **185** C8
St Michael's Ct 22 DN19 . . **12** A8
St Michael's Dr 15 DN8 . . **15** B7
St Michael's Gate PE1 . . **226** C4
St Michael's La
11 Wainfleet St Mary
PE24 . . . . **102** D1
Wainfleet St Mary PE24 . . **115** D8
St Michael's Mount 18
HU14 . . . . **3** B7
St Michael's Rd
Grimsby DN34 . . . . **190** D4
1 Louth LN11 . . . . **198** C5
16 Wittering PE8 . . . . . . **172** B1
St Michaels Terr 7
LN1 . . . . **234** B3
St Michael's Way 1
NG34 . . . . **120** C8
St Michaels Wlk 8
NG34 . . . . **212** C6
St Nectan Cl 9 HU3 . . . . **180** A4
St Nicholas Ave HU4 . . . **179** C2
St Nicholas CE (Controlled)
Prim Sch PE21 . . . . **209** B4
St Nicholas CE Prim Sch
DN39 . . . . **12** A1
St Nicholas Cl
4 Barkston NG32 . . . . . **130** B8
Boston PE21 . . . . **209** B3
St Nicholas Dr DN37 . . . **190** C6
St Nicholas Gdns HU4 . . **179** C2
St Nicholas Prim Sch
PE12 . . . . **160** A8
St Nicholas Rd
Boston PE21 . . . . **209** B3
Thorne/Moorends DN8 . . . **15** A8
St Nicholas St LN1 . . . . **234** A4
St Nicholas Way
10 Lutton PE12 . . . . **160** A8
9 Spalding PE11 . . . . . **214** A5
St Norberts RC Prim Sch
DN17 . . . . **16** D7
St Norbett's Cath Prim Sch
PE11 . . . . **214** C4
St Olaf's Dr DN32 . . . . . **191** D6
St Olave's Dr 17 PE6 . . **175** A1
St Paul Rd DN21 . . . . . . **197** B7
St Paul's Ave 4 LN3 . . . **203** E7
St Pauls Cl PE24 . . . . . **102** D7
St Paul's Cl PE13 . . . . . **169** E2
St Pauls Gdns DN16 . . . **185** B5
St Paul's Gdns PE10 . . . **213** D4
St Paul's La 2 LN1 . . . . **234** B3
St Pauls Prim Sch
PE11 . . . . **214** F6
St Paul's Rd
Gainsborough DN21 . . . . **197** B7
Peterborough PE1 . . . . . **225** F7
Scunthorpe DN16 . . . . . . **185** B6
Spalding PE11 . . . . **214** F5
St Pauls St HU2 . . . . . . **180** E8
St Paul's St 5 PE9 . . . . **219** C5
St Pega Cl 17 PE6 . . . . **166** F1
St Pega's Rd
Glinton PE6 . . . . **174** A6
Peakirk PE6 . . . . **220** E8
St Peter at Arches 6
LN2 . . . . **234** B3
St Peter at Gowts CE
(Controlled) Prim Sch
LN5 . . . . **201** E1
St Peter-in-Eastgate CE
(Cont) Inf Sch LN2 . . . . . **234** C3
St Peter & St Paul CE Prim
Sch PE24 . . . . **102** D7
St Peter & St Paul Lincs
Cath High Sch LN6 . . . . . **205** B7
St Peter's Ave
8 Cherry Willingham/
Reepham LN3 . . . . **203** E7
Cleethorpes DN35 . . . . . **192** E6
Kingston upon Hull
HU10 . . . . **178** E6
Lincoln LN6 . . . . **204** D2
Scunthorpe DN16 . . . . . . **185** B3
St Peter's CE Jun Sch
PE13 . . . . **170** E1
St Peters CE Prim Sch
Cleethorpes DN35 . . . . . **192** F6
Dunston LN4 . . . . **95** C6
St Peters Cl DN21 . . . . . . **40** B5
St Peter's Cl
Burgh le Marsh PE24 . . . **102** D8
4 Holton le Clay DN36 . . **195** D2
St Peter's Cres 5 DN36 . . **36** C8
St Peters Ct 9 PE9 . . . . **219** B4

St Peter's Dr 4 LN10 ... 97 D5
St Peters Gr 2 DN37 ... 23 E1
St Peter's Gr 14 DN21 ... 29 C3
St Peter's Hill
4 Grantham NG31 ... 211 A4
14 Stamford PE9 ... 219 B5
St Peter's La 7 LN12 ... 64 C2
St Peters Rd
11 Bourne PE10 ... 213 C5
Peterborough PE1 ... 226 A2
St Peter's Rd 12 DN21 ... 29 C3
St Peter's Sch DN10 ... 39 B1
St Peter's St PE9 ... 219 B4
St Peter's Way PE6 ... 217 A2
St Pierre Ave NG31 ... 211 E7
St Polycarp's Dr PE12 ... 168 B3
St Quintins Cl 5 HU9 ... 181 C8
St Rumbold's St LN2 ... 234 B2
St Sebastians CE (Aided) Prim Sch NG31 ... 129 E5
St Simon's Dr 9 LN3 ... 203 E7
St Stephen's Sh Ctr HU1 ... 180 D6
St Stephens St HU2 ... 180 D6
St Swithins Cl 1 PE20 ... 135 A4
St Swithuns Sq LN2 ... 234 B2
St Thomas CE Prim Sch PE21 ... 208 F1
St Thomas Ct
Boston PE21 ... 208 F2
Long Sutton PE12 ... 216 B5
St Thomas Dr PE21 ... 208 E2
St Thomas Moore RC Prim Sch PE1 ... 226 D4
St Thomas Moore Rd HU4 ... 179 A4
St Thomas More RC Prim Sch HU4 ... 179 A4
St Thomas Rd 2 PE11 ... 214 D2
St Thomas' Rd 13 DN36 ... 36 C8
St Tibba Way 12 PE9 ... 163 C1
St Valentines Way PE25 ... 206 B6
ST VINCENT NG31 ... 211 D3
St Vincent Cl 2 PE25 ... 206 A6
St Vincent's Ave DN15 ... 183 A6
St Vincent's Rd NG31 ... 211 C3
St Wilfrid's Cl 18 LN4 ... 95 D4
St William Ct PE12 ... 215 F3
Salacon Way 16 DN32 ... 189 C1
Saladine Ct 24 DN41 ... 23 F5
Salamander Cl DN31 ... 191 B8
SALEBY LN13 ... 75 F6
Salem St 5 PE11 ... 145 B6
Salisbury Ave 2 LN8 ... 47 B6
Salisbury Cl
1 Grantham NG31 ... 210 D5
Morton DN21 ... 40 D3
1 Saxilby with Ingleby LN1 ... 66 D2
2 Scunthorpe DN17 ... 184 C7
Salisbury Dr
2 Canwick LN4 ... 81 A2
Waltham DN37 ... 194 D4
Salisbury Rd PE4 ... 220 F3
Salisbury St
Gainsborough DN21 ... 197 C7
Kingston upon Hull HU13 ... 178 D1
Salix App 1 LN6 ... 204 C8
Sallie Bank La LN1 ... 65 D2
Sallows Rd PE1 ... 226 B6
SALMONBY LN9 ... 86 E8
Salmonby Rd DN17 ... 184 E4
Salsbury Ave DN34 ... 191 B6
Saltash Rd HU4 ... 179 A2
Saltburn Gr 5 DN32 ... 192 A5
SALTBY LE14 ... 138 F1
Saltby Rd
Croxton Kerrial NG32 ... 138 D3
Sproxton LE14 ... 150 C7
Saltergate
Lincoln LN2 ... 234 B2
Peterborough PE1 ... 226 E7
The Willows DN37 ... 188 A1
Salter Gate LN11 ... 51 A1
Saltergate Rd 28 DN17 ... 29 D7
Saltern Dr PE11 ... 214 B5
Saltersford Gr NG31 ... 211 D1
Saltersford Rd NG31 ... 211 D2
Saltersgate PE1 ... 226 F7
Salters' La LN11 ... 48 B4
Saltersway NG34 ... 132 F3
Salters Way 14 PE11 ... 134 E2
SALTFLEET LN11 ... 51 B4
SALTFLEETBY ALL SAINTS LN12 ... 51 C1
Saltfleetby CE Prim Sch LN11 ... 51 B1
SALTFLEETBY ST CLEMENT LN11 ... 51 C2
SALTFLEETBY ST PETER LN11 ... 63 B8
Saltfleetby - Theddlethorpe Dunes National Nature Reserve* LN11 ... 51 E3
Saltfleet La PE11 ... 145 B4
Saltfleet Rd
Saltfleetby LN12 ... 51 D1
Theddlethorpe All Saints LN12 ... 63 E8
Saltford Ave 2 HU9 ... 5 F8
Saltgrounds Rd HU15 ... 2 B5
Salthouse La HU1 ... 181 A6
Saltings The 6 PE34 ... 161 F3
Saltmarsh PE2 ... 230 C4
Saltney Gate PE12 ... 215 A6
Salts Rd PE14 ... 170 F4
Salvesen Rd DN35 ... 189 D1
Salvesen Way HU3 ... 180 A3
Samman Cl HU10 ... 178 D6
Sampey Way 13 NG34 ... 133 B1
Samphire Cl 6 DN36 ... 37 C5
Sampson St DN17 ... 7 A2
Sam Scorer Gall* LN1 ... 234 B3
Samuel Ave DN32 ... 192 B6
Samworths Cl PE5 ... 223 F2
Sanbeds La DN9 ... 27 B2
Sanctuary Way DN37 ... 190 C6
Sandars Rd DN21 ... 53 A8
Sandbeck Arc PE25 ... 206 D3
Sandbeck Ave PE25 ... 206 C2
Sandbeck La DN21 ... 41 B6
SANDBRAES LN7 ... 33 A4
Sandcliffe Rd NG31 ... 211 A7
Sanderlings The 6 PE6 ... 174 A5
Sanders Cl
Lincoln LN1 ... 201 D8
15 Mablethorpe & Sutton LN12 ... 77 A7
Meering NG23 ... 91 C8
Sanderson Cl 1 DN16 ... 183 B1
Sanderson's Bank DN10 ... 26 C2
Sanders View LN1 ... 201 D8
Sandfield Cl DN17 ... 184 D5
Sandfield Dr 3 HU15 ... 2 C5
Sandford PE3 ... 225 B5
Sandford St 8 DN31 ... 188 D1
Sandhill La 1 DN22 ... 52 B3
Sandhill Rd DN14 ... 7 B6
SANDHOLME PE20 ... 136 F4
Sandholme La PE20 ... 136 E5
Sandhouse Cres
3 Scunthorpe DN16 ... 183 C1
Scunthorpe DN16 ... 185 C8
Sandhurst Cres 5 NG34 ... 212 B2
Sandhurst Ct 6 LN12 ... 77 A7
Sandhurst Rd
3 Hampton Vale PE7 ... 230 D1
5 Mablethorpe/Sutton on Sea LN12 ... 77 A7
SANDILANDS LN12 ... 77 A8
Sandilands Cl 22 LN12 ... 77 A7
Sandilands Pit Nature Reserve* LN12 ... 77 A7
Sand La
Barkston NG32 ... 129 F8
Besthorpe NG23 ... 91 C8
Broadholme LN6 ... 66 D1
4 Broughton DN20 ... 19 D3
Caistor LN7 ... 32 E4
Fenton LN1 ... 65 D3
Great Steeping PE23 ... 101 C7
Hougham NG32 ... 118 C5
Manton DN21 ... 30 A5
Marston NG32 ... 118 E1
Messingham DN17 ... 29 A7
Osgodby LN8 ... 45 B3
Spalford NG23 ... 78 D4
Thorney NG23 ... 79 B8
Torksey LN1 ... 65 E5
Wroot DN9 ... 26 C6
Sandlees La NG34 ... 123 B4
Sandlemere Cl 3 HU3 ... 180 A5
Sandon Cl NG31 ... 211 C5
Sandon Rd NG31 ... 211 B5
Sandon Specl Sch NG31 ... 211 C5
Sandown Cl 5 PE11 ... 156 E3
Sandpiper Dr
Kingston upon Hull HU4 ... 179 B1
Peterborough PE2 ... 231 E6
Sandpit Rd 14 PE6 ... 176 A3
Sandra Cres LN4 ... 203 D1
Sand Rd DN17 ... 28 B8
Sandringham Ave 29 PE13 ... 170 D1
Sandringham Cl
5 Stamford PE9 ... 219 B7
3 Whaplode PE12 ... 158 B6
Sandringham Cres DN17 ... 184 F3
Sandringham Ct 4 PE12 ... 215 F3
Sandringham Dr
Londonthorpe & Harrowby without NG31 ... 211 E5
Louth LN11 ... 198 B7
13 Mablethorpe & Sutton LN12 ... 76 F8
Wragby LN8 ... 70 D4
Sandringham Gdns PE21 ... 209 C6
Sandringham Rd
Cleethorpes DN35 ... 192 D4
2 Peterborough PE4 ... 225 C8
Sandringham St 2 HU3 ... 180 A6
Sandringham Way 3 PE6 ... 217 A5
Sandringham Wlk 6 PE11 ... 214 D2
Sands Cl 3 DN17 ... 17 D5
Sands Ct 1 HU14 ... 3 A4
Sandsfield La DN21 ... 197 D2
Sands La
Brantingham HU15 ... 1 F7
Brough HU15 ... 2 C6
Carlton-le-Moorland LN5 ... 92 E1
Ellerker HU15 ... 2 A6
Scotter DN21 ... 29 B3
2 South Ferriby DN18 ... 10 A7
SANDTOFT DN8 ... 16 A3
Sandtoft Cl LN6 ... 204 D6
Sandtoft Rd
Hatfield DN7 ... 15 A4
Sandtoft DN9 ... 16 B3
Sandtone Gdns PE11 ... 214 D5
Sandwell Dr LN6 ... 200 D1
Sandy Bank PE22 ... 98 C1
SANDY BANK LN4 ... 111 E6
Sandy Bank Rd LN4 ... 111 D6
Sandy Cl 1 DN36 ... 37 C5
Sandyford La PE22 ... 113 E3
Sandy Gate
Quadring PE11 ... 144 F7
Sutton St James PE12 ... 169 A7
Sandygate Cl NG34 ... 133 C1
Sandygate La NG34 ... 133 C2
Sandy La
Anderby PE24 ... 77 C3
Belchford LN9 ... 73 A2
Candlesby with Gunby PE23 ... 88 F1
Chapel St Leonard PE24 ... 90 E7
Great Steeping PE23 ... 101 D7
Lusby with Winceby PE23 ... 86 F1
North Willingham LN8 ... 58 C8
Tealby LN8 ... 46 C1
Tydd St Giles PE13 ... 170 A7
5 West Ashby LN9 ... 85 E7
Woodhall Spa LN10 ... 97 E7
Saner St HU3 ... 180 B6
Sansford Gn 5 LN6 ... 205 A6
SANTON DN15 ... 19 B7
SAPPERTON NG34 ... 141 E8
Sapperton PE4 ... 220 F6
Sapphire Cl PE24 ... 89 D2
Sapphire Gr 7 HU3 ... 180 A4
Saracen Cl DN21 ... 197 F2
SARACEN'S HEAD PE12 ... 215 A7
Sarah Gate PE11 ... 145 B8
Sargeants Ct 9 PE22 ... 113 B1
Sargent Cl 4 LN4 ... 95 C4
Sargent's Ct 5 PE9 ... 219 A6
Sargent's Way 15 DN20 ... 31 A5
Sargon Way 3 DN31 ... 188 A3
Sarthe Cl 5 PE20 ... 135 B7
Sassaby Cl HU4 ... 179 C3
Satinwood Cl 10 LN6 ... 200 C1
Satterley Cl LN6 ... 92 D4
Saunby Gr DN35 ... 192 E7
SAUNDBY DN22 ... 52 B7
Saundby Rd DN22 ... 52 B6
Saundergate La PE21 ... 136 D8
Saundergate Pk 11 PE21 ... 136 D8
Saunders St 3 DN31 ... 191 C8
SAUSTHORPE PE23 ... 87 E4
Sausthorpe Rd
Partney PE23 ... 88 A3
Sausthorpe PE23 ... 87 F3
Sausthorpe St 9 LN5 ... 201 F1
Savile St HU1 ... 180 F6
Saville Rd PE3 ... 225 D4
Saville Rd Ind Est PE3 ... 225 D5
Saville St LN5 ... 205 D7
Savory Rd 1 PE13 ... 170 D1
Savoy Ct 7 DN36 ... 195 C6
Sawmill La LN8 ... 70 C5
SAXBY LN8 ... 55 F5
SAXBY ALL SAINTS DN20 ... 10 A3
Saxby Ave PE25 ... 206 D2
Saxby Cliff Rd LN8 ... 55 D4
Saxby Gdns PE1 ... 226 C8
Saxby Gr DN33 ... 191 A3
Saxby Hill DN20 ... 10 B4
Saxby Rd
Bonby DN20 ... 10 B2
Scunthorpe DN17 ... 184 E5
SAXILBY LN1 ... 66 D3
Saxilby CE Prim Sch LN1 ... 66 E2
Saxilby Rd
Lincoln LN1 ... 201 A7
Skellingthorpe LN6 ... 200 A6
Sturton by Stow LN1 ... 66 D6
Saxilby Sta LN1 ... 66 D2
Saxon Cl
7 Barton-upon-Humber DN18 ... 10 F8
10 Metheringham LN4 ... 95 D4
Spalding PE11 ... 214 F2
Saxon Cres DN35 ... 192 E6
Saxon Ct
2 Blyton DN21 ... 41 C5
Scunthorpe DN16 ... 185 B3
Saxondale HU4 ... 179 B7
Saxonfield LN7 ... 33 A4
Saxon Gate 15 PE20 ... 136 C5
Saxon Rd
8 Barnack PE9 ... 172 D3
Peterborough PE1 ... 226 C3
Saxon St 4 LN1 ... 234 A4
Saxon Way
2 Ancaster NG32 ... 120 A2
Bourne PE10 ... 213 C6
17 Caistor LN7 ... 33 B4
3 Horncastle LN9 ... 199 D3
6 Ingham LN1 ... 54 F2
Kingston upon Hull HU13 ... 178 F1
Saxon Wlk 16 PE20 ... 136 C5
Saxony Way 6 PE11 ... 134 F2
Sayer Ct PE2 ... 229 F2
Scalby Gr HU5 ... 179 D8
Scald Gate PE22 ... 115 B8
Scale La HU1 ... 181 A6
Scalesgate Rd PE12 ... 159 B1
Scalford Dr PE1 ... 226 C8
Scallow La DN17 ... 29 D6
Scalp Rd PE21 ... 137 B7
SCAMBLESBY LN11 ... 72 F5
Scamblesby CE (Controlled) Prim Sch LN11 ... 72 F5
Scamblesby Hill LN9 ... 72 E4
SCAMPTON LN1 ... 67 D6
Scampton Airfield LN1 ... 67 E6
Scampton Ave LN6 ... 204 F6
Scampton CE Prim Sch LN1 ... 67 D6
Scampton Cl 3 DN34 ... 191 A5
Scampton Way
Gainsborough DN21 ... 197 E3
Scampton LN1 ... 67 F5
Skegness PE25 ... 206 A5
Scandinavian Way DN41 ... 187 B3
Scarborough Bank PE22 ... 100 B1
Scarborough Cl PE10 ... 142 F2
Scarborough St HU3 ... 180 A4
Scarbrough Ave PE25 ... 206 D4
Scarbrough Espl PE25 ... 206 E3
Scargate La LN4 ... 108 F8
Scarle Cl 1 LN6 ... 205 A2
Scarle La LN6 ... 79 B2
Scarrington Cres HU4 ... 179 B6
Scarrow Cl HU3 ... 180 A7
SCARTHO DN33 ... 194 E8
Scartho Jun & Inf Sch DN33 ... 191 D2
Scartho Pk DN33 ... 191 B2
Scartho Rd DN33 ... 191 D2
SCAWBY DN20 ... 30 E8
Scawby Cres LN6 ... 204 F7
Scawby Prim Sch DN20 ... 30 E8
Scawby Rd
Brigg DN20 ... 196 A2
Broughton DN20 ... 19 E2
Grimsby DN33 ... 191 A3
Scawby DN20 ... 31 A7
Scunthorpe DN17 ... 184 E5
Schiphol Way DN38 ... 21 E5
Schofield Cl 7 DN19 ... 11 C8
School Cl
1 Maxey PE6 ... 173 C7
Peterborough PE3 ... 225 A5
School Cres
Anwick NG34 ... 109 B1
1 Scothern LN2 ... 68 F4
5 Surfleet PE11 ... 145 E3
School Croft DN9 ... 27 B2
School Dr
27 Messingham DN17 ... 29 D7
8 Welton/Dunholme LN2 ... 68 C6
School Hill LE14 ... 150 C7
Schoolhouse La 11 LN11 ... 198 B5
School House La 6 DN10 ... 39 F3
School Houses 9 DN20 ... 19 E4
School La
Addlethorpe PE24 ... 90 D3
Appleby DN15 ... 9 D1
1 Baston PE6 ... 164 E4
Beckingham LN5 ... 105 B4
8 Bicker PE20 ... 135 A4
Binbrook LN8 ... 47 B5
5 Bonby DN20 ... 10 C2
Boothby Pagnell NG33 ... 140 F5
Buckminster NG33 ... 150 F5
Butterwick PE22 ... 126 E3
Cabourne LN7 ... 33 D5
Canwick LN4 ... 81 A4
Claypole NG23 ... 117 F8
7 Colsterworth NG33 ... 151 D7
1 Coningsby LN4 ... 207 C4
5 Croxton Kerrial NG32 ... 138 D4
4 Donington PE11 ... 134 F2
East Keal PE23 ... 100 E6
Edenham PE10 ... 153 F4
4 Glinton PE6 ... 220 C8
18 Goxhill DN19 ... 12 A8
Grayingham DN21 ... 42 E7
Great Steeping PE23 ... 101 E7
Hainton LN8 ... 58 E3
3 Harmston LN5 ... 93 F5
Heighington/Washingborough LN4 ... 203 C2
5 Helpringham NG34 ... 133 D7
2 Irby DN37 ... 34 D7
Kingston upon Hull HU10 ... 178 C8
9 Lincoln LN6 ... 204 F1
5 Lutton PE12 ... 160 A8
Maltby le Marsh LN13 ... 76 A8
4 Mareham le Fen PE22 ... 99 A4
Marston NG32 ... 118 D2
3 Maxey PE6 ... 173 C7
1 New Holland DN19 ... 4 E2
North Cockerington LN11 ... 49 F1
3 North Ferriby HU14 ... 3 A4
4 North Kelsey LN7 ... 32 A4
North Scarle LN6 ... 78 E1
North Somercotes LN11 ... 50 F7
Old Leake PE22 ... 114 A1
Old Somerby NG33 ... 140 E8
Raithby PE23 ... 87 D2
Redbourne DN21 ... 30 F3
Ropsley NG33 ... 131 B1
Rothwell LN7 ... 33 E2
1 Scampton Airfield LN1 ... 67 F5
Sedgebrook NG32 ... 128 F4
Silk Willoughby NG34 ... 121 A1
School La *continued*
Snitterby DN21 ... 43 D5
South Carlton LN1 ... 67 D3
7 South Ferriby DN18 ... 10 A7
Springthorpe DN21 ... 53 E8
2 Sturton by Stow LN1 ... 66 C7
17 Tetney DN36 ... 36 D4
Thistleton LE15 ... 151 C1
Thorpe on the Hill LN6 ... 92 E8
6 Uffington PE9 ... 172 C6
Walcott LN4 ... 109 C7
3 West/East Butterwick DN17 ... 28 D8
2 Willingham by Stow DN21 ... 53 E3
Wilsford NG32 ... 120 C1
School Rd
1 Barnack PE9 ... 172 D3
Newborough PE6 ... 174 E5
Scunthorpe DN16 ... 185 B6
8 South Killingholme DN40 ... 12 E3
West Walton PE14 ... 170 E4
Winteringham DN15 ... 2 A1
School View 10 NG13 ... 128 A5
School Wlk DN35 ... 192 C5
School Yd Mews DN20 ... 196 C4
Schooner Ct HU4 ... 179 B3
Schrimshaw Ct 6 PE25 ... 206 C4
Schrimshire's Rd DN22 ... 52 A1
Scoggins Way 4 NG34 ... 122 D3
Scoldall La PE11 ... 145 E4
Scolding Dro PE6 ... 176 E5
SCOPWICK LN4 ... 95 D1
Scopwick Pl 3 LN2 ... 201 F8
Scorer St LN5 ... 201 F1
Scotenoon PE2 ... 229 E3
Scotgate PE9 ... 219 A5
SCOTHERN LN2 ... 68 E4
Scothern La
Dunholme LN2 ... 68 E5
Stainton by Langworth LN2 ... 69 B4
10 Welton/Dunholme LN2 ... 68 E6
Scothern Rd LN2 ... 68 D3
Scotia Rd PE21 ... 209 F2
Scotia Way PE21 ... 209 F2
SCOTLAND NG33 ... 141 C5
Scotland La NG33 ... 141 B5
Scotney Dr NG31 ... 211 F5
Scotney St PE1 ... 225 E7
Scott Ave DN17 ... 184 C6
Scott Cl
6 Claypole NG23 ... 117 E8
Grimsby DN37 ... 190 F8
Peterborough PE2 ... 231 E6
Scotten Dike Dro PE10 ... 154 E6
SCOTTER DN21 ... 29 B3
Scotter Prim Sch DN21 ... 29 C3
Scotter Rd
Laughton DN21 ... 41 C8
Messingham DN17 ... 29 D5
Scunthorpe DN17 ... 182 C1
Scotter Rd S DN17 ... 184 C3
SCOTTERTHORPE DN21 ... 29 B5
Scotterthorpe Rd DN21 ... 29 B4
Scott Gdns LN2 ... 202 C6
Scottlethorpe PE10 ... 153 E4
Scottlethorpe Rd PE10 ... 153 D3
SCOTTON DN21 ... 29 C2
Scotton Comm Nature Reserve* DN9 ... 27 B1
Scotton Dr 1 LN6 ... 205 A7
Scotton Rd DN21 ... 29 C3
Scott's Cl PE6 ... 164 E3
Scott's Hill 4 NG32 ... 106 C1
Scotts Rd PE6 ... 220 D8
Scott St
Gainsborough DN21 ... 197 C5
Kingston upon Hull HU2 ... 180 F7
SCOTT WILLOUGHBY NG34 ... 132 B4
SCRAFIELD LN9 ... 86 C3
SCRANE END PE22 ... 137 F8
Scrap Bay Rd DN16 ... 19 A3
SCREDINGTON NG34 ... 132 E7
Scredington Rd
Burton Pedwardine NG34 ... 122 B1
Helpringham NG34 ... 133 C7
SCREMBY PE23 ... 88 E2
SCRIVELSBY LN9 ... 98 E8
Scrivelsby Ct DN35 ... 193 A3
SCRUB HILL LN4 ... 111 B6
Scrub La
Authorpe LN11 ... 75 A8
East Halton DN40 ... 12 E5
Withern with Stain LN11 ... 62 D1
Scullery La NG33 ... 141 A5
SCUNTHORPE DN15 ... 183 B5
Scunthorpe CE Prim Sch DN15 ... 183 A4
Scunthorpe General Hospl DN15 ... 182 E2
Scunthorpe Leisure Ctr DN15 ... 183 B3
Scunthorpe Sta DN16 ... 183 A2
Seabank Rd 22 PE13 ... 170 E1
Sea Bank Rd PE24 ... 90 E7
Seabrook Dr DN16 ... 185 A2
SEACROFT PE25 ... 103 E4
Seacroft Cl 13 NG31 ... 211 D7
Seacroft Dr 10 PE25 ... 206 C1

Seacroft Espl PE25.....103 E4
Seacroft Rd
Cleethorpes DN35......193 A5
Mablethorpe/Sutton on Sea
LN12.....64 B3
Seacroft Sq
10 Skegness PE25......103 E4
11 Skegness PE25......116 E8
SEADYKE PE20 .....136 E3
Sea Dyke PE22.....114 B2
Seadyke Rd
Kirton PE20 .....136 E3
Wisbech St Mary PE13.....177 F6
Sea Dyke Way DN36...37 C2
Sea End Rd PE22.....127 A4
Seafield Rd 5 PE13.....170 B2
Seaford Rd DN35.....193 B1
Sea Front Rd
10 Skegness PE25.....103 E4
9 Skegness PE25.....103 E4
Seagate Rd PE12.....216 D2
Seagate Terr PE12.....216 D4
Seagull HU4 .....179 E2
Seaholme Rd LN12.....64 B2
Sea La
Benington PE22.....127 B4
Butterwick PE22.....126 F3
Friskney PE22.....115 C5
Hogsthorpe PE24.....90 C7
Huttoft LN13.....77 A4
Ingoldmells PE25.....90 E3
Leverton PE22.....127 B6
Mablethorpe/Sutton on Sea
LN12.....77 A7
North Coates DN36.....37 B4
Old Leake PE22.....114 C1
Saltfleet LN11.....51 C5
Theddlethorpe St Helen
LN12.....63 E7
Wrangle PE22.....114 E1
Sealey's La PE13.....177 D8
**Seal Sanctuary & Nature
Ctr The** ★ LN12.....64 B5
Seamer Gr 1 DN32.....192 A5
SEARBY DN38.....32 C8
Searby Hill DN38.....32 D8
Searby Rd
Lincoln LN2.....202 B8
Scunthorpe DN17.....184 E4
Searby Wold La DN38...21 E1
Sea Rd
Anderby PE24.....77 B2
19 Chapel St Leonard
PE24.....90 D7
Cleethorpes DN35.....192 F6
Seargeants Cl 1 PE6...174 E4
Searjeant St PE1.....225 E5
Searson Cl PE9.....172 F7
Seascale Wlk DN32.....191 F8
Seas End Prim Sch
PE11.....145 D3
Seas End Rd
Moulton PE12.....146 D1
Surfleet PE11.....145 E3
SEATHORNE PE25.....206 E8
Seathorne Cres PE25...90 F1
Seathorne Prim Sch
PE25.....206 D7
Seaton Cl PE7.....233 D6
Seaton Gr
Grimsby DN32.....192 A5
Kingston upon Hull HU4...179 E5
Seaton Rd
Kingston upon Hull
HU13.....178 F2
Scunthorpe DN17.....184 D8
6 Stamford PE9.....219 B4
Sea View LN11.....51 D3
Sea View Rd PE25.....206 D5
Sea View St DN35.....192 F5
Seawall La DN36.....37 C5
Sebrights Way PE3.....224 F3
Second Ave
Fixborough Ind Est DN15...7 F1
Grantham NG31.....211 F6
Grimsby DN33.....191 B4
5 Scampton Airfield LN1...67 E5
3 Scunthorpe DN17.....184 C6
Spalding PE11.....214 A4
Second Dro
Crowland PE6.....166 E2
Gosberton PE11.....144 C3
Peterborough PE2.....226 D1
Second Dro Ind Est
PE1.....226 D1
Second Marsh Rd
PE14.....170 C3
SEDGEBROOK NG32.....128 E5
Sedgebrook Cl 1 LN2.....201 F8
Sedgebrook Rd NG32.....128 F6
Sedge Cl
6 Barton-upon-Humber
DN18.....3 F1
Leasingham NG34.....121 C7
**Sedge Hole Cl Nature
Reserve** ★ DN9.....27 F2
Sedgemoor Cl 3 LN6...204 E1
Sedge Pl 9 PE12.....167 B8
Sedgewood Way DN15..182 C6
Seed Cl La 4 DN37.....23 F1
Seedlands Cl PE21.....209 B7
Sefton Ave PE13.....170 E1
Sefton St 2 HU3.....180 B4
Segmere St 3 DN35.....193 A5
Segrave Gr HU5.....179 D8

Selbourne Rd 4 DN34..190 E4
Selby Cl LN6.....205 A3
Selby Ct DN17.....184 D7
Selby Rd DN8.....14 F8
Selby St HU3.....180 A5
Selge Way DN33.....190 F3
Selkirk St HU5.....180 A8
Sellers Grange PE2.....230 B4
Sellwood Ct NG34.....212 F7
Sellwood Gdns LN9.....199 B3
Selmeston Ct DN34.....191 C6
Selwyn Ave 16 HU14.....3 A4
Selwyn Ct DN34.....190 F6
Selwyn Rd PE9.....219 A7
Sempers Cl LN6.....92 E8
Sennefleet Rd DN21.....29 B4
Sentance Cres PE20.....136 C6
Sequana Ct HU9.....181 B6
Seraphim App Rd
DN16.....183 E1
Seraphim Rd DN16.....183 F1
Serena Rd 5 PE25.....206 D2
Serlby Gdns PE3.....225 B3
Serpentine Gn Sh Ctr
PE7.....230 D3
Serpentine St 1 LN8....57 D7
Serpentine The PE7.....230 D3
Service Rd DN37.....190 D8
Service Rd 1 18 DN37...190 E8
Service Rd 2 17 DN37...190 E8
Service Rd 3 15 DN37...190 E8
Service Rd 4 8 DN37.....190 E8
Service Rd 5 13 DN37...190 E8
Service Rd 6 14 DN37...190 E8
Service Rd 7 3 DN37.....190 F8
Service Rd 8 9 DN37.....188 A1
Service Rd 9 7 DN37.....188 A1
Service Rd 10 6 DN37..188 A1
Service Rd 12 2 DN37..188 A1
Service Rd 13 4 DN37..188 A1
Service Rd 14 3 DN37..188 A1
Service Rd 15 16 DN37..190 E8
Service Rd 17 DN37.....190 E8
Service Rd 18 DN37.....190 F8
Service Rd 19 4 DN37..190 E8
Service Rd 20 19 DN37..190 E8
Service Rd 21 1 DN37..190 E8
Service Rd 22 3 DN37..190 E8
Service Rd 23 DN37.....190 F8
Service Rd 25 11 DN37..190 E8
Service Rd 26 3 DN37..188 A1
Service Rd No 1 3
DN32.....189 B1
Service Rd No 2 4
DN32.....189 B1
Services Rd DN16.....183 E2
Setchfield Pl PE2.....230 F7
Setterwood Garth 2
HU10.....178 E8
Setts Gn PE10.....213 C2
Sevenacres PE2.....229 E5
Seven Quay Rd DN40...186 E7
Seventh Ave 3 NG31...211 F6
Severn Cl PE4.....221 C1
Severn Rd PE11.....214 F5
Severn St LN1.....201 C4
Severn Way 2 DN37...190 E8
Sewell Cl PE6.....217 E5
Sewell Rd LN2.....234 C3
Sewell's Wlk LN5.....201 E1
Sewer La 3 HU1.....180 F5
SEWSTERN NG33.....150 F4
Sewstern Cl 15 LN4.....81 A1
Sewstern La
Allington NG32.....128 E7
Long Bennington NG23...117 E1
Sedgebrook NG32.....128 D4
Sewstern Rd NG33.....151 B4
Seymour Ave LN11.....198 C4
Seymour Cl 14 LN13.....75 F2
Seymour Pl PE4.....221 F2
Seymour St HU3.....179 F5
Sezanne Wlk 10 PE11...214 C6
Shackleton Cl
Market Deeping PE6.....217 B7
10 Spalding PE11.....214 C2
Shaddys Wlk LN13.....88 E6
Shaftesbury Ave
Birchwood LN6.....200 D2
Grimsby DN34.....191 B7
Shaftesbury Mews 6
DN36.....195 C6
Shaftesbury Way 2
NG23.....91 D5
Shakespeare Ave
Grantham NG31.....211 E6
Peterborough PE1.....225 E4
4 Scunthorpe DN17.....184 C6
Shakespeare Cl 6
HU3.....180 B8
Shakespeare St
5 Gainsborough
DN21.....197 D2
5 Lincoln LN5.....205 E8
Shamfields Rd 3
PE23.....101 A8
Shamrock Cl PE2.....231 C7
Shanklin Dr NG31.....210 E4
Shannon Ave LN6.....205 A5
Shannon Cl 2 LN6.....205 A5
Shannon Rd 8 LN4.....207 D4
Shardloes LN4.....81 E2
Shardloes Rd 9 PE25...103 E4
Sharma Leas PE4.....220 E3
Sharmans Cl 11 LN12...77 A7
Sharman Way PE11.....214 B5

Sharnbrook Ave 1
PE7.....230 C1
Sharpe 35 DN18.....10 E8
Sharpe Rd NG31.....211 C6
Sharpe's Rd PE6.....165 C3
Sharp's Cl PE10.....213 B6
Sharp Wlk LN6.....93 C8
Shawbury Cl 10 LN6...204 C6
Shaw Dr DN33.....191 E1
Shawfield Cl 10 DN3...14 A3
Shaw La PE22.....127 B8
Shaw Rd
Boston PE21.....208 C7
Grantham NG31.....210 D2
Gringley on the Hill DN10..39 C2
Shaws La PE12.....160 B3
Shaws Mews LN11.....198 B5
Shaw St HU9.....181 B7
Shaw Way 4 LN2.....68 C2
Shays Dr 1 LN6.....205 A7
Shearers Dr 12 PE11...214 A2
Shearman's Wath
Thimbleby LN9.....85 C6
West Ashby LN9.....199 A8
Shears Ct DN37.....194 F4
Shearwater PE22.....229 D6
Shearwater Cl
3 Birchwood LN6.....200 E1
Louth LN11.....198 D8
Shearwater Rd LN6.....200 E1
Sheep Cote La DN7.....14 E8
Sheep Dip La DN7.....14 D4
Sheepdyke La 4 DN20...10 C2
Sheepfold St DN32.....191 E7
Sheepgate PE22.....127 A6
Sheep Marsh La DN36...37 B3
Sheep Mkt
2 Spalding PE11.....214 D4
11 Stamford PE9.....219 B5
Sheepwalk
Auborn Haddington & South
Hykeham LN5.....92 E5
Peterborough PE4.....221 E1
Sheepwash La LN4.....81 E4
Sheffield Pk Ave DN15..182 F5
Sheffield St (East) 1
DN15.....183 A4
Sheffield St (West) 4
DN15.....182 F4
Sheffield St DN15.....183 A4
Sheila Cres 4 PE11.....214 A3
Sheldrake Rd 1 NG34...212 B3
Shelford St DN15.....183 A3
Shelley Ave
Grantham NG31.....211 D6
Grimsby DN33.....191 B4
Shelley Cl
3 Mablethorpe/Sutton on
Sea LN12.....77 A7
New England PE1.....225 F8
12 Stamford PE9.....218 E6
Shelley Dr
Lincoln LN2.....202 B6
7 Sleaford NG34.....212 F4
Shelroy Cl DN15.....182 C5
Shelton Rd PE2.....231 D6
Shenley Cl 11 DN7.....14 D3
SHEPEAU STOW PE12...167 F3
Shepeau Stow Prim Sch
PE12.....167 F3
Shepherds Cl PE4.....221 A4
Shepherd's Croft 1
DN9.....27 D7
Shepherd's La NG34.....133 E7
Shepherd's Wlk PE9...163 D1
Sheppard's Dro PE6.....167 B1
Shepperson's Ave
PE11.....144 F5
Shepton La NG34.....142 A8
Sheraton Cl 15 LN6.....204 D7
Sheraton Dr 3 DN36...36 D8
Sherborne Rd PE1.....226 D6
Sherbourne Cl 16
PE20.....135 B7
Sherbrooke St 2 LN2...202 D4
Sherburn Cres DN15...182 D4
Sherburn St
Cleethorpes DN35.....192 F4
Kingston upon Hull HU9..181 D8
Sheridan Cl 1 LN2.....202 C7
Sheridan Rd PE1.....225 F8
Sheriff Way PE21.....208 E7
Sheringham Way PE2...230 C6
Sherwood Ave
Boston PE21.....208 E7
Newark-on-Trent NG24...104 A4
4 Peterborough PE2.....230 F7
7 Wisbech PE13.....170 D1
Sherwood Cl
1 Louth LN11.....198 C4
Stamford PE9.....218 F5
Sherwood Dr
Kingston upon Hull
HU4.....179 A7
Spalding PE11.....214 D6
Waddington LN5.....205 D1
Sherwood Rd
10 Coningsby LN4.....207 D4
Grimsby DN34.....190 F5
3 Mablethorpe/Sutton on Sea
LN12.....64 B4
Sherwood Rise 7
NG32.....119 B7
Sherwood Vale DN15...182 D3
Shetland Way DN40.....186 C2
Shillaker Ct PE10.....213 D4
Shipton Rd DN16.....185 C5

Shire Ave PE11.....214 A5
Shiregate 12 LN4.....95 C4
Shire Gr PE1.....226 C5
Shire La NG23.....117 D8
Shires Orch 6 NG32...138 D4
Shirley Cres DN16.....185 B8
Shivean Gate 5 PE12...157 F7
Shodfriars La 4 PE21...208 F4
Shoe La LN9.....72 C5
Shoemaker's La DN21...29 E5
Shoff Dro PE11.....134 D1
Shoff Rd PE11.....134 D1
Sholt's Gate PE12.....158 C7
Shop Hill 7 PE22.....98 F4
Shop La LN11.....72 D6
Shore Rd
Freiston PE22.....126 D2
Garthorpe & Fockerby
DN17.....7 F5
Shortacres Rd PE2.....230 F7
Short Dro
Gosberton PE11.....144 C5
Pointon & Sempringham
NG34.....143 F4
Thurlby PE10.....164 E8
Shortfen PE2.....230 C4
Short Ferry Rd LN3.....82 F6
Shortfield La PE21.....209 E8
Short Furrow LN5.....107 B8
Short Hollow NG33.....131 C1
Short La
Fotherby LN11.....49 A2
Ingham LN1.....54 F3
Lincoln LN1.....234 A2
1 West Halton DN15.....8 E8
3 Wisbech PE13.....170 A1
Shortleys Rd DN22.....65 B5
Short's Cnr PE22.....112 D3
Short St
2 Cleethorpes DN35.....192 F6
4 Spalding PE11.....214 C4
Short Wheatley La
NG23.....91 D3
Shortwood La
Bullington LN8.....69 F4
Friesthorpe LN3.....57 A2
Shorwell Cl 3 NG31...210 E4
Shotbolt La PE11.....214 F8
Shrewsbury Ave PE2...230 D5
Shropshire Rd 9 LN1...67 E5
**Shrubberies Nature
Reserve The** ★ PE12...216 B5
Shrub Rd PE7.....230 C1
Shrubwood Cl 3
NG34.....122 E2
Shuttlefield La PE20...135 F4
Shuttleworth Ct 12 LN6..93 C8
Sibelius Rd HU4.....179 B4
SIBSEY PE22.....113 B2
Sibsey Ct DN37.....188 A2
Sibsey Drain Bank
PE22.....126 A6
*Sibsey Free (Controlled)
Prim Sch* PE22.....113 A2
Sibsey La 3 PE21.....208 F4
Sibsey Rd
Boston PE21.....209 B8
Fishtoft PE21.....125 F5
Sibsey Trader Windmill ★
PE22.....113 A2
Sibthorpe Dr LN2.....68 F2
Sibthorp St LN5.....201 E1
Sickling Gate Rd PE22..115 B7
Sidebar La NG34.....123 C4
Side La DN33.....195 A7
Side Row NG24.....104 A4
Side St 2 NG32.....128 F7
Sidings Ct 3 HU15.....2 B5
Sidings The
Holbeach PE12.....215 D1
Horncastle LN9.....199 A3
Lincoln LN6.....234 A1
Long Sutton PE12.....216 B4
2 Louth LN11.....198 C6
23 Mablethorpe/Sutton on Sea
LN12.....77 A8
4 Morton PE10.....154 D6
8 Moulton PE12.....157 F6
9 Ruskington NG34.....108 E1
25 Saxilby LN1.....66 D2
Sidlaw Gr LN5.....205 C2
Sidney Chase LN11.....54 F1
Sidney Ct 1 DN35.....192 B8
Sidney Pl DN35.....192 B8
Sidney Rd
Grimsby DN34.....191 B7
5 Scunthorpe DN17.....184 C6
Sidney St
4 Cleethorpes DN35.....189 D1
Cleethorpes DN35.....192 B8
Grantham NG31.....211 A6
Lincoln LN5.....205 E8
Sidney Terr 17 LN5.....205 E8
Sidney Way DN35.....192 B8
Signal Rd NG31.....211 C5
Signhills Ave DN35.....193 A4
Signhills Inf & Jun Sch
DN35.....193 A4
Silica Cres DN17.....184 C5
SILK WILLOUGHBY
NG34.....121 C1
Silt La PE20.....136 E3
Silt Pit La PE21.....137 A7
Siltside PE11.....144 D4
Silverbell DN16.....185 E4
Silver Birch Rise DN16..185 B3
Silvergarth DN32.....192 B5
Silver Hill PE7.....230 D3

**Silverines Mdws Nature
Reserve** ★ LN11.....72 E5
Silver La PE9.....219 B5
Silversides La DN20.....196 A2
Silversides La Cvn Site
DN20.....196 A2
Silver's La PE13.....177 E7
Silver St
Bardney LN3.....83 C4
Barnetby le Wold DN38....21 B4
Barrow upon Humber
DN19.....11 C7
Baumber LN9.....72 A1
Benniworth LN8.....71 F8
Branston LN4.....81 E2
Coningsby LN4.....207 C4
Gainsborough DN21.....197 C4
Holton le Clay DN36.....195 D1
11 Kingston upon Hull
HU1.....180 F6
Lincoln LN2.....234 B2
Minting LN9.....84 C8
North Clifton NG23.....78 C7
Owston Ferry DN9.....28 B2
Peterborough PE2.....230 F7
1 Ruskington NG34.....108 E1
Stainforth DN7.....14 C6
Theddlethorpe St Helen
LN12.....63 E5
3 Waddingham DN21.....43 D7
6 Wainfleet All Saints
PE24.....102 D1
Winteringham DN15.....2 B1
Wisbech PE13.....170 D1
5 Wragby LN8.....70 D5
Silverstone Rd 17 LN6...204 C7
Silvertoft La DN21.....136 B8
Silverwood Rd
8 Bottesford NG13.....128 A5
Peterborough PE1.....225 F5
Silvester Rd PE5.....223 E2
Silvester St HU2.....180 F7
Simons Cl
4 Donington on Bain
LN11.....59 E1
5 Louth LN11.....198 D4
Simon's Gn LN6.....205 C6
Simons Pl DN35.....192 D7
Simon Weir La PE20...135 D8
Simpson Cl
17 Barrow upon Humber
DN19.....11 C8
Chapel St Leonard PE24...90 D6
Sincil Bank LN5.....234 B1
**Sincil Bank (Lincoln City
FC)** LN5.....201 E1
Sincil St LN5.....234 B2
Sinclair Cl PE21.....208 E8
Sinderson Rd DN36.....36 D8
Singerfire Rd PE5.....223 D2
Sir Francis Hill Prim Sch
The LN6.....205 C8
Sir Isaac Newton Cl 3
PE12.....215 E3
Sir Isaac Newton Dr 3
PE21.....208 F1
Sirius Cl 3 HU3.....180 B5
Sir John Nelthorpe Sch
DN20.....196 C3
*Sir William Robertson High
Sch* LN5.....106 E4
Siskin Cl PE10.....143 A3
Siskin Cres DN16.....185 B2
Sissley PE2.....229 E2
Sitwell St HU8.....181 A8
Sixfields Cl LN6.....205 A7
SIXHILLS LN8.....58 E6
Sixhills La LN8.....59 A7
Sixhills Rd LN8.....58 D6
Sixhills St DN32.....191 E7
Six House Bank PE11...144 D1
Six Hundreds Dro
PE20.....123 E3
Six Score Rd PE6.....165 C4
Sixth Ave
Fixborough Ind Est DN15...8 A1
2 Grantham NG31.....211 F6
Scunthorpe DN17.....184 B6
Skaters Way PE4.....221 A4
Skayman Fields 7
LN5.....105 E8
SKEGNESS PE25.....206 E4
Skegness Bsns Ctr
PE25.....206 B2
*Skegness Coll of
Vocational Ed* PE25.....206 C2
Skegness & District Hospl
PE25.....206 B3
Skegness Gram Sch
PE25.....206 C4
Skegness Inf Sch PE25..206 C4
*Skegness (Ingoldmells)
Aerodrome* PE25.....90 D1
Skegness Jun Sch
PE25.....206 C4
*Skegness Motor Racing
Stadium* PE24.....90 A2
Skegness Rd
Burgh le Marsh PE24.....103 A7
Chapel St Leonard PE24...90 D6
Ingoldmells PE25.....90 E3
Partney PE23.....88 B3
5 Wainfleet All Saints
PE24.....102 D1
Skegness Ret Pk PE25..206 A3
Skegness Sports Ctr
PE25.....206 B5
Skegness Sta PE25.....206 C3

Skegness Wr Leisure Pk★
PE25 . . . . .90 E1
SKELDYKE PE20 . . . . .136 F4
Skeldyke Rd PE20 . . .136 D5
SKELLINGTHORPE LN6 . .200 B4
Skellingthorpe Rd LN6 .200 D2
Skelton Dr PE12 . . . .216 C3
Skelton Rd DN17 . . . .184 C7
SKENDLEBY PE23 . . . . .88 D4
Skendleby Nature
Reserve★ LN13 . . . . .88 E6
Skerries Cl [5] LN6 . . .205 A1
Skerry La NG13 . . . . .128 C5
SKIDBROOKE LN11 . . . .51 B3
Skillings La HU15 . . . . .2 C5
SKILLINGTON NG33 . . .151 B8
Skillington Rd NG33 . .151 B6
SKINNAND LN5 . . . . .106 C8
Skinnand La LN5 . . . .106 D7
Skinners La
[6] South Ferriby DN18 . .10 A7
Waltham DN37 . . . . .194 E4
Skinner's La
Middle Rasen LN8 . . . .45 C1
South Kyme LN4 . . . .110 B1
Skipmarsh La
Leverton PE22 . . . . .126 E8
Old Leake PE22 . . . .113 E1
Skippingdale Ind Pk
DN15 . . . . .182 C7
Skippingdale Rd DN15 .182 F6
Skipwith Cres [20] LN4 . .95 D4
Skipworth Way PE25 . .206 C8
SKIRBECK PE21 . . . . .209 B3
Skirbeck Dr [18] LN1 . . .66 D2
Skirbeck Gdns PE21 . .209 B3
SKIRBECK QUARTER
PE21 . . . . .208 D2
Skirbeck Rd PE21 . . .209 A3
Skirmore Rd PE22 . . .114 E5
Skirth Rd LN4 . . . . .109 F6
Skitter Rd DN40 . . . . .5 D1
Skylark Dr DN16 . . . .185 B2
Skylarks Cl [6] PE7 . . .230 D3
Slack The [4] DN17 . . . .16 D8
Slash La LN9 . . . . . . .86 D3
Slate Drift [2] PE9 . . .171 C2
Slate Mill Pl NG31 . . .211 B5
Slate Mill The NG31 . .211 B5
Slay Pit Cl DN7 . . . . .14 F4
Slay Pit La DN7 . . . . .14 F3
Slea Cotts [15] DN37 . .212 D4
SLEAFORD NG34 . . . .212 B4
Sleaford (Aided) RC Prim
Sch NG34 . . . . . . .212 C5
Sleaford Art Studio★
NG34 . . . . .212 D5
Sleaford Coll NG34 . . .212 E4
Sleaford Joint Sixth Form
NG34 . . . . .212 D5
Sleaford Leisure Ctr
NG34 . . . . .212 E4
Sleaford Lollycocks Field
Nature Reserve★
NG34 . . . . .212 E4
Sleaford Mareham Nature
Reserve★ NG34 . . . .212 E2
Sleaford Rd
Ancaster NG32 . . . .120 A2
Barnby in the Willows
NG24 . . . . .104 F5
Boston PE21 . . . . . .208 B4
Bracebridge Heath LN4 . .81 A1
Coningsby LN4 . . . . .207 A4
Cranwell NG34 . . . . .120 F8
East Kirkby PE23 . . . .99 E4
Folkingham NG34 . . .142 D8
Heckington NG34 . . .122 D3
Honington NG32 . . . .119 C2
Leadenham LN5 . . . .106 D2
[14] Leasingham NG34 . .121 D7
Metheringham LN4 . . . .95 B4
[18] Navenby/Wellingore
LN5 . . . . .107 A7
Newark-on-Trent NG24 . .104 A5
North Kyme LN4 . . . .109 E2
Ruskington NG34 . . . .108 E1
Tattershall LN4 . . . . .110 D7
Walcot near Folkingham
NG34 . . . . .132 D2
Sleaford Sta NG34 . . .212 D3
Sleaford Virtual Mus★ [7]
NG34 . . . . .212 C4
Sledge La LN8 . . . . . .59 B8
Sledmere Gr HU4 . . . .179 C5
Sleepers Cl [1] PE12 . .216 B4
Sleights Cl HU3 . . . . .180 A7
Sleights Dr [2] PE14 . .170 F1
Sleights La HU15. . . . . .1 B6
Slessor St [2] LN5 . . . .94 A7
Slipe Dro PE11 . . . . .155 F5
Slipe The PE10 . . . . .213 F4
Slippery Gowt La PE21 .136 F8
Slipway DN35 . . . . . .193 A6
SLOOTHBY LN13 . . . . .89 D5
Sloothby High La
Hogsthorpe PE24 . . . .90 A6
Willoughby with Sloothby
PE24 . . . . .89 F6
Sluice La DN18 . . . . . .9 E8
Sluice Rd
Holbeach PE12 . . . .215 B8
South Ferriby DN18 . . .9 F8
Sutton Bridge PE12 . .161 A6
Whaplode PE12 . . . .147 B4
Small Dro PE12 . . . . .157 E7
Small Dro La PE11 . . .144 E1
Small End Rd PE22 . . .114 E6

Smalley Rd PE21 . . . .209 D4
Smallwood PE3 . . . . .225 B5
Smeeton Ct [6] NG34 . .212 D6
Smeeton's La PE20 . . .146 C7
Smithdale Cl [9] PE11 . .214 C6
Smithfield PE6. . . . . .176 B3
Smithfield Rd DN16 . . .185 D6
Smith Field [10] DN36 . . .36 B1
Smith St
Lincoln LN5 . . . . . .201 C5
Scunthorpe DN15 . . .182 F4
Smithy La
[7] Barnetby le Wold
DN38. . . . . .21 B4
Friskney PE22 . . . . .115 A4
Smooting La [4] LN3 . . .82 A8
Smooting The LN8 . . . .46 C1
Smythe La DN22 . . . . .52 C1
Snaffer's La PE12 . . . .158 C5
Snainton Gr [4] HU5 . .179 D8
Snaith Cl [9] LN6 . . . .204 B6
SNARFORD LN2. . . . . .56 C1
Snarford Rd LN3 . . . . .69 D8
SNELLAND LN3 . . . . . .69 E8
Snelland Rd LN3 . . . . .69 E8
Snetterton Cl [1] LN6 . .204 C7
Snipe Dales Ctry Pk★
PE23 . . . . .86 F3
Snipe Dales Nature
Reserve★ LN9 . . . . .86 E3
SNITTERBY DN21 . . . .43 D5
Snitterby Carr La DN21. . .43 A5
Snitterby Rd DN21 . . . .43 D6
Snowberry Gdns [5]
LN6 . . . . .204 C8
Snowden Cl [1] PE6 . .175 C8
Snowdon Cl [4] LN5 . .205 D3
Snowdonia Ave DN15 .182 D7
Snowdon Rd [3] NG23 . .91 D4
Snowdrop Cl [10] DN41 . .23 F5
Snowdrop Pl [8] PE11 . .214 A5
Snowhills PE7 . . . . . .233 E5
Sods La PE11 . . . . . .145 D5
Soff La DN19 . . . . . . .12 A6
Soke Parkway PE1 . . .221 E1
Soke Rd PE6 . . . . . . .174 D5
Solhem Ave [13] PE21 . .136 D8
Solomon Ct DN35 . . . .192 D5
Solway Ave PE21 . . . .136 E8
Solway Ct [5] DN37 . . .190 E8
SOMERBY DN38 . . . . .21 B1
Somerby Cl
[8] Moulton PE12 . . . .157 F7
[3] Stamford PE9 . . . .219 B7
Somerby Garth [4] PE1 . .226 D8
Somerby Gr NG31 . . . .211 D2
Somerby Hill NG31 . . .211 C2
Somerby Pl NG31 . . . .211 E1
Somerby Rd
Gainsborough DN21 . .197 F5
Ropsley & Humby NG33 . .141 A8
Scunthorpe DN17 . . .184 D5
Somerby Wold La DN38 . .21 C1
Somerden Rd HU9 . . . . .5 F8
Somerfield Dr [9] LN11 . .50 F7
SOMERSBY PE23 . . . . .87 A7
Somersby Ave [9] LN12 . .64 B4
Somersby Cl LN6 . . . .205 C4
Somersby Ct
[15] Louth LN11 . . . .198 B5
North Carlton LN1 . . .67 C4
Somersby Gr NG31 . . .209 B7
Somersby Gr [2] PE25 . .206 D1
Somersby St [5] DN31 . .191 D8
Somersby Way PE21 . .209 B7
Somerset Dr [4] DN15 . . .8 B4
Somerset St HU3 . . . .180 A5
Somerton Dr [3] DN7 . . .14 F3
Somerton Gate La LN5 . .93 D7
Somerton Rd DN40 . . .186 D3
Somervell Rd DN16 . . .185 C4
Somerville PE4 . . . . .220 E5
Somerville Cl [15] LN6 . . .93 E8
Somerville Ct [14] LN6 . . .93 E8
Somerville Rd [1] PE9 . .219 A6
Somes Cl [1] PE9 . . . .172 C6
Somme Cl LN1 . . . . . .201 E7
Sonia Crest DN33 . . . .186 B4
Sophia Ave DN33 . . . .191 C1
Sorbus Cl [7] PE7 . . . .230 D3
Sorbus Ct [5] HU3 . . . .180 D6
Sorbus View [4] HU5 . .179 C7
Sorby Cl PE25 . . . . . .206 E8
Sorrel Cl
[3] Binbrook LN8 . . . .47 C5
[1] Market Deeping PE6 . .217 D6
[2] Stamford PE9 . . . .218 D6
Sorrel Ct LN6 . . . . . .204 C8
Sorrel Dr PE11 . . . . .214 A5
Sorrel Way DN15 . . . .182 C6
Soss La DN10 . . . . . . .40 A5
SOTBY LN8 . . . . .71 E5
Sotby Mdws Nature
Reserve★ LN8 . . . . .71 E5
SOTS HOLE LN4 . . . . .96 C7
Soulby La PE22 . . . . .114 C2
Sour La DN7 . . . . .14 F4
Soutergate [13] DN18 . . .3 F1
South Airfield Rd
NG34 . . . . .120 C8
South Axholme Com Sch
DN9. . . . . .27 D6
South Bank [3] DN17 . . .17 D6
SOUTH BRAMWITH
DN7 . . . . .14 A6
South Brick Lines
NG34 . . . . .120 B8

South Bridge Rd [2]
HU9 . . . . .181 A5
Southburn Ave HU5 . . .179 E7
SOUTH CARLTON LN1 . . .67 D3
South Carr Rd DN20 . . .31 A4
South Church Side [14]
HU1 . . . . .180 F6
Southcliffe Rd [19] DN21 . .29 C3
South Cliff Rd [27] DN21 . .30 B1
SOUTH CLIFTON NG23 . . .78 B5
Southcoates La HU9 . .181 D5
SOUTH COCKERINGTON
LN11 . . . . .62 A8
South Cres
[11] Bottesford NG13 . .128 A5
[1] Chapel St Leonard
PE24 . . . . .90 D7
South Dale LN7 . . . . . .33 B4
South-Dale Cl [3] DN21 . .30 B2
Southdown LN5 . . . . .205 D1
Southdown Rd PE7 . . .233 F5
South Dr
[12] Balderton NG24 . .104 C1
[4] Stow LN1 . . . . . . .66 C8
South Dro
Bicker PE20 . . . . . .134 E4
Helpringham NG34 . . .133 E6
Lutton PE12 . . . . . .149 A1
Quadring NG34 . . . .144 A8
Spalding PE11 . . . . .156 E2
SOUTH ELKINGTON
LN11 . . . . .60 E7
South Ella Dr HU10. . . .178 D7
South Ella Way HU10 . .178 D7
South End
Boston PE21 . . . . . .208 F4
Collingham NG23 . . . .91 C4
SOUTH END DN19. . . . .12 B7
South End
Hogsthorpe PE24. . . . .90 B6
Thorne/Moorends DN8 . .15 A4
South End La DN22. . . . .52 E3
Southern Dr HU4 . . . .179 C5
Southern La LN6 . . . . .92 B7
Southern Rd DN40 . . .186 D7
Southern Way DN40 . .186 C7
Southern Wlk DN33 . . .194 F7
South Fen Rd
Bourne PE10 . . . . . .213 F4
Helpringham NG34 . . .133 D6
SOUTH FERRIBY DN18. . . .10 B8
South Ferriby Prim Sch
DN18. . . . . .10 A7
Southfield
[7] Belton DN9 . . . . .16 E1
[4] Kingston upon Hull
HU13. . . . . .3 E4
SOUTH FIELD HU13. . . . .3 E4
Southfield Ave DN33 . .194 F7
Southfield Cl
[18] Thorne/Moorends
DN8. . . . . .15 B7
Ulceby DN39 . . . . . .12 B1
Southfield Dr
[10] Epworth DN9 . . . .27 D6
[2] Louth LN11 . . . . .198 C4
[21] North Ferriby HU14 . .3 A4
Southfield La
Fishtoft PE21 . . . . . .137 C8
[6] Old Leake PE22 . . .114 A1
Old Leake PE22 . . . .127 A8
Willoughton DN21 . . . .42 D3
Southfield Pl LN9 . . . .199 C3
Southfield Rd
[1] Broughton DN20 . . .19 D3
[13] Crowle DN17 . . . .16 D7
Grimsby DN33 . . . . .194 F7
Holton le Clay DN36 . .195 D1
North Kelsey LN7 . . . .31 F3
Scunthorpe DN16 . . .185 C5
Thorne/Moorends DN8 . .15 B7
[1] Winterton DN15 . . . .8 F5
Southfields
[7] Binbrook LN8 . . . .47 C4
Bourne PE10 . . . . . .213 D4
[3] Sleaford NG34 . . . .212 D3
Southfields Cl [10] PE13 . .170 C2
Southfields Dr PE21 . .231 D5
Southfields Inf Sch
PE2 . . . . .231 D5
Southfields Jun Sch
PE2 . . . . .231 D5
South Furlong Croft [22]
DN9 . . . . .27 E6
Southgate
Kingston upon Hull
HU13. . . . . .178 A1
[12] Pinchbeck PE11 . .156 E8
Scunthorpe DN15 . . .183 B3
South Gate NG34 . . . .212 D4
Southgate Spinneys [3]
NG34 . . . . .120 E4
Southgate Way PE2 . .229 C2
South Gn NG34 . . . . .161 F2
SOUTH GREEN NG34. . .161 E2
South Heath La NG32 . .106 C4
South Holland Ctr★
PE11. . . . . .214 D4
South Humberside Ind Est
DN31. . . . . .188 B2
South Hunsley Sch HU14 . .2 E5
SOUTH HYKEHAM LN6. . . .93 B7
South Hykeham Com Prim
Sch LN6 . . . . .93 B7
South Ing Dro PE11 . . .134 E1
South Ings La PE24. . . .90 B5
South Intake La DN9 . . .40 C7

SOUTH KELSEY LN7 . . . .32 A1
South Kesteven Works
. . . . .210 F3
SOUTH KILLINGHOLME
DN40 . . . . .12 C3
SOUTH KYME LN4 . . . .123 B8
South La
Kingston upon Hull
HU13. . . . . .178 A1
Willingham DN21. . . . .54 A3
Southland Ct DN37 . . .188 A1
Southland Dr [5] LN6 . .205 B4
Southlands Ave
Gainsborough DN21 . .197 B8
Louth LN11 . . . . . . .198 D3
Peterborough PE1 . . .226 A6
Southlands Dr
Grantham NG31 . . . .211 C4
Morton DN21 . . . . . .197 B8
Southlands Gdns DN21 .197 B8
South Leys Sch LN17 . .184 D4
South Lincs Con Ctr
NG31 . . . . .211 A1
South Marsh Rd
Immingham Power St
DN41. . . . . .187 F1
Stallingborough DN41 . .23 F7
South Marsh Rd Ind Est
DN41. . . . . .187 F2
South Mkt Pl [7] LN13 . .75 F2
Southmoor La
Newton on Trent LN1 . . .78 D8
Snitterby DN21 . . . . .43 E5
Southmoor Rd
Crowle DN17 . . . . . .16 C8
Newton on Trent LN1. . .78 D8
South Moor Rd DN10 . . .39 F3
Southoe PE7 . . . . . . .231 D2
Southolme DN21 . . . . .197 D4
SOUTH ORMSBY LN11. . . .74 D2
Southorpe PE9 . . . . . .172 E2
Southorpe La PE21 . . . .42 A7
Southorpe Paddock Nature
Reserve★ PE9 . . . . .172 E1
SOUTH OWERSBY LN8 . . .44 E4
South Parade
Boston PE21 . . . . . .208 C4
[11] Caythorpe NG32 . .119 B7
Gainsborough DN21 . .197 F3
Grantham NG31 . . . .211 B2
Grimsby DN31 . . . . .191 D8
[1] Lincoln LN1. . . . . .201 C4
[5] Saxilby LN1 . . . . . .66 D2
Peterborough PE3 . . .225 E3
Skegness PE25 . . . .206 D2
South Kyme LN4 . . . .123 B8
Spalding PE11 . . . . .214 C3
Thorne/Moorends DN8 . .15 A4
South Parade Jun & Inf Sch
DN31. . . . . .191 D8
South Pk LN5 . . . . . .205 F8
South Pk Ave
Bracebridge Heath
LN5 . . . . .205 F8
Lincoln LN5 . . . . . .201 F1
South Pk Rd DN17 . . .184 D3
South Ramper DN21 . . .44 A5
SOUTH RAUCEBY
NG34 . . . . .120 E4
South Rd
Bourne PE10 . . . . . .213 D4
Chapel St Leonard PE24 . .90 E6
[5] Keadby with Althorpe
DN17. . . . . .17 C6
Mablethorpe/Sutton on Sea
LN12 . . . . .64 C1
North Somercotes LN11 . .50 E7
Sturton le Steeple DN22 . .52 C4
Tetford LN9 . . . . . . .73 F1
SOUTH RESTON LN11. . . .62 D1
SOUTHREY LN3. . . . . .83 D1
South Ridge Cres [2]
DN17. . . . . .184 F3
South Rise LN8 . . . . . .47 C4
South St Mary's Gate [4]
DN31. . . . . .191 D7
South Scaffold La NG23 . .91 E3
SOUTH SCARLE NG23. . . .91 E6
South Scarle La LN6 . . .78 E1
South Scarle Rd NG23 . .91 E6
South Sea La DN36. . . .36 D7
South Side DN15 . . . . .2 A1
SOUTH SOMERCOTES
LN11 . . . . .50 E5
South St
[12] Alford LN13 . . . . .75 F2
[17] Alford LN13 . . . . .75 F2
[10] Barnetby le Wold
DN38. . . . . .21 B4
Bole DN22 . . . . .52 C5
Boston PE21 . . . . . .208 F4
Bourne PE10 . . . . . .213 D4
Caistor LN7 . . . . . . .33 B4
[1] Cleethorpes DN35 . .193 A6
[20] Crowland PE6 . . . .166 F1
Horncastle LN9 . . . . .199 B3
Keelby DN41 . . . . . .23 A5
Louth LN11 . . . . . . .198 B5
Morton DN21 . . . . . .197 C8
[15] North Kelsey LN7 . . .32 A4
Owston Ferry DN9. . . .28 B2
Roxby cum Risby DN15. . .8 F3
Scamblesby LN11 . . . .72 F5
Swineshead PE20 . . .135 B7
West Butterwick DN17 . .28 D8
[17] Winterton DN15 . . . .9 A5

South Terr
Boston PE21 . . . . . .208 F3
[4] Louth LN11 . . . . .198 C5
SOUTH THORESBY
LN13 . . . . .75 A3
South View
Anlaby HU4 . . . . . . .179 B6
Broughton DN20 . . . .19 D4
Holton le Clay DN36 . .195 E1
Humberston DN36. . . .193 A1
Peterborough PE2 . . .230 F7
Yarborough DN34 . . . .191 A6
South View Ave
Brigg DN20 . . . . . . .196 C5
Burringham DN17 . . . .17 D4
South View Cl [4] PE25 . .206 D2
South View Com Prim Sch
PE6 . . . . .166 E1
South View La LN11 . . .62 A7
Southview Leisure Ctr
PE25 . . . . .103 C8
South View Rd PE4 . . .225 D8
South View Way [16] LN2 . .68 E7
Southwell Ave
[3] Kingston upon Hull
HU9. . . . . .5 F8
Peterborough PE4 . . .220 E4
Southwell Cl NG31 . . .210 C5
Southwell Rd [2] PE13 . .170 D1
Southwell's La [1] LN9 . .199 C4
Southwick PE4 . . . . . .221 C1
SOUTH WILLINGHAM
LN8 . . . . .59 A2
SOUTH WITHAM NG33. . .151 A3
South Witham Nature
Reserve★ NG33 . . . .151 F2
South Witham Prim Sch
NG33. . . . . .151 D2
Southwold Cres DN33 . .194 E8
South Wood Dr [10] DN8. . .15 A7
Sovereign Cl
[12] Grimsby DN34 . . . .190 D4
[12] Wisbech PE13. . . .170 C1
Sovereign Pl [1] PE25 . .225 E2
Sovereign St NG34 . . .142 E4
Sow Dale Nature Reserve★
PE23 . . . . .87 A1
Sowers La DN15 . . . . . .9 A5
Spa Bldgs LN2 . . . . .234 B2
Spafford Cl [7] DN21. . . .65 E8
Spa Hill [9] DN21. . . . . .30 B1
Spain Cl [7] PE21 . . . .208 F4
Spain La [5] PE21 . . . .208 F4
Spain Pl PE21 . . . . . .209 A4
SPALDING PE11 . . . . .214 E6
Spalding Bulb Mus★
PE11 . . . . .145 C1
Spalding Comm [6]
PE11 . . . . .214 B1
Spalding Dro
Cowbit PE12 . . . . . .157 A3
Spalding PE12 . . . . .214 E1
Spalding FE Ctr PE11 . .214 D4
Spalding Gate PE12 . .158 B8
Spalding Gram Sch
PE11 . . . . .214 D3
Spalding High Sch
PE11 . . . . .214 F3
Spalding Parish CE Day
Sch PE11 . . . . .214 E2
Spalding Prim Sch
PE11 . . . . .214 B5
Spalding Rd
Boston PE21 . . . . . .208 E3
Bourne PE10 . . . . . .213 E5
Deeping St James PE6 . .165 C1
Gosberton PE11. . . . .145 C5
Holbeach PE12 . . . . .215 A2
Market Deeping PE6 . .217 E5
Pinchbeck PE11 . . . .214 C8
Scunthorpe DN16 . . .185 B8
Wigtoft PE20 . . . . . .135 E1
Spalding Rd Bsns Pk
PE10 . . . . .213 F5
Spalding Sta PE11 . . .214 C4
SPALFORD NG23. . . . . .78 E3
Spalford La LN6 . . . . .78 E2
Spalford Rd LN6 . . . . .78 E3
Spalford Warren Nature
Reserve★ NG23 . . . . .78 D2
SPANBY NG34 . . . . . .132 F4
Spanby Dr [5] LN6 . . .205 A7
Spanning Dr [22] LN13. . .75 F2
Spa Rd
Lincoln LN5 . . . . . .234 C2
[2] Woodhall Spa LN10 . .97 D6
Spark's La PE12. . . . .158 A4
Spark St DN34 . . . . . .191 A7
Sparrowgate Rd PE14 . .170 F1
Sparrow La
[2] Long Bennington
NG23. . . . . .117 D3
Marnham NG23 . . . . .78 A5
Newball LN8 . . . . . . .69 F2
Sparrow Rd [1] PE7. . . .230 D1
Spa St LN2 . . . . .202 B3
Spaw La [5] LN11. . . . .198 B6
Spayne Rd PE21 . . . . .209 A4
Speechley Rd PE7. . . .233 F6
Speechley's Dro PE6. . .174 F7
Speedwell Cres DN15 . .182 C6
Speedwell Ct [7] PE6 . .217 D6
Speight Cl [5] NG24. . .104 B7
Spencer Ave
Peterborough PE2 . . .231 D5

Spencer Ave *continued*
Scunthorpe DN15 . . . . 182 F4
Spencer Cl
3 Long Sutton PE12. . . . . 216 B5
West Walton PE14. . . . . . . 170 E4
Spencer Gdns
7 Butterwick PE22. . . . . 126 E3
Holbeach PE12 . . . . 215 F3
Spencer St
Grimsby DN31. . . . . 189 D1
6 Kingston upon Hull HU2. . . . . 180 E7
9 Lincoln LN5. . . . . 205 E8
Spence St 10 PE23 . . . . 87 F1
Spendla's La PE12 . . . . . 159 F3
Spendluffe Ave 3 LN13 . . 75 F3
Spennymoor Cl 1 LN6 . . . 93 B8
Sperrin Cl 5 LN5 . . . . . . 205 D2
Speyer Ave PE11. . . . . . . 214 C5
Speyside Ct 1 PE2. . . . . . 229 D4
Spice Ave PE21 . . . . 136 D8
Spicer's La PE22 . . . . 127 B5
SPILSBY PE23 . . . . 101 A8
Spilsby Cl 8 LN6 . . . . . . 204 D8
Spilsby Hill PE23. . . . . 100 B8
Spilsby Prim Sch PE23 . . . 88 A1
Spilsby Rd
Boston PE21 . . . . 209 A6
Eastville PE22 . . . . 101 A1
High Toynton LN9. . . . . 86 B4
Horncastle LN9 . . . . 199 E4
Scunthorpe DN17 . . . . 184 E5
Spilsby PE23 . . . . 101 A8
Thorpe St Peter PE24 . . . . 102 B4
Spindelwood Dr PE10 . . . 213 D3
Spindles The PE10 . . . . . . 213 D7
Spindlewood 1 HU15 . . . . . 2 C7
Spinnaker Cl HU9 . . . . 181 C6
Spinners Cl 3 NG34 . . . . 212 E3
Spinney Cl
Immingham DN40 . . . . 186 C4
7 Manby LN11. . . . . 62 C6
9 Ryhall PE9 . . . . 163 C1
Spinney Croft Cl 14 HU14 . . 3 A5
Spinney La
10 Ryhall PE9 . . . . 163 C1
2 Scopwick Heath LN4 . . 108 A7
Spinneys The 5 LN2 . . . . . 68 D7
Spinney The
1 Barnby Dun DN3 . . . . . . 14 A3
13 Barrow upon Humber DN19. . . . . 11 D8
Brigg DN20 . . . . 196 D2
3 Gainsborough DN21. . . . 197 F5
3 Grimsby DN31 . . . . 191 C7
2 Market Deeping PE6 . . 217 B5
7 Swanland HU14 . . . . 3 B7
7 Winthorpe NG24. . . . . . . 104 B7
Spinney Wlk
Kingston upon Hull HU4. . . . . 179 C6
Longthorpe PE3. . . . . 225 B2
Spion Kop La PE20 . . . . . . 135 E3
Spirea App LN6. . . . . 204 C8
Spires The 15 PE20. . . . . . 136 A2
Spire View
1 Bottesford NG13 . . . . . 128 A6
14 Grantham NG31. . . . . . . 211 A5
1 Kingston upon Hull HU13. . . . . 178 E1
Sleaford NG34. . . . . 212 A2
Spire View Rd LN11 . . . . . 198 D5
Spirewic Ave PE25 . . . . . . 206 D8
Spitalgate CE (Controlled) Prim Sch NG31 . . . . 210 D3
Spital Hill
Gainsborough DN21 . . . . . 197 E5
18 Louth LN11. . . . . 198 B5
SPITAL IN THE STREET LN8 . . . . 43 B1
Spital La LN8 . . . . 55 B8
Spital St LN1 . . . . 234 B4
Spital Terr DN21. . . . . 197 D4
Spitfire Ave LN11 . . . . 62 B6
Spittal Hill Rd PE22 . . . . . 126 D4
SPITTLEGATE NG31 . . . . . . 211 A3
Splash La
Ailsworth PE5 . . . . 228 E8
Castor PE5. . . . . 223 E1
Spotfield La PE20 . . . . 136 C7
Spout Hill HU15. . . . . 2 C8
Spout Yd 6 LN11 . . . . 198 B6
Spratt Cl LN9 . . . . 199 D1
Spratton Ct DN34 . . . . 190 C4
SPRIDLINGTON LN8 . . . . 55 F3
Spridlington Rd LN8 . . . . . 56 D3
Spriggs Cl NG34 . . . . 212 C3
Sprignall PE3. . . . . 224 F4
Springbank DN20 . . . . 196 C5
Spring Bank
5 Binbrook LN8 . . . . 47 C4
Grimsby DN34 . . . . 191 A7
Kingston upon Hull HU3 . . 180 D7
Spring Bank W HU5 . . . . . 179 D7
Springbok Cl HU4. . . . . . . 179 D2
Springburn St HU3. . . . . . . 180 A5
Spring Cl 9 LN2. . . . . 68 E6
Spring Ct
Dunston LN4 . . . . 95 C5
Louth LN11 . . . . 198 C5
13 Welton/Dunholme LN2. . . . . 68 D7
Springdale Cl
2 Kingston upon Hull HU9. . . . . 5 D8
Springdale Cl *continued*
Kingston upon Hull HU10 . 178 F8
Spring Dr
9 Balderton NG24 . . . . . . 104 C1
Farcet PE7. . . . . 231 B2
Spring End 3 NG31 . . . . . 129 D5
Springfield PE2. . . . . 231 A7
Springfield Ave
Brough HU15 . . . . 2 C6
7 Hatfield DN7. . . . . 14 E4
Springfield Cl
Branston LN4. . . . . 81 E2
Gainsborough DN21 . . . . . 197 E4
Lincoln LN2 . . . . 234 B4
2 Scunthorpe DN16. . . . . . 185 C6
Springfield Est LN4 . . . . . . 95 D1
Springfield Prim Sch DN33. . . . . 194 D7
Springfield Rd
2 Brigg DN20. . . . . 196 D3
Grantham NG31. . . . . 211 A2
Grimsby DN33 . . . . 191 C1
Kingston upon Hull HU3 . . 179 F6
Parson Drove PE13 . . . . . . 177 D7
Peterborough PE1. . . . . 225 F5
6 Ruskington NG34 . . . . . 108 D2
Yaxley PE7. . . . . 233 F5
Springfield Rise 1 DN20 . . . . 196 E3
Springfields LN8. . . . . 46 B1
Springfields Sh & Events Ctr PE12 . . . . 157 B7
Springfield Way HU10 . . . 178 E7
Spring Gdns
Gainsborough DN21 . . . . . 197 D4
Grantham NG31. . . . . 211 B2
Long Sutton PE12 . . . . 216 B4
13 Louth LN11. . . . . 198 B5
Sleaford NG34. . . . . 212 C5
Spalding PE11 . . . . 214 C3
Spring Gdns E HU4. . . . . . 179 B6
Spring Gdns S HU4. . . . . . 179 B5
Spring Gdns W HU4 . . . . . 179 B6
Spring Gr
Kingston upon Hull HU3. . . . . 180 A7
Terrington St Clement PE34 . . . . 161 F2
Springhead Ave HU5 . . . . 179 A7
Springhead Ct HU10 . . . . 179 A6
Springhead Gdns HU10 . . . . 179 A7
Springhead La HU5 . . . . . 179 A7
Springhead Prim Sch HU10. . . . . 178 E7
Spring Hill
3 Binbrook LN8 . . . . 47 C4
Cherry Willingham/Reepham LN3 . . . . 203 F8
Grantham NG31. . . . . 211 D3
Lincoln LN1 . . . . 234 A3
Spring La
Balderton NG24. . . . . 104 C2
8 Colsterworth NG33 . . . 151 D7
4 Folkingham NG34. . . . . 142 D8
Horbling NG34. . . . . 133 B2
14 Laceby DN37 . . . . 23 F1
5 Leasingham NG34 . . . . 121 B7
4 Wymondham LE14 . . . . 150 B1
Springs La DN22 . . . . 52 A2
Springs Parade DN20 . . . . 196 B3
Springs Rd DN10. . . . . 26 C1
Spring St
Immingham DN40 . . . . 186 D4
Kingston upon Hull HU2 . . 180 D7
Spalding PE11 . . . . 214 D3
Springs Way DN20 . . . . . . 196 B3
SPRINGTHORPE DN21 . . . . . 53 E8
Springthorpe Rd
Corringham DN21 . . . . 41 E1
Gainsborough DN21 . . . . . 197 F4
Spring View 4 LN8 . . . . . . 47 C4
Springville Ave HU13. . . . . 178 F2
Springway Cres DN34 . . . 191 A7
Springwood Cres DN33 . . . . 194 D7
Sprite La LN4. . . . . 109 D5
SPROXTON LE14. . . . . 150 C7
Sproxton Rd
Buckminster NG33. . . . . . . 150 D6
Skillington NG33 . . . . 151 A8
Spruce Cl PE12 . . . . 215 C4
Spruce La DN39. . . . . 12 A1
Spurn Ave DN33 . . . . 194 F8
Spurn Lightship★ HU1 . . 180 F5
Spurr The 7 LN5 . . . . 107 A7
Spyvee St HU8. . . . . 181 A7
Square The
2 Barnack PE9. . . . . 172 D3
Barrowby NG32. . . . . 129 B3
12 Goxhill DN19 . . . . 12 A8
Kingston upon Hull HU13. . . . . 178 E1
18 Kirton PE20 . . . . 136 C5
4 Leasingham NG34 . . . . 121 B7
North Thoresby DN36 . . . . . 36 B1
5 Ryhall PE9 . . . . 163 C1
Toynton All Saints PE23. . . 100 F6
Squires Gate PE4 . . . . 221 D3
Squires Mdw 10 LN11 . . . . 50 F7
Squires The PE2 . . . . 230 F8
Squirrel Chase LN6 . . . . . . 92 D5
Stable La 3 DN18. . . . . 3 E1
Stables Ct 11 PE13 . . . . . . 170 B2
Stable Way 7 LN8 . . . . 57 E7
Stacey Cl 2 PE25. . . . . 90 D3
Stackyard The PE2. . . . . . 229 E5
Stafford Ave NG24 . . . . . . 104 A2
Staffordshire Cres 6 LN6 . . . . 204 D7
Stafford St
3 Boston PE21. . . . . 208 F6
Kingston upon Hull HU2 . . 180 E8
Stagsden PE2. . . . . 229 F4
Stagshaw Dr PE2 . . . . 231 B8
STAINBY NG33 . . . . 151 C5
Stainby Rd
Buckminster NG33. . . . . . . 150 F5
Gunby & Stainby NG33 . . . 151 C4
Staindale Rd DN16 . . . . . . 185 D5
Stainesway LN11. . . . . 198 E7
STAINFIELD
Haconby PE10 . . . . 154 A8
Stainfield LN8 . . . . 83 B8
Stainfield Rd
Kirkby Underwood PE10. . . . . 142 D1
Morton PE10 . . . . 154 B7
STAINFORTH DN7. . . . . 14 C6
Stainforth Inf Sch DN7 . . . 14 C6
Stainforth Kirton La Prim Sch DN7 . . . . 14 C7
Stainforth Moor Rd DN7 . . . . 15 C3
Stainforth Rd DN7 . . . . 14 A5
Stain La LN12. . . . . 63 E3
STAINSBY LN9. . . . . 86 F6
Stainton Ave 6 DN21 . . . . 43 D7
STAINTON BY LANGWORTH LN3 . . . . 69 C4
Stainton Cl 5 DN21. . . . . . 53 A5
Stainton Dr
Grimsby DN33 . . . . 191 A3
8 Immingham DN40 . . . . 186 B4
Scunthorpe DN17 . . . . 184 E4
Stainton Gdns LN1. . . . . . 201 E7
Stainton La LN2. . . . . 69 B4
STAINTON LE VALE LN8. . . . 46 E5
Stallebrass Cl PE2 . . . . . . 231 E5
STALLINGBOROUGH DN41 . . . . 23 E6
Stallingborough CE Prim Sch DN41 . . . . 23 E6
Stallingborough Rd
Immingham DN40 . . . . 186 B2
Keelby DN41 . . . . 23 A5
Stallingborough Sta DN41. . . . . 23 E6
STAMFORD PE9 . . . . 219 D4
Stamford Bsns Pk PE9 . . 219 E6
Stamford Cl 4 PE6 . . . . . . 217 B5
Stamford High Sch PE9. . . . . 219 C4
Stamford Jun Sch PE9 . . 219 B3
Stamford Leisure Ctr PE9. . . . . 219 D6
Stamford Lodge Rd PE6 . . . . 224 C5
Stamford Mus★ PE9 . . . . 219 C5
Stamford Rd
Barnack PE9 . . . . 172 C4
Buckminster NG33. . . . . . . 151 A4
Collyweston PE9 . . . . 171 C2
Colsterworth NG33 . . . . . . 151 E5
Easton on the Hill PE9. . . . 219 A1
Essendine PE9. . . . . 163 D2
Helpston PE6. . . . . 173 C1
Ketton PE9. . . . . 218 A2
Marholm PE6. . . . . 220 A1
Market Deeping PE6 . . . . . 217 A4
Tinwell PE9 . . . . 218 A6
West Deeping PE9 . . . . 173 A7
Stamford Ret Pk PE9. . . . 219 D6
Stamford & Rutland Hospl PE9. . . . . 219 D6
Stamfords Art Ctr★ PE9. . . . . 219 C5
Stamford Sch PE9 . . . . . . 219 C6
Stamford St NG31. . . . . 211 B2
Stamford Sta PE9. . . . . . . 219 C4
Stamford Theatre★ 28 PE9. . . . . 219 C5
Stamford Wlk 25 PE9. . . . 219 C5
Stamp End LN2 . . . . 234 C2
Stamper St 2 PE3 . . . . . . 224 F3
Standard La LN5. . . . . 93 A2
Standish Ct PE2. . . . . 230 D8
Standish Gr PE21 . . . . 209 B7
Standish La DN40. . . . . . . 186 B5
Stane Dr 12 LN4 . . . . 81 A1
Stanfield Rd 2 DN9. . . . . . . 27 D6
Stanford Cl 1 DN37. . . . . . . 23 F1
Stanford Jun & Inf Sch DN37. . . . . 23 E1
Stanford Wlk 4 PE3 . . . . . 225 C4
STANGROUND PE2. . . . . . . 231 C5
Stanground Coll PE7. . . . . 231 C5
Stanholme La DN36 . . . . . . 36 A1
Stanhope Ave 7 LN10. . . . . 97 D6
Stanhope Gdns 1 PE21 . . . . 209 C4
Stanhope Pl DN35. . . . . . . 192 C7
Stanhope Rd LN9 . . . . 199 C4
Stanhope Terr 3 LN9 . . . 199 C4
Stanhurst La DN7 . . . . 15 A5
Staniland Prim Sch PE21. . . . . 208 D4
Staniland Rd PE21 . . . . . . 208 D3
Staniland Way
1 Humberston DN36 . . . . . 36 D8
Peterborough PE4 . . . . 221 A5
Staniwell Rise DN17. . . . . 184 D7
Staniwells Dr 11 DN20. . . . . 19 D3
Stanley Ave 5 LN12. . . . . . . 64 B3
Stanley Cl 2 PE24 . . . . . . 102 D2
Stanley Cres LN4 . . . . 205 F4
Stanley Dr
11 Sutterton PE20. . . . . . . 136 A2
Sutton Bridge PE12 . . . . . . 160 E4
Stanley Gdns 13 DN7. . . . . 14 C6
Stanley Pl 1 LN5 . . . . 201 F1
Stanley Rd
Peterborough PE1 . . . . 226 A3
Scunthorpe DN15 . . . . 182 C3
18 Stainforth DN7. . . . . 14 C6
Stanley St
Bourne PE10 . . . . 213 C6
Gainsborough DN21 . . . . . 197 D2
Grimsby DN32 . . . . 189 C1
Kingston upon Hull HU3 . . 180 C7
Lincoln LN5 . . . . 205 D7
1 Stamford PE9 . . . . 219 C5
Stan Rowing Ct PE2. . . . . 231 C7
Stansfield Gdns DN40 . . . 186 A5
Stansted St 5 DN31 . . . . 188 D1
Stanthaket Ct 12 LN1. . . . 234 B3
Stanton Cl PE10. . . . . 213 E5
Stanton Rd 4 LN12 . . . . . . 77 A8
Stanton's Pit Nature Reserve★ PE10 . . . . 163 C8
Stanton Sq PE7 . . . . 230 D2
Stanton St 7 NG31 . . . . . . 211 A4
Stanwick Ct PE3 . . . . 225 F2
Stapes Garth 1 LN11 . . . . 50 B8
Stapledon Rd PE2. . . . . . . 229 D2
Staplee Way PE1. . . . . 226 F7
STAPLEFORD LN6. . . . . 105 B8
Stapleford Ave LN2 . . . . . 201 F8
Stapleford La
Coddington NG24. . . . . 104 E6
Collingham NG23. . . . . 91 E1
Staple La NG24 . . . . 104 B1
Staple Rd DN40. . . . . 12 F3
Staples La 12 LN5 . . . . 93 F7
Star Carr La DN20. . . . . . . 196 D8
Star Cl PE1 . . . . 226 C3
Starella Gr HU3. . . . . 180 A4
Star Fen Dro NG34 . . . . . . 123 A4
Starham Rd LN7 . . . . 31 C4
Starks La LN8. . . . . 58 D7
Star La
Holbeach PE12 . . . . 215 C7
4 Stamford PE9. . . . . 219 C5
Star La Mews 26 PE9. . . . . 219 C5
Star Lode Dro PE11 . . . . . 144 B1
Star Mews PE1 . . . . 226 C2
Star Rd PE1 . . . . 226 C2
Stathern Rd PE1 . . . . 226 D7
Stathern Wlk NG31. . . . . . . 210 E2
Stather Rd DN15. . . . . 8 A1
Stathers Wlk 3 HU10 . . . . 178 F6
Station App
6 Ancaster NG32. . . . . . . 120 A3
Boston PE21 . . . . 208 E4
Cleethorpes DN35. . . . . 192 F7
11 Donington PE11 . . . . . . 134 E2
Louth LN11 . . . . 198 C6
Station Ave
New Waltham DN36. . . . . . 195 D6
16 South Witham NG33. . . . 151 D2
Wisbech St Mary PE13 . . . . 177 D5
Station Cl 9 NG23 . . . . 91 D4
Station Ct 7 DN7. . . . . 14 D4
Station Field LN6 . . . . 200 B3
Station La
Horncastle LN9 . . . . 199 A3
Searby cum Owmby DN38. . 32 D7
Station Rd
Ailsworth PE5 . . . . 223 C1
Alford LN13 . . . . 75 E2
Algarkirk PE20. . . . . 146 B8
Bardney LN3 . . . . 83 B4
Barkston NG32 . . . . 129 F8
Barlings LN3 . . . . 69 B3
Barnack PE9 . . . . 172 E4
Beckingham DN10. . . . . 52 B8
1 Billingborough NG34 . . 133 B1
Blyton DN21. . . . . 41 C5
Bottesford NG13 . . . . 128 A6
Bourne PE10 . . . . 155 C3
Branston LN4. . . . . 81 E2
Brough HU15 . . . . 2 B5
Burgh le Marsh PE24. . . . . 102 C8
Burringham DN17 . . . . 17 E4
Candlesby with Gunby PE24 . . . . 89 B1
Careby Aunby & Holywell PE9. . . . . 163 A8
Castle Bytham NG33 . . . . . 152 D1
6 Cherry Willingham/ Reepham LN3 . . . . 82 A8
Cherry Willingham/Reepham LN3. . . . . 203 F8
Cleethorpes DN35. . . . . 192 F7
Collingham NG23. . . . . 91 D4
Corby Glen NG33. . . . . 152 D7
Deeping St James PE6 . . . 174 B7
Digby LN4 . . . . 108 E5
Donington on Bain LN11 . . . 59 E1
East Halton DN40 . . . . 12 D7
Epworth DN9. . . . . 27 D7
6 Essendine PE9. . . . . 163 D3
Fulstow LN11. . . . . 49 A7
Garthorpe & Fockerby DN17. . . . . 7 E6
Gedney Hill PE12. . . . . 168 C1
Gosberton PE11. . . . . 145 A5
Grantham NG31. . . . . 211 B3
Grasby DN38 . . . . 32 E6
Great Steeping PE23 . . . . . 101 F6
Grimsby DN37 . . . . 190 C8
Gunness DN15. . . . . 17 E5
Habrough DN40. . . . . 12 F1
Halton Holegate PE23 . . . . 101 B8
Station Rd *continued*
Harby NG23. . . . . 79 B5
Harmston LN5 . . . . 93 E5
Hatfield DN7 . . . . 14 D4
Haxey DN9. . . . . 27 D1
Healing DN41 . . . . 23 F5
Heckington NG34. . . . . 122 E2
Heighington LN4 . . . . 81 E4
Helpringham NG34 . . . . . . 133 D7
9 Hibaldstow DN20. . . . . . . 30 F5
Holbeach PE12 . . . . 215 D2
Holton le Clay DN36 . . . . . . 36 B4
Hubbert's Bridge PE20 . . . 124 E1
Keadby with Althorpe DN17. . . . . 17 D6
6 Ketton PE9 . . . . 171 A3
Kingston upon Hull HU13. . . . . 178 E1
Kirton in Lindsey DN21 . . . . 30 B2
Kirton PE20 . . . . 136 C5
Knaith DN21 . . . . 53 A4
Legbourne LN11 . . . . 61 E3
Lincoln LN6 . . . . 204 D3
Little Steeping PE23 . . . . . 101 D5
5 Long Sutton PE12. . . . . . 216 B4
Ludborough DN36 . . . . 48 E6
16 Mablethorpe & Sutton LN12. . . . . 76 F8
20 Mablethorpe/Sutton on Sea LN12 . . . . 64 B4
Metheringham LN4 . . . . 95 D4
Midville PE22. . . . . 113 E8
1 Misterton DN10 . . . . 40 A5
Misterton LN13 . . . . 89 A6
Morton PE10 . . . . 154 D6
Moulton PE12 . . . . 157 F6
Mumby LN13 . . . . 76 F1
North Kelsey LN7. . . . . 32 B4
Northorpe PE10. . . . . 164 C7
North Thoresby DN36 . . . . . 36 B1
Owston Ferry DN9. . . . . 28 A2
Peterborough PE3 . . . . 225 F2
Potter Hanworth LN4 . . . . . 82 A1
Ruskington NG34. . . . . 108 E1
Scawby DN20. . . . . 30 F7
Scredington NG34 . . . . 132 F7
Scunthorpe DN15 . . . . 183 A2
Sibsey PE22. . . . . 113 C1
Sleaford NG34. . . . . 212 D3
South Kelsey LN7. . . . . 32 D2
South Killingholme DN40. . . 13 A5
South Willingham LN8 . . . . . 59 A1
Stallingborough DN41 . . . . . 23 E6
Stamford PE9. . . . . 219 B4
Stixwould & Woodhall LN10. . . . . 97 A8
Sturton le Steeple DN22 . . . 52 B3
Surfleet PE11. . . . . 145 E3
Sutterton PE20 . . . . 136 A1
Swinderby LN6. . . . . 92 A6
Swineshead PE20 . . . . 123 F1
Theddlethorpe All Saints LN12. . . . . 63 D7
Thorney PE6 . . . . 176 A3
Thornton Curtis DN39 . . . . . 11 F5
Thorpe on the Hill LN6 . . . . 79 E1
Thorpe St Peter PE24 . . . . 102 B3
Timberland LN4. . . . . 96 B1
Torksey LN1. . . . . 65 D6
Tumby Woodside PE22. . . . . 98 F1
Tydd St Mary PE13 . . . . . . 170 C8
Ulceby DN39 . . . . 12 B1
Waddington LN5 . . . . 93 F7
Wainfleet All Saints PE24. . . . . 102 D1
Walkeringham DN10 . . . . . . 40 A3
Waltham DN36. . . . . 195 A5
Waltham LE14 . . . . 138 A1
Whitton DN15 . . . . 1 D3
Wickenby LN3 . . . . 57 B1
Woodhall Spa LN10. . . . . . . 97 D6
Station Rd N PE34 . . . . . . 161 C2
Station Rd S PE34. . . . . . . 161 C2
Station Rd (West) NG31 . . . . 211 A3
Station St
Boston PE21 . . . . 208 E5
Donington PE11 . . . . 134 E2
Lincoln LN5 . . . . 234 A1
Rippingale PE10. . . . . 143 A3
1 Spalding PE11 . . . . 214 D4
Station Terr LN5 . . . . 106 D3
Staunton Ct LN1 . . . . 201 D3
STAUNTON IN THE VALE NG13 . . . . 117 A2
Staunton St 3 LN1 . . . . . 201 D3
Staunt Rd PE22 . . . . 112 E2
Staveley Rd 8 LN13. . . . . . 75 E2
Staverton Cres LN6 . . . . . 200 B1
Staverton Rd PE4 . . . . . . 220 E3
Staves Ct 5 DN36. . . . . 36 D4
Staxton Cl PE6. . . . . 220 A1
Staxton Ct HU9 . . . . 181 D8
Steadfold La PE9 . . . . 218 A3
Steadings The DN15 . . . . 8 B2
Steamer Point Rd LN4. . . . . 95 C7
Steapas Cl 2 PE23. . . . . . 101 D7
Steeles Dr NG24 . . . . 104 C2
Steepers The 4 LN2 . . . . . 68 D2
Steep Hill LN2. . . . . 234 B3
Steeping Ct LN1 . . . . 201 E8
Steeping Dr DN40. . . . . . . 186 A3
Steeping Rd PE23. . . . . . . 101 C6
Steeple Leas 15 NG31 . . . 211 A5
Stells La PE21 . . . . 208 F3
STENIGOT LN11 . . . . 72 D8
Stenigot Cl 3 LN6 . . . . . . 204 C6
Stenigot Gr LN6 . . . . 204 D6

Stenigot Rd **1** LN6 . . . . . 204 D6
Stenner Rd LN4. . . . . . . 207 F6
Stennett Ave **1** PE11. . 156 E2
STENWITH NG32. . . . . . 128 D3
Stephen Cl **3** DN39 . . . 12 A1
Stephen Cres
16 Barton-upon-Humber
DN18. . . . . 10 F8
Grimsby DN34 . . . . . 190 E4
Humberston DN36. . . . 36 C8
Stephen Rd NG24 . . . . 104 A6
Stephenson Ave
Gonerby Hill Foot
NG31. . . . . 210 F8
Pinchbeck PE11. . . . . 214 E8
Stephenson Cl
9 Alford LN13 . . . . . 75 E2
4 Boston PE21. . . . . 208 F1
Yaxley PE7 . . . . 233 D6
Stephenson Ct **5** PE1. . 226 B2
Stephenson Way PE10. . 213 D7
Stephens Way **4** PE6 . . 227 C3
Stephen's Way NG34 . . 212 F3
Sterling Cres DN37. . . . 194 C4
Sterling Pl **8** LN10. . . . . 97 E6
Sterne Ave **9** DN20 . . . . 19 D3
Stevenson Pl **1** DN35 . . 192 D5
Stevenson's Way **33**
DN18. . . . . 10 E8
Stevern Way PE1 . . . . . 226 F4
STEWTON LN11. . . . . . . 61 E5
Stewton Gdns LN11 . . . 198 D4
Stewton La LN11 . . . . . 198 E4
Steyning La PE20 . . . . 135 A7
Steynings The PE4. . . . 221 A3
STIBBINGTON PE8 . . . . . 222 C2
STICKFORD PE22. . . . . . 100 B2
STICKNEY PE22. . . . . . . 113 A8
Stickney CE (Aided) Prim
Sch PE22. . . . . 113 A8
Stickney Farm Pk★
PE22. . . . . 112 F8
Stickney La PE22. . . . . 112 D7
Still Cl PE6 . . . . 217 B5
Still The PE13. . . . . . . 170 E1
Stirling Cl **4** DN21 . . . . 197 E6
Stirling Ct
14 Grantham NG31 . . 210 E2
Heckington NG34. . . . 122 D2
Stirling Dr **12** NG24 . . . 104 C5
Stirling Rd PE9 . . . . . . 218 F5
Stirling St
Grimsby DN31 . . . . . 189 D1
Kingston upon Hull HU3 . 179 F6
Stirling Way
Market Deeping PE6 . . 217 C7
Peterborough PE3 . . . 220 E1
4 Skellingthorpe LN6. . 200 A4
STIXWOULD LN10. . . . . . 97 B8
Stixwould Rd LN10. . . . 97 C7
Stockbridge Pk **3** HU15. . 2 C7
Stockbridge Rd HU15 . . 2 C7
STOCKHOLES TURBARY
DN9. . . . . 16 B2
Stockhouse La PE11. . . 145 B3
Stocking Way LN2 . . . . 202 F6
Stockman's Ave **2**
PE12. . . . . 215 F3
Stockmoor La LN8 . . . . 57 A8
Stocks Hill
4 Belton DN9. . . . . . 16 E1
Castor PE5. . . . . 223 F1
Stockshill Rd DN16. . . . 185 C6
Stocks La LN8 . . . . 56 F3
Stockwell Gate PE21 . . 215 A4
Stockwell Gr **6** HU9 . . . . 5 F8
Stockwell Prim Sch HU9 . . 5 F8
Stockwith Mill★ PE23. . 87 B5
Stockwith Rd
Haxey DN9. . . . . 27 E1
Walkeringham DN10 . . 40 A3
STOKE ROCHFORD
NG33. . . . . 139 F2
Stoke Rochford Hall Con &
Leisure Ctr★ NG33. . 139 F2
Stokesay Ct **8** PE3. . . 225 B1
Stokes Dr NG34. . . . . . 212 B6
Stoksley Wlk DN37. . . . 190 F8
Stonebow Ctr LN2 . . . . 234 B2
Stonebridge PE2. . . . . 230 C5
Stonebridge Lea PE2. . . 230 C5
Stonebridge Rd NG31. . 211 B4
Stone Cl **8** PE10. . . . . 213 C6
Stonecross Rd NG34 . . . 107 E1
Stone Dr LE15 . . . . . . 152 A1
Stonefield La LN2 . . . . 234 B4
Stonefield Pk LN2. . . . . 68 C7
Stonegate
Gedney PE12. . . . . . . 159 D6
Spalding PE11. . . . . . 214 E3
28 Thorne/Moorends
DN8. . . . . 15 A8
Stone Gate
Cowbit PE12 . . . . 157 B1
Weston PE12. . . . . . . 145 F2
STONE HILL DN7. . . . . . 14 F4
Stone Hill DN7. . . . . . . 15 A4
Stone Hill Rd DN7. . . . . 15 A4
Stonehouse Rd PE7 . . . 233 E5
Stone La
Aubourn Haddington & South
Hykeham LN5 . . . . . 92 E6
Burringham DN17. . . . 17 E4
Peterborough PE1 . . . 225 F5
Sutterton PE20 . . . . . 135 F1
6 Waddington LN5. . . 93 F7
Stoneleigh Ct PE3 . . . . 225 B2

Stonemasons Ct **4**
NG31. . . . . 211 B4
Stone Moor Rd **14** LN6. . 93 B8
Stonepit La
Marston NG32. . . . . . 118 C2
8 Skillington NG33. . . 151 A8
Stone Pit La
Skendleby PE23. . . . . 88 D4
Willingham DN21 . . . . 53 F3
Stonepit Rd HU15. . . . . . 2 E6
Stonesby Rd LE14. . . . . 138 E1
Stones Cl **4** PE24. . . . . 90 B7
Stones La
13 Spilsby PE23. . . . . 88 A1
West Keal PE23. . . . . 100 C5
Stones Pl **1** LN6. . . . . 200 E1
Stone Way NG34 . . . . . 212 B6
Stonewell Row LN9 . . . 199 C4
Stoney La DN21. . . . . . . 54 F7
Stoney Way **15** DN36. . . 36 D4
Stoney Yd LN6. . . . . . . 200 A5
Stong's Dro PE11 . . . . 144 F8
Stool Cl Rd **2** DN9. . . . . 16 E1
Storbeck Rd **15** PE13. . 170 D1
Storey's Bar Rd PE6. . . 227 A3
Storey's La PE24. . . . . 102 E7
Storrington Way PE4. . . 221 A3
Stortford St **7** DN31 . . 188 D1
Story St **11** HU1. . . . . . 180 E7
Stothards La **7** DN19 . . 12 A8
Stoton's Gate PE12. . . 158 E2
Stour Ct **7** NG31. . . . . 210 E2
Stourton Pl LN9. . . . . . 199 B4
Stove Ct LE15. . . . . . . 162 A8
Stovin Cres DN15. . . . . . 9 A5
STOW LN1. . . . . 66 C8
Stow LN37. . . . . 190 D8
Stowehill Rd PE4. . . . . 221 D2
Stowe Rd PE6 . . . . . . 164 E2
Stowgate Rd PE6 . . . . 174 A8
Stow Hill LE14 . . . . . . 150 C7
Stow La NG34. . . . . . . 133 A1
Stow Pk Rd
Marton DN21. . . . . . . 65 E8
Stow LN1. . . . . 66 B8
Stow Rd
Scunthorpe DN16 . . . . 185 B7
Sturton by Stow LN1. . . 66 C8
Willingham DN21 . . . . 53 E2
Wisbech PE13. . . . . . 170 E1
Strafford St DN21. . . . 197 D2
STRAGGLETHORPE
LN5 . . . . 105 E3
Stragglethorpe La
Caythorpe NG32 . . . . 118 E8
Fulbeck NG32 . . . . . . 105 E2
Strahane Cl LN5 . . . . . 205 C3
Straight Dro PE7. . . . . 231 E1
Strait Bargate **28** PE21. . 208 F5
Strait The LN2. . . . . . . 234 B3
Strand Cl
Kingston upon Hull
HU2. . . . . 180 E8
8 Mablethorpe/Sutton on Sea
LN12. . . . . 64 B3
Strand Infants Sch
DN32. . . . . 189 B1
Strand Jun Sch DN32 . . 189 B1
Strand St DN32 . . . . . 189 B1
Strand The LN12. . . . . . 64 B3
Stratford Ave DN34 . . . 191 A4
Stratford Dr **5** DN16 . . 183 C1
Stratten Cl **5** NG34. . . 107 C1
Stratton Pk **1** HU14. . . . 3 C6
Strawberry Cl **13** PE13. . 170 C1
Strawberry Fields Dr
PE12. . . . . 147 D6
Strawberry Gdns HU9 . . 181 B7
Strawberry Hill DN37. . . 194 B4
Strawberry St HU9. . . . 181 B7
Strayfleets La PE22 . . . 126 D5
Stray Gn **12** NG34 . . . . 108 E2
Street La
North Kelsey LN7. . . . . 32 B4
North Leverton with
Habblesthorpe DN22 . . 65 A8
Street La Rd DN22 . . . . 52 C1
Street Life Mus of
Transport★ HU9 . . . 181 A6
Streetway PE21. . . . . . 136 E7
Stretham Way **5** PE10. . 213 C7
Stretton Cl **4** LN1. . . . 66 C7
Stretton Rd LE15. . . . . 162 B6
Strickland Rd DN17. . . . . 7 A3
Stricklands Dr **4** PE6. . 175 C8
Strickland St HU3. . . . . 180 C4
Strong's Bank PE12 . . . 158 F4
Strong's Gate PE12 . . . 158 F3
STROXTON NG33. . . . . . 139 E5
Stroxton La NG33 . . . . 139 F5
Stroykins Cl DN34. . . . . 190 F6
STRUBBY LN13 . . . . 63 C1
Strubby Airfield LN13 . . 75 E8
Strubby Cl
9 Birchwood LN6. . . 204 D8
Cleethorpes DN35. . . . 193 A4
Strugg's Hill La PE20. . . 136 B3
Stuart Cl
Peterborough PE2. . . . 231 C6
Scunthorpe DN17. . . . 184 F2
Stuart Ct PE1. . . . . . . 226 B4
Stuart St NG31. . . . . . 211 C3
Stuart Wortley St **1**
DN31 . . . . 189 B2
Stubbs Cl **21** HU15. . . . 2 D5
STUBTON NG23. . . . . . . 118 B7
Stubton Hall Sch NG23. . 118 B7

Stubton Rd NG23. . . . . 117 F7
Studcross DN9. . . . . . . 27 D6
Studio Ct DN12. . . . . . 181 B8
Studley St HU8 . . . . . . 181 B8
Stukeley Cl
Lincoln LN2 . . . . 202 E6
Peterborough PE2 . . . 231 D5
Stukeley Gdns **2** PE12. . 215 C2
Stukeley Hall Dr PE12 . . 215 D2
Stukeley Rd PE12. . . . . 215 D2
Stumpacre PE3 . . . . . . 225 A8
Stump Cross Hill NG34 . . 212 C1
Stumpcross La PE20 . . . 135 B6
Stumps La PE12. . . . . . 157 B7
Sturdy Hill LN11. . . . . . 62 E4
STURGATE DN21. . . . . . 53 F8
Sturgate Airfield DN21. . 53 E6
Sturgate Cl **15** LN6. . . 204 C7
Sturgate Wlk DN21. . . . 197 F3
Sturmer Ct **1** DN16. . . 185 B2
Sturrock Cl **12** NG31 . . 210 E2
Sturrock Way PE3. . . . . 225 C8
STURTON DN20 . . . . 30 F7
STURTON BY STOW
LN1. . . . . 66 C7
Sturton by Stow Prim Sch
LN1. . . . . 66 D8
Sturton CE Prim Sch
DN22. . . . . 52 C2
Sturton Cl **1** LN2. . . . 201 F7
Sturton Dr **2** NG33. . . 191 B4
Sturton La DN20 . . . . . 30 E7
STURTON LE STEEPLE
DN22. . . . . 52 B3
Sturton Rd
North Leverton with
Habblesthorpe DN22. . 52 B1
Sturton Way PE12. . . . . 216 B5
Stutte Cl LN11 . . . . . . 198 E3
Styles Croft **6** HU14 . . . 3 C6
Subway St HU3 . . . . . . 180 B3
Subway The DN16. . . . . 19 A4
Sudbeck La **17** LN2. . . . 68 D6
SUDBROOK NG32 . . . . . 119 E3
Sudbrooke LN2. . . . . . . 68 F2
Sudbrooke Dr LN2 . . . . 202 A7
Sudbrooke La LN2 . . . . 68 E2
Sudbrooke Rd LN2 . . . . 68 F3
Sudbrook Rd NG32. . . . 119 D4
Sudbury Cl LN6 . . . . . . 205 A5
Sudbury Ct PE7. . . . . . 231 F5
Sudbury Pl LN11 . . . . . 198 B4
Suddle Way **19** DN41. . . 23 A4
SUDTHORPE NG32. . . . . 119 C8
Sudthorpe Hill **8**
NG32. . . . . 106 C1
Suffolk Cl PE3. . . . . . . 225 B2
Suffolk Ct DN32. . . . . . 189 C1
Suffolk Rd **10** LN1. . . . 67 E5
Sugar Way PE2 . . . . . . 230 D8
Suggitt's Ct DN35. . . . . 192 B8
Suggitt's La DN35. . . . . 192 B8
Suggitt's Orch DN35. . . 192 B8
Sullivan Rd HU4 . . . . . 179 B4
Summerdale **2** DN18 . . 10 E8
Summerfield Ave
DN37 . . . . 194 E5
Summerfield Cl
Waltham DN37. . . . . . 194 E5
16 Wisbech PE13. . . . 170 C1
Summerfield Ct **3**
NG34 . . . . 212 D6
Summerfield Dr **4**
NG34 . . . . 212 D6
Summerfield Rd PE1. . . 225 F4
Summerfields PE22 . . . 114 B1
Summergangs La
DN21 . . . . 197 D1
Summergates La PE24. . 102 C7
Summergroves Way
HU4 . . . . 179 B2
Summer Hill DN21 . . . . 197 B5
Summer Lesure La
PE12 . . . . 159 F2
Sunbeam Ave LN6 . . . . 204 D1
Sunbeam Rd HU4 . . . . 179 D5
Suncastle★ PE25 . . . . 206 E4
Sunderfleet La LN11 . . . 51 A5
Sunderland Cl **6** LN6. . 200 A4
Sunfield Cres LN6. . . . . 200 D1
Sunfields Cl PE12 . . . . 157 C3
Sunflower Way PE21 . . 208 B4
Sunningdale
Grantham NG31. . . . . 211 C8
Peterborough PE2. . . . 229 E6
8 Waltham DN37. . . . 194 C4
Sunningdale Ave
Brigg DN20 . . . . 196 C5
Spalding PE11. . . . . . 214 C2
Sunningdale Cl
Chapel St Leonard PE24. . 90 E7
1 Skegness PE25. . . 206 D4
6 Woodhall Spa LN10. . 97 C5
Sunningdale Cres **2**
PE25 . . . . 206 D4
Sunningdale Dr
Boston PE21 . . . . . . 208 C6
Chapel St Leonard PE24. . 90 E7
4 Immingham DN40. . 186 D5
Lincoln LN5 . . . . 205 D8
Skegness PE25 . . . . . 206 D4
Sunningdale Gr LN4. . . 203 D1
Sunningdale Rd
5 Hatfield DN7. . . . . 14 F3
Kingston upon Hull HU13 . 178 F2
Scunthorpe DN17 . . . . 184 D4

Sunningdlae Way
DN21 . . . . 197 E6
Sunnybank **11** DN18. . . . 10 E8
Sunny Bank HU3 . . . . . 180 B7
Sunny Bank Gdns DN10 . 39 C2
Sunny Cnr DN33 . . . . . 191 D1
Sunnydale Cl **1** PE11. . 145 D2
Sunny Hill **8** DN21. . . . 30 B1
Sunnymead PE4 . . . . . 220 E6
Sunway Gr DN16 . . . . . 185 B5
SURFLEET PE11. . . . . . 145 C3
Surfleet Bank PE11. . . . 145 F5
Surfleet Lows Nature
Reserve★ PE11 . . . . 145 D3
Surfleet Rd **5** PE11. . . 145 D2
SURFLEET SEAS END
PE11. . . . . 145 F3
Surfside **5** LN12. . . . . 77 A8
Surrey Ct **20** DN32 . . . 189 C1
Surrey Garth HU4. . . . . 179 B4
Surtees St DN31 . . . . . 189 B2
Sussex Ave PE21 . . . . . 208 B4
Sussex Cl **7** LN8. . . . . 47 B6
Sussex Ct DN32. . . . . . 189 C1
Sussex Gdns **16** LN1. . . 67 E5
Sussex Rd PE9 . . . . . . 219 B6
Sussex St DN35 . . . . . 192 B8
SUSWORTH DN17. . . . . . 28 D5
Susworth Rd DN17. . . . . 28 E4
Sutcliffe Ave DN33 . . . . 191 A3
Sutherland Way PE9 . . . 218 F5
SUTTERBY PE23. . . . . . . 87 E7
SUTTERTON PE20. . . . . 136 A3
SUTTERTON DOWDYKE
PE20 . . . . 146 A8
Sutterton Dro LN4 . . . . 110 E1
Suttling Dales La PE22 . 126 B8
SUTTON
Beckingham LN5 . . . . 105 B3
Sutton PE5 . . . . 222 F2
Sutton Branch Line
Walkway & Conservation
Area★ LN12 . . . . . . 76 F6
SUTTON BRIDGE PE12. . 160 D4
Sutton Cl
Heighington/
Washingborough LN4. . 203 A1
15 Nettleham LN2. . . . 68 C2
SUTTON CROSSES
PE12 . . . . 216 C1
Sutton Ct **2** PE25. . . . 206 C3
Sutton Gate PE12 . . . . 159 D1
Sutton Mdws PE13 . . . . 170 C2
SUTTON ON SEA LN12 . . 76 F8
Sutton on Sea Prim Sch
LN12. . . . . 77 A8
SUTTON ON TRENT
NG23 . . . . 91 A8
Sutton Pl **4** DN20. . . . 30 F7
Sutton Rd
Beckingham LN5 . . . . 105 B4
Bilsby LN13 . . . . 76 C4
16 Kirk Sandall DN3 . . 14 A3
Mablethorpe/Sutton on Sea
LN12. . . . . 64 C2
Newton PE13. . . . . . . 170 B6
Sutton St James PE12 . . 159 D2
Terrington St Clement
PE34. . . . . 161 F2
SUTTON ST EDMUND
PE12 . . . . 168 F4
SUTTON ST JAMES
PE12 . . . . 159 D1
Sutton St James Prim Sch
PE12. . . . . 159 C1
Sutton's La PE6. . . . . . 217 D4
Svenskaby PE2 . . . . . . 229 B6
SWABY LN13 . . . . 74 E4
Swaby Cl LN2. . . . . . . 202 A8
Swaby Cres **4** PE25. . . 206 B4
Swaby Dr DN35 . . . . . . 192 D3
Swaby Valley Nature
Reserve★ LN13 . . . . 74 F4
Swadales Cl **1** NG31. . 129 E5
Swain Cl PE2 . . . . 230 F3
Swain's Dro PE13 . . . . 170 C8
Swale Ave PE4. . . . . . . 221 C1
Swale Bank PE11. . . . . 144 D5
Swaledale **10** HU15. . . . 2 D6
Swaledale Pl **2** DN16. . 185 E6
Swale Rd **14** HU15. . . . . 2 D6
Swales Rd **12** DN36. . . . 36 D8
SWALLOW LN7. . . . . 34 B5
Swallow Ave LN6 . . . . . 200 A3
SWALLOW BECK LN6 . . . 205 B5
Swallowbeck Ave LN6. . 205 A4
Swallow Cl
5 Chapel St Leonard
PE24 . . . . 90 D7
4 Gainsborough DN21. . 53 A7
5 Sleaford NG34 . . . . 212 C3
Swallow Ct **6** DN9 . . . 27 D7
Swallow Dr
3 Claypole NG23 . . . 117 E8
15 Healing DN41. . . . 23 F5
Louth LN11 . . . . 198 D8
Swallowfield **4** PE4 . . 220 E4
Swallowfield Dr HU4. . . 179 B2
Swallowfields Ct **2**
PE25 . . . . 206 A4
Swallow Gate Rd LN11. . 51 B2
Swallow Hill PE10. . . . . 164 B7
Swallow La
Tydd St Giles PE13 . . . 170 B8
Wootton DN39 . . . . . . 11 E2
Swallow's Cl **1** NG31. . 210 E7
Swallow Wlk **3** PE6. . . 217 D5
Swanage Wlk HU4 . . . . 179 B4

Swan Cl PE11 . . . . 214 F2
Swan Ct DN21 . . . . . . 197 F5
Swan Dr
Skegness PE25 . . . . . 103 C7
6 Sturton by Stow LN1. . 66 D7
Swanella Gr HU3. . . . . 180 A4
Swan Gdns
Newark PE1. . . . . . . 226 E6
Parson Drove PE13 . . . 177 C2
Swanhill PE8 . . . . 222 A4
Swanhole La PE22. . . . 126 D4
Swanholme Cl LN6. . . . 204 E5
SWANLAND HU14. . . . . . 3 A7
Swanland Butts Cl
HU10. . . . . 178 C6
Swanland Cl **1** DN8. . . 15 B7
Swanland Ct **24** DN8. . . 15 B7
Swanland Dale HU14. . . . 3 B8
Swanland Garth **6** HU14. . 3 A5
Swanland Hill HU14. . . . 3 B5
Swanland Prim Sch HU14. . 3 B6
Swanland Rd HU13. . . . 178 C2
Swan Moor Bank PE22 . . 114 C3
Swannacks View **3**
DN20 . . . . 30 F7
Swan's La LN5. . . . . . . 105 F5
Swanspool PE3 . . . . . . 225 B6
Swan St
1 Lincoln LN2. . . . . 234 B2
Spalding PE11 . . . . . . 214 D4
Swapcoat La PE12 . . . . 216 B5
Swapcoat Mews PE12. . 216 B5
SWARBY NG34 . . . . . . 132 A7
Swarby La NG34. . . . . . 132 A7
SWATON NG34. . . . . . . 133 D4
Swaton La NG34. . . . . 133 C3
SWAYFIELD NG33. . . . . 152 D5
Swayne Cl LN2 . . . . . . 202 C7
Swaythling Cl LN6. . . . . 204 E5
Sweetbriar **3** PE9 . . . . 218 C7
Sweet Briar Cl **6**
DN37 . . . . 194 C5
Sweetbriar La PE4 . . . . 220 F6
Sweet Cl **2** PE6 . . . . . 217 D5
Sweet Dews Gr HU9. . . 181 D8
Sweetlands Way PE11. . 145 B5
Swen Cl **17** LN2. . . . . . 68 D7
Swift Ave LN11 . . . . . . 62 C6
Swift Cl PE6 . . . . 217 D4
Swift Ct **1** PE11. . . . . 214 F2
Swift Dr DN20 . . . . . . 196 A3
Swift Gdns LN2 . . . . . 202 C7
Swift Gn LN2 . . . . 202 B7
Swift Rd DN17 . . . . . . 184 D6
Swiftsure Cres DN34 . . 190 D4
Swift Way PE10 . . . . . . 164 B7
Swinburne La DN17. . . 184 D7
Swinburne Rd DN17. . . 184 D7
Swin Cl PE20 . . . . 135 C6
SWINDERBY LN6. . . . . . 92 A5
Swinderby Cl **1** NG24. . 104 B5
Swinderby Gdns **2**
DN34 . . . . 191 A1
Swinderby Rd
Collingham NG23. . . . 91 E4
Eagle & Swinethorpe LN6. . 79 B1
North Scarle LN6 . . . . 78 F1
Norton Disney LN6 . . . 92 C2
South Scarle NG23 . . . 91 F7
Swinderby Sta LN6 . . . . 92 B7
Swindler's Dro PE12 . . . 157 C6
Swinefleet Rd DN14. . . . 6 B8
Swinegate
Grantham NG31. . . . . 211 A5
Kingston upon Hull
HU13. . . . . 178 E1
Swine Hill NG32. . . . . . 139 C7
SWINESHEAD PE20 . . . . 135 B7
SWINESHEAD BRIDGE
PE20 . . . . 123 F1
Swineshead Rd
Boston PE21 . . . . . . 208 A3
Frampton PE20 . . . . . 124 C1
Swineshead St Marys Prim
Sch PE20 . . . . 135 C7
Swineshead St Pa PE20 . 123 F1
Swine's Meadow Rd
PE6 . . . . 217 D8
SWINETHORPE LN6. . . . 79 B4
Swingbridge Rd NG31. . 210 D2
SWINHOPE LN8. . . . . . . 47 C7
Swinhope Hill LN8 . . . . 47 C5
Swinhope Rd LN8. . . . . 47 B6
SWINSTEAD NG33 . . . . 153 A5
Swinstead Rd
Corby Glen NG33. . . . 152 F7
Counthorpe & Creeton
NG33. . . . . 153 A3
Irnham NG33. . . . . . . 141 E1
Swinster La DN40 . . . . 12 E6
Switchback LN8 . . . . . . 47 C2
Swithin Cl HU13 . . . . . 179 A2
Swynford Cl LN1. . . . . . 65 D2
Sybil Rd **18** PE13 . . . . 170 C1
Sycamore Ave
Grimsby DN33 . . . . . 191 C3
Peterborough PE1 . . . 226 C6
Sycamore Cl
1 Barnetby le Wold
DN38. . . . . 21 B4
4 Birchwood LN6. . . 204 E8
Bourne PE10 . . . . . . 213 A5
2 Broughton DN20. . . 19 D3
Cherry Willingham/Reepham
LN3. . . . . 203 D5

Sycamore Cl *continued*
Croft PE24 102 E4
Hessle HU13 178 C3
Kingston upon Hull HU5 179 C7
5 Scopwick Heath LN4 108 A7
Sycamore Cres 5 LN6 204 E8
Sycamore Ct 3 NG31 210 D2
Sycamore Dr
7 Gainsborough DN21 197 E6
Louth LN11 198 E5
Sleaford NG34 212 D6
3 Waddington LN5 93 E8
Sycamore Gr LN4 81 A1
Sycamore La 2 LE14 150 B1
Sycamores The 5 PE11 214 B1
Sycamore View PE12 168 C2
Sydney Dr 3 PE25 206 A4
Sydney Rd PE2 231 D5
Sydney Smith Sch HU10 179 A5
Sydney St PE21 208 D5
Syd Wilson Ct LN1 201 D7
Syerston Way 5 NG24 104 B5
Sykemouth Dro PE20 124 C1
Sykes Cl
6 Kingston upon Hull HU10 178 F6
15 Swanland HU14 3 B7
Sykes La
Goxhill DN19 5 A2
Saxilby with Ingleby LN1 66 C3
Sykes St 2 HU2 180 F7
Sylvan Ave 5 LN10 97 D6
Sylvden Dr 24 PE13 170 E1
Sylvester St 12 DN21 30 B1
Symmington Cl PE2 230 F8
Sympson Cl LN2 202 E6
Syne Ave 5 PE25 206 D1
Syringa Gn LN6 200 C1
SYSTON NG32 130 A7
Syston Gr LN5 205 D4
Sywell Cl 16 LN6 204 C6

T

Tabor Ct PE7 230 D2
Tadman St HU3 180 D4
Taggs Dr 7 PE25 206 A6
Tait Cl PE1 226 C5
Talbot Ave PE2 230 D6
Talbot Cl 4 PE23 101 A8
Talbot Rd
Immingham DN40 186 D3
Skegness PE25 206 C4
Talbot Wlk DN16 183 B2
Talisman Dr DN16 185 A2
Tallert Way DN33 190 F3
Tall Gables 2 NG22 65 B1
TALLINGTON PE9 172 E7
Tallington Dry Ski Ctr* PE9 172 F7
Tallington Lakes Leisure Pk* PE9 173 A8
Tallington Rd PE9 172 F6
Tall Trees HU13 178 C3
Tamar Ct 5 NG31 210 E2
Tamar Dr 4 DN36 195 D7
Tamarisk Way DN16 185 D5
Tamar Way 3 LN6 205 A2
Tamar Wlk DN17 184 C8
Tame Ct 4 NG34 212 D5
Tamson Way 5 NG34 212 D5
TAMWORTH GREEN PE22 126 E1
Tanglewood PE4 220 F6
Tanglewood Cedar Falls 3 PE11 214 B1
Tanhouse PE2 230 C5
Tanners Ct LN5 234 A1
Tanners' La NG33 152 E8
Tanner's La LN5 234 A1
Tannery Cl
Boston PE21 208 E4
7 Bourne PE10 213 E4
Tannery La 3 NG34 142 D8
Tansley Ct 1 DN15 182 B2
Tansor Garth PE3 225 C5
Tantallon Ct 6 PE3 225 B1
Tapin Cl LN1 201 C6
Tarleton Ave 1 LN10 97 E6
Tarleton Cl 2 DN3 14 A2
Tarragon Way PE10 213 C6
Tarrant PE4 220 E6
Tarran Way PE25 206 B5
Tasburgh St DN32 191 F6
Tasman Cl 7 PE11 214 B2
Tasman Rd 5 PE23 101 A8
TATHWELL LN11 61 B2
Tattersall Cl DN17 184 D5
TATTERSHALL LN4 207 A5
Tattershall Ave DN34 190 F4
TATTERSHALL BRIDGE LN4 110 D7
Tattershall Castle* LN4 207 A4
Tattershall Cl 3 NG31 210 E5
Tattershall Coll Bldgs* LN4 207 A4
Tattershall Dr 10 PE6 217 A5
Tattershall Lakes Ctry Pk* LN4 207 A3
Tattershall Rd
Billinghay LN4 109 F5
Boston PE21 208 D7
Fishtoft PE21 125 C5
Woodhall Spa LN10 97 D5
Tattershall Sta Gall & Pottery* LN4 110 E7
TATTERSHALL THORPE LN4 207 B8
Tattershall Way LN11 198 A8
Tatwin Dr 8 PE6 175 B8
Taunton Cl 2 NG34 212 D7
Taunton Rd HU4 179 A3
Taunton Way DN33 194 E8
Tavella Ct 1 DN9 27 B2
Tavern Cl LN13 89 A6
Taverner Rd PE21 208 D6
Taverners Rd PE1 225 F4
Tavern La 7 PE24 90 B7
Tavistock Cl 15 PE6 176 A3
Tavistock Rd PE11 214 B2
Tawney St PE21 208 F6
Taylor Cl
6 Belton DN9 16 E2
5 Boston PE21 209 D4
Taylor's Ave DN35 192 E4
Taylor's Dro PE12 159 C1
Taylor St DN35 189 D1
TEALBY LN8 46 C1
Tealby Cl 1 DN21 53 A7
Tealby Gr DN33 191 B3
Tealby Rd
Middle Rasen LN8 57 E8
Scunthorpe DN17 184 D5
Tealby Sch LN8 46 D1
Tealby St 11 LN5 205 E8
Teal Cl
4 Brigg DN20 196 A3
3 Skegness PE25 206 A6
Teal Dr DN18 10 E8
Teale St DN15 183 A4
Teal Gr 10 PE12 167 B8
Teal Pl LN7 33 A4
Teal Rd LN4 110 E8
Team Gate DN37 190 C6
Teanby Ct 5 PE3 224 F3
Teanby Dr 8 DN15 9 A5
Teasel Dr PE10 213 D3
Teasles 6 PE6 217 D6
Tedder Dr 3 LN5 93 F7
Teddy's Farm* LN5 105 C4
Tee La DN15 8 B5
Tees Ct DN37 190 E8
Teesdale Cl LN6 200 C2
Teesdale Rd NG31 211 A7
Telford Dr
Newark NG24 104 B6
Yaxley PE7 233 D6
Telford Pl DN34 191 A7
Temperance Ave 5 DN17 29 D7
Temperance La 2 NG23 91 C4
Temper Rd DN16 185 F8
Temperton's La 5 DN9 28 A3
Tempest St LN2 202 B3
Templar Ct DN16 185 B3
Templars Way 2 NG33 151 D2
Temple Bruer Templar Preceptory* LN5 107 C4
Temple Cl
2 Alford LN13 75 E2
4 Belton DN9 16 E2
3 Brough HU15 2 E6
Templefield Rd DN21 42 D4
Temple Gdns LN2 234 B3
Temple Grange PE4 220 F6
Temple La DN37 23 E1
Templeman Dr PE9 163 E5
Templemans La DN36 36 A1
Templemeads Cl 3 PE10 154 D6
Temple Rd
Aslackby & Laughton NG34 142 E5
Welbourn LN5 107 A4
Westcliffe DN17 184 F6
Temples Ct 3 PE6 173 B4
Temple Terr LN11 198 B6
Templeway Cl 5 NG32 119 B7
Templeway Sq 8 NG32 119 B7
Temple Wlk 2 HU15 2 E6
Ten Acre Dro PE11 135 C1
Ten Acre La
Pinchbeck PE11 145 C1
Wyville cum Hungerton NG32 139 B5
Tenens Way PE21 209 A1
Tennyson Ave
Grantham NG31 211 E5
16 Mablethorpe/Sutton on Sea LN12 64 B4
Sleaford NG34 212 D5
4 Thorne/Moorends DN8 15 B8
Tennyson Cl
Benniworth LN8 59 B1
Brigg DN20 196 D2
2 Caistor LN7 33 A3
12 Mablethorpe/Sutton on Sea LN12 77 A7
14 Metheringham LN4 95 C4
Tennyson Dr
Bourne PE10 213 D3
22 Welton/Dunholme LN2 68 D6
Tennyson Gdns LN9 199 D2
Tennyson Gn 3 PE25 206 C2
Tennyson High Sch The LN12 64 C3
Tennyson Rd
Cleethorpes DN35 192 E7
Louth LN11 198 C4
17 Mablethorpe/Sutton on Sea LN12 64 B4
Peterborough PE1 225 F7
2 Ruskington NG34 108 E2
Scunthorpe DN16 185 D7
Tennyson St
Gainsborough DN21 197 D5
Grimsby DN31 191 D8
1 Lincoln LN1 201 D4
Tennyson Way 1 PE9 218 E5
Tennyson Wlk LN3 203 C6
Tensing Rd DN16 185 C5
Tentercroft St LN5 234 A1
Tenter La 6 LN5 107 A8
Tenters The PE12 215 E2
Tern Rd PE7 230 C2
Terrace La PE22 99 C5
Terrace The
Great Ponton NG33 140 A5
Louth LN11 198 D4
10 Spilsby PE23 88 A1
Terrington Pl DN35 192 D4
TERRINGTON ST CLEMENT PE34 161 E3
Terry O'Toole Theatre* LN6 204 D1
TETFORD LN9 73 F1
Tetford Hill LN9 73 E3
Tetford Rd LN9 86 A5
Tethering La DN10 39 A2
TETLEY DN17 16 D6
Tetley Rd DN16 185 C7
Tetley View 3 DN17 16 E6
TETNEY DN36 36 D4
Tetney Blow Wells Nature Reserve* DN36 36 E3
Tetney Cl 6 LN1 201 E8
Tetney La DN36 195 E2
TETNEY LOCK DN36 37 A4
Tetney Lock Rd DN36 36 E4
Tetney Marshes Nature Reserve* DN36 37 C7
Tetney Prim Sch DN36 36 D4
Tetney Rd DN36 36 C7
Tewkesbury Dr 4 DN34 191 C6
Thackeray Ct DN37 190 E8
Thacker Bank LN12 63 B7
Thackers Cl PE8 222 A4
Thackers La LN4 81 D2
Thacker's Rd PE22 112 B2
Thackers Way PE6 217 D5
Thames Cl 3 PE24 90 B7
Thames Cres 5 PE24 90 B7
Thames Ct DN37 190 E8
Thames Meadow Dr 2 PE24 90 B7
Thames Rd
Grantham NG31 210 E2
Spalding PE11 214 F5
Thames St
Hogsthorpe PE24 90 B7
Louth LN11 198 D6
Thary La PE11 145 E4
Thatchers Wlk PE22 113 B2
Theaker Ave DN21 197 F5
THEALBY DN15 8 D4
Thealby La DN15 8 E5
Theatre Royal* LN2 234 B2
THEDDLETHORPE ALL SAINTS LN12 63 D7
Theddlethorpe Com Prim Sch LN12 63 D6
Theddlethorpe Rd LN12 63 F4
THEDDLETHORPE ST HELEN LN12 63 E8
Theodore Rd DN15 182 E4
Theodore St LN1 234 A4
THE PARKS DN7 14 C4
Theresa Cl 8 PE25 206 A4
Thesiger St
2 Grimsby DN32 189 B1
Lincoln LN5 201 F1
Thesiger Wlk 8 DN31 189 B1
THETFORD PE6 164 E5
Thetford Ave 5 PE6 164 E5
THE WILLOWS DN37 190 E7
THIMBLEBY LN9 85 B5
Thimbleby Hill LN9 85 C5
Thinholme La DN9 27 A1
Third Ave
1 Fixborough Ind Est DN15 8 A1
Grantham NG31 211 F7
4 Scampton Airfield LN1 67 E5
2 Scunthorpe DN17 184 C6
Spalding PE11 214 A4
Third Dro
Gosberton PE11 144 B4
Moulton PE12 146 F7
Peterborough PE1 226 E2
Third Hill Rd LN4 81 F3
Third La DN37 35 D3
Third Marsh Rd PE14 170 C3
Thirkleby Cres DN32 192 B4
Thirlmere Ave DN33 194 E7
Thirlmere Cl 8 LN6 205 A2
Thirlmere Gdns 3 PE4 221 C3
Thirlmere Way 1 LN6 200 D1
Thirsk Dr LN6 204 F4
Thistle Cl LN2 202 C8
Thistle Dr PE2 231 C7
Thistlemoor Rd PE1 225 E7
Thistleton La LE15 151 D1
Thomas Cl 7 PE3 224 F3
Thomas Cowley High Sch The PE11 134 F2
Thomas Ct 13 NG34 212 D4
Thomas Gibson Dr LN9 199 D3
Thomas Kitching Way 8 LN3 83 C4
Thomas Magnus Sch NG24 104 A4
Thomas Mid Cott Dr 20 PE20 136 C5
Thomas Rd
10 Balderton NG24 104 C1
Scunthorpe DN17 184 F8
Thomas St
Grimsby DN32 191 F7
Kingston upon Hull HU9 181 B7
Lincoln LN2 234 C2
Sleaford NG34 212 D4
Thomas Sully Cl LN9 199 A4
Thomas Sumpter Sch DN17 184 E7
Thompson Cl
Skegness PE25 206 C5
3 Spalding PE11 214 C3
Thompson Dr 25 DN7 14 D4
Thompsons Gd PE7 230 D3
Thompson's La
Fosdyke PE20 146 E8
Hough-on-the-Hill NG32 119 A5
Thompson St 10 DN15 183 B3
Thonock Cl LN2 201 F7
Thonock Dr 7 LN1 66 C2
Thonock Rd DN21 197 D8
Thoresby Pl DN35 192 E4
Thoresby Prim Sch HU5 180 B8
Thoresby Rd
Fulstow LN11 49 A8
Scunthorpe DN17 184 D5
Tetney DN36 36 D3
Thoresby St HU5 180 B8
THORESTHORPE LN13 75 F4
THORESWAY LN8 46 D7
Thoresway Dr LN2 202 A7
Thoresway Gr 5 DN33 191 A3
Thorgam Ct DN31 191 C7
THORGANBY DN37 47 B8
Thorganby Rd DN35 193 A3
Thorlby Haven 12 PE20 135 A4
Thorley Cres PE2 230 D8
Thorn Bank DN9 26 E4
Thornbury Rd DN40 186 D3
Thorndales La PE22 113 A5
Thorndike Way DN21 197 E3
Thorndyke Mews 7 DN21 197 D3
THORNE DN8 15 B8
Thorne N Sta DN8 14 F8
Thorne Rd
Edenthorpe DN3 14 A2
Sandtoft DN8 16 A3
8 Stainforth DN7 14 C7
Thorne S Sta DN8 15 B7
Thorne Swimming Baths DN8 15 B8
Thorne Waste Drain Rd DN8 15 E8
Thorne Way PE20 136 C4
THORNEY
Thorney NG23 78 F8
Thorney PE6 176 A3
Thorney Heritage Mus* PE6 176 A3
Thorney Rd
2 Crowland PE6 175 C8
Newborough PE6 174 D5
Wisbech St Mary PE13 177 C2
THORNEY TOLL PE13 177 A2
Thorngarth La 9 DN19 11 D8
Thorngate LN5 234 B2
Thornham's Way 8 HU15 2 C7
Thornhill Cres 4 DN17 184 F3
Thornhill Gdns DN34 191 A7
Thornhill La DN22 52 E1
Thornholme Dr DN16 185 A3
Thorniman La PE20 136 E6
Thorn La DN19 12 A8
Thorn Leigh 3 HU3 180 C6
Thornleigh Dr PE2 230 C6
Thornmead PE4 221 B4
Thorn Rd PE7 230 C2
Thorns La NG32 210 A8
Thornton 20 HU15 2 C6
THORNTON LN9 85 C2
Thornton Abbey* DN39 12 B5
Thornton Abbey Sta DN39 12 A5
Thornton Ave
Boston PE21 208 D3
Scunthorpe DN16 185 A7
Thornton Cl
3 Heighington/Washingborough LN4 203 A2
Kingston upon Hull HU13 178 D1
Langriville PE22 124 F8
6 Lincoln LN6 205 A7
Peterborough PE4 221 C3
Thornton Cres
Cleethorpes DN35 192 E4
Horncastle LN9 199 C2
Thornton Ct DN36 195 D8
THORNTON CURTIS DN39 11 E4
Thornton Gdns 21 DN41 23 A4
Thornton Gr 5 DN34 190 E4
THORNTON LE MOOR LN7 44 E7
Thornton Pl DN40 186 B3
Thornton Rd
Barrow upon Humber DN19 11 D6
7 Collingham NG23 91 D4
Goxhill DN19 11 F6
Owersby LN7 44 E7
South Kelsey LN7 32 A1
Spalding PE11 214 F3
Thornton Curtis DN39 11 E4
Thornton St
Barrow upon Humber DN19 11 C7
6 Gainsborough DN21 197 D3
Thornton Way LN3 203 E6
Thornwell La 2 PE23 87 A4
Thornwick Ave HU10 178 E8
Thornwick Cl 2 HU3 180 C5
Thorold Ave
Cranwell & Byard's Leap NG34 107 E1
5 Cranwell NG34 120 E8
Thorold Gdns 1 NG32 130 B8
Thorold Pl 1 DN3 14 A2
Thorold Rd NG32 210 A4
Thorolds Charity CE (Aided) Prim Sch NG32 118 D2
Thorold St
Boston PE21 208 F6
Grimsby DN31 189 C1
Thorolds Way PE5 223 D2
Thorold Way LN5 93 F4
THORPE LN12 64 A1
Thorpe Ave
Lincoln LN1 201 D8
Moulton PE12 157 E2
Peterborough PE3 225 C2
Thorpe Bank PE22 101 B3
Thorpe Camp Visitor Ctr* LN4 207 B8
Thorpe Cl 3 NG24 104 D5
THORPE CULVERT PE24 102 A3
Thorpe Culvert Sta PE24 102 B3
Thorpe Dr NG34 120 E2
Thorpe Dro NG34 120 E3
THORPE FENDYKES PE24 101 F3
Thorpehall Rd 12 DN3 14 A2
Thorpe La
Aubourn Haddington & South Hykeham LN6 93 A8
Brattleby LN1 67 B7
Eagle & Swinethorpe LN6 79 C1
Tealby LN8 46 B1
THORPE LATIMER NG34 133 C6
Thorpe Lea Rd PE3 225 E2
THORPE LE VALE LN8 47 B1
Thorpe Mdws PE3 225 C2
THORPE ON THE HILL LN6 92 E8
Thorpe Pk Rd PE3 225 C3
Thorpe Pl LN4 207 B6
Thorpe Prim Sch PE3 225 B3
Thorpe Rd
Doddington & Whisby LN6 79 E2
Ewerby & Evedon NG34 122 C6
Peterborough PE3 225 B1
Tattershall LN4 207 C6
THORPE ST PETER PE24 102 B3
Thorpes La 3 NG32 138 D4
Thorpe's La PE12 158 B6
THORPE TILNEY LN4 109 C8
Thorpe Tilney Dro
Timberland LN4 97 A1
Walcott LN4 109 C8
Thorpe Wood PE3 224 F1
Thorsby Cl LN5 205 D1
Thorseby Cl PE3 225 B3
Threadneedle St 9 PE21 208 F5
Three Bridge La LN11 63 A7
THREE BRIDGES LN11 63 A7
THREEKINGHAM NG34 132 E3
Threekingham Bar NG34 132 D3
Three Leys La DN22 52 B2
THROCKENHOLT PE12 177 B8
Throstlenest PE7 231 C3
Thrumber Marsh La LN13 76 F1
Thrunscoe Inf Sch DN35 192 F5
Thrunscoe Jun Sch DN35 192 E5
Thrunscoe Rd 7 DN35 192 F5
Thrush Cl 10 NG34 212 B3
Thurlaston Cl PE3 225 B2
THURLBY
Bilsby LN13 76 D2
Thurlby LN5 92 E4
Thurlby PE10 164 C8
Thurlby Cl 4 LN4 203 A2

Thu–Uly 281

Thurlby Com Prim Sch PE10 164 C8
Thurlby Cres LN2 202 B8
Thurlby Fen Nature Reserve* PE10 164 F7
Thurlby Rd
Bassingham LN5 92 F3
Bilsby LN13 76 B3
Gainsborough DN21 197 E4
Thurlow Ct 1 LN2 202 E7
Thurning Ave PE2 231 C6
Thuro Gr PE2 230 A3
Thursfield PE4 221 A4
Thurstan Cl PE10 213 B6
Thurston Gate 2 PE3 225 A1
Thyme Ave
Bourne PE10 213 C5
12 Market Deeping PE6 217 C5
Thyme Ct LN6 205 D8
Tiber Rd LN6 204 C1
Tichbourne Cl 6 HU3 180 C5
TICKENCOTE PE9 171 A8
Tideswell Ct DN15 182 B2
Tilbury Prim Sch HU4 179 B3
Tilbury Rd HU4 179 B3
Tilebarn La PE20 134 F7
Tilia Cl
Kingston upon Hull HU4 179 B2
Scunthorpe DN16 185 D4
Tilia Way 5 PE10 213 E2
Till Bridge La
Marton LN1 65 F8
Scampton LN1 67 A6
Stow LN1 66 A8
Tillbridge Rd LN1 66 D7
Tilley Gate LN11 51 B3
Tilney Ave PE21 208 D6
Tilney The 10 PE12 158 B7
Tilton Ct PE1 226 C8
Timber Hill NG33 151 A4
Timberland DN16 185 C4
TIMBERLAND LN4 96 C1
Timberland Dro LN4 96 E2
Timberland Rd LN4 96 C2
Timberley Dr DN37 190 C7
Time Trap Mus* DN32 191 E7
Timm's La 18 LN5 93 F7
Timms's Dro PE20 134 E8
Timson Ct 5 DN10 52 B8
Tindale Bank Rd DN9 39 C8
Tindall Cl 2 PE13 170 D2
Tindall Way 10 PE24 102 D1
Tinkermere Cl 3 LN2 68 D6
Tinker's Dro PE13 170 D1
Tinker's La
Girton NG23 91 C8
2 Waddington LN5 93 F6
Tinkle St LN11 62 C7
Tin La PE10 213 C5
Tinsley Cl NG23 117 F7
Tintagel Ct 7 PE3 225 B1
Tintagel Way DN36 195 C7
Tintern Rise 4 PE6 175 A1
Tintern Wlk DN37 188 A1
Tinus Ave PE7 230 C1
TINWELL PE9 218 D3
Tinwell Rd PE9 219 A4
Tinwell Rd La PE9 218 F4
Tip La PE24 102 B4
Tirrington PE3 225 A3
Tison Garth HU10 178 F6
Tithe Barn La 9 DN8 15 B8
Tiverton Rd PE3 225 C3
Tiverton St DN35 189 E1
Tivoli Gdns DN32 191 F8
TLS Com Arts Coll DN35 192 D4
Tobias Gr 4 PE9 218 C7
Tobruk Cl LN1 201 D8
Toby's Hill Nature Reserve* LN11 51 C5
Todd La DN21 41 C4
Todds Cl
1 Swanland HU14 3 C6
18 Tetney DN36 36 D4
Todds Ct 26 DN17 29 D7
Todds La 1 DN15 8 A4
Todd's La HU15 2 A8
Todkill's La 7 PE12 160 F4
TOFT PE10 163 F8
Toft Cl PE24 115 D8
Toft Field La PE22 114 A3
TOFT HILL PE22 98 D5
Toft Hurn 1 PE22 98 F4
Toft La
17 Sleaford NG34 212 D4
Toft Newton LN8 56 E7
Toftland PE2 230 C5
TOFT NEXT NEWTON LN8 56 C7
Tofts Rd 10 DN18 10 E8
Toft Tunnel Nature Reserve* PE10 154 A1
Tolethorpe Hall* PE9 163 B1
Tolethorpe Sq 6 PE9 219 B6
TOLL BAR PE9 218 C8
Toll Bar Ave
6 Bottesford NG13 128 A6
New Waltham DN36 195 B6
Tollbar Rd
Great Gonerby NG32 129 B8
Marston NG32 118 C1
Toll Bar Rd
Croft PE24 103 D3
Grantham NG31 211 C3
Toll Bar Sec Sch DN36 195 A5
Tollemache Fields 9 NG33 151 D2
Tollemache Rd (North) NG31 139 F8
Tollemach Rd (South) NG31 139 F8
Tollesby La 33 DN7 14 D4
Tollfield Rd PE21 209 B7
Tollgate
Peterborough PE3 225 A5
Spalding PE11 214 C4
Toll House Rd PE2 230 C7
Toll's La PE12 215 E5
Tom La NG34 120 E5
Tomline Rd 5 DN41 23 A5
Tomline St DN31 189 B1
Tomlinson Ave 4 DN15 182 E3
Tomlinson Cl 3 LN4 207 A5
Tomlinson Way 5 NG34 108 E2
Tom Otter's La LN1 66 B1
Tonbridge 1 DN33 194 E8
Tonbridge Wlk DN33 194 E8
Toneham La PE6 175 F2
Tonglet Cl 3 PE25 206 C1
Tonnant Way DN34 190 D5
Tooley La PE22 114 C2
Tooley St
Boston PE21 209 A3
Gainsborough DN21 197 D3
Toothill Gdns DN34 190 F6
Toot La PE21 209 D4
Topaz Gr 3 HU3 180 A4
Topham Cres 13 PE6 176 A3
Top La
Goulceby LN11 72 C6
Kirk Bramwith DN7 14 A6
Topmoor Way PE4 221 D1
Top Rd
4 Croxton Kerrial NG32 138 D4
Little Cawthorpe LN11 61 E2
Osgodby LN8 45 A2
South Killingholme DN40 12 E3
Thorney NG23 78 F7
Winterton DN15 8 F6
Worlaby DN20 10 D1
Topsgate PE12 159 C7
Torbay Dr DN33 194 E6
Torchil Cl HU10 178 C6
Torfrida Dr PE10 213 B6
Torfrid Cl 14 PE6 166 F1
Torgate Ave LN5 92 F2
Torgate La LN5 93 A2
Torkington Gdns 9 PE9 219 B5
Torkington St PE9 219 A5
TORKSEY LN1 65 E5
Torksey Ave LN1 66 C2
Torksey Dr DN33 191 B3
Torksey Ferry Rd DN22 65 B5
TORKSEY LOCK LN1 65 E5
Torksey Pl 3 DN33 191 B3
Torksey St
14 Kirton in Lindsey DN21 30 B1
Rampton DN22 65 A5
Torold Dr PE7 230 D2
Tor-o-Moor Gdns 2 LN10 97 E6
Tor-o-Moor Rd 9 LN10 97 E6
Toronto St 2 LN2 202 C3
Torpel Way 5 PE6 173 C7
Torrington La
East Barkwith LN8 71 A8
Fleet PE12 159 B5
Legsby LN8 58 C1
Torrington Rd
Lincoln LN2 201 F8
Scunthorpe DN17 184 C8
Torrington St DN32 191 F5
Torr St DN21 197 D4
Torskey Castle* LN1 65 D5
Tortoiseshell Wood Nature Reserve* NG33 152 B2
Tossey La LN11 50 B2
Tothby Cl 1 LN13 75 E3
Tothby La LN13 75 E2
Tothby Mdws LN13 75 E3
TOTHILL LN11 62 E1
Tothill Cl LN6 204 F7
Totnes Rd DN33 194 E6
Tottermire La 5 DN9 27 D7
Touthill Cl PE1 226 A2
Towell Cl PE21 209 B3
Tower Ave
Bracebridge Heath LN4 205 F3
Lincoln LN2 202 D4
Tower Cl
9 Mablethorpe & Sutton LN12 64 B3
Woodhall Spa LN10 97 F7
Tower Cres LN2 202 D4
Tower Ct PE2 230 F8
Tower Dr
Lincoln LN2 202 D4
Woodhall Spa LN10 97 F7
Tower Espl PE25 206 D3
Tower Flats 4 LN2 202 D4
Tower Gdns
Boston PE21 209 A4
1 Lincoln LN2 202 D4
Tower Hill
Kingston upon Hull HU13 178 E1
Westwoodside DN9 27 B2
Tower Hill Dr HU13 178 E1
Tower Hill Mews 2 HU13 178 E1
Tower House La 7 HU12 5 F8
Tower La
Harmston LN4 94 B4
Spalding PE11 214 D3
Tower Rd PE21 209 A5
Tower Rd Prim Sch PE21 209 A6
Tower St
14 Boston PE21 208 F5
Gainsborough DN21 197 D5
1 Kingston Dock Village HU9 181 A5
Towers The 2 PE25 206 D5
Tower View
Kingston upon Hull HU10 178 C5
Sleaford NG34 212 B3
Tow La 5 NG32 117 F1
Towler St PE1 226 A3
Town Bridge 22 PE21 208 F5
Town Dam Dro PE11 144 F8
Town Dam La PE11 134 F2
Town Dro PE11 144 F8
Town End NG32 120 B2
Town Farm Cl 1 PE11 156 F8
Townfield La 5 PE20 135 C7
TOWNGATE PE6 164 F1
Towngate E PE6 217 C7
Towngate W PE6 217 A6
Town Hall Sq DN31 191 E7
Town Hall St 4 DN31 191 E7
Town Hill DN20 19 E4
Town Hill Dr DN20 19 E4
Towning Cl 9 PE6 217 D6
Townley Cl LN9 199 D1
Town Rd
Sleaford NG34 212 B1
Tetney DN36 36 D4
Townsend Cl DN36 193 C1
Townsend Rd 6 PE8 172 B1
Townsend Way LN4 95 C4
Townside DN40 12 D6
Town St
Cottam DN22 65 B6
Immingham DN40 12 E4
South Somercotes LN11 50 E4
Westborough & Dry Doddington NG23 117 F3
TOYNTON ALL SAINTS PE23 100 F6
Toynton All Saints Prim Sch PE23 100 F6
Toynton Cl 3 LN6 205 B4
TOYNTON FEN SIDE PE23 100 F5
Toynton La PE23 101 B6
Toynton Rd DN33 191 B3
TOYNTON ST PETER PE23 101 A6
Trader Bank
Frithville PE22 125 F8
Sibsey PE22 113 A2
Trafalgar Ave
Grimsby DN34 190 D5
Skegness PE25 206 D1
Trafalgar Ct 2 LN4 203 B2
Trafalgar Pk DN36 195 D7
Trafalgar Pl 3 PE21 208 E4
Trafalgar Sq
Long Sutton PE12 216 B4
4 Sutton on Trent NG23 91 A8
Trafalgar St 5 HU3 180 D7
Trafford Est PE14 170 F4
Trafford Pk 25 PE13 170 E1
Trafford Rd
Kingston upon Hull HU10 178 E8
13 Wisbech PE13 170 E1
Trafford St DN15 183 B4
Traffords Way DN20 30 F6
Train Gate 23 DN21 30 B1
Tramway Dr 21 LN12 76 F8
Tranby Ave HU13 178 D2
Tranby Croft HU10 178 C5
Tranby Dr DN32 192 B4
Tranby La
Anlaby with Anlaby Common HU10 178 B5
Swanland HU14 3 C6
Tranby Lodge Gdns HU13 178 C1
Tranby Mdws Pk HU13 178 C3
Tranby Ride HU10 178 C5
Tranmere Cl HU3 180 B5
Travellers Rest Cvn Site NG31 211 B1
Travis Ave 16 DN8 15 B8
Travis CE Fst Sch DN7 14 E4
Travis Cl 14 DN8 15 B8
Travis Gr 15 DN8 15 B8
Traviss Cl 2 DN16 185 B8
Treadgold Ave 10 NG31 129 E5
Treading Bank PE13 169 C4
Treasure La LN11 49 F5
Treece Gdns 10 DN18 3 F1
Tree Cl PE25 206 A5
Trefoil Dr PE25 103 C6
Trehampton Dr 4 DN21 53 A5
Trelawney Cres 2 LN1 201 E8
Tremayne Ave 1 HU15 2 C5
Trenchard Cl DN40 186 E5
Trenchard Rd
9 Ashby de la Launde & Bloxholm LN4 108 A7
3 Mablethorpe/Sutton on Sea LN12 64 B3
Trenchard Sq
2 Scampton Airfield LN1 67 F5
1 Waddington LN5 94 A7
Trent Ct 6 DN37 190 E8
Trentholme Dr 37 DN17 29 D7
Trent La
Beacon Hill NG24 104 A5
Besthorpe NG23 91 B7
Girton NG23 78 B1
Newton on Trent LN1 65 C1
South Clifton NG23 78 B5
Trenton Ave HU4 179 B6
Trent Port Rd DN21 65 D8
Trent Rd
Grantham NG31 210 D2
Keadby with Althorpe DN17 17 D6
Trentside
Gainsborough DN21 197 B8
Keadby with Althorpe DN17 17 C3
Trent Side DN17 7 F1
Trent St
Gainsborough DN21 197 D3
Scunthorpe DN16 183 B2
Trentvale Prep Sch DN17 17 D6
Trent View
Ermine LN1 201 D8
Keadby DN17 17 D5
5 Marton DN21 65 E8
Trent Wlk 13 HU15 2 D5
Tresham Rd PE2 229 D3
Trevitt Cl 1 NG34 212 B7
Trevor Cl 22 DN37 23 F1
Trevose Dr 2 LN6 205 A1
Triangle Dr 9 HU14 3 A4
Triangle The 13 HU14 3 A4
Trienna PE2 230 B5
Trinity Cl
10 Crowland PE6 166 E1
10 Goxhill DN19 12 A8
Trinity Ct 9 DN20 19 D4
Trinity Gr HU13 178 E2
Trinity House La 17 HU1 180 F6
Trinity La LN11 198 D6
Trinity Rd
Cleethorpes DN35 192 E5
Newark-on-Trent NG24 104 A2
Scunthorpe DN16 185 A4
Stamford PE9 219 A6
Wisbech PE13 170 E1
Trinity St
Boston PE21 208 E4
Gainsborough DN21 197 D3
14 Grimsby DN31 189 C1
Kingston upon Hull HU3 180 C7
3 Peterborough PE1 226 A2
Trinity Wlk 1 DN18 3 F1
Tritton Rd LN6 201 D2
Trollope St LN5 234 B1
Trollybus Mus at Sandtoft The* DN8 16 A3
Trondheim Way DN41 187 A2
Troon Cl
Grantham NG31 211 D8
7 Heighington/Washingborough LN4 203 D1
11 Stamford PE9 218 E6
Troon Rd DN7 14 D4
Trotters La 2 NG32 139 C7
Troughton Way 10 PE13 170 B2
Troutbeck Cl
6 Lincoln LN2 202 A8
1 Peterborough PE4 221 D3
Troutsdale Gr HU9 181 F8
Truesdale Gdns PE6 164 E3
Trunch La PE24 90 D5
Trundle La 2 DN7 14 D8
Trunkass La DN37 34 D7
Truro Cl
6 Grantham NG31 210 F5
5 Sleaford NG34 212 C7
Truro Dr LN6 204 B8
Truro Way 2 PE11 214 C4
TRUSTHORPE LN12 64 B2
Trusthorpe Rd 2 LN12 64 C1
Tuckers Nook PE6 173 C7
Tucker's Yd PE2 231 C7
Tudor Ave PE7 230 C1
Tudor Cl
Beacon Hill NG24 104 A4
23 Brough HU15 2 C5
Northorpe PE10 164 C7
Peterborough PE4 221 C2
4 Sutterton PE20 136 A2
1 Toft Newton LN8 56 D5
Tudor Cl (Doglands) LN8 56 C5
Tudor Dr
4 Boston PE21 208 E7
Gainsborough DN21 197 B8
Louth LN11 198 C4
Tudor La 24 HU15 2 C5
Tudor Pk LN9 199 D4
Tudor Pl PE6 217 E5
Tudor Rd LN6 204 D6
Tudor Way PE12 215 D1
Tudworth Field Rd DN7 15 B5
Tudworth Rd DN7 15 A5
Tulip Fields PE12 158 C7
Tulip Rd DN15 183 C3
Tulipwood Ave 11 LN6 200 C1
Tumby PE22 207 F8
Tumby La PE22 98 D2
Tumby Rd LN4 207 E6
TUMBY WOODSIDE PE22 111 F8
Tummel Ct DN40 186 B2
Tunnard St
Boston PE21 208 F6
Grimsby DN32 192 B8
Tunnel Bank PE10 213 F3
Tunnel Rd DN20 196 F7
Turbary Rd DN9 27 B6
Turf Moor Rd 4 DN7 15 A3
Turnberry App DN37 194 C4
Turnberry Cl 1 NG31 211 D7
Turnberry Dr 4 LN10 97 C6
Turnbury Cl LN6 204 B7
Turner Ave 3 LN6 205 A6
Turner Cl 2 LN5 107 B8
Turner Ct LN6 204 B8
Turner's La 17 HU14 3 A5
Turner St
15 Kirton in Lindsey DN21 30 B1
Lincoln LN1 234 A4
Turnor Cl 5 NG33 151 E6
Turnor Cres NG31 211 C5
Turnor Rd NG31 211 F4
Turnpike Cl
Great Gonerby NG31 210 D1
14 Wisbech PE13 170 E1
Turnpike Rd PE9 163 C2
Turnpole Cl 2 PE9 219 D7
Turnstone Way PE2 231 D7
Turpin Cl DN21 197 F5
Turves Rd PE6 175 A2
Tut Hole PE23 100 F7
Tuxhill Rd PE34 161 E1
Tweed Cl LN9 199 D2
Twelve Foot Bank LN4 109 F5
Twelvetree Ave PE4 220 E5
TWENTY PE10 155 C3
Twenty Dro PE10 155 C3
Twenty Foot Bank LN4 110 C6
Twitchell 4 LN1 66 D7
Two Plank La PE11 214 B6
Two Pole Dro PE7 231 F1
Two Sisters Cl 3 PE12 160 E4
Twyford Cl 2 NG33 151 E6
Twyford Gdns 3 PE1 226 D7
Twyning Pl DN35 192 D7
Tydd Low Rd
Long Sutton PE12 160 A3
Sutton Cross PE12 216 B1
Tydd Rd PE11 156 C6
TYDD ST GILES PE13 169 F7
Tydd St Giles Sch PE13 169 F6
TYDD ST MARY PE13 160 B1
Tydd St Mary CE (Aided) Prim Sch PE13 160 A1
Tydeman Cl DN16 185 A2
Tyesdale PE3 225 A4
Tye's Dro PE6 165 D2
Tyghes Cl PE6 217 F5
Tyler Ave DN31 191 A7
Tyler Cres 2 PE22 126 E3
Tylers Cl 30 PE24 90 D7
Tylers Mews PE4 220 F3
Tyndal Rd NG31 210 F5
Tyne Cl 4 LN6 205 A2
Tynedale Ct 5 DN3 14 A2
Tyne St HU3 180 B4
Tyne Way 7 DN37 190 E8
Tyrrell Pk PE1 226 D2
Tyson Cl NG31 211 C6
Tytton Cl 2 PE21 136 D8
Tytton La E PE21 136 D8
Tytton La W PE21 136 D8

U

UFFINGTON PE9 172 C6
Uffington Ave LN6 205 A6
Uffington CE (Cont) Prim Sch PE9 172 C6
Uffington Cl 10 LN6 205 A7
Uffington Rd
2 Barnack PE9 172 D4
Stamford PE9 219 E6
UFFORD PE9 172 F3
UK Coll DN31 191 B8
ULCEBY
Ulceby DN39 12 B1
Ulceby with Fordington LN13 88 C7
Ulceby Cross LN13 88 B8
Ulceby Rd
Scunthorpe DN17 184 D5
South Killingholme DN39 12 C2
Wootton DN39 11 F3
ULCEBY SKITTER DN39 12 C2
Ulceby Sta DN39 12 C2
Uldale Cl LN6 200 C2
Uldale Way PE4 221 D2
Ullswater Ave PE4 221 B2
Ullswater Cl 6 LN6 205 A2
Ulster Ave DN33 191 D2
Ulster Rd DN21 197 D6
Ulverston Rd HU4 179 A3
Ulyett La DN17 28 C8

Unicorn Row 10 DN21 ... 30 B1
Union Pl 1 PE21 ... 208 F5
Union Rd
Lincoln LN1 ... 234 A3
Thorne/Moorends DN8 ... 15 A8
Union St
2 Boston PE21 ... 208 F5
Grantham NG31 ... 211 A5
Holbeach PE12 ... 159 A7
Louth LN11 ... 198 B6
14 Market Rasen LN8 ... 57 D8
Unity Ave HU13 ... 178 F1
Unity Rd DN32 ... 192 C6
Unity Sq 5 LN2 ... 234 B2
University Ct 2 NG31 ... 211 B3
University of Lincoln Brayford (Main Campus) LN6 ... 234 A2
University of Lincoln Derek Crothall Building HU1 ... 180 E6
University of Lincoln Holbeach Campus PE12 ... 215 D4
University of Lincoln Riseholme Campus LN2 ... 68 A2
Upgate LN11 ... 198 B5
Upland Cl LN9 ... 199 A5
Uplands PE4 ... 221 A5
Uplands Dr NG31 ... 211 D6
Upper Burgess St 2 DN31 ... 191 E8
Upper Cl The 8 LN1 ... 66 D7
Upper Ings La DN22 ... 52 D2
Upper Kenyon St 9 DN8 ... 15 A8
Upper Lindum St LN2 ... 234 C3
Upper Long Leys Rd LN1 ... 234 A4
Upper Row NG22 ... 65 A1
Upper Saxon St LN1 ... 234 A4
UPPERTHORPE DN9 ... 27 B3
Upperthorpe Hill DN9 ... 27 A2
Uppingham Rd 6 LN12 ... 64 C1
Upsall Rd 9 PE22 ... 126 E3
UPTON
Upton DN21 ... 53 E5
Upton PE6 ... 223 B6
Upton Cl
Peterborough PE2 ... 231 E5
Peterborough PE3 ... 225 A2
Upton Rd DN21 ... 53 B4
Upton Wlk DN21 ... 197 F3
Urban St LN5 ... 205 D6
Uredale Pl DN16 ... 185 E5
Usher Gall* LN2 ... 234 B3
Usher Gn
4 Lincoln LN6 ... 205 B6
3 Lincoln LN6 ... 205 B7
Usher Jun Sch The LN6 ... 205 B7
USSELBY LN8 ... 45 C4
Utgard Way 4 DN33 ... 191 B2
UTTERBY LN11 ... 48 F4
Utterby Dr DN34 ... 191 C5
Utterby Prim Sch DN36 ... 48 E5

V

Vacherie La LN4 ... 109 F3
Vagarth Cl 15 DN18 ... 3 E1
Valda Vale DN40 ... 186 A4
Vale Ct PE23 ... 101 A8
Vale Dr
Hampton Vale PE7 ... 230 C1
Yaxley PE7 ... 233 D8
Valence Rd PE2 ... 229 F4
Valentine Cl
Boston PE21 ... 209 C3
1 Kingston upon Hull HU4 ... 179 A2
Valentine Rd LN6 ... 201 C1
Vale of Ancholme Sch DN20 ... 196 B4
Vale Rd
Gonerby Hill Foot NG31 ... 210 F8
10 Spilsby PE23 ... 101 A8
Vale The HU10 ... 178 B7
Vale View NG23 ... 117 F5
Vale Wood DN16 ... 185 C3
Valiant Rd
8 Coddington NG24 ... 104 C5
Manby LN11 ... 62 C5
Valletta St HU9 ... 5 E8
Valley Dr HU10 ... 178 B7
Valley La
Long Bennington NG23 ... 117 B4
Swaby LN13 ... 74 E4
Valley Pk View PE2 ... 230 D8
Valley Rd
Grantham NG31 ... 210 C4
1 Waddington LN5 ... 93 E8
Valley View 8 NG24 ... 104 D5
Valley View Dr DN16 ... 185 A2
Valliant St 7 LN5 ... 94 A7
Vampire Rd LN11 ... 62 C5
Vancouver Cres DN17 ... 184 E4
Vanessa Dr DN21 ... 197 C7
Vanessa Rd LN11 ... 198 A4
Vane St HU3 ... 180 D7
Van Gogh Dr 8 PE11 ... 214 B3
Vanguard Ct 4 NG34 ... 212 A3
Vanwall Dr 8 LN5 ... 93 F7
Varah Cl 39 DN18 ... 10 E8
Varlow Rd 8 LN7 ... 33 B4
Varsity Cl 4 DN7 ... 26 A8
Vasey Cl LN1 ... 66 E2
Vaughan Ave
Bottesford NG13 ... 128 B6
Grimsby DN36 ... 192 B4
Vauxhall Rd
12 Boston PE21 ... 209 A5
Bracebridge Heath LN4 ... 205 F2
Veall Ct LN4 ... 207 C4
Veal St DN31 ... 191 C7
Velden Way 5 LN8 ... 57 D7
Venables Cl 13 PE24 ... 102 E7
Venables Way LN2 ... 202 D6
Vence Cl 1 PE9 ... 219 A5
Venom Rd LN11 ... 62 C5
Ventnor Ave NG31 ... 210 E4
Ventura Bsns Pk DN31 ... 188 D2
Venture Way NG31 ... 210 D2
Verdun Cl LN1 ... 201 E7
Vere Rd PE1 ... 225 F7
Vere St LN1 ... 201 F6
Vere Terr DN31 ... 191 C8
Vergette Rd PE6 ... 220 D8
Vergette St PE1 ... 226 B3
Vermont Gr PE3 ... 225 E1
Vermuyden Villas DN8 ... 16 A3
Vernatts Gn PE11 ... 214 C7
Vernon Ave NG31 ... 210 F8
Vernon Rd PE25 ... 206 C4
Vernon St LN5 ... 201 D1
Vicarage Ave 2 DN20 ... 196 F6
Vicarage Cl
5 Collingham NG23 ... 91 D5
4 Cowbit PE12 ... 167 B8
Holbeach PE12 ... 158 D1
Vicarage Cres 4 DN15 ... 8 B5
Vicarage Ct 18 NG34 ... 212 D4
Vicarage Dr LN6 ... 200 B3
Vicarage Dro PE20 ... 134 D5
Vicarage Farm Rd 5 PE1 ... 226 D3
Vicarage Gdns
2 Brough HU15 ... 2 C6
5 Littlefield DN34 ... 191 C6
Scunthorpe DN15 ... 182 F2
1 Wrawby DN20 ... 20 E3
Vicarage La
Beckingham DN10 ... 40 B1
Broughton DN20 ... 19 E1
Cadney DN20 ... 31 D6
3 Carlton-le-Moorland LN5 ... 105 E8
Dunston LN4 ... 95 C6
Elsham DN20 ... 20 F7
Grasby DN38 ... 32 E7
Harmston LN5 ... 93 F5
1 Helpringham NG34 ... 133 D7
1 Immingham DN40 ... 12 E4
3 Kingston upon Hull HU13 ... 178 E1
4 Long Bennington NG23 ... 117 D3
Long Sutton PE12 ... 216 D2
11 Lutton PE12 ... 160 A8
21 Nettleham LN2 ... 68 C2
1 Scawby DN20 ... 30 E8
Scopwick LN4 ... 95 C1
9 Scothern LN2 ... 68 F4
4 Sibsey PE22 ... 113 B1
South Clifton NG23 ... 78 C5
Wainfleet All Saints PE24 ... 102 D1
19 Wellingore LN5 ... 107 A7
Wootton DN39 ... 11 E3
Vicarage Lawn DN34 ... 191 C6
Vicarage Pk 4 DN15 ... 9 D1
Vicarage Rd
3 Heckington NG34 ... 122 E3
Willoughton DN21 ... 42 E4
Wrawby DN20 ... 196 F6
Vicarage Way PE7 ... 233 D5
Vicar La 2 HU1 ... 180 F5
Vicars Ct LN2 ... 234 B3
Vicar's Wlk 6 DN17 ... 16 D7
Viceroy Dr PE11 ... 156 F8
Vickers La 4 LN11 ... 198 B5
Victor Dr 1 LN6 ... 204 C1
Victoria Ave
1 Hatfield DN7 ... 14 E4
Sleaford NG34 ... 212 C3
1 Woodhall Spa LN10 ... 97 D5
Victoria Bank NG34 ... 133 B1
Victoria Cl
Gainsborough DN21 ... 197 F2
2 Marshchapel DN36 ... 37 C2
2 Stainforth DN7 ... 14 C5
Wike Well End DN8 ... 15 B7
Victoria Ct 5 DN15 ... 8 B5
Victoria Dock Prim Sch HU9 ... 181 B6
VICTORIA DOCK VILLAGE HU9 ... 181 C5
Victoria Dr 5 DN18 ... 3 E1
Victoria Gr
Heighington/Washingborough LN4 ... 203 D1
Morton PE10 ... 154 D7
Victoria Mews 18 PE11 ... 214 D4
Victoria Pas LN1 ... 234 A3
Victoria Pier* HU1 ... 181 A5
Victoria Pl
8 Boston PE21 ... 208 F4
3 Bourne PE10 ... 213 E4
Peterborough PE1 ... 225 F4
Victoria Rd
Barnetby le Wold DN38 ... 21 B4
10 Keelby DN41 ... 23 A5
Louth LN11 ... 198 C7
Mablethorpe/Sutton on Sea LN12 ... 64 B3
2 Market Rasen LN8 ... 57 E8
Scunthorpe DN16 ... 185 A5
Skegness PE25 ... 206 B3
Stamford PE9 ... 219 B6
Victoria Ret Pk DN31 ... 189 A1
Victoria St N DN31 ... 189 A1
Victoria St S 4 DN31 ... 191 E7
Victoria St W DN31 ... 191 E7
Victoria St
Billingborough NG34 ... 133 B1
3 Billinghay LN4 ... 109 F6
Grantham NG31 ... 211 A2
4 Holbeach PE12 ... 215 E2
Kingston upon Hull HU13 ... 179 A1
Lincoln LN1 ... 234 A3
Peterborough PE1 ... 226 A5
Peterborough PE2 ... 230 F6
10 Spalding PE11 ... 214 D4
3 Wragby LN8 ... 70 D5
Victoria Terr LN1 ... 234 A3
Victoria Way DN31 ... 188 D2
Victor St
Grimsby DN32 ... 189 C1
Kingston upon Hull HU9 ... 181 C8
Victor Way
Bourne PE10 ... 213 E3
10 Waddington LN5 ... 94 A7
Victory Cl 6 PE12 ... 157 F6
Victory Ct 1 PE11 ... 214 C3
Victory Way
2 Barton-upon-Humber DN18 ... 3 F1
8 Grimsby DN34 ... 190 D4
6 Sleaford NG34 ... 212 A3
Viersen Platz PE1 ... 226 A1
Vigo Cl LN1 ... 201 C7
Viking Cl
6 Bourne PE10 ... 213 C6
Immingham DN40 ... 186 A4
7 Swineshead PE20 ... 135 B7
11 Waddington LN5 ... 93 F7
Viking Sch The PE25 ... 206 B4
Viking Way
32 Metheringham LN4 ... 95 C3
7 Northorpe PE10 ... 164 C8
Spalding PE11 ... 214 F2
Villa Cl PE12 ... 216 A5
Village Farm Dr 5 LN1 ... 66 C7
Village St
Burton Coggles NG33 ... 152 C8
Easton NG33 ... 139 F2
Pickworth NG34 ... 142 A8
Sedgebrook NG32 ... 128 F4
Woolsthorpe by Belvoir NG32 ... 128 D1
Village The PE2 ... 230 B5
Villa La PE20 ... 135 B7
Ville Rd DN16 ... 185 D6
Vincent Cl 3 HU4 ... 179 A2
Vincent Rd DN33 ... 191 B2
Vine Cl 13 NG13 ... 128 A5
Vine Cres 8 PE21 ... 136 D8
Vine Ct 3 NG34 ... 133 B1
Vinegarth 3 DN9 ... 27 E6
Vinehall Rd 3 DN9 ... 27 C2
Vine Rd 2 PE25 ... 103 E4
Vine St
Billingborough NG34 ... 133 C1
12 Grantham NG31 ... 211 A5
Lincoln LN2 ... 234 C2
Spalding PE11 ... 214 D4
Stamford PE9 ... 219 C5
Vine Wlk PE3 ... 225 B4
Vineyard Rd PE1 ... 226 B2
Viney Cl PE1 ... 226 D5
Vinters Way PE22 ... 126 E3
Vintners Cl PE3 ... 225 D3
Violet Cl
4 Humberston DN35 ... 192 E1
9 Morton PE10 ... 154 D6
Virginia Cl 1 PE3 ... 225 A2
Virginia Dr LN11 ... 198 E5
Viscount Rd PE2 ... 231 A6
Viscount Way 6 DN36 ... 36 D8
Vista The 3 PE11 ... 214 D3
Visual Arts Ctr* DN15 ... 183 C3
Vivian Ave DN32 ... 192 B5
Vivian Cl 1 NG31 ... 210 F8
Vixen Cl PE7 ... 233 F6
Voases Cl HU10 ... 178 E6
Voases La HU10 ... 178 E6
Vokes St PE2 ... 230 D8
Vulcan Cres LN6 ... 204 C2
Vulcan Dr 4 LN11 ... 67 F5
Vulcan St 9 LN5 ... 94 A7
Vulcan Way DN7 ... 15 A1
Vyner Cl 18 LN12 ... 64 B3

W

Waby Cl DN37 ... 190 D7
WADDINGHAM DN21 ... 43 D7
Waddingham Pl
5 Habrough DN40 ... 22 E8
New Waltham DN36 ... 195 D5
Waddingham Prim Sch DN21 ... 43 D7
Waddingham Rd LN7 ... 31 F1
WADDINGTON LN5 ... 93 F7
Waddington Dr 1 DN17 ... 184 E3
Waddington La NG23 ... 91 C7
Waddington Pl 4 DN34 ... 191 A5
Waddington Redwood Cty Prim Sch LN5 ... 93 E8
WADDINGWORTH LN10 ... 84 C6
Waddingworth Gr LN2 ... 202 A8
Wade Pk Ave PE6 ... 217 C4
Waggoners Cl 11 DN21 ... 29 C4
Waggoners Way PE10 ... 154 C6
Waggoners Wlk PE22 ... 113 B1
Waggons Way 4 DN7 ... 14 C5
Waincroft Cl PE24 ... 102 E2
Wainer Cl LN6 ... 204 C5
WAINFLEET ALL SAINTS PE24 ... 102 D2
WAINFLEET BANK PE24 ... 102 B1
Wainfleet Rd
Boston PE21 ... 209 D7
Croft PE24 ... 102 D7
Firsby PE23 ... 101 F6
Fishtoft PE21 ... 209 D7
Grimsby DN33 ... 191 B3
Irby in the Marsh PE24 ... 102 B6
Skegness PE25 ... 206 A3
Thorpe St Peter PE24 ... 102 C3
Wainfleet Rd Industrial Est PE25 ... 206 A2
WAINFLEET ST MARY PE24 ... 115 E8
Wainfleet Sta PE24 ... 102 D1
WAINFLEET TOFTS PE24 ... 115 C8
Wainman Rd PE2 ... 230 D5
Wainwell Mews 3 LN2 ... 234 C3
Wainwright PE4 ... 220 E5
WAITHE DN36 ... 36 A3
Waithe La DN37 ... 35 E4
Wakefield Ave DN21 ... 29 D4
Wakefield Cl NG31 ... 210 C4
Wake Rd PE1 ... 226 B2
Wakerley Dr PE2 ... 230 C7
Wakerley Rd 6 DN21 ... 29 C3
Wakes Cl 1 PE10 ... 213 E4
Wake St LN1 ... 234 A4
Walbury Cl 4 LN5 ... 205 D2
WALCOT
Alkborough DN15 ... 8 B8
Walcot Near Folkingham NG34 ... 132 C1
Walcot Bar NG34 ... 132 D2
Walcot Cl LN6 ... 204 F6
Walcot La NG34 ... 142 C8
Walcot Rd
Alkborough DN15 ... 8 B8
Ufford PE9 ... 172 F3
WALCOTT LN4 ... 109 D7
Walcott Prim Sch LN4 ... 109 C7
Walcott Rd LN4 ... 109 E6
Walcott St HU3 ... 180 C4
Walcot Way 2 PE9 ... 218 E6
Walcot Wlk PE3 ... 225 B3
Waldeck St LN1 ... 234 A4
Walden Gdns 1 PE21 ... 208 E4
Waldo Rd LN4 ... 205 F5
Waldorf Rd DN35 ... 193 A1
Waldo Way DN15 ... 8 C1
WALESBY LN8 ... 46 A3
Walesby Cl DN33 ... 194 D8
Walesby Hill LN8 ... 46 B3
Walesby La LN8 ... 46 B2
Walesby Rd
Market Rasen LN8 ... 57 E8
Middle Rasen LN8 ... 45 E1
Scunthorpe DN17 ... 184 E4
Walford Cl 2 NG13 ... 128 A5
Walford Dr LN6 ... 205 A6
Walgrave PE2 ... 230 B4
Walker Ave DN33 ... 194 F8
Walker Cl 1 DN15 ... 8 E7
Walker Dr 4 DN15 ... 9 A5
Walkergate 14 LN11 ... 198 B5
WALKERINGHAM DN10 ... 39 F3
Walkeringham Nature Reserve* DN10 ... 39 E3
Walkeringham Prim Sch DN10 ... 39 F3
Walkeringham Rd
Beckingham DN10 ... 40 A2
Gringley on the Hill DN10 ... 39 D2
WALKERITH DN21 ... 40 B4
Walkerith Rd
East Stockwith DN21 ... 40 B5
Gainsborough DN21 ... 197 B8
Morton DN21 ... 40 D3
Walker Rd PE6 ... 220 D7
Walkers Cl
4 Bottesford NG13 ... 128 B5
Scunthorpe DN15 ... 183 B3
Walker's Cl 5 DN38 ... 21 B4
Walkers Ct 20 DN17 ... 29 D7
Walker St HU3 ... 180 C5
Walkers Way
Barrowby NG32 ... 210 A3
Peterborough PE3 ... 224 F3
Ulceby DN39 ... 12 B2
Walkington Way 18 LN12 ... 77 A7
Walk La
Humberston DN36 ... 36 C7
Irby DN37 ... 34 D7
Langton by Wragby LN8 ... 70 F4
Walks Rd NG34 ... 120 F1
Walks The 4 PE9 ... 171 B1
Walk The DN21 ... 197 F3
Wallace's Dro PE6 ... 176 D4
Walled Gdn The 5 LN5 ... 93 F5
Waller St HU9 ... 181 C8
Walliker St HU3 ... 180 A6
Wallingfen La HU15 ... 1 B8
Wallis Ave LN6 ... 205 B4
Wallis Ct DN33 ... 191 B2
Wallisgate PE12 ... 158 C7
Wallis Rd LN11 ... 198 D5
Walls Ave 5 PE24 ... 102 E7
Wall's La PE25 ... 90 E2
Wall St
Gainsborough DN21 ... 197 D3
Grimsby DN34 ... 191 A7
Walmer St 1 LN2 ... 202 C3
Walmsgate DN34 ... 191 B4
WALMSGATE LN11 ... 74 C5
Walmsgate Gdns DN33 ... 191 B4
Walmsgate Pl 3 DN33 ... 191 B4
Walmsgate Wlk DN33 ... 191 B4
Walmsley St HU3 ... 180 D7
Walnut Cl
5 Newborough PE6 ... 174 E4
14 Ruskington NG34 ... 108 E2
2 Waddington LN5 ... 93 E8
Walnut Cres DN35 ... 192 D2
Walnut Dr 1 DN20 ... 30 F7
Walnutgarth 6 NG34 ... 212 F3
Walnut Gr 3 NG33 ... 151 E7
Walnut Pl LN5 ... 234 B1
Walnut Rd
3 Bottesford NG13 ... 128 A5
Kirton PE20 ... 136 C6
Walnut Way DN17 ... 29 C7
Walpole Bank PE14 ... 170 F7
WALPOLE CROSS KEYS PE34 ... 161 C3
WALPOLE MARSH PE14 ... 170 F8
Walsall Garth HU4 ... 179 B4
Walsham Rd PE7 ... 233 D8
Walsh Gdns 7 DN33 ... 191 B2
Walsingham Ct 3 PE13 ... 170 C1
Walsingham Dr NG33 ... 152 F7
Walsingham Way 13 PE6 ... 175 A1
WALSOKEN PE13 ... 170 E1
WALTHAM DN37 ... 194 D5
Waltham Cl
9 Birchwood LN6 ... 204 C6
2 Dogsthorpe PE1 ... 226 D8
Waltham Grange 5 DN35 ... 192 F3
Waltham Mus of Rural Life* DN37 ... 194 D3
Waltham Rd
Barnoldby le Beck DN37 ... 194 A3
Birchwood LN6 ... 204 B6
Brigsley DN37 ... 194 C1
Croxton Kerrial NG32 ... 138 A4
Grimsby DN33 ... 194 F8
Waltham St 1 HU1 ... 180 F6
Waltham Windmill* DN37 ... 194 E3
WALTON PE4 ... 221 A1
Walton Com Sch PE4 ... 221 A2
Walton Gdns NG31 ... 211 A2
Walton Girls High Sch The NG31 ... 210 F1
Walton Gr DN33 ... 191 C4
Walton Heath Cl 2 NG31 ... 211 D7
WALTON HIGHWAY PE14 ... 170 F3
Walton Infants Sch PE4 ... 221 A1
Walton Jun Sch PE4 ... 221 A1
Walton Pk PE4 ... 221 A1
Walton Rd
7 Leverington PE13 ... 170 B2
Marholm PE6 ... 220 C1
Wisbech PE13 ... 170 E1
Walton St Leisure Ctr HU3 ... 180 A6
Walton St HU3 ... 180 A7
Walton Way 4 NG32 ... 139 C7
Wandell's View HU15 ... 2 C8
Wansbeck Rd 8 NG34 ... 121 B7
WANSFORD PE8 ... 222 A4
Wansford Rd PE8 ... 222 A3
Wanton La PE34 ... 161 F3
Wanton's Cross Gate PE12 ... 159 D2
Wanton's La PE12 ... 159 E2
Wapping La 4 DN21 ... 65 E8
Warbon Ave PE1 ... 225 F7
Warburton Ct DN32 ... 191 F7
Wardall St DN35 ... 192 F6
Ward Cl PE1 ... 226 B3
Ward Cres PE21 ... 209 E4
Wardentree La PE11 ... 157 A8
Wardour Dr NG31 ... 211 F5
Ward's La PE22 ... 114 A3
Ward St DN35 ... 192 C8
Wareley Rd PE2 ... 225 F1
Wares Way DN15 ... 182 B3
WARGATE PE11 ... 145 B5
Wargate Field La PE11 ... 145 C5
Wargate Way PE11 ... 145 B6
Waring St LN9 ... 199 B3
Warley Ave 1 DN16 ... 185 C8
Warley Dr DN16 ... 185 C8
Warley Rd DN16 ... 185 C7
Warneford Gdns HU5 ... 180 A8
Warneford Rd DN35 ... 192 D8

Warping Way DN15 ..... 182 B3
Warren Cl DN21 .... 197 B6
Warren Ct PE7.......... 230 C2
Warrendale 12 DN18 ..... 10 E8
Warren Farm Cl DN40 .... 12 D7
Warren La LN6........... 92 D4
Warrenne Cl 21 DN7 ..... 14 D4
Warrenne Keep 8
PE9 .... 219 B4
Warrenne Rd DN7 .... 14 D4
Warren Rd
North Somercotes LN11 ... 51 A6
Scunthorpe DN15 .... 183 B5
5 Thorne/Moorends
DN8.................. 15 B7
Wothorpe PE9 .... 219 C1
Warren Way NG31 ...... 211 F7
Warth La PE25.......... 206 A5
Warwick Ave DN33...... 191 A4
Warwick Cl
9 Grantham NG31...... 210 D5
4 Hatfield DN7.......... 14 F3
2 Saxilby with Ingleby
LN1................... 66 C2
Warwick Dr 24 DN18 ..... 10 E8
Warwick Rd
7 Chapel St Leonard
PE24.................. 90 D7
Cleethorpes DN35....... 192 D4
Louth LN11 .... 198 B8
Newark-on-Trent NG24 ... 104 B2
Peterborough PE4 .... 221 A2
Scunthorpe DN16 .... 183 C1
Warwick St HU9 .... 181 B7
Wascana Cl HU4 .... 179 B3
Wasdale Cl 2 LN6 ...... 200 C1
Wasdale Gdns 1 PE4 ... 221 E2
Wash Bank PE12........ 167 A5
Washdike Dro PE11 ..... 135 C1
Washdike La
Croft PE24............. 102 E4
Donington PE11......... 135 A1
Stoke Rochford NG33 .... 140 A3
Toynton St Peter PE23.... 101 B6
Wainfleet St Mary PE24 .. 102 C1
Wash Dike La PE22...... 115 A6
Washdike Rd
Algarkirk PE20.......... 136 B1
Kirton PE20 .... 136 A6
Washdyke La
Belton & Manthorpe
NG32.................. 130 A6
Boston PE21 .... 208 B7
Cumberworth LN13 .... 89 E8
Elsham DN20............ 20 D6
2 Glentham LN8.......... 43 F1
Immingham DN40 .... 186 B5
Leasingham NG34 .... 121 B7
Mumby LN13 .... 76 F1
Nettleham LN2........... 68 B2
Old Leake PE22 .... 113 F4
Osgodby LN8 .... 45 A3
Washdyke Rd 7 NG32... 106 C1
Washdyke Ret Pk
DN40.................. 186 C4
WASHINGBOROUGH
LN4 .... 203 D2
Washingborough Prim Sch
LN4.................. 203 C2
Washingborough Rd
Heighington/
Washingborough LN4 .... 81 E4
Lincoln LN4 .... 202 D1
Washinghall La DN17 ..... 7 A2
Washington Cl 6 LN4... 207 C4
Washington Dr 5 LN8 ... 56 D5
Washington St 4
DN21 .... 197 D2
Wash National Nature
Reserve The★ PE12 .... 149 C2
Wash Rd
Fosdyke PE20 .... 146 D7
Kirton PE20 .... 136 D4
Washtub La NG23 .... 91 E6
Washway Rd
Fleet PE12 .... 159 B8
Holbeach PE12 .... 215 C6
Moulton PE12 .... 146 F4
WASPS NEST LN4......... 95 E7
Wassand St HU3 .... 180 C4
Wass La LN8............. 71 E5
Waste Gn La PE20....... 146 C7
Water Bank DN9 .... 26 E5
Waterbelly La PE20 ..... 136 A1
Water End
Marholm PE6........... 220 B1
Peterborough PE7 .... 229 A5
Waterfall Gdns 2 PE6 .. 174 E4
Waterford La LN3....... 203 D5
Waterfront The PE21.... 208 F3
Waterfurlong PE9....... 219 A4
Watergall 1 PE3 .... 220 F1
Watergall Prim Sch
PE3................... 225 B8
Watergate
11 Grantham NG31...... 211 A5
10 Stamford PE9........ 219 C5
Water Gate
Quadring PE11.......... 145 B8
Sleaford NG34.......... 212 D4
Water Hill LN3.......... 82 B7
Waterhouse La HU1..... 180 E5
Watering Dyke Houses
LN2 .... 67 F4
Water La
1 Ancaster NG32....... 120 A2
Bourne PE10 .... 213 D2
Castle Bytham NG33 ..... 152 D1
Water La *continued*
Castor PE5............. 223 F1
6 Colsterworth NG33 ... 151 D7
Gunby & Stainby NG33 ... 151 B5
5 Hagworthingham PE23.. 87 A4
Lincoln LN1 .... 234 A2
4 Lincoln LN6........... 93 C8
1 Long Bennington
NG23.................. 117 D4
12 South Witham NG33... 151 D2
4 Spalding PE11 .... 214 D2
Threekingham NG34 ..... 132 F3
Thurlby LN5 .... 92 E3
Thurlby PE10 .... 164 C8
2 West Halton DN15 ...... 8 E7
Waterlees Rd PE13...... 170 D1
Water Lilly Way PE10.... 213 D3
Waterloo Cl 1 NG32 .... 119 B7
Waterloo Dr
4 Grimsby DN33 .... 191 B2
2 Morton PE10 .... 154 D6
Waterloo La LN6........ 200 B3
Waterloo Paddock
LN5 .... 106 D3
Waterloo Rd
Mablethorpe/Sutton on Sea
LN12................... 64 B4
Peterborough PE1 .... 226 A5
Waterloo St
Kingston upon Hull
HU2................... 180 E8
Lincoln LN6 .... 201 D2
4 Market Rasen LN8 ..... 57 D8
Waterlow Dr 22 DN15 ..... 9 A5
Watermill La 18 LN2 ..... 68 C2
Water Mill La PE23..... 100 F6
Water Mill Rd LN9 ..... 199 B4
WATER NEWTON PE8..... 228 C7
Waters Edge DN20 ...... 196 A3
Waters' Edge Ctry Pk★
DN18..................... 3 F2
Waterside 5 LN4 .... 109 F5
WATERSIDE DN8.......... 14 E8
Waterside
3 Ryhall PE9 .... 163 C1
Thorne DN8 .... 14 F8
Water Side DN15........... 2 B1
Waterside Bsns Pk HU13 ... 3 F4
Waterside Cl 10 PE10... 213 C7
Waterside Dr 4 DN31... 191 D8
Waterside Gdns 5
PE12 .... 215 E2
Waterside N LN5........ 234 B2
Waterside Rd DN18 .... 3 E2
Waterside S LN5........ 234 B2
Waterside Sh Ctr LN2... 234 B2
Waterslade Rd PE7 ..... 233 C4
Water St PE9 .... 219 C4
Waterton Cl 2 PE6 ..... 217 E4
Waterton La DN7 .... 14 D2
Waterwell La NG32...... 120 C4
Waterworks La PE6 ..... 220 B6
Waterworks St
1 Gainsborough
DN21.................. 197 D2
Immingham DN40 .... 186 D5
Watery La
Asterby LN11............ 72 F5
Butterwick PE22 .... 126 F3
Goulceby LN11........... 72 D6
Lissington LN3........... 57 D1
Little Cawthorpe LN11..... 61 E2
Mareham le Fen PE22..... 98 F4
Swaby LN13.............. 74 E4
4 Welton/Dunholme LN2.. 68 E6
1 West Ashby LN9........ 85 E7
Wickenby LN3 .... 70 A8
Watford Ave DN34 ...... 190 F4
Watkin St N DN31....... 188 F1
Watkin St S 2 DN31 .... 188 F1
Watkins La 2 DN22...... 52 B3
Watling Cl
7 Bourne PE10 .... 213 C6
8 Bracebridge Heath
LN4.................... 81 A1
Watson Pk 4 DN10 ...... 52 B8
Watsons Croft 5 DN7..... 14 D6
Watt Cl PE4 .... 221 C2
Watts La LN11 .... 198 C4
Wauldby Cl 4 HU10...... 178 E7
Wauldby View 2 HU14..... 3 B7
Waumsley Way 1 LN13 .. 75 E2
Wavell Dr LN2 .... 202 E4
Waveney Cl 1 DN15 .... 8 B5
Waveney Gr PE4 .... 221 C2
Waverley Ave LN6....... 204 F3
Waverley Gdns
3 Leverington PE13..... 170 B1
Stamford PE9........... 218 F6
Waverley Pl 3 PE9 ..... 218 F6
Waverley St HU1....... 180 E5
Waverly Cl PE10 .... 154 D7
Wayet Rd 6 PE11....... 156 E8
Wayford Cl PE3 .... 225 A2
Wayside Cl
5 Holton le Clay
DN36.................. 195 D2
Scunthorpe DN16 .... 185 A3
Wayside Dr DN36 .... 195 C7
Weatherthorn PE2 ...... 230 C5
Weaver Rd LN6 .... 204 B5
Weavers Croft 11 DN9.... 27 A2
Webb Cl 36 DN18 .... 10 E8
Webb St LN5 .... 205 D8
Webster Ave DN15 ...... 182 E3
Webster Cl 3 LN6 ...... 205 A5
Websters Cl PE6 .... 220 D8
Webster Way NG31 ..... 210 E7
Wedgewood Cl 10 LN6 .. 204 D7
Wedgewood Dr 4
PE11 .... 214 B5
Wedgewood Gr 9
LN6 .... 204 D7
Wedgewood Rd LN6 .... 204 D7
Wedland La PE24 .... 102 D3
WEECAR NG23 .... 78 D1
Weedon Cl PE4 .... 221 D2
Weekes Rd DN35........ 192 F4
WEELSBY DN32.......... 192 A5
Weelsby Ave DN32 ...... 191 F4
Weelsby Gr DN32 .... 191 E4
Weelsby Prim Sch
DN32.................. 192 A8
Weelsby Rd DN32 ...... 191 D5
Weelsby St S DN32...... 192 A7
Weelsby St
15 Grimsby DN31 .... 189 C1
Grimsby DN32.......... 192 A8
Weelsby View DN36..... 195 D8
Weelsby Way HU13 ..... 178 C2
Weeping Elm Way 6
DN16 .... 185 D4
Weeton Way 5 HU10 ... 178 E7
Wegberg Rd LN4......... 95 C7
Weir Cl 3 DN9 .... 27 A2
Weir Farm 3 LN2......... 68 F4
Weir Rd DN9 .... 27 A2
Weirs La PE22 .... 126 D4
Weir St LN5 .... 205 D8
Weir The HU13 .... 178 E1
Welbeck Dr PE11 .... 214 C5
Welbeck Pl 3 DN34..... 190 E4
Welbeck Rd DN35....... 192 C5
Welbeck St HU5 .... 180 B8
Welbeck Way
Louth LN11 .... 198 B6
Peterborough PE2....... 230 D7
WELBOURN LN5 .... 106 F5
Welbourn CE (Cont) Prim
Sch LN5............... 106 E5
Welbourne PE4......... 221 A4
Welbourne La PE12 ..... 215 C4
Welbourne La E PE12 ... 215 C4
Welbourne's Cl 6
NG23.................. 117 D4
Welbourne's La 7
NG23.................. 117 D4
Welbourn Gdns 9
LN2 .... 202 A8
Welbourn Prim Sch
PE4................... 221 A4
Welbourn Rd LN5 ...... 106 A5
Welbourn Wlk HU4 ..... 179 B6
WELBY NG32............ 130 F5
Welby Cl NG34......... 212 B4
Welby Dr 3 PE11 ...... 145 B6
Welby-Everard Ct
NG31 .... 211 B4
Welby Gdns
Grantham NG31......... 211 A6
Holbeach PE12 .... 215 B2
Welby St 6 NG31 ...... 211 A4
Weldon Rd DN21......... 42 E1
Wel Fen La NG23....... 117 E8
Welham St NG31........ 211 B4
Welholme Ave DN32 .... 191 D5
Welholme Jun & Inf Sch
DN32.................. 191 F6
Welholme Rd DN32 ..... 191 E6
WELL LN13.............. 88 E8
Welland Ave DN34 ...... 190 F4
Welland Bank PE6 ...... 166 C1
Welland Cl
Peterborough PE1 .... 226 A7
9 Ruskington NG34 ..... 108 D2
1 Spalding PE11 .... 214 C2
Welland Ct 3 NG31 .... 210 E2
Welland Dr 2 DN15........ 8 B7
Welland Hospl PE11..... 214 F6
Welland Mews PE9 ..... 219 C4
Welland Prim Sch PE1 .. 226 C8
Welland Rd
Borough Fen PE1........ 174 E1
Boston PE21 .... 208 B3
Lincoln LN1 .... 201 D8
Peterborough PE1 .... 226 B8
Spalding PE11 .... 214 D3
2 Wittering PE8........ 172 B1
Welland Way PE6 ...... 217 E4
Wellbeck Cl 4 DN20... 196 D4
Wellbeck Rd DN34 ..... 190 E4
Wellesley Cl 3 LN8 ...... 57 D8
Wellesley Way NG34 .... 120 B8
Wellfield Cl 6 NG33 ... 151 D2
Wellgarth DN32......... 192 B5
Wellhead La LN4......... 95 B7
Well High La LN13 .... 75 D1
WELLINGORE LN5....... 107 A7
Wellingore Rd 5 LN2... 201 F8
Wellington Ave 11 LN12 .. 64 B4
Wellington Cl
7 Heckington NG34..... 122 E2
Skellingthorpe LN6 ...... 79 F6
9 South Killingholme
DN40................... 12 E3
Wellington Ct DN32 .... 192 A8
Wellington Dr 1
NG31 .... 211 D2
Wellington La HU3...... 180 D8
Wellington Rd
2 Beacon Hill NG24..... 104 A4
Boston PE21 .... 209 B4
Mablethorpe/Sutton on Sea
LN12................... 64 B4
Wellington St Wes
HU1 .... 180 E5
Wellington Sq 12 LN5 .... 94 A7
Wellington St
12 Gainsborough
DN21.................. 197 D3
Grimsby DN32.......... 191 F8
Kingston upon Hull HU1 .. 180 F5
Lincoln LN1 .... 201 D4
4 Louth LN11.......... 198 C6
Peterborough PE1 .... 226 B2
7 Scampton Airfield LN1 .. 67 E5
Wellington Way
1 Elsham Wold Ind Est
DN20................... 21 A8
Market Deeping PE6 ..... 217 B7
1 Skegness PE25....... 206 A5
Wellington Yd 4 PE23 ... 88 A1
Well La LN2 .... 234 B3
WELLOW DN32 .... 191 E5
Wellowgate DN32....... 191 D7
Wellowgate Mews
DN32 .... 191 D6
Wells Cl
Grantham NG31......... 210 C5
Heighington/Washingborough
LN4................... 203 E1
Peterborough PE4 .... 220 F3
Wells Cres DN35 .... 192 E2
Wells Ct PE2........... 231 D6
Wells Dr
Bracebridge Heath LN4.... 81 A2
5 Market Rasen LN8 ..... 57 E7
Wells La DN22 .... 65 B7
Wells Rd DN37 .... 23 D4
Wells St
Grimsby DN31 .... 191 B7
Kingston upon Hull HU3 .. 180 A5
Scunthorpe DN15 .... 183 B4
Well St
5 Bishop Norton LN8..... 43 D3
Messingham DN17........ 29 C7
Wellsted St HU3 .... 180 C5
Wells The 18 LN2 .... 68 D6
Wellsyke La LN10 .... 98 A6
Well Turn LN13 .... 75 F1
Well Vale 2 DN33 ...... 194 D8
Well Vale Cl 29 PE24 .... 90 D7
Welmore Rd PE6........ 220 D8
Welsdale Rd LN11........ 59 E2
WELTON
Welton HU15 .... 2 E6
Welton LN2 .... 68 C6
Welton Cl 32 DN18 ...... 10 E8
Welton Gdns LN2 .... 201 F8
WELTON HILL LN2 .... 69 A8
WELTON LE MARSH
PE23 .... 89 B3
WELTON LE WOLD
LN11 .... 60 C6
Welton-le-Wold Nature
Reserve★ LN11.......... 60 D7
Welton Low Rd HU15...... 2 C6
Welton Old Rd HU15 .... 2 E6
Welton Rd
Brough HU15............. 2 C5
Nettleham LN2........... 68 C3
Welton Wold View 9
HU14 .... 3 B7
Welwyn Cl NG31 .... 210 E1
Wembley Rd LN11 .... 50 F7
Wembley St DN21....... 197 C4
Wendan Rd 9 DN8 .... 15 A7
Wende The PE11........ 214 A3
Wendover Cl
19 Humberston DN36..... 36 D8
Messingham DN17........ 29 D7
Rippingale PE10......... 142 F2
Wendover Mews PE10.... 213 E5
Wendover Rd 13 DN17.... 29 D7
Wendover Rise DN35.... 192 E5
Wenlock St HU3 .... 180 C7
Wensleydale Cl 1
NG31 .... 211 A8
Wensleydale Rd DN16... 185 E6
Wensum Cl 4 PE11 .... 214 F5
Wentworth Cl
Heighington LN4 .... 203 E1
4 Skegness PE25....... 206 D6
1 Spalding PE11 .... 214 C1
Willerby HU10.......... 178 F8
Wentworth Cres 2 DN19... 4 E2
Wentworth Dr
Dunholme LN2........... 68 E5
Grantham NG31......... 211 D8
25 Messingham DN17..... 29 D7
2 Saxilby with Ingleby
LN1.................... 66 D2
Wentworth Rd
Grimsby DN34 .... 191 B7
Scunthorpe DN17 .... 184 D2
Wentworth St 1 PE1.... 226 A1
Wentworths The PE12... 216 A4
Wentworth Way
Kingston upon Hull
HU9................... 181 C7
7 Woodhall Spa LN10 .... 97 C5
Werneth Rd DN32....... 191 F8
WERRINGTON PE4 .... 220 F4
Werrington Bridge Rd
PE6 .... 221 B6
Werrington Ctr PE4..... 221 A5
Werrington Gr PE4...... 220 F2
Werrington Gr Cvn Pk
PE4 .... 220 F2
Werrington Mews 5
PE4 .... 221 A3
Werrington Parkway
PE6 .... 220 C5
Werrington Pk Ave 2
PE4 .... 221 A3
Werrington Prim Sch
PE4................... 221 A3
Werrington Sports Ctr
PE4................... 220 F4
Werry's La 4 PE10..... 213 C5
Wesleyan Ct LN2........ 234 B2
Wesleyan Rd PE1 .... 226 A7
Wesley Ave 5 PE34..... 161 F3
Wesley Cl
4 Epworth DN9 .... 27 E6
15 Metheringham LN4..... 95 C4
Sleaford NG34.......... 212 C2
11 Terrington St Clement
PE34 .... 161 F3
2 Winterton DN15 .... 9 A5
Wesley Cres 2 DN35.... 192 E3
Wesley Ct
8 Grimsby DN31 .... 189 C1
8 Kingston upon Hull
HU3................... 180 C5
Wesley Rd
Brigg DN20 .... 196 C3
Scunthorpe DN16 .... 185 E7
9 Terrington St Clement
PE34 .... 161 F3
Whaplode PE12 .... 158 C7
Wesley St 19 DN21 .... 30 B1
Wesley Way LN9......... 199 D3
Wesselow Rd LN4....... 207 F6
Wessex Cl
Peterborough PE2 .... 231 D7
Sleaford NG34.......... 212 B1
West Acridge 16 DN18...... 3 E1
WEST ASHBY LN9......... 85 E7
West Ave
Cranwell & Byard's Leap
NG34.................. 120 B8
Grantham NG31......... 210 D3
6 Stainforth DN7........ 14 C6
West Bank
Crowland PE6 .... 166 E1
Saxilby with Ingleby LN1... 66 C2
Stainforth DN7........... 14 B7
Strubby with Woodthorpe
LN13................... 63 E2
West Bank Rd PE12 ..... 161 A8
West Banks NG34 .... 212 C4
WEST BARKWITH LN8 ..... 70 F7
Westbeck 2 NG34 ...... 108 D2
Westbeck La DN21 .... 42 C5
West Bight 1 LN1 ...... 234 B3
WESTBOROUGH NG23..... 117 E3
Westborough La NG23 .. 117 D4
Westborough Way
HU4 .... 179 B6
Westbourne Ave 3
HU13 .... 178 E2
Westbourne Dr
22 Crowle DN17 .... 16 D7
6 Glinton PE6.......... 220 C8
Westbourne Gdns 5
PE11 .... 214 D3
Westbourne Gr
6 Grimsby DN33 .... 194 F8
Kingston upon Hull
HU13.................. 178 D2
6 Lincoln LN1.......... 201 D3
Westbourne Pk PE10.... 213 B5
Westbourne Pl 2
NG31 .... 210 E4
Westbourne St 5 HU3 .. 180 A4
Westbrecks La DN22 ..... 65 A7
Westbridge Rd PE21 .... 208 A3
Westbrook Ave 1 PE2 .. 230 F7
Westbrooke Cl LN6 ..... 205 B8
Westbrooke Rd LN6 ..... 205 B8
West Brook La NG23 ..... 91 D3
Westbrook Pk Cl 2
PE2 .... 230 F7
Westbrook Pk Rd PE2... 230 E7
Westburn Ave 4 DN19 ..... 4 E2
Westbury Pk 2 DN35 ... 193 A1
Westbury Rd DN35 ...... 193 A1
WEST BUTTERWICK
DN17 .... 28 D8
West Butterwick CE Prim
Sch DN17 .... 28 D8
WESTBY NG33........... 140 F3
Westby Rd
Bitchfield & Bassingthorpe
NG33.................. 140 F2
Burton Coggles NG33 .... 152 C8
WESTCLIFF DN17 .... 184 E7
Westcliffe Prim Sch
DN17.................. 184 D6
Westcliffe Rd
Ruskington NG34........ 108 C2
21 Scotter DN21......... 29 C3
Westcliffe St LN1 ...... 201 D6
Westcliff Gdns DN17 .... 184 F7
West Coates Rd DN31 ... 188 D2
West Cob Gate PE12 .... 157 F6
Westcombe Sq PE1 ..... 226 D4
West Comm Cres
DN17 .... 184 F8
West Comm Gdns
DN17 .... 184 F7
West Comm La DN17.... 184 E7
West Comm N Rd DN17 .. 29 A8
West Comm Sports Hall
DN17.................. 184 E8
Westcroft Dr 3 LN1 ..... 66 D3
West Cross St 24 DN21 ... 30 B1

West Ct 14 DN8 . . . . 15 A7
West–Dale Cres 2
  DN21 . . . . 30 B2
Westdale Dro PE11 . . . . . 134 C2
West Dock Ave HU3 . . . . 180 B4
West Dock St HU3 . . . . . 180 B3
West Dr
  Coningsby LN4 . . . . 110 E8
  Sudbrooke LN2 . . . . 68 F3
West Dro PE12 . . . . 168 C2
West Dro N PE12 . . . . . . 168 C3
West Dro S PE12 . . . . . . 168 C1
WEST ELLA HU10 . . . . . . 178 A8
West Ella Rd
  Kingston upon Hull
    HU10 . . . . 178 A7
  Swanland HU14 . . . . 3 C7
West Ella Way HU10 . . . 178 C7
West Elloe Ave PE11 . . . 214 E6
WEST END PE22 . . . . 126 E6
West End
  Burgh le Marsh PE24 . . . . 102 D8
  Garthorpe & Fockerby
    DN17 . . . . 7 E5
  Gorefield PE13 . . . . 169 E3
  Harlaxton NG32 . . . . 139 B7
  Hogsthorpe PE24 . . . . 90 B7
  Holbeach PE12 . . . . 215 D2
  Ingham LN1 . . . . 54 F2
  Langtoft PE6 . . . . 164 E3
  7 Spilsby PE23 . . . . 87 F1
  Swanland HU14 . . . . 3 B6
  Walcott LN4 . . . . 109 C7
  Winteringham DN15 . . . . . . 2 A1
  Yaxley PE7 . . . . 233 D4
West End Cl
  9 Bottesford NG13 . . . . 128 A6
  Laughton DN21 . . . . 41 B8
West End Cres 9 PE23 . . . 87 F1
West End La DN36 . . . . . . 37 B1
West End Rd
  Boston PE21 . . . . 136 D8
  Epworth DN9 . . . . 27 C8
  2 Habrough DN40 . . . . . . 22 E8
  Kirton PE20 . . . . 136 B7
  Maxey PE6 . . . . 217 A1
  Ulceby DN39 . . . . 11 F1
  Wyberton PE21 . . . . 208 B2
West End Villas 11
  PE9 . . . . 219 A5
Westerdale HU14 . . . . 3 B7
Westerdale Gr HU9 . . . . 181 E8
Westerdale Rd
  2 Grantham NG31 . . . . . 211 A7
  Scunthorpe DN16 . . . . . . 185 D5
Westerdale Way DN37 . . 190 E8
Westerley Cl PE3 . . . . . . 225 C4
Westerly Way 1 PE11 . . . 214 A5
Western Ave
  Brigg DN20 . . . . 196 C5
  Easton on the Hill PE9 . . . 171 C3
  Holbeach PE12 . . . . 215 C2
  Lincoln LN6 . . . . 205 C7
  Peterborough PE1 . . . . . . 226 B7
  3 Saxilby LN1 . . . . 66 C2
Western Cres LN6 . . . . . 205 C8
Western Dr
  Balderton NG24 . . . . 104 C1
  11 Barton-upon-Humber
    DN18 . . . . 3 E1
  9 RAF Cranwell NG34 . . 120 C8
Western Gn DN15 . . . . 2 A1
Western Outway DN34 . . 191 A4
Western Prim Sch
  DN34 . . . . 190 E5
Western Tech Sch The
  DN34 . . . . 190 F5
West Fen Drain Bank
  PE22 . . . . 112 D1
West Fen La PE22 . . . . . . 100 A1
WEST FIELD DN40 . . . . . . 12 C6
Westfield App LN2 . . . . . 203 A8
Westfield Ave
  Boston PE21 . . . . 208 D4
  Greetwell LN2 . . . . 203 B8
  Grimsby DN33 . . . . 191 C3
Westfield Cl
  8 Metheringham LN4 . . . . 95 D4
  Yaxley PE7 . . . . 233 D5
Westfield Dr
  Greetwell LN2 . . . . 203 A8
  22 Messingham DN17 . . . 29 D7
  1 Pinchbeck PE11 . . . . . 156 E8
  3 Skegness PE25 . . . . . 206 B4
  11 Swineshead PE20 . . . 135 B7
Westfield Garth 2
  DN17 . . . . 16 E6
Westfield Gr DN35 . . . . . 192 D6
Westfield La
  Collingham NG23 . . . . 91 B4
  Cumberworth LN13 . . . . . . 89 D8
  Kirk Bramwith DN7 . . . . . . 14 B8
West Field La
  1 Swanland HU14 . . . . . . 3 B6
  Thorpe on the Hill LN6 . . . . 92 E8
Westfield Pk 11 HU15 . . . . . 2 C6
Westfield Rd
  Bardney LN3 . . . . 83 D1
  Barton-upon-Humber DN18 . . 3 C1
  Fishlake DN7 . . . . 14 B8
  13 Goxhill DN19 . . . . 12 A8
  6 Hatfield DN7 . . . . 14 E4
  Kingston upon Hull HU4 . . 179 D5
  Newton PE13 . . . . 169 F5

Westfield Rd *continued*
  Peterborough PE3 . . . . . . 225 E4
  Scunthorpe DN17 . . . . . . 184 B6
  Waltham DN37 . . . . 194 C4
  2 Wisbech PE13 . . . . . . 170 C2
  Yarburgh LN11 . . . . 49 D3
  Yaxley PE7 . . . . 233 D5
Westfield Rise HU13 . . . . 178 D2
Westfields
  1 Alford LN13 . . . . 75 F2
  Easton on the Hill PE9 . . . 171 C3
Westfield St 4 LN1 . . . . . 201 D3
Westfield Villas 5 DN7 . . 14 E4
Westfield Way PE6 . . . . . 164 E2
WESTGATE DN9 . . . . 16 D2
Westgate
  Grantham NG31 . . . . 211 A4
  Grimsby DN31 . . . . 188 F1
  Kexby DN21 . . . . 53 E4
  Lincoln LN1 . . . . 234 A3
  Louth LN11 . . . . 198 A5
  Peterborough PE1 . . . . . . 225 F2
  Scotton DN21 . . . . 29 C1
  Sleaford NG34 . . . . 212 C4
West Gate
  9 Ruskington NG34 . . . . 108 E2
  Wainfleet All Saints
    PE24 . . . . 101 E2
  Weston PE12 . . . . 157 D2
Westgate House★
  LN11 . . . . 198 A5
Westgate Jun Sch LN11 . . 234 A4
Westgate Pk 3 NG34 . . . . 212 C4
Westgate Pl 7 LN11 . . . . 198 B5
Westgate Rd DN9 . . . . 16 D2
West Gn
  Kingston upon Hull HU10 . . . 3 C8
  29 Messingham DN17 . . . 29 D7
West Gr
  7 Colsterworth NG33 . . . 151 E6
  Kingston upon Hull HU4 . . 179 D4
Westhall Cl 1 LN5 . . . . . . 92 C1
Westhall Rd 16 LN2 . . . . . 68 D7
WEST HALTON DN15 . . . . . . 8 E8
West Halton La DN15 . . . . . 8 C8
West Haven La DN9 . . . . . . 4 C1
Westhaven 2 PE9 . . . . . . 171 D3
West Haven Way DN40 . . 186 B8
Westhawe PE3 . . . . 224 F7
West Hill 1 HU13 . . . . 3 E4
Westhill Rd DN34 . . . . . . 191 A5
Westholm 2 LN3 . . . . 203 E5
Westholme Cl LN2 . . . . . 202 D8
Westholme Cl 11 DN15 . . . . 8 A4
Westholme La DN38 . . . . . 21 C5
WESTHORPE PE11 . . . . . . 144 F5
Westhorpe Rd PE11 . . . . 144 F5
Westhouses PE22 . . . . . . 112 F5
WEST KEAL PE23 . . . . 100 C6
Westkirke Ave DN33 . . . . 191 D1
West La
  Baumber LN9 . . . . 72 A1
  Girton NG23 . . . . 78 C1
  Haltham LN9 . . . . 98 C6
  7 Keelby DN41 . . . . 23 A4
  Skidbrooke with Saltfleet
    Haven LN11 . . . . 51 A2
  5 Winterton DN15 . . . . . . 9 B5
Westlaby La LN3 . . . . 69 E8
Westlake Ave PE7 . . . . . . 230 C1
Westland Rd
  Kingston upon Hull
    HU10 . . . . 178 B7
  5 Westwoodside DN9 . . . 27 B2
Westlands Ave
  Grimsby DN34 . . . . 191 C5
  4 Tetney DN36 . . . . 36 D4
Westlands Rd HU5 . . . . . 179 B8
West Lea DN33 . . . . 194 F7
West Leys Pk 7 HU14 . . . . 3 B6
West Leys Rd HU14 . . . . . . 3 B6
Westlode St PE11 . . . . . . 214 C4
WEST MARSH DN31 . . . . . 188 D1
West Marsh Ind Est
  DN31 . . . . 188 F1
West Marsh La
  Barrow upon Humber
    DN19 . . . . 4 B1
  Goxhill DN19 . . . . 5 A3
West Marsh Rd
  Pinchbeck PE11 . . . . 145 E1
  Spalding PE11 . . . . 214 F6
Westmere Prim Sch
  PE12 . . . . 160 E4
West Mid Mere Rd
  DN40 . . . . 12 D3
West Mill 1 PE9 . . . . 171 C2
West Mill Gate 2 LN3 . . . 203 E6
Westminister Way 2
  NG31 . . . . 210 F5
Westminster Cl DN21 . . . . 40 D3
Westminster Dr
  Grimsby DN34 . . . . 191 C6
  12 Hatfield DN7 . . . . 14 C2
  1 Spalding PE11 . . . . . . 214 B1
Westminster Gdns 24
  PE6 . . . . 175 A1
Westminster La 6
  PE10 . . . . 213 B5
Westminster Pl PE1 . . . . 226 F5
Westminster Rd
  5 Broughton DN20 . . . . . 19 D4
  Lincoln LN6 . . . . 204 D4
Westmoor La LN1 . . . . 65 E2
West Moor Rd 1 DN10 . . . 39 F3
Westmoreland Ave 14
  LN1 . . . . 67 E5

Westmoreland Cl 1
  DN9 . . . . 27 A2
Westmoreland Gdns 4
  PE1 . . . . 226 B2
Westmoreland Rd 2
  PE12 . . . . 157 F6
Westoby La DN19 . . . . 11 C7
WESTON PE12 . . . . 157 D7
Weston Gr DN40 . . . . 186 B5
WESTON HILLS PE12 . . . . 157 C3
Weston Hills CE Prim Sch
  PE12 . . . . 157 D7
Weston Hills Rd PE12 . . . 157 B4
Weston Miller Dr 8
  PE13 . . . . 170 D1
*Weston St Mary CE Prim
  Sch* PE12 . . . . 157 E7
Westonville 6 PE9 . . . . . . 171 B1
Westover Dr 4 DN15 . . . . . 8 A4
West Parade
  Grimsby DN31 . . . . 191 C7
  Kingston upon Hull HU3 . . 180 C7
  Lincoln LN1 . . . . 234 A3
  Peterborough PE3 . . . . . . 225 D2
  Spalding PE11 . . . . 214 B4
  Wisbech PE13 . . . . 170 C1
West Parklands Dr 9
  HU14 . . . . 3 A5
Westport Rd 1 DN35 . . . . 193 A1
WEST RASEN LN8 . . . . 56 E8
WEST RAVENDALE
  DN37 . . . . 35 A2
West Rd
  Billingborough NG34 . . . . 133 B1
  Bourne PE10 . . . . 213 B4
  Deeping St Nicholas
    PE11 . . . . 156 D3
  Haconby PE10 . . . . 154 C6
  2 Keadby with Althorpe
    DN17 . . . . 17 C6
  Pointon & Sempringham
    NG34 . . . . 143 A6
  3 Ruskington NG34 . . . . 108 D1
  2 Tallington PE9 . . . . . . 172 F7
  Tetford LN9 . . . . 73 E1
  Thorney NG23 . . . . 78 F8
  1 Tydd St Mary PE13 . . . 170 C8
West Riverside DN40 . . . 186 B8
West Row 4 PE21 . . . . . . 208 E4
WESTRUM DN20 . . . . 196 C1
Westrum La DN20 . . . . . . 196 D2
Westry Cl
  Barrowby NG32 . . . . 210 A3
  1 Leverington PE13 . . . . 170 F1
Westry Cnr NG32 . . . . . . 210 A4
West St Gdns 8 PE9 . . . . 219 A5
West St Mary's Gate 3
  DN31 . . . . 191 D7
Westside Ave NG31 . . . . 139 E8
West St
  Alford LN13 . . . . 75 E2
  Barkston NG32 . . . . 119 A1
  Barnetby le Wold DN38 . . . 21 B4
  Billingham LN4 . . . . 109 F6
  Boston PE21 . . . . 208 E4
  Bourne PE10 . . . . 213 C5
  Brant Broughton LN5 . . . . 105 F5
  Cleethorpes DN35 . . . . . 192 F6
  Clipsham LE15 . . . . 162 B7
  7 Crowland PE6 . . . . . . 166 E1
  Easton on the Hill PE9 . . . 171 C3
  Folkingham NG34 . . . . . . 142 C6
  Gainsborough DN21 . . . . 197 B8
  Hagworthingham PE23 . . . 87 A4
  Helpston PE6 . . . . 173 B4
  Hibaldstow DN20 . . . . 30 F5
  Horncastle LN9 . . . . 199 A3
  Kingston upon Hull HU1 . . 180 E6
  Long Sutton PE12 . . . . . . 216 B4
  11 Navenby/Wellingore
    LN5 . . . . 107 A7
  North Kelsey LN7 . . . . . . 32 A4
  Osbournby NG34 . . . . . . 132 C5
  1 Roxby cum Risby DN15 . . 8 F3
  Scawby DN20 . . . . 30 E8
  Scunthorpe DN15 . . . . . . 183 A3
  Stamford PE9 . . . . 219 A4
  Swaton NG34 . . . . 133 C4
  Thorne/Moorends DN8 . . . 15 A7
  2 Timberland LN4 . . . . . 96 B1
  West/East Butterwick
    DN17 . . . . 28 C8
  West Halton DN15 . . . . 8 E7
  Winterton DN15 . . . . 9 A5
WEST STOCKWITH
  DN10 . . . . 40 C6
West Stonebridge PE2 . . 230 C5
West Syke La LN1 . . . . 66 B7
West Terr DN20 . . . . 196 B3
West Terr St 10 DN17 . . . . 16 D7
WEST TORRINGTON
  LN8 . . . . 58 A1
West Town Prim Sch
  PE3 . . . . 225 E3
West View
  3 Ancaster NG32 . . . . . 120 A3
  15 Bardney LN3 . . . . 83 B4
  Messingham DN17 . . . . . 29 C7
  16 North Ferriby HU14 . . . . 3 A4
  Scunthorpe DN17 . . . . . . 184 B3
West View Cl 3 DN41 . . . . 23 A5
West View Cres 25
  PE24 . . . . 90 D7

Westville Rd PE22 . . . . . . 112 B2
WEST WALTON LN4 . . . . . 170 E4
Westward DN34 . . . . 191 C5
Westward Ho DN34 . . . . . 191 C5
Westward Row LN4 . . . . . 207 A5
Westway 18 LN2 . . . . 68 D2
West Way PE25 . . . . 206 D7
West Wells La 4 DN10 . . . 39 C1
Westwick Dr LN6 . . . . . . 205 B7
Westwick Gdns LN6 . . . . 205 B6
WEST WILLOUGHBY
  NG32 . . . . 119 E2
Westwinds Gdns 19
  DN15 . . . . 9 A5
Westwold Rd 25 LN7 . . . . 33 B4
Westwood 6 DN20 . . . . . . 19 D4
Westwood 5 PE3 . . . . . . 225 C4
Westwood Cl LN6 . . . . . . 205 A8
Westwood Dr
  Bourne PE10 . . . . 213 B4
  3 Kingston upon Hull
    HU4 . . . . 179 B6
  Lincoln LN6 . . . . 205 A8
Westwood Ind Est PE3 . . . 225 D7
Westwood Pk Cl PE3 . . . . 225 C3
Westwood Pk Rd PE3 . . . 225 D2
Westwood Rd DN41 . . . . . 23 F5
WESTWOODSIDE DN9 . . . . 27 A2
Westwoodside CE Prim Sch
  DN9 . . . . 27 B2
West Wr Crescen PE7 . . . 230 C1
Wetherby Cl
  3 Bourne PE10 . . . . 213 C7
  6 Market Rasen LN8 . . . . 57 E7
Wetherby Cres LN6 . . . . 204 F4
Wetherby Way 1 PE1 . . . 226 D6
Wetmoor La LN2 . . . . 56 C1
Weydike Bank PE12 . . . . 159 A4
Weyford Rd 4 DN35 . . . . 193 A1
Weymouth Cl 10 LN5 . . . 205 D3
Weymouth Cres DN17 . . . 182 C1
Weymouth Way PE1 . . . . 226 D6
Whalebone La NG31 . . . . 140 B7
Whale Dro
  Holbeach PE12 . . . . 168 A1
  Whaplode PE6 . . . . 167 E1
Whalley St PE1 . . . . 226 B3
WHAPLODE PE12 . . . . 158 A7
Whaplode CE Prim Sch
  PE12 . . . . 158 C7
WHAPLODE DROVE
  PE12 . . . . 168 B4
WHAPLODE ST CATHERINE
  PE12 . . . . 158 C2
Wharfdale Cl 6 DN15 . . . . 17 E6
Wharfedale Dr 2 LN6 . . . 204 F3
Wharfedale Pl 1
  DN16 . . . . 185 E6
Wharfe La
  Kirkby on Bain LN10 . . . . . 98 C5
  Tattershall LN4 . . . . 207 D6
Wharf Rd
  Crowle DN17 . . . . 16 D7
  Grantham NG31 . . . . 211 A4
  7 Horncastle LN9 . . . . . 199 B4
  12 Misterton DN10 . . . . . 39 F5
  Stamford PE9 . . . . 219 C4
Wharfside Mews 6
  NG34 . . . . 212 D4
Wharf St 20 PE12 . . . . . . 160 E4
Wharf The DN36 . . . . 37 A5
Wharncliffe Rd DN31 . . . 189 C3
Wharncliffe Rd N
  DN31 . . . . 189 B3
Wharncliffe St HU5 . . . . 180 A8
WHARTON DN21 . . . . 41 B4
Wharton Rd DN21 . . . . . . 41 A5
Wharton St DN31 . . . . . . 191 B7
Whattoff Way PE6 . . . . . 164 D4
Whatton's Cl NG32 . . . . . 128 F5
Wheatdale PE2 . . . . 230 A3
Wheatfield Cl
  5 Barnby Dun DN3 . . . . . 14 A3
  Epworth DN9 . . . . 27 F6
  2 Kingston upon Hull
    HU4 . . . . 179 D2
Wheatfield Dr 7
  DN37 . . . . 194 C5
Wheatfield Rd LN6 . . . . . 200 C1
Wheatfields 1 PE12 . . . . 158 B7
Wheatfield PE6 . . . . 164 E2
Wheat Gr 4 NG34 . . . . . . 212 F3
Wheatgrass La NG32 . . . 119 B7
Wheatholme La NG23 . . . . 78 D6
Wheatley Bank PE14 . . . . 170 F1
Wheatley La
  1 Carlton-le-Moorland
    LN5 . . . . 105 E8
  Collingham NG23 . . . . 91 D2
Wheatley Rd DN22 . . . . . . 52 A3
Wheatmere Dro PE12 . . . 157 B5
Wheatsheaf Ave 1
  NG24 . . . . 104 A6
Wheatsheaf Cl
  3 Holbeach PE12 . . . . . . 215 B2
  Sibsey PE22 . . . . 113 B3
Wheatsheaf Ct 8
  PE11 . . . . 166 C6
Wheatsheaf La 4
  NG23 . . . . 117 D4
Wheeldon St 9 DN21 . . . . 197 D3
Wheeler Cl PE21 . . . . 209 A4
Wheeler Prim Sch
  HU3 . . . . 179 F5
Wheeler St HU3 . . . . 179 F6
Wheelwright Cl PE10 . . . . 154 C6
Wheelwrights Ct NG34 . . 109 B1

Wheel Yd PE1 . . . . 226 A2
Whelpton Cl LN9 . . . . 199 D3
Whetstone Ct 1 PE1 . . . . 226 E7
Whichcote Rd PE6 . . . . . 174 C1
Whimbrel Way
  6 Long Sutton PE12 . . . . 216 B4
  New Waltham DN36 . . . . . 195 D7
Whin Moor La HU15 . . . . . . 2 A7
Whins Gate DN17 . . . . 7 A4
Whipchicken Rd PE6 . . . . 167 B3
WHISBY LN6 . . . . 79 E2
Whisby Ct DN36 . . . . 195 E2
Whisby Nature Pk★
  LN6 . . . . 79 F1
Whisby Rd LN6 . . . . 204 A4
Whisby Way LN6 . . . . . . 204 C5
Whiston Cl 5 PE4 . . . . . . 221 D2
Whiston Way 9 DN18 . . . . . 3 F1
Whitacre PE1 . . . . 226 E6
Whitby Dr DN32 . . . . 192 A5
Whitby St HU8 . . . . 181 B8
Whiteacres 3 PE12 . . . . 216 B4
Whitebeam Cl
  4 Hampton Hargate
    PE7 . . . . 230 D3
  Kingston upon Hull HU3 . . 180 D5
Whitebread Rd PE20 . . . . 136 A7
White Croft PE3 . . . . 225 B6
Whitecross Gate PE20 . . 146 D8
Whitecross La NG34 . . . . 121 F1
White Cross La 4
  PE11 . . . . 145 D2
Whitecross St 12 DN18 . . . 10 F8
Whitefriargate HU1 . . . . 180 E6
Whitefriars Cl LN2 . . . . . 202 E6
Whitefriars Rd LN2 . . . . 202 F6
White Gate LN9 . . . . 73 E2
Whitegate Hill LN7 . . . . . 33 C3
Whitehall 5 PE11 . . . . . . 145 C6
Whitehall Cres LN4 . . . . 205 F4
Whitehall Ctry Cotts
  DN35 . . . . 192 A1
Whitehall Gr LN1 . . . . . . 234 A3
Whitehall Rd 6 DN35 . . . 193 A1
Whitehall Terr 1 LN1 . . . 234 A3
White Hart La 1 NG23 . . . 91 C4
Whitehead Cl 5 LN12 . . . . 64 B5
Whitehorse La 10 PE21 . . 208 F4
White House Cl
  29 Hatfield DN7 . . . . 14 D4
  4 Stainforth DN7 . . . . . . 14 C7
White House Garth 19
  HU14 . . . . 3 A5
White House La
  Boston PE21 . . . . 209 D3
  3 West Halton DN15 . . . . . 8 E8
White House Mews 16
  HU14 . . . . 3 A5
Whitehouse Rd 1
  NG34 . . . . 108 E2
White La
  Harmston LN5 . . . . 93 F5
  Thorne DN8 . . . . 15 A8
White Leather Sq
  NG34 . . . . 133 C1
Whitemoor La NG23 . . . . . 91 C3
WHITE PIT LN13 . . . . 74 D4
Whitepit Way LN13 . . . . . 74 D4
Whitepost Rd PE6 . . . . . . 174 F3
White Row La LN12 . . . . . 64 C1
Whites La LN5 . . . . 92 E2
White's Rd DN35 . . . . . . 192 F5
White St HU3 . . . . 179 F5
Whitestone Rd DN17 . . . . 184 C6
*White's Wood Com La Jun
  Sch* DN21 . . . . 197 F4
White's Wood La
  1 Corringham DN21 . . . . 53 A8
  Gainsborough DN21 . . . . 197 F4
Whitethorn Gr 7 LN6 . . . 200 C1
Whitewater PE2 . . . . 229 D6
Whiteways PE2 . . . . 229 D6
Whitewell Cl 4 DN21 . . . . 30 B1
White Wlk HU10 . . . . 178 C6
Whitfield Rd DN17 . . . . . 184 D6
Whitgift 21 DN37 . . . . 23 F1
Whitgift Sch DN37 . . . . . 190 D8
Whitgift Way DN37 . . . . . 190 E8
Whiting Sq PE21 . . . . . . 208 F6
Whitley Cl 5 LN6 . . . . . . 200 A4
Whitley St 11 LN1 . . . . . . 67 E5
Whitley Way PE6 . . . . . . 217 B7
Whitman Cl 9 PE9 . . . . . 172 D3
Whitman Rd DN17 . . . . . 184 C6
Whitsed Rd 8 PE6 . . . . . 174 E5
Whitsed St PE1 . . . . 226 B3
Whittington PE1 . . . . 226 E7
Whittle Cl 2 PE21 . . . . . 208 F1
Whittlesey Rd
  Peterborough PE2 . . . . . . 231 B7
  Thorney PE6 . . . . 175 F1
WHITTON DN15 . . . . 1 D3
Whitton Rd
  Alkborough DN15 . . . . 1 C1
  Whitton DN15 . . . . 1 E2
Whitwell PE4 . . . . 221 E2
Whitworth Way 12 LN8 . . . 57 D7
Whoofer La DN21 . . . . . . 40 E8
Whyalla Cl 2 LN11 . . . . . 50 B8
Whyche The LN4 . . . . . . 109 E5
WICKENBY LN3 . . . . 69 F8
Wickenby Airport LN3 . . . . 69 F1
Wickenby Cl
  6 Grimsby DN34 . . . . . . 190 F4
  Lincoln LN6 . . . . 205 A3
Wickenby Cres LN1 . . . . 201 E2
Wickenby Rd LN3 . . . . . . 57 D1
Wicken La PE22 . . . . 113 F3

Wicken Way PE3 . . . 225 C6
Wickham Rd DN31 . . . 189 C2
Wicklow Ave DN33 . . . 194 E8
Wide Bargate 8 PE21 . . . 208 F5
Widford Gn 8 DN7 . . . 14 D3
Widow Fen La LN13 . . . 76 C3
Wigeon Cl 14 PE12 . . . 167 B8
Wigford LN5 . . . 234 A1
Wigford Way LN5 . . . 234 A2
Wigg La PE24 . . . 90 D8
Wigmore Dr PE7 . . . 231 F5
Wignal's Gate PE12 . . . 215 A2
WIGSLEY NG23 . . . 78 F5
Wigsley Cl 7 LN6 . . . 204 D6
Wigsley Rd
- 6 Birchwood LN6 . . . 204 D6
- Harby NG23 . . . 79 B5
- North Scarle LN6 . . . 78 E3
WIGTOFT PE20 . . . 135 E3
Wigtoft Bank PE20 . . . 135 D1
Wigtoft Rd PE20 . . . 135 F2
Wike Gate Cl 4 DN8 . . . 15 B7
Wike Gate Gr 2 DN8 . . . 15 B7
Wike Gate Rd DN8 . . . 15 B8
WIKE WELL END DN8 . . . 15 B7
Wilberforce Dr 6 HU1 . . 180 F7
Wilberforce House* HU1 . . . 181 A6
Wilberforce Rd PE1 . . . 225 E7
Wilberforce St HU3 . . . 180 D6
Wildfowlers Way PE12 . . . 148 F4
Wildlake PE2 . . . 230 C5
Wildmore Cl LN4 . . . 111 C6
Wildmore Cres PE22 . . . 114 F6
Wildshed La PE24 . . . 102 D7
WILDSWORTH DN21 . . . 40 E8
Wiles Ave 5 PE12 . . . 157 E1
Wiles's La PE20 . . . 135 B4
Wilford Gr PE25 . . . 206 C1
Wilfred Ave NG24 . . . 104 B2
Wilkie Cl DN15 . . . 182 C3
Wilkie Dr NG34 . . . 142 C8
Wilkinson Dr 9 LN8 . . . 57 B8
Wilkinson Rd 7 NG32 . . . 117 F1
WILKSBY PE22 . . . 99 A5
Willan Ct PE2 . . . 230 F8
Willders Garth PE12 . . . 215 F2
Willerby Rd HU5 . . . 179 C8
Willerton Rd 3 LN11 . . . 50 F7
Willesby Rd PE11 . . . 214 E5
Willesden Ave PE4 . . . 225 D8
Willey's La PE24 . . . 90 B8
William Alvey CE Sch NG34 . . . 212 E5
William Barcroft Jun Sch DN32 . . . 192 C7
William Farr CE Comp Sch LN2 . . . 68 D6
William Gn Cl 9 LN12 . . . 76 F8
William Harrison Sch DN21 . . . 197 E2
William Hildyard CE (Aided) Prim Sch PE6 . . . 217 B5
William Law CE Prim Sch PE4 . . . 220 F5
William Lovell CE Sch PE22 . . . 113 A7
Williams Cl 1 PE6 . . . 174 E5
Williams Dr DN39 . . . 12 B1
Williamson Ave PE3 . . . 225 E3
Williamson's Dro LN4 . . . 110 A7
Williamson St
- Kingston upon Hull HU9 . . . 181 C7
- Lincoln LN2 . . . 234 B4
William St
- Cleethorpes DN35 . . . 192 E5
- 2 Grantham NG31 . . . 211 A3
- Kingston upon Hull HU1 . . 180 E5
- 24 Saxilby LN1 . . . 66 D2
- 1 Scunthorpe DN16 . . . 183 B2
William Stukeley CE Prim Sch PE12 . . . 215 D2
William Tow Cl 7 LN12 . . 76 F8
William Way PE25 . . . 206 B2
William Wright Dock HU3 . . . 180 C3
Willingham Ave LN2 . . . 201 F8
WILLINGHAM BY STOW DN21 . . . 53 F3
Willingham Hill LN8 . . . 58 E7
Willingham La LN8 . . . 57 F6
Willingham Rd
- East Barkwith LN8 . . . 58 E1
- Fillingham DN21 . . . 54 D4
- Lea DN21 . . . 53 A5
- Market Rasen LN8 . . . 57 E7
- Marton DN21 . . . 53 B1
- Tealby LN8 . . . 58 A7
Willingham St DN32 . . . 191 E6
Willington Rd PE20 . . . 136 A7
Willing Way DN32 . . . 191 F8
Willis Cl LN1 . . . 234 A4
Willis Terr LN1 . . . 234 A4
Willonholt PE3 . . . 225 C7
Willoughby Meadow Nature Reserve* LN13 . . . 89 B6
WILLOUGHBY LN13 . . . 89 B7
Willoughby Ave 2 PE6 . . . 217 C5
Willoughby Branch Line Nature Reserve* LN13 . . . 89 A7
Willoughby Chase DN21 . . . 197 E1
Willoughby Cl
- Corby Glen NG33 . . . 152 F7
Willoughby Cl *continued*
- Helpringham NG34 . . . 133 E7
- Silk Willoughby NG34 . . . 121 B1
Willoughby Ct PE1 . . . 226 E8
Willoughby Dr 1 PE23 . . . 88 A1
Willoughby Gall The* NG33 . . . 152 F8
Willoughby Gr 5 DN34 . . . 190 F4
WILLOUGHBY HILLS PE21 . . . 209 E7
Willoughby La
- Authorpe LN11 . . . 74 F8
- Muckton LN11 . . . 62 C1
- Waddington LN5 . . . 205 C1
Willoughby Meadow Nature Reserve* LN13 . . . 89 B6
Willoughby Mem Trust Gall* NG33 . . . 152 F7
WILLOUGHBY MOOR NG32 . . . 119 F2
Willoughby Rd
- 16 Alford LN13 . . . 75 F2
- Ancaster NG32 . . . 119 E2
- Aunsby & Dembleby NG34 . . . 132 B4
- Boston PE21 . . . 209 A7
- Bourne PE10 . . . 213 E4
- Cumberworth LN13 . . . 89 E8
- 14 Hibaldstow DN20 . . . 31 A5
- 7 Mablethorpe/Sutton on Sea LN12 . . . 64 C1
- Scunthorpe DN17 . . . 184 E5
- Sleaford NG34 . . . 120 F3
- Stamford PE9 . . . 219 C7
Willoughby Sch PE10 . . . 213 D3
Willoughby St 1 DN21 . . . 197 D3
WILLOUGHTON DN21 . . . 42 D4
Willoughton Prim Sch DN21 . . . 42 D4
Willoughton Rd 3 PE25 . . . 206 D2
Willow Ave
- 4 Misterton DN10 . . . 39 F5
- Peterborough PE1 . . . 226 B7
Willowbrook Dr DN20 . . . 196 E3
Willow Cl
- 12 Barnetby DN38 . . . 21 B4
- Gainsborough DN21 . . . 197 B7
- 10 Heckington NG34 . . . 122 E3
- Horncastle LN9 . . . 199 A5
- 6 Laceby DN37 . . . 23 E1
- 17 Saxilby LN1 . . . 66 D2
- Scopwick LN4 . . . 95 D1
- Skellingthorpe LN6 . . . 200 B3
Willow Ct
- 3 Bracebridge Heath LN4 . . . 81 A1
- Heighington/Washingborough LN4 . . . 203 C2
- 1 Sleaford NG34 . . . 212 E3
Willow Dr
- 14 Barton-upon-Humber DN18 . . . 3 F1
- 9 Bourne PE10 . . . 213 C7
- 27 Brough HU15 . . . 2 C5
- 2 Coningsby LN4 . . . 207 D4
- Kingston upon Hull HU10 . . . 178 D8
- Louth LN11 . . . 198 C8
- 35 Messingham DN17 . . . 29 D7
Willow Dro PE6 . . . 174 E6
Willowfield Ave 12 LN2 . . . 68 D2
Willow Gdns 2 DN19 . . . 11 D8
Willow Gr
- 1 Keadby with Althorpe DN17 . . . 17 D6
- 7 Scawby DN20 . . . 30 F8
- Scunthorpe DN16 . . . 185 C7
Willow Hall La PE6 . . . 227 D6
Willow Holt PE7 . . . 230 C3
Willow La
- Billinghay LN4 . . . 109 E6
- 3 Cranwell NG34 . . . 120 F8
- Dunston LN4 . . . 95 C6
- 6 Goxhill DN19 . . . 5 A1
- Grantham NG31 . . . 210 F2
- Ruskington LN4 . . . 109 B3
Willowmead Cl DN15 . . . 182 C6
Willow Pk DN37 . . . 194 B4
Willow Rd
- Lincoln LN6 . . . 204 F2
- Stamford PE9 . . . 218 D7
Willow Row PE11 . . . 214 E5
Willow Row Bank LN11 . . . 62 F6
Willows Cl PE13 . . . 160 A1
Willows Ct LN4 . . . 207 A4
Willows La PE22 . . . 125 F7
Willows Prim Sch DN37 . . . 190 E8
Willows The
- 6 Cranwell NG34 . . . 107 F1
- 5 Crowland PE6 . . . 166 E1
- Glinton PE6 . . . 220 D8
- Kingston upon Hull HU13 . . . 178 E4
Willow Tree Cl DN40 . . . 186 D5
Willow Tree Gdns LN6 . . 204 C8
Willow Wlk PE11 . . . 214 E5
Will Row LN12 . . . 63 C5
WILL ROW LN12 . . . 63 C5
Wilmington Dr 18 LN12 . . . 77 A8
WILSFORD NG32 . . . 120 C1
Wilsford La NG32 . . . 120 A2
Wilson Cl
- Ingoldmells PE25 . . . 90 D3
Wilson Cl *continued*
- 8 North Ferriby HU14 . . . 3 A4
Wilson Ct LE15 . . . 162 A8
Wilsons Cl DN15 . . . 183 B3
Wilson St
- Cleethorpes DN35 . . . 192 D8
- Gainsborough DN21 . . . 197 B5
- 4 Kingston upon Hull HU9 . . . 181 B7
- Kingston upon Hull HU10 . . . 178 E6
- Lincoln LN1 . . . 234 A4
WILSTHORPE PE9 . . . 164 C4
Wilton Ave 14 PE24 . . . 90 D7
Wilton Cl PE3 . . . 225 C4
Wilton Dr PE3 . . . 225 C4
Wilton Rd DN36 . . . 192 D1
Wilton Rd Ind Est DN36 . . . 195 F8
Wilton Road Ind Est DN36 . . . 192 D1
Wilton St HU8 . . . 181 B8
Wiltshire Ave DN15 . . . 8 B4
Wiltshire Rd HU4 . . . 179 E2
Wilyman Cl 21 LN12 . . . 77 A7
Wimberley Cl 3 PE12 . . . 157 D7
Wimberley Way
- 8 Pinchbeck PE11 . . . 156 E8
- 3 South Witham NG33 . . . 151 D2
Wimbishthorpe Cl 3 NG13 . . . 128 A6
Wimborn Ave DN34 . . . 191 B6
Wimborne Dr 7 PE1 . . . 226 E7
WINCEBY PE23 . . . 86 E3
Winceby Ave DN31 . . . 191 B8
Winceby Gdns LN9 . . . 199 D4
Winchcombe Ave DN34 . . . 190 E4
Winchelsea Prim Sch The NG34 . . . 108 D1
Winchelsea Rd 14 NG34 . . . 108 E1
Winchester Ave DN33 . . . 191 A3
Winchester Cl 3 LN4 . . . 81 A2
Winchester Ct 9 LN6 . . . 93 B8
Winchester Dr
- Bottesford DN16 . . . 185 C3
- Heighington/Washingborough LN4 . . . 203 C1
- 6 Mablethorpe/Sutton on Sea LN12 . . . 64 A3
Winchester Rd
- Grantham NG31 . . . 210 E4
- 13 Hatfield DN7 . . . 14 D4
- 8 Wainfleet All Saints PE24 . . . 102 D2
Winchester Way
- Peterborough PE3 . . . 225 E1
- Sleaford NG34 . . . 212 C7
Wincolmlee HU2 . . . 181 A7
Windass Ct HU13 . . . 178 E1
Windermere Ave
- 4 Grimsby DN33 . . . 194 E7
- Lincoln LN6 . . . 205 A2
Windermere Cres DN36 . . . 192 E1
Windermere Rd LN2 . . . 202 D8
Windermere Way PE4 . . . 221 C3
Windgate Way PE8 . . . 222 A6
Windlass Cl 16 DN8 . . . 15 A8
Windle Dr PE10 . . . 213 E2
Windlesham Ave DN33 . . 194 D7
Windmill Cl
- Holbeach PE12 . . . 215 B2
- 4 Waddington LN5 . . . 93 F6
Windmill Dr
- Burgh le Marsh PE24 . . . 102 D8
- 13 Heckington NG34 . . . 122 E2
Windmill Gdns 3 PE13 . . . 170 E2
Windmill La
- 5 Alford LN13 . . . 75 F2
- Gosberton PE11 . . . 144 F6
Windmill St PE1 . . . 225 F5
Windmill View 3 LN1 . . . 234 A4
Windmill Way HU13 . . . 178 F1
Windrush Dr PE4 . . . 221 D1
Windsmoor Rd 15 LN8 . . . 47 B6
Windsor Ave
- Holbeach PE12 . . . 215 F2
- Kingston upon Hull HU10 . . . 178 E7
- 3 Peterborough PE4 . . . 225 C8
Windsor Bank PE21 . . . 209 A3
Windsor Cl
- Collingham NG23 . . . 91 D4
- 6 Keelby DN41 . . . 23 A5
- 1 Sleaford NG34 . . . 212 B2
- 4 Stamford PE9 . . . 219 B7
- 6 Sudbrooke LN2 . . . 68 F2
Windsor Cres
- Boston PE21 . . . 209 A4
- 1 Crowle DN17 . . . 16 C7
- 4 Ingoldmells PE25 . . . 90 D3
- Scunthorpe DN17 . . . 184 F2
Windsor Ct
- 7 Grimsby DN31 . . . 189 C1
- 12 Hatfield DN7 . . . 14 C2
Windsor Dr
- 19 Caistor LN7 . . . 33 B4
- Grantham NG31 . . . 211 E5
- Peterborough PE2 . . . 231 D6
- Spalding PE11 . . . 214 D2
- Wisbech PE13 . . . 170 D2
Windsor Gdns PE12 . . . 216 C5
Windsor Gr 1 DN19 . . . 5 A1
Windsor La DN17 . . . 16 C7
Windsor Mews LN11 . . . 198 C5
Windsor Pk Cl 5 LN6 . . . 204 F1
Windsor Rd
- Cleethorpes DN35 . . . 192 C5
- Crowle DN17 . . . 16 C7
- Louth LN11 . . . 198 B8
- Yaxley PE7 . . . 233 F6
Windsor Terr 11 PE21 . . . 209 A5
Windsor Way
- Barnetby le Wold DN38 . . . 21 B5
- Broughton DN20 . . . 19 E4
Wine Hill La LN11 . . . 51 B5
Winfrey Ave PE11 . . . 214 D4
Wingate Parade DN37 . . . 190 E8
Wingate Rd DN37 . . . 190 D8
Wingate Way PE10 . . . 213 E7
Wing Dr PE21 . . . 209 C4
Wingfield PE2 . . . 229 F3
Winn Ct DN35 . . . 192 E5
Winniffe Gdns LN2 . . . 202 D7
Winn La 4 LN9 . . . 86 B8
Winnowsty La LN2 . . . 234 C3
Winn St
- Lincoln LN2 . . . 234 C2
- 2 Scunthorpe DN16 . . . 183 B2
Winship Cl 4 HU3 . . . 180 C5
Winslow Dr DN40 . . . 186 B5
Winslow Gate PE12 . . . 159 B8
Winslow Gr 2 DN34 . . . 190 F4
Winslow Rd
- 4 Boston PE21 . . . 209 C4
- Peterborough PE3 . . . 225 C3
Winsover Rd PE11 . . . 214 B3
Winston Ave DN34 . . . 191 B6
Winston Dr PE25 . . . 206 B6
Winston Gdns PE21 . . . 209 A7
Winston Rd PE23 . . . 100 F8
Winston Way
- 5 Brigg DN20 . . . 196 D4
- Farcet PE7 . . . 231 C2
Winterbeck Cl 5 NG13 . . . 128 A6
Wintergold Ave PE11 . . . 214 A5
WINTERINGHAM DN15 . . . 2 A1
Winteringham Foreshore Nature Reserve* DN15 . . . 2 B1
Winteringham La DN15 . . . 8 E8
Winteringham Prim Sch DN15 . . . 2 A1
Winteringham Rd DN15 . . . 9 B6
Wintern Ct DN21 . . . 197 D2
Winter's La
- 9 Long Bennington NG23 . . . 117 D4
- Long Sutton PE12 . . . 160 A3
WINTERTON DN15 . . . 9 A5
Winterton CE Inf Sch DN15 . . . 9 A5
Winterton Comp Sch DN15 . . . 9 A6
Winterton Cty Jun Sch DN15 . . . 9 A5
Winterton Rd
- Roxby cum Risby DN15 . . . 8 F2
- Scunthorpe DN15 . . . 183 B4
- Winteringham DN15 . . . 9 B8
WINTHORPE
- Langford NG23 . . . 104 B8
- Skegness PE25 . . . 206 C8
Winthorpe Ave PE25 . . . 206 D8
Winthorpe Cl 17 LN6 . . . 204 D7
Winthorpe Gr 16 LN6 . . . 204 D7
Winthorpe Prim Sch NG23 . . . 104 C8
Winthorpe Rd
- Birchwood LN6 . . . 204 D7
- Grimsby DN33 . . . 191 B3
- 4 Kingston upon Hull HU13 . . . 179 A3
- 8 Newark NG24 . . . 104 B7
Winthorpe Way
- Ingoldmells PE25 . . . 206 D8
- Skegness PE25 . . . 90 E1
Winton Rd 11 LN5 . . . 107 A8
Wintringham 26 HU15 . . . 2 C6
Wintringham Rd DN32 . . 191 E6
Wintringham Sch DN32 . . . 191 E4
Winwick Pl PE3 . . . 225 C5
Winyates PE2 . . . 229 F3
Winyates Prim Sch PE2 . . . 230 A3
Wire Hill La LN8 . . . 70 E5
Wirral Ave 7 DN34 . . . 190 F4
WISBECH PE13 . . . 170 B1
Wisbech Rd
- Long Sutton PE12 . . . 216 E1
- Thorney PE6 . . . 176 A3
- Walpole PE14 . . . 161 C1
- Walsoken PE14 . . . 170 E2
- Wisbech St Mary PE13 . . . 177 A2
Wiseholme Rd LN6 . . . 200 B2
Wiseman's Gate 1 PE12 . . . 157 D7
Wiske Ave 7 HU15 . . . 2 D5
WISPINGTON LN9 . . . 84 E6
Wistaria Rd PE13 . . . 170 E1
Wisteria Ave LN4 . . . 81 D2
Wisteria Dr DN41 . . . 23 F5
Wisteria Rd PE7 . . . 233 D4
Wisteria Way
- Bourne PE10 . . . 213 B7
- Scunthorpe DN16 . . . 185 E4
- Werrington PE4 . . . 221 B3
Wistow Gr HU4 . . . 179 D5
Wistow Way PE2 . . . 229 D6
Witchford Cl 2 LN6 . . . 204 B6
Witchford Rd 3 LN6 . . . 204 B6
Witham HU9 . . . 181 B7
Witham Bank
- Dogdyke LN4 . . . 110 D8
- Timberland LN10 . . . 97 C3
Witham Bank E 4 PE21 . . . 208 E6
Witham Bank W PE21 . . . 208 E6
Withambrook Pk NG31 . . 211 F7
Witham Cl
- Lincoln LN6 . . . 205 D5
- 11 Ruskington NG34 . . . 108 D2
- Stamford PE9 . . . 219 C6
Witham Ct
- 2 Boston PE21 . . . 208 E6
- Lincoln LN6 . . . 201 D1
Witham Dr 6 DN15 . . . 8 B5
Witham Gdns PE21 . . . 208 E6
Witham Gn PE21 . . . 208 E6
Witham Hall Prep Sch PE10 . . . 163 D7
Witham/Haven Mouth Nature Reserve* PE22 . . . 137 F6
WITHAM ON THE HILL PE10 . . . 163 D7
Witham Pl
- Boston PE21 . . . 208 E5
- Grantham NG31 . . . 211 C2
Witham Rd
- Gunby & Stainby NG33 . . . 151 C4
- 5 Long Bennington NG23 . . . 117 D4
- Thistleton LE15 . . . 151 C1
- Woodhall Spa LN10 . . . 97 B5
WITHAM ST HUGHS LN6 . . . 92 D5
Witham St Hughs Prim Sch LN6 . . . 92 D5
Witham St 3 PE21 . . . 208 F5
Witham Town PE21 . . . 208 E6
Witham View LN4 . . . 203 A2
Witham Way
- Peterborough PE4 . . . 221 D1
- Westborough NG23 . . . 117 F3
WITHCALL LN11 . . . 60 C2
WITHERN LN13 . . . 63 A1
Withern Rd DN33 . . . 191 A3
Withington St 1 PE12 . . . 160 E4
WITTERING PE8 . . . 172 B1
Wittering Airfield PE8 . . . 171 F1
Wittering Cl 5 LN6 . . . 204 D6
Wittering Prim Sch PE8 . . . 172 B1
Wittering Rd PE9 . . . 172 D3
Witty St HU3 . . . 180 A3
Wivell Dr 1 DN41 . . . 23 A5
Woad Farm Rd PE21 . . . 209 B4
Woad La
- Fishtoft PE22 . . . 137 C7
- Grimsby DN31 . . . 188 A2
- Long Sutton PE12 . . . 216 E5
Woburn Ave LN1 . . . 201 E6
Woburn Cl
- Louth LN11 . . . 198 B7
- 4 Market Deeping PE6 . . 217 A5
- Peterborough PE3 . . . 225 A1
Woburn Dr
- Grantham NG31 . . . 211 F5
- Thorney PE6 . . . 176 A2
Woburn Gr 1 LN10 . . . 97 C5
Woburn St HU3 . . . 179 F4
Woffindin Cl 12 NG31 . . . 129 E5
Woldcarr Rd HU3 . . . 179 F6
WOLD NEWTON LN8 . . . 47 F7
Wold Rd
- Barrow upon Humber DN19 . . . 11 D7
- Kingston upon Hull HU5 . . 179 C8
- Wootton DN39 . . . 11 C2
- Worlaby DN20 . . . 10 E1
Wolds Cl 5 DN17 . . . 16 D7
Wolds Leisure-De Aston Sports Ctr LN8 . . . 57 E7
Wolds The DN21 . . . 43 D6
Wold View
- 1 Brigg DN20 . . . 196 D4
- 25 Brough HU15 . . . 2 C6
- Caistor LN7 . . . 33 C4
- Fotherby LN11 . . . 49 A2
- Holton le Clay DN36 . . . 195 C2
- 3 Nettleham LN2 . . . 68 D2
- Rothwell LN7 . . . 33 F2
Wolf La PE13 . . . 169 F1
Wolfreton Ct HU10 . . . 178 E6
Wolfreton Dr HU10 . . . 178 F6
Wolfreton Garth HU10 . . . 178 D8
Wolfreton La HU10 . . . 178 F8
Wolfreton Mews HU10 . . . 178 F7
Wolfreton Rd HU10 . . . 178 F7
Wolfreton Sch HU10 . . . 178 C7
Wolfreton Villas HU10 . . . 178 F7
Wolla Bank Nature Reserves* PE24 . . . 77 D1
Wollaston Rd
- Cleethorpes DN35 . . . 192 E6
- Peterborough PE3 . . . 225 C6
Wolseley Cl PE7 . . . 233 D6
Wolsey Dr 6 DN19 . . . 11 C7
Wolsey Rd NG24 . . . 104 A6
Wolsey Way LN2 . . . 202 D8
Womersley Rd DN31 . . . 189 C2
Wong Gdns NG32 . . . 210 A4
Wong Row 10 NG31 . . . 211 A5
Wongs La PE24 . . . 102 B7
Wong The LN9 . . . 199 B3
Woodale Cl 2 DN15 . . . 182 C6

Woodapple Ct 4 DN41... 23 E6
Woodbank
  1 Deeping St Nicholas PE11...166 C6
  Skellingthorpe LN6...200 A5
Woodbine Ave DN20...196 C4
Woodbine Contemporary Arts★ PE12...168 A3
Woodbine St PE2...231 A8
Woodbridge Rd NG34...212 E6
Woodbridge Rd Ind Est NG34...272 E6
Woodburn Way 15 LN10...97 C5
Woodburn Cl LN1...201 E8
Woodburn View 13 LN1...201 E8
Woodbyth Rd PE1...226 A6
Wood Carr La DN9...16 C2
Wood Cl DN33...194 F7
Woodclose Rd DN17...184 D6
Woodcock La LN1...200 C8
Woodcock St LN3...180 A4
Woodcote Cl PE1...226 A7
Woodcroft Cl 9 PE6...217 A5
Woodcroft Rd
  Marholm PE6...220 A3
  4 Saxilby LN1...66 C2
Wood Dr 4 HU14...3 A4
Wooden Beck Hill DN10...39 E2
Wood End NG33...131 A1
WOOD ENDERBY PE22...98 F6
Woodfield 7 PE9...171 B1
Woodfield Ave LN6...200 C1
Woodfield Cl
  9 Birchwood LN6...200 C1
  15 Humberston DN36...36 D8
  Spalding PE11...214 F2
Woodfield La HU13...178 C1
Woodfield Rd
  Gainsborough DN21...197 F5
  Peterborough PE3...225 D3
Woodgarr Ave 4 DN17...17 D6
Woodgate PE6...173 C4
Woodgate La
  Beckingham LN5...105 C4
  Kingston upon Hull HU5...179 F8
  Maxey PE6...217 A1
Woodgate Rd
  Kingston upon Hull HU5...179 F7
  Leverington PE13...170 A2
  7 Moulton PE12...157 E1
Woodgates Cl 13 HU14...3 A5
Woodgates La HU14...3 A6
Woodgates Mount 3 HU14...3 A5
Woodhall Cl PE21...208 C5
Woodhall Cres 9 LN1...66 C2
Woodhall Dr
  Lincoln LN2...201 F8
  Waltham DN37...194 C4
Woodhall Rd
  Horncastle LN9...199 A3
  Roughton LN9...85 C3
Woodhall Rise PE4...220 F6
WOODHALL SPA LN10...97 E5
Woodhall Spa Cottage Mus★ LN10...97 D6
Woodhead Cl 4 PE9...219 D7
Woodhill Ave DN21...197 E6
Woodhill Cl 2 HU10...178 E7
Wood Hill Rd DN21...29 B3
Woodhill Rise HU13...178 C2
WOODHOUSE DN9...16 E3
Woodhouse Gn Rd DN7...14 B8
Woodhouse La
  2 Belton DN9...16 E3
  Hatfield DN7...14 D2
  Holbeach PE12...159 A8
  Moulton PE12...146 E1
Woodhouse Rd DN16...185 E8
Woodhouse St HU9...181 D7
Woodhurst Rd PE2...231 D6
Wood La
  Bardney LN3...83 B4
  Beckingham DN10...52 A8
  Croxton Kerrial NG32...138 A6
  Gringley on the Hill DN10...39 C2
  1 Lincoln LN6...93 A8
  Lincoln LN6...204 A1
  Little Cawthorpe LN11...61 F2
  Louth LN11...198 D4
  Moulton PE12...158 A7
  Norton Disney LN6...92 B3
  Quadring PE11...135 C1
  South Kyme LN4...109 F1
  South Kyme LN4...123 B8
  South Scarle NG23...91 F7
  Sturton le Steeple DN22...52 A3

Thurlby PE10...213 C1
Woodland Ave
  1 Bourne PE10...213 B5
  22 Brough HU15...2 C6
  15 Crowle DN17...16 D8
  Gainsborough DN21...197 B7
  Skellingthorpe LN6...200 B2
Woodland Dr
  8 Broughton DN20...19 D4
  5 Elsham DN20...20 F7
  Grantham NG31...211 F7
  Kingston upon Hull HU10...178 C6
  6 Woodhall Spa LN10...97 E6
Woodland End HU4...179 C5
Woodland Lea 2 PE6...173 B4
Woodland Rise LN11...198 A6
Woodlands
  Langford NG24...104 B8
  Long Sutton PE12...216 D4
  5 Louth LN11...198 C6
Woodlands Ave
  Immingham DN40...186 C5
  15 Keelby DN41...23 A4
  6 Spilsby PE23...87 F1
Woodlands Cl 5 DN19...11 C7
Woodlands Dr
  1 Colsterworth NG33...151 E7
  Grantham NG31...211 C4
Woodlands La 14 HU15...2 C6
Woodlands Prim Sch DN33...191 A2
Woodlands Rd HU5...179 B7
Woodlands Rise 7 HU14...3 A5
Woodlands The
  3 Market Deeping PE6...217 B5
  Peterborough PE1...226 E5
  1 Stallingborough DN41...23 D6
Woodland View
  2 Barnetby le Wold DN38...21 B4
  Lincoln LN2...234 C3
  Scunthorpe DN15...182 C3
Woodland Way 16 DN9...27 E6
Woodland Wlk 1 DN35...192 E1
Woodman's Ct 4 PE22...98 F4
Woodmill Bank PE12...159 F2
WOODNOOK NG33...140 C7
Woodpecker Cl LN6...200 A3
Woodpecker Ct PE4...221 E2
Woodpecker Way DN21...42 E8
Wood Rd 24 LN13...75 F2
Woodrow Pk DN33...191 D1
Woodrush Rd LN4...202 C8
Woods Cl 14 NG23...117 D3
Woodside
  Boston PE21...208 E1
  Branston & Mere LN4...81 D2
  Kingston upon Hull HU13...178 D1
WOODSIDE DN9...26 D6
Woodside Ave NG34...212 C6
Woodside Cl 1 PE10...164 C8
Woodside Ct NG34...212 D7
Woodside E PE10...164 D8
Woodside Falconry & Conservation Ctr★ LN3...69 D3
Woodside La DN9...26 D6
Woodside Rd DN20...136 B5
Woods La 2 DN40...12 F2
Wood's La
  Kingston upon Hull HU1...180 E5
  3 Pinchbeck PE11...145 D2
Woodsley Ave DN35...192 E5
Woods Mdw 1 DN20...30 F6
Wood St 3 DN32...191 F8
Woods Terr DN21...197 C7
Woodstock Rd DN16...183 D1
Woodstock St 4 LN1...201 D4
WOODSTON PE2...230 E7
Woodston Ind Est PE2...230 E6
Woodston Prim Sch PE2...230 E7
WOODTHORPE LN13...75 D7
Woodthorpe Ave PE21...209 C4
Woodvale Ave LN6...204 C6
Woodvale Cl 14 LN6...204 C6
Wood View
  Bourne PE10...213 C5
  1 Messingham DN17...29 D7
  3 Swanland HU14...3 B7
Woodville Gdns E 3 PE21...208 D3
Woodville Gdns W 2 PE21...208 D3
Woodville Rd PE21...208 D4
Woodward's La
  Little Sutton PE12...160 B3
  Long Sutton PE12...216 F1

Wood Way LN11...198 E5
Woodyard The 4 NG32...119 B7
Woolcroft Cl 2 PE13...170 A1
Woolfellhill Rd PE6...174 F1
Woolgard PE3...225 A3
Woolley's La
  Castle Bytham NG33...152 A4
  North Witham NG33...151 F4
Woollin Ave DN17...185 A6
Woolram Wygate PE11...214 C5
WOOLSTHORPE BY BELVOIR NG32...128 D1
WOOLSTHORPE-BY-COLSTERWORTH NG33...151 D7
Woolsthorpe La
  Belvoir NG32...138 D7
  Bottesford NG13...128 C4
Woolsthorpe Manor★ NG33...151 D7
Woolsthorpe Rd 3 NG33...151 D7
Woolwich Dr 2 HU4...179 B2
WOOTTON DN39...11 F3
Wootton Ave PE2...231 A6
Wootton Ct DN17...184 C8
Wootton Dr PE2...230 F6
Wootton Rd
  Grimsby DN33...191 A3
  Wootton DN39...11 F2
Wootton St Andrews CE Prim Sch DN39...11 E3
Worcester Ave DN34...191 A4
Worcester Cl
  11 Birchwood LN6...204 D7
  7 Bracebridge Heath LN4...81 A2
  5 Louth LN11...198 C5
  Scunthorpe DN16...185 A2
Worcester Cres 4 PE9...219 B6
Worcester Rd
  Grantham NG31...210 D4
  4 Wisbech PE13...170 D1
Wordsworth Cl
  3 Grantham NG31...211 E6
  Peterborough PE4...225 E8
Wordsworth Ct
  5 Grimsby DN32...189 C1
  13 Sleaford NG34...212 F4
Wordsworth Gr PE10...213 D3
Wordsworth Rd
  North Greetwell LN3...203 C6
  Scunthorpe DN17...184 D6
Wordsworth St 6 LN2...234 B3
Workhouse La
  Algarkirk PE20...136 B1
  Hogsthorpe PE24...90 C7
Workington Ave 8 HU4...179 B6
WORLABY
  Maidenwell LN11...74 A4
  Worlaby DN20...20 D8
Worlaby Prim Sch DN20...20 D8
Worlaby Rd DN33...191 B1
World's End Rd PE13...160 A1
Worldwide Way DN41...187 C2
Wormgate PE21...208 F5
Worship St HU2...180 F7
Worsley PE2...230 A4
Worsley Cl
  1 Holton le Clay DN36...195 C2
  Immingham DN40...186 D4
Worsley Rd DN40...186 D4
Worthington La NG32...128 D1
Wortley's La PE21...208 A2
Wortley St DN16...183 A2
WOTHORPE PE9...219 B2
Wothorpe Mews 3 PE9...219 B4
Wothorpe Rd PE9...219 B4
WRAGBY LN8...70 E5
Wragby Prim Sch LN8...70 D5
Wragby Rd
  Bardney LN3...83 C4
  Holton cum Beckering LN8...70 C7
  Lincoln LN2...234 C3
  Lissington LN3...57 E2
  Reepham LN3...68 F1
  Scunthorpe DN17...184 D5
Wragby Rd E
  Greetwell LN2...203 A8
  Reepham LN3...68 E1
Wragby St 3 DN32...191 F7
WRAGHOLME LN11...50 A8
Wragholme La LN11...50 A8
Wragholme Rd LN11...50 A8
WRANGLE PE22...114 C1
Wrangle Bank PE22...114 B4

WRANGLE BANK PE22...114 C4
WRANGLE LOWGATE PE22...114 D2
WRANGLE LOW GROUND PE22...114 D4
Wrangle Prim Sch PE22...114 D2
WRAWBY DN20...20 E4
Wrawby CE Prim Sch DN20...20 E4
Wrawby Rd
  Brigg DN20...196 D4
  Scunthorpe DN17...184 E5
Wrawby St DN20...196 C3
Wray Cl 9 DN37...194 C5
Wray St 20 DN21...30 B1
Wren Cl
  Deeping St Nicholas PE11...166 B6
  11 Healing DN41...23 F5
  15 Market Deeping PE6...217 C5
  Scunthorpe DN16...185 B2
  4 Sleaford NG34...212 B3
Wren Cres DN33...191 B2
WRESSLE DN20...19 F4
Wressle Rd DN20...19 E3
Wright Ave PE2...231 D5
Wright's Dro PE6...175 B7
Wrights Gdns DN10...40 A3
Wrights La 5 LE14...150 C1
Wright's La
  Friskney PE22...115 A5
  Sutton Bridge PE12...160 E4
Wright St HU2...180 E7
Wrightsway LN2...202 D5
WROOT DN9...26 C6
Wroot Rd DN9...26 A3
Wroot Travis Charity Prim Sch DN9...26 D5
Wroxall Dr NG31...210 E4
Wroxham Ave DN34...190 E5
Wroxham Cl 7 LN6...205 A2
Wrygarth Ave 7 HU15...2 C5
Wulfram Dr NG31...211 E2
Wulfric Sq PE3...225 C8
Wyatt Ave 13 DN20...19 D3
Wyatt Cl LN4...96 B2
Wyatt Rd LN5...205 D7
Wybeck Rd DN15...183 A6
Wybers Way DN37...190 D6
WYBERS WOOD DN37...190 C6
Wybers Wood Jun & Inf Sch DN37...190 C8
Wybert Cres 5 PE21...136 D8
Wybert La PE21...136 F8
WYBERTON PE21...136 D8
Wyberton Low Rd 1 PE21...208 D7
Wyberton Prim Sch PE21...136 E7
Wyberton Roads PE20...137 A7
Wyberton W Rd PE21...208 C2
Wyche Cr 13 PE6...166 F1
Wycliffe Gr PE4...220 E5
Wydham Pk PE2...229 D6
Wye Pl PE4...221 C1
Wygate Mdws PE11...214 B5
Wygate Pk PE11...214 A5
Wygate Rd PE11...214 B4
Wyggeston Ave 22 NG13...128 A6
Wyggeston Rd 21 NG13...128 A6
WYKEHAM PE12...145 F1
Wykeham La
  Burgh on Bain LN8...59 C6
  Weston PE12...145 F1
Wykes La PE11...135 A2
Wykes Rd
  Donington PE11...135 B1
  Yaxley PE7...233 D4
Wyke St HU9...181 D7
Wyke The 8 PE11...214 A3
Wylson Cl 5 NG34...120 F8
Wyman Way PE2...229 F5
Wymark View DN33...190 F3
Wymersley Rd HU5...179 A8
WYMONDHAM LE14...150 B1
Wyndham NG31...211 C5
Wyndham Rd 9 DN36...195 C6
Wyndham St HU3...180 C7
Wynmoor Rd DN17...184 F7
Wyredale Rd DN16...185 D5
Wythes La PE21...126 C2
Wyton Cl 8 LN6...204 B6
Wyvern Cl 16 DN17...16 D8
WYVILLE NG32...139 C4
Wyville Rd
  Grantham NG31...210 A1
  Little Ponton & Stroxton NG31...139 E8
Wyville Wlk LN6...204 F7

Y

YADDLETHORPE DN17...184 E3
Yale Cl LN4...203 D1
YARBOROUGH DN34...191 A7
Yarborough Cl 3 DN36...195 C2
Yarborough Cres
  17 Broughton DN20...19 E4
  Lincoln LN1...201 E6
Yarborough Ct DN15...182 B2
Yarborough Dr 3 DN31...191 D8
Yarborough Leisure Ctr LN1...201 E7
Yarborough Prim Sch DN34...190 F7
Yarborough Rd
  Boston PE21...136 E8
  Brigg DN20...196 D3
  Grimsby DN34...190 F6
  Keelby DN41...23 A5
  1 Lincoln LN1...234 A4
  Scunthorpe DN16...19 A4
  9 Skegness PE25...206 A6
Yarborough Sch LN1...201 E7
Yarborough Terr LN1...234 A4
YARBURGH LN11...49 E4
Yarburgh Rd LN11...49 E2
Yarde The 2 PE10...213 E2
Yardley Way 2 DN34...190 D4
Yarmouth Ave
  Grantham NG31...210 D4
  3 Kingston upon Hull HU4...179 A3
Yarra Rd DN35...192 F6
Yarrow Rd DN34...190 F7
Yarwell Cl PE2...230 D7
Yarwell Rd PE8...222 A3
Yawling Gate Rd PE22...114 F5
YAWTHORPE DN21...42 A2
YAXLEY PE7...233 E6
Yaxley Jun Sch PE7...233 E6
Yew Dr DN16...185 B2
Yews La 4 DN37...23 E1
Yew Tree Cl 1 PE10...213 C6
Yewtree Dr HU5...179 B7
Yew Tree Gr 1 PE21...209 C2
Yew Tree Way 1 NG24...104 C5
Yew Tree Wlk PE3...225 A2
York Ave
  Lincoln LN1...201 D4
  Scunthorpe DN16...185 B4
York Cl LN4...203 D1
York Gdns
  2 Gosberton PE11...145 B6
  30 Wisbech PE13...170 D1
York House Rd 6 NG34...120 C8
York Pl DN35...192 C4
York Rd
  5 Binbrook Tech Pk LN8...47 B6
  Brigg DN20...196 D4
  Hatfield DN7...14 D4
  Kirton in Lindsey DN21...30 C1
  Mablethorpe/Sutton on Sea LN12...64 D1
  Peterborough PE1...225 F6
  RAF Cranwell NG34...107 C1
  Sleaford NG34...212 C6
  9 Stamford PE9...219 B6
York Ride 4 PE12...216 B5
York St (Boston United FC) PE21...209 A5
Yorkshireside DN17...7 A3
York St
  Boston PE21...209 A4
  Grimsby DN31...191 C8
York Terr 3 DN10...40 A5
York Way
  5 Bracebridge Heath LN4...81 A2
  Grantham NG31...210 C5
Youlgrave Ave 6 LN12...77 A8
Younger's La PE24...103 A8
Young Pl DN35...192 B7
Youngs Ave 9 NG24...104 C1

Z

Zara Cl PE21...209 C6
Zetland St HU3...180 A5